M000239078

Samba

Steve Litt, et al.

SAMS

Unleashed

Samba Unleashed

Copyright ©2000 by Sams Publishing

International Standard Book Number: 0-672-31862-8

Library of Congress Catalog Card Number: 99-067308

Printed in the United States of America

First Printing: April 2000

01   00   99   4   3   2   1

Trademarks

Warning and Disclaimer

ASSOCIATE PUBLISHER
Michael Stephens

ACQUISITIONS EDITOR
Angela Kozlowski

DEVELOPMENT EDITOR
Clint McCarty

MANAGING EDITOR
Charlotte Clapp

PROJECT EDITOR
George E. Nedeff

COPY EDITOR
Bart Reed

INDEXER
Heather McNeill

PROOFREADER
Matt Wynalda

TECHNICAL EDITORS
Steve Epstein
Rob Rati
Dallas Releford

TEAM COORDINATOR
Pamalee Nelson

INTERIOR DESIGN
Gary Adair

COVER DESIGN
Aren Howell

COPY WRITER
Eric Borgert

PRODUCTION
Darin Crone
Tracy Thomas

Contents at a Glance

Contents

About the Lead Author

Steve Litt is the author of *Rapid Learning, Secret Weapon of the Successful Technologist,* and *Troubleshooting: Tools, Tips and Techniques* and a contributing author to *Red Hat Linux 6 Unleashed* and *Linux Unleashed, Fourth Edition*, as well as Webmaster of Troubleshooters.Com and lead content provider of the Linux Library, Code Corner, and Troubleshooting Professional Magazine subsites. A software developer for over 10 years, Steve switched to Open Source to escape the workarounds and Blue Screens of Death bestowed by popular "development environments." Quickly recognizing Samba as a vital key to Open Source server acceptance, he documented it first on Troubleshooters.Com, then as chapters in *Unleashed* books, and now in *Samba Unleashed.*

Steve is an Executive Committee Director for Linux Enthusiasts and Professionals of Central Florida (LEAP-CF), and he frequently gives technical presentations. He lives in Central Florida with his wife, Sylvia, and their three children, Brett, Rena, and Valerie. He can be reached at the Troubleshooters.Com Web site.

Contributing Authors

Mike Harris obtained a degree in Real-time Systems Design in 1993 and has since been working professionally in various sectors of the IT industry. He is a strong Linux advocate, having fallen in love with UNIX. He has suffered for his sins and worked with Windows NT for several years as well. He co-founded Psand Limited in 1996 to promote Linux and Open Source software to a wider audience in the U.K. and now works as a virtual consultant for Internet applications and Open Systems. He recently escaped the dreariness of southern England to live in Barcelona, where the wine is better and cheaper.

Kevin Long is originally from Oxford, England, where he started working with business computers in 1979. He has been employed in the Los Angeles area for the past six years in construction engineering. He runs a 30-client network of Windows 9x and NT workstation systems, all tied into a 200-client WAN of NT and Linux/Samba servers for file- and-print, database-backed Apache intranet services. The Windows clients are maintained by Perl scripts and batch files and have 65 engineering applications, including CAD, that are integrated into the network somewhat holistically.

Daniel Robbins resides in Albuquerque, New Mexico and is the Chief Architect of the Gentoo Project, CEO of Gentoo Technologies, Inc., and the mentor for the Linux Advanced Multimedia Project (LAMP). Daniel has been involved with computers in some fashion since the second grade, when he was first exposed to the Logo programming language as well as a potentially dangerous dose of Pac Man. This probably explains why he has since served as a Lead Graphic Artist at Sony Electronic Publishing/Psygnosis. Daniel enjoys spending time with his wife, Mary, who is expecting a child this spring.

Jaron J. Rubenstein began his computer career early in life by destroying systems in new and unique ways, only to hack them back together before his father got home (sometimes). Today, Jaron is Director of Technology for Logicept, a premier Web applications development firm located in New York's Silicon Alley. Logicept's tools of choice are Open Source technologies, including Samba, Linux, GNU tools, Apache, and Perl. Jaron can be reached via Logicept at `www.logicept.com`.

Bryan J. Smith holds a Bachelor of Science in Computer Engineering from the University of Central Florida. Originally born in Illinois, his facination with computing began when he received a PCjr at the age of 9. By 1993, he was hacking GNU, Linux and other Open Source software, integrating Samba into corporate LANs as early as 1995. With a 'dual-role' background in both IT and engineering, he has managed dozens of computing platforms at engineering firms such as Post, Buckley, Schuh & Jernigan, and Coleman Aerospace. His current employer, semiconductor technology and design startup Theseus Logic, relies heavily on Open Sourse software for both its networking and engineering capabilities. Mr. Smith currently lives near Orlando with his wife Lourdes.

Glenda R. Snodgrass is lead consultant and managing partner of The Net Effect, LLC, a consulting firm in Mobile, Alabama. She has spent most of the past five years instructing local area businesses in commercial uses of the Internet, conducting numerous beginner- and intermediate-level seminars and workshops, and consulting with and training employees of local industries on intranet development. Glenda is an avid Linux enthusiast with extensive background in database design and management. She holds a B.A. from the University of South Alabama in Mobile, and a *ma trise* from Université Paris I Panthéon-Sorbonne in Paris, France. When not in front of the computer, Glenda can be found on trails across the Southeast, riding endurance on her Arabian gelding, Lakota, with her Dobie, Bailey, for company.

Dedication

To my father, Walter Litt, for a lifetime of love, knowledge, and inspiration.

Acknowledgments

First and foremost, I thank my loving wife, Sylvia, for her continued support and encouragement of my writing career, and for taking care of our six-year-old triplets and everything else in our family while I locked myself in the office writing this book. Sylvia, 10 years ago I showed you a three-page table of contents and told you I was going to write a book, and you were enthusiastic. Thank you, and I love you. Thanks also go out to our children, Brett, Rena, and Valerie, for their calm and patient acceptance of my 100+ hour workweeks.

A huge thank-you goes out to the outstanding team Sams Publishing assembled for *Samba Unleashed*: Acquisitions Editor Angela Kozlowski, who performed magic with the book's logistics and personnel, Development Editor Clint McCarty, whose audience-centered vision kept this book on track, copy editor Bart Reed, who converted my techie talk to professional prose, technical editors Steve Epstein, Rob Rati, and Dallas Releford, who tested every script and configuration and made numerous suggestions to improve the book, and Executive Editor Don Roche, whose friendly enthusiasm convinced me to write *Samba Unleashed*. Further thanks go out to Project Editor George Nedeff and Team Coordinator Pamalee Nelson. A very special thank-you goes out to the top-notch team of contributing authors who did such a great job on many of *Samba Unleashed*'s toughest chapters: Mike Harris, Kevin Long, Daniel Robbins, Roman Rochelt, Jaron Rubenstein, Bryan Smith, and Glenda Snodgrass.

Thanks to Andrew Tridgell for creating Samba, and to the entire Samba extended family, including the Samba Team with CVS upload privileges, and everyone who has contributed good patches, features, coding, and ideas. Special thanks to two Samba people, Jeremy Allison and Jerry Carter, for consistently answering my questions and giving me encouragement. Thanks to all those who administer and contribute to the Samba mailing lists.

I owe a very deep debt of gratitude to Richard Stallman. Without the GNU GPL he wrote so long ago, this would be a much less pleasant world today. Kudos to the entire GNU and FSF organizations. A warm thank-you goes out to all software authors offering software with legally available, reproducible, and modifiable source code.

Thanks to my LUG, Linux Enthusiasts and Professionals of Central Florida, for all the advice, tips, and encouragement. If I appear knowledgeable, it's because I have a 56Kbps connection to 50+ other brains on the LEAP-CF mailing list.

Thank you to all my teachers, instructors, professors, mentors, book authors, friends, and fellow experimenters, too numerous to name, who have taught me everything I know. A special thanks to the two who have taught me the most, my parents, Walter and Connie Litt. Thanks to Jeff Jones, Sid Carter, Dave Burns, and Paul Watkins for their consistent interest and help with my career over the years.

Each of us stands on the shoulders of those who came before. The shoulders I stand on are numerous, broad, strong, and enduring. I thank you all.

—Steve Litt

Tell Us What You Think!

As the reader of this book, *you* are our most important critic and commentator. We value your opinion and want to know what we're doing right, what we could do better, what areas you'd like to see us publish in, and any other words of wisdom you're willing to pass our way.

As an Associate Publisher for Sams Publishing, I welcome your comments. You can fax, email, or write me directly to let me know what you did or didn't like about this book—as well as what we can do to make our books stronger.

Please note that I cannot help you with technical problems related to the topic of this book, and that due to the high volume of mail I receive, I might not be able to reply to every message.

When you write, please be sure to include this book's title and author as well as your name and phone or fax number. I will carefully review your comments and share them with the author and editors who worked on the book.

Fax: 317.581.4770

Email: michael.stephens@macmillanusa.com

Mail: Michael Stephens
          Associate Publisher
          Sams Publishing
          201 West 103rd Street
          Indianapolis, IN 46290 USA

Introduction

Where were you when you realized Open Source would triumph? I was on the phone with Don Roche of Sams Publishing. Don told me in very numeric terms of the huge demand for a *Samba Unleashed* book. The numbers he discussed couldn't be attributed to Open Source advocates or hobbyists. The numbers were obviously produced by mainstream professional IT people. Why the sudden mainstream interest in Samba?

A few minutes into the phone call I understood the demand. Samba is the gateway between the proprietary desktop and Open Source back ends. The readers clamoring for this book contemplated replacing or augmenting their proprietary servers with Open Source. The tide had turned, Open Source was advancing, and Samba was the battlefield. I accepted Sams' offer to write *Samba Unleashed* and began organizing a book to meet the needs of a huge audience of IT professionals wanting to implement Samba in formerly proprietary environments.

As a member of this audience, you need much more than a technical treatise on Samba. Your Samba implementation must conform to your organization's standards, politics, and prejudices. You may need to overcome resistance from within your organization. You need a Samba implementation strategy custom-made for your environment. You need information to integrate Samba with your existing networks, systems, and corporate culture—quickly, correctly, and with a minimum of experimentation.

Samba Unleashed is structured to address these needs. Part I, "Introduction to Samba," discusses Samba's relationship to the Windows and TCP/IP environments. The discussion includes Samba installation. Because many readers are much more familiar with UNIX than Windows, or vice versa, Part I is designed to fill any knowledge gaps.

Part II, "Creating a Turnkey Samba System," is the technical heart of *Samba Unleashed*. After reading Part II, you'll be able to set up a Samba server to match a technical specification. Starting with a proof of concept and a chapter that seeks to simplify the seemingly complex subject of Samba access, Part II delivers straightforward information on Windows 98, NT, and 2000 Samba clients, UNIX Samba client utilities, Samba printers, SWAT, Samba security, Samba PDCs, Samba backup strategies, and Samba troubleshooting.

Part II also contains a chapter on Samba server-side automation (SSA). SSA is Samba's mechanism that enables a Windows user to trigger a UNIX process on a Windows file, from an icon click, or from within a batch file or other Windows program. This chapter presents several detailed examples of practical tasks best done with server-side automation, complete with the necessary code and procedures. SSA is a subject rarely covered in Samba books and documentation, but as you'll see later in the book, it's a vital missing link for a wide variety of environment-dependent networking tasks.

The final chapter in Part II is "Samba Learning Tools." This chapter helps you construct several tools to find any Samba information you might need from the source code, man pages, and other sources. These tools are exactly what you need to become increasingly expert in Samba, and to stay current with Samba progress. To my knowledge, there is nothing like this chapter in any other Samba book.

After reading Part II, you'll be able to set up a Samba server to match any technical specification. Part III, "Enterprise Samba," delivers the information necessary to actually create such a specification in the large-scale technical environment usually known as *the enterprise*.

The chapters in Part III were written by contributing authors chosen especially for their use of Samba in computing environments with thousands of users and huge investments in popular proprietary networking software. Such environments use multiple servers in separate buildings, usually in different cities or countries.

Part III discusses the procedures, politics, and nuts and bolts of tasks such as adding Samba to an existing NT network, replacing an NT server with a Samba server, Samba backup and security in the enterprise, and Samba file transfer enterprise apps. There are also chapters on incorporating Samba in an enterprise's software development department and using Samba in the automatic configuration and installation of Windows software.

Enterprise computing adds political, business, and strategic challenges to the technical tasks normally associated with computer networking. Once you've finished Part III of this book, you can combine its information with your own enterprise experience to successfully introduce Samba into your large computing environment.

Part IV, "Advanced Samba," is a group of four chapters that delivers advanced theory and concepts related to local and cross-subnet browsing, WINS, and Samba optimization. Although there are many Samba installations for which this information is not necessary, those needing this information will find Part IV essential.

Part V, "Special Uses of Samba," is dedicated to the fact that Samba's use goes far beyond the enterprise. Part V delivers solid examples of Samba use in the educational computer lab and the home (including the home office). It also discusses the use of Samba in departmental servers and from the point of view of the value added reseller. As a niche example, there's a chapter that discusses the procedures and details of implementing Samba in the litigation-support department. Each chapter discusses the optimization of Samba to take advantage of the business, technical, and economic properties of the environment.

Part V also contains a chapter titled "Using Samba as an Open Source Migration Strategy." This chapter goes to the root needs of the professional IT audience described in the beginning of this introduction.

Samba Unleashed is organized to serve the large audience needing to interface Windows to Open Source. Upon completion of this book, you'll be in an excellent position to successfully implement Samba in your present work environment, turning that environment's unique technical, business, political, and economic challenges into opportunities.

Sams Publishing scoured the globe for the best possible contributing authors, producing a world-class team of industry experts. We have security experts, large-computing experts, Windows experts, and UNIX experts, all sharing a common Samba expertise. The result is so good that each chapter proudly bears the name of its author.

If you are, or soon will be, professionally responsible for implementing Samba, take confidence in the fact that this book was built from the ground up specifically for you. Technical facts are delivered in an organized fashion for the purpose of quick and easy assimilation. Recognizing that technology is the tip of the iceberg, we've included voluminous information custom-made to help you integrate Samba into your technological, political, business, and economic environment.

Samba has a reputation for complexity. *Samba Unleashed* has been constructed with a single priority—to make your professional Samba installation easy and successful.

Introduction
to Samba

PART
I

In This Part

Choosing Samba

by Steve Litt

CHAPTER 1

Samba is a file and print server that enables Windows client computers to read, write, and print files on a Linux, BSD, or UNIX server. This simple definition, although accurate, is just the tip of the iceberg.

Samba's Free Software license and its ability to run on Linux give Samba the economic edge over rivals Microsoft NT and Novell NetWare. Samba is extremely reliable, as are the operating systems on which it runs. Unlike some other systems, Samba servers and networks run for months or years without rebooting. Beyond these advantages, Samba offers a strategic path toward vendor independence and scalability.

Samba is a port of the SMB (session message block) protocol to non-Windows servers. It began in early 1992 with Andrew Tridgell releasing code to link DOS computers running DEC Pathworks with non-DEC servers. By the mid-1990s, it had developed into an SMB protocol server named *smbserver*. The name was changed to Samba in 1994. When Microsoft enhanced the SMB to CIFS (Common Internet File System), Samba followed suit, copying features almost as fast as Microsoft could put them into NT. Samba's popularity has skyrocketed hand in hand with that of Linux.

Samba Defined

Samba is a software suite whose primary purpose is enabling UNIX, Linux, BSD, Linux-type operating systems, and non-UNIX operating systems to act as file and print servers. It can also serve some of the other functions of Microsoft NT Server, including functioning as a login server, profile server, and primary domain controller. The Samba suite includes several client utilities that enable access to Windows shares from a non-Windows computer.

The Role of the File Server

A *file server* is a computer that stores files for other computers. File servers are a necessity for any organization with more than a few computers.

> **Tip**
>
> A *client computer* is a computer that the user interacts with. It has a keyboard, mouse, and graphical interface, and sometimes it has programs installed on it. The intent is that all data created by the user is stored on the server computer. Client computers are often called *desktop computers* or *workstations*.
>
> A *server computer* is a computer whose job is storing data. Often, server computers also store programs. Typically multiple client computers (as few as two and as many as hundreds) are wired up to one or a small number of server computers to form a network.

File servers enable file sharing. They reduce the risk of data loss by providing a single backup point for all data and by putting all data under the control of an experienced network administrator. When the application software resides on the file server, users can transparently move from one client computer to another without disruption to their work.

File servers must handle file ownership, security, and locking. *Ownership* simply refers to who created the file, unless an administrator has changed the ownership. *Security* refers to the permissions given to the file's owner, members of the owner's group, and others. Typically the file's owner can read and write the file to make further modifications. Often, the owner's group has those same rights, and others can only read the file. Often, data privacy dictates that read permissions be given only to select groups of users. Samba provides ways to handle all these requirements.

File locking refers to the principle that although many people may be able to modify a file, only one can modify it at a time. For instance, three employees might want to collaboratively write a marketing plan. But if it's possible for two to write it at the same time, the one saving it last would overwrite the changes of the one saving it first. To prevent such an occurrence, Samba can lock files so only the first person accessing it has the ability to write the file. Subsequent users are given a read-only copy. Once the first user closes the file, another user with proper permission may open the file for writing.

Samba's Implementation of Print Server Functionality

Samba also serves as a print server. Print servers enable numerous users on numerous desktop computers to print to one printer, without their pages becoming intermixed. This has the obvious advantage of reducing printer expenditures. It allows the organization to purchase one (or a few) high-speed, highly reliable printers for a tiny fraction of the cost of purchasing cheap printers for each desktop. This, in turn, slashes repair and tech support costs.

Samba provides highly reliable print services.

Components of the Samba Suite

The Samba Suite consists of server-specific files, client utilities, and other utilities. The server-specific files, consisting of daemons, the `smbpasswd` utility, and `smb.conf`, enable a UNIX or UNIX-like computer to act as a file and print server. The client utilities enable a UNIX or UNIX-like computer to access SMB shares on a Samba server or on a Windows box. These include `smbclient`, `smbmount`, and `smbumount`. Other utilities include diagnostic `nmblookup`, the `smbtar` front end to `smbclient`, and the `smbprint` script enabling SMB print shares to be accessed from `/etc/printcap`.

Server-Specific Files

File-serving capabilities are provided by the smbd and nmbd daemons and their configuration file, smb.conf. nmbd is the NetBIOS name server that provides NetBIOS over IP naming services to clients. It normally runs at bootup. smbd is the server that provides SMB/CIFS services to clients and likewise is normally started at boot time.

> **Note**
>
> Upcoming versions of Samba will incorporate many daemons in addition to smbd and nmbd.

The third file vital to Samba's file service is smb.conf. smb.conf is a configuration file that defines the behavior of smbd and nmbd.

Additionally, the smbpasswd utility handles input of encrypted passwords and also assists in joining an NT domain.

Client Utilities

The Samba server enables access to the server's files from Windows Explorer or the Windows command line. Client utilities do the reverse, enabling access to Windows directories and files from a non-Windows computer. The most important of these utilities is smbclient, an ftp-like interface that enables command-driven puts, gets, ls, and the like. smbclient can also print to a shared Windows or Samba printer. Many of the other client utilities do their work by calling smbclient or they share common source code with smbclient.

The smbfs utilities, consisting of smbmount and smbumount, enable the mounting of shares on a non-Windows machine. They're typically used to make a shared Windows directory seem like part of the UNIX file system. In the upcoming Samba version 2.0.6, the mounting and dismounting can be accomplished with the standard UNIX mount commands. smbfs has the disadvantage of running only on Linux.

The smbsh utilities provide another method of mounting and dismounting Windows shares. smbsh runs on many platforms, but unfortunately some compiler issues are presently preventing its complete adoption.

Other Utilities

Although the smbprint script and the smbtar program could be thought of as client utilities, their method of use deserves special attention. The nmblookup utility is a diagnostic program whose use transcends client/server differentiation.

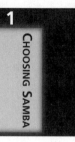

smbprint is a shellscript for printing to a Samba printer. It's a front end to smbclient that can be used directly to print to Samba printers. smbtar is a front end program to smbclient that enables easy backup of Samba shares and/or shared Windows directories. nmblookup is a diagnostic that helps with tough NetBIOS problems.

Samba Interconnects Linux, UNIX, and Windows

Samba is a file server that runs on a computer running Linux or some other UNIX OS variant. It enables Windows client computers to communicate sufficiently with the Linux or UNIX server to read and write files on that server.

Microsoft Windows is presently the most popular operating system. Windows comes in several flavors, including NT Server, NT Workstation, Windows 98, Windows 95, and Windows for Workgroups 3.11. Microsoft is scheduled to introduce Windows 2000, the next version of NT, in late 1999 or early 2000. As of October of 1999, the versions used extensively on desktop computers are Windows 98, Windows 95, and Windows NT Workstation.

The popularity of Windows comes from its ease of use and the large number of applications that it can run. Windows is widely entrenched as the most popular desktop operating system and likely will remain so for the next few years.

Windows NT (both Workstation and Server, and the various Windows 2000 editions) is widely perceived as the most reliable version of Windows. Windows 95 and 98 often hang with heavy use, requiring frequent rebooting. Most users consider this a small price to pay for the convenience offered by Windows. It should be noted that even Windows NT is perceived by many as less reliable than UNIX and its variants, including Linux and BSD.

Although convenience is the top selling point for a desktop computer, reliability is king for servers. Rebooting a server requires notification of the many users who might be accessing the server. In many organizations, the server cannot be rebooted during business hours. Today's mobile workforce with dialup connections often requires 24×7 server usage. For these reasons, many organizations choose UNIX or a UNIX variant for their servers.

UNIX servers are nothing new. They've provided email, Web, and other "Internet" services for years. However, until the widespread adoption of Samba, file access between the Windows and UNIX world was convoluted, often revolving around FTP (File Transfer Protocol). Samba enables UNIX files to appear native to the Windows desktop machine via Windows Explorer, Network Neighborhood, or the net use and net view commands. It's this role as bridge between Windows and UNIX that makes Samba so popular.

Pure-UNIX Networks Use NFS

Samba is most useful in Windows/UNIX integrated environments, where it's the only useful choice for file sharing. Other, more established choices exist in pure-UNIX (including UNIX workalikes) environments, the most popular being NFS (Network File System). Samba is rarely seen in pure-UNIX environments. This may change with time, given Samba's consistent feature development.

Samba on Non-UNIX Operating Systems

UNIX is not the only highly reliable server operating system. The Samba file server has been ported to VMS and MVS. Samba has also been ported to OS/2, StratOS, Amiga, and BeOS. It's also been ported to Windows NT and NetWare, but in the case of these two operating systems, one would likely choose the native file server.

Samba Benefits

Samba offers several advantages. Among them are reliability, licensing, independence, modularity, better talent, and less cost. All these advantages lead to a reduction in expense and busywork in the IT department. Samba's advantages are increasingly being recognized in corporate IT, resulting in a snowballing migration to Samba.

Reliability

Samba runs on operating systems widely perceived as more stable than Windows NT Server. These include UNIX and UNIX-like operating systems such as Linux, BSD, AIX, HP-UX, many versions of SUNOS and Solaris, and UNIXWARE. Samba also runs on the enterprise workhorses VMS and MVS.

A computer program is only as stable as the operating system it runs under. The Samba hosts UNIX, Linux, BSD, AIX, MVS, and VMS are all known to be highly reliable operating systems. Samba, itself, is seen by most administrators as having high reliability.

The result of this enhanced reliability is often counted in weeks, months, or even years, along with vastly reduced data loss and corruption. Additionally, most of these operating systems enable the reconfiguration and restarting of almost any service without rebooting the machine itself.

For all these reasons, those wanting to combine high reliability with a Windows front end choose Samba.

Licensing

Software licensing is increasingly seen as a "hassle" by system administrators and their managers. There's a trend toward increasingly complex licensing terms. Some such licenses are complex enough to require review by the legal department. All this license reading is time consuming, worrisome, and certainly not within the organization's core competency.

Several companies now make a good living selling "license tracking" software designed to prevent inadvertent violation of software licenses. Such software isn't cheap, but the alternative is often manual tracking. This can mean the network administrator must take affirmative steps to limit who can use the software, or otherwise risk license violations.

Violation of licensing provisions can be costly both monetarily and in terms of one's career. Software licensing is often seen as a sword hanging over the IT department's head. Even an inadvertent violation can result in legal action.

Many software licenses, including those of the most popular commercial network operating systems, require a per-user fee. Although provisions vary, this typically means that in addition to the purchase price of the network operating system, a fee must be paid for every client computer connected to the server. As new client computers are added, new fees must be paid and new paperwork must be tended to.

Contrast this with a Linux/Samba server combination. Both are "free software" covered by the GNU GPL license (this is a free software and Open Source license). This means it's perfectly legal to install multiple copies of Linux and Samba, without informing anyone, without paying anyone, and without worrying about how many computers are connected to them. In fact, it's very easy to obtain a 100% Open Source CD containing Linux and Samba together (as well as Apache and Sendmail and networking software). Such a CD can be legally installed on unlimited computers.

Tip

The term *Open Source* is a common term referring to software whose license states that the software must be accompanied by its source code. Although there is no official definition for the Open Source term, a very widely accepted definition exists at www.opensource.org/osd.html. Throughout this document we have tried to conform to that definition in our use of the term Open Source.

The term *free software* applies to a type of license that requires more than just the inclusion of source code. It also requires that all source used by the free software–licensed program is itself free software and that no free

continues

source–licensed source code can be used in software that is not free software. Free software is designed from the ground up to prevent any proprietary use of itself. Note that free software adheres to the Open Source definition at www. opensource.org/osd.html. By its nature, free software can be always be legally copied, as long as the source code is supplied with the copy. You can learn more about free software at the Free Software Foundation's Web site (www.fsf.org).

The GNU GPL is a standard software license that implements free software. GNU is a software project devoted to creating a free software UNIX clone. In fact, many Linux utilities, including the compiler and the editors, came from the GNU project. For this reason, many people refer to the operating system commonly called Linux as *GNU/Linux*.

GNU stands for *GNU's Not UNIX*. GPL stands for *General Public License*.

Therefore, the Linux/Samba combination's licensing provisions eliminate numerous headaches for the administrator, managers, and the organization.

There's one other trait of Open Source software that's just starting to be recognized as an advantage. Because the source code is open to all, there are more eyes inspecting it. Many Open Source projects, including the Samba project, have incredibly large development "staffs." Although common sense tells us too many cooks spoil the broth, in fact the results to date indicate that Open Source licensing, with its huge development community, produces more reliable software. Even when there are bugs, they're often fixed in a few days.

Ability to Evaluate

With the Open Source licensing comes another powerful benefit—the ability to evaluate. There's no need to negotiate an evaluation copy of the software and no temptation to "temporarily" load illegal copies of software onto evaluation machines.

Caution

Never make illegal installations of commercial software, even if the installation is intended to be temporary or for evaluation only. There are severe penalties associated with such copyright violations.

The vendor could easily find out. Vendors and software associations sponsor "whistleblower" type programs, where an employee with a problem with the company or a problem with you could report your activities.

Evaluations should be done in a vendor-authorized fashion or with legally copyable software.

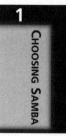

Many Linux distribution CDs contain only Open Source software. With such a CD, it's perfectly legal to use that CD to load Linux and Samba (in other words, a complete file server) on 5, 10, or 100 machines.

Such ability to evaluate reduces the need for excessive research normally associated with the purchase of expensive software, thus reducing implementation time and cost.

Independence

Throughout the history of software, many organizations have felt uncomfortable with the degree of control wielded by their software vendors. Many believe their software vendors create interoperability roadblocks to force them to buy additional software. Others perceive part of the cost of software resulting from their being "locked in" to a vendor's software, thus lacking competitive alternatives.

Samba makes Linux a real alternative to Windows NT and Novell NetWare, thus filling the needs of organizations wanting to achieve a greater level of independence from their software vendors.

Going with the Flow

Linux is growing rapidly in the network operating system arena. Extrapolating over time, if this trend continues, Linux will overtake Microsoft Windows NT in the marketplace, at which time network software vendors will make Linux compatibility their top priority. Samba enables the organization to adopt Linux early.

More Modular, Easier to Understand

Modularity has its rewards. Modular software is easier to produce and less susceptible to bugs. Even when there are problems, modular software is much easier to troubleshoot.

The value of modularity doesn't stop there. A modular system is easier to document, easier to teach, easier to understand, and easier to work with.

Modular systems are easier to enhance because it's obvious where the enhancement belongs and where it doesn't. On the other hand, nonmodular systems eventually collapse under the weight of their entanglements and workarounds.

Samba is particularly modular, consisting of a program called nmbd, which interacts with the NetBIOS interface, smbd, which does the rest of the file server work, and smb.conf, a configuration file that tells smbd and nmbd exactly what to do. The server portion of the Samba Suite also includes smbpasswd, which enables entry of Samba encrypted passwords and assists in joining a Samba server to an NT domain. Knowing those four main components means you know most of Samba's file service. Samba's architecture is modular and understandable.

Additionally, the Samba Suite comes with several client utilities, including a program called `smbclient`, which allows a person to access Windows shares from a UNIX machine. These utilities are also modular and easy to understand.

Better Talent

Although it may be easier to find people capable of administering NT and NetWare systems, those people might not be of the same caliber as typical UNIX administrators. UNIX networking is true to networking principles, making its knowledge applicable to other operating systems. Windows NT knowledge, especially taught by some certification mills, may consist more of OS-specific workarounds. To take it a step further, learning Samba is an excellent way to learn Windows networking principles.

Central Administration

Using commodity hardware for servers is very attractive for small businesses, departments, and branch offices. However, as a business grows and these commodity servers multiply, administration becomes a nightmare. A single, high-power UNIX machine running Samba can replace thirty commodity NT or NetWare boxes. This is especially attractive for organizations that already own the high-power UNIX box and aren't maxing it out.

This type of centralization also delivers a cost savings because those servers' licenses can be used elsewhere instead of buying more licenses.

Cost Considerations

What is the real cost of proprietary software? Start with its price and then add the per-seat licensing fees. Add in the labor expended in license tracking, as well as possibly the cost of license-tracking software. Then there's the cost of vendor dependence—being forced to buy only software compatible with the vendor's software. Now, compare this with the Open Source development process, which is widely perceived to produce better products, thereby reducing costs.

Samba Disadvantages

Samba's not perfect. Disadvantages include the lack of directory services, the need to hire additional expertise, the shortage of technologists capable of supporting Samba and UNIX, the lack of a legally responsible party, and corporate politics. Additionally, most midsize and large businesses need at least one Windows NT server anyway, so why bother with alternatives?

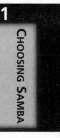

NT Servers Are Often Needed in Addition to Samba

File and print serving capability was one of the factors limiting the encroachment of Linux on NT turf, but others still remain. Many organizations have applications requiring SQL Server on the back end, and others use MS Exchange. These are not the only examples. Given that NT Server must remain for the foreseeable future, why bring in a second OS and file server technology? This must be weighed against the Samba benefits.

No Directory Services (Yet)

Novell NetWare has had NDS for a while now, and it's working great. Directory services immensely reduce administration work and headaches as well as yield a more organized network. Windows 2000 promises to have directory services soon.

Samba's implementation of LDAP (Lightweight Directory Access Protocol) directory services is still experimental.

Additional Expertise Needed

The introduction of Samba and Linux means an entirely new technology to support, with the need to obtain additional expertise. Given the high price of good talent, this is a serious issue.

Mitigating this is the fact that UNIX-aware administrators tend to have a better grasp on networking concepts than many NT administrators, especially those trained in certification mills. UNIX administrators are often quite capable of handling NT Server issues and are often more productive in multiplatform environments.

Nobody to Support the Software

Samba is free software, so essentially there's no vendor to support it. Unlike proprietary software, there's no 800 number to dial for immediate tech support.

That being said, Linux has won media awards for technical support excellence. This has come about due to mailing lists and newsgroups. Since then, commercial service organizations have begun supporting Linux and its apps in the traditional tech-support manner.

Given that most commercial software vendors' support leaves much to be desired, this disadvantage is more a matter of perception than fact.

Nobody to Sue

The GNU GPL license very strongly disavows any warrantee or responsibility. Samba is produced and maintained by a number of private individuals spanning the globe. If a Samba failure causes massive data loss and business loss, who can be sued? Nobody. The acceptance of Open Source software effectively means you're on your own legally. The only remaining question is, who would you sue if software from a large software vendor caused data loss and damage? Such vendors have huge legal departments. Would it be prudent to sue them, especially given that their license agreements likely disavow any warrant of merchantability or fitness?

The choice comes down to which software lessens the likelihood of such damage.

Politics

No one ever got fired for buying _____ (fill in the blank). The names have changed over the years, but the answer has always been a large commercial outfit. Samba is not such an outfit.

In fact, many organizations have either written policies or unwritten rules forbidding Open Source software. Such policies have varying stated reasons. Often the background motivation is simply "playing it safe."

It's often easier to wait than to try to buck such a political trend. Open Source software has been proving itself a high-quality alternative. The media and upper management are watching this closely. If Open Source continues to provide a superior alternative to commercial software, political barriers to Samba will crumble.

Enlisting Support

Samba is not yet considered a mainstream technology, so choosing Samba isn't quite a "no brainer." A successful Samba implementation requires support from inside your company as well as from outside your company—from upper management, middle management, fellow technical employees, and users.

Existing Samba Sites

Your best resources in the advocacy or administration of Samba are administrators at existing Samba sites. They're your best allies. They're living proof that Samba works, and they're excited about it. They can email, phone, or personally demonstrate Samba to your management team or even help you demonstrate it.

Linux User Groups

The place to meet Samba administrators is at Linux user groups. Linux user groups, commonly called *LUGs*, exist in every major city. Some cities have multiple LUGs.

Attending LUG meetings is easy and painless. Find your nearest LUG using a search engine query on LUG and your city, go to the LUG's Web site to find out the date and location of the next meeting, and then show up.

LUGs generally welcome everyone. Those presently working with Linux are welcomed for obvious reasons. Windows users are also welcome, as they can often influence the adoption or evaluation of Linux in the corporate IT department.

You'll find no shortage of Samba experts at your local LUG. Many will be system administrators working with large networks including both NT and Samba file servers. They'll know the ins and outs, the security issues, and the little tricks to make Samba perform.

Samba administrators at LUGs love Samba and want to see it implemented in other organizations. They'll often bend over backwards to help you introduce and maintain Samba in your organization.

Helpful Advocates

Helpful advocates abound in email, newsgroups, and user groups. These people love Samba and consider it their duty to help others promote it. They're a great source of information and support.

Upper Management

Ultimately nothing succeeds without support from upper management. These people generally have less of a technological bias; they simply want the software that meets today's needs and tomorrow's strategies.

Massive Samba implementation should not be attempted without upper management support. Until that support is gained, Samba is best brought in at the departmental or task level, where it can be self-contained. Also, care should be taken not to offend the IT department.

Upper management responds to business benefits. Reduced cost is one such benefit, but only if it can be demonstrated that the total cost is reduced. Saving a few dollars on server software won't cut it here.

Perhaps the best benefits to discuss with upper management are reduction of project failures and dead-end prevention.

Reducing Failed Projects

The cost of projects never completed is staggering. Even when projects reach completion, they're usually late and over budget. The primary cause of abandoned, late, or over-cost projects is typically unexpected factors and problems.

This is where Samba, Linux, and UNIX shine. They're well known and well documented. UNIX is over 30 years old. Samba and Linux, although younger, have made their source code available to all wanting to see it. Although such source code might not serve as documentation for the purposes of project management, it does guarantee that no problem long remains undiscovered or unrepaired.

The availability of source also makes documentation easier and ensures a rich supply of Samba experts. In the ultimate worst case, source availability gives an escape route from any trap or dead end. The organization can hire programmers to add a "must have" feature. Although this is unattractively expensive, many IT departments have wished for just this option when dealing with commercial software.

The theoretical benefits of Open Source are, in fact, demonstrated by its consistently solid performance. UNIX, Linux, and Samba have few of the intermittent and unexplained problems that plague so much of today's software.

In short, choosing Samba and UNIX or Linux helps prevent failed projects.

Preventing Dependence on a Single Proprietary Technology

Large commercial software outfits have a long and rich history of locking their customers into their software. They do this simply by taking advantage of incompatibilities between their software and that of competitors. This fact is not lost on upper management.

The Samba project is a study in interoperability. Coming from behind, it has consistently added interfaces to Windows features and protocols soon after Microsoft introduced them. Although Samba is not a guarantee against getting boxed in, it certainly lessens the danger.

Technical Management

Although upper management concerns itself with matters of strategy, technical management must bend technology to make those strategies happen. It's a big job, often undertaken with too little money, too few good technologists, and too much political flack.

The key to technical management buy-in is making their lives a little easier.

Loosening the Budget Squeeze

Some managers have adequate budgets to fulfill their automation responsibilities. Some don't. Even the ones with adequate budgets often encounter unexpected and expensive unbudgeted technological demands.

Such budget squeezes are made for Samba. For example, take a 20-person satellite office that's newly created and must have a file server. NT Server with 20 user licenses is expensive and requires a substantial hardware investment to run efficiently. On the other hand, a hand-me-down PC can be outfitted with Samba at no cost. With NT Server, the manager begs for funds and whines that the server was unbudgeted. With Samba, he simply reports that the job is completed.

> **Note**
>
> Obviously a high-quality server with a RAID array and quality backup facilities is preferable and should go in the next year's budget. However, it's nice to know a reasonable file server can be quickly rolled out at the salvage cost of yesterday's high-power desktop machine.

Limiting Licensing Hassles

Although network administrators often set up and enforce licensing, the ultimate responsibility rests with technical management. It's their heads that are on the block if the company is caught in a licensing violation.

Every copy of every piece of commercial software has a license, usually with voluminous fine print. Anything that can reduce licensing hassles helps the technical manager.

Being free software, Samba and Linux can be legally copied on as many machines as desired. Such copies require no further attention to licensing.

Limiting Embarrassing Glitches

Samba, Linux, and UNIX have well-earned reputations for reliability. Once set up correctly, they tend to perform consistently day after day. This limits embarrassing glitches.

Technical managers have enough to do without unpleasant surprises. Consistently reliable systems are a big selling point.

Suggesting Samba Implementation Tactics and Strategies

Technical managers might not be familiar with Samba, UNIX, or Open Source software. They might not understand the workings of Samba or why it's inherently so reliable. They may have heard that it's difficult to set up (this book will disprove that myth).

Explain Samba to technical management. Explain what it is, why it costs nothing, what it can do, what it can't do, and how to work around what it can't do.

Explain how to implement it. Different implementation strategies fit different organizations. Some find it best to dive right in, whereas others find it better to start with an isolated temporary server in a relatively unimportant area. Many organizations first use Samba in the software development department, where there's plenty of talent to make sure it works right.

Fellow Technical Employees

Lucky is the technologist who works a mere 50-hour week. Most technologists work more and then are on call for those inevitable emergencies. Technical employees love reliable systems, and they're in a position to know how reliable Samba is. Samba is an easy sell for fellow technical employees.

The one fly in the ointment is a perception that Windows skills are more marketable than UNIX or Linux skills. Although right now there are more jobs in the Windows world, there's considerable evidence that UNIX and Linux salaries outpace those of equivalent Windows positions. There are more than enough jobs to go around for those proficient in Linux and UNIX.

Eliminating Most Crashes and Downtime

The only thing worse than a tough 60-hour week is a tough 60-hour week followed by a two-day emergency. With slimmer staffs and more users with less training, the technologist's life is often an exercise in fire fighting. Fire fighting is the bane of the technical employee's existence. The employee is grateful for any relief from emergencies.

Enter Samba reliability. Fewer emergencies, less unscheduled downtime, the ability to plan and schedule, and, of course, less overtime. Most technologists do not dispute that UNIX, Linux, and Samba are more reliable than their Windows NT counterparts, and they're in a position to truly appreciate that reliability.

More Fun, Less Frustration

Most technologists chose their profession for the fun. The excellent salary is a consequence of the choice, not the main reason. The better the technology, the more the fun.

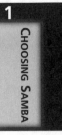

Good technology produces predictable results based on logic and good design. Quirky and intermittent systems are not good technology, and they're not fun. Most technologists resent the need for workarounds to compensate for inadequate design. The technology can be difficult. That's half the fun. But to be fulfilling, it must follow the laws of cause and effect.

Samba is highly modular, primarily consisting of the `nmbd` `netbios` interface, the `smbd` daemon, the `smb.conf` configuration file that tells `smbd` and `nmbd` what to do, the `smbpasswd` program, and several client utilities that run completely independent of `smbd`, `nmbd`, `smb.conf`, and `smbpasswd`. Samba is a straightforward and consistent technology, so it's fun to use.

> **Note**
>
> As previously mentioned, Samba versions currently under development have additional daemons, but the modularity principle remains the same.

Users

Users just want to do their work. They're not technologists, and they seldom care about how "cool" the technology is. To the extent a technology helps them do their work, they like it. To the extent it holds them back, they loath it.

Demonstrating OS Transparency

Users prefer consistency, so any change must be either transparent or obviously beneficial to the user. User support depends on it. Things we take for granted as trivial, such as icon appearance or printer names, are a big thing for an employee expending brain power on accounting problems rather than technology problems.

Samba does a great job of mimicking NT Server, so it's not difficult to make the new Samba system look like the existing NT system. To the extent that anything changes, make sure there's adequate user training.

Take nothing for granted. Even problems having nothing to do with Samba will be blamed on Samba. Try not to install Samba concurrently with application software upgrades because the upgrade's bugs and glitches may be blamed on Samba.

Fewer Crashes and Hang Hassles

Users are the ones saddled with crashes, hangs, and blue screens of death. Each such mishap frustrates the user, creates rework, and in extreme cases slows work to a crawl.

Convincing users that a Samba server will reduce crashes goes a long way toward obtaining their support. If Samba has been used successfully in other parts of the organization, word gets out. Make sure to publicize all successes, and make sure users know the extent to which Samba is responsible for decreased crashes.

Alliance-Building Tactics

Alliances are vital in any project or endeavor. Build alliances for your Samba project. Start by finding successful Samba installations, hopefully local ones. Get all the information you can and make sure you still think Samba is right for your organization. Organize a field trip for key technologists and managers to see the technology in action and get your questions answered. Document the benefits as you see them and then document press reports for added credibility. Creating a Samba demonstration can be highly effective.

Finding Successful Installations

The quickest path to success is via imitating others who have achieved your goal. Reports of success give confidence to technologists and management. Documenting the implementation strategies of successful implementations boosts the likelihood of success.

Your acquaintances at Samba-enabled organizations are usually eager to help. They like Samba and want to see others like it. Many consider Samba's alternatives quirky and difficult, and they desire to make Samba popular so that they won't ever need to return to those alternatives. These acquaintances can serve as mentors throughout the process.

The best place to find local successful installations is at your local Linux user group. Every large city has one, and they can be found quite easily on the Internet.

Making Field Trips

"I'll believe it when I see it" is more than a phrase—it's the way most of us make decisions. One picture is worth a thousand words. Technologists seeing a successful Samba installation feel good about signing onto the project. Managers seeing the installation feel confident that they're making the right decision.

The field trip is the ideal place to find out the real facts about Samba, minus the marketing hype. What problems did you have? How did you handle them? Is your system really more reliable? Has it caused interoperability problems with proprietary software?

Field trips to one or more successful installations generate enthusiasm that's hard to put down.

Documenting Benefits

For those not attending the field trip(s), documentation is the next best thing. Document Samba benefits from technological and business points of view as well as from the user point of view. Address any additional costs or cost savings. If there are revenue ramifications (increased uptime of revenue producing systems), that should be documented as well.

Documenting Press Reports

The technology press likes Samba. Unbiased reports and comparisons are a strong component of internal support and enthusiasm. Big, well-known magazines are ideal. Be sure to find articles from magazines the boss reads. A couple hours of Internet research or a trip to the library will yield the information.

Managers rely heavily on information outside the organization to make informed decisions. Giving the boss Samba press reports is an excellent vehicle for enlisting his or her support.

Demonstrating the Technology

This also falls into the "I'll believe it when I see it" category. Get three machines with network cards. Install Linux/Samba on one and Windows (whatever flavor used in your organization) on the other two. Hook them together with a 100Mb hub and Cat 5 cable.

Who can resist the following demo? Change the desktop coloring or layout on one Windows computer and note that its coloring or layout has changed identically on the other Windows computer. This is a truly great demo for any organization desiring uniformity on the desktop. Explain how this can be used to enforce polices, too.

> **Note**
>
> The described demo is actually a little more complicated, because the sequence of logging into and out of each desktop must be right so that one desktop's configuration doesn't "clobber" the changes in the other. This is discussed further in the "Setting Up Roaming User Profiles" section of Chapter 16, "Using Samba As Your Windows 98 Logon Mechanism."

It's no secret this can be done with NT. The point is that Samba can do almost anything NT can do, and do it more reliably and probably at a lower cost.

You also can demonstrate the server hosting an application and/or data for the application. On applications such as MS Access, be sure to correctly configure the `oplocks=` parameter.

Making the Decision in Steps

Not all IT departments roll out their first Samba installation on a mission-critical project. Most view prudent strategy as implementing Samba in steps.

Start with a Proof of Concept

Samba is not for every organization. It's essential to discover any problems precluding Samba for your organization. Will it do what needs to be done? Research goes only so far in answering this question. Eventually, you roll up your sleeves and try it.

Samba makes trying it trivially easy. Unlike other software, there's no need to negotiate an evaluation copy or risk loading an illegal copy on an evaluation machine. Just take an Open Source–only Linux distribution CD and install it on all necessary machines for the proof of concept.

The best proof of concept starts without connection to the existing network. This eliminates any possible damage through error. Once the concept has been proved, it can be expanded and revised. Later, it can be added to the existing network.

The "Backwater" Server

The next step is to place a Samba server where it won't be noticed and doesn't affect much, and where expectations are not high. Examples include as a test server in the software-development department, as a temporary server for a temporary project, and as an unbudgeted special favor used by just a few people.

This serves the same function as a software beta test, allowing for the discovery of issues in a noncritical, low-pressure environment. Failures here can be buried while successes can be announced.

Move Up to a Departmental Server

The next step is using Samba in a visible but limited and self-contained environment. Often, a department needs its own server, with limited interaction with the enterprise-wide WAN. Sometimes a branch office needs a server. These are ideal places for first implementations.

Most of the installation and configuration is done in the administrator's work area. The system can be tested there. By making the Linux box a DHCP (Dynamic Host Configuration Protocol) server in addition to a Samba server, many client configuration issues can be avoided. Assuming all network and electrical wiring has been completed, installing and testing the new server can take a few hours.

Some system administrators prefer to do this work at night when there's no interference. Others like to do it in the day so that they have access to desktop users' passwords and can explain and work out any perceived problems with the users. The interruption to the user is in the neighborhood of 5 to 10 minutes. Most users consider this a small price to pay for understanding how to use the new system.

Make or Procure an Add-On Enterprise Server

The next step involves the Samba server being accessed throughout the enterprise. This has the advantage and disadvantage of high visibility. If it goes off without a hitch, the visibility is an advantage. If there are problems, it's a disadvantage. The purpose of the proof of concept, backwater, and departmental stages is to gain the experience needed to ensure success.

The first enterprise Samba server is preferably a simple file server lacking authentication capabilities. Authentication can be done on one of the many NT servers in the organization. As the number of Samba servers increases and confidence builds, Samba servers can be used as login servers for Windows 9*x* machines. Also, NT machines can use Samba's new PDC (primary domain controller) capabilities. Samba PDC is very difficult to implement in a mixed NT Server/Samba environment, so it's best attempted only for very good reason and with sufficient experience.

Move on from There

Most organizations will be quite happy using Samba to increase reliability and decrease cost, while keeping their NT servers for domain control, Microsoft back-end tools, and other jobs Windows NT does well. Occasionally, organizations want to go further.

Given the industry's history of large vendors "locking in" their customers and getting them "over a barrel," some organizations consider throwing out most or all of their proprietary software. Samba is a key component in that transition, with PDC support enabling Samba to function as both a file server and an NT and Windows 9*x* login device.

Of course, such organizations will sooner or later eliminate Windows on the desktop, at which time, there will be little further need for Samba. UNIX has NFS, after all.

However, the truth of the matter is that Windows desktops will be around for at least the next few years. As long as Windows desktop machines exist, Samba will be there.

Summary

Samba is a file and print server capable of storing files on UNIX, Linux, BSD, and several other platforms as well as serving them to Windows client machines via Network

Neighborhood and the Windows net command. Samba has significant advantages, including reliability, licensing, vendor independence, adherence to the trend, modularity, availability of highly skilled talent, and cost reduction.

Samba isn't perfect. It doesn't yet have directory service, it requires expertise in additional skills, and there's nobody to sue if things go wrong. Also, a perception exists that there's nobody to support Samba, but that perception is rapidly being replaced by the perception of superior service as IT personnel learn to take advantage of mailing list and newsgroup support available for Open Source software.

Samba implementation is like any other project or endeavor in that support must be enlisted. Such support includes people at existing successful Samba implementation sites, upper management, technical management, technologists, and users.

Samba is not right for every organization, so there's a need to approach it in stages, starting with a proof of concept, moving on to a "backwater server" implementation, then to a departmental or branch office server implementation, and finally as part of the enterprise-wide network.

Files and Directories: Windows Properties and UNIX Permissions

by Steve Litt

IN THIS CHAPTER

Samba's role as a file server requires it to store files on a UNIX (or other non-Windows) box, while giving the appearance that the files are on a Windows box. This necessitates Samba storing all Windows (DOS, for practical purposes) file attributes on the UNIX computer. Most of these attributes are stored in the UNIX file's or directory's permissions.

A full understanding of Samba requires understanding of UNIX file and directory permissions, DOS file and directory attributes, and how they map to each other. Additionally, it requires the administration technique of assigning groups to projects and users to groups. These must be understood from the Windows, UNIX, and Samba points of view. Samba adds quite a bit of functionality over and above the UNIX group access paradigm.

After reading this chapter, you'll thoroughly understand the aforementioned information and be ready to tackle other file-serving prerequisites such as networking.

UNIX File and Directory Permissions

UNIX and all its workalikes (such as Linux, BSD, AIX, HP-UX, and the like) have a simple ownership model for file and directory access. Although simple, this model works well and is remarkably flexible.

Every UNIX file is assigned an owner and a group. The owner has a set of permissions (some combination of read, write, and execute), the group has a different combination of the previously mentioned permissions, and "other" people have yet another combination. In addition, there are special permissions such as set user ID, set group, and sticky bit, which fine-tune access to directories and files.

Permission Types

UNIX permission types are simple. The big three are read, write, and execute (run as a program). In addition, there are some special permissions that will be discussed later in this section. Table 2.1 enumerates the three main permission types.

TABLE 2.1 File Permission Numbers

Number	Meaning
1	Execute permission
2	Write permission
4	Read permission

The permission to access the file is determined by the sum of the preceding permissions. For instance, 7 is a combination of all three, whereas 5 is read and execute but not write, 6 is read and write but not execute, and 4 is read only.

Permission Recipient Classes

There are three classes of permission recipients: user, group, and other. Each of these three permission-recipient classes can have a different permission to access the file. The permissions for a particular recipient class are set by a chmod command with the proper permission in that recipient class's digit. There's also a fourth permission (pseudo class) used by the chmod command. All of this will be discussed in the section titled "The chmod Command." These permission classes are enumerated in Table 2.2.

TABLE 2.2 File Permission Recipient Classes

Number	Meaning
1's place	Other users.
8's place	The user is in same group as the file.
64's place	The user is the owner of the file.
512's place	Used for special permissions.

The following command, with comments, shows the preceding information graphically:

```
chmod 4754 helloscript
#      ||||
#      |||`other has read only
#      ||`-group has read and execute
#      |`--user has read, write and execute
#      `---execute file as file's user (dangerous)
```

The special permissions use an octal digit, the one in the 512's place. Table 2.3 enumerates the special permission numbers.

TABLE 2.3 Special Permissions

Number	Meaning
1	Sticky bit
2	Set group
4	Set user ID

Once again, the special permissions are set with the 512's digit of the chmod command. A more detailed discussion of these special permissions follows.

Sticky Bit

The sticky bit can be applied to directories or to files. When applied to a file, the file is saved in memory after first access, thus making it quickly available.

A directory marked with the sticky bit prevents the deleting and renaming of any files and/or directories within that directory, unless the user is the owner of the sticky bit–marked directory or the owner of the file to be deleted or renamed (unless the user is a privileged user such as root).

The sticky bit is very OS and distribution dependent, so it needs to be investigated locally before use.

Set Group ID

Used with a program (not a shellscript), this permission allows the program to be executed as a member of the file's group, giving the program the program's group permissions to all files and directories, thus allowing it more latitude. Of course, this also dilutes security and should be used only as a last resort. It should also be used very carefully, especially with powerful groups.

Set group ID can be very handy with directories. Let's say you have a directory for a specific project called myweb, whose directory is /data/myweb. You create group myweb and add all users needing access to /data/myweb to that group. You set the ownership of /data/myweb so its group is myweb.

But there's a problem. When any user creates a file in /data/myweb, the file's group is the user's primary group, not myweb. Therefore, various members of group myweb cannot modify each other's files without excessively loose permissions (such as chmod 777).

This is where set group ID comes in. Instead of simply setting permissions of /data/myweb to 770 (read and write for user and group), do a set group ID as follows:

```
$ chmod 2770 /data/myweb
```

Now any file created in /data/myweb has a group designation of myweb, regardless of the user's primary group. All users of group myweb can now read and write each other's files in the /data/myweb directory. Naturally, /data/myweb must have group myweb as its group:

```
$ chown  root.myweb /data/myweb
```

Set User ID

Used with a program (not a shellscript), this permission allows the file to be executed as the user named as the owner of the file. Of course, this also dilutes security and should be used only as a last resort. It should also be used very carefully. When used with a file whose owner is root, this is referred to as `suid root` or `setuid root`. Unless used with extreme care, this represents a major security breach. There's usually a better way to accomplish the same goal.

A Set User ID and Set Group ID Example

As an ordinary user, in a directory available to all (this is vitally important to this example), create the following `testset.txt` file:

```
This is testset.txt
```

Set that file as inaccessible to all other normal users with this command:

```
$ chmod 700 testset.txt
```

Now, only the owner can read this file. Next, as the same user, create a Perl program called `testset.pl` to read that file:

```
#!/usr/bin/perl
open(INF, "<testset.txt");
my(@lines) = <INF>;
close(MYINPUTFILE);
print "@lines\n";
```

Set this program as executable to all and set all permissions to owner with the following command:

```
$ chmod 755 testset.pl
```

Now run the program with the following command (notice that you see the contents of `testset.txt`):

```
$ ./testset.pl
```

Now open a second session logged in as a different ordinary user and try the program again. Note that you do not see the contents of the file. That's because the user ID you're presently using has no permission to read `testset.txt`. From the file owner's session, make the Perl program set UID with the following command:

```
chmod 4755 testset.pl
```

An `ls -l testset.pl` command should now yield the following:

```
-rwsr-xr-x   1 myuid  myuid    109 Oct  5 09:44 testset.pl
```

The s in the owner executable permission's place indicates the file has been set suid.

2

FILES AND
DIRECTORIES

Run the program as the non-owner user, and you see the text. This happens because the file has been set to the owner's UID, executes as that UID, and therefore has all rights to `testset.txt` as defined by the `chmod 700 testset.txt` command performed earlier.

Next, as the file's owner, remove the set UID (suid) and replace it with a set group (sgid) with the following `chmod` statement:

```
$ chmod 2755 testset.pl
```

An `ls -l testset.pl` command should now yield the following:

```
-rwxr-sr-x   1 myuid  myuid    109 Oct  5 09:44 testset.pl
```

Note that now the s has moved to the group executable permission's place, indicating that the file has been set sgid.

As a non-owner ordinary user, run `testset.pl` again, and notice you do not get the contents of `testset.txt`. This is because `testset.txt` has all rights for owner but no rights for group. To enable the set group to work, simply give `testset.txt`'s group read rights with the following `chmod` command:

```
$ chmod 740 testset.txt
```

Verify that you once again can see the contents of `testset.txt`. The reason you can read the contents now is because the `testset.txt` file now enables read permission to its group, and the program that reads it (`testset.pl`) is a member of the same group as `testset.txt` and has sgid set.

To verify that the true cause of these changes was the set UID and the set group, you can remove all set UID and set group permissions from `testset.pl`. Notice that once again the other user cannot see the contents of `testset.txt` when running `testset.pl`. Here's the command to remove the set group:

```
$ chmod 755 testset.pl
```

Therefore, you've shown that a user without read rights to a file (in this case, `testset.txt`) can gain read rights to that file through an executable set UID to a user with read rights to that file or a group with read rights to that file.

Used with executables, set UID and set group are serious potential security breaches. Imagine what happens if an executable file grants any old user write rights to `/etc/passwd`. Although nobody would do such a thing, some set UID and set group programs are flexible enough that a determined user can use his power to gain write access to a file he has no business accessing.

The `ls -ldF` Command

Create a directory called `test` and set its permissions as follows:

```
$ mkdir -m777 test
```

Now view the directory permissions of directory `test` with the following command:

```
$ ls -ldF test
drwxrwxrwx   2 username username  1024 Oct 5 10:27 test/
```

Notice the `drwxrwxrwx`. Here's a breakdown of its meaning:

```
drwxrwxrwx
||||||||||`-Other executable
|||||||||`--Other writeable
||||||||`---Other readable
|||||||`----Group executable
||||||`-----Group writeable
|||||`------Group readable
||||`-------Owner executable
|||`--------Owner writeable
||`---------Owner readable
|`----------Directory
```

> **Note**
>
> The exact file mode of the newly created directory depends on the mode of its existing parent directory. Specifically, if the parent directory is `sgid` (a 2, 6, or 7 in the 512's place), the mode of the newly created directory will be `drwxrwsrwx`.

A `chmod 7777 test` command will change the permissions output of `ls -ldF test` to `drwsrwsrwt`. The s designation in the owner and group executable places indicates it's set user id and set group, and the t in the other executable place indicates the sticky bit is on.

The `chmod` Command

The `chmod` command is used to change file permissions in UNIX. The `chmod` command has two methods of use—numerical and symbolic. The symbolic method has the advantage of changing a specific element of the mode without changing the others, and is also easier to understand. The numerical method has the advantage of completely defining the mode, thus guaranteeing the mode to be in a known state.

Using Numbers

Once again, remember the numerical equivalents of the three common file permissions, as shown in Table 2.4.

TABLE 2.4 File Permission Numbers

Number	Meaning
1	Execute permission
2	Write permission
4	Read permission

As mentioned previously, the three user classifications for the purpose of file permissions are user, group, and other. The chmod command can take an octal number as an argument to define all file permissions of a file. The lowest order octal digit defines the permissions of other, the next highest order digit defines group permissions, and the next highest order digit defines user permissions. An even higher order digit is used for special properties of the file. Following is a diagram elaborating on this:

```
$ chmod 4754 helloscript
#        ||||
#        |||`other has read only
#        ||`-group has read and execute
#        |`--user has read, write and execute
#        `---execute file as file's user (dangerous)
```

Each of the three lower-order digits is the sum of the numerical permission equivalents listed in Table 2.4.

Therefore, 7 means execute, read, and write permission. 4 is read only, 6 is read and write but no execute, and 5 is read and execute. Note that to execute a file (that is, run it as a program), it must have both read and execute permissions. It's possible to have write-only permission. In such a case, the file cannot be read or executed, but it can be written by any method not requiring a read (which leaves out many editors).

Start by creating the following helloscript file using vi or some other editor:

```
#!/bin/bash
echo  "hello world"
```

Now determine its permissions with the following command:

```
$ ls -l helloscript
```

The preceding command outputs something similar to the following:

```
-rw-rw-r--   1 myuid  myuid     40 Oct  5 08:42 helloscript
```

In the preceding output, notice that the file lets the file's owner (user `myuid`) and its group (group `myuid`) read and write the file, but others can only read the file. Now note the failure when trying to execute it with the following command:

```
$ ./helloscript
```

The file must be executable. Set it readable and executable for the owner only with the following command:

```
$ chmod 500 helloscript
```

An `ls -l helloscript` command now produces the following:

```
-r-x------   1 myuid  myuid     40 Oct  5 08:42 helloscript
```

Now running `helloscript` produces output. Notice that it will not run unless both read and execute permission are included.

Note that the file is now write protected. Here's what happens when an attempt is made to write it with an `echo` command:

```
$ echo "echo hello again" >> helloscript
bash: helloscript: Permission denied
```

Because the write permission's number is 2, you can add write permission by adding 2 to the 5, thereby giving the file's owner read, write, and execute permission, like so:

```
$ chmod 700 helloscript
```

Now the previous `echo` statement will successfully add a line to `helloscript`.

An interesting exercise is `chmod 200 helloscript`. This enables the file's owner to write to the file using any method not requiring a read. This leaves out the `vi` editor, because `vi` must read the file before writing it. However, an `echo "hello world" >> helloscript` command will succeed because the file is writable by the owner. The owner cannot read or execute the file, because it has neither read nor execute permissions.

Most file permission modifications can be accomplished quite easily with the numeric form of `chmod`. To make `chmod` even easier for the casual user, it can be used with symbolic arguments.

Using Symbols

The numeric form of `chmod` is powerful, and it's easily understood by any person familiar with UNIX with knowledge of octal arithmetic. However, it's not intuitive to or easily remembered by the Windows system administrator with occasional UNIX duties. The symbolic form of the chmod command is more appropriate for such users. The command looks like this:

```
$ chmod recipient_class [+ - =] permission
```

For instance, the following adds write permissions for the file's group:

```
$ chmod g+w myfile
```

If the group already had write permission, the preceding command did nothing. But if it did not, the preceding command added write permission for the group. Permissions can be revoked, as shown by the following command to remove write permissions from the group:

```
$ chmod g-w myfile
```

Multiple permissions can be added or subtracted:

```
$ chmod o-rwx myfile
$ chmod g+rwx myfile
```

The preceding gives read, write, and execute permissions to the group, but revokes read, write, and execute permissions from other users (except the owner, of course). Likewise, multiple recipient classes can be given to or revoked from a permission:

```
$ chmod go-w myfile
```

The preceding removes write permission from group and other users. Going a step further, multiple permissions can be granted to multiple recipient classes. The following grants read and write permission to the user and group:

```
$ chmod ug+rw myfile
```

Occasionally it's desirable to set all three recipient classes (user, group, and other) to one set of permissions. The special recipient class identifier a does that. The following command adds read and write permission to user, group, and other:

```
$ chmod a+rw myfile
```

The previously discussed symbolic chmod commands add or subtract permissions rather than setting them. To exactly set the a permission, use the equal sign:

```
$ chmod ug=rw myfile
```

The preceding command sets permissions for user and group to read and write. It removes any existing executable permission for those two recipient classes. Because recipient class other isn't mentioned, its permissions are untouched.

Special permissions can be manipulated using the symbolic form. For instance, the following sets the sticky bit:

```
$ chmod +t myfile
```

The following does a set UID (sets suid):

```
$ chmod u+s myfile
```

The following does a set group (sets sgid):

```
$ chmod g+s myfile
```

The following revokes both the set UID and the set group:

```
$ chmod ug-s myfile
```

Default File-Creation Mode: umask

There's a per-session variable that determines the file permissions of newly created files.

> **Caution**
>
> Before using any umask command with an argument (thereby changing the directory creation default for the session), use the umask command and memorize the result. After completing all experiments, use an umask command to restore the original value. If for some reason you cannot remember the original value, log out and log back in, after which the default umask value will be reinstated.

That variable can be read or written by the umask command. Here's an example:

```
$ umask 022
```

Like the chmod command, the argument is a three or four digit octal number, with the least significant digit applying to other, the next significant digit applying to group, and the next significant digit applying to user. However, each digit represents the permissions *not* given the file. For instance, the script

```
#!/bin/sh
umask 027
touch mytestfile
ls -l mytestfile
```

yields the following output:

```
-rw-r-----   1 username username   0 Oct  5 14:04 mytestfile
```

The 0 in the most significant digit of the preceding umask command means no permissions are removed for owner, whereas the 2 in the 8's digit means write permission (2) is removed, and the 1's digit's value of 7 means all permissions are removed, yielding a file that's read-write for the owner, read-only for the group, and inaccessible for others. Notice that umask does not allow automatic setting of the executable permission.

As mentioned, the umask value is set on a per-session basis. It's set at login according to the value in /etc/profile.

DOS File Attributes

DOS has four file attributes: read-only, archive, hidden, and system. Archive files are files that have changed and *need* archiving, not files that have already been archived and have not changed since. DOS files do not have an "executable" attribute—their file extensions determine executability.

For files, the read-only and archive attributes map completely to Samba, by default, whereas the hidden and system attributes require smb.conf changes for support. In the case of directories, Samba directories are normally neither read-only nor archive.

Read-Only

A file with the read-only attribute cannot be written to or erased by the DOS shell, or by normal Windows or DOS applications. However, certain applications can modify or erase such files. An example is Windows Explorer, which upon a delete request on the file prompts for verification of deletion of a read-only file.

Archive

A file with the archive attribute set *needs to be archived*. All newly created files have the archive attribute set. Upon being backed up by a backup program, the archive attribute is cleared.

Hidden

Hidden files do not show up in normal directory listings or the Windows Explorer program in its default configuration. They are completely accessible by filename but cannot be found by browsing.

Hidden files can be edited by normal applications but cannot be deleted. The purpose of hidden files is to keep out the curious.

System

System files are very much like hidden files. System files do not show up in normal directory listings or the Windows Explorer program in its default configuration. They are completely accessible by filename but cannot be found by browsing.

System files can be edited by normal applications but cannot be deleted. The purpose of system files is to keep out the curious.

The system attribute is meant to designate files vital to the operating system.

Executable Status Determined by File Type

UNIX determines executability by the existence or absence of the execute permission. Windows and DOS determine executability from the file type (file extension). The following file extensions indicate executable files:

- `exe`
- `com`
- `bat`

Other files cannot be executed.

Windows Access Control Lists

Each file and directory on a Windows system has an Access Control List (ACL). An ACL is a list of users and/or groups having access to its files and directories and defining the type of access each user and group has to the file or directory. There is no such thing in UNIX, where access is determined by user ID and group membership. Fortunately, Samba expands the UNIX control mechanism to allow multiple group access to a directory but not to an individual file.

ACLs are most evident while converting from an NT file server to a Samba file server.

Windows 9x Share Permissions

Windows 9x computers can share their directories and printers. The type of access control is set in the Access Control tab of the Network Neighborhood Properties dialog box. Access control can be either share level, meaning a single password accesses that share for any user, or user level, meaning that only certain users can access shares. The access control level is global for all shares on the Windows 9x computer.

In addition, each share can be shared as a read-only share, a full share (meaning both read and write), or a "depends on password" share, meaning one password suffices for read-only access, whereas another password allows the user read-write access.

Windows 9*x* shares are created by right-clicking the directory, choosing Share off the pop-up menu, and filling out the dialog box. If the system-wide access control level is user level, the dialog box has a list of users who can access the share as well as buttons for adding, removing, and editing such users.

UNIX User and Group Strategies

Access to system resources is determined by user IDs and group memberships. This exactly mirrors real life, where access and privileges are determined either by one's identity (for instance, season tickets to football home games), or by membership in a group (for instance, student discounts at the computer store). In the case of group membership, such membership is determined by one's identity (for instance, student #3432 has passed the entrance requirements and paid his tuition). Once again, notice the exact parallel between user and group on the network, and real life. The reason network access is so universally determined by user and group is precisely because it so closely mirrors real life. There are many strategies for mapping between resources, user IDs, and groups.

The User's Primary Group

The user's primary group is the group ID in his /etc/passwd entry. Unless affirmative steps are taken to avoid it, files created by a user have a group ownership defined by their primary group. As you'll see later in this book, the primary group has Samba ramifications.

User Private Groups (Used by Red Hat)

Upon user creation, Red Hat Linux automatically creates a group with the same name as the user, and it uses that new group as the user's primary group.

As you continue to read about User Private Groups, you'll notice that this is not a feature of Red Hat. It's simply a strategy where each user is given a primary group named after his username, and the system default umask is set to 002 instead of 022.

Advantages

Typically groups are mapped to projects, such that a user on many projects is assigned to many groups. As explained in the "Set Group ID" section of this chapter, by setting a directory's group to the group name and doing a set group on the directory, all files written to such a directory will bear the group designation of the directory itself, meaning all people in that group can write all files in that directory, regardless of which user created them.

To accomplish this magic, the system's default umask must be set to 002 instead of the usual 022. This is because newly created files need write permission at the group level so that group members can write each other's files. But if the umask default is 002, and the users' primary groups are set to user or some other generic group, everyone will be able to write everyone else's home directory files—clearly not a desired outcome. To get around this, the User Private Groups methodology creates a primary group named the same as the user ID for each new user ID, after which the system-wide default umask value in /etc/profile can be set to 002.

Disadvantages

The User Private Groups methodology creates a group for each new user. On a network with thousands of users, there will be thousands of groups. This makes group maintenance difficult.

Tips

The use of User Private Groups is not necessary for straight-Samba installations, because Samba adds functionality over and above UNIX for handling multiple groups and forcing group ownership of files and directories.

The Group-Per-Project Strategy

The group-per-project strategy is used universally to control access to files for specific projects and groups of people. As discussed earlier in the "User Private Groups (Used by Red Hat)" section of this chapter, a new project called myweb might be given directory /data/myweb and group myweb. With suitable manipulations (an example is the User Private Groups strategy discussed earlier), access to such a directory can be granted on a group basis.

Advantages

The group-per-project strategy is ubiquitous, extending across the operating system. NetWare has raised this strategy to an art form.

Having a group for each project is a sensible way to implement security, because it enables the administrator to enable and disable user access, as the users enter and leave the project, by adding or deleting the user from the group.

Disadvantages

UNIX has only one group per directory, meaning that two different groups cannot be granted access by group. Take this example: The Human Resources department is assembling a super-secret handbook. All HR people need read permission to the handbook, but only a select few writers require write permission. So what group owns the directory, `hr_personnel` or `handbook`?

Additionally, without going the "User Private Groups" route, file administration becomes difficult. Luckily, Samba enables multigroup access to directories via their `valid users=`, `write list=`, and `force group=` attributes.

Samba User and Group Strategies

Samba's access control mechanisms are amazingly versatile. At a directory level, there's almost no access scenario that cannot be realized.

Best of All Worlds

Samba enables multigroup access to directories, without the need of set group ID or `umask` commands or any of the gyrations necessary to accomplish this in UNIX.

The User Gets a Single Directory Tree

Samba has a share called `[homes]` that enables each Samba user access to a directory. By default, that directory is the user's home directory (`/home/username`). This can be problematic because the dot files (`.profile`, `.bash_profile`, and so on) are accessible through Samba. A Windows user might not realize the importance of these files and delete or corrupt them.

Keeping the User Away from Dot Files

Including a simple `path=%H/smbhome` in the `[homes]` share will redirect the share to a `smbhome` directory below the user's home directory. The `%H` is a replacement symbol for the user's home directory, so the effect is the `smbhome` subdirectory below the user's home directory.

Additionally, server-side automation is used to create that directory if it doesn't exist, because, of course, it won't exist when a new user logs in. Server-side automation is discussed in Chapter 14, "Using Samba Server-Side Automation." To test this feature without using server side automation, log into the UNIX box as a user, and create the directory inside that user's home directory with the following command:

```
$ mkdir -m700 smbhome
```

The Group-Per-Project Strategy

This is the Samba version of the "group-per-project" philosophy that works so well in every environment. It's trivially simple when members of a single group need to create, delete, read, and write files and directories inside the project's directory.

> **Tip**
>
> Permissions to read, write, create, and delete a file do not confer permissions to change its attributes. Only the file's owner can change the file's attributes through Samba.
>
> Because of an undocumented feature of the `create mask=` attribute, even the owner might not be able to change the attributes from Samba. Specifically, if the `create mask=` attribute removes user write permission, the owner cannot remove a read-only attribute from a file.
>
> This can be especially disconcerting because the owner can change the file to read-only through Samba but cannot change it back. Never remove user write permission in the `create mask=` attribute.
>
> `create mask=` also affects a user's ability to change file attributes on a Samba-served file. Specifically, `create mask=` must have an odd number in the other position for access to the hidden attribute, must be odd in the group position for access to the system attribute, and must be odd in the user position for access to the archive attribute. Access to the hidden and system attributes require `map hidden=yes` and `map system=yes`, both of which are no by default.

In the following sections, assume you have a directory called `/data/ourdir` and a group called `ourgrp`. Given these assumptions, here is a synopsis of the procedure to implement a share accessible by group `ourgrp`:

- `mkdir /data/ourgrp`
- `chown root.ourgrp /data/ourgrp`
- `chmod 0770 /data/ourgrp`
- Create the Share

`mkdir /data/ourgrp`

The directory must be created. This will be the directory devoted to the project. Note that project members can easily create subdirectories and trees below this directory. Any such directories have a group of `ourgrp`, so once again their contents are available to all group members.

`chown root.ourgrp /data/ourgrp`

This sets the directory's group to `ourdir`. This is necessary so group members can access the directory in UNIX. As discussed later in Chapter 7, "Determining Samba Access," with a few exceptions Samba accessibility is limited by UNIX accessibility.

chmod 0770 /data/ourgrp

Once again, this enables group members to access the directory's contents. Now that you've set the directory's group to `ourgrp`, the rightmost 7 bestows read, write, and execute permissions to members of group `ourgrp`. Note that it is not necessary to do a set group ID because Samba's `force group=` parameter accomplishes the same purpose.

Create the Share

As user root, add the following share to the `/etc/smb.conf` file and then restart Samba:

```
[ourdir]
path=/data/ourdir
read only=no
valid users=@ourgrp
create mask=770
directory mask=770
force group=ourgrp
```

The brackets indicate that the share's name is `ourdir`. The `path=` statement points to the directory. The `read only=no` setting enables all users of this share to have read/write access, but the `valid users=` command limits access to members of group `ourgrp`. The @ sign preceding the word `ourgrp` indicates that the name is a name of a group rather than a user. This is necessary because the `valid users=` command is normally used to specify users, not groups.

Both `create mask=770` and `directory mask=770` are necessary to ensure that the group has full rights to the directory. This is necessary because access to the directory is granted on the basis of group, not user. The default value of these two parameters would not allow writing to the directory.

Because the `force group=` command is used exclusively to specify groups, no @ sign is necessary. The `force group=` statement is Samba's equivalent to "set grouping" a directory in that it forces all files created in that directory to have group `ourgrp`.

Multiple Groups Can Share Directory Trees

Multiple groups accessing a single directory is a frequent requirement. Often, some groups require read-write access, whereas others require just read-only access. This is easy to accomplish in Samba.

First, create directory `/data/ourdir` and give it `chmod` attribute `0770`. (Owner is root; group is `ourgrp`.)

Next, create the following share in `smb.conf` and then restart Samba:

```
[ourdir]
path=/data/ourdir
read only=yes
valid users=@ourgrp,@writegrp
write list=@writegrp
create mask=770
directory mask=770
force group=ourgrp
```

This is very similar to the previous setup for one group access to the directory. Here are the differences:

- `write list=` is added to grant write access to some groups.
- `read only=` is changed to `yes` to prevent writing by all others.
- `valid users=` now lists more than one group.

Note that this works correctly regardless of the system-wide `umask` setting. This directory will be read-only to any users or groups not enumerated in `write list=`. Only users or groups enumerated in `valid users=` have access to the directory. The `force group=` parameter ensures that all files created through Samba in this directory are group `ourgrp`, so they can be written and read by everyone in `valid users=` and written by everyone in `write list=`. Note that the @ sign before the group names labels them as groups instead of users.

Both `create mask=770` and `directory mask=770` are necessary to ensure that the groups have full rights to the directory. This is necessary because access to the directory is granted on the basis of group, not user. The default values of these two parameters do not allow writing to the directory.

These principles will be further elaborated on throughout this book.

Mapping DOS File Attributes to Samba Permissions

Samba maps excellently to DOS file attributes. By default, toggling the DOS archive attribute toggles the user executable bit on the UNIX side, and toggling the DOS read-only attribute toggles the user write permission on the UNIX side. By default, system and hidden files are not supported. UNIX files beginning with a dot (for example, `.bash_history`) show up in Windows as hidden files but cannot be adjusted to a non-hidden status in Windows.

Hidden files are supported by adding the `map hidden=yes` attribute to the share and making the `create mask=` attribute odd in the 1's place. System files are supported by adding the `map system=yes` attribute to the share and making the `create mask=` attribute odd in the 8's place. Archive files are supported by default because `map archive=` is yes by default, and create `mask=` is odd in the 64's place by default. If either of these defaults is defeated, archive files are not supported. Read-only files are supported as long as `create mask` enables the write permission (that is, 2, 3, or 7) in the 64's place (user). Because the default `create mask=` is 744, this is normally enabled.

Setting Read-Only from DOS Removes the UNIX User Write Permission

The DOS read-only attribute is directly related to the UNIX write permission for the file's user (owner). Upon a file called `test.txt` being created in Samba, its DOS attributes will typically be A (archive). An `ls -l` command in UNIX will reveal its permissions to be something like `-rwxr--r--`, depending on the exact nature of the share. Setting it to read-only from Windows changes the UNIX permissions to `-r-xr--r--`. The user write attribute is removed.

Note that if the file is `-rwxrw-r--` on the UNIX end, setting it to DOS read-only through Samba removes *all* write permissions from the UNIX side. Subsequent removal of the DOS read-only attribute restores *only* the user write permission.

The change can also be made from the UNIX end. Removing the file's user write permission causes the file to acquire the DOS read-only attribute. The group and other write permissions do not affect the DOS read-only attribute.

Setting the Archive Attribute from DOS Sets the UNIX User Executable Permission

The DOS archive attribute is directly related to the UNIX execute permission for the file's user (owner). Upon a file called `test.txt` being created in Samba, its DOS attributes typically will be A (archive). An `ls -l` command in UNIX will reveal its permissions to be something like `-rwxr--r--`, depending on the exact nature of the share. Removing the archive attribute from Windows changes the UNIX permissions to `-rw r--r--`. The user executable attribute is removed.

Note that if the file is `-rwxr-xr-x` on the UNIX end, removing the DOS archive attribute through Samba removes *only* user executable permissions on the UNIX side. Subsequent restoration of the DOS archive attribute restores *only* the user write permission. (Note the behavior difference relative to the read-only attribute.)

The change can also be made from the UNIX end. Removing the file's user execute permission causes the file to lose the DOS archive attribute, whereas restoring the user executable permission restores the DOS archive attribute. The group and other executable permissions do not affect the DOS archive attribute. The UNIX execute permission does not affect the executable status on the Windows end, because Windows deduces executability from the file extension.

Setting the System Attribute from DOS Sets the UNIX Group Executable Permission

The DOS system attribute maps to the UNIX group permission similarly to the relationship between archive and the user executable permission. This mapping is not supported by default. To support it, add `map system=true` to the share and make sure that `create mask=` is an odd number in the 8's place (group). Because the default `create mask=` value is `744`, this requires an explicit `create mask=`.

Setting the Hidden Attribute from DOS Sets the UNIX Other Executable Permission

The DOS hidden attribute maps to the UNIX *other* permission similarly to the relationship between archive and the user executable permission. This mapping is not supported by default. To support it, add `map hidden=true` to the share and make sure that `create mask=` is an odd number in the 1's place (*other*). Because the default `create mask=` value is `744`, this requires an explicit `create mask=`.

Configuring Default New File Permissions

Default UNIX file permissions for files created through Samba are configurable at the share (directory) level in `/etc/smb.conf` using the `create mask=` and `force create mode=` parameters of `smb.conf`. Note that these parameters affect the permissions of regular files, *not* directories.

Setting `create mask=`

This `smb.conf` parameter uses a "bitwise and" to decrease the UNIX permissions derived from the DOS attributes. In fact, the DOS-to-UNIX conversion returns ones (1) in the group and other read and write permissions. The user permissions are mapped to the DOS attributes. The `create mask=` parameter defaults to `744`, which allows newly created Samba files to be read, but not written, by group and other on the UNIX side. To enable adjustment of the DOS hidden and system attributes, the 8's (group) and 1's (other) digits must enable execute, meaning they're odd. Setting `create mask=700` prevents all but the file's owner from reading it, which is exactly what you want in single-user shares. 711 is necessary to enable hidden and system adjustment. For shares gaining access by group, create mask=770 is what you want. 771 is necessary for adjustment of the hidden DOS attribute. Setting create mask=0 makes all newly created files inaccessible on the UNIX side and read-only non-archive on the Windows side. This is undesirable, but it further clarifies the functioning of create mask=.

> **Caution**
>
> If the create mask= parameter removes write permission from the owner, the owner cannot use Samba to remove a read-only attribute from the file, even if he previously set that read-only attribute using Samba.

As mentioned, create mask= decreases UNIX permissions from Samba's DOS-to-UNIX mapping. To increase those permissions, use the force create mode= parameter of smb.conf.

Setting force create mode=

This smb.conf parameter uses a "bitwise or" to increase UNIX permissions from those obtained in Samba's DOS-to-UNIX mapping. The default for this parameter is 0, because it's seldom desirable to allow access to Samba files from the UNIX box. A value of 777 would make all newly created Samba files universally accessible to all users. A value of 760 guarantees that every newly created Samba file is readable and writable on the UNIX side, to members of the file's group.

Note that force create mode= takes precedence over create mask= in any conflicts between the two parameters.

Configuring Default New Directory Permissions

Default UNIX file permissions for directories created through Samba are configurable at the share (directory) level in /etc/smb.conf using the directory mask= and force directory mode= parameters of smb.conf. Note that these parameters affect the permissions of directories, *not* regular files.

Setting directory mask=

This smb.conf parameter uses a "bitwise and" to decrease the UNIX permissions derived from the DOS attributes. In fact, the DOS-to-UNIX conversion returns ones (1) in every permission. The user permissions are mapped to the DOS attributes. Because under normal circumstances Samba directories are read-write and non-archive, this attribute completely determines the UNIX permissions of directories newly created through Samba. A Samba directory can be made read-only, after creation, with a chmod command on the UNIX side.

This parameter defaults to 0755, which allows newly created Samba directories to be read and browsed (executable), but not written, by group and other on the UNIX side.

Setting directory mask=700 prevents all but the file's owner from reading it in UNIX, which is just what's needed for a share accessible to a single user. For shares accessed by group, directory mask=770 is the proper setting. Setting directory mask=0 makes all newly created directories inaccessible on the UNIX side and read-only non-archive on the Windows side. This is undesirable, but it further clarifies the functioning of directory mask=.

As mentioned, directory mask= decreases UNIX permissions from Samba's DOS-to-UNIX mapping. To increase those permissions, use the force directory mode= parameter of smb.conf.

Setting force directory mode=

This smb.conf parameter uses a "bitwise or" to increase UNIX directory permissions from those obtained in Samba's DOS-to-UNIX mapping. The default for this parameter is 0, because it's seldom desirable to allow access to Samba directories from the UNIX box.

Note that this parameter has limited value, because its function can be replicated with directory mask=. Because the DOS-to-UNIX directory mapping creates directories with all bits set, UNIX permissions of newly created Samba directories can be completely controlled with directory mask=.

Note that force directory mode= takes precedence over directory mask= in any conflicts between the two parameters.

Summary

In its role as file server software, Samba must map Windows (DOS) attributes to UNIX permissions and must handle varied project-to-group-to-directory mapping strategies to implement adequate security for an organization's varied and changing needs.

UNIX has three main permissions: read, write, and execute. Every UNIX file or directory has an owner (individual user) and a group. A distinct combination of the three main permissions is given to each file's or directory's owner (user), group, and all others (other). Special permissions such as set group ID enable access via group membership. However, such access frequently requires other "tweaks." One such tweak is the setting of the

global default `umask` to `002` instead of `022`, which has security ramifications if normal users share a primary group. The User Private Group strategy implemented in modern Red Hat installations clears up these security ramifications, but at the expense of creating a new group for every user.

Samba adds considerable functionality over and above native UNIX by use of such `smb.conf` parameters as `valid users=`, `write list=`, `force group=`, `create mask=`, `force create mode=`, `directory mask=`, and `force directory mode=`. Correct use of these parameters enables access by multiple groups to single directories and enables the granting of specific write permissions based on group. This is all done without the `umask` workarounds or other "tweaks" necessary in UNIX.

Windows files have four attributes: read-only, archive, system, and hidden. Only read-only and archive are mapped by Samba, by default, although hidden and system can be accomplished with `smb.conf` changes. Much of the file access and security in Windows is accomplished with Access Control Lists (ACLs), which are not available in UNIX and Samba. However, Samba's ability to map multiple groups with multiple access levels to single directories can be used to accomplish all but the most arcane file security configurations.

The next chapter discusses the widely accepted networking standard in the non-Windows world—TCP/IP networking.

TCP/IP Networking Review

by Steve Litt

In This Chapter

CHAPTER 3

As mentioned in previous chapters, Samba is software for sharing files and printers over a network. Samba works only in the presence of a functioning network—and not just any network. Samba works only with TCP/IP networks. That's not to say it can't interface with Windows machines that are part of a NetBEUI network or other machines that are part of an IPX/SPX network. Modern Windows 9x and NT machines have TCP/IP built in, with no need to obtain a TCP/IP stack from a third party.

Because Samba depends so heavily on TCP/IP, a working knowledge of TCP/IP networking is essential to understanding Samba. This chapter reviews the basic principles of TCP/IP networking.

A single computer is great for doing word processing, playing games, or keeping the books for a one-person company. However, a single computer can be used only by a single person at a single location. No email, no Internet. To give a file to somebody else, it must be copied to a removable disk and walked, driven, or mailed to the other person. Single computers can use only printers directly hooked to them, meaning everyone who prints must have a printer. And if the user's printer is busy, he must wait unless he can put the other file on a removable disk and bring it to a computer whose printer is not busy.

Networking was devised to solve the aforementioned problems. It enables file sharing, email, printer sharing, and Internet use.

Those are the features. The benefit is collaboration between people in different rooms, buildings, states, and even countries. The writing of this book is a perfect example. The main author lives in the state of Florida, and the contributing authors are from all over the world.

Examples in This Chapter

All the examples in this chapter use server `mainserv`, located at `192.168.100.1/255.255.255.0` as the Samba server. All domain names end in `.cxm`. The use of the public IP address and the bogus first-level domain name limits problems if they somehow "escape" onto the Internet.

The user is called `username`, a name unlikely to be confused with genuine users on your system. These examples have been checked on a Celeron-equipped machine running Red Hat Linux 6.0.

If you're following along with this chapter's examples, it's easiest to create a user called `username`.

> **Caution**
>
> Before attempting any of the examples in this chapter, be sure to back up your existing `smb.conf`! This is true for all configuration files.

Networking Terminology

The first step in learning TCP/IP networks is getting a handle on the terminology. Computer networking is a complex topic with many systems, subsystems, technologies, and models. This section explains the following common networking terms:

- ICMP
- ISO/OSI Networking Model
- Broadcast
- Ethernet
- TCP/IP
- IP Address
- Subnet
- Netmask
- UDP
- DHCP
- DNS

Although these are only a few of the network terms, understanding these few terms provides an excellent foundation of networking knowledge.

ICMP (`ping`)

IMCP stands for *Internet Control Message Protocol*. It's a very low-level protocol used by `ping` and `traceroute`. It's also used to deliver messages such as "host unreachable."

On the other hand, `ping`, one of TCP/IP networking's most fundamental diagnostic tools, is used to test connectivity between two networked computers.

ISO/OSI Network Model

The ISO/OSI Network Model is a seven-layer model of networking, the lowest level being the hardware and wire, and the highest being the network-enabled application, such as `telnet` or `ftp`.

ISO stands for *International Standards Organization*, whereas OSI stands for *Open Systems Interconnection*.

Broadcast

Many network topologies consist of multiple computers connected to a single wire. How can information be sent to a single computer?

Often it isn't. Instead, the information is broadcast to all computers on the wire, and each computer "listens" for information intended for it.

An analogy is a raffle. The number is drawn from the hat. No attempt is made by the person drawing the number to "go to" the person with the matching number. Instead, the number is called out to the entire audience. The person with the matching number acknowledges the announcement.

Ethernet

Ethernet is a very low-level network protocol. It breaks up files and other network transmissions into small groups of ones and zeros. These groups are called *packets*. Each computer participating in an Ethernet network has a network interface card (NIC) inside. Each network interface card contains a unique Ethernet address (sometimes called a *MAC address*).

Each packet contains the Ethernet address of the network interface card in the intended destination computer. The packet is given to all but acted upon only by the intended destination computer (the equivalent of yelling "that's my number" at a raffle).

The Ethernet protocol also defines the hardware transporting it. We've already discussed network interface cards. Ethernet packets travel over thin and thick coax cable as well as twisted pair, including Category 5 cable. They can also travel through properly equipped and configured bridges and routers.

Ethernet commonly supports two transmission speeds: 10 megabit per second (Mbps) and 100 megabit per second. In addition, there's a 1 gigabit per second (Gbps) speed that's also available. Ethernet also exists, but it's uncommon and expensive as of this writing. 100Mbps Ethernet is very fast, approaching the speed of modern hard disks, and it's therefore adequate for large file transfer. This becomes important in Samba, where, essentially, the network acts as a hard disk.

10Mbps Ethernet is slower but still sufficient for all but the largest and most intensive file transfers. 10Mbps Ethernet is also less expensive. Network interface cards and hubs supporting it are much less costly, and it can be run on wire that's less expensive than the Category 5 wire required for 100Mbps Ethernet.

The speed of the Ethernet medium doesn't tell the whole story, and it often isn't the bottleneck. The process on the client computer and the server computer can bottleneck the transfer, especially when the server must process data from numerous clients (which is the case in a typical Samba network). The wire can also "clog up" with packets. When packets are on the wire simultaneously, they can collide. These collisions result in re-requests and re-transmissions, clogging up the system with even more packets, leading to more collisions. Such a scenario leads to an avalanche, and can bring the entire network down.

TCP/IP

TCP/IP is the most common network protocol in the non-Windows world. Like Ethernet, TCP/IP is transmitted in packets. Unlike Ethernet, it's normally routed rather than broadcast.

TCP/IP encapsulates Ethernet, with TCP/IP packets wrapping themselves around Ethernet packets. TCP/IP packets are sent over the wiring of a network, occasionally routed by a router or switch, until they arrive at the destination subnet (defined later). Once they arrive at the subnet, lower-level protocols (such as Ethernet) are used to deliver these packets to their exact destinations.

TCP/IP is by far the most widely used network protocol. The entirety of the Internet runs on TCP/IP. Even Windows networks can now communicate using TCP/IP, and it looks like they're starting to favor that over the NetBEUI protocol formerly favored by Windows.

Every TCP/IP packet has an IP address, which is very much like the address on an envelope. At each step along the network, the packet is directed toward the final destination defined by that address.

IP Address

IP addresses are four-byte numbers used as destination addresses. IP addresses are written in the "dotted decimal" notation, with decimal representations of each byte separated by dots (for example, 192.168.100.1). IP addresses are discussed at greater length in the "IP Addresses" section of this chapter.

Subnet

In the old days, the word *subnet* referred to all the computers hooked to a single wire. To get packages from one wire or wire system to another, a router, switch, or bridge was required.

Although all this is still true, subnets in the TCP/IP world typically refer to groups of computers (hooked to a common wire or wire system) that have the most significant bits of their IP addresses in common. For example, a subnet might consist of all computers in an organization whose IP addresses begin with `192.168.100`. This would include `192.168.100.1`, `192.168.100.2`, `192.168.100.121`, and so on.

Subnets are discussed at greater length in the "Subnets and Netmasks" section of this chapter.

Netmask

On its own, an IP address does not specify how much of itself is the subnet address and how much is the computer's address within the subnet. The netmask serves that purpose. It's basically the number bits that define the subnet, whereas the remaining bits define the computer within the subnet.

Netmasks are discussed at greater length in the "Subnets and Netmasks" section of this chapter.

UDP

UDP stands for *User Datagram Protocol*—a fast, simple, and stateless protocol often used with IP instead of TCP. It maintains no permanent connection. It does not handle packet loss or corruption, instead passing that task up to the application.

DHCP

DHCP stands for *Dynamic Host Configuration Protocol*. This is best interpreted backward: DHCP is a protocol to configure hosts dynamically. In this usage the word *host* means "computer." It's simple to set up a DHCP server on a UNIX or UNIX-like box. Once the server is set up, a computer that's set up as a DHCP client and possesses a hostname will use the DHCP server's information to configure itself upon bootup. Among the configuration information that the server can give (if so configured) is the following:

- `option subnet-mask <ip_address>`
- `option router <ip-addresses>`
- `option domain-name-servers <IP addresses>`
- `option host-name <string>`
- `option domain-name <string>`
- `option ip-forwarding <0 or 1>`

- option broadcast <IP address>

- option static routes <IP addresses>

- option netbios-name-servers <IP addresses>

- option netbios-node-type <1, 2, 4 or 8>

- option netbios-scope <string>

The last three are vitally important to Samba, which uses NetBIOS for its name service.

The DHCP Advantage

Each desktop computer has a lot to keep track of. IP address, WINS server, DNS server, NetBIOS mode (which determines how much network traffic Samba activities trigger), and many other items. This is easy with 10 desktop computers. It's doable with 100. But add more, and it's next to impossible.

DHCP does all this for you. Give the Windows desktop a name, set it to be a DHCP client, and plug it in. Simple. A functioning DHCP server makes quick Samba success much more likely.

Windows DHCP Clients

Configuring a Windows desktop computer to gather its configuration from DHCP is a snap. On each Windows client, access the network properties (right-click on Network Neighborhood and then choose Properties). Fill in a unique computer name on the Identification tab as well as the name of the workgroup (presumably the same workgroup as the Samba server). Then, on the Configuration tab, click the TCP/IP protocol for the Ethernet adapter and then click the Properties button to access the TCP/IP properties dialog box.

On the TCP/IP Properties dialog box, click the IP Address tab and its Obtain IP Address Automatically radio button. Then click the WINS Configuration tab and its Use DHCP for WINS Resolution radio button. Click the OK button on the TCP/IP properties dialog box, click the OK button on the Network Properties button, put in the Windows CD when asked, and then reboot when prompted.

Configuring NT Clients

The DHCP configuration is almost the same on a Windows box. Fill in the computer name and workgroup name on the Identification tab and then switch to DHCP on the Protocols tab.

Linux DHCP Clients

To configure a Linux box as a DHCP client, change BOOTPROTO="none" to
BOOTPROTO="dhcp" in /etc/sysconfig/network-scripts/ifcfg-eth0. If this file
contains no BOOTPROTO line, insert BOOTPROTO="dhcp".

Note that the IP address change set in motion by this change may require changes to
other files needing to know the box's IP address—most notably DNS configuration files.

Linux DHCP Servers

DHCP server software comes with most Linux distributions, and either comes with
or can be obtained for most other UNIX and UNIX-like operating systems. Once the
software is installed, setting up a DHCP server is a three step process:

1. Create or modify dhcpd.conf.
2. Create dhcpd.leases if it doesn't exist.
3. Restart the dhcpd daemon.

The best way to find out whether the dhcpd.conf and dhcpd.leases files exist, as well as
where the software expects them, is to run dhcpd in the foreground with this command:

```
$ dhcpd -f
```

If either file doesn't exist, this command will gripe about it and tell you where it expects
to find the file. For further DHCP information, consult *Red Hat Linux 6 Unleashed* and
Linux Unleashed, Fourth Edition, as well as the man pages for dhcpd and dhcpd.conf.

The following is a plain-vanilla sample dhcpd.conf to ease you into this topic.
This particular example serves up client IP addresses in a pool of 192.168.100.200
through 192.168.100.240. 192.168.100.1 is the default router, DNS server, WINS
(netbios-name-servers), and datagram (netbios-dd-server) server. This configuration
enables IP forwarding, sets the domain name to domain.cxm, and sets the WINS lookup
order to an H node via the option netbios-node-type 8; line. This dhcpd.conf gives
clients a Class C netmask of 255.255.255.0. Here's the plain-vanilla dhcpd.conf:

```
subnet 192.168.100.0 netmask 255.255.255.0 {
    range 192.168.100.200 192.168.100.240;
        option subnet-mask 255.255.255.0;
        option broadcast-address 192.168.100.255;
        option routers 192.168.100.1;
        option domain-name-servers 192.168.100.1;
        option domain-name "domain.cxm";
        option ip-forwarding on;
        option netbios-node-type 8;
        option netbios-name-servers 192.168.100.1;
        option netbios-dd-server 192.168.100.1;
    }
```

DNS

DNS stands for *Domain Name Services*. It's a distributed system for correlating names to IP addresses, and vice versa. At present, DNS isn't too important in Samba because, currently, Windows and Samba use NetBIOS for name resolution. However, Windows 2000 enables name resolution via DNS, so it will become much more important.

For further information on DNS, consult *Red Hat Linux 6 Unleashed* and *Linux Unleashed, Fourth Edition*, as well as the named man page.

The ISO/OSI Seven-Layer Networking Model

The ISO/OSI seven-layer networking model serves to explain and define networking. Although no set of software completely and accurately implements this model in its entirety, it still serves as an important source of understanding. Here's a list of the layers:

- *Layer 1: Physical*   This is the hardware, the wiring, and the network topology.
- *Layer 2: Data Link*   This is the layer that splits the data into frames that are sent on the Physical layer.
- *Layer 3: Network*   This layer routes packets from sender to receiver, using the Data Link layer. The most common protocol at this layer is IP.
- *Layer 4: Transport*   The Transport layer provides correct connections so the Network layer can route packets, and it also arranges for the packets to arrive uncorrupted and in correct order. TCP is a common Transport layer protocol, as is UDP.
- *Layer 5: Session*   The Session layer handles security and creation of the session, using the Transport layer for the connection.
- *Layer 6: Presentation*   This layer handles format conversions, compression, and the like, and it also conducts disparately formatted data from the Application layer to the Session layer.
- *Layer 7: Application*   This is the application as seen by the user; ftp, telnet, and various mail programs are all part of the Application layer.

IP Addresses

TCP/IP uses IP addresses to route packets. IP addresses are four bytes long, yielding a theoretical upper limit of 4,294,967,296 (over four billion) destination addresses. In practice, special use of certain numbers and suboptimal divisions into subnets decreases that number markedly. IP addresses have become a scarce commodity.

IP addresses are assigned to computers (or to organizations to use on their computers) by ARIN (American Registry for Internet Numbers) for IPs in North America, South America, the Caribbean, and sub-Saharan Africa. RIPE NCC registers IP addresses in Europe, the Middle East, and parts of Africa. APNIC registers names in the Asia Pacific area. IP addresses are assigned individually or in a block (a series of consecutive numbers).

Because Samba uses TCP/IP networking, IP addresses are a vital component of understanding Samba.

Subnets and Netmasks

Subnets are important in TCP/IP communications because TCP/IP packets cannot cross to another subnet without going through a bridge, router, switch, and so on. This is true even if the two subnets exist on a common wire.

Every IP address conveys two pieces of information:

1. The address of the subnet
2. The address of the computer within that subnet

Some subnets are huge, with all but the first byte identifying the computer. Others are small, with only the last byte identifying the computer. Obviously, the existing subnet space can be carved into more subnets if each subnet is small.

Modern IP addresses do not need to split the subnet on byte boundaries but can, in fact, split on any bit. This is called *classless addressing*, and such IP addresses are called *classless addresses*.

There's nothing within the IP address to specify where the subnet/computer split occurs. That job falls to a second number, called the *netmask*. The netmask is a number that modifies a computer's IP address. It specifies how many bytes are devoted to the subnet. In fact, it's an IP address to be bitwise and'ed to the IP address to yield the subnet address. This netmask (also called *subnet mask*) is typically appended to the network address with a slash or input as a data piece in a file. As a simple example, let's take a look at the following:

`192.168.100.5/255.255.255.0`

This is a typical Class C situation, with the first three bytes specifying the subnet and the final byte specifying the computer within the subnet. Note that bitwise and'ing the preceding subnet with the preceding IP address yields `192.168.100`, which is the network address of the subnet.

Netmasks can also be written as the number of address bits (not bytes) consumed by the subnet. For instance, here's the same subnet mask written as a number of bits:

`192.168.100.5/24`

Note that 24 bits are 3 bytes, so it's the equivalent of `255.255.255.0`. Once again, a bitwise and of the two yields `192.168.100`.

It's obvious that an organization or department or other subnet needing only four IP addresses could split on a nonbyte boundary. Let's say it needs addresses `192.168.100.32` through `192.168.100.35`. This can be accomplished as follows:

`192.168.100.32/255.255.255.252`

Here it is stated another way:

`192.168.100.32/30`

Class A, B, and C Addressing

In the old days, there were three classes of networks (subnets), as shown in Table 3.1.

TABLE 3.1   The Original IP Address Classes

Class	*Subnet determination*
Class A	First byte determines subnet.
Class B	First two bytes determine subnet.
Class C	First three bytes determine subnet.

A Class A network could use up to 16,777,216 addresses, a Class B 65,536, and a Class C 256. This class system resulted in many organizations getting more IP addresses than they needed, thus creating a scarcity of IP addresses for others. To relieve the pressure, classless addressing was instituted.

Classless Addressing

In the early days of the Internet, it was inconceivable that IP addresses would ever become scarce. After all, there were theoretically 4,294,967,296 of them. Even subtracting those that end in `255` (those are typically used for broadcast addresses), those that end in `0` (they typically represent networks), and the private IP addresses (discussed later in this section), there were still in excess of three billion.

But the Internet exploded, requiring huge numbers of new IP addresses. Also, various noncomputer devices required IP addresses because they were hooked to networks and the Internet. And last but not least, the utilization of IP addresses was extravagantly inefficient.

IP addresses were given away in blocks. Class C blocks had 256 addresses, Class B blocks had 65,536 addresses, and Class A blocks (and there are less than 256 of those in the whole system) contained 16,777,216 addresses.

Therefore, an organization needing three addresses often got a block of 256, an organization needing 300 got a block containing 65,536, and an organization needing 100,000 got 16,777,216.

Several years ago, it became apparent that IP addresses needed to be distributed more efficiently, so blocks were no longer distributed on byte boundaries. This put an end to the Class A, B, and C addressing designations, which were based on byte boundaries.

Perhaps the simplest example of a classless addressing scheme is to create a subnet of four numbers (let's say `192.168.100.0` through `192.168.100.3`). This corresponds to an IP address of `192.168.100.0` and a netmask of `255.255.255.252`. The first three bytes are typical network/netmask relationships, so let's look at only the final byte:

Property	*Value*
IP for lowest number (0)	00000000
IP for highest number (3)	00000011
Bitwise and with this number	11111100

Therefore, in the preceding example, the netmask would be `255.255.255.252`, or stated as the number of bits for subnet addressing, `30`.

Now take the example of a four-number subnet in the range `192.168.100.32` through `192.168.100.35`. Once again, let's consider only the last byte:

Property	*Value*
IP for lowest number (32)	00100000
IP for highest number (35)	00100011
Bitwise and for subnet	11111100

Once again, the netmask is `255.255.255.252`, the only difference being the subnet part of the address, which is `192.168.100.32`.

These were simple examples, but exactly analogous methods can be used to figure netmasks for blocks split inside any of the bytes of an IP address.

This is classless addressing. It enables allocation of IP blocks to fit the needs of an organization, thereby conserving scarce IP addresses.

IPV6

To avoid the IP address shortage that's sure to arrive with increasing Internet and connected appliance use, a new system of addressing has been devised. It's called *IPV6*, and it uses 16-byte addresses instead of 4-byte addresses. This yields a theoretical maximum of 3.4e+38 (256^{16}) destination addresses, which should tide us over for awhile.

The Public IP Addresses

Because of the scarcity of IP addresses, three large series of IP addresses have been declared "public," meaning they can be used by anyone, but only within an organization. They cannot (or rather should not) be used on the Internet or between organizational entities. They are as follows:

- 10.0.0.0 through 10.255.255.255
- 172.16.0.0 through 172.31.255.255
- 192.168.0.0 through 192.168.255.255

The first is a Class A, whereas the second could be described as 16 consecutive Class B's. The third is intended to be 256 consecutive Class C's, but it could also be used as a single Class B.

Private IP addresses are useful and appropriate inside an organization. The examples in this book use private IP addresses to prevent "real" IP addresses from inadvertently being sent to the Internet.

Giving Your Network Card an IP Address

Network cards have built-in Ethernet addresses, but they must be assigned IP addresses in software. This is done different ways in different operating systems—and even in different versions and distributions of the same operating system.

This section contains subsections demonstrating assigning IP addresses and other TCP/IP properties in:

- Windows 9*x*
- Windows NT
- Linux

In the case of Linux, several different methods are discussed.

Configuring Your Windows 9*x* TCP/IP Properties

In Windows 9*x*, the IP address is assigned as outlined in the following sections.

Installing the Network Card and Drivers

If not done already, you should physically install the network card inside the computer. Using the CD or floppy disk provided by the network card's manufacturer, follow the manufacturer's instructions to install the card's driver software.

You do not need IPX/SPX or NetBEUI protocols to use Samba, so unless you have an excellent reason to keep those protocols (such as wanting the client to act as a NetWare client), delete them (likewise for any NetWare clients).

If the installation did not install a TCP/IP protocol, click the Add button on the Network dialog box's Configuration tab and choose Protocol, Microsoft, TCP/IP.

If, for some reason, the installation did not install Client for Microsoft Networks, click the Add button on the Network dialog box's Configuration tab and choose Client, Microsoft, Client for Microsoft Networks.

If File and Printer Sharing for Microsoft Networks is not installed, click the Add button on the Network dialog box's Configuration tab and choose Service, File and Printer Sharing for Microsoft Networks.

Bindings

Bindings are what connect adapters to protocols, and protocols to clients and services. They must be properly enabled. There's a Bindings tab on adapter and protocol dialog boxes, including those for the Ethernet adapter and the TCP/IP protocol.

On the Ethernet Adapter Bindings tab, be sure you bind TCP/IP to the Ethernet Adapter.

On the TCP/IP protocol Bindings tab, be sure you bind to Client for Microsoft Networks, and to File and Printer Sharing for Microsoft Networks if you intend the Windows workstation to share its directories or local printer with other computers.

A successful installation includes the following:

- Client for Microsoft Networks (client)
- Ethernet Adapter (adapter)
- TCP/IP Ethernet Adapter (protocol)
- File and Printer Sharing for Microsoft Networks (services)

Configuring the IP Address

Now that the hardware and drivers are in place, the next step is to configure the IP address for the Windows computer. If your server is running DHCP server software, the easy way is to configure your client as a DHCP client, in which case all IP information is obtained from the DHCP server. Otherwise, you should hardcode the information in the TCP/IP Properties dialog box.

Configuring as a DHCP Client

Choosing to make a desktop computer a DHCP client enables that computer to receive the following information (in addition to an IP address) automatically from the DHCP server:

- `option subnet-mask <ip_address>`
- `option router <ip-addresses>`
- `option domain-name-servers <IP addresses>`
- `option host-name <string>`
- `option domain-name <string>`
- `option ip-forwarding <0 or 1>`
- `option broadcast <IP address>`
- `option static routes <IP addresses>`
- `option netbios-name-servers <IP addresses>`
- `option netbios-node-type <1, 2, 4 or 8>`

To configure the client as a DHCP client, access the Network dialog box by right-clicking Network Neighborhood and choosing properties or by double-clicking Network on the Control Panel.

> **Note**
>
> Changing any network configuration in Windows requires the Windows instal-lation CD as well as a reboot after the change. Be sure that you have your Windows installation CD handy and that you're in a position to reboot.
>
> Sometimes you can forgo the CD by clicking a "Skip File" button one or several times, but if the changes actually require a new file, this will lead to problems.

Click the Identification tab, put a network-unique name in the Computer Name field, and put the name of your workgroup in the Workgroup field. Things tend to go better when names do not contain spaces. The computer description field is information text and can contain anything.

Click the Configuration tab, choose TCP/IP protocol, and click the Properties button. You'll be brought to the TCP/IP Properties dialog box.

Click the IP Address tab and click the Obtain an IP Address Automatically radio button. Next, click the WINS Configuration tab and click the Use DHCP for WINS Resolution radio button. There are many other tabs on the TCP/IP Properties dialog box, but a properly configured DHCP server should make modification of those tabs unnecessary.

Click the OK button on the TCP/IP Properties dialog box; then click the OK button on the Network dialog box, and insert your Windows install CD and reboot as requested.

When the machine reboots, its IP address should be one of those in the pool defined by the DHCP server. Use the Windows `route print` command to ascertain that. If there are problems, you can use `c:\windows\system\winipcfg.exe` (`c:\winnt\system32\ipconfig.exe` on NT machines) to release and renew the DHCP lease. Note that this is a command-line program, so read the help given with the `/?` argument. If there are problems, be sure to look at the server also.

Hardcoding the IP Address

You can manually fill in the information supplied by the DHCP server at each client not served by DHCP. To configure the client, access the Network dialog box by right-clicking Network Neighborhood and choosing Properties or by double-clicking Network on the Control Panel.

Click the Identification tab, put a network-unique name in the Computer Name field, and put the name of your workgroup in the Workgroup field. The Computer Description field is information text and can contain anything.

Click the Configuration tab, choose TCP/IP protocol, and click the Properties button. You'll be brought to the TCP/IP Properties dialog box.

Click the IP Address tab and click the Specify an IP Address radio button. Fill in the desired IP address and netmask in their respective fields.

Next, click the WINS Configuration tab and click the Disable WINS Resolution radio button. Then, fill in the desired default gateway on the Gateway tab.

On the DNS Configuration tab, assuming you need DNS on the Ethernet network (as opposed to on Dial-Up Networking), list the desired DNS Server IP's and Domain suffixes in the appropriate list fields.

Click the OK button on the TCP/IP Properties dialog box; then click the OK button on the Network dialog box, insert your Windows install CD, and reboot as requested.

When the machine reboots, its IP address should the one you hardcoded. Use the Windows `route print` command to ascertain that. If there are problems, you can use `c:\windows\system\winipcfg.exe` (`c:\winnt\system32\ipconfig.exe` on NT machines) to release and renew the Ethernet and the DHCP lease. If there are problems, be sure to look at the server also.

IP Self-Testing

After the Windows desktop machine has been rebooted, test its new IP address. You can see the effective IP address by running `c:\windows\system\winipcfg.exe`, (`c:\winnt\system32\ipconfig.exe` on NT machines), choosing the Ethernet Adapter from the list, and viewing the contents of the read-only IP Address and Subnet Mask fields. You can view routing information via the `route print` command (executed in a DOS box).

Once you're sure you have the intended IP address, ping it from a DOS box on the Windows machine. If it pings there, ping it from another machine on the network. Once you have the correct IP address for the machine and you can ping it from anywhere on the subnet, everything's okay.

Configuring Your Windows NT TCP/IP Properties

In Windows NT, do your administrative work as user Administrator. The IP address is assigned as outlined in the following sections.

Installing the Network Card and Drivers

If not done already, physically install the network card inside the computer. Using the CD or floppy disk provided by the network card's manufacturer, follow the manufacturer's instructions to install the card's driver software.

You do not need IPX/SPX or NetBEUI protocols to use Samba, so unless you have an excellent reason to keep those protocols (such as wanting the client to act as a NetWare client), delete them from the Network dialog box's Protocols tab. Likewise, delete any unnecessary NetWare clients from the Services tab.

If the installation did not install a TCP/IP protocol, click the Add button on the Network dialog box's Protocols tab and choose TCP/IP Protocol from the list. Then click the OK button.

If, for some reason, the installation did not install Workstation, Computer Browser, and NetBIOS Interface on the Services tab, add them.

Bindings

Bindings are what connect adapters to protocols, and protocols to clients and services. They must be properly enabled. NT has its own Bindings tab on the Network dialog box. This tab has a tree interface. There are actually three trees. The tree displayed depends on whether All Services, All Protocols, or All Adapters is chosen from the Show Bindings For list.

Start with the All Services tree. Make sure both the NetBIOS Interface and the Workstation are bound to the WINS client.

On the All Protocols tree, make sure both the TCP/IP protocol and the WINS Client (TCP/IP) are bound to the Ethernet Adapter.

Finally, on the All Adapters tree, make sure the Ethernet Adapter is bound to the TCP/IP protocol and the WINS Client (TCP/IP). Because of the work you did on the All Services tree, the WINS Client (TCP/IP) should be further bound to both the NetBIOS Interface and the Workstation.

A successful installation includes the following:

- Workstation (service)
- Ethernet Adapter (adapter)
- TCP/IP (protocol)
- NetBIOS Interface (service)

Configuring the IP Address (NT)

Now that the hardware and drivers are in place, the next step is to configure the IP address for the Windows NT computer. If your server is running DHCP server software, the easy way is to configure your client as a DHCP client, in which case all IP information is obtained from the DHCP server. Otherwise, you should hardcode the information in the TCP/IP Properties dialog box.

Configuring NT As a DHCP Client

Configuring a desktop NT computer as a DHCP client enables that computer to receive the following information (in addition to an IP address) automatically from the DHCP server:

- `option subnet-mask <ip_address>`
- `option router <ip-addresses>`

- option domain-name-servers <IP addresses>

- option host-name <string>

- option domain-name <string>

- option ip-forwarding <0 or 1>

- option broadcast <IP address>

- option static routes <IP addresses>

- option netbios-name-servers <IP addresses>

- option netbios-node-type <1, 2, 4 or 8>

- option netbios-scope <string>

To configure the client, access the Network dialog box by right-clicking Network Neighborhood and choosing Properties or by double-clicking Network on the Control Panel.

> ### Note
>
> Changing any network configuration in Windows NT may require the Windows NT installation CD as well as a reboot after the change. Be sure that you have your Windows NT installation CD handy and that you're in a position to reboot.
>
> Sometimes the CD isn't requested, and other times you can forgo the CD by clicking a "Skip File" button one or several times, but if the changes actually require a new file, skipping the file(s) will lead to problems.

Click the Identification tab, put a network-unique name in the Computer Name field, and put the name of your workgroup in the Workgroup field. Life is easier if the names do not contain spaces.

Click the Protocols tab, choose TCP/IP Protocol, and click the Properties button. You'll be brought to the TCP/IP Properties dialog box.

Click the IP Address tab and then click the Obtain an IP Address Automatically radio button. Next, click the WINS Address tab. Choose the proper adapter from the Adapter list, fill in the IP address of the DHCP server in the Primary Wins Server field, and, if desired, add another potential WINS server in the Secondary WINS Server field.

Leave the Enable DNS for Windows Resolution, Enable LMHOSTS Lookup, Import LMHOSTS, and Scope ID settings alone, unless you have a good reason to change them. You may want to temporarily blank them out for troubleshooting reasons, but be sure to remember their original contents.

Click the OK button on the TCP/IP Properties dialog box; then click the OK button on the Network dialog box, insert your Windows install CD, and reboot as requested.

When the machine reboots, its IP address should be one of those in the pool defined by the DHCP server. Use NT's `route print` command to ascertain that. If there are problems, you can use `c:\winnt\system32\ipconfig.exe` to release and renew the Ethernet and the DHCP lease. If there are problems, be sure to look at the server also.

Hardcoding the NT IP Address

You can manually fill in the information supplied by the DHCP server at each client or at certain clients. To configure the client, access the Network dialog box by right-clicking Network Neighborhood and choosing Properties or by double-clicking Network on the Control Panel.

Click the Identification tab, put a network-unique name in the Computer Name field, and put the name of your workgroup in the Workgroup field.

Click the Protocols tab, choose TCP/IP protocol, and click the Properties button. You'll be brought to the TCP/IP Properties dialog box.

Click the IP Address tab and click the Specify an IP Address radio button. Fill in the desired IP address, netmask, and default gateway in their respective fields. Be sure to choose the proper adapter from the adapter list.

On the DNS tab, assuming you need DNS on the network (as opposed to on Dial-Up Networking), list the desired DNS Server IP's and Domain suffixes in the appropriate list fields.

Click the OK button on the TCP/IP Properties dialog box; then click the OK button on the Network dialog box, insert your Windows install CD, and reboot as requested.

When the machine reboots, its IP address should be the one you hardcoded. Use the `route print` command to ascertain that. If there are problems, you can use `c:\winnt\system32\ipconfig.exe` to release and renew the Ethernet and the DHCP lease. Note that this is a command-line program, so read the help given with the `/?` argument. If there are problems, be sure to look at the server also.

IP Self-Testing

After the Windows desktop machine has been rebooted, test its new IP address. You can see the effective IP address of the adapter from a DOS box by running `c:\winnt\system32\ipconfig.exe`. You can view routing information via the `route print` command (executed in a DOS box).

Once you're sure you have the intended IP address, ping it from a DOS box on the Windows machine. If it pings there, ping it from another machine on the network. Once you have the correct IP address for the machine and you can ping it from anywhere on the subnet, everything's okay.

Configuring Your Linux TCP/IP Properties

The Linux population is skyrocketing. Linux is now found in many departments and organizations. For that reason, we'll discuss IP configuration in Linux.

> **Caution**
>
> Most configuration programs, including `linuxconf` and `lisa`, write to text configuration files. They aren't always clear on which files are being written. Although these configuration utilities usually "do the right thing," for the sake of safety, you might want to back up your `/etc/` tree before using them. Some administrators use the RCS revision control program to accomplish this.

Different Linux distributions come with different configuration tools. Using these tools is easier—*much* easier for beginners. Nevertheless, the fallback plan is always editing configuration files. Linux users are fortunate that their entire operating system can be configured by editing text files.

This section will discuss four IP configuration methods:

- `netconf`
- `lisa`
- COAS
- Configuration files

Using `netconf`

`netconf` is part of `linuxconf`, a software project not affiliated with any specific Linux distribution. However, because it ships with Red Hat Linux, it's often mentioned in the same sentence as Red Hat. The `netconf` tool has the huge advantage of being text based, meaning there's no necessity for a working X system. It's a CURSES app, so it has easy-to-use menus and other components manipulated by cursor keys. However, the CURSES nature of it prevents its use in a teletype-only `telnet` session (such as from Windows).

`linuxconf` is a single-point configuration tool. It calls `netconf` to configure the network, so for the rest of this section, I'll refer only to `netconf`.

Start `netconf` by typing **netconf** on the command line of a Red Hat or other `linuxconf`-enabled Linux box. You'll see a menu. Depending on the version of `netconf`, this menu has various choices. Typically, it's divided into client tasks, server tasks, and misc. Most of what you'll be doing is in the client tasks category.

`netconf`: Basic Host Information

First, choose (by cursoring down and pressing the Enter key) Basic Host Information. There's a field to fill in the hostname (with domain appended), after which there's a scrollable list to define any and all network adapters. Let's assume you have one adapter. The following paragraphs discuss how you fill it out.

To begin, verify that the Enabled checkbox is checked. If you want the Linux box to receive its configuration information from a DHCP server, select the DHCP radio button in the Config Mode radio button set. Otherwise, select the Manual radio button.

The Primary Name + Domain field typically contains the computer's hostname appended with the domain, just like the Host Name field at the top. The Aliases (opt) field typically contains the hostname without the domain.

Input the IP address and netmask in their respective fields, unless you selected DHCP for the Config mode. Typically, the Net device and Kernel module will have already been correctly input by installation procedures, and they are typically best left as is.

When the Basic Host Information screen is completed, tab to the Accept button and press Enter.

`netconf`: Name Server Specification

Choose Name Server Specification (DNS) from `netconf`'s main menu. This brings you to a screen to define what DNS server(s) this DNS client uses. This is the type of information that ends up in `/etc/resolv.conf`. This is *not* a definition of server capabilities of this box.

Enter the IP addresses of any nameservers this machine queries for DNS. If the machine, itself, has a working DNS server, then its own IP can be included. Also, input any search domains.

netconf: Hostname Search Path

This determines the correct search order between the hosts file, NIS, and DNS. Choose the radio button corresponding to the one you want. If you don't know, leave it as is (hosts, dns is usually a safe choice).

netconf: Other Menu Choices

The previously mentioned netconf menu choices are usually sufficient, but if the IP address is changed occasionally, this necessitates other changes, especially in certain server capabilities.

Using lisa

Older versions of Caldera Linux used lisa. It's still available in Caldera 2.2, and it's still an excellent tool. Like netconf, lisa is a CURSES-enabled console application.

lisa starts with a main menu containing Verbose System Analysis, Software Package Administration, System Configuration, and Start LISA Help System. All are very useful and handy, but to set the IP address choose System Configuration, which brings up another menu. Choose Network Configuration from that menu; then choose Configure Network Access and then Configure Network Card. This runs a wizard that queries for various NIC configuration items, including its IP address and netmask. If you get any of these wrong, just run the wizard again.

If this Linux box performs any server activities, you may need to change other lisa parameters. This isn't hard because it's a very user-friendly program.

Caution

Various prompts in lisa imply that an ongoing edit can be aborted with the Esc key. In fact, this is not always true. Generally speaking, the Esc key only aborts changes made on the present screen.

Using COAS

COAS stands for *Caldera Open Administration System*. On the KDE menu, choose COAS, Network, Ethernet Interfaces. A "Welcome to COAS" splash screen will appear, telling about use and help in COAS. Click OK to get to the Ethernet Interface Configuration dialog box.

Choose the proper network device (probably eth0); then change the interface address, network mask, broadcast address, and default gateway, as appropriate. Click OK. A prompt will ask you whether you want to save the information or discard it. Choose Save unless there is a problem with the session, in which case choose Discard. If you discard, go back in to verify that all changes were indeed discarded.

Editing the Configuration Files

Linux (and most UNIX workalikes) gives the option of configuration by editor. This means that if you can get up a kernel capable of running the ubiquitous vi editor, you can configure your system.

Of course, you need to know which files to edit and what to do with them. This section explains how to set the IP address in the configuration files.

There's also a potential problem in that direct editing of these files could conceivably get them out of sync with automated configuration utilities such as linuxconf, lisa, and COAS. Fortunately, most of these utilities usually seem to accurately go back and forth with ASCII configuration files.

Different UNIX and Linux systems are different, so your mileage may vary. The following list of IP address configuration files is based on a Red Hat 6.0 installation. In this list, the change to /etc/sysconfig/network-scripts/ifcfg-eth0 actually changes the IP address. The remaining files may require changes in order to keep them consistent with the new IP address. Here are the files to change:

- /etc/sysconfig/network-scripts/ifcfg-eth0
- /etc/sysconfig/network-scripts/ifcfg-eth0:0
- /etc/hosts
- /etc/sysconfig/network
- /etc/named.conf
- /etc/smb.conf
- /etc/resolv.conf
- /etc/dhcpd.conf
- /etc/dhcpd.leases

Note

The locations of the files in the preceding list are correct for Red Hat Linux, but some of the file locations vary between Linux distributions and according to installation methods.

`/etc/sysconfig/network-scripts/ifcfg-eth0`

`/etc/sysconfig/network-scripts/ifcfg-eth0` defines the `eth0` NIC interface. To the extent that you have other network cards, you may need to modify files named `ifcfg-eth1`, `ifcfg-eth2`, and so on.

Set the `IPADDR=` line to the desired IP address. Set the `NETMASK=` line to the desired netmask. Set the `NETWORK=` line to the `IPADDR=` line bitwise and'ed with the `NETMASK=` line. Typically, the `BROADCAST=` line is set to the highest possible computer number on the network.

The following is a sample `ifcfg-eth0` file:

```
DEVICE=eth0
IPADDR=192.168.100.1
NETMASK=255.255.255.0
NETWORK=192.168.100.0
BROADCAST=192.168.100.255
ONBOOT=yes
```

Note that this is the file that actually changes the machine's address. The rest of the file changes identified in this section simply serve the purpose of keeping consistency with this change.

`/etc/sysconfig/network-scripts/ifcfg-eth0:0`

There may be many files named `ifcfg-eth0:1`, `ifcfg-eth0:2`, and so on. These are virtual IP files containing information for ranges of virtual IPs hung off the interface (in this case, `eth0`). They can be hung off any device. They can even be hung off `localhost`, but that's a very bad idea. These virtual IP addresses are typically used in virtual Web hosting. Here's an example of an `ifcfg-eth0:0` file declaring a virtual IP range from `192.168.100.101` through `192.168.100.110`:

```
IPADDR="192.168.200.101-110"
NETMASK="255.255.255.0"
```

`/etc/hosts`

This file lists hosts, their aliases, and their IP addresses. At a minimum, it must list `localhost` and the machine's hostname. This file must be changed when your Ethernet card's IP address changes. Here's a trivial example of an `/etc/hosts` file:

```
127.0.0.1        localhost    localhost.localdomain
192.168.100.1    mainserv.domain.cxm    mainserv
```

`/etc/sysconfig/network`

`/etc/sysconfig/network` defines certain aspects of networking for the operating system. To the extent that it contains IP addresses, and to the extent that those IP addresses

3

TCP/IP
NETWORKING
REVIEW

require changes after an IP change to a computer, those changes must be made. The following is a sample `/etc/sysconfig/network` file:

```
NETWORKING=yes
FORWARD_IPV4=false
HOSTNAME=mainserv.domain.cxm
DOMAINNAME=domain.cxm
GATEWAY=192.168.100.254
GATEWAYDEV=eth0
```

Notice the `GATEWAY=` line. This does not necessarily need a change. If that gateway is not the specific machine that's been changed, and if the changed IP does not represent a subnet change, it's not necessary to change the `GATEWAY=` line of `/etc/sysconfig/network`.

/etc/named.conf

`named.conf` is the primary DNS server configuration file. It lists every domain it expects to see as well as what file to call for DNS configuration on that domain. It does the same for reverse domains (`in-addr.arpa`). Look at your `named.conf`, and if any IP addresses contained in it pertain to the IP address you changed, change those addresses. This includes the backwards ordered IPs in the `in-addr.arpa` domain.

> **Note**
>
> These steps needn't be taken if the machine whose IP was changed is not a DNS server and is not in the domains listed in `named.conf`.

Beyond that, look in every file referenced by `named.conf` to see whether those files contain IP addresses needing to be changed after the machine's IP address is changed. Note that the referenced files can be found in the directory identified on the `directory` line of the `options` section, unless the referenced files have a complete path. In the following example, for instance, file `named.local` can be found in the `/var/named` directory (this is an example of a `named.conf` file):

```
options {
        directory "/var/named";
};

zone "." {
        type hint;
        file "named.ca";
};

zone "0.0.127.in-addr.arpa" {
        type master;
        file "named.local";
```

```
};

zone "100.168.192.in-addr.arpa"
  type master;
  file "named.192.168.100";
};

zone "200.168.192.in-addr.arpa"
  type master;
  file "named.192.168.200";
};

zone "localhost" {
  type master;
  file "named.local";
};


zone "domain.cxm" {
  type master;
  file "named.domain.cxm";
};


zone "troubleshooters.cxm" {
  type master;
  file "named.troubleshooters.cxm";
};
```

/etc/smb.conf

`smb.conf` is the configuration file for the Samba server. Sometimes `smb.conf` contains IP addresses, in which case they should be checked after the Samba server's IP address has changed.

/etc/resolv.conf

This file configures the DNS client on the Linux box, telling the client which DNS servers to query and which domain names to search. Note that the DNS server may be on the same box.

Problems with reverse DNS hang or slow certain operations and severely curtail access via `telnet` and `ftp`. A bad `/etc/resolv.conf` can cause such symptoms, as can a reverse DNS problem in DNS server configuration files.

Such hangs can be temporarily worked around by renaming `/etc/resolv.conf` to something else. Here's a small sample `/etc/resolv.conf`:

```
search domain.cxm
nameserver 192.168.100.1
```

If any of the `resolv.conf` nameservers are the box you've changed the IP for, that IP must be changed in `/etc/resolv.conf`.

/etc/dhcpd.conf

`dhcpd.conf` is the configuration file for the DHCP server. Here's a small example:

```
subnet 192.168.100.0 netmask 255.255.255.0 {
    range 192.168.100.200 192.168.100.240;
        option subnet-mask 255.255.255.0;
        option broadcast-address 192.168.100.255;
        option routers 192.168.100.1;
        option domain-name-servers 192.168.100.1;
        option domain-name "domain.cxm";
        option ip-forwarding on;
        option netbios-node-type 8;
        option netbios-name-servers 192.168.100.1;
        option netbios-dd-server 192.168.100.1;
}
```

If the changed IP address is that of the DHCP server, a router, DNS server, NetBIOS name server, or datagram server, or if the subnet is changed, appropriate changes must be made to `dhcpd.conf`.

/etc/dhcpd.leases

This file keeps track of which DHCP clients have been assigned which IPs. If the changed IP address is that of the DHCP server, a router, DNS server, NetBIOS name server, or datagram server, or if the subnet is changed, appropriate changes must be made to `dhcpd.leases`. Because `dhcpd.leases` is created by the DHCP server, perhaps the easiest solution would be to simply delete this file, replace it with an empty file, and let the DHCP server repopulate it. Here's a small, fictional example of a `dhcpd.leases` file:

```
lease 192.168.100.203 {
        starts 4 1999/10/07 13:12:22;
        ends 5 1999/10/08 01:12:22;
        hardware ethernet 00:a0:c9:e7:1d:63;
        uid 00:a0:c9:e7:1d:63;
        client-hostname "DESK1";
}
lease 192.168.100.201 {
        starts 4 1999/10/07 10:45:23;
        ends 4 1999/10/07 22:45:23;
        hardware ethernet 00:00:e7:4d:5d:51;
        uid 00:00:e7:4d:5d:51;
        client-hostname "P2300";
}
```

Connectivity Testing

Without network connectivity, nothing works. This includes Samba. It's surprising how often this fact is forgotten in the heat of battle.

Connectivity is simply the ability of two computers to receive each other's packets on the network. It says nothing about understanding the packets or about specific applications such as Samba, ftp, telnet, DNS, or email. Connectivity is the road those applications travel down. If that road is blocked, it makes no difference whether the applications are in shape to travel—they have no place to go.

ping is the tool of choice in determining network connectivity.

ping

ping is used not only to give a yes or no answer to whether there's connectivity but also to troubleshoot connectivity problems to the source.

ping 127.0.0.1

This command verifies the internal TCP/IP stack and the localhost interface. If this fails, there's a problem with the network card or the computer's TCP/IP software. In almost all cases, if the TCP/IP software is installed correctly and working, and networking is enabled at the OS software level, this will work, regardless of the network card, wiring, hubs, other computers, and so on.

If this ping command fails, look at the outputs of the /sbin/ifconfig command to make sure that the eth0 interface is up and running and has the IP address you think it has. Also, use the route command to make sure there's a route to the IP address. Then troubleshoot accordingly.

The following is a typical output for the lo interface from the /sbin/ifconfig command:

```
lo        Link encap:Local Loopback
          inet addr:127.0.0.1  Mask:255.0.0.0
          UP LOOPBACK RUNNING  MTU:3924  Metric:1
          RX packets:20447 errors:0 dropped:0 overruns:0 frame:0
          TX packets:20447 errors:0 dropped:0 overruns:0 carrier:0
          collisions:0 txqueuelen:0
```

The output of a typical /sbin/route command, shown without the Metric and Ref columns for brevity, looks like this:

3

TCP/IP NETWORKING REVIEW

```
Kernel IP routing table
Destination     Gateway         Genmask         Flags   Use Iface
192.168.100.1   *               255.255.255.255 UH        0 eth0
255.255.255.255 *               255.255.255.255 UH        0 eth0
192.168.100.0   192.168.100.1   255.255.255.0   UG        0 eth0
192.168.100.0   *               255.255.255.0   U         0 eth0
127.0.0.0       *               255.0.0.0       U         0 lo
default         192.168.100.254 0.0.0.0         UG        0 eth0
```

ping serverIP

Once there's a known valid TCP/IP stack, verify the network interface card as well as its software and drivers by pinging its IP address from the command line. The success of this command is not affected by wiring, hubs, or other computers. If this command succeeds from the command line of the Samba server, you can pretty much assume that the server is capable of connecting to a network in its subnet.

If this command fails, look at the outputs of the /sbin/ifconfig command to make sure that the eth0 interface is up and running and has the IP address you think it has. Also, use the route command to make sure there's a route to the IP address. Then troubleshoot accordingly.

The following is a typical output for the eth0 interface from the /sbin/ifconfig command:

```
eth0      Link encap:Ethernet  HWaddr 00:A0:C9:B1:C2:D3
          inet addr:192.168.100.1  Bcast:192.168.100.255  Mask:255.255.255.0
          UP BROADCAST RUNNING MULTICAST  MTU:1500  Metric:1
          RX packets:13880 errors:0 dropped:0 overruns:0 frame:0
          TX packets:111761 errors:0 dropped:0 overruns:0 carrier:0
          collisions:465 txqueuelen:100
          Interrupt:5 Base address:0xe400
```

The output of a typical /sbin/route command, shown without the Metric and Ref columns for brevity, looks like this:

```
Kernel IP routing table
Destination     Gateway         Genmask         Flags   Use Iface
192.168.100.1   *               255.255.255.255 UH        0 eth0
255.255.255.255 *               255.255.255.255 UH        0 eth0
192.168.100.0   192.168.100.1   255.255.255.0   UG        0 eth0
192.168.100.0   *               255.255.255.0   U         0 eth0
127.0.0.0       *               255.0.0.0       U         0 lo
default         192.168.100.254 0.0.0.0         UG        0 eth0
```

Notice the 192.168.100.1 with the UH flags. U means the route is up, which is a good sign. H means the interface is a host, as opposed to a gateway or subnet. Once again, this is a good sign.

ping otherIP

By using the ping command on a computer with a known good network connection on the same subnet, you verify the wiring, subnet, and your machine.

ping thirdIP

If the previous test didn't work, was the problem in the supposedly good computer or in wiring? By using a ping command on a third computer with known good connectivity on the same subnet, you have a tiebreaker.

ping serverIP from the Other Box

As a final touch, ping the server from a client on the same subnet. Once again, success verifies the wiring between them.

ping othersubnetIP

Sometimes intersubnet connectivity is necessary. By using ping commands to connect to known good machines on the other subnet, you test the router and any routes on the machines.

ping Stoppers

Many things can prevent ping from working (in other words, stop connectivity). Here are some of the many problems that can block connectivity:

- A bad network interface card
- A bad cable
- A bad hub
- A bad or misconfigured router
- A misconfigured firewall
- A proxy in the way
- A VPN client intercepting TCP/IP stack data before it gets there
- A TCP wrapper in the way

In all these cases, it's often handy to have some spare Cat 5 wires, a spare speed-switching hub, and a spare Linux machine with two or three network cards suitable to replicate the function of a router.

Mismatched Subnet or Route

Many connectivity problems are as simple as subnet mismatches. A machine on one subnet cannot ping a different subnet without a router or equivalent piece of hardware.

If two machines are intended to be on the same subnet, make sure they really are.

Sometimes the "router" is inside the machine being pinged. Take the case of a virtual hosting Web host with virtual IPs, and those IPs being on a subnet other than the one connected to the Internet or intranet. Given proper routing, machines on the Ethernet card's subnet should be able to ping the virtual IP addresses. However, without the proper routing, that just won't happen.

Mismatched Network Speeds

Some network cards are 10Mbps, some are 100Mbps, and some automatically switch between the two. Likewise, some hubs are 10Mbps, some are 100Mbps, and some automatically switch. Some hubs that switch can switch at each wire, whereas others can only switch as a whole.

Connectivity cannot be achieved if there are speed mismatches. A 10Mbps NIC cannot communicate with a 100Mbps hub, and vice versa. A hub that switches at each wire is a great troubleshooting tool, because it can connect two hosts at differing speeds, thereby identifying speed-mismatch problems.

Bad Hub

You can't connect through a bad hub. First, make sure the hub is powered up. If a hub is suspected, often a simple hub swap is the easiest test. When hubs are stacked, it becomes a little more difficult. Often, on-the-fly rewiring at the hub stack narrows the problem to the root cause. Sometimes wiring can temporarily be routed around the entire hub stack to test whether *any* of the hubs have a problem.

Bad Cable

Obviously, a bad cable disables any kind of connection. If two machines cannot ping each other but they can each ping their own network cards, this is a distinct possibility.

For short cable runs, the obvious test is to swap the cable. For longer runs, you might want to physically move the computer to a different wire or connect a known good computer (configured for the same subnet) to the questionable cable.

The hub is a convenient place to test all wires as well as the hub itself.

Bad or Misconfigured Router

Routers are designed to pass packets between subnets. Often, routers consist of Linux boxes with two network cards and the necessary routing and IP forwarding to route packets between the two subnets.

If the router is a Linux box, you should see whether the router itself can ping boxes on each of the subnets. If so, it's probably a simple routing problem or IP-forwarding problem in the router.

If the router is a specialized piece of equipment, temporarily connect each of its subnets to a Linux box and see whether that box can ping boxes on the subnet. If so, the router is probably at fault.

A Misconfigured Firewall

Firewalls are meant to protect from unwanted access. Sometimes, they do too good of a job. Devise tests to check for connectivity on either side of the firewall to determine whether the firewall is to blame.

Bad Network Interface Card

Obviously, a bad network card prevents connectivity. Sometimes, the problem is hardware, and sometimes it's the drivers for the card or another item of software configuration. Either way, a same-machine ping is pretty accurate at determining whether this is the problem.

Other Stoppers

Other problems can disrupt connectivity. Among them are having a proxy in the way, a VPN client intercepting TCP/IP stack data before it gets to its destination, and having a TCP wrapper in the way.

`nslookup` (Linux)

`nslookup` is a utility designed to test DNS lookups. Here's the simplest form of `nslookup`:

```
$ nslookup computername
```

This uses DNS to look up the IP address of the computer named `computername`. It uses the nameserver identified in `/etc/resolv.conf` to do the work. Sometimes, it's desirable to make sure you're using a good nameserver. In such a case, you can use the two-argument form:

```
$ nslookup computername dnsserverIP
```

Both the one- and two-argument forms can be used to reverse resolve IP addresses into names. In the two-argument version, the IP to be resolved to a name (reverse DNS resolution) is the first argument.

Here are examples of single-argument forward and reverse lookups using `nslookup`:

```
$ nslookup desk1
Server:   mainserv.domain.cxm
Address:  192.168.100.1
```

```
Name:    desk1.domain.cxm
Address:  192.168.100.2

$ nslookup 192.168.100.2
Server:  mainserv.domain.cxm
Address:  192.168.100.1

Name:    desk1.domain.cxm
Address:  192.168.100.2
```

If it hangs, there's probably a problem.

Note that there's also an interactive `nslookup` mode that runs if it's given no arguments. You can research this more on the `nslookup` man page.

`nslookup` tests only DNS name resolution. NetBIOS lookups, which are discussed in the next chapter, are tested with other commands.

route print (Windows)

This command gives routing information on the Windows box, including the IP address of the box and any routes that are in effect. Here's an example:

```
C:\WINDOWS> route print

Active Routes:

1234567890123456789012345678901234567890123456789012345678901234567890
Network Address          Netmask Gateway Address        Interface Metric
        0.0.0.0          0.0.0.0   192.168.100.1 192.168.100.201      1
      127.0.0.0        255.0.0.0       127.0.0.1       127.0.0.1      1
  192.168.100.0  255.255.255.0 192.168.100.201 192.168.100.201      1
192.168.100.201 255.255.255.255       127.0.0.1       127.0.0.1      1
192.168.100.255 255.255.255.255 192.168.100.201 192.168.100.201      1
      224.0.0.0        224.0.0.0 192.168.100.201 192.168.100.201      1
255.255.255.255 255.255.255.255 192.168.100.201         0.0.0.0      1
```

Routers, Routing, and IP Forwarding

A router is a device that connects two different subnets. Normally, there's no communication between different subnets.

An excellent router can be made from an old Linux box with two network cards. One NIC is configured for an IP address on one subnet, and one for an IP address on the other. Once the proper routing and IP forwarding are configured, the Linux-based router passes information between the two subnets.

Some routers are created just for the purpose of routing and are not built from commodity computers. When a router fails or is misconfigured, connectivity between the subnets it serves is broken.

Name Resolution

Computers are great with numbers. People tend to forget numbers but are great with names. Various name resolution schemes exist to translate between the names we can easily remember and the numbers computers can deal with, and vice versa. The two most applicable to Samba are DNS and NetBIOS.

DNS

DNS stands for *Domain Name Service*. It's a worldwide distributed service, with a few top-level servers delegating authority over first-level domains (such as `.com`, `.org`, `.net`, `.mil`, and so on) to many other computers. Those computers, in turn, delegate authority to many others. In addition, first-level domains are subdivided by second-level domains (`linux.com`, `microsoft.com`, `troubleshooters.com`, `mcp.com`, and so on).

Windows NT 4.0 gives the option to use DNS for Windows name resolution instead of NetBIOS. Windows 2000 uses DNS exclusively for name resolution. Therefore, DNS name resolution is becoming more important.

NetBIOS

NetBIOS name resolution is the old Windows way, and it's still the exclusive name-resolution method in Windows 9*x*. NetBIOS name resolution will be discussed in detail in the next chapter, "Windows Networking Review."

Summary

Samba is a file and print server software that runs on functioning TCP/IP networks. Therefore, a basic knowledge of TCP/IP networking is essential to understanding Samba.

The most basic understanding of networking comes from a very basic understanding of the ISO/OSI Network Model, which contains these seven layers that pass information between adjacent layers:

- Layer 1: Physical
- Layer 2: Data Link
- Layer 3: Network

- Layer 4: Transport
- Layer 5: Session
- Layer 6: Presentation
- Layer 7: Application

TCP/IP splits files and other data into packets that are sent to the destination named in an IP address. IP addresses are four-byte numbers written in a dotted decimal format. Although these four-byte numbers theoretically yield over four billion addresses, special numbers and inefficient allocation have made them scarce.

To combat that scarcity, IP addresses are now allocated in "classless" groups, where the border between the network address and the computer within the network is not made on a byte boundary. Additionally, three groups of "private addresses" have been defined as addresses that can be used by any organization, as long as they do not "escape" outside the organization's borders. These private addresses often serve the organization's internal needs. Last but not least, a new addressing scheme called *IPV6* is being implemented. This scheme uses sixteen-byte numbers, thus increasing the existing number of IP addresses by a factor of 256^{12}.

An IP address consists of a network address and the number of the computer within that network. A second piece of information is required to specify how much of an IP address belongs to each component. That piece of information is the netmask, sometimes called the *subnet mask*, which simply defines the number of bits devoted to the network (netmask) part of the IP address. Netmasks can be written as the number of bytes (for example, /24) or as a dotted decimal number with ones in the network bits and zeros in the computer bits (for example, /255.255.255.0).

Giving each computer's network card an IP address is an important part of nuts and bolts networking. The easiest way to do this is to create a DHCP server and make most of the other computers DHCP clients. DHCP servers automatically assign IP addresses to DHCP client–enabled computers plugged into their subnets.

IP addresses can also be configured on a machine-by-machine basis. Windows machines have a single prescribed method for doing this, but UNIX and Linux machines offer many choices. Some of the most popular are netconf (linuxconf, primarily found on Red Hat machines), lisa (Caldera), COAS (Caldera), and editing text configuration files (works on all UNIX and UNIX workalikes, including Linux). On Red Hat 6 installations, those files are as follows:

- /etc/sysconfig/network-scripts/ifcfg-eth0
- /etc/sysconfig/network-scripts/ifcfg-eth0:0

- `/etc/hosts`
- `/etc/sysconfig/network`
- `/etc/named.conf`
- `/etc/smb.conf`
- `/etc/resolv.conf`
- `/etc/dhcpd.conf`
- `/etc/dhcpd.leases`

Note

File locations can vary with Linux distribution and installation methods.

Note that `ifcfg-eth0` is the one that actually changes the IP, with the remainder sometimes needing modification for consistency with the changed IP.

The most basic networking criteria is connectivity, which is tested by the `ping` command. Connectivity depends on functioning network interface cards, associated drivers and software configurations, correct and functional hubs, network cabling and other hardware, correct use of routers and routing when connectivity must span subnets, and many other factors. Besides `ping`, the Linux `nslookup` and `route` commands and the Windows `route print` command are helpful.

At a higher networking level, name resolution translates back and forth between names and IP addresses. There are many forms of name resolution. The two most topical to Samba are DNS and NetBIOS.

TCP/IP networking is only part of the Samba networking story. Because Samba is primarily an imitation of Windows NT and Windows 9*x* networking, it must interface with Windows-specific networking—and that's covered in the next chapter.

3

TCP/IP
NETWORKING
REVIEW

Windows Networking Review

by Steve Litt

IN THIS CHAPTER

CHAPTER 4

Samba is (usually) a UNIX-hosted fileserver for networks of Windows machines, so knowledge of Windows networking is necessary. While it's possible to approach Samba from a Unix-only orientation, sooner or later such an approach proves insufficient. As Samba takes over ever more of Windows NT server functionality, a basic understanding of Windows networking becomes increasingly important. Today Samba functions as a logon mechanism for Windows 98, Windows NT and Windows 2000. It mimics Windows ACL (Access Control List) functionalities. It interoperates extensively with Windows using Remote Procedure Calls (RPC).

The purpose of this chapter, therefore, is to present a review of the most common and necessary Windows networking concepts. The "Other Windows Networking Information Sources" section at the end of this chapter points to extremely detailed reference information on the subject.

Windows Networking Terminology

The first step in understanding Windows networking is mastery of the terminology. The following subsections cover the most important terms. Where practical, the terminology has been organized by functionality.

SMB-Related Terminology

SMB stands for *Server Message Block*, a Microsoft fileserver standard. Andrew Tridgell created an SMB server to run on UNIX boxes. That server grew up to be Samba.

The SMB standard is ubiquitous to all Windows networking. SMB uses the NetBIOS standard defined in RFC 1001 and RFC 1002 (discussed later this chapter). NetBIOS is basically a complete implementation of name resolution suitable for a Local Area Network. NetBIOS is implemented over one of several protocols, including NetBEUI, IPX, and TCP/IP. Samba uses NetBIOS over TCP/IP exclusively. The term *NBT* basically means NetBIOS over TCP/IP, which is how the name-resolution portion of Samba works.

Samba's TCP/IP centricity is not a major restriction because TCP/IP is quickly becoming the standard. Modern Windows clients (Windows 95 and later) come with functioning TCP/IP stacks and therefore don't need NetBEUI. It is therefore often recommended that modern clients be configured *not* to use NetBEUI, the mechanism that came with 16-bit Windows.

NetBEUI stands for *NetBIOS Extended User Interface*. NetBEUI is a network protocol (like IPX and TCP/IP) used in Windows networking. It's fast being replaced by TCP/IP, but it's still used occasionally in Windows, especially in networks containing some 16-bit Windows boxes. Given that Windows 95 came out five years ago, such networks are becoming rare.

TCP/IP stands for *Transmission Control Protocol/Internet Protocol*, and it's fast becoming the network protocol of choice. The Internet uses TCP/IP.

Samba's one and only networking protocol is TCP/IP. It does not "talk" NetBEUI or IPX. Fortunately, because modern versions of Windows and NetWare are also capable of "talking" TCP/IP, this is not a problem.

TCP/IP is discussed extensively in Chapter 3, "TCP/IP Networking Review."

CIFS stands for *Common Internet File System*. After Samba came into being, Microsoft enhanced SMB, renaming it CIFS. Soon Samba incorporated the changes. At present, CIFS is well supported in Samba.

CIFS is often thought of more as a name change than as an entirely new protocol.

DHCP

DHCP stands for *Dynamic Host Configuration Protocol*, but it's best understood backwards: DHCP is a protocol for the configuration of hosts dynamically.

DHCP is a very handy accessory to Samba because it automatically gives any Windows computer plugged into its subnet an IP address, a subnet mask (netmask), a NetBIOS node type, and much more information. This reduces both setup and troubleshooting time on Samba networks. Using DHCP configuration also comes in very handy when troubleshooting suspected Samba client problems.

DHCP is discussed extensively in Chapter 3.

Windows Name Resolution Terminology

Name resolution is a critical component in the SMB protocol and in Samba. Because pre-2000 Windows uses NetBIOS instead of DNS for name resolution, a vocabulary has built up around Windows name resolution. Understanding that terminology is important for masterful Samba administration, and may be new to the administrator coming from an exclusively UNIX background.

Name resolution order is the order in which the Samba server attempts name resolution. Name resolution can be accomplished by WINS, `lmhosts`, broadcast, or host, all of which are defined in this section. The `smb.conf` parameter `name resolve order=` parameter tells the Samba server which methods to use and in which order to use them, for the server's own queries. It does not affect queries by other hosts. Take a moment to

4

WINDOWS NETWORKING REVIEW

contemplate the difference between this and a NetBIOS node type, which tells an SMB *client* which order to resolve names.

Here's the default for this parameter:

```
name resolve order = lmhosts host wins bcast
```

If the Samba server tends to often have DNS problems, you might want to take host out of the picture with the following `smb.conf` parameter:

```
name resolve order = lmhosts wins bcast
```

The *NetBIOS node type* determines the order in which the Samba client asks for name resolution. There are four NetBIOS node types corresponding to four different lookup methodologies:

- b-node (1). Broadcast only
- p-node (2). Unicast only
- m-node (4). Broadcast first, unicast on failure
- h-node (8). Unicast first, broadcast on failure

The numbers in parentheses are the corresponding `dhcpd.conf` option `netbios-node-type` values. The node type can easily be set from DHCP.

These apply to the individual client machine, not to the Samba server. H-nodes are widely considered optimal.

The term *broadcast* refers to communications sent to all other computers on the subnet. It is one of the four name-resolution methods accepted by the `resolve name order=` `smb.conf` parameter. NetBIOS name-claiming and resolution can be achieved by broadcasting packets across the subnet (and through routers on a multisegment network). This is not necessarily the best option, because the broadcast traffic can seriously impact the performance of larger networks. NetBIOS broadcasts originate from ports 137, 138, and 139.

Broadcast NetBIOS name resolution is a great fallback position, because it's so easy, reliable and straightforward. Well-configured Samba installations use broadcast as just that—a fallback position.

WINS stands for *Windows Internet Name Service*. It's a name-resolution service that does not rely on broadcasts. Samba browse servers depend on access to a WINS server to do their work. WINS is accomplished by a WINS server. The WINS server can be located either on an NT box, or on a Samba server using the `wins support=yes` `smb.conf` parameter.

> **Caution**
>
> It's vital to distinguish between the `wins support=yes` smb.conf parameter, which configures the Samba server to be a WINS server, and the `wins server=<ip address>` smb.conf parameter, which configures the Samba server to use a different box as a WINS server. If both of these options are enabled, problems will result. This is so important it will be mentioned several times throughout this book.

Browse servers are not WINS servers—they're WINS clients. However, it's very easy to have Samba run both WINS server software (via the `WINS support=` attribute) and browse server software (via attributes such as `local master=yes`, `preferred master=yes`, and `domain master=yes`).

As mentioned, Samba can serve as a WINS server, but it's tricky to do right, and Samba's WINS doesn't support all NT WINS features, especially WINS replication. If your network has an NT server, it's better to let that server run the WINS service.

`lmhosts` is a file on computers supporting NetBIOS name resolution. This file is used for hard-coded quick name lookup. It's in the directory `/etc` on a Red Hat Linux box. It's at `C:\WINNT\System32\Drivers\Etc` on a typically configured Windows NT Server machine. Here's a sample `/etc/lmhosts` file off a Red Hat 6 Linux Samba server:

```
127.0.0.1 localhost
192.168.100.1 mainserv
192.168.100.203 p2300
192.168.100.2   desk1
```

> **Note**
>
> The exact location of the `lmhosts` file depends on the exact operating system, distribution and configuration. On a stock Red Hat system it's in the `/etc` directory. On a stock Caldera OpenLinux system it's in the `/etc/samba.d` directory. To determine your default `lmhosts` location, observe that `nmbd.c`, puts the filename as constant `LMHOSTSFILE`, which is defined in Makefile. A stock Makefile straight from Samba.Org places `LMHOSTSFILE` at `$(LIBDIR)/lmhosts`, which evaluates to `/usr/local/samba/lib/lmhosts`.

Obviously, `lmhosts` provides an incredibly quick lookup, but it's very manual in nature. It's often placed in front of WINS—and certainly in front of broadcast—in the name resolve order. It's handy to place the most-used and least-changing names in `lmhosts` to gain the most benefit from the least work.

Host is one of the name resolution methods that can be listed in `name resolve order=`. This is a resolution method that uses the host's name-resolution methods. This includes NIS, DNS, and the `/etc/hosts` file. This works only with names having the SMB server resource tag `<20>`.

DNS stands for *Domain Name Service*. It's a method of name resolution. Name resolution is the conversion back and forth between IP addresses and names (such as `mcp.com`). The beauty of DNS is that it's a distributed system in which each computer can have many slave computers sharing the load and assuming the load in fault situations while still providing a single point of configuration for each zone (for the purpose of this chapter, consider a *zone* to be similar to a domain name).

> **Note**
>
> Both *Red Hat Linux 6 Unleashed* and *Linux Unleashed, Fourth Edition* contain excellent chapters on DNS. Both books are written by Billy Ball and David Pitts.

Until recently, DNS had very little impact on Samba because Windows networking used NetBIOS for name resolution instead of DNS. Modern Windows operating systems give the option of using DNS, and now Windows 2000 focuses on DNS for name resolution. Therefore, DNS will become much more important in the Samba world.

Browsing Terminology

Browsing is the act of seeing shares from a Windows client, and navigating those shares. Browsing is one of the most complex facets of the SMB and CIFS protocols. It is also one of the most important SMB/CIFS functionalities because it's the only way a non-sophisticated user can access his or her shares. A large plurality of Samba problems involve browsing. It's vital to understand browsing and its terminology.

A *browse* is a list of visible SMB shares. It is also called a *browse list*. There will likely be other SMB shares available for use, but not visible. When you double-click a server in Network Neighborhood, the display you get is a browse list. You can also get a browse list using the `net view` command. Here's an example:

```
C:\>net view \\mainserv
Shared resources at \\MAINSERV

Sharename    Type        Comment
------------------------------------------------------------
username     Disk        Home directory of username
homes        Disk
```

```
lp          Print
printers    Print
The command was completed successfully.

C:\>
```

Master browsers store and distribute browse lists. There are two types of master browsers: *Local master browsers* (LMB), which handle browse lists for a single workgroup (usually confined to a single subnet), and *Domain master browsers* (DMB), which handle browse lists for an entire domain (usually multiple subnets).

Only one Local master browser should exist for each workgroup (once again usually one per subnet). The way that's enforced is by the system conducting a browser election. A *browser election* is an election just like electing a president. Certain "candidates" (computers) get preferential treatment.

Every box running for office (`local master=yes`) is evaluated on its OS level (`os level=`). An `os level=65` defeats all Windows candidates, although it's possible for another Samba server to beat `65`. `255` is the maximum.

> **Note**
>
> The `local master=`, `os level=`, `preferred master=`, and `domain master=` mentioned in this section are all `smb.conf` parameters.

A few extra votes are given to any candidate that's a preferred master (`preferred master=yes`), although the main function of the `preferred master=` Samba parameter is that it calls for a browser election every time Samba is restarted on it.

Whenever a Samba client needs a browse list, it queries the local master browser. The local master browser then sends back the list. This entire transaction can be seen using the `tcpdump` program. This is discussed in detail in Chapter 22, "Troubleshooting Samba."

The DMB is the computer which stores and distributes browse lists throughout the domain, which typically encompasses several subnets. There's one domain master browser per domain. It can be either a Windows NT server or a Samba server. If there's an NT server doing WINS resolution or acting as a PDC, it's recommended that you not use a Samba server for the domain master browser. To make a Samba box the domain master browser, give it the `smb.conf` attribute of `domain master=yes`.

> **Note**
>
> Election to Domain master browser does not automatically ensure election to Local master browser. It is possible for a Domain master browser to not assume LMB duties on its subnet. Since the election criteria for LMB and DMB are so similar, in practice the DMB is usually also the LMB for its subnet.

The DMB frequently distributes the current browse list to the LMBs.

The `remote announce=` parameter is used to enable `nmbd` to announce itself periodically to specific workgroups on specific IP subnets. Although this sounds like a great solution to some of the Windows 9*x* Network Neighborhood browse problems, in fact, by itself, this parameter does not help with that problem. Its use is much more restricted and specialized.

`remote announce=` is an `smb.conf` parameter which is used primarily to enable a Samba server to appear in a browse list of machines in a different subnet.

Here's the syntax:

```
remote announce=Ipaddress/workgroupname
```

Here's an example:

```
remote announce=192.168.200.255/WEBGROUP
```

Note that the announcements are typically sent to a broadcast address. However, in ultra-stable networks, they can be sent to the subnet's browse master.

remote browse sync

The `remote browse sync=` is an `smb.conf` parameter that enables `nmbd` to request periodic browse list synchronization with other Samba (not NT) servers on other subnets. Here's the parameter to request synchronization with the master browser on subnet `192.168.200.0/24`:

```
remote browse sync=192.168.200.255
```

UDP

UDP stands for *User Datagram Protocol*—a fast, simple, and stateless protocol often used with IP instead of TCP. It maintains no permanent connection. It does not handle packet loss or corruption but instead passes that task up to the application.

UDP packets can be sent either broadcast or unicast, named Broadcast UDP and Unicast UDP, respectively. Certain SMB communications rely on UDP.

Workgroup

In the physical world, a *workgroup* is a group of people working together and sharing the load.

In Windows networking, a *workgroup* is a group of boxes serving a "workgroup" of people. This is *not* the same as a UNIX group, because one person can belong to many groups, whereas one machine belongs to exactly one workgroup.

In simple Windows networking, login is done at the workgroup level, but it's done against a replicated copy of the workgroup's user/password lists. Therefore, if you request access to a resource on the ACCOUNTING server, ACCOUNTING will validate your request with its copy of the password list. If two minutes later you request access to the DEVELOPMENT server, DEVELOPMENT will validate your request.

Although this is workable in a modest group of machines, administration becomes unwieldy on large networks.

Therefore, to summarize, workgroups work together to validate requests from each other. Workgroups also provide the framework for browsing. *Browsing* is simply the act of seeing a list of a box's shares. Here's an example of a browse from a Windows client to a Samba server on a Linux box:

```
C:\>net view \\mainserv
Shared resources at \\MAINSERV

Sharename    Type         Comment
--------------------------------------------------------
username     Disk         Home directory of username
homes        Disk
lp           Print
printers     Print
The command was completed successfully.

C:\>
```

Domain

Domains are like workgroups that authenticate on a central server (or a central server with some backup servers). Administration is easier because passwords and authentication are in one place.

4

WINDOWS
NETWORKING
REVIEW

> **Note**
>
> Windows NT authentication is based entirely on domains. Large Windows networks are based on domains. Most Windows LANs bigger than a single subnet have authentication based on domains. PDCs and BDCs are domain based. Domains are very important in the SMB/CIFS protocol.

Domain authentication is managed by a domain controller, which keeps track of who can access what across all clients and servers in the domain. Therefore, when a client computer asks a server for a resource, the server hands off the request to the domain controller, which tells the server yes or no. The server acts accordingly.

PDC and BDC

PDC stands for *primary domain controller*. A PDC is a CIFS fileserver capable of handling logins from Microsoft Windows NT clients. Note that this is very different from handling Windows 98 logins, which has been available in Samba for a long time.

Samba has had experimental code supporting PDCs for quite a while. As of Samba version 2.0.5a, it became official.

PDC support is a giant coup for Samba, because it enables Samba use without an NT server. That being said, if the network has NT servers anyway, it's still best to let those NT servers assume the PDC role.

BDC stands for *backup domain controller*. As the name implies, it's a domain controller that acts as a backup to the PDC. If the PDC goes down, any one of the BDCs can pick up the slack. As of this writing, Samba is not a good choice to act as a BDC. However, the code is written, and Samba will soon reliably fill this function.

RPC

RPC stands for *remote procedure call*. Without going into detail, RPC is used for establishing trust relationships. To quote DOMAIN-MEMBER.txt (and you should read that document if you're interested in domain technicalities), "domain-level security is passed down the authenticated RPC channel in exactly the same way that an NT server would do it."

As Samba takes over an increasing array of NT functionalities, RPC becomes more important because it's a primary method of communication between Samba and Windows NT servers.

Resource Domain and Master Domain

A *resource domain* is a domain especially created to house the organization's resources, such as printer queue definitions, file shares, and application back ends.

Contrast the resource domain with a *master domain*. Typically, the master domain houses everything but the resources, and it does the validation. The resource domain containing the resources trusts the master domain to validate users.

A single master domain can be trusted by multiple resource domains. Sometimes geographical or organizational factors require multiple master domains. In such a case, each master domain has one or more resource domains trusting it, and the two master domains trust each other. Alternatively, a one-way trust can be configured between the master domains.

Domain Trust Relationship

A *trust relationship*, or *domain trust relationship*, is a relationship between two separate domains—call them DomainA and DomainB. Normally, a user would need an account (login) on each, with the possibility of different names and passwords and all the trouble that that brings. The trust relationship solves this problem.

Each domain trusts the other, basically saying "if he could get into the other domain, I trust him in mine." For example, the user logs in to DomainA and then accesses DomainB, which lets gives him access based on the fact that DomainA let him in. Trust relationships must be properly set up; otherwise, as you can imagine, security problems can spread.

Figure 4.1 shows a simple one-way trust relationship between a master domain and a resource domain.

4

WINDOWS
NETWORKING
REVIEW

FIGURE 4.1

A simple one-way trust relationship between a master and resource domain.

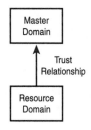

Figure 4.2 shows a trust between two masters domains in different cities, each of which have a trust relationship with a resource domain local to them. Notice that this is still a modular and manageable situation, and it still would be even if several resource domains maintained trust relationships with each master domain.

FIGURE 4.2

A two-way trust relationship between two masters.

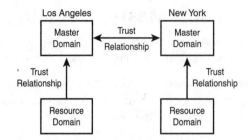

Contrast that with a *complete trust relationship*, where everyone trusts each other. Such a situation is typically the result of fast growth, lack of planning, or suboptimal corporate politics. Figure 4.3 shows a complete trust relationship.

FIGURE 4.3

A complete trust relationship.

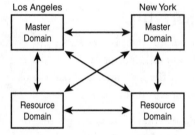

SID

SIDs are security IDs that are attached to every object in a domain. Security ID's are the basis for deducing rights through ACLs (discussed in next section). SIDs are one of the formerly NT exclusive implementation now included in Samba.

ACL

ACL stands for *access control list*. In the Windows world, every file and directory has an access control list. An access control list is a list of which users and groups can perform what operations on the file or directory.

Modern Samba implementations simulate ACLs quite well. The `smb.conf` parameter `nt acl support=` enables this simulation.

Even if the administrator chooses not to use ACL support, Samba has fine enough control to simulate ACLs on a directory level through various masks and force parameters, which are discussed in several of this book's chapters.

NetBIOS Overview

NetBIOS is a programming API for working with networks. It forms the backbone of Windows name resolution. It's defined by RFC 1001 and RFC 1002, written in 1987. These are available at `http://ietf.org/rfc/rfc1001.txt` and `http://ietf.org/rfc/rfc1002.txt`.

RFC 1001 defines the following services for NetBIOS use:

- Name Service
- Session Service
- Datagram Service
- Miscellaneous functions
- Nonstandard extensions

Miscellaneous functions include Reset, Cancel, Adapter Status, and Unlink. Nonstandard extensions include Find Name for Token Ring implementation. We'll leave miscellaneous functions and nonstandard extensions alone, concentrating on the Name, Session, and Datagram Services instead.

Name Service

The Name Service deals with naming services—the translation of names to numbers and finding machines and other resources by name. Names are applied for by various resources. Names can either be *unique* (meaning only one resource can have a certain name at a time) or *group* (meaning multiple resources can have the same name).

RFC 1001 5.2 lists three primitives associated with the NetBIOS Name Service:

- Add Name
- Add Group Name
- Delete Name

Add Name is used by a resource wanting exclusive use of the name. It bids for the name. If another resource has the name, it defends its name and the Add Name request is rejected. Otherwise, the requesting resource succeeds in getting the name and in the future defends it.

Add Group Name is used by a resource willing to share the name with others.

Delete Name is used to give up use of a name. RFC 1001 5.2 goes out of its way to explain that this request is not done when the user simply powers down the computer, and that the standard must support such behavior. Fortunately, modern operating systems

such as Windows 9*x*, Windows NT, and Linux/BSD/UNIX require orderly shutdowns, so this is not as much of a problem as with older operating systems.

There are various types of numbers, each with its own number. As an example, a `<1d>` name identifies a local master browser. It's important to note the distinction between unique names, which are owned by a single computer, and group names, whose ownership is shared by all.

The following name/number combinations must be unique:

- `computer_name<00>`. The workstation service name on the WINS client.
- `computer_name<03>`. This is the Messenger Service name on the WINS client.
- `computer_name<06>`. The name registered by RAS when started on a RAS (Remote Access Service) server.
- `computer_name<1f>`. Network DDE. Appears only if Network DDE services are running.
- `computer_name<20>`. Name of the Server Service on the WINS client.
- `computer_name<21>`. RAS Client Service. Not to be confused with `<06>`, the RAS server.
- `computer_name<be>`. Network monitoring agent. Only appears if the service is started. Names less than 15 characters are padded with plus signs.
- `computer_name<bf>`. Network monitoring utility (a part of Microsoft Systems Management Server). Names less than 15 characters are padded with plus signs.
- `username<03>`. User names. This is used to receive `net send` messages.
- `domain_name<1b>`. This is the name of the domain master browser. WINS queries to this *name<number>* return the IP of the domain master browser that registered the name.
- `domain_name<1d>`. Registered by the local master browser for the subnet. There can only be one local master browser for each subnet. Backup browsers use this *name<number>* to communicate with the local master browser. The existence of this name and number indicates that the Samba server has won a local master browser election, after which it's much more likely to show up in a Network Neighborhood browse.

Group Name Types

The following name/number combinations are intended to be nonunique group names:

- `domain_name<00>`. The Workstation name to receive LAN Manager broadcasts.
- `domain_name<1c>`. A list of domain controller addresses (up to 25), one of which is the PDC.

- domain_name<1e>. Used by browsers to elect a master browser. WINS returns the requesting client's broadcast address upon a query for a name ending with #1e.

- __MSBROWSE__<01>. Registered by each subnet's local master browser for each sub-net. WINS returns the requesting client's broadcast address upon a query for __MSBROWSE__ #01.

Name List Example Using `nmblookup`

The following `nmblookup` command and its output show some of names in the workgroup (note that the server's name is `mainserv`, and the `[global]` section contains `workgroup=39`):

```
$ nmblookup -SR mainserv
Sending queries to 192.168.100.255
192.168.100.1 mainserv<00>
Looking up status of 192.168.100.1
received 8 names
        MAINSERV        <00> -          M <ACTIVE>
        MAINSERV        <03> -          M <ACTIVE>
        MAINSERV        <20> -          M <ACTIVE>
        ..__MSBROWSE__ . <01> - <GROUP> M <ACTIVE>
        TEST39          <00> - <GROUP> M <ACTIVE>
        TEST39          <1b> -          M <ACTIVE>
        TEST39          <1d> -          M <ACTIVE>
        TEST39          <1e> - <GROUP> M <ACTIVE>
num_good_sends=0 num_good_receives=0

$
```

This is the result of an `nmblookup` command on the Samba server, which rigged the browser election with `os level=65`, `preferred master=true`, `local master=true`, and `domain master=true`, and, of course, it's serving as a WINS server with `wins support=true`. Its workgroup name is `TEST39`.

The results are that `TEST39` came back as a `<00>` (broadcast reception), `<1b>` (domain master browser), `<1d>` (local master browser), and `<1e>` (browser elections). `MAINSERV`, the NetBIOS name and hostname of the server, came up with `<00>` (workstation), `<03>` (messaging), `<20>` (Server Service), and, of course, `__MSBROWSE__ <01>` (local master browser).

Session Service

NetBIOS provides Session Service. The Session Service handles the connection between the two computers, with primitives such as Call, Listen, Hang Up, Send, Receive, and Session Status. It's a "virtual wire."

The Session Service is intended to provide a highly reliable method of communication between two specific resources. Sessions are sequenced, meaning packets are placed in

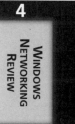

the right order by the service. The RFC goes into detail about the session's error detection and handling.

Datagram Service

NetBIOS provides Datagram Service. The first sentence of RFC 1001 5.4 is "The Datagram Service is an unreliable, nonsequenced, connectionless service."

Why use unreliable datagrams when you can use the highly reliable Session Service? The most obvious reason is that you cannot broadcast a session—it's a link between two specific NetBIOS names.

However, datagrams also support sending to a specific name. Of course, that name can be a group name, in which case it's really a multicast. Also, even datagrams sent to a unique name carry one advantage—the fact that they're nonsequenced and connectionless make them stateless. They're perfect for quick-and-dirty tasks.

Datagram Service primitives are Send Datagram, Send Broadcast Datagram, Receive Datagram, and Receive Broadcast Datagram.

CIFS Overview

CIFS stands for *Common Internet File System*. It's an enhancement of the SMB protocol.

CIFS uses the TCP/IP protocol, with NetBIOS over TCP/IP for naming services. CIFS is connection oriented. Packets are ordered, and there's sufficient error handling to properly handle lost connections. SMB is stateless with regard to connections.

Making a Connection

When a user operating an SMB client makes a connection through Network Neighborhood, `net use`, or `smbclient`, a connection sequence occurs. Here's how it works:

1. Negotiate the protocol.
2. Set up the session.
3. Accomplish the tree connect.

Negotiate the Protocol

The client sends a request to negotiate a protocol listing the protocols it knows. The server then responds by picking the most sophisticated of the client's protocols that it can handle.

Set Up the Session

A *session* is a connection between the two machines. Sessions support error handling and packet sequencing. The client requests the session, including a username and password.

The server validates the user and password (or hands off the validation to a password server). If the validation succeeds, the server returns a session ID to the client.

Of course, depending on the level of guest access, even a failed validation can return a session ID.

Tree Connect

The client then requests a tree connect, authenticated by the session ID. The server checks to see whether the user has the right to access the share and, if so, returns a tree ID. This tree ID is used in all subsequent accesses to the share.

Other Windows Networking Information Sources

This chapter has obviously just scratched the surface. Although this information suffices for building normal Samba networks, you'll need more information for large networks or diverse networks with many domains and platforms.

RFCs

RFC 1001 and RFC 1002 are the ultimate authority on NetBIOS. When the information doesn't show up elsewhere, look at the RFCs. You can find them at
`http://ietf.org/rfc/rfc1001.txt` and `http://ietf.org/rfc/rfc1002.txt`.
IETF.org is the official site for RFCs, so look there for any RFCs you may need.

Distribution Text Documents

Within `/usr/doc/samba-2.0.3/docs/textdocs` (obviously, your Samba version number may vary, and different distributions may organize the docs a bit differently), find the documents listed in Table 4.1.

TABLE 4.1 Samba Distribution Text Documents

Document Filename	Subject
BROWSING-Config.txt	Browser configuration
BROWSING.txt	More browsing information
BUGS.txt	Gotchas
DOMAIN.txt	Domains
DOMAIN_CONTROL.txt	More about domains

continues

4

WINDOWS
NETWORKING
REVIEW

TABLE 4.1 continued

Document Filename	Subject
DOMAIN_MEMBER.txt	Joining a domain
GOTCHAS.txt	More gotchas
HINTS.txt	Some hints
NTDOMAIN.txt	NT domain information
Recent-FAQs.txt	Miscellaneous good info
UNIX-SMB.txt	Interacting UNIX with Samba
cifsntdomain.txt	Heavy, source-level documents

Note that the documents in Table 4.1 are only the ones related to Windows networking. There are many other documents in this directory that are just as useful. Familiarize yourself with them.

Distribution HTML FAQs

The Samba server FAQ is /usr/doc/samba-2.0.3/docs/faq/Samba-Server-FAQ.html (filename and directory may vary). It contains a plethora of often-asked questions with answers. The Samba meta-FAQ is /usr/doc/samba-2.0.3/docs/faq/ Samba-meta-FAQ.html.

Source Code

Some of Samba's source code can give you a feel for the product. Start with local.h to see the various compiled-in defaults. includes.h sheds light on system dependencies and what's included in the product. nameserv.h is probably the best documentation for this chapter's subject. You might also find the various rpc*.h files interesting. Because the #defines tend to be toward the top, you might want to scan the tops of all the files like this:

```
$ head -n100 *.h | less
```

This is a little like hitting the Scan button on your car radio.

Other Information Sources

Be sure to view the Samba.org Web site, including the documents on the "download" part of the site.

For live answers to questions you can't find elsewhere, there's the Samba.org mailing list and the comp.protocols.smb newsgroup.

Summary

A thorough understanding of Samba requires an understanding of Windows networking. This becomes increasingly true as Samba takes over more and more Windows NT functionality such as logon services (PDCs and BDCs), Windows security functionalities such as SIDs and ACLs. Upcoming versions of Samba will interoperate with Windows in ways unimaginable a year ago. This chapter defines the Windows networking terminology, and gives an overview of the Windows networking technology required for Samba administration.

Windows networking is based on the SMB protocol, later renamed CIFS. This protocol was, until Windows 2000, dependent on NetBIOS. While Windows NetBIOS can operate on top of the NetBEUI, IPX/SPX or TCP/IP protocols, Samba uses SMB/CIFS only over TCP/IP, which is rapidly becoming the standard.

CIFS makes connections between systems in three distinct steps:

1. Negotiate the protocol.
2. Set up the session.
3. Accomplish the tree connect.

NetBIOS is the networking API that helps with name resolution. NetBIOS has three primary services: Name Service, Session Service, and Datagram Service. NetBIOS names include several unique names and several group names, each of which has several numbered categories. NetBIOS is defined by the RFC 1001 and RFC 1002 documents.

Trust relationships occur between domains. They can be one-way or two-way relationships. A one-way trust occurs when one domain allows a user access to its resources because the user authenticated on the other. A two-way trust occurs when both domains "feel that way" about each other. Domain trust relationships enable a single point of login, instead of replicating authentication information over several domains.

As seen in this chapter, Windows networking can be rather complex. Fortunately, Samba encapsulates much of this complexity in its `smbd` and `nmbd` daemons, and places most configuration in a single place, `smb.conf`.

4

WINDOWS
NETWORKING
REVIEW

Installing Samba

by Mike Harris

IN THIS CHAPTER

Once you've decided to use the power and flexibility of Samba in your network, the next question is where to get it and how to install it on your existing system. This chapter aims to guide you through the process of procuring and installing Samba on your network server or workstation. I'll try to cover as many different approaches as possible without overwhelming you with information.

There are a myriad of different versions of UNIX and Linux available out there. If this chapter attempted to explain installation specific details for every variant, it would most likely be the size of this entire book! What you'll find are the details needed to install Samba in a generic fashion with specific explanations for three popular UNIX/Linux variants (namely Red Hat Linux, Caldera OpenLinux, and Debian GNU/Linux) along with guidelines as to several other operating systems to aid you. If you have one of these three systems, you'll be halfway home already. If not, don't worry; this chapter should contain sufficient information to get you started as well as pointers to different resources that should help you along the way.

Samba is a very neatly packaged product; the source code configuration script is professional and complete and can successfully identify system-specific information in many cases. A word of advice: Before you start, make sure you have the latest versions of your system's libraries and development tools. The GNU suite of tools are very good, and most people usually find success with them.

This chapter assumes that you understand the use of the basic UNIX commands (`ls`, `man`, `mkdir`, `cp`, `cd` and `su`), have knowledge of the use of the system's development tools (such as the compiler `cc` or `gcc` and a `make` utility), and know how to use one of the system's text editors (such as `vi` or `emacs`). Every example will give command-line instructions for reference. Note that some of the command-line parameters for the utilities vary on different systems; therefore, I suggest you refer to the manual pages for the command if your system is not explicitly covered here. For example, to find out more about your system's `tar` utility, type the following:

```
% man tar
```

Examples in This Chapter

This chapter uses the example of a very small local area network that consists of two machines. The first machine (`PERSEUS`) is a server system running a version of Linux; this will be the Samba server. The second machine (`WIN98_2`) is running Windows 98 and will be used to test whether the Samba machine is working correctly. The two machines are members of the workgroup `MYGROUP` and are on the same Class C IP network. Table 5.1 summarizes the IP setup.

TABLE 5.1 The Network Setup Used in This Chapter

Machine	IP Address
WIN98_2 (Windows 98 client)	192.168.100.10
PERSEUS (Samba Server)	192.168.100.2

A single user account is created on both the Windows 98 client and the Samba server. The username is username, and the password is identical for both systems.

The Windows 98 machine is configured with share-level access control and has the following networking components:

- Client for Microsoft Networks
- TCP/IP bound to the Ethernet card
- File and Printer Sharing for Microsoft Networks

Figure 5.1 shows a snapshot of the Network control panel for this machine.

FIGURE 5.1

The network configuration for the Windows 98 machine.

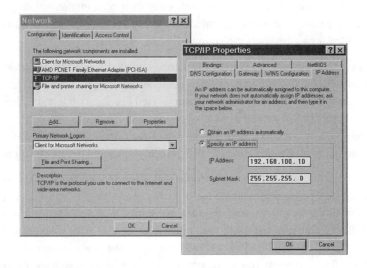

Software Versions

Table 5.2 shows the software versions used for the examples in this chapter.

TABLE 5.2   Software Versions for the Chapter's Examples

Software	Version
Windows 98	Original release
Red Hat Linux	6.0
Caldera OpenLinux	2.3
Debian GNU/Linux	2.1

At the time of this writing, the latest available stable release of Samba is version 2.0.6; this is the version used in the upgrade examples. The latest development version is 2.1.

When to Use the Version Already Installed

Until recently, Samba has not been included as a package available for commercial Linux systems. Certain propriety UNIX variants offer their own implementation of the SMB/CIFS protocol. However, Samba is available for many UNIX platforms and can be compiled for virtually all the common major variants.

Most Linux variants should come with Samba already installed or available to install on the installation CD. How recent the version of Samba you have will depend on how recent your version of Linux is. For example, Red Hat Linux 6.0 and Caldera OpenLinux 2.3 both come with a version of Samba greater than 2.0; this is the version that you should be running (see the section "When to Use the Latest Stable Release"). Debian GNU/Linux 2.1, however, comes with version 1.9.18, which you should definitely upgrade.

Samba 2.0 is the release that most people will want to be running on their systems because it now incorporates stable facilities for encrypted password support (essential for newer Windows clients) and includes the Samba Web Administration Tool (SWAT). Rather than potentially wrestling with older releases that offer weaker implementations of SMB/CIFS, you should always consider running the latest version. You'll also inevitably find that when you need support or help with Samba, most people are running the latest version and will be unlikely to support multiple older versions.

When to Use the Latest Stable Release

If your existing installation performs all the functionality you need, it's unlikely that you'll see the benefit in running the latest release. Upgrading could cause unwanted disruption to your users and extra work for you. However, if you have a support query, you'd be well advised to be running the latest version of the software before contacting support companies or posting to newsgroups.

You may want to use the latest version of Samba, if it contains functionality that could improve your network and services over the current installed version. For example, Red Hat Linux 6.0 comes with Samba 2.0.3 preinstalled. Although this is good, dependable release of Samba, there are some benefits to running a later release. If your Samba server is primarily running as a network application server to Windows clients, the Level-2 oplocks support provided by Samba 2.0.5 and later versions would help to speed up application serving to your clients.

A good place to start to find out what benefits you might gain from upgrading is the `whatsnew.txt` file in the top-level directory of each distribution of Samba. You can also find a copy of the latest version of this file at `http://us3.samba.org/samba/whatsnew/samba-2.0.6.html`.

All in all, you should carefully weigh the benefits gained from upgrading against the potential disruption to your network. In actuality, the impact on the user end of the network is usually minimal (especially if done in the evening when your discerning users and financial directors have gone home).

When to Use the Development Version

You may be interested in testing some of the cutting-edge features of Samba—for example, the primary domain controller (PDC) support that's currently available in the latest versions.

If you fancy being on the cutting edge of Samba development, you might consider running the latest development version. This is obtainable from the Internet in "gzipped" `tar` archives and from the CVS service (see "Accessing the CVS for the Latest Development Version," later in this chapter). Before you do this, consider the following points:

- You should never run the latest version in a live environment unless it's absolutely necessary because a critical bug-fix or feature is implemented.
- If you want to test groundbreaking new features, you should be running a test server separate from your live Samba servers.
- Samba is constantly under development. Therefore, the source packages will probably be updated daily and many changes could occur between releases. You'll have to watch for the latest release to see what's new.

- Configuration file parameters can come and go almost daily. If you're testing something experimentally (such as the PDC support), you'll need to keep an eye out for configuration changes.

- The source package will inevitably not be tested thoroughly on every platform. Therefore, you might have problems with compiling, installing, and running. Very often with development versions you'll find that one will be broken, the next one working, and then the next broken again. This can be frustrating and time-consuming.

- You should almost certainly subscribe to one of the development mailing lists. This will give you all sorts of cutting-edge information that can help with your configuration. If you can help, feel free to contribute. The more the merrier!

Installing an Updated Samba on Red Hat Linux

At the time of this writing, the version of Samba provided with Red Hat Linux is 2.0.3, which should be suitable for most installations. However you may have a need to upgrade to use the latest package.

As well as the source archives, Samba is also available for Red Hat Linux in the form of binary RPM package files (RPM stands for *Red Hat Package Manager*). By far, the greatest benefit of using the provided RPM is that all files and directories are correctly created for you in locations that integrate into Red Hat Linux's file structure. This removes the need to modify the system's configuration and therefore helps maintain the system's integrity. As a bonus, a working sample configuration file (/etc/smb.conf) is also provided.

Installing a Red Hat Samba Binary RPM

With Red Hat Linux, Samba is provided as a binary RPM on the installation CD (CD 1). Also, the latest versions of the Samba binary RPM package can usually be obtained from http://updates.redhat.com.

The Samba RPM contains all the files required for Samba and SWAT. With Red Hat 6.0, the version of Samba is 2.0.3.

Before installing Samba, you need to make sure that the Red Hat Linux installation CD is mounted on /mnt/cdrom. Use a shell as root and type the following:

```
% mount /mnt/cdrom
```

If this command fails, you may need to use the full form, which is as follows:

```
% mount -t iso9660 /dev/hdc /mnt/cdrom
```

> **Note**
>
> Your CD-ROM drive might be installed an a different part of the EIDE bus or it might even be a SCSI device. Be sure to consult your local configuration.

Testing for the Presence of Samba on Red Hat

First, you need to check whether Samba has been installed on your system. Use the `rpm` command to do this from a terminal window as any user:

```
% rpm -q samba
```

This will return one of the following messages:

```
package samba is not installed
```

or

```
package samba-2.0.3 is installed
```

Installing the RPM

If Samba is already installed, great! You can move on to configuring and testing the installation. If not, you need to install it first. For this, you need to be logged in as `root` with the Red Hat installation CD mounted. Next, issue the following command:

```
% rpm -i /mnt/cdrom/RedHat/RPMA/samba
```

This should install Samba and all its files in the correct locations for the Red Hat distribution.

Installing Using GnoRPM

As an alternative installation, you can also use the graphical packages installed with Red Hat 6.0 if you have access to an X Server for the system. Probably the best package is GnoRPM, which comes with the Gnome environment. You'll need to run GnoRPM as `root`, and you can do this from the Gnome menu under the System group of applications or from the command line, like this:

```
% gnorpm &
```

Gnome RPM is a very useful utility that presents all installed packages in a logical tree structure. You also have the advantage of being able to review a package's contents before installing. To install Samba using GnoRPM, click the Install icon on the menu bar of GnoRPM. The Install pop-up window appears. In the Install window, click Add and select the file `/mnt/cdrom/RedHat/RPMS`. Click Add and then Close in the file browser windows that pops up. Then choose Install to install the package.

Figure 5.2 shows a picture of GnoRPM running with the Install option selected and a file browse window open.

FIGURE 5.2

Installing Samba on Red Hat using GnoRPM.

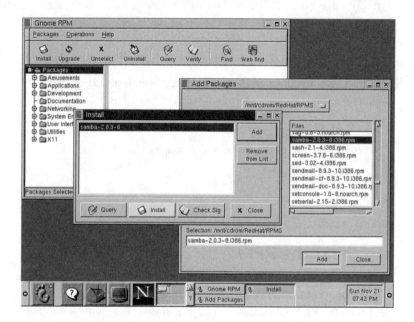

Fixing Red Hat's Samba RPM

Red Hat's default installation of Samba is pretty well complete and ready to run. The only issue is that, for some reason, the Web-based administration tool SWAT is commented out in the file `/etc/inetd.conf`. This means that you're unable in the first instance to access it from your Web browser. To fix this, choose your favorite editor and log in as `root`; then open `/etc/inetd.conf` and move to the end of this file. You should see a line similar to the following:

```
#swat      stream  tcp     nowait.400      root /usr/bin/swat swat
```

Remove the leading # character from the line and save the file. Now you need to restart the `inetd` daemon by executing as `root`. Here's an example:

```
% /etc/rc.d/init.d/inetd restart
```

Starting and Stopping the Samba Daemon

To start Samba following installation, use this command:

```
% /etc/rc.d/init.d/smb start
```

Here's how to stop Samba again:

```
% /etc/rc.d/init.d/smb stop
```

Installing from Source over Red Hat's Samba

This method allows you to install a later (or earlier) version of Samba to fit exactly over the default installation. It assumes that you already have Samba installed from the Red Hat installation CD. By using this method, you can save time and effort reconfiguring your system and make everything slightly less complicated. Logged in as user root, use the following steps:

1. Before you start, back up the existing configuration files that came with your Red Hat distribution:

   ```
   % cp /etc/smb.conf /etc/smb.conf.backup
   % cp /etc/smbusers /etc/smbusers.backup
   % cp /etc/rc.d/init.d/smb /etc/rc.d/init.d/smb.backup
   ```

2. Stop the Samba daemons:

   ```
   % /etc/rc.d/init.d/smb stop
   ```

3. Remove the existing Samba package to avoid any conflicts between the different versions:

   ```
   % rpm -e samba
   ```

4. Next, you need to obtain your source distribution and go to the directory where you want to install it. (This is usually /usr/local/src on a Linux system, but it may vary depending on your site. I generally use /usr/local/sources to store my archived software and /usr/local/src to contain my uncompressed packages for installation.)

   Change to the following directory:

   ```
   % cd /usr/local/src
   ```

5. Uncompress the archive file using the tar utility:

   ```
   % tar xvfz /usr/local/sources/samba-2.0.6.tgz
   ```

   This will create a directory named samba-2.0.6 (or something similar, depending on the version you're using) below /usr/local/src. The source files for building Samba are located in the source subdirectory:

   ```
   % cd samba-2.0.6/source
   ```

5

INSTALLING
SAMBA

6. Now when you configure Samba, you pass parameters to the configure script to make the installation place its files in Red Hat-friendly locations:

```
% ./configure --with-pam --with-smbmount \
              --prefix=/usr --sysconfdir=/etc/ \
              --localstatedir=/var/log/samba \
              --libdir=/etc/ \
              --with-lockdir=/var/lock/samba \
              --with-swatdir=/usr/share/swat \
              --with-privatedir=/etc/
```

7. Follow this with the usual make commands:

```
% make; make install
```

8. Now restore the backup copies of the configuration and system files you made in step 1:

```
% mv /etc/smb.conf.backup /etc/smb.conf
% mv /etc/smbusers.backup /etc/smbusers
% mv /etc/rc.d/init.d/smb.backup /etc/rc.d/init.d/smb
```

9. Test the configuration:

```
% testparm
```

10. Finally, restart the service:

```
% /etc/rc.d/init.d/smb start
```

Modifying Red Hat to Use Samba's Default Location

For one reason or another, let's suppose you've decided to install Samba in it's usual location (/usr/local/samba) and reconfigure Red Hat Linux to use this version. There are several reasons for doing this, as highlighted earlier. The most common reason is a general systems policy for putting all additional software under /usr/local (this is the UNIX tradition). Another would be so that you can have several versions of Samba installed for testing purposes. Logged in as user root, follow these steps:

1. Before you start, back up the existing configuration files that came with your Red Hat distribution. As root, type the following commands:

```
% cp /etc/smb.conf /etc/smb.conf.backup
% cp /etc/smbusers /etc/smbusers.backup
% cp /etc/rc.d/init.d/smb /etc/rc.d/init.d/smb.backup
```

2. Stop the Samba daemons:

```
% /etc/rc.d/init.d/smb stop
```

3. Remove the existing Samba package to avoid any conflicts between the different versions:

```
% rpm -e samba
```

4. Next, you need to obtain your source distribution and go to the directory where you want to install it. (This is usually `/usr/local/src` on a Linux system, but it may vary depending on your site. I generally use `/usr/local/sources` to store my archived software and `/usr/local/src` to contain my uncompressed packages for installation.)

   Change to the following directory:

   ```
   % cd /usr/local/src
   ```

5. Uncompress the archive file using the `tar` utility:

   ```
   % tar xvfz /usr/local/sources/samba-2.0.6.tgz
   ```

   This will create a directory called `samba-2.0.6` (or something similar, depending on the version you're using) below `/usr/local/src`. The source files for building Samba are located in the `source` subdirectory:

   ```
   % cd samba-2.0.6/source
   ```

6. Configure Samba using `with-pam` and `with-smbmount`, which are suitable for the Red Hat system:

   ```
   % ./configure --with-pam --with-smbmount
   ```

7. Follow this with the usual `make` commands:

   ```
   % make; make install
   ```

8. Now restore the backup copies of the configuration and system files you made in step 1:

   ```
   % mv /etc/smb.conf.backup /usr/local/samba/smb.conf
   % mv /etc/smbusers.backup /usr/local/samba/smbusers
   % mv /etc/rc.d/init.d/smb.backup /etc/rc.d/init.d/smb
   ```

9. Use your favorite editor to edit the file `/etc/profiles`. Add the following lines to the end of this file:

   ```
   PATH=$PATH:/usr/local/samba
   MANPATH=$MANPATH:/usr/local/samba/man
   ```

10. Edit the script used to start the Samba daemon in `/etc/rc.d/init.d/smb` and make the following changes (line numbers are prefixed by L and are in brackets). Specifically, edit the line

    ```
    (L17) [ -f /etc/smb.conf ] || exit 0
    ```

    to read as this:

    ```
    (L17) [ -f /usr/local/samba/lib/smb.conf ] || exit 0
    ```

11. Create the `locks` directory and set the correct permissions:

    ```
    % mkdir /usr/local/samba/var/locks/
    % chmod 755 /usr/local/samba/var/locks/
    ```

12. Test the configuration:

    ```
    % testparm
    ```

13. Finally, restart the service:

    ```
    % /etc/rc.d/init.d/smb start
    ```

Installing an Updated Samba on Caldera OpenLinux

At the time of writing, the version of Samba provided with Caldera OpenLinux is 2.0.5, which should be suitable for most installations. However, you may have a need to upgrade to use the latest package. Updated packages can be obtained from `http://support.calderasystems.com`.

As well as from the source archives, Samba is also available for OpenLinux in the form of binary RPM package files. By far the greatest benefit of using the provided RPM is that all files and directories are correctly created for you in locations that integrate into OpenLinux's file structure. This removes the need to modify the system's configuration and therefore helps maintain the system's integrity. As a bonus, a working sample configuration file (`/etc/samba.d/smb.conf.sample`) is also provided.

Installing Caldera's Samba Binary RPM

With Caldera Linux, Samba is provided as three separate RPM archives on the installation CD (CD 1). The three RPM files are for the Samba core daemons and utilities, the Samba documentation, and SWAT. The version of Samba that's provided with OpenLinux 2.3 is 2.0.5.

You may install Samba using the `rpm` command from a shell or by using the graphics KDE Package Manager from X Server.

Testing for the Presence of Samba on OpenLinux

First, you need to check whether Samba has been installed on your system. Use the `rpm` command to do this from a terminal window as any user:

```
% rpm -q samba
```

This will return one of the following messages:

```
package samba is not installed
```

or

```
package samba-2.0.5-1 is installed
```

Installing with the `rpm` Command

If Samba is already installed, great! You can move on to configuring and testing the installation. If not, you need to install it first. For this, you need to be logged in as `root`. Before installing Samba, you need to make sure that the Caldera OpenLinux installation CD is mounted on `/mnt/cdrom`. Use a shell as `root` and type the following:

```
% mount /mnt/cdrom
```

If this command fails, you may need to use the full form:

```
% mount -t iso9660 /dev/hdc /mnt/cdrom
```

> **Note**
>
> Your CD-ROM drive might be installed an a different part of the EIDE bus or it might even be a SCSI device. Be sure to consult your local configuration.

Then issue the following commands:

```
% rpm -i /mnt/cdrom/Packages/RPMS/samba-2.0.5-1.i386.rpm
% rpm -i /mnt/cdrom/Packages/RPMS/samba-docs.2.0.5-1.i386.rpm
% rpm -i /mnt/cdrom/Packages/RPMS/swat.2.0.5-1.i386.rpm
```

This will install Samba and all its files in the correct locations for the Caldera distribution.

Installing with the KDE Package Manager

The KDE desktop environment includes its own graphical application for software installation—the KDE Package Manager. As an alternative installation, you can use this application. You'll need access to an X Server for the Samba server. You can run the binary, `kpackage`, from the command line as `root`:

```
% kpackage &
```

The KDE Package Manager is a very useful utility that presents all installed packages in a logical tree structure. You also have the advantage of being able to review a package's contents before installing.

The simplest way to use `kpackage` to install Samba is by using the KDE File Manger (`kfm`). The method to achieve this many vary depending on how OpenLinux was installed on your system. In general, simply follow these steps:

1. Make sure the OpenLinux installation CD is in your CD-ROM drive on your Samba server.

5

INSTALLING SAMBA

2. Double-click the CD-ROM icon on your KDE desktop. This will bring up a `kfm` browser window showing the contents of the CD-ROM drive.

3. Using `kfm`, navigate to the directory file `/auto/cdrom/Packages/RPMS/`.

4. Scroll through the list of icons to install until you find the file `samba-2.0.5-1.i386.rpm`.

5. Single-click this icon, and the corresponding file will be opened by `kpackage`.

6. Click the Install button.

7. Repeat steps 4 through 6 for the files `samba-docs-2.0.5-1.i386.rpm` and `swat-2.0.5-1.386.rpm`.

Figure 5.3 shows a screen of OpenLinux with `kfm` and `kpackage` running, ready to install the Samba package.

FIGURE 5.3

Installing Samba on Caldera using KDE Package Manager.

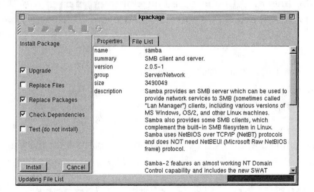

Fixing Caldera's RPM

There are a number of small changes you'll need to make to get your basic Samba installation working correctly for Caldera. The first issue you should address concerns SWAT. You'll find that you're unable to access it from your Web browser. This is due to a minor typo on Caldera's part, but it can be easily fixed. As `root`, edit the file `/etc/hosts.deny` and change the line

```
swat:ALL EXCEPT 127.0.0.2
```

to read as this:

```
swat:ALL EXCEPT 127.0.0.1
```

You can also add any number of IP addresses after this line of clients that want to access SWAT remotely. Alternatively, you can forego Caldera's security consciousness and simply remove this line altogether, thus leaving it open to everyone.

Now that you have SWAT running, you need to make some minor changes to the default configuration because it's not quite what it should be. Using your favorite editor, log in as root and modify the [homes] section of the default smb.conf file (located in /etc/samba.d) to read as this:

```
[homes]
read only = no
browseable = no
```

After saving this file, restart the Samba daemon as root:

```
% /etc/rc.d/init.d/samba restart
```

Everything should now be working sufficiently to test a basic Samba network and begin developing your configuration.

Installing from Source over Caldera's Samba

This method allows you to install a later (or earlier) version of Samba to fit exactly over top of the default installation. It assumes that you already have Samba installed from the Caldera installation CD. By using this method, you can save time and effort reconfiguring your system and make everything slightly less complicated. You'll need to be logged in as root to do the following:

1. Before you start, you should back up the existing configuration files that came with your Caldera distribution. As root, type the following commands:
   ```
   % cp /etc/samba.d/smb.conf /etc/samba.d/smb.conf.backup
   % cp /etc/samba.d/smbusers /etc/samba.d/smbusers.backup
   % cp /etc/rc.d/init.d/samba /etc/rc.d/init.d/samba.backup
   ```

2. Stop the Samba daemons:
   ```
   % /etc/rc.d/init.d/samba stop
   ```

3. Remove the existing Samba package to avoid any conflicts between the different versions:
   ```
   % rpm -e samba; rpm -e swat; rpm -e samba-docs
   ```

4. Next, you need to obtain your source distribution and go to the directory where you want to install it. (This is usually /usr/local/src on a Linux system, but it might vary depending on your site. I generally use /usr/local/sources to store my archived software and /usr/local/src to contain my uncompressed packages for installation.)

   Change to the following directory:
   ```
   % cd /usr/local/src
   ```

5. Uncompress the archive file using the tar utility:
   ```
   % tar xvfz /usr/local/sources/samba-2.0.6.tgz
   ```

5

INSTALLING
SAMBA

This will create a directory named `samba-2.0.6` (or something similar, depending on the version you're using) below `/usr/local/src`. The source files for building Samba are located in the `source` subdirectory:

```
% cd samba-2.0.6/source
```

6. Now when you configure Samba, you pass parameters to the configure script to make the installation place its files in Caldera-friendly locations:

```
% ./configure --with-pam --with-smbmount \
              --prefix=/usr --sysconfdir=/etc/samba.d \
              --localstatedir=/var/log/samba.d \
              --libdir=/etc/samba.d \
              --with-lockdir=/var/lock/samba.d \
              --with-swatdir=/usr/share/swat \
              --with-privatedir=/etc/samba.d
```

7. Follow this with the usual make commands:

```
% make; make install
```

8. Now restore the backup copies of the configuration and system files made in step 1:

```
% mv /etc/samba.d/smb.conf.backup /etc/samba.d/smb.conf
% mv /etc/samba.d/smbusers.backup /etc/samba.d/smbusers
% mv /etc/rc.d/init.d/samba.backup /etc/rc.d/init.d/samba
```

9. You now need to make symbolic links for the Samba daemons:

```
% ln -s /usr/bin/smbd /usr/sbin/smbd
% ln -s /usr/bin/nmbd /usr/sbin/nmbd
% ln -s /usr/bin/swat /usr/sbin/swat
```

10. Test the configuration:

```
% testparm
```

11. Finally, restart the service:

```
% /etc/rc.d/init.d/samba start
```

Modifying Caldera to Use Samba's Location

For one reason or another, let's suppose you've made the decision to install Samba in the default location defined by the Samba package (`/usr/local/samba`) (as opposed to Caldera's default location), and now need to modify OpenLinux to access Samba there rather than the default. Here are the steps to follow:

1. Back up the existing configuration files that came with your Caldera distribution. As root, type the following commands:

```
% cp /etc/samba.d/smb.conf /etc/samba.d/smb.conf.backup
% cp /etc/samba.d/smbusers /etc/samba.d/smbusers.backup
% cp /etc/rc.d/init.d/samba /etc/rc.d/init.d/samba.backup
```

2. Stop the Samba daemons:

```
% /etc/rc.d/init.d/samba stop
```

3. Remove the existing Samba package to avoid any conflicts between the different versions:

```
% rpm -e samba; rpm -e swat; rpm -e samba-docs
```

4. Next, you need to obtain your source distribution and, as root, go to the directory where you want to install it. (This is usually /usr/local/src on a Linux system, but it might vary depending on your site. I generally use /usr/local/sources to store my archived software and /usr/local/src to contain my uncompressed packages for installation.)

Change to the following directory:

```
% cd /usr/local/src
```

5. Uncompress the archive file using the tar utility:

```
% tar xvfz /usr/local/sources/samba-2.0.6.tgz
```

This will create a directory named samba-2.0.6 (or something similar, depending on the version you're using) below /usr/local/src. The source files for building Samba are located in the source subdirectory:

```
% cd samba-2.0.6/source
```

6. Now when you configure Samba, you pass parameters to the configure script for it to be compatible with Caldera:

```
% ./configure --with-pam --with-smbmount
```

7. Follow this with the usual make commands:

```
% make; make install
```

8. Now restore the backup copies of the configuration and system files made in step 1:

```
% mv /etc/samba.d/smb.conf.backup /usr/local/samba/lib/samba.d/smb.conf
% mv /etc/samba.d/smbusers.backup /usr/local/samba/lib/samba.d/smbusers
% mv /etc/rc.d/init.d/samba.backup /etc/rc.d/init.d/samba
```

9. You now need to make symbolic links for the Samba daemons:

```
% ln -s /usr/bin/smbd /usr/sbin/smbd
% ln -s /usr/bin/nmbd /usr/sbin/nmbd
% ln -s /usr/bin/swat /usr/sbin/swat
```

10. Edit the file /etc/rc.d/init.d/samba. Make the following changes (line numbers are prefixed with L and are in brackets):

```
(L7)    DAEMON_S=/usr/local/samba/bin/$NAME_S
(L9)    DAEMON_N=/usr/local/samba/bin/$NAME_N
(L42)   ssd -K -p /usr/local/samba/var/lock/$NAME_N.pid -n $NAME_N #-x
➥$DAEMON_N
(L43)   ssd -K -p /usr/local/samba/var/lock/$NAME_S.pid -n $NAME_S #-x
➥$DAEMON_S
```

11. Add the following to `/etc/config.d/shells/bashrc`:

    ```
    (L28)    _q="$_q /usr/local/bin
             /usr/X11R6/bin /opt/bin /opt/teTeX/bin /usr/local/samba/bin"
    ```

12. If you use the C shell, change `/etc/config.d/shells/csh.cshrc`:

    ```
    (L40)    set path=($_p $_q /usr/local/samba/bin)
    ```

13. Make changes to `/etc/man.conf` by inserting the following line somewhere near the top of the file:

    ```
    MANPATH /usr/local/samba/man
    ```

14. Test the configuration:

    ```
    % testparm
    ```

15. Finally, restart the service:

    ```
    % /etc/rc.d/init.d/samba start
    ```

Installing an Updated Samba on Debian GNU/Linux

At the time of writing, the version of Samba installed with Debian GNU/Linux 2.1 is version 1.9.18. You're definitely advised to upgrade your Samba to the latest stable version.

Debian comes with several programs for managing package installation in the `.deb` file format. These are `dpkg`, `dselect`, and `apt`. Because `dselect` is a quite complicated console-based application and `apt` is primarily aimed at installing over the Internet, I'll deal solely with `dpkg` in this section.

Installing over Debian's Samba

This method allows you to install a later (or earlier) version of Samba to fit exactly over top of the default installation. It assumes that you already have Samba installed from the Debian installation CDs. By using this method, you can save time and effort reconfiguring your system and make everything slightly less complicated. You'll need to be logged in as `root` to do the following:

1. Before you start, you should back up the existing configuration files that came with your Debian distribution. As `root`, type the following commands:

    ```
    % cp /etc/smb.conf /etc/smb.conf.backup
    % cp /etc/smbusers /etc/smbusers.backup
    % cp /etc/init.d/samba /etc/init.d/samba.backup
    ```

2. Stop the Samba daemons:

   ```
   % /etc/init.d/samba stop
   ```

3. Remove the existing Samba package to avoid any conflicts between the different versions:

   ```
   % dpkg -r samba; dpkg -r samba-doc
   ```

4. Next, you need to obtain your source distribution and go to the directory where you want to install it. (This is usually `/usr/local/src` on a Linux system, but it might vary depending on your site. I generally use `/usr/local/sources` to store my archived software and `/usr/local/src` to contain my uncompressed packages for installation.)

   Change to the following directory:

   ```
   % cd /usr/local/src
   ```

5. Uncompress the archive file using the `tar` utility:

   ```
   % tar xvfz /usr/local/sources/samba-2.0.6.tgz
   ```

   This will create a directory called `samba-2.0.6` (or something similar, depending on the version you're using) below `/usr/local/src`. The source files for building Samba are located in the `source` subdirectory:

   ```
   % cd samba-2.0.6/source
   ```

6. Now when you configure Samba, you pass parameters to the configure script to make the installation place its files in Caldera-friendly locations:

   ```
   % ./configure --prefix=/usr --sysconfdir=/etc/ --libdir=/etc/ \
     --localstatedir=/var/log/ \
                 --with-lockdir=/var/lock/ \
                 --with-swatdir=/usr/share/swat \
                 --with-privatedir=/var/samba
   ```

7. Follow this with the usual `make` commands:

   ```
   % make; make install
   ```

8. Now restore the backup copies of the configuration and system files made in step 1:

   ```
   % mv /etc/smb.conf.backup /etc/smb.conf
   % mv /etc/smbusers.backup /etc/smbusers
   % mv /etc/init.d/samba.backup /etc/init.d/samba
   ```

9. You now need to make symbolic links for the Samba daemons:

   ```
   % ln -s /usr/bin/smbd /usr/sbin/smbd
   % ln -s /usr/bin/nmbd /usr/sbin/nmbd
   ```

10. Test the configuration:

    ```
    % testparm
    ```

5

INSTALLING
SAMBA

11. Edit /etc/services and append the following entry to the file:

```
swat    901/tcp
```

12. Edit /etc/inetd.conf and append the following entry to the file:

```
swat    stream    tcp    nowait.400    root    /usr/bin/swat swat
```

13. Force your system to reread inetd.conf after amending it:

```
/etc/init.d/netbase reload
```

14. Finally, restart the Samba service:

```
% /etc/init.d/samba start
```

Modifying Debian to Use Samba's Location

For one reason or another, let's suppose you've made the decision to install Samba in the default location specified by the Samba package (/usr/local/samba) as opposed to Debian's default location. You will need to modify Debian to access Samba there, rather than the default. Here are the steps to follow:

1. Before you start, you should back up the existing configuration files that came with your Debian distribution. As root, type the following commands:

```
% cp /etc/smb.conf /etc/smb.conf.backup
% cp /etc/smbusers /etc/smbusers.backup
% cp /etc/init.d/samba /etc/init.d/samba.backup
```

2. Stop the Samba daemons:

```
% /etc/init.d/samba stop
```

3. Remove the existing Samba package to avoid any conflicts between the different versions:

```
% dpkg -r samba; dpkg -r samba-doc
```

4. Next, you need to obtain your source distribution and go to the directory where you want to install it. (This is usually /usr/local/src on a Linux system, but it might vary depending on your site. I generally use /usr/local/sources to store my archived software and /usr/local/src to contain my uncompressed packages for installation.)

   Change to the following directory:

```
% cd /usr/local/src
```

5. Uncompress the archive file using the tar utility:

```
% tar xvfz /usr/local/sources/samba-2.0.6.tgz
```

   This will create a directory named samba-2.0.6 (or something similar, depending on the version your using) below /usr/local/src. The source files for building Samba are located in the source subdirectory:

```
% cd samba-2.0.6/source
```

6. Configure Samba with no parameters (this should be fine for Debian):

```
% ./configure
```

7. Follow this with the usual make commands:

```
% make; make install
```

8. Now restore the backup copies of the configuration and system files made in step 1:

```
% mv /etc/smb.conf.backup /usr/local/samba/lib/smb.conf
% mv /etc/smbusers.backup /usr/local/samba/lib/smbusers
% mv /etc/init.d/samba.backup /etc/init.d/samba
```

9. You now need to make symbolic links for the Samba daemons:

```
% ln -s /usr/local/samba/bin/smbd /usr/sbin/smbd
% ln -s /usr/local/samba/bin/nmbd /usr/sbin/nmbd
```

10. Create the locks directory with correct permissions:

```
% mkdir /usr/local/samba/var/locks
% chmod 755 !$
```

11. If you plan to use encrypted passwords, you'll need to create an smbpasswd file:

```
% cd /usr/local/src/samba-2.0.6/source/script
% cat /etc/passwd | sh mksmbpasswd.sh > /usr/local/samba/private/smbpasswd
```

12. Modify your search path for binaries by editing /etc/profile and appending /usr/local/samba/bin to the PATH setting. Here's an example:

```
PATH="/usr/bin:/usr/sbin:/bin:/usr/X11/bin:/usr/local/samba/bin"
```

13. Edit /etc/manpath.config and append the following line:

```
MANDATORY_MANPATH=/usr/local/samba/man
```

14. Test the configuration:

```
% testparm
```

15. Edit /etc/services and append the following entry to the file:

```
swat    901/tcp
```

16. Edit /etc/inetd.conf and append the following entry to the file:

```
swat    stream    tcp    nowait.400    root    /usr/bin/swat swat
```

17. Force your system to reread inetd.conf after amending it:

```
/etc/init.d/netbase reload
```

18. Finally, restart the Samba service:

```
% /etc/init.d/samba start
```

Installing Samba from Source

Those of you more accustomed to the Windows world of binary packages might find the idea of compiling and installing something from source somewhat daunting at first.

Luckily, it's not actually as difficult or complicated as it may first appear to be. Many source distributions are very well packaged and can be built and installed with a minimum amount of difficulty. The key point here is to make sure the development tools (that is, your compiler, linker, and make utility) are up-to-date and installed correctly. You'll also need to be aware of which libraries you've installed and which libraries are required by the package you're installing.

Samba does not require any out-of-the-ordinary libraries except if you're planning on an advanced configuration with SSL support or other features. The only exception to this is PAM (Pluggable Authentication Modules), which is often employed by Linux variants (notably Red Hat and Caldera). For this, you'll need to obtain the PAM libraries, which are usually available in package form from your OS manufacturer.

What Different Forms Are There?

The most common form Samba occurs in is as a gzipped tar file. For this, you'll need the UNIX tar (tape archiver) utility, which normally comes with most distributions of UNIX and Linux. The tar utility comes in several different versions, and the parameters in each may vary. The most common difference is whether support for gzip (GNU Zip) compression is built in. If tar supports the z parameter, gzip compression is built in; if not, you'll need to have the gzip utility. If you don't have gzip, it's available from www.gnu.org.

Gzipped tar packages can be obtained from the host of Samba http and ftp servers around the world. For your closest Samba mirror, check www.samba.org.

Binary packages for many platforms are available but are often not up-to-date. Nevertheless, it's worth checking samba.isca.uiowa.edu/samba/ftp/Binary_Packages.

CVS (Concurrent Versions System) is a source tree management tool for version control. The core Samba development team has write access to this tree, and it's available in read-only form over the Internet. This is the place where you'll get the absolutely latest source code available. To access the Samba CVS, you'll need to have the cvs utility installed. There's also http access available. Visit cvs.samba.org/cvs.html for more information.

Accessing the CVS for the Latest Development Version

CVS is a version control system that allows for tracking of source code and logging of when and by whom updates are made. The Samba team runs a CVS server that holds the latest-breaking source distribution of Samba. If you really want the latest stuff, this is where to go. The Samba CVS can be found at cvs.samba.org/cvs.html.

There are two methods for accessing CVS. The first is via a utility called cvsweb, which allows browser access and can be reached from the Samba CVS site. The second is the more traditional method—using an anonymous cvs client. This second method is explained in this section. You'll need to have the cvs utility, which you should have as a standard development tool for your system, and an Internet connection. Follow these steps as root:

1. Create a symbolic link called samba to an uncompressed version of the latest Samba development source you have:

```
% cd /usr/local/src
% ln -s ./samba-2.1/ ./samba/
```

2. Connect and log in to the CVS server:

```
% cvs -d :rpserver:cvs@cvs.samba.org:/cvsroot login
```

Log in with the password cvs. If your login attempt fails, make sure you're in a directory that contains a subdirectory named samba.

3. Execute the following command:

```
% cvs -d :pserver:cvs@cvs.samba.org:/cvsroot co samba
```

This will update the contents of the subdirectory samba with the latest samba sources. Because the source is not in compressed format, this might take some time if you're connecting by modem.

4. Log out from the CVS system:

```
% cvs -d :pserver:cvs@cvs.samba.org:/cvsroot logout
```

Whenever you want to update this with the latest sources, you can simply perform the following steps:

1. Change to the CVS source directory:

```
% cd /usr/local/src/samba
```

2. Connect and log in to the CVS server:

```
% cvs -d :rpserver:cvs@cvs.samba.org:/cvsroot login
```

Log in with the password cvs. If your login attempt fails, make sure you're in a directory that contains a subdirectory named samba.

3. Execute the following command:

```
% cvs update -d -P
```

4. Log out from the CVS system:

```
% cvs -d :pserver:cvs@cvs.samba.org:/cvsroot logout
```

5

INSTALLING
SAMBA

Configuring and Running the Source Install

Obtain your source distribution by one of the methods described previously and, as `root`, go to the directory where you want to install it. This is usually `/usr/local/src` on a Linux system, but it might vary depending on your site.

I generally use `/usr/local/sources` to store my archived software and `/usr/local/src` to contain my uncompressed packages for installation. These are the directories I'll use in this example. You should modify them for your site.

Uncompressing the Source

Change to the source install directory:

```
% cd /usr/local/src
```

Uncompress the archive file using the `tar` utility:

```
% tar xvfz /usr/local/sources/samba-2.0.6.tar.gz
```

or

```
% gzip -dc /usr/local/sources/samba-2.0.6.tar.gz | tar xvf -
```

This will create a directory named `samba-2.0.6` (or something similar, depending on the version you're using) below `/usr/local/src`. The source files for building Samba are located in the `source` subdirectory. Change to this directory:

```
% cd samba-2.0.6/source
```

Configuring and Building Samba

Now you need to configure Samba for your system:

```
% ./configure
```

Next, compile and install Samba:

```
% make
% make install
```

Samba will now be installed in the default directory: `/usr/local/samba`. Refer to the section "Installation-Specific File Locations" for details of the installed directory structure.

Configuring Your System to Recognize Samba

Once Samba has been installed in `/usr/local/samba`, you'll need to change some of your system's configuration files to tell it where to look for the binary files when the Samba service is started upon booting and for normal execution from a shell. Also, you'll probably want to include the location of the manual pages in the system's MANPATH variable so that you can find out information about the Samba binaries.

Configuring the PATH and MANPATH Variables

You must modify your system's PATH and MANPATH variables in order for it to be able to find the binary files for execution and manual pages. These are normally set in a file such as /etc/profiles, /etc/bashrc, or /etc/csh.cshrc, depending on your system.

For sh- and bash-based systems, add the lines

```
PATH="$PATH:/usr/local/samba/bin"
MANPATH="$MANPATH:/usr/local/samba/man"
```

and make sure a line similar to the following appears after them:

```
export PATH MANPATH
```

For csh- and tcsh-based systems, add the following lines:

```
setenv PATH = "${PATH}:/usr/local/samba/bin"
setenv MANPATH = "${PATH}:/usr/local/samba/man"
```

Configuring the Daemon Processes

In order to guarantee that Samba is always running, even if you reboot your server, you need to configure your system to start the Samba smbd and nmbd daemon services automatically upon startup. Normally the services are started in a file such as /etc/rc, /etc/rc.local, /etc/rc.d/rc.local, or /etc/rc.d/init.d/smb, depending on your version of UNIX or Linux. If you're unfamiliar with the location of such a file, you should consult your system's documentation.

There are many different ways in which the system services can be started, depending on your system, the shell in force and the mechanism by which they are handled. There is no single, simple method for handling this that will definitely work on all systems, but the following example should cover most of them.

Create a file called rc.samba and place it in the /etc or /etc/rc.d directory. This file should contain, at minimum, the following lines:

```
#!/bin/sh
/usr/local/samba/bin/smbd -D
/usr/local/samba/bin/nmbd -D
```

The first line specifies the shell used to execute the script (in this case, sh). The second line starts the SMB service as a daemon process, and the third line starts the NetBIOS naming service as a daemon process.

Configuring SWAT

Two entries are needed in different files to access SWAT. The first file is /etc/services (this is the usual location for nearly all UNIX and Linux systems). It defines what TCP or UDP services are available from different ports on your system. SWAT usually runs on port 901, so as root you need to add this entry:

```
swat      901/tcp    # Add swat service used via inetd
```

The second file you need to modify is /etc/inetd.conf. This file defines which programs handle different network service requests made to the inet daemon. As root, add the following entry:

```
swat      stream  tcp    nowait.400      root /usr/bin/swat swat
```

Configuring the `inet` Daemon to Run Samba

On some systems, you might want to have the Samba daemons smbd and nmbd running as inet services rather than daemons. This action means that they do not run continuously but rather are dynamically run when a request for their services is made.

This action is the same for the ftp daemon and other Internet services, and it's configured by placing entries in /etc/inetd.conf. You need two entries: one for smbd, and one for nmbd. Append or modify the following entries in /etc/inetd.conf for your system:

```
netbios-ssn    stream   tcp    nowait    root    /usr/sbin/tcpd /usr/sbin/smbd
netbios-ns     dgram    udp    wait      root    /usr/sbin/tcpd /usr/sbin/nmbd -a
```

Although you have the advantage of using less memory when running the Samba services as processes of the inet daemon, be aware that you will experience slower network response times than if running them as system services. This is generally useful only for sites that rarely use their Samba services.

Installing Multiple Versions of Samba

It may be necessary to have multiple versions of Samba installed on the same server at the same time and to be able to swap between them easily. For example, suppose you have a working environment running on the current stable release but want to experiment with the latest development version, which implements some new features. You want to keep each installation intact with its respective configuration and evaluate the differences in functionality between them. A simple change to the configuration prior to installation makes this easy.

In this example, you have successfully installed Samba, as described, but now want to experiment with the latest development version without corrupting your existing installation. Here are the steps you should follow:

1. Go to your compile directory and "untar" the new version; then go to the `source` subdirectory:

```
% cd /usr/local/src
% gzip -cd /usr/local/sources/samba-2.1.tar.gz | tar xvf -
% cd samba-2.1/source
```

2. Now, when you issue the configuration command, you pass a parameter to tell it to install somewhere different:

```
% ./configure --prefix=/usr/local/samba-2.1
```

3. Continue to compile and install:

```
% make
% make install
```

You can now simply switch between versions by using a symbolic link to the actual source directories.

4. Rename your existing Samba-installed directory name:

```
% mv /usr/local/samba /usr/local/samba-2.0.6
```

5. Link to the version you want to use currently:

```
% ln -s /usr/local/samba-2.1 /usr/local/samba
```

In this way, your system configuration files can remain as they are, and you can simply change between the two (or more) installation directories by using the following method:

```
% rm -f /usr/local/samba
% ln -s /usr/local/samba-2.0.6 /usr/local/samba
```

With respect to Samba daemons, I recommend using a simple shell script to stop the daemons, swap the directories, and restart the daemons. Here's an example:

```
#!/bin/sh
/etc/rc.d/init.d/smb stop
rm -f /usr/local/samba
ln -s /usr/local/samba-2.0.6 /usr/local/samba
/etc/rc.d/init.d/smb start
```

Installation-Specific File Locations

It's a well-known fact that each different proprietary UNIX version has its own way of arranging directory structures and methods of system configuration. This has been the bane of UNIX and one of the reasons why it lost a lot of prestige in the 1980s. Because each flavor of UNIX is specific (not just considering System V and BSD differences), specific knowledge is required for each variant. Microsoft, therefore, has gained a lot of ground on UNIX.

Unfortunately, to a lesser degree, Linux suffers a similar dilemma. Although the nature of Linux has meant that many things are standardized and common throughout the various distributions, each choose a slightly different location for various files and a slightly different organization of system configuration files. Luckily, with Linux, these variations are not too great, and any experienced administrator of one distribution should be able to quickly adapt to a different one.

Samba's Default File Locations

With no site-dependant configuration options specified, Samba installs itself into the directory /usr/local/samba. Table 5.3 shows the default directory structure for Samba.

TABLE 5.3   The Default Samba Directory Structure

Directory	Description
bin/	Binary files (including administrative binaries and daemons)
lib/	Where the configuration files smb.conf and smbusers will be stored
lib/codepages/	Where codepages for international language support are stored
man/	Manual pages
swat/	The Samba Web Administration Tool (SWAT)
var/	Directory where state information such as log and lock files will be stored
private/	Where Samba stores the smbpasswd files and ID files

Several key configuration files are associated with Samba, as shown in Table 5.4.

TABLE 5.4   Samba Configuration Files

File	Description
smb.conf	The main configuration file for Samba in Windows INI format
smbpasswd	The password list for Samba, similar to /etc/passwd
smbusers	A map of Windows-to-UNIX usernames (for example, Administrator to root)

Sample File and Directory Locations on Linux Distributions

Table 5.5 shows the default locations of the key Samba directories and resources for the three Linux distributions covered in this chapter.

TABLE 5.5 Locations of Samba Files on Linux Distributions

File Type	Red Hat Linux	Caldera OpenLinux	Debian GNU/Linux
smb.conf	/etc	/etc/samba.d	/etc
smbpasswd	/etc	/etc/samba.d	/var/samba
Lock files	/var/lock/samba	/var/lock/samba.d	/var/lock
Log files	/var/log/samba	/var/log/samba.d	/var/log
Client binaries	/usr/bin	/usr/bin	/usr/bin
Samba daemons and admin binaries	/usr/sbin	/usr/sbin	/usr/sbin
SWAT	/usr/share/swat	/usr/share/swat	Not installed

Testing Your Installation

Before unleashing your Samba server into your production environment, you should seriously consider testing the configuration and its interaction with other CIFS clients on your network. The advantages of this are two-fold. Firstly, it will help you get a clearer understanding of exactly how the CIFS and Samba work and how Samba interacts clients. It may even help you better understand the way Windows clients use CIFS. Secondly, it will help you be better prepared for going live. By making sure you fully understand what is happening, you will be able to reduce the impact on your users and save your own reputation.

This section will help you test and diagnose problems with your Samba installation.

Setting Up the Test Environment

You should prepare the following minimum configuration before proceeding:

- A simple LAN with your Samba server and at least one Windows client (preferably Windows 9x or NT 4 Workstation)
- User accounts on both the Samba server and the Windows client that are identical in login name and password
- The TCP/IP protocol and Microsoft Networking Service running on the Windows client
- IP addresses and netmasks on both machines that place them in the same Class C subnet

A Basic Network Configuration

A basic test for ensuring that TCP/IP is running correctly is to issue a ping command between the Windows client and the Samba server. Either from a shell prompt on your

5

INSTALLING SAMBA

Samba server or from a command prompt (DOS) on your Windows machine, use the ping command to see whether TCP/IP is working between the two machines. For example, if your Samba server has an IP address of 192.168.100.2 and your Windows 98 machine has an IP address of 192.168.100.1, on your Windows 98 machine, you would bring up the DOS prompt and type the following:

```
C:> ping 192.168.100.2
```

This should yield the following or a similar response:

```
Reply from 192.168.100.2: bytes=32 time<10ms TTL=255
```

A Basic Configuration File for Testing

Here's an example of a very simple smb.conf file that should be suitable for testing whether Samba is working correctly on your server and can be accessed by Windows clients on a simple LAN:

```
[global]
    workgroup = MYGROUP
    encrypt passwords = Yes
[homes]
    read only = No
    browseable = No
[public]
    path = /tmp
    guest ok = Yes
```

This file will enable you to view a per-user homes share and a public directory available to all users. In this example, the machine is called PERSEUS, and it's located in the MYGROUP workgroup.

Creating a Test User

In order to test your connection to your Samba server, you'll need to create a user account, which is used by the CIFS protocol to connect to the server's services. This account needs to exist as both a UNIX user account and in the Samba accounts database (the smbpasswd file).

To create a UNIX user account, log in to your Samba server as root and enter the following commands:

```
% useradd -d /home/username1 -s /bin/false -n username
% passwd username
```

Having created the user account, you need to add it to the smbpasswd file:

```
% smbpasswd -a username
```

Testing Locally on Your Samba Server

Before jumping into the seat of your Windows test workstation, it's a good idea to check whether all is working fine on the Samba server itself. There are several tests you can run with the Samba server acting as both server and client. If your configuration doesn't work locally, you can be sure it won't work on another Windows machine.

Using `testparm` to Verify `smb.conf`

The `testparm` utility inspects your configuration and will notify you of errors. With your `smb.conf` file as shown previously, running the command

```
% testparm
```

will yield the following output:

```
[username@perseus samba]$ testparm
Load smb config files from /etc//smb.conf
Processing section "[homes]"
Processing section "[public]"
Loaded services file OK.
Press enter to see a dump of your service definitions
```

Pressing Enter will dump your configuration in its entirety (notice the many extra parameters that form the defaults for Samba).

Using the `smbclient` Command to Test Samba Locally

The `smbclient` command can be used to access shares from remote machines running the SMB/CIFS protocol. In this instance, you'll connect from the Samba server to the Samba server to make sure that the services are running correctly on the local machine. As your test user account, from a shell prompt type the following command:

```
% smbclient //perseus/public
```

You'll be asked for a password. Enter your UNIX password. The response from the Samba server PERSEUS logged in as user `username` yields the following:

```
[username@perseus local]$ smbclient //perseus/public
Added interface ip=192.168.100.2 bcast=192.168.100.255 nmask=255.255.255.0
Password:
Domain=[MYGROUP] OS=[Unix] Server=[Samba 2.0.6]
smb: \>
```

Try listing the files with the `ls` command. You should get something similar to this:

```
smb: \> ls ~*
    ~SAM1dcd.tmp                          0  Wed Nov 10 08:25:01 1999
    ~WRI1e85.tmp                          0  Wed Nov 10 08:28:05 1999
    ~WRI1ed1.tmp                          0  Wed Nov 10 08:29:21 1999
    ~WRI21b8.tmp                          0  Wed Nov 10 08:41:44 1999
                44197 blocks of size 65536.12486 blocks available
    smb: \>
```

To exit, use the `quit` command.

5

INSTALLING SAMBA

If you have a similar experience to what's shown here, that means you have a working Samba configuration and that your server is successfully sharing and connecting to CIFS services. The next thing to do is check with a Windows machine.

Testing with Samba and a Windows Client

Once you've tested locally on your Samba server and are sure everything is working correctly, it's time to try the connection between a Windows machine and the Samba server. The simplest configuration is with one Samba server and one Windows 9x client.

Using the `smbclient` Command to Test a Windows File Share

On your Windows machine, create a simple file share. Here's an example:

1. Open My Computer.
2. Right-click on the C: drive icon (or a different one if C: doesn't exist) and select Sharing from the pop-up menu.
3. Select the Shared As option, as shown in Figure 5.4, and click OK.

FIGURE 5.4

Configuring a Windows 98 machine for sharing.

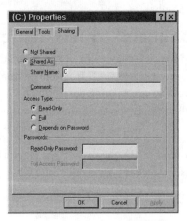

Now, from a shell on your Samba server logged in as any user, use the `smbclient` command to connect to the Windows 9x share you just created.

Using a Windows 9x or NT4 Workstation Client to Test a Samba Share

With your Samba machine connected to the same local LAN and Samba running with the preceding configuration file, open Explorer or Network Neighborhood on your

Windows machine. You should be able to view the file share as shown in Figure 5.5. (It can sometimes take a while for Windows 9*x* clients to refresh their browsers.) You should be able to access the Samba server directly by using the following method:

1. Click Start

2. Select Run.

3. Enter ***MACHINENAME*** in the command box and click OK.

An Explorer-style window should appear with two file shares: one for public, and one for your user (username). Figure 5.5 shows Explorer 5.0 on Windows 98 displaying a basic file share.

FIGURE 5.5

Viewing a Samba share with Windows 98.

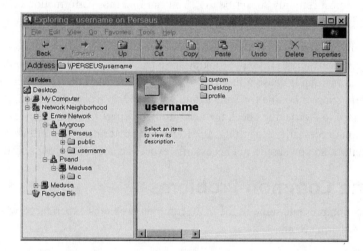

Troubleshooting Tips

If you're experiencing a problem with Samba, first look through the list of common problems, later in this section, to see whether it's covered.

There's an awful lot of documentation provided with Samba, which should always be referred to for greater detail and troubleshooting. The documentation normally resides under /usr/doc on a preinstalled system and can also be found in the docs directory under the Samba source.

You can also reference a number of resources on the Internet.

Where to Look If Something Doesn't Work

The Samba Web site contains late-breaking information about Samba and a wealth of other resources. The main site can be found at `www.samba.org`, and it's mirrored in many locations throughout the world.

The Samba FAQs (frequently asked questions) documents can be found in the `docs` directory under the Samba source tree. On a preinstalled system, these will usually be under `/usr/doc/samba` or a similar location.

The Samba digest is sent out regularly, and it acts as a kind of tips, tricks, problems, and solutions magazine for Samba users. If you're the administrator of a Samba network, you should almost certainly subscribe to it. You can find more information on subscribing to this and other Samba-related mailing lists at `http://lists.samba.org`.

The main newsgroup on the Internet for Samba-related discussions is `comp.protocols.smb`. If you're looking for a particular solution, it's worth subscribing to this newsgroup because it has a lot of information. The newsgroup acts as a kind of voluntary support hotline for Samba, and you could do worse than posting a query there. Be advised to thoroughly check the newsgroup postings for your query before posting so as not to unnecessarily clog things up. Remember that interaction in Internet newsgroups is voluntary, so you should not necessarily expect an answer to your question.

Some Common Problems

This section presents some of the more common problems experienced when installing and configuring Samba.

SWAT Doesn't Work. I Can't Access Port 901.

Check that you have an entry in `/etc/services` similar to this:

```
swat    901/tcp
```

Also, check that you have an entry in `/etc/inetd.conf` similar to this:

```
swat    stream    tcp    nowait.400    root    /usr/bin/swat swat
```

You'll need to restart the `inet` daemon in order for these changes to take effect.

My System Uses TCP Wrappers.

Modify your entries in `/etc/inetd.conf`. Here's the entry to use for `smbd`:

```
netbios-ssn    stream    tcp    nowait    root    /usr/sbin/tcpd /usr/sbin/smbd
```

Here's the entry to use for `nmbd`:

```
netbios-ns   dgram   udp   wait   root   /usr/sbin/tcpd /usr/sbin/nmbd -a
```

Finally, Here's the entry to use for `swat`:

```
swat   stream   tcp   nowait.400   root   /usr/sbin/tcpd /usr/bin/swat
```

My Samba Server Can Connect to Services Locally but Clients Cannot.

Check your hostname–to–IP address mappings in `/etc/hosts` to make sure that the hostname is not pointing at your loopback device.

I Receive an Error When Configuring `--with-pam`.

When you try to run the configure script with `--with-pam`, you get the following error:

```
Checking configure summary
Configure: error: summary failure. Aborting config
```

In this case, you need the PAM libraries installed. These are located in the `/lib` directory on Linux systems. Try the following command:

```
% ls -l /lib/libpam*
```

This should yield output similar to the following:

```
lrwxrwxrwx   1 root      root           11 Jun 24 14:50
      /lib/libpam.so -> libpam.so.0*
lrwxrwxrwx   1 root      root           14 Jun 24 14:50
      /lib/libpam.so.0 -> libpam.so.0.66*
-rwxr-xr-x   1 root      root       111662 Apr 17  1999
      /lib/libpam.so.0.66*
-rw-r--r--   1 root      root        48092 Apr 17  1999
      /lib/libpam_misc.a
lrwxrwxrwx   1 root      root           16 Jun 24 14:50
      /lib/libpam_misc.so -> libpam_misc.so.0*
lrwxrwxrwx   1 root      root           19 Jun 24 14:50
      /lib/libpam_misc.so.0 -> libpam_misc.so.0.66*
-rwxr-xr-x   1 root      root        41619 Apr 17  1999
      /lib/libpam_misc.so.0.66*
```

If you do not get this output, you'll need to install the libraries for PAM.

I Can't Log in to SWAT when Using PAM.

In this case, check whether the file `samba` exists in your PAM configuration directory (commonly `/etc/pam_d` or `/etc`) and contains the following two lines:

```
auth      required      /lib/security/pam_pwdb.so nullok shadow
account   required      /lib/security/pam_pwdb.so
```

5

`smbclient` Yields an Authentication Error when Connecting to Samba Server Using Encrypted Passwords.

The command `smbclient //hostname/share` fails with the following error:

```
session setup failed: ERRSRV - ERRbadpw
(Bad password - name/password pair in a Tree Connect
 or Session Setup or invalid.)
```

In this case, you need to create a correct `smbpasswd` file using the `mksmbpasswd.sh` script:

```
% Cd /usr/local/src/samba-2.0.6/source/script/
% cat /etc/passwd | sh ./mksmbpasswd.sh > /var/samba/smbpasswd
```

Also, you need to set the password for the user who you're trying to connect as:

```
smbpasswd username
```

How Do I Run Samba As a Process in `inetd`?

Running Samba as an `inetd` process, not as a daemon, is possible. For networks where it's used occasionally, loading on demand uses less memory but network performance will be slower. If you're sure you need this functionality, add these entries into `inetd.conf`:

```
netbios-ssn    stream    tcp    nowait    root      /usr/sbin/tcpd /usr/sbin/smbd
netbios-ns     dgram     udp    wait      root      /usr/sbin/tcpd /usr/sbin/nmbd -a
```

Having added these entries, the Samba daemons will only be run on demand. When the server receives a TCP or UDP request that corresponds to the netbios-ssn (port 139) or netbios-ns (port 137), it will automatically start the smbd and nmbd services respectively. Other internet services such as telnet and ftp operate in exactly the same fashion.

How Can I Test Whether the `smbd` and `nmbd` Services Are Running from `inetd`?

In this case, use the `telnet` command. Here's an example:

```
% telnet hostname 137 (for smbd)
% telnet hostname 139 (for nmbd)
```

Successful connections will not yield errors. This means that the services are being started by `inetd`.

I Have the `smbfs` Tools on My System and Want to Upgrade.

The `smbfs` tools (`smbmount`, `smbumount`, and `smbmnt`) are a separate set of tools that are built on the Samba libraries but are not actually part of Samba. For this reason, on many systems, they are installed in a separate package (usually called `smbfs`).

The Samba source distribution does include these utilities, and you may build and install them to update your system by using the `--with-smbmount` parameter upon configuration. Here's an example:

```
% ./configure –with-smbmount
```

Summary

We have covered many topics in this chapter from downloading and compiling the Samba source from the CVS archive through to configuring and testing a Samba installation. The following is a summary of the most important points that have been made:

- Read all the documentation. There are many useful tips that can be gathered from Samba's documentation, the SWAT manual pages and from the Samba Web site.

- If your distribution of UNIX comes with a recent version of Samba or a binary package can be obtained, use this version unless it is absolutely necessary to have a newer version for reasons of functionality.

- Stick to using the current stable version. The latest development version can be unstable and you may have problems with compilation.

- If you do decide to use the latest development version, you should subscribe to at least one of the Samba mailing lists to follow current status and developments.

- Review whether you will overwrite your system's default Samba installation or whether you will be using Samba's default location.

- If using both stable and development versions of Samba on the same server, plan where you will store the two versions and implement a simple scripted method to swap between them.

- Create a test environment before unleashing your Samba server on an unsuspecting production environment. Make sure that you understand the concepts, its operation and how to troubleshoot problems.

- Start with a simple configuration. Samba will work with a configuration file of three lines. Do not try to implement every piece of functionality at first. Start simple and gradually build your site configuration.

5

INSTALLING
SAMBA

- Document everything you do. Keep a journal of your experiences with Samba and how different configurations behaved in your network. This will make an invaluable resource for future support and installations.

This has been a long and involved chapter that has only covered three distributions in detail. If your UNIX or Linux system is one of those that hasn't been covered, you would be well advised to follow through with the instructions for installing Samba on one of the covered systems, just for an example.

Creating a Turnkey Samba System

PART

II

CHAPTER 6

Creating a Simple Samba Proof of Concept

by Steve Litt

Samba servers are simple and modular. They consist of the `smbd` and `nmbd` daemons and the `smb.conf` configuration file, which tells those daemons how to act. Many of the problems encountered by Samba users are traceable to their viewing of Samba as a black box, as well as the fact that their configuration files are much too complex. This tendency is exacerbated by the huge "sample" `smb.conf` files provided with distributions.

Samba becomes much more approachable when started with a proof of concept. Once you're successful with a proof of concept, it's very easy to add features. Starting with a proof of concept reduces troubleshooting time and can speed Samba configuration, especially with unfamiliar parameters. Experimenting and building stepwise with a proof of concept on a spare Linux machine is often the quickest and safest route to putting a configuration into production.

This chapter starts with the simplest possible `smb.conf` and incrementally builds on that to create a Samba server useful in a small office setting.

Examples in This Chapter

All examples in this chapter use server `mainserv`, located at `192.168.100.1/` `255.255.255.0`, as the name of the Samba server. Substitute the name of your server. The user is called `username`, a name unlikely to be confused with genuine users on your system. These examples have been checked on a Celeron-equipped machine running Red Hat Linux 6.0. This machine has an HP printer connected to its one and only parallel port.

If you're following along with this chapter's examples, you'll find it easiest to work on a small network consisting of a Linux Samba server and a Windows client. That way, no production machines are impacted. Because the examples in this chapter come from a Red Hat machine, a Red Hat server is ideal. It's easiest to create a user called `username`.

> **Caution**
>
> Before attempting any of the examples in this chapter, be sure to back up your existing `smb.conf`!

The examples in this chapter assume a Windows client with encrypted passwords enabled. The newer Windows clients all default to encrypted passwords. If your client does not default to encrypted passwords, most of the examples will still work if you change yes to no in the examples' `encrypt passwords=` parameters.

> **Warning**
>
> Many examples in this chapter will not work unless /home/username is chmod 755. Although this is a security breach in real life, username is a "bogus user" intended for reproducing these examples, and it has no valuable data. Therefore, in this case, it's okay. If you intend to follow along with the examples in this chapter (and that's highly recommended), make sure to use chmod 755 /home/username.

Backing Up Your Existing `smb.conf`

Practically speaking, the Samba server's entire behavior is specified by the `smb.conf` file. Therefore, it's absolutely essential that you back up this file before changing it. Be sure to back up your existing `smb.conf` before starting the examples in this chapter.

The location (and even the name) of `smb.conf` is distribution dependent. The most common place to find `smb.conf` is in the /etc directory. On default Caldera 2.3 setups, it's in the /etc/samba.d directory.

Basic Structure of `smb.conf`

Most non-comment lines of `smb.conf` are key/value pairs that look like this:

```
propertyname=propertyvalue
```

Here, `propertyvalue` can be a text string, a number, or a boolean such as yes, no, true, false, 1, and 0. It can also be a dotted decimal representation of an IP address or a directory or file. Both `propertyvalue` and `propertyname` may contain spaces. `propertyname` is always case insensitive.

These key/value pairs describe either Samba as a whole (if they're in the [globals] section) or a particular share (directory or printer) if they follow the name of a share in square brackets.

The Three Samba-Defined Shares

A *share* is a directory or printer accessible through Samba. Every share in `smb.conf` starts with the share's name in square brackets. That share's definition continues until the next name in brackets or until the end of the file.

The behavior of most shares is entirely defined by the information following them. However, there are three shares whose behavior is partially defined by Samba itself. Those shares are [global] (which isn't really a share at all), [homes], and [printers].

> **Note**
>
> There are actually other Samba-defined shares, including [netlogon], which is discussed in Chapter 16, "Using Samba as Your Windows 98 Logon Mechanism."

[global]

The [global] share is an exception to the rule that shares must start with a name between square brackets. Any statements from the start of the file to the first name enclosed in square brackets are treated as being in the [global] section, even if there's no line containing the word [global].

The [global] section is not really a share. Instead, it's a section to place information about Samba as a whole, such as whether passwords should be encrypted or whether the Samba server is a domain master. Additionally, properties that would normally appear in a share, such as whether the share can be browsed remotely, can be put in the [global] section, in which case they become defaults for all shares not explicitly specifying them.

[homes]

The [homes] share automatically maps to the user's home directory, and it shows that directory as the user's name in Network Neighborhood. The beauty of [homes] is that because the user already has an account on the UNIX box, he or she will almost certainly have a home directory, so no path needs to be defined. [homes] shares usually work immediately, so they're very handy.

One problem with the [homes] share is that it exposes UNIX user configuration files (the ones beginning with dots) to the non–UNIX-savvy Windows user. This problem can be eliminated by using substitution characters and server-side automation, but for the purposes of this chapter, the [homes] directory points to the user's home directory—dot files and all.

[printers]

The [printers] share exposes, to the Windows Network Neighborhood, every printer in the /etc/printcap file. This is handy because it eliminates the need for the administrator to find names in the printcap file and assign them to Samba printer shares.

Testing `smb.conf` and Restarting Samba

Get in the habit of doing two things immediately upon finishing a change to Samba:

- Test smb.conf.
- Restart Samba.

Testing `smb.conf`

Testing smb.conf is as easy as typing this command:

```
testparm
```

This outputs success or failure messages, waits for a carriage return, and then outputs voluminous information about the values (including values arrived at by default) in the [global] section. Here's an example of the output for the first part of testparm output:

```
$ testparm
Load smb config files from /etc/smb.conf
Processing section "[netlogon]"
Processing section "[profile]"
Processing section "[homes]"
Processing section "[printers]"
Processing section "[cdrom]"
Processing section "[ourdir]"
Loaded services file OK.
Press enter to see a dump of your service definitions
```

Notice the line Loaded services file OK. That does not necessarily mean you're out of the woods, because shares can load simply by ignoring errors. Instead, ascertain that there are no error messages. The absence of error messages is highly indicative of an smb.conf file with the legal parameter names and values in legal locations. It doesn't imply the Samba setup will work, just that the file uses all legal syntax.

However, any errors reported by testparm almost guarantee that at least one share will not work. testparm-reported errors should always be corrected before continuing on.

Note

You may see testparm warnings saying a share name is more than eight characters and may cause errors on older clients. If you know that all your clients can handle share names greater than eight characters, it's safe to let this go. However, because an older client can be added to your network at any time, consider limiting share name length to eight characters or less, thereby eliminating this warning message.

Finally, `testparm` tests the file, itself, not Samba's state. This means Samba doesn't need to be restarted to run `testparm`. This makes troubleshooting and preventative maintenance much quicker.

Restarting Samba

Changes to `smb.conf` can be tricky because some take effect without restarting Samba, and some do not. To achieve a known state, it's best to restart Samba at the conclusion of modifications to `smb.conf`. The command to restart Samba is OS, version, and distribution dependent. There are three common `restart` commands. For example, you *can* Restart Samba in Red Hat installations as follows:

```
# /etc/rc.d/init.d/smb restart
```

You can restart Samba in Caldera installations as follows:

```
# /etc/rc.d/init.d/samba restart
```

Finally, you can restart Samba in Debian installations as follows:

```
# /etc/init.d/samba restart
```

If your server is not one of the preceding types, look at your Linux or UNIX version/distribution's initialization code to determine how to restart Samba.

Placing the server's Samba `restart` command in a shellscript is a real timesaver as long as it doesn't create a security breach.

Setting Up the Simplest Possible Samba

It could be a game show question: What's the simplest possible `smb.conf`? Here it is:

```
[homes]
```

That's it. A one-line file. All other information is defaulted. Try it. Back up your original `smb.conf` and create this single-line `smb.conf`, run `testparm`, and then restart Samba:

```
# testparm
Load smb config files from /etc/smb.conf
Processing section "[homes]"
Loaded services file OK.
Press enter to see a dump of your service definitions
#

# /etc/rc.d/init.d/smb restart
Shutting down SMB services:                    [  OK  ]
```

Creating a Simple Samba Proof of Concept

CHAPTER 6

157

6

CREATING A SIMPLE
SAMBA PROOF OF
CONCEPT

```
Shutting down NMB services:               [  OK  ]
Starting SMB services:                    [  OK  ]
Starting NMB services:                    [  OK  ]
#
```

Test this setup from the server's command and note the output. Assuming the server's hostname is mainserv, here's the command and its output:

```
# smbclient -NL mainserv
Added interface ip=192.168.100.1 bcast=192.168.100.255 nmask=255.255.255.0
Domain=[WORKGROUP] OS=[Unix] Server=[Samba 2.0.3]

        Sharename      Type      Comment
        ---------      ----      -------
        homes          Disk
        IPC$           IPC       IPC Service (Samba 2.0.3)

        Server                   Comment
        ---------                -------
        MAINSERV                 Samba 2.0.3

        Workgroup                Master
        ---------                -------
        WORKGROUP
#
```

This output proves a functioning Samba server. You can access your files with the FTP-like interface of the smbclient program.

> ### Caution
>
> Once in the interactive smbclient interface, you should use no commands other than ls (directory listing) and quit (leave smbclient). Other commands, especially put and rm, can destroy data.

Assuming the server's hostname is mainserv and an existing uid is username, here's an smbclient session that produces a directory listing of the .b* files in user username's home directory:

```
$ smbclient '//mainserv/homes' -Uusername
Added interface ip=192.168.100.1 bcast=192.168.100.255 nmask=255.255.255.0
Password:
Domain=[WORKGROUP] OS=[Unix] Server=[Samba 2.0.3]
smb: \>> ls .b*
  .bash_logout         H      24  Mon Jul  5 14:10:52 1999
  .bash_profile        H     230  Mon Jul  5 14:10:52 1999
```

```
.bashrc               H      124  Mon Jul  5 14:10:52 1999
.bash_history         H    24458  Fri Oct  8 07:13:52 1999

              61906 blocks of size 32768. 13688 blocks available
smb: \> quit
#
```

In the preceding session, note that user `username`'s password must be interactively typed at the password prompt.

> **Note**
>
> The Windows browsing and access commands might not work on the one-line `smb.conf`. The defaults on this one-line `smb.conf` file may restrict it to access through `smbclient`. The next section, "Setting Up the Simplest Windows-Friendly Samba," implements fixes granting reliable access and browsing on the Windows client.

Note the results of the proper `net view` command on the Windows client (as mentioned, your mileage may vary):

```
C:\WINDOWS>net view \\mainserv
Shared resources at \\MAINSERV

Sharename    Type         Comment
-------------------------------------------------------
username     Disk         Home directory of username
homes        Disk
The command was completed successfully.

C:\WINDOWS>
```

The Windows command-line browse of server `mainserv` found that it contains shares `username` and `homes`. Due to the nature of the [`homes`] share, those two are really the same share. If the [`homes`] share included a `browseable=no` line, only `username` would show up.

Finally, try accessing the share with this command:

```
$ net use z: \\mainserv\homes
$ dir z:
```

On Windows clients with plain-text passwords, the preceding may succeed, but it will definitely fail with an "invalid password" type error on Windows clients using encrypted passwords.

Early Windows 9*x* and NT defaulted to plain-text passwords. Later versions defaulted to encrypted passwords. Samba defaults to plain-text passwords. This means the one-line smb.conf is configured for plain passwords, thus making it incompatible with Windows clients configured for encrypted passwords. In such a case, the solution is to set the Windows box for plain passwords or to enable Samba to use encrypted passwords. The next section describes the latter.

Even on a client with plain-text passwords, the [homes] share declared in the one-line smb.conf probably will not be visible in Network Neighborhood. Network Neighborhood, especially the version in Windows 9*x*, has a difficult time recognizing Samba shares. However, those difficulties can be solved, as discussed in the next section.

Setting Up the Simplest Windows-Friendly Samba

Let's replace the one-line smb.conf with a four-line smb.conf that's friendlier to Windows clients and then note the improvement. Here's the four-line smb.conf file:

```
encrypt passwords=yes
netbios name=mainserv
workgroup=mygroup
[homes]
```

Note that testparm declares this a legal file. Restart Samba. Before exercising this setup, let's briefly discuss it.

encrypt passwords=yes

This line sets Samba to use encrypted passwords, thereby making it compatible with Windows 98, Windows 95 OSRV3 and later, and later NT versions. On these machines, this should be set to yes. On earlier Windows versions, it should be set to no. If you seem to have trouble with passwords, try switching this parameter.

> **Note**
>
> Choosing encrypted passwords on the Samba server means the Samba server must have access to an encrypted password file. You can add your Windows username to the encrypted password file with the command smbpasswd -a username. You'll be prompted for the password, after which that user will be in the encrypted password file.

Note that there's also a Registry tweak to enable plain passwords. It's a DWORD set to 1, and if it doesn't exist, you need to create it to perform this Registry tweak. Here it is on Windows 9*x*:

```
HKEY_LOCAL_MACHINE\System\CurrentControlSet\Services\VxD\VNETSUP
➥/EnablePlainTextPassword=1
```

On Windows NT it's this:

```
HKEY_LOCAL_MACHINE\system\CurrentControlSet\Services\Rdr\Parameters
➥\EnablePlainTextPassword=1
```

This is explained in much more detail in the Win95.txt and WinNT.txt documentation files that come with Samba. Look at those files before attempting any Registry tweak.

> **Caution**
>
> Registry tweaks are very risky—you can potentially lose data or cause the machine not to boot. Therefore, you should be very careful when tweaking the Registry.

To summarize, the encrypt passwords= parameter determines whether encrypted passwords are used on the server. If they're used on the client, they must be used on the server, and vice versa. If plain text is used on the client, it must be used on the server, and vice versa. Encrypted passwords require an encrypted password file that can be written to with the smbpasswd -a username command.

netbios name=mainserv

Windows NT can now use DNS for name resolution, and Windows 2000 always uses DNS. However, many Windows systems still use NetBIOS for name resolution. This means that the Windows client may not be able to access your Samba server by name via hostname or DNS. The smb.conf parameter netbios name= yields a reliable method for Windows clients to locate your Samba server by name. It's best to make the NetBIOS name identical to the hostname.

workgroup=mygroup

Windows clients have a much easier time finding computers and shares in the same workgroup as theirs. Although it's relatively easy to make other workgroups visible, this easy proof of concept is best done in a single workgroup. Therefore, you should substitute your Windows client's workgroup name for the mygroup in this example.

Note that the Windows setup often defaults to workgroups containing spaces, which causes problems in Samba. If at all practical, you should change your Windows workgroup to something without spaces (and hopefully something that's fairly short). The Windows workgroup can be changed on the Identification tab of the Network Properties dialog box, which is accessible through the Control Panel.

Creating the Encrypted Password

Assume a Windows user `username`. Also, assume that the username is already valid on the UNIX box. Now, issue the following command:

```
smbpasswd -a username
```

When prompted, input the same password as the one on the Windows box. You may get the following message instead of the password prompt:

```
startsmbfilepwent: unable to open file /etc/smbpasswd
```

Don't worry about it. This means that the `/etc/smbpasswd` file didn't exist before, so the `smbpasswd` program created it before storing the information for user `username`.

Exercising the New Configuration

Let's review what's happened. We've changed the one line `smb.conf` to this four-line one:

```
encrypt passwords=yes
netbios name=mainserv
workgroup=mygroup
[homes]
```

The first line has a value of `yes` or `no` to match the client's encryption or lack thereof. The second line enables Windows clients to easily find the server by name, whereas the third line is set to the same workgroup as the Windows client to make it easy to browse to.

After restarting Samba, Navigate Network Neighborhood as follows:

```
Network_Neighborhood\entire_network\workgroupname\servername\homes
```

Typically, this should work well. If it does not, try the following:

```
$ net view \\servername
$ net view /workgroup:workgroupname
$ net use * \\servername\homes
```

Then go to Start, Find, Computer and find the server by name. Wait 30 seconds and again try to navigate to the share in Network Neighborhood. This time, it will probably work because the `net use /workgroup:workgroupname` and Find Computer commands most likely triggered a browser election.

If there are problems, troubleshoot. Troubleshooting is covered in the next section.

You'll notice that two shares are visible: `[homes]` and `[username]`. You'll also notice they point to the same directory. This is true because they're really both the `[homes]` share, which has no `browseable=` parameter and has therefore defaulted to `browseable=true`. Also, you'll notice you cannot write anything to these directories. Absent any `read only=` parameter, the share has defaulted to read-only status.

At this point, you've created a four-line `smb.conf` that can easily be navigated in your Windows client's Network Neighborhood. Before continuing on to further `smb.conf` enhancements, let's briefly discuss some simple Samba tests.

Performing the Simplest Possible Samba Tests

Like anything else pertaining to computers, troubleshooting is usually necessary. Luckily, there are many simple tests to quickly narrow the scope of any problem. Several such tests are reviewed in this section.

smbclient -NL localhost

When issued from the command prompt of the server, this command ignores network problems and concentrates on the Samba setup itself. It lists any browseable shares. If this command doesn't work, try substituting `127.0.0.1` for `localhost`. If neither works, it's likely there's a Samba problem on the server, and it's time to troubleshoot your `smb.conf`. Here's an example of the command and a typical output:

```
$ smbclient -NL localhost
Added interface ip=192.168.100.1 bcast=192.168.100.255 nmask=255.255.255.0
Domain=[MYGROUP] OS=[Unix] Server=[Samba 2.0.3]

        Sharename      Type      Comment
        ---------      ----      -------
        homes          Disk
        IPC$           IPC       IPC Service (Samba 2.0.3)

        Server                   Comment
        ---------                -------
        MAINSERV                 Samba 2.0.3
        P2300                    P2300 Steves Main Computer

        Workgroup                Master
        ---------                -------
```

```
        MYGROUP                P2300
[root@mainserv username]#
```

This test proves browseability but not necessarily accessibility.

smbclient '//localhost/homes' -Uusername

Rather than listing browseable shares, this command enables access to the named user's (in this example username) home directory. From there, the smbclient internal command ls can be used. This test proves accessibility to the user's home directory but not necessarily browseability. Here's an example of a session that produces a listing of the .b* files in user username's home directory:

```
$ smbclient '//mainserv/homes' -Uusername
Added interface ip=192.168.100.1 bcast=192.168.100.255 nmask=255.255.255.0
Password:
Domain=[WORKGROUP] OS=[Unix] Server=[Samba 2.0.3]
smb: \>> ls .b*
  .bash_logout         H      24  Mon Jul  5 14:10:52 1999
  .bash_profile        H     230  Mon Jul  5 14:10:52 1999
  .bashrc              H     124  Mon Jul  5 14:10:52 1999
  .bash_history        H   24458  Fri Oct  8 07:13:52 1999

          61906 blocks of size 32768. 13688 blocks available
smb: \> quit
#
```

testparm

The testparm command is too easy not to use every time an smb.conf file is changed. This five-second test often reveals problems that would have resulted in half-hour problem searches, especially as smb.conf gets more complex. This command should be used every time. Here's an example of testparm finding the global parameter encrypt passwords= in the [homes] share:

```
$ testparm
Load smb config files from /etc/smb.conf
Processing section "[homes]"
Global parameter encrypt passwords found in service section!
Loaded services file OK.
Press enter to see a dump of your service definitions
```

testparm is much more handy than just a go/nogo test of smb.conf. It can tell you the values of every Samba global parameter as well as whether those global parameters were acquired via an smb.conf parameter or via defaults. To obtain a list of all parameters, use this command:

```
$ testparm -s | grep =
```

The `-s` argument suppresses the pause for carriage return. Also, `grep =` finds only lines with the equal sign parameters. To see the list sorted by parameter name, do this:

```
$ testparm -s | grep = | sort -f
```

This sorts the lines in a case-insensitive manner. Often you'll want the value of a single parameter, such as the NetBIOS name. This can be done as follows:

```
$ testparm -s | grep -i "netbios name"
```

Notice the quotes surrounding the two-word search criteria. The `-i` argument performs a case-insensitive search for the string.

All in all, `testparm` is an extremely powerful yet simple Samba diagnostic tool.

net use z: \\mainserv\homes

This command, when issued from the Windows command prompt, attempts to access [homes] and set it to drive letter Z:. If Z is already used, you can use a different letter. Of course, you'll substitute your Samba server's name for `mainserv`. If this command fails, try substituting the Samba server's IP address for its name.

If successful, this command proves the Samba share is accessible from Windows, regardless of any problems you may be having in Network Neighborhood, which can be a little quirky in its Samba share handling, especially in Windows 9x.

If this command fails, it's an excellent indication that there's a username or password discrepancy, or even a connectivity problem. What's more, if it hasn't been already ruled out, this might also indicate a problem on the Samba server itself.

ping

`ping` tests connectivity. It doesn't test Samba. But because Samba requires an intact network over which to travel, if `ping` does not work, neither will Samba. Connectivity problems must be resolved before Samba troubleshooting begins.

Here's what a successful `ping` command looks like:

```
$ ping desk1
PING desk1.domain.cxm (192.168.100.2): 56 data bytes
64 bytes from 192.168.100.2: icmp_seq=0 ttl=255 time=0.5 ms
64 bytes from 192.168.100.2: icmp_seq=1 ttl=255 time=0.2 ms
64 bytes from 192.168.100.2: icmp_seq=2 ttl=255 time=0.2 ms
64 bytes from 192.168.100.2: icmp_seq=3 ttl=255 time=0.2 ms

--- desk1.domain.cxm ping statistics ---
4 packets transmitted, 4 packets received, 0% packet loss
```

```
round-trip min/avg/max = 0.2/0.2/0.5 ms
[root@mainserv username]#
```

Here's the result of a UNIX-style `ping` to a foreign subnet without the benefit of a router:

```
[root@mainserv username]# ping 192.168.101.1
PING 192.168.101.1 (192.168.101.1): 56 data bytes
```

Note that it hangs after the first attempt.

Here's the same `ping` command at a Windows command prompt:

```
C:\WINDOWS>ping 192.168.101.1

Pinging 192.168.101.1 with 32 bytes of data:

Request timed out.
Request timed out.
Request timed out.
Request timed out.

Ping statistics for 192.168.101.1:
    Packets: Sent = 4, Received = 0, Lost = 4 (100% loss),
Approximate round trip times in milli-seconds:
    Minimum = 0ms, Maximum =  0ms, Average =  0ms

C:\WINDOWS>
```

Here's the result of what would have been a legitimate `ping`, except that the wire from the hub to machine `desk1` has been disconnected:

```
$ ping desk1
PING desk1.domain.cxm (192.168.100.2): 56 data bytes
```

Just like a bad subnet, it hangs.

`ping` is a low-level connectivity test that can be done both from the UNIX command prompt and the Windows command prompt. It can be used to test the local loopback interface, the local network interface card, as well as connectivity to another computer. Here's the command for testing the local loopback interface:

```
$ ping localhost
```

or

```
$ ping 127.0.0.1
```

Note that on a Windows machine, it tests four times and then quits. On a UNIX box, it keeps testing until the user presses Ctrl+C.

Once you can ping `localhost`, the next step is to see whether you can ping your own network card. This verifies a working network interface, without worrying about wiring, hubs, other computers, and routes. Assuming the local computer's network interface card is `192.168.100.1` and is called `mainserv`, here's how you would ping locally:

```
$ ping mainserv
```

or

```
$ ping 192.168.100.1
```

Once the local network interface is a "known good" card, the next step is to ping a different machine:

```
$ ping desk1
```

or

```
$ ping 192.168.100.2
```

Once connectivity is verified by this successful ping, it's time to start testing Samba interoperability between the two machines.

Note that using a name argument instead of an IP address introduces another variable: name resolution (DNS). The purest test of connectivity is to ping the IP address of the machine in question.

Encrypting Passwords

There's a program called `tcpdump` that intercepts packets on the wire. If it's running during the first `net use` command of a resource on a plain-text-password Windows client, `tcpdump` will capture the username and password. This is the argument for password encryption. Any text transmitted "as is" over the wire is not private.

Unfortunately, there's also a security risk inherent with encrypted passwords. With encryption, password hashes are stored on disk. A cracker could create a modified client capable of using those hashes to break in. This takes more "technical talent" than intercepting clear-text passwords on the wire, but it is possible. This hole can be closed by making the `/etc/passwd` and `/etc/smbpasswd` files `chmod 700` and, of course, owned by `root`.

Therefore, at first glance, password encryption is desirable.

When *Not* to Encrypt Passwords

Password encryption creates problems in certain situations, including password synchronization, PAM authentication, and the use of very early Windows clients.

Samba Password Synchronization

Samba offers methods for synchronizing UNIX passwords with those entered from
Windows Samba clients. Unfortunately, some of these methods do not work with
encrypted passwords.

Therefore, if Samba password synchronization doesn't work, try it with plain-text
passwords.

If PAM Authentication Is Needed

PAM stands for *pluggable authentication module* and is a series of security modules. For
reasons similar to those explained for Samba password synchronization, PAM sometimes
doesn't work with encrypted passwords.

Early Windows Clients

Early Windows 3.*x* clients cannot perform password encryption; therefore, they cannot
communicate with a Samba server set up for password encryption.

Getting Rid of the homes Directory in Network Neighborhood

As previously mentioned, the homes and username (assuming your Windows username is
username) directories show up in Network Neighborhood (or in net view \\mainuser),
and they're really the same physical directory. However, only the username directory
should show up. This can be fixed with the browseable parameter.

Add browseable=no below [homes] to get rid of the homes directory in Network
Neighborhood. Your smb.conf now looks like this:

```
encrypt passwords=yes
netbios name=mainserv
workgroup=mygroup
[homes]
browseable=no
```

As always, Samba must be restarted.

Network Neighborhood does not instantly respond to external changes. It must be
refreshed. Network Neighborhood's screen can be refreshed—either use the View,
Refresh menu choice or press the F5 key.

Note that the homes directory has now disappeared from Network Neighborhood, leaving
only username (or whatever username you're using).

Demonstrating That the Word [global] Is Optional

A fact that's rarely documented is that the [global] designation is optional. Most Samba documentation mentions the placement of the [global] designation before any parameter statements.

Users of the SWAT browser-based smb.conf-configuration utility know that [global] is optional. SWAT removes any [global] lines. In fact, any noncommented parameter statements between the top of the file and the first instance of a bracketed share name are interpreted as part of the [global] section by Samba.

Adding [global] Above encrypt passwords=

Looking at the smb.conf file we've developed so far, you can see that it doesn't have a [global] section. After you add [global] to the top, the file will look like this:

```
[global]
encrypt passwords=yes
netbios name=mainserv
workgroup=mygroup
[homes]
browseable=no
```

After adding this line, run testparm and notice that its output does not change. Restart Samba, refresh Network Neighborhood, and then note whether everything's the same.

Nothing has changed because the [global] line is optional. Anything from the top of the file to the first bracketed name is considered part of the global section already, so adding [global] changes nothing.

Changing [global] to [garbage]

Change [global] to [garbage] and then run testparm. Note that the output contains errors:

```
[root@mainserv /etc]# testparm
Load smb config files from /etc/smb.conf
Processing section "[garbage]"
Global parameter encrypt passwords found in service section!
Global parameter netbios name found in service section!
Global parameter workgroup found in service section!
No path in service garbage - using /tmp
Processing section "[homes]"
Loaded services file OK.
Press enter to see a dump of your service definitions
```

Creating a Simple Samba Proof of Concept

CHAPTER 6

169

6

CREATING A SIMPLE
SAMBA PROOF OF
CONCEPT

[garbage] is the name of an ordinary share, so Samba interprets all the global parameters as part of a normal share, thus resulting in the "found in service section" error messages.

Restart Samba and refresh Network Neighborhood. You might not be able to access the share, depending on whether you're using encrypted passwords and certain other factors. However, there can be no doubt that [global] is a "reserved" word whose purpose is delineating the global section.

Putting [global] at the Bottom of the File

It's not technically necessary for [global] to be at the top of smb.conf. For instance, make an smb.conf like this:

```
[homes]
browseable=no
[global]
encrypt passwords=no
netbios name=mainserv
workgroup=mygroup
```

Now run testparm and note that it once again produces the original results. In other words, the only use of [global] is to place global data below other shares. In fact, you can have two different [global] sections and keep more global data at the top of the file.

However, it's very uncustomary in the Samba world to place global data anywhere but at the top. For maximum readability and understandability, never have global data below other shares. The main use of [global] appearing anywhere but the top involves the use of file includes.

The remainder of this book will place all global configuration data before any shares.

Making homes Writable

Using the following smb.conf, restart Samba:

```
encrypt passwords=yes
netbios name=mainserv
workgroup=mygroup
[homes]
browseable=no
```

Assuming you're logged in as username, your home directory shows up as username in Network Neighborhood. Attempt to create a directory inside of directory username in Network Neighborhood. You get an "access denied" error and cannot make the directory.

This isn't surprising. The default for read only= in any share is yes, so in the absence of an explicit read only=no, [homes] will be read-only.

> **Note**
>
> The `read only=` parameter has three inverse synonyms: `writeable=`, `writable=`, and `write ok=`. Therefore, `read only=no`, `writeable=yes`, `writable=yes`, and `write ok=yes` all mean the same thing and perform the same function.
>
> The `read only=` parameter is a "first among equals," because both `testparm` and SWAT report this property as `read only=` rather than `writeable=`, `writable=`, or `write ok=`.

Adding `read only=no` Below `[homes]`

So, `smb.conf` now looks like this:

```
encrypt passwords=yes
netbios name=mainserv
workgroup=mygroup
[homes]
read only=no
browseable=no
```

Restart Samba, refresh Network Neighborhood, and once again try to create a directory in `username`. Notice that now you can add it.

The ability to write to a Samba share is controlled by its `read only=` parameter. In the absence of this parameter (or one if its inverse synonyms), the default is `read only=yes`.

Adding a Share Parameter Globally

Samba's parameter defaults greatly ease the administrative workload by reducing the size and complexity of the `smb.conf` file. There may be times when you find yourself "undoing" one of these defaults in most shares and wish another default for that parameter had been picked. Such situations are easily accommodated with global share parameters—that is, share parameters placed in the global section.

Example: Global `read only=yes`

This simple `smb.conf` prevents writing to the share and enables the `homes` directory (as well as `username`) to show up in browses:

```
encrypt passwords=yes
netbios name=mainserv
workgroup=mygroup
[homes]
```

Restart Samba and note that in Network Neighborhood, both `homes` and `username` show up (they're really the same share). Also note that you cannot create a directory in either. The default for the `browseable=` and `read only=` parameters is yes.

Previous examples got rid of `homes` with `browseable=no` and made `[homes]` read/write by inserting `read only=no`. This time, you can defeat those defaults by inserting the same lines in the global area. The difference is that when they're in the global area, they serve as the default for all shares, although they can be overridden inside any specific share.

Here's `smb.conf` with `read only=no` inserted at the top:

```
read only=no
encrypt passwords=yes
netbios name=mainserv
workgroup=mygroup
[homes]
```

Restart Samba and note that you can now create directories in the `username` directory via Network Neighborhood. The global `read only=no` applies to all shares, including `[homes]`.

Example: Global `browseable=no`

Not all global share parameters are that simple. This example shows how a global `browseable=no` removes browseability not only from `[homes]` but from `IPC$` as well, thus causing unexpected consequences.

Remove `read only=` and add `browseable=no` to the top of the file. This is how `smb.conf` looks now:

```
browseable=no
encrypt passwords=yes
netbios name=mainserv
workgroup=mygroup
[homes]
```

Restart Samba and browse Network Neighborhood. Previous experience with the `browseable=` parameter in the `[homes]` share leads to the expectation that the `homes` directory will disappear from Network Neighborhood, leaving only the directory named after your username, `username` in this example. However, that's not what happens. In fact, neither `homes` nor `username` is visible. Here's the explanation: The global `browseable=no` removes browseability not only from `[homes]` but from `IPC$` as well. Without a browseable `IPC$`, the `username` representation of `[homes]` is not browseable either.

> **Note**
>
> IPC$ is a special share used in browsing and other Samba internals. It's a special interprocess communication share that handles browse lists. Source code `ipc.c` and `smb.h` provide excellent documentation on the subject.

The absence of IPC$ is verified by the `smbclient` browse command:

```
$ smbclient -NL mainserv
Added interface ip=192.168.100.1 bcast=192.168.100.255 nmask=255.255.255.0
Domain=[MYGROUP] OS=[Unix] Server=[Samba 2.0.3]

        Sharename      Type      Comment
        ---------      ----      -------

        Server                   Comment
        ---------                -------
        MAINSERV                 Samba 2.0.3

        Workgroup                Master
        ---------                -------
        MYGROUP
$
```

IPC$ is not there.

The situation is rectified by moving the `browseable=no` from the top to the bottom of the file, under [homes]. After Samba restarts, the `smbclient` browse shows the desired result (username but not homes):

```
$ smbclient -NL mainserv
Added interface ip=192.168.100.1 bcast=192.168.100.255 nmask=255.255.255.0
Domain=[MYGROUP] OS=[Unix] Server=[Samba 2.0.3]

        Sharename      Type      Comment
        ---------      ----      -------
        IPC$           IPC       IPC Service (Samba 2.0.3)

        Server                   Comment
        ---------                -------
        MAINSERV                 Samba 2.0.3
        P2300                    P2300 Steves Main Computer

        Workgroup                Master
        ---------                -------
        MYGROUP                  P2300
$
```

IPC$ is once again visible. The username directory is now visible in Network Neighborhood.

Adding the [printers] Share

The [printers] share easily and quickly makes visible and available the server's printcap file printers.

> **Note**
>
> Chapter 8, "Configuring Printer Shares," contains much more detailed information on [printers] and other printer shares, including heavy troubleshooting information.
>
> It's possible the examples in this section of this chapter will not yield successful results. That's okay, because after finishing Chapter 8, you'll be able to set up any kind of Samba printer and troubleshoot any kind of Samba printer problem.

smb.conf Changes

Create the following smb.conf:

```
encrypt passwords=yes
netbios name=mainserv
workgroup=mygroup
printcap name=/etc/printcap
printing=bsd
[homes]
[printers]
print ok=yes
path=/var/spool/samba
```

Note the addition of the printcap name= and printing= global parameters as well as the addition of the [printers] share, with the print ok=yes parameter.

printcap name=

printcap name= is the file containing the list of print queues. Samba defaults this parameter to lpstat. Linux installations typically have this file at /etc/printcap, which is what it should be on Linux installations. Whatever OS, version, and distribution you have, this parameter should point to your system's printer list.

This parameter is the way Samba reaches out and deduces what printers are available and makes them visible and useable as shared printers.

printing=

This parameter tells Samba which printing system to use. Note that the Red Hat 6 Samba installation defaults this parameter to sysv. This creates a problem, because Red Hat

Linux 6.0 uses a bsd printing system, not a sysv printing system. Therefore, the parameter printing=bsd is necessary to print correctly on a Red Hat 6/Linux-hosted Samba server.

> **Note**
>
> The use of a wrong printing= parameter can be compensated by the explicit use of correct print command=, lpq command=, lprm command=, lppause command=, lpresume command=, queuepause command=, and queueresume command= parameters. Sometimes it can be compensated for with just the explicit use of the print command= parameter. Certainly, the easiest course of action is to use the correct printing= parameter.

[printers]

[printers] is a special share that's heavily manipulated by Samba. When Samba sees this share, it uses the file named in printcap name= to enumerate all the system's printers, and it makes them available in browses. It then takes possession of the file to be printed (that file has been given by the client, presumably Windows), stores it temporarily in the directory pointed to by path=, and then via the print command= parameter (which probably includes the lpr shell command) submits it to the proper printer's queue.

print ok=

The single factor identifying a share as a "printer" instead of a "directory" is the existence of a print ok=yes parameter in it. Because [printers] is a printer share, it must have a print ok=yes parameter.

path=

The path in a printer share is a temporary holding area for the file to be printed. It can be in any directory with 1777 permissions, but it's typically put in a "standard" directory. On Red Hat installations, that standard is /var/spool/samba. See your OS and Samba documentation to find the suggested place to put this directory.

Testing

A much more detailed treatment of testing and troubleshooting printers is contained in Chapter 8. This chapter gives a few tips on testing a simple [printers] section.

Creating a Simple Samba Proof of Concept

CHAPTER 6

175

6

CREATING A SIMPLE
SAMBA PROOF OF
CONCEPT

Testing Your Printer Queue

Samba's [printers] share won't print without a working printer queue. Assuming the printer exposed by this share is lp, try printing a file to lp in UNIX. Be sure to use a DOS format file. DOS files delineate lines with a carriage return/linefeed character combination.

Most printers are set up to treat a carriage return/linefeed combination as a newline character, not just a linefeed character. Most Linux files delineate only with linefeeds, so if they're printed on such a printer they soon scroll off the right of the paper.

Samba printers must be "plain-text" printers that do nothing but pass bytes through to the printer. The printer definition is on the Windows side.

Therefore, a DOS-style file must be printed to the printcap printer. The best way to do this is to "binary ftp" your Windows autoexec.bat or config.sys file (or some other short text file) to your UNIX home directory. Remember, the ftp must be binary. Now you have a carriage return/linefeed–delineated file. Now use your OS's standard print command to print it. In Linux, it looks like this, assuming your printcap printer is called lp:

```
$ lpr -P lp autoexec.bat
```

Assuming the printcap printer is plain text, it will not formfeed at the end of file, so the page will still be in the printer. To formfeed it out, send a formfeed to the printer. Here's how to do it in Linux:

```
$ echo ^L | lpr -P lp
```

The formfeed character in the preceding command is made by holding the Control key, tapping the V key, then tapping the L key combination.

Assuming your autoexec.bat file printed correctly, you're ready to test with smbclient.

Testing [printers] with smbclient

This test verifies whether Samba can interact with the printer tested in the previous example. Once again, assume a plain-text printcap printer called lp and assume you still have your binary copy of your Windows machine's autoexec.bat file. The following command finds which printers [printers] exposes:

```
$ smbclient -NL mainserv
Added interface ip=192.168.100.1 bcast=192.168.100.255 nmask=255.255.255.0
Domain=[MYGROUP] OS=[Unix] Server=[Samba 2.0.3]

        Sharename      Type      Comment
        ---------      ----      -------
        homes          Disk
        printers       Printer
```

```
IPC$          IPC       IPC Service (Samba 2.0.3)
lp        Printer

Server                Comment
---------             -------
MAINSERV              Samba 2.0.3
P2300                 P2300 Steves Main Computer

Workgroup             Master
---------             -------
MYGROUP               P2300
$
```

Note the `lp` sharename representing the `lp` print queue defined in the `printcap` file. If the share works, the following command sends the previously acquired `autoexec.bat` file to `lp`, after which it's printed:

```
$ smbclient '//mainserv/lp' -Uusername%whatever -c "put autoexec.bat"
Added interface ip=192.168.100.1 bcast=192.168.100.255 nmask=255.255.255.0
Domain=[MYGROUP] OS=[Unix] Server=[Samba 2.0.3]
putting file autoexec.bat as \autoexec.bat (4.31082 kb/s) (average 4.31083 kb/s)
$
```

In the preceding command, the `whatever` following the `%` sign is the `username`'s password. As before, the file is still stuck in the printer. The following command formfeeds it:

```
$ echo ^L | smbclient '//mainserv/lp' -Uusername%whatever -c "put - f"
Added interface ip=192.168.100.1 bcast=192.168.100.255 nmask=255.255.255.0
Domain=[MYGROUP] OS=[Unix] Server=[Samba 2.0.3]
putting file - as \f (0.0673489 kb/s) (average 0.0673491 kb/s)
$
```

In the preceding command, a formfeed is piped into `smbclient` via the `echo` command, so `smbclient` sees the formfeed in its `stdin`. Also, `-c` means that a command will follow—that command being `put - f`. The dash (`-`) represents `stdin`, and the `f` following it means "call `stdin` file `f`," thereby fulfilling the need for `smbclient`'s internal `put` command to operate on a file. The result is that the formfeed is passed to the printer, which then formfeeds the `autoexec.bat` file sent to it previously.

Testing the Raw Print Share from Windows

So now it's clear that the Samba printer works, at least from `smbclient` on the UNIX side. Now print directly to that share from Windows, without using any Windows printer definitions. Capture that printer share to a nonexistent LPT port (call it `lpt9:`). Then copy a file to that LPT port and echo a formfeed to that port:

```
C:\>net use lpt9: \\mainserv\lp
The command was completed successfully.

C:\>copy c:\autoexec.bat lpt9:
        1 file(s) copied

C:\>echo ^L > lpt9:

C:\>
```

The formfeed character is made either by pressing the Ctrl+L keystroke combination or entering 012 on the keypad while holding down the Alt key.

Testing with a Windows Printer Definition

The preceding examples are great for testing and are intellectually interesting, but they don't do anything for the average Windows user. Now that you've proved you can hit the Samba printer from Windows, hook that printer share to a Windows printer definition by going to Start, Settings, Control Panel, Printers, Add Printer. In the resulting wizard, choose Network Printer and then fill in \\mainserv\lp in the Network Path or Queue Name field while leaving the Print from MS-DOS Based Programs option set to No. Next, choose the printer manufacturer and printer model and, in general, do what you'd do to install your printer locally. If the wizard tells you that you already have a driver, be sure to keep the existing driver. Next, it asks for the printer name. Use testprinter to prevent mixing it up with real printers. On the same screen, be sure to indicate that you don't want it as your default printer.

Now the wizard asks if you'd like to print a test page. Unfortunately, the Windows printer test page and the accompanying "troubleshooter" usually aren't sufficient to troubleshoot, so answer "no" to the test page.

Now go into a Windows application and print a single page, choosing testprinter as the printer. The page should print just as it would from a local printer. If not, troubleshoot it. Chapter 8 contains voluminous printer-troubleshooting information.

Discussion

A *printer share* is a Samba share that contains a print ok=yes (or printable=yes) statement. Its path serves as a holding pen for files waiting to be printed—a sort of queue before the print queue. The [printers] share is a special printer share that reads the printcap file (whose location is pointed to by the printcap name= parameter), and it reveals the printer queues in a browse. Those printers can be accessed either from UNIX via smbclient, from Windows via capturing a printer port, or from Windows via a Windows printer definition linked to the printer share.

Making a Universally Accessible Directory Share

The [homes] share provides an easy way to access your home directory, but it's only one of many directory access and sharing possibilities. Another simple share is one that has no accessibility restrictions. This share can be called anything, but we'll call it [everyone].

> **Warning**
>
> Many examples in this chapter will not work unless /home/username is chmod 755. Although this is a security breach in real life, username is a "bogus user" that's intended for reproducing these examples, and it has no valuable data. Therefore, in this case, it's OK. If you intend to follow along with the examples in this chapter (and that's highly recommended), make sure to use chmod 755 /home/username.

This section serves as an illustration of the factors affecting shares. The procedure, devoid of experiments and examples, is as follows:

1. Create directory /home/username/test with 777 permission.
2. Create smb.conf share [everyone] with path=/home/username/test and read only=no.
3. Restart Samba.

The remainder of this section builds such a share to illustrate the relationship of UNIX permissions and owners to the Samba parameters as well as the [global] section and the effect of share parameters placed in the [global] section.

Inserting [everyone] at the Bottom of the File

Insert [everyone] at the bottom of a simple smb.conf. It should now look like this:

```
encrypt passwords=yes
netbios name=mainserv
workgroup=mygroup
[homes]
[everyone]
```

Restart Samba and browse to everyone in Network Neighborhood. The directory now has the following characteristics:

- It's read-only.
- It points to /tmp.
- It's readable by all.

The Directory Is Read-Only

The everyone directory is read-only because Samba defaults to read-only unless specifically told otherwise by a read only= parameter (or reverse synonym) in smb.conf. No files or directories can be created inside it.

The Directory Points to /tmp

The files inside this directory may appear unfamiliar. A directory listing of the /tmp directory on the UNIX box shows that everyone points to the UNIX box's /tmp directory. Unless told otherwise by a path= parameter in smb.conf, Samba defaults to path /tmp.

The Directory Is Readable by All

All users can access this directory. Absent a valid users= statement, Samba defaults to access by all. It's usually not a good idea to have a directory accessible by everyone, except in all but the smallest network environments, but it's often reasonable to have printers accessible to all users.

Setting the [everyone] Share's Path

A share to directory /tmp has little value. In this section, we'll change the share to point to /home/username/test, and explore some of the issues and pitfalls associated with setting the path of a share.

Making a No-Permission Directory

The relationship between Samba parameters and UNIX permissions can be illustrated by making a no-permission directory below /home/username called test. This assumes a username user with a home directory of /home/username.

Logged in as user username, create the new directory with no permissions:

```
mkdir -m0 /home/username/test
```

Verify the success of the operation with an `ls -ldF` command, whose output should be the line after the following command:

```
$ ls -ldF /home/username/test
d---------    2 username username     1024 Sep 25 14:52 /home/username/test/
$
```

The directory has no permissions. It's owned by user `username`. On a Red Hat–style Hat User Private Group setup, the group is `username`; otherwise, it may be a generic group such as `user`. Any attempt to switch to this directory with a `cd` command fails with a "permission denied" error. There's no executable permission, so you can't switch to it.

Configuring the `[everyone]` Path in `smb.conf`

Configure `[everyone]` as follows:

```
[everyone]
path=/home/username/test
read only=no
```

According to `smb.conf`, this share allows complete read and write access to `/home/username/test`. However, attempts to see it through Network Neighborhood or any other client are met with an error message, because under normal circumstances Samba cannot grant more access to a directory than that given by UNIX. Because in UNIX the share has no permission for read, write, or execute, it cannot be navigated.

Changing the User Permission to Read and Execute

The problem is partially resolved by giving read and execute permissions to the directory's owner, `username`:

```
$ chmod 500 /home/username/test
```

The result can be verified with the `ls` command:

```
$ ls -ldF /home/username/test
dr-x------    2 username username     1024 Sep 25 14:52 /home/username/test/
$
```

Now you can navigate inside directory `everyone`.

> **Note**
>
> Both read and execute permissions are necessary. Read is necessary to see files inside the directory, whereas execute is necessary to `cd` into the directory. Samba must be able to `cd` into the directory to see its contents.

Attempts to create a file or directory inside directory everyone fail with an "access denied" error. Although `smb.conf`'s `read only=no` parameter in the `[everyone]` share would normally grant write access to the directory, the UNIX write permission is missing, thereby restricting this directory to read access. Samba respects the more restrictive UNIX permissions.

chmod 700 /home/username/test

Write permission enables `username` to create and change files and directories inside the share. The UNIX permissions are no longer restricting the Samba configuration. But what about other users?

chown root.root /home/username/test

So far, this is a contrived example. `username`, the same user whose logged in on the Windows machine, owns the `/home/username/test` directory. To better simulate real life, change the directory's owner and group to `root` with this command:

```
$ chown root.root /home/username/test
```

This simulates the more general situation of universal access.

The ownership change prevents access from Network Neighborhood, as can be verified from Windows. `/home/username/test` has no permissions for `group` or `other`, meaning that it's now accessible only by user `root`. UNIX permissions once again hold the share back from its intended universal access.

chmod 777 /home/username/test

The intended use of this share is read/write access for everyone, so there's no harm giving it universal access in UNIX. Now all users can read and write the share from Network Neighborhood.

This roundabout demonstration has shown that the default path of shares is `/tmp` (on most systems), that shares default to browseable, and that Samba accessibility is the lesser of Samba access and UNIX permissions.

Changing the Workgroup on the Samba Side

Up to this point, the `workgroup=` parameter on the Samba side has had the same value as that listed on the Identification tab of the Windows client's Network Properties dialog box. This makes browsing through Network Neighborhood almost a sure thing.

Samba also enables browsing of other workgroups. However, due to features of Network Neighborhood, this is often tricky. Changing the workgroup to `test2` yields this `smb.conf`:

```
encrypt passwords=yes
netbios name=mainserv
workgroup=test2
[homes]
```

After restarting Samba and refreshing Network Neighborhood, browse from Network Neighborhood to Entire Network and notice that the new `test2` workgroup probably does *not* appear. It's also likely that you'll see the Samba server under its former workgroup, even though the workgroup changed. This is all part of the same problem: Windows Explorer's quirkiness in recognizing new and different workgroups.

> **Note**
>
> Windows Explorer (and therefore Network Neighborhood) in Windows NT is much more capable of finding workgroups than is the Windows 98 version. It's likely that if you're using NT, you'll see the `test2` workgroup in Network Neighborhood.

Access Does Not Require Browseability

Not being able to see `test2` and/or `mainserv` in Network Neighborhood does not mean they're inaccessible in Windows. This Windows command accesses the `[homes]` share as the drive Z:

```
$ net use Z: \\mainserv\homes
```

Browseability Tweaks

The Windows command-line `net` utility is much more capable of browsing.

The following Windows 98 command often finds the Samba server. In many cases, it also enables it to be seen in Network Neighborhood after a 30-second delay:

```
net view /workgroup:test2
```

Here's the Windows NT version of this command:

```
net view /domain:test2
```

If these commands don't enable `test2` to show up in Network Neighborhood, you can use heavy artillery in your `smb.conf`.

Caution

Do not add the following parameters to `smb.conf` if your network is live and contains a master browser. The following example is best followed on a small, encapsulated network with a single Samba server and no other SMB protocol servers.

Add the following lines to the top of your simple `smb.conf`:

```
wins support=yes
os level=65
local master=yes
preferred master=yes
domain master=yes
```

Restart Samba, wait 30 seconds after the restart completes, and then note that the new workgroup is now navigable in Network Neighborhood.

The `preferred master=` parameter invoked a browser election, and the others ensured that the Samba server would win this browser election. Chapter 9, "Working with Windows 98," presents a complete treatment of the subject of browseability in Windows 98 environments and discusses how these lines make the workgroup browseable.

The Samba Access Hierarchy

Samba has an access hierarchy that helps you understand and troubleshoot Samba. At the top level, Samba must work on the server, and there must be connectivity between the Samba server and the Windows client before the Windows client can access the server's Samba shares.

Same-Box Samba

As mentioned, if Samba doesn't work on the Samba server (the *same box*), it certainly won't work elsewhere. Same-box Samba must be working before other troubleshooting is attempted.

Correct Configuration

`smb.conf` must be correct. Although it's difficult to ascertain correctness, there's a very easy method of determining `smb.conf` syntax legality. Run `testparm` to prove whether `smb.conf` is legal and to see what shares it declares.

Daemon

Obviously, Samba won't work if it isn't running. These two commands can be used to test whether the smbd and nmbd daemons are running:

```
ps -ax | grep smbd
ps -ax | grep nmbd
```

Here's a possible output of two such commands:

```
[root@mainserv username]# ps -ax | grep smbd
13492 ?        S      0:00 smbd -D
[root@mainserv username]# ps -ax | grep nmbd
13503 ?        S      0:00 nmbd -D
13504 ?        S      0:00 nmbd -D
13559 pts/0    S      0:00 grep nmbd
[root@mainserv username]#
```

Notice that two nmbd daemons are running. That's okay. In a large installation, there can be many copies of either or both daemons running. That's perfectly okay. Also notice that one of the grep commands found itself.

If both daemons are not running, restart Samba. There's no use continuing troubleshooting until the daemons can be run.

Local Accessibility

Interestingly enough, it's usually easier to access a share than it is to see it in a browse. Here's the command and session for locally accessing user username's [homes] share:

```
$ smbclient '//mainserv/homes' -Uusername
Added interface ip=192.168.100.1 bcast=192.168.100.255 nmask=255.255.255.0
Password:
Domain=[TEST2] OS=[Unix] Server=[Samba 2.0.3]
smb: \> ls .b*
  .bash_logout                  H      24  Thu Sep  2 15:52:43 1999
  .bash_profile                 H     230  Thu Sep  2 15:52:43 1999
  .bashrc                       H     124  Thu Sep  2 15:52:43 1999
  .bash_history                 H    8003  Sun Oct 10 08:30:30 1999

            61906 blocks of size 32768. 13687 blocks available
smb: \> quit
$
```

Note that the resource in the preceding command could have been //mainserv/username instead of //mainserv/homes. If the user is username, the two are equivalent.

If the share was meant to be writable, smbclient's internal put command could have been used to test the writability of the share. Obviously, extreme care must be taken not to overwrite an existing file.

Local Browseability

As mentioned before, browseability is more complex than mere accessibility. First, shares might be deliberately marked as "not browseable," in which case the correct behavior is not to enumerate them in a share. Beyond that, depending on items such as browse masters and browser elections, browses might not be visible, especially on Windows clients.

Local browseability is much more consistent, usually depending only on smb.conf parameters. Here's the test for same-box browseability for server mainserv from the command line of mainserv:

```
$ smbclient -NL mainserv
Added interface ip=192.168.100.1 bcast=192.168.100.255 nmask=255.255.255.0
Domain=[TEST2] OS=[Unix] Server=[Samba 2.0.3]

        Sharename      Type      Comment
        ---------      ----      -------
        homes          Disk
        IPC$           IPC       IPC Service (Samba 2.0.3)

        Server                   Comment
        ---------                -------
        MAINSERV                 Samba 2.0.3

        Workgroup                Master
        ---------                -------
        TEST2
$
```

Note that the output lists homes as browseable, so it is.

Same-Box Samba: A Discussion

The same-box tests test Samba itself. Passing all these tests means Samba, itself, is working correctly. The remaining question is whether it can convey that information to clients, which requires network connectivity and Samba accessibility from Windows.

Connectivity

Connectivity is necessary to every operation over a network, including Samba, so resolving all connectivity problems is a prerequisite to troubleshooting Samba problems on a remote client computer.

Connectivity is best tested with the ping command. If the Windows client can ping the address of the Samba server, and the Samba server can ping the address of the Windows client, you have good connectivity. Otherwise, troubleshoot.

Connectivity troubleshooting usually takes the form of pinging `localhost` and the local network interface from the command line of each machine to determine whether the problem is local to the respective machines. If both machines seem okay, you should troubleshoot the wiring, hubs, and so on. If the machines are on different subnets, check the routing and routers.

Windows Network Samba Access

Access from the Windows client only works after you have Samba working locally on the server and good connectivity to the server. Once that's accomplished, troubleshooting moves to the client.

Windows Command-Line Accessibility

Share access from the Windows command line is very straightforward. Here's the command used to test connectivity for user `username` to the `[homes]` share on server `mainserv`:

```
C:\WINDOWS>net use * \\mainserv\homes
V: connected to \\MAINSERV\HOMES.


C:\WINDOWS>dir v:.b* /ah

 Volume in drive V is USERNAME
 Directory of V:\

BASH_~5V ___          24  09-02-99  3:52p .bash_logout
BASH_~4E ___         230  09-02-99  3:52p .bash_profile
BASHR~QU ___         124  09-02-99  3:52p .bashrc
BASH_~10 ___       8,003  10-10-99  8:30a .bash_history
          4 file(s)         8,381 bytes
          0 dir(s)    448,462,848 bytes free

C:\WINDOWS>
```

It's rare that this fails with successful connectivity and Samba server local access. In those rare cases, it's a tough troubleshooting problem. Chapter 22, "Troubleshooting Samba," provides extensive troubleshooting information and help.

Windows Command-Line Browseability

As stated several times before in this chapter, Network Neighborhood, especially as implemented in Windows 98, often has trouble finding browseable shares. This is especially true after a workgroup name has changed.

> **Tip**
>
> Windows Explorer and Network Neighborhood are not reliable enough for troubleshooting. If a browse does not show up in Network Neighborhood, troubleshoot it on the command line until it's successful there. Only then should any Network Neighborhood troubleshooting be attempted.

Assuming a Samba server called `mainserv` and a Windows login of `username`, this is the command of choice for testing browseability:

```
C:\WINDOWS>net view \\mainserv
Shared resources at \\MAINSERV

Sharename     Type          Comment
-------------------------------------------------------
username      Disk          Home directory of username
homes         Disk
The command was completed successfully.

C:\WINDOWS>
```

The preceding example shows a successful test. If the sought-after share does not appear, check whether there's connectivity and whether it appears on the server's `smbclient -NL mainserv` command. If it's browseable on the server and there's connectivity, it's time to troubleshoot the browseability issue. Chapter 9 contains a detailed treatment of this subject.

There's another browseability test that looks for the browseable shares by workgroup instead of by server. This command has the added side effect of sometimes starting a Samba browser election, which often enables Network Neighborhood browseability after 30 seconds. Here's the command, assuming the Samba server's workgroup is `test2`:

```
c:\windows>net view /workgroup:test2
```

On the Windows NT command line, this would be written a little differently:

```
c:\windows>net view /domain:test2
```

Windows Explorer Browseability

The final browseability test is in Windows Explorer (via Network Neighborhood). Samba is of little use without Network Neighborhood browseability.

The bad news is that Network Neighborhood, especially as implemented by Windows 9*x*, is unreliable for browsing workgroups other than the client's (if that workgroup has never before been browsed on the client).

The good news is that once browsed in Network Neighborhood, a workgroup generally remains browseable.

The issue of browseability is explored in Chapter 9.

Putting It All Together: A Departmental Server

Using the information in this chapter, you can put together the [homes], [everyone], and [printers] shares, together with enough global information to make Windows browsing easier, into a practical server for a small office. Listing 6.1 shows what a small-but-practical small-office smb.conf file looks like.

LISTING 6.1   A Small-Office smb.conf File

```
encrypt passwords=yes
netbios name=mainserv
workgroup=mygroup

#Printer Share Globals
printcap name=/etc/printcap
printing=bsd

#Browseability Improvement Globals
wins support=yes
os level=65
local master=yes
preferred master=yes
domain master=yes

[homes]
read only=no
browseable=no

[printers]
print ok=yes
path=/var/spool/samba
```

The preceding smb.conf file gives every user access to his or her home directory from Network Neighborhood, and it gives everyone access to all Linux printers. Note that although this setup is practical for a very small office, it can be improved in terms of both features and security. However, it's certainly impressive what a 22-line smb.conf can do.

Summary

It's vitally important that you back up the existing smb.conf before changing the file. smb.conf is comprised of sections headed by names in brackets and parameters in the form of *parametername=parametervalue*, with *parametername* being case insensitive. The three major Samba-defined shares are [global], [homes], and [printers]. [global] is not a share at all. It's simply a section. All uncommented parameters from the top of the file to the first bracketed name are considered in the [global] section, whether or not the actual text [global] exists.

Immediately upon changing smb.conf, the testparm program should be run to test smb.conf for legal syntax. Once smb.conf is legal, restart Samba using the proper command for your system.

The simplest possible smb.conf is a single [homes] line. the following four-line smb.conf is the simplest practical smb.conf that can reliably be used with a variety of Windows clients:

```
encrypt passwords=yes
netbios name=mainserv
workgroup=mygroup
[homes]
```

In the preceding file, workgroup= must be set to the workgroup of the Windows client(s), netbios name= must be set to the server's hostname, and encrypt passwords= must be set to yes if the Windows boxes encrypt passwords (otherwise, set it to no).

A simple and informative test of browseability and a functioning Samba involves this command from the server:

```
$ smbclient -NL localhost
```

To test access to a share, use this command:

```
$ smbclient '//localhost/sharename' -Uusername
```

The server name can be substituted for localhost to include the name service in the test and to include connectivity (if done from a different machine).

Besides its role in giving a go/nogo ruling on the legality of smb.conf, testparm gives parameter values—both those specified in the file and those incorporated by default. This command yields the parameters in alphabetical order:

```
$ testparm -s | grep = | sort
```

Unfortunately the preceding command mixes global parameters with share parameters, but it's very useful with small smb.conf files. To pinpoint the value of a particular parameter, use a command like this one to find the NetBIOS name:

```
$ testparm -s | grep -i "netbios name"
```

The ping command is used to test connectivity. It can be used locally to test the network card, tested on localhost to test the TCP/IP stack itself, or across the network to test connectivity with other hosts.

The Windows command line provides a rich set of tests, including this accessibility test:

```
$ net use z: \\servername\sharename
```

These browse tests are also available:

```
$ net view \\servername
```

```
$ net view /workgroup:workgroupname
```

```
$ net view /domain:workgroupname
```

Note that the third command is an NT command, whereas the second command is the Windows 98 version.

Decisions on encrypting passwords include whether to encrypt. Solutions include setting the encrypt passwords= parameter and possible tweaks to the Windows Registry to disable encryption.

Samba accessibility is determined by the lesser of Samba parameters and UNIX permissions. When placed in the [global] section, share parameters become the defaults for all shares but are able to be overridden individually within the shares.

The [printers] share requires correct global printing= and printcap name= parameters, share parameters print ok=true and browseable=no, and a path= pointing to a directory with the proper permissions (1777), which is intended to temporarily house files to be printed. Several other printer-configuration parameters can be used to enable printing on unusual systems, but the correct choice of the printing= and printcap name= global parameters usually produces a working printer share.

Samba has a very simple access hierarchy. Basically, Samba shares and browsing must be accessible on the server and connectivity must be achieved between the client and server before the client can access shares. This fact forms the basis of much of this book's troubleshooting.

This chapter started with a one-line smb.conf and incrementally built upon it to create a setup that's suitable for a small office. Using a proof of concept helps with both troubleshooting and figuring out tough Samba concepts. Often, a spare Linux box that's all yours is the best troubleshooting tool of all.

CHAPTER 7

Determining Samba Access

by Steve Litt

Samba implements security in its role as a fileserver: who sees what, who reads what, who writes what. Samba implements a rich set of options in the mapping between users, groups, and directories. This chapter completely identifies the relationships of these options, including which options take precedence in varying situations.

> **Note**
>
> This chapter does not cover `security=share`, because most administrators wanting to control access do not choose share security.

The Question Everyone's Asking

One criticism of Samba is that with so many options, its configuration is hard to understand. Given a share configuration, who has what privileges? How are conflicting options resolved? How can this information be used to custom-build a share for a specific purpose?

Samba access information is widely available in bits and pieces. This chapter gathers the information in one place, thereby answering the question "How do I determine Samba access?"

This chapter is prioritized to answer the access question, not to enumerate `smb.conf` parameters in alphabetical order or in order of most common usage.

Examples in This Chapter

All examples in this chapter use server `mainserv`, located at `192.168.100.1/255.255.255.0`, as the name of the Samba server. You can substitute the name of your server. The user is called `username`, a name unlikely to be confused with genuine users on your system. These examples have been checked on a Celeron-equipped machine running Red Hat Linux 6.0. This machine has an HP printer connected to its one and only parallel port.

If you're following along with this chapter's examples, you'll find it easiest to work on a small network consisting of a Linux Samba server and a Windows client. That way, no production machines are affected. Because the examples in this chapter come from a Red Hat machine, a Red Hat server is ideal. It's easiest to create a user called `username`.

All examples assume encrypted passwords. If your configuration uses plain passwords, change all `encrypt passwords` instances to no.

Caution

Before attempting any of the examples in this chapter, be sure to back up your existing `smb.conf`!

The examples in this chapter assume a Windows client with encrypted passwords enabled. The newer Windows clients all default to encrypted passwords. If your client does not default to encrypted passwords, most of the examples will work if you change yes to no in the examples' `encrypt passwords=` parameters.

The Sample Directory for This Chapter

Many of the examples in this chapter use directory `/home/username/test`. Also, many examples in this chapter will not work unless `/home/username` is `chmod 755`. Although this may be a security breach in a business setting, `username` is a "bogus" user intended for reproducing these examples, and it has no valuable data. Therefore, in this case, this setting is okay. If you intend to follow along with the examples in this chapter (and that's highly recommended), make sure you use `chmod 755 /home/username`.

Use `oplocks=no` in This Chapter

The `oplocks` setting defaults to yes for an excellent reason: Opportunistic locking boosts performance. Samba shares accessed only through Samba are usually excellent candidates for opportunistic locking.

Throughout this chapter, files are accessed through both Samba and UNIX. Leaving opportunistic locking in its default "enabled" status would create situations where the client and server perceive different copies of the file. Therefore, all examples in this chapter contain `oplocks=no` in the global section of `smb.conf`.

The Three Levels of Users and Groups

Internally, Samba tracks users and groups at three levels:

- *Requested* user and group (%U and %G)
- *Effective* user and group (no substitution variables)
- *Service* user and group (%u and %g)

> **Tip**
>
> Memorize these three terms. They are vital to understanding Samba access. What's more, they're used throughout this chapter.

The requested user and group are the user and group requested by the client. Use the following command as an example:

```
$ smbclient '//mainserv/test' -Uusername
```

In the preceding command, the requested user is `username`, and the requested group is the primary group of `username`.

The effective user and group is the same as the requested user and group, unless access is gained as guest, in which case the effective user is defined by the `guest account=` parameter and the effective group is the primary group of the defined user. The effective user and group are used for most Samba validation.

The service user is the same as the effective user and group, unless changed by `force user=` and/or `force group=` parameters. The `force user=` parameter changes the service user to its value and changes the service group to the primary group of its value. The `force group=` parameter changes the service group to its value, overriding any changes made to the service group by any `force user=` parameter.

admin users=

The `admin users=yes` parameter is intended to provide complete administrative access (that means `root`) within the tree defined by the share's path. This is one of a tiny handful of situations in which Samba increases access over that provided by UNIX file permissions.

Make sure `/home/username` has 755 permissions. Then, as `root`, create subdirectory `test` under `/home/username`. The subdirectory should be owned by `root`, have group `root` or some other very exclusive group, and have no permissions for `user`, `group`, or `other`.

Start with this `smb.conf`:

```
encrypt passwords=yes
oplocks=no
workgroup=mygroup
netbios name=mainserv

[test]
path=/home/username/test
admin users=username
```

> **Note**
>
> In the preceding code, substitute the workgroup of the Windows clients for `mygroup` and then substitute the Samba server's hostname for `mainserv`. This is true for all the examples throughout the chapter, and it won't be mentioned again.

One would normally expect the `[test]` share in the preceding `smb.conf` to be completely inaccessible due to the ownership and lack of permissions for subdirectory `test`. But in fact, because of the `admin users=username`, user `username` is able to read, but not write or create, anything within the share. You can verify this by placing a file in the directory (as `root` from the server), after which `username` can see the file in Network Neighborhood. Commenting out `admin users=username` and restarting Samba disables all access to the share.

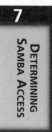

Add `read only=no`

The previous setup granted user `username` read access to everything in the share, even though the path of the share is owned by `root` and has no permissions. The fact that the share's `read only=` parameter defaults to `yes` disables write access, even for the admin user. Specifying `read only=no` enables complete read, write, create, and delete access. Here's the `smb.conf`:

```
encrypt passwords=yes
oplocks=no
workgroup=mygroup
netbios name=mainserv

[test]
path=/home/username/test
read only=no
admin users=username
```

Add `write list=username`

The previous example used `read only=no` to enable write access to the share, regardless of UNIX permissions. The problem is that this share may need to be a read-only share. Substituting the `write list=username` parameter for the `read only=no` parameter grants write access to `username` without granting it to everyone. The following `smb.conf` enables full access to the `root`-owned, no-permission `test` directory:

```
encrypt passwords=yes
oplocks=no
workgroup=mygroup
netbios name=mainserv
```

```
[test]
path=/home/username/test
admin users=username
write list=username
```

The `admin users=username` parameter grants user `username` full access to the directory declared inaccessible by UNIX permissions, but it does not override Samba restrictions, as is shown in some of the following examples.

Add `valid users=root`

Add the `valid users=root` parameter. Next, note that `username` can no longer access the share:

```
encrypt passwords=yes
oplocks=no
workgroup=mygroup
netbios name=mainserv

[test]
path=/home/username/test
valid users=root
admin users=username
write list=username
```

Although the `admin users=username` parameter overrides UNIX permission restrictions `username` would normally experience, it does not override Samba restrictions.

You can restore access of user `username` by changing the `valid users` line to this:

```
valid users=root,username
```

Add `invalid users=username`

Similarly, changing the `valid users` line to an `invalid users` line restricting user `username` prevents any access to the share:

```
encrypt passwords=yes
oplocks=no
workgroup=mygroup
netbios name=mainserv

[test]
path=/home/username/test
invalid users=username
admin users=username
write list=username
```

Deleting the `invalid users=` line once again enables `username` complete access to the share, regardless of UNIX permissions.

Discussion of `admin users=`

The `admin users=` parameter eliminates all access restriction, for the named user, caused by UNIX permissions. It does not in any way eliminate Samba-based restrictions such as `read only=yes`, `valid users=`, and `invalid users=`.

To completely enable a user's administrative rights in a share, eliminate his or her UNIX permission restrictions with `admin users=username`, grant write permission with `write list=username`, name the user on any `valid users=` parameter in the share, and remove the user from any `invalid users=` parameters.

> **Note**
>
> The combination of the `username=` list and the `only user=yes` parameter creates a similar restriction as `valid users=`. The `valid users=` method is much preferred because the `username=` parameter is used primarily to accommodate antique clients that cannot supply a username.

The `admin users=` parameter is a serious security relaxation to be used only with the most trusted administrator. Not only must the administrator be trusted in the traditional sense of the word, but he or she must also be trusted to follow excellent security procedures, including not leaving his or her Windows terminal operational during breaks.

`hosts allow=`

The purpose of the `hosts allow=` parameter is to prevent access from large groups of IP addresses, typically restricting access to a single subnet. This parameter defaults to an empty string, which does not restrict by IP address.

This parameter provides an excellent security enhancement on networks with well-defined subnets. It restricts share access to certain IP addresses. This prevents access from the Internet or from internal subnets with no need to access the information.

The `hosts allow=` parameter eliminates Samba share access by nonlisted IP addresses, no matter what other UNIX or Samba permissions they have.

> **Note**
>
> The combination of `interfaces=` and `bind interfaces only=` implements a similar IP address restriction as `hosts allow=`.

7

DETERMINING SAMBA ACCESS

hosts allow=127.0.0.1

Change the owner of /home/username/test back to username and then change its permissions to 777. As root, delete all files from inside /home/username/test. Then verify that the following smb.conf grants user username full access to the [test] share via Network Neighborhood:

```
encrypt passwords=yes
oplocks=no
workgroup=mygroup
netbios name=mainserv

[test]
path=/home/username/test
admin users=username
read only=no
```

Now add the following line to the [test] share:

```
hosts allow=127.0.0.1
```

The share is now completely inaccessible from Windows because the Windows IP address is not 127.0.0.1 (from the server's point of view). This parameter has overridden the liberal privileges contributed by the UNIX permissions, the Samba read only=no and admin users=username parameters, and the lack of a valid users= parameter.

> **Note**
>
> The inaccessibility may take the form of Samba repeatedly asking for and rejecting a password, rather than telling the reason for inaccessibility. Such behavior makes troubleshooting difficult, but it also makes it difficult to hack into the system.

You can verify whether the share is accessible from the server if the following line, issued from the server's console, is successful:

```
$ smbclient '//127.0.0.1/test' -Uusername
```

hosts allow=192.168.100.

This parameter includes a specific subnet. Assuming the Windows client is on the 192.168.100 subnet, access from the Windows box is restored by adding its subnet to the existing hosts allow= parameter to produce this parameter:

```
hosts allow=127.0.0.1, 192.168.100.
```

7

DETERMINING
SAMBA ACCESS

The trailing dot is essential, because it defines the number as a subnet. Without that trailing dot, the Windows box does not gain access.

The `hosts allow=` parameter can also accept the EXCEPT keyword to rule out one or more computers or subnets in the larger subnet. Assuming the Windows client is at 192.168.100.201 (the client IP can be verified by the `route print` Windows command), you can rule out that client with the EXCEPT keyword by changing the `hosts allow=` parameter to the following:

```
hosts allow=127.0.0.1, 192.168.100. EXCEPT 192.168.100.201
```

Testing `hosts allow=`

The `testparm` utility features an easy method for testing the effects of `hosts allow=` and `hosts deny=` (discussed later this chapter) by inputting the Samba server's NetBIOS name and the IP address whose access is to be tested. Assume the server's name is main-serv and assume the following parameter appears in the [test] share:

```
hosts allow=127.0.0.1, 192.168.100. EXCEPT 192.168.100.201
```

Given this, here are two `testparm` sessions to test IP addresses 192.168.100.201 and 192.168.100.202:

```
$ testparm mainserv 192.168.100.201
Load smb config files from /usr/local/samba/lib/smb.conf
Processing section "[test]"
Loaded services file OK.
Deny connection from mainserv (192.168.100.201) to test

$ testparm mainserv 192.168.100.202
Load smb config files from /usr/local/samba/lib/smb.conf
Processing section "[test]"
Loaded services file OK.
Allow connection from mainserv (192.168.100.202) to test
$
```

It would be nice if multiple `hosts allow=` lines could be recognized in a share; however, you can use the `testparm` utility to show that the last one overwrites any earlier ones in the share. All allowed hosts, subnets, exceptions, and so on must be placed in a single `hosts allow=` line, suitably delimited with commas.

Discussion of `hosts allow=`

The `hosts allow=` parameter provides absolute rejection of Samba access from disallowed IP addresses, regardless of the user's Samba privileges or UNIX permissions. If `hosts allow=` prevents access from a given IP address, no user or group can gain access from that IP address.

`hosts deny=`

The `hosts deny=` parameter is the mirror image of `hosts allow=`. Anything named in this parameter is restricted; everything else is *not* restricted by this parameter.

`hosts deny=windowsClientSubnet`

Make sure `/home/username/test` is owned by `username` and `chmod 777`. Then, create the following `smb.conf` and verify accessibility by the `username` user to the `[test]` share, like this:

```
encrypt passwords=yes
oplocks=no
workgroup=mygroup
netbios name=mainserv

[test]
path=/home/username/test
read only=no
```

Now, assuming the Windows client is on subnet `192.168.100`, add the following line to the `[test]` share:

```
hosts deny=192.168.100.
```

Once again, the trailing dot is vital. Change the subnet to match that of your particular Windows client. The share now becomes inaccessible.

The share can again be made accessible from the client by adding an EXCEPT clause:

```
hosts deny=192.168.100. EXCEPT 192.168.100.201
```

The preceding line assumes the Windows client is at IP address `192.168.100.201`.

Dueling `hosts deny=` and `hosts allow=` Parameters

According to the `smb.conf` man page, when `hosts allow=` and `hosts deny=` contradict, `hosts allow=` takes precedence. This can be confirmed by creating the following `smb.conf`:

```
encrypt passwords=yes
oplocks=no
workgroup=mygroup
netbios name=mainserv

[test]
hosts allow=192.168.100.201
hosts deny=192.168.100.201
path=/home/username/test
read only=no
```

The preceding assumes there's a Windows client at 192.168.100.201. Access is allowed from Network Neighborhood, and the testparm mainserv 192.168.100.201 command confirms this. The hosts allow= parameter has won.

However, there's more to this. Change the hosts allow= and hosts deny= parameters as follows:

```
hosts allow=192.168.100. EXCEPT 192.168.100.201
hosts deny=192.168.100. EXCEPT 192.168.100.201
```

The share is still accessible from 192.168.100.201. The EXCEPT clause from the hosts deny= parameter has overridden the EXCEPT clause from the hosts allow= parameter.

Note that the following lines produce a share accessible from 192.168.100.201:

```
hosts allow=192.168.200.
hosts deny=192.168.100. EXCEPT 192.168.100.201
```

In the preceding conflict, hosts deny= wins. The hosts allow= statement would appear to rule out anything from the 192.168.100 subnet, but the EXCEPT clause of the hosts deny= statement enables access from 192.168.100.201. Next, consider this conflict:

```
hosts allow=192.168.100. EXCEPT 192.168.100.201
hosts deny=192.168.200.
```

192.168.100.201 gains access, so hosts deny= has prevailed.

In general, any conflict between these two parameters results in the least restrictive result. However, given the number of combinations possible, any conflict between these two should be investigated (or better yet, avoided).

Discussion of hosts deny=

The hosts deny= and hosts allow= parameters restrict by IP address. IP addresses ruled out by these parameters cannot access the share, no matter what other access is granted by other parameters. Access ruled out by these two parameters is irrevocably ruled out, whereas access not ruled out goes on to be evaluated by other parameters.

In conflicts between these parameters, the result is usually the least-restrictive possible. Such conflicts should be avoided. If, for some reason, a conflict is necessary, its results should be investigated rather than simply assumed.

Guest Access

Certain low-security shares, especially printers, are appropriate for guest access. Guest access enables users without accounts on the server access to these shares. What happens is that the effective user (see the earlier section "The Three Levels of Users and Groups") is changed to the guest account (guest account=), and the effective group is set to the primary group of the guest account.

Guest access creates a security problem if done incorrectly. What's more, guest access becomes extremely complicated when used with parameters such as force user= and force group=. This chapter does not completely explain such cases, nor would the use of guest access with these parameters be prudent in most cases. Instead, this section illustrates some of the more common aspects of guest access.

The Guest-Only Share

Consider this smb.conf:

```
encrypt passwords=yes
oplocks=no
workgroup=mygroup
netbios name=mainserv

[test]
guest ok=yes
guest only=yes
path=/home/username/test
read only=no
```

The read only=no parameter is necessary in order to deduce the service username and group by creating (putting) a file. You can "put" a file by running smbclient and then using its built-in put command, as shown in the following session:

```
$ smbclient '//mainserv/test' -Uusername
Added interface ip=192.168.100.1 bcast=192.168.100.255 nmask=255.255.255.0
Password:
Domain=[MYGROUP] OS=[Unix] Server=[Samba 2.0.5a]
smb: \> put test.txt
putting file test.txt as \test.txt (5.8588 kb/s) (average 5.85938 kb/s)
smb: \> quit
$ ls -ldF /home/username/test/test.txt
-rwxr--r--   1 nobody    nobody           6 Oct 26 08:48 junk.txt*
$
```

The guest only=yes parameter forces the effective user to the guest account= parameter and the effective group to the primary group of that user. Lacking force user= and force group= parameters, the service user and group are the same as the effective user and group.

Many systems, including the one in the preceding example, default guest account= to nobody. This user can be overridden at the share level by explicitly specifying a different value for guest account=.

Removing the guest ok=yes parameter disables the guest only=yes parameter, resulting in the effective user and group being the requested user and group.

The default value of the global map to guest= parameter is never. This normally disables guest access, but in the case of a guest-only share, it means on any successful access the effective user and group are converted to the guest account user and primary group. Before trying the next example, make sure that guest ok=yes has been put back if you've removed this parameter. Now attempt access with a bad password and then a bad username, as shown in the following two commands:

```
$ smbclient '//mainserv/test' -Uusername%phonypass
Added interface ip=192.168.100.1 bcast=192.168.100.255 nmask=255.255.255.0
session setup failed: ERRSRV - ERRbadpw (Bad password - name/password pair in a
Tree Connect or Session Setup are invalid.)
$
```

```
$ smbclient '//mainserv/test' -Uphonyuser%phonypass
Added interface ip=192.168.100.1 bcast=192.168.100.255 nmask=255.255.255.0
session setup failed: ERRSRV - ERRbadpw (Bad password - name/password pair in a
Tree Connect or Session Setup are invalid.)
$
```

The previous commands failed because map to guest= defaults to never. This default value allows only a legitimate user/password combination; then it changes the user to the one specified by the explicit or default guest account= parameter.

Setting map to guest=bad user results in a failure when a legitimate user is requested but the password is wrong. If a nonexistent user is specified, it enables access as the guest account.

Setting map to guest=bad password enables guest account access if either the user is nonexistent or the user exists but the password is wrong.

The guest-only share has the advantage that all users are the same user and the same group. Therefore, all users can read, write, and even change attributes to each other's files. However, given the lax security of guest-only shares, they're practical only for the most wide-open, no-security environments. For more secure shares, similar benefits can be realized with the force user= and force group= parameters, which are discussed later in this chapter.

7

DETERMINING SAMBA ACCESS

To summarize, access to a guest-only share is either granted as the guest account or not granted at all. If access is granted, the effective user and group are changed to the value of guest account= and that value's primary group. The conditions under which access is granted depend on the global parameter map to guest=. It's impossible to use guest access instead of a valid user/password combination to gain access to a share with a valid users= parameter.

The Guest OK Share

Consider this smb.conf:

```
encrypt passwords=yes
oplocks=no
workgroup=mygroup
netbios name=mainserv

[test]
guest ok=yes
path=/home/username/test
read only=no
```

In spite of the guest ok=yes parameter, guest access is not enabled because of the default global map to guest=never parameter. A correct user/password combination gains access as that user, whereas any bad combination fails. If the share contains a valid users= list, a correct user/password pair fails unless the user is listed in valid users=. A global map to user=never parameter disables all guest access except in guest-only shares.

Inserting map to user=bad user in the [global] section enables guest access if the client requests a nonexistent user, but it fails if the client requests an existing user with a nonmatching password. If the client requests an existing user with a matching password, access is granted as the requested user.

Inserting map to user=bad password in the [global] section enables guest access for bad logins caused either by nonmatching passwords for existing users or nonexistent users. Once again, if the client requests an existing user with a matching password, access is granted as the requested user.

To summarize, access to a guest OK share is either granted as the guest account or the requested username, or it's not granted at all. The conditions under which the username changes to the guest account depend on the global parameter map to guest=. No guest OK share (as opposed to a guest-only share) grants guest access if there's a global map to guest=never parameter. It's impossible to use guest access instead of a valid user/password combination to gain access to a share with a valid users= parameter.

The result of the guest access determination is one of the following:

- Access as the requested user
- Access as the guest account
- No access

In the first case, the effective user and group are the requested user and group. In the second case, the effective user is the guest account and the effective group is the primary group of the guest account. In both cases, the service user and group are set to the effective user and group, with the service user and group further determined by any `force user=` and `force group=` share parameters.

force user= and force group=

The `force user=` and `force group=` parameters modify the service user and group, which would otherwise match the effective user and group. This section of the chapter investigates how Samba uses the effective user and group, together with the user and/or group as changed by `force user=` and `force group=`, to determine access and the state of created files.

> **Tip**
>
> Here's the easy way to remember the function of `force user=` and `force group=`: The service user and group determine all UNIX interaction, whereas the effective user and group determine all Samba interaction.

force user=

The `force user=` parameter changes the service user to the parameter value for the purposes of interacting with UNIX. It also changes the service group to the primary group of the forced user. This means that any new file created in a Samba session on the share has the forced user as its owner and the forced user's group as its group. It also means that the permissions of any file in the share, or the share itself, are evaluated from the viewpoint of the forced user and the forced user's primary group. However, the forced user and group are *not* used in evaluation of any Samba security. Take a look at this example:

```
encrypt passwords=yes
oplocks=no
workgroup=mygroup
netbios name=mainserv
```

```
[test]
force user=myuid
valid users=username
create mask=700
path=/home/username/test
read only=no
```

Using the preceding `smb.conf`, note the results of accessing the share first as username, putting a file, and then attempting to access as user myuid:

```
$ smbclient '//mainserv/test' -Uusername
Added interface ip=192.168.100.1 bcast=192.168.100.255 nmask=255.255.255.0
Password:
Domain=[MYGROUP] OS=[Unix] Server=[Samba 2.0.5a]
smb: \> put test.txt
putting file test.txt as \test.txt (5.8588 kb/s) (average 5.85938 kb/s)
smb: \> quit
$ ls -ldF test/test.txt
-rwx------  1 myuid    myuid           6 Oct 26 12:39 test/test.txt*
$
```

In the preceding access, user username passed user validation and put the file, whose ownership was set to forced user myuid and the primary group of myuid. The following example features an attempt to do the same thing as user myuid: •

```
$ smbclient '//mainserv/test' -Umyuid
Added interface ip=192.168.100.1 bcast=192.168.100.255 nmask=255.255.255.0
Password:
Domain=[MYGROUP] OS=[Unix] Server=[Samba 2.0.5a]
tree connect failed: ERRSRV - ERRbadpw
➥(Bad password - name/password pair in a
➥Tree Connect or Session Setup are invalid.)
$
```

The preceding access failed because the valid users= parameter attempts to match the effective user, not the force user=/force group= modified service user.

The forced user is also used in evaluating file permissions. Note that create mask=700 means that the file was created with no permissions for group or for other, as demonstrated by the ls command. However, in spite of that fact, a subsequent session by user username is able to read and overwrite the file:

```
$ smbclient '//mainserv/test' -Uusername
Added interface ip=192.168.100.1 bcast=192.168.100.255 nmask=255.255.255.0
Password:
Domain=[MYGROUP] OS=[Unix] Server=[Samba 2.0.5a]
smb: \> more test.txt                    .
getting file /tmp/smbmore.3330 of size 21
➥as /tmp/smbmore.3330 (2.92954 kb/s) (average 2.92969 kb/s)
This is a test file.
smb: \> put test.txt
```

```
putting file test.txt as \test.txt (5.8588 kb/s) (average 5.85938 kb/s)
smb: \> quit
$
```

Because the `force user=` parameter works with UNIX, yet Samba restrictions are evaluated according to the effective user and group, `force user=` is used to make multiuser UNIX file permissions look like DOS ownerless files.

force group=

The `force group=` parameter changes the service group to the parameter value, for the purposes of interacting with UNIX. If the service group is changed by a `force user=` parameter in the same share, `force group=` overrides that change. This can be thought of as changing it again, except this behavior happens no matter which of these two parameters come first in the `smb.conf` share.

This means that any new file created in a Samba session on the share has the forced group. It also means that the permissions of any file in the share, or the share itself, are evaluated from the viewpoint of the forced group as well as the user. However, the forced group is *not* used in the evaluation of any Samba security. Take a look at this example:

```
encrypt passwords=yes
oplocks=no
workgroup=mygroup
netbios name=mainserv

[test]
force group=myuid
valid users=username
create mask=770
path=/home/username/test
read only=no
```

Once again, when user `username` puts a file to this directory, that file has owner `username` but group `myuid`. In order for all users of this share to have complete UNIX access to created files, the create mask must be `770`, thus giving the group full rights. Attempting to access this share as a member of the `myuid` group, which is not included in the `valid users=` statement, fails because Samba evaluates the effective user and group, not the service user and group.

> **Note**
>
> Remember not to place the characters @, +, or & in front of the group name in `force group=`. Because `force group=` takes a group as a value, there's no need to inform Samba that the value is a group, and it's an error to preface the group name with @, +, or &.

Testing with `preexec`

The examples so far for demonstrating `force user=` and `force group=` used file creation to deduce user and group names. A more informative method is to use the `preexec=` server-side automation parameter to write to a log. Because this method occurs only when a share is connected to, the access method must reliably connect and disconnect. This is best done with the `smbclient` command. Take the following `smb.conf` as an example:

```
encrypt passwords=yes
oplocks=no
workgroup=mygroup
netbios name=mainserv

[test]
force user=nobody
force group=ftp
create mask=770
path=/home/username/test
preexec=  "echo preexec  %T  u.g=%u.%g, U.G=%U.%G >> check.log
read only=no
```

> **Note**
>
> Remember that %U and %G are the requested user and group. The effective user and group are what determine Samba-level access. In the absence of guest access, the effective user and group are equal to the requested values.
>
> Also remember that %u and %g are the service user and group. These are used in determining UNIX-level access.

Run and exit `smbclient '//mainserv/test' -Uusername` using various usernames, all the while running `tail -f /home/username/test/check.log` to observe the results. Here's an example with accesses by users `username` and `myuid`. In both cases, the share user and group were set to those prescribed by the `force user=` and `force group=` parameters, as shown in the following `check.log` output:

```
[root@mainserv username]# tail -f test/check.log
preexec 1999/10/26 14:01:51 u.g=nobody.ftp, U.G=username.username
preexec 1999/10/26 14:02:36 u.g=nobody.ftp, U.G=username.username
preexec 1999/10/26 14:02:51 u.g=nobody.ftp, U.G=myuid.myuid
```

Working with UNIX Permissions

Except for shares with an `admin users=` parameter, access to the share is the lesser of the Samba privileges and the UNIX permissions. Samba has been developed to respect the restrictions placed by UNIX file permissions. Note that in certain situations (force user=, force group=, and guesting), your actual username might not be what was originally requested. This topic is examined later in the chapter. This section investigates Samba's usage of UNIX permissions in the absence of force user=, force group=, and guesting.

The first example is a completely writable, accessible share. First, make the UNIX directory completely accessible:

```
$chmod 777 /home/username/test
```

Next, make the share completely accessible:

```
encrypt passwords=yes
oplocks=no
workgroup=mygroup
netbios name=mainserv

[test]
path=/home/username/test
read only=no
```

You can verify that this share is read and write accessible to any legitimate user.

chmod 0

Removing all UNIX permissions makes the share completely inaccessible:

```
$ chmod 0 /home/username/test
```

After you issue the preceding command, any client access to the share errors out with an "access denied" error.

Because Samba respects restrictions placed by UNIX file permissions, it does not grant any type of access to this share.

chmod 444

The next step is to give all users UNIX permission to read the share:

```
$ chmod 444 /home/username/test
```

Surprisingly, the share still cannot be read from Network Neighborhood, nor can it or any files or directories inside it be read by the dir command, whether on \\mainserv\test or on a drive letter assigned to that share. Although smbclient '//localhost/test' -Uusername appears to work, with an ls command producing an empty listing with no error, in fact any attempt to read a file in the share or write a file to the share results in an "access denied" error. This directory is *not* readable.

It's not readable because the lack of an executable permission makes it inaccessible. In fact, it's just as inaccessible after a chmod 666. Read and write permission on the directory do not make up for the lack of an executable permission.

chmod 111

Once again, the share cannot be read from Network Neighborhood. The Windows command-line share \\mainserv\test acts the same way. However, this behavior is Samba client dependent. smbclient can read (via its more command) an existing read-enabled file, and it can modify (via its put command) an existing write-enabled file. It cannot, however, create a new file in such a directory.

chmod 555

You can solve the problem by making the share read and execute, like this:

```
$ chmod 555 /home/username/test
```

The share is now accessible from the Windows client. The access is read-only because the UNIX permissions do not include the write permission. Any attempt to create or delete a file in the share fails. Note, however, that an existing write-enabled file in that directory *can* be edited and modified.

> **Note**
>
> The preceding discussion points to a fundamental difference between Samba read-only shares and share directories marked read-only in UNIX. If the share directory is chmod 555 and contains a file that's chmod 777, that file can be modified through Samba. No files can be added to or deleted from the directory, but writable files can be modified.
>
> Contrast this with the read-only restriction through Samba's read only=yes parameter. The use of the read only=yes parameter prevents modification, deletion or creation of any file, anywhere in the share's tree.

chmod 777

Complete access to the share is enabled by adding the write permission:

```
$ chmod 777 /home/username/test
```

Access is now complete, with read and write capabilities for all users. Because Samba access is the lesser of UNIX permissions and share parameters, and the share parameters grant read/write access to all, this share is writable by all.

> **Note**
>
> The exception involves shares containing the `admin users=` parameter, because that parameter overrides the lack of UNIX permissions.

UNIX Permissions: Summary

Except for shares containing the `admin users=` parameter, Samba access is the lesser of Samba parameters and UNIX permissions. Samba has been designed to work with UNIX security, not to defeat it.

The handling of writable files inside read-only directories is SMB client dependent, with Network Neighborhood and Windows command-line representations of the share refusing to modify the file. On the other hand, `smbclient` allows modification of the file via a `put` command. The Windows SMB clients handle the situation more like Samba's `read only=` parameter, whereas the `smbclient` client handles it more like UNIX, where a directory's read-only status does not protect contained files from modification.

Similarly, Windows SMB clients and `smbclient` handle a read-enabled file within executable-only UNIX directories differently. The former prohibits reading of the contained file, whereas the latter (`smbclient`) reads the file via its `more` command.

The preceding differences and dependencies lead to considerable confusion in determining the UNIX portion of file access. Because of the potential for confusion and the client dependencies, it's usually best for Samba-accessible directories to have UNIX permissions at least as permissive as the desired permissions of their contained files.

The customary way to enforce Samba security is by restricting access through `smb.conf`, not by restricting UNIX permissions. Restricting access through `smb.conf` yields a much more predictable result.

read only=

The `read only=` parameter defines whether the share, as a whole, can be written to. The default value is yes, meaning the share is read-only. Setting the share to `read only=no` grants write access to the share as a whole, unless preempted by UNIX file permissions. The following share is read-only because the default for `read only=` is yes:

```
[test]
path=/home/username/test
```

The following example does exactly the same as the preceding example. It simply explicitly specifies the default value:

```
[test]
path=/home/username/test
read only=yes
```

> **Tip**
>
> Samba's default for this parameter is yes. However, if `read only=no` is placed in the global portion of `smb.conf`, then all shares default to `read only=no`.

> **Tip**
>
> The `read only=` parameter has three inverse synonyms: `writeable=`, `writable=`, and `write ok=`. Therefore, the following four statements mean exactly the same thing:
>
> - `read only=no`
> - `writeable=yes`
> - `writable=yes`
> - `write ok=yes`
>
> Using more than one of these in a single share is an error.

Changing the value of this parameter makes the share writable:

```
[test]
path=/home/username/test
read only=no
```

The preceding example defines a share that's writable by all.

The `read only=` parameter defines writability at the share level, assuming the service user or group has the proper UNIX permissions to write the share. Both `read only=yes` and `read only=no` can be overridden on a user-by-user basis with the `read list=` and `write list=` parameters.

read list= and write list=

The purpose of the `read list=` parameter is to restrict access to read-only for shares that would otherwise be read/write. This version of the [test] share is read/write due to the `read only=no` parameter:

```
[test]
path=/home/username/test
read only=no
```

User `username` can both read and write this share from the Windows client.

Add `read list=username`

Now consider adding `read list=username` to the share:

```
[test]
read list=username
path=/home/username/test
read only=no
```

Now user `username` can no longer write the share. Other users still can write the share because their names are not on the `read list=` line. Note that this line can take a comma-delimited list of users and/or groups.

> **Tip**
>
> You can place groups in this parameter, and in most other parameters designed to take users, by prepending one or more characters to the group's name:
>
> - *+groupname* matches to a UNIX group named *groupname*.
> - *&groupname* matches to an NIS group named *groupname*.
> - *+&groupname* tries to match a UNIX group named *groupname*. If that fails, it tries to match an NIS group named *groupname*.
> - *&+groupname* tries to match an NIS group named *groupname*. If that fails, it tries to match a UNIX group named *groupname*.
> - *@groupname* means the same as *&+groupname*.

To summarize, the `read list=username` parameter reduces the access of user `username` from the write access of the share to read/only. Note that this parameter authenticates against the effective user and group, not the service or requested values.

Add `write list=username`

Adding `write list=username` once again restores write access to `username`:

```
[test]
read list=username
write list=username
path=/home/username/test
read only=no
```

The `write list=` parameter overrides the `read list=` parameter. However, the main purpose of `write list` is to grant write access on a per-user basis to an otherwise read-only share:

```
[test]
write list=username
path=/home/username/test
read only=yes
```

The preceding example gives write access to username in spite of the fact that read only=yes. The write list= parameter is extremely useful in multigroup access of a share.

Add `valid users=root`

So far, this chapter's examples have centered around shares available, at least on a read-only level, to all users. The valid users= parameter defines one or more users or groups (effective users and groups, to be precise) allowed access to the share to the exclusion of all others. Adding valid users=root to the [test] share restricts access to user root, as shown in the following share:

```
[test]
read list=username
write list=username
path=/home/username/test
read only=yes
valid users=root
```

The preceding share errors out when user username tries to access it, in spite of username being on the read and write lists. The parameters read list= and write list= do not come into play until after the user has gained access to the share.

Discussion

The read list= parameter restricts the listed users and groups to read-only access in shares that otherwise grant read/write access. The write list= parameter grants write access to the users and groups in shares otherwise restricted to read-only access. If the two parameters conflict, the write list= parameter prevails.

Neither is capable of gaining the named user access if that user's access is blocked by a valid users= or invalid users= parameter. These two parameters use the effective user and group to make their determinations.

Browseability

Browseability is a totally different property from accessibility. For instance, a share can be browseable but not accessible, or it can be accessible but not browseable.

A share is browseable when it shows up in browse lists. Take a look at this example:

```
encrypt passwords=yes
oplocks=no
workgroup=mygroup
netbios name=mainserv
```

```
[test]
valid users=myuid
path=/home/username/test
```

This share is browseable because the `browseable=` parameter defaults to yes, meaning that to keep a share out of browse lists it must be explicitly specified as `browseable=no`. The following command shows the browse list for the preceding `smb.conf`:

```
$ smbclient -L mainserv -Uusername
Added interface ip=192.168.100.1 bcast=192.168.100.255
➥nmask=255.255.255.0
Password:
Domain=[MYGROUP] OS=[Unix] Server=[Samba 2.0.5a]

        Sharename      Type       Comment
        ---------      ----       -------
        test           Disk
        IPC$           IPC        IPC Service (Samba 2.0.5a)

        Server                    Comment
        ---------                 -------
        MAINSERV                  Samba 2.0.5a

        Workgroup                 Master
        ---------                 -------
        MYGROUP
$
```

The `test` share is plainly visible as a "Disk" type share. However, due to the `valid users=myuid` parameter, this share is not accessible to user `username`, as shown by this attempted access:

```
$ smbclient '//mainserv/test' -Uusername
Added interface ip=192.168.100.1 bcast=192.168.100.255 nmask=255.255.255.0
Password:
Domain=[MYGROUP] OS=[Unix] Server=[Samba 2.0.5a]
tree connect failed: ERRSRV - ERRbadpw (Bad password - name/password pair in a
➥Tree Connect or Session Setup are invalid.)
$
```

Adding `browseable=no` to the `[test]` share has no effect on access, but it does eliminate browseability, as shown in this example command on the share with `browseable=no`:

```
$ smbclient -L mainserv -Uusername
Added interface ip=192.168.100.1 bcast=192.168.100.255 nmask=255.255.255.0
Password:
Domain=[MYGROUP] OS=[Unix] Server=[Samba 2.0.5a]

        Sharename      Type       Comment
        ---------      ----       -------
        IPC$           IPC        IPC Service (Samba 2.0.5a)
```

7

DETERMINING
SAMBA ACCESS

```
        Server          Comment
        ---------       -------
        MAINSERV        Samba 2.0.5a

        Workgroup       Master
        ---------       -------
        MYGROUP
$
```

The [test] Disk share is now missing. It's now neither browseable nor accessible.
Deleting the valid users= parameter from the [test] share does not make it
browseable but rather makes it accessible:

```
$ smbclient '//mainserv/test' -Uusername
Added interface ip=192.168.100.1 bcast=192.168.100.255 nmask=255.255.255.0
Password:
Domain=[MYGROUP] OS=[Unix] Server=[Samba 2.0.5a]
smb: \>
```

Browseability and accessibility are two completely different properties that have nothing
to do with each other. A share can be browseable and accessible, browseable and in
accessible, nonbrowseable and accessible, or nonbrowseable and inaccessible.

Working with Browseability Quirks

Test browseability with this command from the server's console or an FTP to the server:

```
smbclient -NL servername
```

The further you get from the server, the more factors intervene. The Windows client
sometimes has trouble finding the server, and Windows 98 Explorer is often very quirky
with browsing. Not seeing a share in Windows 98 Explorer does not necessarily mean
the share is not browseable. To maximize the likelihood of a browseable share showing
up in Windows Explorer, and on a Windows box in general, perform the following tasks:

- Make sure the value of the smb.conf global workgroup= parameter is the same as
  the Windows client's workgroup on its network identification tab.
- Make sure smb.conf contains a netbios name= parameter whose value is the hostname of the server. Using the default often isn't enough.
- Make sure the share really is browseable by using smbclient -NL servername.

The following is a Windows browseability test from the command line (instead of
Explorer):

```
net view \\servername
```

The preceding command should present the server's visible shares, but sometimes it doesn't. The following command shows a browse list based on a workgroup:

```
net view /workgroup:workgroupname
```

The preceding works only on Windows 9*x*. It often triggers a browser election, which after 30 seconds can make the share visible in Explorer. The following is the Windows NT version of the preceding command:

```
net view /domain:workgroupname
```

Browseability is discussed extensively in Chapter 9, "Working with Windows 98."

Accessibility Flowchart

The smb.conf man page makes Samba accessibility look incredibly convoluted. However, Samba accessibility is, in fact, fairly simple when viewed properly. This section contains a series of diagrams that help make Samba accessibility determination simple.

The Top-Level Flowchart

At the top level, Samba access is straightforward. A client requests a share as a user with a primary group (%U and %G). Any hosts allow= and hosts deny= parameters prescreen by IP address. Then Samba's authentication process checks that the user ID exists, the password matches the user, and then it incorporates any guesting. If either user authentication or guest access succeeds, the effective user and group contain either the requested user and group or the guest account and its primary group.

The effective user and group are checked against any valid users= or invalid users= parameters, and if they pass that check, they're evaluated for Samba write access. They're also run through a processes to deduce the service user and group (%u and %g) based on the effective user and group.

The service user and group are checked against UNIX file permissions to determine the readability and writability of a file. That readability and writability are and'ed with the Samba write access to determine whether the file or directory is readable and whether it's writable. However, if the user is one of those in any admin users= list, all files within the share's tree are accessible to the degree specified by Samba, regardless of the service user and group and the file permissions. The service user and group also become the owner and group for newly created files. Figure 7.1 is a flowchart of the top-level access determination.

FIGURE 7.1

Top-level access flowchart.

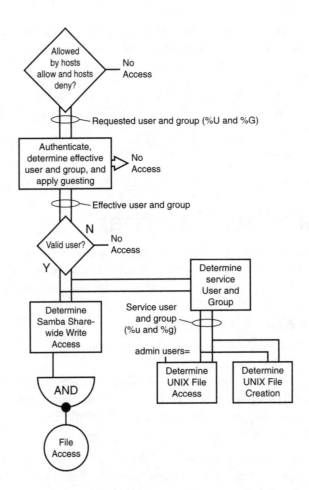

Authentication, Guesting, and Effective User/Group Determination Flowchart

The Samba authentication process checks the username and password, and if either (or both) is bad, then depending on the values of guest ok=, guest only, and map to guest=, it either denies access or grants access as guest. Even if an existing user/password combination is submitted, if the share is both guest only=yes and guest ok=yes, access is switched to guest.

The effective user and effective group are set to the requested user and requested group unless guest access is granted, in which case the effective user is the value of `guest account=`, and the effective group is the primary group of the `guest account=` user. Figure 7.2 charts this logic.

FIGURE 7.2

Authentication, guesting, and effective user/group flowchart.

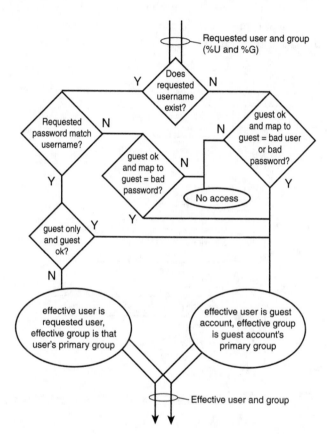

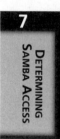

Service User and Group Determination Flowchart

The service user and group are set to the effective user and group. If there's a `force user=` parameter, the service user is changed to that parameter, whereas the service group is the primary group of the new service user. If there's a `force group=` parameter, the service group is changed to that parameter, as shown in Figure 7.3.

FIGURE 7.3

Service user/group determination flowchart.

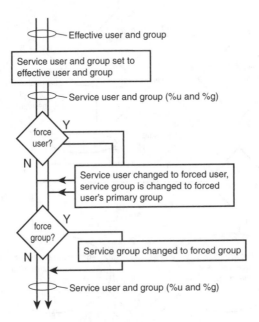

Samba Share-Wide Write Access Flowchart

If the effective user or group is on the `write list=` parameter, it's read-write. Otherwise, if it's on the `read list=` parameter, it's read-only. If `read only=` is set to yes, it's read-only; otherwise, it's read-write. Figure 7.4 makes this much clearer.

FIGURE 7.4

Samba share-wide write access flow-chart.

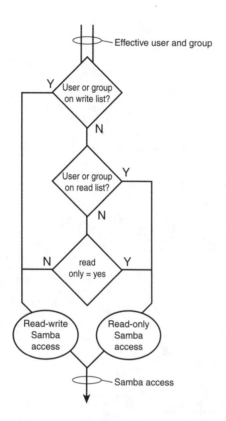

UNIX File Access Determination Flowchart

With its exceptions and Samba client dependencies, UNIX file access is too complex to diagram completely. However, this is not a problem because anyone familiar with UNIX administration instinctively understands UNIX file permissions. Figure 7.5 is a simplified diagram for any readers not intimately familiar with UNIX.

FIGURE 7.5

Simplified UNIX file access determination flowchart.

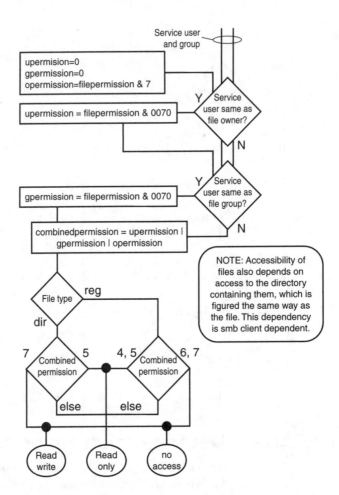

UNIX File Creation

In general, file and directory permissions for Samba-created files are the permissions as per the DOS attributes, and'ed with the appropriate mask and then or'ed with the appropriate force mode. The file's owner is the service user, and the file's group is the service group. Figure 7.6 explains the calculations in greater detail.

FIGURE 7.6

Simplified file and directory creation flowchart.

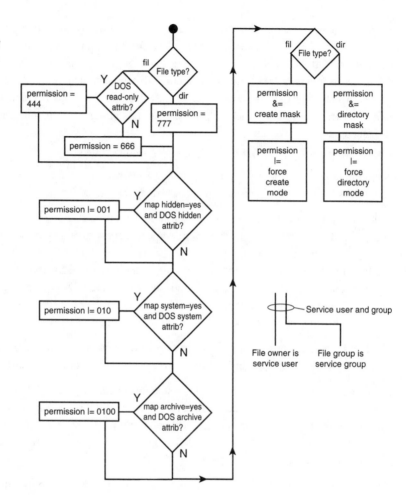

7

DETERMINING
SAMBA ACCESS

Summary

Samba access is simpler than it first appears if viewed from the perspective of the requested user and group, the effective user and group, and the service user and group. The effective user and group are used in all Samba security evaluations, whereas the server user and group are used in all UNIX security evaluations (unless `admin users=yes`).

A client requests a share, submitting a username and password. If the request passes the screening of any hosts allow= or hosts deny= parameters, it's evaluated for authentication and guesting. At this stage, there are three possible outcomes: access as the requested user, guest access, and no access. The exact outcome depends on the requested username and password as well as the guest ok=, guest only=, and map to guest= parameters. The effective user and group are the requested user and its primary group, unless guest access is granted, in which case the effective user is the user defined in the guest account= parameter, and the effective group is the guest account user's primary group.

Next, the effective user and group are screened against any valid users= parameters, and unless they pass the screening, access is denied.

If they pass the screening, the service user and group are set to the effective user and group and then changed by any force user= and force group= parameters. The force group= parameter overrides the group change created by force user=. Note that a share can feature both these parameters, either one, or neither. From this point forward, Samba access is based on the effective user and group, whereas UNIX access and file creation are based on the service user and group. The ultimate file access is the lesser of the Samba and UNIX permissions.

The Samba permissions are for the share as a whole and at this point are either read-only or read-write, depending on the write list=, read list=, and read only= parameters.

If the effective user or effective group is listed in the admin users= share, all permissions to the file are granted, because at the UNIX level the server is operating as root. Otherwise, the UNIX permissions are evaluated in typical UNIX fashion, based on the server user and group. At this stage, UNIX can fail to provide even read permission, thus causing an access failure.

UNIX access can sometimes be tricky, especially when seen though the filter of Samba. In cases where a directory has only executable permission, whereas a file inside it has read-write permission, some Samba clients allow reading and writing of the file, and some don't. Such a setup is not something an administrator would normally strive for. Also, a read-only directory means something different in UNIX than in Samba. The read only=yes parameter prevents all file creation, deletion, and modification within the share's tree. A chmod 555 directory, however, allows modification of the writable files it contains, although it won't permit creation or deletion.

The Samba and UNIX file accesses are compared, with ultimate access being the lesser of the two. Most Samba administrators prefer Samba to have the tighter security and set it up to minimize the permissions UNIX must grant.

New file creation bases the file's or directory's user and group on the service user and group. Directories created through Samba have modes based on the directory `mask=` and `force directory mode=` parameters. Files created through Samba have modes based on the DOS attributes as well as the `map archive=`, `map system=`, `map hidden=`, `create mask=`, and `force create mode=` parameters.

Browseability and accessibility are completely different properties. A share can be browseable and accessible, browseable and inaccessible, nonbrowseable and accessible, or nonbrowseable and inaccessible. Browseability is governed by the share's `browseable=` parameter. However, some clients have bugs that sometimes disrupt browsing on shares that should be browseable. Methods for coping with those bugs are covered in Chapter 9.

This chapter has covered all common access determinations in `security=user` (and therefore `security=server` and `security=domain`) situations. Exotic situations are best handled with experimentation on a test jig server.

Configuring
Printer Shares

by Steve Litt

IN THIS CHAPTER

Samba can be used for network printing. Although it's possible to connect a dedicated printer to each user's machine, that would be a support nightmare in all but the smallest workplaces. The expense would dictate cheap printers for each user, thus reducing reliability. Samba is used to connect many Windows computers to a single high-quality, heavy-duty printer.

Samba printing is conceptually simple, as shown by Figure 8.1.

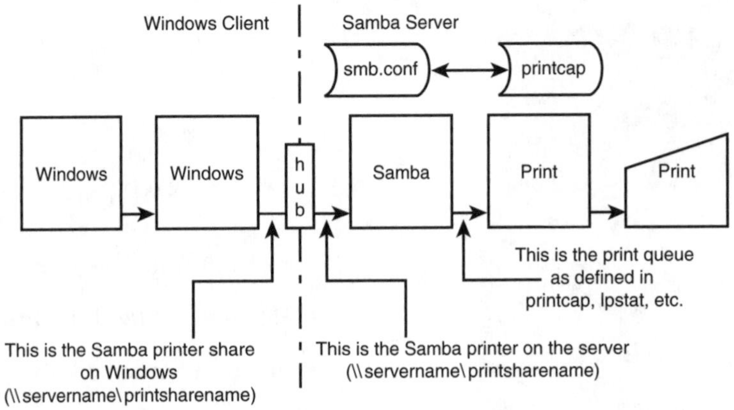

FIGURE 8.1

Samba printing architecture.

Samba printing is controlled almost entirely by the configuration of the smb.conf file and is also dependent on the setup of the server's print queues.

At the conclusion of this chapter, you'll know how to set up and troubleshoot complex Samba printer networking.

Examples in This Chapter

All examples in this chapter use a server named mainserv, located at 192.168.100.1/ 255.255.255.0. The user is called username, a name unlikely to be confused with genuine users on your system. These examples have been checked on a Celeron-equipped machine running Red Hat Linux 6.0. This machine has an HP printer connected to its one and only parallel port. The name of the plain-text printcap printer used in these examples is lp_text, whereas the name of the dedicated Samba printer share is lp_samba.

If you're following along with this chapter's examples, it's easiest to create a user called username and use the same printcap and Samba printer names as the ones in the examples.

> **Caution**
>
> Before attempting any of the examples in this chapter, be sure to back up your existing `smb.conf`!

Defining Your Linux Printer

Samba cannot print to a printer inaccessible from the computer on which it runs. The first step is to set up a print queue that works with your server's command line.

It Must Be a Plain-Text Printer

Because Samba is intended to be used with Windows clients and because the Samba printer is intended to appear as just another hardware printer, a Windows printer definition must exist between your Windows applications and the Samba printer. Because the Windows printer definition does all necessary translation of fonts and graphics for the target printer, the Samba printer share must faithfully pass bytes to the printer.

That means defining the printer as a text printer. There's no printer driver or filter, no banner pages or end of document formfeeds, and no converting linefeeds to carriage return/linefeed combinations (fixing stair steps). All of this is done on the Windows box before the file gets to the Samba server. The Samba server must simply pass bytes.

You may already have a printer defined, and it may have a printer driver. That's not a problem. In this chapter's examples, you'll create a new print queue hooked to the same piece of hardware.

Using `vi` to Edit `/etc/printcap`

By far the easiest way to install the new print queue is to insert it at the bottom of `/etc/printcap` with an editor. You can use tools such as Red Hat's `printtool` to do this, but it's much harder, and the only way `printtool` can suppress formfeeds is to create a plain-text filter, configure it correctly, and link it to the print queue. That's too much work just to avoid inserting seven lines in a file.

> **Caution**
>
> *Always* back up your `/etc/printcap` file before editing it. The file uses a difficult format and is easy to corrupt and hard to re-create.

8
CONFIGURING
PRINTER SHARES

Note

This procedure only applies to BSD-type printing. If your UNIX box uses a type of printing other than BSD, consult your system documentation in order to construct a printer queue.

As user root, edit /etc/printcap (or whatever printcap file you have) and insert the following lines at the bottom of the file:

```
# LOCAL TEXT PRINTER
lp_text:\
        :sd=/var/spool/lpd/lp_text:\
        :mx#0:\
        :lp=/dev/lp0:\
        :sf:\
        :sh:
```

The first line is a comment. The second line is the name of the printer. The backslash at the end is a line-continuation character. This definition continues until a line not ending in a backslash is encountered.

The third line is the spool directory. The fourth line indicates that any size file can be printed, no matter how large. The fifth line indicates that the local printer is device /dev/lp0. The sixth line indicates that formfeeds are suppressed. That's what keeps it from printing a formfeed at the end of each print job. The seventh and final line indicates that the header is suppressed. Without this line, a banner would be printed before every print job. Note that the final line does not end in a backslash because it's the end of the queue definition.

The spool directory must be properly created with the correct permissions all the way down the path:

```
$ ls -ldF /var
drwxr-xr-x  21 root     root          1024 Jul  5 13:50 /var/
$ ls -ldF /var/spool
drwxr-xr-x  16 root     root          1024 Sep 10 04:11 /var/spool/
$ ls -ldF /var/spool/lpd
drwxrwxr-x   5 root     daemon        1024 Oct 12 10:20 /var/spool/lpd/
$ ls -ldF /var/spool/lpd/lp_text
drwxrwxrwx   2 root     lp            1024 Oct 12 11:15 /var/spool/lpd/lp_text/
```

Now test your new printer from the UNIX box with this command:

```
$ echo "^Mhello world^L" | lpr -Plp_text
```

The ^M control character brings the "print head" back to the left in order to compensate for any previous stair stepping. The ^L control character formfeeds the printer at the end.

Exactly one sheet of paper should emerge from the printer. If a blank page follows the one reading "hello world," you haven't correctly inserted `:sf:` in the queue definition in `/etc/printcap`.

> **Tip**
>
> Control characters such as ^M and ^L can be created on UNIX systems as Ctrl+V Ctrl+M and Ctrl+V Ctrl+L keystroke combinations. In the Windows command line, they are created by pressing their key combination: Ctrl+M and Ctrl+L. ^M is the ASCII carriage return character, whereas ^L is the ASCII formfeed character.

Samba behaves the same way if the print queue points to a printer across the UNIX network. Such a `printcap` entry might look something like this:

```
lpnet:\
        :sd=/var/spool/lpd/lpnet:\
        :mx#0:\
        :sh:\
        :rm=192.168.100.1:\
        :rp=lpsmb:
```

In such a case, the print job travels from Windows to the first UNIX computer via Samba and then on to the printer on the second UNIX computer via UNIX networking. Although this practice is easy and fairly common, for simplicity of explanation, the remainder of this chapter omits mention of such double-jump printing.

Printing Systems

There are many printing systems, and each uses a different configuration method, a different print command, and so on. The correct printing system is specified in the `printing=` global `smb.conf` parameter. At present, these are the available options:

- BSD
- SYSV
- AIX
- LPRNG
- HPUX
- QNX
- PLP
- SOFTQ

Because most Linux systems use BSD printing, that's by far the most common. When in doubt, consult your system documentation.

Don't Trust the Defaults

The defaults for your Samba system might not be right for your operating system. As an example, the Samba that comes with Red Hat Linux 6.0 and Caldera OpenLinux 2.2 defaults to `printing=sysv` and `printcap name=lpstat` instead of the needed `printing=bsd` and `printcap name=/etc/printcap`. Debian comes preconfigured with the required `printing=bsd` and `printcap name=/etc/printcap`.

You can run `testparm` into a `grep` command to find your printing defaults. Here's the output on a Red Hat 6 with nothing but `[homes]` in `smb.conf`:

```
$ testparm | grep -i print

        load printers = Yes
        printcap name = lpstat
        printer driver file = /etc/printers.def
        min print space = 0
        print ok = No
        printing = sysv
        print command = lp -c -d%p %s; rm %s
        printer name =
        printer driver = NULL
        printer driver location =
$ testparm | grep -i lp

        lpq cache time = 10
        printcap name = lpstat
        print command = lp -c -d%p %s; rm %s
        lpq command = lpstat -o%p
        lprm command = cancel %p-%j
        lppause command = lp -i %p-%j -H hold
        lpresume command = lp -i %p-%j -H resume
        queuepause command = lpc stop %p
        queueresume command = lpc start %p
$
```

Without an accurate `printcap name=` parameter, the `[printers]` share doesn't know about the system's print queues, so it doesn't offer up printers to browse lists because it won't know about them. However, a dedicated print share is able to work despite an inaccurate `printcap name=` parameter because its name is explicitly defined. Contrast the preceding with an inaccurate `printing=` parameter, which causes even a dedicated Samba printer to fail. However, the insertion of the correct `print command=` parameter often reenables printing. Here's an excellent print command for BSD-type printers:

```
print command = lpr -P %p %s; rm %s
```

It's best to specify the correct values for printing= and printcap name= in smb.conf. If in doubt, consult your system's documentation.

The Easiest Practical Linux [printers] Share

Once you get a single page with "Hello World" in the upper-left corner using the operating system's print command, it's time to build the easiest practical [printers] share. Print shares are effected by many factors, including the smb.conf print share configuration, the print queue the print share points to, permissions on spool directories, and other factors. This is why it's essential to prove that a simple [printers] share works, before constructing a complex custom print share.

Changes to [global]

Insert the following parameters in the [global] section:

```
printcap name=/etc/printcap
printing=bsd
```

The preceding global parameters are highly system dependent. The preceding example is correct for Samba on a Red Hat 6 Linux box. Check your system documentation to find out what kind of printing system your computer uses and the file in which it keeps print queue information.

The printcap name= parameter points smbd to the printer queue configuration file so it can list all print queues in the [printers] section. The printing= parameter tells smbd which type of printing system the box has. This can affect the command used to print, the interpretation of the printcap file, and other types of functionality.

As mentioned previously, an incorrect printing= command can often be overcome by a custom print command= parameter in the print share. However, the right way to do it is to use the right value for printing=.

Another global parameter, load printers=, defaults to yes. However, if you know your printcap name= is correct and your print queues still aren't listed in the browse, place a load printers=yes line in the global section of smb.conf.

The [printers] Share

Do whatever's necessary to create the following [printers] share:

```
[printers]
print ok=yes
path=/var/spool/samba
browseable=no
```

8

CONFIGURING
PRINTER SHARES

Save the file, verify its legality with `testparm`, and restart Samba. The following paragraphs provide a brief description of the share you've created.

`[printers]` is a special share that looks up all print queues in the print queue configuration file (`/etc/printcap`, for instance) and makes those printers available to the browse list.

The `browseable=no` setting in `[printers]` affects the browseability of a resource called `printers`, not the browseability of the individual print queues. Setting it to `no` suppresses a share called `printers` from appearing in the browse list while still making the individual print queues available as Samba shares.

The `print ok=yes` setting is what makes a printer share a printer share. Because `[printers]` is very definitely a printer share (although a special one), it must be defined as `print ok=yes`.

The `path=/var/spool/samba` setting tells Samba where to temporarily house files to be printed. It's sort of a queue before the print queue. Files go from the SMB client to `/var/spool/samba`. From there, the `[printers]` print command (which in this case is a default) picks them up and sends them to the proper print queue. Of course, the print queue has its own queue directory, `/var/spool/lpd/lp_text`, if you're using the `lp_text` print queue described in the "Using `vi` to Edit `/etc/printcap`" section of this chapter.

> **Note**
>
> Be sure to record the file permissions of your spool directory before making any changes to those permissions. Samba printing is extremely sensitive to those permissions. Red Hat and Caldera installations give `/var/spool/samba` permissions `drwxrwxrwt`. That means everyone can read, write, and execute and the sticky bit is set. Setting the sticky bit limits the ability of users to delete each others' print jobs.

Testing with `smbclient`

After creating the `[printers]` share and inserting the proper printer-related parameters in the `[global]` section, it's time to test. Your first tests are from the UNIX box. Start by checking your browse list with `smbclient`:

```
$ smbclient -NL mainserv
Added interface ip=192.168.100.1 bcast=192.168.100.255 nmask=255.255.255.0
Domain=[MYGROUP] OS=[Unix] Server=[Samba 2.0.3]
```

```
Sharename        Type        Comment
.........        ....        .......
homes            Disk
IPC$             IPC         IPC Service (Samba 2.0.3)
lp               Printer
lp_text          Printer

Server                   Comment
.........                .......
MAINSERV                 Samba 2.0.3

Workgroup                Master
.........                .......
MYGROUP
$
```

You'll notice that the newly created `lp_text` print queue shows up. So far so good. Now print to `lp_text` with the following command:

```
$ echo "^MHello World^L" | smbclient "//mainserv/lp_text"
➥ -Uusername%whatever -c "put - f"
```

Once again, the control characters are created with the Ctrl+V key. If all is well, this command should print a single sheet of paper with the words "Hello World" in the upper-left corner. If not, skip to the troubleshooting section of this chapter.

Testing with the DOS `echo` Command

Now run the following command from a Windows command prompt:

```
C:\>echo Hello^L > \\mainserv\lp_text
The command was completed successfully.

C:\>
```

The ^L control character is the ASCII formfeed character created in Windows with the Ctrl+L keystroke combination. Again, "Hello World" should appear on the upper-left corner of the single sheet of paper leaving the printer.

If it doesn't work, once again run the `smbclient` tests described in the preceding section of this chapter. If they now fail, troubleshoot the problem entirely on the server. If they still succeed, this is a Windows-centric or communications problem. Verify connectivity with `ping`. If `ping` reveals connectivity, troubleshoot at the Windows level. This chapter contains a section on troubleshooting Samba printers.

Creating a Windows Printer for `lp_text`

Successfully printing a byte stream to the \\mainserv\lp_text share proves that the share works and is ready to be linked to a Windows printer.

8

CONFIGURING
PRINTER SHARES

> **Note**
>
> A Windows printer driver cannot be linked to a share already mapped to an LPT port. A `net use` command reveals any such links, which can then be unlinked with the `net use lpt9: /delete` command, assuming `lpt9` was the port linked to the share.

Here are the steps for creating a Windows printer definition for the share:

1. Double-click the printer in Network Neighborhood. Click OK when asked if you want Windows to set up the printer. You'll be brought to the first screen of the Add Printer Wizard.

2. Choose Yes or No, as appropriate, when asked if you print from MS-DOS programs. Choose Yes.

3. On the next page, click the Capture Printer Port button and choose lpt9, unless it's taken, in which case choose the next lower port number. Note that the port does not need to correspond to a hardware printer port.

4. Choose the proper printer manufacturer and model. If asked, keep the existing driver rather than replacing it.

5. Call the printer `lp_win`.

6. Decline to print a test page. The Windows test page and Windows printer troubleshooter are of little value on Samba printers.

7. Print a small document to `lp_win` from Microsoft Word or the WordPad app that ships with Windows. Troubleshoot accordingly. Verify that you can still copy files directly to `\\mainserv\lp_text` and have them print out.

8. Open a short but complex document (containing fonts) in a Windows app (Word or PowerPoint serves the purpose) and print it, choosing `lp_win` as the printer. If it prints out the same way as it would on a local printer, you're done. Otherwise, troubleshoot as necessary, keeping in mind that a short document printed OK. Remember that the problem may be in Windows, not Samba.

Working with a Trivial Dedicated Printer Share

Once the [printers] share serves up print queues capable of linkage with a Windows printer, it's easy to create a dedicated print share. Dedicated print shares have the advantage of mapping a single printer to one or more users or groups. Create the following print share in `smb.conf`:

```
[mysmb_lp]
print ok=yes
path=/var/spool/samba
browseable=yes
printer=lp_text
valid users=username
```

Much of the preceding share definition is familiar from the [printers] share previously discussed. This section only discusses the differences.

The browseable= parameter was no in the special [printers] share, but it's yes in this share. That's because smbd itself places all print queues in the browse list for the [printers] share, and in that share the browseable= parameter affects only the name printers. Contrast this with ordinary share [mysmb_lp], where you need to see the name mysmb_lp in the browse list. To do that, browseable= must be set to yes.

The [mysmb_lp] share includes the printer=lp_text line, which was absent in the [printers] share. Every print share must be linked to a print queue, network printer, or Samba printer (a Windows printer accessible via SMB). The [printers] share listed all print queues as shares. The [mysmb_lp] share, on the other hand, must be told which print queue to send its printed material. The printer=lp_text line tells Samba to send all print jobs sent to [mysmb_lp] to the lp_text print queue.

Last but not least, a single valid user was assigned to [mysmb_lp]. Although this could be done to the [printers] share, it's not customary. The valid users=username line makes [mysmb_lp] printable only by user username. Sometimes a printer is intended to be used by everyone. In that case, simply remove the valid users= parameter from the share. Sometimes a printer is intended to be accessible even by people having no login. In such cases, use the guest ok=yes parameter in the share.

Testing

Testing procedures on the [mysmb_lp] share are the same as on the [printers] share using lp_text as the UNIX print queue. Make sure the [mysmb_lp] share is browseable using the smbclient -NL \\servername command, and then print "Hello World" with the following command:

```
$ "^MHello World^L" | smbclient "//mainserv/mysmb_lp"
➥ -Uusername%whatever -c "put - f"
```

Once again, ^M and ^L are control characters made by pressing Ctrl+V followed by the respective control character, and whatever is the password for username.

8

CONFIGURING
PRINTER SHARES

Once "Hello World" prints from smbclient, verify printability with these two commands from a Windows command line:

```
C:\> net use lpt9: \\mainserv\mysmb_lp
C:\> echo Hello World^L > lpt9:
```

Finally, create a Windows printer attached to mysmb_lp. Instructions are in the "Creating a Windows Printer for lp_text" section, earlier in this chapter.

Important smb.conf Printer Parameters

This section discusses several important options that apply to Samba printers. You can use SWAT to find important printer options. You can also use the following shellscript:

```
#!/bin/sh
testparm -s | grep -i print > temp.txt
testparm -s | grep -i lp >> temp.txt
cat temp.txt | sort | less
```

Printer Command Type Parameters

A category of parameters known as the *printer command type parameters* map print queue functions to shell commands. They are all share parameters. If they are not explicitly declared for a share, the smbd program supplies a default.

However, it's a little more complicated than that, because the default supplied depends on another parameter—the printing= parameter—that defines the type of printing system on the machine (BSD, AIX, LPRNG, PLP, SYSV, HPUX, QNX, or SOFTQ).

What makes this tricky is that testparm reports the SYSV defaults, regardless of the actual printing= parameter value.

Theoretically, none of the printer command type parameters are necessary in a system falling neatly into any of the categories BSD, AIX, LPRNG, PLP, SYSV, HPUX, QNX, and SOFTQ. In an ideal world, it's best to try not to use these printer command type parameters. However, it's nice to know they exist for the purposes of troubleshooting and configuring Samba printing on odd-duck systems. In practice, only print command= is commonly specified explicitly.

All these parameters use Samba substitution characters such as %s (the "temporary" name of the file to be printed) and %p (the print queue on which to print it).

> **Tip**
>
> If you're interested in global and share initialization as well as other initialization, here are some excellent source code starting points:
>
> In source/param/loadparm.c, see the following:
>
> init_locals(void), the top comments on how to add a service, struct global, static struct Globals, struct service, static struct sDefault, the various static struct enum_list arrays, parm_table, static void init_globals(void).
>
> Ever wonder how testparm checks shares and outputs error messages? Look at static BOOL service_ok(int iService). lp_load() reads in a services file, such as smb.conf, and stores it in the proper data structures.
>
> The source/include/smb.h file also yields helpful information:
>
> See the various STYPE_ defines. See the LP related enums (search for LPQ_). See the various FLAG_ defines. See enum security_types and enum printing_types. See the various OPLOCK_ defines. See the MAP_TO_GUEST defines at the end of smb.h.
>
> File source/include/local.h defines many important constants:
>
> See the WORKGROUP, GLOBAL_NAME, GLOBAL_NAME2, HOMES_NAME, PRINTERS_NAME, MAX_OPEN_FILES, LOCKDIR, GUEST_ACCOUNT, DEFAULT_PASSWD_CHAT, and MINPASSWDLENGTH defines.

8

print command=

This is a share parameter, whose default depends on compilation parameters. It can get tricky. For instance, on a Red Hat 6 standard setup, this parameter's default is lp -c -d%p %s; rm %s, at least according to testparm. However, this is not necessarily the real default. Consider this tiny smb.conf on a Red Hat Linux 6 box:

```
encrypt passwords=yes
netbios name=mainserv
workgroup=MYGROUP
printcap name=/etc/printcap
printing=bsd
 [mysmb_lp]
path=/var/spool/samba
print ok=yes
browseable=yes
printer name = lp_text
#print command=lp -c -d%p %s; rm %s
```

As you can see, the commented-out print command is simply the default according to `testparm`. This printer works perfectly, but when the print command is uncommented, it stops working. Such problems occur rarely, but it's good to understand that under certain circumstances the reported default `print command=` parameter may in fact not be the one actually used by the daemons.

The `smb.conf` man page sheds some light on this matter. The actual default changes depending on the value of `printing=`, as shown in Table 8.1.

TABLE 8.1   Default Printer Commands

Operating System	*Default* `print command=`
BSD, AIX, QNX, LPRNG, PLP	`lpr -r -P%p %s`
SYS or HPUX	`lp -c -d%p %s; rm %s`
SOFTQ	`lp -d%p -s %s; rm %s`

The `testparm` program is not sophisticated enough to deduce the `print command=` value from the `printing=` parameter; instead it reports the SYSV default. Likewise, although SWAT correctly identifies the present value based on `printing=`, clicking the Default button sets the `print command=` value to the default for SYSV, in spite of the `printing=` parameter.

The `print command=` parameter points to the shell command capable of printing the file. Notice that most versions of this command end with `rm %s`, so the temporary file is deleted after it's successfully spooled to the print queue.

lppause command=

This is a share parameter that defaults to `lp -i %p-%j -H hold` for SYSV, and `qstat -s -j%j -h` for SOFTQ. See `init_locals()` in `source/param/loadparm.c` for other defaults. The program connected to this parameter should take the printer name (`%p`) and job number (`%j`) as arguments and pause the appropriate print job.

lpq command=

This is a share parameter. On SYSV-compiled systems it defaults to `lpstat -o%p`. See `init_locals()` in `source/param/loadparm.c` for defaults on non-SYSV operating systems. The program connected to this parameter should take the printer name (`%p`) as an argument and output printer status information.

lpresume command=

This is a share parameter. On SYSV-compiled systems it defaults to `lp -i %p-%j -H resume`. See `init_locals()` in `source/param/loadparm.c` for defaults on non-SYSV operating systems. The program connected to this parameter should take the printer name (%p) and job number (%j) as arguments and continue printing the job, which was presumably paused earlier by the lppause command.

lprm command=

This is a share parameter. On SYSV-compiled systems it defaults to cancel %p-%j. See init_locals() in source/param/loadparm.c for defaults on non-SYSV operating systems. The program connected to this parameter should take the printer name (%p) and job number (%j) as arguments, delete the print job, and output printer status information.

queuepause command=

This is a share parameter. On SYSV-compiled systems it defaults to lpc stop %p. See init_locals() in source/param/loadparm.c for defaults on non-SYSV operating systems. The program connected to this parameter should take the printer name (%p) as its argument and pause the entire print queue. Note that this pauses the whole queue and stops queued jobs from printing, as opposed to the lppause command, which pauses one job and lets other jobs through.

queueresume command=

This is a share parameter. On SYSV-compiled systems it defaults to lpc start %p. See init_locals() in source/param/loadparm.c for defaults on non-SYSV operating systems. The program connected to this parameter should take the printer name (%p) as its argument and resume the queue so that queued jobs start printing again. Note that this resumes the whole queue, as opposed to the lpresume command, which resumes only one job.

Miscellaneous Printer Parameters

Several other parameters determine the behavior of printers. Some, such as load printers=, lpq cache time=, min print space=, and postscript=, are excellent candidates for leaving at their default values. Others, especially printing= and printcap name=, have defaults so dependent on compile time defines that leaving them at their default values spells disaster. Also in the latter category are the three printer driver parameters. Parameters such as print ok= and printer name= must be set by their very natures.

load printers=

This is a global parameter defaulting to yes. This determines whether [printers] will be able to load and therefore offer to the browse lists all the printers listed in the queue configuration file (that is, printcap).

lpq cache time=

This is a share parameter defaulting to 10. It's uncommon to see this parameter used. See the `smb.conf` man page for further details if necessary.

min print space=

This is a share parameter defaulting to 0. This number is the amount of free disk space, in kilobytes, that must be free in order to spool a print job. 0 means always spool. If the number is higher than the amount of free disk space, when you print from a Windows program it will report a disk full condition and place the Windows printer's status to offline printing. The Windows printer will come to the foreground.

After fixing the problem by increasing disk space or by reducing this parameter and restarting Samba, pull up the window for the affected Windows printer, go into the menu, choose File, and then uncheck Use Printer Offline.

postscript=

This is a share parameter defaulting to no. A yes value forces the printer to interpret the print file as PostScript.

If this parameter is used on a non-PostScript printer, it will not print. Usually it errors gracefully with a single page saying "No way to print this type of input file," or something to that effect.

print ok=

This is a share parameter defaulting to no. This parameter specifies whether a share is a printer share. If [printers] does not have print ok=yes, testparm issues a warning. All shares intended to be printer shares must have this parameter set to yes. All printer shares intended to execute server-side automation must also have this parameter set to yes.

printcap name=

This is a global parameter defaulting to a value set in source/include/includes.h. Defaults to lpstat on any system defined at compile time as SYSV. Note that setting printing= to BSD does not change this, because printcap name= is not adjusted in the init_locals() function of source/param/loadparm.c. For safety's sake, always explicitly specify this parameter in the [global] section of smb.conf.

printer driver=

This is a share parameter with no default. Used to tell Windows the exact name of the printer driver to use in order to automate the setup of printer drivers on the Windows machine. This is discussed in the "Automatic Windows 9x Printer Driver Installation" section, later in this chapter.

printer driver file=

This is a global parameter whose default is set at compile time. Specifies the location of the Windows printer driver definition file, used to automate the setup of printer drivers on Windows machines. Set this explicitly if you're automating printer setup. This is discussed in the "Automatic Windows 9*x* Printer Driver Installation" section, later in this chapter.

This parameter differs from `printer driver location=` in that the latter specifies a directory containing driver files, whereas the former is a file telling which drivers need which driver files.

printer driver location=

This is a share parameter with no default. This parameter tells clients of the print share the location of the special `[printer$]` share, which holds the `.drv`, `.dll`, and `.hlp` type files that Windows needs to configure the printer.

This parameter differs from `printer driver file=` in that the latter specifies a file telling which drivers need which driver files, whereas the former is a directory containing driver files.

printer name=

This is a share parameter having no default on most compiles. It should always be explicitly specified on printer shares other than `[printers]`. This specifies which print queue or network printer the share sends print jobs to.

printing=

This is a global parameter whose default value is compilation dependent. To determine your default, you can run `testparm` without a `printing=` parameter in your `smb.conf`. To see how Samba sets this default, see the following lines in `include.h`:

```
#if (defined(STAT_STATVFS) || defined(STAT_STATVFS64)) && !defined(SYSV)
#define SYSV 1
#endif

#ifndef DEFAULT_PRINTING
#ifdef SYSV
#define DEFAULT_PRINTING PRINT_SYSV
#define PRINTCAP_NAME "lpstat"
#else
#define DEFAULT_PRINTING PRINT_BSD
#define PRINTCAP_NAME "/etc/printcap"
#endif
#endif
```

Without going into too much detail, unless AIX, HPUX, or QNX are defined in `local.h` or in some other way, `DEFAULT_PRINTING` is undefined and SYSV is defined, which means that `DEFAULT_PRINTING` will be `PRINT_SYSV` (printing=sysv).

Automatic Windows 9*x* Printer Driver Installation

Many methods exist for installing printer drivers and printer definitions on a Windows computer. The manual method using Add Printer in the Printers folder or double-clicking a printer share is easy. Printers can be installed with preconfigured printers on OS image installations. Also, with Windows 9*x* clients, the drivers can be installed by Samba. This is not easy, and it's not right for every occasion, but sometimes it's handy.

This section uses a HP LaserJet III installation to reproduce the instructions in the `PRINTER_DRIVER.txt` file that comes with every Samba distribution. Because most printers are compatible with the PCL on LaserJet III printers, this should be reproducible at most installations.

Automatic printer installation is a three-step process:

1. Create `[printer$]`.
2. Build the driver list and `printers.def`.
3. Add three new parameters to `smb.conf`.

Create [printer$]

First, make the following share in `smb.conf`:

```
[printer$]
path=/data/pdrivers
public=yes
read only=yes
browseable=yes
```

Then create the `/data/pdrivers` directory, giving all user permissions and all permissions but write to `group` and `other`:

$ mkdir -m755 /data/pdrivers

Restart Samba and test with `smbclient -NL servername` to verify that share `printer$` is now visible. Note that it might not be visible in Windows. That's OK.

Build the Driver List and `printers.def`

Next, build the drivers and `printers.def` file in directory `/data/pdef`. Make it readable and executable by all, but writable only by user `root`.

From the `c:\windows\inf` directory of a working Windows 9*x* machine, use `ftp` in ASCII mode to transfer files `MSPRINT*.INF` to the server and then move them to `/data/pdef`. If any of the printers involved have updated drivers or if the printer manufacturer supplied drivers, these should be installed first, after which they'll be available as one of the `OEM*.INF` files. Make sure to `ascii ftp` any applicable `OEM*.INF` files as well (there are none in this example because HP LaserJet III is supported completely by Windows).

Now that `/data/pdef` contains the necessary `.inf` files, run this command from the `/data/pdef` directory:

```
$ make_printerdef MSPRINT.INF "HP LaserJet III" >> printers.def
```

> **Caution**
>
> All activities calling for Windows printer driver names, such as "HP LaserJet III," must be typed absolutely correctly with respect to spacing and capitalization; otherwise, failure occurs.

Upon receiving a "printer not found" error, repeat the process with other `MSPRINT*.INF` files until the command works. In fact, it will work for `MSPRINT3.INF` on Windows 98.

When the command works, it does two things: It puts the proper entry in the `printers.def` file, and it lists on `stderr` the Windows driver files that must be copied to your `[printer$]` directory.

In the case of this HP LaserJet III example, using the `.INF` files from the Windows 98 version from 1998, here is the output of the command:

```
# make_printerdef MSPRINT3.INF "HP LaserJet III" >> printers.def
Found:HPPCL5MS.DRV
End of section found
CopyFiles: @HPPCL5MS.DRV,UNI,FINSTALL
Datasection: UNI_DATA
Datafile: HPPCL5MS.DRV
Driverfile: HPPCL5MS.DRV
Helpfile: UNIDRV.HLP
LanguageMonitor: (null)
```

```
Copy the following files to your printer$ share location:
HPPCL5MS.DRV
UNIDRV.DLL
UNIDRV.HLP
ICONLIB.DLL
FINSTALL.DLL
FINSTALL.HLP

[root@mainserv pdef]#
```

Now, either paste this list from the screen to a file or copy the list for further reference. Copy all these files to /data/pdrivers. The easiest way might be to temporarily set the mode of file /data/pdrivers to 777, and temporarily set read only=yes, make the [printer$] share write accessible to Windows via a net use command, and then perform the copy via Samba. Note that because these are binary files, a Samba copy works excellently.

> **Caution**
>
> Case matters! Be sure that all the files ending up in /data/pdrivers are, letter for letter, the same case as on the list. Double-check their case after the copy.

Add Three New Parameters in `smb.conf`

First, add this global parameter:

```
printer driver file=/data/pdef/printers.def
```

This parameter tells Windows to look in the specified file to find the files to download for your particular printer. If you look through printers.def, you see that for each supported printer type (just one in this example) there's a colon-delimited line containing the exact printer name, followed by various necessary files.

Next, add these two lines to the print share you want to enable for automatic installation:

```
printer driver=HP LaserJet III
printer driver location=\\%h\PRINTER$
```

The first line indicates that this particular print share goes to an HP LaserJet III printer. It must, of course, agree exactly with the name in the /data/pdef/printers.def file so that the correct drivers are downloaded. The next line tells Windows that after it reads which files to download from the /data/pdef/printers.def file, it can find those files in share \\%h\PRINTER$. Here, %h evaluates to the server hostname, so it's the path of the [printer$] share (or /data/pdrivers).

Check your work very carefully. Any errors in the automatic printer installation `smb.conf` parameters may cause Windows clients to hang upon printer installation, thus corrupting the entire Windows OS and requiring a reboot. This fact was verified on a test setup incorporating a Windows 98 client and a Red Hat 6.0 server with Samba 2.0.3.

Once all parameters are correct, restart Samba.

Using the New Setup

If you've read about automatic printer installation, you've probably noticed every author saying in one way or another "your mileage may vary." First, any configuration errors in the parameters or the setup discussed in this section might corrupt or disable a Windows session. Second, the documentation states this only works for Window 9*x*. I have confirmed this fact using a Windows NT 4 test client.

Keeping the preceding in mind, if you're still game, navigate through Network Neighborhood until you see the printer to which was added the `printer driver=HP LaserJet III` and `printer driver location=\\%h\PRINTER$` parameters and then double-click it. If all goes well and you have a Windows 98 machine, it should ask you whether you want to print from DOS and what you want to name the printer and then set it up. If it hangs, corrupts the OS, or anything else weird, you'll need to do some `smb.conf` troubleshooting.

Troubleshooting Printer Problems

Samba printer troubleshooting is easy when approached modularly. The first set of tests determine the general position of failure: print queue, Samba share, Samba share as seen on the client, or the client's printer definition, as shown on Figure 8.2.

FIGURE 8.2
Samba printer troubleshooting diagram.

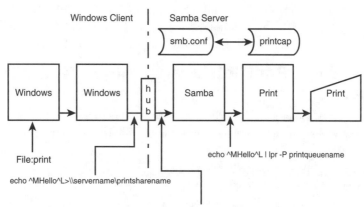

8

CONFIGURING
PRINTER SHARES

Diagnostic Tools

The Samba distribution comes with several excellent diagnostic tools. Others can be made quite easily. Samba is wrongly viewed by many as a huge black box. These tools yield enough test points to easily and quickly fix Samba problems.

testparm

The `testparm` program is so easy to use that it should always be run at the first sign of trouble. If it reports any problems, fix them before going on.

A DOS-Compatible Text File

Because most hardware printers require both a carriage return and a linefeed to correctly print lines, create a DOS-compatible text file. Create a short text file in `vi`, placing carriage return (Ctrl+M) characters at the end of each line. Below the final line, place a single formfeed character (Ctrl+L).

Such a file prints correctly on a straight byte feed printer queue (a plain text printer, in other words), and the file formfeeds the page after printing its contents.

Injecting a Print Job Directly to the Print Queue

A print job can be injected directly to the print queue with the proper command. On BSD systems, use something like this:

```
$ echo ^Mhello^L | lpr -P printqueuename
```

Alternatively, a DOS-type file with a trailing formfeed can be injected directly to the print queue like this:

```
$ lpr -P printqueuename dos.txt
```

Injecting a print job directly to the queue gives a go/nogo status on the print queue, without Samba, connectivity, and Windows muddying the waters. If you use a printing system other than BSD, consult your system documentation for the proper command.

Injecting a Print Job Directly from UNIX to the Print Share

The primary use of `smbclient` in printer troubleshooting is to inject a print job to the Samba server from the Samba server's command line. Here's the command to accomplish this:

```
$ echo "^Mhello^L | smbclient "//servername/printsharename"
➡-Uusername%password -c "put - f"
```

In the previous script, note that username should be a very low-privilege user. The man page for smbclient states that the password typed after the percent sign is not visible to ps commands, but it does become part of the environment, which may be insecure on some systems.

Another way to use smbclient is to print an existing file. The file must be a DOS-type file with lines ending in a CRLF combination, and ideally it should terminate with a formfeed character. Here's the command to print such a file:

```
$ smbclient //servername/printsharename" -Uusername%password
➥-c "put dos.txt"
```

Once again, use a low-privilege user because someone might see what you type. The man page for smbclient states that the password typed after the percent sign is not visible to ps commands, but it does become part of the environment, which may be insecure on some systems. For the ultimate security, run smbclient interactively, input the password, and then "put" the file. Here's such a session:

```
$ smbclient '//mainserv/smb_lp' -Uusername
Added interface ip=192.168.100.1 bcast=192.168.100.255 nmask=255.255.255.0
Password:
Domain=[MYGROUP] OS=[Unix] Server=[Samba 2.0.3]
smb: \> put dos.txt
putting file dos.txt as \dos.txt (3.01845 kb/s) (average 3.01847 kb/s)
smb: \> quit
$
```

The preceding session is the most secure test for injecting a print job directly into the printer share from the UNIX command line.

Injecting a Print Job Directly from Windows to the Print Share

On the Windows side, the print share is available as \\servername\printsharename. Therefore, a simple echo injects a print job to the share on the Windows client:

```
C:\WINDOWS>echo Hello^L > \\mainserv\smb_lp
```

Alternatively, autoexec.bat can be copied to the share. Sometimes Windows responds with a message asking whether you want to overwrite the share. As long as you're sure it's a print share, feel free to answer yes, after which it will print. The following is such a session, using server mainserv and print share smb_lp:

```
C:\WINDOWS>copy c:\autoexec.bat \\mainserv\smb_lp
Overwrite \\mainserv\smb_lp (Yes/No/All)?y
        1 file(s) copied

C:\WINDOWS>
```

8

CONFIGURING
PRINTER SHARES

Assuming your `autoexec.bat` does not end in a formfeed character, you'll need to form-feed the printer with an `echo ^L \\servername\printsharename` command. To eliminate the "overwrite" prompt, the copy can be done in two steps. In the first step, a `net use` command maps the printer share to an unused printer port. The printer port doesn't need to be an actual hardware port, hence the use of `lpt9:` in this example. The second step involves copying the file to the printer port. Here's the session:

```
C:\WINDOWS>net use lpt9: \\mainserv\smb_lp
The command was completed successfully.

C:\WINDOWS>copy c:\autoexec.bat lpt9:
        1 file(s) copied


C:\WINDOWS>
```

Once again, assuming your `autoexec.bat` does not end in a formfeed, you'll need to formfeed the printer with an `echo ^L \\servername\printsharename` command.

Picking Off the Print Job Between Samba and the Print Queue

Rather than injecting a print job and seeing what comes out of the printer, sometimes it's helpful to create a test point and probe what's in the pipeline. The `print command=` parameter of `smb.conf` is ideal for this purpose. Different `print command=` parameters accomplish different things. The most fundamental is to see whether the job even reached the test point. This is an excellent test point:

```
print command = echo "%T: Printer=%p, User=%U, File=%s,
➥`ls -hs %s`"    >> /tmp/test5.log;rm %s
```

> **Caution**
>
> Use extreme care when changing the print command on live production systems. Users can silently lose their print jobs. If it's impossible to do these tests on a test jig system, try to find a time when no users are on the system. If possible, temporarily place a `hosts allow=` parameter on the share so users error out when trying to access the share while you're troubleshooting it.

The preceding print command writes a log record, then deletes the print file to prevent accumulation. The log file, in this case named `test5.log` to minimize the chance of conflict with any other file, should be written in a universally accessible directory such as `/tmp` to maximize the chance that the record will be written. The purpose of the final `ls` statement in backquotes is to get the file size. The following is an example of the contents of the log file:

```
1999/10/16 18:09:30: Printer=lp_text, User=username,
⇒ File=wincli.WkkTXD,  12k wincli.WkkTXD
1999/10/16 18:10:07: Printer=lp_text, User=username,
⇒ File=wincli.1QoP0S,  12k wincli.1QoP0S
1999/10/16 18:10:25: Printer=lp_text, User=username,
⇒ File=wincli.91LRb4, 1.0k wincli.91LRb4
```

If the file is not found, it's either because the print file never got there and therefore couldn't trigger the print command or possibly because the log file could not be written. Try precreating the log file and giving it all permissions for everybody. If the file is not written by subsequent prints, it's probably because the print file never got that far.

Once log records are observed, `rm %s` can be temporarily removed so the print files are not deleted. Remember that these files should show up in the directory of the share's `path=` parameter. If these files do not show up, check the directory's permissions. Typically, they're 1777 so everyone can write the files.

Once written, the print files can be sent to the print queue via the proper shell command (`lpr -P printqueuename filename` in BSD-type printing systems). Once these files can be printed, the command used to print them can be inserted in a custom `print command=` parameter (with appropriate substitution characters such as `%s` and `%p`). This almost always works.

The `print command=` parameter is so flexible that it can be used for almost any printer diagnostic purpose. Shellscripts can be constructed to examine every intricacy of the print situation. There's no limit to its usefulness when used creatively.

ping

`ping` tests connectivity, so it's the tool of choice if writing to the share on the server succeeds but writing to the share on the client fails. Any time connectivity is suspect, `ping` is the tool to use.

Test Jig `smb.conf`

Often the easiest and quickest way to find a problem is by building an `smb.conf` designed to exercise the one share and print queue and then testing by making changes. This obviously is impractical on a production system, but if the problem can be reproduced on a Linux box, then the test jig can be placed there.

Samba Printer Troubleshooting Strategies

In an ideal world, every diagnostic test rules out half the remaining problem scope. In such an idealized world, a system with 16,384 hardware and software components can be troubleshot with 14 tests. Often such a binary search is a goal to work toward, thus saving immense amounts of time.

8

CONFIGURING
PRINTER SHARES

In other situations, it's better to preserve brainpower and test in a linear fashion. This is best when there are few components. One situation in which a linear search pays off handsomely is in pinpointing the bad subsystem in a Samba printer. Referring to Figure 8.2, the problem is restricted to seven major components: the Windows app, the Windows printer definition, the wire and hub, Samba, the printer queue, and the printer. A seven-component subsystem is ideal for linear search.

Once the problem has been isolated to, say, Samba, it's a different story. A `wc` (word count) of the output of the `testparm` command on a `[homes]`-only `smb.conf` reveals 193 lines containing equal signs, which roughly approximates the number of parameter names. Many can take several values, and most have interdependencies. This is the equivalent of thousands of components. Here, a binary search is just what is needed. As mentioned previously, using a test jig `smb.conf` on a nonproduction machine often cuts hours or days off the time it takes to arrive at a solution.

Often the deciding factor in troubleshooting productivity is the choice of what tests to perform. The decision of what test to take next is a quadruple tradeoff between ease, likelihood, even divisions, and safety. Obviously, do not perform unsafe tests. Easy tests such as the `testparm` utility are often good choices, even if they rule out little, because they cost little time. If the last 20 Samba printer problems you've encountered existed because of the wrong `printing=` and `printcap name=` parameters, they make an excellent choice as a first test, based on likelihood, even if they rule out little.

Quick Predefined Diagnostic

Predefined diagnostics are flowcharts, where each test determines which test to take next. Some are oriented more toward a binary search, whereas others are oriented more toward a linear search.

Predefined diagnostics have three advantages: They save brainpower, they provide a common frame of reference between troubleshooters, and they're extremely efficient in the 80 percent of problems that fall in 20 percent of solutions. The granddaddy of all Samba predefined diagnostics is the 10-step diagnostic defined in the `DIAGNOSIS.txt` file that comes with Samba. It's referenced continuously in the Samba.org mailing list and the `comp.protocols.smb` newsgroup. A predefined diagnostic for Samba printer troubleshooting is detailed in the following subsections.

Are There Syntax Errors in `smb.conf`?

Running a `testparm` command takes 10 seconds, so start there. If it shows errors, fix them. This is vitally important because undetected `smb.conf` errors create very tricky problems that might not be immediately noticed in a production system.

testparm | grep -i print

Many printer problems are caused by the wrong `printing=`, `printcap name=`, and/or `print command=` parameters. This 10-second command lists every parameter with the word `print`. Be sure the parameters all make sense and fix any obviously wrong parameters.

Is There Connectivity?

Another easy test is to `ping` the server from the client, or vice versa. Without connectivity, there's no network printing.

smbclient -NL servername

Is Samba working? What shares are visible? Run the `smbclient -NL servername` command from the server console or a telnet session to the server. This is another 10-second command. If it fails, the server is likely to have serious Samba problems that must be solved before going on.

echo Hello^L > \\servername\printqueuename

Here's another 10-second test—this time performed on the Windows client. If this test succeeds, it rules out everything but the Windows printer definition and the application. Therefore, if it succeeds, stop and troubleshoot these items. If it fails, you've ruled out the application and Windows printer (assuming there's only one problem), so go on to the next step.

smbclient '//servername/printsharename' -U myuid, put dos.txt

The previous step ruled out the Windows printer definition and Windows application, assuming there's a single problem.

Successfully printing a DOS-style file from the server's console rules out Samba (at least the print share), the printer queue, and the printing hardware as suspects. If this succeeds but the previous test (echoing the "Hello" to the share on the Windows machine) failed, a connectivity or name resolution problem is most likely the problem. Try both with IP addresses instead of server names. Redo the `ping` test. Also, issue a `net view \\servername` command. If that fails but `ping` succeeded, you have a NetBIOS name resolution problem, most likely due to global parameters in `smb.conf`. Fix connectivity and/or name resolution before continuing.

If this `smbclient` print test fails, the print job is getting lost in Samba, the print queue, the print device, or in the printing hardware. Continue on to the next test.

8

CONFIGURING
PRINTER SHARES

echo ^MHello^L | lpr -P printqueuename

This is another 10-second test. If it fails, there's a print queue, print device (that is, /dev/lp0), or printing hardware problem. Check the cables and try sending another print queue to the same device.

If the echo piped to lpr succeeds, the print queue and printing hardware are good, so the job is getting lost in Samba. It's time to look at Samba.

Search for the Missing Print File

Print a text file with a unique string inside using the command copy uniquestring.txt \\servername\printsharename. Look for this file in the directory denoted in the print share's path= parameter. Use grep if there are a lot of files in that directory.

Look in the queue directory for the associated print queue, as noted in the printcap file's :sd= statement. If you find the file anywhere, try printing it from the UNIX command line to see what's going wrong. Otherwise, continue.

Verify Permissions in the Share's Directory

Each print file is created as the user on the Windows machine. Therefore, each user must be able to create files in the path= directory. The proper permissions for this directory are drwxrwxrwt, otherwise known as 1777. If the permissions are different, log in as the user in question and see whether you can create a file in this directory. If you cannot, that's the problem. Record the existing permissions and then issue this command:

```
$ chmod 1777 /var/spool/samba
```

Obviously, the preceding command should be changed to match the path= parameter in the printer share. Log into the UNIX box as the user in question and verify that you can now write a file there.

Create a Test Point with the print command= Parameter

If you've gotten to this point and there's still no resolution, it's time for the heavy artillery. The previous tests, which probably took less than five minutes in total, were all nondestructive tests safely done on a live system. None of the tests (as opposed to solutions for found problems) involved changing smb.conf or even restarting Samba. This test is different.

The trick here is to install a print command= parameter whose sole purpose is to uncover information—What's the username? What's the filename? Where's the file? Here's one such print command:

```
print command = echo "%T: Printer=%p, User=%U, File=%s,
➡ `ls -hs %s`"   >> /tmp/test5.log;rm %s
```

Make Your Own Diagnostics

If you get to this point and still have a problem, devise your own diagnostic tests. Refer to the smb.conf man page, the documentation that comes with Samba, and the samba.org Web site. Troubleshooters.com contains an excellent description of generic troubleshooting processes at www.troubleshooters.com/tuni.htm.

Other Cool Samba Printer Tricks

The existence of Samba as well as printers connected to UNIX, Linux, and BSD boxes presents excellent opportunities for saving work and time. Two of the most prominent are server-side automation and direct printing on big, repetitive print jobs.

Server-Side Automation

A frequent requirement is to create or process a file in Windows, send it to a UNIX box, and have it further processed by UNIX. This is easily achievable by creating a pseudo printer whose job is to do the UNIX part of the process, with its print command= pointing to the UNIX program, complete with %s representing the file to be processed. The Windows process can then simply copy the file to the pseudo printer's share, and the rest will be taken care of. This is called *server-side automation*, and it's discussed in greater detail in the Chapter 14, "Using Samba Server-Side Automation."

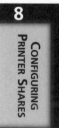

Big, Repetitive Print Jobs

Consider a large, repetitive print job. A company policy manual comes to mind. There's no reason to go through the trouble of opening the source document, choosing the correct printer, and printing it. By capturing the print file on a previous Samba printer write, that file is available for further submissions to the print queue without involving Windows, the source document, or even Samba.

This saves time for the user and eliminates the risk of corruption of the source document. Spooling the print job from a robust UNIX, Linux, or BSD server reduces the risk of the print job crashing or being interrupted by an operating system crash. Using server-side automation, the policy manual print job can be started by clicking a "print policy manual" icon on the user's Windows desktop.

Printing to Windows Printers

There's often a requirement to print to a Windows printer from UNIX or Linux. The printer must be physically connected to the Windows box. Additionally, a Windows printer definition must be created for the printer. The Windows printer definition can be a Generic/Text Only definition or an actual driver for the printer. In the case of the Generic/Text Only definition, the driver function is performed by a printer filter on the UNIX end.

All the methods discussed here use smbclient at some level, all require a password for the printer, and if sharing is user based instead of share based, all require a username. These examples assume share-based sharing is used on the Windows box.

> **Tip**
>
> Always restart the lpd daemon after changing your printcap file.

Printing Straight Through `smbclient`

The simplest method of printing to a printer connected to a Windows printer is to print to its share through smbclient. This requires no print queue and no entry in the printcap file; just a command is needed. Here's an example that assumes the Windows machine is called winclient and its printer definition is named GENERIC:

```
$ echo "^Mhello^L" | smbclient "//WINCLIENT/GENERIC"
➥ -U%SHAREPASS -I192.168.100.201 -c "put - f"
```

This sends bytes to the Windows printer definition, which sends them on to the printer. In this case, it sends them straight through because on the Windows end the printer has been defined as Generic/Text Only.

This is an easy one-minute test. It's much quicker and easier than the other methods discussed. Do not work toward the more complex print methods until this test prints correctly.

Printing Straight Through with `smbprint`

Samba comes with a shellscript called smbprint. Its purpose in life is to be a print share input filter capable of passing the print job to smbclient. A printcap entry using smbprint looks like this:

```
lpsmb:\
        :sd=/var/spool/lpd/lpsmb:\
        :mx#0:\
        :sh:\
        :if=/usr/bin/smbprint:\
        :af=/var/spool/lpd/lpsmb/acct:\
        :lp=/dev/null:
```

Like all spool directories, `/var/spool/lpd/lpsmb` must be `chmod 1777`. The print job is sent through the filter `smbprint`, but instead of continuing on to `lp`, it is picked off and sent to the Windows box via the `smbclient` call in the last line of `smbprint`. Because `lp` is superfluous, it's assigned to `/dev/null`.

`smbprint` runs environment assignments in a file called `.config` in the `spool` directory. These environment assignments define the server, service, user, password, and IP address necessary to access the remote printer. Because they're environment assignments, they need not be in a specific order. Here's an example of a `.config`:

```
server=WINCLIENT
service=GENERIC
password=''
hostip=192.168.100.201
user=''
```

Many Samba distributions have `smbprint` scripts not matching the latest `smbclient` syntax. Some use this `smbclient` command:

```
/usr/bin/smbclient "\\\\$server\\$service" $password -U $server
➡ -N -P >> $logfile
```

Modern `smbclient` software works much better by putting the password after the user, separated by a percent sign. Worse still, the preceding `smbclient` command has no `-I` argument specifying an IP address, making it difficult to reach most Windows clients.

Sometimes `smbprint` must be modified to be practical as a `printcap` filter. Because various filters use the original `smbprint`, if you need to modify `smbprint`, be sure to copy it to a file of a different name and then modify it. Reference the copy in `printcap`. Here's how this looks after modernizing the password placement, including an IP address, and incorporating a user instead of using the server name as a user:

```
/usr/bin/smbclient "\\\\$server\\$service" -I $hostip
➡ -U $user%$password -N -P >> $logfile
```

Here's a compatible `.config`:

```
server=MAINSERV
service=GENERIC
hostip=192.168.100.201
user=""
password=""
```

This method requires having a plain-text copy of the password in `.config`, which is a clear security problem. It's therefore best if the printer has a low-security password or no password at all. If the Windows machine's sharing is user based, the printer should belong to a low-security user.

8

CONFIGURING PRINTER SHARES

This type of setup can be used for printing to a Windows printer definition specifically for the printer, as long as the output of the application is readable by the printer and not PostScript (unless the printer is PostScript or special filters are in place).

The `lpr` command is used to print to a printer, just like any other queue.

Printing with a Filter

Here, `printcap` defines a filter to drive the printer; therefore, on the Windows side, a Generic/Text Only printer is used. This method seems to work much better over a wider range of applications. Here's a sample `printcap` print queue configuration:

```
lpwin98:\
        :sd=/var/spool/lpd/lpwin98:\
        :mx#0:\
        :sh:\
        :if=/var/spool/lpd/lpwin98/filter:\
        :af=/var/spool/lpd/lpwin98/acct:\
        :lp=/dev/null:
```

Similar to the `smbprint` example, this example prints through the input filter, but this time it's a real filter designed to drive the specific printer. It's beyond the scope of this book to discuss print filters, but here's the basic idea behind what's going on: The filter determines that the printer is an SMB-type printer and diverts it to `smbprint` as a postfilter after converting the data to the printer's native format.

The `lpr` command is used to print to a printer, just like any other queue.

Summary

Samba can be used to print documents across the network, usually initiating the print job from a Windows application and printing on a computer attached to a UNIX, Linux, or BSD box. Because the Windows boxes typically contain the necessary print drivers to translate the application's print output into the printer's native print language, the UNIX print queue typically passes all bytes straight through to the printer with a simple `/etc/printcap` entry, something like this:

```
lp_text:\
        :sd=/var/spool/lpd/lp_text:\
        :mx#0:\
        :lp=/dev/lp0:\
        :sf:\
        :sh:
```

Several printing systems exist throughout the UNIX world. Samba directly supports these eight with its `printing=` global parameter:

- BSD
- SYSV
- AIX
- LPRNG
- HPUX
- QNX
- PLP
- SOFTQ

Picking the right one usually enables printing without resorting to hand-tuning the various print command type parameters. Another vitally important global parameter is the `printcap name=` parameter, which points to the definition of print queues. This is typically `/etc/printcap` for BSD-type printing systems (BSD, Linux, and others) and `lpstat` for SYSV printing systems. The intended mapping between the print system type and the `printcap` name can be found in the `init_locals()` function of source file `source/param/loadparm.c`.

A simple series of Samba print shares is made with the `[printers]` share, which lists all print queues as Samba printers. Here's a BSD printing system example:

```
### Other global parameters are above this point
printcap name=/etc/printcap
printing=bsd
[printers]
print ok=yes
path=/var/spool/samba
browseable=no
```

The path must have the correct permissions, typically `chmod 1777`.

Once the share is working correctly, a Windows printer definition can be created for the share by double-clicking it in Network Neighborhood and filling out the Windows Printer Wizard.

Dedicated print shares work almost identically, except they must name their print queue with the `printer=` parameter. Dedicated printers often have only certain valid users. Here's a typical example:

```
### Other global parameters are above this point
printcap name=/etc/printcap
printing=bsd
```

8

CONFIGURING PRINTER SHARES

```
[mysmb_lp]
print ok=yes
path=/var/spool/samba
browseable=yes
printer=lp_text
valid users=username
```

Several important `smb.conf` parameters are concerned with printing. For instance, `printing=` and `printcap name=` are global parameters that should be specified in every `smb.conf`. Every printer share must include `print ok=`, and every printer share except `[printers]` must contain `printer name=`. The `print command=` parameter is often necessary in print shares, although a correct choice of the `printing=` global usually makes it unnecessary, except as a troubleshooting tool. The `lppause command=`, `lpq command=`, `lpresume command=`, `lprm command=`, `queuepause command=`, and `queueresume command=` parameters are similar to `print command=` in that they define commands for specific printing operations, but they're specified less frequently. The `printer driver=`, `printer driver file=`, and `printer driver location=` parameters are used in automatic printer driver installation, which works only on Windows 9x clients. The `load printers=` parameter, which defaults to yes, enables print queues to be listed in browses. The `lpq cache time=`, `min print space=`, and `postscript=` parameters are seldom changed from their defaults.

Samba printer troubleshooting is simple and straightforward. It's simple to inject print jobs at every major point along the Samba printing cascade, thereby seeing where the chain is broken. Table 8.2 shows those injection points.

TABLE 8.2 Troubleshooting Injection Points

Injection Point	*Command*
Share, Windows side	`copy dos.txt \\servername\printsharename`
Share, UNIX side	`smbclient "//servername/printsharename -Uusername%password -c "put dos.txt"`
Print queue	`lpr -P printqueuename dos.txt`

The `print command=` parameter can be changed to provide a test point to pick off and examine the print job before it's sent to its print queue. This is a typical `print command=` test point:

```
print command = echo "%T: Printer=%p, User=%U, File=%s,
➡ `ls -hs %s`"   >> /tmp/test5.log;rm %s
```

The `testparm` and `ping` commands also play important roles in Samba printer troubleshooting. Another excellent troubleshooting strategy is to reproduce the problem using a test jig `smb.conf` on a nonproduction machine (probably a cheap Linux box) and then troubleshoot by repeatedly modifying `smb.conf`.

Although Samba is usually used to print to UNIX-connected printers from Windows, it can also be used to print to Windows-connected printers from UNIX. This can be done straight through an `smbclient` command, by printing to a special print queue using `smbprint` as a filter, or by printing through a print queue with a printer-specific filter that also serves to send output to the Windows printer. All three use `smbclient` at some level.

Samba printing increases print reliability while decreasing cost, and it's very easy to set up and maintain.

## CHAPTER 9

Working with Windows 98

by Steve Litt

IN THIS CHAPTER

Samba's primary purpose is to serve files to Windows clients. The majority of those Windows clients are Windows 98. This statistic can be expected for at least the next couple of years.

This chapter reveals important opportunities, limitations, and tips for maximizing the utility of Samba on Windows 98 clients.

Client Setup

Windows clients require a certain amount of configuration to participate in file sharing. The client configuration is simple but must be done right. This section discusses the important points of Samba Windows 98 client configuration.

Have Your Installation CD Handy

Many Windows 98 configuration changes ask for the installation CD in order to copy new drivers to the hard disk. Occasionally you can click the Skip File button to skip the files, but this runs the risk of creating an operating system in an inconsistent state. Always be sure to have your Windows OS installation CD handy.

If you've upgraded your OS, be sure to have the upgrade disk or files. If the installation warns that it's trying to copy an older file over a new one and asks whether you want to keep the existing newer one, it's usually safest to keep the existing newer one.

The last step of any change to a Windows 9x network configuration is to reboot. Always proceed with the reboot after you finish Windows configuration changes.

Network Dialog Box

All Windows 98 networking configuration is done through the Network dialog box or one of the dialog boxes it calls. Although this dialog box is titled "Network," you can think of it as a "Network Properties" dialog box. You can access the Network dialog box by clicking Start, Settings, Control Panel and then from the Control Panel double-clicking the Network icon.

Alternatively, you can right-click Network Neighborhood on the desktop or in Windows Explorer, and from the pop-up menu choose Properties. Either way the Network dialog box appears. It has three tabs titled Configuration, Identification, and Access Control.

Access Control Tab

The Access Control tab, shown in Figure 9.1, enables you to choose share- or user-based sharing of the Windows computer's resources.

FIGURE 9.1

The Access Control tab of the Network dialog box.

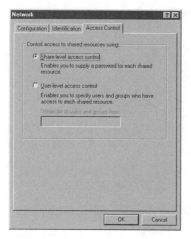

If you choose User-Level Access Control, you must input a resource from which to obtain a list of users and groups. This is done by inputting the workgroup and making sure that workgroup has a WINS server.

> **Note**
>
> WINS stands for *Windows Internet Naming Service*. It's a NetBIOS name resolution service that does not rely on broadcasts. There's a section entitled "WINS Server" later in this chapter, and WINS is covered extensively in Chapter 34, "Windows Internet Naming Service (WINS)."

User-level access control is very tricky and is only practical on a network with a functioning primary domain controller (PDC). Primary domain controllers are thoroughly discussed in Chapter 17, "Using Samba as the NT Primary Domain Controller."

Identification Tab

The Identification Tab is used to configure identifying properties of the computer, specifically the computer's name, the workgroup in which it's a member, and a text "Computer Description" field for human reference. Figure 9.2 shows the Identification tab of the Network dialog box, with its three input fields.

The Computer Name field is where you type the name you give your Windows computer. This must be input even if the Windows computer is a DHCP client (discussed later this chapter). The computer name must be unique on the network.

FIGURE 9.2

The Identification tab of the Network dialog box.

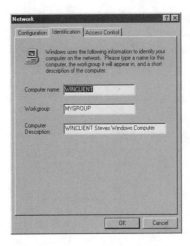

Input the workgroup of the computer into the Workgroup field. Although Windows clients can see servers and clients on other workgroups when everything is properly configured, by far the most reliable setup is to have the Windows client in the same workgroup as the Samba server that serves it. Therefore, if possible, make this name the same as the Samba server's workgroup= global parameter.

Note that the Windows installation program often creates multiword workgroups (based on the user's company name). The workgroup is best left as a single word and in all caps.

Obviously, certain setups require the Windows client to see file servers from other workgroups. Enabling this type of visibility is covered later in this chapter.

The Computer Description field is text for humans only, and it can contain anything.

Configuration Tab

The Configuration tab of the Network dialog box is by far the most involved of the three tabs. It is used to configure the primary logon method, whether and how files and printers are shared, and a list of networking components, each of which can itself be configured. The Configuration tab of the Network dialog box is shown in Figure 9.3.

This dialog box consists of a list of network components with Add, Remove, and Properties buttons to add, delete, and change members of that list. Below the list and buttons is a drop-down list box for the primary network logon. Below that is the File and Print Sharing button.

Primary Network Logon

Typically this drop-down list box gives you two choices: Client for Microsoft Networks and Windows Logon. The former should be used because the latter fails to report network errors and is, therefore, most practical on non-networked computers.

FIGURE 9.3

The Configuration tab of the Network dialog box.

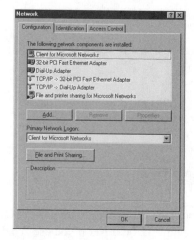

File and Print Sharing Button

Pressing this button brings up a dialog box with two check boxes:

- I want to be able to give others access to my files
- I want to be able to allow others to print to my printer(s)

This is for sharing the Windows client's resources from other computers. It works for Samba and for Windows peer-to-peer networking. Check these options if you want to let others on the Windows client. Otherwise, leave them unchecked for security's sake.

The Following Network Components Are Installed

This is a list of four types of components: clients, adapters, protocols, and services. They communicate to each other like this:

```
Client or Service<==>Protocol<==>Adapter
```

The relationships between specific clients and services and protocols and adapters are defined in the Bindings tabs of the various dialog boxes.

Ethernet Adapter

Adapters interface directly to hardware. For instance, Figure 9.3 shows an adapter called *32-bit PCI Fast Ethernet Adapter*. It embodies the properties of an Intel EE Pro 100+ network card. Highlighting it and clicking the Properties button brings up the Ethernet Properties dialog box, which has three tabs: Driver Type, Bindings, and Advanced.

Driver Type Tab

The Driver Type tab is shown in Figure 9.4.

9

WORKING WITH
WINDOWS 98

FIGURE 9.4

The Driver Type tab of the Ethernet Properties dialog box.

This is a dialog box in which you choose the driver type to use (16-bit ODI, 16-bit NDIS, 32-bit NDIS, and so on). Choose the 32-bit driver if you use Windows 98. The 16-bit drivers are suited for Windows for Workgroups.

Bindings Tab

The Bindings tab of the Ethernet Properties dialog box is where the linking between different networking software components takes place. These linkings are a fundamental part of network configuration. Figure 9.5 shows the Bindings tab of the Ethernet Properties dialog box.

FIGURE 9.5

The Bindings tab of the Ethernet Properties dialog box.

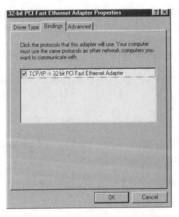

As mentioned earlier, the networking components talk to each other in this configuration:

```
Client or Service<==>Protocol<==>Adapter
```

The Bindings tab enables you to bind the adapter to one or more protocols. It should be bound to the TCP/IP protocol. Unless there's a very specific reason to do otherwise, the NetBEUI and IPX/SPX protocols should *not* be installed. However, if they need to be installed, they should be bound to the adapter.

Advanced Tab

This tab enables you to configure some properties proprietary to the hardware, including network speed (10Mb, 100Mb, auto, and so on). This tab is different for different network cards.

TCP/IP -> Ethernet Protocol

Protocols relate to networking itself. For instance, the list in the Network dialog box shown in Figure 9.3 lists a protocol called *TCP/IP -> 32-bit PCI Fast Ethernet Adapter*. The protocol is TCP/IP. The arrow and reference to the adapter show a binding to the adapter. Highlighting this protocol and clicking the Properties button brings up the Ethernet Properties dialog box, which contains the following seven tabs:

- IP Address
- WINS Configuration
- Gateway
- DNS Configuration
- NetBIOS
- Advanced
- Bindings

IP Address Tab

The IP Address tab of the TCP/IP Properties dialog box is shown in Figure 9.6.

FIGURE 9.6

The IP Address tab of the TCP/IP Properties dialog box.

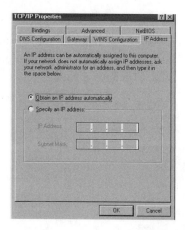

9

WORKING WITH
WINDOWS 98

This tab enables you to either set the client to obtain an IP address automatically (via DHCP, discussed later this chapter) or to specify an IP address. Selecting the latter also involves inputting an IP address and subnet mask in the fields provided.

WINS Configuration Tab

The WINS Configuration tab of the TCP/IP Properties dialog box is shown in Figure 9.7.

FIGURE 9.7

The WINS Configuration tab of the TCP/IP Properties dialog box.

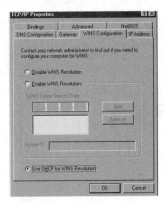

This tab has an interdependency with the IP Address tab. If the IP Address tab is set to obtain an IP address automatically, the Use DHCP for WINS Resolution radio button is enabled. Otherwise, one of the other two is enabled.

WINS resolution enables more efficient NetBIOS name resolution. This is discussed in Chapter 34. If there's a WINS server on the network, by all means set your client for WINS resolution if the IP address is hard-coded on the IP Address tab.

Gateway Tab

The Gateway tab defines a default gateway computer to use for the Windows client. The default gateway should be a machine with an interface on the Windows client's subnet, and interfaces for other subnets. That way the Windows client can communicate with other subnets through the default gateway machine. Figure 9.8 shows the Gateway tab.

Set the gateway to your subnet's "exit point."

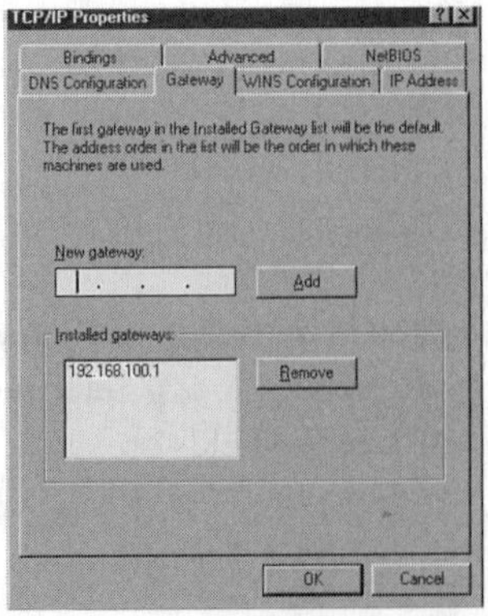

FIGURE 9.8

The Gateway tab of the TCP/IP Properties dialog box.

DNS Configuration Tab

The DNS Configuration tab of the TCP/IP Properties dialog box is shown in Figure 9.9.

FIGURE 9.9

The DNS Configuration tab of the TCP/IP Properties dialog box.

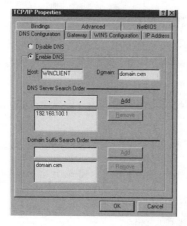

This is the Windows 9*x* equivalent of `/etc/resolv.conf` on a Linux box. Assuming there's a DNS server on the network (and there should be), enable the Enable DNS radio button. The Host field should contain the name of the Windows client and should match the Computer Name field on the Identification tab of the Network dialog box. The Domain field should contain the DNS domain the Windows client belongs to. This domain is probably the domain of the subnet.

> **Note**
>
> It's unfortunate that the word *domain* is used both for the DNS entity associated with a subnet and for the Windows/NetBIOS entity associated with a group of Windows computers sharing a common authentication mechanism. The preceding paragraph refers to a DNS type domain. Most other references in this chapter refer to a Windows domain.

The DNS Server Search Order section lists servers to search for, and the order in which they should be searched. This is very similar to the list of name servers in `/etc/resolv.conf`. IP addresses can be added to the bottom of this list or deleted from anywhere on the list. To add a number to the bottom of the list, type in that number in the DNS Server Search Order input field and then click the Add button. To delete a number, highlight the number and then click the Remove button. There's no cut and paste on this list, so reordering must be done by adding and removing.

The Domain Suffix Search order section lists the various domain suffixes to be appended to the hostname by the DNS server. This list is maintained in the same manner as the DNS Server Search Order list described in the previous paragraph.

NetBIOS Tab and Advanced Tab

These two tabs are typically left as is. The NetBIOS tab typically has its input areas grayed out. If not, be sure to enable NetBIOS over TCP/IP, because NetBIOS over TCP/IP is the basis of Samba.

The Advanced tab contains esoteric protocol configuration data and should typically be left alone.

Bindings Tab

The Bindings tab of the TCP/IP Properties dialog box is shown in Figure 9.10.

FIGURE 9.10

The Bindings tab of the TCP/IP Properties dialog box.

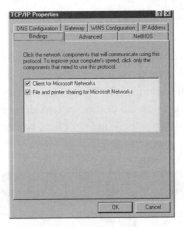

As mentioned earlier, the networking components talk to each other in this configuration:

```
Client or Service<==>Protocol<==>Adapter
```

The TCP/IP protocol must talk to the network adapter on one end, and it must talk to the Client for Microsoft Networks (client) and the File and Printer Sharing for Microsoft Networks (service) on the other. The former is bound on the network adapter's dialog box, whereas the latter two are bound on the Bindings tab of the dialog box for the TCP/IP protocol, as shown in Figure 9.10. Be sure both of these are checked.

Client for Microsoft Networks

The Client for Microsoft Networks Properties dialog box is shown in Figure 9.11.

FIGURE 9.11

The Client for Microsoft Networks Properties dialog box.

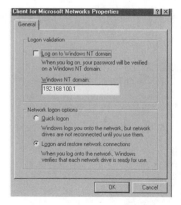

The check box Log on to Windows NT Domain must be checked if a Samba server is used as a login server (this is discussed at length in Chapter 16, "Using Samba as Your Windows 98 Logon Mechanism."

> **Tip**
>
> The Samba server does *not* need to be a PDC in order for you to check this box. The Log on to Windows NT Domain check box must be checked if you want your Windows 98 machine to log in on a Samba server (or an NT server).

If authentication is done on a different machine, the Windows NT Domain input field must contain the IP address of the logon server. Otherwise, it can be blank.

Be sure to enable the radio button Logon and Restore Network Connections. This enables permanently mapped drives and printer ports to remain mapped between reboots.

File and Printer Sharing for Microsoft Networks

The File and Printer Sharing for Microsoft Networks Properties dialog box is shown in Figure 9.12.

On this dialog box you can set certain SMB protocol properties, typically Browse Master and LM Announce. *LM Announce* is the Windows equivalent of the `lm announce=` global `smb.conf` parameter. Leave it at no unless there are OS/2 machines on your network. The Browse Master property defaults to Automatic and should probably be left that way unless there's always a browse master available on another host (the Samba server, for instance). In that case, it's safe to set it to Disabled. On the other hand, on peer networks where you want to have a particular client be the browse master, this

9

WORKING WITH
WINDOWS 98

property should be set to Enabled. In typical situations, you can't go wrong leaving this property at its default setting (Automatic).

FIGURE 9.12

The File and Printer Sharing for Microsoft Networks Properties dialog box.

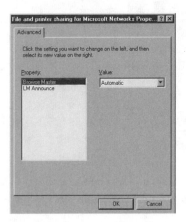

The Difference Between Accessing and Browsing

As an administrator, it's important that you be able to explain to users the difference between browsing and accessing. A share can be accessible and browseable, accessible and nonbrowseable, inaccessible and browseable, or inaccessible and nonbrowseable. In other words, they are completely independent.

Browseability refers to the share showing up on a client's list of shares. Such a list is called a *browse list*. Network Neighborhood is an excellent example of a browse list. The reason users can navigate to a share is because the share is included in the list. Another example of a browse list is the output of either of these Windows commands:

```
C:\WINDOWS>net view \\servername
```

or

```
C:\WINDOWS>net view /workgroup:workgroupname
```

Nor are browse lists limited to Windows SMB clients. The following Linux command produces a browse list:

```
$ smbclient -NL servername
```

A share on a browse list might not be accessible. Attempts to use it could result in an "access denied" error. On the other hand, a share that's accessible can be accessed, whether or not it's browseable. The only effect browseability has on access is that if the share is browseable, it can be navigated to instead of explicitly named. Nonbrowseable shares must be explicitly named. Imagine the following share defined in `smb.conf` on the Samba server:

```
[test]
read only=no
browseable=no
path=/home/username/test
```

In this share, the `browseable=no` parameter guarantees that this share does not show up in Network Neighborhood or in any `net view` command. It must be named explicitly. The most common method is filling in the dialog box brought up by the Tools, Map Network Drive menu command from Windows Explorer. The dialog box has a field for the drive letter, a field for the share (the field is labeled "Path"), and a check box enabling the drive mapping to be persistent (that is, it can survive Windows reboots). If the Samba server were named `mainserv`, the path field would contain `\\mainserv\test`. This method of mapping has the advantage that the mapping can be made persistent.

A nonpersistent drive mapping can be made from the command line, like this:

```
C:\WINDOWS>net use z: \\mainserv\test
```

The share can also be used without mapping to a drive letter:

```
C:\WINDOWS>copy c:\autoexec.bat \\mainserv\test
```

Note that older applications, especially DOS and 16-bit Windows applications, cannot directly use a share and must use a mapped drive letter.

Theoretically, browseability depends completely on the share's `browseable=` parameter (or the default value of that parameter if not explicitly specified in the share). However, many SMB clients have trouble seeing shares that should be browseable. One of the most finicky clients is Windows Explorer, especially the Windows 9*x* version of Windows Explorer. Windows Explorer's browseable shares being invisible is a common occurrence. This creates problems because novice users know only one way to find the share—via Windows Explorer.

The `net view \\servername` and `net view /workgroup:workgroupname` Windows command-line commands are much more likely to show the share. Browseability problems are usually caused by timing and election problems.

A further problem is the inability to resolve the Samba server's NetBIOS name. Fortunately, this problem is eliminated by a global `netbios name=` `smb.conf` parameter. Always hard-code this parameter in `smb.conf` for this reason. Unless you have a good reason to do otherwise, make sure the `netbios name=` parameter's value is the hostname of the Samba server.

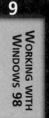

The Timing Problem

Problems seeing a browseable share in Windows Explorer stem from timing problems. Typically, once the share is visible, it is visible forever (or until a major configuration change). Windows clients keep their own copies of browse list data. Once that local list is updated, further visibility of the browseable share is ensured.

These timing problems occur with new workgroups. This problem can be reproduced by changing the `workgroup=` parameter on a working Samba server. To experiment with the timing issue, set `workgroup=test11` and restart Samba. Typically you cannot see the shares in Windows Explorer, although you can map drives to them.

Elections

Browse lists are controlled by browsers. Each subnet has a local browser. If the subnet does not have a browser, Windows Explorer (Network Neighborhood) will not see its shares.

How is one and only one computer selected to be the subnet's browser? The way that rule is enforced is by the system conducting a "browser election." It's an election just like the presidential elections—certain "candidates" get preferential treatment.

Any box that's set to function as a domain master browser (`domain master=yes`) becomes the local master browser of its subnet. If no domain master browser exists on the subnet, every box running for office (`local master=yes`) is evaluated on its OS level (`os level=`). The highest number wins. A value of `os level=65` beats any Windows computer, so if you want the Samba box to win, give it a value of `65`. Just make sure all other Samba boxes on the subnet have lower values (typically `0`).

Therefore, setting `local master=yes` and `os level=65` pretty much wins the election if there are no boxes on the subnet trying to act as domain masters. However, there's one remaining trouble spot: There's no guarantee when the election will take place.

This means that if `smbd` and `nmbd` are restarted, there's an undefined period of time during which there is no election and no subnet browser. Therefore, Network Neighborhood browsing fails to show the shares on the Samba server. This undefined time can easily extend to more than an hour.

Compounding this problem is the fact that it only occurs on clients that haven't accessed the particular workgroup before. This makes the problem appear highly intermittent, thus leading to long and unproductive diagnostic activities.

Fortunately there's a global `smb.conf` parameter that initiates a browser election upon restart. By specifying `preferred server=yes`, an election is called immediately upon restart. Because elections take up to 30 seconds to win, this means a browser is elected within 30 seconds of completion of the daemon restart.

> **Caution**
>
> Be *absolutely* sure only one server per subnet is set to `preferred server=yes`. Servers with this setting not only call an election upon restart but also call them periodically. If there are more than one, they repeatedly call browser elections, each taking 30 seconds to resolve. The result is excessive network traffic, and many 30-second gaps with no browser.

Forcing an Election from the Samba Server

Create the following `smb.conf` (of course, back up the existing `smb.conf`):

```
workgroup=MYGROUP
netbios name=MAINSERV
encrypt passwords=yes

os level=65
local master=yes
preferred master=yes
wins support=yes

[test]
browseable=yes
path=/home/username/test
```

Restart Samba and wait one minute. Now, on a screen that's constantly visible, run the following command from the directory containing `log.nmb`:

```
# tail -n0 -f log.nmb
```

The command appears to hang because `-n0` indicates that the bottom of the log should not be shown. Instead only lines added to the bottom of the log are shown after the command is run. Now, from a different terminal, restart Samba. The following output appears below the `tail -f` command, almost instantly:

```
[1999/11/06 12:33:26, 0] nmbd/asyncdns.c:start_async_dns(150)
  started asyncdns process 7937
[1999/11/06 12:33:26, 0] nmbd/nmbd.c:sig_term(68)
  Got SIGTERM: going down...
[1999/11/06 12:33:26, 0] nmbd/nmbd.c:sig_term(68)
  Got SIGTERM: going down...
[1999/11/06 12:33:27, 1] nmbd/nmbd.c:main(684)
  Netbios nameserver version 2.0.5a started.
  Copyright Andrew Tridgell 1994-1998
[1999/11/06 12:33:27, 0] nmbd/asyncdns.c:start_async_dns(150)
  started asyncdns process 7968
```

The log has recorded the SIGTERM and then the restarting of nmbd. Count slowly to 30. After approximately 30 seconds, the following output appears:

```
[1999/11/06 12:33:50, 0]
➥nmbd/nmbd_become_lmb.c:become_local_master_stage2(406)
    *****

    Samba name server MAINSERV is now a local master browser
➥for workgroup MYGROUP on subnet 192.168.100.1


    *****
```

The preceding output records the results of the browser election. Now comment out the preferred master=yes parameter and restart Samba again. Note that now evidence of the browser election doesn't appear in log.smb in 30 seconds, because there's no election. Depending on other activities of the Samba network, such an election could take an hour or more to be completed.

The preceding experiment clearly shows the role of preferred master=yes as a method of triggering a browser election upon restart (and subsequently from time to time). The local master=yes parameter declares the server as a "candidate" for election to browser. If this parameter were no, the Samba server would be completely ineligible for election to browser. Therefore, this parameter nominates the server. Because this parameter defaults to yes, it isn't strictly necessary, and it serves a documentation role in this example.

To win, this server must beat other servers on the subnet. The competition is based on the os level= parameter, with the highest winning. Ties are broken in various ways. The value of 65 guarantees this server beats all Windows boxes.

The wins support=yes line isn't strictly necessary, but without it, numerous error messages appear in log.nmb, thus causing a potentially confusing interpretation. This parameter makes the box a WINS server.

If the Samba box is the only file server on the subnet, it should have these four global parameters:

```
os level=65
local master=yes
preferred master=yes
wins support=yes
```

Otherwise, whatever server is intended to be the subnet browser should have those parameters (or the Windows equivalents). If there's some reason why it's impractical to insert the preferred master=yes line, it's sometimes still possible to trigger a browser election from Windows clients.

Forcing an Election from a Client

Sometimes the following command triggers a browser election:

```
C:\WINDOWS>net view /workgroup:workgroupname
```

Sometimes an election can be forced by doing a "find computer" on the Samba server's NetBIOS name and navigating down the shares of the found computer. Neither of these practices are as reliable as including the four `smb.conf` parameters discussed in the previous section.

Windows Command-Line Access to Samba Shares

Windows 98 is popular because of its ease of use. One important aspect of that ease of use is the point-and-click functionality offered by such programs as Windows Explorer and Network Neighborhood. All Samba setups should make access easy for unsophisticated users. However, point-and-click is not the only Samba access method available to Windows clients.

The Windows command line has a rich and robust set of Samba access commands in the `net use` and `net view` commands. These commands are vital for automated use of Samba shares and for troubleshooting.

Browsing from the Windows Command Line

There are two command-line commands for browsing the Samba server. Here's an example of the first:

```
C:\WINDOWS>net view \\mainserv
Shared resources at \\MAINSERV

Sharename    Type        Comment
-------------------------------------------
test         Disk
The command was completed successfully.

C:\WINDOWS>
```

The preceding command shows all browseable shares of the Samba server called `mainserv`. This is much more reliable than Network Neighborhood. Here's the second browse observation command:

```
C:\WINDOWS>net view /workgroup:workgroupname
```

This is somewhat more reliable than Network Neighborhood and, depending on a wide variety of network factors, may trigger a browser election, thereby enabling the shares to appear in Network Neighborhood.

Once again, by far the most reliable method of making a subnet-unique Samba server's shares visible is to include these four lines:

```
os level=65
local master=yes
preferred master=yes
wins support=yes
```

Directories

Samba directory shares, whether browseable or not, can be accessed with the `net use` Windows command-line command or by the Map Network Drive tool from Windows Explorer. The writeability of such shares is determined by various `smb.conf` parameters (see Chapter 7, "Determining Samba Access," for details).

Also, 32-bit Windows programs (including the Windows 9x command line) can access shares directly by the `\\servername\sharename` notation, as follows:

```
C:\WINDOWS>copy autoexec.bat \\mainserv\test
```

Older programs can access the share through a mapped drive. Drive mapping occurs either in Windows Explorer, where the mapping can be made persistent, or from the command line, where the mapping is lost upon reboot. The following command maps the `test` share to drive Z:

```
C:\WINDOWS>net use z: \\mainserv\test
```

The following command finds the next available drive letter and maps it to the share. It's shown with its output:

```
C:\WINDOWS>net use * \\mainserv\test
V: connected to \\MAINSERV\TEST.

C:\WINDOWS>
```

To delete the drive mapping, use the following command:

```
C:\WINDOWS>net use v: /delete
```

Occasionally, the preceding command does not disconnect the share. This can be determined by the `net use` command with no arguments. If the share is still shown, it can be disconnected with the following command:

```
C:\WINDOWS>net use \\mainserv\test /delete
```

Printers

All printers are very similar in that they can be used directly:

```
C:\WINDOWS>copy autoexec.bat \\mainserv\myprint
```

The preceding command prints `autoexec.bat` on the Samba printer, although occasionally it asks you to confirm overwriting the previous file. This happens when the Samba printer's spool directory (its `path=` parameter) contains a file by the same name. If that file can't be deleted by the user, an "access denied" error occurs. Otherwise, answering yes prints the file.

> **Note**
>
> Always use `read only=yes` in print shares, whether they're intended to be real printers or server-side automation pseudo printers.

The print share can be mapped to an LPT port, even one that doesn't exist in hardware:

```
C:\WINDOWS>net use lpt9: \\mainserv\test
The command was completed successfully.

C:\WINDOWS>
```

Interestingly enough, by specifying a drive letter instead of an LPT port, you can use the same share as a directory share. However, it cannot be used as both simultaneously.

Other Types of Command-Line Samba Access

The `net diag /status` command prints the NetBIOS names, similar to the UNIX Samba `nmblookup` utility. Here's a sample session of the `net diag /status` command:

```
C:\WINDOWS>net diag /status

Please enter the remote computer's NetBIOS name, or press ENTER to examine
a local adapter's status.


Remote adapter status:

Permanent node name: 0000E84C5D31

Adapter operational for 0 minutes.
64 free NCBs out of 64 with 64 the maximum.
0 sessions in use
254 sessions allocated
```

```
0 packets transmitted 0 packets received.
0 retransmissions 0 retries exhausted.
0 crc errors 0 alignment errors
0 collisions 0 interrupted transmissions.
name 1 WINCLI            status 04
name 2 MYGROUP           status 84
name 3 WINCLI         _  status 04
name 4 WINCLI            status 04
name 5 MYGROUP         - status 84
name 6 USERNAME        _  status 04
The command was completed successfully.

C:\WINDOWS>
```

The net config command prints a brief configuration message. The following is an example:

```
C:\WINDOWS>net config
Computer name                \\WINCLI
User name                    USERNAME
Workgroup                    MYGROUP
Workstation root directory   C:\WINDOWS

Software version             4.10.1998
Redirector version           4.00
The command was completed successfully.

C:\WINDOWS>
```

The netstat utility yields a lot of diagnostic information. You can learn about it via netstat /?. Some of the important uses of netstat are shown here in Listing 9.1.

LISTING 9.1   netstat Command Usage

```
C:\WINDOWS>netstat -n

Active Connections

  Proto  Local Address          Foreign Address        State
  TCP    192.168.100.201:1126   192.168.100.1:139      TIME_WAIT

C:\WINDOWS>

C:\WINDOWS>netstat -r

Route Table

Active Routes:

    Network Address       Netmask  Gateway Address        Interface Metr
          0.0.0.0         0.0.0.0  192.168.100.254  192.168.100.201     1
        127.0.0.0       255.0.0.0        127.0.0.1        127.0.0.1     1
```

```
    192.168.100.0    255.255.255.0   192.168.100.201  192.168.100.201   1
  192.168.100.201  255.255.255.255         127.0.0.1        127.0.0.1   1
  192.168.100.255  255.255.255.255   192.168.100.201  192.168.100.201   1
        224.0.0.0        224.0.0.0   192.168.100.201  192.168.100.201   1
  255.255.255.255  255.255.255.255   192.168.100.201          0.0.0.0   1

Active Connections

  Proto  Local Address        Foreign Address          State

C:\WINDOWS>

C:\WINDOWS>netstat -s

IP Statistics

  Packets Received                      = 1105
  Received Header Errors                = 0
  Received Address Errors               = 753
  Datagrams Forwarded                   = 0
  Unknown Protocols Received            = 0
  Received Packets Discarded            = 0
  Received Packets Delivered            = 355
  Output Requests                       = 393
  Routing Discards                      = 0
  Discarded Output Packets              = 0
  Output Packet No Route                = 0
  Reassembly Required                   = 0
  Reassembly Successful                 = 0
  Reassembly Failures                   = 0
  Datagrams Successfully Fragmented     = 0
  Datagrams Failing Fragmentation       = 0
  Fragments Created                     = 0

ICMP Statistics

                          Received   Sent
  Messages                3          41
  Errors                  0          0
  Destination Unreachable 0          38
  Time Exceeded           0          0
  Parameter Problems      0          0
  Source Quenchs          0          0
  Redirects               0          0
  Echos                   0          0
  Echo Replies            0          0
  Timestamps              0          0
  Timestamp Replies       0          0
  Address Masks           0          0
  Address Mask Replies    0          0
```

9

WORKING WITH
WINDOWS 98

continues

LISTING 9.1   continued

```
TCP Statistics

    Active Opens                 = 8
    Passive Opens                = 0
    Failed Connection Attempts   = 0
    Reset Connections            = 0
    Current Connections          = 0
    Segments Received            = 127
    Segments Sent                = 139
    Segments Retransmitted       = 0

UDP Statistics

    Datagrams Received   = 110
    No Ports             = 118
    Receive Errors       = 0
    Datagrams Sent       = 213

C:\WINDOWS>
```

The `netstat` program is a great diagnostic tool. You can learn more about it with the `netstat /?` command. The `nbtstat` program is even more useful because it deals with NetBIOS. Here's the command for learning the names on the local client:

```
C:\WINDOWS>nbtstat -n


Node IpAddress: [192.168.100.201] Scope Id: []
        NetBIOS Local Name Table

    Name              Type        Status
    ---------------------------------------------
    WINCLI        <00>  UNIQUE     Registered
    MYGROUP       <00>  GROUP      Registered
    WINCLI        <03>  UNIQUE     Registered
    WINCLI        <20>  UNIQUE     Registered
    MYGROUP       <1E>  GROUP      Registered
    USERNAME      <03>  UNIQUE     Registered

C:\WINDOWS>
```

The `nbtstat` program can also be used to find names on a remote host. The following example lists the names on the server:

```
C:\WINDOWS>nbtstat  -n -a mainserv


        NetBIOS Remote Machine Name Table

   Name            Type        Status
   ---------------------------------------------
   MAINSERV    <00>  UNIQUE    Registered
   MAINSERV    <03>  UNIQUE    Registered
   MAINSERV    <20>  UNIQUE    Registered
   ..__MSBROWSE__.<01>  GROUP  Registered
   MYGROUP     <00>  GROUP     Registered
   MYGROUP     <1C>  GROUP     Registered
   MYGROUP     <1D>  UNIQUE    Registered
   MYGROUP     <1E>  GROUP     Registered

MAC Address = 00-00-00-00-00-00
C:\WINDOWS>
```

Some names are kept in cache. These are visible with the nbtstat -c command:

```
C:\WINDOWS>nbtstat -c


Node IpAddress: [192.168.100.201] Scope Id: []
            NetBIOS Remote Cache Name Table

   Name            Type     Host Address    Life [sec]
   --------------------------------------------------
   MAINSERV    <00>  UNIQUE   192.168.100.1      360

C:\WINDOWS>
```

Wondering how well your WINS resolution is working? Try the nbtstat -r command:

```
C:\WINDOWS>nbtstat -r



NetBIOS Names Resolution and Registration Statistics
----------------------------------------------------

Resolved By Broadcast    = 0
Resolved By Name Server  = 6
Registered By Broadcast  = 1
Registered By Name Server = 8
C:\WINDOWS>
```

The route command is a vital troubleshooting tool that enables the observation and manipulation of routes. A detailed description is beyond the scope of this chapter, but you might want to look at the route /? command.

Finding the Elusive Share

Browseability assumes a larger-than-life importance because most casual Windows users perceive nonbrowseability in Windows Explorer as evidence that it doesn't exist. They have no idea about mapping a drive to a share they cannot see or using command-line access to shares. Browseability problems must be resolved quickly.

The first question is whether the share should be seen at all. If it contains `browseable=no`, `browsable=no`, or `browse ok=no` or defaults to `browseable=no` due to a `browseable=no` parameter in `[global]`, it's not intended to be seen.

You can confirm the intended browseability on the Linux host with this command:

```
$ smbclient -NL servername
```

If the preceding command does not show the browseable share, the Samba configuration is doing something unexpected, and this must be investigated. If the share does show up with this command, the Windows environment must be investigated, along with the existence of a subnet browser.

First, see whether the share shows up using either of these commands:

```
C:\WINDOWS>net view \\mainserv
```

or

```
C:\WINDOWS>net view /workgroup:mygroup
```

Next, see whether it shows up in Network Neighborhood using one of the two following commands:

```
C:\WINDOWS>net view \\mainserv
```

or

```
C:\WINDOWS>net view /workgroup:mygroup
```

Now try listing the share's directory:

```
C:\WINDOWS>dir \\mainserv\test
```

If it cannot be accessed at all, that says something entirely different.

WINS Server

WINS stands for *Windows Internet Naming Service*. It's a NetBIOS name resolution service that does not rely on broadcasts. Samba browse servers depend on access to a WINS server to do their work. WINS is covered extensively in Chapter 34.

When set up correctly, WINS makes the network more efficient by reducing broadcasts. However, it can cause problems if used incorrectly. First, there must be only one WINS server per subnet. Second, everything must be set up correctly; otherwise, it's possible WINS can actually increase network traffic.

The BROWSING.txt file describes WINS servers in some detail.

DHCP

DHCP stands for *Dynamic Host Configuration Protocol*. It's a wonderful tool for configuring any host connected to the Samba server, and it reduces the likelihood of client/server Samba incompatibilities. Read DHCP-Server-Configuration.txt in the Samba documentation as well as the dhcpd and dhcp-options man pages. Here are the most important options for Samba compatibility:

- option broadcast-address 192.168.100.255;
- option netbios-name-servers 192.168.100.1;
- option netbios-dd-server 192.168.100.1;
- option netbios-node-type 8;

> **Note**
>
> option netbios-node-type refers to the NetBIOS node type of client. A value of 1 corresponds to a NetBIOS B-node, which resolves names via broadcast only. 2 corresponds to P-node, which uses unicast only. 4 corresponds to M-node, which tries broadcast first and then unicast upon broadcast failure. Finally, 8 configures the client to an H-node, where unicast is tried first and then broadcast upon unicast failure.

This is a fundamental Samba configuration option.

Samba Client Programming

Many Windows programs access their data from a Samba server. Sometimes old DOS programs must access data on Samba servers, thus requiring preexisting drive mappings. Often, requirements state that Windows programs must "kick off" processes on a UNIX server. Fortunately, all this is possible using Samba.

9

WORKING WITH
WINDOWS 98

netuse.pl

The program `netuse.pl`, shown in Listing 9.2, is a trivial example of programming using a Samba share. It first calls subroutine `&mapdrive($driveletter)` to map the drive letter and save that letter; then it calls `&usedrive($driveletter)` to use that mapping. In this case, it simply creates an inelegant directory listing of the share. Then `&deldrivemap($driveletter)` is called to delete the drive mapping. It does not attempt to break the actual share connection, because there may be other programs using that share.

LISTING 9.2 The `netuse.pl` Program Maps and Uses a Drive Letter and Then Deletes It

```
use strict;

my($driveletter) = ' ';

sub mapdrive
  {
  if($_[0] eq ' ')
    {
    my($output) = `net use \* \\\\mainserv\\test`;
    print "\nmapdrive():\n$output\n";
    $output =~ m/(.)\: connected to/;
    my($driveltr) = $1;
    $_[0] = $1;
    }
  }

sub deldrivemap
  {
  my($driveltr) = $_[0];
  my($delcmd) = "net use $driveltr: /delete /yes";
  print "\ndeldrivemap($driveltr)\n" . `$delcmd`;
  }

sub usedrive
  {
  my($dir)= $_[0] . ":\\";
  opendir(SHARE, $dir);
  my(@files) = readdir(SHARE);
  closedir(SHARE);
  print "\nusedrive($dir)\n@files\n";
  }

&mapdrive($driveletter);
&usedrive($driveletter);
&deldrivemap($driveletter);
```

The preceding program has no error-checking or code to escape from odd states. One such state occurs if the share had formerly been a printer and had been changed to a directory share since the last Windows client reboot. Another involves the rare situation where all drive letters have been consumed. And, of course, another odd state would be when the share is inaccessible. A production program would test for all these and more.

This sample program was written in Perl due to Perl's wide use, advanced parsing abilities, and its ability to capture spawned program output with the backtick operators.

Such programming can be done in any language. For instance, in DOS C, Perl's backtick operator can be simulated with a system call, as in this tiny stub DOS C program:

```c
#include<stdio.h>
#include<process.h>
void main(void)
  {
  system("net use * \\\\mainserv\\test > test.tst");
  }
```

The program can then read and parse file `test.tst` to deduce the file letter.

Triggering a Server Process from Windows

Server-side automation is discussed extensively in Chapter 14, "Using Samba Server-Side Automation." One technique discussed is the pseudo printer, which uses a print share to run a UNIX process. For instance, assume there's a UNIX process called `import_phone_charges.pl`, which imports phone charges into the accounting system. Furthermore, assume there's a Windows C program that accumulates phone charges into a file suitable for import on the UNIX side. The following share can be made in `smb.conf`:

```
[lpphone]
print ok=yes
path=/home/username/test
print command=./import_phone_charges.pl %s; rm %s &
```

From the Windows side, once the accumulator program completes and closes the file, it simply copies the file to the share with a statement like the following C example:

```c
system("copy phone.tmp \\\\mainserv\\lpphone");
```

Naturally, there must be code in the Windows program to make sure the system call succeeded and did the right thing.

Networked Start Menu Icon Groups

Often there's a series of icons that are necessary for many users. Often it's impractical to have roaming profiles or other "standardized desktops." Samba offers a great solution— networked Start menu icon groups.

Suppose that several icons are needed for the phone charge system, and there's a desire to have those icons centrally administered by user `username`. You could create the following share:

```
[icongrps]
path=/home/username/icongrps
read only=yes
write list=username
```

Naturally, the `icongrps` directory must have read and execute rights for all users, and all directories above it must be executable to facilitate navigation.

Next, make the phone charge icon group directory while logged into Windows as `username` (because that's who is on the `write list=` parameter). Navigate Windows Explorer into the `icongrps` share and create a directory called `phonchrg`.

Now drag the `phonchrg` directory to the Windows Start button. This places a shortcut to the `phonchrg` directory in the top level Start menu. Any method of placing a shortcut to the directory in the Start menu functions equally well. Observe how clicking this shortcut on the Start menu opens the directory.

Now place the icons. Assume the three Windows-side programs for the phone charge system are `accum.exe`, `validate.exe`, and `input.exe`. Create shortcuts to these three programs in the `phonchrg` directory, which you opened in the preceding paragraph. The easiest method is to highlight the three executables, copy them to the Clipboard, and then right-click in the `phonchrg` directory and select Paste Shortcut. Any changes to the shortcut's name and icon can be made by right-clicking the icon and picking Properties from the pop-up menu.

Because this share is read-only to anyone except `username`, other users cannot accidentally delete the icons. Users pick the phone charge shortcut off the Start menu to bring up the shortcut directory, which remains persistent. The icons in that directory are then clicked to run the programs.

Troubleshooting Windows 98 Samba Clients

The first two steps are to check continuity with ping and to determine whether the problem is common to all Windows 9*x* clients. You must resolve all connectivity issues before troubleshooting Samba.

If the problem is common to all Windows 9*x* Samba clients, the root cause is on the Samba server, and troubleshooting must be done there, with the help of the smbclient program. If the problem is unique to one client, you can exploit the differences between that client and working clients.

If the problem occurs with a group of Windows clients, synthesize the commonalties of the nonworking clients, synthesize the commonalties of the working clients, and exploit the differences between the two groups.

Browseability problems can be maddening. The first step is to make sure the share is intended to be browseable in smb.conf; then confirm browseability on the server with smbclient -NL servername. Once browseability is confirmed on the server, try the net view \\servername and net view /workgroup:workgroupname commands on the Windows side. If those commands show the shares but Windows Explorer doesn't, it's probably a browser election problem that can be fixed as described earlier in this chapter. However, if the share does not show up in one or both of these commands (but does show up in smbclient -NL servername), there's a serious protocol problem, either on the client or the server, that needs solving. This is where comparison with other clients is vital.

For protocol problems, check whether smbclient -NL clientname returns results. If not, that's further evidence of a basic protocol problem. Many such protocol problems occur in attempts to share client resources at the user level. Windows 9*x* is not very good at this, requiring a legitimate PDC on the network. See whether the problem goes away after changing to share-level access control in the Access Control tab of the Network dialog box. Then, troubleshoot accordingly.

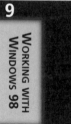

Summary

Samba's most common use is serving files to Windows 98 clients. This requires the Windows client be set up properly. This can be done manually via the Network dialog box and the TCP/IP Properties dialog box, or dynamically via DHCP.

Browsing is often a challenge in Windows 98, especially on Windows Explorer. Browsing and access (mapping drives and so on) are totally independent properties. Browseability is verified by the `browseable=` share parameter and the `smbclient -NL servername` command. On the Windows client, it's verified by the `net view` commands. If something is visible in `net view` but not in Windows Explorer, it could be a browse master problem. The following lines start a browser election upon Samba restart and predispose the Samba server to win the election:

```
os level=65
local master=yes
preferred master=yes
wins support=yes
```

Browser elections take approximately 30 seconds. They can be observed with the following command:

```
$ tail -n0 -f log.nmb
```

The preceding command must be run from the directory containing `log.nmb`—typically `/var/log/samba` or `/usr/local/samba/var`. Sometimes browser elections can be triggered from a Windows 9*x* client with the following command:

```
C:\WINDOWS>net view /workgroup:workgroupname
```

There should be only one preferred server and one WINS server per subnet.

Samba shares are typically browsed from one of the two `net view` commands:

```
C:\WINDOWS>net view \\servername
```

or

```
C:\WINDOWS>net view /workgroup:workgroupname
```

Actual access is done by copying directly to and from the share or by modifying it in place:

```
C:\WINDOWS>notepad \\servername\sharename\filename.ext
```

Some programs, especially older 16-bit programs, cannot access a file that way. In such a case, they can access the file on a mapped drive letter. Such a drive letter can be specified and mapped:

```
C:\WINDOWS>net use z: \\servername\sharename
```

Alternatively, the `net use` command can be used to find the next unused drive letter and map it, as shown in the following example:

```
C:\WINDOWS>net use * \\servername\sharename
```

Printers can be mapped to LPT ports, whether or not those ports exist in hardware. The following is an example of mapping `lpt9:` to a print share:

```
C:\WINDOWS>net use lpt9: \\servername\printsharename
```

Other types of command-line access to Samba include the `net diag /status`, `net config`, and `nbtstat` commands. The `netstat` and `route` commands also provide information helpful to Samba troubleshooting.

DHCP is an excellent method for easing client configuration and reducing Samba errors. DHCP information can be found in the `dhcpd.conf` and `dhcp-options` man pages as well as in `DHCP-Server-Configuration.txt` in the Samba documentation.

A rich variety of client-side programming can be used to access data on Samba shares, and even to trigger a UNIX process (via a server-side automation pseudo printer).

The thrust of Samba Windows client troubleshooting is to verify connectivity and determine whether the problem is limited to a single client, a group of clients, or all clients. In the latter case, the investigation centers on the Samba server, whereas in the former two, the investigation centers on exploiting differences between working and nonworking clients.

CHAPTER 10

Working with Windows NT

by Mike Harris

IN THIS CHAPTER

Working with a network of solely Windows 3.*x* and Windows 9*x* clients is reasonably simple for Samba. As you've seen in Chapter 9, "Working with Windows 98," Samba can fully support file and printer sharing, logon authentication, logon scripts, roaming user profiles, and system policies. At the time of writing, the implementation for the support of Windows 98 clients in Samba is complete and very mature.

Windows NT clients present different issues to Samba because the level of the CIFS (Common Internet File System) protocol that they implement is more complicated than that for Windows 98. At the time of writing, Samba supports around 80 percent of the functionality needed for Windows NT Server or Workstation clients and is well on the way to providing primary and backup domain controller functionality as well.

Currently Samba supports file and printer sharing, domain logons, logon scripts, roaming profiles, and system policies but lacks some of the support for distributed SAM databases and RPCs (remote procedure calls) that real NT systems have. This means that some remote administration activities, such as the use of Server Manager and User Manager to administrate remote Samba machines via RPCs, is not functional. The development project is furious, and day by day more functionality and support is added. It will arrive soon.

This chapter assumes that you have a medium level of experience as an NT administrator and are aware of the following technologies and Windows terminology: primary domain controller (PDC), backup domain controller (BDC), Windows Internet Naming Service (WINS), replication, WINS replication, domain logons, domain member servers, system policies, and user profiles.

You should clearly understand how to set up and maintain a Windows NT domain that includes at least one PDC and a WINS server. They need to be *au fait* with using Windows NT tools such as Windows NT Explorer, User Manager for Domains, Server Manager, and WINS Manager.

Different Windows NT Versions

The evolution of NT has been (and still is) a somewhat rocky road. Originally, NT was a joint venture project between Microsoft and IBM to create a DOS replacement that was known as OS/2. OS/2 was a complete rewrite of an operating system: a 32-bit and architecturally different replacement for the (even then) antiquated and limited DOS, which was running on nearly all PCs worldwide. OS/2 solved many of the problems (for instance, memory restrictions) that had plagued the aged operating system; it also had a built-in GUI known as Presentation Manager. OS/2 1.3 was the original main stable release available from both IBM and Microsoft, packaged under their own names but identical. OS/2 1.3 incorporated an early version of the SMB protocol, known by various names, and introduced the concept of *workgroups*.

All was fine until Microsoft and IBM began to disagree over the choice of GUI being used. OS/2 had been using the Presentation Manager, which was favored by IBM. Microsoft had been toying with GUIs for its DOS product range and had a produced a GUI program to run on top of DOS: Microsoft Windows.

The acrimonious split lead to IBM following the OS/2 product line through versions 2.0, 2.1, 3, Warp 4, and on. Microsoft, meanwhile, coupled OS/2 together with the Windows 3.1 GUI and took the reins on enhancing (and possibly overcomplicating) the SMB protocol and released Windows NT Advanced Server 3.1—the first real NT incarnation.

Apologies go to anyone still running NT 3.1 out there, because it will not be covered within the scope of this chapter—nor unfortunately will OS/2. However, file and printer sharing and browsing will work between Samba and both these platforms.

Windows NT 3.5

NT 3.5 was widely regarded as the first NT that was actually a serious server operating system and notably "Microsoftesque" in comparison to its previous incarnation, Windows NT Advanced Server 3.1. NT 3.5 had a number of shortcomings and instabilities and was quickly followed by NT 3.51. NT 3.5 works in much the same manner as 3.51 and is generally little used due to the availability of the more stable and functional successor.

> **Caution**
>
> Samba does not provide domain support for Windows NT 3.5 or, currently, OS/2.

Windows NT 3.51

NT 3.51 is possibly the most popular NT version. Following the installation of several of Microsoft's service packs (probably to Service Pack 5), 3.51 is a stable and reliable client/server environment. Many organizations still use NT 3.51 because they haven't yet made the move to version 4, generally for reasons of software and retraining costs. With the ever-impending release of Windows 2000, which uses a different network model from the previous NT releases, it would appear that the decision not to move to version 4 has been a wise one.

> **Caution**
>
> On NT 3.51, the default network protocol installed is NetBEUI (NetBIOS Extended User Interface). Because Samba runs on UNIX, which utilizes the TCP/IP protocol, it can only support running the name resolution protocol NetBIOS over TCP/IP. You'll therefore need to make sure that TCP/IP is installed on your NT 3.51 servers as well.

10

WORKING WITH WINDOWS NT

Windows NT 4

Windows NT version 4 was the first version of NT to come packaged with the Windows 95–style interface. There were many improvements over 3.51 for speed and architecture of the operating system, but for the most part the major difference was the interface.

This interface difference radically affected the way in which roaming profiles were handled under NT 4 and introduced the use of system policies and the System Policy Editor. From a network administrator's viewpoint, this is the major difference between running NT 4 clients and NT 3.5x clients on the same network. When a user who was previously logged into an NT 3.5x workstation logs into a NT 4 workstation, the user profile that's downloaded is completely different. User profiles must be set up for both operating systems for every user.

Realizing the Internet age had arrived, Microsoft changed the default network protocol for NT 4 from NetBEUI to TCP/IP with NetBIOS over TCP/IP (or *NBT* for short).

> **Caution**
>
> Windows servers that exist in Novell IPX/SPX networks will need TCP/IP installed in addition to being able to communicate with Samba servers running under UNIX.

Windows NT 4 Service Packs

In possibly many administrators' minds, Windows NT service packs are the bane of installing Windows NT networks. There have been numerous (at the time of writing, Service Pack 6 has recently been released). Each Service Pack aims to bug-fix and enhance certain functionality of the operating system. Some service packs (for example, Service Pack 2) have been known to break rather than fix the operating system and are usually avoided. The service packs of note are 3 and 5.

Service Pack 3 introduced a change that greatly affected the operation of Samba—the introduction of encrypted passwords. Releases of Samba prior to version 2 did not fully support this and the usual process was to make a Registry change on the NT 4 SP 3 machines to support plain-text passwords. This is a major task, and it lowers the security of a network. The solution is to always use Samba 2 configured with support for encrypted passwords.

> **Caution**
>
> A recent issue with the use of Service Pack 6 and Samba has been noted. NT 4
> with Service Pack 6 applied has problems with accessing upper TCP ports. This is
> has been reported in article Q245678 in the Microsoft Knowledge Base and a
> hot-fix Q245687i.EXE is available from Microsoft and also at
> www.windrivers.com. The problem is fixed in NT 4 Service Pack 6a.

Windows NT 4 Option Pack

The Windows NT 4 Option Pack is sometimes confused by people as being Windows NT
4 Service Pack 4; however, this is not actually the case. The Option Pack contains mainly
updates to the Web-serving capabilities of Windows NT. Its installation should not affect
the interoperation of NT and Samba servers.

Examples in This Chapter

This chapter uses the example of a very small local area network of four machines.
There's a Windows Workgroup (MYGROUP) containing an NT 4 workstation (NT4WKS_1),
an NT 4 server (NT4SRV_1), and a Windows 98 workstation (WIN98_2). There's also an
NT domain (MYDOMAIN) controlled by a Windows NT 4 PDC (NT4PDC_1) and containing
one other NT 4 Workstation client (NT4WKS_2).

The forth machine is a Samba server (PERSEUS), which will be configured initially to be a
member of the Workgroup MYGROUP and share files with NT4WKS_1. Later, it will be added
instead to the MYDOMAIN domain and share files with NT4WKS_2. Table 10.1 shows a summary of machine name–to–IP address mappings.

TABLE 10.1   Chapter Network Configuration

Workgroup	IP Address
NT4WKS_1 (NT Workstation)	192.168.100.3
WIN98_2 (Windows 98 client)	192.168.100.10
NT4SRV_1 (NT WINS server)	192.168.100.6
NT4PDC_1 (NT PDC and WINS server)	192.168.100.5
NT4WKS_2 (NT domain member)	192.168.100.4
PERSEUS (Samba server)	192.168.100.2

All NT machines run Windows NT version 4 with Service Pack 5. The Windows 98
machine runs the original release of Windows 98.

10

**WORKING WITH
WINDOWS NT**

A local user account, username, exists on NT4WKS_1, NT4WKS_2, and NT4SRV_1 with "log in locally" capabilities.

A domain user account, username, exists in the MYDOMAIN domain, is a member of the Domain Users group, and (for the purposes of testing) has "log on locally" authorization.

Elections and Timing: A Better Client

Every machine that's part of a CIFS network utilizes a mechanism known as a *browse list*. The browse list holds a list of workgroups, machines, and resources that are available over the network. The browse list is maintained over the NetBIOS (Network Basic Input/Output System) protocol and, for this reason, the names are often referred to as *NetBIOS names*.

NetBIOS is a broadcast protocol that only runs on a local LAN and cannot be routed between different subnetworks. In a WAN, it needs to be layered on top of another network protocol that supports routing.

> **Caution**
>
> Because Samba only supports NetBIOS over TCP/IP and not over NetBEUI, for example, it's a requirement that you run TCP/IP within your Windows network to correctly interoperate with Samba.

Local Master Browsers and Browser Elections

When a client first joins a CIFS network, it sends out a broadcast request to see whether there's a local master browser (LMB) present on the network. If one doesn't exist, it will itself try to become one. The LMB maintains the list of NetBIOS names for the workgroup. Clients query the LMB to obtain or update their own lists of names.

From time to time (or if the current LMB becomes unavailable), clients will broadcast again to become the LMB themselves. If several clients are on the network, they will fight it out to see who becomes the LMB. Different types of clients have advantages over others. For example, a Windows NT Server machine will always win over a Windows 3.*x* or 9*x* client.

This process is known in the CIFS world as *browser election*.

> **Caution**
>
> LMBs suffer from the limitation that they can only work within their local sub-net and therefore are unsuitable for browsing in WAN environments.

Domain Master Browsers and Phantom Workgroups

A special type of master browser, known as a *domain master browser* (DMB) exists in Windows NT domains. Once a DMB is established on the network, LMBs will contact it to update its browse list.

The one major advantage a DMB has is that it can collate the browse list over subnet-works. However, browse list updates between LMBs and the DMB do not take place very regularly. Therefore, in a configuration over several subnets, it can take up to an hour to establish a complete and accurate browse list at the DMB.

The fact that the browse list takes such a long time to update means that the information that a user sees in Network Neighborhood is likely to be untrustworthy. A common prob-lem experienced by users is of *phantom workgroups* and other NetBIOS names such as workstations and printers. These are usually NetBIOS names registered with one LMB on a network segment that have become unavailable since the last update. It may take some time for the LMB responsible for the phantom to update the DMB and, in turn, for the update to filter down to the other LMBs on the network.

This frustrating situation can be avoided by the use of a centrally managed browse list server on the network using WINS.

WINS

Because NetBIOS itself does not support a routing mechanism, problems occur when resolving NetBIOS names over a WAN. It's critical that the name resolution functions correctly, because failure will lead to spurious results when browsing the network. Signs of incorrectly functioning name resolutions are often seen when machine names appear or disappear randomly while you're browsing.

To solve this problem, WINS (Windows Internet Naming Service) is used. WINS centrally manages NetBIOS name–to–IP address resolution even across subnets.

Each client on the network registers its NetBIOS name with the WINS server. The WINS server, therefore, holds a directory of NetBIOS name–to–IP address mappings. When a client wants to contact another client, it contacts the WINS server to obtain its IP address.

Because WINS has this ability to resolve NetBIOS names across network segments, which would otherwise not be possible, it's recommended that there always be at least one WINS server running in any CIFS network. In this manner, WINS servers are similar to DNS servers.

> **Caution**
>
> WINS is supported under Samba in both server and client modes. As a client, all is fine and dandy. As a server, however, Samba cannot provide support for WINS replication and consequently there should only ever be one Samba server configured as a WINS server and none at all if there's an NT Server machine running WINS present in the network. Having more than one Samba WINS server or a mixed Samba/NT WINS network may result in spurious browser results.

Preventing the NT Client from Winning a Browser Election

Internally, each client communicating over NetBIOS holds a number representing the type of NMB machine it is. The higher the value of this number, the more chance the machine has of winning the browser elections. This number is represented by Samba in the [global] section of the smb.conf file by the parameter os level.

With Samba version 2, this value defaults to 0, which means Samba will always lose the browser election against any other machine. This setting is normally what you would desire in a network where NT servers (and notably PDC or BDC machines) are present.

Setting this value to 2 means that Samba will win over Windows or DOS/LAN Manager clients but lose to Windows NT machines. Setting the value to 65 means that Samba will always win the elections and gain control as the browse master.

Making Sure NT Wins the Election

Before you see how to prevent NT from winning browser elections, let's briefly look at preventing Samba from competing in any way. The following entries in the smb.conf file will make Samba never attempt to participate in browser elections (this would be the desired setting on any network with PDCs or NT Server machines running WINS):

```
domain master = no
local master = no
preferred master = no
os level = 0
```

Making Sure Samba Wins the Election

To make sure that Samba wins the browser elections, set the following parameters in your smb.conf file and restart the Samba service:

```
domain master = yes
local master = yes
preferred master = yes
os level = 65
```

The parameter os level = 65 means that Samba will beat all current types of NT servers. You should only make Samba compete and win elections if it's running in a network where there are no other NT servers (for example, a network of Windows NT Workstation and Windows 9x clients with one or more Samba servers). You should never set more than one Samba server to this os level parameter either because it will result in a continuous battle for control and generate a lot of network traffic and possibly spurious browser results.

Probably the most common Windows network that Samba is added to is one where there's a primary domain controller (PDC) and possibly other BDCs and NT servers. In this environment, it's critical that Samba abandon any ideas of having control over a domain or browse lists. There are three essential reasons for this:

- Windows NT Server expects to win browser elections against any other machine except other NT Server machines.

- There can only be one PDC in any domain. Because Samba cannot currently support BDC functionality, promoting Samba to a PDC will have disastrous results.

- Samba cannot perform WINS replication; therefore, Samba should never be configured as a WINS server when NT WINS servers are present.

Forcing a Browser Election from NT

The browstat command (available with the Windows NT 4 Resource Kit) provides statistics and information regarding the status of the browse lists and masters on a Windows NT network. It can also be used to force browser elections.

Election Results

After the various parties have canvassed for who will lead and maintain the network and be the master browser, you need to find out who won that election. This can be useful in diagnosing problems with phantom workgroups and WINS.

Checking Whether WINS Is Working

Use the `nbtstat` utility from the command prompt in Windows NT to view how NetBIOS names on the network have been resolved. Here's an example:

```
C:>nbtstat -r
NetBIOS Names Resolution and Registration Statistics
-------------------------------------------------
Resolved By Broadcast            = 3
Resolved By Name Server          = 10

Registered By Broadcast          = 1
Registered By Name Server        = 8
```

What you're looking for are entries under `Resolved By` and `Registered By Name Server`. This indicates that WINS is acting on the network to resolve NetBIOS name resolution queries and that machines are registering their NetBIOS names with the server. You may also see some `Broadcast` values; these would have been created by the WINS server initially when it first joined the network and advertised its services.

Checking Whether Samba Has Won the Election

Use the Samba utility `nmblookup` to find out who is the domain master browser. Here's an example:

```
[root@perseus /]# nmblookup -M -
querying __MSBROWSE__ on 192.168.100.255
192.168.100.2 __MSBROWSE__<01>
```

The IP address returned (`192.168.100.2`) matches that of the Samba server `PERSEUS`; therefore, you now know that you have control over the network. If the IP address did not match the Samba server, you would be able to ascertain which machine had won and take steps to reduce its chances of doing so—perhaps by increasing the `os level` parameter in the `smb.conf` file to `65`.

Using the Windows NT net Command

The `net` command under Windows NT is a useful command-line tool that can be used to test and diagnose SMB/CIFS networks. With it, you can perform from the command line virtually all the normal operations available in the Windows NT Explorer interface. It's an important command to be familiar with because it's very useful for writing login scripts that automatically map network drives and printers. It has several useful parameters and is reasonably well documented in the standard Windows NT help pages. We'll look at a few of the command forms suitable for testing your SMB/CIFS network with Samba.

Connecting to and Listing Network Resources

The net use form of the net command is used to connect to and disconnect from network resources (such as file and printer shares) as well as to view lists of current connections.

Connecting to a Samba Share

To connect to a Samba or other share over the network and map this connection to a local hard drive, use the following form of net use:

```
C:\>net use p: \\perseus\public
The command completed successfully.
```

Alternatively, to make a persistent connection (one that's reconnected every time the user logs in), use this:

```
C:\>net use p: \\perseus\public /persistent:yes
The command completed successfully.
```

Connecting to the Home Share

You can use the special parameter /home of the net use command to connect to your home share. This is specified by the special [homes] share in the smb.conf file. This command will only work if you have domain logons enabled and the client is a member of a domain that the Samba server is controlling. For more information, see Chapter 17, "Using Samba as the NT Primary Domain Controller."

The form of the command is simply this:

```
C:\>net use u: /home
The command completed successfully.
```

To connect to your home share on a Samba server that's not acting as a domain controller, use the following syntax for net use:

```
net use u: \\perseus\%username%
The command completed successfully.
```

This is a very useful line to include in a network logon script for your NT clients; the %username% variable is a special system variable provided by NT.

Connecting As Another User

You may also attempt to connect to a share as a different user from the one you're currently logged in as by using the following form of the command:

```
C:\>net use p: \\perseus\public * /user:perseus\username
Type the password for \\perseus\public:
The command completed successfully.
```

This command might not work because you may not necessarily be allowed to have a session open from two different logins at the same time. Another problem can occur in which the currently logged-in user credentials will swap to that of those specified in this implicit command, thus rendering previously available shares unusable.

Disconnecting from a Resource

To disconnect from a network resource, use the /delete parameter of the net use command. Here's an example:

```
C:\>net use p: /delete
p: was deleted successfully.
```

Listing Connections

You can also view a list of all network connections that are mapped to local directories. Here's an example:

```
C:\>net use
New connections will be remembered.


Status       Local     Remote                     Network

-------------------------------------------------------------------------
OK           P:        \\Perseus\public           Microsoft Windows Network
OK           U:        \\Perseus\root             Microsoft Windows Network
The command completed successfully.
```

Viewing the Browse List

As discussed previously in this chapter, the Browse List maintains a list of NetBIOS servers that are available to a client in a Windows network. In addition to this, it also provides details of what resources (in the form of file and printer shares) are available to be connected to from the client over the network.

The net view form of the Windows NT net command can help you find out what servers are available, what resources are offered from each server, and which ones are currently in use by the client.

Viewing Server List

You can view the list of NetBIOS names for servers offering servicing over SMB/CIFS by simply typing this:

```
C:\>net view
Server Name              Remark
-----------------------------------------------------------------------
\\NT4WKS_1
\\PERSEUS                Samba 2.0.6
\\WIN98_2                Under VMWARE
The command completed successfully.
```

Viewing Resource Lists

To find out what resources are available from a server on the network and which (if any) are currently in use by the client, use the following form of the net view command:

```
C:\>net view \\PERSEUS
```

Figure 10.1 shows an NT workstation (NT4WKS_1) connected to a Samba server (PERSEUS) with local drives P: and U: mapped and viewed under My Computer. The net view command has been issued under a command prompt.

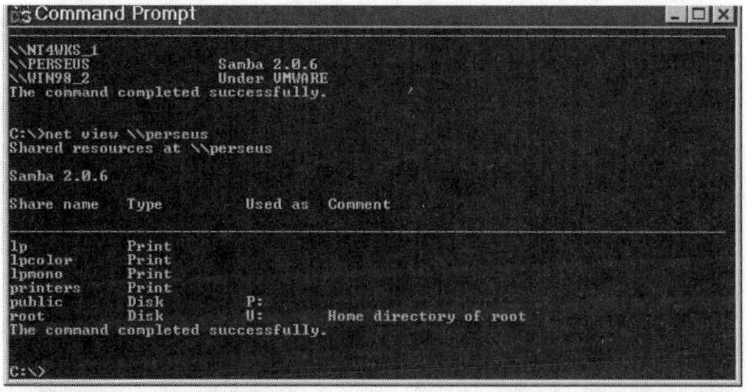

FIGURE 10.1

Use of the net
view *command.*

Synchronizing Clocks

A common requirement in medium-to-large networks is to make sure that all machines show the same time. This is done in order that file creation dates are correct across the entire network. If this is not the case inconsistencies can arise during file comparisons and database updates.

A common problem is often seen with Windows Roaming Profiles where the clocks of two workstations are different. If changes are made to (for example) the Desktop on the first machine whose clock is behind the others, when the user logs into the second workstation and the profile on the network is compared with the local profile, the second workstation may *think* that its local profile is newer and does not realize the changes made to the Desktop on the second machine.

10

WORKING WITH
WINDOWS NT

In Windows networks, an NT machine can act as a *time server*, and clients (such as other NT Servers or any other compatible CIFS client) can synchronize their own clocks with it by use of the net time command.

Setting Your Samba Server to Be a Time Server

To set your Samba server to be a time server for your Windows network, use the time server parameter in the global section of smb.conf:

```
time server = Yes
```

You'll need to restart the Samba daemons for the changes to take effect.

Synchronizing Your Client's Clock with Your Samba Server

To check the clock on your Samba server (or for that matter, any other SMB/CIFS server on the network), you can use the net time command from the command prompt in Windows 9*x* or NT:

```
C:\>net time \\perseus
Current time at \\PERSEUS is 11/19/99 1:23 PM
```

You can also use this command to synchronize the clock of any Windows 9*x* or NT machine with your Samba server. Here's an example:

```
C:\>net time \\perseus /set /yes
Current time at \\PERSEUS is 11/19/99 1:24 PM
The command completed successfully.
```

Tip

You could include this command in a logon script for all Windows clients to make sure that all your machines' clocks are set equally.

Remote Authentication of Samba by NT

Under the workgroups model in Windows networks, user authentication is distributed among all clients, and access to resources is controlled locally. This was the model implemented (and encouraged) in software such as Windows for Workgroups 3.11 and is a cheap, reasonably simple and effective way of sharing resources in a small office network. This model is known as *share-level access control* and requires that a user provide a valid username and password pair to access every shared resource.

The problem is that if there are any more than a few resources shared in a workgroup, the number of usernames and passwords to remember becomes unwieldy and the quality of service soon drops with increased user confusion. For this reason, this model should only ever be used in workgroups of no more than 10 machines, with no more than a couple of file or printer shares each.

In the share-level access control method, security is decentralized in that each workstation has to maintain it's own password list for all resources that it shares. Whereas in a Windows NT domain, all access control is governed by the user accounts database stored on the Primary and Back-up Domain Controllers and which is centralized so that all clients access the same security information. Now, in this model, only one username and one password have to be remembered by each user to access all the resources available to him or her on the network. The administrator also has the power to disable logins and upgrade (or downgrade) the level of access rights. This is one of the primary advantages of using NT domain control over share-level access control.

Samba's normal out-of-the-box behavior is to use the underlying UNIX security system (the password file or NIS) to control access to shared resources over SMB/CIFS. This behavior is fine and very secure, but it means that an administrator has the responsibility of maintaining synchronization of the user accounts on both the Samba server and any NT server. In this mode (with the parameter `security=user` set), Samba will behave much as if it were a standalone NT server, and it's suitable in a peer-to-peer network with NT Workstation and Windows 98 clients. This is the required mode if Samba is to be used as a PDC.

Remote Authentication and User Accounts

With Samba, it's possible to specify the use of an NT server or domain for login authentication that bypasses all local login authentication by UNIX.

The impact of this is that it's no longer necessary to have matching passwords between the NT server and the Samba server to access the home directory and other shares. In addition, the account need not even have a password set or have a valid login shell for UNIX (for example, the login shell is set to `/dev/null` in `/etc/passwd`). As long as the username is listed in `/etc/passwd` on the Samba server and the UNIX home directory exists, the home share can be viewed on any client that's a member of the domain. There's obviously a security issue here, and it's crucial that the NT Server machine can be trusted to authenticate in this manner.

Furthermore, the user account does not even have to exist in the UNIX password file for the user to access resources available to the Everyone group on the NT Server machine. This is useful if the Samba server is to be sharing only publicly available file shares and printers. The user will obviously not have a home share available when he or she accesses the server.

Using an NT Server As a Password Server

To use an NT Server machine as a password server in a network where there's no PDC present, use the following settings in your smb.conf file:

```
workgroup = MYGROUP
security = server
password server = NT4SRV_1
```

In this configuration, NT4SRV_1 is a standalone NT server on a LAN comprised of Windows NT Workstation and Windows 98 clients. When one of the clients accesses a file share on the Samba server, it queries NT4SRV_1 for authentication.

Using an NT PDC As a Password Server

In a Windows NT domain, authentication is provided from a PDC and (if present) any number of BDCs. To use domain controllers as password servers for remote authentication, use the following settings in your smb.conf file:

```
workgroup = MYDOMAIN
security = domain
password server = NT4PDC_1 NT4BDC_1 NT4BDC_2
```

In this configuration, Samba will, in turn, query the PDC and then the BDCs for authentication.

From version 2.0.6 of Samba, the password server parameter has been enhanced to allow automatic discovery of domain controllers for a given domain. This is the normal behavior for a Windows client, and it makes the Samba administrator's life easier. If you are using version 2.0.6 or later, use the following in smb.conf:

```
workgroup = MYDOMAIN
security = domain
password server = *
```

This way, Samba will find the first (or nearest) available PDC or BDC to authenticate the client's request.

Samba As a PDC

Support for Samba to act as a primary domain controller has been available for awhile but is not quite complete nor is supported yet by the Samba team. At the time of writing, there's still a little way to go. Nevertheless, it can be achieved at the administrator's own risk. The basic settings for an smb.conf file to support PDC functionality are identical to those for supporting login functionality on Windows 9x clients:

```
workgroup = SAMBADOMAIN
security = user
domain logons = yes
```

For more information on Samba as a PDC, refer to Chapter 17.

Support for Samba as a backup domain controller is not presently available, and Samba should never be configured if there's a PDC already present in the domain.

Some Network Illustrations

You've received a lot of information so far in this chapter, and much of it can be confusing when it's not actually applied to a real-life situation. In order to clarify what has so far been discussed, the following examples of real-life NT/Samba network configurations should help.

There are three basic network models discussed in this section. The first is a simple peer-to-peer network that contains only client machines (Windows NT Workstation and Windows 98) and one Samba server. This model serves to highlight the interaction between Samba and NT clients as well as introduce how WINS can improve the use of browse lists.

The second network model is again a peer-to-peer network. This time, however, an NT Server machine is included in the network and is configured to run WINS. This model highlights the importance of Samba not competing to be a DMB or a WINS server against an NT server, and it introduces an example of remote authentication of Samba by NT.

The third and final network model uses a Microsoft domain with an NT Server machine acting as both a PDC and WINS server. This third model highlights again how Samba should behave in such a scenario and how it can become a domain member server.

Microsoft usually advises that Windows networks of any more than a handful of work-stations should be built upon the third model described above and incorporate a PDC. However, the first two models are in some way simpler and should help to explain some of the background of the interaction between Samba and NT machines on a Windows network. All three should aid your overall understanding of Windows NT workgroups and domains as a network administrator, so it's suggested that you study them all.

10

WORKING WITH
WINDOWS NT

Windows NT Workstation and Samba Peer-to-Peer Network

This simple network has workstations running Windows NT 4 Workstation (some may actually be running Windows 98 instead) and a Samba server. We'll look at the pitfalls associated with this form of peer-to-peer network and how you can make it more robust. This form of solution would be suitable for a small office network, but it's not really recommended. However, it serves to highlight the issues associated with browser elections and WINS very well.

In reality, it's unlikely that this type of network would be used, and it would be better if there were a least one NT Server machine in the network.

Two workstations—one NT 4 Workstation (NT4WKS_1) and one Windows 98 (WIN98_2)—are configured on the local area network, and both are running only the TCP/IP protocol stack. The Samba server is called PERSEUS, and all machines are members of the Workgroup MYGROUP.

Without WINS Serving

Samba is configured with the following parameters:

```
encrypt passwords = yes
local master = yes
domain master = no
preferred master = no
os level = 0
```

Without any WINS servers configured, you'll find that you're able to browse the network perfectly fine. There's likely to be a delay in building the full browse list as the NT workstations vie to be browse master. Once the dispute has been settled, browsing will work fine, but there is one caveat: One of the machines is now the domain master browser, but which one? To find out, use the Samba nmblookup utility:

```
[root@perseus bin]# nmblookup -M -
querying __MSBROWSE__ on 192.168.100.255
192.168.100.3 __MSBROWSE__<01>
```

This is the IP address of the workstation NT4WKS_1, so you know that it's the browse list master. You can also show that WINS is not resolving names by using the NBTSTAT command from the NT command prompt:

```
C:>nbtstat -r

NetBIOS Names Resolution and Registration Statistics
-------------------------------------------------

Resolved By Broadcast          = 1
Resolved By Name Server        = 0

Registered By Broadcast        = 8
Registered By Name Server      = 0
```

Now the problem is that NT4WKS_1 is simply a normal NT Workstation machine. Therefore, if the user goes to lunch and shuts the computer down, the master browser is lost and another election will have to take place. Before this occurs (usually a period of 300 seconds), if another user chooses to browse the network in Windows Explorer, it will hang as requests are being directed to the now *dead* machine. This can be annoying and frustrating for users and can lead to trouble for the IT support people.

A better method is to use a machine that's permanently running as the domain master—in this case, the Samba server.

With Samba WINS

In order to better the network configuration in a peer-to-peer workgroup environment, you need to run a WINS server. A WINS server will keep the NetBIOS names list. All client machines should point to the WINS server for the browse list lookups.

In order for this to work, you should remember the following points:

- If there are no native Microsoft WINS servers in the network, use a Samba server and make this the domain master as well.

- If there are native Microsoft WINS servers in the network, never make Samba a WINS server or a domain master.

- Never make more than one Samba server a WINS server, because replication is not currently supported.

Samba is configured with the following parameters:

```
encrypt passwords = yes
local master = yes
domain master = yes
preferred master = yes
os level = 65
wins support = yes
```

10

WORKING WITH
WINDOWS NT

All NT Workstation clients are configured with the WINS server pointing at the Samba server. In Control Panel, Network, Protocols, TCP/IP, Properties, WINS, the WINS server points at PERSEUS (IP address 192.168.100.2). Figure 10.2 shows this configuration under NT Workstation 4.

FIGURE 10.2

Configuring NT Workstation to use WINS Server.

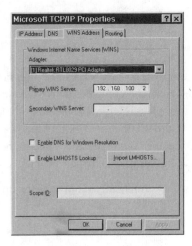

You can check that PERSEUS (IP address 192.168.100.2) is the master browser by using nmblookup:

```
[root@perseus bin]# nmblookup -M -
querying __MSBROWSE__ on 192.168.100.255
192.168.100.2 __MSBROWSE__ <01>
```

Also, you can use the nbtstat command from the NT command prompt to check that WINS is working okay:

```
C:>nbtstat -r
NetBIOS Names Resolution and Registration Statistics
----------------------------------------------------

Resolved By Broadcast          = 0
Resolved By Name Server        = 2

Registered By Broadcast        = 0
Registered By Name Server      = 6
```

Notice how the statistics have moved to Name Server. This is Samba doing its WINS magic!

Now, you no longer have the browser issue as long as the Samba server remains running. If the WINS option is disabled, the Samba server will still win the elections. If the

Samba server is shut down, normal broadcast elections will happen and one of the NT Workstation machines will temporarily take on the role. Once the Samba server comes back online, it will force the election and take over once more.

Windows NT Server and Samba Peer-to-Peer Network

The next step from a small peer-to-peer Windows network is the introduction of a Windows NT Server machine, but without Windows domain control. Although this is not necessarily likely in a real-world scenario, it nevertheless serves to illustrate the interaction between Samba and NT servers. When an NT Server machine is present, you should make this the WINS server as well and abandon all ideas about using Samba for this purpose. You should also make sure Samba loses any browser elections to the NT box. By using this method, you greatly reduce the network traffic created by browser elections and keep your NT box happy. Because Samba cannot participate in WINS replication, you also give yourself the opportunity to add more NT-based WINS servers in the future.

A Simple Workgroup Addition

Based on the same sample network in the last section, this example uses a small workgroup called MYGROUP that has a Windows 98 workstation (WIN98_2) and a Samba server (PERSEUS). Also, an NT 4 Server machine (NT4SRV_1) will be added to the network that holds user account information and runs WINS.

Configuring Samba

The following parameters need to be set in the [global] section of smb.conf:

```
security = server
encrypt passwords = Yes
password server = NT4SRV_1
domain master = No
preferred master = No
local master = No
os level = 0
wins support = No
wins server = NT4SRV_1
domain logins = No
```

This configuration uses the Access Control List (ACL) on NT4SRV_1 (the NT server) from PERSEUS (the Samba server) to authenticate user connections using the password server parameter. For more information regarding this setup, refer back to the section "Remote Authentication of Samba by NT." The critical setting is security=server which indicates to Samba to use the server specified in password server for user account authentication.

10

WORKING WITH
WINDOWS NT

Note that configuring Samba in this way means that the user account need not necessarily exist on the Samba server for a client to connect to its resources. This means that user accounts can be maintained solely by using User Manager for Domains on the NT server. However, because there is no UNIX user account on the Samba server, there will be no home directory and consequently no home share available to clients. This type of configuration is ideal if the Samba server is only sharing public and not user-specific resources.

Testing the NT WINS Server

First, you need to make sure that the NT server is actually the DMB for the workgroup MYGROUP; you can again use the nmblookup command from UNIX:

```
[root@perseus /root]$ nmblookup -M -
querying __MSBROWSE__ on 192.168.100.255
192.168.100.6 __MSBROWSE__<01>
```

The IP address 192.168.100.6 is that of the NT server NT4SRV_1, so you now know that all's well and that it's winning the browser elections.

Running the nbtstat command under the NT command prompt should yield the result that NetBIOS name resolution and registration is being handled by the WINS server and not through broadcasts. Here's an example:

```
C:>nbtstat -r

NetBIOS Names Resolution and Registration Statistics
-------------------------------------------------

Resolved By Broadcast          = 0
Resolved By Name Server        = 1

Registered By Broadcast        = 0
Registered By Name Server      = 8
```

If any names have been resolved or registered via broadcasts, check that they're correctly pointing at the WINS server for resolution.

Windows NT PDC and Samba Domain Member

Probably the most common Windows network that Samba is added to is one where there's a primary domain controller (PDC) and possibly other BDCs and NT servers. In this environment, it's critical that Samba abandon any ideas of having control over a domain or browse lists. There are three essential reasons for this:

- Windows NT Server expects to win browser elections against any other machine, except other NT servers, to become the DMB.

- There can only be one PDC in any domain. Because Samba cannot currently support BDC functionality, promoting Samba to a PDC will have disastrous results.

- Samba cannot perform WINS replication; therefore, Samba should never be configured as a WINS server when NT WINS servers are present.

A Simple Domain

In the sample network, you have a small domain called MYDOMAIN that has a Windows NT 4 Server PDC (NT4PDC_1) and an NT 4 Workstation machine (NT4WKS_2). You're going to move the Samba server out of the MYGROUP workgroup (from the previous example) and add it to the MYDOMAIN domain, thus making it a full-fledged domain member server.

Configuring Samba for Domain Membership

Samba is configured to use the security=domain model. This often causes confusion among new users of Samba in that they think this implies domain control capabilities; in truth, it implies *domain membership*. For more information regarding Samba domain controllers, refer to Chapter 17. The password server parameter points at the NT PDC, which means that authentication is passed through to this machine rather than using the smbpasswd file. If you cannot trust the security of your NT server, this is probably not such a good idea. Under Samba 2.0.6, this parameter may be configured to read password server=*, which performs the default NT functionality of searching for the domain's PDC.

Logging in as root and using your favorite editor to edit your smb.conf file, configure Samba as follows:

```
encrypt passwords = Yes
domain logins = No
security = domain
password server = *
wins support = No
wins server = NT4PDC_1
os level = 0
domain master = No
preferred server = No
local master = No
```

Adding the Samba Server to Your Domain

First, stop the Samba service:

```
% /etc/rc.d/init.d/smb stop
```

On your NT PDC (in this case, NT4PDC_1) using Server Manager for Domains, add the Samba machine name as an NT Server or Workstation machine.

Joining the NT Domain

Log on to your Samba server as root and execute the following command to join the NT domain:

```
% smbpasswd -R wins -j MYDOMAIN -r NT4PDC_1
```

You should get a message returned similar to this:

```
[root@perseus source]# smbpasswd -R wins -j MYDOMAIN -r NT4PDC_1
1999/11/16 16:24:04 : change_trust_account_password:
Changed password for domain MYDOMAIN.
Joined domain MYDOMAIN.
```

> **Tip**
>
> If you have problems with this operation (for example, it hangs up), try adding a single line to your /etc/hosts file before executing the command. Here's an example:
>
> ```
> 192.168.100.5    NT4PDC_1
> ```

In Figure 10.3, you can see Server Manager on NT4PDC_1 showing properties for the shared resources on the Samba server PERSEUS, which has successfully joined the MYDOMAIN domain.

FIGURE 10.3

Using Server Manager to view properties of a Samba member server.

Troubleshooting Windows NT Samba Clients

This section is aimed at helping administrators identify problems with their SMB/CIFS networks, and it covers some of the more useful NT and UNIX command-line tools.

There's also a subsection on the NT Network Monitor utility, which can produce a wealth of information that's normally way in excess of most people's needs. Nevertheless, it's a powerful tool.

Command-Line Utilities for Troubleshooting

In addition to the `net` command under NT, there are a number of other useful commands available to UNIX and NT administrators to help test and troubleshoot issues with SMB/CIFS networks and Samba in particular. These utilities generally allow you to obtain a greater amount of detailed information about the exact nature of how your network is operating than their GUI-based counterparts may.

The Windows NT `nbtstat` Command

With the `nbtstat` command, you can display statistics about NetBIOS-over-TCP/IP connections on the network.

The `-r` parameter allows you to see how NetBIOS names are being resolved and registered, and it can help you find out whether your WINS servers are working correctly:

```
C:\>nbtstat -r
NetBIOS Names Resolution and Registration Statistics
----------------------------------------------------

Resolved By Broadcast     = 0
Resolved By Name Server   = 5

Registered By Broadcast   = 11
Registered By Name Server = 1
```

The `-c` parameter displays the NetBIOS Remote Cache Name table, and the `-R` parameter allows you to clear the table:

```
C:\>nbtstat -c
           NetBIOS Remote Cache Name Table

    Name           Type      Host Address    Life [sec]
 --------------------------------------------------------

PERSEUS       <20>  UNIQUE     192.168.100.2      120

C:\>nbtstat -R
Successful purge and preload of the NBT Remote Cache Name Table.

C:\>nbtstat -c
No names in cache
```

10

WORKING WITH
WINDOWS NT

The -n parameter displays the list of local NetBIOS names registered with a server:

```
C:\>nbtstat -a win98_2 -n

        NetBIOS Remote Machine Name Table

   Name              Type        Status
   ---------------------------------------------
MAC Address = 00-50-56-81-64-02
WIN98_2         <00>  UNIQUE        Registered
MYDOMAIN        <00>  GROUP         Registered
WIN98_2         <03>  UNIQUE        Registered
WIN98_2         <20>  UNIQUE        Registered
MYDOMAIN        <1E>  GROUP         Registered
USERNAME2       <03>  UNIQUE        Registered
```

The -s parameter displays a list of active NetBIOS connections:

```
C:\>nbtstat -s

               NetBIOS Connection Table

Local Name          State    In/Out  Remote Host        Input   Output
----------------------------------------------------------------------
NT4PDC_1     <00>  Connected  Out    PERSEUS      <20>   9KB     11KB
NT4PDC_1           Connected  In     WIN98_2      <00>   5KB     11KB
NT4PDC_1           Connected  In     PERSEUS      <00>   483B    2KB
NT4PDC_1     <03>  Listening
NT4PDC_1     <03>  Listening
ADMINISTRATOR <03> Listening
ADMINISTRATOR <03> Listening
```

In all these examples, the -a parameter can be used to specify a remote machine name to query.

The Samba `nmblookup` Command

The `nmblookup` command can be used to discover exactly what's happening with the NetBIOS network.

It has several useful command forms; one of the most useful informs you of which severs are broadcasting themselves as DMBs on the network. It can be very useful for detecting rogue machines that are causing phantom workgroups to appear on the network. Here's an example:

```
[mike@perseus chapter10]$ nmblookup -M -
querying __MSBROWSE__ on 192.168.100.255
192.168.100.5 __MSBROWSE__<01>
192.168.100.10 __MSBROWSE__<01>
```

If your PDC is at IP address 192.168.100.5, you have a problem because someone else thinks he or she is a DMB, too. This could lead to phantom workgroups appearing in certain segments of the network. 192.168.100.10 turns out to be a Windows 98 machine that took control when it was left running during a reboot of the PDC; you should disable this ability for it to become a DMB in the future.

The nmblookup command can also tell you more information about which names are registered with a host or WINS server—for example, you can explicitly look at the rogue machine to find out what it thinks is going on:

```
[mike@perseus chapter10]$ nmblookup -STR win98_2
querying win98_2 on 192.168.100.5
192.168.100.10 win98_2<00>
Looking up status of 192.168.100.10
received 6 names
        WIN98_2        <00> -           M <ACTIVE>
        MYDOMAIN       <00> - <GROUP> M <ACTIVE>
        WIN98_2        <03> -           M <ACTIVE>
        WIN98_2        <20> -           M <ACTIVE>
        MYDOMAIN       <1e> - <GROUP> M <ACTIVE>
        USERNAME2      <03> -           M <ACTIVE>
num_good_sends=0 num_good_receives=0
```

Lastly, you can do a recursive query on the WINS server to discover what names it has registered:

```
[mike@perseus chapter10]$ nmblookup -STM -
querying __MSBROWSE__ on 192.168.100.255
nt4pdc_1, 192.168.100.5 __MSBROWSE__<01>
Looking up status of 192.168.100.5
received 11 names
        NT4PDC_1       <00> -           M <ACTIVE>
        NT4PDC_1       <20> -           M <ACTIVE>
        MYDOMAIN       <00> - <GROUP> M <ACTIVE>
        MYDOMAIN       <1c> - <GROUP> M <ACTIVE>
        MYDOMAIN       <1b> -           M <ACTIVE>
        MYDOMAIN       <1e> - <GROUP> M <ACTIVE>
        NT4PDC_1       <03> -           M <ACTIVE>
        ADMINISTRATOR  <03> -           M <ACTIVE>
        NT4PDC_1       <06> -           M <ACTIVE>
        MYDOMAIN       <1d> -           M <ACTIVE>
        ..__MSBROWSE__. <01> - <GROUP> M <ACTIVE>
num_good_sends=0 num_good_receives=0
```

Windows NT Network Monitor

The Network Monitor Utility is a useful Windows tool for diagnosing network problems. It presents a graphical interface to every item of traffic occurring on a Windows network and offers the ability to filter to exactly which types of network traffic need to be monitored. It offers the ability to view to the finest detail exactly what's happening during any network transaction and monitors not only SMB and NetBIOS but also TCP/IP, Novell IPX/SPX, and AppleTalk traffic (among others). It's capable of producing an overwhelming quantity of details, which (for most people) is way in excess of what's required. It is, however, useful for detecting network errors and for checking which machines are communicating during a network transaction.

Network Monitor has two parts to it: the Server part, which can only be installed on an NT Server machine, and the Client (or Agent) part, which can be stored on an NT Workstation machine.

Installing Network Monitor

Network Monitor is available on the Windows NT 4 Server CD-ROM and on the Microsoft Systems Management Server CD-ROM. It's treated as a Network Service and can be installed through the Network Control Panel (select Start, Control Panel, Network, Services, Add, Network Monitor Tools and Agent). Figure 10.4 shows this service ready to install.

FIGURE 10.4

Installing the Network Monitor under Windows NT.

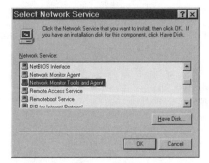

Using Network Monitor

Figure 10.5 shows the Network Monitor running on the server NT4SRV_1, which is monitoring the Samba client PERSEUS and a Windows 98 client, WIN98_2.

In the second window on the left side, the first entry (*BROADCAST) is the initial NetBIOS machine name's broadcast from the NT server. The second line shows communication between NT4SRV_1 and PERSEUS, all of which is generated by passthrough authentication when WIN98_2 accesses a file share on PERSEUS (see the section "Remote Authentication of Samba by NT" for details of this method). The third line shows a basic share-access request between WIN98_2 and NT4SRV_1.

Having acquired sufficient data (a very small amount is normally sufficient), you should run Network Monitor, start the capture, perform the desired network request immediately, and then stop the capture. In this way, you'll have less data to sift through.

FIGURE **10.5**

*Using the
Windows NT
Network Monitor.*

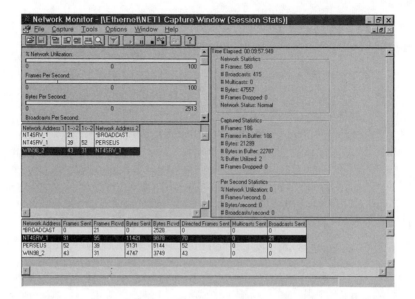

You may then view the data for diagnostic purposes. For example, Figure 10.6 shows the
details of a capture from a remote authentication session initiated by a user (USERNAME2)
in the domain MYGROUP trying to access a share on the Samba server PERSEUS. The Samba
server uses the password server=NT4SRV_1 parameter and does not hold the user
account locally.

FIGURE **10.6**

*Diagnosing pass-
word authentica-
tion with Network
Monitor.*

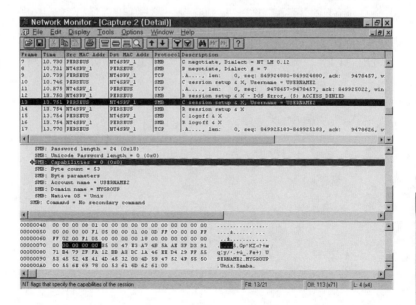

Summary

Samba is a powerful tool that can cope with the stresses and strains of being involved in a Windows NT environment. Samba has the capability to successfully act as a file and printer server to Windows NT Workstation and Server clients and can even provide WINS and domain logon facilities for small networks.

With medium-to-large environments, Samba can live happily as a domain member server and seamlessly provide sharing to clients on the network. Using remote authentication to an NT PDC means that administration overhead is minimized and password synchronization is unnecessary. This is perfect for heterogeneous network environments where users require a mixture of UNIX and Windows applications to be available but also need the ability to share files between the two environments.

A good example is any organization that uses powerful UNIX tools for CAD applications and the usual suite of Office applications for day-to-day work. Running an X Server application (such as WRQ Reflection or SCO Vision) on a Windows NT workstation, a user will be able to access the UNIX tools he or she needs while still having the use of Word and Excel from the same console. The user will be able to access the same file space in both the X environment and the Windows environment, providing him or her with a common workspace where files can be transferred.

In a domain environment, Samba also makes an excellent file and printer server for replacing an NT box. Samba does not require client licenses to be accessed, and it's now widely accepted that an operating system such as Linux is more reliable and a better performer than NT. The overall cost of adding extra NT servers to a network can be greatly reduced by the addition of Linux servers running Samba. It also allows the reapplication of older UNIX servers and improves their overall cost of ownership.

Working with Windows 2000

by Mike Harris

IN THIS CHAPTER

Windows 2000 is the latest generation of the Windows NT operating system. Known for a long time as *Windows NT 5*, Microsoft decided to change the name in 1999. However, Windows 2000 should still be considered to be "NT 5" from a technical viewpoint.

One of the advantages of renaming the product in this way is that Microsoft can move closer to its Holy Grail of finally merging the DOS and NT product lines—something it has been trying to achieve since the mid-1980s, when it first embarked on the OS/2 project with IBM.

Windows 2000 is a very new product (not yet released at the time of writing) and there is much to learn about it. It will take time for there to be sufficiently skilled IT professionals around to fully understand and utilize all the new functionality, detect problems, and stabilize it.

Samba itself is constantly under development, and at the time of writing, concerted efforts are underway to improve its interoperability with Windows 2000. This is a difficult process, and one not helped by the lack of detailed documentation provided by Microsoft about the internal workings of Windows 2000. But it will happen. By the time Windows 2000 is being seriously accepted within IT environments, Samba should be able to support its new functionality.

With the exception of the new network functionality of Windows 2000, the interoperation of Samba and Windows 2000 is largely similar to that of previous versions of NT. Therefore, this chapter will not reiterate ground already covered in the previous chapter, "Working with Windows NT." Refer to that chapter for more information regarding browsing, NetBIOS, and WINS operation. Using these two chapters together will give you a full picture of how Windows 2000 works.

Different Windows 2000 Versions

Microsoft has produced four different versions of Windows 2000 to scale into different areas of a network. The lowly Windows 2000 Professional is designed for the desktop, whereas the mighty Windows 2000 Datacenter Server is designed for multiprocessor servers performing transaction processing. A brief description of each version is discussed here.

Windows 2000 Professional

Windows 2000 Professional is the version designed for desktop users and effectively replaces Windows NT Workstation. It appears to be the intention of Microsoft to tempt Windows 98 users to this version as well and therefore end the dual product line. Professional, like NT Workstation before it, has cut back on support for network serving and cannot act as a domain server.

Windows 2000 Server

Windows 2000 Server is the direct descendant of Windows NT 4 Server and, as such, will perform the same role as its predecessor in the network. Server has the ability to act as a file and print server as well as an authentication server for user and other resource accounts. Server will suit the role of a domain controller in a small-to-medium-sized network.

Windows 2000 Advanced Server

Windows 2000 Advanced Server is not the direct descendant of NT 3.1 Advanced Server but rather is similar in comparison to NT 4 Server Enterprise Edition. Advanced Server is basically identical to Server except that it has support for a larger number of processors. Advanced Server would be suitable for the domain controller in a large network.

Windows 2000 Datacenter Server

Windows 2000 Datacenter Server is Microsoft's attempt at persuading us that it can compete in the larger-scale mini-computer and mainframe environments of the transaction-processing world. Once again, Datacenter Server is essentially the same as Server but can scale to support up to 64 processors. At present, there does not seem to be a sensible reason for using this version of Windows 2000. In my opinion, time and testing are required to prove that Windows 2000 is much more stable than its predecessors for companies to begin deploying Datacenter Server in their mission-critical transaction-processing applications.

What's New in Windows 2000

Windows 2000 has many changes and some improvements, not the least of which is the great change in the way networking is implemented. Microsoft, in what appears to be a change of heart, has decided to embrace some standard network technologies that have previously mainly been used with UNIX. The main additions are discussed in this section.

The most important change to note is that in a pure–Windows 2000 network (that is, a network with no Windows NT servers or clients), all authentication of resources is performed through Microsoft's Active Directory Service (ADS), with the NetBIOS protocol and WINS becoming obsolete. A pure–Windows 2000 server natively running ADS will not support NetBIOS/WINS clients. This includes all previous versions of Windows, Windows NT, OS/2, and more relevant to this book, Samba.

Active Directory Service

Microsoft's Active Directory Service (ADS) is built on the Lightweight Directory Access Protocol (LDAP), which in itself is a *lightweight* implementation of the X.400 Directory Services specification. ADS uses a tree structure to store all information about a network. All resources on the network (including computers, users, file shares, and printers) are given a place (or node) on the tree, depending on their organizational location.

In ADS, one server is chosen to be the domain controller for the entire ADS domain. This server effectively controls resources and authorization to access them for the very top level (or *root*) of the tree. Other ADS servers join the domain by taking over the control of branches below the top level of the tree.

The latest development versions of Samba contain some experimental support for LDAP, and various free implementations of LDAP for UNIX are available on the Internet.

For example, the Open-LDAP Web site at www.openldap.org is the source for a completely free implementation of LDAP for UNIX, and the University of Navarra has produced a FAQ for integrating Samba and LDAP. This can be found at www.unav.es/cti/ldap-smb-howto.html.

Distributed File System

The Distributed File System (DFS) is another attempt by Microsoft to throw off the shackles of its legacy systems. It is intended that DFS replace the existing highly limited and unwieldy system of network share–to–local drive mappings.

DFS provides clients with a single network file structure tree, where file shares can be accessed, without the need to remember which server they are stored on or what network drive has been mapped to it. A DFS manager provides the ability to map network file shares onto nodes of the DFS directory tree and handles client operations invisibly through the use of a redirector.

DFS is essentially the Microsoft equivalent of NFS under UNIX, and anyone familiar with NFS should have no problems understanding and maintaining DFS services under Windows 2000.

The latest development versions of Samba provide experimental support for DFS.

Windows Internet Naming Service (WINS)

As mentioned earlier, Microsoft has done away with the use of WINS and NetBIOS in a pure–Windows 2000 environment. Because all authentication is now controlled through the use of ADS and because ADS runs a form of the LDAP protocol over TCP/IP, it is no longer necessary for Windows 2000 networks to support the CIFS (Common Internet File System) protocol or any of its derivatives.

This means that, at present, a Samba server will not be able to communicate with a Windows 2000 server running in native ADS mode over the network. Initially, this may appear to be a major issue for existing Samba servers, but this is not so. Development for support of Windows 2000 is already underway, and native support under UNIX for LDAP is already available.

> **Tip**
>
> Microsoft seems to have taken LDAP and enhanced it, adding it's own propri-etary code. Therefore, at the time of writing, Microsoft's version of LDAP might be incompatible with existing LDAP servers that are already in use.

Although an issue for Samba, this is actually a greater issue for sites that already have Windows or Windows NT installed. Remember that unless all servers are migrated to Windows 2000 (a large, complex, difficult and costly process), full support for ADS can't be used. This means that Samba will have at least a few years of longevity in the corporate environment and, by which time, UNIX support of Windows 2000 will be complete.

Internet Domains and Windows Domains

One of the most confusing things about CIFS (and in particular Windows NT) is the use of the term *domain* to mean a workgroup that has centralized authorization by a primary domain controller. In the UNIX world, the term *domain* has always been used in the sense of an Internet domain name, and this dual meaning has previously caused confusion for newcomers to Samba and NT alike.

With the advent of Windows 2000 and ADS, Microsoft has effectively dropped the use of the domain/workgroup module in favor of using Internet domains to group computers. In fact, Microsoft's DNS server integrates with and is used to resolve naming for ADS domains and hostnames. Because WINS is used to resolve NetBIOS names to Internet names, this explains why it has now become redundant.

Something that all Samba and NT administrators should be aware of is that Windows 2000 hostnames now appear in the same format as Internet hostnames (`machine.dept.domain.com`) and the domain name is determined by which point in the ADS tree the computer has been joined.

Microsoft Management Console

Microsoft Management Console (MMC) first made its appearance in the early betas of NT 5 and then later in Internet Information Server 4. MMC is an application that orders configuration of all services and resources into a hierarchical tree structure. Each different service has an MMC template that utilizes MMC to administrate the attributes relevant to that service. Its appearance represents only a change for Windows administrators and does not affect Samba's interaction with the operating system.

Kerberos Version 5

Windows 2000 implements version 5 of the Kerberos protocol, as defined in the Internet Engineering Task Force RFC 1510, and can utilize it for secure authentication. Kerberos was named after the three-headed dog that guards the gate to Hades in Greek mythology and was designed to be a very strong security model for distributed authentication over networks.

Kerberos utilizes a *ticket server* that issues users with keys to access resources on a per-user, per-resource, and per-session basis. The user wishing to access a resource makes a request to do so to the ticket server, which provides the user with a key for the resources encrypted with a public key, for which the user (and only that user) has a private key with which to decrypt it. The user needs to be correctly authenticated with permission to access the resource, hold the correct private key, and have the correct public session key to access the resource in question. All communications that take place between ticket server, user, and resources are encrypted.

Microsoft has implemented the ticket server in the form of the Kerberos Key Distribution Center (KDC). Kerberos does not initially directly affect the operation of Samba, and Samba contains experimental support for version 4 (but not, at the time of writing, version 5) of Kerberos.

Kerberos has been around since the mid-1980s in the UNIX world, and many implementations of Kerberos are available for UNIX on the Internet.

Network Illustrations

To better illustrate the differences in Windows 2000 from previous versions of NT with respect to network management and the way in which Samba can and cannot interoperate with it, this section provides three network examples.

The first example shows how a Samba server can be simply configured to interact with a workstation running Windows 2000 Professional. The example uses a simple peer-to-peer workgroup network model and shows that Samba can be placed in a Windows 2000 environment.

The second example looks at how to make a Samba server be a full-fledged member of a Windows 2000 domain and authenticate user accesses using passthrough authentication to a Windows 2000 domain controller.

The third example covers the issues involved in using Samba as a PDC for Windows 2000 Professional clients, whether or not it can be achieved, and how to do it.

For more information, these examples should be cross-referenced with those examples in the previous chapter.

Windows 2000 Setup Requirements

Before Windows 2000 can interact with Samba or any other client or server that uses the NetBIOS protocol, it must be configured to run in compatibility mode.

To do this, you must make sure your Windows 2000 system (server or workstation) has NetBIOS over TCP/IP enabled. To enable this, log into the Windows 2000 system as an administrator and follow these steps:

1. Right-click My Network Places and select Properties. The Network and Dial-Up Connections window will appear.
2. Select the local area connection for the Ethernet network that your Samba server is connected to. Right-click and select Properties. The Local Area Connection Properties dialog box will appear. Note that if you only have one local area connection, select it.
3. Highlight Internet Protocol (TCP/IP) and click Properties. The Internet Protocol (TCP/IP) Properties dialog box will appear.
4. Click the Advanced button in this dialog box. The Advanced TCP/IP Settings dialog box will appear. Select the WINS tab.
5. Make sure that the Enable NetBIOS over TCP/IP radio button is selected and click OK. Close all other dialog boxes.

Figure 11.1 shows the Advanced TCP/IP Settings dialog box with NetBIOS over TCP/IP enabled.

FIGURE 11.1

Enabling NetBIOS over TCP/IP on Windows 2000.

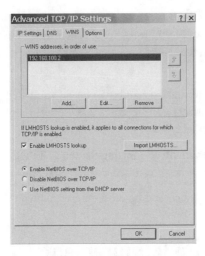

A Windows 2000 and Samba Peer-to-Peer Network Without WINS

This simple example has a network that contains two computers—one running Windows 2000 Professional (W2KWKS-3) and one running Samba (PERSEUS). They are both members of the Windows Workgroup MYGROUP, and domain controllers are now configured.

No WINS server will be running and, consequently, all name resolution and registration requests will be done via the use of NetBIOS broadcasts. To achieve this, Samba is configured with the following values in smb.conf:

```
workgroup = MYGROUP
encrypt passwords = yes
local master = yes
domain master = no
preferred master = no
os level = 0
```

Once the Samba daemon has been restarted to realize these parameters, the services should be easily browseable from the Windows 2000 client. Figure 11.2 shows the Samba server PERSEUS being browsed from the Windows 2000 Explorer.

As with Windows NT, the nbtstat command can be used under Windows 2000 to show how name resolution is being handled. Figure 11.3 shows the result of this command in a network where no WINS server exists.

FIGURE 11.2

Browsing a Samba server using Windows 2000.

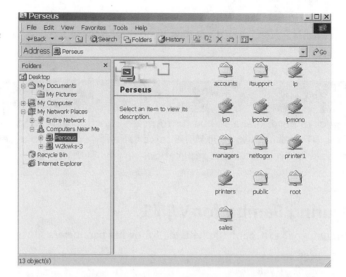

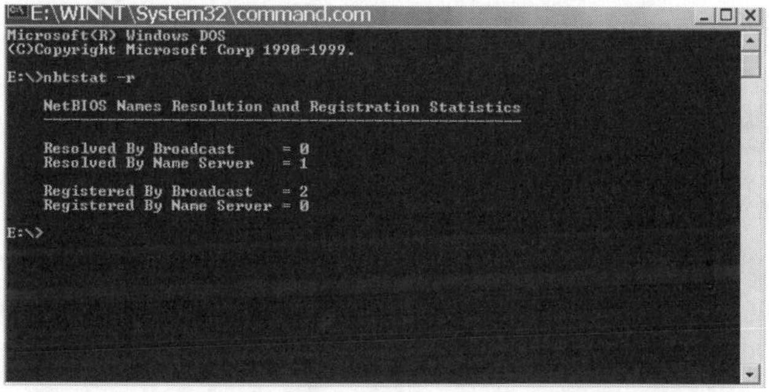

FIGURE 11.3

The nbtstat *command under Windows 2000.*

Notice how the output of the WINS command shows that names have been registered and resolved by means of *broadcasts* rather than by use of the name server (WINS).

A Windows 2000 and Samba Peer-to-Peer Network with WINS

The benefits of using WINS in your network for NetBIOS name resolution have been widely discussed in the previous chapter. In short, with a WINS server in your network, NetBIOS names are registered, managed, and resolved through a central point—a WINS server. This leads to the ability to browse between different subnets, faster resolution of NetBIOS names on the network, and a reduction in the occurrence of "ghost" NetBIOS names appearing in network browsers, such as Network Neighborhood.

Samba can be configured as a WINS server for Windows 2000 clients in exactly the same way as for NT. Here, you'll see how to do this and how to check whether it's working correctly.

> **Caution**
>
> Remember to *never* make Samba perform the function of a WINS server if a Windows NT or Windows 2000 WINS server already exists in your network— Samba does not support WINS replication.

Configuring Samba for WINS

First, configure your `smb.conf` file with the following parameters set:

```
workgroup = MYGROUP
encrypt passwords = yes
local master = yes
domain master = yes
preferred master = yes
wins support = yes
os level = 65
```

Note that as well as enabling WINS support, this also forces Samba to win all browser elections for the network (by use of the `domain master`, `local master`, and `preferred master` parameters), thus ensuring that the Samba server is the domain master browser (DMB). Also, `os level` is set to `65` so that the Samba server is guaranteed to win browser elections over all Windows 2000 clients.

You'll need to restart your Samba service for changes to take effect and the WINS server to come into action.

Configuring Windows 2000 to Use Samba WINS

You'll need to configure your Windows 2000 clients to look to the Samba WINS server for name resolution. This can be achieved by the following method:

1. Right-click My Network Places and select Properties. The Network and Dial-Up Connections window will appear.

2. Select the local area connection for the Ethernet network that your Samba server is connected to. Right-click and select Properties. The Local Area Connection Properties dialog box will appear. Note that if you only have one local area connection, select it.

3. Highlight Internet Protocol (TCP/IP) and click Properties. The Internet Protocol (TCP/IP) Properties dialog box will appear.

4. Click the Advanced button in this dialog box. The Advanced TCP/IP Settings dialog box will appear. Select the WINS tab.

5. Under the WINS Addresses... pane, click the Add... button to display the TCP/IP WINS Server dialog box.

6. Enter the IP address of your Samba WINS server under WINS Server and click the Add button.

Figure 11.4 shows the TCP/IP WINS Server dialog box pointing to the sample server PERSEUS at IP address 192.168.100.2.

FIGURE 11.4

Defining the WINS server under Windows 2000.

Checking That Samba Is Running WINS

Once the Windows 2000 workstation is restarted, the nbtstat command can be used again on the workstation to prove that name resolution is taking place using WINS and not broadcasts. With the Windows 2000 Professional workstation having been rebooted, Figure 11.5 shows the result of running nbtstat.

FIGURE 11.5

Using nbtstat under Windows 2000 with a Samba WINS server.

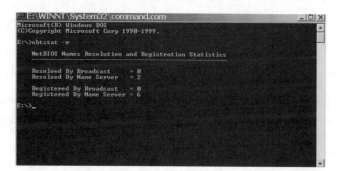

If you compare this output to that shown in Figure 11.3 previously, you can see that name registration and resolution are now performed by the WINS name server as opposed to via broadcasts.

A Windows 2000 Domain Control and Samba Domain Member

This example shows you how to make a Samba server a member of a Windows 2000 domain.

One important note to remember is that neither Samba nor Windows NT support a great deal of the networking enhancements under Windows 2000. Because of this, Windows 2000 needs to run in a backward-compatibility mode, and a large majority of the Windows 2000 administration might not function fully with Samba systems.

This example uses a Windows 2000 domain called `mydomain.com`. This domain also has a backward-compatible NetBIOS domain name, `MYDOMAIN`. A single Windows 2000 server (`W2KPDC-1`) is configured as the domain controller for Active Directory, thus behaving like a primary domain controller for NT and Samba clients. The Samba server `PERSEUS` will be added to this domain.

Configuring a Windows 2000 Server to Support Samba and NT

As discussed in the "What's New in Windows 2000" section of this chapter, a Windows 2000 server running in its native network mode does not support the NetBIOS protocol or WINS and therefore does not support Windows NT or Samba clients.

For this reason, when you install Windows 2000 Active Directory Services, it's important that you do so with backward-compatibility support for Windows NT.

On a newly installed Windows 2000 domain controller, which will need to be the first server for the domain, controlling the top node of the Active Directory tree, you need to run the program `dcpromo` from the Windows 2000 command line. This will start the Active Directory Installation Wizard, which will guide you through the installation.

When you reach the Permissions stage of the wizard, make sure that you select the option Permissions Compatible with Pre–Windows 2000 Servers. Failing to do this will require the deinstallation and reinstallation of Active Directory on the server. Figure 11.6 shows the Permissions stage with this option selected.

> **Caution**
>
> If your Windows 2000 server already has ADS installed without NT backward compatibility, you'll need to first deinstall it and then follow the preceding instructions to reinstall it. To deinstall ADS, run `dcpromo` from the Windows 2000 command line.

FIGURE 11.6

Installing ADS with backward compatibility for NT and Samba.

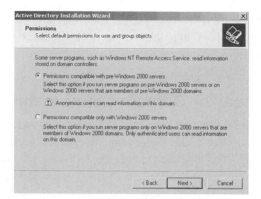

Installing WINS Under Windows 2000

If you're not using an existing Windows NT or Samba WINS server on your network, you'll need to install WINS on your Windows 2000 server to support the correct operation of name resolution.

The following method describes how to do this:

1. Open the Control Panel and then select Add/Remove Programs.
2. Select Add/Remove Windows Components from the menu on the left side.
3. Select Networking Services from the list and click Details.
4. Check the Windows Internet Naming Service (WINS) entry in the list found in the Networking Services dialog box and then click OK.

Figure 11.7 shows the Networking Services dialog box with WINS selected for installation.

FIGURE 11.7

Installing WINS on a Windows 2000 server.

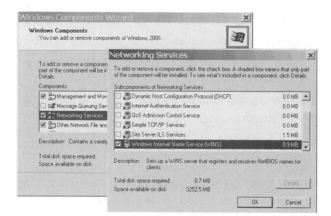

You'll also need to make sure NetBIOS over TCP/IP is enabled and that your Windows 2000 domain controller is configured to point to the correct WINS server (in this example, itself). Refer to the sections "Windows 2000 Setup Requirements" and "Configuring Windows 2000 to Use Samba WINS," earlier in this chapter.

Configuring Samba for Domain Membership

Configuring Samba for membership in a Windows 2000 domain is exactly the same as configuring it for membership in a Windows NT domain, as described in Chapter 10, "Working with Windows NT." You'll need to include the following parameter settings in your smb.conf file:

```
workgroup = MYDOMAIN
security = DOMAIN
password server = *
wins server = W2KPDC-1
wins support = no
local master = no
preferred master = no
domain master = no
domain logons = no
```

As discussed in the "Remote Authentication of Samba by NT" section of the previous chapter, the password server parameter is set to *. This causes Samba to search for the first available domain controller to resolve authentication queries. On versions of Samba before 2.0.6, you'll need to specify a list of domain controllers separated by commas. Here's an example:

```
password server = W2KPDC-1
```

This parameter coupled with security = DOMAIN forces Samba to use passthrough authentication of client requests to the Windows 2000 domain controller W2KPDC-1.

Adding the Samba Client in Windows 2000

The next stage is the adding of the Samba client in the Active Directory database of Windows 2000. This is the Windows 2000 equivalent of adding a computer in Server Manager.

This task is achieved by the use of the Microsoft Management Console for Active Directory Users and Computers. Follow these steps to do this:

1. Start Active Directory Users and Computers from the Administrative Tools program group on the Start menu.

2. Right-click the Computers folder on the left and then select New, Computer from the pop-up menu. The New Object – Computer window will appear.

11

WORKING WITH
WINDOWS 2000

3. Enter the Samba server name (in this instance, PERSEUS) under Computer Name.

4. Check the Allow Pre–Windows 2000 Computers to Use This Account check box and click OK. The computer will be added to the domain.

Figure 11.8 shows the details for adding the Samba server PERSEUS to the MYDOMAIN domain.

FIGURE 11.8

Adding a Samba server to a Windows 2000 domain.

Caution

If you do not allow pre–Windows 2000 computers to use the account, you'll be unable to join either Samba or NT clients to the domain using the computer name. If you make a mistake, you can simply delete the computer and add it again.

Joining the Windows 2000 Domain

Having added your Samba server in Active Directory Users and Computers, you can now join the domain. This is achieved in the same way as joining Windows NT domains—by using the smbpasswd command as follows:

```
% smbpasswd -R WINS -j MYDOMAIN -U Administrator -r W2KPDC-1
2000/01/14 14:13:15 : change_trust_account_password:
Changed password for domain MYDOMAIN.

Joined domain MYDOMAIN.
```

Having joined the domain, you now need to start (or restart) the Samba daemons in order for the server to register itself with WINS. For example, here's what you would do under Red Hat Linux:

```
% /etc/rc.d/init.d/smb start
```

Having started the Samba daemons, you should find that your Samba server has been registered with WINS on your Windows 2000 server. The WINS manager can be found under Administrative Tools on the Windows 2000 Start menu. Right-click Active Registrations in WINS and select Find Name…. Then enter the name of your Samba server. Figure 11.9 shows the WINS entries for the Samba server PERSEUS.

FIGURE 11.9

Viewing WINS registration for Samba under Windows 2000.

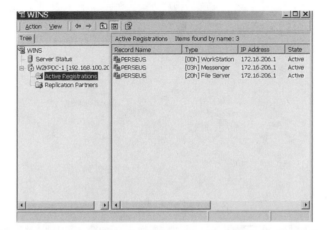

Adding a Samba Server into Windows 2000 DNS

Although not crucial to the interoperation of Samba and Windows 2000, DNS is used heavily under Windows 2000 as the backbone for its Active Directory services. For this reason, it's useful to add your Samba server to the DNS database for Windows 2000. This can be achieved using the following steps:

1. Start DNS from the Administrative Tools program group of the Start menu.

2. Select the Windows 2000 domain (in this example, mydomain.com) and then right-click and select New Host…. The New Host dialog box appears.

3. In New Host dialog box, enter the name and IP address of your Samba server and check the Create Associated Pointer (PTR) Record check box.

4. Click the Add Host button.

Figure 11.10 shows the New Host dialog box completed for the Samba server PERSEUS.

Management of a Samba Client from Windows 2000

You can use a few of the Windows 2000 administration tools to view (but not modify) information about your Samba server. The only tools that I have found to work with a Samba 2.0.6 server are the new Computer Management tool and Server Manager.

FIGURE **11.10**

Adding a server to
Windows 2000
DNS.

The use of the Computer Management tool is limited with Samba 2.0.6 because it cannot support much of the functionality of Windows 2000; however, you are able to view the shares available on the server. Figure 11.11 shows the shares available on the Samba server PERSEUS.

FIGURE **11.11**

Viewing Samba
shares under
Windows 2000.

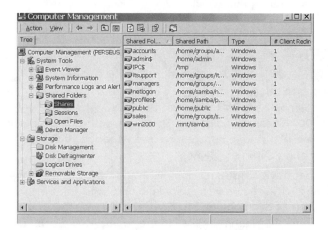

You can also use Server Manager under Windows 2000. It has been provided for backward compatibility with Windows NT domains. To start it, you'll need to run the srvmgr command from the Windows 2000 command line. Figure 11.12 shows the MYDOMAIN domain.

A Samba Domain Controller and Windows 2000 Clients

This next network example illustrates how an administrator might configure his or her network so that the Samba server is acting as a primary domain controller (PDC) to Windows 2000 clients. In reality, there's likely to be a need for a Samba server to support a network of mixed Windows NT and Windows 2000 clients, and possibly Windows 9*x* clients as well. This kind of scenario will arise in any network where Windows 2000 is being evaluated as a possible upgrade to Windows 9*x* and Windows NT.

FIGURE 11.12

Using Server Manager under Windows 2000.

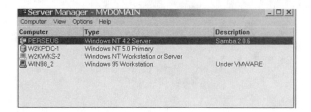

This simple example uses a network that contains two computers—one running Windows 2000 Professional (W2KWKS-3) and one running Samba (PERSEUS). PERSEUS will be configured as the PDC for the domain MYDOMAIN. W2KWKS-3 will then be made a member of the domain, joined from within Windows 2000. PERSEUS will also be acting as a WINS server.

> **Caution**
>
> The examples in this section are based on the use of the latest development versions of Samba 2.1, also known as *Samba TNG* (The Next Generation), and Windows 2000 Release Candidate 3. Therefore, you should be aware of changes that may have occurred in both Samba and Windows 2000 between the time of this writing and their final releases.
>
> Note also that there are several changes in the way that daemons are handled under Samba TNG—the previous two daemons, smbd and nmbd, have been broken down into 12 daemons, which mirror the system services under Windows NT. Refer to the file source/README in the Samba TNG distribution for more information on these changes and how to use the new daemons.

Chapter 10 provides more general information on the setting up and troubleshooting processes. Also, Chapter 17, "Using Samba as the NT Primary Domain Controller," provides a more detailed explanation of Windows NT domains and how Samba can perform the role of PDC.

Windows 2000 Client Setup Requirements

In order for your Windows 2000 client to be able to interact correctly with your Samba domain controller, you'll need to configure the networking properties of the client to support NetBIOS over TCP/IP and to look for your Samba server for WINS resolution.

The methods for configuring both of these options have been discussed previously. Refer to the "Windows 2000 Setup Requirements" and "Configuring Windows 2000 to Use Samba WINS" sections to ensure your Windows 2000 client is configured accordingly before proceeding.

Configuring Samba for Domain Control

Samba needs to be configured to have control over the domain to handle domain logons. Here are the `smb.conf` entries on the Samba server PERSEUS:

```
workgroup = MYDOMAIN
encrypt passwords = Yes
announce version = 4.0
domain logons = Yes
wins support = Yes
preferred master = Yes
local master = Yes
domain master = Yes
os level = 32
```

With the parameters `local master`, `preferred master`, and `domain master` set to yes and `os level` set to 32, Samba is guaranteed that it will win all browser elections to become a domain master browser over all Windows clients except Windows 2000 domain controllers. WINS support has also been enabled, and the `announce version` parameter has been set to `4.2` so that Samba announces itself as a Windows NT primary server to clients.

> **Caution**
>
> Do not succumb to the temptation to make `announce version` equal to `5.0` just because your Samba server is controlling Windows 2000 clients. Samba is still behaving as a Windows NT PDC, and doing so will mean you won't be able to run User Manager for Domains and may experience other problems.

Making Samba the Primary Domain Controller

Under the development version of Samba TNG, Windows NT domain control is now handled more in line with native NT systems. For this reason, you not only have to configure Samba to handle domain logons in `smb.conf` but you also have to create a machine account for your Samba server and join it to its own domain. This functionality is identical to what occurs on a Windows NT PDC.

You first need to create a UNIX user account for the machine account. Here's an example:

```
% useradd -c 'Samba ODC fir MYDOMAIN' -M -s /bin/false -n PERSEUS$
```

Note that the dollar sign ($) is important because this is the method by which machine accounts are differentiated from user accounts under Windows NT. Therefore, you must include it.

Having created an account for the server, you can then use the Samba `smbpasswd` command to add the server to the domain and then join the domain:

```
% smbpasswd -a -m PERSEUS
Password changed for user PERSEUS$

% smbpasswd -j MYDOMAIN
Joining Domain as PDC
Joined domain MYDOMAIN.
```

Adding the Windows 2000 Client to a Samba Domain

Having correctly configured your Samba server for domain control and to become both a domain member and the PDC for the domain, you now need to add a machine account for your Windows 2000 client to join the domain. This time, however, you only need to add the machine account using the UNIX `useradd` command, and a Windows 2000 client is able add its own workstation trust account and produce a random-based password. Here's an example:

```
% useradd -c 'Windows 2000 Workstation' -M -s /bin/false -n W2KWKS-3$
```

Joining the Samba Domain from Windows 2000

To join the Samba domain from the Windows 2000 client, follow these steps:

1. Log in locally to your Windows 2000 client as Administrator.
2. Right-click the My Computer icon and select Properties from the pop-up menu. The System Properties dialog box will appear.
3. Select the Network Identification tab from this dialog box and click the Properties button. The Identification Changes dialog box will appear.
4. In this dialog box, select Domain under Member Of and enter the name of the domain. Figure 11.13 shows the Identification Changes dialog box completed for joining the Windows client to the MYDOMAIN domain.
5. After a short wait, it's likely that a second dialog box will appear to allow you to enter the administrator account name and password for the Samba domain. Figure 11.14 shows the Domain Username and Password dialog box completed for joining the Windows client to the MYDOMAIN domain.

FIGURE 11.13

Joining a Samba domain from Windows 2000.

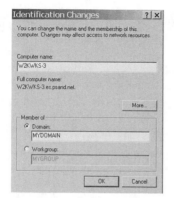

FIGURE 11.14

Entering the Samba domain's administrator name and password.

6. After another short wait, your Windows 2000 client should successfully join the Samba domain and display a welcome message, as shown in Figure 11.15.

FIGURE 11.15

The Windows 2000 welcome message displayed upon the Windows client joining the Samba domain.

Once you've successfully joined the Windows client to the Samba domain, Windows 2000 will ask you to reboot the client workstation in order to put the changes into effect. After rebooting, you'll then be able to log into the domain with a valid Samba account (note that you must make sure this account has a valid, enabled entry in the smbpasswd file).

Accessing Your Samba Domain Controller from Windows 2000

Having joined the Samba domain and logged into your Windows 2000 client, you can use several of the Windows 2000 utilities to monitor your domain membership and Samba server.

> **Caution**
>
> Note that you will fail in any attempts to use the new Windows 2000 adminis-
> tration tools, such as Active Directory Users and Computers, to administer a
> Samba domain. This is due to the fact that Samba does not currently support
> Microsoft's Active Directory Services and consequently the tools are unable to
> interact with the server. Care should be taken not to use these tools on a Samba
> server because they may cause it to fail due to unrecognized network requests.
>
> Similarly, you're likely to experience problems attempting to run other network
> administration tools such as WINS Manager and DNS Manager because Samba
> does not currently support the network requests made by these applications.

You may use the Server Manager application that's included in the Windows 2000
Administration Tools pack on the Windows 2000 Server installation CD for backward
compatibility with older Windows NT servers and domains. Figure 11.16 shows Server
Manager running on a Windows 2000 Professional client viewing the Samba domain
MYDOMAIN.

FIGURE 11.16

*Server Manager
under Windows
2000 for a Samba
domain.*

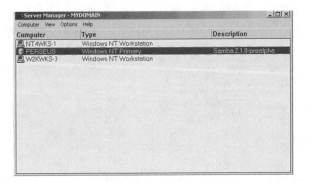

You'll also be able to use User Manager for Domains from your Windows 2000 clients to
list user accounts and view properties for them. At the time of writing, Samba does not
currently support the modification of entries. Figure 11.17 shows User Manager running
the Windows 2000 client W2KWKS-3 for the Samba domain MYDOMAIN.

You're also able to browse a Samba server from within Windows 2000 using Windows
Explorer. Figure 11.18 shows the file shares currently available on the Samba server
PERSEUS to the user Administrator, who is logged into the domain MYDOMAIN from the
Windows 2000 client W2KWKS-3.

FIGURE 11.17

Using User Manager under Windows 2000 to view a Samba domain.

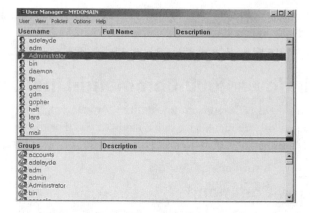

FIGURE 11.18

Browsing a Samba domain controller from Windows 2000.

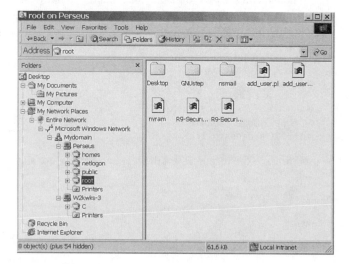

Troubleshooting Windows 2000 and Samba

This section aims to provide you with information to help you troubleshoot and diagnose problems with Windows 2000 and Samba.

First, a number of the command-line utilities are covered that are available under Windows 2000 to provide information about the status of the network and to manipulate connections to network resources.

Second, there's a short section of answers to common problems that you might encounter when working with Windows 2000 and Samba.

Because the network interoperability of Samba and Windows 2000 running in compatibility mode is virtually identical to that of Samba and Windows NT, you should refer to the previous chapter for more information and tips on troubleshooting.

Using Windows 2000 Command-Line Utilities

Virtually all the Windows NT command-line utilities for gathering information and manipulating the network are identical under Windows 2000. For this reason, this section covers command-line examples only. Refer to Chapter 10 for a more detailed explanation.

The net view Command

The net view command can be used to display information about the NetBIOS servers and services available on the network. For example, in its most basic form, this command produces a list of all servers available:

```
C:\>net view
Server Name            Remark
-------------------------------------------
\\PERSEUS              Samba 2.0.6
\\W2KPDC-1
\\WIN98_2              Under VMWARE
The command completed successfully.
```

It can also be used to view the resources available on a server. Here's an example:

```
C:\>net view \\perseus
Shared resources at \\perseus

Samba 2.0.6 Server

Share name    Type        Used as  Comment

--------------------------------------------------------
accounts      Disk                 Accounts Department
Administrator
              Disk                 Samba 2.0.6 Server
itsupport     Disk                 Samba 2.0.6 Server
lp            Print
lp0           Print
lpcolor       Print
lpmono        Print
managers      Disk                 The bosses
netlogon      Disk                 Samba 2.0.6 Server
printer1      Print                Samba 2.0.6 Server
printers      Print                Samba 2.0.6 Server
public        Disk                 Samba 2.0.6 Server
```

```
sales       Disk                Samba 2.0.6 Server
win2000     Disk                Samba 2.0.6 Server
The command completed successfully.
```

The net use Command

As with Windows NT, you can use the `net use` command to connect to and disconnect from network resources. Here are examples:

```
C:\>net use p: \\perseus\public /persistent:yes /yes
The command completed successfully.

C:\>net use p: /delete
p: was deleted successfully.
```

You can also view which network connections are in use. Here's an example:

```
C:\>net use
New connections will be remembered.


Status      Local    Remote              Network

-------------------------------------------------------------------------------
OK          P:       \\perseus\public    Microsoft Windows Network
OK                   \\perseus\IPC$      Microsoft Windows Network
The command completed successfully.
```

The nbtstat Command

The `nbtstat` command gives you the ability to determine how NetBIOS name resolution is taking place and helps you diagnose whether WINS is working correctly. For example, the following command shows that name resolution is being used and consequently WINS is working:

```
C:\>nbtstat -r

    NetBIOS Names Resolution and Registration Statistics
    ----------------------------------------------------

    Resolved By Broadcast     = 1
    Resolved By Name Server   = 4

    Registered By Broadcast   = 9
    Registered By Name Server = 1

    NetBIOS Names Resolved By Broadcast
---------------------------------------------
        MYDOMAIN        <1E>
```

The same command can also be use to determine information about the NetBIOS names on your Samba server and the status of the name registration. Here's an example:

```
C:\>nbtstat -n -a PERSEUS

Local Area Connection:

Node IpAddress: [192.168.100.200] Scope Id: []

        NetBIOS Remote Machine Name Table

    Name            Type        Status
    -------------------------------------------
    PERSEUS     <00>  UNIQUE    Registered
    PERSEUS     <03>  UNIQUE    Registered
    PERSEUS     <20>  UNIQUE    Registered
    MYDOMAIN    <00>  GROUP     Registered
    MYDOMAIN    <1E>  GROUP     Registered

    MAC Address = 00-00-00-00-00-00
```

The netstat Command

Finally, the netstat command can be used to diagnose the types of network connections being made between a Windows 2000 server and other clients and servers on the network. For example, the following output for the W2KPDC-1 Windows 2000 domain controller shows an established NetBIOS-SSN connection to the Samba server PERSEUS. This is the NetBIOS Session service, and it shows that a connection exists to the Samba smbd daemon:

```
C:\>netstat

Active Connections

  Proto  Local Address         Foreign Address           State
  TCP    W2KPDC-1:ldap         W2KPDC-1.mydomain.com:1068  ESTABLISHED
  TCP    W2KPDC-1:ldap         W2KPDC-1.mydomain.com:1069  ESTABLISHED
  TCP    W2KPDC-1:ldap         W2KPDC-1.mydomain.com:1071  ESTABLISHED
  TCP    W2KPDC-1:ldap         W2KPDC-1.mydomain.com:1088  ESTABLISHED
  TCP    W2KPDC-1:1063         W2KPDC-1.mydomain.com:ldap  CLOSE_WAIT
  TCP    W2KPDC-1:1068         W2KPDC-1.mydomain.com:ldap  ESTABLISHED
  TCP    W2KPDC-1:1069         W2KPDC-1.mydomain.com:ldap  ESTABLISHED
  TCP    W2KPDC-1:1071         W2KPDC-1.mydomain.com:ldap  ESTABLISHED
  TCP    W2KPDC-1:1088         W2KPDC-1.mydomain.com:ldap  ESTABLISHED
  TCP    W2KPDC-1:ldap         W2KPDC-1.mydomain.com:1098  ESTABLISHED
  TCP    W2KPDC-1:ldap         W2KPDC-1.mydomain.com:1670  ESTABLISHED
  TCP    W2KPDC-1:ldap         W2KPDC-1.mydomain.com:1672  ESTABLISHED
  TCP    W2KPDC-1:ldap         W2KPDC-1.mydomain.com:1778  TIME_WAIT
  TCP    W2KPDC-1:ldap         W2KPDC-1.mydomain.com:1779  TIME_WAIT
```

```
TCP    W2KPDC-1:1026        W2KPDC-1.mydomain.com:1100   ESTABLISHED
TCP    W2KPDC-1:1026        W2KPDC-1.mydomain.com:1270   ESTABLISHED
TCP    W2KPDC-1:1098        W2KPDC-1.mydomain.com:ldap   ESTABLISHED
TCP    W2KPDC-1:1100        W2KPDC-1.mydomain.com:1026   ESTABLISHED
TCP    W2KPDC-1:1270        W2KPDC-1.mydomain.com:1026   ESTABLISHED
TCP    W2KPDC-1:1424        W2KPDC-1.mydomain.com:ldap   CLOSE_WAIT
TCP    W2KPDC-1:1670        W2KPDC-1.mydomain.com:ldap   ESTABLISHED
TCP    W2KPDC-1:1672        W2KPDC-1.mydomain.com:ldap   ESTABLISHED
TCP    W2KPDC-1:1777        perseus.mydomain.com:netbios-ssn   ESTABLISHED
TCP    W2KPDC-1:1780        W2KPDC-1.mydomain.com:microsoft-ds   TIME_WAIT
TCP    W2KPDC-1:1781        W2KPDC-1.mydomain.com:epmap   TIME_WAIT
TCP    W2KPDC-1:1782        W2KPDC-1.mydomain.com:1092   TIME_WAIT
```

Some Common Problems

A few of the more common problems that might arise when you're working with Windows 2000 are covered here. Remember that if you're experiencing problems while using a large and complex Samba configuration file, you would greatly benefit from creating a temporary minimal configuration, making sure it works, and then building up from there.

Also, remember that if you're using the latest Samba TNG development sources, you're likely to experience certain problems because the code is in a constant state of flux. You're well advised to subscribe the Samba-NTDOM mailing list at lists.samba.org and to ensure that you regularly update the source from the CVS archive. For more information regarding this, refer to "Accessing the CVS for the Latest Development Version" in Chapter 5, "Installing Samba."

I Want to Run User Manager and Server Manager but Can't Find Them

These two utilities are provided for compatibility with previous NT versions and are not on the Start menu, although they are installed with Windows 2000 Server (but not Professional).

Server Manager can be started from the Windows 2000 command line as srvmgr. Similarly, usrmgr will start User Manager.

User Manager Doesn't Work for Windows 2000 Domains

That is correct. You should use the Active Directory administration tools, such as Active Directory Users and Computers, to administrate Windows 2000 domains.

Running User Manager Informs Me That I Can't Manage the Windows 2000 Domain on My Samba Server

Check the value of the parameter `announce version` set in your `smb.conf` file. If this has been set to `5.0`, User Manager will believe the machine is running Windows 2000 and will give this error.

Unset `announce version` and leave it at its default value.

I Cannot Join the Windows 2000 Domain

When you add a computer to a Windows 2000 domain that's running Windows NT or Samba, make sure you check the box Allow Pre–Windows 2000 Computers to Use This Account. If you forgot to do this, you need to delete the computer account and add it again.

Summary

With Windows 2000, Microsoft has made a radical change in its network architecture by moving closer toward a model with more in common with UNIX than previous versions of Windows 9*x* and Windows NT. The introduction of ADS, DFS, and native DNS architecture has basically made CIFS redundant. However, this is only the case in a Windows 2000–only environment (and it will be awhile before this is the case).

It may be tempting to think that the use of ADS, which is based on LDAP, and its close coupling with DNS would improve the ability for Windows 2000 and UNIX to interoperate. However, at present, this seems not to be the case because Microsoft's implementations are not necessarily compatible with the standard UNIX ones. It's almost certain that over the next few years there will be a lot of effort toward making the two interact, and not necessarily using Samba.

The good news is that Microsoft has provided backward-compatibility support for its Windows NT platform and, consequently, Samba as well. Samba can operate well in a Windows 2000 domain, acting as an NT file server, and it can serve as a PDC to Windows 2000 clients, although interaction with the Windows 2000 domain model is currently some ways off.

For these reasons, Samba will be able to play a useful role in any Windows 2000–oriented network for some time to come.

CHAPTER 12

Samba Client Utilities

by Steve Litt

When you have a troubleshooting need, a need to back up Windows clients, or a need to initiate a file transfer to or from a Windows client, the Samba client utilities can often provide your solution. The most used utilities are `smbclient`, `smbmount`, `smbstatus`, `smbtar`, `smbprint`, and `nmblookup`, as briefly described in Table 12.1.

TABLE 12.1   Common Samba Client Utilities

Utility	Use
smbclient	Used to Upload and download information to/from an SMB server, as well as many troubleshooting tasks
smbmount	Used to mount SMB shares in a Linux filesystem
smbstatus	Used to view open connections and files on a Samba server
smbtar	Used to back up SMB shares, typically on Windows computers
smbprint	Used to access remote printers via UNIX and Linux print filters
nmblookup	Used to diagnose name resolution `nmbd` problems

All these utilities are discussed in this chapter.

Using `smbclient`

The `smbclient` utility is the Samba suite's SMB client program. It's an incredibly versatile and useful tool. `smbclient` is an essential troubleshooting tool as well as the most basic and reliable client for accessing SMB shares on Samba boxes, Windows 9*x* boxes, and Windows NT boxes. `smbclient` is the tool of choice for printing to printers attached and configured to Windows boxes.

`smbclient` implements an ftp-like interface for transmitting and receiving files, and it does other file and directory operations. Via the -T and -c command-line arguments, `smbclient` can perform the ftp-like operations without entering an ftp-like session.

Using `smbclient` as a Diagnostic Tool

The `smbclient` utility is the most important tool for testing browseability on UNIX platforms. It can also test accessibility by accessing a share. Because it's used on the server box itself, it's the most reliable view of the state of the Samba server. This eliminates most occurrences of the nightmare that occurs when a test yields erroneous results. A great troubleshooting strategy involves getting Samba to work perfectly with `smbclient` and other Samba client utilities such as `nmblookup` (discussed later in the "Using `nmblookup` for Diagnostic Testing" section of this chapter). After that, get it to work with Windows command line utilities, and finally with Windows Explorer.

Testing Browseability with `smbclient -L`

The most basic diagnostic use of `smbclient` is to reveal a browse list. When used this way, it requires neither a username nor a password (except on NT). The basic command takes this form:

```
$ smbclient -NL servername
```

`servername` can be either a Samba server or a Windows client. Both yield valuable information. The `-N` option tells `smbclient` not to ask for a password. If the `-N` option is given when a password is necessary, the command simply fails. The `-L` option tells `smbclient` to list all browseable shares (think of *L* as standing for *list*). The following is an example listing shares of a Samba server:

```
$ smbclient -NL mainserv
added interface ip=192.168.100.1 bcast=192.168.100.255 nmask=255.255.255.0
added interface ip=192.168.200.101 bcast=192.168.200.255 nmask=255.255.255.0
Domain=[MYGROUP] OS=[Unix] Server=[Samba 2.0.6]

        Sharename      Type       Comment
        ---------      ----       -------
        temp           Disk
        IPC$           IPC        IPC Service (Samba 2.0.6)
        lp             Printer
        lp_text        Printer

        Server                    Comment
        ---------                 -------
        MAINSERV                  Samba 2.0.6

        Workgroup                 Master
        ---------                 -------
        MYGROUP
$
```

The preceding command reveals the explicitly declared [temp] share, the printers lp and lp_text, the server name and workgroup name, and the IPC share IPC$. [homes] is not revealed because it has a browseable=no parameter.

The following command queries a Windows 98 client:

```
$ smbclient -NL wincli
added interface ip=192.168.100.1 bcast=192.168.100.255 nmask=255.255.255.0
added interface ip=192.168.200.101 bcast=192.168.200.255 nmask=255.255.255.0

        Sharename      Type       Comment
        ---------      ----       -------
        MY MUSIC       Disk
        MENUDATA       Disk
        PRINTER$       Disk
```

```
LOCALIII        Printer
IPC$            IPC         Remote Inter Process Communication

Server                  Comment
----------              -------
DESK1
MAINSERV                Samba 2.0.6
WINCLI                  WINCLI Steves Windows Computer

Workgroup               Master
----------              -------
MYGROUP                 MAINSERV
$
```

The preceding session reveals two shared directories, MENUDATA and MY MUSIC, as well as the local shared printer LOCALIII and the special shares IPC$ and PRINTER$.

NT is different. To view an NT server's shares, your command must include a username and password:

```
$ smbclient -L desk1 -U username%userpassword
added interface ip=192.168.100.1 bcast=192.168.100.255 nmask=255.255.255.0
added interface ip=192.168.200.101 bcast=192.168.200.255 nmask=255.255.255.0
Domain=[MYGROUP] OS=[Windows NT 4.0] Server=[NT LAN Manager 4.0]

        Sharename       Type        Comment
        ----------      ----        -------
        ADMIN$          Disk        Remote Admin
        IPC$            IPC         Remote IPC
        C$              Disk        Default share
        NTdata          Disk        NT Data Directory

        Server                  Comment
        ----------              -------

        Workgroup               Master
        ----------              -------
$
```

The preceding reveals the NTdata share as well as special shares ADMIN$, IPC$, and C$.

The purpose of the -L option is to show all browseable shares. Therefore, this smbclient option performs the valuable function of testing browseability. It's the most accurate test of browseability.

Testing Accessibility with smbclient //servername/sharename

Browseability and accessibility are independent of each other. A share can be browseable and accessible, browseable and inaccessible, unbrowseable and accessible, or unbrowseable and inaccessible.

Accessibility of a share on a Samba server is revealed by the following command and session:

```
$ smbclient '//mainserv/temp' -Uusername%userpassword
added interface ip=192.168.100.1 bcast=192.168.100.255 nmask=255.255.255.0
added interface ip=192.168.200.101 bcast=192.168.200.255 nmask=255.255.255.0
Domain=[MYGROUP] OS=[Unix] Server=[Samba 2.0.6]
smb: \> ls o*
  orbit-myuid                    D        0  Fri Sep 24 14:30:19 1999
  orbit-root                     D        0  Sun Oct 17 19:28:54 1999

          61906 blocks of size 32768. 8509 blocks available
smb: \> quit
$
```

Once you're in the smbclient session, writability can be tested with smbclient's put command.

smbclient is also excellent for testing access to a Windows 98 share, as shown by the following session:

```
$ smbclient '//wincli/menudata' -U%sharepassword
added interface ip=192.168.100.1 bcast=192.168.100.255 nmask=255.255.255.0
added interface ip=192.168.200.101 bcast=192.168.200.255 nmask=255.255.255.0
smb: \> put test.txt
putting file test.txt as \test.txt (10.2534 kb/s) (average 10.2539 kb/s)
smb: \> ls
  .                              D        0  Thu Dec 17 08:50:28 1998
  ..                             D        0  Thu Dec 17 08:50:28 1998
  a.mnu                          A      149  Thu Dec 17 00:49:38 1998
  test.txt                       A       21  Sun Nov 21 17:05:42 1999

          36189 blocks of size 32768. 20688 blocks available
smb: \> more test.txt
getting file /tmp/smbmore.15986 of size 21 as /tmp/smbmore.15986 (6.83571 kb/s)
(average 6.83594 kb/s)
This is a test file.
smb: \> quit
$
```

In the preceding session, writability was proven by "putting" file test.txt, and readability was proven by the directory listing and the more command to show the contents of test.txt. Because Windows 9*x* user-level sharing doesn't work, no username is needed. Instead, you should input the share's password (not a user's password) in the usual location of the user's password.

A similar command syntax can be used for NT. Assuming an NT computer shares a directory, using share name NTdata, here's a session that writes and reads the share:

```
$ smbclient '//desk1/NTdata' -Uusername%userpassword
added interface ip=192.168.100.1 bcast=192.168.100.255 nmask=255.255.255.0
```

```
added interface ip=192.168.200.101 bcast=192.168.200.255 nmask=255.255.255.0
Domain=[MYGROUP] OS=[Windows NT 4.0] Server=[NT LAN Manager 4.0]
smb: \> put test.txt
putting file test.txt as \test.txt (4.10148 kb/s) (average 4.10156 kb/s)
smb: \> ls
  .                                   D        0  Sun Nov 21 17:13:37 1999
  ..                                  D        0  Sun Nov 21 17:13:37 1999
  test.txt                            A       21  Sun Nov 21 17:13:37 1999
  username.txt                        A        0  Sun Nov 21 15:08:41 1999

            64259 blocks of size 8192. 40423 blocks available
smb: \> more username.txt
getting file /tmp/smbmore.15996 of size 0 as /tmp/smbmore.15996 (0 kb/s)
➥(average 0 kb/s)
smb: \> quit
$
```

The `smbclient` Command Set

Typing **help** at the smbclient command prompt brings up a list of commands valid within the smbclient environment:

```
]$ smbclient '//mainserv/username' -U username%user
added interface ip=192.168.100.1 bcast=192.168.100.255 nmask=255.255.255.0
added interface ip=192.168.200.101 bcast=192.168.200.255 nmask=255.255.255.0
Domain=[MYGROUP] OS=[Unix] Server=[Samba 2.0.6]
smb: \> help
ls              dir             du              lcd             cd
pwd             get             mget            put             mput
rename          more            mask            del             open
rm              mkdir           md              rmdir           rd
prompt          recurse         translate       lowercase       print
printmode       queue           cancel          quit            q
exit            newer           archive         tar             blocksize
tarmode         setmode         help            ?               history
!
smb: \>
```

Help for each command is available by typing the command after the **help** keyword or its **?** synonym, as shown here:

```
smb: \> ? more
HELP more:
        <remote name> view a remote file with your pager

smb: \>
```

Many commands are obvious. For example, ls lists the contents of the current directory on the share. dir is a synonym for ls. du is similar to the UNIX du (disk usage) command. cd changes the directory. (Note that any attempt to change directories outside of the share's path fails, leaving the directory unchanged.) pwd returns the location of that current directory. lcd changes the directory on the local machine, thus enabling a different set of files to be put and a different destination for get. Finally, quit, q, and exit are three synonyms that exit the smbclient environment.

The four main file-transfer commands are get, mget, put, and mput. All four commands transfer a file as a binary image unless the translate command has enabled CR/LF<->LF translation. put transfers a single file from the current directory (or directory navigated to by the lcd command) of the machine running smbclient to the share and any subdirectory navigated to with the cd command. get transfers in the opposite direction.

mget and mput work with wildcards and, depending on the state of directory recursion set by the recurse command toggle, might recurse directories looking for eligible files. The recursion state also determines the output of the ls command. Note that recursion is off at the start of any smbclient session. Transfer of each file is prompted unless the prompt command has toggled the prompt state to off. The newer command sets a date state to the date of a local file, thus enabling mget to get *only* files newer than that file. The newer command controls files eligible for tar c and ls also. To eliminate the date restriction, issue the newer command with no arguments.

mkdir and md are synonyms that make a directory below the current one in the share. rmdir and rd are synonyms that remove a directory from the current directory in the share.

Several commands operate on a file. rename takes two arguments: the old name first and then the new name. rm and del are synonyms that delete the named file or wildcard without prompting. The more smbclient command outputs the contents of the file to the screen, one screenful at a time, using the spacebar to "screenfeed" or the Enter key to "linefeed" the file's text.

The mask command installs a file mask that determines which files are displayed by the ls command. However, directories are displayed whether or not they conform to the mask. The lowercase command toggles the lowercase state, which is off by default. When the lowercase state is on, a get command on an uppercase file stores it as lowercase locally.

If the share is a print share, several printing commands can be run. The queue command shows the print queue. The cancel command takes a print queue ID as an argument and cancels that print job. The printmode command takes an argument of "text" or "graphics" and sets the print mode appropriately. The print command takes a filename as an argument and prints that file.

The `tar` command enables extracting a local tar file to the share or creating a local tar file from the share. Here's a command that creates a file, called `backup.tar`, of all `.txt` files on the local directory:

```
smb: \> tar c backup.tar *.txt
```

> **Caution**
>
> The argument immediately after the c must *never* contain a wildcard. Otherwise, the created file on the local directory will contain a wildcard and will be very difficult to rename.
>
> The argument directly after the c is intended to be the name of the local `tar` file to be created.

The `tarmode` command sets the `tar` command's archive bit behavior to `full`, `inc`, `reset`, or `noreset`. The `blocksize` command sets the block size of created tar files.

The `tar` command can be used to populate a share with files from a local tar file, using the following syntax:

```
smb: \> tar x backup.tar
```

Creating and extracting `tar` files can also be done with the `smb.conf` option `-T`. Here's an example:

```
$ smbclient '//mainserv/temp' -Uusername%whatever -Tc test.tar wargames
```

The preceding command creates a backup called `test.tar` on the current directory of the local machine. That backup contains everything under the `wargames` directory of the share. To back up the entire directory, change `wargames` to `*`.

Restoring from a local `tar` can be done as follows:

```
$ smbclient '//mainserv/temp' -Uusername%whatever -Tx all.tar wargames
```

The preceding command restores subroutine `wargames` from local `all.tar`, which contains a backup of the entire share. To restore the entire share, change `wargames` to `*`.

The `archive` command sets the archive state to one of the following four, according to the command's argument:

0   Ignore archive bit

1   Only get archive files

2   Only get archive files and reset the archive bit

3   Get all files and the reset archive bit

> **Note**
>
> The customary way to back up a share using `tar` is to use the `smbtar` utility, which is covered in the "Using `nmblookup` for Diagnostic Testing" section later in this chapter.

The `history` command displays the command history of the `smbclient` session. The `setmode` command can be used to set the DOS read-only, system, hidden, and archive attributes of a file in the share.

Using `smbclient` to Print to Remote Printers

A byte stream can be printed to a remote printer using `smbclient`. A text file can be printed as shown in the following example:

```
$ smbclient '//wincli/localiii' -c "print test.txt"
```

In the preceding example, the printer must be manually form-fed unless the file `test.txt` ends with a formfeed character. Also, the print job *stair-steps*, meaning that each new line starts to the right of the end of the previous line. This can be fixed with CRLF<-->CR translation, as done in the following command.

```
$ smbclient '//wincli/localiii' -c "translate; print test.txt"
```

The following is a quick way to formfeed the printer:

```
$ echo ^L | smbclient '//wincli/localiii' -c "print -"
```

> **Note**
>
> The `^L` in the preceding command is the formfeed character (Ctrl+L), produced in UNIX by the Ctrl+V Ctrl+L keyboard sequence.

The following command prints whatever you type to the remote printer:

```
$ cat | smbclient '//wincli/localiii' -c "translate; print -"
```

Note that to end the typing session, you press the Ctrl+D end-of-file keyboard combination.

> **Note**
>
> The preceding printing methods print straight text. Although it's possible to pipe input from a print filter into `smbclient`, the customary way of printing graphical or formatted material to the printer is to use a print filter in a print queue.

`smbclient` Automation

The `smbclient` print commands are one form of `smbclient` automation. The `-T` command-line option supports automation, as does the `-c` option. The `-c` option enables the running of any of the `smbclient` session commands discussed in the preceding section. One example is the following, which marks a file on a Windows 9*x* client as read-only, system, hidden, and archive:

```
$ smbclient '//wincli/menudata' -U%sharepass -c "setmod test.txt rash"
```

The following command copies a file, with CRLF translation, to the Windows client:

```
$ smbclient '//wincli/menudata' -U%sharepass -c "translate; put menu.dat"
```

The preceding might be especially handy in the case of a server-side automation process that runs a UNIX process outputting a UNIX text file. If the last step in the process were the preceding command, the user could find the report, suitably translated to DOS text style, on his local disk. Naturally, this would require some variable substitution for the client name.

Troubleshooting `smbclient`

The `smbclient` program works exceedingly well, but it can have problems, especially if any servers or clients are misconfigured. If `smbclient` fails to gain access to the share, you should first double-check the obvious:

- Is the share declared in `smb.conf` or in a Windows share?
- If it's a share-mode rather than a user-mode share, make sure the password input to `smbclient` is the password for the share, not a user.
- If the problem involves `smbclient -NL computername`, make sure you use the following command if the computer is a Windows NT or 2000 computer:

  `smbclient -L -Uusername%password`.

Here are three quick preliminary steps to take:

- Use `ping` to test for connectivity.
- Use `testparm` to test for a legal `smb.conf`.
- Use `ps ax | grep -i mbd` to test for running daemons.

The next step involves the following additional `smbclient` parameters:

- Use `-I` IP address.
- Use `-U` with a different known good user.
- Use `-W` with various workgroups.
- Use the IP address as the server name after the double slash.

If you can get the command to work, exploit the differences between the command form that worked and the command form that didn't.

Using `smbmount` to Mount SMB Shares as UNIX Directories

The `smbmount` command mounts an SMB or CIFS share as a Linux directory. It works *only* with Linux.

> **Note**
>
> The syntax of `smbmount` changed completely in Samba 2.0.6. The expectation is that the new syntax will remain in force for quite some time. This chapter discusses only the 2.0.6 syntax. If you're running a previous version of `smbmount`, consult your man pages and the no-argument `smbmount` command.

> **Caution**
>
> The default build of Samba does not yield `smbmount`. To obtain the `smbmount` command, the `./configure` command must include the `--with-smbmount` argument.

The `smbmount` command has a long and interesting history. It was originally a contribution that was not integrated completely into Samba. The `smbsh` commands were designed to take its place, but the `smbsh` commands ran into trouble after Linux began compiling with glib-2.1. After that, the Samba project took `smbmount` under its wing and applied rapid changes to the product. Those changes were so rapid that the documentation lagged behind. Therefore, you should always run `smbmount` without arguments and follow the syntax described therein.

The simplest possible use of `smbmount` is as follows:

```
# smbmount //wincli/menudata /mnt/temp
```

The preceding command works only as `root`. It mounts share `menudata` from Windows 98 box `wincli` to mount point `/mnt/temp`. When asked for the password, you should answer with the password of the share if it's a share-mode host. The contents of the share can subsequently be viewed with the normal `ls` command:

```
$ ls -ldF /mnt/temp/*
```

Notice that the files appear to have `root` as the owner. Files in `/mnt/temp` can be edited, regardless of their apparent ownership. This is because Windows 98 clients have no ownership. Therefore, because the mount was done as `root`, that's the ownership that shows up on the files in the `ls` command. This becomes a little confusing when you're mounting a Linux Samba-hosted share. (This subject is discussed in more detail a few paragraphs from here.)

To unmount the share, run the following command:

```
# smbumount /mnt/temp
```

The preceding doesn't work if any user is using the directory or has it as the current directory.

Mounting a Windows 98 Share with `smbmount`

The preferred way to use `smbmount` is from the `mount` command, as shown in this command to mount a Windows 98 share on a Linux file system:

```
# mount -t smbfs //wincli/menudata /mnt/temp -o password=whatever
```

> **Note**
>
> Running the `smbmount` command without arguments outputs a listing of usage information for `smbmount`. At the bottom of that listing is a syntax line showing the `-o` argument and its associated options, (such as username=<string>), preceding the service and mount point. Although this frequently works, it's more reliable to have the service and mount point come before the `-o` and options.

The preceding command mounts the share as an `smbfs`-type file system. File links enable `smbmount` to be called by the preceding command. Once again, `password=whatever` is the password of the share on a share-mode host, not the password of the accessing user.

Mounting a Windows NT Share with smbmount

The following is the command to mount an NT-hosted share called `ntdata`, which is shared as user `ntuser` with password `whatever`:

```
# mount -t smbfs //desk1/ntdata /mnt/temp -o username=ntuser%whatever
```

Notice that unlike Windows 98, NT typically uses user-level security, meaning both a user and a password must be provided. The preferred syntax is `username=username%password`. Obviously, the user must be allowed access to the share by the NT box.

Mounting a UNIX Share with smbmount

Finally, the following command mounts `//mainserv/homes`:

```
# mount -t smbfs //mainserv/homes /mnt/temp -o username=username%whatever
```

Because the `[homes]` share exposes the home directory of the logged in user, the preceding command mounts the home directory of `username`, on server `mainserv`, to mount-point `/mnt/temp`. All files in this share belong to `username` even though performing an `ls -1dF /mnt/temp/*` indicates that they belong to root. Once mounted by `username`, any files in this share that are writable by `username` are also editable by any user accessing this mount point.

In other words, if `root` had previously run the preceding command, user `myuid` could edit `username`'s files in `/mnt/temp`. It's very similar to `smbclient`.

Disappearing Mounts

For several months a sparsely intermittent problem has been reported on mailing lists and newsgroups. Mounts done with `smbmount` intermittently disappear, as if they had been unmounted. This has either been fixed in 2.0.6 or 2.0.6 has greatly decreased the frequency of occurrence. If you get this symptom with previous versions, upgrade your version and it will probably go away. If you get this symptom with the latest version and cannot find a logical reason for it, report it on `samba@samba.org`.

Using smbmount Within fstab

The `smbmount` program can be used in `/etc/fstab` to mount an SMB share upon bootup. The following is an fstab entry to mount a Windows 9*x* share:

```
//wincli/menudata    /mnt/menu    smbfs    password=whatever 0 0
```

Because the preceding mount is a share mode, it only needs a password, hence the absence of a username. Rather than rebooting, you should test this share as follows:

```
$ mount /mnt/menu
$ ls -ldF /mnt/menu/*
$ umount /mnt/menu
```

The following `fstab` entry mounts Windows NT share `ntdata` to `/mnt/ntdata`:

```
//desk1/ntdata    /mnt/ntdata    smbfs    username=username%whatever 0 0
```

The following `fstab` entry mounts the Linux share `//mainserv/music`:

```
//mainserv/music   /mnt/music    smbfs    username=myuid%whatever 0 0
```

All the preceding commands must be done as user `root`.

Troubleshooting `smbmount`

The first step in troubleshooting `smbmount` is to run the equivalent `smbclient` command with the same username and password. If `smbclient` is successful, you should take an extremely close look at the syntax of the `smbmount` command. However, if the equivalent `smbclient` command fails, troubleshoot that first.

Command-Line Syntax

Here's the basic command-line syntax of `smbmount`:

```
# smbmount //server/share /mountdir -o option1=value1,...
```

The preferable syntax uses the `mount` command:

```
# mount -t smbfs //server/share /mountdir -o option1=value1,...
```

In the preceding commands, symbolic links enable the mount command to call `smbmount`, via `smbfs`. In both cases, the share comes first, then the mount directory, then the comma-delimited options list, with each option consisting of a key, an equal sign, and a value. Some documentation suggests placing the options first, but placing them last seems to produce reliable results more often.

A brief discussion of the various options follows.

username=<arg>

This is the equivalent of the user in `smbclient`. It is this user that's compared against any `valid users=` parameters. Note that once mounted, this user's access to the share determines *everyone's* access to the share.

This user is *not* reflected in the ownership revealed by the `ls -l` command. The "owner" indicated by that command defaults to `root` and is changeable by the `uid=` option.

The password can be included by appending `%` and then the password. For greatest security, let the program prompt for a password and enter it manually.

password=<arg>

This is typically used for a single password on a share-mode mount. For greatest security, let the program prompt for a password and enter it manually. To enter a password on the command line for user-mode security, you should use the `username=username%password` syntax.

uid=<arg>

This is how you change the apparent file owner in mounted `smbfs` shares. However, read and write access to the files is determined by `username=`, not `uid=`.

gid=<arg>

This is how you change the apparent file group in mounted `smbfs` shares. However, read and write access to the files is determined by the primary group of `username=`, not `gid=`.

debug=<arg>

This is the level of messages sent to `stdout`. Anything above `2` outputs much too much information, masking legitimate error messages and creating a performance problem. Levels greater than `2` should be used only for debugging.

ro and rw

These options determine whether the share is mounted as read-only or read-write, although `rw` cannot override a `read only=yes` in `smb.conf`. The default is `rw`. The `ro` option makes access to the share read-only.

Other Options

Other options are handy if the defaults don't work or if a finer-level of control is desired. For example, the `guest` option removes the password prompt. The `port=<arg>` option sets the remote SMB port number, in case the standard 139 does not work. The `fmask=<arg>` and `dmask=<arg>` options are the file and directory creation masks, respectively. The `ip=<arg>` option specifies the destination host or IP address, and it's handy if for some reason the name resolution doesn't yield the correct value. Similarly, the `workgroup=<arg>` option specifies the workgroup on the destination, which can overcome certain problems.

The `netbiosname=<arg>` option can hard code a netbios name if the default (the local hostname) does not work.

The `sockopt=<arg>` option specifies TCP socket options, and the `scope=<arg>` option specifies the NetBIOS scope.

Using `smbstatus` as a Quick Check

The `smbstatus` program lists connections and locked files, which is very similar to the status screen in SWAT. Here's an example of the output of `smbstatus -d` (`-d` is verbose) for a simple Samba server with files `test.txt` and `steve3.txt` from share `[homes]` being edited and share `[netlogon]` connected:

```
$ smbstatus -d
using configfile = /usr/local/samba/lib/smb.conf
lockdir = /usr/local/samba/var/locks
Opened status file /usr/local/samba/var/locks/STATUS..LCK

Samba version 2.0.6
Service      uid      gid      pid      machine
-------------------------------------------------
username     username username  1881    wincli
➥  (192.168.100.201) Wed Nov 24 04:41:33 1999
netlogon     username username  1881    wincli
➥  (192.168.100.201) Wed Nov 24 04:47:20 1999

Locked files:
Pid    DenyMode   R/W       Oplock           Name
-------------------------------------------------
1881   DENY_NONE  RDONLY    EXCLUSIVE+BATCH  /home/username/test.txt
➥  Wed Nov 24 04:41:37 1999
1881   DENY_NONE  RDONLY    EXCLUSIVE+BATCH  /home/username/steve3.txt
➥  Wed Nov 24 04:52:16 1999

Share mode memory usage (bytes):
   1048264(99%) free + 224(0%) used + 88(0%) overhead = 1048576(100%) total
#>
```

Another cool feature of `smbstatus` is its ability to enumerate smbd processes via the `-p` option:

```
# smbstatus -p
1881
#
```

This is handy for various scripts.

smbstatus Options

The -b option gives brief output. The -d option gives verbose output, adding to the default output lines that show the config file location, the lock directory location, and the full pathname for the lock file.

The -L and -S options are opposites in that -L prints only locks, whereas -S lists only shares.

As mentioned previously, -p prints a list of smbd processes and nothing else. The -s option followed by a filename uses that filename as the configuration file (smb.conf equivalent). The -u option followed by a username restricts output to that relevant to the user specified in the -u option.

Using smbtar to Back Up Clients

The smbtar script is a simplified command-line front end to the tar capabilities of smbclient. It's used to back up client computers from the server.

The Downside of Client Backup

Although a centralized backup of client computers sounds great, it's not without its problems. Once the administrator backs up files from client computers, it's perceived that backing up the client computers is now the responsibility of the network administrator. The administrator takes on the task of making sure the client computers are turned on and properly connected to the network before every backup. If a file is stored on a client but outside the share being backed up, the administrator must explain why it cannot be restored.

Contrast this with a policy of keeping all important data on server shares. The user is responsible for getting the data to the server, so the administrator only needs to back up the server or its data tree. This way, the administrator is not required to walk from client to client, turning them on.

Backing Up and Restoring from Windows 98 Shares

The following is a simple command for backing up all files (*.*) in the menudata share's tree (this share is on the wincli Windows 98 box). Note that the /dev/fd0 device can be replaced by a tape device, any other device, or a file. Here's the command:

```
$ smbtar -s wincli -x menudata -p whatever -t /dev/fd0 *.*
```

In the preceding command, note that "all files" is represented by *.*. Using just * backs up only subdirectories and their contents and misses files with extensions in the root of the share.

Caution

It's never a good idea to place passwords in shell commands, because they can be sniffed out and the ps ax command might show them in plain text.

It might seem that you could remove the password and percent sign, in which case you would expect the program to prompt for a password. Unfortunately, the program fails silently if it's not given a password.

However, tar backup can be accomplished by smbclient in such a way as to prompt for the password. Here's how:

```
$ smbclient '//mainserv/menudata' -Uusername -Tc /dev/fd0 *.*
```

The following command is used to restore the data to the share. Note that the -r (restore) option has been added and the file list (*.*) has be en removed. Here's the command:

```
$ smbtar -r  -s wincli -x menudata -p whatever -t /dev/fd0
```

The smbtar client utility is an easy way to back up and restore selected shares on Windows 9*x* clients, from the command line on a single UNIX box. Its power and flexibility makes this difficult task less difficult.

Backing Up and Restoring from Windows NT Shares

Backing up from an NT share differs from Windows 98 in two ways:

- NT shares can implement user mode sharing.
- The file list contains both *.* and *.

The following is the command for backing up the contents of share ntdata on NT box desk1:

```
$ smbtar  -s desk1 -x ntdata -u username%whatever -t /dev/fd0 *.* *
```

In the preceding command, note that the username and password are given in the -u option rather than the -p option being used.

> **Caution**
>
> In the preceding command, note that the file specifier is `*.* *`. If it had been set to `*.*`, it would have backed up files in the share's root but missed subdirectories. If it's had been set to `*`, it would have backed up the subdirectories but missed the files in the share's root. Note that `*.* *` cannot be used in Windows 98 shares, because doing so makes two copies of the subdirectories in the `.tar` file.

The following command is used to restore the data to an NT share:

```
$ smbtar -r  -s desk1 -x ntdata -u username%whatever -t /dev/fd0
```

The `smbtar` client utility is an easy way to back up and restore selected shares on Windows NT clients, from the command line on a single UNIX box. Its power and flexibility makes this difficult task less difficult.

Backing Up and Restoring from Samba Server Shares

The following command backs up the `umenu` share on Samba server `mainserv`:

```
$ smbtar -s mainserv -x umenu -u username%whatever -t /dev/fd0 *
```

In the preceding command, notice that the UNIX-centric `*` file specifier is used. The following command restores from backup:

```
$ smbtar -r -s mainserv -x umenu -u username%whatever -t /dev/fd0
```

The `smbtar` client utility can be used to back up Samba shares on other UNIX boxes, although UNIX provides more straightforward methods to do this.

Using smbprint as a Print Queue Filter

The `smbprint` script is not used for printing from the command line. SMB printing from the command line is done with `smbclient`. The `smbprint` script is used as a filter within a `printcap`-specified print queue, thus enabling a UNIX print command to transparently print to a Windows (or other SMB-connected) printer, as follows:

```
lpsmb:\
        :sd=/var/spool/lpd/lpsmb:\
        :mx#0:\
```

```
:sh:\
:if=/usr/bin/smbprint:\
:af=/var/spool/lpd/lpsmb/acct:\
:lp=/dev/null:
```

The preceding is a rather useless exercise because there's no print filtering to match the hardware printer. However, many filters call `smbprint` if the printer is found to be an SMB printer.

The main thing to remember about `smbprint` is that it isn't a script for sending a file to the printer from the command line. Instead, use `smbclient` for sending a file to the printer from the command line.

Using `nmblookup` for Diagnostic Testing

The `nmblookup` utility is the best diagnostic tool for NetBIOS names. Because NetBIOS naming is tightly integrated with all aspects of Samba, `nmblookup` is an extremely powerful tool. It can find the hosts and their names on the network, find the browser, and perform many other tests. Several of the tests in `DIAGNOSIS.txt` involve `nmblookup`.

`nmblookup` and Browser Elections

One way to see browser elections is to use `tail -f log.nmb`. For a Samba system that has not been restarted recently, a better method is to use `nmblookup`. The following syntax tells which machine (if any) is acting as browse master:

```
$ nmblookup -SM -
```

This is discussed in the section on `nmblookup` options (specifically the `-M` option), later in this chapter.

`nmblookup -B servername __SAMBA__`

This is Test 4 in `DIAGNOSIS.txt` and, as such, is very important in the Samba world. If it does not return the correct address of the Samba server (`mainserv` in the following example), then there's a serious problem. Here's an example:

```
$ nmblookup -B mainserv __SAMBA__
querying __SAMBA__ on 192.168.100.1
192.168.100.1 __SAMBA__<00>
$
```

nmblookup -B clientname '*'

This is Test 5 in DIAGNOSIS.txt. It's designed to test the client's Windows networking software. Here's an example:

```
$ nmblookup -B wincli '*'
querying * on 192.168.100.201
192.168.100.201 *<00>
$
```

A problem here would typically not impact the client's ability to hit the server but instead would impact the client's ability to share its own directories.

nmblookup servername -S '*'

This command queries the server for all names. It can often be applied to clients also. It uses broadcast, so it runs outside of WINS, although the results can vary. Here's an example:

```
$ nmblookup mainserv -S '*'
querying * on 192.168.100.1
192.168.100.1 *<00>
Looking up status of 192.168.100.1
received 9 names
        MAINSERV        <00> -          M <ACTIVE>
        MAINSERV        <03> -          M <ACTIVE>
        MAINSERV        <20> -          M <ACTIVE>
        .._MSBROWSE__. <01> - <GROUP> M <ACTIVE>
        MYGROUP         <00> - <GROUP> M <ACTIVE>
        MYGROUP         <1b> -          M <ACTIVE>
        MYGROUP         <1c> - <GROUP> M <ACTIVE>
        MYGROUP         <1d> -          M <ACTIVE>
        MYGROUP         <1e> - <GROUP> M <ACTIVE>
num_good_sends=0 num_good_receives=0

$
```

nmblookup -T '*'

This is a great little diagnostic for looking up all names in WINS. However, it looks up the names through reverse DNS, so unless these names are resolved through DNS or /etc/hosts, it only yields numbers. With clients getting their IP addresses through DHCP, it's highly unlikely to have their names resolved through DNS or /etc/hosts. Here's an example:

```
$ nmblookup -T '*'
querying * on 192.168.100.255
wincli.domain.cxm, 192.168.100.201 *<00>
desk1.domain.cxm, 192.168.100.10 *<00>
```

12

SAMBA CLIENT
UTILITIES

```
desk2.domain.cxm, 192.168.100.204 *<00>
mainserv.domain.cxm, 192.168.100.1 *<00>
$
```

The `nmblookup` Command Options

`nmblookup` has a rich set of command options, making this a versatile debugging tool. This section discusses all the options. Table 12.2 outlines many of these command options.

TABLE 12.2 The `nmblookup` Command Options

Command Option	Behavior
-d debuglevel	Set nmblookup's debug level
-B broadcast IP	Use broadcast, explicitly naming a broadcast address
-U unicast IP	Use unicast, explicitly naming the IP address of the WINS server
-M	Locate the master browser
-S	Looks up all names on an explicitly specified IP address
-T	Uses reverse DNS to convert outputted IP addresses to names
other options	
-R	Makes the request recursive
-h	Displays help
-r	Corrects a Windows 95 bug
-A	Looks up a node status
-i	Handles NetBIOS scopes
-s	Explicitly specifies a nondefault `smb.conf` file

-d debuglevel

This option determines the detail of the debug messages printed to `stdout` by the `nmblookup` command. Anything above 2 is obnoxiously verbose and should be used only for troubleshooting, typically piped into `less` or into a file or `grep` command.

-B broadcast IP

This should not be necessary under default conditions, because the default broadcast address is typically correct. However, if `nmblookup` commands that should succeed fail, you might want to explicitly set this option to the broadcast address of the subnet.

-U unicast IP

This option sends the query directly to the WINS server at the unicast address. The `-U unicast IP` option plus the `-R` option are necessary for querying a WINS server.

-M

This is how you find the master browser. Start with this command:

```
$ nmblookup -SM -
querying ____MSBROWSE___ on 192.168.100.255
192.168.100.1 ____MSBROWSE___<01>
Looking up status of 192.168.100.1
received 9 names
        MAINSERV        <00> -          M <ACTIVE>
        MAINSERV        <03> -          M <ACTIVE>
        MAINSERV        <20> -          M <ACTIVE>
        .._MSBROWSE__.  <01> - <GROUP> M <ACTIVE>
        MYGROUP         <00> - <GROUP> M <ACTIVE>
        MYGROUP         <1b> -          M <ACTIVE>
        MYGROUP         <1c> - <GROUP> M <ACTIVE>
        MYGROUP         <1d> -          M <ACTIVE>
        MYGROUP         <1e> - <GROUP> M <ACTIVE>
num_good_sends=0 num_good_receives=0

$
```

The preceding shows a Samba machine as the master browser. The following shows a total lack of a master browser:

```
$ nmblookup -SM -
querying ____MSBROWSE___ on 192.168.100.255
querying ____MSBROWSE___ on 192.168.200.255
name_query failed to find name ____MSBROWSE___
$
```

Here's the result when an NT box is the master server:

```
$ nmblookup -SM -
querying ____MSBROWSE___ on 192.168.100.255
192.168.100.10 ____MSBROWSE___<01>
Looking up status of 192.168.100.10
received 10 names
        DESK1           <20> -          M <ACTIVE>
        DESK1           <00> -          M <ACTIVE>
        MYGROUP         <00> - <GROUP> M <ACTIVE>
        DESK1           <03> -          M <ACTIVE>
        MYGROUP         <1e> - <GROUP> M <ACTIVE>
        INet~Services   <1c> - <GROUP> M <ACTIVE>
        IS~DESK1        <00> -          M <ACTIVE>
        ADMINISTRATOR   <03> -          M <ACTIVE>
        MYGROUP         <1d> -          M <ACTIVE>
        .._MSBROWSE__.  <01> - <GROUP> M <ACTIVE>
num_good_sends=0 num_good_receives=0

$
```

The -M option (combined with -S to find the name) is vital in determining which box (if any) is the master browser. Without a master browser, Network Neighborhood browsing problems usually occur for any resources in workgroups outside the client.

```
$ nmblookup -U mainserv -R 'desk2'
```

-S IP

This option performs an additional lookup on any returned IP addresses to grab the names. This is the way you find the name list on client computers, as shown in the following session example, which looks up all names on client wincli:

```
$ nmblookup -Umainserv -RS 'wincli'
querying wincli on 192.168.100.1
192.168.100.201 wincli<00>
Looking up status of 192.168.100.201
received 6 names
        WINCLI          <00> -          M <ACTIVE>
        MYGROUP         <00> - <GROUP> M <ACTIVE>
        WINCLI          <03> -          M <ACTIVE>
        WINCLI          <20> -          M <ACTIVE>
        MYGROUP         <1e> - <GROUP> M <ACTIVE>
        USERNAME        <03> -          M <ACTIVE>
num_good_sends=0 num_good_receives=0

$
```

Combined with the -M option, this option is a vital window into the browsing system.

-T

This option translates IP addresses into names using reverse DNS lookup (including the hosts file). However, it's only as accurate as reverse DNS. Consider using the -S option instead, because that's a pure NetBIOS system. On the other hand, if NetBIOS is suspect, -T might be a valuable system check.

Other nmblookup Command Options

The nmblookup command has several other options which are not as important or frequently used as those previously discussed. The following is a list of those options:

The -R option sets recursion on and, when used, is typically used in querying a WINS server (together with the -U option).

The -r option can correct an obscure Windows 95 bug. If necessary, read about it in the nmblookup man page.

The -A option looks up a node status on a name after translating the name to an IP address. This is an alternative to the -S option, but -S is typically more reliable.

The `-i` option takes a NetBIOS scope as an argument, and handles NetBIOS scopes. Read the `nmblookup` man page for details.

The `-s` option takes a filename as an argument, and specifies a non-default Samba configuration file. If the system uses a different `smb.conf` file than the compiled default one, the `-s` option tells `nmblookup` where to find it.

The `-h` option prints a brief help and syntax message.

Using `smbpasswd` for Security

The `smbpasswd` command works with encrypted passwords.

An existing encrypted password can be changed by the `root` user with the following command:

```
# smbpasswd username
```

The `smbpasswd` program then prompts for the password and a confirming password; then it and changes the password. To change an encrypted password as an ordinary user, use the following syntax:

```
# smbpasswd -Uusername
```

The program then prompts for the present password, the new password, and a confirming password. The preceding syntax can also be used by the `root` user.

Using the `-a` option, the `root` user can add new users to the encrypted password list. The new user must have an existing UNIX account. If the new user has no UNIX account, use the `useradd` script or some other method to add the user to the UNIX system. The `root` user then uses the following syntax to add the new user to the encrypted password file:

```
# smbpasswd -a username
```

The program then queries for the password and a confirming password. The `-a` option is a must when inputting a new user to the encrypted password list. If used by a non-`root` user, this syntax produces a syntax error, but it's a perfectly valid syntax for the `root` user.

An `smbpasswd` account can be temporarily disabled, by the `root` user only, with the following command:

```
# smbpasswd -d username
```

The preceding command sets a flag in the `smbpasswd` file. However, in pre-2.0 Samba, doing this destroys the password, necessitating inputting the password again

12

SAMBA CLIENT
UTILITIES

upon re-enabling the account. However, in modern Samba versions, the account is re-enabled with the following command, run as `root`:

```
# smbpasswd -e username
```

By placing the `-D` option followed by a debug level in the command, you enable debug messages up to that level to be written to `stdout` during the `smbpasswd` command. This is handy in troubleshooting what went wrong. This option is available to all users. Here's an example that sets the debug level up to `10` for the duration of the `smbpasswd` command:

```
# smbpasswd -D 10 username
```

There's a null password option, but using it is a bad idea from a security point of view. If you really want to use null passwords, read the `smbpasswd` man page first.

The remote machine option uses the `-r` argument. The `-r` option is used to change the user's encrypted password on a remote server. This is usually used in conjunction with the `-j` (join) option. Note also that the `-U` option is often used to specify a specific username on the remote machine.

The `-R` option determines the resolve order among `lmhosts`, `host`, `wins`, and `bcast`. The `-h` option prints help. The `-s` (script) option suppresses `smbclient`'s `stdout` and takes its input from `stdin` in order to more easily work with scripts.

smbpasswd and NT Domains

The `smbpasswd` command is an integral part of the process of joining a Samba server to an NT domain. This is beyond the scope of this chapter, so see Chapter 24, "Adding a Samba Server to an NT Network," for more details. The `smbpasswd` command looks something like this:

```
$ smbpasswd -j NTdomainname -r PDCserverName
```

Also note that the `-m` (machine account) option is related to joining an NT domain.

Other Client Utilities

There are other, rarely used Samba client utilities, including `smbwrapper` and `smbsh`, as well as some really obscure ones. These can be researched on their respective man pages if you happen to find them necessary.

Summary

Samba has several client utilities that are useful in share access and troubleshooting. The most versatile is `smbclient`, which can be used to view UNIX and Windows 9*x* browse lists, as shown in the following command:

```
$ smbclient -NL servername
```

When this command is used to view a browse list from an NT box, the usage is as follows:

```
$ smbclient -L servername -Uusername%userpassword
```

The `smbclient` command can also be used to access a share via an ftp-style interface. The `smbclient` session is initiated as follows:

```
$ smbclient '//server/share' -Uusername%userpassword
```

The `smbclient` environment has a huge command set, most of which is defined in this chapter. Use the `help` or `?` keyword from within the environment to find these commands and what they do. One command is `tar`. The preferred way to use `smbclient` to back up and restore via `tar` involves the use of `smbclient`'s `-T` option, as follows:

```
$ smbclient '//server/share' -Uuser%pass -Tc tarfile.tar filespec
```

In the preceding command, the argument after the `-Tc` option must not contain a wild-card, because a file with that wildcard would be created. Instead, it must be the name of the `tar` file containing the backup data. A subsequent restore would look like the following:

```
$ smbclient '//server/share' -Uuser%pass -Tx tarfile.tar filespec
```

In the preceding command, if `filespec` is not specified, the entire `tarfile.tar` file is restored to the share.

`smbclient` can print to a remote printer with any of the following types of syntax:

```
$ smbclient '//box/printshare' -c "print test.txt"
```

```
$ smbclient '//box/printshare' -c "translate; print test.txt"
```

```
$ cat | smbclient '//box/printshare' -c "translate; print -"
```

```
$ echo ^L | smbclient '//box/printshare' -c "print -"
```

The `-c` option executes the next argument, a string in quotes, as if it were input at the `smb: \>` prompt.

The `smbmount` client utility is used to mount SMB shares at Linux mount points. It works *only* with Linux. The preferred syntax uses the `mount` command, as follows:

```
# mount -t smbfs //box/share /mountpoint -o password=whatever
```

The preceding works with Windows 9*x* shares. For NT and UNIX shares, use the following:

```
# mount -t smbfs //box/share /mountpoint -o username=username%whatever
```

Use the `umount` command to unmount such shares. The mount can be specified in `fstab` in the following manner:

```
//box/share    /mountpoint   smbfs     password=whatever 0 0
```

The preceding is a Windows 98 share. Other shares require a user as well as password. When you're troubleshooting `smbmount`, the first step is to see whether an equivalent `smbclient` succeeds.

The `smbstatus` command gives a quick list of connections and open files. The most common and informative form of the command is this:

```
$ smbstatus -d
```

The `smbtar` script is a front end to `smbclient`'s `tar` facilities, but it unfortunately requires the password on the command line. If security is an issue, use `smbclient` instead. Otherwise, you can use `smbtar`, being careful to use the correct file specifications, which are *.* for Windows 9*x*, *.* * for NT, and * for UNIX. The following command backs up an entire Windows 98 share to floppy:

```
$ smbtar -s wincli -x share -p sharepassword -t /dev/fd0 *.*
```

Substitute whatever device should contain the data. The command to restore the preceding backup is as follows:

```
$ smbtar -r -s wincli -x share -p sharepassword -t /dev/fd0
```

The `smbprint` script is used as a print filter in print queues and is also called from various printer-specific print filters.

The `nmblookup` command is the prevalent name-resolution diagnostic tool. For example, the local browser can be found with the following command:

```
$ nmblookup -SM -
```

Numerous other helpful `nmblookup` tests exist and are detailed in this chapter. Tests 4, 5, and 6 in `DIAGNOSIS.txt` use `nmblookup`.

The `smbpasswd` command handles encrypted passwords. The `root` user can add new users to the encrypted password system (after they've been given UNIX accounts) with the following command:

```
$ smbpasswd -a username
```

Also, the `root` user can change an existing password for a user with the following command:

```
$ smbpasswd username
```

A normal user can change another user's password (or his own) with the following command:

```
$ smbpasswd -Uusername
```

In the preceding command, the normal user must input the user's old password, thus preventing security violations. The `smbpasswd` utility can be used to join an NT domain with the following command:

```
$ smbpasswd -j NTdomainname -r PDCserverName
```

However, it's not quite that simple, so see Chapter 24 for more details.

Whenever you have a troubleshooting need or a need to back up Windows clients or to initiate a file transfer to or from a Windows client, you should investigate the Samba client utilities.

Using Samba Web Administration Tool (SWAT) for Samba Configuration

by Steve Litt

SWAT is a Samba configuration program with a browser interface. It's primary intended use is for easy configuration of the `smb.conf` file. It fills that need beautifully and goes on to perform excellently as a Samba information source. SWAT has been bundled with every version of Samba since version 2.0.

> ### Use the Proper SWAT Version
>
> Be sure to use the version of SWAT that came with your version of Samba. There have been cases reported where a version mismatch between SWAT and Samba caused problems. See this chapter's "Compiling and Installing SWAT" section, which covers SWAT compile and install instructions. Also, see Chapter 5, "Installing Samba", for details on how to compile and install both SWAT and Samba.

SWAT has a few security issues that are easy to defuse. This chapter fully explains how to safely use SWAT.

Procuring SWAT

SWAT has the advantage of being distributed with Samba, so most of the time if you have Samba, you have SWAT. SWAT made its debut with Samba 2.0 and needs at least Samba 2.0 to work. SWAT can be procured from your Linux distribution CD or from the Internet.

From Your Linux Distribution CD

Different distributions have different installation methods. Red Hat and Caldera are listed here. The general method is to look for a file starting with `sam` or `swa` in the directory containing the installation files.

Red Hat

The Red Hat installation CD has an RPM file for all of Samba, including SWAT, so it's most likely that SWAT was installed with the distribution. The file is located in the CD's `RedHat/RPMS` directory and has a filename similar to `samba-2.0.3-8.i386.rpm`, where `2.0.3` is the version number, `-8` is a subversion, and `i386` denotes the target to be an Intel processor.

However, if for some reason SWAT and only SWAT needs reinstallation, from the install CD's `RedHat/RPMS` directory you can use this command to reinstall:

```
$ rpm -Uvh samba-2.0.3-8.i386.rpm
```

Of course, your RPM file will be a different version, so it has a different name.

> **Caution**
>
> Always back up `smb.conf` and `/etc/rc.d/init.d/smb` before running the `rpm` program against Samba's RPM file. Any kind of uninstall activity deletes these files, and there's also a chance of them being overwritten by an install or upgrade.

Caldera

The Caldera installation CD has a SWAT-specific RPM file in its `Packages/RPMS` directory. The file has a name similar to this:

```
swat-2.0.3-0b.i386.rpm
```

Once again, `smb.conf` and `/etc/rc.d/init.d/smb` should be backed up before any installation. From the CD's `Packages/RPMS` directory, run the following installation command:

```
$ rpm -ivh swat-2.0.3-0b.i386.rpm
```

Naturally, change the filename to the one on your CD.

From the Internet

SWAT is part of the Samba package, which can be procured from the Samba.org Web site. See Chapter 5 to determine exactly which file to download. Note that although it's possible to cruise the FTP tree for only the necessary files, it's most likely easier to download all of Samba, given the rich dependencies of the system.

Compiling and Installing SWAT

See Chapter 5 for a complete discussion on creating a source tree from your `.tar.gz` file as well as for various installation options. This section assumes you've already done that and just want to recompile and reinstall SWAT.

The `swat` executable is all that's needed to run SWAT. From the `source` directory, you can re-create the `swat` executable with this command:

```
$ make bin/swat
```

Once that's complete, copy the `bin/swat` executable to the location of your other Samba executables. Also, make sure to use `chmod a+x` to make the new copy of `swat` executable for all.

13

USING SWAT
FOR SAMBA
CONFIGURATION

Always Back Up `smb.conf` Before Using Swat!

Never run SWAT without first backing up your `smb.conf` file. SWAT's purpose is to modify the `smb.conf` file, and it does so quickly and with no recourse. SWAT's modifications include removal of all comments and removal of all explicitly specified parameters that are set to a default value. Older versions of SWAT remove the `[global]` label. One wrong click can completely and irretrievably change your `smb.conf`. SWAT has no "undo" feature.

Backing up `smb.conf` allows you to use SWAT in complete confidence.

SWAT Buttons Depend on `smb.conf` Permissions

With a properly "permissioned" `smb.conf`, you can safely log in as a non-root user to view, but not change, `smb.conf`. Specifically, the Commit Changes and Delete buttons are not presented to non-root users if `smb.conf` is not writeable by group. However, having `smb.conf` group writeable enables any user to use SWAT to modify `smb.conf`. It doesn't matter which group the user is in. The permissions for "other" (non-owner, non-group) don't matter in SWAT. Table 13.1 presents a summary.

TABLE 13.1   SWAT Accessibility and `smb.conf` Permissions

Permission	Functionality
600	No read capability for non-root
640	Read but no write for non-root
660	Non-root reads and writes

The `root` user experiences full SWAT functionality with any file permissions, even `000`.

An ordinary user not expecting this kind of power from a `660` permission can be unpleasantly surprised after accidentally rewriting `smb.conf`.

> **Note**
>
> The preceding description is for `smb.conf` files whose owner and group are root. If a non-root group is chosen for `smb.conf`, only members of that group are granted group permissions to the file, which means that making the file `chmod 660` does not give all users write access. It only gives users in the `smb.conf` file's group (and root, of course) write access.

The Version 2.0.6 "Can't See What You Can't Edit" Philosophy

Starting with Samba version 2.0.6, users without permission to write `smb.conf` cannot see the Globals, Shares, and Printers navigation buttons, so they cannot see global, printer or share parameters. While this can be considered a security enhancement, it eliminates the use of SWAT in "look but don't touch" mode. Whether the new behavior is an advantage or disadvantage depends on whether your environment faces more risk from malicious crackers, or from innocent mistakes by genuine administrators.

If you would like to revert 2.0.6 (and presumably newer) SWAT versions to the former behavior where seeing didn't depend on write access, it can be done by modifying source file `web/swat.c`.

In that source file's `void show_main_buttons()` function you'll see the following source:

```
if (have_write_access) {
        image_link("Globals", "globals", "images/globals.gif");
        image_link("Shares", "shares", "images/shares.gif");
        image_link("Printers", "printers", "images/printers.gif");
}
if (have_read_access) {
        image_link("Status", "status", "images/status.gif");
        image_link("View Config", "viewconfig",
    ➥"images/viewconfig.gif");
        }
```

As you can see, the preceding code shows the three navigation buttons if and only if you have write access. It can be reverted by moving the three `image_link()` calls to the second `if` statement, and since that leaves the first `if` statement empty, it can be deleted. The following source shows the code to revert to showing buttons to those with read access:

```
if (have_read_access) {
        image_link("Globals", "globals", "images/globals.gif");
        image_link("Shares", "shares", "images/shares.gif");
        image_link("Printers", "printers", "images/printers.gif");
        image_link("Status", "status", "images/status.gif");
        image_link("View Config","viewconfig",
    ➥"images/viewconfig.gif");
        }
```

Note that in the preceding code the `if(have_write_access)` statement and its code block have been completely eliminated. Also important to note is that this modification does not give the user write privilege, as the read-only user does not have the `Commit Changes`, `Create Share`, `Delete Share`, `Create Printer` or `Delete Printer` buttons.

SWAT Security Concerns

SWAT is convenient, but the administrator must address some security issues. The three most pressing security concerns are `smb.conf` permissions, persistence, and clear passwords.

The basic problem is that anyone who can write `smb.conf` can have his way with the entire server, via the `smb.conf root preexec=` parameter (explained later in this section). Such unauthorized write access can be gained from SWAT's unique use of the root group id, or from the fact that it persists on all of a box's browser sessions. The SWAT user forgetting to close all browsers before lunch empowers others to hack `smb.conf` in his absence. Since SWAT uses clear passwords, they can be sniffed off the wire if SWAT is operated from a host other than the Samba server.

Wrong `smb.conf` Permissions

The ability to edit `smb.conf` is a master key to the server. Due to the `root preexec=` and `root postexec=` commands being run as root, one of these commands can be configured to commandeer the system by copying a hacked `passwd` file over `/etc/passwd` or creating an suid root copy of `bash` or `sh`.

> **Caution**
>
> SWAT's ability to edit `smb.conf` is related to its file permissions. If `smb.conf` is group `root`, the file's group permissions are granted to all users, regardless of the users' actual group. This special case can grant unintended write permissions to `smb.conf`. This special case is elaborated throughout this chapter.

One would think that an `/etc/smb.conf` owned by root, group `root`, and chmod `660` would not be accessible to rank-and-file users. But in fact it is—via SWAT. SWAT operates as group `root`, so for any logged-in user, it gets its permissions from the group permission of `smb.conf`, if `smb.conf`'s group is set to `root`. Interestingly enough, if `smb.conf` has a group other than `root`, users who are members of that group have `smb.conf`'s group permissions through SWAT, whereas users not in that group get `smb.conf`'s "other" permissions.

Whether or not you use SWAT, you should always patch this hole. Either remove group write permission from `smb.conf` or change the file's group to a group other than root. A user logging into SWAT as a user in `smb.conf`'s group gets group permissions, even though users not in group `root` get group permissions through Samba if `smb.conf`'s group is `root`. Naturally, if you're changing `smb.conf`'s group, make it a group populated only by the most trusted people, because the ability to modify `smb.conf` confers the ability to commandeer the system.

Never allow a Samba installation to exist without an `smb.conf`. In such a situation, anyone can come in through SWAT and create an `smb.conf`, complete with a dangerous `root preexec=`.

To summarize, there are two ways to fix this problem. You can make `smb.conf` owner `root`, group `root` with no write permissions for group or other. The other solution is to make `smb.conf` owner `root` and set its group to a very trusted group, and give `smb.conf` write permissions for that trusted group. That way, only `root` and members of the trusted group can edit `smb.conf`. In all cases, there should be no write permission for "other."

Persistence

SWAT has a Web-based interface. Once user and password authentication has taken place, the user can come and go from the SWAT interface as desired. Merely leaving SWAT to access other Web sites does not close the SWAT interface. A short trip to the cafeteria can give someone enough time to point the still-open browser at SWAT and continue editing `smb.conf`.

Even closing the browser isn't always enough. Most of us may have several copies of the browser open at once. It's intuitive to simply close the copy with which SWAT was accessed, but in fact any other copies of the browser can still access SWAT without further authentication. It's not until all copies of the browser are closed that subsequent SWAT access is reauthenticated.

Always close *all* copies of your browser upon completion of a SWAT session. Because this is so hard to remember, you may want to restrict access to browsers on the server. This is done with a TCP wrapper and is discussed in the section "The High-Security Setup," later in this chapter.

Clear Passwords

SWAT logins transmit passwords over the wire as clear text. Because `ftp` and `telnet` also transmit clear passwords, this isn't quite the security hole that it seems to be. Nevertheless, it's a security compromise. You may want to limit this compromise with a TCP wrapper, as described in the section "The High-Security Setup," later in this chapter.

SWAT Security Summary

The default Samba configuration is not secure. Security can be beefed up as follows:

- Remove group write permissions from `smb.conf` or change its group to a trusted, non-root group.
- Make a policy to close *all* open browsers upon leaving the workstation.
- Except in low security situations, use a TCP wrapper to limit SWAT usage to specific secure IP addresses..

Enabling SWAT

SWAT does not come enabled in default Samba installations. Given its security considerations, this is a good thing. Setting up SWAT is very easy. The process is as follows:

1. Modify `/etc/services` to enable SWAT as port 901.
2. Modify `/etc/inetd.conf` to start SWAT from `inetd`.
3. Restart `inetd`.

`/etc/services` Changes

Associate SWAT with port 901. Most Linux distributions have this line toward the bottom of `/etc/services`, thus only requiring the removal of the # character. The line should look like this:

```
swat     901/tcp      # Add swat service used via inetd
```

`/etc/inetd.conf` Changes

SWAT is started through `inetd`, so it must be configured into `inetd.conf`. This can be done in a manner restricting access to a few hosts (high security) or giving access to all hosts (low security).

The Low-Security Setup

Red Hat Linux defaults to the low-security setup. This setup enables access from any browser capable of reaching the server's Web server. To implement low security, include the following line in `/inetd.conf`:

```
swat   stream tcp   nowait.400  root /usr/local/samba/bin/swat swat
```

Before doing this, be sure to search for existing lines that start SWAT:

```
cat /etc/inetd.conf | grep -i swat
```

The low-security setup is a wonderful convenience that enables you to modify `smb.conf` from any browser. However, it should be used only where physical security limits the people who can access it via a browser, and only when those people are all known to be trustworthy. Given the mischief that can be made with `root preexec=`, this should never be used on an Internet-connected system. Instead, use the high-security setup.

The High-Security Setup

Caldera defaults to the high-security setup. It uses a TCP wrapper to limit IP addresses accessing SWAT. This should be used in all but the most trusting, nonconnected environments. Here, the entry in `inetd.conf` is different:

```
swat  stream  tcp  nowait.400 root  /usr/sbin/tcpd /usr/sbin/swat
```

Note that column 6 is `/usr/sbin/tcpd` instead of `/usr/local/samba/bin/swat`. This is a TCP wrapper that enables the limitation of accessing hosts. This limitation is achieved on the default Caldera setup with the following line in `/etc/hosts.deny`:

```
swat:ALL EXCEPT 127.0.0.2
```

The combination of the TCP wrapper and `hosts.deny` forces access to come through `127.0.0.2`:

```
$ lynx http://127.0.0.2:901
```

Because it's not `127.0.0.1`, `http://localhost:901` does not work. This configuration requires all SWAT activity to originate from the server, either on the console or through `telnet` or a secure shell.

Starting SWAT

Once SWAT has been installed and set up, all that's left is to restart `inetd` to start SWAT. Use `ps ax | grep inetd` to find `inetd`'s process ID. Then, as `root`, restart `inetd`:

```
# kill -1 PID
```

If the location of the process ID file is known, `grep` isn't needed:

```
# kill -1 $(cat /var/run/inetd.pid)
```

> **Note**
>
> Remember to use backticks (grave accents), not single quotes, around the `cat` command.

13

Last but not least, close all instances of your browser, and run SWAT from `http://` `whatever:901`. URL component *whatever* can be an IP address or a domain name, or, if security permits, `localhost`. When asked for a username and password, enter them. Figure 13.1 shows the authentication window in a Linux Netscape session.

FIGURE **13.1**

The SWAT authen-tication window.

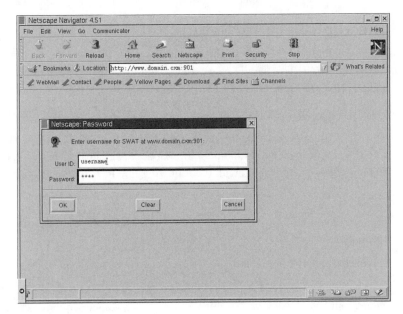

Troubleshooting

Like everything else in life, SWAT sometimes fails on the first try. Luckily, it's not difficult to troubleshoot.

First, round up the usual suspects. Make sure you accurately performed the steps in this section. Make sure you closed all browser windows before attempting access. If you're using a high-security setup, make sure you're accessing a URL not forbidden by `hosts.deny` or `hosts.allow`. Close all instances of your browser and then reopen the browser before attempting the access. Make sure you explicitly specify `http://` in the URL and make sure `inetd`'s PID matches the contents of its `inetd.pid` file and that it's running.

Observe the symptoms. Do you get the username and password prompt? Maybe you simply have a user ID problem. If SWAT times out, maybe your `inetd.conf` line is wrong or nonexistent.

If you've implemented the high-security configuration, temporarily implement the low-security configuration and see whether it makes a difference. If not, you've ruled out a large area. If it made a difference, exploit the differences.

Make sure Samba itself is running. Check for the daemons with `ps -ax | grep mbd`. Also, check the legality of `smb.conf` with `testparm`.

Often, more can be learned by accessing SWAT from Lynx on the command console. The following is a Lynx session piped to a file, from which the various screen control characters were removed. Notice that it deliberately errors out the first request and then asks for a username on the retry. This is normal. Also note that on the screen the text does not scroll down neatly. The Username and Password prompts can overwrite existing text, which is hard to distinguish from a computer hang. If you see the Username prompt, respond by typing your username. Then type the password when you see the Password prompt.

You can pipe the Lynx session to a log file and then from a different session do a tail `-f` on the file. Here is such a session:

```
lynx http://127.0.0.2:901 > lynx.log
Getting http://127.0.0.2:901/
Looking up 127.0.0.2:901.
Making HTTP connection to 127.0.0.2:901.
Sending HTTP request.
HTTP request sent; waiting for response.
Alert!: Access without authorization denied -- retrying
Retrying with access authorization information.
Looking up 127.0.0.2:901.
Making HTTP connection to 127.0.0.2:901.
Username for 'SWAT' at server 127.0.0.2:901':username
Password:****
Sending HTTP request.
HTTP request sent; waiting for response.
Samba Web Administration Tool (p1 of 2)
Home Globals Shares Printers Status View Config Password Management
```

Most important, continue systematically ruling out parts of the system.

The Navigation Buttons

Seven navigation buttons appear across the top of the SWAT screen. These are graphical buttons and do not appear raised. If you're using Lynx, they're words that appear across the top of the console. The seven buttons are Home, Globals, Shares, Printers, Status, View, and Password. Figure 13.2 shows these buttons at the top of the SWAT home page, as shown through Netscape Navigator.

FIGURE 13.2

*The SWAT home
page.*

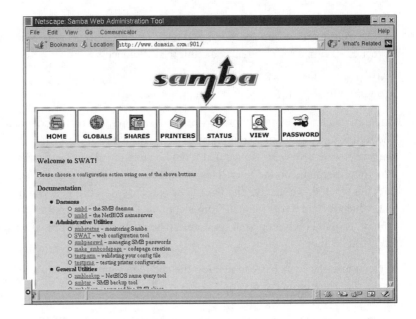

The Home button leads to SWAT's home page, which contains links to various help files. The Globals button brings up a screen to edit parameters in the [global] section. The Shares button brings up a screen to add, delete, or edit non-printer shares. The Printers button brings up a screen to add, delete, or modify printer shares.

The Status button brings up a screen showing active connections, active shares, and open files. If you're logged in as root, it has buttons to restart daemons and kill active connections.

The View button brings up a parameter listing similar to the output of testparm. The Password button brings up a screen to modify passwords, including those of others. However, unless you're logged into SWAT as root, any attempt to modify passwords of other users silently fails.

Using SWAT for Information

Although SWAT configuration might not be for everyone, few fault its amazing potential for gathering Samba and smb.conf information. When used to gather information, it's usually essential to run SWAT in a way that precludes smb.conf modification. Even so, you should always back up smb.conf before running SWAT.

Do Not Log in as root

Never log into SWAT as root when using SWAT to gather information. Logging in as root enables you to change smb.conf, which is not the goal.

Whomever you log in as, make sure you do not see the Commit Changes and Delete buttons. If you see these two buttons, exit immediately and set smb.conf's ownership and permissions in a SWAT-secure way. Figure 13.3 shows the Globals page for a nonwriting user.

FIGURE 13.3

The SWAT Globals page, as seen by a read-only user.

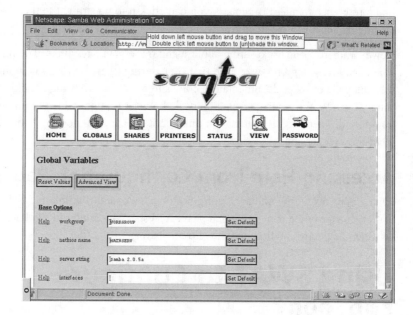

Viewing Current Samba Options

Click the View button to get a view of the Samba system. You'll notice it's very similar to the output of testparm but easier to read. The information is also similar to the contents of the parameter fields in SWAT's Globals and Shares screens.

View Toggle Button

Near the top of the View screen, just under the large words Current Config, you'll see a gray button called either Normal View or Full View. This is the view toggle button, which toggles between full view, where every global option is enumerated, and normal view, where only those globals not set to the Samba default are listed.

This toggle is great for evaluating what your smb.conf is really doing.

Searching for a specific parameter involves a simple Web browser find operation. However, it's not as quick and easy as a `testparm` into a `grep`.

The Front Page Help File Links

If SWAT had nothing but these links, most of which are to HTML format man pages, it would still be worth its weight in gold. Man pages are incredibly easier to read in a scrollbar-enabled Web browser than in a `less` session with paging and screen repaints. Better still, the Web pages linked to SWAT's home page are hyperlink-enabled, so if you find a reference to `guest account`, you can click it to go straight to the description of the `guest account=` parameter.

However, there's one tricky thing about using these man page links. The links open the man page in a second browser. The first time during a session that a help link is clicked, the man page or other documentation comes to the front. After that, clicking these links simply changes the contents of the help file browser session, which might not be in the foreground. Therefore, if you click a link and it appears that nothing happens, click your other browser session.

Accessing Help from Configuration Pages

Each parameter setting on each configuration page contains a link to the description of that parameter in the `smb.conf` man page. It's especially handy to flip back and forth between the documentation and the current settings of the file.

Using SWAT to Configure `smb.conf`

SWAT provides an easy way to configure `smb.conf`. If proper backup and security are practiced, it's also very safe. This section details the use of SWAT in configuring `smb.conf` and other Samba administration.

The seven navigation buttons appearing across the top of the SWAT screen serve as a "menu" for SWAT. If you're using the Lynx text-based browser, these buttons are simply words that appear across the top of the console. The seven buttons are Home, Globals, Shares, Printers, Status, View, and Password. They were described previously in the section titled "The Navigation Buttons."

Signing on as `root` or a Privileged User

As mentioned before, with a root group and owner and file permissions of 640, SWAT cannot change parameters logged in as anyone but `root`. Setting such a file to 660 constitutes a serious security breach. However, if `smb.conf`'s group is changed to a group containing a small number of trusted individuals, it's safe to give `smb.conf` permissions of 660 because only members of that group can use SWAT to modify `smb.conf`.

Either way, to modify the file you must log in as a user capable of modifying it. If the Commit Changes button shows up, you know you can modify the file. Figure 13.4 shows the Globals page, with the Commit Changes button, as seen by root.

FIGURE 13.4

The SWAT Globals page, as seen by root.

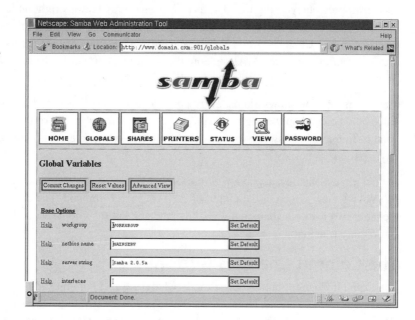

Must Restart Samba to Enable Changes

Some `smb.conf` changes are effective without restarting Samba. Others are not. To prevent problems with configuration and troubleshooting, make it a habit to restart Samba upon completion of changes. This places Samba in a known state.

It's also vital to run `testparm` upon completion of changes. The 10 seconds it takes can save an hour of troubleshooting in the event of a silly `smb.conf` mistake.

Configuring Global Options

The SWAT user can change any global parameter from the Global Variables screen. The Global Variables screen is accessed by clicking the Globals navigation button.

The global variables are critical to the functioning of the Samba server as a whole. Some global variables are rather complex in nature. Using SWAT, with its drop down pick lists and hypertext help links, makes global variable configuration much more straightforward.

The View Toggle Button

As shown previously in Figure 13.4, there are three gray buttons right under the words Global Variables near the top of the page. The three buttons, from left to right, are labeled Commit Changes, Reset Values, and Advanced View. Note that depending on previous work during the SWAT session, the rightmost button may be labeled Basic View. That's because this button is a toggle, called the View toggle button.

The advanced view shows almost every possible global parameter and its value. The value may come about through an explicit declaration in smb.conf or through a Samba default. In the case of synonym (or inverse synonym) parameters, only the primary synonym parameter is shown.

At first glance, the advanced view of the Global Variables screen looks like the full view of SWAT's View screen or the output of the testparm command. The difference is that the latter two list both share and global parameters, but the Global Variables screen shows only true global parameters.

The Commit Changes Button

The Commit Changes button does exactly what it says: It commits any changes made on the Global Variable screen to smb.conf. There is no way to "undo" these changes after they're committed, which is why it's recommended that you back up smb.conf before using SWAT. Any changes made on the Global Variable screen must be committed before you leave this screen. If you click the View navigational button before clicking the Commit Changes button, all your changes are lost.

The Commit Changes button can be used like the Save button in a word processor—to save your work every few minutes or every few configuration changes. That way, if you make a mistake, it can be undone with the Reset Values button without you losing much work.

SWAT makes the simplest possible smb.conf given the changes made. Any specified parameters that match the default for that parameter are simply left out of the file. Older versions of SWAT even removed the [global] name heading, although 2.0.5a no longer does that. All comments are removed from the file.

Although removing explicitly declared default parameters and comments might, upon first thought, appear to reduce the readability of the smb.conf file, the usual effect is to increase readability. Without all the comments and needless defaults cluttering up the file, the parameters that give the setup its personality stand out.

The Reset Values Button

The Reset Values button undoes any changes made in this screen since the last commit or since the screen was entered—whichever occurs last. The way present-day SWAT works, this isn't strictly necessary, because simply moving out of the screen accomplishes the same objective. If later versions of SWAT remember parameters between screen changes, this button will become more important.

The Help File Links

Every parameter's input field has a help link to its left. Each of these links point to that parameter's section in the smb.conf man page. Having that help a click away when deciding on a parameter saves you time and reduces mistakes. These help links should be used whenever you have any uncertainty or curiosity.

The Set Defaults Buttons

Each parameter has a raised, gray Set Default button at the extreme right of the line. When clicked, this button writes the default value of the parameter in the parameter's input field. If this is done in error, it can be backed out with the Reset Values button. Note that SWAT simply deletes any parameters set to the default value from smb.conf.

The Set Default button might not do the obvious. When one parameter's default depends on another parameter's value, the Set Default button yields the default of the dependent parameter based on the *default* value of the independent parameter. This is especially noticeable in the printer command–type share parameters.

Configuring Directory Shares

The SWAT user can change any share parameters from the Share Parameters screen. The first step in accessing the Share Parameters screen is to click the Shares navigational button. That brings up the SWAT Share Parameters page in the choose share state, as shown in Figure 13.5.

FIGURE 13.5

The SWAT Share Parameters page in the Choose Share state, as seen by root.

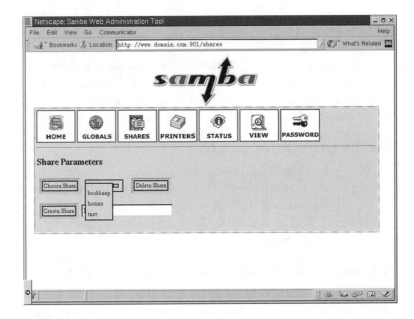

This is where you add, delete, or modify a share. Because there are many shares, one must be chosen for delete and modify operations. Clicking the drop-down list box between the Choose Share and Delete Share buttons brings up a list of available shares. In Figure 13.5, this drop-down list box contains shares bookkeep, homes, and test.

Adding a Share

Type the new share's name (without brackets) in the text box to the right of the Create Share button and then click the Create Share button. This creates a totally default share. The share is then configured by following the instructions in the upcoming "Changing a Share" section.

Deleting a Share

Make sure you really want to delete the share, because there's no undo feature. To proceed with the deletion, pick the share from the drop-down list box between the Choose Share button and the Delete Share button. Then click the Delete Share button to irretrievably delete the share.

Changing a Share

To modify a share, pick the desired share from the drop-down list box between the Choose Share button and the Delete Share button. Then click the Choose Share button. You'll be brought to the SWAT Share Parameters page in the Modify Share state, as shown in Figure 13.6.

FIGURE 13.6

The SWAT Share Parameters page in the Modify Share state, as seen by root.

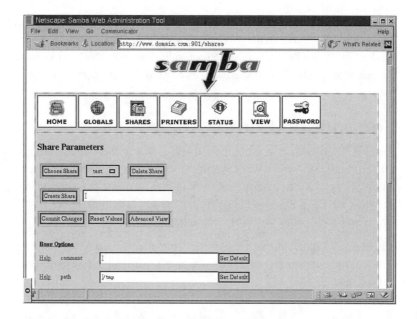

This screen has an input field for each share parameter. Each parameter's input field is preloaded with the present value, taking into account program defaults and defaults created by the placement of the share parameter in [global], as well as the parameter's specified value within the share. Boolean shares have yes/no drop-down list boxes, whereas all other parameters have text boxes. Each parameter has a link to its man page information on the left and a Set Default button to the right. Note that the Set Default button sets the default to the smbd program default, even in the case of the share being set to a different value in the [global] section.

If a Set Default button is clicked erroneously, the result can be backed out by retyping the correct value in the field or by clicking the Reset Values button near the top of the page. Note that clicking Reset Values backs out all changes made since the last commit or since the page was entered. When unsure whether you want to back out, use the Set Default button. It's best to place the field's contents in the paste buffer before clicking the button. That way, it's easy to retype the contents into the field if need be.

As shown previously in Figure 13.6, the page contains a Commit Changes button, a Reset Values button, and a View toggle button that is titled either "Advanced View" or "Basic View," depending on its state. The advanced view shows the value of every parameter the share can have, whereas the basic view shows only the most common share parameters. The latter is great for setting up a simple share, and the former works well for troubleshooting and setting up sophisticated shares. The availability of help next to each parameter makes the job easy.

13

USING SWAT
FOR SAMBA
CONFIGURATION

Every few changes, click the Commit Changes button to write the changes to `smb.conf`. This is very much like frequently saving a word-processing job. If a mistake is made, it can be backed out by clicking the Reset Values button, which backs out all changes since the last commit (or since the screen was entered if the Commit Changes button has not been clicked).

Configuring Printer Shares

Clicking the Printers navigation button brings you to the Printer Parameters screen. The Printer Parameters screen works identically with the regular share screens, in that you pick a printer share to modify or delete, or else you type in the name of a printer share and click the Create Printer button. In the modify state, this screen has the same Commit Changes, Reset Values and View toggle buttons.

The major difference is that the Printer Parameters screen has printing-specific parameters that don't appear on normal shares, and it's missing a few parameters appearing on a normal share.

Using SWAT for Samba Password Administration

Click the Password navigation button to get to the Server Password Management screen shown in Figures 13.7 and 13.8.

FIGURE 13.7

The top view of the SWAT Password Management page, as seen by root.

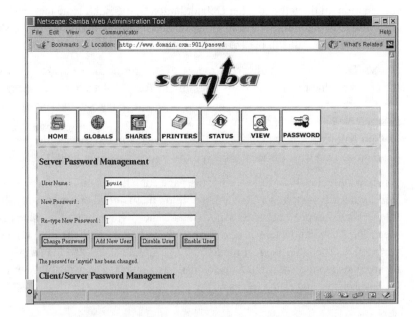

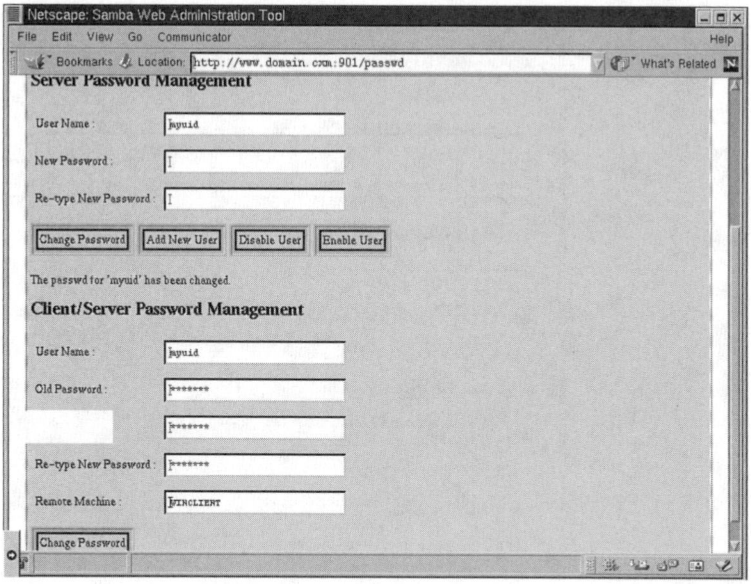

FIGURE **13.8**

*The bottom view
of the SWAT
Password
Management
page, as seen
by* root.

This page has two sections labeled "Server Password Management" and "Client/Server Password Management." The Server Password Management section changes the Samba encrypted password (smbpasswd) on the local server, whereas the Client/Server Password Management section changes the Samba encrypted password on other SMB servers on the network. As root, you can add, disable, or enable users.

You may find it easier to administer passwords from the UNIX command line.

Using SWAT to Administer Samba

Clicking the Status navigation button brings up the Server Status page. From this page daemons can be killed and restarted, connections viewed and terminated, and open files viewed. While all of this could be done from the UNIX command line, SWAT's Server Status page provides a convenient command center for SWAT administration. The SWAT Server Status page is shown in Figures 13.9 and 13.10.

13

USING SWAT
FOR SAMBA
CONFIGURATION

FIGURE **13.9**
*The top view of
the SWAT Server
Status page, as
seen by* root.

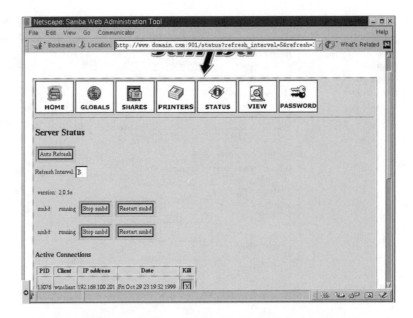

FIGURE **13.10**
*The bottom view
of the SWAT
Server Status
page, as seen
by* root.

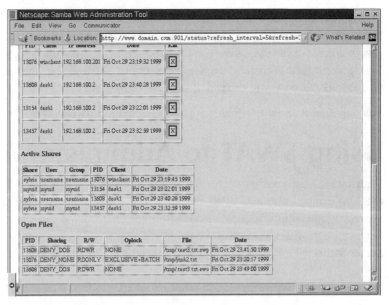

This page serves as a Samba command console.

Refresh Button and Interval Text Box

The manner in which this page stays up-to-date is configurable. The Refresh button is a toggle, labeled either "Auto Refresh" or "Stop Refreshing." The Refresh Interval field is a text box when the button is labeled "Auto Refresh" and a nonwriteable label when the button is labeled "Stop Refresh."

To set the refresh rate and start auto-refreshing, input the number of seconds between refreshes and then click the button. The default refresh rate is 30 seconds, which is an excellent compromise between currency and readability. Refreshes clear the screen and move to the top of the page. Frequent refreshes (every 5 to 10 seconds) can be disturbing.

In the non-refresh mode (when the button is labeled "Auto Refresh"), the page can be refreshed with the browser's reload feature or by clicking the Status navigation button.

Daemon Buttons

The daemon buttons are labeled "Stop smbd," "Restart smbd," "Stop nmbd," and "Restart nmbd." The two labeled "Stop" are actually toggles that are relabeled "Start" when clicked and "Stop" when clicked again. The "Restart" buttons stop then restart their respective daemons. Therefore, when you click the Restart button, its corresponding stop/start toggle is labeled "Stop."

These buttons perform a similar function as the Samba restart script (/etc/rc.d/init.d/smb on Red Hat machines).

Active Connections Table and Kill Button

The Active Connections table lists all client connections to the Samba server, with one row per client session (a box can run several smbclient sessions). Each row has the process ID, the client's NetBIOS name, the client's IP address, and the date and time the connection was initiated.

At the right end of each row is a kill button that terminates the connection. Because this also closes any open files, it should be used in emergencies only. Typically, this is used to remotely administrate when a user has left a document up on his or her screen and gone home for the day.

Active Shares Table

The Active Shares table has a row for each share access. This, and the Open Files table, are critical information for troubleshooting user problems. This is where you can deduce

13

USING SWAT
FOR SAMBA
CONFIGURATION

whether a user has locked a file and gone home, or whether a share is in use prior to deactivating that share, or a host of other administrative tasks necessary in multiuser networks. Each row of the Active Shares table contains the following information:

- Share
- User
- Group
- PID
- Client
- Date

The PID, client, and date are actually information corresponding to rows in the Active Connections table. Note also that the user and group are the service user and group (%u and %g), meaning they're affected by `force user=` and `force group=`.

Open Files Table

The Open Files table lists open files. It has a row for each access to each file opened. Each row contains the following information:

- PID
- Sharing
- R/W
- Oplock
- File
- Date

The PID column is the connection's PID. The Sharing column indicates the DOS sharing bitmap, such as `DENY_DOS`, `DENY_NONE`, and so on. The R/W column indicates whether the file is opened as read-write or read-only. The Oplock column indicates what kind of oplock the accessing application has placed on the file. This is extremely handy for diagnosing problems involving Visual C++ and MS Access as well as problems where "old versions" of files seem to come back. The File column lists the complete path of the file, and the Date column lists the date the file was opened. Note that the date is *not* the connection date.

Summary

SWAT is a browser-interfaced configuration application for Samba administration, with heavy emphasis on configuring `smb.conf`. SWAT has been bundled with Samba distributions since Samba version 2.0. It's bundled with most Linux distributions because they bundle Samba. It can be compiled with SWAT source code.

To enable SWAT, modify `/etc/services` to enable SWAT as port 901, modify `/etc/inetd.conf` to start SWAT from `inetd`, and then restart `inetd`. If you're specifying a TCP wrapper in `inetd.conf`, also make the proper changes to `/etc/hosts.deny` or `/etc/hosts.allow` (the former being preferred in the Caldera default installation).

SWAT usage is intuitive. Seven navigation buttons appear across the top of the screen (or top of page if you're using Lynx). These buttons are graphical rather than raised gray, and they're labeled from left to right: Home, Globals, Shares, Printers, Status, View, and Password.

Clicking the Globals navigation button brings up a page in which to modify global parameters. Clicking the Shares navigation button brings up the Share Choice page, where a new share can be added or an existing share can be selected for deletion or modification. Clicking the Choose Share button after selecting the share off the drop-down list brings up the Share Parameter page, where all share parameters are available for modification.

Both the Global Parameter and Share Parameter pages contain a button to toggle between advanced view and basic view. In most cases, any parameter set to the Samba default value is simply deleted from `smb.conf`, thus yielding a very simple file. Comments are also deleted.

SWAT has some additional functionality. A certain level of live system administration is available via the Status navigational button. A listing of all parameters can be gained by clicking the View navigational button. Also, password administration is available via the Password navigational button.

SWAT is an unparalleled source of information, both for the local configuration and for Samba itself. A wide variety of hyperlink-enabled, HTML-enabled man pages and other documents are available from SWAT's home page. On the Global Parameters and Share Parameters pages, to the left of each parameter is a link to its part of the `smb.conf` man page, once again fully hyperlink-enabled HTML.

SWAT is one of the few tools that correctly identifies the value of certain defaulted parameters. A great example is the standard Red Hat setup, which comes with `printing=sysv`. That setting changes the effective value of `print command=`. The `testparm` utility does not recognize that change, but the correct value is shown in SWAT's print command field. However, clicking the Default button changes that value to the same value as shown by `testparm`.

SWAT must be used safely. Always back up smb.conf before using SWAT. SWAT can completely and irretrievably change a carefully crafted smb.conf. A wrong permission can give a normally read-only user write privileges.

SWAT must be used securely. In any but the most encapsulated, trusting environments, use TCP wrappers to restrict SWAT to 127.0.0.2 so it can't be used over an intranet or the Internet.

Make sure smb.conf is set up so that most users do not get write access. For an smb.conf whose owner and group is root, this means chmod 640. Perhaps a better alternative is to chown the file to a group of a few trusted people and make the file chmod 660. That way, members of that group log in as themselves to modify the file, and the root password never goes over the wire. It's important to remember that because of the power of the root preexec= and root postexec= parameters, anyone who can change smb.conf can overwrite /etc/passwd or create an suid root copy of bash, sh, or other shells.

Even with all these safety procedures in place, everyone using SWAT must remember to close *all* browser sessions after finishing their SWAT work. Otherwise, during a short break, a mischievous coworker can come to their workstations and access SWAT without authentication. The original authentication is persistent as long as any copies of the browser remain open. Once all copies have been closed, reauthentication is required.

When used with a little care and intelligence, SWAT is a major timesaver, a great information source, and a handy troubleshooting tool.

CHAPTER 14

Using Samba Server-Side Automation

by Steve Litt

In This Chapter

Server-side automation (SSA) refers to a Samba client triggering a UNIX process. Typically the Samba client is on a Windows box. The two main uses of server-side automation are to perform initialization and finalization for share access and to trigger jobs on the UNIX box from the Windows client.

Examples in This Chapter

All examples in this chapter use a server named `mainserv`, located at `192.168.100.1/255.255.255.0`. The user is called `username`, a name unlikely to be confused with genuine users on your system. These examples have been checked on a Celeron-equipped machine running Red Hat Linux 6.0.

The client in the examples is a Windows 98 machine called `WINCLI` at `192.168.100.201`, with password encryption.

If you're following along with this chapter's examples, it's easiest to create a user called `username`.

Caution

Before attempting any of the examples in this chapter, be sure to back up your existing `smb.conf`!

Three Types of Server-Side Automation

Here are the three types of SSA:

- Exec methods
- Pseudo printer methods
- Magic script methods

Exec methods use the `preexec=`, `postexec=`, `root preexec=` and `root postexec=` parameters. Because they are invoked at share connection and disconnection, they are best for share initialization and finalization.

Pseudo printer methods use the `print command=` parameter in a print share to run a nonprinting process, thus enabling Windows processes to kick off a UNIX process after passing data to it.

Magic scripts use the `magic script=` parameter to define a filename which, when written to a share, is used as a script. That script's output is sent to the file defined by the `magic output=` parameter. Magic scripts are an extremely powerful technology that's still experimental and does not work in some environments.

The Variable Substitution Strings

Variable substitution strings give SSA its configurability and flexibility. When used in a server-side automation statement, these parameters are replaced by their values. Table 14.1 shows the most common variable substitution strings.

TABLE 14.1   The Variable Substitution Strings

String	Description
%s	The name of the file passed to a print share
%T	Current date and time
%u	Current service username
%g	Primary group name of %u
%H	Home directory of %u
%U	Session username
%G	Primary group name of %U
%d	Current server process's server ID
%L	Server's NetBIOS name
%S	Current service name
%P	Current service root directory
%p	Path of service's home directory
%R	Selected protocol level after protocol negotiation
%I	Client machine's IP address
%m	Client machine's NetBIOS name
%a	Remote machine's architecture
%M	Client machine's Internet name
%h	Internet hostname Samba is running on
%N	Name of your NIS home directory server
%v	Samba version

14

USING SAMBA
SERVER-SIDE
AUTOMATION

The remainder of this section contains a more detailed discussion of these parameters. All of these variable substitution strings are highly useful for troubleshooting. Most are also useful for directory creation and navigation, file manipulation, and many other Server Side Automation activities. Note that the %u, %g, %H, %U, and %G replacement strings involve complex user and group determinations explained in Chapter 7, "Determining Samba Access".

%s is replaced with the name of the file passed to a print share. %s is only valid in print shares. It's vital in pseudo printer SSA because all passed data comes through the file named by this parameter. The following print command parameter appends the file "printed" in Windows to a log file:

```
print command=cat %s >> all.log; rm %s
```

Note that the preceding command deletes the file after appending it. It's the responsibility of the print command to delete the print file after using it. This is a simple example of pseudo printer server-side automation, and it's discussed in detail in the "Pseudo Samba Printer Server-Side Automation" section, later in this chapter.

%T is replaced with the date and time in the following form:

```
yyyy/mm/dd hh:mm:ss
```

The hours are in 24-hour time. This parameter can be used in any of the three forms of SSA. It's highly useful in any kind of diagnostic or logging. Because it sorts from earlier to later, it can also be used as a record key in applications not likely to have more than one new record per second.

%u is replaced with the current service username. As explained in the "The Three Levels of Users and Groups" section of Chapter 7, there are three levels of users and groups:

- Requested user and group (%U and %G)
- Effective user and group (no substitution variables)
- Service user and group (%u and %g)

The current services username is the one used to interact with UNIX, as opposed to interacting with Samba.

%u is the force user= user if a force user= parameter exists. If not, it's the guest account= parameter value if guest access was granted. Otherwise, it's the requested user (%U).

This parameter can be used to name or point to files on a per-user basis or to map users to directories.

%g is replaced with the current service group, which defaults to the primary group name of the %u variable substitution string. Once again, this is the group used to interact with UNIX, as opposed to Samba. %g is the value of `force group=` if that parameter exists. If not, it's the primary group of the `force user=` parameter value if that parameter exists. If not, it's the primary group of the `guest account=` parameter value if that parameter exists. If not, it's the primary group of the requested user (%U).

%H is replaced with the home directory of the current service user (%u). This means that this parameter is affected by `force user=`, `force group=`, and guesting. Because `force user=` and `force group=` are usually used to group multiple users or groups into a single user or group, this makes perfect sense (although in the case of guesting there's some uncertainty).

%H is used primarily to define a directory relative to the user's home directory. Home directory dot file protection is an excellent example that's covered later in this chapter.

%U is replaced with the session user, also called the *requested user*. This is the username initially passed from the client. This parameter can be used to name or point to files on a per-user basis or to map users to directories.

%G is replaced with the primary group name of %U. As the primary group of the requested user, this substitution variable can be used to name or identify files and directories on a per-group basis.

%d is replaced with the current server process's server ID. Primarily used in diagnostic logging, this substitution variable could also be used in exotic ways, such as killing its own process.

%L is replaced with the server's NetBIOS name. Not extensively used, this substitution variable could be used as the servername portion of an `smbclient` call, thus setting up a "recursive" SSA. Obviously, any such recursion needs a sophisticated script to deduce when to end the recursion and back out.

%S is replaced with the current service name. The service name is the share name (the name between the square brackets). This can be very handy when several shares share a common directory (path).

%P is replaced with the current service root directory. In other words, it's replaced by the full path of the share's `path=` value. A script could use this to detect whether one is in the root of a share.

%p is replaced with the path of service's home directory. The operation of this substitution variable is very nonintuitive. It does not typically return the same as %P. It sometimes returns the same as %S.

%R is replaced with the selected protocol level after protocol negotiation. In the absence of a global protocol= parameter, it's usually replaced by NT1. If there's a protocol= parameter, it's usually replaced by the value of that parameter. This is useful only in very specialized situations.

%I is replaced with the client machine's IP address. This substitution variable can be used to send a message back to the client machine or even to initiate an ftp transfer to the client machine. It's also useful in diagnostic logging.

%m is replaced with the client machine's NetBIOS name. Once again, this substitution variable can be used to send a message back to the client machine or even to initiate an ftp transfer to the client machine. It's also useful in diagnostic logging.

%a is replaced with the remote machine's architecture, which can be Samba, WfWg, WinNT, or Win95 (for Windows 9*x*). Anything else is replaced by UNKNOWN. It can be used to run different UNIX commands against files created on different clients. For instance, one might remove carriage returns from files created in Windows. Note that the client architecture recognition is imperfect.

%v is replaced by the Samba version. This substitution variable is useful for diagnostics. It may also be useful for passing to canned scripts that work differently for different Samba versions.

%M is replaced with the client machine's Fully Qualified Domain Name (FQDN), sometimes called its Internet name, which can be useful when Samba shares are accessed via the Internet (not recommended).

%h is replaced with the hostname of the Samba server, which is excellent troubleshooting information on networks with multiple SMB servers.

%N is replaced with the server containing your NIS home directory, which is valuable troubleshooting information on networks using NIS.

Exec Server-Side Automation

Exec SSA is used primarily for share connection setup and disconnection cleanup. It occurs only on the specific events of connection and disconnection. Because disconnection is SMB client dependent, it's not always reliable. Because disconnection is unpredictable, any subsequent connection is also unpredictable, at least after the first connection after a client reboot.

The Four Exec Server-Side Automation Commands

Exec SSA is performed by one or more of these four commands:

- `preexec=`
- `postexec=`
- `root preexec=`
- `root postexec=`

The value of each is a command to be run. Most variable substitution strings can be used, with %s being a conspicuous exception. `preexec=` and `root preexec=` are run when the connection is made. `postexec=` and `root postexec=` are run when the connection is broken.

The "root" exec parameters differ in that they're run as `root`, and they can reach outside the share to do their work. This is why `smb.conf` should never be editable by normal users. The root exec commands can easily be configured to replace `/etc/passwd`. These commands can copy `bash` or `sh` to an suid root version. A malicious party can cause a lot of mischief with these parameters.

For the same reasons, care should be taken to avoid any user input to the root version of these commands. It's best to avoid the root versions if possible.

Exec SSA is best for share-maintenance activities needed during connection and disconnection. Pseudo printers and magic scripts are much better for triggering UNIX processes on demand from Windows.

Exec Server-Side Automation Proof of Concept: Log File

The simplest example of exec SSA is the creation of a log file. This is also an excellent diagnostic tool, because it records every connection and disconnection from the share.

Creating an `smb.conf` for Your SSA Proof of Concept

While it's not necessary to create an `smb.conf` file specifically for SSA, using a tiny `smb.conf` invariably eases troubleshooting. Samba has the huge advantage of placing almost all configuration in one file, meaning a complete configuration change is as easy as a file backup, file copy, and daemon restart. However, if your situation does not allow complete `smb.conf` replacement, most of the following examples can be done just using

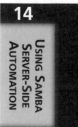

14

USING SAMBA
SERVER-SIDE
AUTOMATION

the share definitions. If you make a new `smb.conf`, be sure to back up your existing `smb.conf`. The following is the recommended proof of concept `smb.conf`:

```
encrypt passwords=yes
workgroup=mygroup
netbios name=mainserv

[test]
path=/home/username/test
preexec =echo Pre :%T: U.G=%U.%G u.g=%u.%g >> test.log
postexec=echo Post:%T: U.G=%U.%G u.g=%u.%g >> test.log
```

This appends the date, time, requested user and group, and service user and group to the file `test.log` in the directory specified by `path=`. The lines in that log file look like this:

```
Pre :1999/10/30 14:40:32: U.G=username.username u.g=username.username
Post:1999/10/30 14:40:34: U.G=username.username u.g=username.username
```

Triggering SSA from Explorer

Navigating to a Samba share in Explorer makes the connection (assuming there was no connection already in effect) and triggers `preexec=`. However, navigating back out does not cause a disconnect. The next section discusses how to disconnect.

Precision Triggering

Windows Explorer and Network Neighborhood cannot disconnect. The `net use` command must be used for that. First, any drive letters mapped to the share must be deleted. You can find the drive letters with the `net use` command, as shown in the following sample session:

```
C:\WINDOWS>net use

Status          Local name      Remote name
-------------------------------------------------
OK              V:              \\MAINSERV\TEST
OK              X:              \\MAINSERV\TEST
The command was completed successfully.

C:\WINDOWS>
```

In the preceding example, both V: and X: are mapped to \\mainserv\test, so they both must be deleted, as shown in the following session:

```
C:\WINDOWS>net use v: /delete
There are open files on the connection. Close all files and quit all programs
related to the connection before you try to delete it.
Do you want to continue this operation? (Y/N) [N]:y
The command was completed successfully.
```

```
C:\WINDOWS>net use x: /delete
There are open files on the connection. Close all files and quit all programs
related to the connection before you try to delete it.
Do you want to continue this operation? (Y/N) [N]:y
The command was completed successfully.

C:\WINDOWS>net use

Status          Local name      Remote name
-------------------------------------------------
OK                              \\MAINSERV\TEST
The command was completed successfully.

C:\WINDOWS>
```

Drives V: and X: were deleted in the preceding session, but the final `net use` command shows there's still a connection. The final step in disconnecting from the share is to delete the share, itself, as shown in the following session:

```
C:\WINDOWS>net use \\mainserv\test /delete
The command was completed successfully.

C:\WINDOWS>net use
There are no entries in the list.

C:\WINDOWS>
```

A `tail -f test.log` command would show the `postexec` triggered immediately upon the preceding `delete` command.

Once there's no connection, triggering a connection is as simple as renavigating to the share in Explorer or issuing the following command from the Windows command prompt:

```
$ net use \\mainserv\test
```

Precedence of Root Execs

Add the following two lines to the [test] share:

```
root preexec=echo rpre %T >> test.log
root postexec=echo rpos %T >> test.log
```

Examining the log file shows that on connection, the `root preexec` is triggered before the `preexec`, whereas on disconnection the `postexec` is triggered before the `root postexec`. This ordering is not sensitive to the placement of the lines in `smb.conf`.

Exec Server-Side Automation Home Directory Protection

Creating log files is interesting and a great troubleshooting aid, but it has little relevance to real-life usage of Samba. A much more common usage of exec SSA is protecting the UNIX contents of the [homes] share. By default, [homes] paths to the user's home directory. That directory contains files a typical Windows user has no business seeing, and under certain circumstances the user can delete them, even if they start with a dot.

There are many ways to protect the contents of the user's UNIX home directory. The method used here is to point [homes] to a directory called samba, below the user's home directory.

The problem is that directory may not exist for new users. The network administrator could create a script to create samba below the new user's home directory. However, an easier way is to use exec SSA to create the directory. For instance, create the following [homes] share:

```
[homes]
read only=no
path=%H/samba
root preexec=mkdir -m 711 %H/samba;chown %u.%g %H/samba
```

In the preceding share, the share points to a subdirectory called samba, below the user's home directory. Before connection, the directory is created by the mkdir command and set to the proper ownership with the chown command.

If the directory already exists with the proper ownership, this command does nothing. A slightly more complex command can be constructed to test for the existence of the directory before using the mkdir and chown commands.

This server-side automation must use the root preexec= rather than preexec= parameter. Use of the latter results in errors.

> **Note**
>
> In testing the preceding share, it's possible to get in a state where there's a connection to [homes] but no samba directory, in which case any attempt at access errors out. This state can be corrected with net use \\mainserv\homes /delete.

Pseudo Samba Printer Server-Side Automation

Many specifications call for a Windows process to trigger a UNIX process. Because exec SSA methods work only on connect and disconnect, using those methods to fulfil that spec would be contrived at best. Fortunately, pseudo printers offer an ideal vehicle for triggering a UNIX process from a Windows process. Better still, the basic function of a print share enables passing a large file from the Windows process to the UNIX process.

A pseudo printer is a real Samba print share, with `print ok=yes` and a path (though usually not `/var/spool/samba`). Just like a "legitimate" print share, the material to be "printed" is passed as a file in the path. A pseudo printer differs in only one respect: Its `print command=` parameter runs the desired UNIX process instead of printing the file.

This chapter gives the following examples of pseudo printer SSA:

- Log file proof of concept
- Single-program pseudo printer
- Multi-program pseudo printer
- Batch record adder

Log File Proof of Concept

This is the simplest possible pseudo printer. It does nothing but write a record to a log file when its share is "printed to." Start with this `smb.conf` share:

```
[pseudo]
print ok=yes
path=/home/username/test
print command=echo Pseudoprinter : %T >> test.log;rm %s
```

The `print ok=yes` line makes this a printer share. The path specifies that the file to be printed, which has a variable substitution string of `%s`, is to be placed in the `/home/username/test` directory. To trigger this share, from your Windows computer input the following command:

```
C:\WINDOWS>echo hello > \\mainserv\pseudo
```

The preceding command "prints" the word "hello" (as a file) to "printer" `\\mainserv\pseudo`. The bottom line in `/home/username/test/test.log` looks like this:

```
Pseudoprinter : 1999/10/30 16:52:18
```

14

USING SAMBA
SERVER-SIDE
AUTOMATION

Taking it one step further, you can record the word after `echo` in the DOS command. To do so, change the `print command=` statement to this:

```
print command=echo Pseudoprinter : %T : $(head -n1 %s) >> test.log;rm %s
```

In the preceding command, `%s` represents the file sent from DOS to be printed, and `head -n1 %s` prints the first line of that file to stdout. Because that command is in parentheses preceded by a dollar sign, its output is used as an argument to the `echo` command. The result is that if you execute the following three commands on the Windows client, you see log output created by the pseudo printer share's `print command=` parameter:

```
C:\WINDOWS>echo Samba > \\mainserv\pseudo
C:\WINDOWS>echo is > \\mainserv\pseudo
C:\WINDOWS>echo terrific > \\mainserv\pseudo
```

After executing the previous three commands on the Windows client, the last three lines of `test.log` look like this:

```
Pseudoprinter : 1999/10/30 18:53:38 : Samba
Pseudoprinter : 1999/10/30 18:53:45 : is
Pseudoprinter : 1999/10/30 18:53:52 : terrific
```

This is an introduction into using the contents of the print file as an input to the UNIX program to be executed.

Single-Program Pseudo Printer

The following pseudo printer copies the last 100 entries from the access log `ldp.cxm` to a file called `/tmp/ldp.cxm`, presumably to be picked up via another Samba share:

```
[pseudo]
print ok=yes
path=/home/username/test
print command=tail -n100 /etc/httpd/logs/ldp.cxm-access_log >
➥ /tmp/dump.rpt &
```

To be practical, a real tail-stripping program would need to strip off a certain date range and would need to convert to the CR/LF DOS file format. However, this serves as an example of a very real use for server-side automation.

Multi-Program Pseudo Printer

It's impractical to add a print share for each needed command. This section shows how to use one print share to run a wide variety of commands in a safe manner. The first line of the print file identifies the command, but it identifies it relative to the `scripts` directory below the pseudo printer's path, thereby preventing the user from trying to run commands in `/usr/bin` (and so on).

All commands to be run by this pseudo printer are located in the `scripts` directory below the pseudo printer's path. Each of these commands takes exactly one argument—the name of the print file. Therefore, all communication between the Windows process and the command occurs in the print file, starting with the second line. Remember, the first line identifies *which* command is run. All these commands are started from the pseudo printer's path, *not* the `scripts` directory below it. Each script or command in the `scripts` directory must assume its current directory is the pseudo printer's path.

The following printer share calls the script named in the first line of the print file, using the print filename as the one and only argument:

```
[pseudo]
path = /home/username/test
print ok = Yes
print command=scripts/$(head -n1 %s |  tr -d '\r') %s;rm %s
```

Examine this part of the `print` command:

```
$(head -n1 %s | tr -d '\r')
```

In the preceding command particle, the `head` command strips off the first line of file `%s`; then the `tr` portion strips off any carriage return from that line to make it UNIX compatible. The dollar sign and parentheses take the output of that command and assign it to a variable suitable for inclusion in the command line. If the first line of the print file is the word `loc`, the preceding command particle evaluates to `loc`. Therefore, script `scripts/loc` is run, and because the argument `%s` follows it, it becomes `arg1` to `scripts/loc`.

The `;rm %s` command deletes the print file to prevent jam-ups, whereas the trailing `&` returns control to Samba immediately to prevent perceived delays on the Windows side.

The next step is to create a script to complete the `print` commands. The following is a script for operating the `locate` command, on the word or phrase in the second line of the `print` command, and write the results to `/tmp/loc.rpt`, which presumably is available to Windows via another share:

```
#!/bin/sh
str=$(head -n2 $1 | tail -n1 | tr -d '\r')
/usr/bin/locate $str | scripts/u2d.pl > /tmp/loc.rpt
```

In the preceding script, note that paths to all executables are explicitly specified in case the normal `$PATH` variable is not available. Note also the `scripts/u2d.pl` filter, which restores carriage returns for DOS compatibility, thereby enabling the Windows Notepad editor to directly access `/tmp/loc.rpt` through a share. There are many such filters available, so pick your favorite. In case you don't have one, here's the code to `u2d.pl`:

```
#!/usr/bin/perl -w
while (<STDIN>)
```

14

```
{
chomp($_);
print $_ . "\r\n";
}
```

The final step is to create a Windows batch file (let's call it ssacmd.bat) to easily access the loc command. This command's first argument is the name of the command to run, and the second argument is the string to pass the command:

```
echo %1 > temp.tmp
echo %2 %3 %4 %5 %6 %7 %8 %9 >> temp.tmp
copy temp.tmp \\mainserv\pseudo
```

The preceding code passes a two-line file to the printer, the first line being the name of the command, and the second being the command tail for the command. To create a report on the results of the UNIX locate postgres command, use this command from the Windows command line:

```
C:\WINDOWS>ssacmd loc postgres
```

Obviously many more features are required to make this useful in a real environment, but it serves as an example of how useful pseudo printers can be.

Adding a Second Command

A second command can be added simply by creating the command in the scripts subdirectory below the pseudo printer. This command adds a single person to a list kept in the people subdirectory below the pseudo printer. This command is called addname and looks like this:

```
#!/bin/sh

newname=$(head -n2 $1 | tail -n1 | tr -d '\r')
if !(grep -iq "$newname" people/people.txt); then
 echo $newname >> people/people.txt;
 sort -f -o people/people.txt people/people.txt;

fi
```

The preceding command checks for the person's name in the file; then, if the person is not already in the file, it adds the person and re-sorts the file. This can be tested with the Windows side ssacmd.bat as shown in the following five commands:

```
C:\WINDOWS>ssacmd addname Zelda Zimmerman
C:\WINDOWS>ssacmd addname Yolanda Yarborough
C:\WINDOWS>ssacmd addname Alex Alexander
C:\WINDOWS>ssacmd addname Edward Edwards
C:\WINDOWS>ssacmd addname Douglas Donnegan
```

> **Note**
>
> If these are run with less than a second or so between them, they error out on an access error of the DOS temporary file `temp.tmp`. This can be prevented by placing a delaying command between `ssacmd` commands.

After the five preceding Windows commands are run, the `people.txt` file looks like this (the command is run from `/home/username/test`):

```
$ cat people/people.txt
Alex Alexander
Douglas Donnegan
Edward Edwards
Yolanda Yarborough
Zelda Zimmerman
$
```

The `addname` example is obviously not ready for prime time. A real application would add names to a database, not a text file. A real application would have record locking for multiuser access. A real application would sort by last name and define when uppercase and lowercase are used. A real application likely would have field separators so there's no ambiguity about whether William Van Gelder's middle name is Van or his last name is Van Gelder. All of these features can be easily added to this example.

Batch Record Adder

The previous examples were trivial uses of pseudo printers in that they used only the first two lines of file. This example uses a longer file, while still retaining the simplicity necessary for an example. To begin, create the following file called `scripts/addnames.pl` (note the plural):

```perl
#!/usr/bin/perl -w
use strict;
my($filename)="people/people.txt";

# GRAB THE EXISTING LIST
open(NAMELIST, "<$filename");
my(@namelist) =<NAMELIST>;
close(NAMELIST);

# GRAB THE ADD LIST, BLOW OFF PROGRAM NAME AT TOP
open(PRINTFILE, "<" . $ARGV[0]);
my(@addlist) = <PRINTFILE>;
close(PRINTFILE);
shift @addlist;
```

14

```
# MERGE, UPCASE, SORT
push(@namelist, @addlist);
for (@namelist) {tr/[a-z]/[A-Z]/;}
@namelist = sort { $a cmp $b } @namelist;

# DELETE DUPS AND REWRITE NAME LIST
my($prev) = 'noname';
my(@out) = grep($_ ne $prev && ($prev = $_), @namelist);
open(NAMELIST, ">$filename");
print NAMELIST @out;
close(NAMELIST);
```

Now create the following adds.txt file on the Windows machine:

```
addnames.pl
Zelda Zimmerman
Ursula Ullman
Tommy Thompson
Steve Shapiro
Rita Rhodes
Felice Fredericks
George Gilmore
```

Notice that Zelda Zimmerman is already in people/people.txt from a prior example. The program leaves only one copy of her name because it has a "delete duplicates" process. Now add the names by copying to the printer share:

$ copy adds.txt \\mainserv\pseudo

The people from the Windows box's adds.txt file are now in the UNIX box's people/people.txt file, converted to uppercase and sorted in alphabetical order.

Once again, this example is not ready for prime time. It needs file or record locking, separate fields for first and last names as well as other information, and a real database to be useful. However, it does give you an idea how a DOS or Windows process can easily update UNIX data.

Printing Directly from Windows Applications

In an ideal world, you could link a Generic/Text Only Windows printer to the pseudo print share and trigger SSA. Unfortunately, most Windows apps, even supposed "text editors," insist on putting font, margin, and spacing information in their print files. Printing to a Generic/Text Only printer does not back out the font, margins, and spacing.

A better link directly from Windows applications is via VBA macros. A VBA macro can export the text to a text file and copy that file to the pseudo printer, all with the click of a single icon.

The following is an MS Word VBA macro, called `pseudoprint`, that can be attached to an icon or key combination. It saves the current file as text file `c:\temp33.txt` and then calls `mybat.bat`, which does the copy to the pseudo printer:

```
Sub pseudoprint()
ActiveDocument.SaveAs FileName:="C:\temp33.txt", _
  FileFormat:=wdFormatText
Shell ("c:\mybat.bat")
End Sub
```

Note that the preceding macro does not change the filename or file format of the current document. We wouldn't want it to. Once the file is written out as pure text, it can be copied to the pseudo printer. The following is a batch file to do the copy:

```
echo addnames.pl > c:\temp34.txt
type c:\temp33.txt >> c:\temp34.txt
copy c:\temp34.txt \\mainserv\pseudo
```

Note that the preceding batch file prepends a line containing the phrase `addnames.pl` to the text file from Microsoft Word. As previously explained in the "Batch Record Adder" section, `addnames.pl` is the program to run on the UNIX side. If the user prepends the program name in the word document itself, you can reduce the batch file to a single `copy` command.

Practical Pseudo Printer Ideas

A pseudo printer can accept an HTML file, and based on various codes in the file, place the file in the proper directory of the Web site. What's more, if there's not already a link to this file from the main page, the pseudo printer can set a link to it.

Many older DOS and Windows processes gather information destined for a UNIX back end. Often, such files are ftp'ed to the server, where either the import process is manually kicked off or it's run regularly as a cron job. Neither is ideal. Instead, consider having the DOS or Windows process copy the completed intermediate file to a pseudo printer share, thereby automatically kicking off the UNIX process. If the UNIX process is configurable, arrange for the head of the intermediate file to have the configuration options. Because those options can be binary copied to the front of the file on the DOS side and removed (and interpreted) by a script on the back end, this is practical even for shrink-wrapped DOS and UNIX applications.

Often non-technical employees need to run UNIX processes. Rather than giving them `telnet` and teaching them to type the commands, link a Windows icon to a batch file that copies the appropriate file to a pseudo printer share. If the UNIX process is a report program, have the employee pick up the resulting report file via Samba.

When tracing reports of intermittent Windows freezes, it's handy to have a log of all bootups. Consider placing a command in the Windows startups of all affected computers to copy a file containing the computer's host-name to a pseudo printer. The UNIX process then tacks on a timestamp and records it in a log. Soon relationships in time and hosts can be seen.

Magic Script Server-Side Automation

Magic scripts are a new, experimental addition to Samba. They're the most configurable because the script itself is provided by the Windows client, meaning that if the client uploads a script to delete everything from the share's tree, there's little to stop it (assuming the user has those permissions). Magic scripts are useful only in low-security environments.

Magic scripts do not always work. Your results will vary. The way they're used is you define a script filename in the `magic script=` parameter and an output file in the `magic output=` parameter. Neither need exist.

The client triggers the automation by copying the script, by the name used in the `magic script=` parameter, to the share. That script is run, with its stdout being redirected to the `magic output=` filename.

As of Samba 2.0.5a, magic scripts often fail. Start troubleshooting by verifying that the scripts uploaded are in UNIX text format (no carriage returns) and that they would work if run on the UNIX box in the share's directory by the user involved. Perhaps the best troubleshooting starting point is creating a script that does nothing but write the word *hello* to a file. Try for a file in the share (assuming the share is writeable) and in a universally writeable directory, such as `/tmp`.

If magic scripts don't work for you, consider using pseudo printers instead. Pseudo printers can do almost everything magic scripts can do, and most of the exceptions are shady in the security department.

smb.conf Includes

While not strictly speaking SSA, `smb.conf` includes can accomplish similar setup tasks as `preexec=` and `root preexec=`. Examples are limited only by the administrator's imagination. A simple example is granting encryption to selective clients. For example, place the following line in the global section of `smb.conf`:

```
include=/usr/local/samba/opt/encrypt.%m
```

Then create files specifying encryption for each client. For instance, a Windows 98 encrypting client called `WINCLI` would have the following `/usr/local/samba/opt/encrypt.wincli` file:

```
encrypt passwords=yes
```

On the other hand, a Windows 95 client named `W95`, lacking encryption, would have the following `/usr/local/samba/opt/encrypt.w95` file:

```
encrypt passwords=no
```

In the previous examples, the file extensions were lowercase, even though the client hostnames were uppercase. Although this is the usual behavior, exceptions are possible. Exceptions can be located by experimentation or with the use of a log file.

Server-Side Automation Security Issues

The top security issue in server-side automation is the power of `root preexec=` and `root postexec=`. Whereas most other server-side automation restricts mischief to the share at hand or to directories having liberal permissions, these two SSA parameters can go anywhere and do anything because they're executed as root.

These two commands should be unconfigurable or minimally configurable by the client. Their functions should be kept simple to avoid nooks and crannies where security breaches can hide. Above all, take all precautions, including those in Chapter 13, "Using Samba Web Administration Tool (SWAT) for Samba Configuration", to prevent users from modifying `smb.conf`. In five minutes of access to `smb.conf`, a mischievous employee with some UNIX knowledge could create a `root preexec=` script to install his or her own `/etc/passwd`, delete the `root preexec=` from `smb.conf`, delete or selectively purge the log files necessary to figure out who did the damage, and restart Samba.

Similarly, avoid calling suid root processes from SSA. If those processes are client configurable, they could be used for mischief. Even a seemingly harmless suid process such as running the database refresh for the `locate` command could lead to denial of service if a Windows batch file repeatedly triggers it.

Summary

Server-side automation (SSA) refers to a Samba client triggering a UNIX process. There are three types of SSA:

- Exec methods
- Pseudo printer methods
- Magic script methods

Magic script methods are experimental and sometimes don't work. Even when they do work, because the client determines the script to be run, they're inherently insecure.

The exec methods, consisting of `preexec=`, `postexec=`, `root preexec=`, and `root postexec=`, are used for setup and teardown of a Samba connection. The `preexec` commands take as values commands to be run at share connection. The `postexec` commands take as values commands to be run at share disconnection.

Because disconnection (and therefore the subsequent connection) is client dependent and hard to predict, these forms of server-side automation should not be used for anything except share setup and teardown. Because the `root exec` commands are run as `root`, they can be an extreme security risk if the client is allowed to determine his or her actions. A person having write access to `smb.conf` could set `root preexec=` to overwrite `/etc/passwd` with his or her own copy or create an suid root version of the shell in his or her home directory.

Pseudo printer methods are the workhorse of server-side automation. A print share is set up with a command that runs a UNIX script instead of submitting the file to a print queue. When the client copies a file to the print share, that file becomes the configuration and data for the process. In this way, a client process can build a file for the UNIX process and then "kick off" the UNIX process to operate on the file.

Samba has a rich variety of variable substitution strings to be used with server-side automation. These are listed in Table 14.1 in this chapter. Among the most important are `%s`, which represents the file passed to the UNIX process of a pseudo printer; `%T`, which is replaced by a sortable timestamp; `%U` and `%u`, replaced by the requested and service username, respectively; `%G` and `%g`, the requested and service groups; respectively, and `%H`, the home directory of the service user. When these and other variable substitution strings are passed to the command being run, extremely configurable, yet safe, scripts can be made.

Although not strictly defined as server-side automation, `smb.conf` includes perform a similar setup function as `preexec=` and `root preexec=`. Such includes should be considered for any user-, group-, or machine-dependent configurations.

Files passed to pseudo printers typically consist of a few lines of configuration information, followed by data, which can be either text or binary. The configuration lines can be picked off by `head` piped to `tail` piped to `tr`. The `tr` process strips any carriage returns. If one pseudo printer is used to run several different scripts, it's important those scripts be in a specific subdirectory and called from the script with a complete path. This eliminates the possibility of a client user submitting a pseudo printer job with a first line of `rm -f *`, for example.

Server-side automation is extremely powerful and configurable, limited only by the administrator's imagination. Whenever there's a need for coordination between Windows and UNIX processes, you should look to server-side automation for help.

14

USING SAMBA
SERVER-SIDE
AUTOMATION

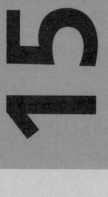

Samba Security

by Kevin Long

IN THIS CHAPTER

Security Principles

Security is the process of preventing intended damage or unauthorized access to a network of computers. Security is constantly in review, and it should never be considered completed. A cross-platform network of Samba servers and Windows clients and servers raises the complexity level of security; however, it also allows for some more creative approaches. Because a Samba server runs without problems for much longer than an NT server, you'll have more time available to pay attention to client configuration. However, you cannot ignore either.

Preinstallation Security Measures

When you download or obtain a Samba package, you'll need to verify its integrity using a variety of signature-checking methods. Here are the two main package types:

- rpm and deb
- Gzipped tar

At the time of writing, no deb packages were available on the Samba FTP site, so this discussion covers only rpm format.

Checking an rpm Package Signature and Checksum

If you're installing a new or updated Red Hat Package Manager (rpm) of Samba, you need to check the package before installing it. The two levels of checking include the checksum and the author. The checksum is simple:

```
rpm --checksig
[root@server RPMS]# rpm --checksig samba-2.0.5a-12.i386.rpm
samba-2.0.5a-12.i386.rpm: md5 GPG NOT OK
[root@server RPMS]#
```

Does GPG NOT OK mean this file has a problem? Well, not exactly. rpm supports MD-5 signatures, Pretty Good Privacy (pgp) available at www.cryptography.org/getpgp.htm, and now GNU Privacy Guard (gpg) —go to www.gnupg.org/download.html). Not all rpm versions have been signed with gpg at this time. If you do not have gpg installed with the right public keys, you'll need to skip that part (although this, in itself, is a potential security hole).

It's worth the effort to install or obtain gpg and start collecting the public keys of the developers or vendors you'll be dealing with; it's a simple procedure.

To do this for Red Hat, download the public keys from Red Hat's site and add them to your public key "key ring." The public key used to sign rpm files is available at www.redhat.com/about/redhat2.asc. Save this file to disk; then invoke gpg to import it to your public key ring:

```
gpg --import redhat2.asc
```

You can then verify it again, like so:

```
[root@server root]$ rpm -K /mnt/cdrom/RedHat/RPMS/samba*.rpm
/mnt/cdrom/RedHat/RPMS/samba-2.0.5a-12.i386.rpm: md5 gpg OK
/mnt/cdrom/RedHat/RPMS/samba-client-2.0.5a-12.i386.rpm: md5 gpg OK
/mnt/cdrom/RedHat/RPMS/samba-common-2.0.5a-12.i386.rpm: md5 gpg OK
[root@server root]$
```

Note that you don't have to perform the signature verification as root. You can just as easily add the public keys to a lower-level user account's key ring. You can also verify an rpm without checking the key:

```
[root@server RPMS]# rpm --checksig --nogpg samba-2.0.5a-12.i386.rpm
samba-2.0.5a-12.i386.rpm: md5 OK
[root@server RPMS]#
```

This way, the error message is skipped. Note that --checksig is actually the -K option. You can get slightly more verbose output by using v with it, too:

```
[root@server RPMS]# rpm -Kv --nogpg samba-2.0.5a-12.i386.rpm
samba-2.0.5a-12.i386.rpm:
MD5 sum OK: 28232b0e2bca295e9f51285de1a4269b
[root@server RPMS]#
```

You can get even more complete verification information by using the display debug (-vv) option:

```
[root@server RPMS]# rpm -Kvv samba-2.0.5a-12.i386.rpm
D: New Header signature
D: Signature size: 149
D: Signature pad : 3
D: sigsize       : 152
D: Header + Archive: 1740143
D: expected size   : 1740143
samba-2.0.5a-12.i386.rpm:
MD5 sum OK: 28232b0e2bca295e9f51285de1a4269b
gpg: Signature made Mon 27 Sep 1999 04:38:55 PM UTC using DSA key ID DB42A60E
gpg: Can't check signature: public key not found
[root@server RPMS]#
```

This also details gpg failure when a public key cannot be found. For source code files, there are no signatures to check.

15

SAMBA SECURITY

Checking Existing Packages

Signature checking is used on packages that have not yet been installed. You can verify an existing installed Samba rpm by using the verify options:

```
rpm -v
```

This produces no output; it simply verifies the package. Here, no news is good news, because only errors would generate output. This is nice to know, but you may want more in-depth information about your package. If so, run this instead:

```
rpm -Vvv
```

Here's what you get:

```
[username@server username]$ rpm -Vvv samba-2.0.5a-12
D: opening database mode 0x0 in //var/lib/rpm/
D: record number 6572760
D:    YES     A pam = 0.68-7      B pam >= 0.64
D:  requires: pam >= 0.64 satisfied by db packages.
D:    YES     A samba-common = 2.0.5a-12  B samba-common = 2.0.5a
D:  requires: samba-common = 2.0.5a satisfied by db packages.
D:  requires: /sbin/chkconfig   satisfied by db file lists.
D:  requires: /bin/mktemp   satisfied by db file lists.
D:  requires: /usr/bin/killall   satisfied by db file lists.
D:  requires: fileutils   satisfied by db packages.
D:  requires: sed   satisfied by db packages.
D:  requires: /bin/sh   satisfied by db file lists.
D:  requires: ld-linux.so.2  satisfied by db provides.
D:  requires: libc.so.6  satisfied by db provides.
D:  requires: libcrypt.so.1  satisfied by db provides.
D:  requires: libdl.so.2  satisfied by db provides.
D:  requires: libnsl.so.1  satisfied by db provides.
D:  requires: libpam.so.0  satisfied by db provides.
D:  requires: libreadline.so.3  satisfied by db provides.
D:  requires: libtermcap.so.2  satisfied by db provides.
D:  requires: /bin/csh  satisfied by db file lists.
D:  requires: /bin/sh  satisfied by db file lists.
D:  requires: /usr/bin/awk  satisfied by db file lists.
D:  requires: libc.so.6(GLIBC_2.0)  satisfied by db provides.
D:  requires: libc.so.6(GLIBC_2.1)  satisfied by db provides.
[username@server username]$
```

This gives you more information about the compiled requirements of the rpm package. Everything checks out—but you already knew that from the lack of errors with the simple -v option.

You can get more detail about an installed package by using the -qip option:

```
[root@server RPMS]# rpm -qip samba-2.0.5a-12.i386.rpm
Name        : samba               Relocations: (not relocateable)
Version     : 2.0.5a                           Vendor: Red Hat Software
```

```
Release     : 12            Build Date: Sat 25 Sep 1999 05:12:36 PM UTC
Install date: (not installed)         Build Host: porky.devel.redhat.com
Group       : System Environment/Daemons   Source RPM: samba-2.0.5a-12.src.rpm
Size        : 5012565               License: GNU GPL Version 2
Packager    : Red Hat Software <http://developer.redhat.com/bugzilla>
Summary     : Samba SMB server.
Description :

Description follows…

 [root@server RPMS]#
```

Some important notes in the description field include references to WHATSNEW.txt, a document that details changes and security fixes in this package/release of Samba and references to the status of encrypted password support (required for NT SP3 and 98 clients) as well as the status of PAM support.

Finally, you can get a program listing by adding the l option:

```
[root@server root]$ rpm -ql samba | grep bin
/usr/bin/addtosmbpass
/usr/bin/convert_smbpasswd
/usr/bin/mksmbpasswd.sh
/usr/bin/nmblookup
/usr/bin/smbadduser
/usr/bin/smbpasswd
/usr/bin/smbstatus
/usr/bin/smbtar
/usr/sbin/nmbd
/usr/sbin/samba
/usr/sbin/smbd
/usr/sbin/swat
[root@server root]$
```

You can also get a configuration file listing:

```
[root@server root]$ rpm -ql samba | grep etc
/etc/logrotate.d/samba
/etc/pam.d/samba
/etc/rc.d/init.d/smb
/etc/smbusers
/etc/smb.conf
[root@server root]$
```

Compile-Time Options

If you're not using a package and are instead compiling from source, security-specific compile-time options include specifying a guest account other than the default of "nobody." You can also override the guest account settings for an individual service (if the account "nobody" is unable to print, for example). Therefore, this might not be needed.

SSL Support

Samba can be compiled with SSL (Secure Socket Layer) support, but this feature cannot be used by Windows clients.

SSL is a mechanism that allows fully encrypted and authenticated access between computers. It makes use of Certificate Authorities (CA's) to restrict and verify connection attempts.

Currently, only two clients support it—smbclient, which comes with the basic Samba package, and Sharity, found at `www.obdev.at/Products/Sharity.html`. Sharity, is commercial software. If you want to run an SSL server with non-Windows clients, you'll need to review the document `SSLeay.txt` and obtain the latest SSL source. You can also run an SSL-enabled Samba server as a regular Samba server at the same time by using the `SSL hosts resign = ip address range` option. This forces specified hosts or subnets to be forced into non-SSL mode. All other hosts will be forced into SSL mode.

Security Resources

The place to start reading about security is the Samba documentation; on a Red Hat system, this is the `docs/textdocs` directory of your installation.

The `NT_Security.txt` document details how to manipulate access control lists (ACLs) when using an NT client connected to a Samba file server. It requires an understanding of native NT ACLs so that an effective comparison can be made with the ACL "emulation" Samba provides.

The `cifsntdomain.txt` document provides detailed information on the network activity surrounding a domain logon, including the SMB transact pipes. Unless you're a developer, this document is for information only.

The `Security_level.txt` document describes, in detail, the `security` = options of the global section in `smb.conf`.

`UNIX_SECURITY.txt` is a short document that covers the topic of the [home] service.

The `Recent-FAQs.txt` document covers any recent security issues as well as common questions asked about Samba.

The `htmldocs/smbpasswd.5.html` document is different from the man page for `smbpasswd` and goes into considerably more detail on the topic of the LANMAN versus NT hashes used in password protection. LANMAN is the original password scheme used by LAN Manager networks. It was developed jointly by Microsoft and IBM. It is the underlying password mechanism used by Windows 9x clients, and is sometimes referred to as plain text equivalent. An NT hash is a fully encrypted password mechanism developed by Microsoft and introduced to NT with SP3. Both coexist in a mixed-client network.

Security announcements appear on the main Samba web site (the following is the U.S. mirror):

```
http://us1.samba.org/samba/samba.html
```

These announcements are part of the release cycle information.

The Usenet discussion group `comp.protocols.smb` can be found with a searchable front end on dejanews (`www.deja.com`). Be sure to visit the `comp.protocols.smb` discussion forum.

The Samba Kernel Cousins site (`http://kt.linuxcare.com/KC/samba/`) provides information on interaction between current Samba releases and the "adjustments" made by Microsoft to Windows clients.

Finally, `www.ntbugtraq.com` is a site devoted specifically to NT security.

Don't forget to include Microsoft in your security picture. It's important to check both the Microsoft Knowledge Base and the newsgroups shortly after a Windows NT Service Pack or a Windows 9x update is released to see what (if anything) might be broken when connecting to a non-Windows server. Some elements are benign and easily fixable (such as the Windows 98 file write slowdown); others require a big rethink and rollout plan (such as the encrypted passwords switchover). Fortunately, the Samba developers really understand their subject, and it shows in the thoughtful way that workarounds and changes are made. The Microsoft Knowledge Base is available at `www.microsoft.com`, under the Search option. Input your topic and elect to search only the Knowledge Base.

Samba Configuration Components Security Parameters

Configuration file security is provided by restricting access to the `/etc/smb.conf` file. Make sure only `root` can modify the file.

User access can be blocked by IP range as well as by eliminating any guest access, unless it's required for your application. You can run multiple NICs in a Samba machine and allow only correct ranges to connect to specific services.

Share permissions must be set with appropriate group access to prevent unauthorized connection.

If you have NT clients and NT ACL emulation is enabled, you can implement more granular file permissions.

Provide least privilege access to the server by restricting services. As this server's primary purpose is to Windows clients, traditional UNIX login shells are probably not needed. Remove them by setting the shell portion of /etc/passwd to /bin/false. This is doubly important because the typical Windows network, in which users are allowed to choose their own passwords, is a hotbed of weak, "crackable" words. Try to keep the peace yet enforce some level of elevated security by following the recommendations in the passwords section.

Password-Related Security Parameters

Your password options are determined by your environment. Is your environment Samba only or a combination of Samba and NT PDC? If you're using a PDC for authentication, your only options are to review the security policies of that domain controller. If you don't have that access privilege (for example, you're running an unauthorized Samba server), you need to review what it is you're trying to accomplish and how it fits into your company's infrastructure.

Assuming all is well in your company's infrastructure and you have control over the contents of your password files, you'll need to secure these files. The two to deal with are /etc/passwd and /etc/smbpasswd (note that you may have smbpasswd in another location). /etc/smbpasswd needs to have restricted access to read-write for root only. /etc/passwd can have its security boosted by enabling shadow passwords. You can turn an existing password system into a shadow password system by running the pwconv utility:

```
pwconv /etc/passwd
```

This converts a regular password file into a shadow password file. Conversely, the pwunconv utility reverses this action. Similar utilities exist for group files: grpconv and grpunconv. Be sure to run the check utilities pwck and grpck on the password and group files first to catch any errors.

Review password security when open on the wire—are you using LANMAN "plain-text equivalent" or NT hash encrypted? For Windows clients, NT Service Pack 3 and Windows 98 introduced encrypted passwords. Windows for Workgroups and Windows 95 remain with "plain text equivalent" passwords. This change was made to get away from a password mechanism called the *LANMAN hash*, originally invented by IBM. It has a reputation for breaking easily.

You can read more about the LANMAN hash and the other password-protection mechanisms used by Samba in the `smbpasswd.5.html` document in the `html` section of `docs`. You should at least aim to have a password policy for your network that avoids dictionary words and eight-character passwords. The LANMAN hash breaks a windows password into two seven character pieces, so an eight character password would be handled as a seven character password and a one character password. Ideally, your passwords should be seven or fourteen characters. The Open Solution Providers document `www.osp.nl/infobase/ntpass.html` goes into detail on this subject.

You can review your existing password base effectiveness by running John the Ripper from `www.openwall.com/john/`. This is a password-ripping program that attempts to decrypt passwords. Grab the latest sources and then compile and install the program. Run it on your password files and see which passwords are cracked within a day. This gives you a starting point for detecting weak accounts.

Password Synchronization

Password synchronization is needed to keep matching username/password pairs on your NT and Samba servers. This allows users to change their passwords (which can be set as mandatory in the password-aging option of the user accounts on your PDC) from the Windows clients, thus alleviating the need for a UNIX shell prompt. Here are the parameters in `smb.conf`:

```
unix password synch = yes
passwd program = /usr/bin/passwd %u
passwd chat = *New*UNIX*password* %n\n *ReType*new*UNIX*password* %n\n
*passwd:*all*authentication*tokens*updated*successfully*
```

Changing Passwords from Windows NT

If you're not using `security = server` to authenticate login requests against a domain controller, your users can still manually synchronize their passwords on a Samba server by pressing Ctrl+Alt+Del and choosing Change Password. They'll need to first change the domain password and then repeat the exercise, this time changing the domain to the format \\servername, as shown in the dialog box. The Samba server will not appear in the drop-down list.

This will initiate a password chat session on the Samba server.

440 | *Creating a Turnkey Samba System*

PART II

Using `passwd chat debug`

If passwd chat fails, you can enable passwd chat debug:

```
passwd chat debug = True
```

`passwd chat debug` allows `passwd chat` scripts to be debugged, but it has the side effect of recording plain-text passwords in the smbd log file. If you use this for development, make sure it's set to `false` (the default) when you're done and the log is cleared. You might also need to check and clear rotated logs.

PAM-Based Password Synchronization

Pluggable Authentication Modules (PAM) provide a method of increasing flexibility in authentication methods. It's a complex issue that's best covered by the documentation that comes with PAM itself. In short, having PAM support in an application means you can pick and choose authentication methods and databases without having to recompile the application. The PAM module takes care of that.

You can verify whether your Samba installation has been compiled with the `--with-pam` option by using `ldd`:

```
[root@server root]$ ldd /usr/sbin/smbd
    libnsl.so.1 => /lib/libnsl.so.1 (0x40018000)
    libreadline.so.3 => /usr/lib/libreadline.so.3 (0x4002f000)
    libdl.so.2 => /lib/libdl.so.2 (0x40051000)
    libcrypt.so.1 => /lib/libcrypt.so.1 (0x40054000)
    libpam.so.0 => /lib/libpam.so.0 (0x40081000) << here it is
    libc.so.6 => /lib/libc.so.6 (0x40089000)
    libtermcap.so.2 => /lib/libtermcap.so.2 (0x4017c000)
    /lib/ld-linux.so.2 => /lib/ld-linux.so.2 (0x40000000)
[root@server root]$
```

This shows that PAM is compiled into this version of Samba, and here's the related Samba config file for PAM:

```
[root@server root]# cat /etc/pam.d/samba
auth     required        /lib/security/pam_pwdb.so nullok shadow
account required        /lib/security/pam_pwdb.so
[root@server root]#
```

Here's the master configuration file for PAM for a Red Hat system:

```
[root@server root]# cat /etc/pam.d/login
#%PAM-1.0
```

```
auth       required    /lib/security/pam_securetty.so
auth       required    /lib/security/pam_pwdb.so shadow nullok
auth       required    /lib/security/pam_nologin.so
account    required    /lib/security/pam_pwdb.so
password   required    /lib/security/pam_cracklib.so
password   required    /lib/security/pam_pwdb.so nullok use_authtok md5 shadow
session    required    /lib/security/pam_pwdb.so
session    optional    /lib/security/pam_console.so
[root@server root]#
```

pam_smb information from www.csn.ul.ie/~airlied/pam_smb/ can be used to see how PAM works with the SMB protocol.

The pam_ntdom page can be found at http://core.ring.gr.jp/pub/net/samba/ pam_ntdom/. It allows UNIX/Linux users to authenticate using an NT domain controller. Although this may seem like an unusual use, it performs a valuable function in reducing or consolidating separate user account databases.

Implementing Access Restrictions

Are the shares in your network browseable? To prevent curiosity when users are navigating the Network Neighborhood, you can hide services by setting browseable = no in your service configuration.

IP ranges to allow and deny can be set in the global section and can also be service specific. Global settings override service settings. Here are examples:

```
Hosts allow = iprange1, iprange2
```

```
Hosts deny = iprange1, iprange2
```

You can verify the correct operation of the settings using the hostname option of testparm:

```
Usage: testparm [-sh] [-L servername] [configfilename] [hostname hostIP]
        -s                      Suppress prompt for enter
        -h                      Print usage
        -L servername           Set %L macro to servername
        configfilename          Configuration file to test
        hostname hostIP.        Hostname and Host IP address to test
                                against "host allow" and "host deny"
```

Exercise caution with SWAT--plain-text passwords are sent over the wire and are subject to sniffing. Refer to Chapter 13, "Using Samba Web Administration Tool (SWAT) for Samba Configuration."

15

SAMBA SECURITY

User Accounts, Groups, and Directory Services

Samba works with the Lightweight Directory Access Protocol (LDAP). Using directories is the way to go according to Novell and Microsoft, and there's some merit to the concept of a unified user account and information database. Novell's NDS has been around for several years, and it's a seasoned product. Microsoft has made much of its competing Active Directory product and, at the time of this writing, it nearly exists. Meanwhile, in the real world, freely available standards-based solutions have been developed, and the one that has come to prominence is LDAP. Integration with Samba is not mentioned on the Samba Roadmap document. With the advent of Microsoft LDAP implementations and Active Directory, the landscape shifts. The phenomenal success of Samba may cause the sights to be set higher, growing it into what NT should have been (see www.unav.es/cti/ldap-smb-howto.html).

Service-Level Security Options

Samba allows security to be defined at the service level, allowing you to choose authentication methods and varying levels of user access, from required to guest. Each attempted connection to a Samba server goes through authentication steps before being granted.

Here are the six steps of username/password validation:

1. Match supplied username/password to UNIX username/password. If the client has passed a username and password pair, and that pair is validated by the UNIX system's password programs, then the user is connected as that username.

2. Check the password against the username previously supplied by the client. If the client has previously registered a username with the server and now supplies a correct password, the connection is made.

3. The client's NetBIOS name and any previously used usernames are checked against the password. If they match, the connection is made.

4. If the client has previously supplied a correct and validated username and password pair and has passed the validation token, that username is used. This allows the client to connect to multiple shares without prompting for a username/password at each attempt.

5. If a `user` = field is set in the `smb.conf` file for the service and the client has supplied a password that matches one of the usernames from the `user` = field, the connection is made as the user specified. If a group is specified using `user` = @groupname, the name expands to a list of names in the specified group.

6. If the service is a guest service, the connection is made as the user in the `guest account` = setting for that service, regardless of the supplied password.

Guest Access Issues

You might want to allow guest logins to your server for users who do not have accounts (for example, for printing resources or information shares). Because Samba always needs a valid account of some nature, the "accountless" login has to be mapped.

`map to guest` applies to security modes user, server, and domain, and allows logins to be mapped to the defined guest user account. Three modes are available: never, bad user, and bad password. The default is never, which rejects all user logins with incorrect or invalid passwords.

Bad user mode rejects user logins for valid accounts when the password is incorrect. If the user account doesn't exist, a guest login is generated, which is mapped to the guest account.

Bad password mode takes user logins that have incorrect passwords and treats them as guest logins, mapping them to the guest account.

guest ok = yes

If `guest ok =` is set to `yes`, guest logins will be permitted on the service and the permissions will be those of the guest account. The default is `guest ok = no`.

guest account = ftp

Whenever a guest login is made, the account is mapped to the user specified in `guest account =`. For security, this account will exist in the password file but will not be able to log in. This is usually "nobody," but on some systems that account might not be able to print. If your Samba server is also an anonymous FTP server, you can use the `ftp` account that's typically made when installing the service. However, due to the frequency of security alerts on the most common anonymous FTP server packages, you might find it better to provide select guest login points for accountless distribution.

Security Problems

The `homes` service allows Samba to dynamically generate shares in the format `\\servername\%U`, which is perfect for storing users' mailboxes, browser caches, and so on. It's also the users' regular UNIX home directory. You must not use any guest parameters in this service because doing so opens up all home directories to guest logins, which is definitely not what you want.

15

SAMBA SECURITY

Samba Security Levels

Samba can emulate different types of Windows "servers" at different levels of security. The simplest harks back to Windows for Workgroups, the most complex is the current NT domain level, or domain member.

security = share

This setting is analogous to Windows for Workgroups sharing. Each share point or service has a predefined password. smbd always uses a valid UNIX user account to act on behalf of the client, even in security = share.

security = user

In user-level security, a valid username/password pair must be supplied to connect to resources. If you have NT clients that use encrypted passwords, you'll need this level of security.

security = server

This mode allows you to use another server's account resources, such as a PDC.

security = domain

If you've used smbpasswd to add the Samba server to a domain, you can use domain level security. Passwords must be encrypted. Samba will attempt to validate the username/password pair by passing it to an NT domain controller (PDC or BDC). This is the same behavior as an NT server that has joined a domain and has services authenticated against domain accounts. It's important to note that a valid user account must still exist on the Samba server for it to map file access to. This is in contrast to security = server, which dynamically generates accounts.

Security Risks and Breaches

Most Linux distributions and default Windows installs are set to moderate to low security levels. You will always need to modify the environment to bring security into place on both your Samba servers and your windows clients. There are also configuration errors that are possible with Samba that reduce security levels unnecessarily.

The Gratuitous Breach: hosts equiv=

This is not the same as the hosts allow UNIX service access file. hosts equiv, when set, specifies a file that contains names of hosts and users who will be granted access without needing to specify passwords. This has no place in a secured network.

admin users =

When admin users are specified, they can perform file operations as `root`. In the unlikely event this is what you want, you can follow some NT conventions and offer the services as hidden shares. For example, if you want access to the `/etc` file system, you could share it as `etc$`, and it would not appear in service lists. Keep in mind that if you are logging into an NT workstation's local Administrator account and using Administrator as a passthrough account, the local SAM of the workstation is a potentially "crackable" doorway into `root` access on your server.

Abuse Potential: wide links = yes

Links within the share point are always permitted; the `wide links = yes` setting controls whether links that go outside the share point can be followed.

User Manipulable suid root Executables

Guard against suid `root` executables as you would with any UNIX-type system.

Beefing Up Security

Allow encrypted passwords. NT SP3 introduced mandatory encrypted passwords, which offer greater protection than the LANMAN hash.

Remove unneeded services from your `inetd.conf` file. Research each entry if you are unfamiliar with it's function, then decide whether to remove it. You can modify your `inetd.conf` file and then reload it without rebooting the server. I recommend you do this from the server terminal itself, to avoid being cut off from your network connection. You should also install protection programs, such as Tripwire, to monitor your server. Tripwire and other security tools for UNIX can be found at `http://ciac.llnl.gov/ciac/ToolsUnixSysMon.html`.

Preventing Shell Logins

Samba servers are typically installed to replace NT servers in an all-Windows environment. Unless you have specific applications that require conventional UNIX logins, you can boost the security of your Samba server by setting all regular user accounts to have a login shell of `/bin/false`. Coupled with the removal of all plain-text password login services, such as `ftp`, `telnet`, and `rlogin/rsh`, this diminishes greatly the ease with which intruders can poke around the file system.

Diagnostic Tools for an SMB Network

You can get `tcpdump-smb`, an extension to `tcpdump`, from the Samba Web site. It's used to investigate SMB networking problems over NetBEUI and TCP/IP. Look in the Downloads section. Typically, it must be run as `root` due to the hardware access level and the information it provides. Here's an example:

```
[root@server root]# /usr/sbin/tcpdump port 139
```

This captures all SMB packets going to the machine running `tcpdump` and provides pages of output for you to go through. Use it when you have specific problems to investigate (preferably repeatable problems) and all other simple diagnostics have failed.

To debug name resolution problems, use port 137. For browse packet problems (such as an incorrect or deficient Network Neighborhood browse list), use port 138.

To investigate current user and file access, use `smbstatus`. User accounts get mapped to a process ID (PID). File and service access is then correlated with that PID. To get a user account PID, issue the following:

```
smbstatus | grep username
```

Note the PID returned. You can then issue

```
smbstatus | grep pid
```

to find all the files and locks associated with that account.

To solve the user problem of a file that is reported as locked when the user believes it is not in use, first find the file's associated PID:

```
smbstatus | grep filename
```

Then, go back and see which user is associated with the current file access. Sometimes there's no existing file access. For example, the user could be encountering a stale lock, which would probably have freed itself in the time it took for the user to walk over to discuss the problem with you.

Log files of Samba events are kept in individual logs, by machine name, and the regular system message log file, with the format `smb.`*`computername`*, where *`computername`* is the NetBIOS name of the computer that has made a Samba connection.

If you're experiencing a specific, repeatable problem (for example, a "server is too busy" error message from a client that's trying to connect to a Samba server), you can watch what happens dynamically in the Samba message log:

```
tail -f /var/log/log.smb
```

This reveals the culprit:

```
connection denied from 192.168.1.5
Gethostbyaddr failed for 192.168.1.5
```

Now you can tell that name resolution is not functioning correctly for Samba.

Client-Side and Server-Side Security Working Together

The Windows design requires you to exercise a combination of client-side and server-side security methods, from the application of system policies on windows 9*x* and NT, to the ACL locking and user group levels of NT alone. Samba is the correct place to store lockdown scripts and policy files

Using System Policies to Improve Security

System policy files are covered in greater detail in Chapter 27, "Samba Enterprise Backup Strategy," in regard to their location and how they're applied. From a security perspective, you can use them to "lock down" a Windows 9*x* machine, in some respects making it behave more like NT by preventing access to the machine's configuration and enforcing mandatory network logons that eliminate access to the machine without a valid logon. The idea of a mandatory domain logon is a good one in a network of reasonable size. The question used to be, "How do you work when the server goes down?" The reply is, "Use Samba so it doesn't!" Enforced logons prevent uninvited guests from using your computers to investigate your network; however, they don't prevent someone with a DHCP-enabled box from plugging into an outlet, configuring the domain name, and playing around. The biggest advantage here is bringing NT-like protection to your 9*x* computers. Coupled with a BIOS configuration that prevents a user from booting to a floppy, you get a workable, although not high, level of security.

System Policies—Windows 95/98

Designate a master policy-editing machine and create your policy files on it. If you have a mixed-OS network, you'll need an NT machine and a 9*x* machine. The policy editor is the same executable for both NT and 9*x*, but it will only produce policy files that work with the generating OS—NT policies must be created using NT, and 9*x* policies must be created using 9*x*.

Your policy files will be stored in the `netlogon` share of the Samba server, to be used automatically when Samba is a PDC or referred to when Samba is part of a domain. Use differently named files for NT clients and 9*x* clients. Here's the `smb.conf` entry for the `netlogon` service:

```
[netlogon]
comment = Network Logon Service
path = /home/netlogon
guest ok = yes
writable = no
share modes = no
```

Use the policy editor in conjunction with application and OS template files to control Windows behavior. See Figure 15.1 for an example that provides an option profile for download limits.

FIGURE 15.1

Security-related policy settings.

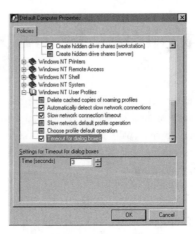

Create a policy file—9*x* example, Samba as the PDC.

The file needs to be named `config.pol`, and stored in the `netlogon` share. When 9*x* encounters a policy file of this name in the netlogon share it is automatically run at the time of logon.

Create a policy file—9*x* example, NT PDC, Samba as part of the domain.

The file should be named `9xconfig.pol`, and stored in the `netlogon` share of the Samba server. It will not automatically run at logon (as it is not in the same share as the login server. To work around this, you will need to specify the file in the manual update path for policies).

Create a policy file—NT example, NT PDC, Samba as part of the domain.

The file will be named `ntconfig.pol`, and stored in the `netlogon` share of the Samba server but will not automatically run at logon. To work around this, you will need to specify the file in the manual update path for policies).

Summary

Security is a process that's never completed. Implementing security requires a disciplined approach and attention to detail. Because it's extra work that's somewhat nitpicking, security can be perceived as an irritation—however, it's very necessary. People implementing Samba generally come from two camps: from UNIX or from Windows. The UNIX camp should have a good grasp of the security already configured on the server but might become exasperated when faced with 50 PC clients that all need individual security configurations. The Windows camp is amazed to find that a malicious intruder can literally destroy a server using a 300-baud phone line connection. Education is required on both sides. Studying UNIX/Linux security issues, regularly monitoring security sites, and applying vendor- and developer-released patches are essential server-maintenance tasks. System policies, which prevent clients from reconfiguring the PCs and which bring order to a chaotic situation, are almost mandatory as the number of clients goes up.

When you're reviewing security of a Samba server or any Windows-based network, a client-security strategy must be involved from the start. Using a Samba logon server and Windows 9*x* clients coupled with policies provides some similar benefits to an all-NT network, although in a compromised manner. Using an all-NT network with a PDC and Samba server allows you to take advantage of the NT domain model. Although there's a lot of public criticism of Windows security, you can mix and match elements until you get a network that's adequately protected.

You're correct to be nervous about security. The greater the dependence on computers for actual work, the higher the cost of unexpected downtime. Security lapses come both from within an organization and from without, and an effective security policy acknowledges these two weak points. Always take care to boost safety while avoiding alienation of the user, and implement a policy that balances concerns.

15

SAMBA SECURITY

CHAPTER 16

Using Samba as Your Windows 98 Logon Mechanism

by Steve Litt

IN THIS CHAPTER

No file server is complete without the ability to provide logon services, including authentication, logon scripts, and server-based client desktop configuration control. Samba can be configured to provide all these services.

Samba can be configured as an NT primary domain controller (PDC), a process which is discussed in the next chapter. This chapter discusses the simpler case of providing logon services for Windows 9*x* clients.

Gathering Necessary Documentation

Creating a Windows 9*x* logon server is simple if the right documentation is handy. This chapter forms the primary documentation for configuring a Samba server as a logon server. Beyond that, you should assemble the following documents:

- DOMAIN.txt
- DOMAIN_CONTROL.txt
- DOMAIN_MEMBER.txt
- BROWSING.txt
- BROWSING-Config.txt

All these documents are found in the docs/textdocs directory of your source distribution or binary distribution.

The documentation strategy is to use this chapter as the primary guide to configuring Samba as a Windows 9*x* logon server. In odd circumstances where this chapter's examples do not yield a working logon server, consult the text documents.

DOMAIN.txt

This document contains terse but explicit instructions for setting up a logon server and roaming profiles. It also contains information for setting up Windows NT roaming profiles and sharing profiles between Windows NT and Windows 98. This document also contains a small amount of domain theory.

DOMAIN_CONTROL.txt

Although not directly related to the Windows 9*x* logon service, this document offers information on configuring Samba as a Windows NT primary domain controller. This is background information that can, in some cases, enhance your understanding of Windows 98 logon servers.

DOMAIN_MEMBER.txt

Once again, although not directly related to the Windows 9*x* logon service, this document offers information on configuring a Samba server to work with a NT PDC by joining its domain. This also is background information that can, in some cases, enhance your understanding of Windows 98 logon servers.

BROWSING.txt

This document covers most browsing issues. As is the case in the Samba world in general, browsing problems can accompany Windows 98 logon service.

BROWSING-Config.txt

This document contains technical details of browser configuration and WINS. This may prove helpful in some situations.

Windows 98 Domain Terminology

Before proceeding into the conversion of a Samba server into a Windows 9*x* logon server, a few terms need to be defined:

- Workgroup
- Domain
- NetBIOS
- WINS
- Roaming Profiles
- Network System Policies

Workgroup

A *workgroup* is a group of client computers, typically with one or more servers, that can talk to each other.

Domain

A *domain* is like a workgroup, except it adds authentication (logon services) to the workgroup's abilities.

NetBIOS

NetBIOS is an application programming interface (API) for interfacing to a network. This API is used throughout the Windows world.

The NetBIOS API can run atop at least three protocols: TCP/IP, IPX, and NetBEUI. Samba's NetBIOS support works only with the TCP/IP protocol.

NetBIOS is used primarily for name resolution in Windows networking.

WINS

WINS is a piece of software capable of name resolution without using broadcasts. This improves network efficiency.

Roaming Profiles

A *profile* is data that defines the look and feel of a Windows computer. Normally, profiles reside exclusively on the Windows computers they define. However, using a server such as Windows NT or Samba, profiles can be stored on a server in such a way that changes to the look and feel made on one computer "roam" to other computers. Roaming profiles are implemented on a per-user basis. Roaming profiles are discussed in great detail in the "Setting Up Roaming User Profiles" section later in this chapter.

Network System Policies

A *system policy* is a definition of which programs and configuration tools are offered the user and which are not. Policies can be granted on a per-user, per-group, or per-computer basis. Default policies can be made for all users not otherwise defined or all computers not otherwise defined.

In a manner very similar to roaming profiles, policies can be made "universal" across a domain. Doing so gives you the opportunity to set up networks of truly homogeneous "appliance" computers.

Domain Logon Principles

Domain logons operate on a set of principles defining their reasons and advantages. These principles involve the advantages of central administration of authentication, passwords, logon scripts, thin client setup, and the like.

Why a Single Point of Logon?

Without a logon server, each box authenticates against its own list, which can basically be modified by any user. Even if logons could be restricted, the administration of 30 or more such clients would be an administrative nightmare. By using a Samba server to authenticate Windows 9*x* logons, the administration can be done on the server.

Centrally Administrated Logon Scripts

Network administration is never easy. The ability of the administrator to centrally configure logon scripts, rather than visiting each workstation individually, is a powerful timesaver. It's also a security advantage, because the logon scripts can be made read-only.

Logon scripts can be based on users, groups, or other factors.

Central Administration of Thin Clients

Most users are not power users and don't need control over their machines. They
appreciate their computer being an appliance.

By filling the role of logon server, the Samba server can administer roaming profiles. The
Samba server can give the client computer its desktop, its Start menu, its user profile, and
almost its entire personality. The user can simply use it. Roaming profiles are discussed in
great detail in the "Setting Up Roaming User Profiles" section later in this chapter.

This is also great for an administrator. There's no need to repair attempted configurations
by users, no need to visit individual machines, and client profiles can be backed up and
restored like any other files.

Password Synchronization

A client computer user might be tempted to use different passwords on different computers. This invariably leads to forgotten passwords, passwords written on the bottom surface
of the desk, or an equally serious security gaffe. By synchronizing the user's password on
the server, this problem is eliminated.

The user can still change the password from any client to which he or she is logged on
simply by changing the Windows networking password along with the local machine
password from the Windows 9*x* Password Properties dialog box.

Security Issues

A normal Windows computer allows anybody to log on to it. All a person needs to do is
to create a new username and password, and he's in. The use of the Samba server for
authentication prevents access by anyone not in the `smbpasswd` file.

Creating a Windows 98 Domain Logon

Logon servers and roaming profiles can be very complex. If you're building your first
Windows 9*x* logon server, it's best to keep variables to a minimum. Make your first one

with a single Windows 98 client and a single Linux Samba server. This eliminates extraneous problems, including the possibility of non–WINS-enabled clients messing things up.

Start with a Trivial Non-Logon Server

Very similar to a "Hello World" computer program, the following `smb.conf` proves that Samba works, that there's no problem with connectivity, and so on.

The following sample `smb.conf` makes these assumptions:

- There's a single Windows 98 client and a single Linux Samba server on a single, working subnet.
- The client's workgroup is set to `MYGROUP`. If not, `workgroup=` should be set to the client's workgroup.
- The Linux server's hostname is `mainserv`. If not, `netbios name=` should be set to the hostname of the Linux server.
- The client uses encrypted passwords. If not, `encrypted passwords=` should be changed from `yes` to `no`.

Back up your existing `smb.conf` and create the following trivial `smb.conf`:

```
[global]
netbios name=mainserv
workgroup=MYGROUP
encrypt passwords=yes

[homes]
read only=no
```

Restart Samba and make sure you can pull up the server and the `homes` directory in Network Neighborhood. If not, troubleshoot until you can.

Once this basic setup works on the client, continue by configuring your logon server.

Make a Non-Scripting Logon Server

The next step is to make a logon server that does authentication but no scripting. This involves the following steps:

- Configure the `[global]` section of `smb.conf`
- Make sure `security=` is not `share`
- Make `wins support=yes`
- Make `domain master=yes`
- Make `domain logons=yes`

- Create the user in `smbpasswd`
- Test with `smbclient`
- Test with Network Neighborhood
- Prove genuine remote authentication
- Explore simultaneous Windows and Samba server password changes

Configure the `[global]` Section of `smb.conf`

Add the following three lines to the `[global]` section of `smb.conf`:

```
wins support=yes
domain master=yes
domain logons=yes
```

Explanations of each of these parameter changes follow.

Make Sure `security=` Is Not `share`

Logon servers don't work with share security because share security does not validate users. If the `testparm` program, when run against the `smb.conf` file described in this chapter, shows that `security=` defaults to `share`, `security=user` needs to be explicitly specified in the `[global]` section. Older Samba software defaulted this parameter to `share`, whereas newer versions default to `user`.

Make `wins support=yes`

WINS provides proper NetBIOS name resolution. This is critical for proper function as a Windows 98 logon server. The `wins support=yes` line makes the Samba box a WINS server. Do *not* include a `wins server=` line.

Make `domain master=yes`

Even though the server described in this chapter is not a true NT domain, it needs certain types of domain functionality, including that of a domain browser. This line makes the server a domain browser.

> **Caution**
>
> Do not make `domain master=yes` if there are NT servers acting as PDCs, BDCs, or domain master browsers (DMBs). Doing so would cause browser wars and other serious problems.

Make domain logons=yes

This is the line that declares the Samba box to be a logon server. More configuration is required, but this is the basic switch that turns on the logon service.

Create the User in smbpasswd

This is an easy step to forget. To authenticate user username, the server must have that user in its smbpasswd file. Here's the command to do this:

```
# smbpasswd -a username
```

The preceding command must be done as root.

Test with smbclient

Restart Samba. The least challenging test is smbclient. Before continuing, make sure the following command can gain you access to the [homes] share:

```
$ smbclient '//mainserv/username' -U username
```

Test with Network Neighborhood

The first step is to configure Windows to authenticate from mainserv, which is in workgroup mygroup. Next, follow these steps:

1. Make sure you have your Windows installation CD handy.
2. Start the Network dialog box by right-clicking Network Neighborhood and choosing Properties or by double-clicking Network from Control Panel.
3. Choose the Configuration tab.
4. Click the Client for Microsoft Networks option in the Network Component list and then click the Properties button. This brings up the Client for Microsoft Networks Properties dialog box.
5. Check the Log on to Windows NT Domain check box. This is true even though there's no NT box on the network and your Samba box is not operating as a PDC.
6. Type the name of the workgroup in the Windows NT Domain text box. This example uses MYGROUP for the workgroup. For this example, the Samba machine and the Windows client should be in the same workgroup.
7. Make sure the Logon and Restore Network Connections radio button is enabled.
8. Click the OK button on the Client for Microsoft Networks Properties dialog box and then click OK on the Network dialog box.

9. Supply the Windows Install CD and click OK as needed. The computer reboots, and when it comes up again, a third field appears on the logon dialog box, as shown in Figure 16.1.

FIGURE 16.1

The Windows Remote Authentication Logon dialog box.

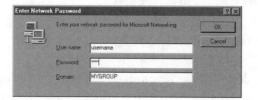

10. Fill in the username and password as usual. Type the client's and server's workgroup in the Domain field, as shown in Figure 16.1. Windows should start, logged in as the proper user.

Prove Genuine Remote Authentication

It's conceptually possible that even though a three-field logon screen is presented, the authentication is really local. This is very simple to test. Change the server password with the `smbpasswd` command; then log off and log on to the Windows PC. If the logon now fails, you've proven remote authentication.

> ### Note
>
> In the preceding experiment, inputting the password newly edited in `smbpasswd` does not get you in, because you're asked for a new Windows-side password, and that new password fails because of the existing Windows-side password.
>
> The next section demonstrates how to change the Samba server password to match the Windows password.

Now that the point has been proven, use `smbpasswd` to reset the password to its original value and confirm that once again you can log in to Windows.

Explore Simultaneous Windows and Samba Server Password Changes

The previous section changed the Samba password using the `smbpasswd` command, and it ran into the snag that the local Windows password wasn't changed at the same time. This section demonstrates how to change both. It's done from the Windows side. First, assume both the Windows and the Samba password for user username are set to pas1. This enables the smbclient usage:

```
$ smbclient '//mainserv/homes' -U username%pas1
added interface ip=192.168.100.1 bcast=192.168.100.255 nmask=255.255.255.0
added interface ip=192.168.200.101 bcast=192.168.200.255 nmask=255.255.255.0
Domain=[MYGROUP] OS=[Unix] Server=[Samba 2.0.6]
smb: \>
```

Now change both the Windows and the Samba server passwords simultaneously from the Windows side. Double-click the Passwords icon in Windows Control Panel and click the Change Passwords tab. The dialog box is shown in Figure 16.2.

FIGURE 16.2

The Passwords Properties dialog box.

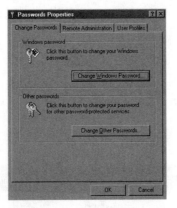

Now click the Change Windows Password button to access the Change Windows Password dialog box. Highlight *and* check Microsoft Networking in the service list, as shown in Figure 16.3.

FIGURE 16.3

The Change Windows Password dialog box with Microsoft Networking highlighted and checked.

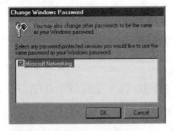

Click the OK button to access the Old and New Password dialog box, which is also titled "Change Windows Password" in its title bar. On the Old and New Password dialog box, fill in the old password (pas1, in this example) and type **passwd2** into the New Password and Confirm New Password fields, as shown in Figure 16.4.

FIGURE 16.4

The Old and New Password dialog box.

Click the OK button on the Old and New Password dialog box. A message box appears that states "The Windows password has been successfully changed," as shown in Figure 16.5.

FIGURE 16.5

The Success message box.

Click OK on the message box and close all the other password change boxes. Now try your old password in `smbclient`:

```
$ smbclient '//mainserv/homes' -U username%pas1
added interface ip=192.168.100.1 bcast=192.168.100.255 nmask=255.255.255.0
added interface ip=192.168.200.101 bcast=192.168.200.255 nmask=255.255.255.0
session setup failed: ERRSRV - ERRbadpw (Bad password - name/password pair in a
Tree Connect or Session Setup are invalid.)
$
```

The preceding `smbclient` session shows that the old pas1 password fails. Using the new passwd2 password succeeds, as shown in the following session:

```
$ smbclient '//mainserv/homes' -U username%passwd2
added interface ip=192.168.100.1 bcast=192.168.100.255 nmask=255.255.255.0
added interface ip=192.168.200.101 bcast=192.168.200.255 nmask=255.255.255.0
Domain=[MYGROUP] OS=[Unix] Server=[Samba 2.0.6]
smb: \>
```

Log out of and back in to Windows and note that the new password works. The Windows and Samba passwords were both changed by a single action on the Windows client.

> **Note**
>
> Note that the preceding procedure does not change the UNIX password unless password synchronization is undertaken with the `unix password sync=yes` parameter in place.

Adding a Logon Script to the Logon Server

The preceding section described how the Samba server can be used for Windows 9x authentication through adding three [global] statements in smb.conf and changing to NT domain logons in the Client for Microsoft Networks Properties dialog box.

This section describes the process of enabling logon scripts. Because of the numerous possible missteps that can derail logon scripts, and because troubleshooting such missteps can be time-consuming, this section builds a practical logon script in small steps. The first step involves creating the simplest possible logon script.

Creating the Simplest Possible Logon Script

The first step is to create a [netlogon] share to house the logon scripts. Add the following lines to smb.conf:

```
[netlogon]
path=/data/dos/netlogon
read only=yes
guest ok=no
oplocks=no
write list=@username
```

It's read-only and non-guesting for security reasons. This example gives members of the primary group of user username (which in this case is group username) write access, thus enabling the use of Windows editors via Samba to create logon scripts having the proper carriage return/linefeed line terminations. Alternatively, the vi editor could be used on the server to carefully add ^M to the end of every line.

Note the use of path=/data/dos/netlogon. The primary purpose of this share is to provide a path for logon scripts. The path does not need to be user- or group-dependent, because individual files and directories within it can be made user- or group-dependent. This path should *not* include the [homes] directory, based on the following entry in DOMAINS.txt. This is the quote from DOMAINS.txt:

Luke Kenneth Casson Leighton's DOMAINS.txt Quote

[lkcl 26aug96 - we have discovered a problem where Windows clients can maintain a connection to the [homes] share in between logons. The [homes] share must NOT therefore be used in a profile path.]

The preceding cautionary note in DOMAINS.txt refers to roaming profiles, not the [netlogon] directory. Also, the entry is dated August 1996, meaning the problem may have been fixed. Nevertheless, prudence dictates that neither [netlogon] nor the profile directory include the path specified by [homes] in its path. It's customary to avoid the [homes] path in the [netlogon] and [profile] (discussed later this chapter) shares.

The final smb.conf task is to define the file used as a logon script. Place this line in the [global] section:

```
logon script=test.bat
```

The preceding line states that file test.bat, which will be found in the special [netlogon] share, is the logon script for clients authenticating to the server. Note that logon scripts are always located relative to [netlogon].

A share isn't much good without its directory. In this example, the [netlogon] share is in /data/dos/netlogon. Create the directory with permissions 711 up the tree and 775 for the netlogon subdirectory itself. Make the netlogon subdirectory's group the same as username's primary group so that user username can edit scripts via Samba.

> **Caution**
>
> If directory /data or /data/dos exists, do not change its ownership or permissions. As long as the [netlogon] share is executable by all, all the way up the tree, it works.

Here are the commands for creating the directory for this share, assuming it must be created from scratch:

```
$ mkdir -m711 /data
$ mkdir -m711 /data/dos
$ mkdir -m775 /data/dos/netlogon
$ chown root.username /data/dos/netlogon
```

So far, the [netlogon] share has been created both in smb.conf and in the file system, and the logon script has been declared to be test.bat in the [netlogon] share's root directory. Now create the simplest possible script that positively gives evidence of itself—a single call to the DOS choice command:

```
c:\windows\command\choice.com
```

When run with no command-line arguments, choice.com stops and prompts the user to press the Y or N key:

```
[Y,N]?
```

At this point, the sample `smb.conf` should look like this:

```
[global]
netbios name=mainserv
workgroup=MYGROUP
encrypt passwords=yes

wins support=yes
domain master=yes
domain logons=yes
logon script=test.bat

[netlogon]
path=/data/dos/netlogon
read only=yes
guest ok=no
oplocks=no
write list=@username

[homes]
read only=no
```

Save `smb.conf` and run `testparm` to make sure it's a legal file. Fix any problems revealed before going further.

Once `testparm` produces no error messages, restart Samba and then log off and log back on to the Windows client. See whether you're presented with the [Y,N]? prompt, and if so press either Y or N to see the rest of the script execute. If you do not see the prompt, it's time to troubleshoot.

Moving the Script to a Subdirectory

Create the subdirectory like this:

```
# mkdir -m775 /data/dos/netlogon/scripts
# chgrp username /data/dos/netlogon/scripts
```

The preceding is valid on Red Hat machines set up with User Private Groups. If your username user's primary group is not username, substitute its value for username in the preceding command.

Next, create the following `test.bat` batch file in the `/data/dos/netlogon/scripts` directory:

```
echo This is test.bat in ./scripts
c:\windows\command\choice.com
```

The `echo` statement in the preceding script marks the script so that the output makes it evident that this script is the one coming from the `scripts` subdirectory. Now modify the `logon script=` parameter to include the subdirectory, as follows:

```
logon script=scripts\test.bat
```

Using Samba as Your Windows 98 Logon Mechanism

CHAPTER 16

465

16

USING SAMBA AS
YOUR WINDOWS 98
LOGON MECHANISM

> **Caution**
>
> Be aware that the `logon script=` command uses a DOS-type backslash as a directory separator rather than a UNIX-type forward slash. Use of a forward slash appears to run a logon script, but in fact it does not run the intended script. This can be very hard to troubleshoot.
>
> This is such a common slipup that it's recommended that you deliberately use a forward slash and note how it prevents the logon script from running. Always look at the slashes in the `logon script=` parameter if the logon script appears not to run.

Save `smb.conf`. Test it with `testparm` and fix it as necessary. When `smb.conf` passes `testparm`, restart Samba, log off, and then log back on to the Windows machine. If everything is correct, the proper logon script operates, requiring a press of the Y or N key.

Creating a User-Specific Logon Script

A single logon script for all users is unlikely. The most common case is for each user to have a logon script. This is easy once you have a working `test.bat`. Create the following `username.bat`:

```
echo This is user username
c:\windows\command\choice.com
```

Pick another user. For the sake of this example, the user will be called `otheruser`. Be sure to substitute whatever other user you have available. Next, create the following `otheruser.bat`:

```
echo This is user otheruser
c:\windows\command\choice.com
```

Finally, change the `logon script=` parameter as follows:

```
logon script=scripts\%U.bat
```

Restart Samba. Then log out and log on to the Windows machine as `username` and as whatever other user you substituted for `otheruser`. Note that the logon script is user dependent.

Creating a Useful Logon Script

The primary challenge of creating logon scripts is that they execute in the black box of logging on, thus presenting a difficult troubleshooting challenge. This section presents an example of a script that "should" work as well as the steps necessary to troubleshoot it. This example has been tested on a Pentium II 300 running the original Windows 98 OS.

Start by changing `username.bat` to the following:

```
net use z: \\mainserv\homes /yes
explorer z:
```

The preceding batch file "should" map drive letter `z:` to `\\mainserv\homes` and then open a graphical directory of that drive. Indeed, navigating to and double-clicking `\\mainserv\netlogon\scripts\username.bat` performs exactly as expected. But when logging out and logging back on as `username`, the graphical directory to `z:` does not appear. A `net use` command reveals that neither `z:` nor `\\mainserv\homes` is used. The only used resource is `\\mainserv\netlogon`, and it's not mapped to a drive letter. It's as if the script never ran.

The most reliable way to determine whether the script has run is to insert the following command into the logon script:

```
c:\windows\command\choice
```

Inserting the preceding command stops the logon script and prompts for Y or N, so you know that the script is running. However, its commands are ineffectual. It works when double-clicked in Windows Explorer but not when run as a logon script. Something is very different when it's run as a logon script, so a "peephole" into the running script is needed.

Log files always provide a great peephole. Remove the call to `choice` and add various log file appends, as follows:

```
net use > c:\test.log
net use y: \\mainserv\homes /yes >> c:\test.log
net use >> c:\test.log
explorer y:
```

Log out and log back on as `username`; then examine `c:\test.log`. The following is what you see in that log file:

```
Status        Local name     Remote name
OK            Z:             \\MAINSERV\NETLOGON
The command was completed successfully.
The command was completed successfully.
```

The log file reveals that the first `net use` command shows that drive `z:` was already in use—it was mapped to special share `\\mainserv\netlogon`. Because drive `z:` is not present after the logon is completed, a logical conclusion is that a part of the logon process deletes that drive mapping.

It seems odd that the second `net use` command without arguments produces no output instead of a resource listing. However, odd behavior is expected because the mapping to the `[netlogon]` special share was overwritten.

The obvious next step is to change all the z: instances in the logon script to y:. Once that's done and a fresh `username` logon is completed, a graphical directory of y:, mapped to \\mainserv\homes, pops up. The logon script works. Further confirmation comes from the log file, which now looks like the following:

```
Status          Local name     Remote name
OK              Z:                  \\MAINSERV\NETLOGON
The command was completed successfully.
The command was completed successfully.


Status          Local name     Remote name
OK              Y:                  \\MAINSERV\HOMES
OK              Z:                  \\MAINSERV\NETLOGON
The command was completed successfully.
```

This time everything works, and the second `net use` command without arguments produces the expected results. The output redirection to c:\test.log is for diagnostic purposes, so the redirection can be removed once the logon script works properly.

The primary challenge of logon scripts is the fact that they operate in a black box. The c:\windows\command\choice command is the best way to determine whether the script runs. Writing to a log file is one of the best ways to "peer inside" the running of the logon script.

Logon scripts can be user specific or group specific, or they can even rely on other parameters, depending on the replacement variable used to name the file. Once again, the major challenge is troubleshooting.

Troubleshooting Windows 98 Domain Logons

Domain logons can be a little tricky. However, generally speaking, if your Samba server is correctly configured and the previous instructions are followed, your problems will be minor. Make sure you're conversant with information sources, check the obvious, make sure the client is set to authenticate against an NT domain, and see whether the logon script runs.

Information Sources

Domain logons require some subject matter expertise. Information sources include the distribution Samba documentation, newsgroups such as comp.protocols.smb, Web sites such as www.samba.org, and mailing lists such as samba@samba.org as well as the Samba project's other fine mailing lists.

Check the Obvious

Start by taking five minutes to run through DIAGNOSIS.txt and fix any problems there. It's tough to get domain logons working on a defective Samba setup.

Is Windows Set to Log On to an NT Domain?

The clients must have their Client for Microsoft Networks set to "Log on to Windows NT Domain" and must also be set to "Log on and Restore Connections." The Windows NT Domain field on the Client for Microsoft Networks dialog box must be set to the domain of the server.

Does the Logon Script Run?

It's sometimes hard to see whether the logon script runs. Place the following command at the top of the script to unequivocally prove whether it runs:

```
c:\windows\command\choice.com
```

If you need to peer inside a logon script, have its commands write to a log file. While on the subject of logon scripts, remember that a logon script that changes directories or drives without changing back appears to hang, thus requiring the user to press Esc.

Does net use Work?

Verify the readability of \\server\netlogon with the net use command.

Symptoms and Solutions

When the logon script appears to hang, immediately check whether that script changes directories or drives without changing back. If so, that's why.

If the logon script does not run, check whether the logon script= parameter uses backslashes. If it does not use them, it will not run.

It's normal for Windows NT clients to be unable to log on to a server configured according to this chapter. NT clients require a primary domain controller (PDC). PDCs are covered in Chapter 17, "Using Samba As the NT Primary Domain Controller."

Setting Up Roaming User Profiles

If roaming profiles weren't so valuable in creating homogenous, appliance-like clients, we wouldn't bother with them. They can seem extremely temperamental. Of course, they're really not temperamental because they constantly follow their own logic. However, that logic involves so many variables that when something goes wrong, it can seem like an intermittent problem. Once again, roaming profiles can be extremely valuable in certain departments and enterprises, so this chapter explains how to use them with a minimum of trouble.

The personality of a Windows 98 computer can be made to change according to which user is logged in. These personality differences are called *profiles*.

Caution

Roaming profiles can trash your favorite computer's settings, including MS Word's smart quotes feature, and even the video resolution, thus overdriving your monitor. While experimenting with roaming profiles, always work with a user other than the username under which you normally work.

With a Samba server acting as a logon server, these profiles can be stored on the server itself. This allows the user to have his profile "roam" with him to any computer he uses, as long as that computer has the same Samba server as a logon server.

The profile includes color combinations, lists of previously accessed files, video settings, and even the Start menu and policies. In many respects, a user can have every computer on the network act just like the one he usually works on. This can be a great convenience.

However, it's not for everyone. If the computers have significantly different hardware, the profile may choke on some setting or force the user to downgrade his settings. In certain cases, even video resolution can be defined by the roaming profile. There can be problems if the user changes his environment on two computers at once, because one environment will overwrite the other.

Roaming user profiles are most advantageous in homogeneous environments in which unsophisticated users view their computers as appliances to complete their work rather than as malleable tools to use imaginatively.

Setting up roaming profiles requires several major steps, each of which consists of many minor steps. The major steps can be done in different sequences, depending on the situation. This section's example sets up roaming profiles after an initial investigation of test jig systems, the Samba 2.0.6 profile path fix, and the timing issues that are so critical to successfully implementing roaming profiles.

Note

Roaming profiles are complex, and troubleshooting them can be challenging, to say the least. If you encounter problems, be sure to read the section titled "Troubleshooting Roaming Profiles," later in this chapter.

Start with a Test Jig System

Because of the complexity of roaming profiles and policies, and because of the potential harm they can cause if implemented incorrectly, your first attempt should not be on a live system. Instead, do it first on a test jig system comprised of a Linux/Samba server and two cheap Windows boxes.

The Samba 2.0.6 Profile Path Fix

The `logon path=` parameter defines the location of roaming profiles. However, in Samba 2.0.6, that parameter is ignored in the placement of the profile files and directories, which instead are placed in the home directory. This is due to a fix that changed `/home` to point to the home directory instead of the logon path. Unfortunately, it assigned the logon path to the home directory regardless of the value of `logon path=`.

This change can be reverted in `source/smbd/ipc.c`. There are two calls of the following syntax:

```
pstrcpy(p2, lp_logon_home());
```

One is at line 2481, and one is at line 2517, both in the `api_RnetUserGetInfo()` function. To bring back the functionality of the `logon path=` parameter, change each to the following:

```
pstrcpy(p2, lp_logon_path());
```

Once these changes have been made, `make` the executable and `make install` or copy the executables to the proper place.

This fix might adversely affect the `net use h: /home` command. Roaming profiles still work without this fix, but they're thrown right into the user's home directory.

The remainder of this chapter assumes this fix has been made.

Roaming Profile Timing

Roaming profiles are extremely time dependent. Their behavior is predictable only to the extent that all computers' clocks are synchronized. The rest of the roaming profile section assumes both Windows clients and the Linux/Samba server are synchronized to within 10 seconds. It also assumes that both clients are configured to be in the same time zone and that their daylight savings time flags are configured the same.

If a logon server is used, the clients are set up with Client for Microsoft Networks configured to "Log on to NT Domain," and the Users Can Customize... radio button is checked in the Password Properties dialog box's User Profile tab, then a copy of the profile is kept on the logon server and a local copy is kept on the client.

Upon logging off, the cached profile is written locally and immediately thereafter is written to the logon server. This is done regardless of the timestamp on the logon server's existing copy. So, upon logoff, the logon server has a profile slightly later than the local copy.

Upon logging on, the local profile date stamp is compared with the logon server's copy, and the later of the two is used and cached locally. That cached copy, with any modifications during the session, are once again written to the server upon logoff.

> **Note**
>
> If, upon logging on, the client finds no profile on the server, it writes its profile to the server immediately.

Here's a timing problem example. Clients A and B have been logged off for an hour. At 8:00, client A logs on and begins work. At 8:10, client B logs on, changes the desktop scheme from its formerly obnoxious "large pumpkin" scheme, and logs off at 8:20, writing those changes to the server. Client A logs off at 8:30, writing its unchanged cached profile to the server. Client B's scheme change is overwritten by Client A's inaction.

If both clients had changed the scheme, the first one to log off would have had its changes overwritten. Here's another example. Client A logs on at 9:00 and changes the profile but keeps working. Client B logs on at 9:30, getting the old profile since client A has not yet logged off and written the changes to the server. Client A finishes at 10:00 and logs off, writing the changes to the server. Client B finishes at 10:30 and logs off, writing its profile, which was the original, to the server, thus overwriting client A's changes.

Any time a client computer changes a user's profile, steps should be taken to ensure that that particular client is the only one logged in as that user, and that the changes are immediately written by logging off.

Things get hairy if there's a time discrepancy. For instance, if both clients are set to the same time but one is Eastern time and one is Pacific time (three hours behind), modifications on the Pacific time computer are always recognized on the Eastern time computer, but changes on the Eastern time computer are never recognized on the Pacific time computer. Actually, *always* and *never* aren't quite accurate, because if the Pacific computer has been logged off for more than three hours when changes are made and recorded (via logoff) on the Eastern time computer, then the profile is transferred to the Pacific time computer.

Similar anomalies occur if there's a discrepancy between the clients' clocks. If client A is set to the right time, but client B is set an hour fast, then client B's changes are recognized by client A, but client A's changes are overwritten by client B. Once again, if client B has been logged off for more than an hour before client A makes its changes and then logs back off, client A's changes transfer to client B.

A server with the wrong time does not stop the transfer of profiles, but it can interfere with the server setup of profiles.

Most of the rest of this chapter involves various examples of roaming profile configurations. If these are to be done in a reasonable amount of time, the two client computers and the server computer must be synchronized to within a few seconds. Always wait an interval that's much longer than the discrepancy between the clocks between logging off one client and logging on the other.

When any kind of roaming profile problems occur, immediately investigate time sync. Make sure all clients have the same time to within a few seconds, and that all clients are set to the same time zone and daylight savings settings. Make sure the server is set to within a few seconds of the client computers' time. Any time there's a suspicion that roaming profile problems involve timing, carefully note the timestamp of USER.DAT (in the root of logon path=) after logging off each client. If one client seems to write an earlier or later file, fix that problem before troubleshooting roaming profiles.

It's easy to make a timing mistake. The tiny time displays in clients' system trays can match perfectly, yet mask a time mismatch. To save hours of troubleshooting time, always double-check these elements of client time sync:

- Time
- a.m./p.m. designator
- Date
- Time zone
- Daylight savings designator

smb.conf Changes

Start with this simple baseline logon server smb.conf, making sure it functions as a logon server:

```
[global]
netbios name=mainserv
workgroup=MYGROUP
encrypt passwords=yes
```

```
wins support=yes
domain master=yes
domain logons=yes

[homes]
read only=no
```

Once the preceding `smb.conf` is verified to work and authenticate against the server, add the [profile] share.

> **Note**
>
> The preceding does not contain the [netlogon] share for simplicity's sake as well as to demonstrate that it's not necessary for roaming profiles. However, there's nothing wrong with including it. Note also that the [netlogon] share *is* necessary for networked system policies, which are discussed later in this chapter.

Add the [profile] Share

The [profile] share is traditionally where the profiles are kept. Unlike [netlogon], it's not a special name recognized by Samba. It could be named anything, but usually it's called [profile]. Its purpose is to serve as a target for the logon path= parameter.

Add the following share to `smb.conf`:

```
[profile]
path=/data/dos/profile
read only=no
create mode=600
directory mode=770
browseable=no
guest ok=no
```

The path must be executable all the way down, with the final directory set as chmod 777 so that new users can create their own profile directories in it. For the same reason, the read only=no setting is used. The create mode and directory mode parameters reflect the fact that the user must read and write files within his profile directories. The browseable=no setting reflects the fact that this share is used only for logons and should not be visited by the curious. Guesting in the profiles would be insecure, hence the guest ok=no setting.

Now that the repository of profiles has been defined, the next step is to point to it with the logon path= parameter.

`logon path=\\mainserv\profile\%U`

Insert the following in the `[global]` section:

```
logon path=\\mainserv\profile\%U
```

The preceding statement deserves some special attention. First, notice that it uses backslashes and not forward slashes. If profile problems occur, always verify that this parameter uses the Windows-style share designation, because using the wrong slashes is a common oversight.

> **Caution**
>
> Use of forward slashes instead of DOS style backslashes causes the logon script not to work. It's an incredibly common mistake, and often necessitates overly-long troubleshooting sessions. Always double-check the slashes on your `logon path=` parameter.

Next, notice `%U` at the end. That's a subdirectory under the `[profile]` share. How is the subdirectory made? Typically, such subdirectories are created with a `root preexec=` server-side automation, but in this particular case, `smbd` does it automatically, hence the lack of `root preexec=`.

Do Not Use `[homes]`

The `logon path=` parameter must never include the `[homes]` share. For instance, the following would be taboo:

```
logon path=\\mainserv\homes\profile\%U
```

The reason is stated in the following quote from `DOMAINS.txt`:

> **Luke Kenneth Casson Leighton's `DOMAINS.txt` Quote**
>
> [lkcl 26aug96 - we have discovered a problem where Windows clients can maintain a connection to the `[homes]` share in between logons. The `[homes]` share must NOT therefore be used in a profile path.]

The preceding cautionary note in `DOMAINS.txt` is dated August 1996, meaning the problem may have been fixed. If it has been, that fact was never widely published and `DOMAINS.txt` was never updated. Therefore, prudence dictates that the value of `logon path=` not contain the `homes` share.

Create the Profile Directory

If it hasn't been done yet, create the profile directory, which in this example is /data/dos/ profile. Make sure it's executable all the way up the path and that the profile subdirectory is mode 777. It should be owned by root, with the root user's primary group as its group.

Enable Profiles on the Windows Client

Choose Passwords from the Windows Control Panel to access the Password Properties dialog box; then click the User Profiles tab. Check the Users Can Customize... radio button, leaving everything else unchecked, as shown in Figure 16.6. You do not want desktop icons or the Start menu customized, in case anything fails. Once the system is rock solid, you can add those items to the roaming profiles.

FIGURE 16.6

The User Profiles tab of the Passwords Properties dialog box.

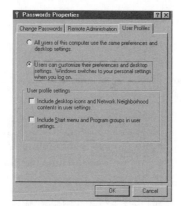

Click the OK button. When asked to restart the computer, click Yes.

Note

The restart done by Windows after changing the User Profiles tab of the Passwords Properties dialog box is not sufficient to completely enable user profiles, and it can leave the computer in an inconsistent state. In this inconsistent state, the Domain field is often not offered upon logon. To achieve a consistent and correct state, when the machine comes back up, shut it down and then power it back up.

Make a slight configuration change (maybe change the desktop scheme); then log out and log back in again as username. So far, all profiles are kept on the client.

Preparing to Test

As mentioned earlier, make sure all computer times are synchronized to within 10 seconds. Also, make sure all clients have the same time zones and the same daylight savings setting.

Log off all clients. For good measure, reboot the clients you'll be testing.

Run testparm and make sure smb.conf is a legally configured file.

Finally, restart Samba to incorporate the changes and leave the system in a defined state.

On the server, verify the existence of a test user or create one. For this example, the new user is called username. Run smbpasswd -a username on that user to give the user a known password.

Testing the Profiles

Go to the profile directory (/data/dos/profile, in this example). See whether the user already has a directory. If so, go into that directory and note the date on USER.DAT. The following is the best command to use:

```
$ ls -l --full-time USER.DAT
```

The --full-time option enables reading of timestamps in the future. Without it, future timestamps show the year instead of the time, as follows (assume the command was issued 11/26/1999):

```
-rw-------   1 username username   458784 Nov 27  1999 USER.DAT
```

If your UNIX implementation doesn't have --full-time, use something else to read future timestamps.

If there's not yet a /data/dos/profile/username subdirectory, change to the /data/dos/profile directory. Log on to the test user name (username, in this example) on the client and watch as the subdirectory is created (if it wasn't there) and watch as the timestamp changes for USER.DAT. That timestamp should be accurate to within 10 seconds. If not, fix it. It's important to get roaming profiles working with a single client before attempting multiple clients.

Once the first client is synced, perform the following experiment:

1. Log in and log out from the client.
2. Copy USER.DAT to OLD.DAT.
3. Log in and verify that the correct screen scheme comes up.

4. Change the scheme to another scheme. High contrast white is an excellent choice for this experiment.

5. Log off the client, log back on, and verify that the new scheme "sticks." Log off the client again.

6. Rename USER.DAT as NEWER.DAT.

7. Copy OLD.DAT to USER.DAT.

8. Wait long enough to overcome any time-sync discrepancy between the client and server. A good indication is that the system time is later than the timestamp on NEWER.DAT.

9. Use the touch command to update the date of USER.DAT (touch USER.DAT).

10. Log on to the client and verify that the old scheme is displayed on the client. This proves that the schemes are being written to and received from the server.

The preceding test gives you a hint on how to set up client environments from the server.

Now that roaming profiles have been tested with one client, test them with two (call them A and B). Assume they've been checked and found to be completely synced, in all ways, to within 10 seconds. Now follow these steps:

1. Log off all clients using the test user (username). Leave them logged off for more than the time discrepancy between the clients. Note that although A and B have been synced, others might not have been. If USER.DAT appears to be in the future, rename it.

2. Log on to A, change the scheme to high contrast black, and log off. Wait a longer period than the time discrepancy between the clients.

3. Log on to B and verify that its scheme is now high contrast black, as set by client A.

4. Set the scheme on B to red, white, and blue and then log off. Wait a longer period than the time discrepancy between the clients.

5. Log on to A and verify that the scheme is now red, white, and blue.

Mandatory Profiles

Mandatory profiles are profiles unchangeable by the user. In other words, they're dictated by the system administrator. Basically, you can make a normal profile mandatory by renaming the USER.DAT file to USER.MAN. Beyond that you need to change the directory owner and directory and file permissions so the user cannot rename USER.MAN back to USER.DAT, and cannot modify the file via a share or UNIX command line access to the UNIX box. The entire tree for the user's profile must be modified for read-only access. A script can be created to do all this work while adding a user.

Mandatory profiles are important because they take the thin client concept to a new level.

Including Desktop Icons and Start Menu Choices

The real purpose of roaming profiles is to set up a series of uniform clients to act as appliances. This is best accomplished by having a profile specify the desktop icons and Start menu selections.

From the User Profiles tab on the Passwords Properties dialog box (refer back to Figure 16.6), check both the "Include Desktop Icons and Network Neighborhood Contents…" check box and the "Include Start Menu and Program Groups…" check box. Do this for both client A and client B.

Caution

Be aware that checking these boxes can trash a client's existing desktop icons, Network Neighborhood contents, Start menu, and program groups for any user subsequently logged in on that client. That's why it's vitally important that this task be done as the test user and that while those check boxes are checked, only the test user logs in or logs out.

This is tested (using the test user) by adding a shortcut to the desktop and menu on A, logging off, verifying that the shortcut shows up on B, and then adding another shortcut to the desktop and to the menu on B, logging off, and verifying that the new shortcut shows up on A. This must be done with the same respect for timing issues as the tests discussed earlier.

Roaming System Policies

When it comes to converting a hodgepodge collection of clients into a consistent fleet of disciplined appliances, this is where the rubber meets the road. First, the pitfalls of roaming system policies should be examined, as is done in the following section.

Caution

Because roaming system policies modify the local Registry, they can permanently lock out some or all users. *Never* modify policies for Default Computer or Default User unless you're positive that's what you really want to do. No examples in this chapter require modifications in these two areas. All examples in this chapter use experimental user username.

Using Samba as Your Windows 98 Logon Mechanism

CHAPTER 16

479

16

USING SAMBA AS
YOUR WINDOWS 98
LOGON MECHANISM

Roaming System Policy Potential Pitfalls

As long as there's some user with rights to use the network and the `poledit` program, policy errors can be backed out (although with difficulty).

If you must change Default User, make sure to first create a fully privileged administrative user who can change the Registry and policies. That admin user should have the DOS prompt, regedit, and the Start menu Run command enabled *explicitly* (blank in the tri-state check box). If you must change Default Computer, make sure to first add a fully privileged administrative computer that can change the Registry and policies.

It's highly recommended that any experimentation be done on a test jig network lacking valuable data. Once a sound knowledge has been gained and perfected by practice, it's reasonable to use roaming policies on a live network.

In the event of a complete lockout, try the following:

1. Shut down Samba.

2. Use `ftp` to load `\\server\netlogon\CONFIG.POL` onto a standalone Windows 98 box with `poledit` privileges.

3. Rename `\\server\netlogon\CONFIG.POL` as `\\server\netlogon\CONFIG.OLD` on the UNIX box.

4. Use `poledit` to edit the local `CONFIG.POL`, setting at least one existing user and one existing computer on `Windows 98 System/Shell/Restrictions/Remove run Command` and all settings in `Windows 98 System/Restrictions` to the blanks state. These are tri-state check boxes, with checked meaning "restrict and change local policy to restrict," unchecked meaning "do not restrict and change local policy to unrestricted," and grayed meaning "use local value and leave local value as-is."

5. Save the policy to the standalone machine's hard drive.

6. Use `ftp` to send the new policy up to `\\mainserv\netlogon\CONFIG.POL`. Set it to mode `744` and set its owner to the administrative user. If there's an administrative group, set it to that group also.

7. Back up `\\mainserv\netlogon\CONFIG.POL` so that you don't need to go through all this again.

8. Log in to the administrative computer as the administrative user and fix everything with `poledit`.

9. Start Samba.

Enabling Networked System Profiles

Begin by making sure roaming profiles work perfectly. Once they do, perform the steps outlined in the following sections.

Fix `smb.conf`

Networked system policies require the special `[netlogon]` share. If it isn't yet in `smb.conf`, insert it as follows:

```
[netlogon]
path=/data/dos/netlogon
read only=yes
guest ok=no
oplocks=no
```

Be sure the `oplocks=no` setting is in place; otherwise, there may be problems with mismatches between local cached copies and the network copy.

Create `CONFIG.POL`

Log in to one of your PCs as a user other than `username`. Obviously, that user must be set up on the Samba server. Run `poledit` on the windows box, choose File, New Policy from the menu. Then choose Edit, New User from the menu and type in **username** and click the OK button. A new icon for `username` appears in the window. Double-click that icon to see the policy tree.

It's a typical Windows tree, with expanding nodes going down to leaf nodes. Each leaf node has a tri-state check box. A check mark means "enable this policy and overwrite the local policy with it." A blank means "disable this policy and disable it on the local policy." A grayed box means "ignore this policy and do not update it in the local policy."

To tightly restrict clients logged in as `username`, place check marks in the following:

- `Windows 98 Network/Sharing` Check all options.
- `Windows 98 System/Shell/Restrictions` Check the "Remove 'Run' Command" and "Don't Save Settings at Exit" options. You may want to check others for greater security. Checking "Disable Shutdown Command" means the Windows client computer cannot be cleanly turned off or rebooted without logging in as a different user. This may encourage unsafe shutdowns/reboots using the power switch or reboot switch—clearly, an unintended consequence.
- `Windows 98 System/Desktop Display/Color Scheme` You can pick one color scheme for this user. This is helpful in determining whether the policy has been in force, but it's not necessary for security.
- `Windows 98 System/Restrictions` Check all options except "Only Run Allowed Windows Applications." The selection of all but this option disables the user's use of Registry-editing tools and access to the DOS prompt. The lack of access to Registry tools makes it extremely difficult for a user to "back out" the policy, especially if the default user is not allowed to change the Registry (but remember the previous cautions).

If it's desired to limit this user to a few specific apps, the "Only Run Allowed Windows Applications" option can be checked and those apps input; however, keep in mind this will substantially slow troubleshooting.

Once the changes are complete, back up any existing \\server\netlogon\CONFIG.POL and save it as \\server\netlogon\CONFIG.POL.

Enabling Client Download and Upload of Policies

On each client computer subject to networked system policies, use poledit to enable remote updates. From the menu, choose File, Open Registry and then double-click Local Computer and make sure that Windows 98 Network/Update/Remote Update is checked. Because this is usually the default, chances are you can simply cancel out of this poledit session.

This can be done directly in regedit by navigating to HKEY_LOCAL_MACHINE\System\ CurrentControlSet\Control\Update, and within that "directory" ensuring that the item UpdateMode is a dword valued 0x00000001. However, do not use regedit! The poledit program is much safer and can be installed from the Windows 98 installation CD.

Test

Restart Samba, log on as username, and verify that the DOS prompt is no longer accessible and that the Run option is no longer part of the Start menu.

To back out the changes, use poledit on \\server\netlogon\CONFIG.POL (while logged in as the same user who created it) to blank out all the check boxes you checked for username and then log in on all clients that the policy affected. Then use poledit again to gray out all those check boxes, thereby leaving everything pretty much as it was.

Summary: Networked System Policies

Networked system policies are perfect for enforcing a standard appliance client on the network. However, they must not be approached lightly—a single slip can lock out all access. Managing networked system policies is a legitimate system administration duty. Such policies are not something for the newbie or wannabe to use (on a live network, that is).

Roaming Profile Areas of Concern

Serious challenges must be addressed before implementing roaming profiles. None of these challenges is a show stopper, but each one must be known and addressed so it doesn't bite you later.

Best Suited to Homogeneous User Communities

Roaming profiles are not well suited to a community of power users requiring custom desktops. They're especially ill suited to environments where users routinely change their own desktops, Start menus, and so on. Timing issues and other overwrite issues almost guarantee heavy help desk activity in such an environment.

Roaming profiles are best used in environments containing relatively naive users who view their computers as appliances.

Video Sync

Under certain circumstances, a user updating his video resolution on one client updates it on other clients via his roaming profile. If he updates his brand-new 21-inch monitor system to 1600×1200 and then logs into a system with a 10-year-old 14-inch standard VGA monitor, that monitor can be overdriven. Overdriven monitors can sustain physical damage.

Clock

Under certain circumstances, changing the clock on one system might force a clock change on another.

Dial-Up Networking

Dial-Up Networking is part of the profile and can be adversely changed in certain circumstances.

Policies

Policies can lock out all users. Recovering from a total policy lockout was covered in the "Roaming System Policies" section. It's always a good idea to back up the latest known good copy of CONFIG.POL.

Start Menu Items

A carefully crafted set of Start menu items can be trashed by roaming profiles. Unless the machine has that same Start menu system under another user or the default user, restoring the menu system is a tedious, manual job.

Application Defaults

Application defaults are part of the profile. Carefully crafted application defaults, such as turning off smart quotes in MS Word, can be undone by roaming profiles. Once again, without the correct profile under another user, there's little hope of restoring the defaults in an automated fashion.

Minimizing Risk with Profile Tree Backups

If the [profile] tree and the [netlogon] trees are backed up regularly, they can be restored to their prior states. However, because of timing issues, the restored trees must be run through a script that runs touch on all files, bringing them up to the system date, so that they won't be overwritten by the local profile.

Settling Special Windows 95 Concerns

There are certain concerns for Windows 95 that can be read in the DOMAINS.txt file that comes with your Samba distribution.

Roaming Profile Benefits

Given the numerous challenges of roaming profiles, why would anyone want to implement them?

Roaming profiles bring order to an otherwise chaotic network. They enable a user to "feel at home" on any PC on the network. They make the client computers more like appliances and less like user-configurable computers.

With the addition of networked system policies, they form an additional layer of security by preventing users from "freelancing" their configurations and preventing use of unauthorized programs. They reduce help desk traffic by implementing a standardized interface.

Chapter 40, "Niche Example: Using Samba in the Litigation Department," describes the type of environment where tightly regulated profiles and policies are mandatory.

A well thought out system of roaming profiles and policies can exist even in environments with some power users. The policies can be made to exclude those power users by giving them their own profiles that basically say "let the local machine decide." Problems with profiles clobbering each other can be minimized by good practices, including logging off and logging on immediately after any important changes.

Roaming profiles aren't for everyone. But in those cases where homogeneity, security, and order are called for, they're important problem solvers.

Troubleshooting Roaming Profiles

First, run DIAGNOSIS.txt and fix any problems. Then address the big three trouble sources: timing, timing, and timing. On the clients check the following:

- Time
- a.m./p.m. designator
- Date

- Time zone
- Daylight savings designator

If all the clients are in the same time zone, make sure the server's time is matched to that of all the clients. In a test setup, all boxes should be within 10 seconds of each other. In a live environment, they should be within a minute or so of each other.

Once you dispense with the basics and timing issues, if you still encounter problems, make sure you understand everything in this chapter.

A trivial error that causes many problems is the use of forward slashes where there should be backslashes in logon path= and logon script=. If there's a problem with Samba not recognizing the value of logon path=, verify the source code change in the section titled "The Samba 2.0.6 Profile Path Fix."

If you suspect a browsing problem, you might want to guarantee that the Samba box is a local browser with the addition of these three lines to the [global] section of smb.conf:

```
os level=255
preferred master=yes
local master=yes
```

Summary

Using Samba as your Windows 98 logon mechanism yields many benefits, including security, ease of administration, and the ability to homogenize the interfaces of clients across the network.

The simplest nonscripting Samba logon server looks like this:

```
[global]
netbios name=mainserv
workgroup=MYGROUP
encrypt passwords=yes

wins support=yes
domain master=yes
domain logons=yes

[homes]
read only=no
```

You would then create the user with smbpasswd -a username and restart Samba. All that remains is to enable logging in to an NT domain on the Client for Microsoft Networks Properties dialog box. Once Samba authentication is working, Samba passwords can be changed from the client, along with the client's version of the password. However, this does not change the UNIX password unless password synchronization is undertaken with the unix password sync=yes parameter in place. In addition, some other steps must be taken.

Adding a logon script requires the addition of the following line to `[global]`:

```
logon script=scripts\%U.bat
```

Then you would create the `[netlogon]` special share:

```
[netlogon]
path=/data/dos/netlogon
read only=yes
guest ok=no
oplocks=no
```

Of course, any path can be used. Finally, create the directory for `[netlogon]`. Make it mode `775`. Then create the `scripts` directory below it, once again mode `775`, and make sure both directories have a group to which Samba administrators belong.

Roaming profiles help yield consistent user interfaces for a given user throughout the network, although sometimes this can be more of a curse than a blessing. Power users typically should not have roaming profiles, whereas users whose jobs require "appliance" computers typically should have them. Roaming profiles are extremely sensitive to any desynchronization between clients.

To create roaming profiles on an existing Samba logon server, add the following line to `[global]`:

```
logon path=\\mainserv\profile\%U
```

Also, add the following share to `smb.conf`:

```
[profile]
path=/data/dos/profile
read only=no
create mode=600
directory mode=770
browseable=no
guest ok=no
```

Create the directory and then test it. Note that Windows 98's Passwords Properties dialog box must be set to recognize distinctive users. Be *absolutely* sure that all the machines' clocks are synchronized in all ways, including time, date, daylight savings, and time zone. Never configure roaming profiles on a live system unless you've thoroughly gone through the process on a test system.

Networked system policies are implemented by placing the properly configured `CONFIG.POL` in the `[netlogon]` share. Once again, never configure roaming system policies on a live system unless you've thoroughly gone through the process on a test system.

When there's a need to centralize authentication, profiles, and policies for networked Windows 9*x* computers, Samba does the job.

Using Samba as the NT Primary Domain Controller

by Daniel Robbins

IN THIS CHAPTER

Samba and PDCs

The ability to set up Samba as a primary domain controller has been an extremely desired feature of this popular network connectivity tool. This chapter begins by reviewing what a primary domain controller is and what a Windows NT domain is. It then explains the role a primary domain controller plays in a Windows NT environment. After that, the chapter delves into the inner workings of PDCs, where you'll take a look at an experimental version of Samba called *SAMBA_TNG*, which provides PDC support.

PDC support in Samba is, unfortunately, not quite ready for prime time (as of February 2000). If you're in need of a fully functional production-quality primary domain controller, your best bet right now is to use a Windows NT or 2000 product. Preliminary support for Samba acting as a primary domain controller appeared over a year ago. Since then, this preliminary support has been removed and then added back. In Samba releases, such as version 2.0.6, primary domain controller support is not advertised, although some exists. This is because the Samba development team believes that the PDC support that does exist in 2.0.*x* versions of Samba is not production quality and contains several bugs. Therefore, the Samba development team strongly cautions against using any Samba 2.0.*x* version as a primary domain controller, due to its instability. Take this into account before banking on a Samba PDC solution. Remember, PDC support is currently in the alpha stage, so some development still needs to be done.

PDC Functionality Overview

In a domain, domain controllers are responsible for authenticating users as well as performing other miscellaneous tasks. Every domain has at least one primary domain controller and any number of optional backup domain controllers. All the domain controllers in the same domain will actively replicate changes in their security database to one another so that all have the same data regarding which accounts exist and what their privileges are.

In an official Windows NT network, only NT servers can play the role of domain controller. When a server is set up, the administrator can choose whether the machine should serve as a primary domain controller (PDC), a backup domain controller (BDC), or a standalone server. The differences between all three are quite simple—a PDC acts as the primary authentication authority for the domain, whereas BDCs act as secondary authentication authorities, allowing the domain to continue operation even if the PDC goes down. Standalone servers, on the other hand, *use* the distributed security database but do not perform any role of authenticating client logins. Effectively, they are domain members, very similar to a Windows NT workstation that happens to be running Windows NT Server; this allows more advanced server software to be deployed on these machines.

When you look at PDCs and BDCs in the real world, you can get a better grasp of how they operate. Rather than simply serving as backups to the PDC, BDCs also share the load of authenticating all login and security database requests. Although adding a BDC to a domain is supposed to increase stability (by providing a certain amount of redundancy), the opposite can be true. If a PDC goes down, it can take a good amount of time for the client machines to recognize this fact (possibly up to an hour or more). During this time, a percentage of machines in the domain will be unable to find a domain controller. For example, if a domain contains one PDC and one BDC, bringing down one domain controller would cause approximately half the client machines to be unable to authenticate for about an hour. This is something to keep in mind when you're designing NT networks; when you're in the testing stages, make sure to test your domain controllers to see how they perform under such conditions.

> **Note**
>
> Although Windows NT Server 4.0 makes the distinction between primary and backup domain controllers, under Windows 2000, there is no such distinction. Domain controllers cooperatively replicate the active directory between domain controllers and handle unexpected domain controller downtime much more reliably. Again, to get a good idea how Windows 2000 will perform in your environment, it's always best to do a lot of testing.

This isn't to say that Windows NT domains are bad things—in fact, they're great if they're configured correctly and their strengths and weaknesses are properly understood. It's for this reason that the Samba development team has put such a tremendous effort toward adding mature PDC (as well as BDC) support to Samba. If Samba can participate in a domain to the same extent that a Windows NT server can, UNIX machines can then effectively replace Windows NT and 2000 servers without any loss of functionality, other than the ability to run Windows-based server software. Obviously, many "UNIX heads" salivate at the possibility of replacing Windows NT and 2000 servers with work-alike UNIX machines running Samba, and with good reason.

Client Workstations Overview

In a domain, *client workstations* are the machines regular users are allowed to use. These include Windows NT Workstation and 2000 Professional but can also include Windows 95, 98, and even UNIX machines. To be considered part of the domain, these client machines must be configured to authenticate against the domain's domain controllers. In turn, the domain controllers and other domain members grant these machines a certain level of trust in accessing shared resources. This does *not* mean that once a user has successfully logged into an NT Workstation machine that it is part of a domain or that the user has full access to of the domain's resources. However, it does mean that, to some extent, the domain has granted the user certain privileges to access resources on the network. If a user logs in as "guest," he or she might get only basic privileges, whereas logging on as "administrator" would allow full access to all resources and domain administration from a client machine. Exactly what kind of access is granted depends on the contents of the domain's security database and the permissions on the domain's shares, printers, and directories.

Secure and Insecure Workstations

Before setting up a domain, you need to understand the security implications of client workstations. For example, Windows NT Workstation and 2000 are designed to be *secure* clients; that is, they're designed to enforce the domain's security. In Figure 17.1, you can see a Windows NT Workstation login dialog box. In this dialog box, you can see that the user has the choice of two domains to log into. The first domain, GENTOO, is an actual domain in the sense discussed in this chapter; if the user chooses GENTOO, the workstation will check with one of GENTOO's domain controllers to verify that the user has rights to log into this machine. It's worth noting that under Windows NT and 2000, a failure to authenticate against one of GENTOO's domain controllers will result in an inability to log into this particular machine. The user will be stuck at this screen until he or she provides a valid username and password. The only alternative for the user would be to select NTBOX, which is the local client workstation's name, from the drop-down list. If this machine is configured to have a local account, the user can log into the machine (with a valid username and password) and use it as a standalone workstation only. Regardless, as you can see, without a valid domain or local account, the user is out of luck and unable to use the machine. For this reason, Windows NT and 2000 are considered secure clients.

Contrast this with Windows 95 and 98, which are *insecure* clients. You're probably familiar with the dialog box that 95 or 98 presents to allow a user to log into a Windows network. At this point, the user can simply click the Cancel button and be granted full access to the local machine! It doesn't matter whether the user has supplied a valid local or domain account; by design, Windows 95 and 98 allow any user to use the machine, with or without supplying a password. In fact, the act of logging into a Windows 95 machine is a convenience feature rather than a security feature. By logging in through the initial dialog box, a user can supply a username and password that will be used to attempt to connect to network resources such as shares and printers. However, the local machine has no such security features and can be used or abused by anyone who is able to sit in front of it.

FIGURE **17.1**
*Windows NT
Workstation login
dialog box.*

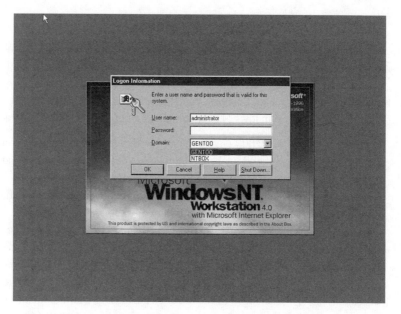

In addition to Windows NT and 2000, UNIX machines can be configured to be secure members of a domain. With the proper setup, a UNIX machine can be configured to authenticate all login requests against an existing domain. Because of UNIX's flexibility, a number of hybrid approaches are also possible. For more information on setting up a UNIX machine as a member of a domain, see Chapter 18, "Password Synchronization and Administration." In Figure 17.2, you can see a diagram of a domain that consists of two domain controllers and three workstations. Although all are considered part of the domain, the Windows 95 box does not effectively enforce domain security, thus allowing the machine to be easily tampered with.

FIGURE **17.2**
*A diagram of a
small, multiplat-
form domain.*

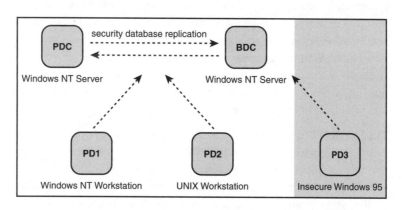

Domain Logons Overview

Domain logons are definitely the fundamental feature of a domain. In combination with secure clients, they effectively expand the security "umbrella" from a single server or group of servers to cover the entire organization. Although domain logons have been covered extensively in this chapter, this time you'll take a look at them from an administrator's perspective, under both Windows NT and Samba, looking at the benefits of each method.

In a pure–Windows NT/2000 environment, the fact that secure clients can perform domain logons is a tremendous help. Practically speaking, this means that an administrator can control all access to an organization's computing infrastructure simply by using User Manager for Domains on one of the NT servers. Remember, any change the administrator makes on a PDC or BDC is automatically replicated to the other servers. What's more, because all secure domain members will authenticate against either a PDC or BDC, the administrator literally controls all access to the domain from a single program. Because a domain can consist of thousands of machines, this is a tremendous benefit. The administrator does not need to worry about any password synchronization issues because all his or her changes to the security database are automatically propagated throughout the entire organization. All this functionality is handled by the Windows NT `netlogon` service.

Using Samba, domain logons provide a similar appeal. With a properly configured Samba PDC, all user accounts can be managed from a single machine. All changes to the `smbpasswd` file will be automatically propagated to other domain controllers. For this reason, the combination of a Samba PDC and secure clients (such as Windows NT and 2000), make for a very secure and easy-to-manage network environment.

User Profiles Overview

If domain logons constitute a domain's primary security feature, the domain's special handling of profiles is its primary convenience feature. As you might know, a profile consists of all your personal user settings as well as such things as your desktop background, items in the Start menu, certain Control Panel settings, and the contents of your desktop. Basically, a user profile contains almost all items customizable under Windows. In addition, many programs store their settings in a user profile, including Microsoft Outlook and Microsoft Internet Explorer.

The fact that Windows creates a new profile for each user of the machine means that every user gets to customize Windows the way he or she likes it. When a user logs back into the machine, his or her settings appear as the user left them, with the right icons and files on the desktop and the proper menu items in the Start menu. Although you might be used to using profiles only on standalone Windows machines, domains actually allow for the possibility of what are called *roaming profiles*. Practically speaking, roaming profiles allow you to log into any Windows machine in the domain and be greeted with your familiar desktop, wallpaper, and so on. This is a tremendous help for users who do not have their own desktop computers or frequently log in on secondary machines. Roaming profiles provide a level of consistency and familiarity that helps to ease the inconvenience of not being able to use the same machine to access the domain.

The implementation of roaming profiles is actually quite simple. When roaming profiles are enabled, a successful logon to a domain PC will cause the user's profile to be downloaded to the local machine. Upon logout, any updates to the profile will be uploaded to the server. As mentioned, Microsoft Outlook and Internet Explorer use this functionality extensively. This fact means that users' mailboxes and Internet favorites will automatically follow them from machine to machine. The downside of this design is that storing all this data in a user's profile can make the profile very large. This can slow down the domain logon process significantly. For this reason, you might want to test roaming profiles to see how they perform in situations where users have a very large Outlook mailboxes or large Internet Explorer caches.

It's also important to understand that roaming profiles do not do away with the need to install software on each client machine. For example, Outlook and Internet Explorer must be installed individually on each client PC in order for the respective program's settings to be used at all. Nevertheless, roaming profiles are a tremendous feature, adding familiarity and convenience to a domain. In addition, roaming profiles also allow user settings to be centrally backed up. If a client machine crashes, the users' personal settings and possibly their mailboxes are not lost. This is only possible because roaming profiles are stored centrally on a server.

In addition to roaming profiles, *mandatory profiles* provide another domain-related profile feature. Mandatory profiles are very similar to roaming profiles, but they are read-only. This means that any changes a user makes to the desktop will be discarded after the user logs out. Therefore, mandatory profiles are very handy when desktop consistency is essential—for example, in a campus computer lab.

> **Note**
>
> When you're using roaming profiles, it's essential that all the computers in your domain agree on the correct time because Windows NT uses this information to determine whether the local or roaming profile is more recent. Because Windows NT will use what appears to be the most recent profile, any major time discrepancies will cause Windows to select the wrong profile, causing changes to be unintentionally discarded.

17

USING SAMBA AS THE
NT PRIMARY DOMAIN
CONTROLLER

For more information on profiles, refer to the Microsoft Knowledge Base article "Guide to Windows NT 4.0 Profiles and Policies," a six-part series consisting of IDs Q161334, Q185587, Q185588, Q185589, Q185590, and Q185591.

Logon Scripts Overview

Logon scripts constitute another feature of Windows domains. When configured, they allow a DOS `.bat` or `.cmd` script to be downloaded from the domain controller and executed locally. This script typically maps network shares to drive letters and also could be used to synchronize the workstation's time so that it matches that of the domain controller.

Home Drives Overview

Mapping home drives is another feature of logging into a domain. Quite simply, this feature allows a specific network share to be mapped to a specific drive letter upon login. This setting is settable on a per-user basis.

Samba PDC Sources

As mentioned earlier, the PDC support in Samba is continuously being developed. For this reason, it's of no great help to provide you with a cookie-cutter approach to setting up Samba as a full PDC—no such standard method exists. Therefore, this section is going to provide you with the resources and knowledge you'll need to think for yourself and to do the proper research and testing to ensure that, regardless of the Samba version you're using, your Samba PDC performs well. Because you'll be using experimental Samba functionality, it's essential that you are up-to-date on current Samba developments and that you regularly read the Samba mailing lists. In particular, it's essential that you join or at least monitor the `samba-ntdom` mailing list to keep track of what's going on in PDC development. The `samba-ntdom` mailing list can be browsed and searched under the "Archives" section at `www.samba.org`. In addition, you may want to take a look at Lars Kneschke's detailed SAMBA_TNG instructions located at `www.kneschke.de/projekte/samba_tng/`.

Because Samba's PDC support is in development, you may need to do some fishing for the latest version of Samba. The Samba team is very clear on the fact that although some PDC support exists in version 2.0.*x* of Samba, this support is not particularly stable. Therefore, until Samba 3.*x* is available, you'll need to use CVS to check out the most recent development sources. CVS, the Concurrent Versions System, is a tool used to provide source code control for complex development projects. More information on CVS can be found in Chapter 5, "Installing Samba." CVS is available on the Web from `www.sourcegear.com/CVS/`.

Currently, there are three CVS trees that you should be familiar with—SAMBA_2_0, SAMBA_HEAD, and SAMBA_TNG. Each one contains a different developmental version of Samba, with various features. Additionally, to make things more confusing, the purpose of these CVS trees can and does change over time. SAMBA_2_0 contains the current developmental version of Samba. SAMBA_2_0 has the benefit of being the most recent stable version of Samba, and it has the ability to be used in production environments. The disadvantage to using SAMBA_2_0 is that the only domain feature it supports is domain logons, and it does not support Windows NT printing.

Next is SAMBA_HEAD, which contains the next major release of Samba (currently dubbed *pre-3.0.0*). Unfortunately, although it's a very efficient file server and supports NT printing, SAMBA_HEAD has no PDC support. Also, because it's being actively developed, it can at times be unstable. SAMBA_HEAD will eventually be transformed into the next major release of Samba. Unfortunately, at the time of this writing, SAMBA_HEAD cannot be used as a PDC.

That's where SAMBA_TNG comes in. SAMBA_TNG (or *Samba, The Next Generation*) is the version of Samba that's being designed with full PDC support in mind. Specifically, SAMBA_TNG is designed to act as a primary domain controller in Windows NT 3.51, 4.0, and 2000 domains. In addition, Windows NT 3.51 and 4.0 backup domain controller emulation is currently working. SAMBA_TNG does not stop there—it also supports the following Windows NT tools, which allow Samba to be remotely managed from a Windows NT server:

- User Manager for Domains
- Server Manager for Domains
- Event log
- Service Control Manager
- Registry Editor

Although SAMBA_TNG provides for almost full compatibility with Windows NT administration tools, it also comes with its own administration tool, called `rpcclient`. `rpcclient` is a UNIX Windows network administration tool that provides identical functionality to the listed Windows NT–based programs. With that being said, it seems like SAMBA_TNG would be the obvious choice for implementing a PDC; unfortunately, SAMBA_TNG is on CVS for a reason. As of the time of this writing (February 2000), SAMBA_TNG is currently a *pre-alpha* release. This means that you should not rely on SAMBA_TNG in a production environment and should treat it as a prototype until you've been explicitly told otherwise by the Samba development team or have tested it under heavy stress with excellent results. You're also again encouraged to monitor the `samba-ntdom` mailing list to keep abreast of what CVS trees currently contain PDC support. This is especially important because as

SAMBA_TNG becomes more and more stable, it's very likely to be combined with the SAMBA_HEAD tree! Samba development sure is exciting, isn't it?

Checking Out SAMBA_TNG

Regardless of which CVS tree you check out, the underlying process is identical. After installing CVS, create a directory with the exact same name as the CVS tree you plan to check out (in this case, SAMBA_TNG). This is not necessary, but it's strongly recommended. You'll see why in a moment.

Once you've created the directory, `enter` it. Then, type the following command at the prompt:

```
cvs -d :pserver:cvs@cvs.samba.org:/cvsroot checkout -r NAME_OF_TREE samba
```

Replace `NAME_OF_TREE` with the name of the tree you would like to check out (for example, SAMBA_TNG). When prompted for a password, type **cvs**. After this, CVS will begin checking out the entire source tree. Its contents will be deposited in a nondescript directory called `samba`. That's why you need to perform this task *inside* a well-labeled directory—if you're checking out multiple source trees, they will all end up in a directory called `samba`, and you'll have trouble figuring out which source tree is which.

Once this process is complete, you'll have a new directory called `SAMBA_TNG`, which contains another directory called `samba`. Take a look inside the `samba` directory. If you've looked at the Samba sources before, you'll find the overall structure of the files familiar. Here are a couple files you'll want to read for late-breaking information related to this particular development version of Samba:

```
SAMBA_TNG/samba/WHATSNEW.txt
SAMBA_TNG/samba/source/README.txt
```

`WHATSNEW.txt` should always be in the main `samba` directory, whereas `source/ README.txt` sometimes exists and sometimes doesn't. Study these files! They often contain information that is not available anywhere else. Because Samba developers are focusing on the Samba code, they do not spend much time, if any, updating the "official" Samba documentation in `docs` until the code has been officially released. This means that your sole source of information will be the existing (often outdated) documentation, the `WHATSNEW.txt` and `source/README.txt` files, and the `samba-ntdom` and other mailing lists. Be patient! You have a lot of studying ahead of you.

Compiling SAMBA_TNG

Now you're ready to compile the tree. One thing you should avoid is using your checked-out version of Samba as your development directory. Ideally, this directory should be copied to another location, and the copy should be used to compile the new version of Samba. To automate this process, I've created the following script, called compile, which resides in the SAMBA_TNG directory, next to the samba directory itself:

```
#!/usr/bin/env bash
TMPDIR=/tmp
SAMBAVERS=SAMBA_TNG
if [ -d ${TMPDIR}/${SAMBAVERS} ]
then
        rm -rf ${TMPDIR}/${SAMBAVERS}
fi
mkdir ${TMPDIR}/${SAMBAVERS}
# the following line works under Linux
cp -a samba/* ${TMPDIR}/${SAMBAVERS}
# under BSD, comment out the line above, and uncomment this line below
#cp -R samba/* ${TMPDIR}/${SAMBAVERS}
cd ${TMPDIR}/${SAMBAVERS}/source

# the following line should contain ./configure
➥with all the options you normally use
./configure --libdir=/usr/local/etc --localstatedir=/var
➥--with-swatdir=/usr/local/share/swat --with-lockdir=/var/spool/lock
➥--with-privatedir=/usr/local/private
make
# if you have a dual processor machine, use make

➥-j4 to compile samba using both processors
```

This particular script, when run in the SAMBA_TNG directory, will copy the contents of the samba directory to /tmp/SAMBA_TNG. It will then change to the source directory, configure Samba for compilation, and then build Samba by calling make. After this script completes, you'll probably want to enter /tmp/SAMBA_TNG/source and run make install to install Samba on your system. Be sure to back up any production version(s) of Samba before doing this, however! This script is particularly useful because it's very likely that at a later date you'll need to update your CVS tree and recompile Samba as new features are added or bugs are fixed. Keeping this script handy will eliminate some of the drudgery involved in this process, and it also eliminates possible errors and inconsistencies in ./configure flags.

Updating the Tree

Because SAMBA_TNG is a moving target that's being aggressively developed, changes are often committed to CVS hourly. This means that a feature that's currently not functional might be fixed in a matter of days or even hours. Because of the liquidity of the source code, you'll need to update your CVS tree on a regular basis just to keep up with recent updates. For this reason, in addition to the preceding compile script, I also created the following script, called `cvs-update`, in the SAMBA_TNG directory:

```
#!/usr/bin/env bash
cvs -d :pserver:cvs@cvs.samba.org:/cvsroot update -r SAMBA_TNG
```

When run, this command updates your checked-out CVS source so that it's current. Running the `compile` script will allow you to automatically recompile this new version. After that, you just need to issue a `make install` in the `/tmp/SAMBA_TNG/source` directory and then restart some daemons to get the new version running. Actually, the current version of SAMBA_TNG forgets to do some tasks during the `make install` process. Here's what to do to correct this limitation. First, change to the samba directory (wherever it was installed) and then create the following directories:

```
mkdir private
mkdir profiles
mkdir netlogon
```

The `private` directory needs to have an empty `smb.conf` file in it, so type the following command:

```
touch private/smb.conf
```

Also, the `private` directory should be secure, so if you created it by hand, type the following to allow non-`root` access:

```
chmod go-rwx private
```

In the next section, you'll use the `profiles` share to store user profiles. It's best if all users can create files in this directory, so type the following command to allow full access to `profiles`:

```
chmod 1777 profiles
```

Finally, Samba is fully installed.

Samba as PDC

Now that you have Samba correctly installed, it's time to set it up to be a PDC so that it can allow proper domain logins. Add the following lines to your `smb.conf`:

```
[global]
domain logons = yes
domain master = yes
```

```
security = user
workgroup = YOURDOMAIN
encrypt passwords = yes

[netlogon]
path=/usr/local/netlogon
writeable=no
guest ok=no
```

Before continuing, now would be a good time to use the *testparm* command to verify whether all the smb.conf settings are correct. All these settings are required in smb.conf for basic PDC functionality. The first setting, domain logons, allows Windows 95 and 98 clients to log into this domain. The domain master setting tells the nmbd daemon to be a master browser for the domain. User level security is a requirement on a PDC, so security=user is included. In addition, the workgroup option now specifies the name of your domain. Of course, encrypted passwords are required because you're emulating a modern Windows NT server.

The netlogon share should point to an existing directory, and it should be read-only for all users but Administrator. As you might guess, it's used during the login process, and it will contain login scripts as well as system policies. You'll learn more about this a bit later.

Now that smb.conf has been correctly configured, it's time to start or restart the daemons. If you're using SAMBA_TNG, you'll notice that in addition to smbd and nmbd you have a host of other daemons. This is because SAMBA_TNG uses a new, modular architecture. The primary benefit of this architecture is that, in the future, you'll be able to "mix and match" different daemons from different versions of Samba, thus allowing you more choices as to what kind of functionality is enabled on your network. Here's a quick overview of what daemons to start for a particular situation.

Daemon	When to Run It	Purpose
smbd	All the time	File sharing service
nmbd	All the time	Browsing service
srvsvcd	If you want browsing to work	Server service
wkssvcd	If you want browsing to work	Workstation service
lsarpcd	If you use encrypted passwords	lsarpc service
netlogond	If you use encrypted passwords	netlogon service
samrd	If you use encrypted passwords	Changing passwords from NT
winregd	If you use encrypted passwords	Password changing from NT
spoolssd	If you need NT printing	Spool service
svcctld	If you want to remotely start or stop services	Service control

The basic rule when deciding whether to run a daemon is to run them all unless you specifically know that you do not need certain ones. Now that the daemons are started, it's time to create trust accounts. Trust accounts are user accounts that Samba and NT use for individual machines on the network. Samba and NT use trust accounts to determine domain membership. If the trust account isn't properly set up for a client machine, that client machine will be refused access to the domain. With the proper setup of a trust account, a machine will be able to participate in the domain. Not only does this mean that a client machine will be given the opportunity to access domain shares and services, but it could mean that the client machine (if it's a Windows NT machine) can also assist in providing browsing functionality to the network. To create the trust accounts, you'll need to collect the NetBIOS names of all your client machines and your *server*. Then, on your Samba machine, you'll need to create new user accounts in /etc/passwd, using these rules:

Attribute	Setting	Purpose
username	machinename$	Samba requires an additional trailing $.
shell	/bin/false	This is not a login account, prevent interactive login under UNIX.
home dir	/nonexistent	These accounts do not need home directories.
comment	"Samba Trust Account"	This is a memory aid.

If your version of Linux or UNIX has an adduser command, lines similar to the following four should create the required UNIX accounts. Since we used a shell command to add these accounts, we need to type in $ as \$ to prevent shell variable expansion. This problem can be avoided by using the vipw command to add the entries to /etc/passwd manually. For example, if you have a Samba server called freebox and three client machines called ntbox1 through ntbox3, you would create *four* new accounts— freebox$, ntbox1$, ntbox2$, and ntbox3$:

```
$ useradd -s /bin/false -d /nonexistent -c "Samba Trust Account"  freebox\$
$ useradd -s /bin/false -d /nonexistent -c "Samba Trust Account"  ntbox1\$
$ useradd -s /bin/false -d /nonexistent -c "Samba Trust Account"  ntbox2\$
$ useradd -s /bin/false -d /nonexistent -c "Samba Trust Account"  ntbox3\$
```

This would also be a good time to add any user accounts to /etc/passwd that Samba will need, if you have not done so already.

If you're setting up SAMBA_TNG, type the following command, which tells Samba to join its own domain:

```
smbpasswd -j YOURDOMAIN
```

smbpasswd should then tell you that you have successfully joined YOURDOMAIN. The next step is to set up the encrypted samba password file, smbpasswd. To do this, you'll make liberal use of the smbpasswd command. Using the sample names freebox, ntbox1, ntbox2, and ntbox3 as PDC and clients, you would type the following commands:

```
smbpasswd -a -m freebox
```

This adds an encrypted machine account entry to the smbpasswd file. After each command, you should see output that looks like this:

```
Added user freebox$.
Password changed for user freebox$
```

If you receive an error, make sure you added the proper accounts to /etc/passwd first. The final smbpasswd step is to add encrypted machine accounts for all your clients:

```
smbpasswd -a -m ntbox1
smbpasswd -a -m ntbox2
smbpasswd -a -m ntbox3
```

Again, this would be a good time to add any encrypted user accounts, if you have not done so already, by typing the following command:

```
smbpasswd -a newuser
```

If you've reached this point, everything has been set up properly on the Samba side to allow client machines to join the domain. Both Windows NT and Windows 95/98 require additional configuration steps to actually join the domain. I'll show you how to do this for both Windows NT and Windows 95/98 boxes.

Joining a Domain from Windows NT Workstation

Once the Samba machine trust account is set up properly, it's very easy to get a Windows NT Workstation machine to join a domain. As you can see in Figure 17.3, it's a simple process. First, open up the Network control panel. Click the Identification tab to view the current domain and workgroup settings. The computer name and workgroup name should be displayed. This is a good time to do a quick check—you should have created a UNIX user account called computername$ and a smbpasswd machine account entry by typing **smbpasswd -a -m computername** (without $). If you did, joining the domain will generally happen without any problems. Click on the Change... button, and the Identification Changes dialog box will appear. Select the second radio button, labeled Domain:, and type in the name of your domain. Do *not* create a computer account in the new domain; you've already done this earlier by creating the machine trust account. After clicking OK, you should be welcomed to the new domain. After exiting out of all the dialog boxes, a reboot will be necessary. After the machine restarts, you should be able to log into the domain by using the Windows NT login dialog box, shown previously in Figure 17.1.

FIGURE 17.3

*Configuring
Windows NT to
become a domain
member.*

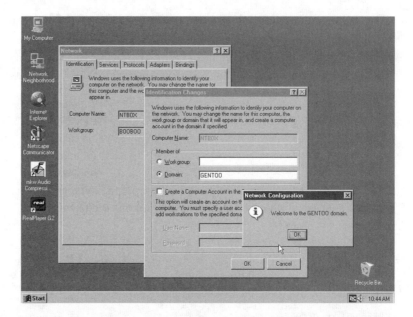

Caution

After you configure a Windows NT machine to join a domain, you will need to restart the machine. After the machine restarts, remember to select the proper domain from the NT login dialog box, where you type in your username or password. Otherwise, you will be logging into the local machine rather than your brand-new Samba domain!

Note

If you join an NT Workstation machine to a Samba domain and then "unjoin" it (by switching back to a workgroup), you'll have problems rejoining the domain at a later date. To get around this problem, you need to manually delete the machine trust account from the smbpasswd file with a text editor and then re-create the entry by typing **smbpasswd -a -m machinename**. After that, rejoining the domain should work flawlessly. This situation happens because when a machine trust account is first created, the password is set to a special "dummy" value to allow the machine to initially join the domain.

Joining a Domain from Windows NT Server

If you would like to configure a standalone NT Server machine to join your Samba domain, first complete all the steps listed in the previous section, "Joining a Domain from Windows NT Workstation." Then, you need to log on locally to do a quick change to the local system policy so that Windows NT Server will grant anyone rights to log on locally. By default, NT Server is configured to only allow Administrator logons, so this step would be required even if you were trying to join a Windows NT–based PDC. To do this, simply use the User Manager for Domains to grant Everyone or Authenticated Users the right to log on locally. After that, you should have no problem logging into your Samba-based domain.

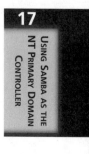

Joining a Domain from Windows 95/98

Joining a domain from Windows 95/98 is also very easy. Remember, doing so will not make the Windows 95/98 machine more secure; it will just allow the machine to participate in the domain and browse the domain, access shares and printers, and so on. As you can see in Figure 17.4, to join a domain, you open the Network control panel. Double-click the Client for Microsoft Network component, and the Properties dialog box will appear.

FIGURE 17.4

Configuring Windows 95 to participate in a domain.

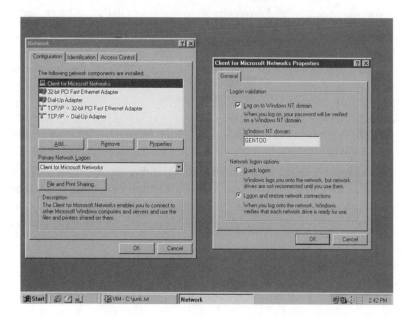

Under the Login Validation section, check the Log into Windows Domain option and type the name of the domain into the Windows NT Domain text box. You'll also want to make sure that the Logon and Restore Network Connections option is checked. After accepting all these changes and rebooting Windows, you'll be able to log into the domain by typing an appropriate username, password, and domain into the Windows network login dialog box. This procedure is also touched upon in Chapter 16, "Using Samba as Your Windows 98 Logon Mechanism."

Implementing Logon Scripts

Implementing logon scripts is very easy. Simply add the following option to the [global] section of your smb.conf:

```
logon script = myscript.bat
```

A good way to test logon script functionality is to create a simple sample script, such as the following one. This particular script will output "Hello Client!" to the screen and then run Windows Notepad:

```
rem my sample script
echo Hello Client!
notepad.exe
```

When clients log into your domain, the myscript.bat file will be downloaded from the netlogon share and executed locally. For this reason, make sure you save myscript.bat inside your netlogon share! Also note that because this is a Windows batch file, it will need to be in DOS text format. The easiest way to do this is to create and edit this file on a Windows machine and then copy it over to your UNIX box using Samba before placing it inside your netlogon share.

You can also take advantage of Samba's % macros in the script name. For example, if you have separate scripts for each user, you might want to have the following entry in your smb.conf:

```
logon script = %U.bat
```

Samba's % macros are covered in detail in the smb.conf man page, in the "Variable Substitutions" section.

For example, if drobbins were to log into this domain, a script called drobbins.bat would be executed. Also, be sure to take advantage of the fact that Windows will map the netlogon share to drive Z: for the duration of the logon process. This means that you can place additional scripts and executable programs in netlogon and refer to them in your batch file, as follows:

```
z:\dothings.exe
```

As you can see, it's very easy to create very intricate login scripts this way.

Mapping Home Drives

Home drive mapping is a very simple process. Use the following commands to accomplish home drive mapping, which should be placed in the [global] section:

```
logon home = \\%L\%Ulogon drive = h:
```

The logon home parameter specifies the location where the user's particular home directory exists. Because %L expands to the name of the PDC and %U specifies to the name of the user, this will cause the user's home directory to be mapped to a share matching the user's name on the PDC—a perfect match for the [homes] section. The second option actually causes the home share to be mapped to a drive letter upon login to make it easier for users to access their data.

Mapping Groups and Users

One of the challenges that Samba faces is its ability to integrate two security systems into one—in particular, the UNIX password database and the Windows security database. Windows NT's security system has a number of different default groups that users can belong to. Belonging to these groups defines a particular user's privileges on the system. Obviously, Windows NT has User Manager for Domains to manage such relationships, but how exactly does Samba do it? Of course, Samba uses the smbpasswd file, but smbpasswd stores only user and machine accounts, not group information.

Samba defines NT groups by using two new global options: domain group map and local group map. Before diving into specifics, it's important that you have a good general understanding of what these options do. First, domain group map provides a means of associating a UNIX group with a Windows NT domain group so that when a user is in a specified UNIX group, Samba considers the user part of the NT domain group. This gives you an easy, convenient way of adding users to an NT domain group that uses your existing /etc/group file.

Here's how domain group map works. Placed in the [global] section, domain group map points to a group mapping file, as follows:

```
domain group map = /usr/local/samba/domaingroup.map
```

> **Note**
>
> The domaingroup.map, localgroup.map, and domainuser.map files must be readable by all users! Make them world readable by typing these two commands:
>
> ```
> chmod ugo+r domaingroup.map
> chmod ugo+r localgroup.map
> ```

This file should contain mapping information in the following format:

```
UNIXgroup = NTgroup
```

For `domain group map` to work properly, the specified UNIX group must exist. After Samba is restarted, you can add your users to the particular Windows NT group by simply adding them to the appropriate UNIX group. This is easily done by editing `/etc/group`.

One of the caveats regarding the use of the `domain group map` option is the fact that if you want to add a UNIX user to standard NT group, the spelling in the `domaingroup.map` file must exactly match the name of the group in User Manager for Domains. Because not everyone has his or her own NT server to reference, I've included the following `domaingroup.map` file as a reference, which defines all of the standard Windows NT groups:

```
domadmin = "Domain Admins"
domguest = "Domain Guests"
domuser = "Domain Users"
```

To use this data, simply add it to your `domaingroup.map` file and then create the `domadmin`, `domguest`, and `domuser` groups. After adding the `domain group map` option to your `smb.conf` and restarting Samba, edit `/etc/group` to add users to these particular groups. When you do so, they will automatically be considered members of the corresponding NT group.

The `local group map` option works almost identically, except that it points to a file that maps UNIX groups to NT local groups. When a user is a member of an NT local group, he or she will be considered a member of that group on your Samba PDC. Here's a sample `localgroup.map` file that defines all the standard Windows NT groups:

```
ntadmin = Administrators
ntuser = Users
ntguest = Guests
ntpuser = "Power Users"
ntaccop = "Account Operators"
ntsysop = "System Operators"
ntpriop = "Print Operators"
ntbackop = "Backup Operators"
ntreplic = "Replicator"
```

After entering this data into your `localgroup.map` file, add the following line to your `smb.conf` global section:

```
local group map = /usr/local/samba/localgroup.map
```

Now, create the nine groups listed previously (`ntadmin`, `ntuser`, and so on), restart Samba, and edit `/etc/group` to add whomever you want to these groups. Samba will then consider these people members of the corresponding NT local group. Now, not only do you have NT users but NT groups as well! What's more, Microsoft servers will now have an easier time getting along with your security database.

One additional option can also help with this process. Of course, one of the areas where Windows NT and UNIX differ is in the use of usernames. Typically, UNIX usernames are eight characters or less in length, whereas NT usernames can be much longer, and even contain spaces! Obviously, this isn't possible under UNIX, but suppose you want to be able to have these nice, big usernames in your Samba security database. You can do this by using the `domain user map` option. It's specified similarly to the previous two options:

```
domain user map = /usr/local/samba/domainuser.map
```

In addition, the format of the `domainuser.map` file is also very similar:

```
UNIXuser = NTuser
```

After you set up this file, any UNIX user you specify will be known from NT as the corresponding NT user. You might be wondering which account should be added to the `smbpasswd` file. Good question! Simply add the UNIX user, and Samba will perform the translation automatically. This way, you don't need a UNIX user account for the NT user in `/etc/passwd`, which is what you're trying to avoid in the first place.

Roaming and Mandatory Profiles

Roaming profiles are not too hard to implement. The first step is to add the following information to your `smb.conf`:

```
[global]
logon path = \\%L\profiles\%U.pds[profiles]
        comment = user profiles
        path = /usr/local/samba/profiles
        create mode = 0600
        directory mode = 0700
        force group = %G
        force user = %U
        writeable = yes
        browseable = yes
```

By adding this information to Samba, you'll now have a new share called `profiles`. Make sure your `profiles` directory allows full access by enabling read, write, and execute permissions for all users:

```
chmod 1777 /usr/local/samba/profiles
```

The `logon path` parameter specifies that Samba should find the user's profile inside the `profiles` share, in a directory called `<username>.pds`.

Thankfully, once the `profiles` share has been set up properly, the next time `<username>` logs out, his or her local profile will be automatically uploaded to the share specified in `smb.conf`. The next time the user logs in, the roaming profile will be automatically downloaded from the share to the local machine.

Mandatory profiles involve just a simple twist on this particular setup. When you copied the user's local profile to the `profiles` share, you probably noticed a file called `NTUSER.DAT`. Simply renaming this file to `NTUSER.MAN` will enable mandatory profiles. After this change, any modifications made to the current profile will be discarded upon logout.

Testing Profiles

A simple test is available to verify whether your profiles are being sent to and down-loaded from the Samba server. The first step is to make certain the NT client's clock is synchronized with the clock on the server, with respect to time, date, daylight saving time, and time zone. This is because profile synchronization is time based, as explained in Chapter 16.

Once the client and server are in synch in terms of time, log on and off the client twice, noting the Windows desktop settings. With the client logged off, copy `NTUSER.DAT` in your profile directory to `NTUSER.DAT.OLD`. Then, with the `chown` command, change the owner and group of `NTUSER.DAT.OLD` to be the same as those of `NTUSER.DAT`.

Now log on a third time, change the Windows theme to a recognizably different theme, and then log off. Log on and off once more and then verify that the new theme is still in effect. Copy `NTUSER.DAT` to `NTUSER.DAT.NEW`. Then, with the `chown` command, change the owner and group of `NTUSER.DAT.OLD` to be the same as those of `NTUSER.DAT`.

> **Tip**
>
> Wait one minute before proceeding further to ensure that the server's `NTUSER.DAT` file is newer than the cached copy on the client.

In the `profiles` directory, notice and remember the time on file `NTUSER.DAT` as well as the owner and group. Copy `NTUSER.DAT.OLD` to `NTUSER.DAT` and then verify that `NTUSER.DAT` now has a time later than before the copy. Also verify that the owner and group on the file are the same as before the copy. Once these facts have been verified, log on again and notice that the theme has reverted to the original theme because of your copy on the server. If the theme has reverted, you've proven that profiles work on your system.

Summary

This chapter looked at Samba's functionality as a primary domain controller. Beginning with an introduction to domains in general, it investigated various aspects of domain controller functionality as well as how Windows NT and 95/98 differ in how they enforce domain security. After reviewing the current state of affairs regarding Samba PDC development, this chapter showed you how to properly check out a developmental version of Samba via CVS. Then, two scripts were presented that help you easily compile and update your CVS source tree. After this, the chapter covered SAMBA_TNG installation and configuration, detailing the steps required to set Samba up as a PDC.

CHAPTER 18

Password Synchronization and Administration

by Daniel Robbins

IN THIS CHAPTER

What Is Password Synchronization?

In the days of single servers running entire departments and organizations, password synchronization was not much of an issue. Generally, these systems contained one central database of users and passwords, and because all programs ran on one server, authentication was performed against one database.

Today, however, we often find ourselves faced with relatively complex multivendor networks that somehow need to work together as one cohesive whole. Often, these environments consist of multiple servers or networking systems, each with their own distinct password database. In order for these various systems to work together, there needs to be some synchronization of user/password databases. Otherwise, users are faced with the task of remembering a number of unique passwords for the various servers in an organization.

This is only one side of the problem—if multiple distinct password databases are a pain for users (and they are), they're a tremendous burden for system administrators, who are often faced with the task of keeping these databases in sync manually. Obviously, a better solution is needed. After all, should various operating systems be able to share their security information automatically?

One of Samba's major benefits is its ability to unify an organization's UNIX and Windows environments into a consistent whole. However, this goal could not be fully realized if there wasn't a way to integrate the user and password databases on these separate systems. When I refer to "password synchronization," this is what I'm talking about: the ability to take two or more systems, and from a user/password database perspective, configure them to work together rather than independently. When password synchronization can occur automatically, it's a tremendous benefit to the organization, increasing the reliability and manageability of the organization's network (not to mention user productivity). Indeed, the promise that Samba holds to administrators would not be complete if Samba did not include a number of ways to "work together" with your Windows systems; fortunately for us, it does.

Tackling the Password-Synchronization Challenge

Tackling the password-synchronization challenge requires a lot of planning. When you're dealing with user/password databases, educated decisions need to be made. I recommend that you read this entire chapter and familiarize yourself with the options that Samba provides you with. After you have a good grasp of what options are available, you'll need to make some decisions.

Research, Research, Research

After studying what password synchronization options are available, you need to define a goal. Do you want to manage users centrally from your UNIX server or from your Windows NT server? What are the tradeoffs to each approach? Is there a preferred administration tool that's available on one platform that isn't available on the other?

After answering these questions, now look at your network from your users' perspective. What client operating system do they use primarily? How many passwords does a typical user need to remember to access all the resources on your network? Do you want to unify all these password databases or just certain ones? What about future growth? What do you see your users requiring in the next two years, and can you use certain password synchronization strategies to make these transitions easier both for you and your users? Planning is definitely the key to a good transition.

A Careful Design

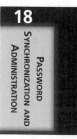

The preceding questions should help give you a vision about how your network *could* work. Maybe you'll identify particular Samba features described in this chapter that you know you want to implement. Your next step is to develop this design on paper and then continue to research the particular features you want to implement. Draw diagrams of how your new environment would operate. In your diagrams, you'll want to identify all the password databases in your network and how they're going to hook together, if at all.

An Action Plan

Your new network design can be perfect and your research flawless, but without a proper plan of implementation, you'll be in trouble. Remember that you're attempting to synchronize user and password databases—not a trivial task. A poorly planned transition could result in users being locked out of their important files for extended periods of time. Careful planning during this time will not only help you to end up with a wonderfully synchronized network in the end, but it will keep your users happy during the transition.

You'll want to identify any tools or techniques that you can use during the transition to minimize hassle or downtime. Also, the ordering of steps during the transition can be critical. You should incorporate testing into your plan and take steps to find possible flaws in the system before your users do. The last thing you want is a series of unexpected phone calls or personal visits from your users in the late afternoon or early morning.

Password Functionality of Common Platforms

It's a good idea to have a basic working knowledge of the functionality of various platforms when it comes to password authentication. The following sections provide an overview.

Windows 95/98

Because Windows 95 and 98 do not have any kind of secure user database, they should not be used to store user account information. Windows 95 and 98 are exclusively client operating systems, allowing users to connect to network shares as needed. If, for example, you have a single UNIX server and all Windows 95 and 98 clients, you'll definitely want to centrally manage everything from UNIX—it's your only option.

Windows NT Workstation

Windows NT Workstation has an internal user and security database that it uses to authenticate users for access to any of its own shares and/or printers. Because of NT's enhanced security and reliability, it's generally a better choice for a client network operating system than Windows 95 or 98.

Although Windows NT Workstation is an ideal network client, it doesn't provide what is needed to be a server, at least when it comes to password synchronization.

Windows NT Server

Windows NT Server has its own user and security database and is able to share this database with other NT servers and workstations, forming what's called an *NT domain*. Changes made on any NT server are propagated to the other NT servers so that the domain user database will remain consistent even as it's changed. This kind of distributed security model is the preferred configuration for an exclusively NT network.

UNIX/Samba System

As you might guess, UNIX/Samba offers the most possibilities as well as the most complexity when it comes to password synchronization. Thanks to Samba, UNIX can interact with Windows clients and servers in a number of powerful ways. Because so many options are available, choosing the correct method can be somewhat overwhelming. I'll quickly mention the possibilities in the next few paragraphs before covering them in detail later in the chapter.

As a client, a UNIX/Samba system can become part of an existing NT domain. Through the use of a pluggable authentication module (PAM), the UNIX/Samba system can use an NT server for some of its password authentication (local logins, telnet/ftp sessions, and so on). Of course, a UNIX system can also use its own internal password database exclusively or hook into a UNIX distributed password database, such as NIS.

As a server, a UNIX/Samba system can manage its own password database. It can have one database for Samba and another for everything else, or these two databases can be synchronized. It's also possible for the Samba server to become part of an NT domain and use the security database of an existing NT network just for Samba authentication— or even for *all* authentication, if desired. To top it all off, Samba now offers experimental support for "being in charge" of its own NT domain, thus becoming a primary domain controller! This is covered in Chapter 17, "Using Samba as the NT Primary Domain Controller."

As you can see, the options can be overwhelming. Fortunately, this chapter will provide you with a good, clear grasp of all that Samba offers when it comes to password synchronization.

Password Synchronization Between UNIX and Samba

Samba offers a tremendous number of options when it comes to user authentication. First, Samba can run in one of two modes: either an encrypted password mode or a nonencrypted password mode. In the encrypted password mode, Samba will insist that the passwords it accepts from Windows clients be encrypted. In the nonencrypted mode, Samba will allow plain-text authentication, which is less secure. For this reason, you should run Samba in encrypted password mode if at all possible.

Why did I bring this up? When Samba is configured to use nonencrypted passwords, it can simply use the usernames and passwords stored in /etc/passwd for authentication. However, things gets a bit more complicated when Samba is running with encrypted passwords, which just so happens to be the recommended arrangement. In this case, Samba can't use your UNIX system's own differently encrypted password to verify the SMB/CIFS challenge it receives over the wire. What this means is that in encrypted password mode, Samba needs an additional password file, called smbpasswd. When set up this way, your UNIX system now has *two* password databases—one for Samba and one for regular UNIX items. This means that you need to be concerned about password synchronization between both files on the UNIX box itself! Be aware of this as you familiarize yourself with Samba's configuration file options.

Using Samba Password Synchronization

We're now ready to explore configuration file options in depth. All the following options should appear in the [global] section of smb.conf. It's recommended that you familiarize yourself with *all* these options before implementing any, because it's common for several to be used in conjunction with one another.

encrypt passwords =

Samba has two methods for sending SMB passwords over the network—one is called *encrypted passwords*. Using this method, Samba will not send any passwords over the network as plain text, where they could be easily intercepted and recorded by a third party via the use of a packet sniffer on your network. Obviously, this is a great advantage, and for this reason, it's recommended that you use encrypted passwords with Samba if at all possible. If you have any machines on the network running Windows NT with Service Pack 3 or later, encrypted passwords are required by default on the Samba side so that Samba and NT get along (although the Windows NT Registry can be hacked to use unencrypted passwords—we'll cover this later). Most versions of Windows 95 and all versions of Windows 98, NT 4.*x*, and 2000 work great with encrypted passwords, so unless you need to share files with relatively ancient Windows software, encrypted passwords should be your first choice. The only time you should consider nonencrypted passwords is when you fully understand the tradeoffs involved (that is, you've carefully reviewed all the information in this section) and are comfortable with the choice. All new Samba users should attempt to use encrypted passwords if at all possible.

When not using encrypted passwords, Samba can simply use your /etc/passwd or /etc/shadow file as its password store. However, with encrypted passwords enabled, Samba requires an additional file called smbpasswd. This is simply because the password hash stored in /etc/passwd or /etc/shadow is of a different type than Samba uses internally for encrypted passwords, so the standard UNIX hash is unusable for this purpose. What this means is that when in encrypted password mode, your UNIX system will have two independent password files, and they won't necessarily be synchronized. This does add a bit of additional complication because now Samba requires the smbpasswd file to authenticate users; however, encrypted passwords are almost always well worth it because of their added security.

Understanding How smbpasswd and /etc/passwd Interact

When Samba uses encrypted passwords, it requires the use of a file called smb-passwd. However, even though this file exists, Samba still needs the appropriate user accounts for your CIFS/SMB users to exist in your standard UNIX password file (/etc/passwd). You may wonder why this is. The answer is quite simple: A user must exist in /etc/passwd so that Samba can set the permissions on the user's files correctly, and the user must exist in smbpasswd so that he or she can be authenticated using CIFS/SMB-encrypted passwords. If the user account only existed in smbpasswd but not in /etc/passwd, the user could be authenticated, but Samba could not assign the proper ownership to any files this user created or modified! Remember, for a UNIX system to set file ownership of a file to a particular user, the corresponding user must be defined in /etc/passwd. In this particular area, you can see the challenges that Samba faces in integrating two disparate systems (UNIX and Windows). Fortunately, Samba tackles this challenge extremely well.

Samba offers several possibilities for keeping these files automatically in sync; for more information, see unix password sync, passwd program, and passwd chat. These three options, when set correctly, will cause Samba to automatically change a user's UNIX password when the CIFS/SMB password has been changed, thus keeping the two files in sync if any password changes occur. For example, these options allow the administrator to be able to change a particular user's password using the smbpasswd command, at which point Samba will automatically change the user's UNIX password by calling passwd directly. This is quite a useful feature; it allows your users to have consistent passwords under the UNIX and Windows environments.

Advanced Encrypted Password Topics

This subsection is for those who would like to delve a bit deeper into the inner workings of encrypted and nonencrypted passwords. Although this is not required reading for the configuration of Samba, it is recommended for intermediate-to-advanced readers.

First, I'll contrast the advantages of encrypt passwords = yes with the advantages of encrypt passwords = no, for those who may be considering using nonencrypted passwords.

The main advantage of nonencrypted passwords is the fact that Samba will use the standard UNIX password database to perform all authentication, thus eliminating the need for the smbpasswd file. This can simplify your Samba setup. The downside of this is that passwords will be sent over the wire in plain text, and Windows NT does not work well with plain-text passwords. Such an arrangement will mess up browsing in security =

user mode and cause NT to repeatedly prompt the user for his or her password for each connection. That's definitely something you want to avoid. In addition, with Windows NT 4.0 Service Pack 3 and later, NT will not allow the use of plain-text passwords without a Registry modification. We'll cover how to make this modification later. However, it's probably best if you simply go ahead and use encrypted passwords if you have an NT network.

Here are the various settings that must be made to enable plain-text passwords on various Microsoft operating systems. This is normally accomplished by the use of the regedit program. For each operating system, the name of the new Registry value should be set to `EnablePlainTextPassword` with a `DWORD` value of `00000001`. The appropriate locations for this new value vary by operating system.

Operating System	Registry Setting
Windows 2000	[HKEY_LOCAL_MACHINE\SYSTEM\ CurrentControlSet\Services\LanmanWorkStation\ Parameters]
Windows NT	[HKEY_LOCAL_MACHINE\SYSTEM\ CurrentControlSet\Services\Rdr\Parameters]
Windows 98	[HKEY_LOCAL_MACHINE\System\ CurrentControlSet\Services\VxD\VNETSUP]
Windows 95	[HKEY_LOCAL_MACHINE\System\ CurrentControlSet\Services\VxD\VNETSUP]

unix password sync =

Now that we've explored the complexity and significance of the smbpasswd file, I'm going to introduce you to some Samba functionality that's designed to make your life much easier. To begin, `unix password sync` defaults to `False`; however, when it's set to `True`, Samba will automatically synchronize a user's UNIX password with any changes made to the existing Samba password contained in smbpasswd. Therefore, with this option enabled, the use of the smbpasswd command will cause *both* /etc/passwd and the smbpasswd file to be updated, thus totally eliminating password synchronization hassles in certain instances!

Let's explore a scenario where `unix password sync` comes to the rescue. Let's say you're an administrator of a hybrid Windows/UNIX network; not only do users connect to shares on your UNIX Samba server, but they also frequently use ftp and telnet to get into the UNIX system directly. In addition, of course, you're using encrypted passwords to increase network security. In this particular example, when a user uses telnet or ftp, he or she will be authenticated based on the password in /etc/passwd. On the other hand, when a user connects to a CIFS/SMB share, he or she will be authenticated using `smbpasswd`. You've just run into your first password synchronization challenge; it would be nice if these passwords remained consistent without any manual trickery by you, the system administrator. The recommended solution in this instance would be to enable `unix password sync`, allowing Samba to update `/etc/passwd` manually. Then, you would create a shell alias for users so that when they type **passwd**, `smbpasswd` is executed in its place. Now, when a user changes his or her shell password, the CIFS/SMB password will automatically change, too. Quite elegant, isn't it?

There are some important points to note about this command. First, if you're not using encrypted passwords, `unix password sync` is unnecessary and should not be used, because the `smbpasswd` file is not used in this configuration. Second, the `unix password sync` configuration option works in conjunction with several other configuration options: `passwd program`, `passwd chat`, `min passwd length`, and `passwd chat debug`. These options are described later, and you should review them fully before you enable `unix password sync` on a production server. Third, you should adequately test the syncing of passwords to ensure that your `passwd program` and `passwd chat` strings are set appropriately. After this works for you, make sure it works for your users and that your `smbpasswd` alias is operating properly so that this change is transparent to the users.

smb passwd file =

Use this option to set the fully qualified path to the Samba encrypted password file, `smbpasswd`. The default for this option is determined at compile time, but it's often `/etc/smbpasswd` on a typical system. If you're running two or more CIFS/SMB servers with separate encrypted security databases on the same machine, you'll need to use this option to force at least one `smbd` service to use a file at an alternative location.

passwd program =

`passwd program` is a configuration option that's used in conjunction with `unix password sync`; it specifies what program is used by Samba to set the new UNIX password. `passwd program` defaults to `/bin/passwd` and should contain the *fully qualified* path to an appropriate UNIX password-change program. In addition, the string `%u`, if used, will be replaced with the username whose password is currently being changed. For this reason, on a UNIX system, you'll probably want to set `passwd program` to `/bin/passwd %u`.

You need to understand the steps that Samba takes when a password change happens via the use of the `smbpasswd` command. Let's review them now:

1. `smbpasswd` is called by a username `bob`.
2. Samba runs the command `/bin/passwd bob` with `root` permissions (this example uses `passwd program = /bin/passwd %u`).

3. If successful, Samba proceeds to change the CIFS/SMB password in `smbpasswd`. If it's not successful, the password change aborts at this point and neither password is changed.

To reiterate a bit, Samba attempts to change the password in `/etc/passwd` first. It's possible that the password change will not be successful. Why? Because many standard UNIX password-change programs check the password to make sure it's relatively "hack proof," consists of an adequate number of characters, isn't based on a dictionary word, and so on. This can make things a bit tricky, but in either case Samba will handle the situation gracefully. Simply make sure you inform your users of your UNIX password policy so that they'll have an easier time choosing a valid password.

A word of caution: Some clients, such as Windows for Workgroups, capitalize a password before it's sent. In this case, you may need a creative solution to get password changing to work properly from Windows for Workgroups. Here are two possibilities:

- Use a modified `/bin/passwd` program that automatically "decapitalizes" passwords.
- Simply set a department policy that all users with Windows for Workgroups machines must have passwords that contain no lowercase characters.

passwd chat =

Essential to the use of the `passwd program =` option is `passwd chat`, which contains a "script" that Samba should use with your local `passwd` executable to change passwords. Remember that most `passwd` programs do not simply accept command-line arguments; they also prompt the user for input from the terminal. This setting allows Samba to say the right stuff at the right time. Let's look at how this works.

The `passwd chat` string contains pairs of alternate *expect* and *send* strings; that is, when the `passwd` executable prints a string that matches an expect string, Samba will print the corresponding send string. In this way, Samba will be able to properly communicate with a program that was designed to interact with a human being at the terminal.

Here's the default setting for this command:

```
passwd chat = *old*password* %o\n *new*password* %n\n
➥*new*password* %n\n *changed*
```

The first step in understanding this sequence is knowing how to determine which characters are part of the expect string and which are part of the send string. The simple rule of thumb for this is that the expect and send pairs are separated by whitespace. If an expect or send string contains whitespace, it must be enclosed in double quotes.

The second and final step in understanding the passwd chat string involves understanding the special macros that can be used in the string:

Macro	Description
%o	Old password
%n	New password
\n	Line feed
\r	Carriage return
\t	Tab
\s	Space
*	Matches any character sequence
"."	By itself, represents an empty string

Note that when the "." string is used as an expect or send sequence, no string will be expected or no string will be sent, respectively.

passwd chat debug =

passwd chat debug is an essential tool for debugging the proper operation of your passwd chat script, but it can be dangerous if enabled on a production server. This is because passwd chat debug, when set to True, will cause the passwd chat sequence to be output to your log.smb file. This will mean that users' passwords will show up in plain view in your log file, which could possibly be read by one of your users. For this reason, after you've verified the proper operation of passwd chat using passwd chat debug, you should stop smbd, delete or safely back up your log.smb file, disable the passwd chat debug option in smb.conf, and start smbd again. As you might guess, this option defaults to False.

update encrypted =

update encrypted is a configuration file option that helps you to transparently migrate from an already functional nonencrypted password Samba environment (using a UNIX password database) to one that uses smbpasswd to authenticate users. You might want to do this if you finally upgraded the last ancient CIFS/SMB client on your network (that did not work properly with encrypted passwords) and now want to switch over to encrypted passwords to take advantage of the increased security that this setting provides.

Here's the normal way you would want to use this option to switch from nonencrypted passwords to encrypted ones:

1. Add update encrypted = yes to smb.conf and restart Samba.

2. Inform your users that you're making a network reconfiguration and would like everyone to log in at least once during the next week. When a user logs on, a new entry will be added to the smb.conf file containing his or her encrypted password.

3. At the end of the week, verify that all your users have an entry in the new smbpasswd file. After this is done (and possibly after nudging some stragglers), you'll now have a fully functional smbpasswd file and you're ready to switch Samba into encrypted mode.

4. Add encrypt passwords = yes and *remove* the update encrypted line from smb.conf. Restart Samba.

5. Samba will now use encrypted passwords over the network.

Why is this option needed? Simply because there's typically no way to convert the standard UNIX password database to an smbpasswd database. For this to happen, Samba must have access to the user's original plain-text password.

add user script =

The add user script configuration file option provides a very handy way to integrate Samba with an already existing Windows NT network. If your site has a Windows NT network with an already existing user database that you plan to use for authentication (in security = server or security = domain mode), this option will allow users to be created on the fly on the Samba server. Remember, even if you're using an existing Windows NT security database, the Samba server needs to have matching local users in its UNIX password database simply so it can set the proper permissions on files that these users may create or modify on your Samba shares. It can be a tiresome task to add a large number of new users to your UNIX password database, not to mention the hassle of synchronizing these two databases as new accounts are created or deleted.

Fortunately, Samba frees you from this by providing the add user script option. By setting up add user script correctly, no user intervention will be required to "sync up" user account information on the Samba side. What this means is that nearly all user account administration can be done under Windows NT Server, which may be a tremendous benefit in ease of use when Samba is added to an already existing NT network where administrators may have varying degrees of UNIX and Samba expertise.

Let's look at how this system works. If add user script is set to point to a fully qualified path of a script that will add a user to the system, when this user attempts to access a Samba share, the following things will happen:

- The user will be authenticated with a password server (such as Windows NT Server).

- If the user is authenticated, the UNIX password database will be checked to see whether that particular user exists under UNIX.

- If the user does exist, he or she will be granted access to the share and Samba will proceed as normal.

- If the user does not exist, the add user script will be called, as root, and the user will be added to the system. Then, he or she will be granted access to the share and Samba will proceed as normal.

This option defaults to the empty string. Here's a sample setting:

```
add user script = /usr/sbin/add_user %u
```

"%u" will be replaced with the current username.

Remember that the add user script option can do much more than simply add users to your UNIX system; for example, you may want add user script to send out an email to a new user, welcoming him or her to the server and explaining appropriate usage policies for the system. You may think of other creative ways to use the add user script option to enhance your computing environment.

delete user script =

delete user script allows users to be automatically deleted from your UNIX system. This option only works with the security = domain setting, unlike add user script, which works with both domain and server security settings. However, you should use this option with caution!

With that being said, delete user script provides an easy way for Samba to automatically remove user accounts from the UNIX password database that have already been deleted from Windows. Note that delete user script does not need to be used, even if you've enabled add user script.

> **Tip**
>
> The delete user script option only works if a user who has already been deleted from the Windows security database attempts to access a Samba share. If this does not happen, the user will not be deleted from the Samba database. This means that the delete user script option is not perfect and some periodic maintenance of the UNIX password database may be required to remove deleted users.

Here's how it works. When Samba is running in `security` = `domain` mode and an SMB/CIFS share is accessed, Samba will attempt to authenticate the user by contacting one of its password servers. If the authentication fails and a specific error code is returned by the Windows server indicating the user has been deleted, Samba will search for that particular user in the UNIX password database and call `delete user script` to delete the user if he or she exists. This script will be run as `root`. Here's a sample setting of this parameter:

```
delete user script = /usr/sbin/del_user %u
```

"`%u`" will be replaced with the username being deleted. This option defaults to an empty string.

> **Caution**
>
> The use of the `delete user script` option could cause a breach in security, allowing newly created users to read and modify files that they do not own. This could happen because when a user is deleted, his or her UNIX user ID is available again for use by any new user who may be created. For this reason, you might want to make your `delete user script` option scan your files for any items belonging to the deleted users and set the ownership on these files to nobody. This will prevent any new user who happens to be assigned a recycled user ID from accessing files that aren't his or hers. You might also want to consider using `delete user script` as a method to simply notify yourself or another administrator (via `sendmail`) of a user who needs to be deleted. Then, you or the other administrator can perform this deletion manually for security purposes.

password server =

`password server` is used to list one or more NetBIOS names of CIFS/SMB servers that will be used to authenticate users when Samba is in `security` = `server` or `security` = `domain` mode. It should only be used in combination with these security modes and should never point to itself. Therefore, if you aren't using either of these modes, simply remove this option.

In `security` = `domain` mode, Samba will try each server listed until it finds one that responds. This allows for very redundant network configurations. Note that the password servers in this case must consist of NetBIOS names of primary or backup domain controllers that are in the same domain as your Samba server. How to make Samba part of your NT domain is covered in Chapter 24, "Adding a Samba Server to an NT Network."

> **Tip**
>
> In Samba 2.0.6 and later, new `password server` functionality has been added. When in `security = domain` mode, `password server` can be set to `"*"`, which will cause Samba to automatically locate an active domain controller for authentication, just like Windows NT does.

In `security = server` mode, password server will still get the job done, but it won't be as robust. If the password server that Samba selects for authentication loses network connectivity, Samba will be unable to authenticate any more users. This is due to a deficiency in the protocol used, so unfortunately there's nothing the Samba team can do about this. In addition, if you're using Windows NT as your password server, you'll need to make sure it accepts connections directly from your Samba server. This is because your Samba server connects directly to the Windows NT machine during the authentication process.

> **Tip**
>
> Password servers must be listed by their NetBIOS names. IP addresses will not work.

machine password timeout =

As a security feature, Windows NT machines will change their machine account passwords every week. When a Samba server is in `security = domain` mode, this option can be used to change this time interval. `machine password timeout` accepts a value in seconds, and it defaults to `604800`, which is a week. The machine account is stored in the same directory as the `smbpasswd` file and has the name `DOM.SMBSRV.mac`, where `DOM` is the domain and `SMBSRV` is the NetBIOS name of your Samba server.

min passwd length =

This setting, which defaults to `5`, sets the minimum password length that Samba will accept when `unix password sync` is enabled.

null passwords =

`null passwords` controls whether accounts with no passwords set will be automatically denied. The default is `no`, which means that users will not be allowed to log in if they have no password set. Setting this option to `yes` will enable user login with a null password.

`password level =`

The `password level` configuration option exists to handle buggy CIFS/SMB clients, such as Windows for Workgroups, that sometimes send passwords over the wire in uppercase and sometimes leaves them as is. This makes things tricky for Samba. `password level` tells Samba to try a variety of uppercase/lowercase combinations of the received password to see whether any of them work. If one is the valid password, the user will be authenticated. This setting, which defaults to 0, will cause Samba to attempt to authenticate the user using the password as is, and if that doesn't work, attempt to authenticate the user using a password in all lowercase letters.

A `password level` setting of 1 will cause Samba to try every permutation of the password, which contains one uppercase letter as well as the default lowercase password. If the `password level` option is set to 2, it will try all the passwords in `password level` 1 in addition to all combinations that contain two uppercase characters. For example, when "BOB" is received as a password, the following permutations will be attempted with a password setting of 2:

- BOB
- bob
- Bob
- bOb
- boB
- BOb
- BoB, and so on

Tip

The `password level` configuration option is a hack at best, and it can have a dramatic negative impact on Samba performance and security at higher settings. There's a simple trick that can be used to get Samba working with Windows for Workgroups without using `password level`—simply let the few users you have that are still using Windows for Workgroups know that their passwords should be entered in uppercase. If their passwords contain only uppercase characters, authentication should always work even with a `password level = 0` setting (the default).

Using PAM-Based Password Synchronization

A pluggable authentication module (PAM) is an authentication system that's gaining popularity on UNIX, and especially Linux systems. PAM was designed to address a shortcoming in the UNIX environment—typically, individual programs such as `login` and `passwd` were hard-coded to perform their authentication functions one way, by using the UNIX password database. This was fine if the UNIX password database met your needs, but if it didn't and another authentication system was needed, you were out of luck. Typically, in such situations, a new version of every program that authenticates users (`login`, `passwd`, and so on) would have to be hand-coded in C to work with any new authentication system. The tremendous amount of programming required to implement any new system was a great deterrent to administrators desiring to improve upon the standard UNIX authentication mechanisms.

This is where PAM comes in. With PAM, the authentication mechanisms of programs such as `login` can be dynamically reconfigured or upgraded by the system administrator. For PAM to work, all programs that perform authentication must be made "PAM aware," and this requires modification to the programs' source code. Fortunately, this only has to be performed once, because once a program is PAM aware, it now uses PAM libraries to perform authentication instead of using its own internal code. Fortunately, many modern UNIX-like operating systems and distributions, such as Linux, come with PAM support built in. On these systems, you have several more options available to you to integrate UNIX and Windows.

18

PASSWORD
SYNCHRONIZATION AND
ADMINISTRATION

PAM Review

Before we begin reviewing PAM, it's important that you know whether PAM is supported under your operating system. Many modern Linux distributions, including Debian 2.2, Red Hat, Caldera, and SuSE include PAM support. In addition, PAM is supported under FreeBSD 3.1 and later. PAM is used under Solaris 2.6 and later, but its implementation differs from Linux-PAM, the implementation covered here.

When PAM is enabled on your system, you'll have either an `/etc/pam.d` directory or an `/etc/pam.conf` file. More modern versions of PAM use the `/etc/pam.d` directory, and I'll refer to the `/etc/pam.d` directory in the following text.

Inside the /etc/pam.d directory are a number of text files; each one contains PAM configurations for a particular application. Here's a directory listing from a SuSE Linux 6.2 /etc/pam.d directory:

```
total 17
-rw-r--r--   1 root      root            231 Jul 23 06:34 chfn
-rw-r--r--   1 root      root            231 Jul 23 06:34 chsh
-rw-r--r--   1 root      root            580 Jul 23 06:23 ftpd
-rw-r--r--   1 root      root             94 Jul 23 06:40 imap
-rw-r--r--   1 root      root            501 Jul 23 06:34 login
-rw-r--r--   1 root      root            444 Jul 23 01:48 other
-rw-r--r--   1 root      root            231 Jul 23 06:34 passwd
-rw-r--r--   1 root      root            311 Jul 29 08:40 ppp
-rw-r--r--   1 root      root            263 Jul 23 06:23 rexec
-rw-r--r--   1 root      root            450 Jul 23 06:23 rlogin
-rw-r--r--   1 root      root            292 Jul 23 06:23 rsh
-rw-r--r--   1 root      root            110 Jul 23 06:33 samba
-rw-r--r--   1 root      root            317 Jul 22 19:08 su
-rw-r--r--   1 root      root            108 Jul 23 06:34 su1
-rw-r--r--   1 root      root             60 Jul 23 06:34 sudo
-rw-r--r--   1 root      root            265 Jul 23 07:37 xdm
-rw-r--r--   1 root      root             67 Jul 23 06:40 xlock
```

As you can see, there are a number of configuration files, and you'll recognize a number of the program names, including Samba. Let's take a look at the samba PAM configuration file:

```
#%PAM-1.0
auth      required        /lib/security/pam_unix.so
account   required        /lib/security/pam_unix.so
```

This file tells Samba to authenticate users by using the UNIX password database, and it will be used when Samba is in encrypt passwords = no mode. This file can always be changed to authenticate users differently.

Note the existence of the others file. This is the default PAM configuration file, and it will be used for PAM-aware applications that do not have their own configuration files in /etc/pam.d. Note that the name of the config file in /etc/pam.d is normally the name of the PAM-aware program, but not always—this file name is compiled into the program itself.

Covering the contents and all the options available in PAM configuration files is beyond the scope of this section, but I can direct you to some great online resources. You'll definitely want to visit http://www.kernel.org/pub/linux/libs/pam/, the main Linux PAM page. It contains configuration file documentation, a very detailed overview of PAM, and an FAQ. It's recommended that you spend some time exploring your /etc/pam.d directory and studying the documentation to get a feel for how PAM works.

> **Caution**
>
> Modifying anything in the `/etc/pam.d` directory can be a dangerous undertaking. It's very possible that you could lock yourself out of your machine in the process. Before beginning, make sure you know how to boot your system in single-user mode or have a boot disk that you can use to access your `root` file system in the case of an emergency. It's always best to keep a couple `root` shells open while you modify the `/etc/pam.d` directory, just in case.

pam_smb

`pam_smb`, available from `http://www.csn.ul.ie/~airlied/pam_smb/`, is a PAM module that will allow you to configure any UNIX service to authenticate against a Windows server. This means that `login`, `passwd`, `pppd`, and others can all use a Windows NT server as their password server. All that's required is the proper compilation and installation of this module and the careful modification of your PAM configuration files. You can configure PAM to use `pam_smb` for only certain services or your entire system.

pam_ntdom

`pam_ntdom`, available at `ftp://ftp.samba.org/pub/samba/pam_ntdom/`, is a variation on `pam_smb`; it uses the NT domain authentication protocol to perform its password checking. It's very similar to `pam_smb` but is used in situations where your UNIX machine is part of an NT domain you're using for authentication. With `pam_ntdom`, you can turn a UNIX box into a full-fledged member of an NT domain, which is an interesting concept!

Using Password-Change Scripts

Depending on what Samba features you're using, you may have a need to create a new `passwd` script or program for either your users or Samba itself (via the `passwd program` option). In this section, I'll highlight several approaches to this problem. Before you try them, however, make sure there isn't already a simpler way to perform the same function. If your system uses PAM, you may be able to modify the behavior of `passwd` itself to meet your needs. Try the simpler approaches first before considering the more complicated ones.

Using expect

One of the tricky things about the `passwd` program is that it needs text to be entered at the keyboard. Although Samba's `passwd chat` option can help get around this, there are times when it might not be sufficient. In these cases, you may want to look into a program called expect, which allows you to create your own scripts that you can use to automate interactive programs. Of particular interest is a sample script that comes with expect, called autopasswd:

```
#!usr/bin/env expect -f
# wrapper to make passwd(1) be non-interactive
# username is passed as 1st arg, passwd as 2nd

set password [lindex $argv 1]
spawn passwd [lindex $argv 0]
expect "password:"
send "$password\r"
expect "password:"
send "$password\r"
expect eof
```

This expect script will, as mentioned in the preceding comments, allow autopasswd to be a noninteractive command, thus making it easier to use from scripts. If you do not have expect already installed on your system, it can be downloaded from http://expect. nist.gov/. It's definitely a handy tool.

Writing Your Own passwd Program

Although more intimidating, it's possible to write your own password program to perform your specific needs. This is a time-consuming option, so before pursuing it, you should be absolutely sure your current passwd program doesn't meet your needs. Remember, with expect you can change passwd's interface, and with PAM (if on your system), you can change passwd's authentication methods. If neither PAM nor expect (or both in combination) meet your needs, your own passwd program may be on the horizon. Try to only write a key section of code in C, and code the rest in some form of scripting language such as sh, Perl, or Python. This is generally a faster approach than writing the whole thing in C. If you're looking for source code examples, you'll find sample passwd programs in the Linux-PAM tarball available from http://www.kernel. org/pub/linux/libs/pam/. It's often better to base your work on already functional source code rather than create your own from scratch.

Summary

We've covered a lot of ground in this chapter. Beginning with an explanation of password synchronization, I then defined the password-synchronization challenge that modern multiplatform networks present. After we took a look at the password functionality of the Windows and UNIX environment, I then addressed the issue of how to synchronize passwords on the Samba server, itself, between the UNIX password database and the smbpasswd file.

In the second half of the chapter, I presented an in-depth explanation and discussion of the various Samba password-synchronization options available for `smb.conf`. Following that, we took an introductory look at pluggable authentication modules and what they offer to the UNIX environment. In closing, I provided some useful information to help you create your own password-change scripts, including an introduction to `expect`.

smb.conf Global Parameters

by Steve Litt

IN THIS CHAPTER

This chapter discusses the global `smb.conf` parameters. Where appropriate, references to relevant chapters of this book are included. This chapter is not a substitute for the `smb.conf` man page, nor vice versa.

This chapter, the `smb.conf` man page, and the other chapters of this book are all necessary for proficient use and administration of Samba.

Getting Your Own Information

There's no single source of information on `smb.conf` parameters. Other sources of parameter information include SWAT, the `smb.conf` man page, the `testparm` utility, Samba documentation, and source code.

From SWAT

SWAT is the Web-based configuration program packaged with Samba. Unless you want to actually change `smb.conf`, log in as a non-`root` user. In any event, *always* back up `smb.conf` before going into SWAT. The SWAT program is covered extensively in Chapter 13, "Using Samba Web Administration Tool (SWAT) for Samba Configuration."

In advanced view, SWAT's "globals" page shows the operating values of almost every parameter and has a help link next to each.

Unlike the `smb.conf` man page, SWAT arranges the parameters in categories similar to those in this chapter, which helps in grouping.

From the `smb.conf` Man Page

The `smb.conf` man page can be accessed from the `man smb.conf` command or from the front page of SWAT. The SWAT option has the additional benefit of enabling links from parameter references to parameter definitions. Other than the source code, this man page is considered the most authoritative source of information on the parameters.

From `testparm`

The `testparm` command yields information on default values of global parameters. Combined with the `grep` command, it can be used to look up the default value of a single parameter. Here's an example:

```
$ testparm -s | grep -i "domain master"
        domain master = No
$
```

It can also look up entire groups of parameters:

```
$ testparm -s | grep -i print
Processing section "[printers]"
        load printers = Yes
        printcap name = /etc/printcap
        printer driver file = /usr/local/samba/lib/printers.def
        min print space = 0
        print ok = No
        printing = bsd
        print command = lpr -r -P%p %s
        printer name =
        printer driver = NULL
        printer driver location =
        print ok = Yes
[printers]
        print ok = Yes
$
```

Unfortunately, `testparm` does not say which section it found the parameter in or whether it was a default, and occasionally it gets the wrong defaults (especially when dealing with the various printer commands). Nevertheless, it's an important tool in gaining parameter information.

From Samba Documentation

Samba distributions come with several text files detailing the use of parameters in achieving specific results. A quick search of Samba's text document directory can be done from that directory, like this:

```
$ grep -i "domain logons" *
```

Such a command brings up several references in files, listing the filenames and showing the references within the filenames. It may not find all instances if a word wrap occurs in the string.

From Source Code

The ultimate authority on parameters and their behavior is the source code. It can be searched for parameter names, which once found can be followed down the code. A good way to start is with a recursive `grep` on the source directory:

```
grep -ir "domain admin" * | less
```

Among the many lines found are two in `param/loadparm.c` relating parameter names to variables:

```
"domain admin group", &Globals.szDomainAdminGroup
```

```
"domain admin users", &Globals.szDomainAdminUsers
```

Note that for brevity, the preceding lines were shortened. Now `szDomainAdminGroup` can be "grepped," once again yielding three references to `param/loadparm.c`.

Global Base Parameters

The global base parameters define the basic properties of the Samba server. These include `workgroup=`, `netbios name=`, `netbios aliases=`, `server string=`, `interfaces=`, and `bind interfaces only=`.

workgroup=

The default is `WORKGROUP` on Linux setups, which is set at compile time. This parameter specifies the workgroup the server belongs to. Typically, this should be set to the same workgroup as the clients the server serves. Doing so makes the server much more "find-able" on the client machines.

If for some reason the workgroup must be different, other steps must be taken to make the server available for browsing, especially on Windows 9x hosts. This subject is discussed extensively in Chapter 9, "Working with Windows 98".

If `security=domain`, the workgroup represents the Windows domain.

netbios name=

This parameter determines the name of the Samba server in the NetBIOS world. If not specified, it's set to the server's DNS name. This can cause difficulties in the presence of certain DNS problems, and under certain other situations. It's best to explicitly specify this parameter as the server's hostname in `smb.conf`.

For trouble calls from users saying "I can't find the server," check to make sure this parameter is specified in `smb.conf`.

netbios aliases=

The default is an empty string. This is a list of other names by which the server appears on browse lists. This functionality is disabled if the Samba server is a logon server or browser.

If tempted to use this capability, think carefully to make sure it's a solution and not a workaround or symptom fix. In general, it's better to have a one-to-one correspondence between names and entities.

server string=

The default for Samba is %v. This is a server identification string for the benefit of users; it has no technological effects. It shows up in browse lists such as Windows Explorer and Find Computer, as well as the net view /workgroup:workgroupname DOS command. Note that this is the global equivalent of the comment= share parameter.

interfaces=

The default is an empty string. This parameter enables multisubnet browsing. If the server serves more than one subnet, it must identify all served subnets with this parameter. Here's an example of a two-subnet server serving both the 192.168.100 and 192.168.200 subnets:

```
interfaces=192.168.100/24 192.168.200/24
```

See bind interfaces only= as well. Chapter 33, "Cross-Subnet Browsing," elaborates on the intricacies of multiple subnets. Chapter 17, "Using Samba As the NT Primary Domain Controller," and Chapter 34, "Windows Internet Naming Service (WINS)," are also required reading for cross-subnet browsing.

bind interfaces only=

The default is false. If it's set to true, files are served only to the subnets listed in interfaces=. Note that the customary and preferred way to restrict by IP is to use the hosts allow= and hosts deny= global parameters. bind interfaces only= also binds nmbd ports 137 and 138 to the interfaces= subnets as well as 0.0.0.0.

See interface= as well. Chapter 33 elaborates on the intricacies of multiple subnets. Chapter 17 and Chapter 34 are also required reading for cross-subnet browsing. If this parameter is used for security purposes, see Chapter 15, "Samba Security," as well.

Global Security Parameters

Samba has a rich and configurable security model. Different environments require different security setups. Some security is implemented on a share-by-share basis. Other security is implemented for the server as a whole. The global security parameters govern the security of the Samba server as a whole.

encrypt passwords=

The default is no. Password encryption is a fundamental factor in Samba operations. It must match the encryption status of its clients. Older Windows clients used plain-text

passwords, whereas newer Windows clients default to encrypted passwords but can be set to plain-text passwords with a Registry tweak. See `ENCRYPTION.txt` for details.

If this parameter is set to `yes`, the encrypted passwords are kept in an `smbpasswd` file (typically in `/etc`, `/etc/samba` or `/usr/local/samba/private`), which is updated by the `smbpasswd` command. This setting has effects on PAM (Pluggable Authentication Module), password synchronization, and many other Samba components.

> **Tip**
>
> On networks where some clients encrypt and some don't, both can be accommodated with this statement:
>
> ```
> include=/usr/local/samba/opt/encrypt.%m
> ```
>
> Here, `%m` is replaced by the client name. A file for each client is then created, with a single line containing the appropriate `encrypt passwords=` parameter.

hosts equiv=

The default is `none`. This is a security risk—do not use it! This parameter enables hosts listed in a certain file to access the server without needing a password. If you're running an ultra-low security system and feel you must have this feature, read about it in the `smb.conf` man page.

map to guest=

The default is `Never`. Unless `security=share`, logins must present valid usernames. The one other exception is that if the share allows guests, the share can be accessed as `guest` using the `guest` user ID. Even if the share allows guests, it allows guest access according to the `map to guest=` parameter, which can take one of three values:

- `Never`
- `Bad User`
- `Bad Password`

If it's `Never`, no share is guest accessible unless it's `guest only=yes`. If `map to guest=Bad User`, clients requesting a nonexistent user get in as `guest`, but clients with legitimate usernames who have forgotten or mistyped their passwords cannot get in as `guest`. If `map to guest=Bad Password`, any wrong password—whether the username is bad or the password is mistyped—gets in as `guest` *silently*. This means that incorrectly typing a password leaves one with a completely different set of rights than usual, with no apparent explanation. Here's a quote from the `smb.conf` man page:

Helpdesk services will *hate* you if you set the "map to guest" parameter this way :-).

In the preceding quote, the phrase "this way" refers to Bad Password.

A complete flowchart of the guesting process is contained in Chapter 7, "Determining Samba Access."

min passwd length=

The default is 5. This is the minimum plain-text password length Samba accepts in UNIX password changes (with Unix password sync). Password synchronization is elaborated in Chapter 18, "Password Synchronization and Administration." Chapter 15 is also a good resource.

null passwords=

The default is no. If enabled, it allows users with zero-length passwords to access the server. This is a bad idea except in very-low security situations.

passwd chat=

The default is *old*password* %o\n *new*password* %n\n *new*password* %n\n *changed*. This is a chat script for changing the UNIX password when the Windows password is changed.

Here, %o and %n stand for old and new passwords, and \n, \r, \t, and \s are a newline character, a carriage return, a tab, and a single space (which comes in handy when a space would otherwise delineate an argument), respectively. If unix password sync=yes, the part of this process that changes the password in smbpasswd is executed as root.

Password synchronization is covered in Chapter 18. Security in general is covered in Chapter 15.

Receive/response scripts are difficult to debug. Therefore, when changing this parameter, it's often good to have passwd chat debug=yes.

passwd chat debug=

The default is no. This parameter prints the conversation between Samba and the password programs in the smbd log at debug level 100. This creates a vital test point in what would otherwise be a black box.

19

smb.conf GLOBAL PARAMETERS

> **Caution**
>
> This puts passwords in the log! Use this option only when other users are off the system, and use only a bogus user created just for this purpose. When the password chat is working, set passwd chat debug=no and delete the bogus user.
>
> To prevent other users from connecting to Samba (and thus possibly getting their passwords written in the log), you may want to back up smb.conf and create a temporary debug smb.conf file with a single service accessible only from your computer's IP address.

passwd program=

The default is /bin/passwd. This parameter specifies the program called when a password is changed, thus defining the nature of password synchronization. If unix password sync=yes, the part of this process that changes the password in smbpasswd is executed as root. All commands defined in or called by passwd program= must include full paths. See Chapters 15 and 18.

password level=

The default is 0. This parameter specifies the number of characters in the password that are allowed to be uppercase, assuming a failure of a case-sensitive match and a match to a 100% lowercase version. Intuitively, one might think this means "the first X characters," but in fact what it really means is "the number of permissible uppercase letters."

For instance, if this parameter is set to 1, SAMBA matches SAMBA (via an exact match), Samba, sAmba, saMba, samBa, sambA, and samba (via an all-lowercase comparison). Setting it to a large number increases comparisons in a factorial manner, thus hurting performance.

The default of 0 has this special meaning: First compare the password case sensitively "as is" and then convert the requested password to all lowercase to see whether it matches a UNIX password. In other words, SambaUnleashed would match SambaUnleashed, and any case combinations in the password request would match sambaunleashed on the UNIX uid password.

> **Note**
>
> This behavior varies between distributions and depending on the setting of encrypt passwords=. Investigate it on your own system.
>
> One excellent use for this parameter is troubleshooting a situation where logging in fails. By setting this parameter longer than the password, case problems can quickly be ruled out (or in). Because large numbers here have serious performance consequences, do this when usage is light.

password server=

The default is an empty string. This parameter assigns a *different* server to check passwords, accepting its authentication results. Never set this parameter to the Samba server containing this parameter, because that sets up a loop and can severely disrupt Samba. With `security=domain`, a list of PDCs (primary domain controllers) or BDCs (backup domain controllers) can be the value of the parameter. A list may also be applied when `security=server`, but the first failure terminates the password-authentication search. Because this parameter assigns remote authentication, it does not work with `security=user` or `security=share`.

This parameter is significant in Chapter 15, Chapter 17, Chapter 18, and Chapter 24, "Adding a Samba Server to an NT Network."

root directory=

The default is `/`. All share paths are relative to the value of this parameter. All commands are relative to the value of this parameter. Files outside this tree cannot be accessed. This might be true even of soft links, according to the `smb.conf` man page.

Although this sounds like a great security precaution, it can present problems if the `passwd` and `smbpasswd` files are outside this tree or if the `print` command–type files (such as `lpr`, `lpq`, and so on) or any other processes called in `smb.conf` parameters are outside this tree. In such cases, those files must be mirrored inside the tree.

A properly configured Samba server is very secure. Unless there's a real need for extra security, it's best to leave this parameter at its default.

security=

The default is `user` for Samba 2.0 and above and `share` for earlier versions.

The `security=share` setting requires only a valid password, not a valid username, to access shares. The UNIX server embarks on a very complex process to find a username to go with the requested password. In such situations, it's very difficult to know which username the client was logged in under.

The `security=share` setting is best reserved for low-security servers where everyone can access everything. A print server is a good example. Anything more complex than that should use one of the other security models.

The `security=user` setting requires the client to provide a valid username with a matching valid password. The combination is validated against the UNIX system's password authentication system if `encrypt passwords=no` or against `smbpasswd` if `encrypt passwords=yes`. The user thus authenticated can access any shares for which he or she is a valid user, to the extent that `read only=`, `read list=`, and `write list=` allow.

19

smb.conf GLOBAL
PARAMETERS

The `security=server` setting is like `security=user`, except that instead of authenticating passwords locally, the responsibility is delegated to another server via the `password server=` parameter. If that authentication fails, the server reverts back to `security=user`, in which case, if encrypted passwords are used, it must have a valid `smbpasswd` file.

The `security=domain` setting, the newest security model, is meant to implement NT domains. It's used when the Samba server has been joined to an NT domain, either as a PDC or with another machine enabled as the PDC. Like `security=server`, `security=domain` differs from `security=user` only in its handling of authentication.

See Chapters 15, 17, 18 and 24 for more about the `security=` parameter.

smb passwd file=

The default is decided at compile time. On new installations, let this parameter use the default. The main use of this parameter is to handle situations in which a new `smbd`, with a new default location for the `smbpasswd` file, is installed. In such cases, this parameter enables that file to be used. Alternatively, the file could simply be moved.

Note that this setting is recognized not only by the `smbd` daemon but also by the `smbpasswd` utility. This setting also determines the location of the `MACHINE.SID` file.

unix password sync=

The default is `no`. A value of `yes` enables Samba to, upon a change to the encrypted password file, attempt to similarly change the UNIX password for the user. Obviously, this must be done as `root`. This conceivably allows all UNIX box password changes to be done via `smbpasswd`.

Chapter 18 discusses this parameter.

update encrypted=

The default is `no`. This parameter is used to ease the transition from plain-text passwords to encrypted passwords. If set to `yes`, every successful plain-text login writes the encrypted password to `smbpasswd`. Once most users have logged on to the `update encrypted=yes` server, the clients and the server can be switched to encrypted passwords, and this parameter can be switched back to its default, `no`.

Chapter 18 discusses this parameter.

use rhosts=

The default is `no`. This is a major security risk—do not use it! When set to `yes`, this parameter allows each user to have a `.rhosts` file—in his or her home directory—specifying computers and users that can log in without a password.

username level=

The default is 0. Similar to password level=, this parameter defines the number of case combinations permissible in matching a username. 0 means "try all lowercase and then try all lowercase except for the first character." The behavior of this parameter may be affected by distribution and encrypt passwords=.

> **Note**
>
> One excellent use for this parameter involves troubleshooting a situation in which logging in fails. By setting this parameter longer than the username, case problems can quickly be ruled out (or in). Because large numbers here have serious performance consequences, do this when usage is light.

username map=

The default is none. This is used when client usernames do not match the usernames on the Samba server. Such a situation might occur when Samba is operational on a production UNIX server and it's impractical to give every Windows user a UNIX login. However, when possible, it's preferable to have a one-to-one correspondence between Windows and UNIX users on the Samba server.

This parameter points to a file containing maps between the requested username and the granted username. It can also be used to map multiple users to individual users for the purpose of file sharing. Almost the same result can be obtained with the force user= parameter, which is a much more customary method.

Global Logging Parameters

Log files are powerful troubleshooting tools. They're especially valuable in sparse intermittents or "events." Log files also provide a "smoking gun" useful in bringing crackers and script kiddies to justice. Samba provides a wide range of logging configurations, all controlled by its logging parameters.

Chapter 22, "Troubleshooting Samba," contains many tips for debugging with log files.

log file=

The location of the Samba log files is typically compiled. This parameter can be used to change that location. This can be handy during specific troubleshooting sessions in an effort to isolate a problem. This file can contain variable substitution characters.

log level=

Also known as `debug level`. The default is `0`, unless it's specified otherwise on the command line when running the daemons. According to the man page for the `syslog=` parameter, log levels can be thought of as follows:

0   Errors

1   Errors and warnings

2   Errors, warnings, and notices

3   Errors, warnings, notices, and information

4+   All of these, plus debugging information

As levels go up, so does the amount of debugging information written to the log. As mentioned, the log level can be defaulted on the command line. Additionally, it can be stepped up by increments of 1 at runtime by sending the daemon a `SIGUSR1`, and similarly stepped down with `SIGUSR2`. The `smbd` and `nmbd` log levels can therefore be set to separate levels.

max log size=

The default is `5000`, meaning a 5MB maximum log size. When the log goes over that amount, it's renamed and a new log is started.

status=

The default is `yes`. This parameter should be left alone. Setting it to `no` serves no purpose and would disable the `smbstatus` program.

syslog=

The default is `1`. This parameter specifies what level of Samba messages are sent to `syslog`. The default of `1` specifies errors, whereas `2` would specify errors and warnings. This does not effect what's written to the Samba logs, only what's written to the system logs.

Only messages with debug levels *less than* this value will be sent to `syslog`. Here are the `syslog` levels:

0   LOG_ERR

1   LOG_WARNING

2   LOG_NOTICE

3   LOG_INFO

4+   LOG_DEBUG

syslog only=

The default is no. If set to yes, this parameter sends debug information *only* to syslog, not to the Samba debug logs.

timestamp logs=

The default is no. At higher log levels, the timestamping can obscure pertinent information. Setting this parameter to yes stops timestamps from being written to the log.

Global Protocol Parameters

There's seldom a reason to change the global protocol parameters. Their defaults match most situations. However, the protocols Samba uses to communicate can be custom designed for a particular environment using the global protocol parameters.

It's often prudent in troubleshooting to temporarily comment out explicitly specified global protocol parameters to see how the symptom changes. This is discussed in Chapter 22.

Care should be taken when explicitly specifying these parameters. All too often they needlessly show up in smb.conf due to "example" smb.conf files or due to experimentation. Explicit specification of these parameters must be done only with good reason.

announce as=

The default is NT, which is a synonym for NT Server. This parameter specifies the type of server that the Samba server calls itself in browse lists. Here are the valid values:

- NT Server
- NT Workstation
- Win95
- WfW

There's little reason to change this, and changing it could prevent Samba servers from functioning as browsers.

announce version=

The default is 4.2. This parameter specifies the nmbd version announces itself as. Unless clients require a lower version server or some other very unusual situation occurs, let this parameter use its default.

max mix=

The default is `50`. Always let this parameter default. It specifies the maximum outstanding SMB operations permitted.

max packet=

This is a synonym for `packet size=` and is depreciated. Remove it from `smb.conf`.

max ttl=

The default is `259200`, meaning three days (in seconds). This parameter specifies the maximum time to live for `nmbd` packets (except for WINS packets, which are governed by `max wins ttl=`). Always let this parameter default.

max wins ttl=

The default is `518400`, meaning six days (in seconds). This parameter specifies the time to live for WINS `nmbd` packets. Non-WINS packets are governed by `max ttl=`. This should always be left at its default, so it should not be specified from `smb.conf`.

max xmit=

The default is `65535`. This parameter specifies the maximum packet size used by Samba. Performance can sometimes be enhanced by tuning this parameter. According to the `smb.conf` man page, values below `2048` are likely to cause problems.

min wins ttl=

The default is `21600`, meaning six hours (in seconds). Leave this parameter at its default value. This specifies the minimum time to live for WINS `nmbd` packets, much the same as `max wins ttl=` specifies the maximum.

name resolve order=

The default is `lmhosts host wins bcast`. This parameter can greatly effect the performance of the Samba system because it impacts the speed at which NetBIOS names are resolved as well as the traffic that resolution creates. Although broadcast resolution is most likely to yield results, it's slow and traffic producing by nature. At the opposite end of the spectrum, `lmhost` is a simple file lookup. The host method uses whatever methods are available to the host, usually a combination of `/etc/hosts` and DNS or NIS. WINS is the SMB protocol's own resolution method. The default is excellent because it queries the quickest methods first. On a system with a defective WINS server, you would eliminate WINS from the list. Likewise, if DNS were defective on a server, you'd likely remove `host`.

This subject is discussed in detail in Chapter 34.

nt acl support=

The default is yes, meaning Samba attempts to map UNIX permissions onto NT access control lists. This is a relatively new feature that brings Samba closer to the functionality of NT. Let this parameter default unless you have a good reason to do the opposite.

nt pipe support=

The default is yes. Except when debugging Samba source code, this should be left at the default. It enables or disables connections from NT clients to specific IPC$ pipes. See ipc.c and smb.h for further information.

nt smb support=

The default is yes, and it should be left that way. However, there have been some reports that setting this to no increases performance. This is being investigated and will presumably be resolved in an upcoming Samba version. In a performance analysis, you may wish to *temporarily* set this parameter to no and see the effect. If performance speeds up, give all pertinent information to the Samba project (www.samba.org). Unless the performance improvement is major, set it back to yes for production systems.

protocol=

The default is NT1. This parameter specifies the SMB protocol. Leave it at its default because protocol negotiations with clients set this parameter at the appropriate protocol.

read bmpx=

This parameter defaults to no, and it should be left at no. If set to yes it would enable the rarely used and somewhat antiquated "Read Block Multiplex" SMB.

read raw=

The default is yes. A yes value enables raw reads of 65,535-byte packets for better performance. Some clients cannot handle such packets, in which case either the clients must be upgraded or this parameter set to no. Setting it to no degrades performance.

time server=

The default is no. A yes value enables nmbd to advertise itself as a time server, thereby enabling the Windows net time command to obtain the date and time from the Samba server. Note that regardless of this parameter's value, a Windows client can always obtain the date and time from the Samba server with the net time \\sambaservername command.

19

smb.conf GLOBAL
PARAMETERS

write raw=

The default is yes, and it should be left at yes. When troubleshooting very old clients, it may be prudent to set this temporarily to no and see whether the symptom changes. However, leaving it at no is not a viable long-term solution.

Global Tuning Parameters

Tradeoffs exist between performance and many other factors. Some Samba environments perform better with nondefault tuning. Those defaults are changed with the tuning parameters.

The defaults for these parameters create a reasonably efficient Samba server. When building a new smb.conf, the prudent course of action is to let all these parameters default until a solid, stable, and tested environment is created. If politically feasible, it's best to run the defaults in production for an appropriate shakedown period. Only after a solid, functional state has been reached should performance tuning be attempted.

An important fact often forgotten in the heat of battle is that optimizing something that's not a bottleneck does little good. The first step in any tuning expedition is finding the performance bottleneck(s).

change notify timeout=

The default is 60. This is the number of seconds between "scans" of directories for the purpose of satisfying a "ChangeNotify" request. The larger this number, the fewer the resources that need to be spent scanning directories. Therefore, unless there's a reason to quickly notify clients of changes to directories, this parameter is best left at its default or even raised to a higher number.

> **Note**
>
> Obviously, any directory changes initiated in Network Neighborhood are immediately reflected in Network Neighborhood, so the usefulness of this parameter is limited to changes initiated on the server or other clients.
>
> This parameter has no effect on the use of a new or changed file but rather only on its appearance in a browse—and even that is subject to question because there have been reports of Network Neighborhood not refreshing quickly, even when this parameter has a value of 1. No matter how high this parameter is set, refreshing the Network Neighborhood screen immediately shows any changes.
>
> Except in *very* special circumstances, let this parameter default.

deadtime=

The default is 0, which means "never disconnect inactive clients." This setting represents the number of minutes of inactivity before a client is disconnected, the intent being to prevent inactive clients from sapping system resources. Because most clients have a reconnection feature, this should not cause a problem with clients running applications. A client is considered "inactive" if it has no files open.

Windows Explorer does not close a connection it has opened, even if Windows Explorer is closed. In the absence of a net use /delete command, the connection remains active. This is one reason for the use of this parameter.

getwd cache=

The default is no. Setting this parameter to yes can yield performance benefits if wide links=yes. The level of performance enhancement depends on many factors and should be tested on the target system.

keepalive=

The default is 0, meaning no keepalive packets are sent to clients. The default is usually functional, but if difficulties arise in detecting live clients, this can be set to the interval in seconds to send keepalive packets.

lpq cache time=

Default is 10, meaning that the results of a specific lpq command are cached for 10 seconds, and all further invocations of that exact command are satisfied from the cached result, rather than a rerunning of another lpq command. Depending on the speed of your lpq command, this number may need to be increased to prevent performance degradation or decreased to promote timely accuracy. A value of 0 means the lpq command is run every time such a command is issued, which could present problems if a program issues these commands frequently. A value of 0 could open the door to a brute-force "denial of service" attack.

max disk size=

The default is 0, meaning "no maximum disk space." This parameter specifies, in MB, the upper limit of the disk size reported to applications. It does *not* limit the size of files or the amount of disk space available to the user, as long as the program used to create the files does not base its file creation and/or expansion on a disk size inquiry.

19

smb.conf GLOBAL
PARAMETERS

This is not a tool to limit disk usage—quotas are the tool of choice for that. Use of this parameter puts client perception of the disk in an inconsistent state, because the client can have 500MB on a 100MB disk. The purpose of this parameter is to trick old applications that cannot deal with large disks. Do not use this parameter for any other reason. Note that because it's a global parameter, all shares abide by it, including parameters "pathed" to other partitions.

max open files=

The default is 10000. This represents the maximum open files a process can have for a given client. Note that UNIX limitations are lower, making this number irrelevant in most cases. This can be seen in the following output to log.smb:

```
$ tail -fn0 log.smb
[1999/11/11 07:28:27, 1] smbd/server.c:main(628)
  smbd version 2.0.5a started.
  Copyright Andrew Tridgell 1992-1998
[1999/11/11 07:28:27, 1] smbd/files.c:file_init(216)
  file_init: Information only: requested 10000 open files, 1014 are available.
```

read prediction=

The default is no. Note that this parameter is disabled in version 2 and may be depreciated or removed later. Do not specify it in Samba version 2 and above. In earlier versions, this parameter performed a form of read caching.

read size=

The default is 16384. This is the number of bytes at which certain Samba functions begin their writing activities, even though they haven't received all the data from a previous read. Read about this parameter in Chapter 35, "Optimizing Samba Performance," and the smb.conf man page before attempting to change it from its default.

shared mem size=

The default is 1048576. This parameter is the number of bytes of memory shared between smbd processes. If it's set too high, it wastes the consumed memory.

The number asked for is not necessarily the number of bytes received. If smbd cannot allocate this number of bytes of shared memory, it repeatedly requests an amount that's 0.8 times the last request until the memory is allocated. Obviously, such an outcome is not ideal. Check memory usage with the appropriate ps or top command. If there's a need to explicitly specify this parameter, read Chapter 35 first.

socket options=

The default is TCP_NODELAY. This is a tuning parameter that best matches socket options with the optimal options for your network. This parameter provides an excellent tuning opportunity if used right. This parameter should be left at its default on newly configured systems and adjusted only when the system has reached a high level of stability.

If Samba is suspected of a performance bottleneck, read about this parameter on the smb.conf man page and read your system documentation about socket options, including the setsockopt man page. Also, read Chapter 35.

stat cache size=

The default is 50, and it should be left as is. This is the size of the stat cache.

Global Printing Parameters

The vast majority of printing parameters are share parameters. A few affect the system as a whole and cannot be broken down by share. These are global printing parameters and include load printers=, printcap name=, and printer driver file=.

load printers=

The default is yes, which means that all print queues are listed in the [printers] share, whereas no means none of the print queues are listed in the [printers] share unless they're specifically named in an auto services= parameter.

printcap name=

The default varies with the compile and runtime setting of the printing= parameter. Always explicitly specify this parameter if there's a [printers] share. This parameter specifies where Samba can acquire the list of print queues to list in the [printers] share.

printer driver file=

The default varies with compile. Always explicitly specify this file if Samba provides drivers for printers; otherwise, do not specify this parameter.

Global Filename Handling Parameters

Different operating systems have different filenaming conventions. In addition, different human languages have different characters. The filename-handling parameters provide compatibility across computer operating systems and human languages.

character set=

The default is an empty string. This parameter defines the character set used for *file-names*. This parameter is tightly dependent on the `client code page=` parameter. If there's a need to name files with characters other than the standard English letters, numbers, and punctuation, read the `smb.conf` man page for this parameter as well as `client code page=`.

If the computer users in the organization are comfortable with English letters, it's probably easiest to let this parameter default.

coding system=

This parameter further defines Japanese code page 932. It has no effect if `client code page=` is set to anything but `932`. The `smb.conf` man page has further details.

client code page=

Default is `850` (MS-DOS Latin 1). This default also works with clients using code page 437 (MS-DOS Latin U.S.). Set this parameter to be compatible with the code page used by the clients. This parameter is tightly integrated with the `valid chars=` and `character set=` parameters. If there's a need to change this parameter, read the `smb.conf` man page for all three of these parameters. There's an `smb.conf` order dependency between this and `valid chars=` (specifically, `client code page=` must be declared first).

mangled stack=

The default is `50`, meaning that 50 mangled filenames are stored. Decreasing this parameter can speed performance but possibly lead to mangling errors. Likewise, increasing it decreases performance but can reduce mangling errors. See the `smb.conf` man page for further information.

stat cache=

The default is yes, and it should be left at yes.

strip dot=

The default is no. If set to yes, this parameter strips any dots off the end of filenames ending in a dot. This is sometimes useful for accessing CD-ROMs having files ending with a dot or accessing UNIX directories containing files ending in a dot.

Global SSL Parameters

The Secure Sockets Layer (SSL) parameters are effective only in Samba versions compiled with the SSL libraries and if the configure option `--with-ssl` was given at configure time.

Because SSL is a heavy encryption method, it's not enabled by default in Samba binaries.

SSL is relatively new to Samba. Thoroughly read the smb.conf man page for each of these.

SSL support in Samba is in a state of flux. Throughout most of 1999 it had used the *SSLeay* library. SSLeay is a free implementation of SSL (Secure Socket Layer). Samba is now moving toward the *OpenSSL* library. The OpenSSL library is an extension on the SSLeay library. Because different people will read this book at different times, the best approach is to use the learning tools in this book's chapter 23, "Samba Learning Tools."

The default is no, which disables Samba's SSL. If it's set to yes, SSL is enabled.

ssl CA certDir=

The default is /usr/local/ssl/certs, meaning that the directory contains the Certification Authorities (CA) files. Changing the value of this parameter changes the location to look for CA files.

Note that trusted Certification Authorities can also be defined using the ssl CA certFile= parameter.

ssl CA certFile=

The default is /usr/local/ssl/certs/trustedCAs.pem, meaning that the file contains certificates of trusted Certification Authorities. Changing the value of this parameter changes the file to search for CA certificates.

As an alternative to ssl CA certdir=, ssl CA certFile= is simpler for setups with a single CA.

ssl ciphers=

Ciphers are used during SSL negotiation. Don't change this parameter without good reason and complete knowledge.

ssl client cert=

The default is /usr/local/ssl/certs/smbclient.pem, meaning that this file contains a certificate to be presented to a server by smbclient.

ssl client key=

The default is /usr/local/ssl/private/smbclient.pem, meaning that this file contains the private key for smbclient.

ssl compatibility=

The default is no, meaning "do not attempt to configure SSLeay for bug compatibility with other SSL implementations." Formerly, there were no SSL implementations besides SSLeay, so the default of no was always safe. With changes brought on by the transition to OpenSSL, and future changes, it's best to consult the technical@samba.org mailing list.

ssl hosts and ssl hosts resign=

Both parameters default to empty strings. ssl hosts= lists the only hosts forced into SSL mode, whereas ssl hosts resign= lists the only hosts not forced into SSL mode. If ssl hosts resign=192.168.100.44, every other host communicates only through SSL mode. If ssl hosts=192.168.100.44, every other host communicates through non-SSL mode. Note the similarity to hosts allow, hosts deny, and so on.

ssl require clientcert=

The default is no, meaning the server does not terminate connections from clients not having a valid certificate. Setting it to yes requires client certificates.

ssl require servercert=

The default is no, meaning the client (using smbclient) does not terminate connections from servers not having a valid certificate. Setting it to yes requires server certificates.

ssl server cert=

Defaults to an empty string. If this parameter is not empty, it points to a file containing the server's certificate.

ssl server key=

Defaults to an empty string. If this parameter is not empty, it points to a file containing the private key of the server.

ssl version

Defaults to ssl2or3. This parameter specifies the SSL protocol as follows:

ssl2or3 Dynamic negotiation of SSL v2 or v3

ssl2 SSL v2

ssl3 SSL v3

tls1 TLS v1

Global Domain Parameters

All these parameters are listed as experimental in the smb.conf man page distributed with Samba 2.0.6. They do work to a limited extent in that version, but none of the 2.0.x branch serves domains particularly well. The recommended Samba branch for domain control is the Samba TNG (The Next Generation) branch. Refer to Chapter 17 for details on the following parameters:

- allow trusted domains=
- domain admin group=
- domain admin users=
- domain groups=
- domain guest group=
- domain guest users=
- domain logons=
- machine password timeout=

Global LDAP Parameters

LDAP stands for *Lightweight Directory Access Protocol*. LDAP is a directory service designed to unify administration, authentication, and naming across large networks. Samba is quickly progressing to the point where it supports LDAP, thus giving Samba servers directory services similar to those offered by NetWare and promised by Microsoft.

As of Samba 2.0.6, Samba LDAP support is still experimental. The implementation is better in the head branch and in the SAMBA_TNG branch. There have been many reports, on the Samba mailing lists, of successful Samba LDAP installations. However, given the experimental and changing nature of LDAP in Samba, the implementing LDAP in Samba will be difficult for awhile.

On 1/21/2000, a Samba-technical mailing list message entitled "[SAMBA-TNG] watch out: new LDAP schema may be introduced soon" by Luke Kenneth Casson Leighton indicated that a new developer would be working on an NT5 compatible LDAP schema, meaning that those using the prior schema would need to convert. This is an example of some of the near-term difficulties. Obviously, sooner or later LDAP will become a stable part of Samba.

Because of the rapid changes to LDAP, this book does not cover LDAP's specifics. When you need LDAP information, your best avenue is to use the various learning tools in Chapter 23.

The parameters listed in this section experimentally support a password database stored on an LDAP server back end. These options are only available if your version of Samba was configured with the `--with-ldap` option.

Further information is available in the `smb.conf` man page. Here are the parameters:

- `ldap filter=`
- `ldap port=`
- `ldap root=`
- `ldap root passwd=`
- `ldap server=`
- `ldap suffix=`

Global Login Parameters

An important feature of a full-blown file server is the capability to function as a login server. This means authenticating, setting up, and executing a login script. This also includes housekeeping associated with the addition and deletion of users.

The global login parameters are Samba's way of defining Samba's login server activities.

`add user script=`

The default is an empty string, meaning "run no script when a user is added." If this parameter is not empty, it's a full pathname to a script to be run as `root` to perform the necessary housekeeping for adding a UNIX user when a validated Windows user who has no valid UNIX username logs in. Such a script must obviously be accessible only to user `root`.

This feature works only with `security=server` or `security=domain`, with certain other circumstances. See Chapters 15 and 18 for usage and requirements.

delete user script=

The default is an empty string. Unlike `add user script=`, this parameter works only when `security=domain`. This script, which is run as `root`, is called when a non-authenticated (by the domain) user accesses the Samba server. The purpose is to delete any UNIX user accounts that have been deleted from Windows authentication.

Although this sounds like a great timesaver, problems can ensue on UNIX boxes used for anything besides Samba. The best course might be to have this script delete the UNIX user and send an email to the administrator, who can then decide whether to delete the user's home directory.

This feature works only with `security=domain`, with certain other circumstances. See Chapters 15 and 18 for usage and requirements.

logon drive=

This works only with NT workstations, and only if the Samba server is a logon server. In that case, this parameter can take a value of a drive letter and trailing colon, which will then be the drive mapped to the home directory. For details, see Chapter 17.

logon home=

The default is `\\%N\%U`. This enables a `NET USE H: /HOME` command, which can be essential in setting up roaming profiles. See `DOMAINS.txt` and Chapter 16, "Using Samba as Your Windows 98 Logon Mechanism," Chapter 17, "Using Samba as the NT Primary Domain Controller," and Chapter 10, "Working with Windows NT," for details.

logon path=

The default is `\\%N\%U\profile`. This parameter specifies the location of roaming profiles. If roaming profiles are used, it's best to explicitly specify this parameter. See `DOMAINS.txt` and Chapters 10, 16, and 17 for details.

19

smb.conf GLOBAL
PARAMETERS

logon script=

There is no default, meaning there are no logon scripts. This parameter specifies the location, relative to special share [netlogon], of the login script to be used on the Windows client. This script must be a legitimate Windows batch file. All path designations, including that of the parameter value itself, must use DOS-style backslashes rather than forward slashes. The file must terminate lines using carriage return/linefeed characters.

Individual users can be given individual login scripts by including the %U macro, as in login script=scripts\%U.bat.

If the script changes the current directory or current drive without later switching back, it may appear to hang, thus requiring the user to press the Esc key.

Global Browse Parameters

These parameters determine which server serves up browse lists for its subnet. This functionality is referred to as being a *master browser* or *browse master*. In the case of domains, in which a server serves up browse lists for a workgroup, this functionality is referred to as being a *domain master browser* or *domain browse master*.

Because each subnet is limited to one master browser if it is to work correctly, these browsers are chosen in an election very similar to a presidential election. Election analogies are used in the following parameter explanations.

browse list=

The default is yes. Leave the parameter at its default. Setting this parameter to no would disable Samba's sending a browse list upon receipt of a NetServerEnum call, which is almost never a good idea. Note, however, that setting it to no does not disable all browsing, as evidenced by the net view \\servername and smbclient -NL servername commands. The bottom line is it's best to let this parameter default.

domain master=

The default is no. If set to yes, this parameter causes nmbd to appoint the server as the domain browser (this server will win a browser election). This can present problems if a Windows PDC is on the same workgroup, in which case it will also be the domain browser. This conflict causes problems. If NT servers exist, this parameter should remain no and domain browser responsibility should be delegated to NT servers.

lm announce=

The default is auto. Unless OS/2 clients exist, this parameter can safely be set to no, in which case it will never send LANMAN broadcasts. The auto setting sends no such broadcasts unless one is heard, in which case it begins sending them. Setting this parameter to yes forces the server to send LANMAN (LAN Manager) broadcasts.

If LANMAN broadcasts are sent, they're sent at a frequency determined by the lm interval= parameter. In most situations, the best policy is to leave this parameter out of smb.conf, thus enabling the default.

lm interval=

The default is 60, meaning LANMAN broadcasts are sent every 60 seconds if and only if lm_announce=yes or lm_announce=auto and the server receives a LANMAN broadcast. Note that a value of 0 disables LANMAN broadcasts regardless of lm_announce.

This parameter is meaningless if these broadcasts do not occur, either because lm_announce=no or because lm_announce=auto and there are no OS/2 clients. Unless there are OS/2 clients on the network and problems are encountered, it's best to leave this parameter out of smb.conf, thus enabling the default.

local master=

The default is yes. This parameter is the election equivalent to "throwing your hat in the ring," in that it indicates the server is running for election as browse master. If this parameter is set to no, the server cannot become the subnet's browse master.

os level=

The default is 0. This default "sabotages" the election, guaranteeing it will be lost (unless every client declines to be browse master). Each type of server on the network advertises an OS level, with the highest-numbered server winning the election (subject to a few other variables). The following are the levels at which Windows servers broadcast themselves:

- Windows 9*x* and workgroups are 1
- NT Workstation is 16
- NT Server is 32

At present, a value of 33 "rigs" an election for a Samba server, unless another Samba server has a higher value. This parameter can be set all the way up to 255, which certainly "rigs" the election. A value of 65 is often recommended in Samba documentation.

preferred master=

The default is no. Setting this parameter does two things:

- Calls for an election on nmbd startup (and periodically after that).
- Puts a few extra ballots in the ballot box. This server has a slight advantage over others with the same os level= setting.

It's important to have only one preferred master in any workgroup, because if there are several preferred masters, the constant elections they call will decrease performance and browseability.

The way to use this parameter is to decide on a single Samba machine to be the local browse master and give it the following settings: local master=yes, os level=33 (or higher), and preferred master=yes.

Global WINS Parameters

WINS stands for *Windows Internet Naming Service*. It's a name resolution service, used extensively in Windows, that does not rely on broadcasts. Windows 2000 does not use WINS, so eventually WINS will go away. But as long as any Windows 9*x*, Windows NT, or Windows for Workgroups clients remain on a network, WINS support is needed.

The global WINS parameters define the properties of the WINS server. This book devotes the entirety of Chapter 34 to WINS. Detailed information on all these parameters can be found there.

dns proxy=

The default is yes, meaning the Samba WINS server will attempt to use DNS to look up any names not found in WINS searches.

wins proxy=

The default is no. If enabled, this parameter enables the server to respond to broadcast name queries on behalf of other hosts. This can be used to resolve names of multiple clients with minimal per-client setup. See Chapter 34.

wins server=

The default is an empty string, meaning that this server does not delegate WINS resolution to a different server. If the value of this parameter is set to the IP address of a WINS server, it delegates WINS resolution to that server. This is an essential part of cross-subnet browsing.

This parameter does *not* enable WINS on the server on which it resides. The `wins support=` parameter does that. The value of the `wins server=` parameter should never be set to the IP address of the machine on which it resides.

wins support=

The default is `no`. If set to `yes`, this parameter makes the Samba server a WINS server also. If this parameter is set to `yes`, there should be no `wins server=` parameter in `smb.conf`. Use only one WINS server per subnet.

Global Locking Parameters

Multiuser operating systems require locking to prevent users from overwriting each other's file changes, which would result in file corruption. Unfortunately, locking is very slow and inefficient. Samba provides many levels and degrees of locking in order to balance file integrity with performance. Several parameters adjust *opportunistic locking*, a feature that enables aggressive caching on the client in certain situations.

Several global and share parameters control the type and degree of locking. The global locking parameters are listed in this section. Chapter 35 covers several aspects of these parameters.

kernel oplocks=

The default is dependent on the system. Let this parameter default. If this parameter is set to `yes`, some aspects of oplocks are handled in the kernel, making it possible for SMB/CIFS, NFS, and local file access to cooperatively use oplocks. See the share parameters `oplocks=` and `level 2 oplocks=` as well.

ole locking compatibility=

The default is `yes`. If the UNIX lock manager crashes or other problems arise when you're using OLE, try changing the value of this parameter.

Global Miscellaneous Parameters

This section contains global parameters that cannot be categorized elsewhere.

auto services=

The default is an empty string. Special shares `[homes]` and `[printers]` normally automatically list several services. If either of these special shares don't exist, some of the services they would normally reveal can be turned on with this parameter. For instance, the parameter

```
auto services=username lp
```

enables username's home directory and the lp print queue to appear on browses (and to be used). Special care should be taken, because in the absence of other parameters, it makes username's home directory browseable to everyone, not just to user bogususer.

Note that preload= is a synonym for auto services=.

default service=

The default is pub. This is the service given the user requesting a nonexistent service. If the default service doesn't exist, an error is generated.

The value of this parameter should not be encased in brackets.

> **Note**
>
> It has been observed that the default may fail, even if a valid [pub] share is defined, and even if testparm reports the default for this parameter as pub. Explicitly specifying default service=pub cures this problem.

dfree command=

The default is to use internal routines. Various systems use different methods for reporting disk space. On occasion, they malfunction, in which case this parameter can be used to specify a command to return the number of bytes on the disk and the number of bytes available. See this command in the smb.conf man page as well as your system documentation if it becomes necessary to make such a command.

homedir map=

The default is auto.home. This parameter enables NIS (Network Information System) map extraction under certain circumstances. See the smb.conf man page.

lock dir=

The default is defined at compile time. Contrary to the smb.conf man page, this parameter does not always default to /tmp/samba. A default source compile on a Red Hat 6 machine yields a default of /usr/local/samba/var/locks. This parameter can be used to change that default. The lock directory contains status information, including daemon pids.

message command=

The default is none. If enabled, this parameter specifies a command to forward a WinPopup-type message. The command should end in "&" so that it returns immediately;

otherwise, clients can hang. The filename should be erased. Note that it's possible, though not customary, to use this for server-side automation.

> **Caution**
>
> This parameter has been identified as a denial of service vulnerability in Samba versions prior to 2.0.5 and must be removed from such versions.

NIS homedir=

The default is no. If set to yes, this parameter enables the returned home directory to reside on a server other than the Samba server. This can be slow, and it requires working NIS as well as the Samba server being a login server.

panic action=

The default is an empty string. When this parameter is not empty, it specifies a command to be run when either smbd or nmbd crashes, typically something to alert the developer or administrator of the crash.

preload=

This is a synonym for auto services=.

remote announce=

Defaults to an empty string. This parameter is used so that the Samba server shows up on browses of remote workgroups. The command structure is as follows:

```
remote announce = IP1/WORKGROUP1 IP2/WORKGROUP2
```

If left out, the workgroup name after the slash defaults to that specified in the workgroup= parameter. In certain cases, this parameter enables the server to show up in browses it cannot otherwise show up in.

remote browse sync=

The default is none. If the value is set to an IP address or a space-delimited list of IP addresses, master browsers on those subnets are requested to synchronize browse lists, thereby enabling them to see the server sending the request. See the smb.conf man page for more details, as well as Chapters 17 and 24.

19

smb.conf GLOBAL
PARAMETERS

smbrun=

The default is decided at compile time. This parameter can point to a command capable of executing programs on Samba's behalf.

socket address=

The default is an empty string, meaning "any address." The value can be changed to limit listening to a specific IP address.

time offset=

The default is 0. The value is the number of minutes to add or subtract (if the number is negative) to the client time.

unix realname=

The default is no. If this parameter is enabled, the real name field from the `passwd` record is sent to the client.

Summary

The global `smb.conf` parameters are a vital link in understanding the functionality and possibilities of Samba. Several chapters of this book explain specific ways these parameters can be used. To the degree possible, the Samba administrator should be familiar with every one of these parameters. To gain the broadest understanding, this chapter, the `smb.conf` man page, and the chapters of this book should be read.

smb.conf Share Parameters

by Steve Litt

IN THIS CHAPTER

Share parameters are what give each Samba-accessible printer and directory its personality. This chapter discusses most share parameters in a different way than the `smb.conf` man page. It's best to read both, because knowledge of the parameters is essential in imaginative use of Samba.

Name Mangling

Name mangling controls the mapping of filenames between the client's and the server's operating systems. Some clients require 8.3 filenames. Most clients' filenaming is case insensitive.

A mangled name is a short Windows filename that differs from the long one. Typically, it ends in a tilde and two hex digits, although this can be controlled with parameters. Here's an example of a mangled filename:

```
V:\>DIR TH*.TXT

 Volume in drive V is BOGUSUSER
 Directory of V:\

THISI~FA TXT              0  10-20-99  1:08p thisisalongname.txt
        1 file(s)              0 bytes
        0 dir(s)     407,076,864 bytes free

V:\>
```

The rules of name mangling are complex. Without a specific reason to manipulate these parameters, it's best to leave them at their defaults.

The defaults can be found by examining an `smb.conf` without these parameters. Here are the results of a `testparm` command on a `[homes]`-only `smb.conf` in a user's home directory:

```
$ testparm ./smb.conf | grep -i case

        default case = lower
        case sensitive = No
        preserve case = Yes
        short preserve case = Yes
        mangle case = No
$
```

case sensitive=yes/no

The default is no. This determines whether file lookups are case sensitive. In this case, no means a client request for a file is satisfied by any file with the right sequence of letters, regardless of their case. Although this places an additional search and match burden on the server, it's more compliant with typical Windows clients, which are case insensitive.

Setting this parameter to yes can make prediction and understanding of the results of dir commands extremely convoluted. Also, setting this to yes creates some very strange anomalies, including the inability to create new files from the right-click popup menu in Windows Explorer. Additionally, setting this parameter to yes complicates the function of other name-mangling parameters. In the descriptions of the remainder of the name-mangling parameters, it's assumed that case sensitive=no.

Note that the smb.conf man page lists this as a global parameter when, in fact, it's a share parameter.

default case=upper/lower

The default is lower. If it has no other way to determine the case of a filename or part of a filename, Samba relies on this parameter to decide.

mangled names=

The default is yes, which attempts to map non-8.3 names to mangled 8.3 names. If this is set to no, no name mangling takes place for the share, and long names are simply truncated to make short names.

mangling char=

The default is ~. As mentioned earlier, mangled filenames typically end in a tilde and two hex digits. That tilde is the mangling character. If the share is set to mangling char=^, mangled filenames would end in a caret and two hex digits instead of a tilde and two hex digits.

preserve case=yes/no

The default is yes. This determines whether case is preserved on filenames not conforming to the old DOS 8.3 standards. Case preservation of filenames that do conform to those standards is governed by short preserve case=. The mangle case= parameter does not affect preserve case=. Here's an example that uses preserve case=yes:

```
V:\>copy con: SambaUnleashed.txt
hello
^Z
        1 file(s) copied

V:\>dir sambaunleashed.txt

 Volume in drive V is BOGUSUSER
 Directory of V:\
```

```
SAMBA~K7 TXT            7  10-20-99  6:17p SambaUnleashed.txt
        1 file(s)               7 bytes
        0 dir(s)      407,076,864 bytes free

V:\>
```

short preserve case=yes/no

The default is yes. This determines whether files conforming to the old DOS 8.3 standards will have their case preserved. Here's an example using short preserve case=yes and mangle case=no:

```
V:\>copy con StEvE.txt
Overwrite StEvE.txt (Yes/No/All)?y
hello
^Z
        1 file(s) copied

V:\>dir steve.txt

 Volume in drive V is BOGUSUSER
 Directory of V:\

StEvE   txt            7  10-20-99  6:12p StEvE.txt
        1 file(s)               7 bytes
        0 dir(s)      407,076,864 bytes free

V:\>
```

mangle case=yes/no (S)

The default is no. If this is set to yes, it creates a mangled short name for 8.3 names with mixed case.

The following are examples using short preserve case=yes and mangle case=yes:

```
V:\>copy con: StEvE.txt
hello
^Z
        1 file(s) copied

V:\>dir steve.txt

 Volume in drive V is BOGUSUSER
 Directory of V:\

STEVE~-0 TXT            7  10-20-99  6:23p StEvE.txt
        1 file(s)               7 bytes
        0 dir(s)      407,076,864 bytes free

V:\>
```

```
V:\>copy con: steve.txt
hello
^Z
        1 file(s) copied

V:\>dir steve.txt

 Volume in drive V is BOGUSUSER
 Directory of V:\

steve    txt          7  10-20-99  6:26p steve.txt
         1 file(s)              7 bytes
         0 dir(s)     407,076,864 bytes free

V:\>
```

After switching `mangle case=no`, the same two copies produce the following results:

```
V:\>copy con: StEvE.txt
hello
^Z
        1 file(s) copied

V:\>dir steve.txt

 Volume in drive V is BOGUSUSER
 Directory of V:\

StEvE    txt          7  10-20-99  6:29p StEvE.txt
         1 file(s)              7 bytes
         0 dir(s)     407,076,864 bytes free

V:\>


V:\>copy con: steve.txt
hello
^Z
        1 file(s) copied

V:\>dir steve.txt

 Volume in drive V is BOGUSUSER
 Directory of V:\

steve    txt          7  10-20-99  6:31p steve.txt
         1 file(s)              7 bytes
         0 dir(s)     407,076,864 bytes free

V:\>
```

Share Printing Parameters

Print shares depend on various commands to do their work. The default value of those commands depends on the value of the `printing=` share parameter, which is often placed in the global section. On common printers, correct identification of the `printing=` share removes the necessity of explicitly specifying these printing parameters. However, on unusual servers, they're vital to Samba's portability.

lppause command=

The default is set at compile time and is further influenced by the `printing=` parameter. The `testparm` and SWAT interpretations of the default are not necessarily accurate. The actual default can be deduced by the values in SWAT input fields, assuming those values were not explicitly specified in `smb.conf`. Because $PATH at runtime is unknown, it's recommended that you place the entire path in the command. Typically, this parameter needn't be explicitly specified if the `printing=` parameter is set correctly.

This specifies the command that's called when a request to pause a specific print job is received. The printer name (`%p`) and job number (`%j`) should be part of the value of this parameter in order to specify which job on what printer. Note the difference between this and `queuepause=`, which pauses the entire queue.

lpq command=

The default is set at compile time and is further influenced by the `printing=` parameter. The `testparm` and SWAT interpretations of the default are not necessarily accurate. The actual default can be deduced by the values in SWAT input fields, assuming those values were not explicitly specified in `smb.conf`. Because $PATH at runtime is unknown, it's recommended that you place the entire path in the command. Typically, this parameter needn't be explicitly specified if the `printing=` parameter is set correctly.

This parameter specifies the command to return print queue information. In environments where this command takes excessive time or resources, the global `lpq cache time=` parameter should be increased.

lpresume command=

The default is set at compile time and is further influenced by the `printing=` parameter. The `testparm` and SWAT interpretations of the default are not necessarily accurate. The actual default can be deduced by the values in SWAT input fields, assuming those values were not explicitly specified in `smb.conf`. Because $PATH at runtime is unknown, it's recommended that you place the entire path in the command. Typically, this parameter needn't be explicitly specified if the `printing=` parameter is set correctly.

This parameter specifies the command to resume a print job paused by the lppause= parameter. The printer name (%p) and job number (%j) should be part of the value of this parameter in order to specify which job on what printer. Note the difference between this and queueresume=, which resumes the entire queue.

lprm command=

The default is set at compile time and is further influenced by the printing= parameter. The testparm and SWAT interpretations of the default are not necessarily accurate. The actual default can be deduced by the values in SWAT input fields, assuming those values were not explicitly specified in smb.conf. Because $PATH at runtime is unknown, it's recommended that you place the entire path in the command. Typically, this parameter needn't be explicitly specified if the printing= parameter is set correctly.

This parameter specifies to the command to delete a print job. The printer name (%p) and job number (%j) should be part of the value of this parameter in order to specify which job on what printer.

print command=

The default is set at compile time and is further influenced by the printing= parameter. The testparm and SWAT interpretations of the default are not necessarily accurate. The actual default can be deduced by the values in SWAT input fields, assuming those values were not explicitly specified in smb.conf. Because $PATH at runtime is unknown, it's recommended that you place the entire path in the command.

Unlike the other printer command–type print parameters, this parameter is occasionally necessary even if the printing= parameter is set correctly.

This parameter specifies the command to print the job. The command should include the printer name (%p) and the name of the file to be printed (%s). Note that the filename is seldom meaningful outside the Samba printing system. Because the file is not deleted, this command should include rm %s at its conclusion, appended to the remainder of the command with a semicolon.

This command can be used to execute commands having nothing to do with printing. This subject is covered in Chapter 14, "Using Samba Server-Side Automation."

printer driver location=

This parameter is used in automatic printer driver installation. It specifies the directory containing the actual Windows 9x printer drivers. It must be used in conjunction with global parameters printer driver file=, printer driver=, and share [printer$].

The procedures for setting up automatic printer driver installation are in Chapter 8, "Configuring Printer Shares." Explicitly specify this parameter if you're setting up automatic printer driver installation. Otherwise, do not specify this parameter.

printing=

Although it's a share parameter, this parameter is typically specified in the global section so that all printers default to it. This parameter should always be explicitly specified in smb.conf because its value affects the values of the various command parameters for printing. Although a wrong value of printing= can be compensated for by explicitly specifying several of the print commands, it requires major troubleshooting. On common systems, a correct value for this parameter eliminates the need to hardcode any of the printing command parameters, although the print command= parameter often needs to be specified on uncommon systems.

Because this is a share parameter, it can be explicitly specified in a print share connected to a remote print queue on a server with a different type printing system. Therefore smb.conf on a Linux system has printing=bsd in the global section but may have printing=hpux in a print share linked to a printer hung off an HP server.

queuepause command=

The default is set at compile time and is further influenced by the printing= parameter. The testparm and SWAT interpretations of the default are not necessarily accurate. The actual default can be deduced by the values in SWAT input fields, assuming those values were not explicitly specified in smb.conf. Because $PATH at runtime is unknown, it's recommended that you place the entire path in the command. Typically, this parameter needn't be explicitly specified if the printing= parameter is set correctly.

This parameter specifies the command that's called when a request to pause the entire print queue is received. The printer name (%p) should be part of the value of this parameter in order to specify the print queue to pause. Note the difference between this and lppause=, which pauses a single print job.

queueresume command=

The default is set at compile time and is further influenced by the printing= parameter. The testparm and SWAT interpretations of the default are not necessarily accurate. The actual default can be deduced by the values in SWAT input fields, assuming those values were not explicitly specified in smb.conf. Because $PATH at runtime is unknown, it's recommended that you place the entire path in the command. Typically, this parameter needn't be explicitly specified if the printing= parameter is set correctly.

This parameter specifies the command to resume a print queue paused by the queuepause= parameter. The printer name (%p) should be part of the value of this parameter in order to specify which print queue to resume. Note the difference between this and lpresume=, which resumes a single print job.

Share Security Parameters

Samba has an incredibly rich and configurable security system. Access to a share can be granted on the basis of user or group, and it can be read-only or read/write on the basis of the user or group. Each share's security is controlled by its security parameters.

Chapter 7, "Determining Samba Access," presents a detailed discussion of the use of these security parameters as well as their preferences and priorities.

admin users=

The default is no. Setting this parameter can open a major security hole, because a user specified in this parameter has root UNIX permissions within the share's path and the tree below it. However, as explained in Chapter 7, admin users= is subject to Samba restrictions.

If specified, the value of this parameter is a comma-delimited list of users being granted root permissions to the share. Here's an example:

```
admin users=netadmin, webadmin
```

alternate permissions=

This has been depreciated as of Samba 2.0. Remove it from smb.conf on Samba 2.0 and later.

create mask=

The default is 744. This parameter is a three- or four-digit octal number specifying the maximum permissions given a newly created file (not directory) in the share. If it's three digits, the most significant digit is assumed to be 0. This number is bitwise and-ed with the permissions Samba maps from the DOS attributes of the file.

This parameter also controls the ability to set DOS parameters. The 1's place must be odd to enable map hidden=yes. The 8's place must be odd to enable map system=yes. The 64's place must be odd to enable map archive=yes and must be 2, 3, or 7 in order for the file owner to toggle the file between read-only and read-write.

When setting up a share to be writable by entire groups, you should set this parameter to 770 in order to ensure full access to the group (or 771 if `map hidden=yes`).

Note that another parameter, `force create mode=`, specifies the *maximum* permissions of newly created files. Note also that the `directory mask=` parameter specifies the minimum permissions for newly created *directories*, not files.

Notice that `force create mode=` takes precedence over `create mask=` in any conflict between the two parameters. Here's an example:

```
create mask=777
```

The preceding enables the DOS attribute–to–UNIX permission mapping to determine the file's permissions. In practice, this gives group and other read and write permissions, whereas execute permissions are dependent on the system and hidden DOS attributes. User write permission is dependent on the DOS read-only attribute, whereas the user execute permission is dependent on DOS archive attribute. Here's another example:

```
create mask=700
```

The preceding ensures that created files are accessible only by their creator, and it's appropriate in single-user shares where privacy is desirable. Note that because this removes executable permission, it disables any possible hidden or system attribute mapping. Here's another example:

```
create mask=711
```

The preceding keeps the privacy of 700 but enables system and hidden attribute mapping. Here's another example:

```
create mask=511
```

The preceding causes problems because without user write permission, the read-only attribute cannot be removed. Here's one more example:

```
create mask=770
```

The preceding is the correct value for shares granting access by group. If you want to map the DOS hidden attribute, 771 is your value of choice.

directory mask=

The default is 755. This parameter is a three- or four-digit octal number specifying the maximum permissions given a newly created directory (not file) in the share. If it's three digits, the most significant digit is assumed to be 0. This number is bitwise and-ed with the permissions Samba maps from the DOS attributes of the file.

Note that another parameter, `force directory mode=`, specifies the *maximum* permissions of newly created directories. Note also that the `create mask=` parameter specifies the minimum permissions for newly created *files*, not directories.

When setting up a share to be writeable by entire groups, you should set this parameter to 770 in order to ensure full access to the group (or 771 if `map hidden=yes`). Here's an example:

```
directory mask=771
```

force create mode=

The default is 000. This parameter is a three- or four-digit octal number specifying the maximum permissions given a newly created file (not directory) in the share. If it's three digits, the most significant digit is assumed to be 0. This number is bitwise or-ed with the permissions Samba maps from the DOS attributes of the file.

Use this parameter to set the sticky bit on files. It can also be used to set the file's SETUID and/or SETGROUP permissions, although this is typically a bad idea.

Note that `force create mode=` takes precedence over `create mask=` in any conflict between the two parameters. The following example sets the hidden and system DOS attributes for newly created files:

```
force create mode=011
```

force directory mode=

The default is 000. This parameter is a three- or four-digit octal number specifying the maximum permissions given a newly created directory (not file) in the share. If it's three digits, the most significant digit is assumed to be 0. This number is bitwise or-ed with the permissions Samba maps from the DOS attributes of the file.

Use this parameter to set the sticky bit on directory. It can also be used to set the file's SETUID and/or SETGROUP permissions, although this is typically a bad idea.

Note that `force directory mode=` takes precedence over `directory mask=` in any conflict between the two parameters. Here's an example that sets the hidden and system DOS attributes for newly created files:

```
force directory mode=011
```

> **Note**
>
> Although the Samba documentation suggests that a value of 7000 will set UID, GID, and the sticky bit, in fact, on some implementations, it does not.

force group=

The default is none. This parameter can be set to the name of a single group. It's neither necessary nor permissible to place @ in front of the group name. Any connection complying with `valid users=` and other tests has its service group changed to the value of this parameter. Therefore, any files or directories it creates have this group ID. All UNIX group permissions are based on this group.

However, parameters such as `read list=`, `write list=`, and `valid users=` look at all the user's groups. This is useful in setting up shares writeable by some groups but just readable by others:

```
[test]
path=/test
read only=yes
valid users=@ourgrp,@writegrp
force group=@ourgrp
write list=@writegrp
```

In order for the preceding share to function properly, directory /test must be at chmod 770 (or optionally higher permissions for "other") and must have group ourgrp. Note that because only the owner of the file can change its attributes, this does not guarantee the ability to change attributes. See Chapter 7 for more details of this parameter.

force user=

The default is none. This parameter can be set to the name of a single user. Any connection complying with `valid users=` and other tests has its username changed to the value of this parameter. It also has its group changed to that group's primary group, subject to further change by the `force group=` parameter. Therefore, any files or directories it creates have this user ID and group. All UNIX user permissions are based on this user and group.

This can be handy in creating a share accessible to multiple groups, with access including the changing of attributes. However, it loses the information of the original creator of the file, and it may have some security ramifications. The following is a share in which all newly created files have a single owner so that everyone can modify the files or their attributes:

```
[test]
path=/test
force user=testuser
valid users=@ourgrp,@writegrp
write list=@writegrp
read only=yes
map hidden=yes
map system=yes
create mask=711
```

guest account=

The default is set at compile time and is usually `nobody`. Under certain circumstances (see global `map to guest=`), in an unsuccessful Samba access, the user is converted to a guest user. This account should have no real login and miniscule rights on the system. User `ftp` is often suggested as an excellent choice.

This parameter should be explicitly declared in the global section so that all guest-accepting shares have the right guest account. Then, any shares requiring a different guest account can be changed at the share level. Here's an example:

```
guest account=ftp
```

guest ok=

The default is `no`. If it's set to `yes`, access can be granted according to the `map to guest=` parameter. If `security=share`, guest `ok=yes` eliminates the need for a password. If the `security=` parameter is anything other than `share`, the mapping to the guest account is governed by whether the client request's user ID was bad or whether the client request's password was bad, as governed by global `map to guest=`.

guest `ok=yes` is recommended only for low-security situations, especially printers. Here's an example:

```
guest ok=yes
```

guest only=

The default is `no`. If this is set to `yes`, only guest access is allowed, and all authenticated access is converted to guest access.

hosts allow=

The default is `none`, allowing any host access if it submits an authentic user and password for the share. If this is set to an IP address, a list of IP addresses, or an IP list with exceptions, only the named hosts or subnets can access the share. Note that this restricts access over and above user authentication. This is an excellent security enhancement on an internal network never accessed from the outside. Here's an example:

```
hosts allow = 192.168.100. EXCEPT 192.168.100.40
```

The preceding allows access from the `192.168.100` subnet, except for the host at `192.168.100.40`. This parameter has many other useful forms of syntax. Consult the `smb.conf` man page. Also note that this parameter can be used in conjunction with the `hosts deny=` parameter for finer control of which hosts can access the share.

The host restrictions can be tested with the special `testparm` syntax:

```
$ testparm serverHostname IPtoTest
```

hosts deny=

The default is `none`, meaning that this parameter places no restrictions on access. It's used to pinpoint hosts or subnets not permitted to access the share. In any conflict with `hosts allow=`, `hosts allow=` takes precedence. This is handy for eliminating an entire subnet except for the one or two hosts listed in `hosts allow=`. Here's an example:

```
hosts deny=192.168.200.
```

invalid users=

The default is `none`. If this is specified, it indicates a user, list of users, or group or group list not allowed in the share. Use this to keep out a few users or groups while letting in the population at large.

Groups are specified by prepending @, &, or + in front of the name. @ means match an NIS netgroup (or if that's not found, a UNIX group). & means match only to an NIS netgroup, whereas + means match only to a UNIX group. The symbols can be combined, so &+mygroup means the same as @mygroup, whereas +&mygroup tried to find a UNIX group called mygroup before trying to find the NIS mygroup NIS netgroup.

Here's an example of the `invalid users=` parameter:

```
invalid users=cracker,@clerks
```

only user=

The default is no. When this is set to yes, only users declared in the `username=` parameter are allowed entry. On anything but the oldest of clients and protocols, such a function is better performed by `valid users=`.

read list=

The default is an empty string, meaning that no user's write privileges are reduced if the share has `read only=no`. This parameter can be set to a comma-delimited list of users and groups who are not allowed write access to the share, in spite of the share having a `read only=no` parameter.

Inclusion in this parameter does not grant read access to a user or group excluded by `valid users=` or `invalid users=`. In any conflict between `read list=` and `write list=`, `write list=` prevails. Here's an example:

```
read list=phil,@clerks
```

read only=

The default is yes, meaning the share cannot be written to. Setting it to no grants write access to anyone able to access the share. Per-user and per-group control can be implemented with the read list= and write list= parameters. Here's an example:

```
read only=no
```

> **Note**
>
> This parameter has three inverse synonym parameters: write ok=, writeable=, and writable=. Only one of the four should be used in a share. The following are identical statements:
>
> ```
> read only=yes
> writeable=no
> writable=no
> write ok=no
> ```
>
> testparm returns a value for read only=, so most examples in this book use read only= rather than its inverse synonyms.

revalidate(S)

The default is no. This parameter has no effect unless security=share. If so, setting revalidate=yes means that each time the client accesses a different share, it needs to supply the password again. Although this beefs up security a little bit, those whose priority is security do not use security=share. Here's an example:

```
revalidate=yes
```

username=

The default is the guest account if the share is guest service; otherwise, it's the name of the service. This parameter is a comma-delimited list of users. Some older clients and protocols supply a password but no username. In such cases, Samba marches down the list of users specified by this parameter, looking for a match to the client-supplied password. Obviously this is slow, and if two users have the same password, a user can end up authenticated as the wrong user.

With ancient protocols such as COREPLUS and client operating systems such as Windows for Workgroups rapidly growing extinct, the need for this parameter decreases. Additionally, there are other ways to handle such situations. Here's an example of this parameter:

```
username=alfred, betty, charlie, deborah
```

Note that this parameter does not, by itself, restrict which users can access the share. The `valid users=` and `invalid users=` parameters do that. Also, if `only users=yes`, access is restricted to the `username=` list.

valid users=

The default is an empty string, meaning that any user has access to the share. If this is specified, it's a comma-delimited list of users and groups allowed to access the share. This parameter does not in any way specify whether the access is read-only or read-write. The `read only=`, `read list=`, and `write list=` parameters do that. Any user or group not specified in a nonempty `valid users=` parameter cannot in any way access the share, regardless of the `read list=` and `write list=` parameters.

An opposite parameter, `invalid users=`, specifies a list of users not granted access.

Groups are specified by prepending @, &, or + in front of the name. @ means match an NIS netgroup (or if that's not found, a UNIX group). & means match only to an NIS netgroup, whereas + means match only to a UNIX group. The symbols can be combined, so `&+mygroup` means the same as `@mygroup`, whereas `+&mygroup` tries to find a UNIX group called `mygroup` before trying to find the NIS `mygroup` NIS netgroup.

An obvious point that bears repeating is that when the share contains a `force user=` or `force group=` parameter, share access is determined by the user or groups of the original client request, not those specified in the `force user=` and `force group=` parameters. Here's a `valid users=` example:

```
valid users=@ourgrp,@writegrp
```

write list=

Default is an empty string, meaning no user has any special write privileges. This parameter takes a comma-delimited list of users and/or groups as a value. Each of those users or groups is granted write privileges, despite the use of `read only=yes` or `read list=` inclusion of the user or group. However, if the user or group is absent from a nonblank `valid users=` parameter, inclusion in the `write list=` parameter does not grant any type of access. In any conflict between `read list=` and `write list=`, `write list=` prevails.

Groups are specified by prepending @, &, or + in front of the name. @ means match an NIS netgroup (or if that's not found, a UNIX group). & means match only to an NIS netgroup, whereas + means match only to a UNIX group. The symbols can be combined, so `&+mygroup` means the same as `@mygroup`, whereas `+&mygroup` tries to find a UNIX group called `mygroup` before trying to find the NIS `mygroup` NIS netgroup.

The write list= parameter is a vital component in granting different access levels to different groups. The following is an example that grants read-write access to group writegrp but read-only access to group ourgrp and no access to anyone else:

```
[test]
path=/test
read only=yes
valid users=@ourgrp,@writegrp
force group=@ourgrp
write list=@writegrp
```

Note that for this to work, directory /test must be readable, writeable, and executable in the 8's (group) digit, and the directory must have ourgrp as its group.

Share Filename-Handling Parameters

Different operating systems have different filenaming conventions. The share filename-handling parameters allow interoperation of such operating systems. Note that much of this information was covered previously in the "Name Mangling" section of this chapter.

case sensitive=

The default is no. This is best left at the default unless there's a very good reason to do otherwise (see the "Name Mangling" section earlier in this chapter). Note that although the man page says otherwise, SWAT proves this parameter to be a share parameter.

default case=

The default is lower (see the "Name Mangling" section earlier in this chapter).

delete veto files=

The default is no. The no setting means that any attempt to delete a directory containing one or more nonvetoed files or directories fails. This enables "safeguarding" directories containing mostly vetoed files from unintended deletion.

Setting this parameter to yes means that an attempt to delete a directory containing one or more non-vetoed files recursively attempts to delete what it can. Leave this at its default unless there's a very good reason to do otherwise.

hide dot files=

The default is yes, meaning that UNIX files beginning with a dot behave as hidden files in Windows, with one exception: They cannot be unhidden from Windows. If this parameter is set to no, files beginning with dots are treated as normal files in Windows.

hide files=

The default is an empty string. If defined, this parameter is a forward slash–delineated list of wildcard file specifications that are invisible but accessible to the client throughout the share's directory tree.

These files cannot be made visible with the DOS `attrib` command or the Network Neighborhood file properties.

This parameter adversely affects performance due to match checking. The following example hides any files throughout the share's tree ending in `.job`:

```
hide files=/*.job/
```

mangle case=

The default is `no` (see the "Name Mangling" section earlier in this chapter).

mangling char=

The default is ~ (see the "Name Mangling" section earlier in this chapter).

map archive=

The default is `yes`, meaning that the file's owner has control of the archive DOS attribute from the client. Setting it to `no` removes that control. Because the archive attribute maps to the executable permission of the file's user, the user digit (64) of the create mask must be odd for client archive attribute control. Here's an example:

```
map archive=no
```

map hidden=

The default is `no`, meaning that the file's owner does not have control of the DOS hidden attribute from the client. Setting it to `yes` enables that control. Because the hidden attribute maps to the executable permission of the file's *other* digit, the *other* digit (1) of the create mask must be odd for client hidden attribute control. Here's an example:

```
map hidden=yes
```

map system=

The default is `no`, meaning that the file's owner does not have control of the DOS system attribute from the client. Setting it to `yes` enables that control. Because the system attribute maps to the executable permission of the file's group, the group digit (8) of the create mask must be odd for client system attribute control. Here's an example:

```
map system=yes
```

mangled map=

The default is an empty string. When used, this parameter enables mapping of 8.3-compliant names on the DOS side with longer UNIX names on the UNIX side. Here's an example:

```
mangled map = (*.html *.htm)
```

This makes UNIX .html files show up as .htm files in Network Neighborhood. However, it does *not* make .htm files created in the share show up as .html files in UNIX.

Before using this parameter, you should consider the confusion it can cause.

mangled names=

The default is yes (see the "Name Mangling" section earlier in this chapter).

preserve case=

The default is yes (see the "Name Mangling" section earlier in this chapter).

short preserve case=

The default is yes (see the "Name Mangling" section earlier in this chapter).

veto files=

The default is an empty string. If defined, this parameter is a forward slash–delineated list of wildcard file specifications that are invisible and inaccessible to the client throughout the share's directory tree.

> **Caution**
>
> A visible directory containing nothing but vetoed files can be deleted without any prompting, thus misleading the user about what's being deleted! You can verify this by placing a directory called temp in a share, putting several .txt files in the temp directory, and placing this parameter in the share definition:
>
> ```
> veto files=/*.txt/
> ```
>
> *continues*

20

smb.conf SHARE
PARAMETERS

The `temp` directory shows up as an empty directory, and assuming the user has permission to delete the directory and all the files in it, the user can delete it from Network Neighborhood, at which time the contained `.txt` files are silently deleted.

Note that this dangerous behavior *cannot* be turned off by the `delete veto files=` parameter.

Any directory containing veto files should contain at least one nonvetoed file permissioned such that it cannot easily be deleted.

Share-Tuning Parameters

There's a tradeoff between performance and data integrity. The share-tuning parameters enable optimizing of that tradeoff.

max connections=

The default is `0`, meaning there's no limitation on connections to the share. A positive number in this parameter serves as the maximum number of connections allowed to the share. Limiting connections on a first-come, first-serve basis is usually an example of fixing the symptom but leaving the underlying cause intact. Generally, if a share is important enough to access, it's important enough to access immediately, rather than wasting time with repeated attempts hoping someone has logged off. This is especially true because there's no clean way to "log off" a service accessed in Windows Explorer except to exit Windows Explorer and then do a `net use \\server\service /delete` from a command prompt.

Although this parameter may provide some relief in an extreme emergency, when access to a share taxes resources for an entire server, the big picture should be viewed, including finer access specification, human policies and procedures, and, if huge levels of access are truly needed, server hardware and software limitations.

strict sync=

Default is `no`, meaning that Samba ignores Windows sync calls. Because sync calls suspend the kernel, they're very expensive. Many Windows apps, including Windows 98 Explorer, call for sync when a call to flush the buffer contents is what's needed. Setting this parameter to `yes` can cause serious performance degradation.

There's no clear benefit to setting this parameter to `yes`, although it may be appropriate as a troubleshooting test for corrupt data problems.

sync always=

The default is no. If and only if strict sync=yes, setting sync always=yes ensures an fsync() call following each write to make sure the data is immediately written to disk. Typically, this would only be done when writing important data to an undependable share or when the underlying system is undependable.

Share-Locking Parameters

Without locking, multiuser access to files would quickly cause corruption. The share-locking parameters facilitate a balance between locking and performance in a wide variety of environments.

blocking locks=

The default is yes, which means that if a client byte range lock cannot be immediately granted, periodic retries occur throughout a timeout period. If this is set to no, the request is immediately failed. Here's an example:

```
blocking locks=no
```

fake oplocks=

The default is no, meaning that rather than faking oplocks, the server grants them only when the requester would be the only one accessing the file (or in the case of a level 2 oplock, only when nobody's writing the file).

Changing this parameter to yes causes the server to always grant oplocks to a file. Obviously this can cause corruption in a file being written by multiple clients and can cause inconsistent states on processes even if only one client is writing the file while another is reading it.

This parameter should be enabled *only* when it's guaranteed that all access is read-only. A CD-ROM is an example. It can also be enabled if there's a procedural guarantee that this file will never be simultaneously accessed. Under such conditions, fake oplocks=yes can significantly improve performance.

level2 oplocks=

The default is no in Samba 2.0.5a, but this is planned to change to yes in a later release. Level 2 oplocks are read-only. Multiple clients supporting level 2 oplocks can maintain read-only oplocks until one of them writes the file, at which time the others are notified, break their oplocks, and discard their read-only cache. Setting this parameter to `yes` speeds access to files normally read but not written, such as executables. Here's an example:

```
level2 oplocks=yes
```

As of 2.0.5a, the share must have `oplocks=yes` and the global kernel oplocks must be disabled in order for level 2 oplocks to be enabled.

locking=

The default is `yes`, which enables locking by the server. Setting this parameter to `no` causes the server to answer all lock requests with "success" and tell all clients that the queried lock is clear. Naturally, this causes corruption on any read-write file. The `smb.conf` man page recommends leaving this parameter at its default.

oplocks=

Default is `yes`, which enables opportunistic locking. Opportunistic locking enables aggressive caching on the client side; therefore, it can cause corruption if a connection or computer goes down. For this reason, opportunistic locking should be enabled only in reliable environments. Here's an example:

```
oplocks=no
```

Note that certain files can be excluded from opportunistic locking in a share with `oplocks=yes` by using the `veto oplock files=` parameter.

share modes=

The default is `yes`. The DOS operating system uses share modes `DENY_DOS`, `DENY_ALL`, `DENY_READ`, `DENY_WRITE`, `DENY_NONE`, and `DENY_FCB`. Setting this parameter to `yes` enables Samba compatibility with the DOS share modes. Setting it to `no` disables that compatibility and can break any DOS or Windows app using these modes. Therefore, this parameter must always remain at its default value.

strict locking=

The default is `no`, meaning that lock checks are done only when the client software requests it. Switching this to `yes` causes Samba to lock-check every read and write request, thus slowing performance.

File locking is vital in preventing data corruption. Most well-written multiuser applications incorporate their own locking mechanism or else ask for lock checks whenever necessary. Either way, the client software has everything under control.

However, if the client software is poorly written, it might not submit lock check requests correctly. In such cases, this parameter should be changed to yes to limit corruption.

Frequent file corruption using a new application or a new version of an application might give you cause to set this parameter to yes. If corruption substantially decreases, the application software vendor should be made aware of the problem.

veto oplock files=

The default is none. This parameter lists slash-separated, wildcard-enabled file specifications for which oplocks are not enabled, even if oplocks=yes for the share. This is typically done for files experiencing heavy client contention. Here's an example:

```
veto oplock files = /*.SEM/
```

Server-Side Automation Parameters

Server-side automation enables the startup of UNIX processes via Windows client activities. The following parameters facilitate server-side automation.

magic output=

The default is <magic script name>.out. This is the output file for the share's magic script (see the magic script= parameter for details).

magic script=

The default is an empty string, meaning that magic scripting is disabled. If the value of this parameter is a filename, that file is executed after the file is accessed and then closed from an SMB client.

> **Caution**
>
> This creates a huge security hole if implemented incorrectly. If the client can write or create the script file, he or she can delete everything in the tree, view the contents of /etc/passwd, and cause all sorts of other mischief.
>
> A much safer method of server-side automation that accomplishes all the goals of magic scripting, except having the client author the script, is to use the print command= parameter of a printer intended to accomplish server-side automation.

20

smb.conf SHARE
PARAMETERS

Note also that as of 2.0.5a, this parameter is considered experimental, and the documentation cautions that it might not work. The output of the magic script is defined by the `magic output=` parameter.

preexec=

The default is `none`. When defined, this parameter serves as a command to be run when the share is first connected to by a given client. Unlike magic script and print command server-side automation, it cannot be run at will.

This parameter is best used for initialization of the share, and it's especially good for things like creating a directory if it isn't there and hiding dot files and the like.

postexec=

The default is `none`. When defined, this parameter serves as a command to be run when the share is disconnected. Disconnection is often not a simple thing—it may involve exiting Windows Explorer and then from a Windows command prompt running the following command:

```
$ net use \\servername\sharename /delete
```

Unlike magic script and print command server-side automation, it cannot be run at will.

This parameter is best used for cleaning up the share.

print command=

Although not intended to be used this way, print shares are extremely useful for server-side automation. The share's `print command=` parameter calls the script to be run, complete with the `%s` substitution macro naming the file to be "printed." This file can have a header containing all necessary configuration information for the process, followed by the data. Because a data file is passed instead of a "magic script," this is inherently more secure. However, because any client can pass any data to the print share, the script or program to be run must limit damage no matter what's passed to it in the file.

root preexec=

The default is `none`. This parameter does everything `preexec=` does, except it does these tasks as `root`. This is especially helpful in working outside the share or in working with files in a way not permitted by the user's permissions. Naturally, running anything as `root` has security implications, so caution should be used. The existence of `root preexec=` and `root postexec=` is one of the many reasons `smb.conf` should be off limits to everyone but the administrator.

root postexec=

The default is `none`. This parameter does everything `preexec=` does, except it does these tasks as `root`. This is especially helpful in working outside the share or in working with files in a way not permitted by the user's permissions. Naturally, running anything as `root` has security implications, so caution should be used. The existence of `root preexec=` and `root postexec=` is one of the many reasons `smb.conf` should be off limits to everyone but the administrator.

Miscellaneous Share Parameters

The share parameters that don't fit neatly into categories are listed in this section.

available=

The default is `yes`. The effect of switching this parameter to `no` is to "comment out" the entire share. This is handy for troubleshooting. It can also be handy when a share must be "out of commission" for a time. A perfect example is when the share's path partition is being expanded.

Inserting `available=no` and restarting Samba "comments out" the share. It can be made available again by deleting the parameter from the share. Here's an example:

```
available=no
```

browseable=

The default is `yes`, meaning the share shows up on browse lists such as Network Neighborhood, `smbclient -NL servername`, and `net view \\servername`. Browseability is very different from accessibility. A share may be accessible via a call to `smbclient` or `net use`, without showing up on browse lists. Likewise, a share may show up on browse lists yet not be accessible if the `valid users=` parameter doesn't match the client's passed username.

Automatic shares such as `[homes]` and `[printers]` reveal their shares with `browseable=no`, whereas `browseable=yes` merely enables directories called `homes` and `printers` to show up. Here's an example:

```
browseable=no
```

delete readonly=

The default is `no`, meaning that read-only files in Samba shares cannot be deleted. Setting this parameter to `yes` allows the client to delete read-only files. Although generally dangerous and not a good idea, this may be necessary for applications run by users other than the file's owner. Those users cannot change the read-only attribute of the file to change it. Here's an example:

```
delete readonly=yes
```

Note that in certain circumstances, you may want to use `force user=` to force all newly created files in the share to a single user and enable all users to access the files as that user. In such a circumstance, all users can change the `readonly` attribute.

dont descend=

The default is an empty string. The value can be set to a list of directories within the share that will report being empty even though they're not. This is done either to hide the contents of those directories or to prevent recursive access to a recursive directory (created by a symbolic link). Note that recursion can also be prevented with `follow symlinks=no`. Here's an example on a share accessing the `/tmp` directory:

```
dont descend=kfm-cache-503
```

Note that the use of wildcards does not produce the intended result.

dos filetime resolution=

The default is `no`. This is a workaround for certain Visual C++ problems. If Visual C++ repeatedly reports a file as having been changed, investigate this parameter. Here's an example:

```
dos filetime resolution=yes
```

dos filetimes=

The default is `no`, meaning only the owner of a file can explicitly change a file's date and time. Setting this parameter to `yes` enables any user with read and write permissions on the file to change its date and time.

> **Note**
>
> The preceding description refers to changing the date and time without modifying the file itself. All modifications of the file's contents change the file date and time, regardless of the user or the state of the dos `filetimes=` parameter.

fake directory create times=

The default is no. When this is set to yes, all newly created directories have a create time of midnight, 1/1/1980. The reason for doing this is a Visual C++ workaround (see the smb.conf man page for details).

follow symlinks=

The default is yes, meaning Samba follows symbolic links wherever they go, including out of the share or up the tree, thus causing recursion. Setting this parameter to no prevents following those symbolic links, tightens up security, and prevents recursion. Note that recursion can also be prevented by the dont descend=yes parameter.

fstype=

The default is NTFS. The value of this parameter is the string returned to a client querying for file system type. Here's an example:

fstype=FAT

set directory=

The default is no. The Digital Pathworks system has a command called setdir that can be used to change directories. setdir can be used to change directories if and only if this parameter is set to yes. This parameter has no function or meaning except on Pathworks systems.

status=

The default is yes, and this parameter should be left at the default. Setting this parameter to no would disable logging of connections to a status file, thereby preventing smbstatus from reporting on the connection. Note that the smb.conf man page says this is global, but SWAT demonstrates otherwise.

valid chars=

The default is an empty string. This parameter can be used to add characters considered valid in filenames. If client code page=yes, then valid chars= must follow client code page= in the share. See smb.conf man page for more information.

volume=

This parameter is used to "rename" the share's volume name. This is useful in installation media where the installation procedure demands a certain volume name.

wide links=

The default is no. The smb.conf man page contains the following description of this parameter:

> This parameter controls whether or not links in the UNIX file system may be followed by the server. Links that point to areas within the directory tree exported by the server are always allowed; this parameter controls access only to areas that are outside the directory tree being exported.

The purpose of this parameter is to allow the following of symbolic links, but only within the share's tree. However, this parameter does not always perform as advertised.

Note, however, that on a Red Hat 6 machine using Samba 2.0.5a, it's possible to create the following share:

```
[test]
path=/test
read only=yes
wide links=no
```

Then, you can do this:

```
ln -s /etc/named.conf /test/named.sym
```

File named.sym from the [test] share can then be edited from Network Neighborhood, showing the contents of /etc/named.conf, which is outside of the share's tree.

If you observe this problem with wide links=, the same outcomes can often be accomplished with follow symlinks=no, which does work.

Summary

Samba has a rich variety of configuration choices for shares. These choices are implemented with share parameters. Share parameters come in several categories, including printing parameters, security parameters, filename-handling parameters, tuning parameters, locking parameters, server-side automation parameters, and several miscellaneous parameters.

Samba is almost magical in the wide range of functions it can be configured to accomplish. A thorough working knowledge of these parameters enables the Samba administrator to imaginatively implement any needed functionality.

Samba Backup Strategies

by Daniel Robbins

IN THIS CHAPTER

In this chapter, we'll take a look at the different ways that backups can be approached in a Samba environment. One of the beauties of Samba is that it provides so many options when it comes to backups. The downside of this is that choosing a backup method can be confusing, simply because there are so many options. This chapter will provide you with the necessary background knowledge so that you'll have a good understanding of what you need in a backup system, and what system will work best for your organization.

Review of Terminology

Before we delve into technical specifics, it would be a good idea to review some terminology and basic concepts. A good place to start is the definition of a full, incremental, and differential backups and their proper use. If you're familiar with these terms, feel free to skip to the next section.

A *full backup* is a backup that contains every single file and/or directory that exists on the backed-up filesystem. Of course, this normally will take a good amount of space on the target device (such as a DAT tape), but it has the advantage of being easy to deal when it comes time to restore data. At that time, you can easily work with one tape (or archive) and restore any amount of data you would like. For this reason, full backups are preferred if your backup device has the needed capacity and speed to handle them on a regular basis.

An *incremental backup* is a backup that contains every new or modified file since the last full backup. Incrementals are normally used to save space on the backup medium, because normally not all files are backed up. It goes without saying that if you use incremental backups, it's essential that you keep a copy of your last full backup on hand! Incremental backups allow administrators to perform full backups less frequently yet still maintain a good history of modified files.

One of the disadvantages of an incremental backup occurs during the restoration process, which will normally require the administrator to access two tapes instead of one. This, however, is not a major setback, and incremental backups provide a good complement to a backup strategy.

The third kind of backup is called a *differential backup*, and it's not recommended. A differential backup backs up any new or modified files since the last full, incremental or differential backup. Although this saves a lot of space on the backup medium, it can make restorations a hassle and can cause the administrator to have to restore many archives to perform a full restore of all data. For that reason, differential backups are only recommended to supplement an existing full/incremental backup strategy. Also, long strings of differential backups in a row should be avoided.

Backing Up Under Samba

The concept of "backing up under Samba" can be fairly ambiguous and doesn't necessarily refer to any one specific method of backup. In this section, I'll outline all the backup possibilities that Samba makes available to you.

How Samba Makes Backups Easier

How can Samba make backups easier? One fundamental way is that Samba can be used to allow your Windows-based software to back up your UNIX boxes over the network. At the same time, Samba (specifically smbtar or mounting SMB/CIFS shares using smbmount) will allow your UNIX machine to back up any Windows-based systems on your network. Whether your backup device resides under UNIX or Windows, Samba is an incredible help.

Backup Servers

Because you now have a choice, let's look at two different ways to use Samba to unify your organization's backup strategy. For many organizations, it's advantageous to have a single backup device or an entire server or servers dedicated to backing up all other systems on the network. Using backup servers is helpful for at least two reasons: First of all, you do not need multiple backup devices (such as tape drives) for each system you want to back up. This normally means that your organization can purchase one relatively expensive, high-quality backup device rather than depending on several lower-quality devices. Another advantage that's gained by having a backup server is the fact that it's possible to centrally manage the backup process. Rather than having the users in the department responsible for their own data, this task can be handled more reliably by the system administration staff.

Choosing Windows Backups or UNIX Backups

I hope that you've been convinced to try to centrally manage your backup process. Now, the question arises, should UNIX or Windows NT be used as a backup server? Good question. There are different advantages to each option. The following sections discuss the major factors you should consider.

Software Can Make the Difference

In general, Windows provides a more user-friendly interface than the UNIX equivalents. If less-experienced staff will be managing the backup process, this may move you towards choosing Windows NT as a backup server. You may want to select two possible candidates for backup software—one for UNIX and one for Windows—and compare their strengths or weaknesses.

Is Automation Important? How Much?

UNIX normally (but not always) dominates when it comes to automation. However, nearly all Windows backup software provides some form of automation. You'll want to define exactly how automated you want your backup environment to be. Anything beyond intermediate complexity will most likely make UNIX the better choice. However, this complexity requires a competent staff to operate it properly.

Is Your Backup Medium of Choice Supported?

Although most backup technologies are compatible with Windows NT, not all are compatible with UNIX. If you require specific advanced features in your backup hardware or require an advanced backup medium, make sure it's fully supported under your version of UNIX. Do your homework and make sure everything works together.

Platform Selection—Conclusion

These are just suggestions and generalizations. The choice you make will depend on information specific to your site. Remember, there's no "right" choice for everyone. For some, UNIX will be the right choice, and for others, Windows will be the best option.

Using Samba to Export Data for Windows Backup

There are a number of good backup programs for Windows NT that you may want to use to backup your UNIX system. Several of these packages (such as Tivoli ADSM and Veritas Backup Exec) have *backup clients* for various UNIX systems. Some packages, however, are not able to back up anything but another Windows system. Fortunately, Samba can be used to export data from a UNIX system that you would like to back up. However, there are several things you'll need to be careful of when using such a system.

Consider Turning `follow symlinks` Off

The `smb.conf` option `follow symlinks` is enabled by default. This means that Samba will follow any symlink. This can be a problem for backups for several reasons. If Samba follows a symlink, it means that your backup software will also follow the symlink. This can cause your backup software to unintentionally archive files and/or directories outside the share that's being exported by Samba. For example, if there's a symbolic link in the current share that points to the `/usr` directory, backing up that entire share using a Windows-based backup program will also cause your entire `/usr` tree to be backed up! This might not be what you intended. Remember, the Windows software *cannot* detect that it's following a symlink—across a SMB/CIFS share, it appears as just another directory or file.

Another unwanted side-effect that can occur is *recursion*. With `follow symlinks` enabled, an infinite loop can occur that will at best mess up your backup and waste a huge amount of space, and at worst it will cause your backup program to crash or your backup set to become corrupted. *Recursion* can occur when you have a symlink in a SMB/CIFS share that points to one of the symlink's parent directories. For example, consider the following scenario: You've exported an SMB/CIFS share from your Linux server, called `myshare`. You intend to use Dantz Development Corporation's Retrospect program on your Windows NT server to back up the contents of this share. Inside this share, you have a single directory called `foo`. Inside the `foo` directory, you have a symlink called `bar` that points to its parent directory, `foo`. UNIX backup software (for example, `tar`) will handle this situation correctly and back up both `foo` and `bar`. However, something goes very wrong when backing up this structure using Retrospect under Windows NT with `follow symlinks` enabled (which happens to be the default). This is what will get backed up:

```
foo
foo/bar
foo/bar/bar
foo/bar/bar/bar
foo/bar/bar/bar/bar
....
foo/bar/bar/bar/bar/bar/bar/bar/bar/bar
```

Ad infinitum!

Because Windows NT has no concept of a UNIX symbolic link, Samba cannot "tell" Windows NT that `bar` is a symbolic link. To Windows NT, it appears to be a regular directory, which contains another regular directory, and another, and another. Retrospect (or any other Windows backup software) will continue to recurse into this infinite directory tree, faithfully attempting to back up the contents of the share. Instead, it finds itself caught in a trap from which it cannot escape.

If the `foo` directory also contained a 5MB file, the situation would be even worse. For every recursion that Samba performed, due to the symlink problem, you would waste 5MB of uncompressed storage on your tape.

What should be done? Make sure you have `follow symlinks = No` in your `smb.conf` for any share that you plan to back up from Windows, unless you have *absolute* control over the contents of the share. Otherwise, your users can unintentionally (or even intentionally!) cause your Windows NT backup software to crash and burn.

`follow symlinks`—Special Uses

Now that you've been warned about using `follow symlinks`, there's a special case option where you may want it enabled. If you have full control over the contents of the backed-up data, so that you can ensure that there are no recursive symlinks or symlinks pointing to areas of the filesystem that you do not want backed up, then you can do the following. Add an entry to your smb.conf that looks like this:

```
[backup]
        comment = special share for backing up this machine
        path = /home/backup
        force user = root
        read only = Yes
        follow symlinks = Yes
```

After adding this entry, you can restart smbd and then create symlinks in /home/backup to directories that you would like to back up. Your Windows backup software will follow these symlinks and back up their contents. For example, you could create a symlink called usr that points to /usr, another one called myfiles that points to /home/drobbins/ archive, and so on. This way, you can control what gets backed up simply by managing the symlinks in /home/backup. Also, creating the backup set under Windows becomes simpler. Everything is contained under one share, so your Windows software does not have to access multiple shares to perform a single backup.

Backups and force user=root

You'll notice that in the previous smb.conf excerpt the line force user = root was added. This will cause this user ID to be used for all accesses to this share. I include it in the backup share because it ensures that the Windows backup software will be able to read every single file on the UNIX system. This is normally what you'll want when performing a backup. Also, because we're using follow symlinks = Yes in the preceding example, all files and directories that the symlinks point to on this share will be accessed with root privileges. This means that you don't need to modify any possible existing shares that may contain a force user to force all accesses to a particular non-root user.

Do a Test Backup

In general, it's a good idea to perform a test backup to identify any possible problems with your backup scheme. When you're exporting backup data using Samba, test backups are *essential*. You'll want to check to make sure that the preceding issues are handled correctly. In addition, there's another critical issue.

Windows Backup Software

If you're going to use Windows to perform backups, you'll need to choose some software. In this section, we'll review two popular options, Microsoft Backup and Retrospect, and I'll also provide you with some additional resources for further product

research. Please remember that these are only two possibilities, out of many. While each is a popular choice, they may or may not meet your specific needs.

Windows NT Backup

Although this isn't often mentioned, Windows NT Server 4.0 comes with a fully functional tape backup package that can perform full, incremental, and differential backups. If you do not have extremely sophisticated needs, you may want to consider this package. One of the nice things about Backup is that simply enabling your tape drive under Windows NT (by installing the appropriate driver) is all that's needed for Backup to operate.

Retrospect

Retrospect is a very nice and feature-rich backup program produced by Dantz Development Corporation (`http://www.dantz.com/`). Besides having a very nice and easy-to-use interface, it also provides some innovative backup features.

Retrospect has a couple of areas where it really shines. One of them is the backup of laptops—Retrospect handles laptops extremely well and will back them up as they are connected to the network. Retrospect also excels in its support of the Macintosh platform. If you have a good number of Macintosh systems at your site, Retrospect should be your backup software of choice. Although it offers no native UNIX support, Samba will allow Retrospect to back up any number of SMB/CIFS Samba shares.

FIGURE 21.1

Retrospect after backing up a Samba share.

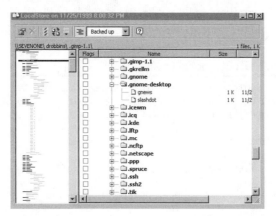

You may be surprised to hear that Retrospect's default mode of operation is incremental. After creating a full backup, Retrospect uses a special system to only add changed or new files in a safe and effective manner. It also backs up the Windows NT Registry and NTFS file permissions. Retrospect is a solid performer.

Other Windows Backup Software

In addition to Retrospect, there are a number of other Windows NT backup solutions that are worth looking into. Of note is Veritas Backup Exec (http://www.veritas.com/), which is a very nice, more traditional software package. If your organization has a very large, multiplatform environment, Tivoli ADSM (http://www.tivoli.com) might be an excellent choice because it supports a very wide range of workstations and mainframes.

Connecting to SMB/CIFS Shares for UNIX Backup

We've just explored the possibility of exporting UNIX data using Samba so that Windows can back it up, but what about the other possibility? Are there ways for UNIX machines to either connect to or mount SMB/CIFS shares so that they can be backed up by UNIX software? There certainly are, and we'll look at two possibilities—smbmount and smbtar—in this section.

smbmount

The smbmount utility is part of the SMBFS but has kindly been included with the Samba source archive. Under Linux, this tool will allow SMB/CIFS shares to be mounted onto a Linux filesystem, thus allowing access to these files as if they were a typical volume. One of the limitations of smbmount is the fact that if you mount an NT share, NT's fine-grained access control permissions will not be preserved. Instead, all files will be owned by the user who mounted the share. Listing 21.1 shows an example use of smbmount.

LISTING 21.1 Sample Output from smbmount

```
bash-2.03# smbmount //enteesrv/c$ /mnt/ntbackup -U administrator
Added interface ip=192.168.1.1 bcast=192.168.1.255 nmask=255.255.255.0
Got a positive name query response from 127.0.0.1 ( 192.168.1.3 )
Password:
bash-2.03# ls /mnt/ntbackup/
AN_PREFS Palm Rescued Document.txt
AUTOEXEC.BAT Program Files TEMP
CONFIG.SYS RECYCLER WINNT
DP_PREFS Rescued Document 1.txt Windows Update Setup Files
IO.SYS Rescued Document 2.txt boot.ini
MSDOS.SYS Rescued Document 3.txt ntldr
My Music Rescued Document 4.txt pagefile.sys
NTDETECT.COM Rescued Document 5.txt
bash-2.03#
```

smbmount's companion program, smbumount, is also available for unmounting shares.

> **Tip**
>
> smbmount-mounted shares have been known to become inactive after a period of several hours of inactivity. For this reason, it's recommended that you mount the shares when needed and unmount them when not in use. Alternatively, simply create a cron job to test to make sure that the share is active, and if not, have the script first smbumount it and then smbmount it again. The script can easily test to see whether the share is properly mounted by testing for the existence of a well-known file or directory inside the mount point.

smbtar

smbtar is another handy utility that comes with Samba. smbtar is actually a shell script designed to use GNU tar to create tar archives. Although this tool is very handy for backing up shares, it does suffer from the same limitation as smbmount—that is, you'll lose any fine-grained security information if you backup an NT share. This makes smbtar handy if you may need a single file restore or if you do not use NTFS on your NT server. If you do use NTFS, however, you would have to restore all file permissions after a full restore—a time-consuming process. Remember this when you consider smbtar for a job and use it accordingly. Listing 21.2 shows some sample output from an smbtar session.

LISTING 21.2   Sample Output from smbtar

```
bash-2.03# smbtar -v -s enteesrv -x c$ -u Administrator -p 's3cr3t' -t
foo.tar
server is enteesrv
share is c$\\
tar args is
tape is foo.tar
blocksize is
Added interface ip=192.168.1.1 bcast=192.168.1.255 nmask=255.255.255.0
Got a positive name query response from 127.0.0.1 ( 192.168.1.3 )
Domain=[WEEBLE] OS=[Windows NT 4.0] Server=[NT LAN Manager 4.0]
 4 ( 2.0 kb/s) \AN_PREFS
 0 ( 0.0 kb/s) \AUTOEXEC.BAT
 649 ( 30.2 kb/s) \boot.ini
 0 ( 0.0 kb/s) \CONFIG.SYS
 324 ( 158.2 kb/s) \DP_PREFS
 0 ( 0.0 kb/s) \IO.SYS
 0 ( 0.0 kb/s) \MSDOS.SYS
directory \My Music\
 26816 ( 1309.4 kb/s) \NTDETECT.COM
 156496 ( 2010.9 kb/s) \ntldr
```

More information on smbtar can be found in the smbtar man page.

Other Windows/UNIX Backup Integration Options

Another way of creating a unified backup solution is through the use of backup clients. A number of enterprise backup solutions offer either Windows or UNIX client software that will allow that particular brand of server software to access files on the system for backup. For example, Tivoli ADSM has a wide selection of client software available from `http://www.tivoli.com/`. In addition, Arkeia (`http://www.arkeia.com`) has a number of clients, ranging from many versions of UNIX to Windows 95/NT to Novell NetWare. Generally, clients such as these are designed to automatically handle system-specific quirks, such as backing up operating system-specific file bits and handling odd filenames.

tar

tar, which stands for *tape archiver*, is the classic UNIX tape backup program. `tar` accepts a number of operation and option flags that affect its behavior. Here are the basic operations available for GNU `tar`:

Operation	Function
c	Create `tar` archive
t	List `tar` archive
x	Extract `tar` archive
r	Append `files` to archive
u	Append only newer files

Each invocation of `tar` needs exactly one operation specified (for example, `tar -c`). Besides operations, there are a number of *options* that affect `tar`'s behavior. Here's a list of the most frequently used options (again, these are for GNU `tar` and may vary slightly on your platform):

Option	Function
U	Unlink file first
--owner=*name*	Added files' owner = *name*
--group=*name*	Added files' group = *name*
p	On extract, keep permissions
f *myfile*, --file=*myfile*	File or tape device to use
z	Use `gzip` to (de)compress

Option	Function
z	Use `compress` to (de)compress
`--use-compress-program=`*app*	Use *app* to (de)compress
-C	Extract
`--exclude=`*glob*	Glob pattern of files to skip
P	Don't strip first / from path
l	Don't cross mount points
-N *date*, `--newer=`*date*	Add files newer than *date*
v	Verbose operation

Because you probably have a good amount of experience with `tar`, I'll just cover a few important tips and tricks relating to its use. There are two things to be careful of. The first is that it can be very risky to use `tar` compression on a tape. This is because `tar` compresses the entire stream of data instead of compressing each file individually. This has a dangerous implication—if you have just one error on your tape, you could lose all data after that error. This will probably happen because once the compressed stream is corrupted, your compression program (for example, `gzip`) will not be able to correctly interpret the rest of the data and will bail out. For this reason, it's recommended that you use hardware compression and avoid `tar` software compression entirely. If there are files that absolutely need compression, it's *much* safer to compress those particular files individually before adding them to the `tar` archive. Then, if you have a hard error in the `tar` archive on that particular file, you'll most likely lose that file rather than the entire backup.

Another word of warning is in order regarding restores: Be careful with symlinks. If you're restoring a large amount of files over an existing filesystem, it's possible that `tar` will extract a file that has the exact same name as a symbolic link already existing on the filesystem. In this case, `tar` will overwrite the file that the symlink points to, by default, rather than the symlink itself. This behavior can be overridden by using the U option, which will cause the symlink to be unlinked (deleted) first before `tar` extracts the file.

dump and restore

`dump` and `restore` comprise another standard suite of backup programs for UNIX. One of the nice things about `dump` is that it's well suited to do incremental backups of filesystems. `dump` selects its files based on the `mtime` (last date modified) of the file.

`dump` performs backups in 10 different levels. A level of 0 tells `dump` to perform a full backup; a level of 1 indicates to `dump` that it should back up any new or modified files since the last level 0 or level 1 backup. This allows not only for incremental backups but for differential ones as well. It's a handy little system for easily dealing with incremental and differential backups.

I'll cover the Linux version of dump and restore in this chapter—if you're using another UNIX-like operating system, the functionality and/or command-line options of dump and restore may vary slightly. Here's a list of commonly used dump command-line options:

Option	Meaning
-0, -1...-9	Perform a level 0–9 dump
-f *file*	Tape or file to write to
-T *date*	Use *date* for incremental dump
-u	Update /etc/dumpdates
-W	List dumpdates for each fs

These options are nowhere near an exhaustive list of dump options but will help you to understand the following examples of how the utility works.

One of the most important things to understand about dump is exactly *how* it keeps track of which files have been backed up and which have not. From the preceding information, you might have gleaned that dump uses an /etc/dumpdates file to keep track of the date(s) that each filesystem was backed up, along with a corresponding dump level. Here's a listing of the contents of my /etc/dumpdates file:

```
/dev/hda10 0 Thu Dec 2 13:12:23 1999
/dev/hda10 1 Thu Dec 2 13:15:42 1999
```

As you can see, this file records the filesystem backed up, the dump level, and the date and time the dump command was executed. Note that these /etc/dumpdates entries were created when I performed the following commands:

```
dump -u -0 -f etc.dump /etc
```

and

```
dump -u -1 -f etc2.dump /etc
```

Review these commands and the options listed so that you get a feel for what these commands perform. Basically, I performed two dumps of my /etc directory—the first one a level 0 dump, and the second one a level 1 dump. What's especially important to notice is the fact that only the filesystem that /etc is on is recorded in /etc/dumpdates. In other words, if I subsequently performed a level 2 dump on my /usr tree, which also happened to be on /dev/hda10, then only modified files after Thu Dec 2 13:15:42 1999 and new files would be backed up! So when using dump, remember that /etc/dumpdates is maintained on a per-filesystem basis rather than a per-directory or per-file basis, as you might assume.

We're now ready to take a look at `restore`, `dump`'s companion. Let's take a look at what command-line options `restore` provides. Remember, this is not an exhaustive list of `restore` options, and it's mainly provided as a means to get you familiar with the proper use of `restore`:

Option	Meaning
`-i`	Run in interactive mode
`-t`	List contents of `dump`
`-x`	Extract specified files
`-f file`	Specify file or tape drive
`-N`	Do a "pretend" restore
`-u`	Unlink files before overwrite
`-v`	Verbose mode

There are two things I want to mention about `restore`. First, if it's used incorrectly, you can destroy data on your filesystem. I recommend that you read the `restore` man page and get very familiar with `restore` before using it on any important data. One way to do this is through the use of the `-N` option, which will cause `restore` to run in a "pretend" mode, where no real files are modified. Another very useful feature of `restore` is it's interactive mode, which provides a shell-like interface that can be used to inspect and modify the archive. Here's some output from a sample session of `restore` in interactive mode:

```
/tmp > restore -i -f etc.dump
restore > ls
.:
etc/

restore > cd etc
restore > ls a*
adjtime
./etc/apache:
access.conf httpd.conf.default mime.types
srm.conf.default
access.conf.default magic mime.types.default
httpd.conf magic.default srm.conf

asound.conf
restore > quit
```

As you can see, this is a very handy feature that `restore` provides.

Other UNIX-Based Backup Solutions

In addition to the preceding solutions, there are a number of other UNIX-based backup solutions that you should consider. All those listed are significantly more complex and feature-rich than the standard UNIX tools described previously.

Arkeia (`http://www.arkeia.com`) provides a very powerful enterprise-class backup solution as well as provides support for a huge number of clients, from personal computers to minicomputers. Arkeia's major claim to fame is its ability to perform multiple backups simultaneously if you have multiple tape drives in your machine. It's a very fast piece of software and sports a number of advanced features that you would expect from an enterprise-class package. Available on the Web site is a fully functional free shareware version, with a suggested price of $20 U.S.

`bru` (`http://www.bru.com`) is a command-line backup program that's similar in functionality to `tar` but with several enhancements. In particular, it supports connecting to and backing up SMB/CIFS shares and is, in general, a much better and more reliable solution than using `tar`. `bru` is especially careful about making sure that the data it writes to tape is not corrupt. In addition to verifying data at the time of backup, `bru` also allows administrators to pick up a completed backup tape, insert it in the drive, and have `bru` verify that the data on it is still intact. This is a nice thing to be able to do, and `bru` makes it easy. Another handy feature is that, unlike `tar`, `bru` allows you to safely use software compression on your files. A 30-day trial version is available from `bru`'s Web site, and BRU Personal Edition is bundled with a number of modern Linux distributions.

`amanda` (`http://www.cs.umd.edu/projects/amanda/`) is another backup system that you may want to take a look at. It's designed to back up large numbers of UNIX workstations as well as Windows 95/NT systems through the use of Samba. It does use each UNIX system's native backup program, such as `tar` or `dump`, to perform the backups, however.

Offsite Backups: `rsync`

`rsync`, as you might guess, is a UNIX program that keeps remote files synchronized. It's a truly excellent tool for the creation of offsite mirrors and backups, allowing for encrypted transmission and very efficient synchronization. Written by Andrew Tridgell and Paul Mackerras, it's available from `http://rsync.samba.org/rsync/` and is distributed under the GNU Public License.

`rsync`, in its most basic use, operates like an enhanced `copy` command and can be used to keep local directory trees synchronized. The first path is considered the *source* tree, and the second is considered the *destination*, similar to `cp` and `mv`. The following sections provide some examples.

rsync Basic Usage

The following command will copy all the files in `/etc` to the directory `/home/drobbins/etcbackup`:

```
rsync /etc/ /home/drobbins/etcbackup
```

However, the following command, without the trailing `/` on the source path, will copy the `/etc` directory itself into `/home/drobbins/etcbackup`:

```
rsync /etc /home/drobbins/etcbackup
```

A more advanced use of this command would be to use it to recursively copy the contents of the `/etc` directory to `/home/drobbins/etcbackup`, in a verbose mode:

```
rsync -av /etc /home/drobbins/etcbackup
```

rsync Network Usage

Still, this is nothing exciting. All these possibilities can be accomplished by using the `cp` command. `rsync` really shines in its ability to copy files over the network. It's particularly good at this because it only transfers the changed portion of files over the wire. This is a tremendous speed and network bandwidth savings. Typically, it means that the first `rsync` operation will take the expected amount of time. However, any subsequent `rsync` operations will take substantially less time, often only several seconds or minutes, even when `rsync` is synchronizing several hundred megabytes of files. Of course, this all depends on how often the data you're using `rsync` on changes, but it always is very efficient at what it does.

Let's look at a true example of `rsync`'s usefulness. Let's say you have `rsync` installed on two machines: `myserver` and `mybackup`. You want `mybackup` to contain a complete mirror of the contents of `myserver`'s `/home` tree. `myserver` also happens to be reached through the Internet, rather than via a private LAN or WAN. What this means is that others could theoretically intercept this data, and you would like some security. The following command, run on `myserver`, would do the trick:

```
rsync -av --partial --delete --rsh="ssh" /home/
➥ drobbins@mybackup.mydomain.com:/home
```

In this example, `rsync` will be instructed to use the `ssh` encrypted shell for its communication, which will make it difficult to near impossible for the data to be intercepted by a third party via the Internet. In addition, notice how the destination path has a username prepended. In this case, ssh will be used to log in as user drobbins to perform the synchronization. The --partial option causes rsync to keep partially transferred files if it's aborted so that it can resume the transfer later. The --delete option tells rsync that it's allowed to delete files under /home on mybackup if the corresponding file has also been deleted on myserver. Note that for the ssh encryption to work, ssh must be set up correctly on both systems, and the user drobbins must be able to log into mybackup from myserver. If that is so, then this option will efficiently synchronize files from myserver to mybackup every time it's run. Putting this command in a cron job would be a great idea.

rsync Servers

rsync can also be run as a standalone daemon, thus allowing other rsync clients to connect to it to read or write files. When in this mode, it's called an rsync *server*. It's a very powerful configuration and might be ideal if you're performing multiple offsite backups or using rsync extensively. When run in a server configuration, rsync does not use rsh or ssh as its transport, but instead it communicates directly with the rsync server.

To use rsync in daemon mode, it needs an /etc/rsyncd.conf file to exist. Here are the contents of a sample file from my system:

```
max connections = 4

[www]
        path=/home/drobbins/public_html
        comment=web export area

[ftp]
        path=/enoch/mirror
        comment=enoch mirror area
```

I use rsync in daemon mode to upload my Web pages as well as synchronize my files with my main FTP mirror. Once the configuration file is in place, I start rsync in daemon mode as follows:

```
rsync --daemon --port=10001
```

This will cause rsync to accept connections to the paths defined in /etc/rsyncd.conf, but only if the remote rsync connects to my machine on port 10001. I use port 10001 because at one time I was behind a firewall that did not allow any remote systems to connect to a port number below 10000. Without this option, rsync will default to port 873, which in most cases will work perfectly.

Suppose I'm ready to connect to the rsync server from my remote machine (in this case, a Web server). The following command will "pull" all changes from my machine to the local Web server:

```
rsync -av --delete rsync://myserver.mydomain.com:
➥10001/www/* /home/drobbins/public_html
```

Let's quickly review this command. First, `-av --delete` tells me that I'm performing a recursive `rsync`, that it's running in verbose mode, and any files that I have deleted from the source will also be deleted from the destination. The source path uses a URL-type syntax to specify the `rsync` server. Note how the port number is specified by using a colon. Also note that the `www` directory is accessed by following `hostname:port` with a slash and the name I assigned to my exported html files. The contents of `/home/drobbins/public_html` will be synchronized with the files residing there.

rsync and You

I think you'll find `rsync` a true UNIX power tool, and I encourage you to learn more about it by studying the `rsync` and `rsyncd.conf` man pages. Remember, the reason why we covered `rsync` in this chapter is because it's an ideal tool for performing offsite backup. Think about ways you could use it in your organization to guard against data loss, possibly by using it to synchronize your data with a mirror at a remote office. And the next time someone asks for an efficient, encrypted offsite backup solution, you can let him or her know you have just the tool for the job.

Choosing the Appropriate Backup Medium

If you haven't looked recently, there are a huge number of competing backup technologies available, ranging from the low-end Zip drive to high-end DLT systems. Although I cannot offer an exhaustive review of the technologies available, I will touch on several different backup options and highlight some new technologies worth looking into. Use this chapter as a starting point for determining the proper backup solution for your organization.

> **Tip**
>
> The *hard error rate* is defined as the frequency of errors occurring on the medium under ideal operating conditions. Generally, higher-quality backup devices will have a better hard error rate. However, you need to be careful and not use the hard error rate as the sole means of comparing different backup technologies—remember that the number refers to the frequency of errors under *ideal* conditions. Certain technologies are more finicky than others and will have a significantly worse "real-world" hard error rate than advertised (for example, a dirty DAT drive can have a horrendously high hard error rate, even though the spec sheet says its hard error rate is 1 in 10^{15}.)

DAT Tape

Probably the most entrenched modern backup medium is DAT tape. Modern drives offer capacities ranging from 8 to 24GB, and they come at a variety of price points. These drives are generally relatively expensive, and they also do not have a sterling reputation as far as reliability. Most of these drives require frequent cleaning and can be quite finicky. If you're in the market for a tape drive, it's recommended that you consider a technology other than DAT, because there are several more-reliable and cost-effective technologies available. With DAT tape, expect a hard error rate of approximately 1 in 10^{15} under ideal operating conditions.

Travan Tape

Travan could be considered DAT's younger and weaker sibling, and it should definitely be avoided for departmental backup. Ranging in capacity from 400MB to 4GB, Travan tapes are significantly more error-prone than DAT tapes. Avoid them if possible.

OnStream Tape

OnStream (`http://www.onstream.com/`) provides an exciting new tape backup technology, offering capacities of 15, 25, and 35GB (uncompressed). OnStream drives feature a number of new technologies to provide very high reliability and good performance, including spatially distributed ECC, variable-speed operation, and other features you would expect from a modern tape system. A number of drives with different performance characteristics are available. All of them offer a hard error rate of 1 in 10^{19}, which is excellent (10,000 times better than DAT). They're also generally less expensive than DAT.

VXA Tape

VXA tape technology (`http://www.vxatape.com/`) is an extremely intriguing tape backup solution, boasting very high recoverability rates. Offering 12 and 33GB native capacities, VXA has its own advanced approach to ensuring extreme reliability. One of the most amazing things about VXA technology is that the tapes are reputed to be able to withstand being boiled in hot water, frozen, and dunked in coffee—and they will still restore perfectly! Using a packet-based technology and dual redundant heads, these drives should definitely be considered if you're very concerned about restorability. In addition, the VXA tape media sports a shelf life of 30 years (the shelf life of other tape technologies, such as DAT, varies by manufacturer). VXA tape offers a hard error rate of 1 in 10^{17}. Although OnStream tape is theoretically 100 times more reliable (according to the spec sheet), VXA handles less-than-ideal conditions with flying colors and therefore will most likely be more reliable than OnStream when the going gets tough. VXA drives and media are reasonably priced and beat DAT significantly when it comes to price/performance. They also offer very good UNIX support, which is another plus.

CDR

Another option, if you have limited backup needs, is to simply use a CD-ROM burner to create periodic backups. The advantage to this system is that you'll have periodic snapshots of your important data sitting on the shelf, and the media can be read by a large number of CD-ROM drives. The downside to this approach is that CDRs have a limited laser life and will wear out after being used extensively. For this reason, it's recommended that you limit accessing your CDR backups unless absolutely necessary, and that you store them in a pristine environment. In addition, it's recommended that you use Verbatim DataLifePlus (http://www.verbatimcorp.com/) CDR media for critical data, because they have a longer laser life.

Other Backup Technologies

I have only touched the surface on the various backup options available, and there are others you should consider. You might want to consider an optical or magneto-optical disk, Exabyte (http://www.exabyte.com/) Mammoth M2 technology, or others. In addition, if you have modest home backup needs, you may want to consider simply purchasing additional IDE drive storage. IBM and Fujitsu drives have a good reputation and high capacities, and they might provide all the extra storage you need. Try to find the best tape technology for your needs; remember, there's no one solution for everybody.

Summary

In this chapter, I began by reviewing basic backup concepts and then covered the various approaches to backups that are available using Samba. After encouraging the implementation of a *centralized* backup solution, I discussed in detail various specifics relating to using Samba to export data for backup by Windows software. After reviewing several Windows backup software options, I then covered two methods of connecting a UNIX machine to a Windows machine so that UNIX can back up Windows data.

In the second half of the chapter, I provided an introduction to the commands tar and dump/restore and then gave you an overview of other UNIX backup solutions. You then were provided with a look at rsync, which allows organizations to easily implement remote offsite backups. Finally, I ended with a review of different backup technologies and provided pointers to additional information.

Troubleshooting Samba

by Steve Litt

IN THIS CHAPTER

CHAPTER 22

For a sophisticated piece of software doing the huge job of helping UNIX and Windows interact, Samba is remarkably easy to troubleshoot. Samba has several troubleshooting advantages not enjoyed by many technologies. This chapter's purpose is to give you the knowledge to exploit every one of the Samba troubleshooting advantages.

Why Samba Troubleshooting Is Easy

Here are some of the reasons why Samba is surprisingly easy to troubleshoot:

- Modularity
- Reliability
- Plenty of Test Points and Tools
- Availability of Test Jig System
- Most Configuration Is Done in One Place
- Intelligent Defaults
- DIAGNOSIS.txt
- Available Source Code
- Subject Matter Expertise Is Easy to Obtain

Each of these advantages is discussed in this section.

Modularity

Modularity is a large part of both product quality and ease of troubleshooting. Samba is modular. The following is a simple block diagram of a Samba system:

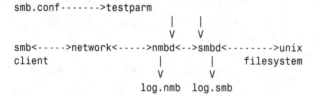

```
smb.conf------->testparm
                        |    |
                        V    V
smb<----->network<----->nmbd<-->smbd<-------->unix
client                  |       |     filesystem
                        V       V
                     log.nmb  log.smb
```

The rest of this chapter refers to the preceding diagram as the Samba system block diagram. It's very simplified, but it's very functional for the purpose of troubleshooting.

Because troubleshooting consists of dividing a system to narrow the scope of a root cause, the modularity of Samba greatly eases troubleshooting.

The Samba Troubleshooting Hierarchy

Referring to the Samba system block diagram, it's evident Samba can be intercepted before the network by accessing it on the server as `localhost`, using `smbclient` and other utilities. If Samba doesn't work locally, that's the problem requiring a fix.

If Samba is accessed from the network, there are a number of different clients from which it can be accessed. From a troubleshooting point of view, the `smbclient` program is the most trustworthy client. The following is the Samba troubleshooting hierarchy:

1. Get it working on `localhost`.
2. Get it working over the wire from a Linux SMB client.
3. Get it working over the wire from a Windows command-line SMB client.
4. Get it working over the wire from a Windows graphical SMB client.

Step 1 bypasses the network for a reading on Samba alone.

Step 2 bypasses Windows clients, which often add problems of their own.

Step 3 bypasses Network Neighborhood and Windows Explorer, which typically are more touchy than Windows command-line SMB clients such as the `net use` and `net view` commands.

Step 4 tests the intended use of Samba.

Many times step 2 is bypassed, instead relying on step 1 to prove that Samba and `nmbd` naming work and relying on `ping` commands to prove network connectivity. That's what `DIAGNOSIS.txt` does. `DIAGNOSIS.txt` is a great example of a series of tests that logically traverse the Samba troubleshooting hierarchy.

This hierarchy is used to narrow the scope of Samba problems, and it often proves the problem is not even a Samba problem. For maximum troubleshooting productivity, the Samba troubleshooting hierarchy must be consciously consulted in all Samba troubleshooting activities.

Plenty of Test Points and Tools

Samba's excellent modularity yields many test points that can be measured or injected. Running the `smbclient -NL localhost` command is an example of measurement. Changing `smb.conf` and observing the result on the client is an example of injection.

> **Note**
>
> The concept of *injection* comes from the electronics world, where it's common to place an audio or radio frequency signal at a point in the circuit and observe whether that signal appears at the output or at a test point. This is called *signal injection*.
>
> The same technique is valuable in Samba troubleshooting. The classic example is requesting a browse list with `net view`, which is the injection, while observing the result with `tcpdump`, which is the measurement. `smb.conf` changes could also be thought of as an injection. An injection is a test whose purpose is to change the system rather than just measure it.

The "Test Points and Testing Tools" section, later in this chapter, discusses many Samba test points and the testing tools that can be used to measure and inject them.

Reliability

The obvious value of reliability in troubleshooting is that it minimizes the need for troubleshooting. Typically, once a Samba system is working properly, it stays that way. Most Samba problems occur after a configuration change.

A more subtle troubleshooting benefit of Samba reliability is that it eliminates most intermittent problems. Intermittent problems (or *intermittents*, for short) typically require a tenfold increase in time to reach a solution.

The opposite of an intermittent problem is a reproducible problem—a problem for which there exists a known reproduction sequence.

Availability of Test Jig System

A test jig network can be had for the price of two hand-me-down computers, a hub, some wires, and a copy of Windows. The copy of Linux and Samba are free. In the case of domain problems, an additional PC must be procured to host a copy of NT Server.

Because the test jig network is a standalone network, it can be configured with the same IP addresses and hostnames as the production systems. Often the production system's symptom can be reproduced on the test jig system simply by transferring `smb.conf`.

The use of a test jig system frees the troubleshooter from the need to protect data from destruction and users from inconvenience. Freed from such needs, troubleshooting can proceed at a much faster rate.

A test jig system provides a great way to explore experimental source code changes. The GNU compiler that ships with all Linux systems is reliable and robust. A wide variety of debuggers can be procured to work with software compiled on Linux systems.

Even in cases where the symptom cannot be reproduced on the test jig system, exploration and experimentation can take place. The economical availability of a test jig system invariably eases Samba troubleshooting.

Most Configuration Is Done in One Place

The `smb.conf` files can get pretty big, especially when NT domains and multiple subnets are involved. Sometimes you hear of an `smb.conf` with hundreds of shares. Nevertheless, having all the configuration in one file makes troubleshooting lightning fast—no flipping between files or having more files open than can fit on a screen. Also, there's no need to back up 17 files before starting.

For experimental configuration changes, `smb.conf` can be open in an editor on one virtual terminal, with another running Samba restarts. This makes troubleshooting test cycles easy and incredibly quick.

Another advantage is that a specific Samba configuration can be implemented with a single file copy. Contrast this with a UNIX/Linux setup, where numerous files must be edited, or a Windows setup, where the administrator must manually navigate a long and involved series of GUI screens.

On a given server, most Samba problems can be reproduced by a specific `smb.conf`. The offending `smb.conf` can be saved for later reproduction, and a simpler `smb.conf` reproducing the symptom can be formulated. If this simplification continues, eventually the problem becomes obvious. If a simplification iteration eliminates the symptom, the troubleshooter is then in a position to exploit the differences between the two `smb.conf` files to nail the root cause.

Iterative `smb.conf` modifications and associated Samba restarts are not practical on a production server during work hours. Often the symptom can be reproduced and troubleshot on an independent test jig system comprised of a Linux/Samba server and one or more Windows clients.

Perhaps the greatest advantage of single-file configuration is that the file can be backed up before troubleshooting begins and restored when necessary. The necessity could be either when troubleshooting inadvertently makes things worse or to reenable symptom reproduction after troubleshooting has eliminated the symptom. Once a version producing the symptom and a version not producing the symptom can be isolated, the solution is a few edits away.

Intelligent Defaults

Samba's parameters have intelligent default values, meaning typically they do not need to be explicitly specified in smb.conf. This makes the smb.conf file short. Any troubleshooting effort is concentrated on those parameters departing from the default values.

Theoretically this could hide an important value from troubleshooting consideration. But more often than not, an smb.conf with comments and defaults deleted makes the problem stand out. The SWAT program deletes comments and parameters explicitly specified to their default values.

Use of Samba's intelligent defaults is a major tool in formulating a minimalistic symptom description.

DIAGNOSIS.txt

Troubleshooting must progress quickly. One method of achieving quick solutions involves the *predefined diagnostic*, a set of tests designed to rule out large sections of root cause scope with minimum expenditure of time and brainpower.

Root Cause Scope

The phrase "root cause scope" in the preceding paragraph refers to the area of the system in which the root cause of the problem might reside. As tests rule out additional areas of the system, the root cause scope shrinks accordingly. Once the root cause is confined to an area small enough to troubleshoot by direct observation, the cause is obvious and a solution can be crafted.

Samba comes with an excellent predefined diagnostic in the form of DIAGNOSIS.txt, which is shipped with the Samba distribution. It's a set of 10 tests designed to run quickly. Also, DIAGNOSIS.txt is designed so that each test requires only the capabilities verified in earlier tests (except testparm, which requires no capabilities other than a running OS). The result is that when a test fails, a defined and suitably narrowed problem has been found.

DIAGNOSIS.txt results form part of a good Samba symptom description. This is discussed in the section titled "Effectively Obtaining Online Help," later in this chapter. DIAGNOSIS.txt can be run in less than five minutes—especially when used as described in the "Effectively Using DIAGNOSIS.txt" section, later in this chapter—and it isolates a high percentage of Samba problems.

Available Source Code

Samba is so easy to troubleshoot that most problems are solved without looking at source code. But when the problem can't be solved with normal troubleshooting methods, source code availability almost guarantees a solution if used by a skilled programmer willing to spend the time required.

Source code viewing and changing is a troubleshooting method not available to users of proprietary software. It's not often necessary, but when the problem can't be resolved or worked around with normal troubleshooting tactics, source code accessibility is the only route to a solution.

This chapter contains source code troubleshooting tips later, in the section titled "Source Code Troubleshooting." Additionally, a set of source code browsing tools are introduced in Chapter 23, "Samba Learning Tools."

Subject Matter Expertise Is Easy to Obtain

Enterprise resource-planning systems exist whose user groups require prior experience before joining. Contrast this with Samba, where anyone can join `samba-technical@samba.org` and regularly see posts by the programmers who created Samba.

Free Samba information can be found all over the Internet. Also, several great books, including this one, are available at prices less than $50.

Better still, Samba is easy to learn on your own. Chapter 23 discusses many tools for Samba self-education. What all this means is that if a particular aspect of Samba has you stumped, it's easy to find the needed information yourself or locate somebody else who has the information.

Effectively Using `DIAGNOSIS.txt`

The `DIAGNOSIS.txt` file contains an incredibly powerful predefined diagnostic useful in Samba troubleshooting. The purpose of a predefined diagnostic is not to solve every problem. Instead, the goal of a predefined diagnostic is to solve a high percentage of problems in a very short time, meaning it must be comprised of quick tests likely to isolate or materially narrow the root cause.

`DIAGNOSIS.txt` serves admirably in this capacity. Unlike some predefined diagnostics that contain flowchart-like jumps, `DIAGNOSIS.txt` is designed to proceed until a test fails, after which that failure, now substantially isolated, is examined by normal troubleshooting tactics. This is true because later tests use only capabilities verified in earlier tests.

Find the location of DIAGNOSIS.txt on your Samba server. It's typically in the Samba distribution's docs/textdocs directory. When preinstalled on Linux distributions, it's typically in docs/textdocs under the Samba documentation directory of your server's documentation tree. You can use the locate command to find it. It's also available online at ftp://ftp.samba.org/pub/samba/docs/textdocs/DIAGNOSIS.txt.

DIAGNOSIS.txt assumes a Samba server named BIGSERVER and a Windows SMB client called ACLIENT. It also assumes a [tmp] share whose path is /tmp and is read only=no with no valid users= specification. In addition, it assumes a guest account= parameter whose value is a genuine UNIX user.

Test 1 is testparm, or if your config file is anything other than the default, testparm configfile. This five-second test reveals any illegal parameter use in smb.conf. There's no use going further if the Samba config file has errors. Note that testparm stops after loading the configuration file. Press Ctrl+C to get out of testparm at that point and check for any error or warning messages interspersed with messages proclaiming the processing of various sections. The errors and warnings are quite clear, so solve each before going to test 2. The following is a testparm example:

```
$ testparm
Load smb config files from /usr/local/samba/lib/smb.conf
Unknown parameter encountered: "beta master"
Ignoring unknown parameter "beta master"
ERROR: Badly formed boolean in configuration file: "bsd".
Processing section "[profile]"
Processing section "[netlogon]"
Processing section "[homes]"
Global parameter domain master found in service section!
Processing section "[printers]"
Processing section "[tmp]"
Processing section "[d]"
Processing section "[lp]"
Processing section "[myuid]"
Loaded services file OK.
Press enter to see a dump of your service definitions
```

The preceding testparm encountered three errors. The first was a line whose parameter name was beta master, which is not a legitimate parameter. The next was a line saying print ok=bsd. That parameter can take only a boolean (1 or 0, true or false, or yes or no). The third was the inclusion of global parameter domain master=yes in the [homes] share. The preceding shows that errors and warnings are interspersed in the shares. To make the errors and warnings more prominent, the lines containing "Processing section" can be removed using the grep command, as follows:

```
$ testparm | grep -v "Processing section"
Load smb config files from /usr/local/samba/lib/smb.conf
```

```
Unknown parameter encountered: "beta master"
Ignoring unknown parameter "beta master"
ERROR: Badly formed boolean in configuration file: "bsd".
Global parameter domain master found in service section!
Loaded services file OK.
Press enter to see a dump of your service definitions
```

> **Note**
>
> For a list of the many possible error, warning, and informational messages of testparm, see the `printf` statements in utils/testparm.c. A quick way to see them in context is to issue the following command from the source directory:
>
> ```
> $ grep -nC4 printf utils/testparm.c | less
> ```

Test 2 is ping BIGSERVER from ACLIENT and ping ACLIENT from BIGSERVER. This is a five-second test that determines network connectivity. If it fails, there's a network problem precluding Samba communications. An excellent first step is to see whether the problem is isolated to ACLIENT or whether all clients exhibit the same lack of connectivity. From there, self-ping each machine as an IP address, as the hostname, and as localhost. Solve all connectivity problems before continuing to test 3.

Test 3 is smbclient -NL BIGSERVER. Note that DIAGNOSIS.txt instructions do not include the N option, which means "don't ask for a password." If it isn't included, simply press Enter on the password prompt. If everything's OK, it displays a list of all BIGSERVER's browseable shares. On error, look at valid users=, hosts allow=, and hosts deny= and make sure guest account= is a valid user. Also check whether smbd and nmbd are running with the ps -ax | grep mbd command. If the cause is still unknown, thoroughly read DIAGNOSIS.txt. Also, try smbclient -NL localhost and smbclient -NL 127.0.0.1 to rule out any name resolution problem. Note, however, that localhost could be disabled by interfaces=, bind interfaces only=, hosts allow=, and so on.

Test 4 is nmblookup -B BIGSERVER __SAMBA__. This tests the nmbd daemon to make sure it's running and listening on UDP port 137. If nmbd is functioning properly, this command prints something resembling 192.168.100.1 __SAMBA__<00>. If it doesn't return the IP address of your Samba server, troubleshoot nmbd and port 137 (netstat -a, netstat -anp |grep 137, ps -ax | grep nmb, and so on).

Test 5 is nmblookup -B ACLIENT '*'. This tests ACLIENT's SMB client software. The -B argument means it does this via broadcast. If this test fails, troubleshoot the client.

Test 6 is `nmblookup -d 2 '*'`. This sets `nmblookup` at debug level 2 and searches the subnet for `<00>` names. This tests for a correct default broadcast address. See `DIAGNOSIS.txt` if this fails, and try to determine what the Samba server's broadcast address is. Look at Samba's `interfaces=` parameter, including `netmask`.

Test 7 is `smbclient '\\BIGSERVER\TMP' -Uusername%password`. The `DIAGNOSIS.txt` test does not include the `-U` argument, instead relying on the user typing in the password of the user performing the command. Unfortunately, if that user is `root`, system security will probably not allow the `smbclient` connection. This test proves the ability to connect to a share, specifically a `[tmp]` share with `path=/tmp` and `read only=no`. Naturally that share must exist for the experiment. The experiment is equally valid with other shares, so a modification of `smb.conf` is not necessary. If this command does not yield the `smb: \>` prompt, investigate the share for `valid users=`, an existing `path=`, and so on. Theoretically, by the time you've gone though the first six tests, most Samba problems have been eliminated, although password encryption and password shadowing problems can show up at test 7. While in the `smbclient` session, test the `smbclient` commands `get`, `put`, `more`, and `dir`.

> **Note**
>
> The first seven tests used SMB clients on Linux boxes. Tests 5 and 6 tested the response of Windows boxes but did not test their client software. This conforms to the Samba troubleshooting hierarchy (`localhost`, Linux-to-Linux network, and then Windows-to-Linux network) discussed earlier. Tests 8, 9, and 10 use Windows SMB clients for testing.

Test 8 is `net view \\BIGSERVER`, which displays a browse list for `BIGSERVER`. Read `DIAGNOSIS.txt` for advice if this fails. Also check whether the correct Samba server hostname is explicitly specified in `netbios name=` and whether `workgroup=` is the same as for the Windows client. If it is not, and if no other machine is acting as the local browse master, try adding the following code to force the Samba server to be a local browse master:

```
os level=255
preferred master=yes
local master=yes
```

If there's not already a WINS server, also add `wins support=yes`.

Test 9 is `net use x: \\BIGSERVER\TMP`, which tests accessibility of the `[tmp]` share. The command should succeed, and you should be able to list directories and read files, as well as write files if `read only=no` for the share. If tests 1–8 succeeded and this test failed, it points an accusing finger at the Windows client software. See `DIAGNOSIS.txt` for details.

Test 10 involves using Windows Explorer to browse the Samba server and to read and write the `[tmp]` share. This often fails even when tests 1–9 succeeded, especially with Windows 9*x* and when the Samba server has a different workgroup than the client, in which case steps must be taken to ensure the existence of a local master browser and to ensure that the correct hostname is assigned to the `netbios name=` parameter.

`DIAGNOSIS.txt` Quick Scripts

`DIAGNOSIS.txt` is quick, requiring less than five minutes to complete. That's good, but it can be improved. Listing 22.1 shows a script called `diagnosis.pl` that performs the first seven tests, plus a new test (1.5) that checks for running daemons, in 30 seconds, outputting the results to `diagnosis.log`. It also checks numerous clients instead of one, and it checks several of the tests both by IP address and by name. Once again, this script just automates the existing `DIAGNOSIS.txt`.

LISTING 22.1   `diagnosis.pl`, Which Automates the First Seven `DIAGNOSIS.txt` Steps

```
#!/usr/bin/perl -w
use strict;

#***** START OF CUSTOMIZATION AREA *****
my($BIGSERVER)="mainserv";
my($BIGSERVERIP)="192.168.100.1";
my($TESTSHARE)="//$BIGSERVER/TMP";
my($USERNAME)="username";

my(@ACLIENTS)=("WINCLI","DESK2");
my(@ACLIENTIPS)=("192.168.100.5","192.168.100.40");
#***** END OF CUSTOMIZATION AREA *****

my($LOGNAME)="diagnosis.log";
my($PASSWORD);

sub writelog
{
  system("echo \'$_[0]\' >> $LOGNAME");
  print "$_[0]\n";
}

sub writeTestHeader
{
  writelog("\n\n\n******** BEGIN TEST $_[0]  ********");
}
```

continues

LISTING 22.1 continued

```perl
sub writeCommandHeader
{
  writelog("\n--- TEST $_[0] ---");
}

sub acquirePassword
{
  my($word);
  print "\n DO NOT ENTER YOUR PASSWORD UNLESS YOU TRUST THIS PROGRAM!\n";
  system "stty -echo";
  print "Password for $_[0]: ";
  chop($word = <STDIN>);
  print "\n";
  system "stty echo";
  return($word);
}

sub dotestparm
{
  &writeCommandHeader(1);
  system("echo > newline");
  my($endflag)="Press enter to see a dump of your service definitions";
  my($line);
  my(@lines)=`testparm < newline`;
  foreach $line (@lines) {
    chomp($line);
    last if $line eq $endflag;
    &writelog($line);
  }
}

sub shareTest
{
  my($tf)="testfile.tmp";
  my($tfback)="$tf\.tst";
  unlink $tfback;
  system("echo First line of test file > $tf");
  system("echo Last line of test file. >> $tf");
  &writeCommandHeader("7");
  my($command)="smbclient \'$TESTSHARE\' -c \"";
  $command=$command . "ls $tf; put $tf;get $tf $tfback;ls $tf";
  $command=$command . "\" -Uusername";

  #CAUTION: Write command before acquiring password!
  writelog($command);
  $command=$command . "%$PASSWORD";
  my($line);
```

```
  #CAUTION: Certain OS's show the password in ps -ax
  my(@lines)=`$command`;
  foreach $line (@lines) {
    chomp($line);
    &writelog($line);
  }
  print glob $tfback;
  my($scratch)=`ls -l --full-time $tfback`;
  writelog($scratch);
  $scratch=`date`;
  writelog("Time is $scratch");
}

sub do1test
{
  my($number, $command)=@_;
  &writeCommandHeader($number);
  &writelog($command);
  my(@output) = `$command`;
  my($line);
  foreach $line (@output) {
    chomp($line);
    &writelog($line);
  }
}

sub main
{
  $PASSWORD=&acquirePassword($USERNAME);
  my($element);
  system("rm $LOGNAME");
  &writelog("Start DIAGNOSIS.txt tests.\n\n");

  &writeTestHeader("1");
  &dotestparm();

  &writeTestHeader("1.5");
  &do1test("1.5", "ps -ax | grep mbd");

  &writeTestHeader("2");
  foreach $element (@ACLIENTIPS) {
    &do1test("2", "ping -c3 $element");
  }
  foreach $element (@ACLIENTS) {
    &do1test("2", "ping -c3 $element");
  }
  &writelog("!!!!! You must manually ping the server from the clients!");

  &writeTestHeader("3");
  &do1test("3", "smbclient -NL localhost");
```

continues

LISTING 22.1   continued

```
&do1test("3", "smbclient -NL $BIGSERVERIP");
&do1test("3", "smbclient -NL $BIGSERVER");

&writeTestHeader("4");
&do1test("4", "nmblookup -B $BIGSERVER __SAMBA__");

&writeTestHeader("5");
foreach $element (@ACLIENTIPS) {
  &do1test("5", "nmblookup -B $element '*'");
}
foreach $element (@ACLIENTS) {
  &do1test("5", "nmblookup -B $element '*'");
}

&writeTestHeader("6");
&do1test("6", "nmblookup -d 2 '*'");

&writeTestHeader("7");
&shareTest();

&writelog("\n\n\n!! DO TESTS 8, 9 AND 10 ON WIN CLIENT !!");
}

&main();
```

Tests 8 and 9 can be run in less than one second using diagnosis.bat, which is shown in Listing 22.2.

LISTING 22.2   diagnosis.bat, Which Automates DIAGNOSIS.txt Steps 8 and 9

```
@echo off
rem ***** START OF CUSTOMIZATION AREA *****
set BIGSERVER=mainserv
set SHARENAME=TMP
set tf=testfile.tmp
set lf=diagnosis.log
rem ***** END OF CUSTOMIZATION AREA *****

dir nosuchfilefersure | sort > crlf

echo ***** START TEST 8 *****            > %lf%
ECHO net view \\%BIGSERVER%             >> %lf%
net view \\%BIGSERVER%                  >> %lf%

echo .                                  >> %lf%
echo .                                  >> %lf%
echo ***** START TEST 9 *****           >> %lf%
ECHO net use x: \\%BIGSERVER%\%SHARENAME% >> %lf%
net use x: \\%BIGSERVER%\%SHARENAME% /Y   >> %lf%
```

```
ERASE X:%tf%
echo This is test 9! > X:%tf%
type X:%tf%                          >> %lf%
dir  X:%tf%                          >> %lf%
net use X: /delete                   >> %lf%
echo .                               >> %lf%
echo THE PRECEDING WAS FILE %tf%     >> %lf%
type %lf% | more
choice /C:Q /N /T:Q,0 Hit Q when done:
```

Using Effective Troubleshooting Process

Effective troubleshooting involves much more than simple mastery of technology. It requires a troubleshooting process optimized to quickly and accurately narrow the scope of the root cause. For a detailed description of a troubleshooting process, see the Universal Troubleshooting Process at `www.troubleshooters.com/tuni.htm`.

This book uses a six-step Samba troubleshooting process:

1. Back up `smb.conf` and any other vulnerable data.
2. Describe and reproduce the symptom.
3. Perform the quick checks.
4. Condense the symptom description.
5. Narrow the scope of the problem.
6. Fix and test.

If practical, reproduce the symptom on a test jig system. This gives you much wider latitude in testing than you'd have with a production system. If using a test jig system is not practical, plenty of nonintrusive tests are available that can be used safely on a production system, including all the tests in `DIAGNOSIS.txt`.

Back Up `smb.conf` and Any Other Vulnerable Data

The `smb.conf` file is likely to change immensely during the course of troubleshooting. Backing it up prevents you from making matters worse (at least from the `smb.conf` point of view). This also makes it unlikely that you'll accidentally lose the ability to reproduce the symptom.

Describe and Reproduce the Symptom

An accurate, detailed, and complete symptom description is the single most effective timesaver in troubleshooting. It can narrow the search scope by a factor of 10 or more. It reduces the risk of fixing the wrong problem or spending hours troubleshooting the wrong section due to a bad assumption.

What's more, it facilitates testing by providing a baseline, so a determination of change can be made upon each troubleshooting test or experiment. The elimination of the symptom is one of the criteria you use to determine that you have arrived at a correct solution. In consulting activities, it can disprove an allegation that you made things worse.

The following are some questions that a good Samba symptom description should answer:

- What do the error messages say?
- In what way(s) is it not serving the purpose?
- When did this start?
- What else happened around that time?
- What are the results of DIAGNOSIS.txt?
- What *specific* sequence of steps is required to reproduce the symptom?
- Can the symptom be reproduced on a standalone test jig system using Linux server and a couple of Windows clients?
- Does the symptom occur with Windows 9*x*, Windows NT, or Windows 2000 clients, some combination, or all?

The final step is to make smb.conf a functional file for the purposes of symptom description, *especially* if you're enlisting outside help. The easiest and quickest way to do that is to run smb.conf through SWAT. This eliminates all comments and parameters that are explicitly specified to the default value. The result is an smb.conf readable to anyone who knows Samba, as opposed to a mess in which the root cause can easily hide.

Caution

Be sure you backed up the original, problem-causing smb.conf before running it through SWAT. SWAT's changes are not revertible.

Perform the Quick Checks

DIAGNOSIS.txt is the ultimate quick check, and it should be used during the symptom description step. Another quick check is to restart Samba (if practical) and reboot the client. Also, check to see whether the symptom happens on all Windows clients. If a problem exists with a specific share, get into the share with `smbclient` to determine whether it's a Windows problem.

Many problems benefit from the three-minute check of substituting a tiny `smb.conf`. If policy allows, this can be done on the system with the problem. Otherwise, do it on a test jig server that reproduces the original problem. The following is an example:

```
netbios name=<hostname of Samba server>
workgroup=<workgroup of Windows clients>
encrypt passwords=<same as on Windows clients>

[homes]
```

If a browsing problem exists, it's often helpful to add the following lines to the top section of the tiny `smb.conf`:

```
os level=255
preferred master=yes
local master=yes
```

Note that you might want to refrain from adding these lines if an NT machine is acting as the local master browser on a production system. Unless there's an existing WINS server, also add `wins support=yes` to the preceding three parameters.

Any authentication problems should immediately be checked for `encrypt passwords=` compatibility and for the existence of the user in the `smbpasswd` system.

Condense the Symptom Description

Many `smb.conf` files were created from huge sample files meant for training, not for real service. This results in overly complex, hard-to-read, and hard-to-troubleshoot `smb.conf` files. Part of this is eliminated by running the file through SWAT to delete comments and explicitly specified default parameters.

Unfortunately, other parameters are often set to nondefault values because the sample file was set that way or because previous troubleshooting tests were not reverted after the root cause was found. It's all too common for 100-line (and longer) `smb.conf` files to be displayed on Samba lists, with the question, "What's wrong?" Answering that with any degree of authority would require either massive analysis or further troubleshooting, neither of which is a likely outcome when the recipient receives hundreds of such symptom descriptions per day. Therefore, it's answered with a guess, with a snide remark, or not answered at all.

Contrast that with a symptom description submission that's 10 to 20 lines long. The problem will most likely be obvious, if not to the submitter, then at least to some recipients on the list.

The process of condensing `smb.conf` is easy. Start by evaluating whether the problem seems to occur on all shares or just some. If the answer is all shares, delete all shares except one representative share. `[tmp]` is a good choice. Restart Samba and see whether the symptom recurs. If so, delete several parameters out of `[global]` and once again restart Samba and see whether the symptom changes. Keep on deleting and restarting until something changes; then add back some of the deleted lines and continue narrowing until you can toggle the symptom with a few lines. To the degree possible, delete all other lines. You want an `smb.conf` embodying the problem. Once you have it, it's easy to submit a symptom description basically saying "I have _____ problem with Samba when using this `smb.conf`, but if I change these parameters, the problem [goes away | changes]." That's a clean symptom description likely to get response. Note also that this type of narrow `smb.conf` is the best way to document a program bug, because otherwise it's likely to be a configuration problem.

The preceding process, with its deletions and reinsertions, requires backing up each `smb.conf`. That's a 10-second process, so it's not a big deal. Be very careful *not* to delete the original, problematic `smb.conf`.

Narrow the Scope of the Problem

Most Samba problems are solved before getting to this step, which is fortunate because this is the time-consuming step. The purpose of `DIAGNOSIS.txt`, the quick checks, and the condensing of `smb.conf` is to enable you to skip over this step—and most of the time it works.

At this point, the question to ask is, "How can I narrow this down just one more time?" It doesn't take very many narrowing steps before the root cause becomes obvious.

The trick here is to think up reasonably safe and quick tests that split the remaining possible scope of the problem in half (or a reasonable facsimile of *half*). Depending on safety, ease, and likelihood, a test that eliminates only 10 percent of the root cause scope might be an excellent test.

The primary challenge of troubleshooting is thinking up these tests. Keep your mind open. Learn more via the learning tools in Chapter 23. Consider the injection and measuring tools you have at hand (described later in the "Test Points and Testing Tools" section of this chapter). Above all, keep asking that one question: "How can I narrow it down just one more time?"

If you find yourself getting a bad attitude, go for a walk. If you're not allowed to do that, walk down the hall for a cup of coffee. Perhaps you can take lunch or work on a different project. However, in the back of your mind, keep asking yourself, "How can I narrow it down just one more time?"

Fix and Test

Fixing is usually easy. Hardware problems are fixed by swapping. On UNIX and UNIX-like systems, software problems are fixed with a configuration change and a subsystem restart. Unfortunately, Windows problems sometimes require a lengthy reboot or occasionally even a reinstall. For the most part, though, once the root cause is known, fixing the problem is trivial.

Then there's final testing. Obviously the symptom must disappear. But that's only the tip of the iceberg. You must verify that you caused no other problems. Most of all, verify that you fixed the root cause rather than strong-arming the symptom.

Consider this problem: User john is a valid user for a share, and that share is read only=no. However, john cannot write to files created by fred, who is also a valid user of the share. Likewise, fred can't read john's files. This problem could be "fixed" by placing all valid users of the share on the admin users= list. It doesn't fix the UNIX permission discrepancies causing the problem, it just gives root privileges within the share. It fixes the symptom, not the root cause.

A property of all symptom strong-arm tactics is that they have unintended side effects. In this case, there's a minor security breakdown. The correct way to solve this would have been to eliminate the permission discrepancies with force user= or force group= plus the correct directory mode= and create mask= parameters. That would have eliminated the need to use the potentially dangerous admin users= parameter.

A further check on the quality of the solution is to verify that the factor you changed is really the cause of the symptom change. This is done by reversing out that one factor (or those few factors) and seeing whether the symptom reverts. We Samba technologists are lucky it takes only a few minutes to make this verification. Most technologies require a long time to perform such a toggle, and as a result it's often not done.

Test Points and Testing Tools

Samba has many test points and testing tools. This chapter uses the following, very simplified Samba system model, which for the rest of the chapter will be called the *Samba system block diagram*:

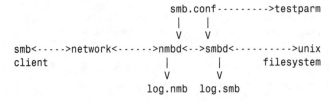

```
                    smb.conf·········>testparm
                       |    |
                       v    v
smb<·····>network<······>nmbd<···>smbd<···········>unix
client                    |        |       filesystem
                          v        v
                       log.nmb  log.smb
```

Like most models, the Samba system block diagram is simplistic. Its value is the creation of an intuitive feel for the high-level structure. The model pretty much lumps authentication in with the daemons, and it has no place for remote authentication (`password server=`). It can be thought of in the same terms as frictionless pucks, massless strings, ideal engines, and resistanceless wire.

You may wish to augment this model with password servers and other real world components.

Intrusive Versus Nonintrusive Testing

A nonintrusive test is one that can be safely done on a production system while users are hammering away on it. An intrusive test is one that makes such action risky.

Nonintrusive tests are typically measurements, whereas intrusive tests are typically configuration changes, restarts, or injections. An *injection* is the creation of a change or the addition of a load, at a test point, for the purpose of observing the change at another point in the system. The stressor tests described in Chapter 35, "Optimizing Samba Performance," are excellent examples of injections. Adding or removing an NT server is another example of an injection.

On production systems, every attempt should be made to use only nonintrusive tests. All `DIAGNOSIS.txt` tests are nonintrusive. `netstat` commands are nonintrusive, as are the various `nmblookup` and `smbclient` commands (unless you write to a share). Other nonintrusive tools include `ping`, `testparm`, `smbstatus`, log file viewing, `net use` (once again, as long as no writes take place), and `net view` commands (although `net view /workgroup:wgname` can trigger a browser election under certain circumstances).

SWAT is nonintrusive if not write enabled. Additionally, it's theoretically nonintrusive to open and save `smb.conf` without making changes, because the file will theoretically be in an identical state from the computer's perception, even though a human would perceive it as having changed radically. Because its software state hasn't changed, restarting would not be necessary. However, you might not want to bet the bank that the new file is perfectly in the same state as the old.

Looking at the source code is nonintrusive. Basically, anything you look at but don't touch is nonintrusive.

All configuration changes are intrusive. Note that some, but not all, `smb.conf` changes can affect the system even if Samba is not restarted. All `smb.conf` changes should be considered immediately intrusive. Samba restarts will most likely generate unrecoverable critical errors on files open when the restart takes place. Because it's advisable to follow any `smb.conf` change with a Samba restart to keep the system in a known state, `smb.conf` changes can be considered potentially harmful.

All system restarts are intrusive. All source code changes are intrusive if the newly compiled program is run. All UNIX file permission changes are intrusive. All changes to the network are intrusive. Even changes to clients can be intrusive.

An intrusive test is not necessarily harmful to a production system. Loosening the permissions on a directory is not likely to cause harm to a heavily used production system as long as it doesn't open up a security hole. Quick network disconnections/reconnections might not be harmful if they're quick enough not to generate critical errors (abort, retry, fail). Removing an unused directory from the file system is not harmful as long as nobody tries to access it.

Many intrusive injection tests simply mimic everyday activity; therefore, they are no more harmful than anything else happening on the production system. An example is performing a `net view \\servername` operation on a Windows client while viewing the result with `tcpdump` or performing a `net view /workgroup:workgroupname` (which can induce a browser election) while viewing `tail -f nmb.log`.

This must all be kept in proportion. Many Windows users consider crashes, problems, and reboots a daily fact of life. Nevertheless, it's best to run all intrusive tests after hours or during maintenance periods.

The ideal solution is to reproduce the problem on an isolated system consisting of a test jig Linux server and one or more test Windows clients. Once the symptom is reproduced there, all tests, whether intrusive or not, can be done at will.

Log Files

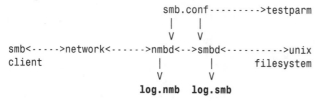

```
                         smb.conf -------->testparm
                            |    |
                            V    V
smb<----->network<------>nmbd<-->smbd<---------->unix
client                      |       |          filesystem
                            V       V
                        log.nmb  log.smb
```

Log files are ideal for many troubleshooting situations. They're the tool of choice for any intermittent problems, acting as a strip-chart recorder for `smbd` and `nmbd`. As shown on the Samba system block diagram, they derive their input directly from `smbd` and `nmbd`, so they provide a great way of seeing inside those otherwise inscrutable daemons.

Log entries are written by the `DEBUG()` calls, with different calls having different levels. By cranking up the daemons' debug level, you can see more entries. The level can be cranked up with a command-line argument when running the daemon or by using the `debug level=` parameter of `smb.conf`. Better yet, you can crank up the debug level at runtime without a restart by sending a `USR1` signal to the running daemon:

```
$ kill -USR1 $(cat /usr/local/samba/var/locks/smbd.pid)
```

You can subsequently crank down the debug level with a USR2 signal. The same can be done to the nmbd daemon by substituting nmbd.pid in the command. You can write shellscripts or Python or Perl scripts to automate the process, or you can set the level up or down by a certain number or set it to a specific debug level. The new debug level can be obtained by running a tail on the log immediately after the signal:

```
$ tail -n2 /usr/local/samba/var/log.smb
```

or

```
$ tail -n2 /usr/local/samba/var/log.nmb
```

nmblookup

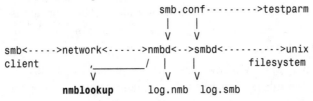

The nmblookup utility is ideal for peering inside the workings of nmbd. It's powerful and versatile. The following example shows nmblookup finding the master browser:

```
$ nmblookup -SM -
querying ____MSBROWSE___  on 192.168.100.255
192.168.100.1 ____MSBROWSE___<01>
Looking up status of 192.168.100.1
received 10 names
        MAINSERV       <00> -            M <ACTIVE>
        MAINSERV       <03> -            M <ACTIVE>
        MAINSERV       <20> -            M <ACTIVE>
        .._MSBROWSE__. <01> - <GROUP> M <ACTIVE>
        MYGROUP        <00> - <GROUP> M <ACTIVE>
        MYGROUP        <1d> -            M <ACTIVE>
        MYGROUP        <1e> - <GROUP> M <ACTIVE>
        SYLITTO        <00> -            M <ACTIVE>
        SYLITTO        <03> -            M <ACTIVE>
        SYLITTO        <20> -            M <ACTIVE>
num_good_sends=0 num_good_receives=0

$
```

In the preceding, __MSBROWSE__ is found on 192.168.100.1. Likewise, the <1d> name is found, indicating a local master browser for group MYGROUP. The next example comes straight out of DIAGNOSIS.txt (test 4) and is used to identify the presence of a Samba server:

```
$ nmblookup -B mainserv __SAMBA__
querying __SAMBA__ on 192.168.100.1
192.168.100.1 __SAMBA__<00>
$
```

The following is DIAGNOSIS.txt test 5, used to test a client's Windows networking software:

```
$ nmblookup -B wincli '*'
querying * on 192.168.100.201
192.168.100.201 *<00>
$
```

The following is used to look up a specific box on an SMB-enabled network:

```
$ nmblookup -U mainserv -R 'desk2'
querying desk2 on 192.168.100.1
192.168.100.40 desk2<00>
$
```

Finally, the following is used to look up all the names on a specific box:

```
$ nmblookup -Umainserv -RS 'wincli'
querying wincli on 192.168.100.1
192.168.100.201 wincli<00>
Looking up status of 192.168.100.201
received 6 names
        WINCLI          <00> -          M <ACTIVE>
        MYGROUP         <00> - <GROUP>  M <ACTIVE>
        WINCLI          <03> -          M <ACTIVE>
        WINCLI          <20> -          M <ACTIVE>
        MYGROUP         <1e> - <GROUP>  M <ACTIVE>
        USERNAME        <03> -          M <ACTIVE>
num_good_sends=0 num_good_receives=0

$
```

Using nmblookup is just one more way to peer into nmbd. It's an excellent way to split up a problem when naming is suspected as a cause. Chapter 12, "Samba Client Utilities," goes into much more detail about the use of nmblookup.

nbtstat

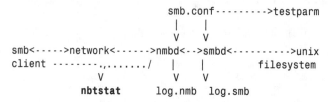

```
                            smb.conf--------->testparm
                              |   |
                              V   V
smb<----->network<------>nmbd<-->smbd<---------->unix
client --------.,......./  |   |          filesystem
          V               V   V
        nbtstat       log.nmb  log.smb
```

nbtstat works on a Windows client and, as such, is a client-measuring utility. However, the property it measures is provided by nmbd. It's the Windows answer to nmblookup. For example, the following command looks up the names on the server:

```
C:\WINDOWS>nbtstat  -n -a mainserv


        NetBIOS Remote Machine Name Table

     Name               Type      Status
   -------------------------------------------
   MAINSERV     <00>  UNIQUE    Registered
   MAINSERV     <03>  UNIQUE    Registered
   MAINSERV     <20>  UNIQUE    Registered
   ..__MSBROWSE__.<01>  GROUP     Registered
   MYGROUP      <00>  GROUP     Registered
   MYGROUP      <1C>  GROUP     Registered
   MYGROUP      <1D>  UNIQUE    Registered
   MYGROUP      <1E>  GROUP     Registered

MAC Address = 00-00-00-00-00-00
C:\WINDOWS>
```

The following command tests the effectiveness of a WINS server's offloading of broadcasts:

```
C:\WINDOWS>nbtstat -r


NetBIOS Names Resolution and Registration Statistics
------------------------------------------------------

Resolved By Broadcast     = 0
Resolved By Name Server   = 6
Registered By Broadcast   = 1
Registered By Name Server = 8
C:\WINDOWS>
```

The nbtstat command can be used to dump and reload the NetBIOS remote cache name table, as shown by the following session, which first dumps the cache with the -R option and then looks at the cache with the -c option:

```
C:\>nbtstat -R
Successful purge and preload of the NBT Remote Cache Name Table.

C:\>nbtstat -c
No names in cache

C:\>
```

The `-n` parameter displays the list of local NetBIOS names registered with a server:

```
C:\WINDOWS>nbtstat -a wincli -n


Node IpAddress: [192.168.100.5] Scope Id: []
          NetBIOS Local Name Table

   Name              Type         Status
------------------------------------------------
WINCLI        <00>  UNIQUE     Registered
MYGROUP       <00>  GROUP      Registered
WINCLI        <03>  UNIQUE     Registered
USERNAME      <03>  UNIQUE     Registered

C:\WINDOWS>
```

To display a list of active NetBIOS connections, use the `-s` option, as follows:

```
C:\WINDOWS>nbtstat -s


          NetBIOS Connection Table

Local Name         State    In/Out  Remote Host        Input   Output
-----------------------------------------------------------------------
WINCLI      <00>  Connected Out    MAINSERV     <20>   96KB    29KB
WINCLI      <03>  Listening
USERNAME    <03>  Listening

C:\WINDOWS>
```

net view

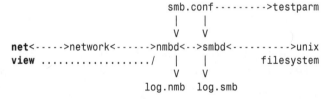

The `net view` command is a command-line browsing client on a Windows box. It "measures" (observes might be more accurate) naming, part of which is provided by `nmbd`. That's why the dotted line to `nmbd` is used in the preceding text diagram. Note that the `net view` command is also an injection test because it induces packet traffic and can even induce a browser election. The following examines the browseable shares of the server:

```
L:\>net view \\mainserv
Shared resources at \\MAINSERV
```

```
Sharename     Type        Comment
-----------------------------------------------------
d             Disk
homes         Disk
lp            Disk        Home directory of lp
myuid         Disk        Home directory of myuid
printers      Print
tmp           Disk
username      Disk        Home directory of username
The command was completed successfully.

C:\>
```

The following command looks at the browseable shares of a fellow client:

```
C:\>net view \\desk2
Shared resources at \\DESK2

Sharename     Type        Comment
------------------------------------------
MYDOCS        Disk
The command was completed successfully.

C:\>
```

The following command lists the computers in the workgroup:

```
C:\>net view /workgroup:mygroup
Servers available in workgroup MYGROUP.
Server name            Remark
----------------------------------------------------
\\DESK2                STEVE LITT
\\MAINSERV             Samba 2.0.6
\\WINCLI               WINCLI Steves Windows Computer
The command was completed successfully.

C:\>
```

The preceding command is also an injection test because it sometimes triggers a browser election. It does not work on NT boxes. NT's equivalent uses the following syntax:

```
C:\>net view /domain:mygroup
```

Once again, net view is an excellent test when naming is suspected. In some cases, it can be used to invoke browser elections. It's very handy as an injection when viewing log.nmb.

net use

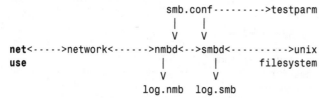

```
                      smb.conf --------->testparm
                          |    |
                          V    V
net<----->network<------>nmbd<-->smbd<---------->unix
use                       |       |      filesystem
                          V       V
                    log.nmb   log.smb
```

net use is a command-line SMB client on a Windows box. It's much more reliable than Windows Explorer. It's used to connect to a share, as follows:

```
L:\>net use \\mainserv\d
The command was completed successfully.

L:\>
```

The more common usage is to actually connect to a drive letter, as follows:

```
L:\>net use y: \\mainserv\homes
The command was completed successfully.

L:\>
```

When used without a share name, net use shows all the client's SMB connections, as follows:

```
L:\>net use

Status        Local name     Remote name
-----------------------------------------------
OK            Y:             \\MAINSERV\HOMES
OK                           \\MAINSERV\D
The command was completed successfully.

L:\>
```

The preceding command shows the results of the two examples that preceded it. An absolutely essential use of net use is to disconnect shares that cannot be disconnected in other ways. Windows 9*x* Explorer connects when you navigate into a share, but it does not disconnect when you navigate back out, or even if you close the Windows Explorer program. Disconnections are especially important on shares with a preexec=, root preexec=, postexec=, or root postexec= parameter. The following disconnects \\MAINSERV\D:

```
L:\>net use \\mainserv\d /delete
The command was completed successfully.

L:\>
```

22

TROUBLESHOOTING SAMBA

Another `net use` command verifies that `\\MAINSERV\D` is no longer connected:

```
L:\>net use

Status          Local name      Remote name
-------------------------------------------------
OK              Y:              \\MAINSERV\HOMES
The command was completed successfully.

L:\>
```

Perhaps the most important use of the `net use` command is in batch files. In the case of diagnostic batch files, `net use` greatly speeds and automates troubleshooting.

smbstatus

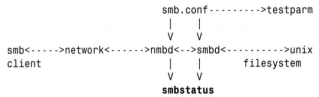

The `smbstatus` utility looks at Samba connections and locked files. It provides a great way to view the results when a Windows process opens a file, and it's an essential tool for tracking locking problems with Windows applications. The most common usage is without arguments:

```
$ smbstatus

Samba version 2.0.6
Service    uid       gid       pid     machine
-------------------------------------------------
d              username username 30180   wincli   (192.168.100.5) Tue Dec 14
➥12:09:42 1999
username       username username 30180   wincli   (192.168.100.5) Tue Dec 14
➥12:00:23 1999

Locked files:
Pid    DenyMode   R/W        Oplock           Name
-------------------------------------------------
30180  DENY_NONE  RDONLY     EXCLUSIVE+BATCH  /d/umenu/menudir/xake.mnu
➥Tue Dec 14 12:10:27 1999

Share mode memory usage (bytes):
   1048360(99%) free + 144(0%) used + 72(0%) overhead = 1048576(100%) total
$
```

Note the readings on deny mode, read status, and oplock. These are handy for diagnosing problems with DOS and Windows applications' share modes. Using the `-d` option puts `smbstatus` in verbose mode, which adds a few lines of server-wide information to the top of the display. Another feature of `smbstatus` is its ability to enumerate `smbd` processes via the `-p` option:

```
# smbstatus -p
30180
#
```

This can provide automated diagnostic scripts in conjunction with `grep`, Python, or Perl.

smbclient

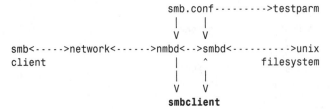

```
                              smb.conf--------->testparm
                                 |    |
                                 V    V
smb<----->network<------>nmbd<-->smbd<---------->unix
client                      |    ^            filesystem
                            |    |
                            V    V
                          smbclient
```

This is perhaps the most widely used diagnostic tool. Its main use is as the most reliable SMB client. The `smbclient` program is therefore the ideal test when other clients fail. You use it to determine whether the other client failed due to browsing problems or due to its own quirks. Of course, the `smbclient -NL servername` syntax, which displays the browse list from `nmbd`, is test 3 in `DIAGNOSIS.txt`. It can be used to inject a print job to a local print share or to a print share on a Windows box, as discussed in Chapter 8, "Configuring Printer Shares." It can also be used to run `tar` on a share, thereby providing a control check for the `smbtar` command. This is discussed in Chapter 12.

The `smbclient` program can be used to read and inject files into a share, using `more`, `get`, and `put`. It can be used as a control check when almost anything malfunctions. `smbclient` is so reliable that if it errors out, it's a safe assumption that something in the Samba configuration or setup is wrong.

The `smbclient` utility is detailed heavily in Chapter 12.

preexec= and postexec=

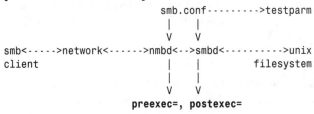

```
                                smb.conf--------->testparm
                                   |    |
                                   V    V
smb<----->network<------>nmbd<-->smbd<---------->unix
client                      |    |            filesystem
                            |    |
                            V    V
                      preexec=, postexec=
```

These parameters provide particularly good ways of finding out what's going on inside a share. The typical diagnostic use of these parameters is writing a log file of a share's uses:

```
preexec=  "echo pre   %T  u.g=%u.%g, U.G=%U.%G >> /tmp/check.log
postexec= "echo post  %T  u.g=%u.%g, U.G=%U.%G >> /tmp/check.log
```

The preceding parameters, when placed in a share, write to a log file every time the share is connected or disconnected. They write the time, the requested user and group (%U and %G), and the service user and group (%u and %g). Of course, other substitution variables can be inserted as needed. This is usually sufficient to diagnose access problems that are not caused by pure authentication.

testparm

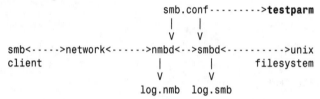

The testparm utility directly tests the smb.conf file, without reference to the network or daemons or Linux file system. testparm does two distinct jobs:

- It runs a syntax test ("lint") on smb.conf.
- It shows the values of all global parameters and the nondefault values of all shares.

First, the results of the syntax test is shown and the user is prompted to press Enter to see a dump of service definitions. After the user presses Enter, all [global] parameters, whether explicitly specified or default, are shown. Then each share is shown with its nondefault parameters.

The following is the syntax:

```
testparm [-s] [-h] [-L servername] [configfilename] [hostname hostIP]
```

If the system uses an smb.conf location other than the one compiled by default, place the full path to that file in the configfilename parameter. The -s option eliminates the "Press Enter..." prompt and the need to press Enter, making it ideal for piping testparm into grep. The -h option prints a help screen. The -L option sets the value of the %L macro to servername, which can be useful for testing include files specified with the %L macro.

Once the smb.conf syntax has been found sound, accessibility from given hosts can be tested with the hostname and hostIP arguments. These are a package deal—don't use one without the other. Using these arguments tests access against hosts deny= and hosts allow=. They do *not* test against the combination of interfaces= and bind interfaces only=. In fact, they report that a host at 192.168.100.5 can access shares in an smb.conf with interfaces=192.168.222.0 and bind interfaces only=yes.

testparm checks smb.conf for legal syntax in five seconds or less. That five seconds invariably finds errors capable of launching a two-hour troubleshooting search. It should be used every time smb.conf is changed, as well as at the start of any troubleshooting session.

Another way to use testparm is to look at the parameters and their values. Although theoretically this information could be gained by browsing smb.conf, smb.conf files are often full of comments, explicitly specified defaults, and duplicate parameters, both identical and conflicting. The testparm program shows you how Samba sees the file. It's often best used with grep. The following example checks for the global value of password level=:

```
$ testparm -s | grep "password level"
```

The output can also be piped to more or less for casual browsing:

```
$ testparm -s | less
```

A specific share can be viewed by specifying trailing context after each find, as shown in the following testparm printout of the [printers] share:

```
$ testparm -s  | grep -E -A20 "^\[printers\]"
```

This section just scratches the surface of the testparm utility's capabilities. Chapter 23 features several scripts for finding the default value of a parameter, finding whether a parameter is of type share or type global, and finding parameter synonyms, all using testparm.

testparm is a nonintrusive test that's extremely quick and often uncovers smb.conf problems that otherwise would have led to hours of wasted time. Use testparm early and often.

SWAT

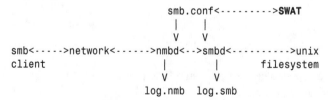

```
                     smb.conf<-------->SWAT
                         |    |
                         V    V
smb<----->network<------>nmbd<-->smbd<--------->unix
client                   |      |        filesystem
                         V      V
                   log.nmb  log.smb
```

The preceding diagram shows the main interaction of SWAT, but SWAT also views and affects smbd via the status screen. SWAT is a *very* intrusive test, so caution should be observed. One of its most valuable uses is putting the smb.conf file in standard form, with comments and explicitly specified default parameters deleted.

strace and Other Debuggers

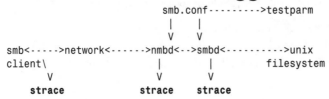

```
                              smb.conf-------->testparm
                                |     |
                                V     V
smb<----->network<------>nmbd<-->smbd<---------->unix
client\                    |       |        filesystem
     V                     V       V
   strace                strace  strace
```

The strace program is a tracer/debugger on Linux. Other operating systems have similar programs. strace traces system calls and signals. This can often be used to detect missing files, blown file opens, and so on. It's hard to detect landmarks because no information exists about what function you're in; however, many debuggers are available that can do this, assuming you compile the program to take advantage of this feature.

strace can be used on any executable in the Linux environment. Like most commands, it's often more informative when filtered through an intelligently crafted grep command.

tcpdump

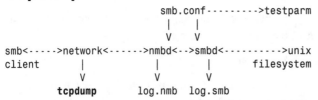

```
                              smb.conf-------->testparm
                                |     |
                                V     V
smb<----->network<------>nmbd<-->smbd<---------->unix
client     |               |       |        filesystem
           V               V       V
         tcpdump        log.nmb  log.smb
```

The tcpdump program is a test probe right into the network's packet traffic. A special, Samba-aware version of tcpdump is available on the Samba.org Web site. tcpdump is handy for identifying communications between clients and servers. An especially handy technique is to run a net use or net view while watching or recording a tcpdump session. If you must view tcpdump in a telnet session, make sure to screen out telnet packets (assuming your telnet is on port 1733):

```
$ tcpdump port not 1733
```

If you want to limit yourself to ports 137, 138, and 139, that can be done as follows:

```
$ tcpdump port 137 or port 138 or port 139
```

It's often preferable not to have tcpdump convert ports and IP addresses into names. This can be done with the -n switch, as shown here:

```
$ tcpdump -n port 137 or port 138 or port 139
```

tcpdump is very handy in exploring browsing problems, because you can see the browse requests and the responses, complete with the actual browse list. However, the default packet data size (`snaplen`) is insufficient to contain even a small browse list. However, it can be increased with the `-s` option, as follows:

```
$ tcpdump -s500 port not 1733
```

The preceding increases `snaplen` to 500 bytes. The `tcpdump` man page says to use the smallest `snaplen` that can accommodate the data. You can determine the adequacy of a snap length by running the following command:

```
$ tcpdump -s100 port 137 or port 138 or port 139 | grep -i snap
```

While that's running, issue a `net view` command from a Windows client and see whether the following error message appears:

```
WARNING: Short packet. Try increasing the snap length
```

Keep increasing the `-s` parameter until those messages disappear.

`tcpdump` is a powerful and sophisticated tool. This chapter just scratches the surface of its capabilities. For further information, refer to the `tcpdump` man page and *Linux Networking Unleashed*.

Various combinations of `tcpdump` and `grep` enable their use as a test probe to pick off very specific information. Add to that just the right injections, such as clients requesting share access or browse lists, and `tcpdump` becomes a very powerful tool.

netstat

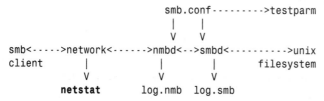

The `netstat` command is handy for investigating the network connections, routing tables, interface statistics, masquerade connections, netlink messages, and multicast memberships that can impact Samba. `netstat -p` is particularly handy because it shows process IDs. `netstat` is a UNIX administration tool. See the man page for more information.

ping

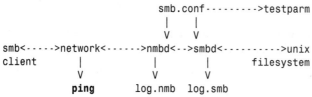

The `ping` program quickly determines network connectivity and is an essential quick check. When `ping` is used in scripts on a UNIX or UNIX-like box, it's best to specify the `-c` option, which determines the number of times it sends packets before quitting. The default is forever, which works poorly in scripts. Note that on Windows boxes, `ping` sends packets four times. The following is an example of a `ping` command using the `-c` option to send packets three times:

```
$ ping -c3 mainserv
```

When used with IP addresses, `ping` proves or disproves connectivity. By then switching to a name, you can investigate name resolution. This works not only with UNIX naming resolution, such as DNS and `/etc/hosts`, but also Windows naming resolution. You can verify this by placing a brand-new name as the value of the `netbios aliases=` parameter in `smb.conf` and then pinging the new name.

If `ping` does not work, here are some things to check:

- A bad NIC
- A bad cable
- A bad hub
- A proxy in the way
- A firewall
- A bad or misconfigured router
- A VPN client intercepting TCP/IP data
- A TCP wrapper in the way

smbpasswd

For the sake of simplicity, the Samba system block diagram used in this chapter does not include authentication. However, the `smbpasswd` utility is excellent for answering certain authentication questions.

For instance, `smbpasswd` can be used to determine whether you are really authenticating against the Samba server, or whether you are just authenticating against a password file somewhere on the local Windows client. Using `smbpasswd` to change the password on the server proves or disproves Samba authentication.

Test Jigs

Although passive troubleshooting using pure measurements is quick, informative, and harmless, it's often not enough. Sometimes it's much quicker to make a change and view the result.

Some servers can be restarted and tweaked regularly. Home systems, very small offices, and software development departments are examples. In each case, it's sufficient to warn the users that a restart will occur in two minutes and will last for one minute, after which they can go to work again.

The cleaner way is to reproduce the symptom on a cheap standalone Linux/Samba/ commodity hardware/Windows network made to be a replica of the production network, complete with the same hostnames and IP addresses and the same Samba version. Many times the symptom can be reproduced on the test jig server by copying the production server's smb.conf to it. In such a case, it can be troubleshot with impunity, restarting every 30 seconds, without worrying about disrupting users.

Test jig smb.conf files can be used either on a production server after hours or on a test jig system. Test jig smb.conf files are simple files designed to verify that Samba is capable of functioning to some degree. Here's the simplest practical smb.conf:

```
netbios name=mainserv
workgroup=mygroup
encrypt passwords=yes
[homes]
```

The preceding assumes the server has hostname mainserv (and both it and its clients are part of workgroup mygroup), has clients with encrypted passwords, and has a UNIX and Samba user who is also on the Windows client.

Another tactic is the test jig share. This is appropriate if trouble occurs on an existing share. Make the simplest possible share, which hopefully does not produce the symptom. Then slowly and stepwise make the test jig share more like the problematic share until the problem is reproduced on the test jig share. Find a single variable that can be toggled to toggle the symptom on both. Problem solved. Of course, such reconfiguring and restarting cannot happen on a production server while users are working.

Samba Troubleshooting by Category

Begin all problem diagnoses by running the predefined diagnostic in DIAGNOSIS.txt. A script capable of running all the tests in 30 seconds and recording the results in a log was detailed earlier in this chapter.

Other approaches common to all problem categories include following a good troubleshooting process, concentrating on dividing the problem, and keeping a good attitude.

Solving Access Problems

If you haven't yet, read Chapter 7, "Determining Samba Access." It gives a clear explanation, including flowcharts, of this complex subject.

The first step is to make sure the problem really is an access problem. An inexperienced computer user might report the loss of a drive mapping or the inability to navigate to a share as an access problem, when in fact it's a browsing problem or a loss of a drive mapping.

It's possible for network problems to be confused with access problems. The `ping` command goes a long way toward clarifying that issue.

Authentication problems can also be confused with access problems. It's sometimes advisable to create a new user and password on the Samba server (both UNIX and Samba encrypted, if that's what you're using) and then attempt to access it with `smbclient`.

Access problems are typically best solved at the `smbclient` level before proceeding to Windows clients.

A very good early test is observing whether the lack of access happens on one share or all shares. Does it happen on one or on all boxes? Does it happen on the server?

For a share access problem, if it's suspected that the problem might be related to UNIX permissions, that can be investigated by adding the user to `admin users=`. A very instructive test is trying to access the share as another user. Temporarily commenting out `valid users=` and `invalid users=` often brings results, after which the root cause can more easily be perused.

Solving Browsing Problems

Browsing problems can be difficult, but methodical use of a troubleshooting process helps immensely. The first step is to get browsing working on the server. Also, make sure some box on the network has taken over as a local master browser. This is done with the `nmblookup -SM -` command:

```
$ nmblookup -SM -
querying __MSBROWSE__ on 192.168.100.255
192.168.100.1 __MSBROWSE__<01>
Looking up status of 192.168.100.1
received 7 names
        MAINSERV        <00> -          M <ACTIVE>
        MAINSERV        <03> -          M <ACTIVE>
        MAINSERV        <20> -          M <ACTIVE>
        ..__MSBROWSE__. <01> - <GROUP> M <ACTIVE>
        MYGROUP         <00> - <GROUP> M <ACTIVE>
```

```
        MYGROUP              <1d> -          M <ACTIVE>
        MYGROUP              <1e> - <GROUP> M <ACTIVE>
num_good_sends=0 num_good_receives=0

[root@mainserv bin]#
```

The local master browser's IP address shows up to the left of the `__MSBROWSE__<01>` symbol, indicating that it's the address of the local master browser. Additionally, the existence of the `<1d>` name indicates that its workgroup (`MYGROUP`) has a local master browser. If it's intended that the Samba server be the local browse master, make sure the following lines are in the `[global]` section of `smb.conf`:

```
os level=65
local master=yes
preferred master=yes
```

Additionally, unless it's intended for one of the Windows boxes or another Samba box to act as the WINS server, insert the following line:

```
wins support=yes
```

In domain situations, there must be a domain master browser. It shows up as a `<1b>` name in the output of the `nmblookup -SM -` command. If no domain master browser exists, steps must be taken to create one, either on an NT box or by inserting the `domain master=yes` parameter in `smb.conf` to force the Samba box to domain master browser status. See Chapter 33, "Cross-Subnet Browsing," for more information.

Solving Authentication Problems

Simple authentication problems are isolated by the `DIAGNOSIS.txt` predefined diagnostic. The most common cause is a mismatch of server and client encryption. Other simple causes include not having the client's logged-in username as a username in UNIX and not having the client's logged-in username in `smbpasswd` (if you're using encrypted passwords). It's also possible that an access problem could look like an authentication problem. Attempt access from several different usernames. As is the case in most troubleshooting efforts, start on the server with `smbclient` and `nmblookup` and then work outward.

Encrypted passwords must be used to get Samba's PDC functionality. Domain authentication gets trickier. If a Samba server has `password server=<IP>`, try changing the IP to a "known good" authenticator, possibly another Samba server or even a test jig Linux/Samba box configured for the purpose of authenticating. Such a switch can isolate the problem to the password server or the Samba server. See whether the authentication problems extend to non-Samba servers. Remember to just keep narrowing the problem down.

22

TROUBLESHOOTING SAMBA

> **Tip**
>
> You may find that using an old Win95(A) machine which does not encrypt passwords along with `encrypt passwords=no` in `smb.conf` to be a quick troubleshooting tool if it is available. If so, try to keep older operating systems such as Win95(A), Windows for Workgroups, and even DOS, on old hand-me-down computers for just this type of testing.

Solving Printing Problems

Print troubleshooting is covered very extensively in Chapter 8, so it won't be discussed in this chapter. For printer problems, turn to Chapter 8.

Solving Performance Problems

This book has an entire chapter devoted to the subject of solving performance problems. See Chapter 35, "Optimizing Samba Performance."

Effectively Obtaining Online Help

Samba is an Open Source program, so it uses the Open Source Support Model. In other words, support is found by joining a community of experts who help each other. However, two individuals, with two identical problems, can submit to a mailing list two separate questions technically the same but worded differently, and one might get 10 answers while the other gets none. It's all in the way the question is asked.

First, it's important to understand who is on these mailing lists. The people answering most of the questions get more than 100 emails a day. Some *substantially* more. They have 30 seconds to decide whether to answer a question. If they don't understand the nature of the question within that time, they'll most likely skip it.

Another trait of the people answering the questions is they do not get paid to answer the questions. They have other motivations. This means they answer what they want and skip the rest. They don't respond to scolding ("I submitted this two weeks ago and nobody answered"). Also, they cannot get fired, because it's not a profession. If they like the email, they'll probably answer. If they don't like it—so many emails, so little time.

Be Part of the Mailing List

The first step is to be part of the mailing lists. This is evident as early as the salutation. Salutations such as "Hello Samba Experts" clearly mark the writer as "outside the group." Salutations such as "Hi everyone," or even no salutation at all, are much better.

Keep in mind that Samba list members are international, so try to keep it dialect free. "Howdy," "hi y'all," and "s'up homie?" are wonderful for local Linux user groups but are a little colloquial for an international mailing list.

In responding to a specific question on the list, it's OK to use the person's name in the salutation.

The next dead giveaway that the writer is an outsider is the phrase "please respond to my personal email at…." In other words, the writer wants free information but won't join the list or contribute. Many Samba mailing list and newsgroup dwellers like to answer the question for a few thousand list subscribers rather than teaching the world one user at a time. "Please respond to my personal email" messages are often skipped.

Finally, correctly and pleasantly answering other list members' questions is the mark of an insider—and insiders are more likely to get their emails answered.

Get to the Point

People with 100+ emails per day appreciate getting the story quick and straight. The best symptom descriptions start with one or at the most two sentences describing what the writer does not like about the behavior of his system. Mention which DIAGNOSIS.txt test failed, both by number and by command. Then quickly mention when it began, what else began around that time, and other symptoms noticed. Give a terse description of the system, including only those components likely to be part of the problem. Quickly describe the outcome of tests performed so far. Maybe ask a couple short questions about the way things work. Finally, include a *condensed* smb.conf and maybe a log listing pruned to show only the pertinent information.

All too often communications start with a sentence such as "I have a Samba problem," followed by a long and detailed description of the system, followed by a 200-line smb.conf complete with comments, commented-out parameters, parameters explicitly specified to default values, and then maybe a voluminous log listing. Interspersed somewhere in there is the perceived misbehavior of the system, but it can't be found in a minute, so the message is most likely skipped.

This brings up the question of whether to attach smb.conf or to include it in the body. Opinions vary, but the bottom line is that if the smb.conf file is big enough to be perceived as a problem in the body, it should probably be condensed. Combine that with the fact that many email clients make it time consuming to open attachments, and attachments reduce the likelihood of a response.

But Don't Be Too Terse

Most of the testy responses on lists are given to those who basically say "It's broke, help." A message needs to mention the operating system, the Samba version, what kind of client is used, and what's aberrant about the behavior of the system. Which DIAGNOSIS.txt test failed? Mention not only the test number but the name because some users haven't memorized the tests by number. Usually information about when the problem started and what else happened around that time is valuable.

Prepare and Learn Before Asking

Consider the following exchange:

> Writer: It keeps asking for a password and won't accept it.

> Responder: Read ENCRYPTION.txt.

The chances for meaningful, detailed responses increase with the preparation of the writer. Anything obvious in the documentation or a scan of the list archives is unlikely to draw an informative response.

Responding to Others' Questions and Posts

Answering others questions is a good thing. It's a great learning tool and improves your image. Be sure to use normal netiquette. Restrict caps locks to acronyms, stick to the technology, and carefully avoid calling others wrong (even if they are).

Common Gotchas, Symptoms, and Solutions

Part of quick and effective troubleshooting is remembering the problems that crop up frequently as well as remembering the solution. However, and this is very important, the assumption of a cause must be tested and proven either true or false. False assumptions are the second worst impediment to speedy solutions, after intermittents.

This section contains some common problems and their causes and solutions.

Config File Changes Sometimes Require a Samba Restart

Some smb.conf changes take effect without a Samba restart, and some don't. Besides intermittents, the common cause of troubleshooting difficulties is the following of an inaccurate assumption. Untested assumptions should be avoided at all cost. It's therefore advisable to restart Samba after every configuration file change. That way, the system is in a known state, and solid conclusions can be drawn. Because repetitive restarts can be so expensive in time and interruption of work flow, always verify the legality of smb.conf with testparm before restarting Samba.

Not All `smb.conf` Misconfigurations Yield `testparm` Errors

One specific instance is that parameters taking a value that must be in an enumeration (type P_ENUM) do not produce errors. This is because in the loading process, lp_do_parameter() in loadparm.c silently ignores any P_ENUM parameter set to a value outside the enumeration, leaving it at the default value. Therefore, the do_global_checks() function finds nothing wrong.

Also, the testparm program does not pay attention to smbd or nmbd. That's normally a fault isolation advantage, but it can let certain errors slip through.

Using Both `wins support=` and `wins server=`

Because you've read this book, you wouldn't do this. However, if you're called in to troubleshoot someone else's Samba server, you might find that both of these were enabled in an effort to make sure WINS is enabled. In modern versions of Samba, testparm catches this.

SWAT Netscape Error Concerning `lpstat`

This happens in older versions of SWAT. When accessing SWAT from Netscape Navigator, an error message like the following appears:

```
sh: /usr/bin/lpstat: No such file or directory HTTP/1.0 401 Authorization
Required WWW-Authenticate: Basic realm="SWAT" Connection: close Content-Type:
text/html  401 Authorization Required You must be authenticated to use this
service
```

This is caused by the printing=sysv compiled-in default causing default printcap name= value to be lpstat instead of /etc/printcap. This has been observed on a Red Hat installation with a distribution Samba and may happen elsewhere. The solution is to explicitly specify printing=bsd and printcap name=/etc/printcap.

Upload Speed Much Slower Than Download Speed

Check the speed, duplex, and setup of the network card. Check for mismatches between NICs and the rest of the network. The NIC's speed and duplex should match the hub it's connected to, and some cards are more sensitive to this than others. Observe whether

22

TROUBLESHOOTING SAMBA

some clients have this problem while others don't, and find out whether a pattern exists with the network cards. Although this symptom could be caused by a slow disk on the server, suspect network cards first.

If you have `null passwords=yes`, try setting it to `no`.

Other Speed Problems

Samba 2.0.5a inadvertently set `socket options=` to no options, instead of the normal `TCP_NODELAY`. This has been reported to severely degrade Samba performance in certain settings. The solution is to explicitly specify `socket options= TCP_NODELAY`.

Mounted Samba Shares Intermittently Drop

This is an aggravating intermittent problem in Samba 2.0.5a (and maybe earlier versions as well). It seems to have disappeared in 2.0.6, though. Therefore, the solution is to upgrade.

Authentication Breaks When Upgrading from Samba 1.*x*

Samba 1.*x* defaults to `security=share`. Samba 2.0 and later default to `security=user`. If you want to use `share`, explicitly define it in Samba 2.*x*.

Roaming Profiles Are Quirky

Perhaps roaming profiles update from one client but not another, or server-based changes to a profile fail to "take hold." Perhaps roaming profiles simply exhibit seemingly intermittent behavior.

If this is the case, synchronize all clocks. Make sure all clocks have the same date, the same time zone, and the same daylight savings setting. The easiest way is via the following command:

```
C:\WINDOWS>net use time \\servername /set /yes
```

See Chapter 16, "Using Samba as Your Windows 98 Logon Mechanism," for details of logon server time-synchronization issues.

Browsing Frequently Doesn't Work

Check for a browser election war. Temporarily set the main Samba box to `preferred master=no`, `local master=no`, `domain master=no`, `os level=0`, and `wins support=no`. Then see whether the problem lessens.

Source Code Troubleshooting

Source code serves as a troubleshooting tool at many levels. The least technical level is finding something otherwise undocumented. How do the `printing=` and `printcap name=` parameters really default?

Another level might be to recompile and reinstall Samba to verify that the installed binary matches the distribution.

A further level involves running the software through a debugger to see what's going on. A slightly more intrusive variation on this theme is the insertion of debugging statements—after backing up the original source, of course.

Finally, the source can be used to correct a bug or make an improvement.

All forms of source code troubleshooting are relatively time consuming, so it's best to attempt to solve the problem via non-code methods first. However, if non-code methods bog down, the fact that Samba is Open Source provides an escape route to problems that would otherwise be insoluble.

The next chapter, "Samba Learning Tools," presents many tools and techniques to make such source searches quick and effective. It also discusses a few techniques for actual coding changes.

22

TROUBLESHOOTING SAMBA

Summary

The success of troubleshooting any system depends on the use of a valid troubleshooting process. The main steps of most valid troubleshooting processes include acquiring and reproducing the system, performing the quick checks, incrementally narrowing the scope of the root cause, and testing the solution.

Every system brings its own unique properties to the troubleshooting process. Samba neatly encapsulates a very complex system that interoperates the UNIX networking, security, and file system with the ever changing and complex Windows networking, security, and file system. The unique properties of Samba troubleshooting are all positive:

- Samba is highly modular.
- Samba exhibits outstanding reliability.
- Samba has plenty of test points and tools.
- Samba and Linux provide an economical means to create a test jig system.
- Most Samba configuration is done in one place, `smb.conf`.

- Samba has intelligent defaults.
- Samba comes with an extremely useful predefined diagnostic procedure described in `DIAGNOSIS.txt`.
- Samba comes with source code.
- Samba subject matter expertise is easy to obtain.

The troubleshooter who uses the preceding properties to his best advantage finds Samba much easier to troubleshoot than much simpler systems. To make Samba troubleshooting easy and uniform, this chapter proposes the following troubleshooting process:

1. Back up `smb.conf` and any other vulnerable data.
2. Describe and reproduce the symptom.
3. Perform the quick checks.
4. Condense the symptom description.
5. Narrow the scope of the problem.
6. Fix and test.

It's important to note that running the `DIAGNOSIS.txt` test occurs in step 2, because information about which `DIAGNOSIS.txt` test failed is an essential part of any Samba symptom description.

The `DIAGNOSIS.txt` file shipped with Samba contains a 10-test, linear, predefined diagnostic in which later tests use only capabilities verified in earlier tests. This predefined diagnostic dramatically narrows the scope of the problem with less than five minutes testing. This chapter provides a script that runs these tests, in many forms, in less than a minute. The outcome of the tests is recorded in a log for analysis. The automated test adds a test numbered 1.5, which checks for running `smbd` and `nmbd` daemons with the `ps` command.

Samba has many test points and testing tools. This chapter uses the following very simplified model of a Samba system:

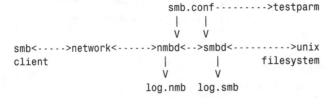

```
                     smb.conf--------->testparm
                         |   |
                         V   V
smb<------>network<------>nmbd<-->smbd<---------->unix
client                    |       |        filesystem
                          V       V
                     log.nmb   log.smb
```

Many Samba diagnostic tools were introduced, each with an ability to measure or inject into a different point of the Samba system. The following are the most important diagnostic tools, all of which were detailed in this chapter:

- nmblookup
- nbtstat
- net view
- net use
- smbstatus
- smbclient
- preexec= and postexec=
- testparm
- SWAT
- strace
- tcpdump
- netstat
- ping
- smbpasswd
- Test jigs

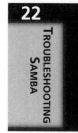

Online help is a substantial advantage to the Samba technologist. It's more of an advantage to some than to others, depending on how they phrase their requests for information. Requests should be framed as being from one member to the other members, not as being from an outsider. The symptom description must tell the most important facts first, because much of the audience has less than a minute to decide what to do with each email. Obvious lack of preparation limits the likelihood of an informative response. And, of course, standard netiquette must be used.

A quick look at any Samba mailing list or newsgroup reveals that Samba troubleshooting can be perceived as very difficult. A closer look at the posts reveals that those having difficulty are not taking advantage of Samba's natural troubleshooting tools, as described in this chapter. Once these tools are known and exploited, most Samba troubleshooting is remarkably simple.

## CHAPTER 23

Samba Learning Tools

by Steve Litt

IN THIS CHAPTER

Samba has an outstanding core group of developers, but that alone is insufficient to explain its phenomenal success. Not even the outstanding product is enough.

A large share of Samba's success is the cadre of thousands of knowledgeable Samba administrators and programmers who find and fix bugs as well as help others get knowledgeable about Samba. The result is huge growth. Most amazing of all is that there are few, if any, formal Samba classes. Instead, Samba administrators and programmers utilize a wide array of powerful learning tools freely available for Samba. This chapter describes some of those tools.

Making Your Own Information Tools

This section describes the creation of information tools. All these tools are contained in a single directory, and they all work correctly only when that directory is the present working directory. The benefit of this is that they form a standalone toolbox not dependent on anything else, and because they're not on the path, they do not clash with identically named scripts outside that directory.

Many of these tools must check that they have one and only one argument. That check can be put in an include file called `syntax1.inc`:

```
[ "$1" != "" ] || { echo NOARG: Syntax: $0 \"parameter name\"; exit }
[ "$2" != "" ] && { echo XS ARGs: Syntax: $0 \"parameter name\"; exit }
```

The preceding can be included at the top of each script. It's called `syntax1.inc`. It exits with a message if called with anything but a single argument.

> **Caution**
>
> Shellscripts are very unforgiving of changes in spacing, line arrangement, and punctuation. Be sure to code these scripts exactly.
>
> Perl and Python are more forgiving and often easier to use. Consider translating these scripts to Perl or Python.

The `testparm`-Based Main Synonym Finder

One challenge of `smb.conf` parameters is the use of synonyms. Although all synonyms are equally valid in an `smb.conf` file, only the main synonym is useful in parsing `testparm` output. Therefore, the first task is to find the main synonym. The following script, called `mainname`, does that quite nicely:

```
#!/bin/sh

. ./syntax1.inc
echo "$1 = 1" > ./temp.conf
testparm -s ./temp.conf > temp1.tmp
echo "$1 = 0" > ./temp.conf
testparm -s ./temp.conf > temp2.tmp

result=$(diff  temp1.tmp temp2.tmp       | \
 head -n2 | tail -n1                      | \
 sed s/\<[[:space:]]*//g                  | \
 sed s/[[:space:]]*=.*$//gi)

[ "$result" != "" ] || result=BADPARAMETER
echo $result
```

The preceding script sets the value of the named parameter first to "1" and then to "0" in an otherwise empty configuration file, and it performs a testparm each time. Note that 1 and 0 are excellent choices because they can represent string parameters, booleans, and even IP address parameters. Even so, there are probably some types of parameters this script will not accurately reveal. printing= is one such parameter. Most P_ENUM type (enumerated-type) parameters fall into this category.

A diff command finds the one and only one changed line, which of course is the main synonym corresponding to the parameter. If a bad parameter name is input, the output is the string BADPARAMETER.

The mainname script often forms the input to other scripts, as in the following example, which determines whether a parameter is global or share:

```
$ ./global.gran "$(./mainname "write ok")"
```

The mainname script is incorporated inside some higher-level informational scripts. Note that there are a few parameters on which mainname malfunctions, including printing=, which it reports as a bad parameter because both 0 and 1 are erroneous values for that parameter, so no change is discerned by testparm.

The testparm-Based Global/Share Distinguisher

The smb.conf man page is not completely accurate in the portrayal of certain parameters as global or share parameters. This is not surprising because there are over 200 possible parameters (not counting synonyms) and because share parameters can be used in the [global] section. Some, such as printing=, usually make more sense in the [global] section.

The most reliable way of deducing whether a parameter is a share or a global parameter is to place it in a share and run testparm, which outputs a specific error message if a global is placed in a share definition. This section describes a script called `global.gran`, which places the parameter (with a legitimate value derived from `testparm` on an empty configuration file) in a share, runs `testparm` on the new config file, detects any error message, and outputs either SHARE, GLOBAL, or BADPARAMETER. Note that this script yields erroneous results if it's not given the primary synonym, so it's usually safest to derive its argument from a call to `mainname`. This is a granular script that can be combined, by a higher level script, with `mainname`. However, certain parameters (`printing=` is an example) yield incorrect results in `mainname`, so occasionally the granular function must be called directly. The following is the `global.gran` script:

```
#!/bin/sh

. ./syntax1.inc

# TEST FOR BAD PARAMETER NAME OR INCOMPLETE PARAMETER NAME
echo > empty.conf
value=$(testparm -s ./empty.conf | grep -i "^[[:space:]]*$1 =")
type="SHARE"
[ "$value" != "" ] || type="BADPARAMETER"

# CREATE TESTING CONF FILE
echo [noshare] > ./temp.conf
echo $value >> ./temp.conf

# DETERMINE GLOBAL OR SHARE
phrase="Global parameter $1 found in service section!"
temp1="$(testparm -s ./temp.conf | grep "$phrase")"
[ "$temp1" != "" ] && type="GLOBAL"

# PRINT THE RESULT
echo $type
```

Once again, the best way to call this is by executing `mainname` as the argument. Note the results of the following three commands:

```
$ ./global.gran "read only"
SHARE

$ ./global.gran "write ok"
BADPARAMETER

$ ./global.gran "$(./mainname "write ok")"
SHARE
$
```

The quotes around `$(./mainname "write ok")` are necessary because `./mainname` `"write ok"` returns the string `read only`, which if not placed in quotes is seen as two separate arguments to `./mainname`.

A simpler command, called `global`, incorporates the call to `mainname` internally:

```
#!/bin/sh
. ./syntax1.inc
./global.gran "$(./mainname "$1")"
```

The following are the results of the preceding command:

```
$ ./global "read only"
SHARE
$ ./global "write ok"
SHARE
$ ./global "printing"
BADPARAMETER
$
```

The final of the three preceding calls demonstrates why the granular function must be available. The `mainname` script cannot accurately process the `printing=` parameter. The proper call for `printing=` is as follows:

```
$ ./global.gran "printing"
SHARE
$
```

The `testparm`-Based Default Displayer

A script can be made to display the default value of a parameter. The script cannot work unless it's passed the primary synonym, so it's a granular script requiring incorporation of `mainname`. The following is the `default.gran` script:

```
#!/bin/bash
. ./syntax1.inc
echo > empty.conf
testparm -s ./empty.conf | grep -i "$1"
```

It's called like this:

```
$ ./default.gran "$(./mainname "write ok")"
```

or

```
$ ./default.gran "printing"
```

In the preceding example, recall that the `mainname` script gives erroneous results for the `printing=` parameter because `printing` cannot be either 0 or 1. For the vast majority of parameters for which `mainname` works, a script can be created to give a simpler command. The following script, called `default`, is an example:

```
#!/bin/bash
. ./syntax1.inc
./default.gran "$(./mainname "$1")"
```

The preceding calls `default.gran` with the primary synonym of `arg1`. The following is the result of running this on the `write ok` parameter using `mainname`:

```
$ ./default "write ok"
        read only = Yes
$ ./default "allow hosts"
        hosts allow =
$
```

The Man Page–Based Synonym Finder

Finding the main synonym from another synonym is quite easy thanks to the translation done by `testparm`. What's much more difficult is finding all synonyms of the main synonym. One way to approach it is to look for instances of the phrase `"synonym for $1"` in the man page, as shown in the following script called `syns`:

```
#!/bin/sh
. ./syntax1.inc
man smb.conf | sed s/^H.//g | grep -iC2 "synonym for \"*$1"
```

The following is an example of its use:

```
$ ./syns "$(./mainname "hosts allow")"
        allow hosts (S)

                Synonym for hosts allow.
$
```

This method is only as reliable as the `smb.conf` man page, whose purpose is not consistent logic.

The preferred method would be to create a small C program that loops through Samba's `parm_table`, outputting the `label` of every array element with the same `ptr` as the desired parameter. It's fairly easy to set up such a program starting with a clone of `testparm`. Be aware, however, that because `parm_table[]` is static, it's not directly accessible outside `loadparm.c`, so you may need to create a small access function in `loadparm.c`.

It's also possible to make a Perl program to parse the table initialization in `param/loadparm.c`, but that's a hack.

Samba-Dedicated Linux Box

The best Samba learning tool is a test jig Linux box running Samba. There's nothing like the `root` password on a nonessential system to bring out the adventurer in us. Some of the quickest learning is done by observing the result of small changes.

Another benefit of a dedicated Linux learning box is the ability to create a share (read-only, one would hope) mapped to the Linux root directory. Then it can be browsed and searched from Windows. Remember to set `follow symlinks=no` to prevent recursion.

Viewing Man Pages in a Browser

The best way to view man pages is in a Web browser. The ability to see large amounts of text and to quickly scroll with a scrollbar is invaluable. It's absolutely essential with huge man pages such as `smb.conf`.

The best way to view "HTML-ized" Samba man pages is using SWAT. SWAT's front page contains links to all the major Samba man pages. Additionally, each parameter on the share, global, and printer pages has a link to its text in a man page.

But sometimes SWAT isn't installed, either because of security concerns or for other reasons. In that case, a CGI script can be written to show man pages in a browser:

```perl
#!/usr/bin/perl -w
use strict;

my($manpage) = $ENV{"QUERY_STRING"};
print `man -C man.conf.man2html $manpage | man2html`;
```

In the preceding script, the "quotes" surrounding the command in the last line are *backticks*. `man2html` is an executable that comes with Red Hat Linux (and maybe other Linux distributions and UNIX versions). On Red Hat Linux 6, it's located in `/usr/bin`. File `man.conf. man2html` is a specially configured copy of `/etc/man.config`. The handlers for `TROFF`, `NROFF`, and `TBL` are changed to `/bin/cat`. Handlers for `EQN` and `NEQN` are commented out, as are the handlers for `REFER`, `PIC`, and `PAGER`. It must also add Samba's man pages to the `MANPATH`.

The preceding script and the `man.conf.man2html` file go in the `cgi-bin` directory for the host, typically `/home/httpd/cgi-bin`. The script can be called anything, so as an example, call it `man.cgi`. Assuming the Linux box is accessible as `http://www.domain.cxm`, the man page for `smb.conf` is accessed as `http://www.domain.cxm/cgi-bin/ man.cgi?smb.conf`. Once again, the Web pages produced by this script are not as good as those available from SWAT. But this script has the advantage of pulling up any man pages, whether they relate to Samba or not.

Read the Source, Luke

As Chapter 6 of the Blue Official Red Hat 5.1 manual states: "Use the Force—read the source!"

This may sound impractical to those not familiar with Open Source software. Many are accustomed to reading proprietary software, which is frequently written first and designed later. Samba source code is very different from the in-house, proprietary software most programmers see.

First, Samba is built very modularly and intelligently. The architecture is clean and strong. Every conceptual building block is coded to stand on its own, to the degree possible. Encapsulation, supposedly difficult in non-object-oriented C, is accomplished very nicely by dividing source files by function and coding "private" variables and functions as `static`. A perfect example is `loadparm.c`, which encapsulates a table holding hundreds of elements, each of which is a nontrivial struct. The table and most functions are static, whereas the few functions required to operate the table are not static and are revealed as externs in `proto.h`.

Form follows function. Samba's data elements and functions are well named and function compliantly with their names. Samba's code is self-documenting, thus relieving the need for gratuitous comments that invariably fall out of sync with the source.

As described in Chapter 5, "Installing Samba," Samba source is available on most Linux distribution source CDs and from the Internet at `www.samba.org`.

All source code searches benefit from keeping a journal of investigated subroutines. This helps one keep the big picture in mind.

Source-Familiarity Tools

This section discusses making a set of source-familiarity tools. They're located in the same directory as the tools previously discussed in the "Making Your Own Information Tools" section. They use some of the same script scraps.

> **Caution**
>
> Shellscripts are very unforgiving of changes in spacing, line arrangement, and punctuation. Be sure to code these scripts exactly.
>
> Perl and Python are more forgiving and often easier to use. Consider translating these scripts to Perl or Python.

The first step in creating the source code–familiarity tools is to create a script scrap, called `setsource.inc`, that defines the location of the source directory:

```
sourcedir=/bldsmb/samba-2.0.6/source
```

The preceding, of course, is for Samba 2.0.6. Also needed is a syntax script scrap to limit these scripts to one argument. The same syntax1.inc used in the testparm tools could be used, but its message mentions "parameter". Instead, make a clone of it with the messages saying "string" instead of "parameter". Call it synstring1.inc:

```
[ "$1" != "" ] || { echo NOARG: Syntax: $0 \"string\"; exit }
[ "$2" != "" ] && { echo XS ARGs: Syntax: $0 \"string\"; exit }
```

grepsrcf

This script takes a single string as an argument and returns all .c and .h files in the source tree (defined by the setsource.inc script scrap) containing that string:

```
#!/bin/bash
. ./synstring1.inc
. ./setsource.inc
find $sourcedir -type f  | grep \.[ch]$ | xargs grep -iEl "$1"
```

The following is an example of its use:

```
$ ./grepsrcf "os level"
/bldsmb/samba-2.0.6/source/param/loadparm.c
$
```

grepsrc

This script is just like grepsrcf, except it also displays the lines possessing the string. This should not be done until the grepsrcf script demonstrates that only a reasonable number of files contain the string. The following is grepsrc:

```
#!/bin/bash
. ./synstring1.inc
. ./setsource.inc
find $sourcedir -type f  | grep \.[ch]$ | xargs grep -iE "$1"
```

The preceding is identical to grepsrcf in every way except that the -l option has been removed from the second grep command. This enables it to display individual lines. The following is an example of its use:

```
$ ./grepsrc "os level"
/bldsmb/samba-2.0.6/source/param/loadparm.c:  {"os level",
➥        P_INTEGER, P_GLOBAL, &Globals.os_level,
➥        NULL,    NULL,  FLAG_BASIC},
$
```

The preceding points to loadparm.c as the source file containing "os level". If that's of interest, loadparm.c can be edited or perused with the less or more command.

23

SAMBA LEARNING TOOLS

cvs.log

The grepsrcf and grepsrc scripts return *where* the string was used, but not *why*. File cvs.log often contains the rationale for changes. The cvs.log command quickly grabs instances containing the string:

```
#!/bin/bash
[ "$1" != "" ] || \
  { echo NOARG: Syntax: $0 \"string\" [context lines]; exit }
[ "$3" != "" ] && \
  { echo XS ARGs: Syntax: $0 \"string\" [context lines]; exit }

context=$2
[ "$2" != "" ] ||  context=0
. ./setsource.inc

#grep -iC$context "$1" $sourcedir/cvs.log | less -N
cat -n $sourcedir/cvs.log |  grep -iEC$context "$1" | less
```

Note that the preceding command scans cvs.log.

grepallf

Sometimes none of the previous searches find the string you were looking for. The grepallf script searches for the string starting at the directory *above* the source directory, because typically the source directory is a subdirectory of the Samba distribution. It searches all files, not just .c and .h files. Because it can output huge volumes, it should be used only after the other scripts fail to find the needed file. The script is coded as follows:

```
#!/bin/bash
. ./synstring1.inc
. ./setsource.inc
grep -iErl $1 $sourcedir/.. | less -N
```

Example: Using the Source Familiarity Tools to Find the Default printing=

The obvious starting place is a search for "printing," which brings up enough data that it must be piped into the less command. Perhaps the most interesting of the bunch is the following from loadparm.c, where it's assigned as the label of a parm_table element:

```
/bldsmb/samba-2.0.6/source/param/loadparm.c:
➥  {"printing",          P_ENUM,     P_LOCAL,
➥  &sDefault.iPrinting,          NULL,  enum_printing,
➥  FLAG_PRINT|FLAG_GLOBAL},
```

A search on `sDefault.iPrinting` brings up only the preceding data, plus one more line from `loadparm.c`:

```
/bldsmb/samba-2.0.6/source/param/loadparm.c:  switch (sDefault.iPrinting)
```

That's probably not where the default value of `printing=` is assigned, because here the parameter determines something else rather than being assigned. Doing a search on just `iPrinting` brings up five lines from `loadparm.c`. It's time to pull up `loadparm.c` in an editor and look for `iPrinting`, keeping in mind that `P_ENUM` and `enum_printing` are also of interest.

The first mention is as an element of a typedef called `service`, so make a note to investigate that later. The next mention is the following at line 410:

```
    DEFAULT_PRINTING, /* iPrinting */
```

This is part of an initiation of a struct. Look up and down to see what that struct is. Sure enough, at line 357 it's `struct service sDefault`. What do you want to bet that the value of `DEFAULT_PRINTING` is being assigned to `sDefault.iPrinting`? So, grep for `DEFAULT_PRINTING`. You get that same line from `loadparm.c` plus several lines from `includes.h`, all of which use `DEFAULT_PRINTING` to the right of a `#define`. Viewing `includes.h`, you see the following starting at line 31:

```
#ifdef AIX
#define DEFAULT_PRINTING PRINT_AIX
#define PRINTCAP_NAME "/etc/qconfig"
#endif

#ifdef HPUX
#define DEFAULT_PRINTING PRINT_HPUX
#endif

#ifdef QNX
#define DEFAULT_PRINTING PRINT_QNX
#endif

#ifdef SUNOS4
/* on SUNOS4 termios.h conflicts with sys/ioctl.h */
#undef HAVE_TERMIOS_H
#endif

#ifdef LINUX
#define DEFAULT_PRINTING PRINT_BSD
#define PRINTCAP_NAME "/etc/printcap"
#endif
```

In the preceding code, if you're running Linux, the printing= parameter is set to the string value of PRINT_BSD, which, as shall be shown later, is the text string bsd. It appears again with this code segment starting at line 683:

```
#ifndef DEFAULT_PRINTING
#ifdef HAVE_LIBCUPS
#define DEFAULT_PRINTING PRINT_CUPS
#define PRINTCAP_NAME "cups"
#elif defined(SYSV)
#define DEFAULT_PRINTING PRINT_SYSV
#define PRINTCAP_NAME "lpstat"
#else
#define DEFAULT_PRINTING PRINT_BSD
#define PRINTCAP_NAME "/etc/printcap"
#endif
#endif
```

Because this code comes later in the includes.h file, it's a pretty good bet that it won't change anything assigned by the code starting at line 31, unless somewhere there's a #undef DEFAULT_PRINTING line. That can be quickly ascertained like this:

```
$ ./grepsrc "#undef[[:space:]]+DEFAULT_PRINTING"
```

The preceding finds nothing. The [[:space:]]+ part means "one or more spaces or other whitespace." So now you can be pretty sure any setting of DEFAULT_PRINTING is done in the section of includes.h starting with line 31. Because it's a Linux box, it's an excellent bet there's a #define LINUX line somewhere. The following command tests that hypothesis:

```
$ ./grepsrc "#define[[:space:]]+LINUX"
/bldsmb/samba-2.0.6/source/passdb/pass_check.c:
➥  #define LINUX_PASSWORD_SEG_CHARS8
/bldsmb/samba-2.0.6/source/include/config.h:
➥  #define LINUX 1
$
```

So it happens in config.h. The final question is whether AIX, HPUX, QNX, or SUNOS4 are defined similarly. The proper grepsrc commands, complete with the regular expression for one or more spaces, shows that they're not.

The last question is, what's the value of PRINT_BSD? It's pretty obvious, but to be sure run this command:

```
$ ./grepallf "#define[[:space:]]+PRINT_BSD"
```

The preceding command brings up nothing, so try this one:

```
$ ./grepsrc "PRINT_BSD"
```

The preceding pulls up a line that's worth investigating:

```
/bldsmb/samba-2.0.6/source/param/loadparm.c:
   {PRINT_HPUX, "hpux"}, {PRINT_BSD, "bsd"},
```

The preceding line turns out to be part of the initiation of enum_printing[].

So that's it. LINUX is defined in config.h. Therefore, the following lines early in includes.h define the values of the printing= and printcap name= parameters:

```
#ifdef LINUX
#define DEFAULT_PRINTING PRINT_BSD
#define PRINTCAP_NAME "/etc/printcap"
#endif
```

The preceding sets the value of DEFAULT_PRINTING to PRINT_BSD, whose value is "bsd". The value of sDefault.iPrinting is set to DEFAULT_PRINTING in the initialization of sDefault in loadparm.c. Finally, in the initiation of parm_table[] in loadparm.c, the record whose label is "printing" is set to sDefault.iPrinting. So in this instance, the default should be printing=bsd.

A verification can be gained by backing up includes.h and temporarily changing

```
#define DEFAULT_PRINTING PRINT_BSD
```

to this:

```
#define DEFAULT_PRINTING PRINT_QNX
```

Perform a make operation and try the resulting testparm against an empty Samba configuration file to see whether the default printing= changes to qnx.

The preceding is a very simple example of source browsing. It would have been easier to use testparm. However, many real-world Samba questions are easiest to answer using the source. The source-browsing tools in this chapter speed such searches.

The Directory Structure

The distribution directory typically "tar-extracts" to something like samba-2.0.6 or whatever's appropriate for the version. For the purpose of discussion, call it distro:

```
distro/
  source/
  packaging/
  docs/
  examples/
  swat/
```

The source subdirectory contains the make files, and in various subdirectories it contains the C code and include files. The docs directory contains all the documentation; the examples subdirectory contains examples, which should obviously be looked at.

However, it's best not to start an actual `smb.conf` with a template using an example from the `examples` tree, because files in that tree explicitly specify far too many parameters. Always let parameters default where practical. Finally, the `swat` directory contains various HTML and images used by SWAT. It does not contain SWAT source, which is instead contained in `distro/source/web`.

manifest

This file in the `distro` directory discusses the files and directories in the distribution. To save grief later on, it's an excellent idea to spend a few minutes looking at these files before taking action. They're very similar to a parts list on a do it yourself project.

roadmap

This file in the `distro` directory discusses the future strategy of the Samba project. This is vitally important because you'll typically map your future Samba usage strategy to the Samba team's future technical strategy. Note that in some releases, especially in "experimental" releases such as the head branch and SAMBA_TNG branch, this file may not be up to date.

packaging/

The `packaging` directory contains files necessary for special configurations, such as building binaries for Red Hat and others. Before building one of these Linux distribution–dependent systems, consider the standard default source code compile consisting of the `./configure`, `make`, and `make install` commands. The standard default source code compile installation method encapsulates Samba in a single tree and enables quick switches between Samba versions. See Chapter 5 for details.

The source Directory

The `source` directory, which is under the `distro` directory, contains all the source code necessary to build Samba. It looks like this:

```
distro/
  source/
    bin/
    client/
    codepages/
    groupdb/
    include/
    lib/
    libsmb/
    locking/
    mem_man/
    nmbd/
```

```
param/
passdb/
printing/
rpc_client/
rpc_parse/
rpc_server/
rpcclient/
script/
smbd/
smbwrapper/
tests/
ubiqx/
utils/
web/
```

This section discusses some of the more important subdirectories under source. It also discusses some important files contained directly in the source directory.

The Make Files

The two best make files to explore are configure and Makefile. The configure file describes all the various build options. You can view them by opening configure with the less pager and searching for string --. This shows the build options and their defaults. Certain options take arguments. You can find these by searching for regular expression --.+=. The configure file creates Makefile from Makefile.in and is described more thoroughly in Chapter 5.

File Makefile is also an excellent learning resource. It can tell you which executables are made and what commands you use to make a single executable. View it with the less pager. The best way to learn from this file is to study the whole thing on one of those rare days when you have too little work.

Some special things to search for are ^install (the caret is the regular expression for "beginning of line"). This shows what's done by the make install command. Searching for clean points out the make clean command and its stronger brothers (realclean, distclean, and the like).

cvs.log

This file contains the change history of Samba and is a vital piece of the puzzle in that it tells *why* changes were made. No source investigation is complete without looking up the appropriate functions and variables in cvs.log.

source/param/

The loadparm.c file in the param/ directory is typically the best place to begin investigations. The source code to load the parm_table[] array is here. parm_table[] is an array of legal `smb.conf` parameters, each with information necessary for use by `smbd`, `testparm`, `swat`, and other programs in the Samba suite. Each array entry is a `struct parm_struct`, which is coded as follows in `smb.h`:

```
struct parm_struct
{
        char *label;
        parm_type type;
        parm_class class;
        void *ptr;
        BOOL (*special)(char *, char **);
        struct enum_list *enum_list;
        unsigned flags;
        union {
                BOOL bvalue;
                int ivalue;
                char *svalue;
                char cvalue;
        } def;
};
```

`label` is the `smb.conf` parameter name synonym, such as `"write ok"` or `"read only"`. `type` is a member of the `parm_type` enum coded in `smb.h`, as follows:

```
typedef enum
{
  P_BOOL,P_BOOLREV,P_CHAR,P_INTEGER,P_OCTAL,
  P_STRING,P_USTRING,P_GSTRING,P_UGSTRING,P_ENUM,P_SEP
} parm_type;
```

`P_BOOL` means "evaluate as a boolean," whereas `P_BOOLREV` means "evaluate as a reverse boolean" (for inverse synonyms, and so on). `P_ENUM` means "evaluate and verify against the enumerated list in the `enum_list` field."

The `class` field is typically `P_GLOBAL` or `P_LOCAL`, which stand for global and share parameters, respectively. There's also a `P_SEPARATOR class` value.

`ptr` is assigned a pointer to the proper value, typically an instance of the `service` struct for share parameters or the `Globals` struct for global parameters.

`special` is a function to be run in association with the parameter. Some parameters that have these functions are `valid chars=`, `include=`, `copy=`, `character set=`, `coding system=`, and `client code page=`.

`enum list` is an enumerated list to check the value of the parameter against, and it's made null except for parameters with type `P_BOOL`.

The loading of this table to default values happens at instantiation with the declaration of `parm_table[]`. The next step is loading it from `smb.conf`. That's accomplished by the `lp_load()` function in `loadparm.c`. `lp_load()` cascades through several function calls, of which `lp_do_parameter()` is of particular interest because this function updates the `sDefault` struct in the case of share parameters in `[global]`, the `Globals` struct in the case of a global parameter, and the appropriate `service` structure in the case of share parameters.

`lp_do_parameter()` first calls the `loadparm.c` function `map_parameter()` to find the index of the first table entry whose label (the `smb.conf` parameter name) is a specific parameter name. Later, it loops through the table again, checking for any other parameters with the same `ptr` elements (synonyms) and updating those the same way the specified parameter name record was updated. This is necessary because the `parm_table[]` is not a "normalized database." If there were a separate synonym table, the second loop would be unnecessary.

`getservicebyname()` returns the service subscript, and it returns the entire service record through a pointer argument.

The `param` subdirectory is an excellent place to start familiarization with Samba. Once an understanding of the contained functions is gained, the `grepsrc` script can be used to find where these functions are used.

Storing Parameter Values

The `parm_table[]` array stores everything about every parameter, *except* its value. A `parm_table[]` element does store a pointer to a value in the `ptr` field. For share parameters, the `ptr` field points to the proper field in an instance of the `service` struct, called `sDefault`. For global parameters, `ptr` points to the proper field in an instance of the `global` struct, called `Globals`.

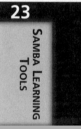

The preceding explains the storage of values for global parameters and for the global default values of share parameters. Values of parameters explicitly specified in share parameters are stored in that share's instance of the `service` struct. These share instances are kept in an array called `ServicePtrs`. It's actually a pointer to `service`, but an array is close enough.

So, here's a simplified description of the evaluation of a share parameter: The parameter's record (element) is found in `parm_table[]`. The displacement of its value into the `sDefault` instance of the `service` struct is found. Then, using the service number, the service's element is found in the `ServicePtrs[]` array. The same displacement is found in the `sServicePtrs[]` element and is evaluated according to the `parm_table[]` element's `type` field.

Most of the preceding is done through macros and function calls, so it may appear different, but from a data point of view first, the share parameter is looked up in its `parm_table[]` entry and then its displacement is found in the known `sDefault` record.

Then, that same displacement is applied to the proper share (service) record, after which that pointer is evaluated according to the rules of `parm_table[parmnumber].type`.

Global parameters are pretty much the same, except they point directly to the `Globals` record, so the displacement arithmetic is not necessary.

include/

The `.h` files are found in the `include` subdirectory. The most valuable to study is `smb.h`. This contains most of the defines, enums, macros, typedefs, and structs used throughout the Samba system. The remainder of the files in this directory are probably better looked at on an as-needed basis and can be found with the `grepsrc` script.

One of the important definitions in `smb.h` is `struct parm_struct`, which comprises each element in `parm_table[]`. `struct parm_struct` has data items of types `parm_type`, `parm_class`, and `enum_list`. All are defined in `smb.h`. `parm_class` and `parm_type` are enumerations, whereas `enum_list` is a struct with a value and name member, designed to map between the two.

smbd

Subdirectory `smbd` contains the many source files for the `smbd` executable. `server.c` has the `main()` function, so an excellent strategy is to start there and descend. This is especially true for file server related code, as opposed to name resolution code.

nmbd

Subdirectory `nmbd` contains the many source files for the `nmbd` executable. `nmbd.c` has the `main()` function, so an excellent strategy is to start there and descend. This is especially true for name resolution code, as opposed to file server–related code.

utils

Subdirectory `utils` contains source code for the various Samba utilities, including `smbrun.c`, `testparm.c`, `nmblookup.c`, `smbpasswd.c`, and many more. `testparm.c` is one of the easiest starting places to learn Samba, because it involves global and share data, and their validation. `testparm.c` also makes an excellent "template" from which to code many new utilities.

web

Subdirectory `web` contains source code for SWAT. The starting point for researching SWAT is `swat.c` in this directory.

Other Interesting Source Code

This list of interesting source code just scratches the surface. The best plan is to use the source-perusing scripts described earlier in this section and track down variables and types.

Testing Your Findings with Source Modifications

The findings in any source exploration are just theories until tested. The ideal test is to change something in the source and determine if the resulting executable's behavior exhibits the expected change. Remember to back up all source files before modifying them, and remember to make the executable. Revert your changes when done, and re-run make to leave the code, directories and files in original condition.

Cloning Existing Programs

If you want to make your own Samba utility, its often best to clone an existing program. The best starting point is often testparm.c. Let's say you want to create a synonym-finding program. You could copy utils/testparm.c to utils/synparm.c. Delete everything from function main() of synparm.c after its call to lp_load() and replace it with a function that calls map_parameter(parmnamestring) to find the parm_table[] index of the parameter. Then, look up the parm_struct element for that index and capture its ptr to another variable. Finally, loop through parm_table[] and output the label field of any elements whose ptr values match the original.

What makes this challenging is that parm_table[] is static, so it's out of scope in your utility source file. You must either find a loadparm.c function to access parm_table[] members or make such a function in loadparm.c.

You can give your new utility program a make file that understands the nuances of the original Makefile but without in any way modifying Makefile, as shown in the following synparm.mak file:

```
include Makefile
PROGS=$(PROGS) /bin/synparm
SYNPARM_OBJ = utils/synparm.o \
              $(PARAM_OBJ) $(UBIQX_OBJ) $(LIB_OBJ)

bin/synparm: $(SYNPARM_OBJ) bin/.dummy
        @echo Linking $@
        @$(CC) $(FLAGS) -o $@ $(SYNPARM_OBJ) $(LDFLAGS) $(LIBS)
```

The preceding make file includes Makefile by reference. Its object and executables are simply clones of testparm (which it was cloned from), with the name testparm changed

23

SAMBA LEARNING
TOOLS

to synparm. If synparm were to be dependent on files other than the ones that `testparm` is dependent on, the `make` file would need to address that fact.

Finally, make synparm with the following command:

```
$ make -f synparm.mak bin/synparm
```

Rather than performing a `make install` operation, just copy the executable to the executable directory.

Experimentation

Experimentation produces some of the quickest and best learning, especially in conjunction with the "Read the Fascinating Manual" technique. If experimentation is the strategy, trivial cases, tiny changes, and exploiting the differences are the tactics.

Trivial Cases

The mammoth "example" `smb.conf` files shipped with every Samba distribution can have the counterintuitive effect of stifling learning. Although these `smb.conf` files are excellent learning tools, a problem arises if those files are used as templates for creating real systems. With so many parameters exposed, the effects of the most important parameters are masked by a pile of other parameters. For example, is the share inaccessible because of a valid `users=`, or `hosts allow=`, or `hosts deny=`, or `interfaces=`?

The best learning takes place in an environment of minimal variables. We're lucky that Samba's defaults are so intelligently thought out. Whenever possible, do your learning with the smallest possible `smb.conf`.

Tiny Changes

Learning occurs when effect is assigned to cause. This is most effective when each change is tiny. Ten tiny changes at 5 minutes apiece take 50 minutes. An equivalent amount of learning using large changes could take hours.

Not only do tiny changes result in faster learning but also more accurate learning. Multivariable changes are often accompanied by guess and superstition. Single-variable changes result predominantly in complete and confident knowledge.

Exploiting Differences

The best understanding takes place when a change of one variable creates a change in the result. By exploiting differences, the exact causation can be determined. This is an extremely powerful troubleshooting tool.

Joining the Samba Project

The ultimate path to Samba knowledge is to be in the inner circle of Samba development.

Here's a direct quote from the Samba.org Web site:

> The Samba Team is a loose-knit group of about 20 people from all over the world who contribute regularly to Samba and have direct write access to the Samba CVS tree.

The Samba team is a pretty select group of people. Therefore, the obvious question is, how does one get on the team?

Again, here's another quote from the Samba.org Web site

> If you want to become a member of the team then the first thing you should do is join the samba-technical mailing list and start contributing to the development of Samba.

As with any list, an introductory period of "lurking" is best. Merely joining the `samba-technical@samba.org` mailing list allows you to see discussions among the top Samba brains in the world. Code is regularly discussed here.

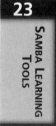

The next step might be to submit bug fixes. As of late 1999, the bug-submission procedures are changing, with `samba-bugs@samba.org` no longer being the preferred place to post bugs. It might be best to ask on `samba-technical@samba.org` where to post your bug.

If you're a C programmer, a good debugger, and knowledgeable in Samba internals, you can post bug fixes you find. Here's a quote from the `BUGS.txt` file:

> The best sort of bug report is one that includes a fix! If you send us patches please use "diff -u" format if your version of diff supports it, otherwise use "diff -c4". Make sure your do the diff against a clean version of the source and let me know exactly what version you used.

There may be only 20 members of the Samba team, but far more regularly contribute. There's no better source of advanced Samba knowledge than `samba-technical@samba.org`.

SWAT as a Learning Tool

SWAT is one of the handiest and most thorough learning tools. It offers access to special hyperlinked, HTMLized man pages, and it shows unspecified parameters accurately, unlike most other tools.

SWAT has the capability to trash a custom-crafted `smb.conf` with a mouse click. When using SWAT as a learning tool, it should be used in a read-only mode. The steps to do this are explained in Chapter 13, "Using Samba Web Administration Tool (SWAT) for Samba Configuration."

The Distribution Documentation

You get much more than source code with a Samba download. Untarring the distribution yields a `docs` directory brimming with Samba information. Major documentation directories include the `docs/textdocs` and `docs/faq` directories.

docs/textdocs

The `docs/textdocs` directory contains many useful files. This section discusses those that make the best learning tools:

- `DOMAIN.txt`
- `DOMAIN_CONTROL.txt`
- `DOMAIN_MEMBER.txt`
- `BROWSING.txt`
- `BROWSING-Config.txt`
- `SSLeay.txt`
- `UNIX-SMB.txt`
- `UNIX_INSTALL.txt`
- `UNIX_SECURITY.txt`
- `cifsntdomain.txt`
- `Application_Serving.txt`
- `Faxing.txt`
- `GOTCHAS.txt`

DOMAIN.txt, DOMAIN_CONTROL.txt, and DOMAIN_MEMBER.txt

These three files spell out, in great detail, using Samba as a logon and authentication server as well as joining it to an existing NT domain. Combined with this book's Chapters 11, "Working with Windows 2000," 16, "Using Samba as Your Windows 98 Logon Mechanism," and 17, "Using Samba as the NT Primary Domain Controller" as well as the information gathering techniques discussed in this chapter, these documents are powerful sources of domain technological information.

BROWSING.txt and BROWSING-Config.txt

Browsing can be a constant source of support challenge in an SMB-enabled network, which is why chapters 32, "Local-Subnet Browsing," 33, "Cross-Subnet Browsing," and 34, "Windows Internet Naming Service (WINS)" are devoted to browsing issues, and chapter 7, "Determining Samba Access,"contains voluminous information on browsing.

The BROWSING.txt and BROWSING-Config.txt files are an excellent additional information source. They are very concise, making an excellent quick lookup. These files discuss all aspects of browsing, WINS, rigging browser elections, and all sorts of WINS and browsing configurations.

SSLeay.txt

If you use SSL or want to in the near future, read this document. It covers including SSL in Samba, certificates, and many other SSL-related subjects. With the advent of OpenSSL, it's likely that this file will be substantially revised for OpenSSL, or possibly renamed.

UNIX*.txt

Files UNIX-SMB.txt, UNIX_INSTALL.txt, and UNIX_SECURITY.txt are excellent resources for administrators who know UNIX but are weaker in Windows or know Windows but are weaker in UNIX. They explain various concerns and considerations from a UNIX point of view. Specific areas of discussion include

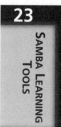

- Usernames, passwords, and file ownership
- File locking and deny modes
- Trapdoor IDs
- Ports and protocols
- An eight-step Samba installation process
- Installation troubleshooting

cifsntdomain.txt

This is a deeply technical discussion of Samba PDC that would take 24 pages if printed on paper. This is an excellent read for the NT domain–savvy reader or the reader who wants to become NT domain savvy. This is very advanced material, written for a reader with a detailed knowledge of C, data structures, Windows networking, and communication protocol.

Application_Serving.txt

If you're interested in installing Microsoft Office on your Samba server, this is the document to read. Note that it was written in 1998, so it will become increasingly out of date unless revised.

Faxing.txt

This document explains how to turn your Samba server into a fax server. It includes source code changes, configuration, and creating a fax queue in /etc/printcap. The installation and configuration instructions are very thorough. Although there are many other faxing solutions, this one is attractive due to being Open Source.

GOTCHAS.txt

This document describes problems when Samba is used as a logon server in an environment that includes NT Server machines. It ultimately advises not to use Samba as a logon server in mixed environments.

docs/faq

This directory contains three FAQs (Frequently Asked Questions). They're rather introductory but a good resource nonetheless. This directory contains three web documents, whose starting points are:

- Samba-meta-FAQ.html
- sambafaq.html
- Samba-Server-FAQ.html

The Samba meta FAQ, Samba-meta-FAQ.html might be the best starting point for those new to Samba. It contains a quick-start section and a standard FAQ that includes "What Is It?," "Where Do I Get It?," and "Who Do I Complain To?" sections. It discusses the basics of SMB/CIFS and the basics of CIFS network design. Its usefulness is slightly marred by the fact that hyperlinks to the text documents do not resolve in the standard distribution file structure. Nevertheless, it's an excellent starting point.

The main Samba FAQ, sambafaq.html gives several questions and answers. Once again, it's primary value is to beginners. That being said, it can probably save a seasoned veteran from at least one silly mistake.

The Samba server FAQ, Samba-Server-FAQ.html is a symptom and solution guide for various server issues. It's a good bet that knowledge of this information can lead to quicker solutions in selected troubleshooting situations.

Man Pages

The ultimate Samba reference is the `smb.conf` man page. This man page describes every `smb.conf` parameter. It's a must-read for anyone determined to gain Samba expertise.

The `smbclient` man page is a vital resource for heavy users of the `smbclient` utility. It gives excellent coverage of this utility.

The `smbpasswd` man page comes in handy for extended use of `smbpasswd`, such as joining an NT domain.

Other man pages, such as `testparm (1)`, `testprns (1)`, `smbd (8)`, `nmbd (8)`, `smbpasswd (5)`, `smbpasswd (8)`, `nmblookup (1)`, `inetd (8)`, and `hosts_access (5)`, can be handy for looking up specific information.

Web Sites, Newsgroups, and Mailing Lists

Voluminous Samba information is available on the Internet. This section covers some of the most pertinent. Many of these resources come from the Samba project under their `samba.org` domain.

RFCs

Much of networking's protocol and behavior is specified by RFCs. RFC stands for *Request for Comments*. RFC 1001 and RFC 1002 are especially vital to Samba because they define the behavior of NetBIOS. RFCs are available all over the Internet. Which site you pick depends on your needs.

`http://ietf.org/rfc/` is the ultimate source of RFCs, from the Internet Engineering Task Force (IETF). All RFCs are listed by number, so if you know the number you're looking for, this is where to go.

`http://www.rfc-editor.org/rfc.html` is where you go if you don't know the number. It has links to various sites capable of finding RFCs when you don't know exactly what you're looking for.

The Samba Web site has RFC 1001 and RFC 1002 at `http://us1.samba.org/samba/ftp/SMB-info/rfc1001.txt` and `http://us1.samba.org/samba/ftp/SMB-info/rfc1002.txt`.

23

SAMBA LEARNING TOOLS

`samba.org` Web Resources

The Samba project's Web resources are available under the domain name `samba.org`. This is your first Internet stop for Samba information. It contains large amounts of Samba information and downloads. The `www.samba.org` URL contains links, organized by region, for all Samba html and ftp mirrors. The Web site is large and its links are not completely hierarchical, so it's sometimes difficult to find what you're looking for. This section lists some of the most commonly sought `samba.org` information. Additionally, the Web site provides a search facility. The search facility is particularly handy for finding information in the email archives.

This Web site has archives for its mailing lists. Those archives are searchable, but the searches frequently don't pull up all the relevant information. This information can also be accessed via `www.deja.com`.

To see the CIFS specification, go to `http://samba.org/cifs/`. It's a series of links to CIFS information, including a Microsoft document at `http://msdn.microsoft.com/workshop/networking/cifs/default.asp?`.

`http://samba.org/cvs.html` is where you get absolutely up-to-the-minute Samba source code. `http://sernet.pair.com` is a Web site run by the Samba project, containing a new `.tar.gz` of Samba 2.1 daily. It's unknown how long this practice will continue, but it exists for the time being. If you find a single file easier to download, this is the place to go.

The Samba project FTP sites can be accessed by clicking one of the FTP mirror links on the Samba home page at `http://www.samba.org`. For instance, clicking the second U.S. mirror brings you to `http://us1.samba.org/samba/ftp/`. From there you can download Samba, as discussed in Chapter 5. You can also download binary versions of Samba, and utilities such as the Samba aware `tcpdump` program. You can also download the latest documentation here.

`samba.org` Mailing Lists

The crown jewels of `samba.org` are its mailing lists. These are the best Samba discussions on the Internet. If you're interested in Samba and NT domains, join `samba-ntdom@samba.org`. This is where technical to highly technical questions on Samba as an NT domain, as well as SAMBA_TNG (the new code branch supporting NT PDC and RPC), are asked and answered. Typically this list stops short of detailed source code discussions.

For detailed source code discussions and highly technical questions and information, join `samba-technical@samba.org`. Much of the discussion and planning of SAMBA_TNG goes on here. This is the list where Samba source code intricacies are discussed, and source level troubleshooting is done. This is where you can listen to the people who develop Samba. This list is the first step toward becoming a part of the Samba project. If you want to become a member of the exclusive Samba team (please remember there are fewer members of the Samba team than there are presidents of industrial countries), this list is where you start.

`samba-announce@samba.org` sends all announcements. There are several other mailing lists. Instructions for subscribing and unsubscribing are contained at `http://lists.samba.org`.

comp.protocols.smb

This is a great Samba newsgroup that yields great information.

Search Engines

Search engines are valuable in tracking down information. Searching on error message text is especially helpful. The `www.deja.com` Web site is especially handy, because you can type in an exact error message and search for newsgroup posts of others who have had the exact same problem.

Summary

There are a wide variety of learning tools for Samba. They include scripts, test jig Linux/Samba boxes, Samba source, SWAT, and various Internet sources, including access to the movers and shakers in the Samba world.

You make some Samba learning tools yourself. This chapter contains a script called `mainname` for finding the main synonym of an `smb.conf` parameter, one called `global` for determining whether a parameter is a global or share parameter, and one called `default` for showing the default value of a parameter. A script called `syns` can sometimes be useful for finding synonyms of a parameter, but because it's based on the imprecise (in wording, not meaning) `smb.conf` man page, it's only partially accurate.

A dedicated Linux Samba server is an ideal learning tool due to its ability to accommodate modifications without the worries of a production server and because it can be used to serve up all its directories, including documentation, as Samba shares suitable for searching in Windows Explorer. A Linux box with a running version of Apache can also be used to serve up man pages in a Web browser. The CGI script to do this is found in this chapter.

Samba's source code is the ultimate learning tool. Samba's source is clean, modular, and easy to read. This chapter contains several scripts used to speed working with source code. These include `grepsrcf`, which finds filenames of all source containing a phrase, and `grepsrc`, which finds not just the filenames but the source lines containing the phrase. Also featured is a script called `cvslog`, which grabs lines out of the `cvs.log` file containing a phrase as well as lines before and after that line so it can be seen in context. If none of the preceding scripts finds the phrase, the `grepallf` script can be used to locate any file in the entire Samba distribution containing the phrase. These tools can take regular expressions and make quick work of source investigations.

Some files especially worth investigating are `configure`, `Makefile.in`, and `cvs.log`. The source tree is contained in a directory called `source` below the distribution directory. Of special interest here is `param/loadparm.c`, `include/smb.h`, `smbd/server.c`, `nmbd/nmbd.c`, `utils/testparm.c`, `utils/nmblookup.c`, `utils/smbpasswd.c`, and `web/swat.c`.

Once source code perusal has led to a hypothesis, that hypothesis can be tested by a change to the proper source file. The original file must always be backed up, and when experimentation is complete, all changes must be reverted unless the experimentation has led to a bug fix or a genuine improvement, in which case you'll want to make a `diff -u` patch.

Another excellent use of the source is the cloning of existing programs. One excellent starting point for utilities is to clone `testparm.c`. Once modifications have been made, a tiny make file can be created for the new program. The tiny make file starts with `include Makefile` so that it complies with everything configured in by the original `./configure` command.

Various types of experimentation are a great source of learning. These include trivial cases, tiny changes, and exploiting differences.

Although most of us never get on the official Samba team, those of us willing to contribute to the Samba project can do so, first in the form of participation in the `samba-technical@samba.org` mailing list, then with patches of bug lists, and finally, possibly by coding programs. This is the way to go beyond the knowledge in any book or Web site.

SWAT is a powerful learning tool due to its access to hyperlinked HTML man files and other documentation as well as its ability to view the content and meaning of `smb.conf`. Other documentation is included with the distribution, including the `textdocs` directory. Man pages round out the docs included with Samba.

The Internet is the research tool of choice. Start with the `www.samba.org` Web site, the `comp.protocols.smb` newsgroup, and the many mailing lists at Samba.org. The RFC files are available at `http://ietf.org/rfc/`. Some Samba experimental code can be found at `http://sernet.pair.com`. Search engines round out the Samba research capabilities of the Internet.

This rich set of learning tools guarantees that an intelligent and hard-working technologist can solve any Samba problems he or she encounters, as well as guaranteeing a steady stream of capable Samba technologists. This is one of the reasons Samba has succeeded in the past and will succeed in the future.

Enterprise Samba

PART

III

IN THIS PART

Adding a Samba Server to an NT Network

by Mitch Adair and Glenda Snodgrass

IN THIS CHAPTER

Reasons for Adding a Samba Server to an NT Network

Why would you add a Samba server to an NT network? Why do you want a Samba server at all? Better still, why have it interact with your NT servers? All valid questions, particularly if you don't already have UNIX and Linux servers in your environment—questions you should ask yourself before you begin. Even if you have Samba servers running now, you may wonder why you would want to go to the trouble of integrating them into an existing NT domain. This chapter tries to answer these questions. We'll go over the reasons for adding Samba servers to your NT network and how to make your Samba and NT servers play nice together. Ultimately this will make your network more reliable, functional, and effective.

The reasons for adding Samba servers are obvious for current UNIX and Linux users. They provide an extremely cost-effective solution for adding extra server capacity. For file and print server duties, older PCs that could never withstand NT can be recycled into reliable and reasonably quick platforms. Indeed, the Samba/Linux combination is renowned for its efficiencies. An old 386 or 486 can generally be turned into a more stable and effective print server, for example, than new and more expensive equipment running NT. Likewise, with the addition of a Samba server, you get a UNIX/Linux box that can be used for other intranet duties—Web server, DNS, mail, and so forth. There should be no problem loading your server up with several of these services and still enjoying the long uptimes—months and even years—and good performance that the combination is known for.

Another consideration is the simple convenience of having all your computers—UNIX/Linux workstations or NT and Windows PCs—able to share files, printing, and information easily over your network. Nearly all UNIX and UNIX-like computers already have this capacity using NFS (Network File System). Most small-to-medium-sized businesses, and even some larger ones, are not predominately comprised of UNIX workstations and servers. Quite the opposite, in fact. In those Windows-centric environments, it makes sense to equip the UNIX workstations and servers with Samba to allow communication between the two. Although NFS implementations exist for the Windows environment, most if not all are commercial applications, adding cost in both outright purchasing as well as installation and support. Therefore, in many instances, it makes more sense to get the UNIX boxes talking the Windows computers' language—with Samba.

Once you've got your Samba servers up and running though, why should you bother with integrating them into your NT domain? That question is largely answered by the reasoning for having NT domain and other network login and information services at all. With the NT domain, you get access to a distributed authentication system that can allow you to access multiple network resources with only a single logon. Network administrators get the benefits of consolidated administration and a consistent authentication scheme among diverse computing resources. In addition, administrators get enhanced security of encrypted passwords over the network, automatic finding of logon resources for clients, and redundancy of a replicated authentication database. In fact, not all of this is currently supported in the 2.0 Samba releases, but support for all features of the NT domain model are planned. In some of these areas, in spite of the hype, the implementation of the domain architecture in NT has not been without its flaws. Still, the domain architecture does have its obvious advantages. Given, too, the limited support for integrating current NT 4.0 into other distributed services, such as NIS/NIS+, and the even lesser likelihood that most Windows-centric shops would want to or be able to use alternatives, if you want distributed authentication and the like in Windows, you have to use the NT domain. If you want the NT domain with Linux and most UNIX flavors, you'll need to use Samba.

Another important point in Samba's favor is that it is Open Source software. For some people, this alone is a major consideration—either for their own philosophical reasons or just because they like to know they have a chance to actually fix their own problems should some crop up. What is perhaps an even more important consideration, however, is that Samba represents an open repository of information on the subject of NetBIOS/Windows networking. Because it needs to interact with other NetBIOS implementations, Samba itself turns out to be a remarkable diagnostic and information-gathering tool on the state of a Windows network. It's almost universally the case that the information provided by Samba logging and diagnostic tools provides a more accurate view of what's happening on the network than most any other tools available, and certainly those available to most Windows users. The documentation provided by Samba is also exceedingly helpful and informative. Perhaps the best thing you get from the Samba package is the knowledge of how all the pieces and protocols really work in a NetBIOS/Windows/CIFS environment.

All these reasons add up to compelling arguments for installing Samba servers on your network and getting them communicating and working together with your existing NT domain. What follows is a comprehensive and understandable explanation of how to do just that.

24

ADDING A SAMBA
SERVER TO AN NT
NETWORK

Joining an NT Domain with Samba 2.0

If you want your Samba server to operate like the NT Server and Workstation machines on your network, you'll need to add them to your NT domain. Without this, the trust relationships between servers and the distributed authentication will not be available to you.

Add the Samba Server NetBIOS Name to the PDC

Oddly enough, your first steps in adding a Samba server to your NT domain will be taken at the console of an NT machine. This is because you have to add the Samba server's name to the Domain Security Access Manager (SAM) database. The SAM database maintains not only lists of users and passwords but also the names and keys of the servers that are allowed to operate and authenticate in the domain. The SAM database of interest resides on the primary domain controller (PDC). This computer is the repository for the master SAM database. The PDC's SAM database is then replicated (read-only) to backup domain controllers (BDCs). This way, if anything happens to the PDC to make it inaccessible, network resources can still be used by authenticating against one of the BDCs. This SAM database is then used by all clients to authenticate against—for example, for logging in to the domain and accessing resources.

So, on the PDC, you or some administrator for the PDC will have to add the name of your Samba server into the SAM database. On NT, this is done using the Server Manager for Domains, which can be started by going to the Start menu and selecting Programs, Administrative Tools (Common), Server Manager for Domains. From there, you should create a machine account for an NT Workstation or Server machine. You should not add the Samba server as a backup or primary domain controller, because in Samba 2.0, at least, this won't work.

Use `smbpasswd` to Join the Domain

Now that you have an account for your machine in the PDC SAM database, go to your Samba server and ensure that Samba is not running. Once Samba has been shut down (specifically, no `smnd` or `nmbd` processes should be running), you can add your Samba server to the NT domain using the `smbpasswd` program. You must run the following command as `root` to join the domain:

```
# smbpasswd -j DOMAIN_NAME -r DOMAIN_PDC
```

If this is successful, the `smbpasswd` program will return the following:

`smbpasswd: Joined domain DOMAIN_NAME.`

This will result in a machine account file being created by `smbpasswd` where Samba keeps its configuration and password files. This file is owned by `root` and is read-only. It will be called `DOMAIN_NAME.MACHINE_NAME.mac`.

Changes to `smb.conf`

Once the account is set up for the NT domain, some changes will need to be made to the default Samba configuration. We'll look at the defaults included in the `examples/smb.conf.default` file with Samba and how these must be changed to allow your server to work in its new NT domain.

Listing 24.1 shows the global settings in the `smb.conf.default` file. Remember that the pound (#) and semicolon (;) characters are used to comment out lines in the `smb.conf` file.

LISTING 24.1   `smb.conf.default`

```
#=========================== Global Settings ===========================
[global]

# workgroup = NT-Domain-Name or Workgroup-Name, eg: REDHAT4
   workgroup = MYGROUP

# server string is the equivalent of the NT Description field
   server string = Samba Server

# This option is important for security. It allows you to restrict
# connections to machines which are on your local network. The
# following example restricts access to two C class networks and
# the "loopback" interface. For more examples of the syntax see
# the smb.conf man page
;   hosts allow = 192.168.1. 192.168.2. 127.

# If you want to automatically load your printer list rather
# than setting them up individually then you'll need this
   load printers = yes

# you may wish to override the location of the printcap file
;   printcap name = /etc/printcap

# on SystemV system setting printcap name to lpstat should allow
# you to automatically obtain a printer list from the SystemV spool
# system
;   printcap name = lpstat
```

continues

24

ADDING A SAMBA
SERVER TO AN NT
NETWORK

LISTING 24.1   continued

```
# It should not be necessary to specify the print system type unless
# it is non-standard. Currently supported print systems include:
# bsd, sysv, plp, lprng, aix, hpux, qnx
;    printing = bsd

# Uncomment this if you want a guest account, you must add this to /etc/passwd
# otherwise the user "nobody" is used
;   guest account = pcguest

# this tells Samba to use a separate log file for each machine
# that connects
    log file = /usr/local/Samba/var/log.%m

# Put a capping on the size of the log files (in Kb).
    max log size = 50

# Security mode. Most people will want user level security. See
# security_level.txt for details.
    security = user
# Use password server option only with security = server
;    password server = <NT-Server-Name>

# You may wish to use password encryption. Please read
# ENCRYPTION.txt, Win95.txt and WinNT.txt in the Samba documentation.
# Do not enable this option unless you have read those documents
;   encrypt passwords = yes

# Using the following line enables you to customise your configuration
# on a per machine basis. The %m gets replaced with the netbios name
# of the machine that is connecting
;    include = /usr/local/Samba/lib/smb.conf.%m

# Most people will find that this option gives better performance.
# See speed.txt and the manual pages for details
    socket options = TCP_NODELAY

# Configure Samba to use multiple interfaces
# If you have multiple network interfaces then you must list them
# here. See the man page for details.
;    interfaces = 192.168.12.2/24 192.168.13.2/24

# Browser Control Options:
# set local master to no if you don't want Samba to become a master
# browser on your network. Otherwise the normal election rules apply
;    local master = no
```

```
# OS Level determines the precedence of this server in master browser
# elections. The default value should be reasonable
;    os level = 33

# Domain Master specifies Samba to be the Domain Master Browser. This
# allows Samba to collate browse lists between subnets. Don't use this
# if you already have a Windows NT domain controller doing this job
;    domain master = yes

# Preferred Master causes Samba to force a local browser election on startup
# and gives it a slightly higher chance of winning the election
;    preferred master = yes

# Use only if you have an NT server on your network that has been
# configured at install time to be a primary domain controller.
;    domain controller = <NT-Domain-Controller-SMBName>

# Enable this if you want Samba to be a domain logon server for
# Windows95 workstations.
;    domain logons = yes

# if you enable domain logons then you may want a per-machine or
# per user logon script
# run a specific logon batch file per workstation (machine)
;    logon script = %m.bat
# run a specific logon batch file per username
;    logon script = %U.bat

# Where to store roving profiles (only for Win95 and WinNT)
#        %L substitutes for this servers netbios name, %U is username
#        You must uncomment the [Profiles] share below
;    logon path = \\%L\Profiles\%U

# Windows Internet Name Serving Support Section:
# WINS Support - Tells the NMBD component of Samba to enable it's WINS Server
;    wins support = yes

# WINS Server - Tells the NMBD components of Samba to be a WINS Client
#        Note: Samba can be either a WINS Server, or a WINS Client, but NOT both
;    wins server = w.x.y.z

# WINS Proxy - Tells Samba to answer name resolution queries on
# behalf of a non WINS capable client, for this to work there must be
# at least one  WINS Server on the network. The default is NO.
;    wins proxy = yes

# DNS Proxy - tells Samba whether or not to try to resolve NetBIOS names
# via DNS nslookups. The built-in default for versions 1.9.17 is yes,
# this has been changed in version 1.9.18 to no.
    dns proxy = no
```

The first change you need to make is setting the correct domain name for your server. You do this by changing the workgroup line

```
workgroup = MYGROUP
```

which is near the top of the file, to this:

```
    workgroup = MY_DOMAIN_NAME
```

You then need to change the security mode over to domain security. Change the line

```
    security = user
```

to this:

```
    security = domain
```

You then need to set what servers you will authenticate against when you log into the domain. To do so, change the line

```
;    password server = <NT-Server-Name>
```

to this:

```
    password server = NT_PDC_SERVER NT_BDC_SERVER NT_BDC_SERVER_2
```

From Samba version 2.0.6, you can also set the `password server` option as follows:

```
    password server = *
```

This setting will allow your Samba server to use broadcasts or WINS to find the first available NT PDC or BDC and authenticate against it. This works in the same way NT and Windows clients do, and it requires less maintenance of the Samba configuration file if the PDC or BDCs change. This could be a big help in preventing surprise and mysterious breakages of your Samba server, such as when somebody changes NT servers and doesn't tell you.

Next, you must make sure you're using encrypted passwords. Change the line

```
;    encrypt passwords = yes
```

to this:

```
    encrypt passwords = yes
```

Then, if you're using WINS, be sure to change

```
;    wins server = w.x.y.z
```

to this:

```
    wins server = 192.168.1.1 [NOTE: this should be the WINS IPnumber]
```

This is especially important if you've set the `password server` = option to `*`.

Now when you restart Samba, you should have a fully functioning member of your NT domain.

Linux and NT Distinctions

Although Samba tries hard to provide a seamless implementation of Windows networking, there are instances where the underlying differences between Linux/UNIX and Windows NT show through. Probably the most prominent are the differing views on security and identity. UNIX and NT security models bear only a passing resemblance to each other, which sometimes requires extra effort on behalf of either OS to make everything work together.

Broadly speaking, the NT security model is governed by Access Control Lists (ACLs), where all components of the server are thought of as *objects* upon which ACL rules, governing who can do what to these objects, are placed. Although there are groups in the NT security model, they are really more like groupings of policies with users; they don't map to a completely separate structure. The lack of separate groups and the mapping of NT ACLs onto UNIX permissions can prove problematic.

UNIX has a separate structure for users and groups. In the "everything is a file" UNIX ideology, permissions are maintained on the file system, with separate read, write, and execute bits for the files `User` (owner), `Group`, and `Other` (everybody else). It's important to keep this in mind. Even when it appears that you can set the same permissions in NT and UNIX (both have a read permission, for example), this is not necessarily the case. Don't just trust that the same or similar names mean the same thing. NT and UNIX work from different security models, and there's no requirement that they treat those names the same way. Samba tries to work around this where it can, by ignoring security bits from NT that don't translate to UNIX, for example, but it can't work around everything. This largely explains the need in current Samba releases for a UNIX/`smbpasswd` account on a UNIX server after it has joined an NT domain. It's currently the only way to properly map groups and permissions in UNIX while the Samba team works to complete NT domain integration.

Another important consideration along these lines is to not break the NT server working as a PDC or BDC when you set up your Samba server. Breaking your network so that nobody can log on or access network resources is not likely to put you or Samba in a very good light. Specifically, Windows NT has problems with servers claiming to be a PDC or domain master browser (DMB) when it thinks it should be one. If you already have NT servers working as PDCs, DMBs, and WINS servers, it's generally best to let them continue. Another server winning a master browser election or claiming to be the primary WINS server when an NT server is already doing the job is likely to wreak untold havoc and misery. Worse, it's possible that everything would continue working fine until the NT server in question gets rebooted, at which point it likely will refuse to resume its duties until your Samba server lets it. Samba works extremely well as a DMB and WINS server, but if you already have an NT server assigned to these functions, don't disrupt it. Be sure to double-check that configuration file.

Replacing an Existing NT Server

Samba servers provide the best value going for serving Windows networking clients. Many people find that once they've used Samba for a while, they want to use Samba to replace NT and Windows computers that are reaching the end of their lives or that have been problematic for some reason. Samba's ability (along with Linux) to run on a wide range of hardware make it a perfect fit in replacing NT servers. However, a few important steps need to be taken to get the replacement right.

Document the Existing Network

There's nothing worse than getting halfway through formatting a hard drive and realizing you needed something important off it. Don't let this happen to you. You'll want to be absolutely positive that you know exactly what features of the present NT server you want to replicate and what information you need to get off it. Its position in the current NT domain is important, too. Is it your WINS server or just a printer server? If it performs a fundamental function, such as WINS or DMB, you'll have to plan for the outage its loss may cause or for a spare to be in place. All the shares, all the printers and their exact names are very important. You don't want to reconfigure dozens of client machines with new share names if you don't have to. Take your time, get all the information ahead of time, and you'll save yourself a lot of headaches.

Set Up the Linux Server

Once you have all the information from the old NT server written down, it's time to duplicate it on your Samba server. All the shares will need their own definitions in the `smb.conf` file. All the printer shares can be loaded, once set up in the `/etc/printcap` file (or a similar file, depending on your UNIX), by using the `load printers = yes` option. To reiterate, be sure you have the settings correct for the responsibility of this server in the domain: The `os level`, `local master`, `domain master`, `domain logons`, and `wins server` options are critical here.

Copy Users and Groups

Once your Samba server is set up correctly for serving shares and printers, you need to move over the user and group information from the NT server. One way to do this, for smaller numbers of users and groups, is to manually add the users and groups and then run smbpasswd (or one of the shell script wrappers, such as mksmbpasswd.sh) to load the smbpasswd file. For a large domain, you might take a look at the pwdump utility on the samba.org site. This program will take an NT SAM database and dump it into smbpasswd format for you. Obviously you'll need to have administrator access to some PDC or BDC and be allowed to dump the database information.

Move Files and Print Spools

Now that users are set up, you can move over the actual files in the shares. Once you're sure the Samba server is a replica of the former NT server, you'll want your server to join the NT domain, as described previously. When your server has successfully joined your domain, you then want to double-check all the config files and test the server to make sure it exactly duplicates the former server. If you run into problems, see the "Troubleshooting" section, later in the chapter. Barring any problems, however, it's time to shut down the old NT server and put your new Samba server in as its replacement.

Security Issues

An important consideration when dealing with NT domains is that they're based on trust relationships. Access to network resources and the fundamental security of all the servers in a domain are tied to each server's understanding of which servers and users it is connected to and what authority those connected have. Once any server in a group of servers in a trust relationship is compromised, it becomes relatively easy to compromise the other servers.

For this reason, it's important to maintain the integrity of the SAM database and be vigilant in the upkeep of the security of the NT and Samba servers. Because someone with elevated privilege on one computer can have elevated privilege on other computers, due to the distributed nature of the authentication database and the trust relationships, to compromise of the SAM database would be a catastrophic blow to the security of the network.

On the UNIX side of things, this means that you must maintain the security of the .mac machine account file and the smbpasswd file, particularly if that file contains a large number or important users in the domain. Also note that since release 2.0.4, NT servers can change UNIX permissions if nt acl support is set to true. This is likely to be dangerous only if you didn't pay attention to permissions on the file system. That can happen though. At all times keep in mind that Samba still works with UNIX security. You must think in terms of both NT security policy in Samba and UNIX security policy. They must match each other; otherwise, you're likely to be surprised when something doesn't work or that users have more privileges than you wanted them to have. As the Samba documentation says, Samba doesn't try to outguess the UNIX admins; it assumes they're knowledgeable enough to get that part right. You must live up to this responsibility if you want to use Samba securely and effectively.

Troubleshooting

Frequently, even when you're sure you got everything right on the first try, problems will crop up. We all make mistakes, and networking with Windows systems is rarely a simple and painless task right from the beginning. The following examples and commands should give you a good appreciation of the diagnostic tools available to you as well as ideas on how to correct the odd gaffe.

Nondestructive Tests

These are observational tests you can perform that should not affect your running network or the current setup of your Samba server. They should provide you with all the information you need to tell how your network is running and what changes, if any, are needed to your Samba configuration.

testparm

This wonderful tool verifies that the syntax of your `smb.conf` file is correct. It also checks whether the paths you've assigned to variables actually exist. Finally, it provides a listing of every value your Samba server would operate with if started—either values explicitly set in the `smb.conf` file or default values. Listing 24.2 shows an example of output from the `testparm` command with an error message.

LISTING 24.2   An Example of Output with an Error Message

```
# testparm
Load smb config files from /usr/local/Samba/lib/smb.conf
Processing section "[homes]"
Processing section "[printers]"
Loaded services file OK.
ERROR: lock directory /usr/local/Samba/var/locks does not exist
Press enter to see a dump of your service definitions
```

```
# Global parameters
[global]
        workgroup = THENETEFFECT
        netbios name =
        netbios aliases =
        server string = Samba Server
        interfaces =
        bind interfaces only = No
        security = DOMAIN
        encrypt passwords = Yes
        update encrypted = No
        allow trusted domains = Yes
        hosts equiv =
        min passwd length = 5
        map to guest = Never
        null passwords = No
        password server = NT_SERVER
        smb passwd file = /usr/local/Samba/private/smbpasswd
        root directory = /
        passwd program = /bin/passwd
        passwd chat = *new*password* %n\n *new*password* %n\n *changed*
        passwd chat debug = No
        username map =
        password level = 0
        username level = 0
        unix password sync = No
        restrict anonymous = No
        use rhosts = No
        log level = 2
        syslog = 1
        syslog only = No
        log file = /usr/local/Samba/var/log.%m
        max log size = 50
        timestamp logs = Yes
        debug hires timestamp = No
        debug pid = No
        debug uid = No
        protocol = NT1
        read bmpx = No
        read raw = Yes
        write raw = Yes
        nt smb support = Yes
        nt pipe support = Yes
        nt acl support = Yes
        announce version = 4.2
        announce as = NT
        max mux = 50
        max xmit = 65535
        name resolve order = lmhosts host wins bcast
        max packet = 65535
        max ttl = 259200
```

continues

LISTING 24.2 continued

```
max wins ttl = 518400
min wins ttl = 21600
time server = No
change notify timeout = 60
deadtime = 0
getwd cache = Yes
keepalive = 300
lpq cache time = 10
max disk size = 0
max open files = 10000
read prediction = No
read size = 16384
shared mem size = 1048576
socket options = TCP_NODELAY
stat cache size = 50
load printers = Yes
printcap name = /etc/printcap
printer driver file = /usr/local/Samba/lib/printers.def
strip dot = No
character set =
mangled stack = 50
coding system =
client code page = 850
stat cache = Yes
domain groups =
domain admin group =
domain guest group =
domain admin users =
domain guest users =
machine password timeout = 604800
add user script =
delete user script =
logon script =
logon path = \\%N\%U\profile
logon drive =
logon home = \\%N\%U
domain logons = No
os level = 20
lm announce = Auto
lm interval = 60
preferred master = No
local master = Yes
domain master = No
browse list = Yes
dns proxy = No
wins proxy = No
wins server = 192.168.1.1
wins support = No
wins hook =
```

```
kernel oplocks = Yes
ole locking compatibility = Yes
oplock break wait time = 10
smbrun = /usr/local/Samba/bin/smbrun
config file =
preload =
lock dir = /usr/local/Samba/var/locks
default service =
message command =
dfree command =
valid chars =
remote announce =
remote browse sync =
socket address = 0.0.0.0
homedir map =
time offset = 0
unix realname = No
NIS homedir = No
panic action =
comment =
path =
alternate permissions = No
revalidate = No
username =
guest account = nobody
invalid users =
valid users =
admin users =
read list =
write list =
force user =
force group =
read only = Yes
create mask = 0744
force create mode = 00
security mask = -1
force security mode = -1
directory mask = 0755
force directory mode = 00
directory security mask = -1
force directory security mode = -1
guest only = No
guest ok = No
only user = No
hosts allow =
hosts deny =
status = Yes
max connections = 0
min print space = 0
```

continues

LISTING 24.2   continued

```
strict sync = No
sync always = No
print ok = No
postscript = No
printing = bsd
print command = lpr -r -P%p %s
lpq command = lpq -P%p
lprm command = lprm -P%p %j
lppause command =
lpresume command =
queuepause command =
queueresume command =
printer name =
printer driver = NULL
printer driver location =
default case = lower
case sensitive = No
preserve case = Yes
short preserve case = Yes
mangle case = No
mangling char = ~
hide dot files = Yes
delete veto files = No
veto files =
hide files =
veto oplock files =
map system = No
map hidden = No
map archive = Yes
mangled names = Yes
mangled map =
browseable = Yes
blocking locks = Yes
fake oplocks = No
locking = Yes
oplocks = Yes
level2 oplocks = No
oplock contention limit = 2
strict locking = No
share modes = Yes
copy =
include =
exec =
preexec close = No
postexec =
root preexec =
root preexec close = No
root postexec =
available = Yes
```

```
        volume =
        fstype = NTFS
        set directory = No
        wide links = Yes
        follow symlinks = Yes
        dont descend =
        magic script =
        magic output =
        delete readonly = No
        dos filetimes = No
        dos filetime resolution = No
        fake directory create times = No

[homes]
        comment = Home Directories
        read only = No
        browseable = No

[printers]
        comment = All Printers
        path = /usr/spool/Samba
        print ok = Yes
        browseable = No
```

ping

If you're having problems accessing or using your Samba server, one of the first things to check is network connectivity. You can use the `ping` program to verify whether you're in contact with PDC and BDC computers as well as other computers in your domain. Otherwise, you'll need to break out the replacement network cards and patch cables.

netstat

The `netstat` utility is very helpful in ensuring you haven't done something really silly, such as not starting up Samba at all. It's very hard for Samba to do its job of logging into the domain and such when it isn't running. You should see settings similar to those shown in Listing 24.3 using `netstat -atu` (a slight Linux-ism meaning "show all TCP and UDP connections and servers").

LISTING 24.3   Sample `netstat` Settings

```
# netstat -atu

Active Internet connections (servers and established)
Proto Recv-Q Send-Q Local Address       Foreign Address       State
tcp        0      0 *:netbios-ssn       *:*                   LISTEN
```

continues

24

ADDING A SAMBA
SERVER TO AN NT
NETWORK

LISTING 24.3   continued

```
udp        0        0 comet.thene:netbios-dgm *:*
udp        0        0 comet.thenet:netbios-ns *:*
udp        0        0 *:netbios-dgm            *:*
udp        0        0 *:netbios-ns             *:*
```

tcpdump

A great tool for diagnosing all sorts of network problems, tcpdump can come in very handy when you're trying to diagnose what is going on between your Samba box and other computers. With enough knowledge of the protocols involved, an expert can frequently tell exactly what is happening and when as well as what to do about it. For those less familiar with protocols, tcpdump can at least indicate what communication is happening and in what order. If that rough knowledge is not enough, you can always take the dumps to your friendly neighborhood guru.

A thorough studying of the tcpdump man page is in order if you want to use tcpdump to its fullest. You should also know that only later or patched versions of libpcap are capable of deciphering the SMB/CIFS protocol. Your best results are likely to be met by "tcpdump-ing" on the particular SMB ports—Name service on UDP 137, Datagram on UDP 138, and Session service on TCP and UDP 139—using the udp port # syntax of tcpdump. The best dumps will be received while using a third machine to look at the traffic between, say, a recalcitrant NT server and your Samba box.

Here's the basic syntax:

```
# tcpdump -n -vv -i eth0 host comet and udp port netbios-ns and host DEATHSTAR
```

tail -f log.nmb

This is a very informative tool when you are having problems using Samba. nmbd will generally, depending on debug level, tell you exactly what it is doing in a broad sense. If all is not right with your Samba server, you might get something like the output shown in Listing 24.4.

LISTING 24.4   Sample Debug Output

```
[1999/12/06 20:28:31, 1] nmbd/nmbd.c:main(747)
  Netbios nameserver version 2.0.6 started.
  Copyright Andrew Tridgell 1994-1998
[1999/12/06 20:33:54, 0] nmbd/nmbd_become_lmb.c:become_local_master_stage2(406)
  *****

  Samba name server COMET is now a local master browser for workgroup
➡THENETEFFECT on subnet 192.168.0.55
  *****
```

```
[1999/12/06 20:33:54, 0] nmbd/nmbd_become_lmb.c:become_local_master_stage2(406)
  *****

  Samba name server COMET is now a local master browser for workgroup
➥THENETEFFECT on subnet 10.7.7.77


  *****
[1999/12/06 20:34:15, 0]
➥nmbd/nmbd_browsesync.c:find_domain_master_name_query_fail(362)

  find_domain_master_name_query_fail:
  Unable to find the Domain Master Browser name THENETEFFECT<1b> for the
➥workgroup THENETEFFECT.

  Unable to sync browse lists in this workgroup.
[1999/12/06 20:34:15, 0]
➥nmbd/nmbd_browsesync.c:find_domain_master_name_query_fail(362)

  find_domain_master_name_query_fail:
  Unable to find the Domain Master Browser name THENETEFFECT<1b> for the
➥workgroup THENETEFFECT.

  Unable to sync browse lists in this workgroup.
```

This means the Samba server was unable to find the master browser NT server and therefore thinks it should become one. This is likely to cause problems and will almost undoubtedly mean you won't be able to authenticate against the PDC. You'll probably want to check the os level, domain master, and local master options in your smb.conf file as well as check for good network connectivity.

If your setup has gone along just fine, you'll likely get an uninteresting display like the following:

```
[1999/12/06 20:04:03, 1] nmbd/nmbd.c:main(677)
  Netbios nameserver version 2.0.6 started.
  Copyright Andrew Tridgell 1994-1998
[1999/12/06 20:04:03, 0] nmbd/asyncdns.c:start_async_dns(150)
  started asyncdns process 10765
```

nmblookup

A great utility for performing name lookups on your network, nmblookup shows which servers claim to be master browsers for domains, which domain a computer is in, and so forth. Here's an example of a name and node status lookup:

```
# nmblookup -S deathstar
querying deathstar on 192.168.0.255
192.168.0.66 deathstar<00>
```

```
Looking up status of 192.168.0.66
received 6 names
        DEATHSTAR       <00> -          B <ACTIVE>
        DEATHSTAR       <20> -          B <ACTIVE>
        THENETEFFECT    <00> - <GROUP> B <ACTIVE>
        DEATHSTAR       <03> -          B <ACTIVE>
        THENETEFFECT    <1e> - <GROUP> B <ACTIVE>
        MITCH           <03> -          B <ACTIVE>
num_good_sends=0 num_good_receives=0
```

Here's a lookup for master browsers:

```
# nmblookup -M -
querying __MSBROWSE__ on 192.168.0.255
192.168.0.55 __MSBROWSE__<01>
192.168.0.3 __MSBROWSE__<01>
```

smbstatus

The `smbstatus` tool can quickly give you a lot of information about which client machines are connected to your Samba server and what they are doing. Here's an example showing one NT PC connected to a Samba server:

```
# smbstatus

Samba version 2.0.6
Service     uid     gid     pid     machine
----------------------------------------------
mitch       mitch   users   28761   deathstar (192.168.0.66)
➥Sun Dec 09 21:28:54 1999

Locked files:
Pid     DenyMode     R/W     Oplock          Name
----------------------------------------------------
28761   DENY_NONE   RDONLY   EXCLUSIVE+BATCH  /home/mitch/drinks.html
➥Sun Dec 09 21:35:15 1999

Share mode memory usage (bytes):
    1048272(99%) free + 216(0%) used + 88(0%) overhead = 1048576(100%) total
```

net use

The `net use` console tool is used to assign drive letters to network shares on Samba servers (or NT/Windows computers for that matter.) Here's an example of assigning a drive for a UNIX home directory:

```
C:\>net use E: \\comet\homes
The command completed successfully.
```

If you use * in place of the drive letter, Windows will use the next available letter. Here's the full syntax:

```
C:\>net use /?
The syntax of this command is:


NET USE [devicename | *] [\\computername\sharename[\volume] [password | *]]
        [/USER:[domainname\]username]
        [[/DELETE] | [/PERSISTENT:{YES | NO}]]

NET USE [devicename | *] [password | *]] [/HOME]

NET USE [/PERSISTENT:{YES | NO}]
```

net view

A simple and quick console tool in NT or Windows 9*x*, net view can be used to check which computers are in a particular domain or workgroup and what shares are available to you on a server. Here's the command syntax:

```
C:\>net view /?
The syntax of this command is:


NET VIEW [\\computername | /DOMAIN[:domainname]]
NET VIEW /NETWORK:NW [\\computername]
```

Here's an example of using net view to browse the local Windows network:

```
C:\>net view
Server Name             Remark

-------------------------------------------------------------------------------
\\COMET                 Samba Server
\\DEATHSTAR
The command completed successfully.
```

Here's a sample net view \\computername of a neighboring Samba server, with the home account of the NT user shown:

```
C:\>net view \\comet
Shared resources at \\comet

Samba Server

Share name   Type        Used as  Comment

-------------------------------------------------------------------------------
lp           Print
mitch        Disk                 Home Directories
The command completed successfully.
```

ipconfig /all

In a console window on an NT box, you can use the `ipconfig` command to get information about the TCP/IP and NetBIOS setup of a PC and its network card:

```
C:\>ipconfig /all

Windows NT IP Configuration

        Host Name . . . . . . . . . : deathstar.theneteffect.com
        DNS Servers . . . . . . . . : 206.202.56.3
                                      206.202.0.3
        Node Type . . . . . . . . . : Broadcast
        NetBIOS Scope ID. . . . . . :
        IP Routing Enabled. . . . . : No
        WINS Proxy Enabled. . . . . : No
        NetBIOS Resolution Uses DNS : No

Ethernet adapter AMDPCN1:

        Description . . . . . . . . : AMD PCNET Family Ethernet Adapter
        Physical Address. . . . . . : 00-50-56-81-00-37
        DHCP Enabled. . . . . . . . : No
        IP Address. . . . . . . . . : 192.168.0.66
        Subnet Mask . . . . . . . . : 255.255.255.0
        Default Gateway . . . . . . : 192.168.0.1
```

nbtstat

The `nbtstat` console tool is extremely helpful on an NT Server or Workstation machine. Much like `nmblookup` and several of the `net <command>` options, `nbtstat` can provide lots of information about what the NT PC thinks the current state of the network is, who is connected to a certain computer, who has a registered NetBIOS name, and so on. For example, `nbtstat -a` shows a list of registered NetBIOS names:

```
C:\>nbtstat -h

Displays protocol statistics and current TCP/IP connections using NBT
(NetBIOS over TCP/IP).

NBTSTAT [-a RemoteName] [-A IP address] [-c] [-n]
        [-r] [-R] [-s] [-S] [interval] ]

   -a   (adapter status) Lists the remote machine's name table given its name
   -A   (Adapter status) Lists the remote machine's name table given its
                         IP address.
   -c   (cache)          Lists the remote name cache including the IP addresses
   -n   (names)          Lists local NetBIOS names.
   -r   (resolved)       Lists names resolved by broadcast and via WINS
   -R   (Reload)         Purges and reloads the remote cache name table
```

```
-S   (Sessions)        Lists sessions table with the destination IP addresses
-s   (sessions)        Lists sessions table converting destination IP
                       addresses to host names via the hosts file.

RemoteName    Remote host machine name.
IP address    Dotted decimal representation of the IP address.
interval      Redisplays selected statistics, pausing interval seconds
              between each display. Press Ctrl+C to stop redisplaying
              statistics.
```

Here's a sample `nbtstat -s` listing with one incoming connection from a Samba client (`COMET`):

```
C:\>nbtstat -s

              NetBIOS Connection Table

Local Name            State    In/Out  Remote Host           Input   Output
- - - - - - - - - - - - - - - - - - - - - - - - - - - - - - - - - - - - - - -
DEATHSTAR             Connected   In   COMET          <00>   486B    913B
DEATHSTAR      <03>   Listening
ADMINISTRATOR  <03>   Listening
```

Windows Explorer and Network Neighborhood

You can also check for proper function using the Network Neighborhood icon on NT/Windows desktops or the Network Neighborhood tree in Windows Explorer. This is the ultimate test, really, to see whether everybody can see your Samba server. Even if everything is working wonderfully with Samba and UNIX clients, for most people, the point is interconnectivity. If every average PC user can't see your Samba box, as irritating as that is, you'll need to find out why.

Destructive Tests

In addition to these relatively cautious probings to find out what's going on with Samba, you can also use some slightly more straightforward methods that might yield quicker results, although perhaps at some cost to your network.

One thing you might try is restarting Samba itself. One notable thing about Windows networking is the large amount of state kept in the protocol—information about which server is a master or local browser, NetBIOS names, and so forth. Not that this seems to reduce network chatter from Windows boxes like you might expect, but it does frequently keep different PCs from synchronizing in any sort of timely manner. Sometimes the only way to get things to settle down is by stopping and restarting the Samba server (by *Samba server*, we mean the Samba processes themselves, of course, not the entire server). An example of this is when an NT PDC thinks another server is in charge and won't start its `netlogon` service. The only way to stop its sulking is by stopping the

Samba server and manually starting `netlogon`. Restarting Samba can also help in getting the most up-to-date browsing information if some large change has occurred.

Another method of discerning problems—one you'd certainly want to avoid except while testing before you put servers in production—is to replace the entire `smb.conf` file with simpler ones. This way, you can try to isolate whatever sorts of problems you are having and see whether they go away or change. This plan of attack is frequently stymied, though, by the way the network will interact with your tests. Even just shutting down the Samba server to change files might seem to cure a problem, when in fact the problem will show up the next time the NT servers are rebooted. These complicated interactions make test configurations hit-or-miss affairs on production networks. You'll probably get best results if you can take lots of `tcpdumps` along with any change or can have better control over external factors, or both.

Summary

Samba servers are ideal additions to established NT networks. They are nearly feature-complete replacements for NT domain members running non-UNIX operating systems. They also are based strongly on the ideas of standard compliance and openness, both in the code itself and in providing administrators with a very complete view of what they are doing and how they are interacting.

In addition to the strong qualities of the Samba platform itself, when combined with a free UNIX, such as Linux, a Samba server provides an extremely cost-effective, reliable, and high-performance system. Whether used in new hardware or for extending the life of older machines, the pair of Samba and Linux generally outperform other solutions while having no (or a small) initial price, and none of the bother and expense of per-client licenses. For anyone seeking to improve the reliability and effectiveness of his or her network, Samba is the clear choice.

## CHAPTER 25

Replacing an NT File Server with Samba

by Mike Harris

IN THIS CHAPTER

This chapter aims to discuss the basic process involved in replacing an NT file server with a Samba file server. It should be used in conjunction with the other chapters in this book, especially Chapter 10, "Working with Windows NT."

Why Replace?

You may be considering the replacement of an NT server with Samba for a multitude of different reasons. If your network is already comprised of UNIX servers and you need your users to be able to share files between the different platforms, then Samba is an ideal solution. If you've recently replaced legacy UNIX applications with more modern Windows-based ones, then deploying your old UNIX servers as Samba servers for your Windows network is a good way of obtaining more mileage from your technology investments.

Linux is becoming increasingly popular as an alternative server platform. This is especially the case with the provision of Internet-oriented services, for which it's ideally suited. If you're using (or planning to use) UNIX or Linux servers to provide email or Web services to your network, the use of Samba may help you utilize the power of your servers and increase the return on your investment.

Cost-Effectiveness

It's true that by running an Intel or Alpha server that's running Samba on Linux you can greatly reduce the cost of software licensing. Not only is this the case when considering the initial savings for the server software—Linux is free, NT Server is not—it's also true because you don't require client access licenses for a Samba server. With Windows NT, Microsoft requires the purchase of a client license for every workstation connecting to a server, whereas with a Linux server running Samba, this is not required (depending on the type of licensing you use).

It's also true that Linux running in text-based console mode on an Intel system will use less memory and resources than NT Server running on the same machine. This implies that the hardware cost for running a Samba/Linux server is lower than for NT.

There's a definite caveat for strong Microsoft shops that do not already run UNIX in their environment, in that there will be obvious retraining costs and a notable learning curve for administrators. You will need to seriously consider whether the benefits from diverging into a new platform can justify the cost of doing so.

With that said, the relative costs of training in a new area are no different from training in the Microsoft world; some courses and certification are at least comparable in price to the equivalent MCSE qualifications.

In addition, expanding your IT staff's knowledge of non-Microsoft platforms could perhaps be important in the future, considering the multitude of emerging technologies. Maintaining a degree of vendor independence is quite often advantageous for any company.

Reliability

Although it's widely agreed upon in both UNIX and Microsoft camps that NT is more unreliable than Linux, it's hard to prove. From personal experience, I have found Linux to be a far more reliable and stable platform for serving than Windows NT. Now this is obviously one person's opinion, and many people will have completely opposite experiences.

Examples in This Chapter

To illustrate the process of replacing an NT server with Samba, from this point forward in this chapter, we'll be using a simple Windows NT–oriented network for an NT domain called MYDOMAIN. This domain contains a Windows NT primary domain controller (PDC), a Windows NT fileserver, and a Windows NT Workstation client. We'll be adding a Samba server to replace the existing file server. Table 25.1 shows the configuration for the network.

TABLE 25.1   Network Configuration for MYDOMAIN

Name	*Function*	*IP Address*
NT4PDC_1	PDC	192.168.100.5
NT4SRV_1	Old file server (NT)	192.168.100.4
NT4WKS_1	Client workstation	192.168.100.7
PERSEUS	New file server (Linux)	192.168.100.2

Four departmental groups are set up for the accounts, sales, managerial, and IT support departments as well as four users, each a member of one of the groups. Table 25.2 shows the usernames and group memberships.

TABLE 25.2   Usernames and Groups for MYDOMAIN

User	*Groups*
username1	Domain Users and accounts
username2	Domain Users and sales
username3	Domain Users and itsupport
username4	Domain Users and managerial

25

REPLACING AN NT
FILE SERVER WITH
SAMBA

On NT4SRV_1, there are four user shares set up for each of the four users, and four shares for each of the four groups. There's also one public share for all users as well as one shared printer. Table 25.3 shows the available shares and user/group permissions.

TABLE 25.3 Shares for MYDOMAIN

Sharename	*NT Group/User Required To Access*
accounts	Accounts
sales	Sales
itsupport	ITsupport
managers	Managerial
public	Domain Users
username?$	Username?
printer1	Domain Guests

The public share has read-only access for all users except for Domain Admins, who also have write access.

There's a standard netlogon share on NT4PDC_1 with login scripts for each departmental group to establish the department-specific connections. For example, here are the connections of the accounts department's login script accounts.bat, located in \\nt4pdc_1\netlogon:

```
net use g: \\nt4srv_1\accounts /persistent:no /yes
net use p: \\nt4srv_1\public /persistent:no /yes
net use lpt1: \\nt4srv_1\printer1 /persistent:no /yes
```

All users in the entire domain have their home shares mapped to drive Z: automatically.

For every command-line example in this chapter, it's assumed that the user is logged in as a Domain Admin on any Windows NT machine and as root or a user with equivalent rights on the Samba server.

The Replacement Process

The complexity involved in replacing an NT fileserver with Samba will vary depending on the size and configuration of the site. The example used here has been greatly simplified, but it illustrates the main issues involved in the replacement process.

We'll start with a completely NT-based network that's comprised of a primary domain controller, a fileserver, and a workstation. We'll next connect a Samba server to the network and make it a domain member. As we move through the chapter, we'll look at basic principles, aspects, and issues relating to moving services from an NT server onto a Samba server. By the end of the chapter, you'll be able to switch off the NT fileserver with the knowledge that the Samba server has fully taken over its new role.

Here are the basic stages:

- Document the existing server.
- Introduce the Samba server into the network.
- Test Samba/NT interaction.
- Migrate user accounts.
- Create directories.
- Create shares.
- Test connections with a test user.
- Copy across files for the test user.
- Migrate logon script for the test user.
- Test the migrated test user.
- Modify the configuration, if necessary.
- Copy across files for all users.
- Migrate logon scripts for all users.
- Go live.

Documenting the Existing Server

In order to make sure that a high level of quality of service to users is maintained, the process of documenting the existing server is an important one. It's essential that you can produce a complete list of all the files and permissions, shares and their access, as well as usernames and groups.

You should create worksheets to document the server, and you should complete them as you proceed. Include columns in which you note whether the share is in use (and therefore needs to be migrated) and when it has been successfully migrated to your Samba server.

Obtaining a List of Shares

As an administrator of an NT server, you should be aware of which file shares are available on the server. However, due to the nature of NT, it's very possible that some unrecorded, hidden shares might exist. The obvious way of checking for which shares are available is by using Windows Explorer, but this does not show hidden shares. By far the best method is to use the net share command from the command prompt on the NT server.

For example, on NT4SRV_1, the command returns:

```
C:\>net share
Share name    Resource                          Remark
-------------------------------------------------------------------------------
username4$    C:\Shares\Users\username4
ADMIN$        C:\WINNT                          Remote Admin
IPC$                                            Remote IPC
C$            C:\                               Default share
Users$        C:\Shares\Users                   Users Share for Home directories
username2$    C:\Shares\Users\username2
username1$    C:\Shares\Users\username1
username3$    C:\Shares\Users\username3
print$        C:\WINNT\system32\spool\drivers Printer Drivers
allgroups$    C:\Shares\Groups
accounts      C:\Shares\Groups\accounts
itsupport     C:\Shares\Groups\itsupport
managers      C:\Shares\Groups\managers
Public        C:\Shares\Public                  Publicly Shared Files
sales         C:\Shares\Groups\sales
printer1      LPT1:                    Spooled  HP DeskJet 340 (Monochrome)
The command completed successfully.
```

This command has produced a full list of shares and their physical locations on the server.

Establishing Which Shares Are in Use

It's a good idea to check which shares are actually being used on your server in order to establish a list of priority and critical shares to migrate. It also might help you eradicate superfluous shares that are no longer in use. Obviously, you should make such checks during the busiest times of the day in order to get an accurate view of share connections.

Although you can use Server Manager to find out this information, you can use the `net share` command on the server to find out more information on each share, including which users are connected to it. For example, the following is the output for the `public` share on NT4SRV_1:

```
C:\>net share public
Share name         Public
Path               C:\Shares\Public
Remark             Publicly Shared Files
Maximum users      No limit
Users              username4         USERNAME1
The command completed successfully.
```

Gathering Share Permissions

You now need to gather a list of file and directory permissions for each shared directory on the NT fileserver.

To find out what access through a share is granted, open up Windows Explorer on the NT fileserver and locate the shared directory. Then right-click the directory name and select Sharing from the pop-up menu. The Sharing tab of the Properties dialog box is displayed. Now click on the Permissions button to display the Access Through Share Permissions dialog box. Figure 25.1 shows this dialog box for the accounts share on NT4SRV_1.

FIGURE 25.1

Viewing share permissions on an NT share.

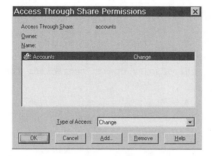

Gathering File and Directory Permissions

You now need to gather a list of file and directory permissions for each shared directory on the NT fileserver.

To find out what permissions are given on a directory or file, open up Windows Explorer on the NT fileserver and locate the shared directory. Then right-click the directory or file-name and select Properties from the pop-up menu. Click the Security tab of the Properties dialog box. Now click the Permissions button to display the Directory or File Permissions dialog box. Figure 25.2 below shows the Directory Permissions dialog box for the C:\Shares\Groups\accounts directory on NT4SRV_1.

FIGURE 25.2

Viewing directory permissions on NT.

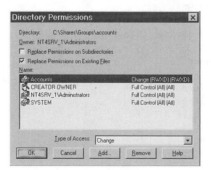

25

REPLACING AN NT FILE SERVER WITH SAMBA

Obtaining a List of Users and Groups

The most obvious way to view the available users and groups is to use User Manager for Domains. To find out information about each user and group, you'll need to double-click each one.

For a large number of accounts, you'll find this a cumbersome method to use; therefore, you may prefer to use the net user command.

To produce a list of all user accounts available on the server, use the following form of net user:

```
Z:\>net user /domain
The request will be processed at the primary domain controller for domain
MYDOMAIN.


User accounts for \\NT4PDC_1

-------------------------------------------------------------------------------
adelayde                 Administrator            Guest
root                     username1                username2
username3                username4                username5
username6
The command completed successfully.
```

The net user command can also be used to find out more information about the user. Here's an example:

```
Z:\>net user username1 /domain
The request will be processed at the primary domain controller for domain
MYDOMAIN.

User name                username1
Full Name                Test User 1
Comment                  Accounts Dept
User's comment
Country code             000 (System Default)
Account active           Yes
Account expires          Never

Password last set        12/6/99 4:14 PM
Password expires         1/18/00 3:01 PM
Password changeable      12/6/99 4:14 PM
Password required        Yes
User may change password Yes

Workstations allowed     All
Logon script             accounts-samba.bat
User profile
```

```
Home directory              \\perseus\username1
Last logon                  12/9/99 3:23 PM

Logon hours allowed         All

Local Group Memberships
Global Group memberships    *Domain Users        *Accounts
The command completed successfully.
```

Putting Your Samba Server Online

Now we'll leave behind the NT server for the moment in order to concentrate on readying the Samba server for the next stage: setting up users and groups. Here, we'll concentrate on making the Samba server a domain member and joining the domain.

If your network configuration does not include a PDC, more examples of configuring Samba for different target environments can be found in Chapter 10.

Configuring Samba

For this example, because there is a PDC in our network, we need to configure Samba to be a domain member. The most important parameters in the smb.conf file that affect the configuration are as follows:

```
[global]
        workgroup = MYDOMAIN
        security = DOMAIN
        encrypt passwords = Yes
        password server = *
        os level = 0
        local master = No
        wins server = NT4PDC_1
        wins support = No
```

Refer to Chapter 10 for a detailed explanation of these parameters.

Here are the parameters of concern:

- security = DOMAIN   This informs Samba that the machine is to be a domain member.
- password server = *   This searches for a PDC in the domain for authentication (in versions of Samba prior to 2.0.6, you'll need to specify a list of the PDC and BDCs, separated by spaces).
- os level = 0 and local master = No   This indicates that Samba will never be involved in browser elections.

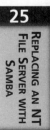

- `wins server = NT4PDC_1` and `wins support = No`   This indicates that Samba will not act as a WINS server and that it resolves NetBIOS names to IP addresses through the WINS server for the domain (in this case, it happens to be the PDC as well).

Adding the Samba Server to the Domain

Now that you've written the basic `smb.conf` file for domain membership of the Samba server, it's time to join the Windows NT domain. This process is the same for Samba as for NT machines in that there are two stages: adding the Samba server into Server Manager on the PDC, and joining the domain from the Samba server.

Log into the domain (in this example, MYDOMAIN) as Administrator and run Server Manager. From the Computer menu, select Add to Domain. The Add Computer to Domain dialog box will appear. Select the Windows NT Workstation or Server option and enter the name of your new Samba server (in this example, PERSEUS). Then click OK. Figure 25.3 illustrates the addition of PERSEUS to the MYDOMAIN domain.

FIGURE 25.3

Adding a Samba server to a domain using Server Manager.

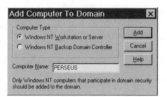

To join the domain, simply issue the following command on your Samba server once you've completed the previous step:

```
[root@perseus source]# smbpasswd -R wins -j MYDOMAIN -r NT4PDC_1
1999/11/16 16:24:04 : change_trust_account_password:
        Changed password for domain MYDOMAIN.
Joined domain MYDOMAIN.
```

After a few minutes, you should find that your Samba server appears as "live" in Server Manager for your domain as a Windows NT 4.2 server, and you'll be able to view properties for it.

If you've provided any shares on your Samba server, you should also be able to browse them in Windows Explorer, given that you have the correct permissions set.

Setting Up Users and Groups on Samba

Now that you've collected all the information regarding your existing NT fileserver and added your Samba server to the domain, you next need to re-create the usernames and groups.

There are several different scenarios, depending on whether you have a PDC in your network, which Samba will utilize for passthrough authentication by using the `password server` parameter in `smb.conf`. By using this configuration, you'll save yourself the extra administrative overhead of having to maintain separate username and password lists for your domain and for the Samba server. If you're not using a passthrough authentication configuration, you should also refer to the section "Creating Users for Non-Passthrough Authentication," later in this chapter.

Access control through Samba requires usernames to exist in the UNIX `/etc/passwd` file, although as you'll see, the username does not need to have a password set or even a login shell.

Setting Up Groups

When you create new users under UNIX, you can also specify group membership to speed up the process. However, it's a good idea to first create the required groups to use. Although using the `password server` parameter in `smb.conf` allows for passthrough authentication of usernames, this facility is not provided for groups. This means that a UNIX group needs to be created for each NT domain group that's being migrated.

You may add groups using the UNIX `groupadd` command, for example:

```
% groupadd accounts
```

Table 25.4 shows the list of UNIX user groups created and their relationship to the original NT domain groups.

TABLE 25.4   NT Domain–to–UNIX Group Mappings

NT Domain Group	UNIX Group
Domain Users	`users`
Domain Admins	`admin`
Accounts	`accounts`
Sales	`sales`
ITSupport	`itsupport`
Managerial	`managers`
Domain Guests	`guests`

In Table 25.4, the standard UNIX group `users` has been used to represent the Domain Users NT domain group, because this is the default primary group for all UNIX users on most systems. For Domain Admins, the temptation might be to use a UNIX group such as `adm` or even `root`. This is likely to cause you security concerns on your system, so a

25

REPLACING AN NT FILE SERVER WITH SAMBA

separate group admin has been used for this functionality. Likewise, the guests UNIX group has been used for Domain Guests; it's unlikely that you'll often use this group for anything other than very public shares and perhaps printers.

The following are the relevant entries as they appear in /etc/group on PERSEUS after they've been added:

```
users::100:
accounts:x:520:
managers:x:521:
itsupport:x:522:
sales:x:523:
admin:x:524:
guests:x:525:
```

Setting Up Users

Use the UNIX useradd command to add users to the /etc/passwd file on your Samba server. Here's an example:

```
% useradd -c 'Accounts Bod' -d /home/username1 \
         -g users -G accounts -s /dev/null -n username1
% useradd -c 'Sales Bod' -d /home/username2 \
         -g users -G sales -s /dev/null -n username2
% useradd -c 'IT Support Bod' -d /home/username3 \
         -g users -G itsupport,admin -s /dev/null -n username3
% useradd -c 'A Manager' -d /home/username4 \
         -g users -G managers -s /dev/null -n username4
```

In these command-line examples, the primary group membership is specified with the -g parameter (in this case, this is users). This is the UNIX equivalent of setting the default group to be Domain Users under NT. Group membership in other groups that will not be the primary are specified with the -G parameter. In this way, we provide the UNIX equivalent of setting group membership of Domain Users and Managers with the default group as Domain Users.

The -s parameter is used to specify a null login shell so that users cannot log on.

The -n parameter is specific to Red Hat Linux systems and prevents a UNIX group from being created with the same name; this is an undesirable and unnecessary function.

The useradd command may vary between UNIX systems and may be called adduser or something similar. For example, some people use /bin/false for the null login shell. There are also several graphical user-management tools available. Consult your system's documentation and manual pages for your variant.

The entries in the /etc/passwd file for the Samba server, following the preceding commands, are as follows:

```
username1:x:1026:100:Accounts Bod:/home/username1:/dev/null
username2:x:1031:100:Sales Bod:/home/username2:/dev/null
username3:x:1032:100:IT Support Bod:/home/username3:/dev/null
username4:x:1034:100:A Manager:/home/username4:/dev/null
```

The following are the relevant entries as they appear in `/etc/group` after the users have been added:

```
users::100:
accounts:x:520:username1
managers:x:521:username4
itsupport:x:522:username3
sales:x:523:username2
admin:x:524:username3
guests:x:525:
```

Creating Users for Non-Passthrough Authentication

If you're not performing passthrough authentication of users connecting to your Samba server by use of the `password server` parameter, you'll need to utilize the file `/etc/smbpasswd` to contain the list of user accounts that may connect. You can do this by using the `smbpasswd` utility on your Samba server. Here's an example:

```
[root@perseus groups]# smbpasswd username3
New SMB password:
Retype new SMB password:
Password changed for user username3.
```

For a site that has many users, it can be a laborious process to have to run the `smbpasswd` utility for every user.

Using the utility `pwdump`, which has been written by the Samba team and is available from `http://us1.samba.org/samba/ftp/pwdump`, you can "dump" the contents of the NT Access Control List (ACL) to produce a file format that can be used for your `/etc/smbpasswd` file. For example, running `pwdump` on `NT4PDC_1` produces the following output:

```
C:>pwdump.exe
Administrator:500:BF4944925A159CC793E28745B8BF4BA6:
        C78813E9AFB03939ED194F53185B50D5:
        Built-in account for administering the computer/domain::
Guest:501:NO PASSWORD*********************:
        NO PASSWORD*********************:
        Built-in account for guest access to the computer/domain::
NT4SRV_1$:1025:*********************************:
        *********************************:::
username1:1026:29CB50F08CB30CC57584248B8D2C9F9E:
        2B4093FAFF2225F25ED3C7032792B0DF:
        Test User 1,Accounts Dept :\\nt4srv_1\username1$:
```

```
username2:1031:29CB50F08CB30CC57584248B8D2C9F9E:
        2B4093FAFF2225F25ED3C7032792B0DF:
        Test User 2,Sales Department:\\nt4srv_1\username2$:
username3:1032:29CB50F08CB30CC57584248B8D2C9F9E:
        2B4093FAFF2225F25ED3C7032792B0DF:
        Test User 3,IT Support :\\nt4srv_1\username3$:
username4:1034:29CB50F08CB30CC57584248B8D2C9F9E:
        2B4093FAFF2225F25ED3C7032792B0DF:
        Test User 4,A Manager:\\nt4srv_1\username4$:
NT4WKS_1$:1036:******************************:
        ******************************:::
PERSEUS$:1038:******************************:
        ******************************:::
```

You should remove the lines beginning with machine names, because these are not needed for Samba in this mode—for example, NT4SRV_1$, NT4WKS_1$, and PERSEUS$ (RIDs 1025, 1036, and 1038, respectively).

Now copy this file over the existing smbpasswd file on your Samba server; you may want to back up the original first. Here's an example:

```
% cp pwdump.txt /etc/password
```

Note that the RIDs (the numbers in the second column of the smbpasswd file) for the user accounts will need to match those of the UNIX user accounts. A modified useradd command should be used that includes the -u parameter to force the user ID to match that of the smbpasswd file:

```
% useradd -c 'Accounts Bod' -d /home/username1 -u 1026 \
        -g users -G accounts -s /dev/null -n username1
```

Creating Directories for Shares

Having added the UNIX users and groups, you're now ready to create the directories that will be shared by the Samba server. In this stage, you'll create each shared directory and assign the appropriate user and group access permissions that correspond with the details gathered from the existing NT fileserver.

In this example, the default UNIX location of /home is been used to store the user directories. Group (departmental) shares are stored in directories under /home/groups and the public share under /home/public. This is a very simple example; you'll want to organize your directory structure in a manner that suits your site's requirements.

Creating Home Directories

On most modern UNIX systems, useradd (or an equivalent command such as mkuser or adduser) not only creates the relevant /etc/passwd and /etc/group entries but also creates the user's home directory under /home.

If the user directories do not already exist, you'll need to create them. It's suggested that you set the group to be users but with no group or world access permissions. Here's an example:

```
% cd /home
% mkdir username1
% chmod 700 username1
% chown username1 username1
% chgrp users username1
```

It's common for a default set of contents to be automatically copied to each new user directory. These files and directories commonly live in the /etc/skel directory on UNIX systems, but this may vary depending on your variant.

You could use this method to create default files that are copied across—for example, a default Windows user profile or a text file labeled README.TXT that explains to every user the new network changes that have occurred.

The following shows the contents for /etc/skel on the server PERSEUS:

```
[root@perseus /root]# ls -l /etc/skel/
total 4
drwxr-xr-x   5 root      root          1024 Jun 24 14:49 Desktop/
-rw-r--r--   1 root      root             1 Dec  7 14:20 README.TXT
drwxr-xr-x   4 root      root          1024 Nov  2 23:13 custom/
drwxr-xr-x   2 root      root          1024 Nov  2 23:14 profile/
```

Creating Group Directories

For every share that was gathered from the NT fileserver that has domain group access, you need to create a corresponding directory on your Samba server. In this example, the permissions for the directory are set giving both root and the relevant group read, write, and execute permissions; no permissions are given to other users not in the relevant group.

As you'll see in the section "Setting Up Shares on Samba," making root the actual owner of the group directory allows the use of an administrators group to override share permissions and to create files.

The command sequence used to create the accounts group share is as follows:

```
% cd /home/groups
% mkdir accounts
% chmod 770 accounts
% chown root.accounts accounts
```

Now that you've created the four group shares for accounts, sales, itsupport, and managers, the contents of /home/groups now appears like this:

```
[root@perseus groups]# ls -l
total 4
drwxrwx---   4 root      accounts    1024 Dec  6 15:40 accounts/
drwxrwx---   2 root      itsuppor    1024 Dec  6 15:38 itsupport/
drwxrwx---   3 root      managers    1024 Dec  6 15:00 managers/
drwxrwx---   3 root      sales       1024 Dec  6 15:05 sales/
```

Creating Public Directories

For a public directory, the creation method is largely similar to that of creating directories for groups. In this example, users who are members of the users UNIX group (Domain Users) get read and execute permissions, and users who are members of admin (Domain Admins) also get write permissions. As you'll see in the next section, "Setting Up Shares on Samba," making root the owner of the public directory will give admin group members write access.

This, for example, would be a public directory for running network application binaries or for managers to distribute corporate information that they have control over:

```
% cd /home
% mkdir public
% chmod 750 public
% chown root.users public
```

The directory now appears like this:

```
drwxr-x---   2 root      users       1024 Dec  6 15:38 public/
```

Setting Up Shares on Samba

Now that you have the users, groups, and directories created on the Samba server, you're ready to configure the sharing.

Note that by far the greatest problem you'll experience is accurately mapping NTFS file and directory permissions to UNIX ones. Because these two systems use very different ways of handling security, there's a limitation to how accurately you'll be able to reproduce the NT permissions under UNIX. This is no cause for concern, because it does not mean that your Samba shares will be any less secure than your NT ones were previously, just that the security model is slightly different and you may need to use some extra parameters in smb.conf to achieve what you require.

User Shares

User shares are the simplest to set up because you initially do not need any information in the [homes] section of smb.conf. For example, [homes] will automatically provide you with shares for every user directory that will be accessible dependant upon which user account is logged in at the time.

However, you'll probably want to modify this section slightly by adding certain configuration parameters pertinent to your site. For example, the [homes] section for PERSEUS contains the following:

```
[homes]
        guest account =
        read only = No
        create mask = 0700
        directory mask = 0700
        browseable = No
```

The parameters create mask and directory mask are both set to 0700, which means that every file and directory created will have user permissions set to read, write, and execute, but all other permissions will be set to no access. This is, in effect, the UNIX equivalent of having share-level access for the user set to change and for Everyone or Domain Users set to no access.

Also useful is guest account, which disables guest access.

Group Shares

When setting up groups, you need to carefully consider what the requirements for access to the share are.

This example has the following requirements:

- Users in the accounts group can access the share with read, write, and execute rights.
- Administrators can also access the share with read, write, and execute rights.
- Files and directories that are created by any user can be read, modified, and deleted by the same user.
- Files and directories created by any user can be read, modified, and deleted by any other member of accounts.

For example, the entry for the accounts share includes the following entries:

```
[accounts]
        comment = Accounts Department
        path = /home/groups/accounts
        valid users = @accounts,@admin
        admin users = @admin
        force group = accounts
        read only = No
        create mask = 0770
        directory mask = 0770
```

The parameter `valid users` is pointing at `@accounts` and at `@admin`. This tells Samba to grant access to the share only to those users who are members of either the `accounts` or the `admin` UNIX group (in `/etc/group`), or both.

The parameter `admin users` is similar to `valid users`, except that users and groups specified in this entry will be granted access to the share as `root`, and all files created will show `root` as their owner. This is obviously a powerful situation to be in, so treat this option with care when deciding the members (if any) of such groups. This is, in effect, the UNIX equivalent of Domain Admins having Change permissions over the share.

In addition, to use `create mask` and `directory mask`, as described in User Shares previously, the parameter `force group = accounts` has been used. This needs some explanation.

Normally, when a file is created under UNIX, its ownership is assigned to the user who created it and the primary group that the user is a member of. The primary group is listed by its ID in the forth column of the user entry in the `/etc/passwd` file. For example, here's the user `username1` who's a member of the accounts group:

```
username1:x:1026:100:Accounts Bod:/home/username1:/dev/null
```

The primary group ID is `100`. Now looking at `/etc/group`, you see that this corresponds to the `users` group:

```
users::100:
accounts:x:520:username1
```

The second entry also shows that the user is a member of the `accounts` group. This is, in effect, the UNIX equivalent of an NT domain user having a primary group of Domain Users and also being a member of Accounts.

The `force group` parameter is set to `accounts`, which means that any files or directories created by any user (even members of `admin`) will be given group ownership by `accounts`, thus allowing all other `accounts` members to read, modify, and delete them.

Public Shares

Finally, we'll look at public file shares. In the following example, the public share requires the following:

- Any user who's a member of `users` can get read and execute access to the share.
- Any user who's a member of `admin` can get read, write, and execute access to the share.

- All files and directories created are readable by all members of `users`.
- All files created can be modified by their owners or other members of the `admin` group.

Here's the share:

```
[public]
        path = /home/public
        valid users = @users,@admin
        admin users = @admin
        force group = users
        create mask = 0750
        directory mask = 0750
```

This entry is very similar to the entry for groups, except it has write permission withdrawn for normal users by the use of `create mask` and `directory mask` set to `0750`.

This time, the `force group` parameter is set to `users`. This means that members of `admin` who have write access as `root` to the share will create files that will have the group ownership set to `users`; therefore, these file will be readable by all users.

This entry is in effect the UNIX equivalent of Domain Users having Read and Execute access to the share and Domain Admins having Change access.

Printer Shares

The moving of printers can be somewhat difficult, because the existing printer is likely already connected to the Samba server and cannot be moved. The simplest solution is to obtain another printer. However, there are a number of other solutions. Here are a couple:

- Set up a printer on your Samba server that prints to the existing printer on your NT server rather than locally.
- Move the printer to the Samba server and share the printer with Samba. Connect to the printer from the existing NT server.

Using one of these methods, you'll be able to support printing from both servers to the same printer during the migration process. Once migration is finally achieved, you can move the printer to its final destination on the Samba server.

You'll need an entry for the printer in your `smb.conf` file, the simplest of which is as follows:

```
[printer1]
        path = /tmp
        print ok = Yes
        printer name = lp
```

Here, `path` represents a temporary spool directory (to which the user must have write permission), `print ok` tells Samba to make the share printable (that is, a print share, not a file share) and `printer name` is the UNIX name for the printer in the `/etc/printcap` file.

Samba also allows the automatic loading of printers by parsing the `/etc/printcap` file. In order to do this, you need to add the following to your `smb.conf` file:

```
[global]
        printcap name = /etc/printcap
        load printers = Yes
[printers]
        path = /tmp
        print ok = Yes
```

> **Tip**
>
> The name and location of the `printcap` file will vary on different systems, and you may need to consult your documentation. On System V systems that use the `lpstat` command, you'll need to set the `printcap name` parameter to `lpstat`.

Testing Before Going Live

Before going live to all users on your network, you should set up several "test" user accounts to be fully functional with your existing NT fileserver and work through your migration process with each user. This will enable you to test and review your configuration of Samba and migration procedures before unleashing them on unsuspecting users and discerning managers.

In this example, four test users (`username1` through `username4`) were already created using the procedures discussed previously. The advantage of these test accounts is that they accurately represent a cross-section of all user accounts for the entire network. Each one is a member of one of the four different departmental groups, and some have special administrator level access. If you can successfully test and approve the migration process for these test users, you can be assured that the same process will work for over a thousand users of the same types. For this reason, it's essential that you strategically create your test user accounts to be an accurate cross-section of all the user accounts on your network. By doing this, you'll render the testing process more valuable and worthwhile.

This section assumes that you've already set up the necessary user accounts, groups, directories, and shares, as described previously, and have configured Samba correctly.

Testing Shares, File Creation, and Permissions

First, make sure that when a test user logs into the Windows NT domain and browses the Samba server, he or she is able to view and access all of the expected shares. The Windows Explorer utility can be used to compare the results of browsing the existing NT fileserver against the new Samba server.

Having confirmed that the user can view the correct shares, you now need to make sure that he or she can successfully create, edit, and delete files and directories in each share and that the permissions that UNIX assigns are correct. You're also checking that the user cannot create, read, or execute anything that he or she should not be able to.

For example, with the test user username1 logged into the domain, you can connect to the user's local share on the Samba server (in this case, \\perseus\username1) and attempt to create a file and directory there using Windows Explorer from the workstation NT4WKS_1.

A quick way to do this is to right-click, select New from the pop-up menu, and then select Folder or Text Document.

Figure 25.4 shows the folder New Folder and the file New Text Document created in the share \\perseus\username1.

FIGURE 25.4

Creating files and directories on a Samba server using Windows Explorer.

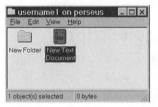

Having created the files, you'll now move to the Samba server to see whether they were created with the correct user and group ownership and permission bits set using the ls command. Here's an example:

```
[root@perseus /root]# ls -l /home/username1/
total 1
drwx------   2 username users          1024 Dec  7 21:08 New Folder/
-rwx------   1 username users             0 Dec  7 21:08 New Text Document.txt*
```

From this example, you can see that the file and directory was created correctly, with owner username1, group users, and permissions for read, write, and execute granted to only the user.

You should repeat the test for any other shares that your test user should have access to. You should also try some that the user should not have access to.

For file shares that you do not have write permissions to, your test user should receive an "Access Denied" error in Windows.

If you experience different results from what you expected, you should return to review your group membership, directory ownership and permissions, and Samba share access and create settings, as described previously.

Testing Printing

To test printing, you need to connect to the printer from your workstation. The simplest way to do this is by using the `net use` command. First, delete any existing connections:

```
Z:\>net use lpt1: /delete
lpt1 was deleted successfully.
Z:\>net use lpt1: \\perseus\printer1 /persistent:no
The command completed successfully.
```

If you can, try sending print jobs to the printer.

Creating a Test Logon Script

Once you're sure your test user accounts can access all the shared resources on your Samba server with the correct permissions and ownership, you should test automatically connecting local devices to the shares using an NT logon script.

Reviewing the Existing Logon Script

First, you need to look for an existing logon script for a user, which is stored in the `netlogon` share of the PDC. The script `accounts.bat` is for members of the accounts department:

```
net use g: \\nt4srv_1\accounts /persistent:no /yes
net use p: \\nt4srv_1\public /persistent:no /yes
net use lpt1: \\nt4srv_1\printer1 /persistent:no /yes
```

You can see from this example that you only need to change the entries for the server NT4SRV_1 to the new PERSEUS.

Creating a New Script

So as not to cause problems, make sure you don't make modifications to the existing logon script, because this will cause you and your users serious problems. Make a copy of the existing logon script before editing and name it something obvious (`accounts_samba.bat`, for example).

Persistent connections (where the user has mapped a network drive and specified it to be restored upon every logon) are sometimes a problem, and it may prove prudent to insert the `net del` command at the beginning of the script to disconnect before attempting to connect to your Samba server. Another good idea is to append a `pause` statement to the logon script so that you have a chance to view the results from running it.

The contents of the modified logon script to connect to the Samba server PERSEUS are as follows:

```
net use p: /del
net use lpt1: /del
net use g: \\perseus\accounts /persistent:no /yes
net use p: \\perseus\public /persistent:no /yes
net use lpt1: \\perseus\printer1 /persistent:no /yes
pause
```

Changing Settings in User Manager

Use User Manager for Domains to modify the logon script for the user to the one you've just created. You may also need to modify the Home Directory entry to map a default drive to the new homes share for the user. Figure 25.5 shows the new user profile settings for user username1 in User Manager.

FIGURE 25.5

A user profile for a Samba user.

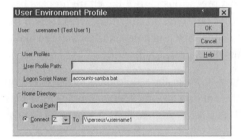

Testing the Logon

If you're already logged in as the test user, log out from the workstation. Now log on as your test user, and the new modified logon script should run. Figure 25.6 shows the results of the script running.

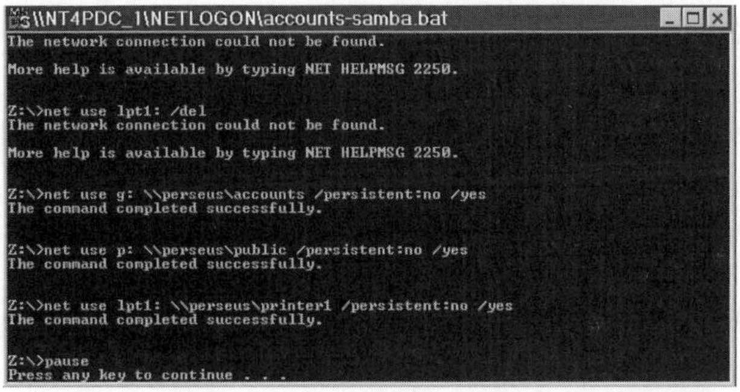

FIGURE 25.6

The modified logon script.

Now you can browse your connected drives by using My Computer. To get more information, you can use the `net use` command from the command prompt:

```
Z:\>net use
New connections will not be remembered.
Status        Local    Remote                     Network
-------------------------------------------------------------------------------
OK            G:       \\perseus\accounts         Microsoft Windows Network
OK            P:       \\perseus\public           Microsoft Windows Network
OK            Z:       \\perseus\username1        Microsoft Windows Network
OK            LPT1     \\perseus\printer1         Microsoft Windows Network
OK                     \\NT4SRV_1\IPC$            Microsoft Windows Network
The command completed successfully.
```

Migrating Files

Once you've successfully tested your Samba configuration with your test user accounts and are certain that the migration will appear to be as seamless as possible to the users, you should start preparing to copy across the contents of the file shares.

This stage is probably the most precarious part of the entire process because the users are using the files. How can the files be migrated smoothly when they're in use? There's no simple solution to this issue, and it very much depends on the size and complexity of your site and the type of shares being migrated.

Remember that you do not have to make the whole move at once. It's quite acceptable (and often prudent) to have the old and new fileservers running side by side during the transition. In this way, you'll be able to migrate some areas before others and to roll back in case of problems.

A good strategy would be to modularize the logon scripts into smaller scripts that handle only a few share connections. This way, the migration can be done in stages, and the administration of script changes will be simplified.

In this example, the users' home directories will be migrated first, followed by the departmental directories and finally the public share.

User Shares

The difficulty with copying over user shares is that the ownership and permissions on each file need to be correct for that user. This could prove a time-consuming task when dealing with a large number of users.

One way to solve the problem would be to use a logon script for the user that copies the files across (as the user) using the DOS xcopy command. This script has to perform the copy only once and therefore needs some way to check whether it has already done so.

An excellent way to achieve this is by using a dummy file placed in the user's home share on the Samba server, which is removed once the copy has been performed. The script checks for the existence of the dummy file. If the file is present, the script performs the copy; if not, the script does not perform the copy. The file could be a part of the standard directory contents for the user that's copied to the home directory for each user created.

The following is an example of a modified logon script called cut-over-user.bat, which is used to migrate the users' home directories for members of the group accounts. The script checks for the existence of the file to_copy.txt in a user's home share on the Samba server and deletes it once copying is complete. The file is an empty file (created with touch to_copy.txt) and is placed in /etc/skel so that it's copied with the correct permissions automatically for every user created. The script is called from the users' group logon script accounts.bat:

```
@echo off
if not exist \\perseus\%username%\to_copy.txt goto skip_copy
echo Your files will now be migrated to the new system.
xcopy /w /c /q /e /k /r /h /z \\nt4srv_1\%username%$\*.* \\perseus\%username%\
del \\perseus\%username%\to_copy.txt
echo Migration Complete, please logoff and logon again
pause
goto end
:skip_copy
echo Already Migrated
pause
:end
```

By using this script, you can easily tell which users are left to migrate by using the find command on the Samba server:

```
[root@perseus /home]# find /home/username? -name to_copy.txt
/home/username2/to_copy.txt
/home/username3/to_copy.txt
/home/username4/to_copy.txt
```

Group Shares

This is possibly the hardest migration because you have to synchronize with all users of the share. You should be careful to fully document who uses what, because the potential repercussions of some users using the old share while others are using the new share are a nightmare. (Imagine having to figure out which copy of which file on the two shares is the most recent!)

The most practical procedure would be to agree on a time (preferably after work hours) to do the migration. In addition, the existing NT share could be made unavailable to users while the files are migrated.

There are many ways to achieve the copying of files, including logging in as a user who's a member of the group and using that account. In this example, the Administrator user has been used and this account is mapped to `root` on the Samba server.

The first stage is to set up the mapping of the NT user Administrator to the UNIX user `root` and give `root` membership in the administrators group on the Samba server. Here are the steps:

1. In `/etc/group`, make `root` a member of your administrators group. Here's an example:

   ```
   admin:x:524:username3,root
   ```

2. Add an entry in the `/etc/smbusers` file to map the NT Administrator account to `root`. Here's an example:

   ```
   root = Administrator administrator admin
   ```

3. Make sure your entry for `username map` in `smb.conf` points to your `smbusers` file. Here's an example:

   ```
   username map = /etc/smbusers
   ```

Now that the administrator is able to connect to the Samba server as `root`, you grant him or her permissions to access the group share on both the old NT and the new Samba fileservers. Here are the steps:

1. Make Administrator a member of the group using User Manager for Domains. This should provide the administrator with, at minimum, read access to the share.

2. For the departmental share on the Samba server, make sure your administrator's UNIX group is in the list for `valid users` and `admin users`. Here's an example:

   ```
   valid users = @accounts,@admin
   admin users = @admin
   ```

3. Log into an NT machine as the domain administrator.

4. Using Windows Explorer, copy the files from the group share on the old fileserver to the new Samba fileserver. This way, the group permissions will be maintained.

5. Logout from the workstation.

6. Using User Manager for Domains, remove the Administrator user from the group.

7. Using User Manager for Domains, change the logon script for the user to connect to the new group share on the Samba fileserver in place of the NT fileserver.

If you're migrating more than one group at a time, you should repeat this process for each one.

Public Shares

Migrating public shares can be performed in much the same manner as that for group shares. There are two basic types of public shares, depending on whether normal users have read-only or read-write access. In the case of the former, it's only important to be concerned with copying the files across during a period when users are not connected to the share to avoid failures due to files being in use. As long as no frequent updates are being made to the public share, you should be able to migrate users at your leisure. For the latter scenario, it's more difficult because you'll need to migrate all users at the same time.

A simple solution to this problem is to create a number of logon scripts that individually handle the mapping of specific shares. In this chapter's example, there's one public share called `public`. Under the `netlogon` share on the PDC, a new `logon.bat` file is created called `map-public.bat`. Here's what this file contains:

```
net use p: /del
net use p: \\nt4srv_1\public /persistent:no /yes
```

This logon script is called from other logon scripts using the DOS command `call`. For example, the logon script for members of `accounts` contains the following:

```
net use g: /del
net use g: \\perseus\accounts /persistent:no /yes
call map-public.bat
```

Therefore, once the files in the public share have been successfully migrated to the Samba server, the only change necessary is to modify `map-public.bat`, like so:

```
net use p: /del
net use p: \\perseus\public /persistent:no /yes
```

Using such a method permits the migration to be executed in a modular fashion, which more accurately mirrors the actual needs of an organization.

Summary

This chapter has shown the complete process involved when migrating from an NT file-server to a Samba fileserver. Although the process has been shown in a particular order, it's intended as a point of reference and should be adapted to suit your particular environment.

By far the most important stage is planning the migration and acquiring the relevant information about the current environment before beginning. The more time you spend here accurately gathering information and discussing with your organization the requirements and potential impact of the move, the smoother the actual migration process should be.

25

REPLACING AN NT
FILE SERVER WITH
SAMBA

As discussed previously, the migration of files is likely to be one of the most perilous areas of the whole process. By modularizing NT logon scripts to handle small parts of the drive-to-share mapping, you can migrate in stages rather than all at once. This undoubtedly will reduce the impact on users and improve the IT department's reputation.

Ideally, "test" user accounts should accurately represent a cross-section of all your user accounts on the network. By proving that migration is successful for these accounts, you're able to prove success for every user account. If you have sufficient facilities at your disposal, setting up an isolated test environment would be advantageous as well. To set up a test network similar to the one discussed in this chapter requires only four systems, and these can be standard desktop systems. Testing in this way will help you gain a clearer picture of how NT and Samba interact and what, if any, potential problem areas may exist in the replacement process.

Samba File Transfer Enterprise Apps

by Steve Litt

IN THIS CHAPTER

With the emergence of client/server apps and Web apps, the use of file transfer apps has decreased. However, file transfer apps are still with us, and they probably always will be. File transfer apps yield certain benefits hard to achieve with real-time application models.

This chapter addresses those aspects of file transfer apps utilizing Samba. Systems comprised entirely of UNIX/Linux/BSD or entirely of Windows do not typically benefit from using Samba.

Even in mixed UNIX/Windows environments, Samba is only one of many possible transport mechanisms for file transfer apps. Email and other TCP/IP-type transports do not use Samba. Even traditional file copy operations from Windows to UNIX can be accomplished in non-Samba ways, such as with FTP. However, Samba offers the intriguing advantages of server-side automation, so you may want to consider using Samba as part of your file transfer app's transport mechanism.

A simple file transfer app consists of a front-end application that interfaces with the user, a back-end application that interfaces with the database, and a transport mechanism to enable communication between the front end and the back end. The transport mechanism is typically comprised of software, protocols, and wire.

You may prefer to think of the front end as a *client* and the back end as a *server*. That's reasonable, but keep in mind that communication is not in real time and is not continuous. Figure 26.1 shows the basic components of a minimal file transfer application.

FIGURE 26.1

Basic file transfer application components.

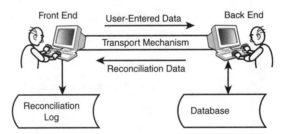

The transport mechanism is typically a set of programs centered around a protocol such as email, Samba, kermit, or FTP.

File transfer apps work very well over dial-up connections. Although we take reliable dedicated lines for granted in most developed countries, dedicated connections to many countries are prohibitively expensive and unreliable, requiring applications to use file transfer techniques. File transfer apps are a great alternative in any situation where dedicated lines are not universally available.

File transfer apps typically use less bandwidth than their Web app and client/server real-time counterparts. On overloaded systems, file transfer apps give back control to the user in microseconds instead of seconds or even minutes. Sometimes these benefits outweigh the benefit of real-time central data access. Additionally, there are situations in which direct access to the central database is not desired, typically for security reasons.

Not all file transfer applications use Samba. Samba is needed only in those cases in which there's a need to copy files from a Windows box to a UNIX box. Even then, FTP can be chosen. However, Samba's server-side automation (SSA) capabilities make it an excellent candidate. SSA is discussed extensively in Chapter 14, "Using Samba Server-Side Automation."

File Transfer Application Structure

File transfer apps come in all shapes and sizes, but they typically link front-end applications from various branch offices to a back-end program at corporate headquarters.

> **Note**
>
> File transfer apps are also finding increased usage in business-to-business electronic commerce. File transfer apps offer a data-exchange mechanism without giving an outside organization direct access to the corporate database, and they're very efficient.

Typically, the front-end program is a multiuser app that outputs a text file for each added, changed, or deleted record. These text files are usually written to an *office collection point*, which may be a standalone box or may be implemented on another box in the office. As will be discussed later, implementing the office collection point on a Linux/Samba server using server-side automation plugs a potentially serious security problem.

The files from the office collection point are then transferred to the *holding area* computer at corporate headquarters. The back end takes files from the holding area, processes and verifies them, and updates the central database. Figure 26.2 shows such an architecture.

In Figure 26.2, the collection points, the holding area, the wires between them, the software running on them, and the wire from the holding area to the back end can all be considered part of the transport mechanism.

Many variations are possible. The office collection point can be eliminated by having the front end transfer files directly to the holding area. The holding area itself can be implemented on the back-end server rather than as a separate computer.

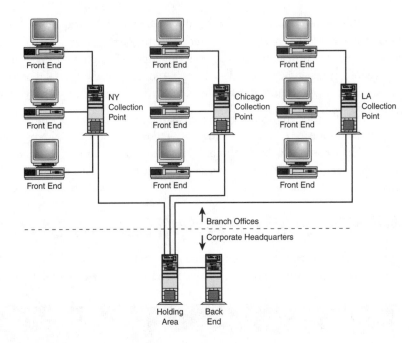

Figure 26.2

A typical file transfer application's system architecture.

The Holding Area

Figure 26.2 shows the holding area as the center of the system. The holding area is typically a standalone machine in corporate headquarters, connected to the machine that is running the file transfer app's back-end program, via a local area network.

The holding area ensures modularity because each office, as well as the back-end program, communicates only with the holding area. This makes it easy to add an office or even change the server on which the back end resides. The holding area can be thought of as a sort of post office, storing messages until the recipient can pick them up.

The holding area can be either active or passive. Active holding areas travel around the enterprise, collecting outgoing messages from offices and delivering confirmations while collecting confirmations out of the back end and delivering messages from offices to the back end. Passive holding areas do not contact other machines, nor do they instantiate file transfers. Instead, they act as servers, providing logons and directories for other machines to access. Each office has a *from* box and a *to* box (relative to the back end).

Each type of holding area has distinctive properties. An active holding area has the following properties:

- It's a program, not a server.
- It has centralized administration.
- It doesn't need to implement server functions.

Contrast the preceding with the properties of a passive holding area:

- It's a server, not a program.
- It requires administration in each office.
- It's more secure: Office and corporate server logons and passwords are not needed.

Generally speaking, use a passive holding area if the communicating entities' (offices, corporations, and so on) security requirements preclude giving out their servers' usernames and passwords. Use an active holding area if central administration is needed. If they require both tight security and central administration, generally the best solution is to use a passive holding area and train the offices to maintain their processes. Alternatively, the front end can be constructed to send files directly to the holding area, or the office collection point's pseudo printers can be made to pass the files on to the holding area.

> **Note**
>
> Pseudo printers are one type of Samba server-side automation (SSA). Server-side automation and pseudo printers are discussed extensively in Chapter 14.

Using an Active Holding Area

An active holding area moves administration to a central location, which is vital if local office technologists cannot be depended upon to set up and maintain systems to exchange files with the holding area on a regular basis (hourly, for instance). However, because the active holding area must proactively log on to the office collection servers and the back end, it must know usernames and passwords for each and store them. This is not ideal from a security point of view. This security compromise can be mitigated to a degree by having the office collection points on servers that do nothing but handle the system's messages.

Active holding areas perform no server functions. They require only the ability to connect to Windows, NetWare, or UNIX/Samba boxes. Therefore, an active holding area is best implemented as a commodity Windows 98 or Linux box with a reliable hard disk and a fast network connection. There's no need for an active holding area to be a server unless there's a desire to trigger Samba server-side automation on the holding area itself.

The active holding area is simply a program that continuously cycles through a configuration file containing logon information for the various offices, logs into each, and performs all necessary move operations, complete with verification. On a well-functioning system, no data stays in the holding area for more than a few minutes, because it's quickly sent on to its final destination. Therefore, there's little point in backing up data on the holding area.

If the back-end program is on a UNIX server and the active holding area is Windows 9*x*, NT Desktop, or 2000, transfers to the back-end program are accomplished via copy operations to Samba shares on the back-end server.

Using a Passive Holding Area

A passive holding area is more secure because, such a holding area doesn't need to know usernames and passwords for other machines. Instead, each office logs on to the holding area and can access only directories belonging to that office. The back end can access all office directories on the holding area. You'll notice that no entity can "reach back" into an office collection point server. However, a passive area requires offices to proactively send messages. Such file transfers could be implemented by an hourly cron job, but if the local-office administrator does not maintain the cron job, it results in delayed or even lost data.

The risk of spotty transfers to the holding area can be mitigated by designing the system so that the front-end program's transmissions write directly to the holding area. However, performing such direct writes securely requires special tactics such as setuid programs or a directory service such as LDAP or NDS.

Passive holding areas are servers and are therefore best implemented on Linux/Samba boxes. Such a box doesn't need to be powerful, because it simply accommodates move operations. It implements a separate security and directory structure, with a to and a from directory, for each office. The following is an example of such a directory for an enterprise with offices in New York, Chicago, and Los Angeles:

```
/hold
    ny
        from
        to
    chi
        from
        to
    la
        from
        to
```

Note that all the `from` directories hold data destined for the back-end program, and all the `to` directories hold receipt-confirmation data sent back to the office.

As an example of directory ownership and permissions, New York's logon to the holding area should enable write access to `/hold/ny/from` and read and write access (the write permission is necessary to delete) to `/hold/ny/to`. The back end should have read and write access to all `from` directories, with only write access to the `to` directories.

As a practical matter, if the passive holding area is implemented with UNIX, Linux, or BSD, it's much simpler to give each office read and write permissions to both its in and out boxes as well as give the back end read and write permissions to all directories. Because the logons to the holding area are special accounts not available to users of the system, the security impact of such permission relaxation is minimal.

So, `/hold/ny` would be owned by user `ny` and group `ftbackend` (the group includes only the back-end program's logon and the people doing the technical administration) and would be `chmod 6770`. Therefore, offices cannot access each other's data, but the back end can access all office directories.

The office data typically comes from the office collection point server. For reasons discussed later in this chapter, it's usually advantageous for the office collection point server to be a Linux/Samba server. However, if it's a Windows box, the passive holding area must be set up as a Samba server or an FTP server. The following is an example of `smb.conf` implementing such a structure on the passive holding area:

```
[ny]
read only=no
path=/hold/ny
force user=ny
force group= ftbackend
valid users=ny,@ftbackend

[chi]
read only=no
path=/hold/chi
force user=chi
force group= ftbackend
valid users=chi,@ftbackend

[la]
read only=no
path=/hold/la
force user=la
force group= ftbackend
valid users=la,@ftback
```

Implementing the Holding Area on the Back-End Server

It's possible to implement either an active or passive holding area on the back-end app's server, rather than on a separate box. This decreases network traffic on the corporate headquarters's LAN and eliminates the need for a $1,000 commodity computer, but it requires giving production server logons to each office. Depending on the situation, this may be viewed as an undesirable security risk.

The Office Collection Point

Referring back to Figure 26.2, each office typically has an office collection point, which may be either a standalone server (preferable) or a directory structure on an existing server. The purpose of the office collection point is to give each instance of the front-end program a fast, local place to dump its outgoing data files. The fact that this directory is write-accessible by every user of the front-end program makes it the primary security challenge in a file transfer enterprise application. A somewhat knowledgeable and malicious user could place a bogus data file in the directory, and unless the data file is recognized as bogus by the back-end program, it goes into the database.

The first step in sealing that security crack is preventing users from seeing valid data files. Unless they know the structure of such files, they cannot manufacture credible counterfeits. Such write-only access can be gained with UNIX file permissions, and especially with the use of Samba server-side automation (pseudo printer) on the office collection point.

> **Note**
>
> Another possible security solution is to set the user ID of the front-end program to a privileged user. Therefore, users on the front end can neither read nor write files created *by* the front-end program, except *through* the front-end program.

If that's not enough security, a CRC verification can be embedded by the front end and verified by the back end. Beyond that, encryption can be implemented. Only the SSA option depends on Samba, so it's the one discussed extensively in this section.

As mentioned, the primary danger point is the directory written to by the front end. Anyone using the file transfer app's front end must have write permission to this directory, meaning they can copy bogus files into it. Unless a mischievous employee understands the makeup of the file, this is not a problem because corrupted files can be removed at the back end.

Samba File Transfer Enterprise Apps

CHAPTER 26

751

26

SAMBA FILE
TRANSFER
ENTERPRISE APPS

However, if a mischievous employee knows the structure of these files, he or she can use a pattern file to add or change amounts, change employee numbers, and the like. The first defense against such mischief is to remove read access from the employee.

One excellent way to do this is with a Samba pseudo printer. The pseudo printer [ftapp] follows:

```
[ftapp]
browseable=no
read only=yes
print ok=yes
valid users=@ftapp
path=/test/ftappqueue
force group=ftapp
force user=ftadm
print command = /test/ftapp.sh %s &
```

The preceding share is very close to being perfectly "write only." The `browseable=no` parameter enforces the default to defend against a `browseable=yes` in the [global] section, guaranteeing this share will not induce curiosity by showing up in browse lists. The `read only=yes` repetition of the default defends against a change instituted in the [global] section and guarantees it cannot be written to as a normal "share." The `print ok=yes` parameter labels it as a printer, enabling files to be written to it by accessing it as a printer. Such files cannot be read, modified, or deleted, because the share is a printer. The `valid users=@ftapp` restricts access to the `ftapp` group. All users of the front end program must be members of that group.

The `force group=ftapp` setting removes user dependence, whereas the `force user=ftadm` setting enables a special user called `ftadm` on the UNIX side with full access to the file. The purpose of that full access is discussed later along with the `print command=` parameter.

The `path=/test/ftappqueue` setting sets up the pseudo printer's spool directory in this example. This is the directory in which "printed" files are held until they're moved or disposed of by the print command. If the `print command=` parameter is set to a do-nothing script, the files remain in this directory. For the sake of the immediate discussion, assume `/test/ftapp.sh` has no commands.

Note the state of the path directory, as shown by the following command:

```
# ls -ldF /test/ftappqueue
drwx-wx---   2 root      ftapp          1024 Jan  6 17:33 /test/ftappqueue/
#
```

The owner is `root`, and the group is the same `ftapp` group that users of this app belong to. But the group has only write and execute permissions; the group has no read permission. Samba allows reading of files in this directory, but UNIX prohibits it. Only root can read the files. Also, the user cannot overwrite the files. The share is `read only=yes`, so the only write access is via printing.

Specific filenames can be delivered to this share by a command such as the following:

```
copy afile.txt \\mainserv\ftapp\whatever.txt
```

or

```
echo Hello > \\mainserv\ftapp\whatever.txt
```

The preceding commands create a file called `whatever.txt` in the share's path. To create a seemingly random, unique filename, map an LPT port to the share and write to that port, like this:

```
net use lpt8: \\mainserv\ftapp
copy whatever.txt lpt8:
```

The preceding command creates a new file with a unique filename in the share. The following DOS commands create a file called `whatever.txt` and a semi-random unique filename on the server:

```
C:\WINDOWS>net use lpt8: \\mainserv\ftapp
The command was completed successfully.

C:\WINDOWS>echo Hello > \\mainserv\ftapp\whatever.txt

C:\WINDOWS> echo Hello > lpt8:
        1 file(s) copied

C:\WINDOWS>
```

The following `ls` command, executed from the share's path directory (`/test/ftappqueue` in this example) shows the results on the server:

```
# ls -ldF *
-rwxr--r--   1 ftadm     ftapp        8 Jan  9 12:48 whatever.txt*
-rwxr--r--   1 ftadm     ftapp        8 Jan  9 12:49 wincli.Jvoovc*
#
```

Caution

Do not copy a filename directly to a printer share directory without appending a filename to the end of the directory. In other words, do not do the following:

```
copy c:\autoexec.bat \\mainserv\ftapp
```

The result might either be a file called AUTOEXEC.BAT on the server or a file with a semi-random unique filename such as `wincli.tG8EZL`, depending on the history of the share connection.

The pseudo printer office collection point discussed so far prevents read access from a Windows box or other SMB client, but not from the UNIX box itself.

The Office Collection Point's `print command=` Parameter

All aspects of the office collection point's pseudo printer share have been discussed except the `print command = /test/ftapp.sh %s &` parameter. Up to this point, `ftapp.sh` has been assumed to be a do-nothing script.

> **Note**
>
> There's no need to put the script in the directory above the pseudo printer's path or to give it a particular name. The script should be executable and readable, but not writable, to members of the `ftapp` group. In a production system, the script is best put where curious eyes will not happen upon it.

Notice the trailing ampersand (&) on the `print command=` parameter. The ampersand runs the command in the background and returns control immediately to the foreground process. This is absolutely essential to prevent logjams caused by repeated use of this pseudo printer.

Because the files are owned by user `ftadm` and group `ftapp`, members of `ftapp` (everyone using this app) can read the files in the printer's spool directory. This makes it easier for malicious employees and others to modify a file and recopy it back into the system. However, the pseudo printer's `print` command script (`ftapp.sh`, in this example) can be used to move the file out of sight of group `ftapp`. The following is such a script:

```
#!/bin/sh
chmod 700 $1
mv $1 ../ftsafe/$1
```

The preceding script changes the file's permissions so that only the owner can access it. Because the share's ownership is forced to the special privileged user `ftadm`, normal members of group `ftapp` can no longer access it. Then the file is moved to a safe directory called `ftsafe`, whose owner and group are `ftadm`.

The preceding `print` command could be modified to send the file on to the holding area. It could also be sent directly to the back end, triggering a server-side automation on the back end to immediately update the central database and send back a confirmation. A different office collection point server-side automation could append the new file's information to a local multirecord file destined for pickup by an active holding area. The possibilities are numerous.

The Confirmation System

Because the front-end program submits data and continues without waiting for success confirmation, the back end must transmit confirmation files for all successful database manipulations. The confirmation is returned to the office that sent the add, change, or delete. At that point, the local-office list of transmitted database manipulations is updated to record the successful add, change, or delete.

This is made possible with the use of a system-wide unique key, typically consisting of an office identifier; other identifying information such as employee number, service date, customer, and so forth; and finally a timestamp. This enables complete matching of confirmations with transmissions.

Reconciling transmissions with confirmations is similar to reconciling a checkbook. Reports must leave sufficient travel time for the transmission before declaring it "unconfirmed." Once this time has passed, the transmission's disappearance must be investigated, similar to investigating a lost check.

A well-designed confirmation system requires the following items of information to be included with the initial transmission:

- Unique message identifier
- Original transmit time
- Original receive time
- Message total (dollars, hours, units, and so on)
- User ID of the person transmitting

The back end must add these pieces of information:

- Confirmation transmit time
- Confirmation receive time
- Status code indicating success or identifying a problem

You can create reconciliation-reporting programs to immediately point out any transfers that were not confirmed in a reasonable amount of time. Proper use of a well-designed confirmation system makes it extremely unlikely that a database update failure will go unnoticed.

Implementing Modularity

Well-designed file transfer applications allow plug-compatible replacement and addition of transport mechanisms. This is typically done by having the front end call a

Samba File Transfer Enterprise Apps

CHAPTER 26

755

26

SAMBA FILE
TRANSFER
ENTERPRISE APPS

`submit_to_database()` function, which writes a temporary file and calls a separate executable program to submit that file to the transport mechanism(s). The use of temporary files is a security risk because users can recover such files to learn about transmission file structure and possibly send a counterfeit file into the system.

Samba server-side automation enables the more secure use of a print process to transfer the file and call the executable (via the `print command=` parameter). On the other end, the back-end program calls an executable to copy all files out of all transport mechanisms into a directory in preparation for parsing and database update.

The confirmations go the other way, with the back end calling a program to submit confirmations to the transport mechanism(s). A pseudo printer might be an excellent choice for such activity, even if both the back end and the holding area are UNIX systems. Unfortunately, a pseudo printer is not designed to deliver a file to a Windows box, so the front-end program's access to confirmations must be through read access to Samba shares. In theory, this enables crackers to create counterfeit confirmations, but, in fact, false confirmations do little harm. Additionally, if the original transfer files contain the user's logon ID, the receiving software attached to the transport mechanism(s) can use the `chown` command to make sure that only the original owner can recover the files.

The important point is that neither the front-end program nor the back-end program can contain any transport-specific information. They must simply interface in a known way to programs designed to submit/retrieve information from any and all transport mechanisms. As new transport mechanisms are brought online, they're adapted with scripts to enable them to work with those interfaces.

Other Samba File Transfer App Security Issues

The configuration discussed in the preceding section makes it difficult for the casual mischievous employee to send bogus information into the system. However, it does little to stop exploits by a knowledgeable and determined cracker, who can easily read and write to such a system. This section discusses some additional security steps:

- Avoidance of temporary files
- Filtering unauthorized messages
- CRC authentication
- Encryption

Avoidance of Temporary Files

It's been mentioned several times so far that knowledge of the structure of transferred files must be kept from users as much as possible. This means temporary files should be avoided as much as possible.

A program crash could leave a temporary file readable and ready to copy for a user intending mischief. Such crashes could even be engineered by the user. Undelete programs present the problem of allowing recovery of deleted temporary files. This is especially true of temporary files on NetWare networks, where the salvage command can be used to bring back various revisions of a temporary file.

The worst place to have temporary files is in end user–accessible areas, especially on the desktop hard disk. Depending on the programming language used for the front-end program, such temp files can often be avoided by the use of a pseudo printer office collection point. The first step is to have the front-end program "print" to the pseudo printer instead of writing a file. This is possible in many development environments. If this is done, no temporary files are written anywhere but the pseudo printer spool directory, where they are exceedingly hard for an end user to access.

Filter Unauthorized Messages

The back-end program is responsible for updating the database with data from the transferred files. Obviously, any transferred file with incomplete, inconsistent, or erroneous information must be dropped, and a log record must be written for later troubleshooting. Erroneous information might take the form of the use of an unassigned employee ID. Incomplete information means the lack of a required field. Inconsistent information could be the breaking of a business rule (for instance, if an exempt employee submits a request for overtime pay). Another form of inconsistency occurs when the file contains evidence that it was not created by the front end, as discussed in the next section.

CRC Authentication

Security requires all input to the system to come through legitimate system front-end programs. The problem is that an employee possessing knowledge of the file structure of the transferred files could easily create a file to perform a deletion, addition, or transfer in Microsoft Notepad and then copy that file to the pseudo printer. Unless the back end has enough information to realize that the front end did not create the file, it goes straight into the database. This requires preventative steps.

This hole can be plugged if the front end submits a CRC (cyclical redundancy check) of each transferred file, with each transferred file. The back end can be fitted with the reverse algorithm to check whether the file was changed in any way because it was created by the front-end program. An editor-induced change of hours, dollars, or employee number would then cause the back-end program to detect the discrepancy between the file's present CRC value and its embedded CRC, drop the record, and write it to a log to be quickly discovered.

CRC authentication does nothing to prevent unauthorized reading of transmitted materials, and it does not stop a hardened cracker with the skill to simulate the CRC algorithm. But it does stop bogus file input by 99.9% of the organization's employees. Often that's enough.

Privacy and Encryption

The ultimate security provision is encrypting all communications. This can be done via front-end encrypting and back-end decrypting of all files. Encryption methods come in all strengths, from simple hard-coded character-for-character translations to public key/private key encryption methods qualifying as munitions under United States law. The selection and construction of an encryption system is beyond the scope of this chapter.

File Transfer App Architectures

File transfer apps can be constructed in architectures limited only by human imagination. This chapter has already covered active and passive holding areas as well as directory-oriented versus Samba pseudo printer office collection points (the latter is better). As stated previously, it's even possible for the front-end program to push the file directly out to the holding area, possibly inducing a Samba pseudo printer to push it on to the back end.

This section covers a few of the more interesting possibilities.

The Instant-Confirmation System

File transfer apps have the advantage of instant transmission, independent of the state of the system outside the front-end program. They can also be given the advantages of a real-time system by implementing "instant" confirmations.

An instant confirmation system depends on the same always-up dedicated lines that a client/server app would rely on. The front end prints to an office collection point Samba pseudo printer, which in turn prints to a holding area Samba pseudo printer, which in turn prints to a back end Samba pseudo printer that updates the database and sends back a confirmation. Similar pseudo printers on the way back send the confirmation instantly. Because Windows boxes cannot serve as Samba pseudo printers, the front end must invoke an algorithm that polls for the confirmation. Although polling would be an extreme CPU hog anywhere else, it's not so bad in the front end, which has its own machine. Such polling is still a network bandwidth hog, so it would be limited to spaced intervals during the time the confirmation is most likely to return.

It's possible to shorten the time for confirmation by eliminating steps in the transport. For instance, if the front-end program operates a pseudo printer on the back end's box, it could proceed very quickly. However, such an architecture requires the front end and back end to know each other's details, thus reducing modularity.

Samba is a vital component in an instant-confirmation system. Samba pseudo printer server-side automation replaces wasteful continuous polling, making instant confirmation practical.

Front End Direct Transmission to Back End

As mentioned in the preceding subsection, it's possible to eliminate the office collection point and the holding area. In such a case, the front end transmits directly to the back end.

In one way, this simplifies and speeds up matters: fewer steps, fewer moving parts. However, it requires a match between the front end and the back end, with the requirement that each knows internal information about the other. This makes piecewise replacement difficult.

Another disadvantage is that the front-end transmit function fails unless there's a working line to the back end. One might think the working line requirement could be gotten around by using email to transport the files. In fact, using email for the transport mechanism more resembles the four-point architecture, with the office's email server acting as the collection point and the back end's email server acting as the holding area.

File Transfer App Troubleshooting

File transfer apps are easy to troubleshoot if and only if the file travel route is well documented. Typically problems are diagnosed by finding how far up the path a file has traveled. Well-designed transport mechanisms do not delete files unless and until the file has been successfully copied to the next point along the route. On such well-designed systems, the troubleshooter simply finds where the file "got stuck" and then finds the cause.

The back end should be constructed to write successful adds, updates, and deletes, as well as rejected transfer files to logs. Examination of such logs often points directly to the cause of problems.

The confirmation system can be used to quickly narrow the scope of problems. It points out any transmissions that do not update the database.

Another useful tool is rerunning a batch and repeatedly deleting half of the submissions until the problem is traced to a single transmission. On systems that concatenate multiple files into a single one, the VI editor is an ideal tool for this purpose.

The back end should not delete transferred input files but rather should copy them, grouped by batch, to a backup location. This ensures the ability to rerun batches after a problem has been found, perhaps a month or two later. Such backup copies should be purged after a suitable time period.

Summary

Fifteen years ago, most enterprise applications were file transfer apps. File transfer apps function well over slow dial-up phone lines. However, file transfer applications incorporate data transmission delays that prevent them from being real-time apps.

The advent of always-up, dedicated phone lines and the Internet, with its virtual private networking protocol, has made possible real-time models such as client/server and Web apps. Real-time user access to a central database is very beneficial. However, there are still many instances when the older file transfer model is the appropriate one.

File transfer apps come in all sizes and shapes. One typical architecture is shown in the block diagram of Figure 26.3.

FIGURE 26.3

A typical, simplified file transfer app block diagram.

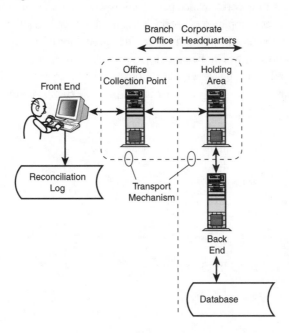

Figure 26.3 shows that the front-end program in the branch office transfers output to the office's collection point, from which it travels to the holding area in corporate headquarters, from which it travels to the back end. The office collection point, the holding area, the communication path between them, and the communication path from the holding area to the back end can all be considered part of the transport mechanism, which also includes various programs, software, and protocols used to transfer files.

The architecture just described is by no means the only possible file transfer architecture. Variations include direct push from the front end to the holding area, or even to the back end itself.

The holding area can either be active or passive. An active holding area runs a program that sequentially connects to each office, collecting and delivering messages. Active holding areas centralize administration.

A passive holding area does not proactively connect to other computers. Instead, it implements a server that provides a logon for each office and for the back end. Each office has its own in and out directory on the server. Each office logs on to the passive holding area to deliver data and collect confirmations. The back end logs on to collect data and return confirmations. Passive holding areas are superior for security because they're not required to know logon information of the computers they serve.

The office collection point provides the front end with a quick place to dump its output files, thereby enhancing the performance perceived by the user. To minimize the likelihood of a malicious user dropping a counterfeit file in the office collection point, it's best implemented as a Samba pseudo printer (server-side automation). The front end writes a report to the pseudo printer, which then quickly moves the information away from areas visible to the front-end user. The server-side automation can also proactively send the data to a passive holding area. The following is one possible Samba configuration for the pseudo printer:

```
[ftapp]
browseable=no
read only=yes
print ok=yes
valid users=@ftapp
path=/test/ftappqueue
force group=ftapp
force user=ftadm
print command = /test/ftapp.sh %s &
```

The following ftapp.sh script moves the file out of view of the user (who is a member of group ftapp):

```
#!/bin/sh
chmod 700 $1
mv $1 ../ftsafe/$1
```

Because of transfer delays, file transfer apps do not offer instantaneous confirmation to the user. Instead, they must implement a separate confirmation system. This system is essentially a duplicate app with confirmations traveling the return path of the data. At the front end, received confirmations are reconciled with records of transmissions, with any transmission that remains unconfirmed after a certain time interval requiring investigation.

File transfer systems can be built to be extremely modular. The front end and back end are built to create and read data files in certain formats as well as to submit and retrieve those files to one or more transport mechanisms via a small external program. In this way, extremely thin interfaces are maintained, and pieces of the system can easily be updated or replaced. Such modularity also reduces dependence on outside vendors for specific DBMSs and middleware.

File transfer apps can be secured by limiting temporary files, especially in areas accessible to end users, and by using pseudo printers on the office collection point box. The back end must filter out any files with inaccurate, incomplete, or inconsistent information. Implementing a CRC check renders any files modified with an editor inconsistent, thereby preventing them from getting into the database. For best security, an encryption system should also be implemented.

File transfer apps are easy to troubleshoot as long as the file travel path is known. That path can be observed to see where files are "getting stuck." Additionally, a well-constructed file transfer system should write logs that can be observed by the troubleshooter.

The confirmation system is an excellent troubleshooting tool, because it quickly informs administrators and troubleshooters of any file transmissions that didn't make it. Batching and batch totaling further narrow problems. Last but not least, the raw files from each batch can be kept and rerun in various combinations and permutations to quickly locate a problem file.

Not all applications are best built as file transfer apps, but a well-constructed file transfer app is reliable, secure, modular, and easy to work on. Samba, and Samba server-side automation pseudo printers in particular, greatly add to the utility of file transfer apps.

CHAPTER 27

Samba Enterprise Backup Strategy

by Kevin Long

The Importance of Backups in the Enterprise

An enterprise backup strategy is designed to enable an enterprise to recover from a disaster such as a fire, flood, or earthquake, to minimize the length of downtime when a less-severe system failure occurs, and to aid in maintaining the integrity of a data set.

In any industry where computers are used for actual work—as opposed to formatting actual work into pretty, word-processed documents—downtime can get very expensive. When you have a Windows-based network of clients and servers, downtime is a way of life, but you can lessen the pain with an effective backup strategy. Because Samba runs on UNIX or Linux, server downtime—the bane of NT admins—is reduced to almost zero, barring hardware failures. This allows you to focus on reducing client downtime to a minimum.

Disaster Recovery

Disaster recovery involves being able to rebuild your infrastructure back to what it was before it was destroyed. The time taken to rebuild must be a known quantity. If it takes six months to rebuild your enterprise computing framework, the backup method may be effectively worthless, because you'll be out of business long before then. You need to be able to replicate a working hardware combination on the server side, restore data sets from backup media, and rebuild client configurations back to the state they were in before the disaster. Your backup media, for this very reason, must exist in at least one separate location. Otherwise, if a fire destroys your server, it will also destroy any backup tapes sitting on top of it. Consumer-grade fireproof safes are good for keeping paper documents protected for a brief time period, but magnetic tapes are much more delicate.

If you have one server with one shared data area and one workstation with two applications, you'll be back in business in about two days after a disaster, assuming next-day shipping of compatible hardware. However, in many industries, a delay of two days could be the end of business. If you have a complex server configuration and several workstations, you need to be able to automatically rebuild the workstations while you concentrate on getting the data back. As a rule of thumb, if it takes more than four hours to get a user productive on a bare-bones Windows machine, and you require more than one hour of hands on preparation time, you're doing something wrong.

Hardware Redundancy

Backup strategies have to take hardware into account, both entire systems and system components, and usually involve some form of redundancy. Good examples of this include using more than one NIC in a server, and storing data on a redundant array of inexpensive disks (RAID). When you use more than one NIC in a SAMBA server, you need to specify which one(s) to use, in the `interface` = line of `smb.conf`.

Protection of Hardware Using Uninterruptible Power Supplies (UPS)

All servers and high priority desktops should be protected with a UPS, but you also need to configure UPS software to stop running tasks and shutdown the system in an orderly manner. In a networked environment, ensure that the hubs and switches are also on a UPS—if a user cannot save files back to the server in the event of a power failure, you will still lose data!

Lower Cost of Servers Allows for Redundant Servers

Despite prepaid benchmark claims, Samba runs well on moderate-to-medium-size hardware and doesn't show deviation under stress. For this reason, you should consider buying two servers for the price of one and synchronizing them to eliminate downtime entirely from your server vocabulary.

The "spare server" idea is particularly appropriate when placing Samba in the enterprise. Samba experts are not as readily available as NT admins. In the event of hardware failure, you'll be hard pressed to call in the local Samba team to fix the server, and "hot swapping" systems with a backup can make a major difference in how rapidly the problems are solved. The good news is that, amazingly enough, Samba (on Linux) will keep running when the hard disk is failing—even the system disk serving logged-in users keeps these users logged in. This is because all the action is going on in RAM, with only the file writes going out to disk. I have personally seen three servers with bad system disk drives where all activity was normal but new logins failed.

Runtimes are typically six to eight months between adjustments (usually networking or security patches), and these rarely require long-term downtime, other than to temporarily stop, upgrade, and start the Samba service. Basically, reboots are for adding new hardware. Here's a script that does an unattended Samba upgrade on an RPM-based system:

```
#!/bin/sh
echo "Updating samba at `date`" > /var/log/smbupdates.log
/etc/rc.d/init.d/smb stop
cp /etc/smb.conf /etc/smb.conf.backup
rpm -Uvh /updatesdir/samba-2.x
cp /etc/smb.conf /etc/smb.conf.replacement-not-used
cp -f /etc/smb.conf.backup /etc/smb.conf
/etc/rc.d/init.d/smb start || echo "failed to restart" >>
➥/var/log/smbupdates.log
```

As with all scripts, verify that the parameters are correct for your system. You also need to read the documents that come with your package update to make sure your `smb.conf` file will still work. Finally, if you're running a secondary server, you should test the update before making it hit the primary live system. In most configurations, unless you have unusual parameters, everything will be fine, and the system will be unavailable for about a minute. You may need to reboot Windows 9*x* clients, but NT workstations will reconnect correctly.

Configuration Backups

You need to back up your configuration files, including the `smb.conf` file as well as your networking configuration and hosts files. It's often simpler to just include your entire `/etc/` directory on the regular tape backups, but you then have to ensure they're secured. A better solution is to keep the system backups and data backups separate, either with two tape drives or with staggered backup procedures.

Server Setup and Preparation Backups

Some time should be spent on automating the build of your server. For example, on a Red Hat system, once the configuration is right, you should create a kick-start file that allows a server to be rebuilt from scratch in about 15 minutes (plus data restoration time). The command to do this is on a Red Hat system is `mkkickstart`. You may need to manually modify the networking section of the generated file.

```
[root@server ]#mkkickstart > ks.cfg
```

This generates the kickstart configuration file, named `ks.cfg`, which you can copy to a boot floppy, or burn onto your install CD-ROM. Refer to the Red Hat documentation on how to install using this kickstart file. Also on Red Hat systems, you can make a system boot disk using `mkbootdisk`:

```
[root@charm /root]# mkbootdisk --device /dev/fd0 2.2.12-20
```

This writes out boot information to the first floppy device (the A: drive) using the kernel image found in /lib/modules. You will need to verify which kernel image you have by issuing

```
[root@server /root]# ls /lib/modules
2.2.12-20
[root@server /root]#
```

and noting the image file that exists. This is important, as Linux systems can often have more than one kernel image, but you need to choose the bootable one.

Client or Desktop Configuration Backups

Unless you enjoy spending hours feeding Windows CDs to set up a new machine or rebuild a failed one, you'll want to leverage your Samba server to store configuration tools, installation points, and software packages. This will require two type of server shares: a hidden or restricted share that only an administrator or administrative account can access and a share that can be read by regular users but is flagged read-only. The following sections describe these in more detail.

Configuration Tools

You will need to build up a toolkit of software scripts and applications that help you automatically configure servers and desktops. These tools will need to function both locally and remotely, and operate in "unattended" or hands-free mode. Create a central location on your server to store these, and share them up to the network with a "hidden" share (sharename$) that also has restrictions placed on access. You do not want to allow users to make unauthorized copies of your software.

ActiveState Perl: WIN32 Desktop Scripting Environment

The ActiveState port of Perl, available at www.activestate.com provides you with WIN32 tools that are beyond compare for managing Windows boxes—from working with the Registry to automating maintenance chores. These come in the base Perl package, and add-ons, in the form of modules that can be installed later. Useful modules are WIN32-AdminMisc and WIN32-NetAdmin, which include tools such as logging on as another user on an NT system (without logging off as yourself), managing groups and user accounts, and an interface to the at service on local and remote computers.

Once you have installed Perl, you can download packages from `www.activestate.com/ packages/zips/`. Unzip, then install them using `ppm`:

```
C:\perlmodules>ppm install Win32-AdminMisc.ppd
Writing C:\Perl\site\lib\auto\Win32\AdminMisc\.packlist
C:\perlmodules>
```

This example shows `Win32-AdminMisc.ppd` being installed from its `ppd` file. Each package has a readme file to cover the installation method used. The ActiveState site and the module maintainer sites include useful examples of code that you can use. `www.roth.net/perl/adminmisc/` details the AdminMisc module's functions.

Software Installation Points: Service Packs and Driver Files

Service packs need to be installed (once tested) to update NT as well as to refresh it after dubious software packages are installed, such as programs of some convenience that aren't from a full-fledged software house. Sometimes these packages need to be installed as Administrator, and they overwrite essential Windows libraries through negligence or lack of attention to detail. Reapplying the service pack fixes Windows.

Example of an Automated Rollout of Windows NT Service Pack 5

The service pack needs to be expanded from its single downloaded file to the network share. From the command line, type:

```
sp5i386.exe /x
```

You'll be prompted for the location, which should be

```
\\servername\sharename$\sp5
```

(Note the use of a hidden share.) The files will be unpacked to that location. Make sure you have plenty of disk space; service packs typically expand to 50MB or more.

Once the files are located, you can verify the install options for this particular service pack:

```
\\servername\sharename\sp5\i386\update\update.exe /?
```

You can safely use the unattended options, and if you haven't experienced problems on your test machine (you have tested it with all your applications, right?), you can skip the undo option. You'll need to research your hardware, specifically the NIC and video card, to see what's appropriate with hardware file replacement. Bigger computer manufacturers usually have a specific recommendation for the sequence of driver installation when applying service packs.

Software Installation Points: Applications

Modern Windows software programs that will be deployed across an enterprise need the capability to be installed without human intervention. This is often accomplished via command-line switches to the `setup.exe` executable or `.inf` file modifications, or a combination of both. Although you can apply switches when running the install program from a CD, the more common method is to create a *software installation point*, which is a network share and path from which the software can be installed on multiple clients. The best types are unattended (or *silent*) installs that don't prompt for information and carry out all the required steps, including reboots, to put the package on a system. You'll need to create a share for these installation points and then subdirectories within that share to contain the installation points. Despite all the noise about long filename support in Windows, it's best to keep the names short and simple. In the case of Windows $9x$ clients, use eight characters or less, with no spaces. Earlier versions of Samba had problems installing 16-bit software (detailed in the Samba FAQs) from share points longer than eight characters for each element.

Once your software installation point has been created and configured, you'll need to make a backup. Because these can get quite large, once your complete set of applications has been built, you should allocate an individual backup to be made of the share.

Vendor-Independent Software Distribution Using `sysdiff.exe`

You may also receive software for a distribution that has no unattended install method and no command-line options. If you have more than one machine to support and both are Windows NT workstations, you can use the `sysdiff` utility to create a package that can be applied to each workstation. `sysdiff` comes with both the NT Resource Kit, `mspress.microsoft.com/prod/books/1318.htm`, and the Microsoft Zero Administration Kit (ZAK), `www.microsoft.com/windows/zak/default.htm?RLD=96`.

You can simply copy `sysdiff` to a hard disk and start using it. `sysdiff` works by taking snapshots of the workstation's hard disk content and Registry before and after the application is installed. You can then compare the two snapshots and create a "system difference" file (hence the name `sysdiff.exe`). This is what should be placed on your server, which can be installed using the scheduler for a truly hands-free software rollout. Even better, use Perl as your intelligent install checker.

To do this, first close all applications except a command prompt set to a directory on the local drive. Then make sure you have a `sysdiff.inf` file. Edit it to include any exclusions, such as folders that have variable or temporary content, and then run `sysdiff` to create the initial snapshot:

```
sysdiff /snap diffname01
```

Once it has completed, install the application as normal and make any configuration changes to it. If you need to reboot after installation, that's okay.

Once the application is installed and completely configured, run `sysdiff` again to make the difference file:

```
sysdiff /diff diffname01 diffname02
```

If this fails, check the Knowledge Base article. The most common reasons for failure are files in use or lack of disk space. Once this is completed, copy the difference file to your "hidden" or restricted access share:

```
copy diffname02 \\servername\sharename\diffdir\diffname02
```

Note that you can quite easily copy using UNC paths instead of drive mapping.

Next, test the difference file:

```
cmd /c sysdiff /apply \\servername\sharename\diffdir\diffname
```

Here, `cmd /c` opens a command window to run the command that will be closed afterwards. Here's a sample Perl script running on Windows NT that checks whether the computer needs the package and installs it if it does:

```
#diffname02 installer
$programdir = 'c:\program files\example application';
if (!-d $programdir) {
`cmd /c sysdiff /apply \\servername\sharename\diffdir\diffname`;
}
```

The routine sets the variable `$programdir` to the directory where it expects to see the applications folders, and if they don't exist, it invokes a command shell that is autoclosing (the `/c` option). The command shell then runs sysdiff, and applies the difference file from the server share. Check the size of your `diff` files, some may be huge and require special time allocations to apply them.

rsync

`rsync` allows you to synchronize data sets across computers. This is similar to the NT Replication service, but it's UNIX based. By coupling `rsync` with `smbmount`, you can mount remote windows file systems and then replicate their content to a local file system ready for backup. `rsync` is freeware available at `samba.anu.edu.au/rsync/`. If you have multiple servers on a WAN, use `rsync` to replicate application install points to each server.

Backing Up an Entire Client Hard Disk

Backing up an entire client hard disk is not a useful disaster recovery method, but it has some benefits. Sometimes you need to take a snapshot of a hard disk for legal reasons. For example, an employee is about to be fired for keeping pornographic items on his hard disk, so before he trashes the hard disk in an attempt to thwart management or the authorities, you can make an image of the disk using `smbclient`.

`smbclient`: The Command-Line FTP of the SMB World

`smbclient` is a tool that comes with the Samba distribution that enables you to connect to and transfer files from remote smb hosts. It is entirely command line oriented, and similar to the command-line FTP utility.

Backing Up an Entire Windows Hard Drive: Windows 9*x*

Backing up an entire Windows hard drive is more readily accomplished if the root of the drive is shared (like the default NT setup) as c$. Once this is done, instructions are the same as for NT.

Backing Up an Entire Windows Hard Drive: Windows NT

You can use `smbclient` to back up an entire Windows hard drive. First, make sure you have the administrative shares enabled on the workstation or server; then connect to one, specifying the IP and username (if not `administrator`). You will be prompted for the administrator's password; then you're given a familiar-looking prompt:

```
[root@server root]$ smbclient //ntbox/c$ -I 192.168.67.15 -U administrator
Added interface ip=192.168.67.1 bcast=192.168.67.255 nmask=255.255.255.0
Password:
Domain=[DOMAIN] OS=[Windows NT 4.0] Server=[NT LAN Manager 4.0]
smb: \>
```

In simple terms, you're on the root of the C: drive of the root machine. Although this is not *strictly* true, it's a fair analogy.

Issue a question mark (?) to see the commands you have available:

```
smb: \> ?
ls              dir             du              lcd             cd
pwd             get             mget            put             mput
```

27

SAMBA ENTERPRISE BACKUP STRATEGY

```
rename      more       mask        del         open
rm          mkdir      md          rmdir       rd
prompt      recurse    translate   lowercase   print
printmode   queue      cancel      quit        q
exit        newer      archive     tar         blocksize
tarmode     setmode    help        ?           !
smb: \>
```

You can use the ? command name at the smb: \> prompt to get more information on a particular command, for example ? ls provides the output:

```
smb: \> ? ls
HELP ls:
        <mask> list the contents of the current directory
smb: \>
```

A simple copy procedure uses the following method, once connected to the remote Windows machine:

```
Smb: \>prompt
```

Prompting is now turned off.

```
Smb: \>recurse
```

Directory recursion (include directories and subdirectories) is now on. Finally, use mget (multiple get):

```
Smb: \>mget
```

The entire contents of the hard disk will now be copied across to your current directory. Make sure it has enough space to store all the files.

smbclient in tarmode

Smbclient tarmode is an interface to the UNIX tar function, that allows you to make and restore Tape Archive (tar) files. The files can be used to backup and restore entire data sets. A tar file is analogous to an uncompressed zip file that includes directory information. Tarmode recognizes windows and DOS archive bit settings. Under windows and DOS, when a file has been modified, the archive bit is set. This assists in making incremental backups of only changed data. The default behavior for tarmode is full, which backs up everything, regardless of the archive bit setting.

```
smb: \> tarmode
```

tarmode is now full, system, hidden, noreset, and verbose.

Alternatively, you can make a tar file:

```
smb: \>tar c remotesystemname.tar
```

This will make a UNIX `tar` file in your local directory of the remote system's `c$` share information.

Dynamic Client Configurations Located on the Server

Backing up your clients' configurations can be greatly simplified if their configurations are dynamically adjusted from a generic base into something more custom at the point of logon. That's what system policies accomplish.

Using System Policies to Configure a Machine at Login

System policies are files listing Registry modifications that are applied upon login. You can contain different parameters in a single file based on named computers, named users, and named groups. You can also dispense with any specifics and use a default computer and default user blanket policy. The policy file is created using the `poledit` program. If you have a mixed network of 9*x* machines and NT workstations, you'll need to create distinct files for each platform, using the target platform to create the policy. Figure 27.1 shows the System policy editor.

27

SAMBA
ENTERPRISE
BACKUP STRATEGY

> **Note**
>
> Be careful about how stringent you make the policies on the Windows 95 computer you're running `poledit` on—you can actually lock it down to such an extent that you can no longer run `poledit` to free it up again!

FIGURE 27.1

The system policy editor with restrictions shown.

System policy files should be served up from the `netlogon` share. If you have Samba running as a PDC, your Windows clients, by default, look for `POLICYFILENAME.pol` and apply it upon login. If you're using NT clients or want to manually adjust and set which policies are used upon logon, you can make a "manual" pointer in the Registry. This might sound less useful than the default "automatic" method, but it has some distinct advantages. If you're performing a phased Office 2000 rollout from Office 97 (or none of the Office versions), you can create "before" and "after" policy files. Office 2000 takes advantage of system policies to a great extent, so your install file can apply the new policy file pointer during its operation. Here's the actual Registry parameter used to point to a Policy filename, modified by a Perl script:

```
#policypath.pl
use Win32::Registry;
Win32::Registry::RegOpenKeyEx
(&HKEY_LOCAL_MACHINE,'System\CurrentControlSet\Control\Update'
➥,NULL,&KEY_ALL_ACCESS,$RegHandle);
Win32::Registry::RegSetValueEx($RegHandle, 'UpdateMode', NULL, REG_DWORD, 2);
Win32::Registry::RegSetValueEx($RegHandle, 'NetworkPath', NULL, REG_SZ,
"\\\\servername\\netlogon\\policy.pol");
Win32::Registry::RegCloseKey($RegHandle);
```

The script uses the `Win32::Registry` module that is part of the base ActiveState Perl application. It opens the Registry key where the policy pointer is located, and sets it to "manually update" its policies on logon from the server and filename specified.

Roaming Profiles

A *roaming profile* is simply the contents of a user's Start menu, the layout and appearance of his desktop, and the currently selected network printers. This information is all contained in the folder `c:\windows dir\profiles\username`, or more accurately, the environment variable `%USERPROFILE%` on Windows NT. On NT, this folder is owned by the creating user (almost like a home directory on a UNIX box) and is copied down from the server upon login and copied back with adjustments upon logoff. The "roaming" part means that a user can walk up to any computer that's participating in the domain and log in to see a familiar desktop and screen layout once all the files are copied from the server. If you're familiar with X Terminals, you know that the concept of a user's desktop being the same from any logon is not a new one; the main difference here is that the bandwidth is sucked up only upon login as the file set comes down the wire. This typically is quick, except when your users start dumping files in `%USERPROFILE%\personal`, the default for many applications. Once the files start to build up in here, a logon to a new machine can take a few minutes—60MB of files in this location (letters to the landlord, graphics files, and so on) leave you with a 20-minute logon time on a 10Mb network!

System policy settings to determine default behavior of downloads and "slow connections" (that is, connections to non–NT servers, amazingly enough). The settings to modify are shown in Figure 27.2

FIGURE 27.2

Slow connections fixes using Policy Editor.

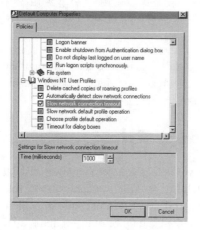

The settings determine how Windows calculates a slow connection. The longer the time-out, the better the chance a server-stored profile will be downloaded, instead of reverting to the locally cached version.

Roaming Profiles in Windows 95

To enable roaming profiles, set the appropriate profile parameters in `smb.conf`. Alternatively, if you're using an NT PDC, enable the profiles in the Control Panel and map a user's home drive in the NT User Manager.

Keeping the login times short with roaming profiles by avoiding caching data within the profile set.

Backing Up the Windows Registry

The Regback utility that comes with the Windows NT Resource Kit allows you to make periodic Registry backups. The following will make a Registry backup to the file `c:\backups\systemname` of the Registry hives `HKLM` (`Hkey_Local_Machine`) and `SYSTEM` and then copy it over to the server share point made to store machine-specific Registry backups:

```
regback c:\backups\%COMPUTERNAME% machine system
copy c:\backups\%COMPUTERNAME% \\servername\sharename\%COMPUTERNAME%
```

Restoring the Registry is accomplished using the `regrest` utility.

Registry patch files (.reg) are usually created by regedit (although they can also be created manually) and need to be backed up as part of the client configuration set. Instead of tweaking configuration parameters, system changes can be compiled into a single .reg file or series of .reg files that can be applied by a script or batch file. To apply registry patches without the accompanying pop up dialog box, use the /s option:

```
C:\regfiles>regedit regfilename.reg /s
```

which applies the registry file, and doesn't provide the usual dialog afterwards. It is often easier to generate registry files from an already configured system, using the export tool in regedit, than it is to write them from scratch.

Backing Up Data Files

One advantage to using a Samba server is that you get the power of UNIX shell programming, coupled with the predictability of Windows applications. Here, *predictability* means that specific files are created and destroyed in the daily operation of those applications, and they allow you to automate the cleanup of old files and redundant files, such as ones left behind in the event of an application or client crash.

The downside is that most Windows applications are heavily file intensive, so your storage requirements will continue to rise, but you stand a good chance of being able to manage this. Here's a sample scenario. AutoCAD creates a copy of a file being opened and renames it as filename.bak. This allows the file to be recovered if problems occur. The file is left on the server and overwritten as needed, but it's not deleted. Although convenient at times, these files are not needed in usual operations and can be removed at night or when file access is not occurring. The following script takes these .bak files and puts them into a tar file each night, named DAY.tar. If a file becomes corrupted, the user or administrator can dig into last night's cache of .bak files and dig out the last known good one. This has limited usefulness, but it gets the files out of the system in a managed fashion. Here's the script:

```
#!/bin/sh
mkdir -m 755 /data/acad-bakfiles
tar --remove-files -cf `find /data -iname "*.bak" -print` >
/data/acad-bakfiles/bak_`date +A%`.tar
```

Samba-Specific Backup Strategies

Samba-specific backup strategies include using rsync, smbclient, and smbmount (a subset of smbclient) and involve copying files and making tar (tape archive) files. These tools are unique to Samba, and require a working and configured Samba install to use them in system recovery.

Multiple-Site Backup Strategies

When you have multiple sites, either on a LAN or dispersed through a WAN, strategic planning, coupled with benchmarking, is the key to success. Unlike local backups, where you can run a backup during the day, if needed, and the users will not notice a performance hit (this is UNIX/Linux, remember?), across-the-wire backups need timing and traffic analysis. If you pull 10GB across a network, you'll need to test how long it takes and how disruptive the wire saturation is. Often, without adequate planning, the backups simply won't finish in time and will grind the network to a halt. Unless the office stops working at 5 p.m. exactly, the backup cannot start running that early. Instead, it will need to be scheduled for a time period when there is little network activity. If one server contains a tape library and the others feed it data during the backup, you'll need to find a way to get the transfer done as rapidly as possible. A good solution is to install a 100Mb cable run in the server room, between the machines, or to run dual NICs subnetted off in their own network so that there's a public "regular" network and a private server pool network.

Finding the Right Person to Do the Backup

The right person to do the job is a machine. It won't forget or get tired or make mistakes. Failing that, try to reduce the requirement for human interaction to simply changing tapes. Program your backup utility to verify the existence of a tape in the drive, the integrity of the tape, and whether last night's tape is being used (and has been for the last two months). Send reminders using `smbclient`:

```
tar -tvf /dev/st0 || smbclient -M workstation < no_tape_in_drive_message.txt
```

Also, send yourself messages when the tape is clearly not being replaced:

```
tar -tvf /dev/st0 monday.txt && smbclient -M adminpc < same_tape.txt
```

Treat the system and the data as two entirely separate entities. In the worst-case scenario, you can talk a user through restoring data files, but you should never be in the position of talking a user through restoring system files.

Making the Directory Structure Fit In

Pay attention to the network resources in the rest of your domain or workgroup. Avoid duplication of efforts, such as software distribution points, and make sure your policy file locations are logical and that your profiles are manageable across subnets. For example, if a user's machine is moved to a different office, review the best location for the profile before he moves to avoid having a "lost" desktop configuration.

Separate User Files and Directories Not Subject to Backups

To reduce the overall size of your daily backups, you can distinguish between slow-moving data sets and rapidly changing ones. Software distribution points and configuration files realistically only need to be backed up when they change, and if you keep a change log, you can determine when that will be. Provided you break those share points into a separated disk or partition scheme, you'll not need to produce elaborate backup scripts or configurations that tiptoe around the static files.

Mistakes Happen

Users delete files, and files get overwritten. The challenge is to anticipate this and develop an effective method of bringing back the files. If you have a backup that runs for four hours from start to completion, beginning at 7 p.m., and a user comes to you at 4 p.m. when a deleted file has been discovered, you won't be able to put last night's tape in the drive and grab just that one file without either overwriting the tape that's left in the tape drive or, if you write protect it, preventing tonight's backup from running. This may be okay, and waiting until the next day, up to four hours into the work day, for the file to return might not be a disaster. If this delay is not acceptable, you'll need two tape drives so that one is always available for restore. Alternatively, you may need two servers, with one replicating to the other, that then stream the data out to tape for disaster recovery only.

Deciding What to Redundantly Back Up

As noted earlier, backing up an entire hard disk is not usually useful. Backing up installed applications (as opposed to application configuration and installation tools) has little value. If someone's copy of Microsoft Word has become corrupted, the fix is to reinstall Word and reapply any configuration changes, not to restore from backup the disk image made of it. However, there is some merit to backing up the Registry of a workstation, because you have a good chance of successfully repairing the PC if you can restore the Registry.

Simple Compression to CD Often Suffices

Sometimes the simplest method is the best. By copying files to a CD burner, you can make quick backups that are easy to store and that have some durability benefits over tape. You can also make multiple copies, at little cost, to store in different locations. CDs are ideal for any configuration scripts and files as well as for software installation points, because you can begin rebuilding workstations from them with little adjustment to the routines while a server is being rebuilt.

When Samba Backups Should Be Distinct from Enterprise Backups

When resources served by a Samba server have different recovery times from the enterprise policy, you should isolate the Samba backups. For example, if you have a Samba unit serving users who need recovered files in a rapid time frame, and the company centralized backup policy is two days to recover single files, you'll need to apply a unique policy to that server. If the rebuild or replacement of a damaged or stolen Samba server would cause undue hardship, the data should be consolidated with the enterprise backup.

Enterprise Backup Hardware

When you start to consider Samba in the enterprise—and particularly with backups, which are so dependant on hardware support—the choices are largely dictated by the underlying operating system. If you're running Samba on conventional UNIX from a large vendor, you'll find few restrictions on how much backup you can buy—from tape libraries to virtually any kind of media. If you're running Samba on Linux, it's more challenging to find a high-end solution that will work with the OS. There's no shortage of folks coding up drivers and support for these systems, but without direct support from the manufacturers and the release of hardware specifications, it can become a real challenge to put together a hardware/software combination. In addition, you'll need to recognize where Samba fits into the larger scheme of your plan. If you use NT domain controllers with NT workstations logging into them and you have Samba in a peripheral role of file or print serving or not as your primary server platform, it's perfectly okay to let NT take care of your data backups with a consolidated tape backup solution.

With a UNIX vendor hardware platform, the backups of Samba data shares can be included in the regular backups of any other data partitions on the server. Underneath the SMB layer, they're regular files with ownership and permissions like any other UNIX file.

With NT as your backup focal point, you'll need to connect to the data shares at the highest level in the tree. This typically requires supplemental (preferably hidden) shares at the top of the data partition. For example, if you have a partition called /d1 with directories under it (for example, /d1/data, /d1/graphics, and /d1/accounts) that are shared out as data, graphics, and accounts, you'll be best served by a top-level share (d1$) at the directory /d1, that the domain admins or backup operator accounts can connect to when performing backups. Having this top-level share is analogous to the admin shares created on NT servers and workstations. It allows domain admins or backup operators to connect to a single share point that encompasses all the data and "sub" shares.

Media Types

There are numerous media choices on the market today. The key ones are

> Quarter-Inch Cartridge (QIC)
> DAT (DDS1-3)
> 8MM
> Digital Linear Tape (DLT)
> Jukeboxes and Changers
> CD Special Data Backup

The following subsections give more detail about each option.

Quarter-Inch Cartridge (QIC)

This media has a bad rap for being too slow, too large, and having too little capacity. However, it has another side: It's dirt cheap and been around for a while, so there's good Linux support for it, even for the worst type—a floppy drive driven on a PC. There's no way this media can be considered for data backups unless you have really small data sets, but as a system and configuration backup unit, it's worth considering. If you have a few drives lying around, you probably also have lots of tapes for them, so you won't lose anything by using them.

DAT (DDS1-3)

The latest version of DAT is DDS-3, and it's the most flexible version, with support for compression. Capacity is limited to 12/24GB compressed. If you have 24GB of data, this is not the tape for you. 12GB of data can be backed up in about three hours. You may need several units to back up disparate data sources if they're greater than 8GB each.

8MM

Manufactured only by Exabyte, these drives have good support on NT, and are available in 3.5, 7.0 and 20GB capacities. The format is proprietary, but common.

Digital Linear Tape (DLT)

Capacities jump to 30 to 70GB (compressed) and throughput is up to five times faster than DAT (5Mbps). Reliability is rated about the same as DAT Mean Time Between Failure (MTBF) figures, but no cleaning or maintenance is required. The units are expensive, but they're the best choice for a single-point, multiple-site backup solution.

Jukeboxes and Changers

Jukeboxes and changers allow many tapes to be put into a server so that backups can be planned for a week at a time, without the need for human intervention to change tapes—a daily task that gets old very quickly. The big question is, though, after a week's worth of successful backups, what happens if there's a fire on Friday afternoon?

CD Special Data Backup

With the current chaos of CD standards, this media type is losing the brief edge it has as a useful backup component. It still has some value, if you can avoid the proprietary extensions that abound. Choose a unit with good throughput that offers standard ISO9660 format as well as a rewritable format. Use it to make quick and simple, multiple copies of static data sets, such as software installation points, configuration files and scripts, and rarely changed libraries.

Enterprise Backup Software

The choices for backup software become more straightforward once your platform and position in the infrastructure has been decided. The following subsections present some scenarios.

Scenario 1

Samba is Linux on i386, file server and PDC for Windows 95 boxes; all data is stored on the Samba server, as well as Windows 95 roaming profiles.

Scripted `tar` works just fine in this scenario. Make sure notifications are sent to you upon backup failure. If your backup is done by a script, email the error output to your regular account. CPIO is also a good choice. It is similar to tar, but the main difference is that files are written out individually. If a file becomes corrupted, or a section of tape is corrupted, CPIO will allow other files to be read from the tape, whereas tar will have a corrupted archive. Compression is greater under CPIO, which allows more data to be put onto a tape, in less time. If you need commercial software, BRU at www.estinc.com/ has been available for Linux for some time and comes with some distributions you can try out.

Scenario 2

Samba is commercial UNIX, file server and PDC for Windows 9*x* boxes, with roaming profiles stored on the Samba server. The server also functions as a regular UNIX system, with UNIX applications running on it, and X-terminals connected to it.

Review whatever backup solution is typical for your system, either from the vendor or a third party. Incorporate Samba data into your data set backups and Samba configuration into your system backups. Often, the commercial software you use will have Windows clients or "agents" that can replicate the desktops.

Scenario 3

Samba is Linux or UNIX, file server in NT domain with NT domain controllers, NT backups. Samba uses NT for it's authentication methods, and is a passive member of the domain.

Share up your data at the top level to NT backup servers. Backup software choices include Backup Exec and ARCServe, which has NetWare, NT, and UNIX versions.

Summary of Other Backup Software Packages

In this summary of software packages, the primary platform is indicated (meaning the server that the software would typically run on). When a client is included, it's a service or agent that allows the client to talk directly to the backup mechanism. This provides some level of disaster recovery without having a full-blown backup server running on each desktop.

Freeware Backup Utilities

Freeware backup utilities run on Linux or other free Unices, and can be used on multiple servers without licensing restrictions.

Amanda

Amanda is available at www.cs.umd.edu/projects/amanda and is described by the authors as the Advanced Maryland Automatic Network Disk Archiver. It is a backup system that allows the administrator of a LAN to set up a single master backup server to back up multiple hosts to a single server's tape unit. Amanda uses native dump and/or GNU tar facilities.

Multiplatform Backup Utilities

Multiplatform utilities include commercial UNIX, Windows, and Linux or freeware Unices. They are licensed software packages, that typically use a license scheme for client agents. You will find good support for "higher end" backup hardware, such as tape jukeboxes and proprietary hardware solutions from hardware vendors.

ADSM from IBM

ADSM (www.storage.ibm.com/storage/software/adsm/adsmhome.htm) provides NT client backup capabilities. If you aren't able to run this on a UNIX system and you use NFS (or something similar) for Linux server backups, you can use modified administrative shares to grab data files.

Arkeia from Knox Software

Arkeia from Knox Software (www.knox-software.com/faq.html) is a Linux solution that has 9*x* and NT clients agents with some disaster recovery features such as registry backups and repair disk utilities. It has a Java-based GUI for consistency across platforms.

Arcserve

Arcserve (www.cai.com/arcserveit) has just released a Linux beta. It has clients and "agents" for many different platforms, including NT and Novell.

Backup Exec

Backup Exec (www.veritas.com/products/) has a long history of NT backup integration and also has UNIX product lines.

Legato Networker

Legato Networker (www.legato.com/Products/html/compatibility-guide.html) has NT and UNIX products.

Yosemite TapeWare

Yosemite's TapeWare (www.tapeware.com/cgi/pages.cgi?name=software|page=enterprise) is a Windows and Novell solution.

Alexandria

Alexandria (`www.avax.com/avax/alexandria.html`) is a UNIX solution with NT clients.

HP Omniback

HP Omniback (`www.openview.hp.com/products/omnibackmixed/general/general.sap?docID=590`) is a cross-platform solution that runs natively on UNIX, NT, and supported distributions of Linux.

Windows-Specific Backup Utilities

Windows-specific utilities are those that have little or no cross-platform capabilities. Usually the only additional supported platform is Macintosh. When storing data on a Samba server in this environment, you must use administrative top level shares to allow the backup utility to store your data sets. By it's nature, the data backup will be done across the network, so you also need to plan traffic and timing strategies to ensure your network doesn't suffer.

Retrospect for Windows

Retrospect for Windows (`www.dantz.com`) runs on 9*x* and NT and includes backup capabilities for Macintosh clients.

Troubleshooting Backup Problems

Each software utility has its own methods of recording problems and logging performance. Here are the main ones to watch for:

- *Media errors and failures*   Especially on DAT.
- *Finish times*   Did the backup run in its time slot?
- *Media integrity*   Did the test restore work?
- *Backup failure strategy*   What's plan B?

Media errors and failures are the most common weak link in a backup strategy. The backups must be tested for integrity as soon as they have been completed. A good solution is to use the backup software to read the tape and log errors, as part of its backup cycle.

Unfinished backups, or backups that run out of time, must also be addressed. You can verify this by using whatever time stamping method your backup software provides. As your data set increases, you will need to revisit this time stamp periodically. A better solution is to have the software alert you when a backup doesn't complete in time. You may be able to switch to a compression method to speed up your backups, or you may need faster hardware. If either of these options is not available (you are already using compression, or your tape unit is top of it's line) you will need to revise your backup strategy.

Media integrity is often overlooked—if the backup completed and can be read by the backup software, everything looks fine, but for extra safety you will need to attempt a read of the tape on a separate unit. Sometimes, DAT tapes appear fine, but cannot be read on another "identical" DAT unit. Your backups should be verified as readable on replacement units, in the event the original units are destroyed in a fire or flood.

Any backup strategy must detail what actions must be performed in the event of backup failure. If the tape failed, when does the next backup occur? Is it immediately once notification is sent, or would that cause too much burden on your network users? What happens if your tape units become obsolete? How long do the tapes last before they become unreadable? The answers to these questions will be specific to your environment, but need to be answered, preferably in a written policy.

Summary

Enterprise backups provide the capability to rebuild Samba servers and Windows clients, restore damaged or lost data sets, and provide recovery from a chaotic state to a normal state. They should be planned to solve a known set of problem scenarios, including dead PCs, new client PCs, dead servers, and natural disasters. Backups are worthless if recovery times are not known or are too long.

As Samba introduces cross-platform configurations to a network, the doors are opened to Windows-based software backup solutions that can dramatically reduce your solution costs.

Finally, the number of enterprise backup software solutions being ported to Linux is rapidly increasing. This greatly aids in consolidating your enterprise backup solution to one platform.

Using Samba to Install, Configure, and Host Windows Software

by Daniel Robbins

At its heart, Samba is about *sharing*. Typically, one begins by first sharing some files, then possibly sharing a printer or two. At this point, some are satisfied with their achievements, while others, driven by a practical need or simply a desire to push Samba to its limits, attempt to share as much as they possibly can. This chapter is for that second group, who are interested in discovering just how closely Samba can integrate itself with Windows. For example, in this chapter, I will teach you the benefits and pitfalls of actually running Windows software directly from an SMB/CIFS share, rather than from a local hard drive. In addition, you will learn the intricacies related to the proper configuration of a Samba-based Windows software development environment, and two ways of using Samba to share CD-ROM data. But before we begin on this grand adventure, it's important that we quickly ground ourselves in the basics.

Basic Principles of Sharing

It is very helpful to set up a Samba SMB/CIFS share that contains copies of the most common software packages that are used at your organization. Doing this will allow you to quickly access the files you need from any networked machine, and install them over the network. Since in this chapter we will be discussing the installation of Windows software, much of which is commercial, it's very important that we take steps to prevent the unauthorized use of such software. One good way to do this is by using the browseable = No configuration option on any shares containing commercial software. This will prevent users from viewing, and thus accessing, the share from the Network Neighborhood. The share will still be accessible from the command prompt and the Run dialog box, however.

While this may be enough security, it often isn't; hiding a share is one thing, and locking it up is another. You are encouraged to lock any administrative shares so that they require administrator rights, thus preventing normal users from poking around at all. This is very easy to do; simply use the valid users = option to grant only your account the privileges to access that particular share. Taking such precautions will allow you to benefit from sharing commercial software for administrative purposes, while at the same time preventing abuse. Now that I've covered the basics, you are ready to learn how to share CD-ROM data using Samba.

Using Samba as a Network CD Server

Every now and then, as a computer professional, you'll see a piece of hardware that seems to have limited usefulness. Perhaps one of the most impractical devices in use today is the CD tower. It normally looks like a large tower and contains several

CD-ROM drives. CD towers are normally used in environments where an administrator wants to give his or her users access to a number of CD-ROMs that the department frequently uses. This sounds like a good idea, but in most circumstances, CD towers are not needed, and a less expensive and more flexible alternative is available.

The Alternative Approach

There's a better way to provide the contents of CD-ROMs to users without using one CD-ROM drive per disc. The CD-ROMs can be either copied to a hard drive or an image can be made of them, which can then be mounted and accessed via the network as if it's the CD-ROM drive itself. You might be wondering why you would want to do this rather than have a pillar of CD-ROM drives whirring away in your server room. The next section provides you with some numbers for comparison.

Cost Analysis

The average CD-ROM drive costs approximately $60 and has a one-year warranty. It can serve up to 650MB of data—one full compact disc. Depending on what kind of CDs you plan to put in the CD-ROM tower, the average CD-ROM storage used may be around 300MB (because not all CDs are 100% full). Based on this average, a CD-ROM drive costs 20¢ per megabyte of data served. And remember that $60 is the cost of the bare drive, not counting the cost of the hard drive enclosure. If you want to serve these CDs over the network, you'll need either a network-enabled enclosure or a server to hook these machines up to. What's more, if you want to serve more than three or four CDs at once, you'll most likely need to use SCSI CD-ROM drives, which have an average cost of $100 or more, plus cabling. A typical six-drive network-enabled configuration would probably cost approximately $2,000. That works out to about $1.11 per megabyte served over the network.

This may not be a major expenditure, but there are a number of reasons to avoid this approach. First of all, CD towers are an unusually expensive way to serve data that can simply be copied to an appropriately-sized hard drive. Consider for a moment that for $140 you can purchase a high-quality Fujitsu 17GB drive, which has the capacity to store approximately 50 average-sized CDs. That works out to approximately 0.8¢ per megabyte of data served. Simply adding such a drive to a server in your department will in almost all cases be a much wiser choice than purchasing multiple CD-ROM drives. The bottom line is quite impressive—it's a 25- to 139-times-cheaper solution!

Another fact to consider is the reliability of CD-ROM drives themselves. Almost all IDE hard drives have a three year warranty and several offer a 48-hour replacement policy via the manufacturer. On the other hand, each CD-ROM drive has a one-year warranty and

28

USING SAMBA WITH WINDOWS SOFTWARE

probably doesn't have a rapid replacement policy. In addition, remember that the probability of a failed device scales linearly with the number of devices—if *one* CD-ROM drive is less reliable than a single hard drive, how much less reliable will 6, 12, or 50 drives be? Remember, you may very well be the one who needs to replace these drives when they fail, and most CD-ROM drives are not very rugged. They are typically one of the first components to fail in a PC.

High-Performance, High-Bandwidth Considerations

A single IDE hard drive might not be adequate in high-performance, high-bandwidth situations, where several users will be regularly reading large amounts of data from multiple CD-ROM images at the same time. This is because a hard drive can only read from one location at once; when multiple users are requesting large amounts of data from multiple CD-ROM images, it will cause the head of the hard drive to jump back and forth between both positions quickly while trying to satisfy both requests. In a sense, a hard drive is similar to a record player; it's very good at handling a single request for data. However, a single hard drive runs into problems when it has to read data from two separate portions at once, thus causing the head to skip back and forth rapidly and seriously degrading performance.

The Software RAID Option

Although CD-ROM towers do not experience this problem (because each CD-ROM drive has its own head that can independently read data), you should seriously consider implementing a software (or even hardware) RAID solution first if extreme performance is needed. Software RAID will outperform a CD-ROM tower, even on highly loaded systems, and it can be more reliable, especially when configured in a RAID 5 configuration. In a RAID 0 or RAID 5 configuration, reads will be distributed evenly over the entire array, thus resulting in greatly enhanced data throughout and much less drive thrashing. Unlike a CD-ROM tower, which becomes less reliable as you add more drives, RAID 5 actually becomes *more* reliable as more drives are added. Also consider that RAID can be used for a multitude of other things besides CD-ROM images. This makes software RAID a very attractive, reasonably priced, high-performance solution. For more information on Linux software RAID, you may want to check out Linas Vepstas's Linux RAID page at `http://www.linas.org/linux/raid.html`.

RAIDZONE

One interesting product you may want to look into is RAIDZONE, which allows standard IDE drives to be used in a very high-performance hardware RAID configuration. Not only is this solution extremely cost effective but it can actually outperform SCSI RAID solutions, because it uses DirectPCI technology, allowing for the IDE drives to interface directly with the 132MBps PCI bus (rather than using the much slower IDE bus). More information on this innovative product can be found at `http://www.raidzone.com/`, and solutions are available with capacities of several gigabytes to one terabyte.

Samba CD-ROM Server Implementation

You may be concerned about the additional complexity of creating images and serving CD-ROM images from a standard hard drive. Fortunately, the process is actually very simple. There are two good ways to get the data from a CD-ROM drive to the hard drive, and several approaches that you might want to use to serve this data to your users via an SMB/CIFS share.

Getting Data from the CD

After clearing off some storage space to house the CD data, you can begin selecting CDs that you would like to copy over to the hard drive. There are two approaches to doing this, and both are simple. One method involves creating a directory on your target volume and recursively copying the data from the mounted CD-ROM using the standard UNIX `cp` command:

```
# cd /pub/cdarchive
# mkdir cdimage1
# cp -ax /mnt/cdrom/* cdimage1
```

This series of commands will copy the contents of a CD mounted at `/mnt/cdrom` to the directory `/pub/cdarchive/cdimage1`. This technique is especially useful if you only need to share a portion of the files from the CD—copy over only the files you need to share.

However, there's another technique you may want to use that is especially handy when dealing with serving entire CD-ROMs over the network, and involves taking a literal binary snapshot of the data on disc.

Assuming your CD-ROM device is `/dev/cdrom`, the following `dd` command will allow you to "rip" the binary data from the CD and save it to a single on-disk file, called `cdimage1.iso`. Note that it's not necessary to actually mount the CD for this command to work properly:

```
# dd if=/dev/cdrom of=cdimage1.iso
```

After I performed this on my Palm IIIx Connected Organizer CD-ROM, my `cdimage1.iso` file on disk was only 22MB! This is because only a fraction of the CD-ROM's capacity was used. It's definitely a waste to dedicate a CD-ROM drive to the task of serving data from a 22MB CD.

28

USING SAMBA WITH WINDOWS SOFTWARE

Mounting the Image

After extracting the ISO image directly from the CD, this ISO image can be mounted at /mnt/cdimage1 by using the following command under Linux:

```
# mount cdimage1.iso /mnt/cdimage1 -t iso9660 -o ro,loop
```

> **Tip**
>
> This command makes use of the *loopback device*, which allows Linux to mount files that contain file system data. If the preceding mount command doesn't work, verify that the loop module is loaded by use of the lsmod command. If you're unable to load this module by typing **modprobe loop**, it's possible that this option was not compiled into your kernel. During kernel configuration, this command is normally found under the Block Devices category and is called Loopback Device Support.

After executing this command, you'll be able to find the CD contents under /mnt/ cdimage1. The advantage to this technique (as compared to simply copying the files over using cp -ax) is the fact that you've captured an exact image of the file system on the CD-ROM, so there's no possibility that files could be accidentally modified or permissions changed during the imaging process. If you need to mount the CD-ROM with alternate permissions, it can be easily accomplished by passing the uid=, gid=, and mode= options to mount. See the mount man page for more information on these options.

Sharing the Data via Samba

After you've placed the data you need on your hard drive or mounted the appropriate file systems, a share has to be configured to serve the data. This can typically be done by creating a standard read-only share, as follows:

```
[disc1]
    public=yes
    path=/mnt/cdimage1
    volume="exact CD-ROM label"
force user=root
    read-only=yes
```

Generally, you can safely use the force user=root option, because you'll want all your users to have full access to the CD. Notice the use of the volume= option to set the name of the CD-ROM as it appears when the disc is inserted under Windows. Some applications (and especially setup programs) rely on this name being exactly the same for proper operation.

There isn't much more to it than that when installing applications from CD to a local drive or when serving out documents or data. However, things become much more complicated when you're actually running applications from a share, which is covered in the next section.

Running Applications from an SMB/CIFS Share

You've learned how to share Windows data from Samba, but how about actually running live applications from an SMB/CIFS share? This seems like a great idea at first, and in many cases it's harmless. For example, running a setup program over the network for the purpose of installing files locally is a common and relatively safe practice. But what about running everyday productivity, development, and business applications from an SMB/CIFS share? Unfortunately, there are some extremely significant drawbacks to such an arrangement. (In fact, I'll spend most of this section trying to convince you *not* to run applications directly from SMB/CIFS shares, at least not on a regular basis.) Although it's possible, and sometimes practical, for an organization to run applications such as Microsoft Office from a single SMB/CIFS share, performance will always be better when they're run locally. Stability will also generally suffer when a large application with a long runtime is executed from an SMB/CIFS share, because network hiccups and major glitches can cause the application to crash and data to be lost.

The Crash Effect

Why all this fuss? To get to the point, if you're running an application from an SMB/CIFS share and you restart Samba, the Windows application will crash every time. Consider this carefully. This means that if you plan to have your users running Windows applications from a Samba share and you restart Samba, all the applications running from the network will crash, possibly bringing down the entire OS with it if the client machine is running Windows 95/98. This creates a difficult-to-administrate environment, and a potentially unstable one. If you do choose to run Windows applications over the network, you should stay away from SWAT's `restart smbd` button, which actually kills and restarts `smbd`. Instead, tell `smbd` to reread its configuration file by sending it a `SIGHUP` command from the UNIX side, typically by typing this:

```
kill -SIGHUP 321
```

In this example, `321` is the process ID of the main `smbd` process. Using a `SIGHUP` command will cause Samba to reread its configuration file after a short period of time, typically at least two minutes. Although your changes to the `smb.conf` file will not take effect instantaneously, using `SIGHUP` will allow any applications running from an SMB/CIFS share to continue proper operation as you add shares, change permissions, and so on.

The Network Load

There's another good reason to stay away from installing Windows applications on network shares—doing so will cause a dramatic load increase on your network infrastructure. This is a serious consideration and is another good reason to install Windows applications on the local hard drive. There will be some instances in which running applications from a network share will be preferred. However, this option should be considered carefully and should only be done if your organization happens to have a relatively fast and very reliable network.

Compatibility Issues

There may be a particular application that you would like to run from an SMB/CIFS share, but it might not be possible. Some programs simply do not support this form of operation and will either refuse to install or, worse, install perfectly but crash periodically. It's *essential* that you contact the manufacturer to find out whether operation from an SMB/CIFS share is supported as well as what issues will need to be addressed if the application is run by more than one user at once. One difficulty is that some programs write data into their own program directories—not only does this create possible corruption and instability problems when multiple users are running the application at the same time, but you may need to keep the share readable and writable to allow the program to even start. When faced with such a program, it's almost always best *not* to use it in any kind of networked configuration. At the very least, make an attempt to receive proper installation instructions from the software developer before installing the software on an SMB/CIFS share.

Compatibility with Development Tools

When using a Samba SMB/CIFS share to store a software development project, extra precautions need to be taken to ensure that your development project compiles correctly. Most development packages have a tool similar to the standard UNIX make command, which is used to recompile and link any updated files. The functionality in make (or nmake, which is included with Visual C++) relies on each file having an accurate modification date setting, and it is critical to make sure that Samba is as Windows-compatible as possible in this area. By default, Samba does do some things that confuse certain make programs, especially nmake. For this reason, the following settings are recommended if you plan to store development projects on a particular Samba SMB/CIFS share:

```
dos filetime resolution = True

dos filetimes = True
```

```
delete readonly = yes
```

```
fake directory create times = yes
```

Each of these options is settable on a per-share basis. The first option above, `dos filetime resolution`, resolves a problem with Visual C++ when oplocks are enabled on a share. Oplocks are enabled by default, and should generally not be disabled. This option tells Samba to use a two second granularity on file timestamps, just like Windows does on DOS and FAT file systems.

The second option, `dos filetimes`, causes Samba to behave in a more Windows-compatible manner. Under Windows, when anyone writes to a file, the timestamp is changed. Under UNIX, the timestamp is changed only when the owner of the file or root writes to the file. Setting this option to true causes Samba to set timestamps identically to Windows. The third option, `delete readonly`, is another option that subtly alters Samba's behavior so that it is more friendly to development tools, in this case `rcs`. Under UNIX, if you do not have read permissions for a file, you can still delete the file if you own it. Under Windows, this is not true. Enabling this option will allow a share to be UNIX-like in this aspect.

The last option, `fake directory create times`, is another option that helps Visual C++'s `nmake` program work correctly. `nmake` uses a directory's creation date when it checks for any new files that need compiling. However, UNIX systems do not store a creation date for directories, so Samba is in a bind. It normally gets around this by using the directory's `ctime` value, which is actually the most recent date that a file was added or removed from this directory. Normally, this subtle difference does not cause any problems. However, Visual C++ gets confused by this, and will not compile programs correctly. Setting `fake directory create times` to `yes` causes Samba to set all directories' create time to January 1, 1980, which makes Visual C++ work correctly.

Because `make` programs rely heavily on an accurate date, it's very important that your UNIX and Windows machines' clocks are synchronized. One easy way to do this is to put the following setting in the global section:

```
time server = True
```

This option will cause `nmbd` to tell Windows Clients that it is a time server. Then, Windows machines can be told to synchronize their clocks with the Samba machine. This is typically done under Windows NT by issuing a `net time` command from the command shell prompt or login script:

```
C:\>net time \\freebox /yes /set
Current time at \\freebox is 2/1/00 12:27 AM

The command completed successfully.
```

Please note that it is not essential that your organization's clocks are set to the correct time, *as long as they all agree with each other.* In other words, every clock in your organization can be ten minutes fast, and as long as every system's clock is synchronized to within a second or two of the others, building files will operate correctly.

In addition to the aforementioned time synchronization method, there are also many other free and shareware time synchronization methods available that you may find more convenient and compatible with other Windows platforms, such as Windows 95 and 98. One particularly good program called Tardis is available from `http://www.kaska. demon.co.uk/`. It provides a number of flexible ways of keeping all your organization's Windows machines in sync with each other. Other similar programs are available; you are encouraged to check your favorite Windows freeware and shareware site for a complete list.

Manageability: The Single Advantage

The one advantage of regularly running applications from an SMB/CIFS share is the fact that they are more manageable. Installing applications on SMB/CIFS shares allows the administrator to easily upgrade and patch any applications in one quick step. In the ideal case, logging all users out of an application, upgrading it, and then installing a new version of the application will perform an instant upgrade on the client machines. In reality, many applications do *not* work this way and require some tweaking or upgrading on the client end. However, some typically smaller applications *can* be easily upgraded using this method. Your applications will likely vary dramatically in their suitability to this arrangement.

Test It Out

After installing an untested program on an SMB/CIFS share, you'll need to test it over and over again. Without putting any valuable production data into the program, see how well it fares in a multiuser environment. What about two users in the same part of the program at the same time, or two users applying changes to the same set of data at the same time? The list of possible disasters is so great that it would be foolish to skip the testing step. Test well and thoroughly—it's far better to find out issues now rather than after you've trained your organization to use the new system.

Success or Failure

All this being said, it's very possible that a number of applications will run very well from an SMB/CIFS share. It's normally (but not always) a sink-or-swim situation—either the application performs well over the network or you find out that it doesn't right away, after initially starting it up. That means that after the proper testing and research, it's definitely possible to run many applications from the network without problems. Some will never work in this configuration. Running directly from a hard drive on a client machine, however, is almost always a sure thing.

Oplocks Review

Oplocks, or *opportunistic locks*, is a system that the SMB/CIFS protocol uses to dramatically enhance performance. When oplocks are enabled (and on modern versions of Samba, they are by default), the client can aggressively cache share data (that is, the client is *not* required to send its changes back to the server but can simply store those changes in its local cache, or *buffer*). This client-side caching speeds things up tremendously, and it's great in this respect.

However, although opportunistic locking ensures that Samba and other SMB/CIFS clients and servers see a consistent view of the data and that the data does not get corrupted, it does not ensure that SMB/CIFS *and* UNIX see a consistent view of the data. For example, if a particular client called CLIENT1 has an oplock on a file named myfile sitting on \\SAMBA1\myshare, all SMB/CIFS clients are ensured a consistent view of the data. However, if significant changes were made to myfile from the UNIX shell, the changes probably would not be immediately reflected on SAMBA1. Such data synchronization issues can lead to data consistency problems, and possibly corruption if you happen to be working on a particular file from "both sides" (UNIX and Windows) at once. At this time, the only UNIX designed to ensure such data consistency with Samba is Silicon Graphics' (SGI's) IRIX 6.5.3f and later. IRIX has been enhanced so that data will always be consistent between the UNIX and SMB/CIFS sides. Such functionality will hopefully be added to other UNIX and UNIX-like operating systems soon.

Installing Microsoft Office on a Share

You're probably familiar with the normal process of installing Microsoft Office from CD—doing so will cause the setup program to install Microsoft Office to run on a particular computer. In addition to this method, there's another way to install Microsoft Office, called an *administrative installation*. This installation method will allow Office to be installed to an SMB/CIFS share, from which Office can be installed on client machines. In addition, client machines can be configured to run Office directly from the server, copying only a minimal set of files to the client machines.

The advantage of such a system is that it allows central updates and management of the Microsoft Office program from the server directly. The drawback of such an arrangement is that it will put a significant load on the your network and your server, depending on its bandwidth, its current load, and the number of users who will be running Microsoft Office over the share.

Initial Office Setup

Several special steps are involved in using Samba in conjunction with an administrative install. The first step required is the creation of a new Samba share for the Microsoft Office setup so that the setup program can write the data to the share. After the setup process is complete, the second step involves *reconfiguring* the share so that it's read-only (protecting it from damage by users) and changing some important file-locking parameters that will allow Microsoft Office to run properly. The final step is to run the Microsoft Office setup program over the network from each client machine. The first step is quite simple and involves creating a standard read/write share on your Samba system. It typically involves adding the following lines to the `smb.conf` file:

```
[office97]
    comment=administrative install
    path=/pub/office97
    read only=No
    force user = root
```

The specific options may vary depending on your current Samba configuration. After this first step is completed, you're ready to start the Microsoft Office setup program by using the following command from a Windows DOS window or by using the Run menu option under the Start menu:

```
D:\SETUP /A
```

In this example, `D` is the drive letter of the CD-ROM drive, `SETUP` is the standard Microsoft Office Setup program, and `/A` is a command-line option that tells Microsoft Office to perform an administrative install. Note that it does not matter which directory this program is run from. You'll specify the installation path during the setup process.

After the setup program begins, you'll be prompted to close all running Microsoft Office applications (if any are running), type in your organization's name, and then choose a destination for the installation. You'll want choose the `office97` share as the destination for the install by clicking the Network button and using the network browser window to select this share. After you've selected the SMB/CIFS share, the Office setup program will automatically map this share to a drive letter for the remainder of the installation. As the setup procedure continues, you'll be prompted for the names of two folders for various Office components. It's safe to accept the defaults, `MSAPPS` and `MsOffice`, for these options. Next, you'll be asked whether you'll have client machines access Microsoft Office via UNC path or via a mapped drive letter. If you choose the drive letter option, all client machines and user profiles will need to have that particular drive letter mapped to your `office97` share. For this reason, the UNC path method is preferred.

On the next screen, you're given the choice of how you would like the Office Setup program to operate when run from a client machine (see Figure 28.1).

FIGURE 28.1

Microsoft Office allows you to choose an installation method.

When Shared Files Installation is set to Server, the setup program will automatically default to installing just the necessary hooks on the client machine to allow Microsoft Office to run from the server, thus saving a lot of disk space but making Office network dependent. The second choice, Local Hard Drive, instructs setup to operate normally, as if it were run from the CD on the client machine. This choice will set up Office to run from the local machine, where it's not network dependent. The third option, User's Choice, will allow the user to select his or her preferred configuration when running the setup program.

After the installation of Office to the administrative share is complete, you need to perform an additional step so that the Samba share operates properly. To do this, you'll need to edit your `smb.conf` file and change the `office97` share to the following configuration:

```
[office97]
    comment=administrative install
    path=/pub/office97
    volume="CD-ROM label goes here"
    read only=yes
    share modes=no
    locking=no
    public=yes
    browseable=yes
    force user = root
```

After either restarting Samba or waiting a short period of time after sending `smbd` a `SIGHUP`, the `office97` share will have these new options enabled. Specifically, these options turn off any kind of SMB/CIFS file locking, set the proper volume name on the share (which should match the CD-ROM name under Windows), and change the share to read-only. The `share modes=no` option enables the setup program to reopen the dynamic link library (DLL) files it needs. After this step, you're ready to begin client installation.

Office Client Installation

Client installation is quite simple. If you told the setup program that client machines would access Microsoft Office by drive letter rather than by UNC path, you'll need to map the drive letter you chose to your `office97` share. After this step, all that's required is to simply run `SETUP.EXE` from the `MsOffice` folder inside the `office97` share. No special options are required like before. During installation, you'll encounter an additional Run from Network Server installation option. If this option is checked, Microsoft Office will run directly from the `office97` share. If you hard-coded `SETUP.EXE` to not allow user selection of this particular option, no such option should appear during install, and the one you selected during the administrative install will be used. The only trick to completing the install is to configure user templates to be installed locally. Workgroup templates, however, can remain on the `office97` share.

More information on installing Microsoft Office 97 on a network can be found in Microsoft Knowledge Base document ID Q159772, "Contents of the `Netwrk8.txt` Readme File." Additional information can be found in the Samba document `Application_Serving.txt`, which can be found in the Samba source tree under `docs/textdocs`.

Summary

This chapter covered a variety of topics related to installing, configuring, and hosting Windows software from an SMB/CIFS share. After covering basic principles of sharing, the chapter explored how to configure Samba to appear as a CD-ROM server over the network and presented the cost benefit of the Samba approach. After reviewing some higher-performance RAID-based application-serving options, the chapter then discussed the benefits and pitfalls of running applications directly from an SMB/CIFS share, providing lots of advice along the way to ensure that the proper precautions are taken. Finally, the chapter ended with a review of oplocks and instructions for how to install and run Microsoft Office from an SMB/CIFS share.

CHAPTER 29

Using Samba in the Small Business

by Roman Rochelt

Samba has an important role to play in the running of a small business. An example of this might be when a small business has more than one operating system running at the same time, and Samba is employed to bridge any communications gap which may exist between dissimilar operating systems.

The Big Picture for the Small Business

Setting up a computer network in a small business brings up many judgment calls for management. Here are some of the possibilities:

- What kind of solution does one go with?
- What kind of service does the proposed solution provide?
- Is the cost of the proposed solution economical?
- How does the competition compare to the chosen solution?
- Does the solution fit with the current configuration?
- What does the application run on top of?

These are all valid questions for somebody running a small business, and they will all be covered in this chapter, with an emphasis on how Samba fits into the picture.

Choosing a Solution for Your Business

There are many choices to consider when choosing a solution for your network. A solution has to be able to meet certain criteria. The three main objectives that come into mind immediately are efficiency, price, and steady performance. Samba deals with all these objectives well and is comparable to a solution such as Windows NT. In this sense, Samba would make an ideal candidate for implementation into a small business.

What Can Samba Do for the Business?

Samba is mainly meant to be a file and print server between a UNIX server and Windows clients. It enables incompatible operating systems to share information. Along with print and file sharing, Samba is also able to authenticate user logins.

Another thing to take into consideration is that Samba can be a replacement for a Windows NT file and print server, thus alleviating the cost of a Windows NT license.

Budget

Budget is very often a critical consideration when dealing with a small business. Unlike an enterprise solution, there's probably not the same amount of funds available. A small business has to often look for a solution that's economical, established, and efficient. Samba provides all three of these characteristics.

Other than the manpower that goes into running and maintaining a Samba server, it's absolutely free. There are no hidden license fees or set number of connections. Samba is freely available for download on Samba's Web site under the GNU general public license.

Other Alternatives

The thought of what other solutions other than Samba are available also has to be taken into consideration. Two other major SMB clients are worth mentioning: Microsoft's DOS network client at

`ftp://ftp.microsoft.com/bussys/Clients/MSCLIENT/`

and the DAVE SMB client for Macintosh:

`http://www.thursby.com`

These alternatives should be used if you have Macintosh or DOS-enabled machines instead of UNIX machines in your business. However, for an SMB client on a UNIX system, Samba is definitely the best option available on the market today.

How Does Samba Fit into the Network?

The question of whether Samba will fit well into your network also arises. If all the computers in the office are all Windows machines or all UNIX machines (or all Mac, all O/S 2, and so on), there's absolutely no need to implement Samba. In fact, it would be pretty ridiculous (Samba would not serve any purpose).

Samba is to be implemented in a network where there are two opposing operation systems in use, with UNIX (or Linux) being one of them. The whole purpose of Samba is to be able to share files between the two opposing operating systems. Samba should be implemented, and is put to its best advantage, when there's no major investment in any particular operating system.

What Does Samba Run on Top Of?

Samba runs on top of a UNIX-type system, which means that it can easily work with Linux. A quick introduction of Linux is detailed next.

Linux

Linux being a freely distributed operating system under the GNU general public license is all well and good, but what does it offer? A free operating system without dealing with the hassles of licensing and financial concerns is great, but can it provide you with the assistance you need to run a small business? This Linux thing would all be for naught if it didn't provide the proper applications and reliability needed for any small business to prosper.

Fortunately, this is not the case with Linux. Linux is known for its excellent reliability. Also, the applications for this revolutionary operating system are quickly becoming available. Many applications are already available, mostly for free. In many situations, Linux even outperforms the Windows operating systems. This makes Linux an excellent solution for the small business.

Important Considerations for the Small Business

In the following sections, some of the advantages and stellar applications of Linux will be discussed. The following topics are discussed:

- Apache
- Sendmail
- Web Access
- Applications
- Reliability
- Flexibility
- Networking

Apache

Apache is a freely available source code implementation of a Web server and is easily implemented into use with Samba. Not only that, it's also the most widely used Web server in the world, according to Netcraft (a company that does Web server software usage surveys on Internet-connected computers). Table 29.1 shows the current statistics for Web server usage, according to Netcraft, as of this writing.

TABLE 29.1 Top Servers

Server	November 1999	Percent
Apache	4,847,992	54.81
Microsoft IIS	2,141,099	24.21
Netscape Enterprise	597,058	6.75
thttpd	176,358	1.99
Rapidsite	165,222	1.87
Zeus	115,307	1.30
CnG	104,979	1.19
WebSitePro	89,324	1.01
Stronghold	77,248	0.87
WebSTAR	67,993	0.77

As you can see, the Apache Web server is installed on over half of all the servers on the Internet, with Microsoft's IIS far behind. Apache is designed to be run under a UNIX/Linux operating system, although it's now available for Windows as a beta (but not as stable).

Sendmail

Email has become one of the most important applications to have in any sort of business environment, whether it be a big or small business environment. Without the use of email, a critical means of communication is been lost. Sendmail is a mail-transport program that handles the intricacies of email. Sendmail is an amazingly powerful application—it's probably also the application with the most complex configuration scheme you'll ever come across. Fortunately, there are also less-complex applications available, such as Sendmail+IDA and qmail. To find out more information about Sendmail and qmail, go to their respective Web sites (www.sendmail.org and www.qmail.org). As is the case with all the applications discussed in this section, they're freely distributed for Linux, and therefore make an ideal candidate for integration with Samba and the small business enterprise.

Web Access

Nowadays everybody needs access to the vast information available on the Internet. The small business is no different. There's a plethora of applications that can contribute to accessing the Web with Linux. Netscape Navigator 4.7 is available for Linux, which

comes with a browser, composer, email client, and Usenet newsreader. It's also possible to download a current version of Adobe Acrobat Reader to view PDF files. The RealPlayer G2 and Flash plug-ins are currently obtainable under beta for Linux (meaning that they might not include all the features of other platforms). Numerous Internet Relay Chat clients such as Kvirc, Xchat, and BitchX are also freely available. Of course, there are also numerous FTP (file transfer protocol) programs available for you to utilize. Gftp is one of the nicer graphical FTP clients available for Linux. Of course, you could always perform file transfers from the shell, but a GUI is often so much more nicer to look at.

Applications

Applications are often the main driving force behind a small business. Included with most Linux distributions are hundreds of software packages (with documentation) ready for use right away.

You will often find that in a small business that there is constant sharing of office document files. There are several strong applications that are capable of handling all this document sharing. StarOffice 5.1 for Linux, which is a complete office suite modeled after Office 97, is available as a free download (it comes on some Linux distributions to save you the hassle of downloading it). StarOffice has a fully integrated set of powerful applications that provide word processing, spreadsheet, graphic design, HTML editor, and mail/news reader options. For users using a Windows operating system, the most common office suite used is Microsoft Office. Corel has also decided to make WordPerfect 8.0 freely available for Linux, which is an excellent commercial-grade word processor. There is still a license fee to use Corel WordPerfect under a Windows platform.

There's also an excellent image-manipulation program for Linux called *The Gimp* (which stands for *graphic image manipulation program*). Many demos, tutorials, and utilities can be found for this program at `http://gimp.org/`.

Along with these applications are also many business applications that are available. Apache and Sendmail have been already mentioned. Some other business applications are Photoshop, MySQL, Oracle, Visual Basic, Perl, and PHP3, just to name a few.

Reliability

It has been said many times that Linux is one of the most stable operating systems available today, making it ideal for a small business solution. Although this statement is true, why would Linux be more stable than other operating systems? One of the reasons is because *programmers* made the decisions on what went into the system. Another reason is because Linux programmers contribute their work as a hobby, and there's not such a strict deadline on the completion of projects.

A Linux system can be continuously run for an indefinite time because it can be upgraded and modified in conjunction with other duties. The only time Linux has to be rebooted is when new hardware is added or the kernel is upgraded. Linux can be consistently counted on to be live and running. Because Linux is such a stable platform it is ideal to run Samba on top of.

Flexibility

One of the main advantages of Linux is that it's very flexible. Linux has excellent support for old hardware. This means that hardware should never become obsolete (unlike installing a new version of Windows or MacOS). This often saves a company from having to purchase new hardware every time there's an upgrade to the operating system.

You can acquire, compile, install, configure, and modify a program to your own needs. A program can often be configured in thousands of different ways to suit your needs. If you just want a basic precompiled package of a program, that can also be done by downloading an rpm (Red Hat's packaging system) or deb package (Debian's packaging system). Everything in Linux is configurable to make it look and feel exactly the way you want it.

Networking

Networking comes naturally to Linux, and thus so does Samba. After all, Linux is based on UNIX, where computer networking more or less developed. Probably all networking protocols in use on the Internet are native to UNIX and/or Linux, so you can expect that UNIX and Linux would network better than any other platforms. Setting up a network on a Linux machine is surprisingly simple, because Linux handles most of the work; you just have to give it the correct addresses. Linux is made for networking. A large part of the Web is running on Linux boxes, especially because of the Apache Web server, which has dramatically defeated its commercial competitors, thus proving the effectiveness and viability of the Open Source approach.

Implementing Samba into Your Networking

Samba is made to run on a UNIX platform and therefore exists happily in a Linux environment. As is the case with a lot of applications for Linux, Samba is freely available under the GNU general public license. Samba is needed because UNIX and Windows systems do not want to converse together without some sort of mediator. In short, Samba acts like an interpreter between the two opposing operating systems so that they're able to converse with each other.

Two of the most useful features of a computer are the ability to share files and the ability to share printers. The advantage of sharing a single printer with multiple users is that you do not have to provide every user with his or her own printer, thus saving the company a lot of money. Sharing files lets your computer access files stored on a different computer.

To accomplish these tasks, computers need to be able to communicate with each other (much like we humans do). As humans, we use our knowledge of language to communicate with each other. Similarly, computers speak their own languages to communicate with each other. The language that Windows computers use to communicate with one another is called *Server Message Block (SMB)*. However, UNIX systems cannot inherently speak this language. Fortunately, this problem has been solved with Samba. Now thanks to Samba, UNIX and Windows (as well as OS/2 systems) can happily communicate with each other and share data and print jobs.

Access from Everywhere

Now that UNIX can communicate with Windows and its SMB protocol, you can share files and printers, back up files to a UNIX/Linux system, and administer users and passwords. You no longer have to walk to the other side of the building to get a file from your coworker who's running a Windows machine (whereas you're running a Linux machine). You can now access that file from your computer, provided that your coworker puts it on a network share. Consider that cool laser printer you always wanted to use but could not— well, now you can (provided you have the rights to print to it). No longer can you complain that you cannot get your work done because you don't have access to a certain resource.

Collaboration and Sharing

Now that users can look at the same files simultaneously over the network even with dissimilar operating systems, this opens the door for collaboration. With the utilization of Samba collaboration and sharing between two dissimilar operating systems becomes easy. Projects can now be shared among a group of users. Users can now get together and share their ideas on an outline without even leaving their computer terminals. All one has to do is update some data and post it on the network for everybody to see, even if the other user has a different operating system. Isn't sharing great? With the employment of Samba this has all become possible.

Restricting Access

Now suppose that you only want to share data with a certain group of people and do not want anybody else to see that data. This, too, can be done with Samba. It's possible to set up a shared directory where only a specified group of people have access. That group can access the directory, but everyone else cannot. This option is set in the `smb.conf` file.

Here's an example of access given to a group of users (the `musicians` group and `roman`, with `roman` having Admin access); everybody else is not allowed access to the share:

```
#Give access to musicians and bill while everybody else can
#not access the share.  Give only roman admin access.
#Only let two people access the share at once
[limited-access]
  path = /homes/limited
  comment = Limited access directory
  writeable = yes
  valid users = @musicians  # the @ sign designates a group
  admin users = roman
  max connections = 2
```

With this share, only the `musicians` group and `roman` have access to this writable directory. `roman` also has administration access to the directory. However, only two people can access this share at one time.

To learn more about restricting access, read Chapter 20, "`smb.conf` Share Parameters."

Revision Control

Revision control allows a group of users a degree of control over what changes are made to a system. It can make creating patches to a project easier, it makes integrating changes easier, and it makes working in a group a lot easier. A tool that enables revision control is Concurrent Versions System (CVS).

RCS/CVS

CVS is the best tool available today for revision control. It keeps track of changes that have been made to a project. Every time a user adds something to a project, that user adds a brief description of the changes made and then "CVS stamps" each change with the time that it was made. The name of the user who made that particular change is also added. This can answer many important questions, such as the following:

- Who made a change to a certain project?
- When was the change to the project made?
- Why was the change to the project made?
- What other changes where made to the project at the same time?

Backup

Backup is the process of copying files or databases so that they will be preserved in case of equipment failure or some other catastrophe. Backup is usually a routine part of the operation of large businesses with mainframes as well as the administrators of smaller business computers. The process of retrieving backed-up files is known as *restoring* them.

29

USING SAMBA IN
THE SMALL
BUSINESS

Backing up your data is a very important task. If a failure or some other catastrophe does occur, you'll be prepared. If backups are done regularly, the loss of data will be extremely minimal and a lot of information will be returned upon a backup restoration.

The Samba client is able to do a file backup and recovery operation through its `smbtar` shellscript, which runs on top of `smbclient`. A more detailed description of backup will be provided later in this chapter.

Setting Up Samba in the Small Business

Samba is an ideal candidate for implementation into a small business. One of the main reasons this is true is because Samba is very cost effective yet still has most of the characteristics of a full-fledged server. Samba is freely available under the GNU general public license, and costs nothing to install. Cost is a significant determining factor in network and server implementation, and certainly is worth consideration. With Samba, there's no need to purchase and implement a pricey NT server. Samba provides a setup that's comparable to the ability and power of an NT server. With the implementation of a Samba server in a small business, the overhead costs drop dramatically.

Setting up Samba obviously requires configuration. The configuration and setup of Samba is done through a file called `smb.conf`. The `smb.conf` file can be configured either by hand (with a text editor), or by the swat program. The `smb.conf` file designates the printer access, global shares, home directories, and group shares.

Printers for Everyone

Setting up a network in a small business environment to use one communal printer is a very economical solution. With Samba, you can set the configuration to allow every user on the network to have access to print to the same printer. A setup like this saves your company from having to purchase more printers. Also, employees no longer have to go to a designated workstation to do their print jobs.

Here is a snippet of a typical printer configuration in a small business environment:

```
[printers]
comment = Shared Printer
path=/usr/spool/public
writeable=no
guest ok = yes
printable = yes
```

This is an extremely simple printer share. The first line tells Samba where the printer spool is to be found. The second line tells Samba that the printer cannot be written to. The third line tells Samba that users logged on as 'guest' are allowed to print. To change this all one has to do is change the yes to a no. The final line tells Samba that this printer is allowed to print.

Making Home Directories That Work

It is imperative that users have their own home directories. This lets users store information and files in their own distinct location.

Home directories are created by the [homes] section of the smb.conf file. Here is an example of a simple home directory snippet:

```
[homes]
comment = Home Directories
valid users = %s
writeable = yes
create mask = 0600
directory mask = 0700
browseable = no
```

This is a very simple and straightforward configuration. The valid users = %s option expands to the users name of the share once a connection is made. The %s option will also restrict users to their own home directories. The second line says that this directory is writeable. The directory mask sets the privileges of the current directory. The create mask line dictates what the privileges will be if the user creates a new directory under that share. The last line indicates that this share is not browseable. One can also create home directories with the use of a tool called SWAT, which will be covered later in this chapter.

Making Project Directories

Project directories are often necessary when a group of users are working together on a project. Suppose you need to create a share that three users can write to and nobody else can access. Without using SWAT this time, here's how you might do it (note that for this to work that you first have to create a directory called musicshare on the server):

```
#A share for three users to share and write to
[Musicians]
comment = Mozart's, Beethoven's and Bach's share
path = /musicshare
valid users = mozart beethoven bach
public = no
writeable = yes
printable = no
create mask = 0765
```

You can easily add more users by adding more names to the valid users parameter. You can even set the directory to be printable by setting the printable parameter to yes.

Samba Maintenance

As with any network system, the maintenance of Samba is critical. Sometimes you might have to add a new user, create a new group share for a new project, create a share for a new printer, and other similar tasks. All these tasks require maintenance of your Samba system. There are different ways of performing maintenance tasks like these. Described in the following sections are four typical ways to perform maintenance on your Samba server (or any other server for that matter).

Minimal Maintenance

One approach to maintenance is *minimal maintenance*. This means that once you've installed and configured your Samba server, it stays that way. Nothing will ever be changed about the configuration of Samba. No new directory shares will ever be created, no new users will ever be added to Samba, and no new printers will ever be added to the Samba configuration. You'll only have access to the original qualifications that where set during the installation of Samba.

This setup is definitely not recommended in a business situation that's constantly changing and growing. However, if the installation of Samba is only meant to give certain people access to certain fixed resources, this is a perfectly viable option (although it might seem like a waste of Samba's options).

Internal Administration

For a small business, having an internal administrator to take care of the configuration of Samba is often the best solution. It's more cost effective than outsourcing the administration tasks, and it still gives the business the option of frequently updating shares, printers, and users.

Outsourcing

Sometimes there's nobody available to maintain the Samba server in a small business, but a minimal-maintenance approach might be unacceptable. This is when a company might look into outsourcing to periodically maintain its Samba server.

Outsourcing is an arrangement in which one company provides services for another company that could also be or usually have been provided in-house. Outsourcing is a trend that's becoming more common in information technology and other industries for services that have usually been regarded as fundamental to managing a business.

There are many companies that offer a service like this. The Samba Web site has a list of companies that offer outsourcing support for Samba. Here's the URL for a list of companies that support Samba:

```
http://ca.samba.org/samba/support/
```

Of course, you should choose the closest mirror site to where you live.

The cost of outsourcing can often be very expensive, but the small business is getting an experienced company that most likely specializes in Samba administration to take care of the Samba network. Outsource companies often charge on a per-call basis. Often, an outsource contract is a 24-hours, 7-days-a-week availability contract, and the response time to a request can often be as little as three hours.

Dual Inside/Outside Admin

Another option is to have both an internal administrator and an outsource contract with a company. In this case, the internal administrator will usually take care of the uncomplicated configuration of Samba while the outsource contractor will take care of the more intricate configurations.

Samba Security

Anytime a service is added to one's machine it becomes open for attack to all sorts of crackers. This section will quickly take a look at some ways to protect a Samba server in the small enterprise. For more in-depth coverage of Samba security refer to Chapter 15, "Samba Security." When administering a Samba network, you have to be extremely careful to ensure that only authorized users can access your network. Samba has many security options that can be configured through Samba's configuration file. The configuration file in Samba is called `smb.conf` and can be found under the `/etc` directory.

The best way of learning about the security features of Samba is to look at examples of Samba configuration files as well as some of the settings that are included in the examples.

There are three common sections in the configuration file:

- `global`
- `shares`
- `printers`

29

USING SAMBA IN
THE SMALL
BUSINESS

global

You can specify many security options under the `global` section of Samba's configuration file. Here's an example of a `global` snippet:

```
[global]

;SECURITY PARAMETERS /etc/smb.conf
;Includes a Global section which defines
;some security parameters like passwords,
;password encryption, guest account access
;and networks that are allowed to access server

workgroup = Musicians            #Name of workgroup
netbios name = Musicians-00      #Netbios Name of Server
invalid users = root bin daemon adm sync \
halt mail mews uucp operator gopher #users not allowed
interfaces = 192.168.1.7/24      #NICs + subnet mask
encrypt passwords = Yes          #Required under NT and Win98
null password = No               #User must have a password
log file = /var/log/samba        #Samba log files located
max log size = 50                #Max size of log file
os level = 33                    #priority of browse master
preferred master = Yes           #Sets as browsemaster
Guest account = visitor          #name for guest account
Hosts allow = localhost, 199.132.1 EXCEPT 199.132.1.69   #Allow all  except  one
```

The `invalid user` option specifies which users cannot connect to the share (if it's under the `global` option, this means every single share there is on the network). One does not want any of their system and superuser accounts to access their shares, as this is a definite security risk to a system.

The default option for Windows 98 and Windows NT SP3 and up is to enable encrypted passwords. All other versions default to a plain-text password-authentication scheme. All the computers on this network just happen to be Windows 98 and NT systems with SP5, so it's wise to enable encrypted passwords. For more information on encryption, look at the `ENCRYPTION.txt` file in the `/docs` directory of the Samba distribution. If no encryption mode is specified, Samba will default to using plain-text password authentication to verify all connections.

The `null password` parameter is set to `No` so as to disallow clients who have a null password from accessing any of the shares. To change this setting (which would be a big security risk), you would switch the `No` setting with a `Yes` setting.

`Guest account` is a username that will be used for access to services, which are specified as `guest ok`. Whenever anybody logs on as `guest`, his or her username will be set to `visitor`.

The `hosts allow` option in this configuration file allows `localhost` to access all the shares. It also allows anybody from the `199.132.1` subnet to access the network, except for the machine with the IP address `199.132.1.69`.

shares

The `shares` section of the `smb.conf` file deals with, ironically enough, sharing files in directories. Here's an example of a simple `shares` snippet with some settings to show some access permissions:

```
[homes]
#gives every user access to their own home directory
#and disallow other users from accessing it
comment = Home Directories #Network Neighborhood comment
path = %H                   #display users home directory
valid users = %S            #only user can access directory
read only = No              #can read/write
create mask = 0750          #permissions when creating new
#directory
browseable = No             #only show user's home directory
#not "homes" folder
```

As mentioned in the comments in the example, this section gives a user access to his or her home directory while disallowing everybody else from accessing it. The `create mask` option specifies what permissions to give when a new directory is created.

Next is an example in which every user is allowed to access a directory as well as to read from and write to it. Well, almost anybody can read and write to it. Users that have been set as "invalid users" in the `global` part of the configuration file are not allowed to access this directory (or any for that matter). Here's the snippet:

```
[everybody]
#Creates a directory that everybody will have access to
#read and write to
comment = Everybody         #Network Neighborhood comment
path = /everybody           #path to everybody directory
read only = No              #allow read/write access
guest ok = Yes              #let anyone access this directory
```

This setup allows access to every user through the `guest ok = Yes` option by being logged in as `visitor`. Also the `read only = No` option gives everybody the right to read from and write to the directory. As you've probably noticed by now, this share has absolutely no security measure. This share would only be good for something like a scratch directory where the data distributed is not important.

printers

The `printers` section works pretty much the same way as the `shares` section. Here's a simple example of what a printers configuration would look like:

```
[printers]
#Allow everybody to print to HP890C printer
path = /usr/spool/public    #path of spool directory
guest ok = yes              #allow everybody to print
printable = yes             #allow print jobs
```

This is almost exactly the same as some of the other examples, except for the `printable` option. This option should be set to `yes` if you want to be able to print from this printer.

As you can see, there are many different configurations to consider when implementing your security and user rights. This was just a very basic explanation of Samba security. A much more in-depth coverage of Samba security is contained in Chapter 15.

Samba Backup

Making copies of program and data files on a network is known as *backing up data* (called *backup* for short). Backing up data is the most important thing you can ever do for your network, no matter how big or small your network is. It doesn't matter if you purchased the best file server you could find and the coolest workstations on the market as well as compiled the newest kernel—without ever backing up your data, your network could become nothing more than a doorstop very easily.

Determining the Worst Acceptable Setbacks

Disastrous failures aside, users often make mistakes. Users regularly delete files by accident. Even network administrators sometimes accidentally do the same (although you'll never get them to admit it). It's possible to print files so that there's always a hard copy available, but having to retype all that data (especially if a lot of data is lost) can be very tedious if not nearly impossible. When an executable file is deleted or corrupted, no amount of retyping will get that file back.

As you know by now, humans make mistakes—and so does hardware. Even though hard disks can have a lifetime of over 100,000 hours, the server disk could possibly experience a head crash (usually at the most inconvenient time, according to Murphy's Law). This head crash would render all your company's information useless. There are a lot of shocks great enough to crash your heads, even though disks can withstand several G's of force. The power also sometimes surges, blowing vulnerable disks left and right.

Another really bad scenario is the possible occurrence of natural disasters. Although not often, earthquakes, floods, and tornadoes do happen.

Worse yet, network operating systems (such as Linux and Windows) have glitches. Mysterious system errors can and will cause files to disappear. What's more, you also have to contend with viruses. They may be rare, buy when they do hit your computer network, they can be responsible for an incredible amount of damage.

Large enterprise companies would never dream of running their minicomputers or mainframes without proper backup systems and procedures. A small business network is no different and should be backed up regularly as well.

The Need to Preserve

Why should you always keep two copies of the same data? The reasoning behind keeping an emergency backup of all your files is pretty obvious. Where would a company be without all its important information? Can you imagine losing a database full of all your company's customer information and not having some sort of backup copy? The results could be absolutely horrendous. The company might not even survive a fiasco like this. How about a project that has been worked on constantly for the last couple months—would you want to start a project like that over again from scratch?

The importance of backing up your data regularly cannot be stressed enough. If this is done regularly, your data will be preserved to the last day or two, and a major disaster will be avoided.

Determining Media Based on Needs

There are many different types of media that can be used for the purpose of backup. The following sections describe the most popular types of media currently used for the purpose of backing up data.

Floppies

Floppies are often used for backing up critical files that are not very large. Backup through floppies is done on a personal computer and is not used as a network backup strategy (can you just imagine how many floppy disks it would take to backup an entire network). Copying small amounts of data to a floppy disk is quick and economical.

Large Removable

Backing up to a Zip, Jaz, or SyQuest drive or similar large removable hard disk is also an option that's used on a personal computer. It can even be used on a network backup sometimes (depending on how much hard drive space your network utilizes). Once a week or so, you should back up your files (at least your own data files and perhaps the entire contents of your hard drive) to an alternative storage device, such as a Zip drive. These devices hold at least one million bytes on a special hard disk. Backing up usually takes awhile (about 45 minutes for the contents of a 500MB hard disk). There are also easily removable drives you can back up to, especially if you have other reasons to use these (for example, for large graphic images that you store offline).

Another option is to back up your server to another hard disk, either removable or fixed (preferably removable so it can be stored offsite). Removable disks are very useful because if the server disk somehow fails, you can simply replace it using the removable disk.

Write Once Read Many (WORM)

Yet another type of backup strategy is to archive your daily backups to a read-only CD. However, you cannot change the data once it's on the disk. The distinct advantage of using CD media is that it can hold a lot of information (650MB) and is very cheap to purchase—even cheaper than tape backup.

CD Rewriteable (CDRW)

The idea behind CDRW backup media is basically the same as that of WORM backup. However, a backup using CDRW is a bit superior because the media is rewriteable (up to about 20 times).

Nine-Track Tape

At one point in time, backing up data with a nine-track tape was the norm. No longer is this true. Nine-track tapes are becoming very rare as backup media. Although a nine-track tape backup is very reliable and fast, the cost and storage capacity of the other options outweigh the advantages of nine-track tapes. This is why you'll rarely see a nine-track tape still utilized as backup media.

8mm Tape

Most backup is still done using 8mm tape. The reason for this is because 8mm tape is very inexpensive, somewhat handy, and easily available. Tape backup sizes can come in very big sizes (up to 40GB) for a very reasonable price. The only disadvantage of a tape backup is that tapes seem to wear out quicker than other types of media.

Determining Types of Backup

There are two main methods of backup: image and file-by-file.

Image backup is quite primitive and not very desirable. When you're performing an image backup, an image of the hard drive is taken. It just copies everything onto the backup media. Because there's not much of an overhead with this method, it's a lot faster than the file-by-file method. Although it's much faster, it's definitely not the most efficient. With the image method, it's not possible to restore a single file without restoring the entire hard drive.

The other method is the file-by-file method. This method is more efficient but is also a bit slower. With this method, data from each file is copied to tape before moving onto the next file. This takes longer to reconstruct, but it's possible to restore individual files with this option. There's also an option to back up selected files (for example, only files that have changed in one day). This is not a possibility under the image backup option.

Determining the Placement of Directories

When you're creating shares for Samba, the placement of directories is a very important task. It's essential to make sure that all your shares are created under one main directory. This way, it's a lot easier to back up your data because all your shares are under one main directory structure.

A good idea is to create all your directories that you want to share under your /home or /data directory.

Creating an Easy, Documented Backup Procedure

If backups are only done occasionally, they will not be effective. A good idea is to back up the files that change every day and to do a full backup once a week (preferably at the end of the week when everybody is gone). If this procedure is rigidly followed, the worst that can possibly happen is that the users would lose one day's worth of work.

If you're using tape as a medium for backup, do not use the same tape cartridge every day. The best method is a generational backup system. Have your tapes marked as Monday, Tuesday, Wednesday, and so on and use them as specified. Save these tapes for about four weeks before you use them again. If it's not possible to have such an elaborate backup procedure, at least try to alternate tapes every day. Remember, tape is cheap. Use it, and use lots of it.

The best time to do a tape backup is on the weekend or at night, when most users are not on the system. This is because open files cannot be backed up. If users are still using a certain file when a back-up is happening, those files are not backed up.

Backing Up from a Windows Machine

Backing up from a Windows machine is very easy if you have a good directory structure implemented and the proper rights to the /home directory (or whatever your directory is that the Samba shares are in).

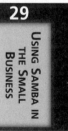

If you have access to the main directory of your Samba shares, the directory is shared, and you have read access to it, you can back up those files from a Windows machine. All you have to do is copy that directory (or only the directories you want) to your backup medium (CDR, CDRW, 8mm tape, or other hard drive).

Using Special User with `preexec=` and `postexec=`

Samba has two really cool features called `root preexec` and `root postexec`. These two functions allow Samba to use certain UNIX commands when a client connects or disconnects from a share. The `preexec` command executes before a client connects to a share, and the `postexec` command executes when a client disconnects from a share.

The advantage of this function is that you can write a simple script that will back up all your data when you connect or disconnect (depending whether you use `root preexec` or `root postexec`) from a share.

Here is an example of a simple `postexec` script that unmounts a CD-ROM while a network is disconnecting:

```
Root postexec = /bin/umount /mnt/cdrom #unmount CDROM
```

It is very easy to tailor a script to perform a routine backup when the network disconnects.

Using Special User Access to the `/home` Tree

As mentioned earlier, to do a full and proper backup to all your Samba shares, you need a user to have access to the `/home` tree (or whatever tree you're using to store Samba shares in). You should create a special user just for this scenario (maybe call the user `backup`). In the `smb.conf` file, make sure that the user you're using to backup files has clear read access to every directory under `/home` (or the directory you're using) so that the user is able to back up everything in that tree. Be extremely cautious and only use that user when performing backup duties.

Samba Administration

No matter how big or small a network is, it has to be constantly maintained. Without constant maintenance, any network will eventually, over time, become useless because new users have not been set up, shares have not been updated, group permissions have not been changed, new printers have not been added, finished projects have not been deleted, and many other ordinary task have not been done.

You can always administer Samba by editing the `smb.conf` file with your favorite text editor and changing the `global`, `shares`, and `printers` sections' text. This method is the way a lot of Samba experts prefer. But for a person who's not a Samba expert and is still learning all the ins and outs of the `smb.conf` file, this method is extremely challenging and frustrating.

Luckily, there's another way of administering Samba without the need of editing the `smb.conf` file with a text editor. A few GUI programs are available that let you administer Samba with a lot more ease than just editing the `smb.conf` file by hand. Here's a list of some of these interfaces:

- Samba Web Administration Tool (SWAT)
- KSamba
- B+B Samba Admin tool
- bbSAT
- smbconftool
- SMBedit
- Smb-mode.el (Emacs mode)
- Webmin
- SMB2WWW Gateway software

The administration tool that's used the most is SWAT, so that's the tool that will be discussed here. You can find more information on the other tools at Samba's GUI page at `http://Samba.org/samba/GUI/`.

According to the Samba documentation:

> SWAT allows a Samba administrator to configure the complex `smb.conf` file via a Web browser. In addition, a SWAT configuration page has help links to all the configurable options in the `smb.conf` file allowing an administrator to easily look up the effects of any change.

So to summarize, SWAT is a Web-based administration tool that lets you make changes to the Samba configuration file through its graphical interface. To bring up SWAT, start up your Web browser and point it to

`http://yourservername:901`

As you can see, SWAT is connected to port 901. Once you've connected, you should see a graphical page like the one at `http://anu.Samba.org/cgi-bin/swat/`.

This is a good Web site for learning how the SWAT utility actually works. It's a fully working version of SWAT and demonstrates how SWAT functions. This is probably one of the best ways to learn SWAT.

The configuration of Samba is done via the icons at top of the screen. Here's a brief explanation of what they do (for a more thorough explanation of SWAT, read Chapter 13, "Using Samba Web Administration Tool (SWAT) for Samba Configuration").

- *Home*   Goes back to SWAT home page
- *Globals*   Edits the [global] section of the server
- *Shares*   Edits the file share section of the server
- *Printers*   Edits the printers section
- *Status*   Gets information about the server
- *View*   Looks at the current smb.conf file
- *Password*   Manages your passwords

SWAT makes it very easy to add shares and printers as well as to edit global parameters. You can also change users' passwords with the SWAT tool (but note that SWAT will only change a user's smbpasswd, not his or her normal UNIX password). An in-depth discussion of SWAT is beyond the scope of this chapter. If you want to learn more about SWAT, refer to Chapter 13.

Summary

In a small business environment where there is more than one operating system platform in use, it is imperative that different systems be able to communicate with each other. Samba provides this communication ability between different operating systems. Once Samba is utilized, file and print sharing between operating systems becomes possible and is easily facilitated.

Security, backup, configuration and maintenance, are of the greatest importance for any network, and Samba is no exception. In this chapter, simple security, backup, configuration and the maintenance of small networks, have all been considered. For the proper utilization of Samba, it is of the utmost importance that the steps that have been laid out be followed exactly.

Stability and price are also important determining factors in the implementation of any small business solutions. This is where Samba's stability, free availability, and ease of implementation shines through, and becomes the best solution for implementation in a small business.

Using Samba in the Software Development Department

by Jaron J. Rubenstein

Samba provides a unique solution for the daunting file sharing requirements of a software development department. Software developers require a unique set of features to be provided in an efficient and reliable manner. Samba implements all these features at a price point that's hard to beat. Through proper configuration and maintenance, Samba provides a variety of features that can fully integrate software development teams with the documentation and source code they need to perform their daily functions.

This chapter is written to address some of the less-technical concerns involved in implementing a Samba server for use by software developers in a collaborative environment. It's written toward a target audience of system administrators planning to implement such a system; however, software developers may also find interest in several of the topics covered in this chapter.

Unique in the Programming Department

There are a variety of issues that make software developers a unique user base for a Samba implementation. Quite often, developers are organized into project-specific teams and need access to the data and source code that their teammates are working on. Instant access to the latest software documentation (that is, requirements documents and design documents) is imperative, and the ability to instantaneously share code revisions and configuration releases is a necessity for an efficient development team.

In most organizations, the software developers are in a separate department from the system administrators. In many cases, software developers fall under a very different organizational hierarchy than the administrators—they may be a different class of users than the standard user base (such as the marketing department, for example) and are generally highly trained technical experts. The following sections outline some of the main features of developers as a user base in order to ensure that these are considered when designing business and technical processes around a Samba installation.

The Users Have Administrator Knowledge

In many cases, software developers have system administration knowledge and/or experience that might affect the efficiency of the administration of the Samba server. This knowledge might prove to be a hindrance when egos collide between developers and administrators. Issues can be avoided by enforcing the policies that are already in place for other development servers in the organization.

Software Developers Sometimes Resent Administrators

In many software development shops, there's a strict dichotomy between the Information Technology (IT) department, where the system administrators usually work, and the software development department. This dichotomy results in a variety of competitive behaviors, including resentment of the system administrators. This is generally a cultural/political issue that enters into play whenever a new system or solution is implemented. Samba is no exception.

Developers are often power users and they grow accustomed to a particular solution, whether it be for file sharing, code editing, or version control. Any attempts to modify this environment is likely to result in the alienation of some portion of the development team. Despite the likely enhancements that the new system will provide, developers are likely to have issues with the fact that something was changed without their input/approval. Because the decision to change systems is often a management-mandated decision, there's little that can be done to rectify this situation.

The Users Need a Strong Degree of Control to Do Their Jobs

Depending on the type of development that the software developers are involved in, they may require a strong degree of control of the Samba server or the files stored on the Samba server. This control may include the ability to add/modify files, create new directory hierarchies, or tweak settings on the Samba server. Policies and tools must be in place to provide this control.

The Users Need a Test Computer

The first time Samba is deployed in a small software department, there's likely to be lots of issues with its configuration and management. With the variety of users in the software development group, there will likely be a lot of hands trying to solve and fix problems. It's best to start with a development-class server that can be configured and adjusted as necessary by the developers. As soon as a preliminary "beta" period has been completed, the finalized configuration can be moved to a production server. In some organizations, this may never happen, and the development-class server may become the best solution.

The Users Are Some of the Highest-Paid Personnel

Not only are software developers among the higher-paid personnel in their company, in many engineering organizations they're often the only nonoverhead personnel. They're the primary users of the server systems provided by the IT department, and their time and productivity are crucial to the success of their organization. In order to ensure that their time is not wasted, the services provided to them must be stable and reliable. This is accomplished by properly configuring and monitoring the Samba server for efficiency.

Source Control

One popular use of file sharing in a software development environment is for the sharing of source code. Source control is an important issue to consider when implementing a Samba server in this environment. Most modern systems for source control are designed to function in a file-sharing environment. Proper configuration and thorough testing will ensure that the services provided by the Samba environment will be safe and stable for the storage of source code and revision-control meta information.

Samba and Open Source Benefits

Samba, and its full source code, are distributed under the GNU General Public License (GPL). There are many benefits to the open source licensing of Samba. Chances are that if you've gotten this far in the book, there's little need to convince you of this. However, a few key points specific to the implementation of Samba as a software development server are in order.

Budget-Friendly Separate Server

Small development groups may find that a low-end Linux server running Samba provides more than enough horsepower to provide for their needs.

Samba Reliability

Samba is reliable. Like most UNIX-based solutions, Samba is a robust, highly configurable solution to the problem of providing print- and file-sharing services to users across an organization. Like most Open Source projects, Samba has been ported to many different platforms and has been tested in an infinite variety of environments. Samba provides the system administrator with the ability to combine the easy-to-use file sharing capabilities of the Microsoft Windows family of products with the robustness and manageability of a UNIX server.

Easily Administered by the Programming Department

A Samba server is easily administrated by programmers who are familiar with its configuration. Programmers can modify directories and files with ease. They can also set up new file shares and fine-tune the Samba server via its basic textual configuration files. If necessary, administrators can drill down to the Samba source code for details on its operation.

Easily Administered by the Network Administrator

Samba provides standard SMB protocol file sharing over a TCP/IP network. Most modern networks are now running TCP/IP as their primary protocol, resulting in little additional concern for the network administrator. Samba is not a bandwidth hog, and its network traffic is linear with usage. Samba can also transcend network segments, making it ideal for users across a corporation.

Can Be Isolated from the Remainder of the System

If desired, steps may be taken to ensure that the Samba server can be completely administered by assigned members of the programming department. This eases the load of the system administrator while putting the software developers in control of their environment.

Properties of a Samba-Served Programming Department

A variety of network architectures, software, and hardware may be present in the software development arena. Some of the most common items are discussed here along with their implications to the Samba installation.

Thick Client, Client-Based Profiles

Developers working on Microsoft Windows workstations are apt to be using a fairly robust development workstation using state of the art commodity hardware. In many organizations, it's not uncommon to have development workstations with hardware specifications very similar to servers.

30

USING SAMBA IN THE SOFTWARE DEVELOPMENT DEPARTMENT

DHCP

Dynamic Host Configuration Protocol (DHCP) offers the ideal solution to the management of IP address allocation. It's employed by many organizations, large and small, to address this concern. In most cases, servers cannot count on a client to have a particular IP address forever.

100BaseT Tree Configuration

With the proliferation of 100Mbps Ethernet throughout the industry, most development networks are based on 100BaseT in a tree configuration. In more advanced, switched networks, this means direct-access to the Samba server for each client machine.

Daily, Reliable Backup

By providing a central repository for all documentation and source code, the Samba server provides the system administrator with a single server to back up. This eases the task of backing up numerous client workstations but introduces a single point of failure to the system. As a result, backups must be performed on a regular basis to ensure source code safety.

Root Password Available to Some Department Members

The control required by some members of the software development department implies that they may require direct, and immediate, access to the Samba server for maintenance and modification of files across projects. As a result, the root password may need to be distributed to key members of the department.

Security Aimed at Outsiders and Mistake Prevention

In the software engineering department, server security is generally geared towards keeping non–project members and outsiders from accessing files. Certain security policies may also be in place to ensure the centralized control of files via read-only shares and other similar measures.

Redundancy

As mentioned earlier, the use of a single Samba server as the repository for project documentation and source code results in the creation of a single point of failure for the software development network. It's often necessary to address this concern by building redundancy into the Samba installation.

Any file server that's going to experience a significant amount of use should have redundant hard disk storage. For most Samba servers, RAID level 5 (RAID 5) storage redundancy is recommended. In RAID 5, data parity information is stored on a different disk than the data. If a disk failure should occur, the data on the failed disk can be reconstructed from the parity information on the other disks. This ensures that all data can withstand a failure of any disk in the array.

> **Tip**
>
> RAID (or *redundant array of inexpensive disks*) is the *de facto* standard for ensuring data integrity and reliability in storage. RAID may be implemented via specialized disk controllers (SCSI, IDE, and so on) or software (many operating systems have RAID support), and it comes in several different configurations (or *levels*).

In a mission-critical Samba installation, one may also want to provide redundancy at the server level. One way to provide this type of redundancy is via a secondary "backup" Samba server. The contents of this server should be synchronized with the primary server on a regular (or real-time) basis. In the event of a failure of the primary server, the backup server could immediately begin taking its place. There are several mechanisms for doing this within Linux. Refer to the Linux High-Availability HOWTO for more information.

Application Documentation

Whether software developers admit to it or not, one of the most crucial parts of their job is writing documentation. Project-related documentation includes requirements documents, design and test manuals, and user documentation. Documentation may also include information on tools used for development and other tool-related information. Documentation requires a unique configuration to ensure that files are stored correctly.

Documentation in HTML Format Is Best

Without a doubt, the best format for application documentation is HTML. By providing application documentation on a Web site and allowing the source of that documentation to be accessed via a Samba file share, you've created a highly efficient documentation-publishing system. Changes are instantly enacted on the Web server, which provides the documentation to intranet and/or Internet users. This "publishing system" ensures that the most recent copies of the documentation is available to all users, around the office and around the globe. HTML documentation is also supported by other operating systems, making it a cross-platform solution. HTML is easy to write (either manually or by using HTML editor applications), and its hierarchical nature makes it the perfect match for application documentation.

Lowercase Filenames

One pitfall in using HTML documentation is that the Apache Web server (and most other Web servers) are case sensitive. Therefore, a URL such as

```
http://docs.mycompany.intranet/object_manual.html
```

is likely to be a different document than the URL

```
http://docs.mycompany.intranet/object_Manual.html
```

Unfortunately, many HTML editors change filenames to capitalized first letters and/or ignore case altogether. It's important that the case of the filename be honored because hypertext links to that document will be case sensitive. Most tools have options to maintain file case when saving. In order to avoid these issues, it may also be a good idea to use only lowercase filenames for HTML documentation.

There are several Samba directives that can be used to set up the ideal environment for file storage and retrieval in order to avoid case-conversion headaches. The following directives can be used to achieve an all-lowercase environment:

- `default case = lower`
- `case sensitive = No`
- `preserve case = No`
- `short preserve case = No`
- `mangle case = No`

Directory Structure

Maintaining a well-developed directory structure will ensure that all HTML application documentation is easy to navigate. The directory structure is best organized on a per-project basis and may contain links to other projects/environments as necessary. One example is the following:

```
/home/www/docs/project2/internal
/home/www/docs/project2/objects
/home/www/docs/project2/user_manual
... etc.
```

Security

Security of application documentation may be of high priority. To ensure that files are kept secure, files should be readable/writable by only the appropriate members of the group. The easiest way to configure this is to specify certain user groups that are allowed access to the file share.

Write Group

By using the `writeable` Samba configuration directive, the administrator can restrict write privileges in a share to a particular user group. This user group might be the users in the documentation department or some other group tasked with writing/editing the documentation. Details of the syntax for the `writeable` directive can be found in the `smb.conf` manual page. Note that a synonym for the `writeable` directive is `write ok`.

Read Group

Although there's not a `readable` directive analogous to the `writeable` directive described in the last section, read access to a Samba share can be restricted in a number of ways. The first is by specifying the users allowed to connect to the share via the `valid users` directive. This directive ensures that only a specified set of users (or user groups) are permitted to access the share. Another directive, the `read only` directive, specifies that users should only be permitted read access to the share. By combining these two directives, you can restrict access to a share such that only a specified list of users will have access, and their access will be read-only. See the `smb.conf` manual page for details of the configuration syntax for these directives.

You should also note that the read/write permissions on a group of files may also be controlled via the standard UNIX ownership and permission attributes. Users who would not normally have permission to access/modify the UNIX files will not be able to read/write the files via the Samba share.

Using Revision Control to Ensure File Integrity

Revision control is another excellent way to ensure integrity and security of software documentation files. By using a revision-control system that performs file locking, one can assure that documents are revised by only a single user at a time. Several popular revision-control systems can operate on a shared file system. One example is the basic GNU RCS (Revision Control System) application suite.

Special Tricks

In addition to sharing source code and documentation for collaboration, there are a number of innovative uses for Samba in the software development department. This section outlines some of these helpful tricks that can be used to further enhance Samba's role in your organization.

Samba Access to Linux Documentation

One great way to use Samba is to share out the Linux system documentation for reference. Other types of documentation, such as software API (Application Programming Interface) documentation, product documents, and so on can also be shared via this method.

The most common way of doing this is to provide a read-only share containing a hierarchical layout of documentation. Users can than map this share to a drive letter, and they've instantly created a documentation drive. This method ensures that all developers are using the same versions of the product and API documentation as tool and library versions change.

Samba Access to Linux Root

Samba may also be used to provide access to the root partition of the Linux file system. This may be useful for easing remote-administration headaches and the system administration of Linux servers. There are some obvious security concerns associated with providing access to the entire server file system via Samba. For example, it probably isn't a good idea to provide this share to untrusted users.

Samba Temporary Directory for Backup

Another popular use for Samba is to provide a temporary directory for backup of crucial workstation files via user-initiated backup. Users can easily connect to a shared temporary directory (either public or user specific) for the purpose of copying important files to that directory for backup. The Samba server could then be backed up periodically, thus providing a safe-house for important data and programs.

Samba Access to Linux Box CD-ROM

Samba can be used to provide CD-ROM services to users. In fact, one popular use of the Samba server is to create CD-ROM jukeboxes by placing several CD-ROM drives in a Linux system and using Samba to make the drives available to users over the network. Not only does this provide easy, centralized access to CD-ROMs, but file-sharing protocols, such as NFS, can be used to provide the same media to users on different systems across your organization.

CD-ROM Images

Linux has the ability to mount files as if they were disk partitions, thus allowing the creation of a number of "virtual" CD-ROMs on a Linux server. These virtual CD-ROMs can then be shared via Samba. There are several advantages to using CD-ROM images instead of actual CD-ROMs, but they all center around faster access speeds.

The first step in providing a Samba-shared CD-ROM image is to create the image file of a CD-ROM. A simple method of creating this image is by using the dd command. The following example creates an image of the CD-ROM in the first SCSI CD-ROM drive with the name cdrom.img:

```
dd if=/dev/scd0 of=cdrom.img
```

Note that it may take quite some time to create this image because up to 640MB of data needs to be transferred. Once a CD image is created, it can be mounted locally by mounting it through the loopback device. The following command utilizes the Linux mount utility to mount the ISO image created in the last step. This example mounts the image at the /mnt/cdrom mount point:

```
mount -o ro,loop=/dev/loop0 -t iso9660 cdrom.img /mnt/cdrom
```

The original contents of the CD should now be accessible via the /mnt/cdrom directory.

The Personal Samba Server

In some environments, setting up a Samba server on a per-developer basis, or for personal home use, is advantageous. This inexpensive alternative to a big UNIX server provides file sharing while maintaining a customized, single-user environment.

Test Jig

For Web software development, Samba can be used to create a Web test jig for developing and testing Web software. Samba can be used to provide file sharing to Windows-based code editors and development environments. These same files can be run through the Linux-based Apache Web server for testing and debugging.

UNIX Information Source

As discussed previously, Samba can also be used on the personal scale for a UNIX information source. Relevant documentation and materials can be shared out for local viewing.

Inexpensive Development Platform

Samba makes for an inexpensive development platform. It reduces the need for large-scale UNIX or Windows NT servers for simple file sharing. It also provides the ideal environment for developing and testing Web and Internet applications that need to run in a UNIX environment but can be developed via a Microsoft Windows client.

Limitations

Although the benefits are numerous, there are also limitations imposed by setting up a personal Samba server. One of these limitations comes in the ease of administration. By setting up numerous small servers instead of one big server, there are additional machines to administrate and maintain. Total cost of ownership (TCO) may increase because many smaller machines can sometimes cost more, in both hardware and software costs, than one larger machine.

Revision Control

Revision control is one of the most important aspects of a mature software engineering department. Revision control is instrumental in the development of medium- to large-scale software products and is employed by nearly all mature software organizations.

Many administrators are familiar with the headaches involved in providing revision-control services to their users. Despite the importance of revision control in software engineering, the products available are surprisingly weak in features and difficult to administrate. The UNIX-based tools generally require command-line interaction or have clumsy X Windows user interfaces. The Windows tools are equally as poor, containing little integrated functionality and even less flexibility. Despite these shortcomings, revision control is a necessary part of software development and its services must be provided to developers.

One redeeming feature of some revision-control systems is their ability to operate on locally shared files. By utilizing a source code share (provided by a Samba server), these tools can generally perform their file revision–tracking, edit-locking, and configuration-management functions transparently. This is because several of these tools store their meta data in files rather than databases. These files are a part of the source code directories and are shared along with the source code.

SourceSafe

Microsoft's Visual SourceSafe is a feature-rich source-control system that's implemented via a Windows client application and a database-backed SourceSafe server. Although

SourceSafe will not operate directly from Samba-shared files, working copies of files can be stored on a Samba share for development purposes. More information about Microsoft Visual SourceSafe can be found on Microsoft's Web page at www.microsoft.com.

PVCS

Merant's PVCS Version Manager product provides cross-platform version control for source code and documentation. There are several different methods of using PVCS Version Manager via a Samba file share. In general, they involve the use of the PVCS client to control the files and a Samba share to access the files. Refer to Merant's online knowledge base for additional information on using PVCS in a Samba environment.

GNU CVS

GNU Concurrent Versions System, or *CVS*, is one of the most popular revision-control systems for online, Open Source, and academic development. CVS is free software that provides advanced tools for source code versioning and merging. Because CVS stores all its meta information as files in the file system (generally in the CVSROOT directory), CVS adapts very well to the Samba file share environment. More information about CVS can be found on the Web at www.cyclic.com.

CVS Client

A CVS client that runs on Microsoft Windows operating systems is available from www.cyclic.com. By providing a Samba share of the CVSROOT directory on the server, clients can easily connect to the share and set local tools to use the shared version of the CVSROOT tree.

Several Open Source and commercial graphical user interfaces (GUIs) are also available for CVS. Refer to the CVS Web site for more information.

GNU RCS

The GNU Revision Control System, or *RCS*, is one of the oldest, and most standardized, applications for revision control. Like CVS, RCS is free software supported by the Free Software Foundation (FSF). It's often the foundation of other version-control products and provides simple versioning on a file-by-file basis. RCS uses special attribute files (which default to the original filename with a ",v" suffix) that store version information. Because all meta information is stored in these files, there's no need for any workarounds to use RCS over a Samba share.

The easiest way to employ RCS via a Samba-shared system is to provide the native RCS utilities on the client and have developers use the applications directly on the Samba files.

Backup in the Programming Department

Without a doubt, the single most important function of a system administrator for a software development department is file backup. By providing a bullet-proof backup scheme, administrators can safeguard their entire development department from hardware failure and operator error. It's not uncommon for developers to accidentally delete entire trees of source code from development servers. This simple mistake can destroy months, even years, of work and result in loss of money. The only way to provide a safety net for these types of problems is via regular file backup.

Done by Network Administrator

File backups should be performed by the network (or system) administrator according to a well-established schedule. The administrator should perform this service for all source code and documentation that's shared to users. Whenever possible, backups should be performed at a period of low to zero usage of the files to ensure file integrity.

Scheduling

Most backup schemes involve two types of file backups: full and incremental. A *full backup* generally involves the archival of files in all specified directories to the archive media (such as DAT tape). A full backup is generally performed on a periodic basis (such as weekly) but less frequently than incremental backups. An *incremental backup* involves the archival of only those files that are new or have been modified since the last backup. Incremental backups are generally performed on a frequent basis (such as daily) and are stored on a separate medium than the full backups.

The frequency of full and incremental backups should reflect the importance of the data to be archived and the frequency of its modification. Most backup schemes perform daily incremental backups (generally around 3 a.m.) and weekly backups (Saturday morning at 3 a.m.). The rationale behind performing backups during the wee hours of the morning is that there's little to no usage of the files at that time. If your development team is spread across different times zones (and even continents), this idle time period may be different for your environment.

High Reliability

In order to ensure high reliability, backups must be performed regularly. Sticking to the previously mentioned schedule is one of the easiest ways to ensure reliability of backups. Further reliability may be introduced into the backup scheme by providing offsite storage of some (or all) of the backups. This offsite storage can be provided in several ways. The most common method is to simply store older full backups in another office or location of the organization.

Recently, Internet-based offsite backup services have become available. These services provide a secure channel for the transmission of encrypted data backups to their data center. They provide a highly reliable offsite data storage environment at their location. Although these services are generally fairly expensive (both in money and network bandwidth), they may prove to be much cheaper than similar data-security measures. They're also much easier to implement in a production environment than, say, mailing or transporting tapes to other locations.

Augmented by Individual Programmers

For backups to be fully effective, developers need to assist in the backup process. One way they can do so is by ensuring that the Samba server always contains the latest releases of software and source code. Another way is by ensuring that backups are performed regularly.

Security in the Programming Department

As with any client/server setup, Samba needs to be configured and maintained in order to ensure file and server security. The exact methods taken to secure the systems vary from organization to organization based on the existing security policies, if any, and the environments that the systems function within. In many organizations, a security committee exists to ensure that policies are followed and systems are secure.

In some instances, particularly in smaller organizations, the security onus rests on the developers themselves. In this case, administrators should take steps to ensure that the Samba servers are kept up-to-date with the latest software and operating system releases and that only select developers have administrator access to the systems.

No security policy can be implemented without thorough evaluation and regular checks for compliance. After the initial installation, and at periodic intervals, the Samba servers should be checked to ensure that they fully implement the security policy. In high-risk

30

USING SAMBA IN THE
SOFTWARE DEVELOPMENT
DEPARTMENT

environments, such as the Internet, the server should be regularly evaluated via security-auditing tools such as SATAN, COPS, and Tiger. Security can also be monitored in real-time with tools such as Tripwire and Swatch.

Services to Disconnect

If the server will function as a Samba server and only a Samba server, all other services on the system should be disabled. Although other services might not be any more or less secure than Samba, they provide openings that could, potentially, be exploited.

In the ideal situation, all services except Samba's `smbd` and `nmbd` daemons, should be disabled. Services such as File Transfer Protocol (`ftp`) and `sendmail` should most certainly be disabled because they're among the most commonly exploited daemons. For most services, simply removing them from the Internet daemon (`inetd`) service should prevent them from being launched in response to incoming connections. Services such as `sendmail` and the Apache web server are generally run as standalone daemons. They should be disabled, as appropriate, in the system initialization scripts or via the appropriate tools for your distribution (such as `chkconfig` for Red Hat Linux).

Services to Place in TCP Wrappers

In the ideal server environment, all non-Samba server services would be disabled and the only shell access to the server would be from the console. In reality, it's often necessary to provide remote login services to the server for server administration and maintenance. In this case, it's strongly recommended that a secure login client be used such as Secure Shell (`ssh`) or Secure Socket Layer Telnet (SSL-Telnet). Both of these remote shells provide a fully encrypted channel for the initial password authentication as well as the login session. Some instances required the use of specific daemons (say, the POP daemon for retrieval of email) on the Samba server. These services, if required to be available, should most definitely be restricted by placing them in TCP wrappers.

Regardless of which remote login client is used, its usage should be limited to a minimal number of developers and should be restricted to a range of IP addresses or, if possible, a specific IP address. This restriction can be implemented via TCP wrappers and serves to further limit the range of users allowed to access the server.

In addition to these restrictions on remote login clients, it may also be desirable to restrict the use of Samba by IP address. In many environments, the set of client IP addresses is well defined and Samba can be configured to restrict access to these IP addresses via the `hosts allow` directive.

Use of Groups

One way to ensure that developers have access to only the files related to their projects is to use the basic user/group system of Samba to divide users into user groups.

Every System Is a Group

One scheme is to divide developers into groups associated with the projects they're working on. In this instance, if there are 10 projects in the organization, there would be 10 groups. Users with multiple projects would belong to multiple groups, but they might need to have separate logins to ensure that files are created under the correct group via Samba.

Forced Password Changes

Most organizational security policies set minimum requirements on the passwords used for system access. Both the quality of the password used (for example, minimum of six characters, must include letters and numbers, and so on) and the frequency with which it must be changed (for example, monthly) may be specified. Changing passwords on a regular basis ensures that a brute-force attack on the password would take longer than the period of time in which the password is valid.

Dial-Up Access

If dial-up users will be granted access to the Samba server, their usage must be restricted to ensure server security. There are generally two environments for dial-up access: access directly to the organization's network via onsite dial-up servers and access to the network via the Internet.

In the first situation, the users' IP addresses will generally be known because they're issued by the dial-up server. In this case, server use should be restricted to that range of IP addresses.

In an Internet dial-up environment, a virtual private network (VPN) should be used to ensure that all communications, including Samba server password authentication, are encrypted over public networks. This encryption would ensure a secure channel between the user's system and the Samba server (and other servers on the corporate network). The use of a VPN would also allow the Samba server to remain on the internal network (inaccessible to the Internet) while still providing file and print services to remote dial-up users.

Server Documentation Is Essential

In any mature system administration environment, documentation is an essential part of the server process. Samba services, server configuration, and the user/group scheme should be well documented in order to ensure that the information is readily available in the event of a security breech, server failure, or some other catastrophe.

No Guarantee of UNIX-Proficient Programmers

The server documentation should be written such that the system can be understood by developers without a thorough UNIX background. Although it would be expected that the administrator utilizing the documentation would be somewhat experienced in UNIX system administration, developers or other personnel may also need access to the documentation.

No Guarantee of Personnel Continuity

One of the most important reasons for documenting the installation and configuration of the Samba server is to ensure that the Samba server can be maintained by other administrators. It's not uncommon for servers of any type to be set up by an administrator who has since left the company. If there's no documentation on that server, future administrators may find it difficult to maintain the server.

There are many stories told of Linux servers running company routers and providing Samba services for years without anyone knowing that they existed. In several cases, the Linux-friendly administrators that configured them are long gone and the systems simply work for years without any attention. They're usually only noticed when hardware failure occurs or a new administrator is hired and questions their existence. Although this is a wonderful concept (set up a server and have it run unattended for years), most organizations would prefer to have documentation and procedures in place for the system's continued maintenance and repair.

Procedures Must Be Easily Done

The procedures listed in the server documentation might include information on upgrading the Samba software, patching the operating system, and adding/deleting/modifying users with Samba access to the system. Each of these procedures should be detailed and explained such that they're relatively simple to perform. If possible, server scripts should be written to simplify maintenance.

Managers Must Have a List of Passwords

Managers should have access to server passwords and documentation to ensure that, in the absence of an administrator, the server can be administered. If an administrator leaves the organization, it's helpful to have password lists to provide to future server administrators.

Administration

System administration can provide a lot of rewards but can also be a stressful position. Providing system administration services to a software development department can be a true test of an administrator's ability. Strict deadlines and long hours can turn software developers into very irate users. Their source code and documentation are the fruits of their countless hours of work and must be protected at all costs. As an administrator, you must ensure that their files are safe, secure, and available to them at all times. Like any server in a production environment, server downtime costs the organization time and money. Lost source code and documentation might not be able to be replaced without incurring immense financial loss.

Summary

As discussed throughout this chapter, Samba provides the ideal solution to the file-sharing needs of the software development department. There reliability of a Samba server can be further enhanced by ensuring regular backup procedures and adding redundancy, making it well suited for both small- and medium-sized software development departments. Since the full source code of Samba is freely available, organizations are ensured that bug-fixes and enhancements will continue through the future.

Through the configuration and implementation methods discussed in this chapter, source code, documentation, and revision-control files can all be stored and accessed via a Samba server. This provides a central repository for all software development resources and allows developers easy access to these resources. When properly configured and maintained, Samba will fulfill all the requirements of an active software development department. Through seamless integration with the existing development environment, Samba will quickly become an indispensable tool for software development in your organization.

Justifying Samba to Management

by Mike Harris

IN THIS CHAPTER

This chapter will deal with issues relating to how to justify the need for Samba in your organization's IT infrastructure to your managers. It contains enough pointers and references to resources on the Internet that you can build a solid case for Samba acceptance.

In some organizations that have strong UNIX serving platforms that need to provide network services to Windows or OS/2 clients, the introduction of Samba should not prove difficult to justify. On the other hand, in the majority of organizations that have been relentlessly battered over the years by the Microsoft marketing machine, it may be much harder to do so. For this reason, this chapter will not be concerned with organizations that rely heavily on UNIX, VMS, or other non-Microsoft systems.

Stages of Samba Acceptance

How far down the road to Samba acceptance you now find yourself depends on what your organization's current IT policy is. Some organizations will already have an idea of the problems they experience with Windows and will be looking for (or implementing) an alternative solution already, whereas some may be completely (perhaps unwittingly) satisfied with their Windows networks. You may even be a strong UNIX shop wishing to introduce Windows-based desktops running X Servers and need to justify Samba and Windows against expensive Sun clients.

Let's look at some of the attitudes towards Samba that you may encounter.

UNIX Is Archaic and Too Complicated

This argument is commonly found in strong Microsoft shops and is normally based on unfounded hearsay and common misconceptions—generally, a lack of knowledge. Your organization may have spent a great deal of money investing in MCSEs who are strongly opposed to the introduction of UNIX because it is likely to threaten their knowledge base. IT people who have only been educated in Microsoft are generally rather frightened by UNIX because it represents a *real* administrator's OS.

Remember that Microsoft is a specialist at one thing above all others: marketing. It has managed to convince many IT professionals and managers alike of a horde of misconceptions surrounding UNIX and Windows, such as the following:

- UNIX is antiquated and built on 30-year-old technology.
- UNIX is difficult to administrate and is command-line oriented.
- UNIX is insecure; NT isn't.

- UNIX does not scale well.
- UNIX is expensive to purchase and costly to maintain.
- Heterogeneous network environments are bad.
- If Windows is used on the desktop, it should be used on the server as well.

The first five, as anyone familiar with UNIX will know, are blatantly untrue. There are plenty of examples available on the Internet that prove these assertions to be unfounded. Find a discarded 486 or Pentium desktop and install the latest Caldera or Red Hat Linux on it and demonstrate how graphical and simple to administrate UNIX really is.

The sixth point assumes that heterogeneous networks are a bad thing. If this is true, why is the Internet so successful? Windows NT itself now normally implements NetBIOS and TCP/IP requests. Is this not a heterogeneous network?

The seventh point does not sit well as a strategy for IT. Network operating systems and desktop operating systems are different products for drastically different uses and should be treated as such. In fact, in my experience, one of the most stable PC office environments I've ever encountered is a Novell NetWare server with Windows 95 clients. Why have so many people ousted Novell for NT?

Find out what the objections are within your organization and answer them individually. Use the same strategy as a defense lawyer might; if you can undermine the prosecution, you're in a much better position to put forth your own case.

Increased Cost-Effectiveness

If cost savings is the major concern for your organization, then consider that UNIX servers are often installed with many extremely useful administration tools and network services.

Linux normally comes with many tools and services that, in the Windows world, do not come with the core product, and you generally have to pay a great deal more for add-ons. Email servers (in the guise of `sendmail`), Web servers (in the guise of Apache), development tools (the GNU suite), remote administration tools (which do not, strictly speaking, exist for NT), scripting tools (the UNIX shells are very, very powerful; unlike the DOS command line), and the `cron` scheduler all come included with Linux and most modern UNIX flavors.

Obviously, Linux is a free operating system and there is no (or comparatively little) initial cost. In addition to this, note that UNIX does not require client access licenses. Once you purchase it, you can connect as many clients as possible to a UNIX server.

NT is normally considered to be a resource-intensive operating system. The main reason for this is that it's strongly tied into the graphical user interface, which is not necessarily an advantageous thing on a server. A basic NT network configuration would see separate servers for a PDC, a BDC, File and Printer services, Internet Information Server, Exchange Server, SQL Server, and more. The proliferation of NT servers in an organization can be mind-boggling—I once worked at a company that administrated 120 NT servers to serve just 1,000 employees!

Most UNIX systems (and especially Linux on comparable Intel hardware) offer much-improved performance and can generally handle many simultaneous user connections while still serving email, Internet, and database services at the same time. The reduction in the number of servers directly effects the costs for remote support, storage space, networking, and the number of IT support staff.

Add to all this the cost of downtime (see the next section, "Improved Reliability") and you'll be able to put a great deal of emphasis on price-reduction by moving to a UNIX/Samba environment.

Once again, there are many comparisons on the Internet of total cost of ownership (TCO) and purchase prices for the different platforms.

Improved Reliability

Fed up with the Blue Screen of Death (BSOD)? You can be sure that a lot of other people in your organization are as well.

Many people have the impression that computers are inherently unreliable—that they crash, have viruses, and need frequent rebooting and software reinstallations. Although this is true in the Windows world, the same cannot be said of the UNIX world.

That is not to say that UNIX systems do not suffer from system hangs—it's just that they're much less common than with Windows-based systems. For example, most UNIX administrators would measure uptime in terms of years; most NT administrators measure uptime in terms of days, weeks, and, at best, months.

The fact that NT servers commonly show the BSOD when invalid network requests are made, unstable applications are run, and viruses are spread is surely not reassuring for an IT department that's required to provide as much uptime to their users as possible.

From a management perspective, downtime is money lost. When a server is not working, workers are not working, invoices are not going out, and Web sites are not running—in short, business is being lost. Perhaps the cost of ownership of, for example, Solaris appears initially greater on paper, but calculate the cost of lost business through NT server downtime and a very different picture will appear.

Another common problem is the number of times NT has to be rebooted following a minor hardware reconfiguration (such as changing the RAS modem type) or applying a patch such as a Service Pack or Hot Fix. There are very few times, with the obvious exception of a kernel rebuild, that a UNIX server ever has to be rebooted.

There are many examples of companies that have switched on and configured their UNIX server and left it running for years. In my own personal experience, I have had Solaris and Linux servers running that I have been able to leave for months and months with the knowledge that no special attention is needed—and certainly no reboots.

Search the Internet for testaments from major companies to the same effect. There are many that have thrown out NT because it just isn't reliable enough.

Reduced Vendor Dependence

Surely being dependant on a single vendor for IT solutions cannot be a good thing. Most of us, when faced with buying a new video player, would shop around for the best machine at a price we could afford. Even if our previous experience with one manufacturer's television was good, we would not necessarily buy a video player from the same manufacturer.

If we're vendor dependant, we're tied into using what the vendor is dictating we should use. This might not necessarily be a direct order from the vendor but, if it is marketed in the right way with sufficient force behind it, we can find ourselves implementing solutions that are overly expensive and technically poor due to having been sold the idea. How many companies over the last few years have experienced the upheaval of upgrading to NT version 4 when version 3.51 was actually a very stable and reliable solution? How many companies migrated from the formerly inexpensive Microsoft Mail Server to the complicated, costly and resource-hungry Exchange Server? How many companies now face an even greater human and monetary cost in the forthcoming furore of Windows 2000?

By being vendor independent, an organization can increase its ability to evaluate differing systems and, through its own experience, make the right technology decisions. If you're running Solaris and NT and you're dissatisfied with the test run on Microsoft Exchange as a mail server (or for that matter, `sendmail`), you have the technical and organizational ability to choose between either solution.

The caveat to vendor independence is that in a multiplatform environment, multiplatform skill sets are required. This will inevitably require either the training of staff in different areas, the hiring of staff with differing skill sets, or, most likely, both. The question is, therefore, what is wrong with this?

If the adoption of Windows 2000 is going to require huge IT budgets for retraining to overcome the myriad of differences from previous versions, could some of this budget be reallocated for training of UNIX and Samba administrators? They certainly should be.

Having a wider variety of skill sets available to your organization can only benefit it. It will help your company make better IT decisions in the future and be more adaptable to emerging technologies.

Removing Microsoft from an Organization

Although for a strong UNIX advocate, this may seem like an excellent suggestion, in reality, it's as dangerous as the "buy only Microsoft" philosophy.

Nobody can deny that Windows is an important platform. Windows has its benefits and its failures, just like any other operating system. You'll need to stem the tide of enthusiasm for such a task and migrate in a controlled and orderly fashion; otherwise, the effect on your organization and its users could be catastrophic.

Do not run before you can walk—start small. Implement solutions that UNIX systems are known to be good for and begin to migrate your NT servers over to Samba. Don't be too keen to switch off all Windows machines just in case you need to roll back your Samba deployment.

Moving too fast could lead to a failure in the migration project and an irrevocable swing back towards Windows. Nevertheless, this is a good sign, and you should take advantage of it. Use it to your benefit to prove that you know the issues involved and can play a major role in the migration.

Total Cost of Ownership

Total cost of ownership is a measure of the entire cost to an organization of owning a system throughout its entire life span, from when it arrives shrink-wrapped and gleaming, to when it is hefted into the local dump with less scrap value than an old tin bathtub.

It's reasonably difficult to accurately calculate cost of ownership—not only the initial purchase price but also the cost for maintenance and upgrades, the cost of staffing and training, the cost of work lost due to downtime, and the cost of decommissioning and replacing it at the end of its life span all have to be taken into consideration.

Some of the more pertinent areas of ownership cost in the Samba and NT arena are discussed in the following sections.

Purchase Price

Windows NT can be purchased at a reasonable price for a server operating system. Many versions of UNIX can initially cost a lot more. However, consider what you're actually able to do with a box with NT Server installed on it against the possibilities that you'll possess with a freshly installed Solaris server. NT includes only the Internet Information Server Web server, and this is only useable following the installation of several Service Packs and additional software.

This comparison should also be made against Linux and FreeBSD, which come with servers for Web, email, databases, news, cluster workstations, schedulers, complete programming and scripting environments, and graphical and remote administration tools. The software is free, and one copy can be used for all your servers. No additional client licenses are needed, and you can use your server straightaway.

Per-Seat Licenses

Microsoft's licensing policy turns an initially reasonable outlay for an operating system into a very expensive option. Because Microsoft chooses to charge for client access licenses for NT, the cost is not just for the server and desktop software.

Remember that client licenses also include those for Microsoft Exchange Server, Microsoft SQL Server, and Systems Management Server. If you start to calculate the entire software cost, including the server operating system and additional server software and client licenses for each one, you'll begin to get a picture of how expensive it really is.

License Tracking

In order to ascertain whether your site is legally complying with client licenses under Windows, you need to use a tool such as License Manager. This is a time-consuming process for sites with many servers and many clients accessing them.

License Violation Contingent Liability

Failing to correctly track licenses could potentially lead to legal action. As an administrator for a large site, you'll have a lot of responsibility to ensure that this situation does not arise.

Downtime and Lost Work

Each time an NT server crashes, the users lose work time through lost or corrupt files and inability to access the system. Troubleshooting servers that frequently crash can be a time-consuming exercise that costs expensive IT time. Recovering corrupt data from backups costs time as well. Loss of customers due to failed systems being inaccesible or incorrect billing directly costs the business, and the business is why you're there in the first place.

All these are hidden costs tied to the reliability of the systems that have been implemented and these costs need to be calculated and taken into consideration when you're evaluating the overall cost of a platform. If you can prove that a Samba/UNIX solution is more stable and reliable than an equivalent NT solution, the figures will speak for themselves.

Generally from a management viewpoint, costs due to lost productivity in an organization are more important than costs of the systems in the first place. A more expensive initial investment will pay off and be justifiable if the overall costs of failure are greatly reduced.

Administrator Salaries

UNIX administrators are expensive. Although it's usually true to say that their salaries can be somewhat higher that their NT counterparts, they will usually be highly skilled individuals with some programming and scripting knowledge.

Remember that almost anyone can become MSCE qualified in a relatively short space of time. This does not necessarily mean that they have a good understanding of what their role entails.

That's not to say that the MCSE is not a valid qualification and that NT administrators are in any way inferior to those from a UNIX background. It's just that the quality assurance of NT administrators cannot be depended upon. Because of the pure nature of UNIX, most administrators will have a good understanding of what administration actually is. Like the old adage says, "You get what you pay for."

Vendor Independence

As discussed previously, by being a little more vendor independent, your organization can increase its flexibility with IT decisions and help protect itself against an uncertain future.

The following sections cover some of the areas in which having a multivendor environment can be of benefit to an organization.

Scalability

NT does not scale well. NT version 4 can support several processors at one time; Windows 2000 is reported (by Microsoft) to support up to 64 (only time and experience will show whether this is a reliable assertion). NT is available for two platforms: Intel and Alpha.

UNIX, on the other hand, scales well. Therefore, Samba scales well. Linux or FreeBSD can run an acceptable server environment on an Intel 80486 desktop with just 16MB of RAM. Linux can be installed on multiprocessor high-powered Pentium servers and the next version is touted to support Intel's new 64-bit Itanium (formerly Merced) processor. Linux will also run on Alpha, MIPS, VAX, SPARC, and PowerPC (to name but a few). Linux was used in the Beowulf project, which produced the world's most inexpensive supercomputer from a cluster of Linux servers running in parallel.

Samba will run on any version of UNIX—Linux, FreeBSD, and Solaris-*x86* on Intel; Solaris on SPARC; DEC-UNIX on Alpha; HP-UX and IRIX on SGI workstations. If this isn't scalability, what is?

Bargaining Position

The investment in a mixed-vendor environment may help protect you against bad technology decisions made by vendors in the future. If you're running several environments and have the option to test multiple solutions at once, you'll be better suited to make the technology decision that's best for your organization.

In addition to this, you won't be too tied to one vendor's perceptions of the technology of tomorrow. If that vendor proposes an upgrade or migration that doesn't suit your organizational or technological requirements, you have the opportunity to change course and evaluate your options. You do not have to be a lamb following the rest to the slaughter!

Overcoming Objections

You can rest assured that there will be objections to your Samba plans. Try not to let them get to you. Instead, research objections and provide a well-reasoned response to each, backed up by relevant information.

Do not retaliate to objections with accusations that question your colleagues' integrity or with derogatory comments about the existing systems. You'll need to make friends (not enemies) and, with time, any well-reasoned response with answers to objections will win through.

The following sections provide a few of the more common objections.

Can't Find Administrators

There are plenty of UNIX administrators out there. Some are probably working in your organization already as NT administrators who formerly worked with UNIX.

Besides this, any competent and skilled administrator will be able to be retrained with a UNIX skill set in a reasonably short space of time. Remember how much time and money your organization spent on Systems Management Server training? And did it ever work properly?

Nobody to Sue

Whereas the argument that no one could be sued for a free piece of software such as Linux or FreeBSD was possibly true in the past, the same cannot be said today. As there are now more and more commercial Linux vendors out there and, in addition, many more hardware manufacturers and solution providers, there are plenty of potential plaintiffs.

When looking at this line of reasoning, one should consider whether it is actually possible to sue an organization for a piece of software. If this were the case, then Microsoft would probably be facing summons from people all over the world. It is much more likely that a firm which provided an IT solution will be sued for poor advice, rather than the actual manufacturers of the hardware and software, unless there is a health and safety issue.

No Support

Commercial UNIX installations come with extensive support contracts. Many Linux vendors now offer support. Hardware vendors, such as IBM, Dell, and Compaq now preinstall and support Linux on their servers. UNIX and Linux are both extensively supported for free on the Internet by the wealth of documentation available (on sites such as Sun) and by the multitude of mailing lists and newsgroups that exist.

Samba is also well supported on the Internet through Web sites, mailing lists, and newsgroups. There are also several companies that now offer support and consulting services.

With the wealth of documentation and the ability to contact the developers of the products directly for answers to software problems, any administrator of Samba should be able to support it without the need for commercial support contracts. However, these do exist if required.

UNIX Is Obsolete and Difficult to Use

The belief that UNIX is a cumbersome, difficult-to-use, and outdated operating system is unfounded and is generally proffered by people with little or no experience with the system.

The most straightforward solution to this case of fear, confusion, and doubt is to arrange a demonstration of just how untrue these assertions are. If you can get hold of a used desktop PC, install one of the modern distributions of Linux on it and try to arrange a time to demonstrate just how good, current, friendly, and simple UNIX actually is.

Anyone willing to make this assertion should also be willing to back it up. Suggest they partake in the demonstration as an opportunity to learn something about a different technology (or, as in the case of Linux, an emerging technology) and try to present it as a willingness to investigate the best technology opportunities for your organization.

Remember that your managers might not be in favor of your using company time for *playing* with UNIX. Show that you can arrange this on your own time and suggest a meeting that does not clash with other important schedules—perhaps during a lunch hour one day.

Remember also to be prepared for the demonstration, plan out what you're going to do and test it beforehand. If your audience is itching to put UNIX down, do not give it an excuse to do so.

Justification Strategy

Now that you've decided to begin implementing Samba solutions in your enterprise, think carefully about how you'll approach it. You may be facing strong opposition and must be able to justify your actions accordingly. Here are some suggestions as to how you might approach this.

Do Not Appear Partisan

The key point here is to show that you're objective and have the interests of your organization at heart. Try to keep personal opinions of how bad Windows or Novell is and how great UNIX and Samba are out of your vocabulary. If your detractors in the organization want to keep their feet firmly in the Microsoft camp, let them. By being obstinate, they will show themselves as unwilling to contribute constructively.

Show that you are simply open to new technology and the different opportunities available to improve infrastructure and that you wish to research the possibilities.

Start Small

Start with one or two Samba servers and a small workgroup of clients. Although Samba can do many things (such as providing roaming profiles and PDC support), do not get overzealous and try to implement *all* the great things Samba can do.

By starting with a small and relatively simple network, you'll be able to concentrate on getting the right stable solution. There's a lot to learn with Samba and the CIFS protocol, and you should not attempt to understand everything right off.

Also, a simple management network will not require too much equipment and will not take up too much of your time (that management might feel would be better used elsewhere). Keep a journal of your activities as a technical reference and to show how much time you've actually spent.

Start in a Self-Administrating Department

Do not decide to run your first Samba tests on an unsuspecting finance department. Any problems will inevitably lead to the immediate cancellation of your experiments. Remember, because it is foolish to make the first NT 4 rollout to the finance department, it's just as foolish to do the same with Samba.

Run your first tests within the IT department itself, in a small subdivision or alongside your normal network. Perhaps serve some noncritical network file or printer shares. It's a good idea to run the test for a few months before venturing out into the rest of your organization's network.

Following this, if you can find a small, non–mission critical department with real everyday users and you have no management opposition, then start implementing Samba here. *Small* is intended to mean a department of around 10 Windows workstations with two printers.

Make Noncritical Servers from Hand-Me-Down PCs

Your Samba intentions are likely to be viewed as a noncritical, blue skies project. Do not expect to be able to send requests for the latest quadprocessor servers to your managers and expect them to be supplied (even though this seems to be the case with NT).

Your first test servers can easily be assimilated from unwanted desktops and servers that you're likely to find scattered around your organization. If you have old out-of-date and out-of-service Novell or UNIX servers, put them to work. Remember that a high-performance Samba server can run under Linux on a low-to-mid range Pentium desktop PC.

Once again, remember not to go replacing critical servers and network services that your users depend on. (Not because Samba will not be able to satisfy their demands, but because you'll likely to be on a learning curve and will be making frequent configuration changes.) Do not let your detractors have the satisfaction of saying, "See, we told you so!"

Provide High-Level Network Services on NT

Samba can act as a WINS server, a domain master browser, a PDC, and a BDC. However, Samba cannot perform WINS replication: Microsoft will not release the information on how to do so. Samba cannot currently fully function as a BDC and support the Microsoft RPC-based tools such as User Manager for Domains.

Don't push it! Let Samba do a subset of NT functionality; stick to file and printer serving at first. Then move on to roaming profiles and login scripts. Save the big stuff for later.

Because NT is designed to provide these services (whether it provides them efficiently or not is a question for debate) and is not usually very cooperative with anything else attempting to provide them, let it have its way for now. Do not bring Samba into direct conflict with NT servers any more than you have to.

Let Samba fit seamlessly into your organization so that people become accustomed to having it around and can see that it's stable and provides a good, if not better, solution. Don't give its detractors the chance to accuse Samba of messing up the network when you tried to make it a WINS server and one existed already.

Track and Present Uptime and Problems

Make sure you keep a log of all the issues involved in your Samba tests as well as the uptime of the Samba services. It would be preferable to run your test side by side against an NT server in a similar role and log its performance as well.

If you can show that there's no quality of service degradation when using Samba and that what was achieved caused no more problems than the normal running of an NT server, you're halfway there.

If most people's grievances regarding NT are well founded, you may well be able to show better reliability on the part of Samba. Then, you'll be even closer.

Well-recorded logs will show that you're carefully considering Samba and that you're willing to evaluate and question your own suppositions. They'll show your peers and management alike that you are open in what you're trying to achieve and that you have the organization's best interests at heart.

Form Alliances with Samba Enthusiasts

Once you subscribe to the various mailing lists and newsgroups out there on the Internet, you should find yourself making contacts with other Samba enthusiasts. There's a wealth of professionals who raise questions daily and contribute answers to these forums and, in addition to being an indispensable resource for information and support, they may help you find people in a position similar to yours.

You may also encounter other Samba enthusiasts in your own organization. Many IT professionals often run their own computers (and sometimes, small networks) at home, and they will often have Linux or another free UNIX flavor installed. Try to find out who they are and discuss your plans with them. It's very probable that they'll be interested in supporting and, perhaps, contributing to your plans. The more people involved and the more information, the better.

Volunteer Samba Information

Don't be hesitant in volunteering the information that you've gathered about Samba to your peers and to management. The more information you can provide, the more respect you'll gain because others will see that you do have a keen interest in Samba and that you know what you're talking about.

An interesting byproduct of this is that, because Samba does expose for you the nitty-gritty of how Microsoft networking actually works, you may find yourself quickly knowing more about how Windows machines interact on a network than your MCSE counterparts. This will help bolster their views that you do know what you're talking about.

In addition to this, give back what you get out of any newsgroups or mailing lists you subscribe to. If you know the answer to someone's question, offer it. The more popular Samba becomes, the more queries will appear on these forums. There are only a limited number of people who are directly involved in Samba, and they cannot answer every question. Become part of the support network yourself; it's a community project!

Make the Promise Come True

It's likely to be insufficient to simply install a few Samba servers, show them working, and simply proclaim that Samba is wonderful, it works fine, and the time is right to migrate the rest of the network.

You'll need to back up your proclamations, not only with hard facts based on performance and reliability, as discussed previously, but with detailed documentation of the systems and tools to help administrate and support them.

If you're the only Samba enthusiast within your organization, who will support it if you leave? This is exactly the question you'll be asked by management. Show that you can provide well thought-out documentation procedures for setting up and supporting the Samba servers as well as useful administration tools to boot.

Admin Scripting

Scripts to automate common tasks (such as user account creation) will be of great benefit to you. Not only will they help you in reducing your workload, they'll also make it easier for other administrators to use your Samba network.

Try to design simple scripts that do common tasks. Here are some examples:

- A script for adding a new user and copy a default profile
- A script for adding a new printer
- A script for adding a new share
- A script for users to change passwords for password synchronization between NT and UNIX
- A script for setting correct user and group permissions on files
- A script for creating a new user group and share

You'll find that some of these already exist as part of your UNIX distribution. Tailoring them is important, because it will enable an NT administrator to start using your scripts without any prior knowledge of the UNIX command line and how to use the `man` utility.

Some scripts, such as ones to change the user's password, could be set up to be triggered remotely from Windows. Therefore, an NT administrator can double-click an icon on his desktop, which fires up a `telnet` window to do exactly the command he requires.

Admin Menu Interface

Administrators coming from an NT world to Samba will be used to graphical administration tools such as User Manager for Domains and Windows Explorer. Whereas administrators with a UNIX background often find graphical tools cumbersome, inflexible, and difficult to learn, NT administrators usually feel the same way about the UNIX command-based equivalents.

You're not going to win many NT people to your cause if you have to explain to them how to use `emacs` or `vi` to edit `smb.conf` and then use `testparm`. You need to provide them with what they're familiar with—graphical administration tools.

For a start, remote administration tools for Samba are excellent, and these should be encouraged because direct console access is not required to use them; this also shows one of UNIX's strengths. The SWAT tool that comes with version 2 of Samba is very comprehensive but can often be a little daunting to all but experienced Samba administrators.

One popular UNIX utility is Webmin, which offers a Samba module among many other things. Webmin runs on virtually every UNIX variant and allows Web-based remote administration of servers, including user account management, printer management, and Samba management—the three main components of day-to-day administration.

It's also reasonably simple to write a Web-based interface to some of your admin scripts. For example, a user needs to change her password and double-clicks an icon that brings up a Web page that allows her to enter her old and new passwords. Using the powerful CGI Perl module that calls your shell, scripts could achieve this effectively without too much extra work.

There are many other graphical administrative tools you could evaluate and test that are X based (and even some Windows-based ones as well). The Samba Web site contains a whole page of links to different projects for GUI-based development tools.

There are also the default administration tools that come with your UNIX system. For example, the CDE Control Panels, Caldera's COAS system, and the `linuxconf` utility with Red Hat Linux (which coincidentally supports console, X, and Web-based administration), to name but a few. You should try these out and evaluate them to establish your favorite.

If you're very adventurous, you could use a relatively simple development environment such as Perl/Tk to provide graphical tools that *wrap* your existing administration scripts, thus making them available to both X and console users.

Admin Documentation

You should document everything, and document it well! Does anyone really do this?

You should. A failure in the documentation could lead to a failure in the system. If you're not around and someone else tries to recover it, this in turn could lead to a failure in your overall Samba project.

You should provide information about general configurations and setups of the systems for technical references and as future information for your successors. In addition, you should produce a document that's procedural. This way, it's simple for a newcomer to turn to the relevant page and implement what he or she needs to do, without having to learn the details of how you configured that rare EISA SCSI card.

Here's a list of some of the procedures and general information that you should consider documenting:

- How to reboot servers and restart any services
- How to add, delete, and edit users
- How to add, delete, and edit printers
- How to reconfigure and restart Samba
- How to install a Samba/UNIX system from scratch
- What to do in the event of a server crash, such as disk recovery

Useful Web Resources

This section contains a list of useful resources on the Internet for finding out more about Samba and UNIX and their advocacy as an alternative to NT. You'll find many facts and figures comparing the scalability, reliability, and cost of ownership of the two platforms as well as a plethora of testimonies from major companies that have successfully kicked out NT and implemented Samba/UNIX solutions.

Microsoft recently felt the need to publish a document on its Web site called *Linux Myths*, which everyone pushing for Linux in their organizations should be aware of. The article contains many instances of sweeping statements and outright misinformation, but it's well presented with the usual Microsoft gloss and is backed up by some case studies. The article can be found at

```
http://www.microsoft.com/ntserver/nts/news/msnw/LinuxMyths.asp
```

Be aware of this article, because your detractors may use it to bring you down. Read it before they do, research the accusations made, and produce the answers to the accusations. Many of the major Linux forums contain intelligent, accurate, and well-reasoned responses to this article.

Samba Advocacy

Obviously, the main Samba Web site contains many links and a lot of information:

```
http://www.samba.org
```

Samba gets a mention and UNIX gets a lot of support in the paper "Providing Reliable NT Desktop Services by Avoiding NT Server," produced by engineers at Lucent Technologies, Bell Labs. You can find this article at

```
http://www.bell-labs.com/user/tal/papers/
```

The link also includes postscript format documents and a PowerPoint slide presentation. It's well worth a look.

Linux Advocacy

The main Linux site, from which everything Linux that's important on the Net can be found, is

```
http://www.linux.org
```

The Corporate Linux Advocate has information and links to resources to justify Linux in a corporate world:

```
http://www.geocities.com/SiliconValley/Haven/6087/
```

A list of some of the companies and organizations using Linux can be found at this site:

```
http://www.m-tech.ab.ca/linux-biz/
```

Also, lots of important technical news and opinions can be gathered from

`http://www.slashdot.org`

The latest online developments regarding Linux can be found at Linux International:

`http://www.li.org`

Some major IT hardware and software suppliers are now openly supporting Linux. Here are a few examples:

`http://www.dell.com/us/en/biz/topics/linux_linuxhome.htm`

`http://www.compaq.com/linux/`

`http://www.ibm.com/linux/`

`http://www.sgi.com/`

`http://platforms.oracle.com/linux/`

`http://www.sybase.com/`

`http://linux.corel.com/`

`http://www.valinux.com/`

UNIX Advocacy

An excellent document that should be read by anyone involved in justifying UNIX over NT in his or her organization is "Microsoft Windows NT Server 4.0 versus UNIX," by John Kirch. It can be found at

`http://www.unix-vs-nt.org/kirch/`

Also, the UNIX versus NT Organization has a lot of useful links at this site:

`http://www.unix-vs-nt.org/`

Other Useful Links

The Webmin Web-based UNIX administration that incorporates a Samba module can be found at

`http://www.webmin.com/webmin/`

The p-synch utility is designed to help synchronize passwords between different platforms (including UNIX and NT). It can be found at

`http://www.psynch.com/`

The KDE desktop environment is an excellent graphical interface for UNIX systems and can be found at

```
http://www.kde.org
```

Likewise, the GNOME project has an excellent window manager for X. It can be found at

```
http://www.gnome.org
```

Summary

Remember that Samba is a server product. Keep your arguments and justifications to your organization's server platform and do not get involved in desktops—this involves a completely different scenario.

It's inevitable that on the road to Samba acceptance, you'll come up against strong opposition from "Microsoftphiles" within your organization. In most strong Microsoft shops, the introduction of Samba also means the introduction of UNIX, and this will probably end up being the area in which you'll experience the most resistance.

The key is to remain objective. Do not climb the UNIX ivory tower to sit face to face with your Microsoft "opponents," because this will not lead to a satisfactory outcome. Conflict will not end in success, and it may give ammunition to your Microsoft-entrenched colleagues. Research your subject well. Management likes facts, figures, and testimonies; provide them. There are plenty available on the Internet. Do not accuse NT of being "garbage." This isn't an intelligent answer and will not gain you respect, because it indicates a biased opinion and a lack of research. When colleagues fire UNIX misnomers and Microsoft hearsay at you, research the facts and provide a well-reasoned answer; you'll get there in the end.

Good luck!

Advanced Samba

PART
IV

Local-Subnet Browsing

by Steve Litt

CHAPTER 32

Network Neighborhood's ease of use stems from browse lists. Browse lists are typically supplied by the local master browser (LMB) on request from the client. Shares can hide themselves from browse lists with the explicit specification `browseable=no`, either in the share or in the global section.

Browsing behavior depends heavily on the configuration of the Samba server. This chapter contains the information necessary to properly configure single-subnet browsing.

The Terminology of Browsing

Understanding browsing starts with understanding some basic terminology:

- A *workgroup* is a group of computers that share common files. These computers are all able to see and use these files. A *domain* is like a workgroup, except it includes authentication in its services.
- *WINS* stands for *Windows Internet Naming Service*. It's a name-resolution service that does not rely on broadcasts. Samba browse servers depend on access to a WINS server to do their work.
- A *subnet* is a group of computers that have the most significant bits of their IP addresses in common. Without serious intervention (from routers and such), `ping` succeeds only between two computers on the same subnet.
- A *browser* is a piece of software that keeps track of the names of browseable shares (called a *browse list*).
- A *local master browser* is the browser that has authority over a given subnet. A *master browser* controls the browse list seen from SMB clients.
- A *domain master browser* has authority over an entire domain, which typically spans subnets. The domain master browser can synchronize local master browsers.

The Difference Between Browsing and Accessing

Browseability and accessibility are orthogonal. A share can be browseable and accessible, browseable and inaccessible, nonbrowseable and accessible, or nonbrowseable and inaccessible.

Nonbrowseable shares that are accessible can be accessed by name, such as a Windows Explorer "map network drive," or via the `net use y: \\servername\sharename` command.

Browsing occurs in the Windows Explorer environment (via Network Neighborhood) and on the Windows command line via this command:

```
net view \\servername
```

The preceding shows a list of browseable shares on the named server. The following command, which works only on Windows 9*x*, displays the hosts in the named workgroup:

```
net view /workgroup:workgroupname
```

The following command is the Windows NT equivalent to the preceding command. It shows the hosts in an NT domain (or workgroup, if the NT network is using workgroups):

```
net view /domain:workgroupname
```

Samba shares are made browseable by including `browseable=yes` in their share definition. However, there may be anomalies on the network that prevent those shares from being seen in various SMB clients, especially Windows 9*x* Windows Explorer.

Browsing Parameters by Example

Several parameters affect browsing. This section discusses their involvement in browsing and gives examples of the effects of changes to these parameters.

workgroup=

The Samba server's `workgroup=` parameter determines the workgroup the server is in. If the server is acting as part of an NT domain or as a PDC, this parameter determines the domain. Assuming the Windows clients are in group `mygroup`, you could code the following simple `smb.conf` and restart Samba:

```
encrypt passwords=yes
workgroup=mygroup
[tmp]
path=/tmp
```

You'll almost certainly be able to browse and read files in the `[tmp]` share. If you cannot, the probable cause is a NetBIOS naming problem, which can be cured by adding a `netbios name=` parameter with the value set at your Samba server's hostname.

Now, as an experiment, change `mygroup` to `test1` and restart Samba. You probably won't be able to navigate to your share in Windows Explorer. Seeing outside the client's workgroup is much more challenging. This is primarily due to the lack of a browser for the new workgroup. Eventually, the problem will most likely resolve itself. The following batch file, called `hurry.bat`, can often hasten correct browsing:

```
net use \\mainserv\tmp
net use \\mainserv\tmp /delete
net view /workgroup:%1
choice /C:~ /N /T:~,40 Please wait 40 seconds...
```

```
net use \\mainserv\tmp
net view \\mainserv
net view /workgroup:%1
echo Your share should now be visible in Network Neighborhood
```

netbios name=

In a perfect world, a Samba server would always default its NetBIOS name to its host-name. Often this is not the case. It's a good idea to explicitly specify the name in a `netbios name=` parameter in the [global] section.

netbios aliases=

This enables the Samba server to be known under other names. For instance, add the following line to the [global] section and then restart Samba:

```
netbios aliases=sylvia brett rena valerie
```

Note that computers named sylvia, brett, rena, and valerie appear:

```
C:\WINDOWS>net view /workgroup:mygroup
Servers available in workgroup MYGROUP.
Server name          Remark
-------------------------------------------------
\\BRETT              Samba 2.0.6
\\DESK2              STEVE LITT
\\MAINSERV           Samba 2.0.6
\\RENA               Samba 2.0.6
\\SYLVIA             Samba 2.0.6
\\VALERIE            Samba 2.0.6
\\WINCLI             WINCLI Steves Windows Computer
The command was completed successfully.

C:\WINDOWS>
```

preferred master=

The major behavior of `preferred master=` is that it calls a browser election upon Samba startup and additionally calls browser elections from time to time. Its minor behavior is that it gives the Samba server a slight advantage in becoming the local master browser in cases where there's a tie for `os level`.

Any given workgroup should have only one preferred master. Multiple preferred masters continually call for elections to "unseat" the others, thereby increasing network traffic and creating frequent 30-second browse blackouts during browser elections.

Create the following `smb.conf`:

```
encrypt passwords=yes
workgroup=test11
[tmp]
path=/tmp
```

Now use `tail -fn0 log.nmb` to observe nmbd activities; then restart Samba from a different virtual terminal. It should produce output something like this:

```
[root@mainserv var]# tail -fn0 log.nmb
[1999/12/02 12:40:58, 0] nmbd/nmbd.c:sig_term(67)
  Got SIGTERM: going down...
[1999/12/02 12:40:59, 1] nmbd/nmbd.c:main(747)
  Netbios nameserver version 2.0.6 started.
  Copyright Andrew Tridgell 1994-1998
```

Wait a full minute and notice that you see no output regarding a local master browser. Now add the following line to the top of `smb.conf`:

```
preferred master=yes
```

Press Ctrl+C to get out of the `tail` command; then rerun it and restart Samba. Notice that the output is the same as last time. However, 30 seconds later, output scrolls again, culminating in a message resembling the following:

```
*****

  Samba name server MAINSERV is now a local master browser for
workgroup TEST11 on subnet 192.168.100.1

*****
```

> **Note**
>
> The preceding message appears only if the Samba server *wins* the browser election. You can guarantee the win by including `os level=255` (see the next section).

os level=

The browser election winner goes to the box with the highest OS level. The Samba server's OS level is specified by its `os level=` parameter. According to `BROWSING.txt`, the OS level for Windows 9x is 1, and the level for NT is 32. Accordingly, `os level=33` would beat everything but another Samba server.

The best course of action is to set the `os level=` parameter very high for the one Samba server you want to win the election and to 0 for all other Samba servers. If you want to let an NT box be the local master browser, set all Samba boxes to 0.

The default level of `os level=` has changed with Samba versions. 2.0.6 defaults this parameter to 20, whereas 2.0.5a defaulted this parameter to 0. In Samba 2.1 it defaults to 32, which ties NT. The maximum value of `os level=` is 255.

local master=

This parameter defaults to yes. If this parameter is set to yes, it enables the Samba server to win a browser election, but does not guarantee that it will. If this parameter is set to no, the Samba server cannot win the browser election. Start with the following `smb.conf`:

```
encrypt passwords=yes
workgroup=mygroup
preferred master=yes
os level=255
[tmp]
path=/tmp
```

Run `tail -fn0 log.nmb` on one virtual terminal and then restart Samba on another. Note that after 30 seconds, the Samba server wins the browser election. Now add the following line to the top of `smb.conf` and restart Samba:

```
local master=no
```

Note that this time the Samba server does not win the browser election.

wins support=

Start with the following `smb.conf`:

```
encrypt passwords=yes
workgroup=mygroup
[tmp]
path=/tmp
```

Restart the server and then shut down or start up a Windows 9*x* client. There's a flurry of error messages resembling the following:

```
[1999/12/02 13:54:12, 0] nmbd/nmbd_incomingrequests.c:
➥process_name_registration_request(224)
  process_name_registration_request: unicast name registration
  request received for name MYGROUP<1e> from IP 192.168.100.40
  on subnet UNICAST_SUBNET. Error - should be sent to WINS server
```

Now insert the following line at the top of `smb.conf`, restart Samba, and boot up or shut down a Windows 9*x* client:

```
wins support=yes
```

The flurry of error messages is gone, because now the Samba server is acting as a WINS server.

> **Caution**
>
> Do not perform the previous exercise if there's another WINS server on the subnet. There should be only one WINS server per subnet.

domain master=

If set to yes, this parameter causes the Samba server to act as a domain master browser. It's typically used in an NT environment or when Samba is used as a logon server. It's not necessary for single-subnet browsing in other situations. This will be discussed in more detail in Chapters 33, "Cross-Subnet Browsing," and 34, "Windows Internet Naming Service (WINS)."

server string=

Place the line `server string=Test Samba Server` in the `[global]` section, restart Samba, and note that the string now appears in Network Neighborhood and other browses. This parameter has no technical use. Its only purpose is to display a meaningful string alongside the server in browse lists, including Network Neighborhood. This can be very handy to end users, and is also handy for troubleshooting.

interfaces=

This parameter is uncommon for single-subnet browsing. Its primary use is on a server serving more than one subnet. If this parameter is used, it must have the correct subnet IP addresses, each followed by a slash, and then the subnet mask as either a number of bits or a dot-delimited address.

By deliberately placing the wrong IP address in this parameter, you can verify that an incorrect value for this parameter caused browsing to fail. After verification, be sure to replace the wrong IP address with the correct one.

load printers=

The default is yes. However, if this parameter is set to no, the print queues from `printcap` do not appear in browses. This can be verified with `load printers=no` at the top of `smb.conf`.

[homes]

[homes] is a special share that reveals the user's home directory, named for the user's username, on browses. This happens regardless of any browseable=no settings in the share. Such browseable=no settings only prevent a share called [homes] from appearing on browses.

auto services=

This parameter can reveal printers and home directories that would normally not be revealed. Create the following smb.conf and reboot Samba:

```
encrypt passwords=yes
workgroup=mygroup
load printers=no
auto services=lp myuid

[printers]
print ok=no
browseable=no

[homes]
browseable=no
```

The browse for the preceding smb.conf is as follows, assuming the Windows user is logged in as username:

```
C:\WINDOWS>net view \\mainserv
Shared resources at \\MAINSERV

Sharename    Type       Comment
-------------------------------------------------
lp           Disk       Home directory of lp
myuid        Disk       Home directory of myuid
username     Disk       Home directory of username
The command was completed successfully.

C:\WINDOWS>
```

Note that printer lp was revealed in spite of the load printers=no parameter. This is because it's listed in the auto services= parameter. Likewise, the home directory for user myuid is listed in spite of the fact that myuid is not the logged-in user. Once again, this is made possible by the fact that it's listed in auto services=. Note, however, that auto services= derives its list of homes and printers from the [homes] and [printers] shares, respectively. Removal of the [printers] share disables the auto services= listing of any printers. Likewise, the removal of [homes] disables the auto services= listing of any home directories.

announce as= and announce version=

These parameters determine how the Samba server's nmbd daemon announces itself. They should be left at their defaults except in extremely unusual situations.

lm announce= and lm interval=

The defaults are auto and 60, respectively, which work for most situations. The auto setting means that no LAN Manager (LANMAN) announce broadcasts will be made unless some are received (from OS/2 clients, usually). An lm announce=no setting means "do not broadcast no matter what," whereas an lm announce=yes setting means "definitely broadcast." Therefore, lm announce=auto performs identically to lm announce=no in the absence of OS/2 clients or other hosts that originate LANMAN broadcasts.

The lm_interval= parameter determines how often the server sends out these broadcasts.

Share-Level Browsing Parameters

The browseable= and comment= parameters effect specific shares.

The browseable= parameter defaults to yes. If it's set to no, it prevents the share in which it's explicitly specified from showing up in browse lists. Experiment by toggling the browseable= parameter for [tmp]. Note that its appearance on browses is toggled. However, it can be accessed with a net use command no matter what browseable= is set to.

The comment= parameter is the share equivalent to the global server string= parameter. Its string value shows up on browses, including net view \\servername.

Browsing Theory

The theory is that the local master browser keeps the browse list. When any client sends a browse request, the local master browser sends the browse list to that client. To see the theory in action, run tcpdump and hit the server with a browse. It's best if you use the special tcpdump program available from the Samba project, because it shows SMB packets in an intelligible form. The first step is to find the right snap length. The snap length is the -s option in tcpdump, and it determines the maximum packet size. For experimentation purposes, you want the snap length to be barely big enough to hold the entire returned browse list. Run the following command:

```
$ tcpdump -s500 port 137 or port 138 or port 139 | grep -i snap
```

Then, from a Windows box, run the following command:

```
$ net view \\servername
```

If you get output from the tcpdump command piped through grep, it means you got the "increase snap length" messages, so increase the snap length. If you do not get output, decrease the snap length. Continue until you have the snap length a few bytes bigger than the minimum necessary to eliminate snap length messages. Now you're ready to pipe the output to a file. Do the following:

```
$ tcpdump -s500 port 137 or port 138 or port 139 > tst.tst
```

The preceding listens on all the Samba ports, dumping the results to a file called tst.tst. Once that's running, from a Windows session, execute the following command:

```
$ net view \\servername
```

Wait 10 seconds from the time the Windows command completes and then press Ctrl+C on the tcpdump command. View tst.tst in the less pager. You'll see several packets going from client to server, and vice versa, that set up the protocol.

Next, you'll see an IP packet from the client to the server containing an SMB packet of type SMBtrans (REQUEST). It's followed immediately by an IP packet from the server to the client containing an SMB packet of type SMBtrans (REPLY). This is a huge packet, and if you look in the hex editor portion of the packet's dump, you'll see the browse list. This is how the Samba server supplies the client with the browse list.

Similarly, you can see an election request from a Windows client as well as the transactions that follow. Start with a Samba server running without benefit of a local master browser (set preferred master=no and restart Samba). Pipe tcpdump for the Samba ports into a file; then run net view /workgroup:workgroupname on a Windows client. Let it run for about 40 seconds and then press Ctrl+C to get out of the tcpdump.

The client hits the server with a flurry of \MAILSLOT\BROWSE requests. After fielding a bunch of these, the server finally sends back (after 17 seconds in the author's setup, for example) a registration packet with __MSBROWSE__ in the SMB packet's name. Note that *sends back* is not quite accurate, because the server broadcasts the packet.

The bottom line is that packet sniffing is an excellent method of troubleshooting and gaining insight into the NetBIOS communication process.

Browsing Troubleshooting

Browsing can be rather tough to troubleshoot. In an effort to simplify it, this section identifies a troubleshooting strategy meant to minimize the time it takes to arrive at a solution by performing the quickest tests first:

- Determine whether `testparm` produces any errors.
- Determine whether the share is browseable on the server's console.
- Determine whether the share is meant to be browseable.
- Determine whether the share is browseable on the Windows command line.
- Resolve naming issues.

The section then goes on to discuss other handy troubleshooting tactics for browsing.

Determine Whether `testparm` Produces Any Errors

The `testparm` program is too quick not to use right away. First, fix any errors or warnings revealed by `testparm`:

```
[root@mainserv /root]# testparm
Load smb config files from /usr/local/samba/lib/smb.conf
Processing section "[homes]"
params.c:Section() - Badly formed line in configuration file: printers
params.c:pm_process() - Failed.  Error returned from params.c:parse().
Error loading services.
[root@mainserv /root]#
```

The preceding `testparm` test found the `[printers]` line lacking the final bracket. All such errors must be corrected. Next, make sure the share in question is revealed in the output. As an example, notice that `[homes]` is revealed in the preceding command.

In one minute, it's been confirmed that `smb.conf` has a legal format and that the share in question exists and is spelled correctly.

Determine Whether the Share Is Browseable on the Server's Console

The next step is also quick. Observe browseability on the server's console as follows:

```
$ smbclient -NL localhost
```

If the preceding command does not reveal the share, check whether the share is meant to be browseable (see the next section).

Determine Whether the Share Is Meant to Be Browseable

If `smbclient -NL localhost` revealed the share, skip this section.

Now you'll see whether the share is operating as designed. Look at the share definition in `smb.conf`. If the share explicitly specifies `browseable=` or `browse ok=`, then the value of the parameter (yes or no) determines the share's browseability. If there's not an explicit specification in the share, is there an explicit specification in a global section? If not, the default value of yes is used.

Normal shares are browseable if and only if the preceding method shows they evaluate to browseable=yes. Note that browseable=no in the global section hides special share IPC$ from browse lists.

Determine Whether the Share Is Browseable on the Windows Command Line

Try the following command from the Windows client:

```
C:\WINDOWS>net view \\mainserv
```

If this command reveals the share but Network Neighborhood does not (you should recheck Network Neighborhood at this time), the problem is probably related to a missing local master browser. If the preceding command says that it was completed successfully but it does not show the share, there's an obscure problem, once again probably having to do with NetBIOS naming, WINS, or a lack of a local master browser. If the command errors out, there's a problem with basic networking or NetBIOS naming. In this case, ping both ways between the client and the server and then resolve any problems standing in the way of ping.

Resolve Naming Issues

If there's any remaining question about connectivity, run ping both directions between the client and the server and then resolve any problems standing in the way of ping.

Next, check NetBIOS naming from the DOS computer with the following command:

```
C:\WINDOWS>nbtstat -n -a mainserv


        NetBIOS Remote Machine Name Table

     Name              Type        Status
   ---------------------------------------------
   MAINSERV      <00>  UNIQUE    Registered
   MAINSERV      <03>  UNIQUE    Registered
   MAINSERV      <20>  UNIQUE    Registered
   .._MSBROWSE__.<01>  GROUP     Registered
   TEST11        <00>  GROUP     Registered
   TEST11        <1D>  UNIQUE    Registered
   TEST11        <1E>  GROUP     Registered
```

```
MAC Address = 00-00-00-00-00-00
C:\WINDOWS>
```

Note the existence of __MSBROWSE__, which indicates a local browse master. The <1D> version of the workgroup name also indicates the existence of a local master browser. If a local master browser didn't exist, these two entries wouldn't appear.

If the preceding command errors out, try it again using an IP address with the uppercase -A option:

```
C:\WINDOWS>nbtstat -n -A 192.168.100.1


        NetBIOS Remote Machine Name Table

     Name              Type         Status
   ---------------------------------------------
   MAINSERV       <00>  UNIQUE      Registered
   MAINSERV       <03>  UNIQUE      Registered
   MAINSERV       <20>  UNIQUE      Registered
   .._MSBROWSE__.<01>  GROUP       Registered
   TEST11         <00>  GROUP       Registered
   TEST11         <1D>  UNIQUE      Registered
   TEST11         <1E>  GROUP       Registered

MAC Address = 00-00-00-00-00-00
C:\WINDOWS>
```

Note, however, that the inability to access the server by NetBIOS name is, in itself, a problem that must be corrected.

Sometimes a browser election can be triggered by the following command, issued from the Windows command prompt:

```
C:\WINDOWS>net view /workgroup:test11

Error 6118: The computer(s) sharing resources in this workgroup
cannot be located. The computer(s) might have been restarted.
Wait a few minutes, and then try again. If the problem
persists, make sure your network-adapter settings are correct.


C:\WINDOWS>
```

In the preceding command, the response indicates an error. The error is caused by a lack of a local master browser. However, the preceding command sometimes has the side effect of triggering a browser election. Often, within 30 seconds of the preceding command, the nbtstat -n -a servername command will indicate the existence of a local master browser.

Here's a UNIX command that determines the local master browser:

```
nmblookup -SM -
```

This command produces the same output as `nbtstat -n -a servername` if a local master browser exists on the Samba server; otherwise, it comments that it failed to find `__MSBROWSE__`.

On the Samba server, the following command can show the registration of the local master browser (and the domain master browser if one's elected) in real time:

```
$ tail -fn0 nmb.log
```

This command outputs to the `log.nmb` file, including the registration of the local master browser.

Other Troubleshooting Tactics for Browsing Problems

There are numerous tactics for troubleshooting browsing problems. This section discusses a few that are most likely to reveal the root cause of the problem.

Creating a Surefire Local Master Browser

A handy tactic is to modify `smb.conf` to force a browser election 30 seconds after Samba restarts. Include these three parameters in the global section:

```
local master=yes
preferred master=yes
os level=255
```

Caution

The preceding command disrupts any existing NT or other Samba local master browser. Use the preceding command only if such a consequence causes no damage or inconvenience.

Restart Samba and then notice via `tail -fn0 servername` that within 30 seconds the Samba server becomes the local master browser.

Toggle `wins support=`

Depending on other factors, `wins support=` may play a part in browsing problems. If it won't compromise the stability of the network or inconvenience users, toggle `wins support=` and restart Samba.

Find a Browseable Share and Exploit the Differences

If one share shows up in a browse list and the other doesn't, exploit the differences. Make changes to the shares to make them more like each other, until you find the single root cause of the browsing problem.

When doing this, it's important to have the local master browser in a consistent state; therefore, be sure to add the three lines previously mentioned to start a surefire local master browser within 30 seconds.

Always Look for Another Test to Narrow the Scope of the Problem

Troubleshooting is about narrowing, not about finding. Finding is the consequence. Continually seek tests to narrow the scope of the problem, and the solution will eventually reveal itself.

Summary

Browsing refers to the act of a client displaying SMB shares in a list. The browseability of a share is determined by its `browseable=` parameter. Contrast this with *accessibility*, which is the ability to read or write files in the share by explicitly naming the share. Shares can be browseable and accessible, browseable and inaccessible, nonbrowseable and accessible, or nonbrowseable and inaccessible. Often, shares intended to be browseable do not show up on browse lists because of problems with the network, the local master browser, or the SMB client.

The global parameters that have the greatest effect on the browsing environment are `workgroup=`, `netbios name=`, `preferred master=`, `os level=`, `local master=`, `wins support=`, and `auto services=`. Some secondary parameters were also discussed in the chapter.

Browsing occurs when a client requests a browse list from the local browse master and then receives that list. This can be seen with the `tcpdump` packet observation program.

When problems occur, one way to minimize the time it takes to arrive at a solution is to start with the easiest tests first and then progress to the harder ones. Here's the approach you would use:

- Run `testparm`.
- Is the share browseable on the server's console?
- Is the share meant to be browseable?

- Is the share browseable on the Windows command line?
- Resolve naming issues.

Chapter 33, "Cross-Subnet Browsing," and Chapter 34, "Windows Internet Naming Service (WINS)," further elaborate on browsing and name server issues.

Cross-Subnet Browsing

by Bryan J. Smith

CHAPTER 33

In the preceding chapter, the concepts behind single-subnet browsing and system resolution were explained. This chapter builds on those subjects and expands into the realm of multiple subnets, with or without multiple workgroups and/or domains. It assumes you're running Samba 1.9.17 or greater, preferably 2.0 for maximum compatibility and options with modern platforms.

First and foremost, the key to proper cross-subnet browsing is a good understanding of all the concepts involved, because its complexity over single-subnet workgroups is exponentially greater. As such, the browser and name services of Samba are covered in greater detail in this chapter than in probably any other. To put it bluntly, the content and depth of this chapter becomes necessarily "dry." If you're on a time schedule or wish to see a working example in action, go ahead and skip directly to the "Proof of Concept: Two-Subnet Domain" section. Then return to the preceding sections when a deeper understanding is necessary.

Networking Review: Subnets

If your organization has numerous departments, possibly even numerous buildings, each with its own servers and/or services, it's highly likely that your organization maintains separate subnetworks (or *subnets*). Subnets are often local area networks (LANs) organized so that most communication between systems only occurs between the systems themselves. At the same time, the use of separate subnets in a network allows for the most efficient communication between them. Communication between subnets is handled by a router using a routable protocol.

IP Subnets and Routing, Ethernet, and Switching

Concepts such as IP subnets and routing are anchored at Layer 3 of the International Standards Organization (ISO) Open Standards Interconnect (OSI) model. NetBEUI, IPX, and IP are all OSI Layer 3 protocols.

Although most subnets are physically separate ethernet LANs, they do not have to be. Ethernet is an OSI Layer 1 and 2 protocol, and multiple subnets (at Layer 3) can exist on the same physical ethernet LAN.

Many new ethernet switches offer, in addition to traditional Layer 1 and 2 ethernet bridging, Layer 3 routing features, which help reduce traffic and overhead on those LANs with multiple IP subnets. The Layer 3 switching capability in ethernet equipment may be well worth the cost for large, physically interconnected LANs with multiple SMB servers and workgroups.

Unlike NetBEUI, IP is a fully routable protocol, which is why most documentation on SMB services recommends you use only TCP/IP on your networks. This chapter assumes that only IP is being used on systems that either offer or use SMB services.

> **Caution**
>
> Enabling NetBEUI or IPX on Windows systems in a network where Samba servers or clients are present will not only introduce multiple, disparate master browsers (one NetBEUI, one IP) but may cause many systems to be inaccessible across subnets (or even on the same subnet).

Finally, understand that this chapter only deals with SMB communication between subnets. Additional requirements for cross-subnet browsing include proper IP subnet setup, IP routing, IP name services (for example, the Domain Name System, or *DNS*), and other non-Samba, IP networking services. Such concepts and details are beyond the scope of this book (and could in fact fill several books) but will be required for proper communication between IP subnets. Macmillan USA offers several excellent books on TCP/IP communications that cover these subjects and will help you further diagnose issues that do not deal with Samba but affect its proper operation.

> **Caution**
>
> Even properly configured Samba servers will fail to communicate if the underlying IP services between networks, such as DNS, routing, and so on, are not properly set up.

As a quick reference, Table 33.1 lists the standard IP subnet classes and available private networks as defined by the InterNIC in its Request for Comments (RFC) documents. Never use a subnet that has not been designated "private" unless it has been registered with the InterNIC for use by your organization.

TABLE 33.1   IP Subnet Classes and Private Networks

Class	Subnets (Number)	Subnet Mask	Max Nodes/ Subnet	Private Subnets
A	1.x.x.x–127.x.x.x	255.0.0.0	16.7 Million	10.x.x.x (1)
B	128.x.x.x–191.x.x.x	255.255.0.0	65,534	172.16.x.x–172.31.x.x (16)
C	192.x.x.x–223.x.x.x	255.255.255.0	254	192.168.0.x–192.168.255.0 (256)
D, E, F	224.x.x.x–255.x.x.x	Varies	Varies	None

Browser and Controller Differentiation

Native Windows servers understand only workgroups and domains, folding into each a set of predefined services for browse lists and authentication control. To these Windows servers, the two are inseparable. Samba servers separate the browse list from authentication control, which provides for a myriad matrix of greater options and greater control over each. As such, even the most experienced Windows server administrator should refamiliarize himself with how browse lists and authentication control are, in fact, separate from one another.

The greatest confusion you'll have in understanding this chapter results from misconceptions regarding the features of workgroups and domains. Remember that, to Samba, a workgroup can extend to offering the same level of services as a native PDC domain by you just setting and/or changing a few options.

Tip

In separating browser functionality from controller functionality, browser-only Samba servers have an advantage over native Windows servers in that the added authentication load of the controller is removed. This increases both reliability and performance because the master browser for a domain does not have to do anything more than manage the list of servers—rather than servers and user accounts (let alone their various authentication services, such as domain logins and so on).

Browser Services

Key to communication in any subnet or between subnets is the maintenance of a list of systems and their capabilities. CIFS/SMB services maintain a browse list of all systems in any workgroup or domain.

Native Windows servers and clients in a workgroup cannot access other systems outside of their subnet. For multiple subnets, Windows introduces the concept of a *domain* (often referred to as a *[Windows] NT domain*, so as to not confuse it with DNS or NIS domains). The domain controller—be it a primary domain controller (PDC) or backup domain controller (BDC)—is responsible for synchronizing the browse lists between all subnets in a domain. Therefore, for native Windows servers, maintaining multiple subnets requires at least one PDC.

Windows NT's Loss, Samba's Gain

Windows NT servers must either be designated standalone, PDC or BDC at installation time. Therefore, servers designated as standalone at installation time can never become domain servers and, therefore, can never offer cross-subnet browsing. That is where Samba can come in and help you. You can use Samba to manage your domain (browser, controller, or both) instead of requiring you to reinstall all of your native Windows servers as PDC/BDCs.

Samba does not make a hard distinction between a workgroup and a server, and this blurred definition can be seen in their options and usage. Samba, in stark contrast to native Windows servers, can maintain browse lists for a small workgroup on its own subnet or an entire enterprise of multiple subnets at the toggle of a few options. Samba still uses the term *domain* on some options to signify their relationship to the browser services normally provided by native PDCs.

Samba's flexible browser services and the various arrangements possible for multiple subnets are the focus of this chapter.

Controller Services

Key to any service of limited access is authentication. CIFS/SMB is no exception and offers varying levels of users and authentication, both standalone (workgroup) and distributed (domain).

Native Windows servers functioning as standalone (or workgroup) servers can only authenticate local users on their subnet. Those servers functioning as PDC/BDC (or domain) servers can authenticate users throughout a domain of one or more subnets. Clients, including standalone servers, must be configured as domain members to take advantage of these cross-subnet services. Again, note the strict tying of browser services to controller services through the workgroup and domain implementations of native Windows servers.

Samba authentication mechanisms feature both the oldest version of LAN Manager (the predecessor SMB server product to Windows NT) protocols and the inclusion of Samba servers in native PDC domains. Stock Samba 2.0 can also serve as a Windows $9x$ PDC server (a Windows NT PDC with additional, nonrelease code) or pass authentication to another server, such as a native Windows server, regardless of its controller status.

Although browsing is the focus of this chapter, with domain control left to other chapters, some authentication issues do arise with Samba browser services. Successful cross-subnet browsing will sometimes require the troubleshooting and elimination of user and other authentication issues first.

Caution

In the stock Samba 2.0 distribution, Samba servers emulating PDC services cannot exchange most authentication information with native PDCs.

Principles of Cross-Subnet Browsing

This section covers the concept of the browse list including how some servers control it, how they share it, how others read from and report to it, and which servers are elected to what in a subnet or multiple subnets. Also covered are NetBIOS names, their resolution and the types and order of their resolution.

The principles covered in this section are crucial to proper communication between subnets with any CIFS/SMB servers. Although you may jump directly to the section "Proof of Concept: Two-Subnet Domain," I encourage you to become familiar with the concepts in this section (possibly in tandem with reading that section). These concepts are hard enough to digest on their own, possibly the hardest in this entire publication. Please take your time and reference back and forth between both sections if you find yourself becoming confused.

Browse List Mastery

The master browser is the CIFS/SMB server that all clients often refer to for name resolution. By default, all Samba servers aspire to be a master browser. In multiple subnets, more than one master browser will exist.

Local Master Browser (LMB)

One master browser exists per subnet, designated as the *local master browser* (LMB). The LMB maintains the browse list for all systems on the subnet. A master browser can also be set to be the *preferred master*. The preferred master will force an election to occur to designate the LMB for the local subnet and, in the absence of a domain master browser (DMB), the entire workgroup (to a very limited extent for multiple subnets).

> **Identifying Browsers in Files and Utilities**
>
> The LMB of each subnet has a NetBIOS type of 1D hexadecimal.
>
> The DMB has a workgroup/domain-unique NetBIOS type of 1B hexadecimal.

Domain Master Browser (DMB)

The *domain master browser* (DMB) handles browse list maintenance and distribution, similar to native PDC/BDC servers. Otherwise, the DMB behaves just like a regular preferred master (and should be configured as one) for a workgroup. Samba can also provide Windows Internet Naming Service (WINS), and its use is highly recommended for cross-subnet browsing.

> **Note**
>
> From the standpoint of Samba's browser services, a workgroup and domain are the same. This means Samba workgroups can span multiple subnets, with or without the use of a DMB or WINS. Of course, cross-subnet browsing is best implemented with Samba by using both DMB and WINS.

33

CROSS-SUBNET
BROWSING

OS Level and Elections

The term *election* was introduced in the preceding paragraphs alongside the preferred master option. By default, the first Samba server (specifically, the first nmbd session) to start is the LMB. Any server with the preferred master option set forces an election both when it starts and on a regular basis if it has not been designated the LMB. The setting of the OS level is the important option for elections, although other options, such as preferred or DMB, can affect the outcome of an election. Table 33.2 lists the default OS levels of various Windows operating systems.

TABLE 33.2   Default Browser OS Level for Each Release of Windows

Windows Release	OS Level
Windows for Workgroups and Windows 95/98	1
Windows NT Workstation	16
Windows NT Server	32

Minimizing Elections and Unnecessary Traffic

Master browser elections, in general, should be minimized because they degrade performance in both single- and multiple-subnet networks. If two systems on the same subnet are configured with the preferred master option set, the losing server in the LMB election will consistently force an election, thus reducing overall network efficiency. Instead of covering the actual resolution and designation of a server as the LMB, which may change from version to version, consider the following rules as good practice for cross-subnet browsing:

- In the absence of a native PDC, designate one system as the DMB in a workgroup. Also designate it as a preferred master. Set its OS level to the highest in the workgroup and greater than 32 to defeat any standalone NT server.

- Designate one system on each subnet, except the subnet where the DMB is located, as the LMB. Also designate it as a preferred master. Set its OS level under the DMB's but greater than 32 to defeat any standalone NT server.

- Designate one system as the WINS server and set all SMB clients and servers to use WINS services with that system's IP address. WINS is discussed in further detail in the next chapter.

- Configure all Windows clients, as well as servers that are on the same subnets as Samba master browsers, to disable the option for Browse Master. In Windows 9*x*, it's an Advanced option under File and Printer Sharing for Microsoft Networks, as shown in Figure 33.1.

FIGURE 33.1

Disabling the Master Browser option in Windows 98.

Master Browser Redundancy

For redundancy, you can designate both a second DMB, preferably on the same subnet as the first, and a second LMB on each subnet. For each, turn off the enable preferred master option and reduce the OS level below the first's respective level. However, still set the OS level greater than 32 to defeat any standalone NT server.

> **Tip**
>
> In general, all Samba servers should have the local master option set, which it is by default. This allows maximum redundancy and failover. Network traffic will not increase as long as the preferred master option is not set on more than one server per subnet.

> **Note**
>
> The latest stock Samba 2.0 code does not offer WINS server redundancy. Only one system in a Samba workgroup/domain should serve WINS, period.

Browser Mastery in a Native PDC

In a domain with a native PDC server, the PDC server is the domain master. Samba servers should not be configured to contest the native PDC as a DMB on any subnet. In addition, Samba should never be used as a WINS server anywhere in a domain controlled by a native PDC. Doing so often will incorrectly reroute domain logons from some poorly coded Windows clients to the Samba WINS server.

33

CROSS-SUBNET
BROWSING

> **Note**
>
> Samba's ability to serve as an LMB to Windows systems alongside a native PDC (controlling the domain and all the systems in it) is only one of the few protocols and functions that work interoperably between the usually proprietary Windows and open-standard Samba interfaces. The same does not hold true for the DMB, the WINS server, and most of the domain controller functionality.

On subnets in a native PDC domain where native Windows servers do not exist, Samba can and will act as the LMB for the subnet. Although Samba can serve browse lists to and receive them from the PDC, Samba cannot act as a redundant domain master. Consider the following rules for Samba servers participating in a native PDC domain:

- The OS level should always be set below 32. Although the OS level may be set above 32 on subnets where the PDC isn't located, it's not recommended.

- On the same subnet as the native PDC, Samba should never have the preferred master option set.

- On subnets with a Windows NT server, Samba should lose the election because the native server's OS level is set at 32. As such, do not enable the preferred master option.

- On subnets without a Windows NT server, Samba can be safely designated as the LMB, including having the preferred master option set (but only on one Samba server per subnet, as mentioned earlier) and the OS level set at a nonconflicting value of 17 to 31.

Name Discovery and Resolution

In addition to understanding the authoritative sources for names in a subnet or work-group/domain, you need to explore how, and in what order, clients (including the masters themselves) resolve names.

NetBIOS Naming Fundamentals

When it comes to evaluating NetBIOS as a system of directory services, you'll find it severely lacking. However, for CIFS/SMB services, there is no alternative. Here are some limitations of Windows file services:

- NetBIOS names cannot exceed 15 characters.

- All NetBIOS names in a workgroup need to be unique.

- All authenticated objects, users, systems, and groups in a domain need to be unique.

Active Directory

Windows 2000 offers a new CIFS/SMB directory infrastructure called *Active Directory* (AD). Although it's still not a globally suitable directory system (for example, it requires some hostname uniqueness), AD does solve some issues with current NetBIOS resolution. AD's protocols and authentication mechanisms are closed standards and will require many months of reverse engineering before Samba is able to interoperate with them.

Tip

In general, to avoid never-ending troubleshooting issues with Windows, always use unique names for everything. This includes never using the same name for any two objects in Windows, even of different types, such as users, groups, systems, and so on. For example, I had a user who could not get a portable data assistant (PDA) device to connect to his NT Workstation machine via Remote Access Services (RAS), even after countless reboots and calls to the PDA vendor's tech support. He humored me by following my suggestion to log on with a different username than his system name, and it worked instantly. This was not exactly something the vendor's support staff could foresee as the root cause.

Multiple Paths of Discovery

For single subnets, especially medium to small ones, NetBIOS name discovery and resolution order are of little concern. However, as a network grows and expands over subnets, both accessibility and traffic generation make these items important.

Native Windows networking defines three major methods of NetBIOS name discovery. Samba runs on UNIX, a network operating system (NOS) with a long tradition and history of system naming and directory services. Samba adds yet another method of resolution as well as complete control over the use and priority of any of the NetBIOS name resolutions.

Broadcast

IP broadcasts are used by default by Windows servers and clients alike for discovery. Without any additional configuration, subnets without a PDC use broadcasts to discover systems and maintain the master browser list of systems. Broadcast is the most inefficient method of browse list maintenance and the least reliable.

The major issue with broadcast is that it usually stops at the router, staying local to the subnet of origin. Samba can expand broadcast capabilities to include *unicast* (that is, a directed broadcast) to another subnet's broadcast address (for example, the .255 octet of a Class C network) or the master server of other subnets. Administrators should consider broadcast to be the "last resort" of discovery and resolution, and the Samba default resolution list reflects this.

> **Caution**
>
> Many routers do not allow unicasts to the broadcast address of a remote network. In such cases, either the router must be configured to allow such broadcasts or the address of the master browser of the network must be known.

lmhosts File

The LAN Manager hosts, or lmhosts, file is the CIFS/SMB equivalent of /etc/hosts for most UNIX name resolvers for traditional IP services. Similar to the static, single-line listing format of /etc/hosts, lmhosts also defines additional parameters for NetBIOS types, such as master browsers and domain servers.

Both Samba and Windows servers and clients can use lmhosts files, although the formats usually differ. Examples of Samba and lmhosts files, including the use of NetBIOS types, follow. The examples feature a designated DMB (or PDC), two file servers on remote subnets, and two local file servers, including one designated as the LMB:

```
#   /usr/local/samba/var/lmhosts
#   Example lmhosts file for Samba
192.168.0.16    wrkgp_dmb#1b
192.168.1.48    subnet1_lmb#20
192.168.2.48    subnet2_lmb#20
192.168.3.48    subnet3_lmb#1d
192.168.3.50    subnet3_svr2#20
192.168.3.128   subnet3_pc1

#   c:\win98\lmhosts
#   Example lmhosts file for Windows 98
192.168.0.16    wrkgp_dmb     #PRE #DOM:workgroup
192.168.1.48    subnet1_lmb   #PRE
192.168.2.48    subnet2_lmb   #PRE
192.168.3.48    subnet3_lmb   #PRE
192.168.3.50    subnet3_svr2
192.168.3.128   subnet3_pc1
```

As with /etc/hosts, lmhosts is a static file and suffers from the same lack of replication and dynamics.

> **Tip**
>
> A domain's lmhosts file for Samba servers can be centralized on an NFS server mounted by all Samba servers. For Windows, a client's lmhosts file can be updated at domain logon by setting domain profiles and logon scripts.

Windows Internet Naming Service (WINS)

The Windows Internet Naming Service (WINS), the preferred method of resolving names across subnets, is a dynamic directory service for NetBIOS systems. If possible, always set up and configure all systems to use a WINS server in a multiple-subnet workgroup/domain implementation. In the case where existing Windows clients are numerous, Samba provides proxying options for relaying non–WINS-aware clients via its LMB designation to the WINS server for the workgroup/domain. The WINS server does not have to be the same server as the DMB for a workgroup.

WINS is covered in greater detail in the next chapter. The basic application of WINS to proper cross-subnet browsing and configuration is used in the examples in this chapter.

UNIX Name Resolution

In addition to the three universally accepted methods of NetBIOS name and discovery, Samba servers offer a fourth method of name resolution. This method involves the use of the underlying UNIX resolver functionality for most IP services. Depending on the version and configuration of your underlying operating system, this resolver functionality could include /etc/hosts, DNS, NIS (Network Information Service, or *yellow pages*), and similar IP directory and name resolution services.

> **Note**
>
> Files for consideration on modern Linux systems include /etc/host.conf, /etc/resolv.conf, /etc/yp.conf, and others. For Solaris 2, see /etc/nsswitch.conf, /etc/resolv.conf, and others. For just about any UNIX system, try a keyword search on the manual for resolve[r] (for example, man -k resolve).

Samba handles the resolver by returning the leftmost name (the bare hostname) as the NetBIOS name. This will require, of course, that all hostnames, or at least the ones that use or provide CIFS/SMB services, adhere to NetBIOS naming limitations, such as having 15 characters or fewer and being unique.

> **Tip**
>
> An extremely powerful use of the UNIX resolver, especially as the primary resolver method for Samba, is on the primary DNS, or one or more secondary DNS servers (the load may be a consideration on the primary DNS) for a corporate WAN. Such a system could and should serve as the DMB, possibly alongside a redundant DMB, for the corporate CIFS/SMB domain.

Applicable Samba Options

The browser is an essential part of any CIFS/SMB network. As such, numerous options affect and are affected by browser configuration. Authentication between systems, for one, can greatly affect proper browsing.

For each of the following options under consideration, any use or example is made in the general context as if it were set under the global section of the `smb.conf` file.

Basic Configuration

At a bare minimum, the workgroup needs to be defined in the `smb.conf` file before anything can happen. Provided there are existing SMB resources on the network, simply setting the workgroup name will allow browsing and resolution to occur (largely via broadcast). Set your network's local- or multiple-subnet workgroup/domain name (again, they are equivalent from the standpoint of this Samba option):

```
Workgroup = MYDOMAIN
```

An optional setting, although required if your hostname exceeds the 15 character limit of NetBIOS, is the NetBIOS name:

```
NetBIOS Name = MYSERVER
```

As another option, any aliases should be defined as well. If this server provides browser (for example, LMB or DMB) or controller services, they will not be made available under any of the NetBIOS aliases, but only under the NetBIOS name in the preceding parameter. Here's an example:

```
NetBIOS Aliases = MYALIAS1 MYALIAS2
```

Browser-Related Options

The following options are directly browser related. Failure to set them properly will most likely result in either inefficiencies or major SMB service disruptions in an existing implementation. Take care in setting these options, because the browser service is probably the most fundamental of all basic SMB services.

- Master browsers (LMB and DMB)
- WINS, proxying, and usage
- Name resolution and order
- Remote unicast announcements and reception

Master Browsers: LMB and DMB

The preceding section on browse list mastery covered the concepts regarding Samba as a master browser. Building on this, the following options are usually appropriately named (for questions and concerns regarding how browsers are selected or used, refer to the aforementioned section, which covers these concepts in much greater detail):

```
Browse List = Yes
Browse Master = Yes
```

The preceding two options should always be set, and they will be, by default. The small memory footprint for `Browse List` is worth the cached name performance, and `Browser Master` ensures that at least one Samba or Windows server offers itself as an LMB in the absence or failure of an appropriately designated one.

The first SMB service to start is usually designated the local master browser (LMB) until an election occurs. `Preferred Master` forces an election to occur when a Samba server first starts, and periodically if it's not elected as the local master. Once an election occurs, `OS Level` is used to select the LMB, where a greater value equals a greater chance. `Preferred Master` should never be used on more than one server on a subnet. To do so would encourage servers to send extra chatter over the wire periodically as they consistently challenged the current master. A Samba server in a domain controlled by a native Windows PDC is configured as follows:

```
#    Example of a Samba server alongside a native PDC
Preferred Master = No   # I will not initiate elections
Domain Master = No   # I will not be a DMB
OS Level = 24   # I will lose to NTS, but not to 9x/NTW
```

`OS Level` defaults to `0` to prevent Samba from disrupting an existing SMB network by activating it. The preceding setting is probably safe on a network run by either a native, standalone NT server or a domain with a native PDC. In the absence or failure of the native NTS on a subnet, the Samba server will serve as a redundant LMB for the subnet.

To guarantee that Samba always initiates and wins browser elections against native Windows servers, thus becoming the LMB, use the following settings:

```
#    I will be the LMB for a subnet, possibly the workgroup
Preferred Master = Yes # I will initiate elections until I win
```

```
Domain Master = No   # I will not be a DMB
OS Level = 48    # I will always win against Windows
```

To properly manage a multiple subnet, a domain master browser (DMB) will be necessary. Again, for networks with a native PDC, Samba should not be enabled to be one, and it's not by default. For networks with multiple subnets, whether they are comprised of Samba servers, native standalone Windows servers, or both, one Samba server should be configured as follows to be the DMB:

```
#       I am always the DMB for an entire domain
Preferred Master = Yes # I will initiate elections
Domain Master = Yes    # I am the root browser of my domain
OS Level = 255         # I will win against everyone
```

WINS, Proxying, and Usage

Usage of the Windows Internet Naming Service (WINS) is highly recommended for multiple subnets. The WINS server can be a native Windows server or a Samba server, but not both—nor can either be redundant to the other. For a more complete introduction to and discussion of WINS, see Chapter 34, "Windows Internet Naming Service (WINS)." Here's an example of a Samba server that announces itself to and gets Browse List information from a WINS server:

```
#   I am a LMB in a workgroup/domain with a WINS server
WINS Support = No     # I am not the WINS server
DNS Proxy = No        # Only valid on the WINS server
WINS Server = 192.168.0.16  # My workgroup/domain WINS
WINS Proxy = Yes      # I will forward broadcasts to WINS
```

The preceding example should be used on Samba servers that act as the LMB for a subnet. Only one Samba server or native Windows server (although Windows does offer some WINS redundancy options) in an entire subnet should serve as the WINS server; therefore, only one server should have the WINS Support option set (or be running the WINS server in the case of a native Windows server).

The latter two options in this example involve the setting of the IP address of the WINS server, which should always be done if a WINS server exists. The WINS Proxy option should be set on the LMB of each subnet. It forwards broadcasts and other NetBIOS requests and announcements to the WINS server, for those systems not aware of the WINS server's existence. This saves you from having to manually configure each and every SMB client with WINS to the WINS server's IP.

Regardless of this setting, newer Windows clients should always be configured with the IP address of the WINS server to reduce unnecessary network traffic.

Caution

Although native Windows servers serving WINS can be configured as secondary WINS servers, the stock Samba 2.0 code currently does not offer such capabilities (nor can it interoperate with native WINS servers). As such, you should never input an IP address into the field for a secondary WINS server if Samba is providing the WINS for a domain.

This is an example of the WINS server for a Samba-managed workgroup/domain:

```
#   I am the WINS server for a Samba-managed workgroup/domain
WINS Support = Yes   # I am the WINS server
DNS Proxy = No       # DNS will not be used for WINS
WINS Server =        # Never set on the WINS server itself
WINS Proxy = Yes     # I will include broadcasts in WINS
```

Samba does not have to have controller services enabled in the same domain, but a Samba server will need to be the DMB in the workgroup/domain. Again, the DMB and WINS server for a domain does not have to be the same Samba server.

Caution

Never configure Samba as a WINS server in a domain with a native PDC. Doing so will often result in poorly coded Windows clients sending login requests to the Samba WINS server.

This last Samba WINS server example is the same as the one before it, except here the `Dns Proxy` option has been set:

```
#   I am the WINS server and a DNS server for a corporate intranet
Wins Support = Yes # I am the WINS server
Dns Proxy = Yes    # I can fall back to DNS for resolution
Wins Server =# Never set on the WINS server itself
Wins Proxy = Yes   # I will include broadcasts in WINS
```

This is a powerful option that should be used on Samba WINS servers that are also primary or, due to load concerns, secondary DNS servers in an organization's intranet. When the Samba WINS server fails to resolve a NetBIOS name from its WINS database or other NetBIOS name resolution functions, the WINS server will attempt to resolve the name via traditional IP Domain Name Services (DNS) lookup.

> **Caution**
>
> Enabling Dns Proxy on networks where a base (that is, leftmost) hostname is
> not unique will definitely introduce NetBIOS resolution issues. All SMB servers
> and clients should also be labeled using 15 characters or less in DNS, not includ-
> ing the node's (or subnet's) respective DNS domain.

> **Note**
>
> When running as a daemon, the setting of the dns proxy option will launch a
> second instance of nmbd.

Name Resolution and Order

The preceding section on multiple paths of discovery covered the various methods of
NetBIOS name discovery and resolution. Name resolution, although often neglected and
left to its default, is very important to performance and efficiency, especially on subnets
and workgroups/domains with large numbers of SMB nodes. This is the default in
Samba 2.0:

```
#   Samba 2.0 default
Name Resolve Order = lmhosts host wins bcast
```

At a the very least, a minimally configured Samba server in a workgroup/domain with
multiple subnets should use an lmhosts file with at least one entry for the DMB server:

```
#   /usr/local/samba/var/lmhosts
192.168.0.16   wrkgp_dmb#1b
```

The server with the NetBIOS name wrkgp_dmb is the DMB, as designated by the
NetBIOS type 1b hexadecimal. If the Samba server is not the LMB for the local subnet,
it, too, can be listed and designated as the LMB for the local subnet with a NetBIOS type
1d hex. All other SMB-aware nodes anywhere on the network can be listed, including the
NetBIOS type 20 hex to designate those nodes with SMB file services.

> **Note**
>
> The format of the lmhosts file for Samba is different than the lmhosts file for
> other SMB server and client operating systems, such as Windows.

Of course, the primary issue with lmhosts is that it's a static file, which introduces and requires additional support for replication and distribution. The most obvious way to solve this is to rearrange the Name Resolve Order to prefer dynamic resolution method (to avoid regular use of the lmhosts file for resolution).

The two obvious choices are broadcast and WINS. Although perfect for smaller, single-subnet workgroups, the former is of little advantage in multiple-subnet workgroups. It also slowly introduces increasing inefficiencies as the number of SMB systems increases. As such, the use of WINS, once again, is recommended for optimal cross-subnet browsing. The following example takes advantage of a WINS server (which is not provided by the Samba server itself):

```
Name Resolve Order = wins lmhosts host bcast
WINS Server = 192.168.0.16
```

The *host* method of resolution uses the underlying operating system IP name resolver, which usually is a combination of /etc/hosts, DNS, and/or NIS/Yellow Pages functions. As in the default, the last-resort method is broadcast, which may be omitted, along with any other undesirable method (although it's best to leave all four, unless subnet chatter becomes detrimental).

Remote Unicast Announcements and Reception

Samba provides for two unicast (or remote subnet-directed broadcasts) options—remote announce and remote browse sync—to announce and query, respectively, NetBIOS names and services in remote subnets. In the absence of a DMB, a WINS, and other proper cross-subnet browse lists, these two options will allow disparate subnets to know about NetBIOS services in each others' networks.

The IP addresses of both options should be either directed to the broadcast address (for example, 192.168.1.255) or the LMB server of each subnet. Here's an example:

```
#   subnet3_pc1, 192.168.3.128
remote announce = 192.168.0.16/MYDOMAIN 192.168.1.255/MYDOMAIN
➥192.168.2.255/MYDOMAIN
remote browse sync = 192.168.0.16 192.168.1.255 192.168.2.255
```

> **Caution**
>
> As a security and/or performance measure, most routers will prevent unicasts to the broadcast addresses of a remote subnet by default. Either consult your router's product documentation regarding its settings or limit the addresses used in the preceding options to the IP address of the subnet's LMB.

33

CROSS-SUBNET
BROWSING

These options can be used to announce and receive information from other workgroups as well. However, their usefulness may be limited because many Windows clients other than Samba itself either cannot understand information from more than one workgroup or expect such information to be handled and presented to them by a native PDC server. This does not prevent Windows clients of different workgroups from accessing each other, but may prevent disparate workgroups from transparently browsing each other in Network Neighborhood.

An example of an issue with Windows 98 is shown in Figure 33.2. Client Holden2 is located in the workgroup SMITHCONCEPTS. Although Holden2 can access the Wally Samba server in the SC2 workgroup, the browse list for the SC2 workgroup is not transposed and hidden from view in the Network Neighborhood tree.

FIGURE 33.2
Windows clients may have problems browsing other workgroups' browse lists.

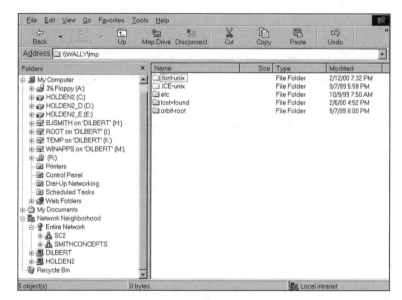

Again, these options should find limited use in most Samba implementations because they simply increase broadcast traffic. Ideal cross-subnet browsing in Samba networks should involve only one workgroup/domain, with a DMB and WINS server. Broadcast should always be considered a last resort for resolution in multiple-subnet networks, for just about any IP service in general.

LAN Manager Support

To properly support the browse lists in older LAN Manager and OS/2 servers and clients, the following options are provided:

```
lm announce = Auto
lm interval = 60
```

The default value of `lm announce = Auto` should suffice for most networks. `Auto` specifies that Samba should wait until it sees a client requiring such services before providing LANMAN-compatible announcements. For large subnets with these clients, the `lm interval` can be increased in order to lower the overhead required in supporting these clients.

Other Considerations

Samba services begin with the NetBIOS browse lists, but they are often useless without proper interface or authentication configuration. A key first step to troubleshooting cross-subnet browsing is verifying that the problems are not interface or authentication related.

Interfaces and Hosts

An often-forgotten key option for successful cross-subnet browsing is `hosts allow` and its inverted synonym `hosts deny`. Although the stock Samba 2.0 empty default is open host access, some binary distributions are compiled with, for security considerations, the empty default for no remote subnet access. Regardless of the default, if the `hosts allow` option is explicitly used, only address ranges listed are valid hosts that can access the services of the Samba server. This is commonly forgotten when adding a new subnet to a domain.

Both the `hosts allow` and `hosts deny` options can take parameters of IP addresses (example: `192.168.0.1`), networks (example: `192.168.0.`), networks with masks (examples: `192.168.0.0/24`, `192.168.0.0/255.255.255.0`) and combinations of any of the preceding (separated by whitespace). The following example includes two equivalent `hosts allow` entries:

```
#    subnet3_pc1, 192.168.3.128
#hosts allow = 192.168.0. 192.168.1. 192.168.2.0/24 192.168.3.0/255.255.255.0
hosts allow = 192.168.0.0/22    # the same as the preceding line
hosts deny =
```

Note

The loopback interface at `127.0.0.1` is always allowed unless it's explicitly listed in `hosts deny`. It's required for most browse list functionality, so it should never be denied access.

33

CROSS-SUBNET
BROWSING

The Interfaces option, along with its associated Bind Interfaces Only option, can also be a source of problems. By default, an empty Interfaces line enables the loopback and primary (for example, eth0 in Linux) network interfaces, with their appropriate subnet masks, as points of SMB services. If the Samba server serves SMB over more than one network interface, then the additional interfaces need to be specified with an explicit use of the Interfaces option:

```
#   Server with two NICs, one on 192.168.2 and one on 192.168.3
Interfaces = 192.168.2.48/24 192.168.3.48/24
Bind Interfaces Only = No
```

Additional care must also be taken when the Bind Interfaces Only option is set. When this option is set, some unicasts and remote broadcasts that are not made on the same subnet as the interfaces, including the "all interfaces" network (0.0.0.0), will be ignored. This can, of course, affect proper browse list creation. Of additional concern is the fact that some Samba services (for example, smbpasswd and SWAT) will fail if the loopback is omitted from the Interfaces line when the Bind Interfaces Only option is set. This system's configuration will allow smbpasswd and SWAT operating when the Bind Interfaces Only option is set:

```
Interfaces = 127.0.0.1/8 192.168.3.48/24
Bind Interfaces Only = Yes  # ignoring remote uni/broadcasts
```

> **Tip**
>
> A common misconception behind the Bind Interfaces Only option is the belief that it will prevent IP source address spoofing. This is simply not the case. Therefore, there's little reason to enable the option for security reasons but you might want to for performance reasons (for example, to ignore remote subnet broadcasts when WINS is used).

Authentication and Services

Because Samba separates NetBIOS names and browsing from SMB authentication and controller services, you're likely to have issues between standalone servers stemming from disparate lists of user accounts (unless controller services, such as a PDC, are available). Refusal of one server, LMB, or subnet resource to cooperate with another server, LMB, or subnet resource can usually be attributed to improper access and/or authentication between the two.

Servers and clients in a browser domain, but not a controller domain, usually maintain a disparate list of user accounts. To allow users to browse resources on other servers, unknown users should be mapped to guest. This is usually safe to set on an internal server (assuming you have not given guest regular user access):

```
map to guest = bad user
```

> **Tip**
>
> Although allowing guest access without authentication reduces security, resources can be individually configured to deny listing in the browse lists or access by guest users. Regardless, it's good practice to evaluate each share for the appropriateness of browsing and guest access.

Windows 9*x* systems allow access without a network logon or by logging in with a null password. To accommodate the browsing of such users, null passwords will need to be enabled:

```
null passwords = yes
```

> **Note**
>
> Again, this will be a security consideration. When troubleshooting cross-subnet browsing, a quick toggle of this option should be attempted when the troubleshooting session has been reduced to "trial and error."

The restrict anonymous option is often set without a full understanding of its true intent and purpose. Setting this option is almost guaranteed to cause issues if the SMB client base of the workgroup/domain does not consist 100% of Windows NT 4.0 clients. In other words, you should never set it:

```
restrict anonymous = no
```

It would not hurt to provide a default service for clients to access in the event of an error or authentication issue:

```
default service = notfound
[notfound]
   path = /tmp/notfound
   browsable = yes
   read only = yes
   guest ok = yes
```

The epitome of authentication is Samba's Security option. This option is explored in much greater detail in other chapters. User-level security should not affect proper browse list creation, but browsing SMB resources across servers may require controller authentication. A Samba server can, of course, delegate authority to another SMB server, including another Samba server, a standalone native NT server, or even a native PDC. Do so with the following:

```
Security = server
Password Server = PDCSVR
```

Care and numerous additional steps must be taken when the domain option for security is used. In general, unless you're familiar with putting a Samba server under native PDC control, avoid blindly doing the following:

```
Security = domain   # must also follow additional steps
Password Server = PDCSVR
```

Proof of Concept: Two-Subnet Domain

By now, you, the reader, should fall into one of two categories in this chapter:

* The reader who skipped directly to this section (possibly reading the introduction on subnets)
* The reader who has read all prior sections and is considering re-reading the previous sections for a better understanding

In either case, you should not "second guess" why you are here nor should you stop reading this section for any reason now. Please continue and explore the example and listings below. Refer back to the previous section when terminology and/or concepts are used that you are unfamiliar with or you need further review on.

The example network used in this "proof of concept" is purposely simple. It covers, in-depth, exactly what is happening between Samba servers on different subnets. It is completely Samba-oriented because adding a PDC into the equation would disallow Samba from becoming the DMB and WINS server.

Physical Topology

Illustrated in Figure 33.3 is a simple working example of two subnets, each with a Samba server acting as the LMB, and one acting as the DMB and WINS server as well. Also, one client has been placed on the same subnet as the DMB.

FIGURE 33.3

Simple, two-subnet network with two Samba servers.

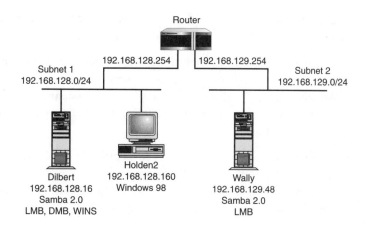

The router used in this example is UNIX based and is anchored at octet 254 on each subnet (that is, `192.168.128.254` for the first subnet and `192.168.129.254` for the second). As such, a simple execution of the address resolution protocol (ARP) on the router results in the following output:

```
[root@router /root]# arp -a
holden2.subnet1.smithconcepts.com (192.168.128.160)
➥at 00:11:22:33:44:55 [ether] on eth0
wally.subnet2.smithconcepts.com (192.168.129.48)
➥at 00:22:44:66:88:AA [ether] on eth1
dilbert.subnet1.smithconcepts.com (192.168.128.16)
➥at 00:33:66:99:BB:EE [ether] on eth0
```

Running ARP on each of the two Samba servers will only show the router and the client in the first subnet, and only the router in the second subnet. This clearly shows that the two subnets are unable to receive each others' local subnet broadcasts. Here's an example:

```
[root@dilbert /root]# arp -a
holden2.subnet1.smithconcepts.com (192.168.128.160)
➥at 00:11:22:33:44:55 [ether] on eth0
router.subnet1.smithconcepts.com (192.168.128.254)
➥at 00:44:88:BB:00:44 [ether] on eth0
```

```
[root@wally /root]# arp -a
router.subnet2.smithconcepts.com (192.168.129.254)
➥at 00:44:88:BB:00:44 [ether] on eth0
```

Network and Samba Configuration

The two server configurations are documented in the following subsections. Only those parameters relevant to browsing are covered. These include the `Browse List`, LMB, DMB options, WINS options, `OS Level`, name resolutions, `Interfaces` lines and the basic workgroup/NetBIOS strings. Remote subnet announcements are not used, nor do they need to be, since WINS and DMB services are used.

You should be able to use these settings almost without modification (except the names, IP addresses and so forth) on two existing Samba servers in order to enable cross-subnet browsing. All other entries for shares and global options not defined in the following should work alongside these settings, provided they do not affect proper operation as discussed in preceding sections.

As far as controller and user authentication is concerned, the Samba servers are set up to do their own user authentication (note the Security = User option). Again, the use of a controller and PDC emulation is beyond the scope of this chapter (which only deals with the browser half of the domain equation).

Subnet 1 LMB, DMB, and WINS Server

The DILBERT Samba server is located on the 192.168.128.0 network. In addition to being the local master browser (LMB) of its own subnet, it serves as the domain master browser (DMB) and provides the Windows Internet Naming Service (WINS) for the workgroup SMITHCONCEPTS. In addition to its browser mastery, the DILBERT server also provides DNS for various subnets and has the Dns Proxy option set for WINS. Here are the settings:

```
Workgroup = SMITHCONCEPTS
NetBIOS Name = DILBERT
Browse List = Yes
Browse Master = Yes
Preferred Master = Yes
Domain Master = Yes
OS Level = 255
Wins Support = Yes
Dns Proxy = Yes
Wins Server =
Wins Proxy = Yes
Name Resolve Order = wins lmhosts host bcast
Hosts Allow = 127. 192.168.128. 192.168.129.
Interfaces = 192.168.128.16/24
Bind Interfaces Only = No
Security = User
```

A simple /usr/local/samba/var/lmhosts file has been created:

```
127.0.0.1          localhost
192.168.128.16     dilbert#1b
192.168.129.48     wally#20
```

In any given UNIX implementation, a good number of configuration files are key to networking interface setup and IP resolution and routing. Instead of listing all files and their settings here, the correct settings and routes for IP, including the default gateway, can be verified with the `netstat` utility (available in most UNIX implementations):

```
[root@dilbert /root]# netstat -r
Destination     Gateway         Genmask          Flags  MSS Window  irtt Iface
192.168.128.16  *               255.255.255.255  UH       0 0          0 eth0
192.168.128.0   *               255.255.255.0    U        0 0          0 eth0
127.0.0.0       *               255.0.0.0        U        0 0          0 lo
default         router.subnet1  0.0.0.0          UG       0 0          0 eth0
```

Subnet 2 LMB Server

The WALLY Samba server is located on the `192.168.129.0` network. It serves as the local master browser (LMB) for the workgroup SMITHCONCEPTS on its subnet. Here are WALLY's settings:

```
Workgroup = SMITHCONCEPTS
NetBIOS Name = WALLY
Browse List = Yes
Browse Master = Yes
Preferred Master = Yes
Domain Master = No
OS Level = 48
Wins Support = No
Dns Proxy = No
Wins Server = 192.168.128.16
Wins Proxy = Yes
Name Resolve Order = wins lmhosts host bcast
Hosts Allow = 127. 192.168.128. 192.168.129.
Interfaces = 192.168.129.48/24
Bind Interfaces Only = No
Security = User
```

A simple `/usr/local/samba/var/lmhosts` file has been created that's similar to the one for DILBERT, except for one option (1d is used to designate WALLY as the LMB):

```
127.0.0.1       localhost
192.168.128.16  dilbert#1b
192.168.129.48  wally#1d
```

Once again, proper verification of IP settings and routing can be performed with the `netstat` utility:

```
[root@dilbert /root]# netstat -r
Destination     Gateway         Genmask          Flags  MSS Window  irtt Iface
192.168.129.48  *               255.255.255.255  UH       0 0          0 eth1
192.168.129.0   *               255.255.255.0    U        0 0          0 eth1
127.0.0.0       *               255.0.0.0        U        0 0          0 lo
default         router.subnet2  0.0.0.0          UG       0 0          0 eth1
```

Client Configuration

The Windows client, a Windows 98 PC named HOLDEN2, has been configured graphically via Control Panel, Networking. Key to its successful browsing is its configuration to use WINS, as shown in Figure 33.4.

FIGURE 33.4

Configuring a Windows 98 client to use a Samba WINS server.

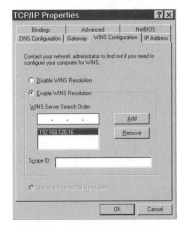

> **Note**
>
> Even if the Windows client is not configured to use WINS, the LMB (DILBERT) would forward broadcasts from HOLDEN2 to the WINS server via DILBERT and its Wins Proxy option setting.

The settings of most Windows clients can be viewed with a hidden utility called WINIPCFG.EXE, located in the Windows directory. If WINS has been properly configured, WINIPCFG will report the Node Type to be Hybrid. Hybrid SMB clients resolve NetBIOS names by first using WINS and then broadcast (if WINS fails).

NetBIOS Logs, Lookups, and Shares

Three major points of information exist on the NetBIOS daemon (nmbd) in Samba: the raw, local nmbd logs, LMB lookups, and the listing of shares in the LMB list.

NetBIOS Daemon Logs

The most chatter is found in the nmbd logs on the DMB server, usually in /usr/local/samba/log/log.nmb. Individual entries are analyzed in the following entry:

```
[timestamp] nmbd/nmbd.c:main(684)
  Netbios nameserver version 2.0.5a started.
  Copyright Andrew Tridgell 1994-1998
```

The preceding entry signals the startup of the nmbd binary. All Samba servers will have at least this single entry in their log.nmb files:

```
[timestamp] nmbd/asyncdns.c:start_async_dns(150)
  started asyncdns process 5079
```

This entry signals the startup of a second nmbd binary, as required for the dns proxy option. This entry will only occur if the dns proxy option has been set. The process number is the actual process ID of the second nmbd binary, as verified with the execution of the ps utility:

```
[root@dilbert /usr/local/samba/log]# ps -eaf |grep nmbd
root      5077     1  0 01:32 ?        00:00:00 nmbd -D
root      5079  5077  0 01:32 ?        00:00:00 nmbd -D
```

The next two sets of entries involve the DMB election. If WINS is used, regardless of whether the WINS server happens to be the DMB, two DMB elections are executed. The first one is for the controlling WINS server, which happens to be the DMB in this example. This entry set is as follows:

```
[timestamp] nmbd/nmbd_become_dmb.c:become_domain_master_browser_wins(342)
➥become_domain_master_browser_wins:
  Attempting to become domain master browser on workgroup
➥SMITHCONCEPTS, subnet UNICAST_SUBNET.
[timestamp] nmbd/nmbd_become_dmb.c:become_domain_master_browser_wins(357)
➥become_domain_master_browser_wins: querying WINS
➥server at IP 192.168.128.16 for domain master browser
➥name SMITHCONCEPTS<1b> on workgroup SMITHCONCEPTS
➥CAST_SUBNET
[timestamp] nmbd/nmbd_become_dmb.c:become_domain_master_stage2(118)
  *****
  Samba server DILBERT is now a domain master browser for
➥workgroup SMITHCONCEPTS on subnet UNICAST
➥SUBNET
  *****
```

The second election held is via broadcast on the local subnet. If WINS is not used, this is the only DMB election held (and the preceding entry set will not occur). Here's the second entry set:

```
[timestamp] nmbd/nmbd_become_dmb.c:become_domain_master_browser_bcast(294)
➥become_domain_master_browser_bcast:
  Attempting to become domain master browser on workgroup
➥SMITHCONCEPTS on subnet 192.168.128.16
[timestamp] nmbd/nmbd_become_dmb.c:become_domain_master_browser_bcast(308)
➥become_domain_master_browser_bcast: querying subnet
➥ 192.168.128.16 for domain master browser on work
➥group SMITHCONCEPTS
```

33

CROSS-SUBNET
BROWSING

```
[timestamp] nmbd/nmbd_become_dmb.c:become_domain_master_stage2(118)
  *****
  Samba server DILBERT is now a domain master browser for
➥workgroup SMITHCONCEPTS on subnet 192.168.128.16
  *****
```

Finally, the DMB will also try to become the LMB on the local subnet. A DMB does not have to be the LMB of its subnet, although it gains a distinct advantage over non-DMB servers in the election. Here's an example:

```
[timestamp] nmbd/nmbd_become_lmb.c:become_local_master_stage2(406)
  *****
  Samba name server DILBERT is now a local master browser for
➥workgroup SMITHCONCEPTS on subnet 192.168.128.16
  *****
```

The preceding entries in `nmbd.log` can be considered the worst case in total length for a system at startup. For the most part, a regular subnet LMB will have little more than the following in its `log.nmb`:

```
[timestamp] nmbd/nmbd.c:main(684)
  Netbios nameserver version 2.0.5a started.
  Copyright Andrew Tridgell 1994-1998
[timestamp] nmbd/nmbd_become_lmb.c:become_local_master_stage2(406)
  *****
  Samba name server WALLY is now a local master browser for
➥workgroup SMITHCONCEPTS on subnet 192.168.129.48
  *****
```

These preceding entries are for WALLY, which does little more than start the NetBIOS daemon and elect itself as the LMB for its subnet.

LMB Lookup and Status

Samba provides for NetBIOS lookups and listings with the utility `nmblookup`. In its most elemental use, `nmblookup` can simply query the local subnet via a broadcast. The LMB will then respond and spill its browse list for the local subnet to the output. Here is the view of the LMB on subnet 1:

```
[root@dilbert /root]# nmblookup -SM -
Sending queries to 192.168.128.255
192.168.128.16 __MSBROWSE__<01>
Looking up status of 192.168.128.16
received 9 names
        DILBERT          <00> -          M <ACTIVE>
        DILBERT          <03> -          M <ACTIVE>
        DILBERT          <20> -          M <ACTIVE>
        .._MSBROWSE__. <01> - <GROUP> M <ACTIVE>
        SMITHCONCEPTS    <00> - <GROUP> M <ACTIVE>
        SMITHCONCEPTS    <1b> -          M <ACTIVE>
```

```
             SMITHCONCEPTS   <1c> - <GROUP> M <ACTIVE>
             SMITHCONCEPTS   <1d> -         M <ACTIVE>
             SMITHCONCEPTS   <1e> - <GROUP> M <ACTIVE>
num_good_sends=0 num_good_receives=0
```

Of particular interest are those entries with the NetBIOS types of 01, 1d, and 1b hexadecimal. They verify the existence of an LMB on the subnet, an LMB for the workgroup and the DMB on the local subnet, respectively. Also note the NetBIOS type of 20 hex on the network identifying a node with SMB shares. Each of these exist on the first subnet with the LMB, DMB, and WINS server DILBERT.

Now here is the view of the LMB on subnet 2:

```
[root@wally /root]# nmblookup -SM -
Sending queries to 192.168.129.255
192.168.129.48 __MSBROWSE__<01>
Looking up status of 192.168.129.48
received 7 names
             WALLY              <00> -        M <ACTIVE>
             WALLY              <03> -        M <ACTIVE>
             WALLY              <20> -        M <ACTIVE>
             ..__MSBROWSE__.    <01> - <GROUP> M <ACTIVE>
             SMITHCONCEPTS      <00> - <GROUP> M <ACTIVE>
             SMITHCONCEPTS      <1d> -        M <ACTIVE>
             SMITHCONCEPTS      <1e> - <GROUP> M <ACTIVE>
num_good_sends=0 num_good_receives=0
```

Note the lack of a NetBIOS type 1b entry in the LMB list in subnet 2. Therefore, the DMB is not located here.

NetBIOS Share Browsing

Before attempting to browse the cross-subnet resources with an actual Windows SMB client, here's how to verify that everything is working on Samba's own SMB client:

```
[root@dilbert /root]# smbclient -NL localhost
Added interface ip=192.168.128.16 bcast=192.168.128.255 nmask=255.255.255.0
Got a positive name query response from 127.0.0.1 ( 127.0.0.1 )
Domain=[SMITHCONCEPTS] OS=[Unix] Server=[Samba 2.0.5a]

        Sharename      Type        Comment
        ---------      ----        -------
        homes          Disk        Home Directories
        tmp            Disk        Default Share
        IPC$           IPC         IPC Service (Samba 2.0.5a)
        Server                     Comment
        ---------                  -------
        DILBERT                    Samba 2.0.5a
        HOLDEN2                    Lourdes' PC
        WALLY                      Samba 2.0.5a
```

33

CROSS-SUBNET BROWSING

```
Workgroup              Master
- - - - - - - - -      - - - - - - -
SMITHCONCEPTS          DILBERT
```

That was fairly easy given that we are on DILBERT, which is looking at itself via the loopback interface. Note that WALLY, located on a completely different subnet, is showing up in the browse list:

```
[root@wally /root]# smbclient -NL localhost
Added interface ip=192.168.129.48 bcast=192.168.129.255 nmask=255.255.255.0
Got a positive name query response from 192.168.128.16 ( 127.0.0.1 )
Domain=[SMITHCONCEPTS] OS=[Unix] Server=[Samba 2.0.5a]

        Sharename      Type      Comment
        - - - - - - - - -   - - - -    - - - - - - -
        homes          Disk      Home Directories
        tmp            Disk      Default Share
        IPC$           IPC       IPC Service (Samba 2.0.5a)
        Server                   Comment
        - - - - - - - - -        - - - - - - -
        DILBERT                  Samba 2.0.5a
        HOLDEN2                  Lourdes' PC
        WALLY                    Samba 2.0.5a
        Workgroup                Master
        - - - - - - - - -        - - - - - - -
        SMITHCONCEPTS            WALLY
```

Running smbclient on WALLY's loopback interface produces similar results as those for the DILBERT loopback run, although some interesting exceptions exist. First off, the *positive name query response* from the DMB server is actually cached in WALLY's LMB list (designed by the 127.0.0.1 loopback address in parentheses). Another difference is the Master entry for the SMITHCONCEPTS workgroup—WALLY instead of DILBERT. Remember that the DMB server is for coordinating LMB servers across subnets, not for serving the clients themselves. Therefore, smbclient only concerns itself with the LMB and simply calls it the "master" in its output.

Now for the "real" test, running smbclient on WALLY to list DILBERT's shares:

```
[root@wally /root]# smbclient -NL dilbert
Added interface 192.168.129.48 bcast=192.168.129.255 nmask=255.255.255.0
Got a positive name query response from 192.168.128.48 ( 192.168.128.48 )
Domain=[SMITHCONCEPTS] OS=[Unix] Server=[Samba 2.0.5a]
        Sharename      Type      Comment
        - - - - - - - - -   - - - -    - - - - - - -
        homes          Disk      Home Directories
        tmp            Disk      Default Share
        IPC$           IPC       IPC Service (Samba 2.0.5a)
```

```
Server            Comment
---------         -------
DILBERT           Samba 2.0.5a
HOLDEN2           Lourdes' PC
WALLY             Samba 2.0.5a
Workgroup         Master
---------         -------
SMITHCONCEPTS     DILBERT
```

Note that there's little difference. WALLY already has a copy of DILBERT's browse list in its browse list. The only two entries that differ are the name query and the reported LMB (master), because the request was actually made on DILBERT this time.

The Transparent Browse Endgame

Of course, Windows users care little about how Samba works with itself. Hence, the endgame of all efforts—the transparent access by Windows clients. The net view command can be used to list the NetBIOS nodes in a workgroup/domain:

```
Servers available in workgroup SMITHCONCEPTS.
Server name            Remark
--------------------------------------------------
\\DILBERT              Samba 2.0.5a
\\HOLDEN2              Lourdes' PC
\\WALLY                Samba 2.0.5a
The command was completed successfully.
```

It can also be used to list the shares available on a particular node:

```
C:\WIN98>net view \\wally
Shared resources at \\WALLY
Sharename    Type        Comment
--------------------------------------------------
bjsmith      Disk        Home Directories
tmp          Disk        Default Share
The command was completed successfully.
```

> **Note**
>
> Note the resolution of the homes share in the preceding smbclient output to the username, bjsmith, in the Windows net view output. The resolution occurs because Windows 9x clients can only handle the authentication of one user.

33

CROSS-SUBNET
BROWSING

This is all shown from the GUI perspective in Figure 33.5.

FIGURE 33.5

*Network
Neighborhood
and Explorer
correctly cross-
subnet browsing
in Windows 98.*

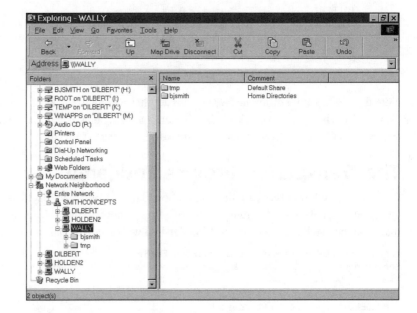

Troubleshooting

There's a good chance that your first attempt at setting up Samba for cross-subnet browsing will fail or that at least a portion of your network will fail to be integrated.

Here are some avenues to troubleshooting issues and solving problems with cross-subnet browsing:

- Run `testparm` on the configuration file.
- Verify whether the NetBIOS daemon is running.
- Verify local services.
- Verify local browsing.
- Verify remote services.
- Verify remote browsing.
- Verify proper NetBIOS naming and resolution.
- Verify proper IP routing.
- Verify proper authentication.

Run `testparm` on the Configuration File

First and foremost, run `testparm` on the `smb.conf` file of all Samba servers under scrutiny. This will quickly identify any typographical errors that may be preventing Samba itself from starting or working properly. Here's an example:

```
[root@wally /root]# testparm /usr/local/samba/var/smb.conf
Load smb config files from /usr/local/samba/var/smb.conf
Processing section "[homes]"
Processing section "[printers]"
Processing section "[tmp]"
Loaded services file OK.
```

Verify Whether the NetBIOS Daemon Is Running

The NetBIOS daemon (`nmbd`) is independent of the main SMB services daemon (`smbd`), and it may stop running altogether while `smbd` continues to execute. As such, all browser list services will halt alongside any name resolution that should be done on the system. A simple execution of the `ps` command should reveal whether `nmbd` is executing:

```
[root@wally /root]# ps -eaf |grep nmbd
root      3364    1  0 01:26 ?        00:00:00 nmbd -D
```

If `nmbd` crashes silently almost immediately after Samba startup, the culprit is usually an incorrect `interfaces` option line. A common mistake is to enter a subnet network/mask combination (for example, `192.168.128.0/24`) instead of an address/mask combination (for example, `192.168.128.16/24`).

Barring the improper setup of the `interfaces` option, the next step is to check the logs of the daemon:

```
[root@wally /root]# tail /usr/local/samba/log/log.nmb
```

Verify Local Services

On a client in the local subnet, verify the existence of local services:

```
[root@subnet2_pc1 /root]# smbclient -NL wally
Added interface ip=192.168.129.192 bcast=192.168.129.255 nmask=255.255.255.0
Got a positive name query response from 192.168.128.16 ( 192.168.129.48 )
Domain=[SMITHCONCEPTS] OS=[Unix] Server=[Samba 2.0.5a]

        Sharename      Type      Comment
        ---------      ----      -------
        homes          Disk      Home Directories
        tmp            Disk      Default Share
        IPC$           IPC       IPC Service (Samba 2.0.5a)
```

33

CROSS-SUBNET
BROWSING

```
Server              Comment
---------           -------
SUBNET2_PC1         Samba 2.0.5a
WALLY               Samba 2.0.5a
Workgroup           Master
---------           -------
SMITHCONCEPTS       WALLY
```

If the shares are not listed, try verifying the existence of shares on the loopback of the system:

```
[root@wally /root]# smbclient -NL localhost
```

If they're now available, the issue is most likely with the `interfaces`, `hosts allow`, or `hosts deny` option.

Verify Local Browsing

On a client in the local subnet, verify the existence of an LMB:

```
[root@wally /root]# nmblookup -SM -
Sending queries to 192.168.129.255
192.168.129.48 __MSBROWSE__<01>
Looking up status of 192.168.129.48
received 7 names
        WALLY           <00> -          M <ACTIVE>
        WALLY           <03> -          M <ACTIVE>
        WALLY           <20> -          M <ACTIVE>
        .._MSBROWSE__. <01> - <GROUP> M <ACTIVE>
        SMITHCONCEPTS   <00> - <GROUP> M <ACTIVE>
        SMITHCONCEPTS   <1d> -          M <ACTIVE>
        SMITHCONCEPTS   <1e> - <GROUP> M <ACTIVE>
num_good_sends=0 num_good_receives=0
```

It's important to verify the existence of both an LMB for the subnet (NetBIOS type 01 hexadecimal) and an LMB that's part of a workgroup/domain (NetBIOS type 1d hex).

If neither exists, try setting the `preferred master browser` option on one Samba server in the subnet.

If only 01 hex is listed, the LMB is not communicating with the DMB of the workgroup/domain. A quick solution to this would be to create a small `lmhosts` file (usually `/usr/local/samba/var/lmhosts`) that lists the IP address of the DMB controller:

```
#    /usr/local/samba/var/lmhosts
192.168.128.16   dilbert#1b
```

A better solution would be to use a WINS server and set every LMB, server, and client to use it.

Verify Remote Services

On a client in a remote subnet, verify the existence of browseable services on the server in the local subnet:

```
[root@wally /root]# smbclient -NL dilbert
```

If services are not being listed, try verifying whether the `hosts allow` and `hosts deny` options are set correctly.

Another solution would be to manually add the server as a system providing file services to the `lmhosts` file:

```
#    /usr/local/samba/var/lmhosts
...
192.168.128.16    dilbert#20
```

Also, verify that either a WINS server is being specified or that your LMB is set up as a WINS proxy. As a last resort, try setting the `remote announce` and `remote browse sync` options in the absence of any communication. Examples of remotely broadcasting and listening are

```
Remote Announce:  192.168.128.16/SMITHCONCEPTS
Remote Browse Sync:  192.168.128.16
```

Verify Remote Browsing

If remote servers are appearing in the local browse list, try sending a NetBIOS name request directly to the remote LMB's IP via unicast:

```
[root@wally /root]# nmblookup -SM -U 192.168.128.16 -
Sending queries to 192.168.128.16
192.168.128.16 __MSBROWSE__<01>
Looking up status of 192.168.128.16
received 9 names
        DILBERT          <00> -          M <ACTIVE>
        DILBERT          <03> -          M <ACTIVE>
        DILBERT          <20> -          M <ACTIVE>
        .._MSBROWSE__. <01> - <GROUP> M <ACTIVE>
        SMITHCONCEPTS    <00> - <GROUP> M <ACTIVE>
        SMITHCONCEPTS    <1b> -          M <ACTIVE>
        SMITHCONCEPTS    <1c> - <GROUP> M <ACTIVE>
        SMITHCONCEPTS    <1d> -          M <ACTIVE>
        SMITHCONCEPTS    <1e> - <GROUP> M <ACTIVE>
num_good_sends=0 num_good_receives=0
```

Then, verify the existence of an LMB (type 01) and an LMB in a workgroup (type 1d).

33

CROSS-SUBNET
BROWSING

> **Note**
>
> You might also try remote broadcast with the -B option (for example, -B 192.168.128.255) instead of -U, although many routers prevent unicasts to the broadcast address of remote networks.

Verify Proper NetBIOS Naming and Resolution

Limitations on the labeling of systems in SMB workgroups were covered in the section "NetBIOS Naming Fundamentals," earlier in the chapter.

Verify that the name resolve order option includes resolution methods that are in use. For example, make sure that your name resolve order option does not solely consist of wins (name resolve order = wins) when WINS is not in use. Try setting the option back to using all methods for resolution:

```
Name Resolve Order = wins lmhosts host bcast
```

Verify Proper IP Routing

Verify that hostnames on different subnets can access at least port 139 between each other:

```
[root@wally /root]# telnet dilbert 139
Trying 192.168.128.16...
Connected to dilbert.subnet1.smithconcepts.com.
Escape character is '^]'.
<terminal hang>
```

Any response, such as the preceding one, indicates port 139 is accessible and routed correctly between networks. If no response is output but browse lists are accessible on the local subnet, your router could be misconfigured and stopping all SMB traffic between subnets.

Verify Proper Authentication

If NetBIOS LMB types 01 and 1d exist in every subnet and at least one subnet has a DMB type 1b, cross-subnet browsing is probably working as desired in your workgroup/domain. In this case, the authentication and/or controller mechanisms most likely become issues. If so, try toggling some of the options discussed in the sections "Applicable Samba Options" and "Other Considerations," earlier in this chapter.

If Samba client–to–Samba server browsing and/or authentication is successful, but Windows client–to–Samba server browsing is not, look into the settings for options security and encrypted passwords.

The logs for services—both the base `log.smb` (usually in `/usr/local/samba/log`) and the client-specific `log.<node>` files—will be of use in troubleshooting authentication and other controller issues.

Other Suggestions

A standard tool in the UNIX hacker's toolkit is `tcpdump`. Use `tcpdump` to directly view IP packets sent on an IP subnet. Ports 138 and 139 are used for nearly all NetBIOS and SMB traffic, with port 137 in limited use by older Windows 95 systems. The following example looks at 1500 byte TCP packets (usually the default for ethernet on most platforms) on the NetBIOS/SMB ports:

```
[root@wally /root]# tcpdump -s1500 port 138 or port 139
```

Summary

The realm of cross-subnet browsing is far from easy to understand. As such, this chapter took a "no holds barred" approach to covering just about every aspect of the browsing services available in CIFS/SMB. Specifically, this chapter covered

- The distinction and separation between browser and controller services in Samba.

- A discussion of the browse list, including the local master browser (LMB), domain master browser (DMB), elections of the LMB and DMB, the communications between nodes on the same subnet and between LMBs, and the optional DMB and WINS servers across subnets.

- NetBIOS naming conventions and resolution, including the four resolving mechanisms Samba can use (`WINS`, `lmhosts`, `hosts`, and `broadcast`) and the options to set their priority (or completely disable them).

- A "proof of concept" example, including the full and relevant `smb.conf` options for the example servers, example `lmhosts` files and a dissection of the `nmbd` logs showing the browser information on each.

- Basic troubleshooting procedures and tips to tracking down and tackling problems with implementing browsing across subnets.

This chapter is far from complete and, barring the creation of a book dedicated to only CIFS/SMB browsing, no single chapter could be. But given the deep discussion of browsing concepts and a basic proof of concept example, you should now be ready to implement a multiple-subnet intranet of Samba and native Windows servers for your organization.

33

CROSS-SUBNET
BROWSING

Windows Internet Naming Service (WINS)

by Mitch Adair
and Glenda Snodgrass

In This Chapter

CHAPTER 34

The Windows Internet Naming Service (WINS) is a mechanism for providing name resolution of NetBIOS/SMB names to TCP/IP addresses. In many ways, it is something like DNS for NetBIOS names but somewhat more automated. More broadly, it also offers a central repository of names on your network, reduced network traffic, faster name resolution, and the capability to provide naming services across complicated, routed LAN and WAN environments. Without WINS, it would be impossible, or nearly so, to use NetBIOS in a large distributed network.

A potential problem with NetBIOS networks, in the absence of WINS (also called a NetBIOS Name Server (NBNS)), is that they broadcast for all name resolutions. This limits the network topologies that will support it and is a burden to the network utilization itself. In short, NetBIOS/SMB is a notoriously chatty protocol, and that not only starves bandwidth but also introduces latency in name resolution and conversion as the network grows. NetBIOS faces a serious upper limit in how many hosts it will support using a purely broadcast model. WINS addresses this problem and provides its solution as well as some other enhanced functionality.

WINS, seemingly a panacea, is not without problems. Most of these come down to implementation and configuration, however. Properly done, a WINS server increases the speed at which Windows Networking/NetBIOS works in resolving names, makes resolution more reliable, and reduces the burdens on your network of NetBIOS resolution through broadcast.

The Cost of Broadcast

For small networks, it is easy to assume that all computers are local, directly connected to the same wire. In a network configuration like this, all hosts can receive the broadcasts of all other hosts. This broadcast mechanism is the default for client computers to resolve NetBIOS names in the absence of a WINS server. This scheme is relatively simple and easy to configure: it means a limited amount of configuration on the clients and no external services to run. This can be contrasted with traditional DNS where names have to be set in a separate server, all clients pointed at that server, and so on.

Network Traffic

Although a simple and relatively effective scheme for smaller networks, the broadcast solution soon turns into a disaster as more hosts are added and networks are interconnected and routed. The addition of computers to the network causes greatly increased broadcast traffic to resolve names and maintain an accurate display of the current network topology. As the network traffic increases, it takes its toll on other network operations, and everything using the network pays the penalty. Traffic is then pushed even farther as requests and connections start to timeout, requiring retransmissions and causing failures.

Additionally, because it is broadcast, these name resolutions are not routable. This is a crippling limitation in a large, distributed network like a corporate WAN or the Internet. Organizations that are expanding their networks would be forced to bridge traffic between networks if they stayed with broadcast, with the previously mentioned problems, as still more hosts are added. In most cases, WINS is a crucial component in using NetBIOS over a routed network.

Slower Browsing

These increases in network traffic then cause browsing slowdowns, which only make the situation worse because latency is increased in the name resolution itself. When the network traffic increases to the point that name resolution broadcasts timeout before they are answered, you start to see hosts drop out of your Network Neighborhood, even though you know they were there just a minute ago. Suddenly people can't work as effectively anymore; they complain about the slow network, slow applications, and slow computers. How can you make it all start working again? WINS may well be the answer.

WINS—Theory and Practice

WINS provides a way of doing NetBIOS name resolution without using broadcasting. With a WINS server on the network, client machines can do a directed name query to a single point on the network (or to multiple points if you are using replicated NT WINS servers). This saves a tremendous amount of traffic because each client would otherwise broadcast for those names, with the resulting consequences mentioned previously. Because an IP address is associated with a WINS server that is known by the client, either through initial configuration or DHCP, WINS is also routable across networks, unlike the broadcast name resolution method.

To properly use WINS, when a client PC is booted it must know two things: its proposed name on the network, which must be configured on the PC, and the IP address of a WINS server. When the client is booted, it then tries to register its name with the WINS server, along with its IP address, either statically configured or dynamically through DHCP. After its name is registered, the client can then request name information from the WINS server to use in browsing and connecting. Because the WINS data includes extra information about what type of name has been registered, through the NetBIOS name_type field, clients can begin to get a complete view of the network(s) around them.

They can see who the Master Browsers are, the Primary Domain Controllers, what workgroups/domains are around them, and so on.

Non-Broadcast Name Resolution Requires WINS

An important consideration for mixed network environments is that WINS is really needed to do non-broadcast name resolution. Although Samba and Windows NT 4 provide mechanisms for DNS lookups to resolve NetBIOS names, this is not really an option for Windows 95/98 client computers. Windows 95/98 computers do not and cannot resolve the fully qualified DNS names of computers as NetBIOS names. All names to them must be the 16-characters-or-less NetBIOS names. The only other way to provide a non-broadcast solution is the use of LMHOSTS, and that is simply not a scalable solution to the problem.

WINS Does Name Validation

WINS also provides name validation for the names registered with it. This means that the WINS server itself is authoritative over which names appear on the network, and duplicate names can be rejected from the database before they have a chance to create confusion on the network. In the absence of name validation, it is possible that different hosts could choose the same NetBIOS name, and then try to "fight it out" between them to see who will register the name.

NetBIOS names must be unique. The general outcome of duplicate names is more havoc than resolution. In most cases, two hosts with the same name will conduct continuous fights to register the name for themselves. The outcome for others on the network is intermittent or erroneous connections to either or both hosts, and an opportunity to share in the costs of continuous broadcast fights for a single NetBIOS name. It is not a pretty scene, and WINS provides a way to avoid it.

Samba-Hosted WINS Cannot Replicate

One potential problem with WINS from the Samba perspective is that it cannot replicate WINS databases between multiple Samba instances or with NT servers. This can be a problem if you have large networks and/or many WINS servers already running NT. In truth, under those circumstances, you should probably be allowing the NT servers to provide WINS and Master Browser services anyway.

Generally, NT is much happier when it is allowed to do Master Browser, WINS, and PDC (assuming that you are running in a domain environment). The three things actually are entirely separate, but it can be extremely difficult getting NT servers to accept that fact and continue doing other useful work. Trying to pull away DMB or WINS from an NT server is likely to result in a nonfunctional server—or even a nonfunctional network—for no real gain. If you already have NT servers providing WINS, let them do that, set up Samba to use the NT WINS servers, and don't look back.

Setting Up WINS in `smb.conf`

Actually configuring Samba to use or be a WINS server is relatively easy, but you do need to have some information about your network and how you want the network to function. Listing 34.1 shows the relevant sections of the `smb.conf` file you will want to look at and configure.

LISTING 34.1   Relevant Sections of `smb.conf` File for Configuring Samba to Use or Be a WINS Server

```
# Browser Control Options:
# set local master to no if you don't want Samba to become a master
# browser on your network. Otherwise the normal election rules apply
;   local master = no

# OS Level determines the precedence of this server in master browser
# elections. The default value should be reasonable
;   os level = 33

# Domain Master specifies Samba to be the Domain Master Browser. This
# allows Samba to collate browse lists between subnets. Don't use this
# if you already have a Windows NT domain controller doing this job
;   domain master = yes

# Preferred Master causes Samba to force a local browser election on startup
# and gives it a slightly higher chance of winning the election
;   preferred master = yes

# Windows Internet Name Serving Support Section:
# WINS Support - Tells the NMBD component of Samba to enable it's WINS Server
  wins support = yes

# WINS Server - Tells the NMBD components of Samba to be a WINS Client
#       Note: Samba can be either a WINS Server, or a WINS Client, but NOT both
;   wins server = w.x.y.z

# WINS Proxy - Tells Samba to answer name resolution queries on
# behalf of a non WINS capable client, for this to work there must be
# at least one  WINS Server on the network. The default is NO.
;   wins proxy = yes

# DNS Proxy - tells Samba whether or not to try to resolve NetBIOS names
# via DNS nslookups. The built-in default for versions 1.9.17 is yes,
# this has been changed in version 1.9.18 to no.
;   dns proxy = no
```

34

WINDOWS
INTERNET NAMING
SERVICE (WINS)

If you already have WINS servers on the network, either Samba or NT, all you should need to do is set the `wins server` variable. If you have a WINS server at IP address 192.168.0.100, for example, you would set the following and be in business:

```
wins server = 192.168.0.100
```

If you also want to act as a WINS proxy (discussed later in this chapter), set the `wins proxy` option:

```
wins proxy = yes
```

Things are slightly more complicated if you want to set up your Samba box as the WINS server. To actually become a WINS server, all you need do is set `wins support`:

```
wins support = yes
```

There are some other considerations here though. A Samba environment should have only one WINS server. So if any other server is currently doing that job, you should not set `wins support` to yes. Also, you should absolutely never set both the `wins support` option and the `wins server` option. This will cause you no end of problems and likely will stop Samba from working entirely.

You may want to consider making the WINS server also the Master Browser for your workgroup. Again this is only if there is not already an NT server providing this job, particularly one also acting as a PDC. It is frequently the case that causing a PDC to lose Master Browser status makes browsing stop working in the Domain. You probably don't want that to happen. If you have an NT WINS/PDC/DMB, you'll likely want to set the previously mentioned options as follows:

```
domain master = no
local master = no
preferred master = no
os level = 0
# set to IP of our NT PDC/WINS server
wins server = 192.168.0.67
```

If no NT servers are acting as DMB and you set up a WINS server, you will probably want to set the options to something like the following:

```
domain master = yes
preferred master = yes
os level = 75
wins support = yes
```

Measuring Broadcast Activity

One way to see the usefulness of a non-broadcast WINS solution is to view the broadcast network traffic passing on your network. After you see the potential bandwidth and latency you can reclaim by eliminating that traffic, you will likely start setting up your WINS server immediately. As a general practice, too, investigating the traffic on your network is a good way to maintain its health and effectiveness. Probably the best way to view this traffic on your network is using a network "sniffer" or packet dumping utility.

Obtaining SMB-Enhanced `tcpdump`

One useful diagnostic tool for examining the NBT and SMB activity on your LAN/WAN is the SMB-enhanced version of `tcpdump`, available from the samba.org site. With this, you can really see what is happening on your network, examine problems, and get a sense for whether your WINS setup has helped relieve some of the traffic and strain. Before you get the sources to this enhanced `tcpdump`, you should note that some Linux distributions now ship with an enhanced `tcpdump` by default. If you are not so lucky to already have this on your box, the sources can be obtained from

```
http://[mirror].samba.org/samba/ftp/tcpdump-smb/
```

where `[mirror]` should be replaced by the mirror closest to you—see `http://www.samba.org` for a complete and current list of mirrors.

For those using ftp, the preceding Web site can be reached with the following:

```
ftp://ftp.samba.org/pub/mirrors/sambaftp/tcpdump-smb/
```

In the `tcpdump-smb/` directory, you can choose to get one of the packaged binaries in the `binaries/` subdirectory (currently limited to Linux RPMs and `Solaris/SunOS4` binaries) or get the sources and compile it yourself. You will need to get the `libpcap` tarball if you don't already have `libpcap` on your system.

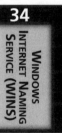

If you are compiling on most Linux systems, you can get one of the `tcpdump` source RPMs (they end in `.src.rpm`) and use that to compile and install. If you want to do it all by hand, or because a binary isn't available to you, you then need to get the `tcpdump-3.4a5-smb.patch` and apply that to the sources for `tcpdump`. You can obtain `tcpdump` sources from

```
ftp://ftp.ee.lbl.gov/tcpdump.tar.Z
```

Using `tcpdump`

You'll want to be familiar with filtering, particularly for a busy network. Still, even the most inexperienced network administrator can use this tool to get an overview of the traffic on the network and learn precisely who is doing what.

An example usage of the tcpdump command is as follows:

Assume that someone on host comet typed the following nmblookup command to find all the Master Browsers on the current subnet.

```
$ nmblookup -M -
Sending queries to 192.168.0.255
192.168.0.55 __MSBROWSE__ <01>
192.168.0.3 __MSBROWSE__ <01>
```

With an unenhanced tcpdump the output is the following:

```
# tcpdump -vv -i eth0
tcpdump: listening on eth0
17:07:19.066769 comet.theneteffect.com.1175 >
 192.168.0.255.netbios-ns: udp 50 (ttl 64, id 21718)
17:07:19.067598 galahad.theneteffect.com.netbios-ns >
 comet.theneteffect.com.1175: udp 62 (ttl 64, id 39148)
```

Not very enlightening, is it? With the SMB enhanced tcpdump, however, the output would be that shown in Listing 34.2.

LISTING 34.2   Sample SMB Enhanced tcpdump

```
# tcpdump -vv -i eth0 -s 1500
tcpdump: listening on eth0
19:14:50.595631 comet.theneteffect.com.1175 > 192.168.0.255.netbios-ns:
>>> NBT UDP PACKET(137): QUERY; REQUEST; BROADCAST
TrnID=0x6903
OpCode=0
NmFlags=0x11
Rcode=0
QueryCount=1
AnswerCount=0
AuthorityCount=0
AddressRecCount=0
QuestionRecords:
Name=`a__MSBROWSE__a NameType=0x01 (Unknown)
QuestionType=0x20
QuestionClass=0x1

 (ttl 64, id 29190)
19:14:50.596341 comet.theneteffect.com.netbios-dgm > 192.168.0.255.netbios-dgm:
>>> NBT UDP PACKET(138) Res=0x110A ID=0x7279 IP=192.168.0.55 Port=138 Length=213
➥Res2=0x0
SourceName=COMET            NameType=0x00 (Workstation)
DestName=THENETEFFECT    NameType=0x1E (Browser Server)
```

```
SMB PACKET: SMBtrans (REQUEST)
SMB Command   =   0x25
Error class   =   0x0
Error code    =   0
Flags1        =   0x0
Flags2        =   0x0
Tree ID       =   0
Proc ID       =   0
UID           =   0
MID           =   0
Word Count    =   17
TotParamCnt=0
TotDataCnt=45
MaxParmCnt=0
MaxDataCnt=0
MaxSCnt=0
TransFlags=0x0
Res1=0x0
Res2=0x0
Res3=0x0
ParamCnt=0
ParamOff=0
DataCnt=45
DataOff=86
SUCnt=3
Data: (6 bytes)
[000] 01 00 01 00 02 00                             ......
Name=\MAILSLOT\BROWSE
BROWSE PACKET
BROWSE PACKET:
Type=0xF (LocalMasterAnnouncement)
UpdateCount=0x80B6
Res1=0xFC
AnnounceInterval=10
Name=COMET              NameType=0x00 (Workstation)
MajorVersion=0x4
MinorVersion=0x2
ServerType=0xC9A03
ElectionVersion=0x10F
BrowserConstant=0xAA55
Data: (13 bytes)
[000] 53 61 6D 62 61 20 53 65   72 76 65 72 00       Samba Server.


  (ttl 64, id 29192)
19:14:50.596489 galahad.theneteffect.com.netbios-ns >
➡comet.theneteffect.com.1175:
>>> NBT UDP PACKET(137): QUERY; POSITIVE; RESPONSE; UNICAST
TrnID=0x6903
```

34

WINDOWS
INTERNET NAMING
SERVICE (WINS)

continues

LISTING 34.2   continued

```
OpCode=0
NmFlags=0x58
Rcode=0
QueryCount=0
AnswerCount=1
AuthorityCount=0
AddressRecCount=0

ResourceRecords:
Name=`a__MSBROWSE__a NameType=0x01 (Unknown)
ResType=0x20
ResClass=0x1
TTL=259200
ResourceLength=6
ResourceData=
AddrType=0x8000
Address=192.168.0.3

  (ttl 64, id 48900)
19:14:50.596647 comet.theneteffect.com.netbios-dgm > 192.168.0.255.netbios-dgm:
>>> NBT UDP PACKET(138) Res=0x110A ID=0x727A IP=192.168.0.55 Port=138 Length=206
➥Res2=0x0
SourceName=COMET              NameType=0x00 (Workstation)
DestName=`a__MSBROWSE__a NameType=0x01 (Unknown)

SMB PACKET: SMBtrans (REQUEST)
SMB Command   =   0x25
Error class   =   0x0
Error code    =   0
Flags1        =   0x0
Flags2        =   0x0
Tree ID       =   0
Proc ID       =   0
UID           =   0
MID           =   0
Word Count    =   17
TotParamCnt=0
TotDataCnt=38
MaxParmCnt=0
MaxDataCnt=0
MaxSCnt=0
TransFlags=0x0
Res1=0x0
Res2=0x0
Res3=0x0
ParamCnt=0
ParamOff=0
DataCnt=38
DataOff=86
```

```
SUCnt=3
Data: (6 bytes)
[000] 01 00 01 00 02 00                              ......
Name=\MAILSLOT\BROWSE
BROWSE PACKET
BROWSE PACKET:
Type=0xC (WorkgroupAnnouncement)
UpdateCount=0x80B6
Res1=0xFC
AnnounceInterval=10
Name=THENETEFFECT     NameType=0x00 (Workstation)
MajorVersion=0x4
MinorVersion=0x2
ServerType=0x80001000
CommentPointer=0xAA55010F
ServerName=COMET


(ttl 64, id 29193)
```

As you can see, with the SMB enhanced `tcpdump`, each of the SMB packets is broken down to show all available data, putting you in a better position to see where your traffic is going and to more quickly identify any problems occurring on the network.

Triggering NetBIOS Name Resolution

You can see NetBIOS name resolution in action when client computers try to obtain a browse list, prior to connection to other computers' network resources. After a client computer actually has done the name resolution, the actual connection and data transfers are conducted using TCP/IP connections, and no more broadcasts are needed. Client computers also have a cache for name resolutions, so it is not always the case that any name resolution attempt will actually call for a broadcast or WINS resolution attempt.

On the whole, however, browsing and connection attempts trigger name resolution, so the best way to see this in action is to make browse and connection attempts. On Samba boxes, this can be done using utilities such as `nmblookup` and `smbclient`. On Windows computers, the same can be triggered using Network Neighborhood or the `net view` commands from a DOS prompt.

Toggling Broadcast

After you have seen the traffic generated by broadcast resolution requests, you will want to see the savings from not having to broadcast for every name request. On a Samba box, you can change this by changing the `name resolve order` parameter in the `smb.conf` file. By removing `bcast` as an option altogether, you ensure that lookups will be made only against WINS or through DNS or LMHOSTS. On Windows computers, you can trigger non-broadcast resolution by either using WINS or even just setting up a test configuration using a temporary LMHOSTS file. Either of these should prove a substantial decrease in network traffic over broadcast and provide the incentive you need to configure your network to use WINS resolution.

name resolve order

Samba provides a mechanism for setting the order in which the various name resolution methods will be consulted. This can also be used to remove one or more of the methods entirely from consideration. This is an important point both for flexibility and in providing the most efficient use of resources. If, for example, you were on an isolated LAN with no DNS, you could remove the `host` option from the `name resolve order` in your `smb.conf` file and DNS and your `/etc/hosts` files would never be consulted at all.

The default for this option is:

```
name resolve order = lmhosts host wins bcast
```

lmhosts

Setting this option enables name resolution using the LMHOSTS file. This is probably the most simple name resolution method for those with small and generally unchanging networks. Additionally, this enables the setting of NetBIOS specific `name_type` information that is important in name resolution on NetBIOS networks.

host

Setting this option enables name resolution using the `/etc/hosts` and DNS, depending on the local setup for TCP/IP name resolution. That is to say, if the relevant `/etc/nsswitch.conf`, `/etc/resolv.conf`, or `/etc/host.conf` allows for it, DNS and or `/etc/hosts` may be used in NetBIOS name resolution. This can be useful if NetBIOS and DNS hostnames are the same. This method does not provide a way of including the NetBIOS `name_type` information, however. So some information is lost in using `host` resolution.

wins

This option enables the WINS name resolution. For WINS to actually work, the `wins server =` or `wins support =` parameter must be filled in with the appropriate information—either a server address, or a `yes` turning on WINS support.

bcast

This option enables the broadcast resolution of NetBIOS name requests. With this set, Samba will broadcast for names on the directly connected network.

WINS and DHCP

You might think that the inclusion of the Dynamic Host Configuration Protocol (DHCP) in Windows products would be a tremendous boon to network administrators. That is certainly the promise: a relatively easy and centrally located method for defining important machine-specific information on each boot; no time-consuming reconfigurations at each individual workstation; much quicker synchronization of all clients to the same network setup when servers and resources change. That is the promise, anyway; in practice, many people have problems, mostly through misconfigurations.

Despite the reasons for the problems and despite the compelling reasons for using DHCP, many wonder if it's impossible, or at least worth the bother. The truth is, it isn't impossible, and it isn't as difficult as most people fear, either. The key is getting the configuration right on the clients as well as the servers. Make sure that your NetBIOS names are unique and make sure that you only use the networking protocols you need to use. SMB networking is sensitive to these client-side considerations. The benefits of a correct setup in this, though, will be a more stable and maintainable network, along with the reduced browsing costs that WINS has to offer.

For SMB clients to be set up properly, they must receive their networking information from the DHCP server. On the DHCP server, there is a configuration file—`/etc/dhcpd.conf`. This is the file that contains all the information clients can use to configure themselves for networking. From the perspective of SMB networking, the important options are the `netbios-name-servers`, `netbios-dd-server`, and `netbios-node-type`. It is important to realize, of course, that all the reset of the information must be correct, or you will be spending a lot of your time trying to troubleshoot odd problems.

Listing 34.3 shows an example `dhcpd.conf` file.

LISTING 34.3   Sample `dhcpd.conf` File

```
subnet 192.168.0.0 netmask 255.255.255.0 {
        # default gw
        option routers 192.168.0.1;

        # network config
        option subnet-mask 255.255.255.0;
        option broadcast-address 192.168.0.255;
```

continues

LISTING 34.3   continued

```
        # DNS domain and servers
        option domain-name "theneteffect.com";
        option domain-name-servers 192.168.0.100;

        # Addresses .50 - .75 availabe for DHCP clients
        range 192.168.0.50 192.168.0.75;

        # 6 hours
        default-lease-time 21600;
        # 12 hours
        max-lease-time 43200;

        # - SMB-specific settings -
    # WINS server
        option netbios-name-servers 192.168.0.100;
        option netbios-dd-server 192.168.0.100;
        option netbios-node-type 8;

}
```

The first sections of this sample config file deal with basic DHCP setup and are pretty straightforward. The last section is the interesting part for WINS setup, however, and demands a bit more attention for proper configuration.

option netbios-node-type

The DHCP server allows you to define what type of NetBIOS node the client machine will be after it acquires its DHCP information. There are many different node types with differing characteristics to match the needs of various types of networks. In short, these differing types of nodes are Broadcast (B), Point-to-Point (P), Mixed Mode (M), and Hybrid (H). It is important that you set the node-type correctly. Failure to do so will likely cause browsing problems—at least.

Broadcast nodes (B-nodes) use, as the name implies, broadcast traffic on their LAN segment to define NetBIOS name resolution. The important point about a true B-node is that it doesn't use other naming services, WINS specifically, even if available, so it is possible for name changes to occur outside the purview of WINS servers using B-nodes in an environment that also has WINS servers. If you actually wanted to set a B-node in the dhcpd.conf, which you don't in a WINS environment, you would set the netbios-node-type option to a 1.

Point-to-Point nodes (P-nodes) use WINS/NetBIOS Name Servers and NetBIOS Datagram Distribution servers (NBDD), in the language of RFC1001, to achieve name resolution without the broadcasting of the B-nodes. They use only directed UDP and TCP and don't listen to the broadcasts of B-nodes at all. To set clients to P-node types from the `dhcpd.conf` file, you would set the `netbios-node-type` option to a 2.

Mixed Mode nodes (M-nodes) are a bit of a combination of P- and B-nodes. They can use both broadcast and directed name resolution. They mostly use WINS/NBNS and NBDD servers but can operate in their absence. Their general methodology is that when a name resolution is needed, they first broadcast for it and then send a directed query. To set clients to M-node types from the `dhcpd.conf` file, you would set the `netbios-node-type` options to a 4.

Hybrid nodes (H-nodes) are much like M-nodes in that they can use both broadcast and directed (WINS) name resolutions. The important difference is that H-nodes do a directed lookup first, and if they can't resolve the name that way, they then try a broadcast. This is the default for Windows clients and is very likely how you want to set them in your configuration. To set clients to H-node type, you would set the `netbios-node-type` option to an 8.

option netbios-name-servers

This sets the address or addresses of your WINS server(s). A critical option, obviously, it can take multiple addresses if you are operating in an NT environment with multiple WINS servers. In the case of multiple WINS servers, the first address is preferred over the second and so on. In a Samba environment, set this to your one WINS server.

option netbios-dd-server

This sets the address(es) of your NetBIOS Datagram Distribution (NBDD) server(s). NBDD servers are capable of distributing NetBIOS datagrams to the various nodes they are in contact with. The connectivity of an NBDD may be greater than that of individual nodes it services, and therefore may be capable of delivering datagrams between nodes that could not otherwise communicate. NBDD servers can be queried for their capability to deliver specified datagrams. Set this to the address of your WINS server in a Samba environment.

lmhosts and Dynamic Addressing

Attempting to implement this in a large, distributed, and dynamic network will make you old long before your time. In short: Don't go there. Although LMHOSTS is a good option in a small and static network environment, it is likely to cause you big problems after the network and number of clients expands. Because each change to the network must be replicated to all LMHOSTS files on all computers, it quickly becomes unmanageable. It may be useful to have one or two fall-back names in an LMHOSTS file, but

34

WINDOWS
INTERNET NAMING
SERVICE (WINS)

even this may cause problems in the future. If you have intermittent failures in browsing and connections, it is not unlikely that stale LMHOSTS information is plaguing your network.

Using WINS as a Proxy

An important method for transitioning your network to WINS-based name resolution can be the use of WINS proxies. Basically WINS proxies act to replicate WINS data through the use of broadcasting. The proxy is set up to do name resolutions using the WINS server. When a broadcast node makes a request for a name, the proxy will request that name from the WINS server.

Assuming that the name is of a computer using WINS name resolution, the WINS server will reply with the address for the name requested by the proxy. The proxy then will cache the name and address locally. If there is no broadcast reply to the originating requesting client, because the requested name is WINS resolvable, then the WINS proxy will answer with the cached address it received from the WINS server. Broadcast nodes can then have access to WINS data without the need for reconfiguration.

Of course, using this scheme still leaves you with all the problems and few of the benefits of WINS resolution. Indeed, it may even increase traffic somewhat as broadcasts are sent and fail initially. As a method for transitioning to pure WINS resolution, however, it can be exceedingly helpful and useful.

If you are going to use WINS proxying, it may be best to use a Samba server in that capacity. Windows clients also have the capacity for proxying, but they are generally configured with smaller name resolution caches, and of course, there is the question of their reliability in general. If you are going to use the proxying feature, best use a server capable of maintaining a cache long enough to reduce unnecessary duplicate requests to the WINS server and redundant broadcast requests that will fail.

Listing 34.4 shows the relevant section of the `smb.conf` file for configuring this.

LISTING 34.4   Configuring `smb.conf` for Proxying

```
# Windows Internet Name Serving Support Section:
# WINS Support - Tells the NMBD component of Samba to enable it's WINS Server
;    wins support = no

# WINS Server - Tells the NMBD components of Samba to be a WINS Client
#       Note: Samba can be either a WINS Server, or a WINS Client, but NOT both
    wins server = 192.168.0.100
```

```
# WINS Proxy - Tells Samba to answer name resolution queries on
# behalf of a non WINS capable client, for this to work there must be
# at least one  WINS Server on the network. The default is NO.
  wins proxy = yes
```

For the WINS proxy to work correctly, the `wins server` parameter must be filled with the address for a WINS server and `wins proxy` must be set to yes.

The WINS Savings

The advantages and benefits of using WINS are fairly obvious: reduced broadcast traffic, stabilized/centralized naming repository, name validation, better browsing performance with faster convergence of names, and better network performance, in addition to making name resolution routable—an essential piece to using SMB/Windows networking over a WAN.

In a Samba environment, the use of WINS is highly recommended for anything but the smallest of networks.

WINS Disadvantages

WINS is not without problems, however. Specific to the Samba implementation, there is no provision for replication of the WINS database. This is a problem for people seeking redundancy and, in the case of large networks, distribution of networking resources close to the clients that will use them. That said, in large distributed networks, it is the case that Samba servers can take advantage of the WINS databases provided by current NT servers.

There is also the additional setup involved with setting up each client to do WINS resolution. Of course, this is an issue for all networking protocols and services. The burden is lessened somewhat in DHCP environments, where there is support for setting the name servers that clients will have access to on boot. Getting rid of legacy issues such as stale LMHOSTS and over-broadcasting generally offers enough improvement to network efficiency that the effort of putting WINS into effect is well worth it.

One other issue is the potential for disruption if WINS is incorrectly or inappropriately configured. Remember, NT servers generally don't like to share. Frequently, if a Samba server takes over the job of an NT server, it isn't uncommon for the NT server to stop working entirely. Don't let this happen to you. It is possible to have WINS servers on a Samba server while an NT PDC continues as PDC and DMB. Generally there is no need for this, though, and no need for the bother of making it work. Be sure of what you are trying to accomplish if you decide to use Samba in this role.

WINS Alternatives

There are alternative solutions to some of the problems that WINS also addresses. Specifically, cross-subnet browsing can be achieved in the absence of a WINS server. Samba specifically has two parameters—`remote announce` and `remote browse sync`— that can be used to provide the same sorts of name propagation across networks and different workgroups.

The `remote announce` option allows you to project a Samba server into workgroups and networks that it wouldn't normally be visible in. With it, you can announce to networks or Browse Masters on that network and have your server appear in the Workgroup browse list. An example to project your Samba server into the ENGR Workgroup on the `192.168.7.0` network would be the following:

```
remote announce = 192.168.7.255/ENGR
```

The `remote browse sync` option, which is purely useful between Samba servers, allows the replication of browse lists on Master Browser across networks. This means that your Samba server and a foreign Samba server could access network resources on each other's distant workgroups. An example that would sync lists between your Samba server and the Master Browser Samba on network `192.168.10.0` would be as follows:

```
remote browse sync = 192.168.10.0
```

Keep in mind that the RFCs (1001 and 1002) that define NetBIOS name servers allow for many more options than WINS actually implements. Keep in mind, WINS is a proprietary Microsoft implementation of a NetBIOS name server; it is not its archetype. It just so happens that NT WINS and the Samba WINS based on it are the most popular and widely used vendor implementations of NBNS.

Making the Decision

The decision of whether to use WINS or one of the WINS alternatives is specific to your network environment. In a Samba environment, it is generally recommended to use WINS regardless, as the most efficient, effective means of name resolution. In truly small workgroups, it may be possible to make LMHOSTS alone work out, but that is a limited and limiting example. The `remote announce` and `remote browse sync` options, although potentially useful, are not as generic as WINS and are mostly Samba specific. In general, the advantages of WINS outweigh any difficulties, and its implementation in larger networks will be a major improvement.

WINS and Windows 2000

With Windows 2000, Microsoft is apparently moving from its own proprietary implementation of NetBIOS name service, WINS, to its own proprietary implementation of

DNS and LDAP, Active Directory. Ostensibly, name resolution and registration will be done using Dynamic DNS updates, hopefully removing an extra layer of traffic in WINS and bringing all naming, for NetBIOS and for the rest of a network's needs, into a single place rather than spread between disparate WINS and DNS resources as it is now.

This does not, of course, mean the end of WINS, although it seems doubtful that Microsoft will spend more time supporting or developing it. The sheer weight of the legacy Windows systems using WINS means that it will still have to be planned for in networks for years to come. NT 4 servers and clients and Windows 95/98 will not have access to Active Directory, so to maintain the benefits of directed name resolution, WINS servers will still be present.

WINS Troubleshooting and Optimization

Sometimes WINS implementations turn out badly, mostly through misconfiguration but also due to client instabilities or incompatibilities. When things aren't working, you can't browse, or the network seems unstable, Samba and most UNIX systems provide many good diagnostic tools for determining problems.

Performance Measurement and Test Points

In the first place, you need to know how your network stands before and after the installation and setup of a WINS server. You should have a good idea of what is going on and what the topology is before you start making changes. You can use the same tools before the change, tcpdump, log files, and database files. After you have made the changes and integrated a WINS server on your network, then you should see what effect that has had—obviously, if you are having problems, but really even if you are not.

tcpdump

One of the best tools for examining your network, as mentioned before, is tcpdump. You need to see whether any particular clients or servers are causing problems. Are they over-broadcasting now? Are they having network connectivity problems? With tcpdump, it is likely that you will be able to tell whether any particular client is causing a majority of problems, or whether your network has more or less activity on it than before. With time and experience, you can tell nearly everything that is happening on the network with tcpdump.

tail -f log.nmb

Samba itself provides good information on what its perspective is on the network. Error messages, connection failures, information about browser elections, and the like all end up in the log files. The `log.nmb` file is a log of all the activity performed by the `nmbd`—the portion of Samba that handles name resolution. When WINS is enabled, `nmbd` can act as a WINS server. When troubles arise, it is frequently good to raise the debug level on the `nmbd` process. This can give a great deal more information on what the `nmbd` server is doing. Although `nmbd` would normally run at a low level of debugging output, during use it can be raised and lowered by sending the process SIGUSR1 and SIGUSR2 signals.

To raise the debug level by one level, use the following command:

```
# kill -USR1 'pidof nmbd'
```

To lower the debug level by one level, use this command:

```
# kill -USR2 pidof nmbd`
```

`/var/lock/samba/wins.dat`

In the `wins.dat` file, you get to see name registration for hosts and workgroups or domains, `name_types`, and associated IP information, along with the date expiration for the entries. If names fail to appear in the `wins.dat` file, it means that either the client is not configured properly to take advantage of WINS or there is some name resolution/network connectivity problem on the network.

The format for the record is as follows:

```
"NAME#name_type" expiration IP_address TTL
```

An important part of this is the `name_type`, which shows what type of registration that name is for. Some important ones (not shown in Listing 34.5) include the following:

`0x00` = Name registration

`0x03` = Unique name registration

`0x20` = Server name registration

`0x1b` = Domain Master Browser

`0x1c` = Primary Domain Controller

`0x1e` = Workgroup/Domain name registration

Listing 34.5 shows an example `wins.dat` for an LMB/WINS server.

LISTING 34.5   Sample `wins.dat` for an LMB/WINS Server

```
VERSION 1 54726
"__MSBROWSE__#01" 947427488 255.255.255.255 e4R
"ADMIN#00" 947427912 255.255.255.255 c4R
"ADMIN#1b" 947427708 192.168.0.100 44R
"ADMIN#1e" 947427916 255.255.255.255 c4R
```

```
"ALDEN#00" 947404864 192.168.0.35 64R
"ALDEN#03" 947404864 192.168.0.35 64R
"ALDEN#20" 947404864 192.168.0.35 64R
"AP#00" 947427087 192.168.2.141  4R
"AP#03" 947427087 192.168.2.141  4R
"AP#20" 947427087 192.168.2.141  4R
"BIZMGR#00" 947426614 192.168.0.144  4R
"BIZMGR#03" 947426614 192.168.0.144  4R
"BIZMGR#20" 947426614 192.168.0.144  4R
"CAIRO#00" 947427708 192.168.0.100 46R
"CAIRO#03" 947427708 192.168.0.100 46R
"CAIRO#20" 947427708 192.168.0.100 46R
"PC54#00" 947416366 192.168.0.54 64R
"PC54#03" 947416366 192.168.0.54 64R
"PC54#20" 947416366 192.168.0.54 64R
"ENGR#00" 947427285 255.255.255.255 c4R
"ENGR#1b" 947429415 192.168.2.80 44R
"ENGR#1e" 947427285 255.255.255.255 c4R
"FRESCO#00" 947427221 192.168.0.101 44R
"FRESCO#03" 947427221 192.168.0.101 44R
"FRESCO#20" 947427221 192.168.0.101 44R
"KINGM#00" 947427285 192.168.0.80 44R
"KINGM#03" 947427285 192.168.0.80 44R
"KINGM#20" 947427285 192.168.0.80 44R
"LUCID#00" 947427743 192.168.0.75 44R
"LUCID#03" 947427743 192.168.0.75 44R
"LUCID#20" 947427743 192.168.0.75 44R
"NDIR#00" 947351986 192.168.0.37 64R
"NDIR#03" 947351986 192.168.0.37 64R
"NDIR#20" 947351986 192.168.0.37 64R
"NEWSPS#00" 947427806 192.168.0.107 44R
"NEWSPS#03" 947427806 192.168.0.107 44R
"NEWSPS#20" 947427806 192.168.0.107 44R
"NWS2#00" 947383168 192.168.0.32 64R
"NWS2#03" 947383168 192.168.0.32 64R
"NWS2#20" 947383168 192.168.0.32 64R
"NWS3#00" 947392884 192.168.0.33 64R
"NWS3#03" 947392884 192.168.0.33 64R
"NWS3#20" 947392884 192.168.0.33 64R
"PROMO#00" 947349546 192.168.0.137  4R
"PROMO#03" 947349546 192.168.0.137  4R
"PROMO#20" 947349546 192.168.0.137  4R
"RECEPTION#00" 947270008 192.168.0.142 64R
"RECEPTION#03" 947270008 192.168.0.142 64R
"RECEPTION#20" 947270008 192.168.0.142 64R
"REMOTE#00" 947346417 192.168.0.78 64R
"REMOTE#03" 947346417 192.168.0.78 64R
"SALES#00" 947427985 255.255.255.255 e4R
"SALES#03" 947427591 192.168.2.186  4R
```

34

WINDOWS
INTERNET NAMING
SERVICE (WINS)

continues

LISTING 34.5 continued

```
"SALES#1e" 947427921 255.255.255.255 e4R
"SALES1#00" 947427980 192.168.0.170   4R
"SALES1#03" 947427980 192.168.0.170   4R
"SALES1#20" 947427980 192.168.0.170   4R
"SALES5#00" 947343370 192.168.0.185   4R
"SALES5#03" 947343370 192.168.0.185   4R
"SALES5#20" 947343370 192.168.0.185   4R
"SALES6#00" 947427591 192.168.0.186   4R
"SALES6#03" 947427591 192.168.0.186   4R
"SALES6#20" 947427591 192.168.0.186   4R
"SERVERS#00" 947427806 255.255.255.255 c4R
"SERVERS#1b" 947427708 192.168.0.104 44R
"SERVERS#1e" 947427806 255.255.255.255 c4R
"TIGGER#00" 947426881 192.168.0.136 44R
"TIGGER#03" 947426881 192.168.0.136 44R
"TIGGER#20" 947426881 192.168.0.136 44R
"UNIXPS#00" 947427079 192.168.0.104 44R
"UNIXPS#03" 947427079 192.168.0.104 44R
"UNIXPS#20" 947427079 192.168.0.104 44R
"VO1#00" 947197565 192.168.0.121 64R
"VO1#03" 947197565 192.168.0.121 64R
"VO1#20" 947197565 192.168.0.121 64R
"VO2#00" 947193692 192.168.0.122 64R
"VO2#03" 947193692 192.168.0.122 64R
"VO2#20" 947193692 192.168.0.122 64R
```

/var/lock/samba/browse.dat

The browse.dat file shows the browse information this Samba server maintains. If the Samba is not configured to be a local or domain browser, then it is likely that only the name of the Master Browser, workgroup/domain, and the Samba box itself will be in browse.dat. If the Samba server is a Master Browser, however, a much fuller picture of the network emerges, with all the computers in the workgroup/domain listed toward the top, and other workgroup/domains with their respective Master Browsers toward the bottom. If workgroups or names are not showing up in the browse.dat file, it is a good indication of some name resolution problem on the network.

Listing 34.6 shows an example browse.dat for a LMB/WINS server.

LISTING 34.6 Example browse.dat for a LMB/WINS Server

```
$ more browse.dat
"ADMIN"                 c0001000 "CAIRO"                      "ADMIN"
"CAIRO"                 400d9a23 "CIFS server (samba2.0.6)"   "ADMIN"
"PC54"                  40412003 ""                           "ADMIN"
"PROMO2"                40412003 ""                           "ADMIN"
```

```
"PC77"              40412003 ""                            "ADMIN"
"TIGGER"            40019a03 "CIFS server (samba2.0.3)"    "ADMIN"
"PC129"             40412203 ""                            "ADMIN"
"RECEPTION"         40412003 ""                            "ADMIN"
"PROM"              40412003 "prom"                        "ADMIN"
"SERVERS"           c0001000 "UNIXPS"                      "SERVERS"
"ENGR"              c0001000 "KINGM"                       "ENGR"
"SALES"             c0001000 "SALES6"                      "SALES"
```

Common Symptoms and Solutions

A common problem with NetBIOS name resolution is having client Windows computers running protocols other than TCP/IP. Because of the election rules involved in NetBIOS, it is entirely possible that Windows clients will have elections for Master Browsers "behind the back" of the Samba servers that are only using TCP/IP. When this happens to a Samba WINS server that is acting as Master Browser, it is entirely possible that all the Samba servers and TCP/IP clients will start having browsing problems, or fail to browse at all. The solution to this is having all your computers running only a single protocol—TCP/IP—and having everybody using WINS resolution. Having a simple policy on this matter will make things work more smoothly.

Other problems may have to do with simple changes to name resolve order and the like. In general, if you have a network where clients are using both broadcast and WINS, and the WINS clients use only that, then the WINS clients will never see the broadcast clients, and broadcast clients won't see WINS clients, unless someone has the wins proxy option on. It should be noted that none of this is a Samba-specific problem but is inherent in the way NetBIOS names are resolved.

In short, keep everyone on the same protocol and name resolution method, and your life will be much easier.

Summary

WINS servers provide an important set of features for Windows Networking/SMB clients and servers. In their absence, the cost of implementing NetBIOS name resolution goes up as machines are added to the network and as the network expands. Eventually, the burden of non-WINS broadcast name resolution impacts the performance and stability of the network itself. Additionally, expansion of the network itself exposes the weakness of the broadcast name resolution. WINS helps to alleviate all these problems, as you have seen. Not only does it improve network responsiveness and help to restore bandwidth, it also provides stability of a centralized name repository and name validation. Add ease of use in large routed networks and the capability to work with DHCP configuration, and it all adds up to a considerably more efficient way of designing and maintaining NetBIOS networks.

Optimizing Samba Performance

by Steve Litt

In This Chapter

CHAPTER 35

A highly publicized benchmark test in early 1999 pitted an NT server against a Linux/Samba/Apache server, both running on identical Dell PowerEdge 6300/400 server hardware. Many were surprised when NT beat Samba in file serving performance by a factor of 2.5 to 1. One result of that test was the publication of many Samba performance tweaks.

Most of these tweaks are discussed in this chapter. However, it's important to evaluate these tweaks in the context of system bottlenecks because some of these tweaks can actually decrease performance in certain situations.

Bottleneck Analysis

Bottleneck analysis is a troubleshooting tactic used when the symptom description includes words such as *too* and *slow* or *insufficient*, as in "my Samba performance is too slow." Bottleneck analysis is based on the fact that the throughput of a system is governed by one or a small number of components. Those components governing the throughput of the system are called *bottlenecks*.

Without Bottlenecks, Everything Would Be Light Speed

Some bottlenecks are intentional. A motor vehicle's gas pedal is a user-adjustable bottleneck designed to govern the speed of a car. Driving a car with no bottleneck between the gas tank and the fuel pump would make life a little too exciting.

Even a car without a gas pedal would have a bottleneck—probably the engine displacement. In every system there's a factor restricting the throughput of the system, because by definition, if such a bottleneck did not exist, the system would have infinite throughput.

Envision a large Samba-served network running on 10Mb wire. Twenty people copy 50MB files to the server. That segment between the server and the first switch bottlenecks the system, in spite of excess capacity in the server's memory, CPU power, and hard disk.

Now replace the 10Mb wire with 100Mb and put fiber between the server and the first switch. Suddenly the wire offers no resistance. Now maybe the CPU bottlenecks. Get a faster CPU and the hard disk can't keep up. It's always something.

Every system has a bottleneck. Otherwise, its throughput would be infinite. Therefore, the question becomes not one of eliminating every bottleneck but rather of what performance is acceptable. And even that question involves bottlenecks.

There's no use souping up a system to accept 1,000 user keystrokes a minute when the world's fastest typists can input only 600. The user is the bottleneck. Likewise, a system capable of creating a report a minute is overkill if it takes the department an hour to read and analyze each.

Every system has a bottleneck. The important question is whether the system's performance is adequate for the users.

The Bottleneck Controls the System

As mentioned in the gas pedal analogy, the bottleneck controls the throughput of the entire system. Serving a large Samba network with a 486 33MHz machine guarantees that the system will be slow. The same can be said of connecting a large Samba system with 10Mb Ethernet or 2Mb wireless.

Bottlenecks typically are not that obvious. Something as obscure as a network card with the wrong duplex setting can bring file transfers to a crawl.

Masked Bottlenecks

Every system has a hierarchy of bottlenecks. Each is masked by the most prominent. Replacing a 486 33MHz machine with a 500MHz Pentium III shifts the bottleneck to the 10Mb wire, resulting in a performance increase much smaller than predicted by the server change. The wire was a potential bottleneck masked by the primary bottleneck—the slow server. Upgrade the wire to fiber, and the bottleneck could shift back to a component of the server, or it could unmask a previously masked suboptimal `smb.conf` parameter.

It's theoretically possible to predict masked bottlenecks through analysis and engineering techniques, but invariably many are discovered only after the removal of a primary bottleneck.

The System Has One or a Few Bottlenecks

In a continuous series flow (such as a single pipe), there's one bottleneck. The only exception is a situation where several points in the system exhibit substantially equal flow restriction. However, this can still be considered a single bottleneck, all components of which need clearing before a significant improvement can be realized. This situation would be encountered if the Samba server and the wire each limited throughput a substantially equal amount. Such occurrences are unusual.

Multiple bottlenecks occur in the presence of noncontinuous flows. Imagine software programs A and B. A provides reports requested by B, and B outputs the proper information based on the report from A and requests additional reports from A based on the output of B. Throughput is delayed by A and then delayed again by B.

Bottleneck Offloading

The classic example of bottleneck offloading is the attorney who can type 120 words per minute, yet still has a 60 word per minute secretary type all the memos. Every second the attorney devotes to typing is a second of legal work that doesn't get billed to the client.

Of course, if secretaries charged as much per hour as attorneys charge, the attorney might decide to do the memo typing. This illustrates the fact that bottleneck offloading often depends on economics.

Caching is the computer world's primary method of bottleneck offloading. Processors and backplanes can be a thousand times faster than hard disks. Every disk write saved, even at the expense of additional work for the processor and memory, is time saved, until the point is reached where the processor or memory becomes the bottleneck.

Samba's primary form of caching is `oplocks=yes`. With opportunistic locking, most "disk writes" can be done locally on the client, with writes to the server occurring relatively rarely. By offloading work from the wire and server to the client, opportunistic locking makes the wire and server appear much faster than they are.

Opportunistic locking is not for everyone. Consider a network wired entirely with fiber and served by a high-capacity minicomputer. Suppose such a network has five 486 33MHz clients with ancient 28ms hard disks. Writing to the wire would certainly be faster than writing to the client's drive. Bottleneck offloading works best when the resources shouldering the load are much faster than the bottlenecked resource.

Compression is another form of offloading. Consider a Samba network whose bottleneck is the wire, with both the client and server underutilized. Suppose the wire would be prohibitively expensive to replace at this time. Further suppose that a few huge Samba transfers consume the bulk of the traffic and that the files being transferred are highly compressible. These files could be routed to a small Windows program that compresses the file and copies it to a Samba server-side automation pseudo printer, which in turn decompresses the file into the correct directory. The result could be a doubling of the apparent capacity of the wire.

Offloading is vitally important because it's a way to increase the apparent throughput of a bottleneck beyond the bottleneck's capacity. Offloading provides an alternative to replacement. Offloading also makes bottleneck analysis a little harder because one needs to consider nonobvious parallel paths.

Bottlenecks Can Move with Usage

A hypothetical server receives heavy data input all day and does statistical analysis all night. The network and perhaps the disk are the bottleneck during the day, whereas the CPU bottlenecks at night.

Any changes in system usage can change the location of its bottlenecks. This is one of the challenges.

Improving Non-Bottlenecks Is Useless and Expensive

The obvious case is installing a multiprocessor-Samba server with a gigabyte of memory and a fast SCSI drive on a network using 2Mb wireless networking. Although nobody would make this mistake, less obvious performance tuning mistakes are made—by very intelligent and thoughtful people—on a regular basis.

Bottlenecks are seldom obvious. Is the disk too slow or are the caching and flushing parameters set wrong? Is the processor too slow or is there too little memory? Could more memory improve disk caching?

Could tweaking the `socket options=` parameter yield a big improvement or only a small improvement that's easier accomplished by adding more memory? Will `fake oplocks=yes` on read-only shares significantly reduce network traffic or just give the administrator one more variable to deal with?

Do you replace the network wiring with higher capacity and more expensive wiring? Do you upgrade the server? Do you change some `smb.conf` parameters?

All these scenarios, even changing the `smb.conf` parameters, cost money. In the case of changing the `smb.conf` parameters, the cost is extra work for an already overworked administrator, as well as the significant risk of reducing the performance or even losing data. Imagine accidentally setting `locking=no` on a heavily used read/write directory.

The conclusion is clear. The first step, finding the bottleneck, comes before implementing the remedy. To do otherwise is costly.

The Bottleneck Leaves Clues

On the factory floor, bottleneck machines are surrounded by mountains of work in a partial state of assembly or completion. Bottlenecks leave similar clues on a network.

Is the server's disk light running continuously without a break? If so, the disk is bottlenecking, which requires either a faster disk or offloading by a better caching program, another disk, or another server. Is a switch collision light continuously flashing? If so, that wire is overloaded. Offload some of its traffic by rerouting some of its traffic. Note that network traffic is sometimes routed through a circuitous path that could be made more straightforward.

35

OPTIMIZING
SAMBA
PERFORMANCE

Does the top program show only 5% idle on the CPU line? If so, that's a dead giveaway that the CPU needs upgrading or steps need to be taken to offload work from it.

Detecting and Verifying Bottlenecks

Bottlenecks are detected using various tools, including CPU and memory analyzers, network analyzers, and other tools, both homegrown and obtained elsewhere. Such tools find the clues left by the bottlenecks.

By definition, bottlenecks control the throughput of the system. This means they can be verified by changing them and watching the effect on system throughput, or whatever symptom caused the search for the bottleneck.

Because it's typically difficult to increase capacity of a suspected bottleneck, it's often easiest to decrease its capacity. If throughput changes proportionally, it's a good bet that that's the bottleneck. If throughput changes only marginally, the search for a bottleneck must continue.

Sometimes it's difficult to vary the capacity of a suspected bottleneck. In such cases, it's often possible to place an extra load on the suspected bottleneck—a sort of reverse offloading.

When a bottleneck is found and verified, the next step is to find the cause of its low performance. This digging for causation can continue through several steps until an anomaly or changed factor is found. Except in rare instances when economics dictates otherwise, bottleneck analysis must descend to the root cause.

Clearing Bottlenecks

There are numerous ways to clear bottlenecks. The choice usually boils down to economics. Here are some of the more common methods of clearing a bottleneck:

- Specification improvement
- Offloading
- Unloading
- Concurrency
- Parallelism

Specification Improvement

The obvious solution is to replace the bottleneck with a unit with greater capacity—for instance, replacing 10Mb wiring with 100Mb wiring or installing more memory, a faster hard disk, or a faster processor. This is an excellent choice if it's economically feasible.

Offloading

As discussed earlier, non-bottlenecks often can take some load off bottlenecks. Caching in the form of opportunistic locking is the obvious example. Implementing compression might be the answer.

Unloading

Many activities are nice but not essential. Often those activities can be curtailed to take the load off a bottleneck. If the network is acting as a bottleneck and it's known that several people run Internet push technology screen savers through the network, that practice can be banned.

Unloading can also be practiced during certain time periods. For years, IT shops have scheduled huge batch jobs late at night so as not to conflict with users.

Concurrency

Requiring one process to wait for another is the kiss of death for throughput. To the extent possible, enable upstream processes to supply bottleneck processes on an as-needed basis by running concurrently.

Parallelism

Five average people can push a stalled car faster and farther than one strong person. What's more, it's easier to find five average people than one strong one.

It's often simple to add a new server for a group of people, thereby removing their traffic from the big server. Ideally, this group should be fairly encapsulated, requiring a minimum of data on the big server. Sometimes the new server is devoted to a certain program or a certain task rather than a group of users.

Such parallelism obviously reduces the load on the main server, but if done right it can also reduce the load on the wire, particularly if a new subnet is created.

With the advent of no-cost Linux and Samba and the ability of the Linux box to access additional subnets for the cost of a network card, such parallelism is now economically feasible.

Work is beginning on adapting Samba to run on Linux clusters. Depending on how it's implemented, this can be the ultimate in parallelism and granular scalability.

Potential System Bottlenecks

A Samba server system can be categorized into major bottleneck types:

- CPU
- Memory
- Disk

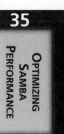

35

OPTIMIZING SAMBA PERFORMANCE

- `smbd/nmbd`
- Network
- Client

Because various components and processes offload and overload bottlenecks, there's a high degree of interdependencies between these potential bottlenecks. This is especially true if the Samba server runs other software such as Web service or batch processes. Nevertheless, division into these categories is an excellent first step in bottleneck analysis.

Obviously, many Samba performance problems are best solved with non-Samba solutions, such as increased memory or changes in network architecture. Other Samba performance problems are best solved with Samba parameter tweaks.

Bottleneck-Analysis Tools

Bottleneck-analysis tools range from simple scripts written by the administrator to sophisticated and costly software and hardware. If your organization can pay for professional analysis tools, that's the easiest and best plan. Professional tools are certainly necessary in order to wring that last 20% of performance out of the system.

This chapter delivers a set of free scripts that can be used to measure and stress various bottlenecks. Although certainly not as accurate as their costly professional counterparts, they are often enough to detect and fix gross bottlenecks.

CPU Bottleneck-Analysis Tools

The CPU is at the center of the server. Unlike other potential bottlenecks, every process uses the CPU. CPUs are extremely fast and are often used to offload from other bottlenecks, so a bottlenecked processor often degrades disk access. A CPU near 100% usage means a zero sum relationship between all processes.

UNIX-like operating systems are very good at distributing time between different processes. The CPU stressors discussed in this section help determine the degree to which the CPU is the bottleneck.

Improving Samba on a CPU-locked server means either upgrading the CPU or moving other processes to another machine.

CPU Stressors

The following C file, called `cpugrab.c`, can be compiled and run on the server's console to grab CPU power:

```
#include<stdio.h>
main(void)
{
```

```
long j;
long billions=50;

for(; billions; billions--)
  {
  printf("%ld billion remaining...\n", billions);
  for(j=1000000000; j; j--);
  }
printf("\nDONE!\n");
}
```

To increase the grab power, call it from the appropriate `nice` command, like this:

```
$ nice -n "-20" ./cpugrab
```

One interesting experiment is to run two copies of this program at `nice` level 0 and note they use approximately the same CPU when viewed in `top`. Then run one at level -20 and one at level 19 and note that the level -20 copy hogs about 95% of CPU, whereas the level 19 copy takes around 4%. The speed of the two copies of the program demonstrate that the level -20 copy gets most of the CPU. By varying the `nice` level, it's possible to examine bottlenecking Samba on the CPU.

CPU-Measurement Tools

A wide range of analysis tools are available to test the CPU. Most also test memory. One Linux-centric tool, `vmstat`, tests CPU usage but is more important in memory usage analysis, so it's included in the section on memory-measurement tools. Most UNIX-like operating systems have one or more equivalents of `vmstat`.

The primary free CPU-measuring tool that's included on most UNIX-like systems, including Linux, is `top`. The `top` program measures and displays several important CPU statistics. *Always* start `top` in secure mode (using `-s`) to prevent yourself or other users from accidentally killing a task or having other destructive accidents. Here's how:

```
$ top -s
```

Within `top`, various keystrokes perform various configurations. The most important ones are shown in Table 35.1.

TABLE 35.1 Most Important Secure Mode `top` Commands

Keystroke	Function
h	Help screen
P	Sort by CPU usage
M	Sort by memory usage

continues

TABLE 35.1   continued

Keystroke	Function
T	Sort by time used
S	Toggle cumulative mode
i	Toggle idle proc display
Spacebar	Update display
s	Set top's refresh period
q	Quit

Note that the secure mode help screen does not show certain commands that are legitimate in secure mode. To learn all the commands, run it in non-secure mode (no -s) and copy the help screen into a text file for reference.

If a program related to Samba uses most of the CPU (smbd for instance), that might be an indication that the program is bottlenecked by CPU. However, it might simply indicate that Linux sees only this program requesting resources and allocates them all to the program. To get a true picture, the CPU must be loaded by some other program.

The cpugrab program discussed previously might be a good tool for providing the parallel load. Experiment with the nice level of cpugrab to maximize the diagnostic value of the test. For instance, at nice level +10, cpugrab grabs about two-thirds of the CPU against FTP but only about half against smbd. That's much better than a test where cpugrab is running at nice level -20, in which case cpugrab hogs about 90% of the CPU against both FTP and smbd. At level -20, both FTP and Samba transfers are seriously bottlenecked and very slow.

The top program shows memory usage in a rudimentary way. However, to get the real "real picture," use vmstat.

Memory Bottleneck-Analysis Tools

Although there may be a few compute-intensive processes that do not use much memory (such as the cpugrab program detailed in the prior section), most real-world programs need large chunks of memory to do their jobs.

UNIX has two levels of memory. The first is semiconductor memory (RAM), which is very fast. The second level is virtual memory, using the swap partition on the disk, which is several multiples slower. UNIX memory algorithms allow virtual memory access to be much faster than one would expect. However, this fast performance disappears when UNIX gets close to using all available memory. A lack of memory can slow apparent disk speed due to increased swap partition use, as well as a decrease in disk caching.

Samba performs much better when using semiconductor memory. If memory is a bottle-neck, move memory-intensive processes to other boxes or schedule them during nonpeak Samba hours. In-house computer programs can be rewritten to use disk space instead of memory, thereby conserving memory. An example is a Perl program that reads an entire file into memory rather than reading it line by line. RAM is becoming a commodity, with prices often suggesting RAM increases rather than conservation.

If memory is a problem, do not use overly large values for `mangled stack=`, `read size=`, and `shared mem size=` (to the degree that it can be avoided).

Memory Stressors

Listing 35.1 is a program called `memgrab.c`. It grabs `ARRAYSIZE` chunks of `CHUNKSIZE` bytes of memory. As set, it grabs 20MB. The memory can be semiconductor, swap, or both. Before using this program, read the caution that follows it.

LISTING 35.1   `memgrab.c`

```
#include<stdio.h>
#include<memory.h>
#include<string.h>
#include<unistd.h>
#define CHUNKSIZE 1000000L
#define ARRAYSIZE 20
#define SLEEPS 10
main(int argc, char *argv[])
  {
  long i;
  int sleeps;
  long mems=0;
  char *bufarray[ARRAYSIZE];
  printf("\n\n");
for(i=0; i < ARRAYSIZE; i++)
    {
    if(bufarray[i]=(char *)malloc(CHUNKSIZE))
      {
      mems += CHUNKSIZE;
      memset(bufarray[i], 'z', CHUNKSIZE);
      sprintf(bufarray[i], "success %ld", mems);
      printf("%s\n", bufarray[i]);
      }
    else
      {
      printf("\n\nBUSTED!!!\n\n");
      break;
      }
```

continues

LISTING 35.1 continued

```
    }
  i--;

  printf("%ld\n", mems);

  for(sleeps=SLEEPS; sleeps; sleeps--)
    {
    long j;
    printf("%ld more sleeps...\n", sleeps);
    for(j=0; j <= i; j++)
      {
      memset(bufarray[j] + 20, 'a' + sleeps % 25, CHUNKSIZE - 20);
      }
    sleep(3);
    }

  printf("\n\n");
  for(; i >=0; i--)
    {
    printf("%s\n", bufarray[i]);
    free(bufarray[i]);
    mems -= CHUNKSIZE;
    }
  printf("%ld\n\n", mems);
  }
```

> **Caution**
>
> Do *not* use the preceding program to run your system out of memory. Doing so
> could cause a crash and possibly lost data. Even at lesser memory levels it could
> still cause problems on certain systems, so to prevent problems, use the smallest-
> possible memory grab necessary to test the throughput change of the system.
> The reason this command is not command-line configurable is to prevent the
> unwary from consuming all system memory.

Within the scope of the preceding caution, the memgrab program can be handy in testing
for memory bottlenecks. Grabbing as little as 20% of remaining memory, as shown in the
vmstat program, can show whether throughput is decreased proportionally. If the
decrease is proportional, memory is the bottleneck.

Note that the border between semiconductor memory and swap memory represents a
major performance step. If all semiconductor memory is used before running memgrab,
the result understates the benefit of adding memory.

The preceding program is designed to test below the virtual memory threshold. Once above
that threshold, the memory writes in the sleep section take a very long time. The purpose of

those writes is to ensure that the allocated memory is not simply written out to virtual memory while all semiconductor memory is made available to other programs under test.

Running the preceding program above the virtual memory threshold thrashes the disk and consumes much of the CPU. For tests in the virtual memory region, you might want to modify the algorithm, possibly by removing the memory writes in the sleep section.

Memory-Measurement Tools

Linux systems use vmstat to track memory—both semiconductor and swap. Other systems use other similar utilities. Here's the command-line syntax for vmstat:

```
$ usage: vmstat [-V] [-n] [delay [count]]
```

The -n option suppresses repeated headers. The -V option prints the version. delay is the refresh rate displayed. If this is not specified, a single row is printed showing the average since boot, which is almost certainly not what's needed. If a delay is specified, a count can be specified so that the program terminates after that number of delay periods. Otherwise, the program can be terminated by typing Ctrl+C.

The program displays the fields shown in Table 35.2, in order from left to right:

TABLE 35.2 The vmstat Display Fields

Keystroke	Function
r	The number of processes waiting for run time
b	The number of processes in uninterruptible sleep
w	The number of processes swapped out but otherwise runnable*
swpd	The amount of virtual memory used (KB)
free	The amount of idle memory (KB)
buff	The amount of memory used as buffers (KB)
cache	Undocumented, probably disk cache memory
si	The amount of memory swapped in from disk (KB/s)
so	The amount of memory swapped to disk (KB/s)
bi	Blocks sent to a block device (blocks per second)
bo	Blocks received from a block device (blocks per second)
in	The number of interrupts per second, including clock
cs	The number of context switches per second
us	The user time as a percentage of the total CPU time
sy	The system time as a percentage of the total CPU time
id	The idle time as a percentage of the total CPU time

* *This field is calculated, but Linux never desperation swaps.*

35

OPTIMIZING
SAMBA
PERFORMANCE

Running the previously discussed `memgrab` program first reduces the `free` figure; then, as the system runs out of semiconductor memory, the `swpd` figure skyrockets. The `si` figure also goes up until `memgrab` stops grabbing memory, at which time the `so` figure goes up. As `memgrab` releases its memory, the `swpd` figure goes down, and once semiconductor memory is released, the `free` figure goes up.

If the `free` figure regularly goes below 5,000 in normal system operation, it's a clue that the system will run much faster with increased RAM. Although memory needs can be filled by virtual memory from the swap disk, doing so is much slower and should only be done occasionally.

Once a good memory snapshot has been taken with `vmstat`, both with and without memory loading, switch back to `top`, which identifies exactly which processes are using the memory.

Disk Bottleneck-Analysis Tools

The hard disk is the slowest regularly used part of a Samba server. Reliable, reproducible disk tests are difficult. Results depend on memory available for cache, operating system parameters specifying how often to write dirty data to disk, and many other factors. If memory testing shows a shortage of memory, fix that problem before attacking disk speed. No drive has sufficient throughput without sufficient memory for cache.

Disk Stressors

The following script, called `diskwhirl.gran`, hits the hard disk very hard, without stressing the wire:

```
#!/bin/sh
counter=50
while [ $[ $counter ]  -ge 0  ]; do {
  echo starting $counter
  nice -n $1 find /usr
  counter=$[ $[ $counter ] - 1 ]
};
done
```

The "grip" the preceding script has on the disk is controlled to some degree by the argument. If it's level `-20`, it gives the `find` command a very high priority; if it's level `19`, it gives the command a low priority. To fully do the job, the script itself should be run from a `nice` command with the same priority level. Additionally, the majority of the output should not appear on the screen, because terminal output slows the process and reduces disk access. Therefore, create script `diskwhirl` to call `diskwhirl.gran`:

```
#!/bin/sh
nice -n "$1" ./diskwhirl.gran "$1" | grep "^starting"
```

The preceding discards all output except that beginning with the word *starting*, which of course pulls up the counter in `diskwhirl.gran`. Run `diskwhirl` on the Samba server and note the effect on various Samba performance-measurement tests.

> **Note**
>
> The preceding `diskwhirl` script is extremely simplistic and might not accurately represent a real system load. Depending on the memory available, iterations might be filled from cache hits, which might not be what you want in a disk test.
>
> The script can be enhanced by running each retrieved filename through `cat` to `/dev/null`.
>
> A serious disk test would include both reads and writes, and it would make those reads and writes different block sizes. However, such tests must be carefully designed to avoid overwriting data, and they're beyond the scope of this book.

Disk-Measurement Tools

If possible, obtain a professional disk-measurement tool. If that isn't practical, there are several ballpark approximations for disk use measurement.

One such approximation is viewing the disk light. If this light is on constantly, it's an indication of disk use saturation. On the other hand, if the light blinks on and off, it's an indication that it can take more throughput. Listening to the disk is another such approximation.

Disk saturation can also be approximated by running a disk stressor, and then running two, and seeing how much the speed of the first is decreased when the second is run. Of course, they should be coded the same and run at the same `nice` level. Such a test might require a less-intensive stressor than the `diskwhirl` script in the previous section.

It's not strictly necessary to measure disk use. If a Samba test is slowed substantially when a disk stressor is run concurrently, it's a good indication that the disk is Samba's bottleneck.

If the disk is the bottleneck, and if Samba is the major user of the machine, Samba tweaks may be used to offload the disk. Make sure to use oplocks to their maximum safe use because they cache on the client. On the other hand, make sure hotly contended files are not "oplocked" with `veto oplocks=`.

smbd / nmbd Bottleneck-Analysis Tools

If a system is bottlenecked at smbd and nmbd, further research is necessary to determine which Samba tweaks to use. This section describes a measuring tool comparing FTP access to Samba access—a crucial distinction. Tools for both large-file transfers and numerous small-file transfers are provided. A crude stressor utilizing the nice level for smbd and nmbd is also described.

smbd / nmbd Stressors

The purpose of a stressor is to restrict the throughput of a suspected bottleneck. One crude way to do this is via the nice level of smbd and nmbd. The following is an example of a script that starts up Samba at the level defined in arg1:

```
#!/bin/sh
/etc/rc.d/init.d/smb stop
nice -n "$1" /usr/local/samba/bin/smbd -D
nice -n "$1" /usr/local/samba/bin/nmbd -D
```

The argument must be in quotes, and it can vary from "-20" to "19". On an unstressed system, this makes very little difference. However, on a reasonably loaded system, it can speed or slow smbd. What this really does is CPU-lock smbd and nmbd, so it's rather crude. However, in conjunction with other tests, it can be informative.

smbd/nmbd-Measurement Tools

One great Samba measurement technique is comparing its file-transfer capabilities to that of FTP. This is really two tests. One involves the megabytes per second for transferring a huge file. The other involves the transfer speed of many tiny files, meant to test the logistics of opening and closing files. Typically, FTP is 5% to 25% faster in transferring huge files, whereas Samba is typically faster by a one-digit multiple in transferring hundreds of small files.

Testing Large-File Transfer

The first step is creating the file to be transferred. Having a file of an exact megabyte-multiple length makes calculations easier. The following program, called makebigfile, makes a file called bigfile.out whose size is arg1 megabytes:

```
#!/bin/sh
dd if=/dev/urandom of=bigfile.out bs=1000000 count=$1
```

The preceding script creates a file filled with random bytes so that disk compression does not play a part. Substituting /dev/zero for /dev/urandom creates an all-null byte ultra-compressible file. If the client computer has a compressed disk, and if client disk writes are a bottleneck, the ultra-compressible file downloads much faster due to fewer client disk accesses.

Once the file is created, a batch file on a Windows PC conducts the test. The Windows batch file shown in Listing 35.2 should be run from its own directory, and that directory must include a file called crlf, which contains one carriage return and linefeed in order to correctly trigger the time command.

LISTING 35.2 Batch File to Test Large-File Transfer Performance

```
echo off

echo open mainserv>          bring.ftp
echo username>>             bring.ftp
echo user>>                 bring.ftp
echo binary>>               bring.ftp
echo get bigfile.out %1.fin>>  bring.ftp
echo quit>>                 bring.ftp

echo open mainserv>          putback.ftp
echo username>>             putback.ftp
echo user>>                 putback.ftp
echo binary>>               putback.ftp
echo put %1.fin %1.fout>>   putback.ftp
echo quit>>                 putback.ftp

echo on

echo > measure.log

echo "starting priming ftp bring" >> measure.log
time < crlf >> measure.log
ftp -s:bring.ftp
time < crlf >> measure.log
echo "finished priming ftp bring" >> measure.log


echo "starting ftp bring" >> measure.log
time < crlf >> measure.log
ftp -s:bring.ftp
time < crlf >> measure.log
echo "finished ftp bring" >> measure.log
```

continues

LISTING 35.2   continued

```
echo "starting ftp putback" >> measure.log
time < crlf >> measure.log
ftp -s:putback.ftp
time < crlf >> measure.log
echo "finished ftp putback" >> measure.log

net use y: \\mainserv\homes

echo "starting Samba bring" >> measure.log
time < crlf >> measure.log
copy y:bigfile.out %1.sin
time < crlf >> measure.log
echo "finished Samba bring" >> measure.log

echo "starting Samba putback" >> measure.log
time < crlf >> measure.log
copy %1.sin y:%1.sout
time < crlf >> measure.log
echo "finished Samba putback" >> measure.log

erase bring.ftp
erase putback.ftp
net use y: /delete
```

> **Caution**
>
> The preceding batch file, and the `.ftp` files it creates, contain the password of the user. This script should be run from an ordinary user created for testing only. Even so, take all proper precautions to see that the script and its passwords do not fall into the wrong hands. Remember that Windows files can be undeleted in certain circumstances.

The preceding script transfers files both ways—first with FTP and then with Samba. The idea is to compare the transfer times in each direction. Because FTP is optimized for pure file transfer, it's typically faster by 5 to 25%. If Samba is much slower than that range, it's time for investigation into Samba's performance.

If both the FTP and Samba transfer rates fall far behind the expected, it's time to investigate the client, the wire, the server's processor, memory and OS configuration, and the server's hard disk.

Testing Multiple Small-File Transfer

Large file transfer speed is not the only criteria. There's a lot of overhead associated with opening and closing files. In order to test a multiple-file transfer, those files must be created. It's important that the files be created in their own directory to minimize the possibility of deleting valuable files when the test files are deleted. The following shellscript creates however many files are specified as arg1, except that there's a maximum number specified by the maxfiles variable:

```
#!/bin/sh
maxfiles=2000
lastfile=$[ $1 ]
[ $[$lastfile] -gt $[$maxfiles] ] && \
   { echo "exceeded max of $maxfiles files"; exit }
[ -d tempdiag ] || mkdir tempdiag
[ -d tempdiag ] || \
   { echo "ERROR: Failed to make directory tempdiag"; exit; }
i=1
while [ $[$i] -le $[$lastfile] ]; do {
  echo "This is small file zzz$i" > tempdiag/zzz$i.txt
  i=$[ $[$i] + 1 ]
};
done
```

The preceding script does not run a test but rather creates a large number of small files suitable for testing the overhead in opening and closing files. The script in Listing 35.3 tests the transfer rate of many small files, in FTP and Samba. It should be run in its own directory on a Windows box. Immediately upon running, its window should be minimized because FTP has excess output that could unfairly slow its progress and skew the results.

LISTING 35.3   Batch File to Test Multiple Small-File Transfer Performance

```
echo off

echo open mainserv>          mbring.ftp
echo username>>              mbring.ftp
echo user>>                  mbring.ftp
echo lcd tempdiag>>          mbring.ftp
echo binary>>                mbring.ftp
echo prompt>>                mbring.ftp
echo mget tempdiag/zzz*.txt>>  mbring.ftp
echo quit>>                  mbring.ftp

echo open mainserv>          mputback.ftp
echo username>>              mputback.ftp
echo user>>                  mputback.ftp
```

continues

LISTING 35.3   continued

```
echo lcd tempdiag>>            mputback.ftp
echo cd tempdiag>>             mputback.ftp
echo binary>>                  mputback.ftp
echo prompt>>                  mputback.ftp
echo mput %1zz*.fou>>          mputback.ftp
echo quit>>                    mputback.ftp

echo on
mkdir tempdiag
erase tempdiag\*.fin
erase tempdiag\*.sin

echo > mmeasure.log
echo "starting priming ftp bring" >> mmeasure.log
time < crlf >> mmeasure.log
ftp -s:mbring.ftp
time < crlf >> mmeasure.log
echo "finished priming ftp bring" >> mmeasure.log

echo "starting ftp bring" >> mmeasure.log
time < crlf >> mmeasure.log
ftp -s:mbring.ftp
time < crlf >> mmeasure.log
echo "finished ftp bring" >> mmeasure.log

rename tempdiag\zzz*.txt %1zz*.fou

echo "starting ftp putback" >> mmeasure.log
time < crlf >> mmeasure.log
ftp -s:mputback.ftp
time < crlf >> mmeasure.log
echo "finished ftp putback" >> mmeasure.log

rename tempdiag\%1zz*.fou %1zz*.fin

net use y: /delete /yes
net use y: \\mainserv\homes

echo "starting Samba bring" >> mmeasure.log
time < crlf >> mmeasure.log
copy y:tempdiag\zzz*.txt tempdiag\%1zz*.sin
time < crlf >> mmeasure.log
echo "finished Samba bring" >> mmeasure.log

echo "starting Samba putback" >> mmeasure.log
time < crlf >> mmeasure.log
copy tempdiag\%1zz*.sin y:tempdiag\%1zz*.sou
time < crlf >> mmeasure.log
echo "finished Samba putback" >> mmeasure.log
```

```
:exitt
erase mbring.ftp
erase mputback.ftp
net use y: /delete
```

Upon reviewing `mmeasure.log`, it's likely you'll find Samba beating FTP by a significant margin. Samba opens and closes files much faster. To repeat, for fair results, the DOS window must be minimized.

> **Note**
>
> Contrary to intuition, the `oplocks=` parameter has little to do with this test's performance.

Network Bottleneck-Analysis Tools

Of all the analysis types discussed, this is the one where purchasing professional tools makes the most sense. It's difficult to stress a network without also stressing the CPU, and it's difficult to provide a controlled level of stress.

Measurement tools are likewise not universally available.

Network Stressors

The ultimate network stressor, at least in the case of 100Mb networking, is to set the system for 10Mb. If throughput decreases by approximately a factor of 10, you know that even at 100Mb the wire was the bottleneck. If throughput decreases by a marginal amount (say, 30%), it's likely that the wire is *not* the bottleneck even at 10Mb. If throughput decreases by a factor of two or three, it's likely that somewhere between 100Mb and 10Mb the wire became the bottleneck.

Note that there's more here than meets the eye. Throughput depends not only on network speed but also on other settings, such as duplex. This makes such evaluation more difficult.

Other stressing methods include flooding the network with unicast packets destined for a host other than the Samba server so that they won't pass through to the server's CPU. A nontechnical way this can be done is to have a couple additional Linux boxes transfer files to each other via FTP, on several virtual terminals on the same subnet. Programs can be written to flood the network with packets, but that's beyond the scope of this book.

35

OPTIMIZING
SAMBA
PERFORMANCE

Network-Measurement Tools

The `tcpdump` program can be used to view network traffic, and, if necessary, its output can be parsed to deduce the source of excess packets. The following command detects Samba usage:

```
$ tcpdump port 137 or port 138 or port 139
```

And the following detects non-Samba traffic:

```
$ tcpdump not port 137 and not port 138 and not port 139
```

Each can be piped into a script that counts packets and multiplies by packet size and continuously outputs a summary.

At each hub, switch, router, network card, and so on, the collision light can be viewed. As mentioned, a professional network sniffer is superior to these methods.

Client Bottleneck-Analysis Tools

The client isn't the first thing most technologists think of when investigating Samba performance. Nevertheless, the client can be a bottleneck, most often relating to client disk writes. Note that Samba performs better with NT clients, whereas NT performs better with Windows 9x clients.

Client Stressors

A simple client stressor is underclocking the CPU and turning off level-two cache (never turn off on-CPU cache). This is practical primarily on newer motherboards that can be clocked from the BIOS screen.

> **Caution**
>
> Be very careful that you do not accidentally *overclock* either the bus or the CPU because that can cause permanent damage to your computer and/or data. Also, it's unlikely but theoretically possible that a major underclock can create sharp square waves, the harmonics of which can harm the system.
>
> Do not change your system's timing unless you know exactly what you're doing.

By setting the bus speed and CPU multiplier to their minimums, plus turning off your level-two cache, it's possible to cut the client's performance in half.

It's interesting to run the large file–measurement script described earlier. (After I cut a 300MHz Pentium II system to 120MHz and eliminated level-2 cache, the transfer from client to server was slightly slower, whereas the transfer from server to client almost halved.) The write speed on the client can be a significant bottleneck.

Clients can also be stressed by running stressor programs in the background while doing Samba transfers.

Client-Measurement Tools

There are various Windows computer performance–measuring programs. Some can be downloaded for free. A standard script combining CPU, memory, and disk activities can also be constructed.

Network Card Setup Problems

Many cases of abysmal Samba performance, especially those where upload and download speeds differ radically, are due to misconfigured network cards. Make sure the NIC is configured with the proper speed and duplex. See whether the same problem exists on computers with different network cards. Be sure all hubs and switches are set up properly.

Standard Samba Performance Tweaks

Thanks to the early-1999 NT versus Linux benchmark test, most Samba performance tweaks are now well published. These are very much like vitamins: Used correctly in the proper way, they yield much improvement, but used incorrectly, they're ineffective or even harmful. Most of the standard Samba tweaks are included in this section.

Oplocks

Samba caching is implemented with *oplocks*, which is short for *opportunistic locking*. Oplocks are turned on with the default `oplocks=yes` parameter setting. Oplocks enable reads and writes, and sometimes even opens and closes, to be accumulated on the client for later writing to the server. Because the wire or the server is likely to be the bottleneck, it's best to leave oplocks enabled. However, in the case of a robust server serving a small number of underpowered clients, there may be a performance gain setting `oplocks=no`, because it might be faster to write to the server every time than to try and cache the data on a slow client computer.

An oplock is granted to the first client opening a file, and that client is granted exclusive access for the duration of the oplock and can therefore aggressively cache the file locally. Some oplock types can even cache the open and close operations on the file.

When a second client opens the same file, the server sends an oplock break message to the client with the oplock. The client with the oplock must then write all its data to disk, and if it has locally cached a large amount of a readable file on disk, it must reread it from disk. If this happens frequently, it can negate all performance benefits of the oplock.

There are several ways to handle this. The first is to turn off oplocks for a share. If most files in the share are under heavy contention, this is the way to go. If only certain files are under heavy contention, they can be excluded from oplocks by the `veto oplocks=` parameter.

Furthermore, there's a share parameter called `oplock contention limit=`, which defaults to 2. This is the highest number of contending clients that does *not* turn off oplocks for the file. This means that it might not be necessary to explicitly turn off oplocks on a heavily contended file. `oplock contention limit=` is a tuning parameter that implements a tradeoff. If it's too low, the performance benefit of oplocks is lost. If it's set too high, the resources spent on the logistics of oplocks may exceed the benefit. The `smb.conf` man page warns not to experiment with this parameter unless you've read and understood the Samba oplock code.

The traditional `oplocks=` share parameter is meant for exclusive access. Contrast that with the `level2 oplocks=` parameter. The `level2 oplocks=` parameter is a read-only oplock. It works like this: Because `oplocks=yes`, the first requesting client gets the oplock with full read/write. Then another client wants to read the file and opens it for read. Instead of sending an oplock break to the first client, Samba tells the first client to downgrade its oplock to a read-only oplock. This way, everyone can cache reads. When any client writes to the file, an oplock break message is sent to all clients accessing the file, after which they reread everything from disk and stop read caching. The `level2 oplocks=yes` parameter setting can greatly speed access to files that are primarily read from rather than written to. However, it can do more harm than good on files with heavy write contention.

The `fake oplocks=` parameter is depreciated in Samba 2. This parameter no longer functions (this can be verified with the source-perusing tools discussed in Chapter 23, "Samba Learning Tools"). It's retained only for backward compatibility. Do not include it in `smb.conf`.

Let the `kernel oplocks=` parameter default. On machines supporting kernel oplocks, this parameter defaults to `yes`, whereas on others it defaults to `no`. Kernel oplocks are oplocks implemented in the OS kernel, meaning that the same locking is recognized by SMB/CIFS, NFS, and the local file system.

To Oplock or Not to Oplock

The bottom line is this: Oplocks should be enabled in the typical situation where the bottleneck is on the network or server. That way, the clients can offload work from the bottleneck to the underutilized client.

However, in atypical cases where the network and the server are underutilized and non-powerful clients are the bottleneck, oplocks should be turned off. Keep in mind, however, that turning off oplocks on 10 clients adds 10 times the offload of each client to the server's load.

In cases of extremely heavy read-write contention for files, turning off oplocks eliminates the logistics of oplocks and may increase performance. Note that the default value of `oplock contention limit=` may make turning off oplocks unnecessary. In cases of heavy read-only contention without write contention, use `level2 oplocks=yes`.

Of course, once you've decided what steps to take, use the performance tests discussed earlier in this chapter.

Locking and Syncing

The `strict locking=` share parameter defaults to `no` because if it's enabled, it checks locking with every file access. This can be a serious performance hit. When disabled, locks are checked only when the client requests the check. So unless the client does not request lock checking when it should, this parameter should remain at its default. In cases where file corruption occurs, this parameter should be set to `yes` long enough to determine whether lack of essential client locking requests caused the corruption.

The `strict sync=` share parameter defaults to `no`. If this is set to `yes`, the server performs a sync operation every time a sync is requested by the client. The sync process is a very time-consuming process of stopping processing until all data is written to disk.

Some clients request syncs when less-expensive flushes would suffice. This problem occurs on Windows Explorer copy operations, resulting in very slow copies if this parameter is set to `yes`. The default `strict sync=no` ignores client requests for a sync. Unless the Samba server crashes, this should not cause corruption. Unless your server is crash prone (and if it's running Samba, it probably is not), leave this at its default. In cases where file corruption occurs, this parameter should be set to `yes` long enough to determine whether lack of essential client locking requests caused the corruption.

The `sync always=` share parameter defaults to `no`. If this is set to `yes`, every write operation from the client is written to disk. Of course, this degrades performance. This parameter is ignored unless `strict sync=yes`. Unless there's a problem with corruption or extremely unstable clients (or an unstable server or network), leave the `sync always=` parameter at its default.

The `locking=` share parameter defaults to `yes` and in almost every case should remain that way. Setting this parameter to `no` causes Samba to report success to every lock operation, essentially eliminating all locking. On files being written to, this is a disaster. However, in a share guaranteed never to be written to (or seldom enough that it's a maintenance operation), it may be appropriate to set `locking=no` because that may speed file reads. Never do this if there's any chance of a file in the share being written to. Unless setting this to `no` yields a huge benefit, leave it at `yes`.

read raw=

This is a highly optimized read operation that improves performance in most situations but can decrease performance in others. It defaults to `yes`. It's a global parameter, so the value chosen must be the best for all clients served by the Samba server.

> **Note**
>
> `read raw=yes` conflicts with `mmap()` support. It's usually best to choose one or the other of these optimizations.

write raw=

This is a highly optimized write operation that improves performance in most situations but can decrease performance in others. It defaults to `yes`. It's a global parameter, so the value chosen must be the best for all clients served by the Samba server. Note that although the `smb.conf` man page says not to tamper with its default, `speed.txt` says in certain situations it could improve performance if changed to `no`.

read prediction=

This is read caching, plain and simple. This parameter defaults to `no`. If it's set to `yes`, read operations on a file opened read/only read large blocks. Those blocks begin and end on 1KB boundaries, and have a maximum size defined by the value of the `read size=` parameter. Unfortunately, this is a global parameter, so it cannot be set on a per-share basis. Setting this parameter to `yes` can greatly improve performance for programs that read sequentially through files in tiny chunks. Such programs are poorly designed.

Setting this parameter to yes can decrease performance for programs that do mostly small random reads on large files.

read size=

Earlier in this chapter, *concurrency* was mentioned as a method of clearing bottlenecks. The read size= global parameter is a perfect example.

Here's a simplified explanation: This parameter defines the number of bytes coming in from the wire before write operations take place, or in the case of SMBreadbraw, the number of bytes read from disk before network transmission begins. The idea is that with extremely large packets, the disk can be working on part of the data while the network is working on the rest. This prevents two separate waits—concurrency.

The smb.conf man page mentions that this works best if the network and wire work at roughly the same speed, and with little benefit if one is much faster. This is true of all concurrency situations. In a two-bucket bucket-brigade situation, if both are equal, the total time without concurrency is double that of each. Total concurrency would reduce that by a factor of two. On the other hand, if one is ten times faster than the other, without concurrency, the time would be 1.1 times the time of the slower one, whereas with total concurrency, it would be 1.0.

The preceding discussion points to keeping this parameter as small as possible. However, there's another side to this situation. Larger values create larger disk writes. A balance must be struck.

You can experiment with this parameter and see whether it affects speed. Note that it's a global parameter. The default is 16384. According to speed.txt, a value over 65536 brings no benefit and needlessly wastes memory.

Note that read size= also serves as an upper limit for the read ahead that's enabled by the read prediction=yes parameter.

max xmit=

This parameter determines the maximum number of bytes the Samba server accepts from the client, and it defaults to the maximum of 65536. Certain clients may perform better with smaller values, but going below 2048 is likely to cause problems. For optimal performance, experiment with this parameter after major bottlenecks have been cleared.

socket options=

The socket options can make huge improvements or degradations in performance. The default of TCP_NODELAY is an excellent starting point. The value of this parameter is a

35

OPTIMIZING SAMBA PERFORMANCE

space-delimited list of possible options, some of which include an equal sign and a numeric value.

If possible, review the socket options in your system documentation (possibly `man setsockopt`) with a network guru who's savvy in the ways of TCP/IP and sockets. Experimentation should be guided by information.

Samba 2.0.5a inadvertently let this parameter default to an empty string, which caused significant performance degradation at many sites. If you're using 2.0.5a, you should either upgrade or explicitly specify `socket options=TCP_NODELAY` (unless you've determined an even better setting).

`log level=`

It's obvious that the more information `smbd` and `nmbd` write to the log files, the slower the performance will be. This is especially important because every log write is flushed to disk. Log levels higher than 2 write voluminous debugging information and should be avoided except when debugging.

`share modes=`

The DOS C `_dos_open()` function looks like this:

```
unsigned _dos_open(const char *filename,
                   unsigned oflags,
                   int *handlep);
```

Here, the `oflags` argument is a group of flags that are bitwise or'ed. Several of these flags specify a sharing mode. The ones recognized by Samba are `DENY_DOS`, `DENY_ALL`, `DENY_READ`, `DENY_WRITE`, `DENY_NONE`, and `DENY_FCB`. Different DOS compilers may have slightly different names for these.

DOS and Windows sharing depends on these share modes. `share modes=yes`, the default, preserves these share modes. The `smb.conf` man page contains this stern warning:

> You should *NEVER* turn this parameter off as many Windows applications will break if you do so.

That being said, this is a share parameter, and if a specific share is accessed only by programs that do not break without share modes, setting this parameter to no can increase performance.

`mmap()` Support

`mmap()` support enables very fast reads on files opened as read-only, and it greatly increases the performance of DOS share modes. However, according to `speed.txt`, it's possible for mmap() support to decrease performance. Unfortunately, this isn't an easy experiment, because mmap() support is compiled in rather than being controlled with an smb.conf parameter.

Most operating systems, including Linux, now include support for mmap() (memory-mapped reads). If your operating system has such support, you can build Samba with mmap() support, which also greatly reduces any performance hit caused by share modes=yes. mmap() support is included by adding the --with-mmap() option to the ./configure step of the build. Alternatively, you can recompile Samba with the -DUSE_MMAP option on the FLAGS line of the Makefile. Note that mmap() can greatly increase the speed of reads on some systems while actually reducing that speed on other systems. Of course, the decision to use mmap() is global.

> **Note**
>
> read raw=yes conflicts with mmap() support. It's usually best to choose one or the other of these optimizations.

wide links=

Earlier versions of Samba defaulted this global parameter to no to gain a little extra security. However, such a setting creates a performance decrease because file operations must then check each file to make sure it's not a link outside the share. As a result, recent Samba versions have defaulted this parameter to yes.

If there's a need to set this parameter to no, setting global parameter getwd cache=yes lessens the performance degradation.

getwd cache=

Contrary to what the smb.conf man page states, this global parameter defaults to yes in modern Samba versions. If you have a noncurrent version, you can test with this command, like so:

```
$ testparm -s | grep getwd
```

When set to yes, this parameter improves performance. It also reduces the performance decrease created by wide links=no.

bdflush and buffermem

Two Linux system tweaks were made famous in the wake of the early-1999 Linux/NT comparison. It's important to remember that they are tweaks to Linux, not Samba, and they have no effect on Samba running on non-Linux operating systems. The two tweaks are the `bdflush` tweak and the `buffermem` tweak. Both `bdflush` and `buffermem` are explained in detail in the `vm.txt` file, which is in directory `/usr/src/linux/Documentation/sysctl` on Red Hat systems.

These tweaks are of limited value because they were intended for a benchmark situation, not for a production situation. Furthermore, they target a system with a gigabyte of RAM and would be inappropriate for a typical commodity box with 64 or 128MB of RAM.

bdflush

The publicized tweak is as follows:

```
$ echo "80 500 64 64 80 6000 6000 1884 2" >/proc/sys/vm/bdflush
```

According to file `/usr/src/linux/Documentation/sysctl/vm.txt`, the defaults for `bdflush` are "40, 500, 64, 256, 15, 30*HZ, 5*HZ, 1884, 2." Read `vm.txt` for a detailed description, but here's the short story on these nine values:

- `nfract` is the percentage of "buffer cache dirty" required to trigger flushing the cache to disk. The higher this number, the more caching takes place. However, cranking it up too high can bottleneck memory. The default of `40` is great for real, live production systems. For a benchmark running on a large memory system, it can be souped up to `80` with the knowledge that this will not affect other processes.

- `ndirty` is the maximum number of dirty blocks to write out in a single `bdflush` wake cycle. Everyone seems to agree on `500`.

- `nrefill` is the number of clean buffers to try to obtain each time `refill_freelist()` is called to get clean buffers. Clean buffers often must be allocated before dirty buffers are written, thus resulting in temporary wastage of memory. The higher this value, the more memory is wasted. The lower this value, the less clean buffers are available, resulting in increasing `bdflush` wakeups. CPU and/or disk bottlenecks would seem to favor higher values of this parameter, whereas memory bottlenecks would seem to favor lower values. In fact, the published suggested tweak matches the default on this variable.

- The `vm.txt` document isn't as clear as it might be on the `nref_dirt` variable, but it appears to be the number of dirty buffers that will cause `refill_freelist()` to activate `bdflush` to write dirty buffers before clean buffers are allocated.

- `dummy1` is unused according to `vm.txt`.

- `age_buffer` is the maximum time a dirty normal buffer can hang around before it's flushed, measured in *jiffies*, which are clock ticks. Alpha machines have 1,024 jiffies per second, whereas other machines have 100. Therefore, a value of `6000` means 60 seconds. Presumably `30*HZ` would be 1,800 in countries with 60Hz current, although this isn't made clear. In a production situation, it's a bad idea to have unwritten data hanging around too long. However, in a benchmark situation, one wouldn't want to needlessly write to disk, thus favoring a large value. Weigh that against the fact that if there are idle periods, it's nice to use those idle periods to write dirty data.

- age_super is the maximum time a dirty superblock buffer can hang around before it's flushed. It's the superblock analogy of age_buffer.
- dummy2 is unused according to vm.txt.
- dummy3 is unused according to vm.txt.

The bottleneck relationship between disk and memory is complex to say the least. Memory offloads work from the disk, whereas the disk, via its swap partitions, offloads memory consumption. The binding is almost tight enough to consider them a monolith, but not quite.

The preceding nine tweak parameters can be used to match disk and memory usage to a specific bottleneck pattern. However, as mentioned several times in this chapter, bottlenecks change with system usage. The defaults for these tweak parameters are reasonable for a production system. The changes recommended in the publicly announced tweaks are optimized for a benchmark test. In an ordinary production situation, it's probably better to leave these parameters alone until other bottlenecks have been dispensed with.

What also must be kept in mind is that the recommendations were for a server with a gigabyte of semiconductor memory. They might be totally inappropriate for a server with 128MB.

buffermem

The tweak recommended is the following:

```
echo "60 80 80" >/proc/sys/vm/buffermem
```

buffermem determines the relationship between total memory and memory used for disk caching. The idea is to make sure memory offloads work from a bottlenecked disk without assuming such a load that it bottlenecks itself. The definition of buffermem, plus a few pertinent declarations, can be found in /usr/src/linux/include/linux/swapctl.h:

```
typedef struct buffer_mem_v1
{
        unsigned int    min_percent;
        unsigned int    borrow_percent;
        unsigned int    max_percent;
} buffer_mem_v1;
typedef buffer_mem_v1 buffer_mem_t;
extern buffer_mem_t buffer_mem;
extern buffer_mem_t page_cache;
```

The preceding should be enough to start the hunt for how this tweak actually functions.

The explanation of the three numbers follows:

- `min_percent` is the minimum fraction of memory devoted to disk cache buffers.
- `borrow_percent` is a percentage threshold. When Linux is short on memory, it borrows back memory from disk cache if disk cache makes up more than this percentage of total memory.
- `max_percent` is the maximum fraction devoted to disk cache buffers.

Once again, the suggested tweaks were for a benchmark on a computer with a gigabyte of RAM and might be totally inappropriate for a production system or a system with significantly less memory.

A Final Word on `bdflush` and `buffermem`

These are very sophisticated operating system tuning parameters. They both determine how often, and under what conditions, data in memory is written to disk. Data remaining in memory for an excessive time is at greater risk of corruption. Do not touch these two parameters unless you know what you're doing, especially on production systems where serious memory or disk problems could cause data loss.

Disk Section Manipulation

Depending on a disk's geometry, certain areas of the platters are faster than others. During the furor over the NT/Linux benchmark test, this was suggested as a possible explanation for NT's victory. Although it's possible to control performance this way in a benchmark, it's of limited practical value in production.

Perhaps a group of very highly used files could be placed on the fastest section of the disk. Such a setup would be hard to maintain.

Client Tweaks

It's relatively simple to see the effects of client bottlenecking by underclocking the client to the minimum and disabling level-2 cache. If the network and server are not overloaded, the speeds of downloads from the server are typically slowed commensurate with the slowdown of the client. Uploads to the client, on the other hand, remain relatively constant.

Caution

Be very careful when underclocking a computer because accidentally changing the wrong variable or overclocking the computer can cause permanent damage. There's a slight possibility that even a correct underclock could create sharp square waves with high harmonics that could cause damage. Disabling level-2 cache could cause timeout-type crashes that could result in data or program losses. Never disable level-1 cache because that would slow the computer to an extent that invites data loss.

In the twenty-first century, it's rarely advisable to spend much time or effort tweaking clients with 386 processors, 8MB of RAM, or DOS or Windows 3.11 operating systems. Even if Samba performance were to be improved, other types of inability would follow. In most such cases, clients should be upgraded or replaced.

Many publicized client tweaks apply to Windows for Workgroups 3.11. It's usually a waste of money to resuscitate this 5-year-old operating system and the ancient hardware it typically runs on.

Because oplocks speed the network and server by caching data on clients, anything that can be done to speed the physical and virtual disk read and write speed (especially write) of the client speeds Samba performance. Client memory upgrades are always a good thing. On older clients, a four- or eight-times memory increase can be had for less than $100.

On a network with a few anemic clients and a fast and robust network and server, turning off all oplocks may improve performance. The same holds true for read prediction.

For further tips on client tweaks, see `speed.txt` and `speed2.txt`.

Summary

There's no set of magic tweaks for Samba performance optimization. Instead, the entire system must be analyzed for bottlenecks, and any solutions must either clear the primary bottleneck, offload work from it, or unload it by removing or rescheduling work.

Bottlenecks on a Samba system can be roughly categorized as follows:

- CPU
- Memory
- Disk
- smbd/nmbd
- Network (including network card settings)
- Client

Complicating the preceding neat categorization is the fact that one category can offload another, but if the offloading goes too far or the workflow moves the bottleneck, the resource shouldering the load can become the bottleneck. Memory and disk are especially pertinent examples because the memory caches the disk, whereas the disk adds to memory with the swap partition. On a single-drive system, any swap partition accesses slow other disk access as the heads move to the swap partition.

A wonderful assortment of diagnostic tools assist those with adequate budgets in isolating bottlenecks. Those lacking funds for such expensive tools can often make due with homemade software tools, many of which are described in this chapter. Some tools measure, whereas others change the capacity of the suspected bottleneck, typically by stressing it with an additional load.

Improving throughput of a non-bottleneck is a useless waste of money, except if that non-bottleneck is later used to offload the bottleneck. Therefore, the bottleneck must be identified before attempting any remedy.

Samba achieves major performance gains by caching data on client computers. This is accomplished with various types of oplocks and the `read prediction=yes` parameter. Such caching is appropriate if the bottleneck is on the server or the network, or if the bottleneck would shift to the network or server if every client relinquished its caching role.

With an unstressed network and server, combined with a small number of anemic clients, performance is enhanced by turning off cache (oplocks and read prediction).

The `read raw=` and `write raw=` parameters often improve performance, but they can hurt performance on certain systems. Compiling in `mmap()` can speed reads, but it can hurt performance, and it also introduces incompatibilities with the `read raw=` parameter.

The `read size=` parameter walks a tightrope with concurrency on one side and caching on the other. Experimentation with this parameter should probably be delayed until major bottlenecks are cleared, unless there's strong evidence in the form of an extreme discrepancy between FTP and Samba access indicating that `smbd` and/or `nmbd` is the bottleneck.

The vital distinction of optimization is that performance is improved only by increasing the throughput of the system bottleneck or by decreasing the bottleneck's workload. Any remedy must accomplish one of those two changes. The decision to widen a bottleneck or to offload, as well as which resource to offload onto, is usually an economic one. Always remember to consider the system as a whole in optimization strategies.

Special Uses of Samba

IN THIS PART

Using Samba as an Open Source Migration Strategy

by Steve Litt

Some practices of the proprietary software industry are not popular. Organizations are increasingly uneasy about complex and changing licensing agreements, high costs, and spotty performance. Many have investigated Open Source software as an alternative.

The question becomes "How do I get there from here?" In other words, how does one migrate from the proprietary software to Open Source software? Usually, the answer involves Samba.

Why the Migration?

Some organizations welcome vendors of proprietary software as strategic partners. Others are uncomfortable with proprietary software and feel it "locks them in." They prefer Open Source software for reasons such as the following:

- Budgetary considerations
- Relief from licensing headaches
- Security and independence

Budget

Open Source software obviously costs less because its licensing explicitly specifies that anyone possessing the source may give it away, and that anyone possessing the binary and wishing to sell it or give it away must include the source with the transaction. Such licensing eliminates all scarcity from the product so that the remaining perceived value is based on the convenience of having someone else compile the code and place it on an easy-to-install CD-ROM.

Because Open Source software allows no-cost distribution and copying of the software, an organization can legally buy a single CD-ROM copy, burn a few dozen copies, and install the software worldwide within its enterprise.

> **Note**
>
> The preceding paragraph is applicable only if all software on the CD-ROM is Open Source. If not, it could be a license violation to copy the CD. Check with the vendor.
>
> Also, many CD-ROMs are bundled with service agreements. Naturally, it's impossible to get service on servers worldwide with the purchase of a single CD and service agreement. Once again, check with the vendor.

The price of the software is just the tip of the iceberg. Open Source software saves large expenses associated with license tracking, and potentially *huge* expenses associated with being "painted into a corner" by proprietary software. The availability of source code always leaves an escape route.

Licensing Headache Relief

Aside from costing money, licensing can be a huge headache. Are we complying? Do we have enough licenses? Are we limiting users to the number required by the license? Is that limitation concurrent or per seat? Has the license changed or will it change on the next upgrade?

Open Source does away with all these questions. Open Source licensing demands only that Open Source code never be taken proprietary (and in certain situations even that requirement can be relaxed).

License Counts

Each license requires tracking to make sure that the numerical limits of the license are being adhered to. This often falls on the network administrator's shoulders, usually with his superiors bearing the ultimate responsibility. It's a headache.

Software is available to help track software licensing. It's costly, and it isn't simple to use. However, it can help reduce the hassles.

Perhaps the ultimate license-tracking reduction is the use of Open Source software. Open Source software licenses allow free copying, as long as all source code accompanies the distribution. No copy tracking is necessary within the organization.

Samba is a great example of this. It can be legally copied to a hundred servers, and there's no need to keep track of how many servers are loaded with Samba or how many users access each one.

License Changes

Licenses can change. Each changed licensing agreement must be read and understood. This is a lot of work.

Although unusual, it is possible for a proprietary software product's new license provisions to become an extreme burden to the customer. The customer is now faced with a tough choice: Keep the current version of the software forever, migrate all work to different software, or live with the unacceptable new licensing. Keeping the old version is a tough choice because the vendor might not continue support of the old version. Without source code, the customer cannot adapt the old version to new software components.

Once again, Open Source software eliminates or lessens these headaches. Although it's possible an Open Source project could go off on the wrong track with a new version, the customer has the source code and can modify it to fit his or her needs—and possibly the needs of similar organizations. If there's a need to migrate out of the existing software, the availability of source code makes doing so a reasonable task.

Stealth Licensing

The previous section mentioned keeping the older version as an alternative to accepting the new license agreement. If the vendor's old license contains a provision that the customer must accept any updates to the license to continue using the product, the alternative of continuing with the old software to avoid the new licensing provisions is eliminated.

Because Open Source software enables copying and full usage, it's unlikely to contain burdensome provisions now or in the future. But if it does, the source availability provides an escape route.

Security and Independence

As late as the 1950s, presidential election ballots were counted by hand. In the early 1970s, evidence of our assets were still kept in bank books hand-written by the tellers. Today, almost every business with more than 10 employees depends heavily on its computers. With proprietary licensing, that gives the software vendors quite a bit of control in their customers' businesses. What can we do if the vendor triples the price on the next version upgrade? In many cases, the answer is "not much."

Open Source software provides relief from that potential nightmare. If the Samba project somehow "went out of business," a few businesses could band together, hire a few programmers, and continue developing Samba under the same GNU GPL license it has always had. Other aspects of the security and independence yielded by Open Source follow.

Certainty of Upgrade Path

There are many examples of "orphan" software—software for which all support has been abandoned by the vendor. No upgrades here. Other examples of uncertain upgrade paths include software available on limited platforms.

Open Source software reduces these risks. With source code available, improvements can be made in-house. If an organization perceives the need to move to a different operating system, it can usually find a port of the Open Source software for that platform. If not, it can modify the source to run on the new platform.

> **Caution**
>
> Almost all licenses for Open Source software forbid modifications to be sold or distributed without full source code being part of the package. Ports and modifications must generally be made available under the same licensing provisions as the original software or not distributed at all outside the organization.

Certainty of Scalability

A particularly tough problem faces the organization that outgrows its server and proprietary software, only to find that there's no bigger server that runs the software. Contrast this with Open Source software, for which the availability of source code makes porting possible, and it's likely the port has already been done.

Additionally, the Linux operating system provides clustering as a scalability option for many applications. If a cluster is used for specific software, hardware horsepower can be boosted by adding more nodes.

Certainty of Data Retrieval

Proprietary software tends to store data in proprietary formats. If the software does not have an "export" function, how can this data be retrieved if the software breaks or stops being useful?

With Open Source software, it's relatively easy to export data to any format, using the software's own source code to read the existing data.

Ability to Add Needed Features

Almost every piece of software is missing at least one key feature. With Open Source, the organization can add that missing feature, often with a minimum of coding.

Take Samba as an example. The `testparm` program is wonderful, but suppose you want to output a tab-delimited list of shares, parameters, and parameter values suitable for parsing with a regular expression. No problem. Such a program can be cloned from `testparm.c`. All parameter checking could be torn out, and a new function added. The new function calls `dump_a_service()` in `loadparm.c`, outputting the information in a proper manner. That function can then be called in a loop to produce the proper output.

If the feature is widely needed, you can contribute it back to the Samba project. Once the Samba project adopts it, your needed feature will be part of the Samba distribution, and you won't need to repeat the modification on subsequent Samba upgrades.

Reliability

There's a perception among at least a few organizations that Windows NT is not reliable enough for their server needs and that Open Source software yields superior reliability. Samba has certainly added to this perception of Open Source reliability.

There's also a perception that Windows NT and its Windows 2000 successor suffer from feature bloat. Those wanting a server—and nothing but a server—often choose Samba as the Open Source alternative.

Some of the perception of Open Source reliability comes from the Open Source development model. Because the source is available, thousands of eyes view every upgrade. No bug can hide for very long under such circumstances.

Part of reliability is support. The Open Source development model means that thousands of people are familiar with the product at a source code level. An organization's technologists can easily familiarize themselves with the source code. Open Source is generally better written and is more modular and readable. Coding is driven by quality, not by marketing.

Samba has contributed heavily to the reputation for coding quality enjoyed by Open Source. Look at the source code that comes with Samba: `include/smb.h`, `include/includes.h`, `param/loadparm.c`, `utils/testparm.c`, `smbd/server.c`, and `smbd/process.c` (the main routine of the `smbd` daemon).

Perceived Rosier Future

Five years ago it would have been unthinkable, but today newspaper and magazine articles discuss Microsoft being broken up as part of the Justice Department proceedings. Even absent such a drastic end, coverage of Microsoft in the press has become much less positive than it used to be. Today, Microsoft is considered more like a normal company—powerful but mortal.

Meanwhile, Open Source is gaining confidence daily. Open Source stocks are rising. Stock brokers are suddenly discussing Open Source as a real option.

It would have been unthinkable a few years ago, but there are individuals and organizations today who believe Open Source is more likely to stand the test of time than any version of Windows. In such organizations, you won't get fired for "buying" Open Source.

Migration Challenges

A complete migration to Open Source software is not without its challenges. Proprietary database management systems (DBMSs) and other back-end software are entrenched development environments that don't run on, and sometimes don't even interoperate with, Open Source.

Perhaps the greatest challenge is the widespread perception that only Windows NT can serve files and authenticate users in a Windows manner. Samba is quickly putting an end to that myth.

Proprietary DBMS

Many applications use DBMSs. Desktop and other applications are created to read and write data from those DBMSs. Although simple SQL statement access should be fairly portable between DBMSs, other activities such as triggers, stored procedures, and low-level record access are typically not as portable and require significant reworking for use with a different DBMS.

If the front-end application is written with such DBMS dependencies, its source code is not available, and it does not support an Open Source DBMS, the proprietary DBMS may be required for the life of the application. Note that several proprietary DBMSs now run on Linux (an obvious plus when choosing software).

Other Proprietary Back-End Software

Other proprietary back-end software (messaging servers, for example) may be tightly embraced by existing applications. If those apps are developed in-house, a significant coding effort might be required to make them compatible with an Open Source alternative. If they're neither developed in-house nor Open Source, there may be no alternative but to keep the back-end software as long as such applications are used.

Development Environments

Many development environments run on only one or a handful of operating systems. Some are optimized to work best with a specific proprietary back-end DBMS or other back-end software. A large prior commitment to a highly proprietary development environment greatly delays any move to Open Source.

An increasing number of proprietary development environments now run on multiple operating systems and work well with a wide variety of back-end software. This should certainly be a factor in future development environment choices. There are also many fine Open Source development programming languages, with Open Source development environments likely to come.

Samba's Extraordinary Role in the Migration

Samba is one of the most frequently traveled paths to Open Source. Samba is what enables Windows and UNIX to share files. Although we typically envision Windows clients accessing shared files on a UNIX server, Samba's smbclient and smbmount utilities also enable a UNIX box to access shared files in a Windows box. Therefore, Samba is quite often the justification for bringing UNIX or Linux into a Windows shop.

Open Source/Windows Connectivity

UNIX, Linux, and BSD would serve primarily as Web and email servers and operating systems for running "big iron" applications without Samba. Samba is the software that allows Windows applications to be stored on Linux disks, Windows apps to trigger Linux apps, and Windows PCs to log in to Linux servers.

Samba is the software that enables Open Source Linux and other Open Source software to interoperate with Windows. Samba is a major justification for bringing Linux into the organization. As Linux proves its quality, its role will go beyond that of supporting Windows.

Complete migration to Open Source would eliminate the need for Samba, as Samba stands right now, because Windows would be a thing of the past. Samba could therefore work its way out of a job. However, if Windows were to become a thing of the past, it would take years—years during which Samba would play a vital role. By that time, Samba would likely have evolved to a role transcending UNIX/Windows connectivity.

Samba Encapsulates Windows Networking Complexity

All Samba configuration is encapsulated in the smb.conf file. An intelligent set of defaults enables an administrator to set up a working server with very few smb.conf lines.

Samba Is Often Perceived as a Better NT File Server Than NT

Many people and organizations view Samba as a more reliable alternative to an NT file server. This isn't surprising. Samba runs on UNIX, Linux, and BSD (to name a few), all of which are considered robust operating systems designed from the ground up for reliable and secure multiuser operations.

Samba itself is very modular, highly reliable, and easy to understand. This stems primarily from the Open Source development model. A large group of contributing developers surround a smaller group of core Samba project developers. All code is open to public scrutiny. This is the ultimate "code walkthrough."

Superior Support

In an IT department comprised entirely of accountants, it would certainly be necessary to have contracted phone support with the file server software's vendor or a competent service vendor. However, that's not true of IT departments comprised of skilled technologists.

Most phone support is less than stellar. A technologist must often speak to several people before reaching someone with as much knowledge as him or herself. Hold times can be over half an hour each. It's not uncommon to have open-ticket problems stretch on for several days.

Contrast this with Samba support. The Internet moves the "help desk software" to the technologist's desk, enabling the technologist to search the Samba project's email lists and archives, the `comp.protocols.smb` newsgroup, and other newsgroups (via `www.deja.com`) for the same symptom and to find out what others did to correct it. If those corrections work, great. Otherwise, he or she can get on the mailing lists.

Armed with the information from the search, the technologist can ask concise and intelligent questions on the subject via appropriate mailing lists and newsgroups. Chances are excellent for receiving an answer within hours.

Open Source software's zero cost and efficient resource use make it ideal for non-production networks whose purpose is testing (often called test jig networks). Samba problems can often be reproduced and troubleshot on cheap and easily configured "test jig" networks. What's more, if none of this works, the source code can also be consulted. As mentioned repeatedly throughout this book, Samba's source code is clean, modular, and easy to understand.

Although an accountant may reach a solution quicker with phone support, a skilled technologist will likely succeed quicker with the Open Source support model. Brief glances at mailing lists `samba@samba.org` and `samba-ntdom@samba.org` as well as the newsgroup `comp.protocols.smb` are typically more complete and responsive than phone support, assuming, of course, the technologist requiring help has done his or her homework and phrased the question well.

If management is not convinced that the Open Source support model yields quicker solutions, Linux phone support organizations with Samba knowledge are available. Phone support levels of service and contract provisions vary, so shop around. Linuxcare (`www.linuxcare.com`) and VALinux (`www.valinux.com`) are excellent starting points in shopping for Samba phone support.

Samba Is an Economical NT File Server Substitute

From a software price perspective, Samba on Linux costs $5 for 10 servers. A Linux distribution containing Samba can be bought for $5 from one of several vendors and legally installed on 10, 100, or even 1,000 servers, as long as the CD contains nothing but Open Source software. Contrast this with NT licenses, whose cost can really add up.

Possible Migration Strategies

Open Source is the up-and-coming thing. Stock market reports constantly speak of Linux, with other Open Source software soon to follow.

Often an organization's technologists are the first to want Open Source. Given that they're the people who must make the system work, this isn't surprising. Several strategies to move to Open Source are discussed in this section.

Stealth Migration

Several "drop-in" file servers use Samba as their file-serving software. Such servers are connected to the wire and, depending on their setup, require a few commands issued on a terminal and a few switches flipped. What's more, sometimes an easy configuration is available via a Web app. Organizations that don't like Open Source may like the idea of a quick, inexpensive, and easily installed file server. It's an appliance that doesn't look like Open Source, but it gets Open Source's foot in the door.

Foot-in-the-Door Strategy .

As mentioned previously, the least "Open Source–sounding" starting point is a drop-in server. Once the drop-in file server shows its worth, the fact that it's Open Source can be publicized in the organization. The next step might be a department server and then a Web or intranet server. Eventually, these servers can replace or augment existing NT servers.

A Department Server

Once Samba has "snuck in" as a file server, it can be used on a real computer as a departmental file server. Such a server holds the files of a single department and supports its users and groups. It can be a standalone server or it can join a domain. Access to different directories is granted through groups encompassing the work functions of the people involved.

A Web Server

The next step is a Web server or intranet server, typically a low-security one. Most Linux distributions default their configurations to run Apache and serve Web pages.

If security is an issue, an additional Linux box can be used as a firewall. With its new ipchains facility, Linux does an admirable job filling this role. Once the Web server is in place, it's easy to outfit it with Samba to serve files.

Replacing or Augmenting Existing NT Servers

The previously mentioned steps for the "foot-in-the-door" strategy were in the frontiers of enterprise computing. As Samba becomes an accepted part of the enterprise, you can use it to replace or augment existing NT servers.

Although using Samba as a PDC is rather challenging in Samba 2.0.*x*, enabling a Samba server to authenticate against an NT server is easier. Using an NT server's WINS service and joining an NT domain is a relatively simple change in `smb.conf` (plus `smbpasswd -j`, and so on). Simple file serving is just as easy (or easier) for a Samba server as it is for an NT server. NT can still be used to host DBMSs as well as perform WINS resolution and domain authentication, but there's little reason to deploy an NT server just to serve files.

Attrition Substitution

As mentioned, there's little reason to deploy NT just to serve files. As NT servers become obsolete, you can replace them with Samba file servers. Move any NT functionalities to other NT servers. As software becomes obsolete, consider replacing it with Open Source (or at least with platform-independent software). Eventually, there will come a time when the last of the proprietary software has become obsolete and the organization runs only on Open Source software.

Open Source Server, Microsoft Client

This is often an easy sell, because there's a general perception that Samba over Linux is a rock-solid file server. The most penny-pinching CFO will appreciate swapping the $5,000 worth of hardware and software necessary to make a good NT file server for a $2,000 commodity computer, as long as the point is successfully made that maintenance will also be less costly.

Keeping One MS Server for NT Compatibility

Naturally, NT performs certain Microsoft-centric tasks better than any Open Source platform. Those few functionalities can be placed on a single NT server in a moderately sized facility or headquarters.

Certainly, it's best to keep WINS resolution, domain authentication, MS Exchange, and MS SQL Server on a genuine NT box. However, you can let Open Source relieve this box of other duties.

This leaves Open Source to do what it does best—file serving through Samba, Web serving through Apache, firewall duties through Linux ipchains (or similar BSD functionality), and UNIX-type heavy-duty data processing.

Keeping Vital Proprietary Software Until It's Obsolete

Most organizations have one or more pieces of mission-critical software that cannot be replaced in the near future. Proprietary back-end software can be kept in place to service those applications.

When those apps are old and need replacement, apps requiring no proprietary support software can be chosen, or maybe the apps themselves can be Open Source.

Complete Migration

The organization demanding full control over the software running its company must choose complete migration to Open Source, other than its in-house developed apps. This is a difficult decision to make, and it's difficult to implement.

Most organizations find that complete Open Source migration cannot be done overnight. Most pure file serving and Web serving can be immediately delegated to Samba and Apache. If a proprietary email and/or messaging software is not tightly integrated with the organization's applications or workflow, the sendmail program can be used as an email server.

Beyond that, specific proprietary applications may remain for some time—maybe years, in fact. Given a desire to migrate completely to Open Source, the company should ensure that these apps' successors are Open Source.

Web App Migration Tagalong

Unless the organization is totally committed to a proprietary Web application development environment such as ASP, a new Web app can be deployed as a package on an appropriately sized server. The Web app can be developed in CGI (using Open Source Perl, Python, C), quick developing PHP, or the Open Source turnkey portal development environment called Zope.

Ban on Proprietary Upgrades

This policy can lead rather quickly to an all–Open Source organization. The recently proposed UCITA legislation adds new urgency to such a policy with its restriction on reverse engineering. At present, there's no ban on reverse engineering. If Microsoft comes out with a new protocol, the Samba project can quickly reverse engineer it and incorporate it in Samba.

If any reverse engineering ban ever becomes law, and if the reverse engineering ban becomes part of international treaties, it could limit the ability of Open Source to interoperate with proprietary software.

A complete ban on reverse engineering could conceivably prevent data export from a proprietary program. Because the data files of most proprietary software that has been released as of this writing, have already been reverse engineered, they have an escape route. Through banning all upgrades to proprietary software, that escape route can be kept open.

Summary

Open Source software isn't for everyone. Some like proprietary software's explicitly specified price deliverable and provisions defined in the contract or license agreement. Others feel "locked in" and inconvenienced by proprietary software for budgetary, licensing, and control reasons. They turn to Open Source to eliminate those problems.

Open Source has proven highly reliable, with an excellent, but different, support model. Because of its source availability, Open Source software guarantees an exit path for data, and it guarantees the ability to add needed features.

Migration can be achieved in many ways, including "sneaking" it in via a drop-in file server or having it ride in on a Web application's coattails. Perhaps the most straightforward method is to fill all file-serving growth needs with Samba. Samba eliminates the need for NT to serve files, leaving NT to do what it does best: run proprietary back ends and perform Windows-specific domain authentication. Note that Samba can act as a primary domain controller, meaning it's possible to do without any NT servers, assuming there's no need for proprietary back-end software that doesn't run on UNIX or Linux.

Using Samba in the Department

by Daniel Robbins

Using Samba in a department is certainly an exciting project, simply because of all the dynamics that exist in a typical department. Not only are there general administrators and IT staff but very likely a larger, organization-wide IT department that may need to be considered. This creates an interesting dynamic, where there are inter- and intradepartmental IT standards. On one hand, there's flexibility, because the department's IT infrastructure must serve those *in* the department first and foremost. At the same time, however, the need of the department to communicate and standardize with other departments in the organization is extremely important. In addition, your department may have typical IT needs, or may have fairly advanced IT needs, in relation to other departments in your organization. No department is identical, yet there's a common requirement for each to be able to communicate and exchange information with anyone in the organization. Understanding this dynamic will help departmental IT staff to steer a clear course for the future, balancing the needs of the department with those of the larger whole.

In this chapter, I hope to prepare the departmental network administrator for issues that he or she may face during the integration of Samba into a department. In addition to technical aspects, I address a number of issues, such as realistically assessing the functionality of each solution and keeping a level head with management.

Defining the Needs of the Department

Before the IT staff can pick an adequate solution for a particular department, a good amount of evaluation and reflection needs to occur. One of the most important parts of this process is defining the IT needs of the department. Your solution should address every IT need in the department so that all members of the department can perform their jobs to the best of their abilities. A number of key points are *very* important to consider before you begin this inventorying process.

Your Desires Are Not Departmental Needs

Yes, it does need to be said—your personal desires are not necessarily the same as the department's needs. Before beginning this process, it is *extremely* important that you look at your own biases when it comes to information technology. Because you're reading this book, it's probably safe to assume that you're a UNIX fan; however, you'll need to put down the pom-poms while you inventory the department's needs. Don't let your personal preference for UNIX-based systems color your decision.

We just touched on the positive aspect of being a UNIX fan, but of course, there are negative components to this position. For example, many UNIX fans tend to have an anti-Microsoft stance, an emotional dislike of the company that Gates built. Don't let this color your evaluation of Microsoft products. Although Windows 95 and 98, due to their instability and dependence on the FAT file system, are not very good choices for a client operating system, there probably will be certain instances where their use will be needed (for hardware compatibility, for example). Also, don't let your dislike of Microsoft drive you away from considering Windows NT. The NT of two years ago is very different from the NT of today; due to increased competition from the Open Source community, Microsoft has had to rapidly whip its premiere enterprise operating system into ship shape. The result of this competitive pressure has resulted in a Windows NT that's significantly more stable than in previous years. As of this writing, Service Pack 6a for NT has been released, and an NT system with Service Pack 6a applied is a very different one than an older machine running with Service Pack 3. Also keep in mind that with the increased popularity of Windows NT, the quality of hardware drivers in general has become significantly better, resulting in a significant reduction in blue screens than in the past. Maybe all of us have a nightmare NT experience from a few years back—now we're challenged to take a look at the NT of today and see how Microsoft has addressed the stability issues. In many areas, there have been dramatic improvements.

Accurately Assessing Technology

This brings us to the topic of *accurately* assessing IT solutions. Compare recent versions of each product to each other. Evaluate them on certified hardware. Remember, the IT world changes rapidly, and the quality of products can improve or even *get worse*. This makes it that much more critical to evaluate a solution that you may have previously evaluated, even less than a year ago. In particular, the Samba team is continually in the process of adding new features and bug fixes to its software, and of course Microsoft is doing the same. The fact that these changes are happening means that Samba and NT are *moving targets*.

There Is a Bigger Picture

We've covered personal bias, and now it's time to look at the organization as a whole. Whatever solution you choose not only must help your department, but it must work well with your organization. Choosing a dramatically different solution than the organization can lead to fracturing of the IT infrastructure and staff, which is a bad thing. Don't be afraid to choose a standard solution approved by the organization as a whole, and you should *supplement* this solution with other technologies, such as Samba, to address individual needs. If your organization runs NT exclusively, switching the department's servers over to Samba might not be a smart move. However, using Samba to integrate UNIX workstations or Linux servers into your existing infrastructure will very likely be perceived as a positive thing. Remember that no department is an island.

The Ultimate Question: Windows or Samba?

Which is the best technology, Windows NT or Samba? The answer is *neither*. Each has its own strengths and weaknesses, and fortunately, NT and Samba work together. Instead of asking yourself whether you should use Windows or Samba, you should probably be asking "Where does Windows make sense, and where does Samba make sense, and how can I integrate these two systems into a larger whole?" Diversity *can* be a good thing, and a hybrid approach in your department will allow your users to benefit from the strengths of both solutions. It will also allow you to consider both UNIX- and NT-based solutions for IT needs, giving you a wider pool of solutions to choose from.

It may turn out that either Samba or NT will be a poor choice for your department, and you won't use one or the other. However, it's more likely that you'll be using each for what it's best at, and using them both to complement each other. Let's review the strengths of both Samba and NT in a server environment and then contrast them with each other, from a departmental perspective.

Expense Issues

Obviously, Windows NT is not free. It costs money, and this may or may not be a critical factor for your department. If your department has a relatively large IT budget, ignore cost and choose the best technology for the job. If cost is an issue, Samba running on a free operating system (such as Linux or BSD) will be the preferred choice. Samba could replace your need for non-free server operating systems or simply *reduce* your use of Microsoft products. Then, you'll only use Microsoft-based products in areas where they're absolutely needed or where they're the best choice, rather then everywhere. All of the sudden, Microsoft is a choice rather than a necessity, and your department can benefit from the cost savings.

Ease of Use

In general, Windows NT requires less skill to administrate. If you have a well-trained UNIX-savvy IT staff, this is not an issue at all. If you're configuring a system that will be administrated by users with limited UNIX experience, NT will be easier for them. In an ideal world, everyone would be comfortable administrating a UNIX box, but that isn't always true.

Windows NT Server PDC Support

Windows NT Server's primary domain controller (PDC) support is very nice, especially if you have lots of Windows NT Workstation machines in your department. Domain support will allow users to log into any Windows NT workstation and have access to their desktop as they left it, as well as their personal files, icons, and preferences. If this sounds like a nice thing, Windows NT Server is the best choice. The Samba team is working on PDC support, but it's not yet completely stable. One solution you may want to consider is possibly setting up a Windows NT server on decent but not expensive hardware, to serve as the PDC and store user profiles and passwords. Then, complement this server with a Samba-based system, a domain member (this Samba functionality works well), storing all the users' home directories. This hybrid approach works well if your users use both Windows and UNIX, because you can synchronize their UNIX home directories and their Windows NT home directories. On every UNIX platform, except SGI IRIX 6.5.3f and later, you could have some data inconsistency problems with this approach, due to a lack of support for kernel oplocks. Under IRIX, the following smb.conf command mand will enable kernel oplocks, resulting in data consistency between the UNIX and SMB/CIFS sides:

```
kernel oplocks = on
```

This is a global setting and will be automatically enabled by Samba if kernel oplock support is available on your platform. For more information on oplocks, see "Oplocks Review" in Chapter 28, "Using Samba to Install, Configure, and Host Windows Software."

Stability Issues

If you're using the nonexperimental features of Samba, you'll find them extremely stable. This has endeared Samba to many administrators, saving them from a sometimes-extremely-unstable NT server, which crashes at least once a week. For this reason, Samba serves as an escape route for those departments that for whatever reason have a hard time keeping Windows NT Server from "blue screening." These nightmare experiences tend to harden even the most Microsoft-loving administrator against NT Server as a choice for mission-critical computing, and not without good reason. That being said, make sure you have the latest Service Pack installed on your NT Server system—give it a fighting chance! Windows NT Server running on *recent* hardware, with a *recent* Service Pack applied, is normally quite stable.

The flip-side to this issue is that certain flavors of UNIX can be unstable, especially Linux when running certain "problem" kernels. Although, in general, Linux is very stable, due to the nature of Open Source development, bad kernel versions do appear from time to time. The 2.2 series of kernels, at least through 2.2.12, have not had a wonderful reputation for stability. They haven't been miserable, but they also haven't been up to the normal high Linux standards. Keep track of Linux kernel development if you do choose a Linux solution. Also, make sure your servers use the most stable kernel available. Although these problem kernel releases do happen every now and then, fortunately the fix for the problem is normally also rapidly forthcoming.

Departmental Issues

Although, as a technology professional, you would hope that all technology-based decisions would be made on the merits of the how the technology solves the issue at hand, that's not always the case. A variety of factors influence what IT decisions are made in a department, and they can range from your relationship with your superiors to their familiarity of Windows. In this section, we'll review a variety of nontechnical challenges that you may encounter as you try to implement Samba in the department, and I provide suggestions on how to get through them smoothly.

Your Superiors

It's very likely that you either have a general department administrator or a higher-level IT manager that you answer to. Depending on your situation, your challenges will be different. However, there's one thing that will be identical—your boss has the final say about any decision, and what he or she says must be carried out. In addition, the relationship and trust level that you and your boss have with each other will often have a dramatic impact on whether your rollout plan will be accepted with no questions or, alternatively, be questioned in every detail.

The Boss Has the Final Decision

You may have the authority to suggest Samba for use in your department, but that may not be up to you. If your boss makes the final decision on the topic, you'll have to present your case for the use of Samba. The first step in this process is to make sure your motivations are legitimate—being a UNIX bigot is not a good reason to suggest throwing away your department's investment in Microsoft software. It will be a much easier process to convince management to supplement your current SMB/CIFS network rather than replace all your servers with Samba. In general, it's best to stay as calm as possible and not rant "Open Source is the future," which in general may communicate to management that you are on an ideological mission. Management wants to know that you have *its* IT infrastructure and *its* users at heart, not your personal ideological goals. Make sure you do. And when you present a solution, focus on how it will benefit the existing IT infrastructure, system administrators, and users. Focus on practical things. You're not only selling management on Samba, but you're also selling it on the fact that you're looking out for the department's best interests. Again, sincerity is key—make sure you're doing the right thing for the right reasons.

A Nontechnical Boss

There are a number of additional challenges that you'll face if you answer to a manager who has little or no technical skills. First, he or she will very likely have little experience with UNIX in general. In addition, he or she will very likely have a lot of experience with Windows software; Windows will be a known entity—something he or she can relate to.

I once had an interesting situation occur when my boss walked into the server room. She looked at the screen of our Linux server—I was in console mode, compiling an application. She noticed that text was flying by very quickly, and because it was all gibberish to her, quickly called me and pointed out that something was wrong. I had to reassure her that everything was working fine, and that there was nothing wrong with the server. Although this may seem silly, it does illustrate a very important point—UNIX is alien territory to a nontechnical person and is very intimidating. This can make nontechnical managers resistant to using it. Yes, I know it's silly and superficial, but it does happen, and often. So what can be done?

If you have enough memory, consider running the X Window System on your server. Choose a nice window manager, such as Window Maker (`http://www.windowmaker.org`) or Enlightenment (`http://www.enlightenment.org`). Make everything look neat. When you compile an application, get into a habit of shrinking or minimizing your xterm window. Yes, again, it's totally silly—but it will make a difference. When a nontechnical manager has no other basis for comparing two technologies, he or she will fall back on a visual comparison. Even with servers, appearance does matter!

Another possibility is to spend some time with your boss to educate him or her about UNIX. This needs to be approached carefully, because some bosses really would rather not learn about UNIX, and if you try to "educate" them about UNIX, it can be interpreted as a manipulative act. Try to determine whether your boss is actually interested in finding out more about this new technology, and don't push.

The Boss Needs Positive Reinforcement

Your boss needs positive reinforcement, especially if he or she is not technically inclined. By positive reinforcement, I simply mean that your superior needs to be told, by you, how Samba is benefiting the department. Ideally, before you started your Samba implementation, you created a list of problems that Samba would solve. As you address each problem, be sure to inform your boss of these improvements, in a humble manner. Has Samba been running without problems for 30 days, a new record for SMB/CIFS services in the department? If so, let your boss know! Do a good job with a Samba transition, and there will be lots of good things to talk about.

Nontechnical bosses may need simpler explanations of your satisfaction with Samba. Don't try to explain difficult concepts (remember, it's your job to understand those), but do try to cut to the heart of the matter and explain the positives in an easy-to-understand way. Instead of saying "by hooking Samba and our UNIX server into the NT password database, I now have one central point of administration," say "Now that we're using Samba, our users only have to remember one password," for example. If he or she wants to know more, explain the details. Otherwise, smile and go on your way.

Stand Up for the Best Technology

As an IT professional, it's your job to promote the best technology that meets the needs of the department. The needs of the department are multifaceted and may include financial needs, performance needs, and even other aspects you may not have considered. Make sure you understand the different kinds of needs that the department has, and their relative priorities, before picking a solution. In particular, understand the needs of the department from your boss's perspective. If you find out that needs have changed, it's your job to select the best technology that meets those current needs. It's frustrating but common for the needs of a department to change *while* you're designing plans for a new technology rollout. Don't take it personally; you'll need to go back to the drawing board and modify your plan to fit the current situation. Keep your eyes on the goal, and the goal is the best technology. Fight hard for it, but not at the expense of your relationship with your boss or coworkers. There's always a polite way to present an idea, even if there's a disagreement.

Know When to Sit Down

It's very easy for an IT professional to fight for the implementation of the best technology for the job, as he or she sees it. It's quite another thing to have to willfully accept a solution that's not yours and may be inferior—this does happen, and may happen to you. The bottom line is that, oftentimes, you may be overruled, or your boss will select another person's proposal. Although difficult, you need to allow your boss to make these decisions, if in fact it's within his or her authority. Sometimes that means admitting defeat or holding off on your department's implementation of Samba. The first rule of thumb is to not take it personally—a thing that's easier said than done. Your boss is making the best decision he or she knows how and wants to be assured that you'll remain supportive even if things don't go your way. Not doing so will very likely cause your boss to perceive you to be selfish—make sure that isn't true. Being overly forceful or irritated after a Samba proposal is rejected will only make the likelihood of a Samba implementation in your department that much more slim. If a solution has been selected that you find truly horrible, and it's one that will make your job miserable, you should look for another job instead of making everyone else around you miserable as well. There's no reason for you to be working somewhere you don't want to be. At the same time, make sure you don't make the decision to leave out of spite or anger. Generally, leaving a job on bad, even "grumpy" terms is not a good thing for you or for the company. If you're actively looking for new work, you'll be so focused on the possibilities for the future that the present IT nightmare won't bother you as much; after all, you won't have to deal with it forever.

Other Departments

One item that makes things interesting working for a department is that you're not alone—there are other departments in your organization. In some organizations, each department will have an identical server setup, client machine setup, and so on. In others, there will be wide variations in implementations among departments. Some departments may have friendly administrators who would be happy to help you out. We'll explore some possibilities when it comes to interdepartmental relations.

Get To Know Your Neighbors

It makes sense to get to know other department system administrators. Make an effort to stop by and visit. Although some organizations have periodic meetings of departmental IT departments, many don't. And although these meetings can be handy, they can't compare to chatting one on one with someone facing similar struggles as you. Practice learning from other departments' experiences, and make yourself available so that other departments can learn from yours. When it comes to Samba, many other departments may never have considered its use; your implementation of Samba may be something that other departments would be very interested in. Of course, they could also have absolutely no interest at all—it all depends on the people. Definitely make an effort to drop by and visit those people who are friendly and willing to share.

Consider Collaboration

Often, what's not possible for one department alone will be practical for two or more departments to pursue as an integrated project. For example, if a particular server would be too expensive for one department, possibly two separate departments could both contribute to the purchase and maintenance of a shared server. This is often a great idea, but there are some pitfalls that need to be carefully avoided. First, before pursuing such a venture, spend a good amount of time with your department's accountant and department head to determine exactly what your department will contribute. Generally, shared computing resources will be maintained by both departments—if not, there needs to be some compensation for the salaries of those maintaining such equipment. Also, consider that your needs may grow in the future, and you might need the full resources of, in this example, the server that you're sharing. Can the server be upgraded? Is the other department entitled to the same amount of use of the resource as your department is? All these things are negotiable and must be clearly delineated *before* the agreement is made and the equipment is purchased. Careful and thoughtful planning and discussion with the other department(s) is essential in having a successful arrangement in the future. With Samba, one server can easily host multiple workgroups or domains. This can be extremely handy if multiple departments need SMB/CIFS file sharing, especially if these needs are modest.It makes a lot more sense to purchase one server than several (that is, one for each department). Also, administration is

centralized. Make sure that any such arrangements are approved by at least both administrators as well as the organization-wide IT group, if any.

A Samba Implementation Plan

Once you have a general idea of what you would like to accomplish with Samba, as well
as the backing of your superiors, it's time to design an official, detailed plan regarding
the transition. In this stage of the game, the more in depth you go, the better, and the
more likely you'll avoid problems during the implementation process. Of any stage of
implementing Samba in the department, this is the last place you want to skimp. Not
only should you create a plan, but you should review it to verify that it accomplishes
your goals and does not interfere significantly with your users' day-to-day work. We'll
review several components of an implementation plan later.

One Goal—Smooth Transition

The one purpose of the implementation plan is to have a smooth transition to Samba.
This means that not only will the final result be what you intended, but the way by which
you made the transition will not adversely affect your users, who need to continue working during this time. There are a couple of possibilities that may help you perform such a
transition, and you might use just one or even all of them. First, consider doing the bulk
of the work off-hours or on the weekend, if the work will interfere with the availability
of critical resources. Inform your users of downtimes significantly in advance and do
your best to work around their schedules.

Another possibility, although somewhat more expensive, is to set up a new server in
parallel with the old; this method allows the existing resources to still remain available
while you "build up" the Samba server. Then, users can be gradually moved over to the
new system at their convenience. You may need some way of synchronizing the data
between Samba and Windows for a period of time, while users are being gradually
moved over. Two really good tools for this purpose are `rsync` and `robocopy`. `rsync`,
written by one of the members of the Samba team, can be used under UNIX to remotely
synchronize two sets of files over the network. You can find out more about it at
`http://rsync.samba.org/rsync/`. The other very handy tool, called `robocopy`, comes
with the Windows NT Workstation and Server 4.0 Resource Kit, which is available from
`http://mspress.microsoft.com`. `robocopy` provides similar functionality under NT.

Identify Areas of Interaction

Now, with your goal in mind (a smooth transition), the next step is to identify areas of
interaction, where Samba will interface with other systems. For example, Samba may

need to interact with an organization-wide data repository. You'll need to plan how this will happen before you start implementing Samba. If you're replacing Windows with a UNIX/Samba solution, you might need to look into replacing other services that Windows provided, such as time synchronization, IMAP mail, and more. Don't just worry about the major services that will need to be "swapped out"—consider them all and make proper arrangements for each network resource. Both intra- and interdepart-mental dependencies will need to be considered.

Plan an Order of Execution

In addition to these strategies, an order of execution needs to be chosen. Many times, the only difference between a successful and a poor implementation of Samba is the order in which the steps of the transition are made. You'll want to order your steps carefully so that you minimize network downtime and plan adequate testing of the new platform. Not only that, but it would be good to make a "fallback plan." A fallback plan is a "half-way" point where you can safely pause the transition if something unexpected occurs. If you run into a problem during your weekend transition, you do not want to have to work until 5 a.m. Monday morning to resolve an unexpected difficulty. Having fallback plans in mind will help you to avoid undue stress, thus allowing you to safely postpone later steps of the transition if necessary.

Training Plans

Of course, with any transition, there's almost always a change in how everyone in the department uses their computers, at least to a certain degree. These users need to be pro-vided with adequate training, in advance, in order for your transition to Samba to be a success. Ignoring this issue can turn a technically perfect transition to Samba into a com-plete nightmare—your users need instruction, and they will track *you* down if they run into any unexpected difficulties with the new system. For some Samba transitions, a departmental email and a one-page instructional handout is all that's required. If you're executing a more extensive transition, you may want to set up a prototype system that users can be trained on, or teach a class on how to use the new system. The more infor-mation you provide your users with, the more productive they will be after the transition is complete, and the more pleased they will be with the solution.

Perform a "Test" Transition

Another great preparation you can do, if you have the necessary equipment, is to perform a "test" transition of a limited number of users to the new system. During this test run, you'll want to record any problems or quirks you find with the new system and incorpo-rate solutions to these problems into your real rollout, thus making it that much more successful. Testing cannot be overemphasized, and it's never a waste of time. If you have the time, plan lots of tests. Be sure to also get users' feedback regarding the ease of use of the new system, as well as other factors not directly related to technical matters. It could be possible that during this time your users will help you to see a new way of organizing shares or configuring the network to make things more efficient and easy to use.

Summary

Samba is an incredibly versatile tool and a wonderful asset to many departments. In this chapter, we focused on the planning, testing, and implementation issues required for a successful departmental transition to Samba, whether on a full or limited basis. First, we covered the topic of accurately assessing the technology, without personal bias, as well as taking into account organization-wide standards. We then took a look at the ultimate question—Windows NT or Samba? The answer turned out to be neither, because they both have advantages and disadvantages. After reviewing some of these key differences, we then took a look at various political issues you may need to deal with in your department, such as dealing with your superiors as well as not scaring nontechnical bosses. I mentioned interdepartmental collaboration as a possibility and provided some things to watch out for. I then ended with an outline of the key components of a Samba implementation plan.

Samba for the Value Added Reseller (VAR)

by Daniel Robbins

IN THIS CHAPTER

Adding Value with Samba

A VAR, or value added reseller, is a reseller that adds value to the hardware it sells by bundling it with additional software and services, as well as support. This chapter looks at different ways for VARs to use Samba to complement their existing solutions, as well as different ways to combine Samba with other technologies to provide enhanced solutions. Samba provides an ideal way for resellers to enhance UNIX products to provide additional functionality at little additional cost. Samba, especially when combined with a free UNIX, provides an attractive solution, allowing servers to be implemented with absolutely no software expense.

Different Types of VARs

Every VAR is unique, and each has its own products and its own balance of hardware, software, and support. However, there tend to be three general categories of VAR, and we'll look at how each can benefit from the use of Samba. The first kind of VAR focuses primarily on hardware sales and supplements hardware sales with some software and support services. The second VAR focuses primarily on service, and hardware tends to be a relatively minor portion of its revenues. The third type of VAR primarily focuses on software sales; this software can be developed in-house, resold, or some combination of the two.

Because every VAR has its own needs, there is no one way that Samba should be used. One benefit of UNIX-based applications is their configurability, and Samba is no exception. Samba can be implemented as a standalone system for some clients, or integrated with other software packages into a complete solution for others. Samba can be used to solve a special-purpose problem (such as serving as a conduit for data exchange between Windows machines) or as a general-purpose solution (such as providing file sharing capabilities for a small business). Because every VAR faces its own technical challenges and goals, this chapter is intended to be a "cookbook" of ideas for VARs interested in leveraging the power and functionality of Samba in some way. Think of this chapter as an idea book; as you read through it, creatively consider new ways of using Samba to help your customers. Because you are a VAR, it is your job to integrate Samba into a larger whole, so use this chapter to flesh out ideas about what you want this larger whole to be, and what technologies you want to use to complement Samba.

Now let's take a look at how each kind of VAR can use Samba to its fullest potential.

The Samba VAR Advantage

Samba provides certain advantages to all VARs, regardless of type. This section looks at these advantages in detail.

Cost Efficiency

Of course, you are well aware of the cost advantages of Samba. However, it's worth taking an in-depth look at exactly how much this can save a VAR. Consider, for example, that a 10-user version of Windows NT Server costs approximately $1,000. If your client simply needs file sharing services, this Windows NT solution ends up being quite expensive. Now, consider a Samba solution—the exact same hardware can provide the exact same functionality, but for $1,000 less. This is a tremendous cost savings and, in the competitive world of VARs, allows your networking solutions to be considerably cheaper than the competition. Samba is especially attractive for medium- to large-sized businesses, where Microsoft license fees definitely do add up. Because Samba is free, the extra money that would be spent on Microsoft license fees can instead be spent beefing up the hardware, adding to your profit margin, undercutting the competition, or all of the above. With software cost eliminated, you are now much more competitive.

When it comes to eliminating software cost, Samba is but one member of a dynamic duo—the other member being free UNIX. Using either Linux (http://www.linux.com/) or a BSD (such as FreeBSD, at http://www.freebsd.org/, or OpenBSD, at http://www.openbsd.org/) provides a completely free solution. In addition, if you are using UNIX for noncommercial or educational purposes, Solaris is also available for no cost. Although not an Open Source operating system, Solaris is a proven, robust solution that runs on both Sparc and Intel hardware. You can find out more about the free promotion at http://www.sun.com/developers/tools/solaris/. Each free UNIX has its own strengths, and you are encouraged to compare and select appropriately. When using a completely free UNIX, you are ensured that there will be no future software upgrade costs as well. This is an important factor to consider when providing file sharing services for an organization, and it is recommended that you calculate a three-year cost comparison covering at least one major operating system level upgrade. For example, if you implement a Windows NT Server solution, consider that in less than two years, you will most likely be upgrading this machine to Windows 2000. Take these costs into account as well.

Reliability

Using Samba means that you are using UNIX, which has a reputation for reliability. This reliability gets passed on to your customers, resulting in more robust solutions and fewer onsite visits. Also, UNIX offers many possibilities in the area of remote maintenance, upgrading, and administration that are simply not available under NT.

Flexibility

UNIX is not only reliable but also flexible, allowing *you* to configure the system to your liking so that it works the way you want it to. Windows NT really doesn't compare to UNIX when it comes to flexibility. For VARs, this flexibility allows you to be creative and use existing tools in exciting ways. You can use programs as building blocks to build a larger, more functional whole, not relying on an operating system developer to perform this task for you. Large, monolithic applications are not often used; in fact, many larger applications, such as postfix and qmail, are internally subdivided into separate single-purpose tools that perform specific jobs. Two great things about UNIX are that your tools never limit you and that there is always more than one way to solve a problem. If something doesn't work quite the way you like it, you can change it, improve it, or replace it.

Alternatives

There may be situations, especially for large clients, where Windows NT Server cannot be avoided. For example, it is possible that certain specialized hardware that you depend on only works under NT. For these situations, consider using a *hybrid* Samba/NT solution to avoid licensing costs. Samba can be used for serving files, and NT can be used where it cannot be avoided. This solution has the additional advantage of providing you and your clients with a choice between UNIX and NT when implementing new technologies and services.

For example, consider a situation in which your VAR provides complete 35mm film recording solutions. Let's assume that the particular film recorder you use only works properly with Windows NT. In this case, NT cannot be avoided, and you must have one NT Server system set up to handle print jobs for the film recorder. However, any other services can be offloaded to a Samba-based system. If, for example, you also need to provide general file sharing service for approximately 2,000 employees, a Samba-based solution would save many thousands of dollars. Remember, Samba can be easily integrated into an NT Server environment using the `security=domain` and `security=server` options. Don't be afraid to mix and match as needed.

ssh Administration

ssh, or secure shell, is a tool that provides a secure, encrypted login session over the network. Available from `http://www.ssh.org/`, ssh is an administrator's dream, allowing you to do anything you could by using telnet but providing a means to do it securely. With `ssh` set up on your system, and `sshd` set up on your client's hardware, you are able to provide a wide variety of remote services for your clients, such as remote administration, troubleshooting, and upgrades.

First, you need to choose which version of `ssh` you want to use. B version 1 has a liberal license allowing for free commercial as well as nonprofit use, whereas version 2 only allows for free noncommercial use. For this reason, a newer non–patent-encumbered version of `ssh`, called OpenSSH, is gaining popularity and is available from `http://www.openssh.com/` or `http://violet.ibs.com.au/openssh` for the Linux (and other UNIX operating systems) port. This version of `ssh` was based on the last free sources from `http://www.ssh.org` and provides a completely free modern `ssh` implementation that is compatible with the original `ssh` version 1.

Whichever version you choose, you will have the best experience if you use the exact same version of `ssh` and the companion daemon program, `sshd`, on client and server, respectively. `ssh` version 1 only works with `sshd` version 1, and version 2 is similarly particular. OpenSSH is probably your best bet because it provides true freedom from licensing issues and has full compatibility with the original `ssh` version 1 from `http://www.ssh.org`. OpenSSH is somewhat trickier to install, however, because it depends on the external openssl library for its encryption services.

After you have `ssh` up and running, you can start exploring different ways of using it to provide world-class support for your customers. Let's take a hypothetical example, in which a particular client is experiencing a technical problem when using your equipment. A simple `ssh mycustomer.company.com` command allows you to remotely connect and perform the proper diagnostics, change some configuration files, and possibly restart `smbd` and/or `nmbd` if necessary. If a security hole or technical problem is found with the current version of Samba, `ssh` allows you to remotely log in and upgrade the client's system without an onsite visit. Under Red Hat Linux, a new Samba RPM could be installed, or Samba could simply be compiled and installed from original source. Under BSD, you can easily upgrade `/usr/ports` (using cvsup, for example) and then compile and install the new Samba. Either way, you can keep your clients up and running, trouble-free, all from the comfort of your office.

Upgrading Samba

The Samba upgrade procedure is simple. First, contact your client and inform him over the phone or via email that the upgrade is going to be performed at a particular time. At that time, simply `ssh` into the correct machine and back up the existing `smb.conf` and associated security files (`smbpasswd`, for example) to eliminate the possible implications of a botched upgrade. To make sure that these files are backed up correctly, it is best to create a shellscript to back up Samba's configuration files. Here is a sample script, written for use with `bash` in a FreeBSD environment (you will need to modify this for your particular installation):

```
#!/usr/bin/env bash

tar czvf /tmp/smb-config-bak.tar.gz /usr/local/etc/smb* /usr/local/private
```

This particular script creates a compressed tarball called `smb-config-bak.tar.gz` in `/tmp` that contains all current Samba configuration and security files. You may want to archive the old version of the Samba executables as well, which allows for an easy rollback in case you discover a bug in the newer version. The following script would do the trick, again for the FreeBSD environment:

```
#!/usr/bin/env bash

U=/usr/local/bin
S=/usr/local/sbin
SMBVERS=`${S}/smbd -V | cut -f2 -d" "`
MYFILES="${S}/smbd ${S}/nmbd ${S}/swat ${U}/smb* ${U}/nmb* ${U}/addtosmbpass
➥${U}/convert_smbpasswd ${U}/testp??? ${U}/make_* ${U}/rpcclient"
tar czvf /tmp/samba-${SMBVERS}-bak.tar.gz ${MYFILES}
```

This script, when executed, creates a file called `/tmp/samba-OLDVERSION-bak.tar.gz`, containing all the current Samba executables. This is a good way of performing a reliable backup of Samba just in case a rollback is needed.

After these scripts have been used to properly back up the current Samba configuration, you are ready to upgrade Samba using your favorite method. After performing the upgrade, both `smbd` and `nmbd` need to be stopped, and the new versions started.

Caution

Stopping and starting `smbd` and `nmbd` will cause any applications currently running from a Samba SMB/CIFS share to crash. For this reason, before proceeding, make sure that no users are currently using a Samba share in this fashion. Generally, it is a good idea for users not to be accessing any files on any Samba share, although the vast majority of programs handle this particular situation well. In general, the fewer people using Samba during a restart, the better.

Complementing Samba

Of course, Samba is not the only thing that will run on your hardware. It is also possible, and worthwhile, to complement the functionality of Samba with several other handy applications, adding even more functionality for your clients. But even more than that, to compete against a Windows NT solution, complementing Samba will likely be required. Today, businesses expect more from a server than just simple file sharing and printing services. The new features expected from a fully functional server can include a Web server, SQL server, mail server, proxy server, and possibly others. So, when offering a Samba solution, remember the big picture—your clients' needs will generally grow over time. Be prepared to provide them with a single integrated solution that will meet their every need, today and in the future. This is especially important for VARs that specialize in software and service.

It is also important to look at your competition. And if you are using UNIX, your competition includes not only other VARs but Microsoft as well. Microsoft is in the business of extending the functionality of its server operating systems, and with good reason. Microsoft is always looking for new ways to integrate its various products to create competitive solutions for many markets. Take Microsoft Small Business Server 4.5, for example.

Using Windows NT Server as a base, Microsoft has created a popular integrated solution for small businesses. Microsoft added value to Windows NT Server by bundling it with a number of software packages from Microsoft's BackOffice family, including SQL Server, Internet Information Server (IIS), Exchange Server, and more. In addition to bundling, Microsoft also added value by creating an easy-to-use administration tool and a simplified installation process. Thus, Microsoft has created a solution that, in a sense, competes with VARs in that many of the normally tricky installation, configuration, and maintenance tasks are now more automated, and the entire system is already integrated. But this is to be expected; after all, Microsoft must continually enhance its solutions for small businesses to remain competitive.

This was a good idea for Microsoft, and you can benefit from this example by applying the same philosophy that Microsoft applied to Windows NT (and BackOffice) to Samba and UNIX. A free UNIX and Samba has a definite price advantage over the approximately $1,000 five-user version of Small Business Server. In competing with Small Business Server, your challenge will be to "round out" the services that your server provides by complementing Samba with other existing UNIX technologies. Then, the next component of this strategy will involve "pulling in," or integrating, these products, so that they can be easily configured and administered using a single consistent interface. In addition, there are certain instances in which you will want to integrate the *functionality* of several products to provide enhanced services. Exactly what you do depends on your needs and the needs of your clients, and there is room for tremendous flexibility—you can thank the UNIX design philosophy for that. However, we will always come back to two key tasks—*rounding out* (combining Samba with other services) and *pulling in* (integrating these services into a consistent whole).

With that being said, we are now going to take a look at a variety of popular UNIX server applications that can be used to accomplish this task so that your UNIX solution can provide comparable functionality to a Microsoft-based solution. We will look at the Apache Web Server, Squid Proxy Cache, and more, as we investigate ways to use and tie these technologies together.

Apache

Apache is probably the best known and most-used Web server in existence today. Available from `http://www.apache.org/` and included with almost every modern Linux distribution, Apache provides a robust environment for serving Web pages and files to the world. In addition, Apache can be an excellent companion to Samba, especially when Samba is used in a corporate environment. In addition to serving pages to the world, Apache can also serve documents to a corporate intranet, for example. The following example focuses on using Apache for an intranet.

Application Integration

Medium- to large-sized businesses often need a corporate directory of some kind. At most businesses, every new employee receives a computer account. This is an ideal time to add the user to a corporate directory, and both functions can actually be performed in one step using a scripting language such as Perl (`http://www.perl.com/`) or Python (`http://www.python.org/`). How does this relate to Apache? Well, after we have updated the corporate directory, which could be stored in an LDAP, SQL, or flat text database (your choice), we can run another script that then generates an HTML company directory that can be accessed by anyone in the department by using a Web browser. By doing this, we are taking three components—account administration, directory services, and intranet—and integrating them into a whole. An automated system like this is easy to maintain, and a little work on the scripts pays off in big ways as your clients benefit from the enhanced functionality that you have created. Let's take a look at the steps needed to design such a system.

We will divide this enhanced user management functionality into three steps. The first task we need to perform is called "user add" and involves adding a UNIX user to the system, setting the correct UNIX and Samba passwords for this user, adding this user's personal information to the corporate directory, and possibly configuring the user's home directory. This program, which we will refer to as uadd, will prompt the administrator to enter information describing the particular user, such as the user's department, phone, fax, email, and Web page.

If a system is designed for companies with 200 or fewer employees, the directory services database can simply consist of plain text files that exist in each user's home directory. In our example system, these informational files will be named .userinfo and will have the following format:

```
lastname: Robbins
firstname: Daniel
fullname: Daniel Robbins
title: Contributing Author
department: Samba
phone: (505) 555-5555
fax: (505) 555-5556
webpage: http://www.gentoo.org
maillists: samba-chat departmental-news
```

This .userinfo file is simple and easy to parse using Perl or Python. Each line contains a single data entry, consisting of an identifier and a data item. The first three lines of .userinfo are self-explanatory and contain the user's first, last, and full names. We include the full name field because there may be times where we want to display the user's proper full name, such as "Dr. Fred Roberts, M.D." Integrating the user's full name into the directory services system will make the Web directory look much nicer— if your name was Dr. Fred Roberts, would you prefer to be listed as "ROBERTS, FRED" or "Dr. Fred Roberts, M.D."?

The following lines have entries for the user's title, department, phone number, and fax number. We then have an entry for the user's Web page. Depending on the functionality of your solution, this Web page could be hosted locally via Apache. In this case, uadd will, in addition to its other tasks, set up the user's public_html directory and create a placeholder Web page.

In addition, uadd will optionally set up a new email address (if you are integrating email into your Samba solution) and allow the new user to be added to any internal email lists. The last line lists any internal email lists that the user should be a member of. This option is part of an email integration option, discussed in the Sendmail/MTA section.

uadd can be as involved as you want and could also possibly send a welcome email to the new user, describing appropriate use policies for the computer system, good local restaurants, and so on. uadd can be implemented as either a command-line utility, X-based application, or Web-based CGI application. The choice is up to you and depends on how intricate you want your solution to be.

After users have been added or modified, these changes need to be propagated in various ways. For example, the company-wide HTML directory needs to be regenerated to reflect the new information, mail lists may need to be regenerated, and so on. Of course, this would be a pain to do manually, so instead we'll create a handy script called ugen. Using Perl or Python, this script will not be trivial, but at the same time, will not be too

38

SAMBA FOR THE VALUE ADDED RESELLER (VAR)

difficult. To help you code this tool, we will review the process that ugen should use to perform its updates:

1. Parse each .userinfo file, one at a time.

2. Gradually create a complete in-memory structure of the data, for later reference.

3. After all .userinfo files have been parsed, you are ready to regenerate any data files.

The three-step process is simple in concept—each .userinfo file needs to be read and parsed by ugen. As the files are being parsed, ugen is merging this parsed data into a single in-memory data structure that will be used later. When all the .userinfo files have been parsed, our Perl or Python script now has a complete up-to-date directory in memory, which can itself be parsed to regenerate any HTML pages. For example, to regenerate a phone list, ugen would perform the following steps to its in-memory data structure:

1. Sort all records by last name.

2. Open existing phonelist.html in overwrite mode.

3. Output beginning part of HTML phone list to phonelist.html.

4. For each name in the list, output HTML for a table row containing Name and Phone.

5. Output final closing HTML to phonelist.html and close the file.

Here are some ideas for things you can create with ugen: HTML phone and fax lists, departmental membership lists, HTML listings of email list membership, and more. Be creative! I have personally designed such a system using Python, and the results were impressive and helpful. Remember to use hyperlinks in the HTML to tie pages together so that users can click on a name in a phone list to receive more detailed information on the individual. And remember, these Web pages do not need to be generated dynamically, although that is certainly an option—the method described here regenerates a static set of Web pages *every time the directory data has been changed.*

The final utility that we need is called umod and will be used to update any individual's .userinfo file. This is an optional utility because you can always edit the .userinfo file by hand and run ugen manually.

Squid Proxy Cache

Now that we've covered Apache and also touched on a means of providing an easy-to-use administrative console as well as directory services, you may be wondering whether a free UNIX solution can go head-to-head with Microsoft's Proxy Server 2, which is included with Small Business Server. Proxy Server actually performs two tasks—it implements firewalling features and Web caching features. In general, most versions of UNIX implement their own kernel-based firewall technology, which can be enabled and configured as needed. Because of the variation in this area, you will need to do a bit of research to find out how to enable firewalling on your system.

While firewalls are used to increase Internet security, Web caching is used to enhance Web surfing performance for an organization. In such a configuration, all the organization's Web browsers are configured to use the local proxy server for all requests. Every request is forwarded to the proxy server, which in turn retrieves the needed data from the Internet and sends it back to the client. This accomplishes two things, the first of which is causing all Web traffic to flow through a single machine, which is handy if you plan to set up a firewall (because with a firewall such an arrangement may be required to allow data through to the outside world). The other major advantage is that, because all Web data is flowing through one machine, there is now the possibility of caching, or creating a local copy of this data, to increase performance. The way this works is simple—if a certain file is requested that is already in the proxy server's cache, this item is simply handed to the client without redownloading it from the Internet, resulting in a huge speed increase for frequently accessed sites. In addition, there is the possibility of content filtering, or blocking of sites. This allows the administrator to block out any sites being misused by employees, resulting in a lack of productivity and so on.

A Web proxy is a great thing, and fortunately, UNIX has a great Web proxy called Squid. Available at `http://squid.nlanr.net/`, Squid is a modern, reliable, and powerful Web proxy that allows your UNIX solution to rival Microsoft's offering. And to top it off, Squid is free to obtain and of course does not have any client licensing fees.

NAT/IP Masquerading

Network Address Translation (NAT), also called IP Masquerading, is an ideal technology for small businesses, allowing multiple machines to share one Internet connection. NAT works by rewriting all outgoing IP packets so that they appear to be coming from the NAT machine. This allows for an ideal modem sharing system in addition to providing a layer of anonymity for company machines using NAT. This system works well for networks that use all internal IPs (such as `192.168.1.`) and have only one official IP, provided by their ISP. Under Linux, IP Masquerading is a kernel compile option. Under FreeBSD, NAT is a simple ppp command-line switch; calling ppp with a `-nat` option, or a `-auto` option on older versions of FreeBSD, will enable this option. Now you have the tools to implement the equivalent of Microsoft's modem sharing service.

MTA/Sendmail

Of course, your job of rounding out your solution's functionality would not be complete if you avoided the incredibly important topic of email. If you are implementing a general-purpose server, email services will most likely be required. Email is now an essential part of almost every business, and with good reason. Under UNIX, you have a variety of choices when it comes to email. Most versions of UNIX come with some version of sendmail (`http://www.sendmail.net/`) enabled. It's a good choice for providing Internet email. Other options include qmail (`http://www.qmail.org/`) and postfix (`http://www.postfix.org`).

If you are implementing a dialup network connection for a client, you will want to complement your existing email solution with *fetchmail* (`http://www.tuxedo.org/~esr/fetchmail`). fetchmail downloads email from an ISP and redelivers each message locally. This allows you to set up company email accounts on an ISP (so that email can always be delivered) and set up fetchmail on your integrated solution so that it pulls down new email periodically and delivers it to the correct mailboxes. This is much better than simply configuring your customers' email clients (such as Microsoft Outlook 2000) to connect directly to an external ISP's mailbox. If you do it the wrong way, accessing mailboxes will be much slower and almost unbearable if the dialup line is saturated with packets. Local mailboxes are definitely a good thing.

Summary

In this chapter, we began by defining what a VAR is, and what different kinds of VARs there are. Then, we looked at the advantages that Samba provides to VARs, starting with cost. Because Samba allows VARs to replace some Microsoft products, there is often a tremendous cost savings associated with using Samba; this savings gets passed on to you and your customers. And another key component to this cost advantage is the existence of free UNIX and UNIX clones, such as FreeBSD, OpenBSD, and Linux, for example. Samba and free UNIX are a dynamic duo when file sharing and printing services need to be implemented effectively and inexpensively.

After discussing the flexibility and reliability of UNIX, two of its additional advantages, we then looked at how to approach a situation where Windows NT cannot be avoided. In the end, we recommended that VARs should seriously consider a hybrid approach, mixing and matching NT and Samba as needed. Samba can be integrated into a Windows NT environment flawlessly, and vice versa, so there is no need to choose just one or the other.

We then covered a key remote administration technology for VARs, namely, ssh. ssh provides a way for a VAR to securely connect to a client's machine to perform necessary administrative tasks. Periodically, ssh may be needed to upgrade Samba to the most recent version. Fortunately, this can all be accomplished without an onsite visit, and we covered how to perform a remote upgrade in detail.

Of course, VARs have competition, not only from other VARs, but also from Microsoft. We took an in-depth look at Microsoft's Windows NT-based Small Business Server solution and discovered two key steps that Microsoft used to target Windows NT for a specific market. Because Small Business Server is a competitor to a UNIX system, we investigated a variety of technologies that can be used in conjunction with Samba so that your UNIX solution can offer similar functionality to Microsoft's solution. We then discussed how Microsoft integrated various disparate network services into a single, manageable whole, and how this is also important for many UNIX VARs. To address this issue, we spent some time describing an integrated system that can be used to pull together account creation and maintenance, directory services, email, and an intranet. Using a similar system, VARs can offer a UNIX-based solution with all the advantages of Microsoft Small Business Server but with no licensing fee overhead.

Using Samba in the Educational Computer Lab

by Steve Litt

Samba is an ideal match for the needs of the educational computer lab. The educational environment has special needs and opportunities that must be exploited to obtain the best automation solutions. The educational environment has significant budget pressures, availability of student workers who can benefit from work-study, a mixture of operating systems and less vendor specific software than typical commercial environments, and special security challenges.

Because it costs nothing and enables the use of Open Source back-end software with commodity Windows front ends, Samba solves a real budget problem in the educational environment. Samba security works well in the educational environment, mapping groups of students to classes and projects, and protecting the Linux home directories. The Linux server itself offers real security options that can be optimized to keep overly inquisitive students out of restricted files, directories and resources. Directories on the Linux back end can be organized for efficient backup, minimizing the chance of catastrophic data loss by large numbers of students.

Of all the benefits Samba offers, perhaps the most significant is the opportunity of student system administration. Although Samba administration is not simple, it follows logical patterns easily taught and learned. Similarly, troubleshooting Samba systems involves logically consistent thought patterns providing a lifetime of benefit. Student workers administering the system gain knowledge far beyond that of students restricted to the mere acquisition of theory.

This chapter examines the creation of an educational computer lab using Samba.

Unique Aspects of the Educational Environment

Here are some of the properties of the educational computer lab:

- Significant budget pressure
- Availability of student workers
- Work-study advantages
- Mixture of Microsoft, UNIX, and Linux
- Independence from specific back-end software
- Special security challenges

The Significant Budget Pressure

Every business has budget pressure; however, most schools go beyond traditional budget pressures. Public grade schools and high schools are supported by taxes, federal money, and state lotteries. There's no profit to plough back into the system, and no venture capitalists or stockholders.

Computer lab expenses can be daunting. Computers become obsolete every three years, and software can be a significant expense. What's more, employees and consultants capable of setting up and running a computer lab don't come cheap.

Whereas private colleges usually have no problem fielding a good computer lab, it's challenging for a state university and very difficult for a community college. Many public K–12 schools either have no computer lab or make due with a hodgepodge of castoff equipment configured by a hobbyists.

The Availability of Student Workers

It's perfectly possible for a 100-seat computer lab to have only one paid employee. With the employee overseeing and teachers or professors providing some guidance, students can build and administer the computer lab without salary.

Student workers come in all skill levels and experience. All are well suited to running a computer lab. Some build from scratch, some configure, and some tutor inexperienced students. Like any organization, students move up the ladder with increasing experience. They do this unpaid work for the work-study advantage.

Work-Study Advantage

The student administering, configuring, or building the computer lab obtains a priceless education. He or she gets much more hands-on experience than students splitting time between class and lab. This student is surrounded by the school's top technology talent and has the type of access to teachers and professors that other students just cannot match. This student also gets a practical balance of classroom studies. Unpaid work in the computer lab is a spectacular opportunity, with the best and brightest students competing to become part of the team.

Mixture of Microsoft, UNIX, and Linux

UNIX computers have been the backbone of college computer studies for a couple of decades. Microsoft Windows is the new "kid on the block" but is quickly becoming the most popular. However, Linux is now starting to give Microsoft a run for its money.

Educational environments typically need connectivity between these three different operating systems, and Samba is a file server capable of serving files to all three.

Independence from Specific Back-End Software

Many corporations have front-end applications that require specific back-end software. Typically, that back-end software is extremely expensive. Many database management systems (DBMSs) are tightly proprietary and fabulously expensive. Various middleware and messaging software also falls into this category.

Because of the budget constraints schools face, they're often free of such expensive, proprietary back-end software. Many have either "rolled their own" or used back-end software that comes with UNIX. The fact that they're not locked into a single vendor's back-end software gives them the freedom to use UNIX or Linux.

Special Security Challenges

All organizations have security challenges. Corporations often fall victim to industrial espionage and theft of intellectual property. Although such security challenges occasionally surface in educational environments, the more common security breaches involve curiosity or inexperience.

Any good student has an abundance of curiosity. The best students have the most. Many top computer science students cannot resist the temptation of trying to see what they're not supposed to see and do what they're not supposed to do. This isn't surprising. Many captains of today's computer industry have considerable experience as crackers. Educational computer labs must have beefed up security to prevent unauthorized access from the best and brightest.

In addition to cracking by students, the system must be protected from the innocent mistakes of the inexperienced. At the basic level, students' access should be limited to a single directory per class so that they cannot delete other students' files. Various group-level securities must be in place to prevent mistakes by student workers from causing too much damage.

Another security problem comes under the heading of *cheating*. If the class rules state that students must not look at each others' homework, those rules must be enforced by security measures.

Samba and Open Source Benefits

Samba is licensed under the GNU General Public License (GPL). This license makes all copying and multiuser use legal, as long as the source is given with any distribution of the binary and as long as Samba's source code is not used in a proprietary product.

The GNU GPL is the strictest (from a reuse-freedom and antiproprietary standpoint) of all Open Source licenses. All Open Source licenses, and especially the GNU GPL, make the source code freely available. This leads to advantages in quality, knowledge availability, and cost effectiveness.

Samba Enables Linux/Windows Integration

By storing Windows files on UNIX or Linux servers, Samba performs the necessary integration between Windows and UNIX or Linux. This yields budget benefits. If the computer lab already has a UNIX server, running Samba there can integrate Windows files with the existing data using the existing backup.

For a new startup computer lab, Samba allows a very inexpensive Linux server to contain files from all the Windows clients. Without the need for large client hard disks, the reduction of client computer costs more than pays for the Linux server.

Samba Reliability

Samba is extremely reliable. Part of this reliability is due to the fine group of programmers who built Samba, and part of the reliability is due to the Open Source development model, which provides thousands of extra hands and eyes for development, troubleshooting, testing, and quality assurance, not only at the binary level, but at the source level. A quick look at any Samba source files shows the result. The code is clean, readable, well organized, and modular.

These same Open Source advantages have made the Linux operating system extremely reliable. Software is only as reliable as the OS on which it runs. The Samba-on-Linux combination is extremely reliable, as are the Samba-on-UNIX and Samba-on-BSD combinations.

It's Easier to Find Talent

There's a perception that it's hard to find Linux and UNIX talent, and there's an element of truth to that perception. With many more technologists employed in Windows than in UNIX and Linux, it's obviously easier to find Windows experience than Linux and UNIX experience. At least in the private industry.

Colleges and universities teach many courses on UNIX administration, development, and system programming. There's no shortage of students with these skills on any college campus. Even in high schools, there's considerable Linux talent. Students with Samba talent are often more capable, because they're more likely to have intimate familiarity with Samba and Linux source code.

39

USING SAMBA IN THE EDUCATIONAL COMPUTER LAB

Combine the preceding with the fact that Linux and Samba are typically more predictable and rule-oriented, and finding good talent for a reasonable price (or free) in an academic environment is easy.

Much More Cost-Effective

A Linux/Samba/Windows computer lab can be built for a trivial sum. The use of the server for file storage means the Windows computers don't require large hard disks. Because many activities are performed on a Linux server, it's often practical to use hand-me-down computers or computers received from charitable contributions.

A Samba server used in an academic setting can be a very inexpensive commodity machine. Because Linux and Samba do not require a graphical interface, big memory and fast processor speed are not required for moderate-sized computer labs. Depending on usage, an inexpensive commodity IDE hard disk might be all that's needed.

Many distributions of Linux can legally be installed for free. Linux comes with a file server (Samba), Web server (Apache), email server (sendmail), and full networking capabilities.

Properties of a Samba-Served Computer Lab

Samba-served computer labs generally rely on thin client, often homogenized by roaming profiles and DHCP. For budgetary reasons, they rely on inexpensive physical layer networking, commodity or hand-me-down clients, and Samba server (unless there's an existing UNIX box to be used as the Samba server), with much of the administration being done by students under the supervision of an employee responsible for the lab.

Thin Client, Roaming Profiles

The Windows clients serve as GUI-enabled, high-horsepower dumb terminals. Data as well as many applications are on the Samba server. Through roaming profiles with restrictive policies enabled, the clients can be kept almost identical. This decreases administration difficulties and beefs up security.

For instance, you could create a (human) policy that all files should be kept on the server. Then you could back up just the server.

DHCP

Part of the thin client philosophy is that Windows clients can be simply attached to the system. A properly configured DHCP server on the Linux box gives all Windows clients their IP, WINS, and DNS configurations. Only the Windows clients' names must be individually configured. The name is most likely a serial number–type string of characters.

Physical Layer Configuration

The budget constraints inherent in most educational environments may preclude 100Mb networking. The problem is that 100Mb traffic can successfully traverse only two hubs, thus eliminating much of the benefit of multilayer setups, as shown in figure 39.1.

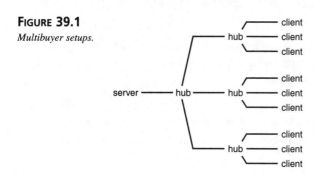

FIGURE 39.1

Multibuyer setups.

Although the server can access any client and any client can access the server, the "100Mb two repeat" restriction prevents clients on different branches from seeing each other. Because 10BaseT has a five-repeat limit, 10Mb hub trees can go three deep. Eight hubs with eight ports and an uplink port can connect a server with 48 clients. Sixteen such hubs can connect a server with 106 clients.

This budget setup would not be appropriate for a lab in which large files are used, because the wire would bottleneck. However, for word-processing training using small files or Visual Basic (VB) training on small VB files (especially if VB itself is installed on the client), this setup can be practical. To the extent possible, set `oplocks=yes`—this enables heavy client-side caching, thus reducing traffic on the wire.

Large files and numerous simultaneous users would swamp the 10Mb budget setup. Heavy use requires 100Mb. Using a 16-port switch at the head and fifteen 100Mb eight-port hubs can serve over 100 users at 100Mb speeds. Be sure the server's hard disk doesn't bottleneck. Use a server with a fast spinning SCSI disk and memory/processor sufficient to transport data to and from the disk. Take any measures necessary to limit packet collisions, and, to the extent possible, set `oplocks=yes`—this enables heavy client-side caching, thus reducing traffic on the wire.

With smaller numbers of users, it's often cheap to go 100Mb. A single 16-port 100Mb hub can connect a server with 15 clients. That hub costs less than one client computer.

Typically eight PCs are connected under the table to each hub, and the uplink wires are run with traditional wiring methods to the central hub or switch.

All Commodity Hardware

All but the most demanding educational computer labs can be built with commodity hardware. The server must have a fast hard disk (a 7200rpm IDE drive should suffice), a network card of the appropriate speed, at least 32MB of RAM (64 or 128MB is better). The processor must be fast enough not to bottleneck the system. A low-grade Pentium suffices in most applications.

The server can have so little RAM and processing power because it runs in text mode, thus eliminating the horsepower requirements usually associated with GUI environments. All horsepower goes toward serving files.

The Windows clients typically can be hand-me-downs or charitable contributions. With the PC doing nothing but running software and drawing screens, a 32MB low-grade Pentium with just enough disk space to hold the OS, virtual memory, and temp files suffices.

Networking hardware is a commodity. Money can be saved if the students make the cables.

Network Administration Is a Course

Network administration is a course available to the top students, and these top students administer the network. Other students in that class practice on a test jig network comprised of a Linux box and a single Windows client.

Server-Installed Applications

Many applications can be installed on the Samba server. Almost all DOS applications can be installed on the Samba server, provided a drive letter is mapped. Many Windows applications can also be installed on the Samba server, although doing so frequently requires specialized procedures and knowledge. This is discussed in detail in Chapter 28, "Using Samba to Install, Configure, and Host Windows Software."

Server-installed software further reduces client administration and disk space use, although it can slow the applications somewhat.

Tight, Self-Contained Security

Except in the college or university setting, computer labs are typically tightly encapsulated, with little connectivity to other subnets in the organization. This prevents curious students from accessing payroll and personnel records.

Possibly Dual-Booting Computers

If the curriculum contains significant UNIX content, the client computers can dual-boot to Linux. Depending on the Linux distribution and how complete an installation is used, this requires an extra 300MB to 2GB of extra disk space. Given the price of today's IDE drives and the availability of hand-me-down multigigabyte drives, this is an inexpensive setup.

If each client's Linux installation has the same hostname as its Windows alter ego, the network can be configured so that DHCP assigns the same IP to each client, regardless of the OS it's running.

Security in the Computer Lab

Students are an inquisitive and creative group, so your network will come under intense scrutiny. Some simple security steps will curtail all but the most determined crackers. Perhaps the first step is to eliminate obvious security holes such as the Samba `hosts equiv=` and `user rhosts=` parameters.

Services to Disconnect

Services started by `inetd` can be commented out in `inetd.conf`. Depending on the exact setup, many can be disconnected. It's often prudent to disconnect `telnet` because it provides a very easy way for script kiddies to install their little gifts, and it's an irresistible attraction for the curious. If it's impractical to disable `telnet`, it can be IP limited via a TCP wrapper.

Depending on your paranoia level, you might want to disconnect `ftp` in `inetd.conf`. Although less threatening than `telnet`, `ftp` can be used for mischief. Depending on the distribution and setup, many other `inetd.conf` services can be done without. For instance, `finger`, `echo`, `shell`, `logon`, `talk`, `ntalk`, `uucp`, `auth` and `bootp` are a few that can, in certain situations, be disconnected. Note that on a Red Hat 6.0 box, neither `echo`, `auth`, `shell`, nor `logon` is necessary to gain normal terminal access.

For services started as daemons, see your runlevel directory. On a Red Hat box, it's at `/etc/rc.d/rc3.d` (where the `3` represents the runlevel). The files in this directory are symbolic links to the daemon starters in `/etc/rc.d/initd`. Those beginning with `S` start daemons, whereas those beginning with `K` kill the daemons. Any of these can be "commented out" by placing an `X` at the front of their filenames. Alternatively, they can be enabled or disabled in Linux Control Panel and other utilities.

Services to Place in TCP Wrappers

The most important service to place in a TCP wrapper is SWAT. This is *especially* true if user root is the only one who can modify smb.conf, because nobody wants his password travelling the wire.

The telnet and ftp utilities are others that should be limited to IP addresses. The object is to keep them away from the general population.

Use of Groups

Every network operating system uses groups to implement security. Groups map literal groups of users to specific network resources such as directories and files. Groups accurately map the "need to know" relationship between network resources and groups of people. In the educational environment, the "need to know" relationship is typically defined by an academic class or project.

Every Class Is a Group

Class assignments are ideally suited to group and user administration. As an example, imagine a class called Math 101. Students receive their assignments from a Web site. They submit their competed or in-progress assignments to a share called [math101a], which through the actions of variable substitution characters and server-side automation path to a unique directory within the math101 tree, as shown in the following share:

```
[math101a]
path=/classes/math101/assign/%U
read only=no
valid users=@math101
root preexec=mkdir -m770 /classes/math101/assign/%U;chgrp
➥ %U /classes/math101/assign/%U &
comment=%U Math101 assignments
```

In the preceding share, the valid users=@math101 line limits access to members of the math101 group. What's actually desired is to limit access to the specific user. This is accomplished by the %U variable in the path= parameter. The valid users= parameter simply prevents those not in the Math 101 class from creating and using directories under this share.

Because the student needs to create and modify files in this share, it's set to read only=no. The root preexec= parameter creates the proper directory if it doesn't exist. Keep in mind that this script runs only on initial connection to the share. If, during student experimentation, the directory is deleted (in UNIX) while the connection is in place, further accesses fail until the connection is broken with a net use \\servername\ math101a /delete command or a client reboot.

The instructor needs read-only access to all the students' assignment shares. This is done with the following share:

```
[math101ia]
path=/classes/math101/assign
read only=yes
valid users=mrbecker
comment= Math101 Instructor Assignment Access
```

The preceding share gives the instructor, Mr. Becker, read-only access to the directory above the student assignment directories. The reason this is read-only is to prevent Mr. Becker from inadvertently deleting or changing anything in the student directories.

Once the deadline for all assignments has passed, share [math101a] is disabled with the addition of the available=no parameter. The instructor accesses the students' work via the [math101ia] share, which can be set to read only=no if appropriate.

This is just one example, and it can be changed depending on policies and the desired level of collaboration among students and between the students and their instructor.

Every Project Is a Group

Using a group for a project is one of computing's most common idioms. It's very useful in academics. Consider the following share devoted to a weather-prediction program project:

```
[weather]
path=/projects/weatherproj/
read only=yes
valid users=@advjava,@weather
write list=@weather
force group=weather
create mask=774
directory mask=-775
comment=Weather Prediction Program Project
```

The preceding share points to /projects/weatherproj, which must be mode 771 and must be group weather. The weather group has read/write access due to its inclusion in the write list= parameter, whereas the entire advanced Java class has read/only access due to its inclusion in valid users= and due to read only=yes. No others are given any access to this share through Samba.

The force group=weather parameter is necessary so that all users in the group can modify files created by all other users in that group. Without that parameter, each newly created file's group would be the primary group of the user. The create mask=774 and directory mask=775 parameters enable different users to modify fellow group members' files at a UNIX permission level. The one thing users cannot do to each other's files is to change the attributes, because only the file's creator (or a user set as its creator with a `chown` command) can do that. To give all users access to attributes, a `force user=` parameter is necessary.

This is just one of many possible setups for a collaborative effort. The exact setup depends on factors such as security, the exact border between "collaboration" and "cheating," and the desired level of secrecy needed for the project.

Limit `smb.conf` Access to a Group

As mentioned in Chapter 15, "Samba Security," anyone who can write to `smb.conf` can create a lot of mischief. Make sure the general populace does not have write access to this file. As mentioned in Chapter 13, "Using Samba Web Administration Tool (SWAT) for Samba Configuration," SWAT has a feature that enables it to write an `smb.conf` that has group write privileges if `smb.conf`'s group is `root`, regardless of the user or the user's group affiliations. Therefore, either use `chmod` to eliminate the file's group write permissions or change its group to a trusted group.

Train the Lab Staff in Security

Because the lab staff is likely to be student volunteers, these students must be trained in security. Ideally, they'll read all of Chapter 15. They should read other security materials, too, including Web sites.

The lab staff should be trained in the importance of observing log files. Whereas an expert cracker can get into the system with little or no trace, the average script kiddie leaves enough evidence to hang himself. Additionally, a log file anomaly can alert the administrator to a break-in.

Backup in the Computer Lab

It's important that the directory structure separate data from operating system files. The latter can be reinstalled from distribution. The decision might be made to provide more a reliable backup (to CD-ROM, for instance) to the data, while backing up the entire hard disk(s) to tape.

Due to budget constraints, backups are typically made by the Open Source program `tar`. All backups should be checked for restorability.

A backup system must be in place. An example is taking incremental backups daily, full backups weekly, and full backups monthly that are saved for several years. This requires seven daily tapes, four weekly tapes, and one tape per month to keep each month. As previously mentioned, there may be a desire to put data on a CD, which is more likely to stand the test of time.

Backup policies must be in place, and they must be followed rigorously. Although the paid lab employee delegates the responsibility, he or she must be responsible for the restorability of backups. Serious problems can result from just a few days of lost data.

All areas of the world experience natural disasters. An offsite backup storage policy must be created and followed.

It's preferable to back up on the UNIX or Linux box, but if software, hardware, or political factors make that impossible, the backup can be made via one or more Samba shares. This must be done when the network is quiet because it creates immense traffic. The following is an example of a read-only share that might be useful in some backup situations:

```
[rootback]
path=/
read only=yes
follow symlinks=no
valid users=@admins
admin users=@admins
```

Read-only access is given to the file system from this share, which can be mapped to a drive letter and subsequently backed up by a batch file that calls any command-line ZIP-file-creation program.

Alternatively, a Windows-based backup program can be used. However, it's highly desirable that the backup program write to an industry-recognized common file format.

Once again, it's best to back up on the UNIX/Linux side.

On a similar subject, it's possible to use the `smbtar` Samba utility to back up shares from Windows client hard disks on the Samba server. However, that's not practical in an educational computer lab. First, `smbtar` runs very slowly on certain setups. Second, once the administrator agrees to back up clients, he or she has taken responsibility for the backup of those clients—responsibility for turning them on and maintaining the shares. The policy must be to store all valuable data on the server.

Details of the Samba Configuration

Computer lab Samba configurations are built for economy and performance. Without an existing UNIX server to be used as the Samba server, a commodity Linux box usually serves as the Samba server, and quite possibly as an HTTP and mail server as well.

For security reasons, guest access is often disabled, and there's no `hosts equiv=` or `rhosts=` parameters. The [homes] share is best provided with some kind of dot file protection, and often it's best to have all student and instructor shares in a single tree that can be backed up as a unit.

Use a Linux/Samba Central Login Server

Linux boxes are cheap and robust. On the low end, you can use a hand-me-down Pentium 150 with 64MB of RAM and a 3GB IDE drive. That's ample for a 10-client network under a moderate load. On the high end, use a modern Pentium with 128 or 256MB of SDRAM on a 100MHz bus, with a SCSI drive or RAID array. When coupled with a fast physical layer, this should handle much heavier loads.

Don't Allow Guest Access to the Network

Guest accounts are a security relaxation designed to allow access to those without accounts. A lab in an educational environment typically has a fixed set of users, so there's no reason these users shouldn't have accounts.

If, for some reason, it's decided to allow guest access, the guest account must be a harmless user with no logon capability. User `nobody` is often used and is the default in some Linux distributions. User `ftp` is often recommended as a good alternative.

No hosts equiv= Parameter

The `hosts equiv=` parameter is a serious security breach, allowing access without a password. It should not exist in the computer lab environment. The same is true of the `use rhosts=` parameter. Although these may be acceptable in a single family residence, they're a break-in ready to happen in a computer lab environment.

[homes]

Students are not IT professionals. They make mistakes the professional would consider silly or reckless. A little goof-proofing goes a long way toward preventing their mistakes from creating disasters.

First and foremost is accidental erasure. Users must be confined to their own areas so they can't erase anyone else's files. Their UNIX home directory files must be protected, either by pointing `[homes]` at a directory below the home directory or by making a `[myhome]` directory with the path `/myhome/%U` and `valid users=%U`.

The `[homes]` share is meant to give individual data space to each Samba user. It normally defaults to the user's home directory. This creates a problem because the user's dot files (`.bash_profile`, for instance) are revealed in Network Neighborhood and can be deleted from there. This is true despite the default `hide dot files=yes` setting, because Windows Explorer can easily be set to show hidden files.

What's more, this cannot be easily undone with `veto files=`. For instance, `veto files=/.*/` vetoes all files in the directory, not just those beginning with a dot.

The best dot file protection is either to path `[homes]` to a directory below the home directory or to create your own `[homes]`-like share. Here's an example of the former:

```
[homes]
read only=no
path=%H/samba
root preexec=mkdir -m 711 %H/samba;chown %u.%g %H/samba
```

Alternatively, a completely different per-user tree can be made. One such example looks like this:

```
[myhome]
path=/d/myhome/%U
valid users=%U
read only=no
root preexec=mkdir -m711 /d/myhome/%U;chown %U.%G /d/myhome/%U &
```

[printers]

The `[printers]` share exposes all print queues to Samba browse lists. Because printers are relatively immune to mischief, the `[printers]` share can usually be configured as typical for Samba installations.

Other Shares

Examples of class assignment, instructor access, and special project shares were presented earlier in this chapter. The primary requirement is that a consistent system be adhered to. Such a system must be consistent with simple data backups and future expansion.

For instance, all data could be kept under the `/d` directory, which presumably would have its own partition. In such an event, per-user "home" directories could be in `/d/myhome/%U`, class directories, their subdirectories could be in `/d/classes/classnumber`, projects could be in `/d/projects/projectname`, and so forth.

Troubleshooting Samba in the Computer Lab

The Samba distribution comes with a predefined diagnostic in the form of `DIAGNOSIS.txt`, located in the text documentation. This is a standard throughout the Samba world, and although it's not always the quickest or most efficient troubleshooting sequence, you can't go wrong using it. In the educational computer lab, always start with that file.

When describing a symptom to others, mention the first step of `DIAGNOSIS.txt` that malfunctioned, and be sure to mention the exact command. Not everyone has memorized every `DIAGNOSIS.txt` step. Also relate the error message or other error condition.

Beyond this, you should consult Chapter 22, "Troubleshooting Samba."

Troubleshooting is often best accomplished by small student teams. It's important that at least one member of the team is familiar with a valid troubleshooting process and is familiar with the contents of Chapter 22.

The number and uniformity of client computers make doubleswapping an excellent trouble-shooting tactic. *Doubleswapping* is the act of trading identical components on a working and a non-working system, to determine if the problem stays with the system or moves with the traded component. Any time a problem occurs on one client computer but not another, doubleswapping is called for. Typically, the first doubleswap is to have two users log out, switch computers, log back in again, and see whether the problem followed the user or the client. If the properly functioning computer is next to the malfunctioning computer, another handy doubleswap is to switch the wires coming into their NICs. Once again, does the problem follow the computer or the wire?

Doubleswapping has built-in redundancy that helps guard against being misled by intermittent problems and false assumptions. If the problem suddenly shows up on both computers or goes away on both, look for a false assumption or an intermittent.

Samba Administration in the Computer Lab

Due to budgetary constraints, Samba (and Linux) administration is sometimes done by students. Due to the nature of school, such student administrators are of limited tenure. That's no problem as long as a method of succession is planned. The ideal is the creation of a basic and an advanced administration class, with students of both classes volunteering to help with administration. This sets up a system of mentoring to ensure an adequate depth of student administrators.

These student administrators must take a Samba class before or concurrently with their basic administration class.

Samba Fringe Benefits

Samba has many benefits directly related to its function as a file and print server. Samba's benefits go deeper. In many ways it benefits the people administering it. It also provides benefits as a result of its quality and stability. This section discusses some of the fringe benefits Samba provides for students, faculty, instructors, administrators, the nation, and the world.

For Students

Students gain a deeper knowledge of networking through Samba administration. Samba interacts with almost every conceivable facet of networking, including TCP/IP, NetBIOS, and security. Hands-on Samba administration gives students incomparable training in these network disciplines as well as in computer network troubleshooting.

Samba is the point of intersection between UNIX and Windows. It gives a unique view of interoperation. It also gives rare insight into the Windows world, which is typically thought of as requiring a series of workarounds. The Samba-wielding student learns the logic of Windows.

For Faculty and School Administrators

Samba is what enables the use of Linux as a Windows file server, and as such it makes life much easier for faculty and administrators. A Linux/Samba server is easier to understand and maintain, with no license hassles. As a fringe benefit, it looks good on a résumé.

Fewer Licensing Hassles

Proprietary software licensing is difficult and is getting even more so. Each software component has its unique license agreement. These agreements are getting complicated enough to be viewed as genuine legal documents.

Penalties for license violations can be extremely high, even if such violations were not deliberate. This often necessitates many employee work hours and expensive license-metering software.

Samba, Linux, Apache, sendmail, and most utilities bundled with the Linux distribution are Open Source software. Such software can be used by unlimited users and can be copied anywhere (as long as the source code is copied with it). No license-tracking software is needed, and no employee salaries are going to tracking licenses. This saves time and headaches.

Easier Maintenance

Samba is easier to maintain than its proprietary cousins. Because Samba is Open Source software, there are not (and cannot be) "secret" features. Everything's revealed in the source code.

That source code is clean and self-documenting. Any good programmer, or even a good administrator with some programming knowledge, can familiarize him or herself with it quite quickly.

However, the main benefit of source code availability is the wide dissemination of knowledge into which the administrator can tap. Samba mailing lists include the general list (samba@samba.org), the geeky list (samba-technical@samba.org), and the NT domain connectivity–centric list (samba-ntdom@samba.org). There's also the comp.protocols.smb newsgroup. The various search engines are quite handy in finding Samba information. An especially handy technique is to search for a specific error message at www.deja.com. You'll find newsgroup posts by people who have encountered, and hopefully solved, your exact problem. These Web techniques usually yield a quicker answer than dialing an 800 number with "your credit card ready." As time goes on, the administrator can form long-distance relationships with others in the Samba community, thus quickening the time it takes to reach a solution.

Easier Understanding

Samba is much easier to understand than its proprietary cousins. A well-chosen set of smb.conf defaults help establish a cause-and-effect relationship between explicitly specified parameters and their results on the client. As a further aid to understanding, the Samba distribution comes with source code.

Heavy Networking on the Résumé

Samba is at the center of almost all networking and interoperability. The Samba expert is a TCP/IP expert and Windows networking expert. To the extent that the Samba expert participates in Samba coding, a detailed internals expertise is developed. Samba expertise enables intelligent discussion and manipulation of all areas of networking. All this is evident to prospective employers.

For the Nation and the World

Samba helps provide all nations with a technologically skilled next generation. Samba provides a clear window into the Windows world, revealing the logic behind Windows in a way a pure Windows-centric course of study never could. It's simpler, with less exceptions and workarounds. Being Open Source, Samba has no secret features or API calls. In fact, the Samba team has uncovered and documented secret features of NT networking. The student trained in Samba has a much better grasp of all networking.

It's a rare student who has access to Windows or NetWare source code. However, every student with a computer and Internet connection has complete access to Samba source code. By studying this high-quality code, students learn about networking, and they gain an example of excellence they can model their work after. Given the shortage of programmers, and the extreme shortage of *good* programmers, this is essential to the technological progress of every nation.

Less Reliance on Huge Software Vendors

We technologists owe much of our world to huge hardware and software vendors. Where would we be without the IBM AT standard or the universal DOS and Windows operating systems? Nobody wants to go back to the days before the IBM PC, when most computer manufacturers had their own system bus, and many had their own operating systems.

However, history also shows it's not good to be at the mercy of a single vendor, as illustrated by the mainframe world of the 1980s.

Samba provides an excellent, and many say *superior*, alternative to the popular proprietary file server systems. As long as Samba exists, the proprietary file server systems must compete on price, quality, and service. In short, Samba safeguards quality computing.

Summary

Educational computer labs have several distinguishing features:

- Significant budget pressure
- The availability of student workers
- Work-study advantages
- Mixture of UNIX, Linux, and Microsoft
- Independence from specific back-end software
- Special security challenges

The budget constraints vary, with well-funded colleges on one end of the spectrum and hard-pressed middle schools on the other. The budget constraints can be overcome with a combination of Open Source software (such as Samba), commodity or hand-me-down hardware, and student design and administration of the network. Such a work-study program not only yields a working network on a surprisingly low budget, but it yields educational and career benefits for the participating students. Samba is a central key in this strategy because it's a major point of interoperation between UNIX and Windows.

Samba is available under the GNU General Public License (GPL), a license that strictly preserves the rights of users to copy and modify the software, without making it proprietary. This license has the effect of putting tens of thousands of eyes on Samba's source code, resulting in a high-quality product with a large population of experts. Linux is available under the same license. These are both ultra-stable products, and when combined, they make a highly reliable file server. Although UNIX is not licensed the same way, it's also extremely reliable and a great host for Samba.

Computer labs are typically comprised of thin clients, often with the profile stored on the server. The TCP/IP setup is often derived as a DHCP client. A significant cost factor is the wiring, including hubs, switches, NICs, and so on. This cost can be reduced by a large factor using 10Mb hardware instead of 100Mb hardware. However, this limits the size and utility of the network, so careful thought should be given to that decision.

An inexpensive Samba server sports a low-end Pentium processor with as little as 32MB of RAM and a large 7200rpm hard disk running Linux in text mode. A faster processor, more RAM, and fast SCSI disk are more suitable for larger labs doing heavier work.

A user's UNIX home directory files should not be exposed by any Samba share, including [homes]. If [homes] is used, it should point to a subdirectory via the %U text-substitution variable and server-side automation to create the directory. Alternatively, a share can be created whose path depends on %U. As with all such shares, it creates the directory with server-side automation.

Given the curiosity of students, security is a vital part of the computer lab. You should disconnect unneeded inetd-started services, disable unnecessary daemons, place TCP wrappers where appropriate, and enforce Samba security with groups. Never allow the populace at large to manipulate smb.conf, because a person with write access to that file can quickly parlay that into a deep security breach. Due to inevitable turnover, the lab staff must be continually trained in security, probably by means of a class. Also, never use Samba's hosts equiv= or rhosts= parameters.

The consequences of data loss in the computer lab are daunting. An appropriate backup policy must be formed and followed. Although a paid employee is ultimately responsible and must oversee backup activities, backup activities can be delegated to students. The ideal backup occurs on the UNIX or Linux box, but if necessary due to special backup hardware or software, the backup can be done from a Windows computer using an appropriate read-only share designed for such a backup.

Troubleshooting in this area is the same as all other Samba troubleshooting, except that because of the uniformity of client computers, doubleswapping assumes a larger role. Because much of the troubleshooting is done by students, they must be trained in the troubleshooting process either by means of a class or through a mentoring system.

Samba provides fringe benefits for the students, faculty, and administrators, as well as for the nation and the world. These benefits derive primarily from the use of a modular, high-quality system whose source code is readily available. Benefits include improved insight into networking (and even Windows networking), the ability to get hands-on source code experience in networking, and a better trained technical populace.

## CHAPTER 40

Niche Example: Using Samba in the Litigation Department

by Steve Litt

IN THIS CHAPTER

This chapter provides an example of a commercial use of Samba. One common activity in the legal industry is the coding of documents in anticipation of litigation. Document coding involves specially trained people (coders) reading documents out of boxes and inputting specific strategic information about the document, such as author, recipients, carbon copies to, and type of document (pleading, memo, and so on).

Each legal case requires different fields. The decision of which information to record is made ahead of time by the attorneys. Because coding is extremely labor-intensive, the data-input program must be fast and reliable. Some of these data-input programs are configurable enough to use in many different legal cases, whereas others are custom-made for a specific case.

Data-input programs can be made in many different ways. They could conceivably be Web apps, although certain logical and numbering rules make that difficult. The data-input programs could be written for the Linux client platform, in which case Samba would not be needed. This is not yet common. The data-input programs could also be client/server apps using ODBC or some other middleware to hit a back-end database. Unfortunately, middleware and DBMSs are often a little too complex and hard to troubleshoot for such intensive data input. Often these data-input programs are simply multiuser, one-tier programs, with the "database" residing on a file server. These are often the most reliable and easiest to troubleshoot. Because DOS apps are inherently easier for touch-typing input, many of these data-input programs are actually DOS programs.

These DOS or Windows one-tier apps need a reliable file server, and Samba is an excellent choice.

Document coding can occur in two different types of environments. One is in an ongoing "coding center," with a permanent network and regular employees doing the coding. The other is a temporary coding center built at the site of the paperwork, for the purpose of recording all the data and going to trial. This might occur, for instance, in a very large merger.

This chapter discusses the effective use of Samba in these one-tier data-input applications.

Document Coding

Document coding is the input process for getting document information into a litigation support database. Litigation support databases are extremely sophisticated programs designed to hold voluminous data, and they allow for maximum flexibility and speed in the data's retrieval (typically in a courtroom setting). Figure 40.1 shows a diagram of the data movement.

FIGURE 40.1
Document coding data travel.

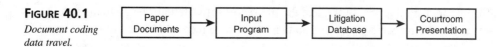

Ongoing coding centers and temporary coding centers can have 5 to 100 people working at once, although numbers over 50 are infrequent.

Once again, a file server is not needed with Web applications or client/server–type input programs. It's only needed with one-tier applications where the input program interacts directly with the central database.

Coding Center Manager Does Network Administration

Typically the coding center manager does most of the administration, with IT professionals ready to provide backup administration and troubleshooting for difficult problems.

Standalone Server

It's not desirable to have the coding center server be connected to the larger LAN. Coders typically do not get email or need to communicate with anyone outside their department.

By keeping their network completely separated from the organization's LAN, troubleshooting and administration headaches are reduced. This also prevents throughput reduction that can occur when coding data leaves the coding center, goes through numerous switches, routers, and hubs, just to come back to the coding center.

Typically the coding center manager needs access to the organization's LAN. This is accomplished with a connection of the manager's Windows client to the organization's LAN.

Performance Issues

Performance is an issue in most coding centers. The importance and urgency of the job plus the payroll for the coding personnel require that the only bottleneck be the typing speed of the coders. This section discusses several performance factors applicable to coding centers.

Constant Database Hits

A coding center puts a very heavy load on the system. There can easily be 50 people coding at one time. Not only does every new record (there's typically one record per document) create traffic, but many field values are chosen from the database. On a one-tier system, this requires pulling numerous records over the wire before choosing one.

The wiring, the server hardware, and the file server software must be up to the task. The rule in the coding center is that the bottleneck must be the typing speed of the coders.

The Wire

100Mb (megabits) is a must, and high-quality switches and hubs are a must. Higher speeds between the server and the first switch may be desirable. Also, data collisions must be kept to a minimum.

Client- Versus Server-Based Data Selection

One-tier programs interact directly with the data. Therefore, selection of one record out of many is done at the client, meaning that voluminous data is passed from the server to the client. The purpose of client/server programs is to make the selection on the server, thereby reducing the load on the wire. Unfortunately, client/server programs have their own problems, often making them impractical for high-volume litigation support input.

Fortunately, a large coding center can be run with a high-end commodity server and good wiring, using a one-tier input program.

Most Litigation Databases Are Vertical Market Apps

The data-input program is simply a vehicle to get the data into a litigation database. Litigation databases are programs that can quickly and easily be queried for data suitable for display in the courtroom. These litigation databases are legal industry vertical market applications. Most data-input programs are either developed in-house or are vertical market applications.

What all this means is that these applications vary widely in terms of their efficient use of the wire and the server.

Coding Centers Are Windows-Centric

A persuasive argument could be made that Linux is the best platform for data input, and that the development of a reliable data-input program is easier on the Linux platform. Use of this platform eliminates the need for Samba.

Most coding centers have Windows clients running the data-input program. This creates a need for a file server. The selection of a file server is based primarily on its performance and reliability as well as on how comfortable the technologists and administrators feel with the server OS.

Seldom Client/Server or Web App

Client/server apps eliminate the transport of hundreds of records to the client when the client needs only one. Client/server programs enable the choice to be made on the server so that only one record is shipped back to the client. Web applications also validate on the server. This server-side validation is obviously superior.

Unfortunately, client/server and Web apps carry their own baggage. They require a DBMS, which requires a whole new set of administration skills. Backup is typically much more than a simple file copy. And with client/server, the client needs frequent ODBC configuration, administration, and troubleshooting. Those are rare skills and are beyond the abilities of the typical coding center manager. Additionally, it's difficult to have a separate DBMS database for each case. One certainly wouldn't want a problem on one case to trash data for all cases.

Web apps typically have problems if the user clicks the browser's "back" button or in any other way steps out of the normal sequence of the application.

Data-input applications are very simple field-input programs, with some field validation and some user choices from the database. They're just temporary stops along the way to the final destination—the litigation database. For these reasons, a one-tier input app is often the best choice. Naturally, this choice requires higher bandwidth network wiring than would be required with client/server or Web apps.

Often Proprietary Data Formats

The data input programs are often written in computer languages with proprietary data formats.

Hardware and Software Costs Are Not an Issue

Permanent coding centers are profit centers attached either to a law firm or to a service bureau used by law firms. An excellent, quality coding center can gain a law firm's business that it otherwise might have lost. Given the billing rates of law firms, the choice of hardware and software is made based on coding speed and quality, not on cost.

Temporary coding centers are assembled for large, high-stakes legal matters such as mergers and acquisitions. Billions can be at stake, so the last thing on anyone's mind is the cost of the network operating system.

Coding Centers Are Profitable

Coding is typically billed to the client, thus making it a profit center rather than a cost center. In the case of service bureaus subcontracting to law firms, coding is their primary source of revenue. Unlike many other IT functions, there's a clear connection between coding and revenue.

Labor Is a Large Cost

It makes little sense to save a little money on the server or the wire, only to have it slow down 20 full-time workers. There's a very simple criteria for "how fast is fast enough." The bottleneck should always be the typing speed of the coders. In a busy coding center, any improvement necessary to achieve this pays for itself in a matter of days or weeks.

Delays Incur a Huge Cost

The ultimate goal of the coding center is trial preparation. If the law firm is unprepared on the trial date, it can carry a huge cost. Coding center delays are extremely expensive.

Paper- Versus Image-Based Coding

There are two types of coding input systems: paper-based and image-based. Both methods can be used as single-tier Samba-hosted applications. They're each described in this section.

Paper-Based

Paper-based systems are the simplest. The coders get a box of paper documents, already Bates stamped. *Bates stamping* is a sequential numbering system that's unique in the case, thus making it the key of choice.

Each paper is read, and the appropriate information is input into the data-input program. After a box is completed, it's recorded as having been input. Then another box is worked on.

Image-Based

Image-based coding is a three-step process that's more automated. Each document is processed by special software that assigns a Bates number and enables an operator to quickly input (via choices, no typing) simple data such as the document type. The Bates number and simple data are contained in barcodes on a header sheet—one header for each document. That paperwork is then scanned by special software that puts the data and image into a database. The coders then code from an image on the screen rather than using paper.

Choosing Samba

As detailed in the previous section, cost is not an issue in choosing the network operating system for a coding center. The only issues are performance, reliability, and ease of maintenance.

Samba is often seen as more reliable than NT and on par with such heavyweights as NetWare. Although NetWare is an excellent choice (keeping in mind that cost is not an issue), an organization whose personnel are familiar with UNIX may feel more comfortable with Samba.

An additional benefit of Samba is quick setup. There's no need to order a license, and hardware requirements are minimal. A technician with a Linux installation CD in his or her drawer can cobble up a new Samba server and have it up and running in an hour. If the /cases directory is mounted to a separate physical hard disk, it can simply be installed on the new server without a data restore. The scripts in this chapter enable the coding center manager to quickly restore all groups and shares as well as to assign users to those groups.

The choice of Samba for a coding center server amounts to this: Without considering cost, is Samba the most reliable choice, and is it the fastest and easiest for the organization's personnel? Often the answer is yes.

A Coding Center Network Strategy

The coding center operates on a self-contained LAN with sufficient power to remove all bottlenecks, except the typing speed of the coders. This section discusses the making of such a LAN.

Wiring

The initial network design should be done by an expert. Although it's typically a standalone network with all wiring confined to the coding center, it's important to maximize bandwidth and minimize data collisions and other problems. All network cards, hubs, switches, and wires should be at least 100Mb. In all but the largest coding centers, wiring can be run on the floor under tables that serve as work areas for the coders. Of course, any wiring on the floor not covered by a table must be taped or covered so as not to be a tripping hazard.

Instant Configuration Clients

The Samba server must be configured as a DHCP server so that Windows clients can simply be given a name and connected to the network. Roaming profiles are also an excellent idea because coders must be restricted to a specific subset of the client machine's capabilities. The client machine is nothing more or less than a very fast data-input device.

Vanilla Windows 98

Windows 98 is a better OS than DOS, and it's an excellent networking client. However, with its Registry and DLL collections, Windows performance can slow down and become quirky with the installation of additional software. Because the client computer's sole purpose is to run the data input program, other applications should not be installed.

The Program Is on the Server

The data-input program is on the server, not on each client. Because many of these data-input programs are developed in-house specifically for a case, administration of per-client input programs would be prohibitive.

If the executable is large and bandwidth is at a premium, the executable can be downloaded once and run from the client. Imagine that the server's name is mainserv, the case's matter number is 123456, and the input program is called 123456a.exe. It could be run from the following \\mainserv\cases\123456\123456.bat file:

```
c:
cd \caseexe
@if exist 123456a.exe goto runn
copy \\mainserv\cases\123456\123456a.exe .
:runn
123456a.exe
```

This limits the executable downloads to one per client. In addition, if a newer version of the executable is created, it can be updated on all clients, like this:

```
c:
cd \caseexe
@if exist 123456a.exe del 123456a.exe
@if exist 123456b.exe goto runn
copy \\mainserv\cases\123456\123456b.exe .
:runn
123456b.exe
```

Samba Configuration

There are many possible ways to set up Samba in coding centers. This section gives an example of one such configuration.

Start by creating /cases, mode 771. The owner is root, and the group is admin. Below that, create one directory for each case, named after the matter number of each case. This scenario assumes six-digit matter numbers. Here's an example:

```
[123456]
path=/cases/123456
read only=no
valid users=@123456,@admin
directory mask=0771
create mask=0771
force group=123456
```

Here's a shellscript (call it addcase) to automatically create such a share when a new case comes in:

```
#!/bin/sh
smbconf=/usr/local/samba/lib/smb.conf;
stat="good";

(grep -iq "\[[[:space:]]*$1[[:space:]]*\]" $smbconf) && \
    stat="[$1] already exists";
[ "$1" != "" ] || stat="Must have one argument";
[ "$(whoami)" != "root" ] && stat="Must run this script as root";

echo $stat;

if [ "$stat" = "good" ]; then
  echo Creating case $1...
  /usr/sbin/groupadd g$1
  mkdir -m771 /cases/$1;
  chown root.g$1 /cases/$1;
  echo "" >> $smbconf;
  echo [$1] >> $smbconf;
  echo path=/cases/$1 >> $smbconf;
  echo read only=no >> $smbconf;
  echo valid users=@g$1,@admin >> $smbconf;
  echo directory mask=0771 >> $smbconf;
  echo create mask=0771 >> $smbconf;
  echo force group=g$1 >> $smbconf;
  /etc/rc.d/init.d/smb restart;
fi
```

> **Caution**
>
> Spacing and punctuation are critical in shellscripts such as the preceding one. Be sure to exactly duplicate the spacing in the shellscript; otherwise, it will fail.
>
> The preceding script may need modification to run on specific platforms.

The preceding shellscript must be run as user `root`. For it to work, `/cases` must be mode 771, owner `root`, and group `admin`. The script checks whether the share already exists, whether there's an argument, and whether it's being run as user `root`. If there's an argument, that argument is not presently a share in `smb.conf`, and the script is being run as user `root`, the script runs.

The shellscript automatically performs all the tasks necessary for adding a new case:

- Adds a group named after the argument with a prepended g.
- Creates and configures the case directory under `/cases`.
- Adds the share to `smb.conf`.
- Restarts Samba.

Note

If restarting Samba causes interference with ongoing coding, remove the code from the script and restart Samba separately on a break. Some applications are more forgiving of a temporary break in Samba than others.

The coding center manager also needs a quick way to place users into groups and take them out again. The following shellscript, called `joincase`, places the user (arg1) into a group (arg2):

```
#!/bin/sh
stat="good";
[ "$(whoami)" != "root" ] && stat="Must run this script as root";

echo $stat

if [ "$stat" = "good" ]; then
  grps=$(id -Gn $1 | tr ' ' ',' ),$2
  cmd="/usr/sbin/usermod -G$grps $1"
  $cmd
  echo ""
  echo User $1 now belongs to the following groups:
  groups $1
  echo ""
fi
```

The following script, called `leavecase`, deletes the user from a specific case:

```
#!/bin/sh
stat="good";
[ "$(whoami)" != "root" ] && stat="Must run this script as root";
```

```
echo $stat

if [ "$stat" = "good" ]; then
  grps=$(id -Gn $1 | tr ' ' ',' | sed s/,$2//g)
  cmd="/usr/sbin/usermod -G$grps $1"
  $cmd
  echo ""
  echo User $1 now belongs to the following groups:
  groups $1
  echo ""
fi
```

Backing Up and Compacting Databases

Databases must be regularly backed up, compacted, and generally maintained. These activities are best done at lunchtime as well as either after quitting time or at dinner time (if the coding center operates more than 8 hours a day).

Daily full backups and maintenance are restricted to cases being worked on. These activities are best controlled by scripts or batch files to minimize downtime. Backups can be done through the individual case shares (@admin is a valid user) or from a central share, like the following:

```
[admin]
path=/cases
read only=no
valid users=@admin
admin users=@admin
```

Regular (though probably not daily) full backups of the entire /cases tree must be created.

The backed up data is vitally important. Restorability of the backups must be confirmed. A system of offsite backups should be maintained.

Security

Security is serious business in a coding center. A single accidental or malicious act could wipe out enough data to cause losses in the millions of dollars—that is, if the data isn't backed up. Much of the data is highly sensitive and could cause great harm if released. The data should be available only to coders presently coding it. Each coder should have a unique user ID, with passwords changed frequently. Passwords must not be shared or revealed. This is accomplished with group-based security.

Each case gets its own directory, share, and UNIX group. Coders are assigned to groups and removed from groups as their need to code specific cases changes. The scripts shown in the "Samba Configuration" section make such additions and removals easy, quick, and practical.

The client PCs should have no floppy drive or other method of copying data out of the system. Legitimate data copying can be accomplished on the network. Clients malfunctioning to the extent that they can't boot from the hard disk should be sent to a technician.

Administration

Once the network is set up, most of the administration is done by the coding center manager. Coding center managers are usually quite technically proficient and are not afraid of the command line. Many have been around since the days of DOS and feel quite comfortable with batch files.

Using the scripts described in this chapter, plus a few UNIX commands such as useradd, passwd and smbpasswd, the coding center manager can do all normal administration. Such administration can be done even more easily and quickly using a UNIX menuing system to call the commands.

Quick and Temporary Coding Centers

Sometimes huge legal matters, such as megamergers, require quick coding of documents at the headquarters of the company involved. In such cases, a temporary coding center is erected right in the company's headquarters. Huge photocopy machines are brought in. Coders are hired, and technical and managerial personnel are flown in. A network is set up, the coding input application deployed, and coders begin coding hundreds or even thousands of boxes of documents. Such projects often have inhuman deadlines, with many coders working as many as 18 hours a day.

Linux/Samba is an excellent choice in such situations. First and foremost, if the server shipped from headquarters is lost, delayed, or fails to work, a server-capable computer can be immediately purchased locally, together with a copy of Linux, including Samba. The server can be up and running within an hour. If the server breaks, another one can be deployed in an hour.

The extreme deadlines of these projects preclude any significant data loss, so backups are typically taken every hour. Backups can be quickly made on a Windows PC's hard drive via a Samba share. The coders then go back to work while the backup is transferred from the Windows PC's hard drive to a CD-ROM via the Windows PC's CD-RW drive.

At the project's conclusion, the server or servers are shipped back to the law firm. In addition, several of the law firm's personnel might hand-carry CD-ROMs containing the data.

Troubleshooting

Here are some distinguishing characteristics of coding center Samba troubleshooting:

- Urgency
- Client uniformity
- Heavy use

These characteristics are discussed in the following subsections.

Urgency

A moderately large coding center with 20 coders wastes 20 hours' wages for every hour that the server is down, but that's not the primary cost. If the outage hurts court preparation, the labor costs are dwarfed. Coding center problems must be fixed immediately.

The first step in that direction involves a consistently followed program of preventative maintenance. All active databases must be regularly compacted or otherwise maintained. Network statistics must be observed to see whether an impending bottleneck will impede progress.

Steps must be taken to make server replacement quick. Regular backups are essential in order to quickly restore to a different computer. Additionally, it's an excellent idea to have the /cases directory mounted to a separate physical hard disk so that in the event of a server failure, it can simply be placed in the new server. Disk mirroring is an additional step in this direction.

A new, tested server should be on the coding center premises, ready to accept the /cases disk and be pressed into action. The coding center manager should maintain a list of users in order to quickly re-create their accounts as well as a list of cases in order to quickly re-create users' smb.conf and group entries.

Not every problem requires a server replacement. Do the quickest tests first. Run testparm on the server to detect any smb.conf problems and use ping from several clients to determine connectivity. If there's a question of connectivity, plug a Windows client directly into the server using a null cable. This rules in or rules out all network wiring. Then narrow it down from there.

Beyond the preceding, take the five minutes necessary to go through DIAGNOSIS.txt. If the server hardware or operating system seems at fault, swap the server and troubleshoot the old server at your leisure.

Client Uniformity

One advantage is the client computer uniformity in the coding center, especially in the older "from paper" coding centers. This makes doubleswaps a quick and efficient troubleshooting tactic. When selective clients have problems, you should determine commonalties and distinctions. The easiest step is to determine whether the problem is limited to a single case. If so, narrow it down to the share, the group, or the input application.

A handy tactic is the doubleswap. Have a person with the problem switch computers with a person not having the problem. See whether the problem stays with the client or travels with the person. This rules out or rules in the Windows client and the wiring to that client. Swapping a client's network inputs is another handy doubleswap.

Heavy Use

5 to 100 users continuously keying information, combined with the client selection from large record sets inherent with single-tier applications, puts the network and server to extremely heavy use. When bottlenecks cause coders to wait for the system, bottleneck analysis must be employed to find and relieve the bottleneck.

The coding center manager should be given the tools to record network statistics as well as some standards by which to measure them. When a trend threatens to slow down the work, the issue must be dealt with before the bottleneck occurs. Such network performance improvement and bottleneck analysis must be done by a network technologist, not the coding center manager.

Summary

Litigation department coding centers are one of many environments where Samba proves valuable. Because of the high stakes and profits in such an environment, Samba must compete on its merits, not its cost. Samba's role in the coding center is to store data pertaining to paper documents that's input by 5 to 100 specially trained people, called *coders*. It's a challenge because of the large amount of simultaneous and continuous input and the fact that many coding input programs operate in the single-tier mode, in which data selection is made at the client from a large dataset shipped over the wire.

The performance objective is to manage bottlenecks so that the main bottleneck is the typing speed of the coders. This is done with fast networks, collision limitation, and a very fast server.

The coding center network is typically a standalone network, without connections to other networks. This increases speed, reliability, and security, and it decreases cost.

Besides managing the activities of the coders, the coding center manager typically does day-to-day network administration with the help of handy scripts.

Because legal cases are completely distinct, input is done on a per-case basis. This implies a directory structure starting with /cases, from which a unique directory for each case is hung, typically named after its matter number. Each case directory is accessible by members of a group named after the matter number, preceded by the letter g, because all-numeric group names are illegal.

The coding center manager starts a new case by running a script that adds the case's group, creates and configures the case directory under /cases, adds the share to smb.conf, and restarts Samba. Depending on the input applications, it may be better to remove the Samba restart from the script and perform it separately. Once the case has been installed, the manager can use scripts to add users to the case's group, after which they can start coding. A similar script can remove users from the group.

Samba servers are very good for quick, temporary coding centers because they set up quickly and can use all commodity hardware as well as all Open Source software (for the server).

Coding center network troubleshooting is distinguished by urgency, client uniformity, and heavy use. A substitute server should be kept ready to go, with case data on a separate drive that can be moved between servers. Preventative maintenance is essential, as is constant monitoring of performance trends. Client uniformity makes doubleswapping easy and practical.

Litigation support coding centers are just one of many practical Samba applications.

## CHAPTER 41

Using Samba in the Home

by Steve Litt

IN THIS CHAPTER

It usually happens at the worst possible time. You need to write two reports before bed-time, and a family member says "I need your computer." He has his own computer, but it doesn't have certain data files, or it isn't loaded with a needed application, or perhaps it's not hooked to the proper printer. Therefore, either you go to bed late or he doesn't get his task done.

This is one of the problems solved by Samba in the home. For the price of a Linux install CD plus a low-end commodity computer (or a hand-me-down computer), every file of every household member can be kept on the Linux server. Files can be shared, collaboration can be accomplished, and household backups can be performed.

This chapter gives examples and instructions for creating a Samba server to share data, printers, programs, and backups in the home.

Printer Sharing

Printer sharing is possible with Windows peer networking, but it's more reliable under Samba. Linux is a robust, multiuser operating system designed from the ground up to handle sharing resources such as printers.

Most families have just one printer. If that's the case in your home, you can connect it to the Samba/Linux box's LPT port and create a plain-text printer queue for it in Linux. Here's an example:

```
# LOCAL TEXT PRINTER
lp_text:\
    :sd=/var/spool/lpd/lp_text:\
    :mx#0:\
    :lp=/dev/lp0:\
    :sf:\
    :sh:
```

The preceding /etc/printcap print queue requires no filter because it's a bytewise passthrough print queue. It suppresses headers and the final formfeed with the :sh: and :sf: lines. The queue can be made with a text editor or with any number of front-end interfaces to /etc/printcap.

The print queue is made available by the following [printers] share:

```
[printers]
print ok=yes
path=/var/spool/samba
browseable=no
```

It's also imperative to have the correct `printing=` and `printcap name=` parameters. Assuming a Linux server is used (a very reasonable assumption for a home Samba network), those values are as follows:

```
printcap name=/etc/printcap
printing=bsd
```

This printer is available to all. It's a bytewise passthrough printer. To make it useful, each Windows client needs its own "Windows printer" to link to the correct printer driver. This can be done in five minutes with the Windows install CD. Alternatively, you can implement automatic Windows 9*x* printer driver installation, as explained in Chapter 8, "Configuring Printer Shares."

There may be a printer that should be available to only certain people, or only to one person. If the printer is intended for use by a single person who always works at a specific computer, it might be best to connect that printer directly to the Windows box and not share it. However, if a group of people must access the printer, you can create a special printer share to access it:

```
[homebiz]
printer=lp_text
print ok=yes
valid users=mommy,daddy
path=/var/spool/samba
browseable=no
```

Often one printer is devoted to the family business, whereas others are available for general use.

Avoiding License Agreement Violations

A home network makes it very easy to share an application. Too easy, sometimes. It's usually illegal to place a proprietary office suite on your network and let all seven members of your household use it. The penalties and fines for such license violations are stiff, and if the wrong person finds out about such misuse, you may be assessed those penalties and fines. Read your license agreement and don't violate it.

Besides being illegal, it's unethical to illegally grant multiuser access to proprietary software. Although we often think of proprietary software as overpriced software from rich, gigantic corporations, some of the best software comes from individuals or small companies who charge very reasonable prices and use their revenues to feed their families.

Allowing several individuals to use a single paid copy of such software is like stealing a birthday present from the software creator's child.

Read all software license agreements and do not circumvent them with a home network.

The Source of Open Source

The exorbitant prices and cumbersome license agreements of some proprietary software has led to the recent popularity of the Open Source movement. Open Source software has no limitations on copying and multiuser access, as long as the software is not used in proprietary software (and some Open Source licenses even allow the practice of taking modifications private).

Open Source is usually associated with the Linux and UNIX platforms, but in fact there's a wealth of Open Source that runs on Windows. The Perl, Python, and TCL/TK interpreters run on Windows. The Java JDK and Java interpreter also run on Windows and can be legally downloaded to run on a multiuser network. Netscape Navigator and Composer are available under an open license that allows multiuser access. Open Source text editors are also available for Windows, and soon there will be office suites.

Open Source and other copy-allowable software provide a great alternative.

File Sharing

File sharing is the premier use of Samba. This section discusses some of the finer points of file sharing.

Kid-Proofing the Home Directories

Kids are kids. They break things. They haven't learned the caution that maturity brings. Many kids are also curious and mischievous. For these reasons, children's Samba access should be separated from their home directories. This can be done either by mapping [homes] to a directory below the home directory or by creating a directory to be the Samba equivalent of [homes]. The following is a remapping of [homes]:

```
[homes]
read only=no
path=%H/samba
root preexec=mkdir -m 711 %H/samba;chown %u.%g %H/samba
```

The preceding remapping limits Samba access to the samba directory below the home directory, thus protecting the dot files and other important files in the home directory. Alternatively, a share can be made to replace the functionality of [homes], as follows:

```
[myhome]
path=/d/myhome/%U
valid users=%U
read only=no
root preexec=mkdir -m711 /d/myhome/%U;chown %U.%G /d/myhome/%U &
```

The preceding share maps to a directory corresponding to the username, below
/d/myhome. This has the advantage of placing it under the /d directory. If all user data is
placed under the /d directory, data backups (as opposed to less critical system backups)
are as simple as backing up the /d tree.

Note that in the previous [homes] and [myhome] shares, server-side automation performed the directory creation.

Other Data Goes in a Single Tree

As much user data as possible should reside in a single tree. Make the root of this tree
/d for the shortest file paths and commands. Home directory equivalents, project directories, and other directories can be placed under this tree.

Having all user data in a single tree makes for more reliable backups. Additionally, this
tree can be mounted to its own partition or even its own physical disk, thereby making
the data less subject to corruption.

Family Sound File Directory

Members of a typical family want to listen to many of the same MP3 and other sound
files. These are large files best not replicated on several clients. Instead, you can grant
household-wide, read-only access to them via a share:

```
[sounds]
path=/d/sounds
write list=mommy,daddy
```

Because the share defaults to read-only, only mommy and daddy can add or delete sounds
through Samba.

The final step is to create a shortcut to the sounds directory in the Start menu. The simplest way to do this is by dragging it from Explorer to the Start button with the Ctrl key
pressed. Once the shortcut is in the Start menu, navigating to that shortcut brings up a
persistent window containing all the sounds.

This same type of usage can be applied to video clips, family photos, and almost any
other resource common to the family that can be legally accessed by all.

File Transfer Directory

There are many ways of transferring files between Windows clients. Often the easiest way is to share a directory on each client. Sometimes that's undesirable for security reasons or because of the client configuration it necessitates. Often it's easiest to transfer files as email attachments.

Sometimes the best choice is to make a central transfer directory to which any family member can copy files and recipients can read them.

If all family members need to read and write to the transfer directory, it's this simple:

```
[xfer]
path=/xfer
read only=no
```

This grants read-write access to all. Note also that this directory is not on the data tree (/d). Files in this directory are by definition in transit and should not be backed up.

It might be desirable to prevent some household members from writing to this directory. That's done by setting read only=no and write list=@xferw, where xferw is a group of people who can write to the transfer directory.

Small Business Trees

For a variety of reasons, it's usually best not to mix data from a small business with personal data. If, for example, Myra Johnson owns Johnson Moving, the following share would accommodate the situation:

```
[jm]
path=/d/jm
valid users=myra
read only=no
comment=Johnson Moving
```

If two members of the family run the business, group access can be provided as follows:

```
[jm]
path=/d/jm
valid users=@jm
force group=jm
read only=no
comment=Johnson Moving
```

Read-only user bobby can be added by rearranging the share:

```
[jm]
path=/d/jm
valid users=@jm,bobby
force group=jm
read only=yes
write list=@jm
comment=Johnson Moving
```

Program Sharing

Most programs that can be legally installed for multiple users on a network are fairly easy to install that way. Many programs do not tweak the Windows Registry or register DLL files but instead simply run when double-clicked. Those types of programs can be installed on the Samba server with a simple copy.

Other programs require some client installation to register DLL files, copy DLL files to the Windows directory, or tweak the Registry. Those take more work. See Chapter 28, "Using Samba to Install, Configure, and Host Windows Software." Also, see the Samba distribution text document `docs/textdocs/Application_Serving.txt`. These sources discuss which software lends itself to network installation, which software doesn't, and what parts of the software need local installation and how to perform that local installation.

Internet Sharing

The same Linux box that gives you file sharing can also share a single Internet phone line connection between all family members. It does this by routing requested packets to the proper client computer, using ipchains. This is not a Samba issue, but you can read more about it in the documentation that comes with your Linux distribution.

Wiring

Although not strictly a Samba issue, no home network can be created without wiring. Wiring methods and strategies depend on whether the residence is owned or rented, and whether the person doing the work knows enough about construction to run the wires in the correct way. Although slow and expensive, wireless networking sometimes works out the best.

Owners Versus Renters

Look at most rental leases, and you'll see that you're not allowed to modify the property. If you do modify it, you must leave the modifications after moving out and pay any costs associated with the owner's later removal of such modifications. Think very carefully before doing major wiring in a residence you rent.

If you decide to run wires from room to room, try for the least invasive method. Sometimes a Cat-5 wire attached to the wall with a couple of small tacks does the trick. This requires minimal patching upon removal.

By far the safest choice in a rental residence is going wireless. It's not fast, and it's not cheap, but there's absolutely no modification to the residence. What's more, when you move, your network moves with you.

Professional Versus Do-It-Yourself

There are many people quite capable of running Cat-5 wire through walls in a safe way that complies with all building codes. Other people have no idea how to do this and might risk creating a fire hazard or even structural damage.

Depending on your knowledge of construction, it might be best to hire an electrician. Be sure to ask the electrician what other wiring should be run through the same wire ways.

If you run wires on the floor, it's vitally important to securely tape them down and keep them away from foot traffic to prevent accidents.

The safest way to go is with a qualified professional or with a wireless setup.

Wireless

Wireless is not fast. One or two megabits per second precludes doing backups or large file transfers over the network. What's more, it's expensive—several hundred dollars per computer.

However, it's the safest and neatest, and if you move to a different house, it moves with you. Give strong consideration to wireless for your family's networking needs. Speed problems can be lessened by proper use of oplocks and other optimizations.

You can learn more about wireless networking at the Linux WLAN Project at `http://www.absoval.com/linux-wlan/index.html`.

Family-Wide Backups

There are typically only one or two people per family with sufficient administration knowledge to perform a backup. In many homes, the majority of work goes without backup for months or years, thus creating a problem after a disk crash or virus attack.

The Samba server provides an opportunity to store all data in a single place, making it available for quick backup. This goes a long way toward the goal of making the client computers more like appliances.

Easy and foolproof backups require the data to be in one or a small number of trees. One strategy is to place all the family's data in the `/d` tree, which can then have its own partition for further insulation from corruption and loss. Alternatively, each person's data can go below his or her home directory. There can be a hybrid system where personal data is stored below the home directory but business and project directory is stored below `/d`.

The /home Directory

All home directories are contained by the /home tree. To back up all home directories, issue this command:

```
# tar -czvf /dev/ftape /home
```

Test the new backup with the following command, done from the root directory:

```
# tar -dzvf /dev/ftape
```

If substantial data is kept in the /home tree, it might be a good idea to mount it to its own partition. Often that partition can be read after a disk crash.

The /d Directory

The easiest directory structure from a backup standpoint is to keep all user data in a tree starting with /d. Once again, this can be backed up easily, like the method described in the preceding section on the /home directory.

For the ideal in crash and corruption protection, mount the /d directory to a single partition on a totally separate hard disk. Such a disk can often be read even after a total system crash. Such a disk can also be physically transferred to a new computer after an upgrade.

Backup Hardware

The optimal backup hardware depends on how long the backup must be kept, the sophistication of the person doing the backup, and the amount of data required in the backup.

Latest Future Need

It's typically recommended that you keep all tax data for seven years, which precludes backing up to floppies because they do not have a seven-year shelf life. Some types of tapes would not be considered reliable after seven years.

CD-ROMs last much longer and should be used for important data that must be kept for years. The high-capacity, removable magnetic disk medium has not been out long enough to get a handle on its shelf life, but it's reasonable to assume this medium falls somewhere between tape and CD-ROM.

Always choose a backup medium with sufficient shelf life for the purpose at hand. The choice of media dictates the choice of backup hardware.

Tape

Tape is wonderful because it's cheap on a per-megabyte basis, and it's reusable. Unfortunately, tape is subject to corruption by magnetic fields and by physical stress involved in using the tape (oxide dropouts).

Tape is best used for noncrucial data that becomes unnecessary after a couple years. It's the preferred method for backing up entire systems.

Tape media vary extensively in reliability and shelf life. Typically commodity-priced tapes and tape drives are insufficient for crucial data, although some of the more expensive technologies are truly robust.

Most commodity-priced tape drives come with drivers and software for Windows but not Linux. Therefore, you can either look for Linux drivers or back up via a read-only Samba share.

CD-W

If your data compresses to less than 650MB, CR-W might be your best choice. Most commodity CR-W and CD-RW (rewrite) drives come with Windows software and Windows drivers, and these drives are fairly new, so backing up on a Windows machine is often easiest. Because much of this software requires you to back up files rather than trees, you may want to back up on the Linux box to a TGZ file and then record that TGZ on the CD.

Rewriteable CDs cost $7 to $10, with write-once CDs priced at a little over $1. A good backup policy might include daily incremental backups to floppy, weekly full backups to rewriteable CDs, and monthly full backups to write-once CDs. Write-once CDs are ubiquitous and should be readable for a long time to come.

Large Removable Disks

Removable disks come in sizes from 100MB to 2GB and more. They vary in reliability and standardization. Try to find a format that's likely to be available for several years. If a media format goes obsolete, your drive breaks, and no more drives are manufactured, all backups are lost.

The ideal large removable disk looks like just another device to the operating system. Driver software for several large removable disks are now available under Linux. This means backups can be done directly on the Linux machine via a shellscript. That's a timesaver, and it minimizes the likelihood of mistakes.

One problem with removable disks is that they're expensive enough to tempt the administrator into cannibalizing older backups. It's important to keep several backups from each year so that if a file silently disappears and its absence isn't noticed for months or years, it can still be retrieved.

Backup Timings

Backup timings depend on the maximum acceptable setback, the medium and its expense, whether or not the medium is rewriteable, and the time involved in backing up. The one constant here is that a backup policy must be made and adhered to.

Worst Acceptable Setback

A household that uses its computers to email friends and family might think nothing of losing two months' worth of data. On the other hand, a household running a thriving mail-order business would be seriously hurt losing three days' worth of data.

Backups should be done often enough that the worst acceptable setback is never reached. In most cases, daily backups are good enough. An incremental backup might take a couple of floppies and five minutes of time. That's a small inconvenience compared to losing more than a day's worth of data.

Occasionally a project is so hot that it calls for hourly backups. The writing of this book is one such example. In such a case, the individual doing the work typically takes responsibility for the hourly backups of the specific work being done. The administrator performs the daily backups.

Incremental Backups

Incremental backups are backups of only the files that have changed since the last backup. This means that a complete backup set comprises a full backup and all successive incremental backups.

Incremental backups have the advantage of being small and taking little time. However, the administrator must keep track of all incremental backups since the last full backup.

Backing Up from a Windows Client

Most commodity backup hardware and software works out of the box with Windows but requires significant work to use in Linux. Backing up from Linux is often worth the extra work, because the proprietary backup software may become obsolete, but it's doubtful tar is going away in the next decade or so.

However, sometimes there isn't time to get the backup hardware to work with Linux. In that case, go for the Windows-side backup. The first step is to create a read-only Samba share encompassing the tree to be backed up. Here's an example for the /d tree:

```
[dback]
path=/d
read only=yes
valid users=@admins
admin users=@admins
```

The admin users=@admins line is in there so that members of the group can back up all directories in the tree, whether or not they would normally have read access. Note that the read only=yes line prevents write access in spite of the admin users=@admins line. See Chapter 7, "Determining Samba Access," for details.

Occasionally there's a need to back up multiple directories. In such a case, a similar read-only directory can be made to the root:

```
[rootback]
follow symlinks=no
path=/
read only=yes
valid users=@admins
admin users=@admins
```

Note the follow symlinks=no line. This eliminates recursion caused by a symbolic link pointing to a directory higher in the tree.

Another method of backing up from Windows is to back up to a file on the Linux box and then use Samba to back up that one file. Such a scenario eliminates the need for a special backup share, because the backup file can be made to the user's home directory. Typically the backup file is a TGZ file.

Backing Up from the Samba Server

Backing up from the Samba server saves bandwidth and, assuming you have the hardware and software to do it, is generally more reliable. Some of the many methods are discussed in the next section, "Backup Software."

Backup Software

Backup software runs the gamut of software types, from proprietary to freeware to Open Source software. Some back up, some compress, and some do both. The tar, gzip, zip, and PKZIP backup programs are all excellent for home network backup. They can be used alone or in combination.

The LZW Software Patent

According to the gzip man page, the Linux "compress" method uses the LZW method of compression. This method is subject to a software patent. The safest course of action may be to avoid using the LZW method of compression in your backups.

The `gzip` man page states that `gzip` uses the LZ77 compression method and that it's more effective than LZW. The `-z` `tar` option uses `gzip` to compress, whereas the `-Z` option uses `compress`. Use the lowercase `-z`.

tar

The `tar` program is the most common backup procedure on Linux. It can back up entire trees into a single file or tape. Using the `-z` option, it can compress. The following command backs up the `/d` tree to tape:

```
# tar -czvf /dev/ftape /d
```

It can then be compare-verified with this command:

```
# tar -dzvf /dev/ftape /d
```

Keep in mind that `tar` normally strips off the leading forward slash, making the backup relative. That's a good thing, because it can be restored to a different directory.

Typically only a single file or a few files are restored. If you need to restore file `/d/myhome/username/abc.txt`, place the following line in a file (call it `x.x`):

```
d/myhome/username/abc.txt
```

The leading slash is removed because that's the way it is in the archive. To restore the file, go to an empty subdirectory and use the following command:

```
# tar -xzvT x.x -f /dev/ftape /d
```

The preceding command restores any files, path and all, relative to the current directory, if they're listed in the file named in the `-T` argument. Wildcards can be used in the file. For instance, here's a line from the `-T` argument file that restores all `.conf` files anywhere in the tree:

```
d*.conf
```

See Chapter 21, "Samba Backup Strategies," and the `tar` man page for further information.

dump

This is made primarily to back up and restore entire file systems, although it can also be used for directories. Restoring a single file is much more involved. The `dump` program has the advantage of sophisticated incremental levels, but `tar` is the more commonly used program. See Chapter 21 and the `dump` man page for further information.

pkzip

PKZIP is a proprietary program from PKWARE, Inc. that backs up to the ZIP format. It runs on Windows and other operating systems. There's a GUI version and a Windows command-line version that can be used in batch files for fine backup control.

The ZIP format is an industry standard that will be readable for years to come. Command-line pkzip is an excellent choice for creating a ZIP file destined for storage on a CD-ROM.

Several other Windows-based programs are available for reading and writing to ZIP files.

zip

Some Linux distributions come with programs called zip and unzip, which are the rough equivalent of the commercial PKZIP program. Their syntax can be seen by issuing the command without arguments. According to the license statement printed with the zip -L statement, these programs can be freely distributed but not modified or sold.

gzip

The gzip program is bundled with most Linux distributions and is used mainly with tar in the form of the -z tar option.

bzip2

This is a compression program using the Burrows-Wheeler block-sorting text-compression algorithm as well as Huffman coding. It compresses slightly better than gzip. To use it with tar, pipe the output of tar into bzip2 and then into a file.

Creating Your Own Shellscript Backup

The following is an example of a shellscript (call it dbup) that backs up tree /d to a file in the home directory, named after arg1, and then verifies that file. It must switch to the root directory for verification because the archive has relative filenames with the front slash stripped. Here's the shellscript:

```
#!/bin/sh
cd
tar -czf $1.tgz /d
cd /
tar -dzf $HOME/$1.tgz
```

The preceding would be invoked like this:

```
./dbup 20000211
```

Here's the same script, but this time it writes to a tape:

```
#!/bin/sh
cd
tar -czf /dev/ftape /d
cd /
tar -dzf /dev/ftape
```

Shellscripts enable the administrator to create sophisticated backups that can be run from a single command.

Backup Storage and Retention

Backups are only as reliable as their storage. No backup medium retains restorability when subjected to undue amounts of dust, liquids, or pollutants. Oxide media, especially tape, must be kept at a reasonable temperature. Magnetic media must always be kept away from magnetic fields, including speakers, televisions, computer monitors, refrigerator magnets, magnetized tools, and the like.

CDs must not be stored in such a way that they warp, and care must be taken not to get them dusty or full of fingerprints. CDs must be left in their cases when not in use.

Always store all backups high off the ground in case of flood—either the natural disaster kind or the kind caused by someone leaving the tub faucet running too long.

Retain backups according to your backup policy. Resist the temptation to cannibalize an older, needed backup to avoid buying more media. Retaining a few backups per year, going back several years, is the best way to recover a file that silently disappeared long ago. This can come in very handy in the case of a tax audit, for instance.

Backing Up the Clients

The `smbtar` utility can be used to back up shares on Windows clients. Chapter 21 contains some information on this, but there are some disadvantages. First, `smbtar` runs very slowly on certain setups. Second, once the administrator agrees to back up clients, he or she has taken on additional responsibility—responsibility for turning clients on and for maintaining the shares. Backups are much more likely to be done if all important data is on the server.

Administration

Administration of the home network involves upkeep of `smb.conf`, some troubleshooting, and backups. There's also wiring and upgrades. Administration of a home Samba network is simple.

Troubleshooting a Home Samba Network

Home Samba network troubleshooting is unusual in that there's less urgency, and there's often no administrator.

Less Urgency

Less urgency is always an advantage because it avoids the mistakes made in the name of haste. The fact that home Samba servers do not require high availability makes it practical to do tests involving the change of `smb.conf`, something that's difficult on large corporate LANs.

Absent Administrator

Counterbalancing the lack of urgency is the fact that the administrator is often absent. If 10-year-old Johnny cannot print his term paper because Samba is malfunctioning and his mother, the household technologist, is at work, his mother will find herself in the position of having to talk Johnny through a troubleshooting session over the phone. Johnny's access to his term paper is determined by the success of that troubleshooting session.

Hopefully, Johnny's mother has previously taken several steps to maximize the chances of a quick solution. The first is an automated diagnostic routine. The following example is a file called `smbtest.bat` that runs many of the Windows-side tests from `DIAGNOSIS.txt`:

```
echo Ping below... > test.log
ping 192.168.100.1 >> test.log
echo Net view below... >> test.log
net view \\mainserv >> test.log
echo Net use below... >> test.log
net use * \\mainserv\homes >> test.log
```

The following example is a file called `smbtest` that runs many of the UNIX-side tests from `DIAGNOSIS.txt`:

```
echo 'testparm -s | head -n20 - BELOW...' > test.log
testparm -s | head -n20 - >> test.log
echo 'PING BELOW...' >> test.log
ping -c3 192.168.100.201 >> test.log
echo 'ps ax | grep -i mbd BELOW...' >> test.log
ps ax | grep -i mbd >> test.log
echo 'smbclient -NL mainserv BELOW...' >> test.log
smbclient -NL mainserv >> test.log
echo 'nmblookup -B mainserv __SAMBA__ BELOW...' >> test.log
nmblookup -B mainserv __SAMBA__ >> test.log
echo "nmblookup -B desk1 '*' BELOW..." >> test.log
```

```
nmblookup -B desk1 '*' >> test.log
echo "nmblookup -d 2 '*' BELOW..." >> test.log
nmblookup -d 2 '*' >> test.log
echo 'smbclient //mainserv/homes -Uusername%user BELOW...' >> test.log
smbclient //mainserv/homes -Uusername%user >> test.log
```

Note that the user must type **q** followed by a carriage return to terminate the preceding script. The q terminates the smbclient session run on the final line of the script.

Good examples of log output should be kept on hand for comparison. Having such a diagnostic script maximizes the chances of an adult successfully walking a child through a repair.

Additionally, checklists should be created and kept handy.

Fringe Benefits

Linux has training benefits outside its file-serving benefits. It offers the family technologist UNIX training, which can translate into serious career enhancements. Good UNIX administrators are in demand and are paid well. In addition, the family technologist learns a great deal about networking, including Windows networking.

For the family technologist who really becomes interested in Samba, there's source code to study and programs to write. Those who love programming and are good at it have great careers ahead of them.

It's also great training for the kids. It's never too early to become a technologist. The child learning Samba administration at age 12 and Samba C programming at age 14 is in a position to do quite well in his or her computer courses.

All this training happens in the home, with no pressure and no expense except the network wiring and hubs and one Samba server.

Summary

Samba gives the entire family access to a set of files and printers, thus eliminating the need for them to use each others' computers or run from one computer to the other with a floppy. All that's needed is an old computer to be used as a server, some wiring, and a Linux install CD.

One problem Linux solves is access to the family's one and only printer. By plugging the printer into the Samba server's LPT port, defining it as a byte passthrough print queue, and then exposing it with the [printers] share, you make it available to all. If you want to have that printer accessible only to some, don't use [printers] but instead make a print share with a valid users= for the desired users. Additional printers can be hung off other LPT ports of the server or off Windows boxes and accessed through Windows peer networking.

Because the Samba printers are bytewise passthrough printers, each client must have a printer driver for each Samba printer. That task can be eased slightly with automated printer driver installation, as discussed in Chapter 8.

Some files are shared, whereas others are available only to one family member. Both have the advantage of a single source for family backups. For that reason, put as many of your family's files as possible in a single tree. This book uses /d because it's short (d stands for *data*).

If there's a [homes] directory, it must point to a subdirectory of the family member's Linux home directory to prevent accidental deletion of dot files. Server-side automation makes sure the directory is created.

Perhaps a better choice is to make a [myhome] share with path=/d/myhome/%U. Server-side automation makes sure the directory is created.

Sounds, such as MP3 and WAV files, can go in their own read-only share to be accessed by all. The same goes for the family photo album, video files, and the like. Administration can be done by a person or group identified in write list=.

Any small businesses can have their own trees, once again in the data tree. They can have one valid user or multiple valid users with a force group= parameter to allow collaboration on files.

Program sharing and a file transfer directory can also be implemented in Samba. It's important not to violate license agreements in such program sharing. Many times Open Source equivalents are available. Open Source software has no limitation on how many users can access it from a server.

Wiring methods depend on the construction skills of the family and whether the residence is owned or rented. Sometimes it's best to have an electrician do the between-rooms wiring. Other times it's best to use a wireless LAN, which, although slow and expensive, eliminates the possibility of construction damage.

Backup is best done on the server, where tar and dump are available and can be used with the gzip compression utility. If the hardware does not work with Linux, a Samba read-only share can be created to expose the data tree(s) to Windows clients. The share should be read-only and tightly restricted with valid users=. Also, the valid user or group must be included in admin users= to enable reading of all files in the tree. Additionally, use follow symlinks=no to prevent following recursive directories.

Administering Samba in the home has the fringe benefit of giving all users hands-on networking experience. It also makes the source code available for any family members wishing to peruse it. It's never too soon for children to learn about technology.

Samba's Future

by Steve Litt

A look at the SAMBA_TNG branch source code reveals PDC code as well as code supporting BDC, LDAP, ACL, and Kerberos. Samba supports Windows 2000 and tracks Windows 2000's changes step for step. With Samba changing dramatically every couple months, it makes little sense to enumerate upcoming features.

It's more relevant—and more difficult—to discuss where Samba is going as a network enabler. Will Samba take NT market share, or vice versa? Will Samba continue to track Windows 2000 changes? What if anti–reverse engineering legislation passes?

Also, will Samba be accepted in the enterprise? Will it unseat NT as the file server and domain mechanism of choice? What will become of Samba if Windows loses control of the desktop? And, of course, the bottom line: Is Samba a good bet for my career and my company?

This chapter discusses ways that you can look into Samba's future, now or any time in the future.

Samba's Past

Future predictions require an extrapolation of the trend between the past and the present, extending out into the future. This information comes primarily from the `history` file in the Samba distribution's `docs` directory.

Samba is a child of the 1990s. It was neither conceived nor realized when Windows 3.0 took the desktop by storm in 1990. Windows had been in development, by a huge corporation, for several years before that. Contrast this with Samba's history.

In December 1991, Andrew Tridgell wrote and published some programs to enable a DEC program called eXcursion to interoperate with Sun servers, with DOS as a front end. After a couple years of semihibernation, the "NetBIOS for UNIX" project was announced December 1, 1993. The product itself was renamed "Samba" in 1994. Making steady progress during the next few years, Samba was ready for prime time in 1998, when Linux took the world by storm. By 1999, many considered Samba the file server of choice.

The bottom line is that in eight years, Samba went from a part-time hobby project of one Ph.D. student to a "best of breed" file server with a development core "staff" of about 20, many more contributors, and a huge installed base. Samba was the Linux file server of choice in the highly publicized Linux/NT benchmark test in early 1999. Samba is progressing with incredible speed. This trend can be expected to extend into the future.

Samba's Future

Samba moves fast. Blink your eyes and another version has come and gone. No matter when you're reading this, you can predict Samba's future with the aid of several tools:

- Leading CVS branch source code
- `cvs.log`
- Man pages
- `testparm`
- Mailing lists (especially `samba-technical@samba.org`)

> **Note**
>
> The *leading CVS branch* refers to the branch undergoing the most advanced development. The leading branch frequently undergoes name changes. It was previously called "the head branch," but that title now belongs to the branch that will become the next stable version. Currently, the leading branch is the SAMBA_TNG branch, but branch naming is likely to continue changing as Samba develops.
>
> There's an excellent description of the various Samba branches in this book's Appendix C, "Samba Code Branches."

The leading branch source code is a wishing well of information. Using the source code browsing tools described in Chapter 23, "Samba Learning Tools," look for keywords in the source. These browsing tools are basically a customized `egrep`. For example, searching early–December 1999 2.1 code for the word *kerberos* yields hits in a comment and in a `DEBUG()` call in `libsmb/clientgen.c`, as well as two comments in `passdb/pass_check.c`. Looking at those files reveals references to `krb5_auth()` and `krb4_auth()`. Searching on regular expression `krb._` reveals a wealth of functions in `passdb/pass_check.c`. Currently, searching on the word *cluster* reveals nothing. However, it's likely this won't long be true.

Features don't spring forth fully grown in a single version. Instead, they're added in the course of time. This means it's likely you can see evidence of features to come in the stable version's `cvs.log`. Specific keywords can be searched or the document can be read starting from a certain date. The former is quicker, but the latter gives a real feel for Samba's progress as well as the rationale for decisions made.

Using the `smb.conf` man page is much the same as `cvs.log`. The easiest way is to look at it is in a Web browser. (See Chapter 23 for a CGI script for viewing a man page in a

Web browser.) Look for a keyword or read the entire man page (this should be done every once in a while). Alternatively, search for the word *experimental*. Because the documentation is typically the last item updated in a new version, it's likely the most up-to-date man page is the one for the stable version.

The `testparm` program is another aid. If you're set up for easy switches between the stable version and the (compiled and running) leading branch, run `testparm` against an empty configuration file on each system, run `diff`, and then look for parameters in the leading branch that are missing from the stable version. Features often make their first appearance as added parameters.

The other way of predicting the future is to ask someone. Get on `samba@samba.org` and ask, "When will so and so be supported?" Often, this brings results, although sometimes it doesn't. If it's a new, geeky feature you're interested in, the question is often best asked on `samba-technical@samba.org`.

Clustered Samba

A message from Jeremy Allison dated December 7, 1999 on the Samba mailing list mentioned that Jeremy had been meeting with someone from the "Linux Cluster Cabal" to make a Linux cluster-optimized version of Samba. This changes everything!

In a highly publicized early-1999 benchmark comparing the performance of Windows NT Server against Samba on Linux, NT beat Linux by a factor of 2.5. This was not surprising because the test was run on a quad-processor machine. Linux is not optimized for multiple processors.

However, Linux is *very* good at clustering. A cluster-optimized Samba (`smbd`, `nmbd`, and whatever other daemons exist by then) would enable big-iron performance at near-commodity prices.

Better still, this solution would be completely scalable. Since the dawn of computers, organizations have outgrown their computer systems, only to find that their upgraded computers could not run their software. A cluster optimized Samba could run on one Linux box or a hundred. A cluster upgrade is as simple as adding machines.

A cluster optimized Samba would go a long way toward taming the obsolescence dragon, at least for file serving. Every year a certain number of new boxes could be added, and 5-year-old boxes could be retired. This limits the "leapfrogging" that typically accompanies discrete upgrades.

Every technology needs a "killer app." Personal computers were a hobby until the invention of the spreadsheet, after which they were indispensable. A cluster-efficient Samba is the killer app for both Linux and Linux clusters. Clusters will no longer be restricted to the realm of weather prediction and film special effects. They'll be a valuable addition to organizations wanting an economical, solid, scalable, and obsolescence-proof file server.

As this chapter is being written, cluster-efficient Samba is an uncoded, unrealized idea. However, given the speed of Samba development, you never know how quickly this idea can become a reality.

More Daemons

As the century begins, the SAMBA_TNG branch consists of many more daemons than the traditional smbd and nmbd. Discussions on samba-technical@samba.org often center around new daemons, how many there should be, how they should be spawned, what functions they should perform, and how they should be modularized. Such activities on the technical list are an example of the design advantages of the Open Source development model. Literally thousands of eyes are going over the initial design and code.

As Samba gains more functionality, it's likely to gain more daemons. What's more, it's likely that those daemons will closely and modularly model specific types of networking functionality.

MSRPC

In late 1999, code was written and modified so that Samba could interoperate with MSRPC (Microsoft Remote Procedure Call) calls. Much of this code is now working reliably in the SAMBA_TNG branch. It's reasonable to expect a much tighter integration with MSRPC in the near future. You can read much more about MSRPC—and RPC over SMB in general—in the book *DCE/RPC over SMB: Samba and Windows NT Domain Internals*, by Luke Leighton (Macmillan Technical Publishing).

The Next Major Stable Release

As of this writing, the next *major* stable release will be Samba 3.0, which will incorporate many of the improvements of the former 2.1 and possibly of the present SAMBA_TNG in a stable version. It's not known to what level Samba 3.0 will incorporate SAMBA_TNG improvements. The new Samba 3.0 will also include all the minor stable release (2.0.*x*) improvements made since the 2.0/2.1 split. The anticipated release date of Samba 3.0 is not known as of this writing.

The Decline of Windows

Perhaps the greatest threat to Samba is the demise of Windows. In the absence of a Windows desktop, there's little reason for an SMB/CIFS technology. Although such a possibility looks remote in the year 2000, nothing lasts forever, including Windows. Like all other technologies, its work will someday be done.

Several Samba possibilities exist at that point. It would be possible for the existing Samba team to rip out the CIFS protocol, replacing it with something better. Another possibility is that the Samba team might decide its work is done and move on.

That's where the GPL license steps in. Anyone can use any Samba code to make any other GPL license software. This means that another group could step in and replace the CIFS protocol. It could also mean that several different developers could build on several different Samba code sections. Look at the Samba source code: There's gold in there.

Samba has a clean methodology for loading, storing, and retrieving parameters from a single file while incorporating intelligent defaults. That's valuable anywhere. Samba's permission model makes user and group sharing of directories very easy—and that's independent of the SMB/CIFS protocol. The list goes on.

Although it's difficult to determine what would happen to Samba in a world sans Windows, this is not really an issue at the time of this writing.

Keeping Your Samba Knowledge Up-to-Date

In an era of ever faster change, rapid time to market and adaptability to change increasingly determine success for products and for people. Samba's Open Source development model has enabled it to move from a handy utility to Windows' primary competition (some say Windows' Waterloo) in a few years. Samba's development branch (SAMBA_TNG at this writing) adds several important features monthly. There is every reason to believe this trend of increasingly quick improvement will continue indefinitely, even if Samba replaces Windows as the top "selling" server product.

Samba's incredibly quick progress creates unique opportunities and challenges for its administrators. No longer can books be relied upon for leading-edge Samba information—you'd need to purchase new Samba books monthly.

The rate of progress even challenges "live" publishing such as HTML and PDF files. Even if there were a piece of documentation that managed to stay current with Samba, it wouldn't help. Not only is Samba's rapid change a challenge to the documentor, but also to the reader. Today's network administrator must employ new methods of accelerated learning in order to keep up. Chapter 23 presents and details the use of many of those accelerated learning techniques. Proficient use of the techniques in Chapter 23 is absolutely vital for continued Samba mastery.

Chapter 22, "Troubleshooting Samba," is also a vital resource for future Samba administration. As time to market decreases (for all software, not just Samba), third party support organizations find themselves increasingly undertrained. Additionally, the continuing flow of new software limits the usefulness of known "fixes." Chapter 22 contains timeless information useful in Samba troubleshooting, and in system-independent troubleshooting. Further system-independent troubleshooting information can be found at the Troubleshooters.Com Web site at `http://www.troubleshooters.com/tuni.htm`.

Beyond what's been mentioned, the best method of keeping current is to read and participate in the various Samba.Org mailing lists. Using the learning techniques in this book, combined with brand new information on the mailing lists, yields a constant state of leading edge Samba knowledge.

Last but not least, view the *Samba Unleashed* Web site once a week. The *Samba Unleashed* Web site, at `http://www.mcp.com/info/0-672/0-672-31862-8/`, contains updates to this book and new Samba information.

Tomorrow's technologist must invent new learning methods to stay current with technology. Because Samba is GNU GPL licensed software, with all the benefits of the Open Source support model, the Samba technologist has a distinct advantage over those technologists supporting proprietary software.

Summary

Samba's mindshare grows monthly. The authors and publisher of this book bet part of their future on the success of Samba. They're confident it's an excellent career move. The multitudes of Samba list members likewise are basing part of their careers on the success of Samba. Samba shows a real potential to become the file server market leader.

Samba's GNU GPL license is the epitome of Open Source licensing. The Open Source development model enables Samba's source code to be "walked through" by thousands of individuals with different agendas and platforms. Bugs are solved quickly. If the Samba team doesn't solve the bug, an individual user invariably will.

The GNU GPL license also enhances an organization's support options. Although phone support can be comforting, a Samba administrator can use mailing lists, source code, and Web searches to get answers to the thorniest problems more quickly than administrators who use proprietary software and are restricted to phone support. What's more, traditional Open Source support channels are not the only ones available. For those organizations insisting on phone support, there are many help desk organizations with Samba knowledge.

Much of Samba's present and future success is due to the universal availability of source code. Few organizations want to use the source code to enhance Samba, and that's not its purpose. In the future, the source will serve as a sort of escrow. It's the bug fixer of last resort. It, combined with the GNU GPL license, is a guarantee that the product will always be freely available. The availability of source code enables use of accelerated learning techniques such as those discussed in Chapter 23.

Samba's future is not without challenges. Windows calls and features must continue to be tracked closely. The Samba team must continually guard against real as well as perceived bugs (even if these bugs are really in a different product), because bugs result in downtime in the enterprise. The stable release of Samba must continue to be a highly reliable product.

Samba already tightly integrates the Windows and UNIX environments, including several methods of UNIX server-side automation. Recent leading branch work on RPC promises even tighter integration to come.

Discussions have begun on how best to make Samba a cluster app. This greatly reduces the objection that a Linux-hosted Samba server doesn't use multiple processors well. A cluster-enabled Samba yields a highly scalable, obsolescence-resistant file server with the traditional reliability of Samba.

In ever-increasing numbers, the world's businesses and technologists are including Samba as a core component in their IT toolset. Samba's future is bright indeed.

Appendixes

PART VI

Samba on Solaris

by Bryan J. Smith

APPENDIX A

IN THIS APPENDIX

Solaris as a Samba Server Platform

This section is designed to provide some background information on Solaris versus both commercial and Open Source UNIX systems. It will aid you in evaluating and deciding whether to use Solaris as a Samba server platform.

An Open Standards, Commercial UNIX

Sun's software products are not fully Open Source. However, when it comes to open standards and support for Open Source software, Sun's software products are almost as ideal as commercial products can be (including recent but limited source code availability). This fact holds true in Sun's operating systems, including its System-V Solaris 2, which includes GNU-ready headers and libraries.

> **Note**
>
> Due to the recent popularity of the GNU/Linux UNIX-like operating system, most other commercial vendors have also pledged full support for open interfaces and other open standards such as GNU cross-compiler (GCC).

Performance

Solaris is not only an efficient workgroup server platform for Samba but is one of the few platforms that brings Windows files and printer services to the enterprise level.

Workgroup Server

Recent studies of workgroup servers give the top Samba performance rankings to SGI's MIPS/Irix platform, with Sun's SPARC/Solaris and IBM's Power/AIX platforms as close seconds. All three perform better than native Windows NT 4.0 servers, even when equivalent costing, but more commodity Intel hardware is used. Unfortunately, Samba is only available for the Irix platform as a binary (a result of Irix not being GCC-ready).

> **Two-Way RISC-UNIX, Four-Way Wintel**
>
> Most two-way RISC systems cost as much as four-way Intel systems. So even when factoring cost in, many RISC UNIX platforms offer higher Windows file server performance than the native "Wintel" platform.

Enterprise and Scalability

From a scalability standpoint, the open standard, GNU-ready nature of Solaris and SPARC hardware, combined with an advanced, multithreaded kernel (briefly discussed later) allows Samba to run and scale well beyond four processors in such systems as Sun's Ultra Enterprise series and even in third-party SPARC systems from licensees (for example, Fujitsu/HAL). This makes it a more ideal choice for high-end servers than completely Open Source operating systems such as FreeBSD and Linux on Intel hardware with more than four processors. Six, eight, and even higher numbers of processors in Solaris shared memory systems are capable of serving out SMB packets that total in the tens of gigabytes per second (GBps).

With such throughput rates, the SMB server bottleneck quickly shifts from the system architecture to the network architecture. So, in addition to the costs of an enterprise-class server, the costs associated with an enterprise-class network infrastructure must not be ignored. Otherwise, most of the additional power offered by a powerful Solaris enterprise server will not be wielded efficiently without a backbone powerful enough for it to serve.

> **Tip**
>
> You should look at servers such as the Ultra Enterprise 10000 to manage your WAN backbone, but it's overkill for a typical fast Ethernet LAN. Look to workgroup server-class systems such as the UE250/450 series, SPARC clones based on AXi and Axmp, or even more commodity Intel-based platforms to serve workgroups at LAN wire speeds.

A

SAMBA ON
SOLARIS

Solaris Versus Open Source

It soon becomes obvious that an Intel-based Open Source UNIX solution may be a more cost-effective Samba platform. However, before committing to such a viewpoint, there are three major considerations that often make Solaris a preferred solution over Open Source operating systems (even for just commodity, workgroup-level performance):

- *Application support*. Solaris supports many enterprise and engineering applications that have yet to be ported to Linux. In the case of engineering, workstations and Solaris computing farms can easily work as a Windows fileserver for an engineering project/team.

- *Native NIS/NFS support*. Solaris supports the latest version of NIS/NFS. If your LAN (or WAN) is littered with UNIX and NIS/NFS, Solaris is the optimal choice to drive both Samba and NIS/NFS on your servers.

- *A scalable, reentrant kernel.* Solaris provides for a scalable operation system, beyond four processors, to enterprise-class servers. For workgroup servers, the Solaris kernel has experienced almost a decade of maturity, resulting in one of the best-performing Samba servers for workgroups (as discussed earlier).

Linux 2.4: NFS and Scalability

The forthcoming Linux 2.4 kernel will feature newer NIS/NFS version support and a more scalable kernel. Regardless, questions and debates will probably still arise regarding its NIS/NFS maturity and its scalability beyond four processors.

Quick Platform Review

This section is not designed as a detailed discussion of the development of Solaris (including SunOS) and its supported platforms. Instead, it's simply a quick platform review that provides minimum version and hardware recommendations for Samba server platforms.

Tip

For more information on the Solaris operating system, see the Solaris 2 FAQ listed in the "Additional Listings and Resources" section later in this appendix.

This section also provides quick insights into recycling older SPARC hardware by using it as a Samba server. IT management should consider using older SPARC systems (for example, sun4, sun4c, sun4m) in a Windows services role via Samba, even if newer SPARC and/or Wintel servers are available.

Tip

Temporarily offloading even the smallest loads onto these older systems can offer greatly improved server performance and lower network contention on the single, more powerful server.

Operating Systems

This appendix focuses heavily on the newer Solaris 2 product. This does not mean that SunOS 4.1 is not covered, but the majority of the appendix takes a Solaris 2 focus, including the upcoming "Quickstart Installation" section.

Solaris 1 (SunOS 4.1)

The popular, historically BSD-based SunOS 4.1 is often, and quite retroactively, labeled *Solaris 1*. Despite their age, being superceded by Solaris 2, and recent discontinuation of production and sales by Sun, SunOS 4.1 systems are still widely used and function as basic Samba servers.

The latest and final release of SunOS 4.1 is 4.1.4. If at all possible (which might be difficult due to hardware-support issues), you should upgrade to version 4.1.4 or to Solaris 2 if the hardware is able to run it sufficiently. Given the fact that Sun no longer sells SunOS upgrades and that the great majority of the installed base of older SPARC hardware is running SunOS 4.1.3, 4.1.3 is also quite an acceptable and accommodating Samba server platform. Of course, you'll want to be sure to apply the latest 4.1.3 patches and updates to fix numerous problems, including date-related bugs (for example, Y2K). Hardware not capable of running at least version 4.1.3 is not ideal for Samba.

> **Note**
>
> That's not to say that pre-4.1.3 systems will not run Samba—many will. However, focus on and support for these older systems will not be on par with more recent SunOS 4.1 and Solaris 2 platforms.

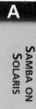

A

SAMBA ON SOLARIS

Solaris 2 (SunOS 5)

The latest release of the System-V–based Solaris is 2.7, which has been marketed as simply *version 7* with the leading "2" dropped (a first with 2.7). If at all possible, an upgrade to Solaris 7 is optimal for Samba services. This might not be possible given some known application incompatibilities and/or lack of official application vendor support for version 7. Solaris 2.6 is quite an acceptable alternative, with the appropriate Y2K and other bug fixes. At the bare minimum, Solaris version 2.5.1 is a stable platform, but it should be updated with the latest patches as well. Versions prior to 2.5.1 should be upgraded to version 2.5.1 or greater, including 2.5 (an original release which varies greatly from 2.5.1). The absolute minimum physical memory consideration for Solaris 2.5.1 and later should be 64MB.

Solaris 8 on the Horizon

At the time of this writing, Solaris 8 is just about to be released.

Caution

It's generally accepted that Solaris 2.5[.0] and earlier do not offer a mature Solaris 2 system. Solaris 2.3 and earlier are riddled with bugs and use what could almost be considered "experimental" kernel releases. 2.5.1 and later implement and utilize both efficient and stable versions of the Solaris 2 kernel design.

Hardware

Other than the operating system recommendations in the preceding section, the only hardware concern is physical memory. For optimal performance, your system should have 0.5MB of physical RAM per SMB client connection. This is in addition to other memory used by the operating system, other daemons, and the applications themselves.

Caution

Solaris 2.5.1+ systems that will function as Samba servers should have a minimum of 96MB of RAM. Consider even more RAM if the same servers function with other network services or with running applications.

SPARC

Of course, actual hardware performance, such as processor(s) and the bus architecture, is also a concern. Even the entry-level UltraSPARC (sun4u) can handle serving a large workgroup. Older MicroSPARC (sun4m) systems are potent Samba servers, especially if accompanied by a large amount of memory (which they usually are). Older SPARC hardware still can be used, but the number of clients and performance will be limited.

Caution

Be aware that 10 million instructions per second (or MIPS, a common rating among processors of the same architecture) should be considered the absolute bare minimum hardware for decent small workgroup Samba performance, and 50 MIPS should be considered the rudimentary starting performance for workgroup services.

Table A.1 provides a basic guide to recycling these older systems for Windows services.

TABLE A.1   Capabilities and Recommendations for Older SPARC Hardware

Platform	Performance / Max Memory	Last Supported OS Version	Samba Recommendation
sun3	10 MIPS, up to 128MB RAM	SunOS 4.1.1, no Solaris 2	Not Recommended (with any OS)
sun4	10 MIPS, 32-128MB RAM	SunOS 4.1.4, Solaris 2.4	<10 Users, NetBSD/Linux instead of Solaris 2
sun4c	30 MIPS, 64MB RAM	SunOS 4.1.4, Current Solaris	Small Workgroups, NetBSD/Linux instead of Solaris 2
sun4m	30-200+ MIPS, 64-640MB RAM	SunOS 4.1.4, Solaris current	Moderate Workgroups, Solaris current (128MB+)
sun4d	Up to 2,000 MIPS, 2GB+ RAM	Solaris current	Large Workgroups

Intel *x86*

For the Solaris 2 operating system, the minimum hardware requirements should be a fast 486 or entry-level Pentium and 96MB of RAM.

Software Requirements and Recommendations

To compile and make Samba on Solaris, you will need several GNU software packages:

- GNU Zip (`gzip`) to uncompress the packages and the Samba source itself
- GNU C Compiler (`gcc`) to compile the Samba source
- GNU Standard C++ Libraries (`libstdc++`) to support GCC compile programs
- GNU Make (`make`) to manage and build the Samba package

All four packages should be available in binary form for both Solaris 1 and 2. Only experienced developers extremely well versed in the design and complications of building GCC from scratch should even attempt to compile GCC from source. Attempting to compile GCC from source will only increase the time it takes to complete your Samba implementation by at least a factor of 10.

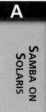

A

SAMBA ON SOLARIS

> **Tip**
>
> For Solaris 1, several SunSITE archives cater to maintaining GNU packages for older versions of Solaris (see the section "Additional Listings and Resources"). For Solaris 2, Sun also subsidizes Sunfreeware.com with ready-to-install binary packages of GNU software.

It's not recommended that you use the UCB development tools included with Solaris 1 to compile Samba. It's also not recommended that you use the premium Workshop C compilers available from Sun to compile Samba under Solaris 1 or 2.

Quickstart Installation

This quickstart is written for the purpose of getting Samba up and running on Solaris 2 systems with minimal effort and reading. It assumes the following:

- If the GNU software listed in the preceding section has not already been installed, it has been downloaded from Sunfreeware.
- Samba has been downloaded.
- Both Samba and the GNU software are to be installed into /usr/local/bin.

For the duration of the quickstart, replace /tmp/download with the path in which the downloaded packages can be found. Also replace *ver* with the version downloaded, *solver* with the Solaris prefix and version, and *arch* with the architecture, as downloaded for your appropriate version of Solaris and architecture from Sunfreeware. For example, replace

pkgadd -v -d gcc-*ver*-*solver*-*arch*-local

with the following for version 2.8.1, Solaris 2.6 and SPARC for GCC:

pkgadd -v -d gcc-2.8.1-sol26-sparc-local

> **Caution**
>
> The GCC 2.8 series is the final traditional release of GCC 2. All 2.9 series releases should be considered "betas" from a GCC 2–compatibility standpoint and are not recommended for use with Samba 2.0 on Solaris 2 at the time of this writing.

> ### The Future of GCC, Version 3
>
> GCC 2.9 series releases are based on Cygnus's egcs compiler, which will be the new design for GCC 3, with Cygnus as its maintainer. The latest version, 2.95.2, is already being used in Linux 2.4 kernel development as well as in new Linux distributions (for example, Linux Mandrake 7.0 and RedHat 6.2).

Installing GNU Support Packages

Skip to the next section on "Installing Samba" if the GNU software has already been installed and set up. Otherwise, continue by running the following commands as root:

```
cd /tmp/download
pkgadd -v -d gzip-ver-solver-arch-local
/usr/local/bin/gzip -d gcc-ver-solver-arch-local.gz
/usr/local/bin/gzip -d libstdc++-ver-solver-arch-local.gz
/usr/local/bin/gzip -d make-ver-solver-arch-local.gz
pkgadd -v -d gcc-ver-solver-arch-local
pkgadd -v -d libstdc++-ver-solver-arch-local
pkgadd -v -d make-ver-solver-arch-local
```

Assuming this is the first-ever set of utilities added to /usr/local, you'll probably need to add /usr/local/bin to your path for the remaining Samba installation procedures to execute correctly, like this:

```
PATH=/usr/local/bin:$PATH
```

Installing Samba

The following installation procedure will cover the majority of Solaris 2 implementations. After the following procedures are completed, the configuration information contained in this book can be further supplemented by additional smb.conf options for Solaris and other Solaris configuration options in the following sections.

Installing and Building Samba

The following will install Samba in /usr/local/src/samba-ver and will install binaries and support files in /usr/local/samba:

```
mkdir /usr/local/src
cd /usr/local/src
/usr/local/bin/gzip -cf /tmp/download/samba-ver.tar.gz | tar xvf -
cd samba-ver/source
./configure -mandir=/usr/share/man
make
make install
```

A

> **Note**
>
> If you've installed many packages into /usr/local and modified your shell environment (for example, MANPATH=/usr/local/man:...) to accommodate them already, you might want to consider using /usr/local/man as the target directory for the installation of Samba man pages. Just modify the mandir option in the ./configure line.

Enabling SWAT

The following will configure the Internet daemon for the Samba Web Administration Tool (SWAT). This procedure kills the currently running inet daemon, installs the line for SWAT in the services and inetd configuration files, and restarts the daemon:

> **Caution**
>
> Because SWAT sends and receives passwords in clear text, it should not be used on publicly accessible systems. Traditional means, such as manual text editing of the smb.conf file, should be used instead.

```
kill -9 `/usr/bin/ps -e | /usr/bin/grep inetd \
         | /usr/bin/sed -e 's/^ *//' -e 's/ .*//'`
chmod 644 /etc/inet/inetd.conf /etc/inet/services
echo "swat  stream  tcp  nowait.400  root \
         /usr/local/samba/bin/swat  swat" >> /etc/inet/inetd.conf
echo "swat  901/tcp" >> /etc/inet/services
/usr/sbin/inetd -s
```

Configuring and Starting Samba

At this time, fire up your favorite Web browser on any local system that this server is accessible to and point its URL to

```
http://sambaserver:901
```

If you haven't read this book's chapters on configuring Samba, do so before starting Samba with the following commands. At a bare minimum, you should continue on to the following sections that discuss some of the smb.conf options available in or recommended for Solaris. However, they will only cover a portion of the basic options that should be set up before Samba is run for the first time, especially if you have a Windows NT Server machine on the same subnet.

To start Samba 2.0 as a daemon that's always running, execute the following commands:

```
/usr/local/samba/bin/smbd -D
/usr/local/samba/bin/nmbd -D
```

A script listing that automates this at startup, as well as at shutdown, can be found at the end of this appendix.

Additional Configuration Options

The following sections cover those smb.conf options that are of particular significance to Solaris and deserve further exploration.

Locking Options

File locking is an integral part of any shared file system service. Locking is often a trade-off between performance and file access/integrity. The balance between the two is quickly (and quite excessively) complicated by the introduction and use of NFS services on the same server.

Samba uses the standard locking mechanisms of the underlying UNIX platform (for example, lockd). The default locking options set in Samba for your particular platform should in no way jeopardize file integrity. Only locking and performance options overridden in the smb.conf file will have any chance of reducing file system integrity. These are performance options you'll have to be familiar with.

Caution

Some NFS clients, primarily those designed to serve Windows clients, require the use a proprietary authentication/locking daemon. This can conflict with Samba and cause simple issues, such as improper file locking, as well as more complex issues that can corrupt data. Sun's pcnfsd (as well as Intergraph's AccessNFS and Microsoft's NT Services for UNIX, which are based on PC-NFS) is a properly behaving NFS locking daemon for Windows clients. Use of Beam & Whiteside's bwnfsd (as well as early versions of Hummingbird's products based on B&W NFS) should generally be avoided in Samba networks.

Tip

If Samba is going to be used for Windows file services, Windows clients should not also be using any NFS client software at the same time. Your life as a system administrator will be drastically less complex if you choose either 100% SMB (Samba server) or 100% NFS (NFS client) for your Windows (and non-UNIX) clients on a given subnet.

Without NFS Clients

Strict locking imposes a stiff performance penalty in order to preserve proper simultaneous local and SMB access. It's largely a client maturity issue, as discussed in the preceding chapters. If the majority of Windows clients are running recent versions, especially Windows NT, disabling strict file locking should improve performance without jeopardizing file integrity. Non-NFS, SMB-only servers should use the following:

```
Strict Locking = No   # Fairly Safe on SMB-only servers
```

Opportunistic locks (oplocks) offer increased performance to shared file access (for example, databases and executables). They're more an issue of the underlying operating system. Solaris 2 supports kernel oplocks. This allows for the safe use of oplocks while preserving local access to the same files. Take advantage of Solaris 2's oplock support with:

```
Kernel Oplocks = Yes  # Solaris 2 kernel supports oplocks
Oplocks = Yes         # Safe for all implementations
```

Solaris 1 does not offer this feature, so its use will depend on whether the server is also being used to host local applications or other services that access the same files. For Solaris 1, disable oplocks with the following:

```
Kernel Oplocks = No   # Solaris 1 kernel does not support
Oplocks = No          # May try YES on SMB-only servers
```

Level 2 oplocks offer additional executable performance for Windows NT clients. Level 2 oplocks, however, are currently not supported on systems that support kernel oplocks. Solaris 2 does not support level 2 oplocks alongside kernel oplocks:

```
Level2 Oplocks = No   # No effect on Solaris 2
```

Caution

It's not recommended that an advanced feature such as kernel oplocks be disabled to enable level 2 oplocks for the small performance gain that it offers. You should always take advantage of Solaris 2's kernel-based oplocks capability.

With NFS Clients

If a Solaris 1 server doubles as an NFS server, or even as an application server, strict file locking should be implemented under Samba. Strict locking is the only way to go with Solaris 1 and NFS:

```
Strict Locking = Yes  # highly recommended for Solaris 1
```

For Solaris 2, if the majority of clients are running more recent versions of Windows 9*x*, or especially Windows NT, then strict file locking can usually be left disabled. Strict locking in Solaris 2 depends on the client base:

```
Strict Locking = No     # Sol 2 with mature 9x/NT clients

Strict Locking = Yes    # Sol 2 with various Win clients
```

The settings for oplocks should not change with the addition of NFS services. Solaris 2 will handle proper oplock interaction between local, NFS, and SMB connections.

> **Note**
>
> Kernel support for oplocks gives Solaris a distinct advantage over Linux and BSD, especially for Samba servers that double as NFS servers or even as applications servers—at least until equivalent support is offered by their respective kernels (which is under development).

Socket Options

Socket options are fairly operating system–specific. They're also important options pertaining to performance.

Solaris 1

The older Solaris 1 OS offers little in the way of socket options for use by Samba. In particular, usage of the `TCP_NODELAY` option is not recommended. It can cause both data corruption and performance issues. Use the following on Solaris 1 Samba servers:

```
Socket Options =
```

Solaris 2

Solaris 2.5.1 and above support all the common socket options as well as many additional, less commonly available options.

Servers that mainly serve their local subnet clients should also minimize TCP services and IP type of service (TOS) delays (`TCP_NODELAY` and `IPTOS_LOWDELAY`, respectively) and reuse local addresses without repeat DNS lookups (`SO_REUSEADDR=1`), which Solaris 2 supports. Here's a good example of a typical Solaris 2 socket option:

```
Socket Options = TCP_NODELAY IPTOS_LOWDELAY SO_REUSEADDR=1
```

A

SAMBA ON SOLARIS

Servers with a great number of clients not on the local subnet (for example, enterprise backbone servers) should maximize IP service throughput (`IPTOS_THROUGHPUT`). Consider using the following on these maximum throughput, backbone Samba servers:

```
Socket Options = IPTOS_THROUGHPUT
```

If the number of clients on the local subnet is small to average, the following Solaris 2–supported socket options should be added if the settings do not tax the bandwidth of the LAN or the memory of the server with additional overhead (which is not likely):

```
Socket Options = ... SO_BROADCAST=1 SO_KEEPALIVE=1
Keepalive =
```

If `SO_BROADCAST` is not enabled, WINS should be properly set up and operating (which is recommended for large subnets and likely required for access from external subnets). Usage of the `SO_KEEPALIVE` socket option removes any requirement and/or benefit of the `smb.conf` keepalive option.

Solaris 2 also supports variable send and receive buffer sizes (`SO_SNDBUF` and `SO_RCVBUF`). These values should be tweaked until optimal performance is achieved for your site:

```
Socket Options = ... SO_SNDBUF=8192 SO_RCVBUF=8192
```

In the case of issues arising from usage of some of the preceding options, debugging is supported. Add the following socket option when problems arise:

```
Socket Options = ... SO_DEBUG=1
```

Additional information and support for socket options in the Solaris operating system is available in the following man pages:

```
man -s 3XN setsockopt
man -s 5 socket
```

Integration with NIS

Many Solaris installations will have to deal with NIS integration issues. The following sections cover some of the most significant NIS features of Samba and using Samba in NIS networks.

NIS+ GNU Autoconf Option

```
./configure --with-nisplus --mandir=/usr/share/man
```

Passwords

Password changing and synchronization become more complex with NIS/NIS+.

Programs and Chat

The NIS/NIS+ password tool yppasswd is used instead of standard UNIX passwd. The interactive chat between the two disparate programs is also different. The following lines should accommodate these changes (Solaris 2):

```
Password Program = /usr/bin/yppasswd
Password Chat = *login*NIS*password* %o\n
        *New*password* %n\n *Re*enter*password* %n\n \n
```

> **Caution**
>
> Most default NIS/NIS+ password programs require a minimum of six characters with mixed letter, case, and/or number requirements. In the case of the latter, Samba might not be able to prevent password string violations from being passed to yppasswd itself. Accommodate this NIS requirement with:
>
> ```
> Minimum Password Length = 6
> ```

UNIX Password Synchronization

With UNIX password synchronization, yppasswd is run as root. On the master NIS Solaris server, the password chat changes to the following:

```
Password Chat = *New*password* %n\n *Re*enter*password* %n\n \n
Unix Password Sync = Yes
```

> **Caution**
>
> When running Samba on Solaris systems that are NIS clients themselves, trying to sync passwords will usually break the preceding settings and usage of yppasswd. This is especially true if the master NIS server is not running Solaris.

> **Tip**
>
> UNIX password synchronization should only be enabled on the master NIS server. To best accommodate clients that do not use the master NIS server, either set up the master NIS server as the SMB logon server or at least access the master NIS server first (among NIS client servers) during user login.

A

SAMBA ON SOLARIS

Linux Master NIS Servers

When `yppasswd` is run as `root` on a Linux system, Linux's `yppasswd` program prompts for the `root` password. Simply adding the `root` password into the widely accessible `smb.conf` file is an obvious security problem. Therefore, exponentially more complex methods must be used to accommodate master NIS servers running Linux.

Logons and Remote Home Directories

Although NIS supports a truly distributed file system (DFS), with home directories spread throughout different servers and NFS automounting each as needed by local services, accommodating SMB services requires additional attention. By default, the `homes` share will share all directories—local or remotely accessible via NIS—on any system in the NIS domain. Unless a means of redirecting SMB shares requests to the actual, physical server on which resources reside is provided, by default, Samba will blindly serve out remote NFS files as if they existed locally on the system. This, of course, triples the amount of traffic generated for each packet exchanged in a NIS domain, because the data physically resides remotely via an NFS mount.

SMB Redirection: Using Domain Logins and NIS Maps

Samba can redirect SMB requests to the actual, physical server where data resides in a NIS domain if the NIS system uses Sun `auto.home` maps (if an automounter is used).

Note

Support for automounter (`amd`)—or a version of `amd` that produces Sun `auto.home` formatted output—and other NIS systems maps are currently being developed.

In addition to the requirement that Sun's automounter be used, the following three options, including domain logons, must be enabled and/or set:

```
Domain Logons = Yes       # and associated other options
NIS Homedir = Yes
Homedir Map = auto.home   # default (current sole support)
```

No SMB Redirection: Limiting Shares to Physical Server

For administrators of NIS systems who either use automounter (amd) or who want to generally avoid potential pitfalls in tying SMB access too closely to NIS, an alternative methodology is explored next.

The simplest way to deal with NIS domains and multiple servers while guaranteeing optimal performance is to only make user shares available on the physical server on which they're hosted. The easiest way to optimize an NIS domain is to organize users on each home server into unique directory names. Specifically, share those directory names instead of using the default homes share. This may include the removal of the default homes share altogether. Here are two examples:

- Arbitrary server X in NIS domain's smb.conf file:

```
#comment out# [homes]
#comment out# path = %H
# Home Directories
[%U]
path=/home/serverX/%U
```

- Arbitrary server Y in NIS domain's smb.conf file:

```
#comment out# [homes]
#comment out# path = %H
# Home Directories
[%U]
path=/home/serverY/%U
```

Note the use of %U instead of %H, which means the username must match the home directory string. It must also be located in the same directory as all other shares on the local system.

> **Note**
>
> The removal of the default homes share and the use of only one system for a given SMB resource have the added side effects of removing two common Windows client pitfalls: security and mapping issues, respectively. Using the default homes share introduces some security issues with some versions of Windows 95 and 98. And by using only one system for an SMB resource, the rampant UNC remapping in Windows 9x/NT icons, shortcuts, and links is completely eliminated.

For existing servers with home directories mapped in various locations, this methodology is still quite applicable. For existing (or future) accounts, simply create the new path

A

SAMBA ON SOLARIS

(used in `smb.conf`) and create symbolic links to the local home directories physically hosted on the server. Remember only to create symbolic links for those home directories actually hosted on the local server.

> **Note**
>
> Now, before your brightest red light goes off regarding symbolic links and NFS automounting, understand that no symbolic links are used for NIS/NFS at all. The symbolic links are only used for SMB organizational purposes, which are followed by Samba down to the actual, physical paths used by the NFS automounter, which further preserves any file locking between SMB and NFS. NIS/NFS are left "as is," and SMB is accommodated as well as its simplistic, non-DFS design allows.

The logon files (including roaming profiles) for each user would be placed in a general area (for example, `/home/logon/%U`) on a single, main logon server (which should probably be the master NIS server anyway). This is not only a good organizational methodology, but it best accommodates NIS domains where there's an actual Windows NT PDC authenticating and serving SMB users and logons (instead of Samba).

> **Note**
>
> It's generally recommended that a user's profile not be located in the user's home directory. Placing it their introduces security issues, especially with certain versions of Windows 95 and 98. Therefore, the preceding alternative methodology provides for yet a third positive side effect.

> **Author's Experience**
>
> I have personally used this alternative methodology to tame SMB on NIS networks in a variety of implementations, including networks both with and without an actual Windows NT PDC. It requires no changes to existing NIS configurations and no changes in current server home directory locations. It also accommodates disparate UNIX platforms (such as Linux, Solaris, FreeBSD, and so on).

Non-Samba Configuration and Considerations

There are several performance and implementation considerations outside of the realm of the Samba configuration itself.

Solaris 2 Priority Paging

Solaris 7 includes a built-in kernel option called *priority paging*. This kernel option is also available in Solaris 2.5.1 and 2.6 with the application of a patch.

In a nutshell, priority paging allows the system to better differentiate between running programs and cached data pages in memory. So when a page fault occurs, priority paging keeps programs from being swapped out of memory before data. This, in turn, keeps services responsive and performing optimally even during intensive I/O. Before the introduction of priority paging, intensive I/O throughput would often result in some programs being swapped out along with data. This would affect Samba performance, mainly responsiveness, significantly because each SMB connection would result in the thread of a new, executing daemon.

In addition to its primary purpose, priority paging tunes many other kernel options to usually accommodating levels for multifunction servers. Therefore, before referencing, changing, and benchmarking the various kernel options available for memory and CPU tuning (not to mention all the reboots involved in such a study), first try enabling the single priority paging option to see whether it increases performance for your setup.

To serve out many services other than Samba, priority paging should be enabled by default. If your server is primarily an SMB server, maximizing the data cache will be hindered by the introduction of priority paging. Regardless of the server's total overall mission and dedication to SMB services, if more than 50 to 200 SMB clients (depending on total memory) are connecting to your server, priority paging should be enabled.

To enable priority paging, add the following line to the `/etc/system` file and reboot afterwards:

```
set priority_paging = 1
```

A

SAMBA ON SOLARIS

> **Note**
>
> Priority paging can be enabled on live file systems without rebooting. See the section "Online Resources for More Information."

Shared `/usr/local` File Systems

It's commonplace to mount the same, single `/usr/local` file system in server farms of same version/architecture Solaris systems. In such implementations, a few issues need to be resolved in order to accommodate Samba in a shared `/usr/local` mount:

- Run `./configure` with the `--prefix=` directive to a directory other than the default of `/usr/local/samba`. Each system will need a unique location to store its own `smb.conf`, directory for log files, and the like, which are located under `/usr/local/samba` by default. Perfectly acceptable alternative locations are `/usr/share/samba` or `/opt/samba`. Here's an example:

  `./configure --prefix=/usr/share/samba --mandir=/usr/share/man`

- Continue to install the Samba source into `/usr/local/src/samba-ver` (or some other directory under `/usr/local`) and preconfigure and precompile/link with `./configure` and `make`, respectively. Then you'll only need to run `make install` on each system to install the binaries, support files, and writeables into locations local to the individual systems themselves (in a directory not under `/usr/local`).

Additional Listings and Resources

As referenced throughout this appendix, listings and additional information on Solaris and Samba on Solaris are provided in the following sections.

Solaris 2 Samba Script

Although a few System-V and/or Solaris startup/shutdown scripts are included with recent Samba tarballs, the following `/etc/init.d/smb.server` listing will probably accommodate about any installation.

LISTING A.1   A Samba Script for Solaris 2 Init Control

```
#!/bin/sh
#     /etc/init.d/smb.server
#     Variables            # Change for your site
_smbdir=/usr/local/samba
_smbconf=${_smbdir}/lib/smb.conf
_logdir=${_smbdir}/var
#     Script
case "$1" in
'start')
        ${_smbdir}/bin/smbd -D -l${_smblog} -s${_smbconf}
        ${_smbdir}/bin/nmbd -D -l${_smblog} -s${_smbconf}
        ;;
```

```
'stop')
        kill -9 `ps -e | /usr/xpg4/bin/grep -E 'nmbd|smbd' \
        | /usr/bin/sed -e 's/^ *//' -e 's/ .*//'`
        ;;
'restart')
        $0 stop
        $0 start
        ;;
'status')
        ps -e | /usr/xpg4/bin/grep -E 'nmbd|smbd'
        ;;
*)
        echo "/etc/init.d/smb.server {start|stop|restart|status}"
        ;;
esac
```

After creating this script, install it with the following commands:

```
chmod 744 /etc/init.d/smb.server
ln -s /etc/init.d/smb.server /etc/rc2.d/S97smb.server
ln -s /etc/init.d/smb.server /etc/rc2.d/K97smb.server
```

Sources of GNU Software

SunSITE archive with GNU software for Solaris 1:

- `http://sunsite.queensu.ca`

Subsidized Solaris 2 GNU software site:

- `www.sunfreeware.com`

Online Resources for More Information

Sun Answerbooks:

- `http://docs.sun.com`

Sun on priority paging:

- `http://www.sun.com/sun-on-net/performance/priority_paging.html`

UseNet Solaris 2 FAQ:

- `http://www.wins.uva.nl/pub/solaris/solaris2.html`

A

Samba on Berkeley Software Design (BSD) UNIX

by Bryan J. Smith

IN THIS APPENDIX

BSD UNIX as a Samba Server Platform

This section is designed to provide some background information on modern Berkeley Software Distribution and Berkeley Software Design (BSD) UNIX and performance. It also serves as an aid in the evaluation of and decision whether to use a modern BSD UNIX variant as a Samba server platform.

A Mature, Proven Platform

Today's BSD UNIX platform draws on over 25 years of code development and maturity. It has survived four major releases (with numerous minor releases), commercial and political interests, and Open Source project forking.

Performance

Open Source BSD UNIX, particularly FreeBSD, runs some of the most powerful, highest-trafficked sites on the Internet. It has been a reliable and consistent performer at just about any task, including handling multiple roles simultaneously. Untouched by the media hype, BSD UNIX runs on thousands of mission-critical servers daily and performs quite brilliantly, regardless of the fact that it rarely gets the respect it deserves.

The Internet's Archive

According to regular press releases, Walnut Creek CD-ROM (Cdrom.com) is the world's busiest Internet site. The daily transfer load usually exceeds 1TB (1 terabyte, or 1 million megabytes). For the most part, all users are served by a single 500MHz Pentium III Xeon server with 4GB of RAM running FreeBSD.

Workgroup Server

When it comes to "bang for the buck," BSD UNIX on the commodity Intel platform tops the list. From basic FTP to dynamic Web content to full NFS version 3 support to Samba itself, BSD UNIX rarely serves a single, monolithic role. Like Linux, a single BSD UNIX server can cover just about any service that any workgroup could want or need. And that's where its performance really shines; not in a monolithic role (where systems can be tweaked to heavily favor a service), but in this "all-in-one" role.

> **Note**
>
> FreeBSD version 3 on Intel is the only Open Source BSD UNIX that supports multiprocessor hardware. In today's Wintel-oriented media, there have been very few studies that have pitted SMP FreeBSD servers against other SMP platforms. There are numerous mission-critical servers running SMP FreeBSD today.

Enterprise and Scalability

At this time, BSD UNIX systems will not be found on systems with more than four processors. This, of course, could very well change as the FreeBSD Alpha port matures. Regardless, uniprocessor BSD UNIX systems are capable of serving large numbers of clients, including controlling a backbone of workgroup servers.

> **Tip**
>
> Unless your WAN backbone requires phenomenal throughput and has the network infrastructure to support it, a serious evaluation of BSD UNIX should be made before it's dismissed as "not an enterprise backbone option."

BSD UNIX Versus Linux

At this time, BSD UNIX has two major advantages over Linux:

- *64-bit journaled file system*. The 64-bit Fast File System (FFS) in most BSD UNIX platforms handles file sizes greater than the 2GB limit of the Linux ext2. Reboots after system crashes also take considerably less time thanks to journaling support.

> **NetBSD, the Universal NAS OS**
>
> Meridan's NetBSD-based Snap! Server, a Network Attached Storage (NAS) device, takes less than 2 minutes to recover after a system crash, whereas Cobalt's Linux-based Cobalt Cube NAS takes more than 10 minutes. With support for dozens of architectures and platforms, NetBSD is an extremely popular OS to power non-*x86* NAS appliances.

- *NFS version 3*. This gives BSD UNIX a distinct performance and maturity advantage over Linux (which only supports version 2 through the 2.2 kernel) in mixed-client environments. For mature and stable NFS services, BSD UNIX should be used over Linux in environments with mixed UNIX and Windows clients.

B

SAMBA ON BSD
UNIX

Linux 2.4 and NFS

The forthcoming Linux 2.4 kernel will feature a new, NFS version 3 server.

Additionally, if you're reading this book in preparation for creating a commercial SMB server product, you'll probably choose to go with BSD UNIX instead of Linux because of the licensing and source code publication issues.

BSD UNIX Versus Commercial, System-V Systems

After AT&T's standardization effort in 1986, the commercial UNIX was destined to be littered with commercial, System V implementations. Regardless, Open Source BSD UNIX is here to stay. Some features that continue to make BSD a popular choice are

- *Commodity costs*. This is obvious. Using commercial software on commodity uniprocessor hardware can easily double a server's cost.
- *Efficiency*. Like a plague, commercial operating systems continue to adopt the requirement of an integrated GUI. This only adds to the basic system requirements of the OS. BSD UNIX Samba servers can run optimally with as little as 16MB of RAM.

Memory Footprint for NAS

Samba network appliances typically only have 16 to 32MB of RAM.

- *Linux compatibility*. The future of UNIX is with Linux. Application compatibility with Linux is a big plus (in addition to the source code overlap).

Linux and BSD : Windows 9*x* and NT

The relationship between Linux and FreeBSD is almost akin to the one between Windows 95/98 and Windows NT/2000, from a binary compatibility perspective.

Quick Platform Review

This section is not designed as a detailed discussion of the development and history of BSD UNIX but rather as a quick review of the platforms commonly used for Samba services.

> **Note**
>
> For more information on the rich history of BSD, see the section "Additional Resources" at the end of this appendix.

Operating Systems

There are three major 4.4BSDLite-based BSD UNIX operating systems available today. Commercial variants, such as BSDi's BSD/OS, and lesser known 4.4BSDLite forks will not be covered.

FreeBSD

Based on the original 386BSD release, FreeBSD become the distribution focused on the commodity Intel *x*86 platform. With version 3, FreeBSD has also been ported to the Alpha architecture. Although version 3 is several revisions deep and quite stable, version 2 is still in widespread use. At the time of this writing, the latest versions were 3.4 and 2.2.8, respectively. Both make excellent Samba platforms.

> **FreeBSD 4.0**
>
> FreeBSD 4.0 was undergoing a feature freeze during this writing.

NetBSD

NetBSD is a resultant flavor from a fork of 386BSD. One of the rare bi-endian-capable operating systems, NetBSD can be, and has been, ported to several dozen architectures. NetBSD makes an ideal embedded OS, especially for plug-and-play hardware with Samba services, because it runs on a variety of low-power chips. The latest version of NetBSD at the time of this writing was 1.4.1.

OpenBSD

OpenBSD was forked from NetBSD in 1995 with the intention of creating the most proactively secure operating system available. This focus has caused its more workgroup-oriented services and features to lag significantly behind NetBSD. This factor, combined with some of the security issues that SMB interfaces introduce (not so much due to Samba but because of the clients connected to it—for example, Windows), usually keeps Samba from being used on most OpenBSD servers.

> ### Canada, the Land of Free Crypto
>
> A Canadian project, OpenBSD is free of the crypto exportation laws of the United States. Ironically, the U.S. Department of Justice (among other U.S. agencies) uses primarily OpenBSD on its servers.

Hardware

Table B.1 gives a very basic overview of the various processor architectures that Open Source BSD UNIX is available on (for which the port is usually named). Entries that include a number in parentheses support multiple vendor implementations and platforms around the processor architecture, each with its own unique names for the ports. Releases that are experimental or not of production quality on a processor series (or amid porting to some of the disparate hardware platforms that use the processor), are marked with an asterisk (*).

TABLE B.1   The All-Platform-Encompassing Expansion of Open Source BSD UNIX

FreeBSD	NetBSD	OpenBSD
i386	i386	i386
alpha *	alpha	alpha
hp300		hp300
m68k (10*)		m68k (4)
mips (4*)		mips (2)
powerpc (3*)		powerpc (2)
sparc (2*)		sparc
arm32		
ns32k		
sh3		
vax		

Minimum Hardware Requirements

Like Linux, use of a graphical windowing environment is completely optional in BSD UNIX. As such, even an entry-level $400 PC can easily serve a moderate-sized workgroup with Samba. If the server is not dedicated solely to SMB services, just factor in 0.5MB and about 10 to 20 million instructions per second (MIPS) per Windows client.

When recycling older systems for Samba duties, look for 100 MIPS performance (for example, a fast 486 or entry-level Pentium) with at least 16MB of RAM. For small-to-moderate workgroups, 32 to 64MB of RAM should be installed.

Non-Intel Platforms

NetBSD will find a home on all major non-Intel platforms. You'll find NetBSD serving two major roles here:

- *Low power.* Largely the focus of network appliances and attached storage, NetBSD will allow you to wield Samba on the smallest hardware form factors.
- *Recycling.* NetBSD and OpenBSD are ideal for recycling older Sun3, Sun4, MIPS DECstation, and other systems into X Terminals. Samba is used for file exchange with Windows. NetBSD is also the preferred NOS upgrade path for older SunOS 4 systems, instead of Solaris 2.

Costs and Power Demote Intel in NAS

Meridan's highly praised Snap! series of network attached storage (NAS) appliances run NetBSD on the low-power, 64-bit MIPS R4000 platform.

Intel i386

Samba will find its mainstay on the commodity uniprocessor *x*86 PC running FreeBSD. All three Open Source BSD flavors are well supported on the Intel i386 platform, largely due to their installed base at major ISPs and Internet sites.

Crusoe Architecture Opens Doors

The new, low-power, *x*86-compatible Crusoe architecture from Transmeta should open an entirely new door for vendors who have traditionally used non-Intel chips because of power considerations.

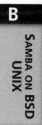

B

SAMBA ON BSD UNIX

Quickstart Installation

This quickstart is written to help you get Samba up and running on FreeBSD version 2 or 3 systems with minimal effort or reading. It assumes the following:

- The standard, basic BSD and GNU development and support tools are installed. This should not be an issue with even the most bare-boned of FreeBSD installations.

- Samba source management will be via FreeBSD's Ports collection file system in `/usr/ports`.
- A recent version of FreeBSD 3, or a late version 2 or early version 3 with the Ports collection updated with a recent tarball (and already extracted into `/usr/ports`), is used.

> **Note**
>
> Administrators fluent with NetBSD or OpenBSD will find the procedure very similar for their respective platforms. In fact, OpenBSD simply uses the same "Ports" collection as FreeBSD, and NetBSD uses a slightly modified and renamed file system structure (for example, `/usr/pkgsrc`) for source code management. For each system, the commands for obtaining, building, installing, and performing post-install cleanup should be almost completely identical.

For the duration of the quickstart, replace `/tmp/download` with the path in which the downloaded packages can be found. Also replace `ver` in the filename with the actual version downloaded.

Installing Samba

The following procedure installs Samba as defined by the FreeBSD Ports `make` file for Samba. This should cover nearly all FreeBSD implementations.

Fetching or Copying the Samba Tarball

If you have a direct connection to the Internet, you can use an automated method to "fetch" the appropriate tarball for your FreeBSD Ports collection. This not only removes the need to hunt for an appropriate download site, but it removes any concerns regarding the download of the correct version supported by the your Ports collection. Here's the command you would use:

```
cd /usr/ports/net/samba
make fetch           # Works on all: Free/Net/OpenBSD
```

If you have no connection or a slow connection to the Internet or if you've already downloaded the appropriate version tarball, you can simply copy it where the Ports collection expects it to reside:

```
cp /tmp/install/samba-ver.tar.gz /usr/ports/distfiles
```

Building Samba

The following will install Samba in its default location on FreeBSD (usually
/usr/local, as is the case with many other ports):

```
cd /usr/ports/net/samba
make
make install
```

> **Note**
>
> Because FreeBSD (and BSD UNIX in general) places such an emphasis on source
> code, the make options set in the Ports collection should cover just about any
> implementation without you needing to run ./configure manually.

> **Caution**
>
> If you do find that you need to change one of the auto-conf defaults, modify
> the Ports collection's make file for the package (in /usr/local/net/samba)
> instead of directly running ./configure in the source tree (usually located in
> ./work/samba-ver/source).

Enabling SWAT

The following will configure the Internet daemon for the Samba Web Administration
Tool (SWAT). The procedure kills the currently running inet daemon, installs the line
for SWAT in the services and inetd configuration files, and then restarts the daemon.

> **Caution**
>
> Because SWAT sends and receives passwords in clear text, it should not be used
> on publicly accessible systems. Traditional means should be used instead (for
> example, manual text editing of the smb.conf file).

```
kill `cat /var/run/inetd.pid`
echo "swat  stream  tcp  nowait.400  root  /usr/local/samba/bin/swat  swat" \
        >> /etc/inetd.conf
echo "swat  901/tcp" >> /etc/services
/usr/sbin/inetd -wW
```

Configuring and Starting Samba

At this time, fire up your favorite Web browser on any local system that this server is accessible to and point its URL to

```
http://sambaserver:901
```

If you haven't yet read about how to configure Samba, do so before starting Samba with the commands that follow. At a bare minimum, you should continue to read the following sections that cover some of the smb.conf options available in or recommended for FreeBSD. However, they will only cover a portion of the basic options that should be set up before Samba is run for the first time, especially if you have a Windows NT Server machine on the same subnet.

To start Samba 2.0 as a daemon that's always running, execute the following:

```
/usr/local/etc/rc.d/samba.sh.sample start
```

> **Note**
>
> The included samba.sh.sample script installed by the Ports collection is a perfectly capable script. Renaming it to or symlinking to it as samba.sh will start and shut down Samba appropriately via FreeBSD's System-V compatibility init scripts for /usr/local/etc/rc.d. Here's the command:
>
> ```
> cd /usr/local/etc/rc.d
> ln -s samba.sh.sample samba.sh
> ```

Additional Configuration Options

The following sections cover those smb.conf options that are of particular significance to FreeBSD and deserve further exploration.

> **Note**
>
> Given the numerous platforms supported by NetBSD (and OpenBSD), there will be some options that are architecturally specific (and not discussed here). Regardless, NetBSD offers many of the same configuration options offered by FreeBSD, as discussed in the following sections.

Locking Options

File locking is an integral part of any shared file system service. The balance between file integrity and performance is a fine one, and it's quickly complicated by the introduction and use of NFS services on the same server. Samba uses the standard locking mechanisms in the underlying mature BSD UNIX kernel, which should not introduce any of its own issues that threaten this integrity.

Tip

Again, FreeBSD versions 2 and 3 (as well as NetBSD and OpenBSD) are probably much better choices for mixed SMB and NFS environments than Linux (through at least kernel version 2.2) from a file-locking and integrity standpoint.

Caution

There are some issues with connecting to BSD UNIX servers with both the SMB and NFS protocols from Windows clients. In general, this should be avoided at all costs—either go 100% with Samba or not at all on any given subnet of Windows clients.

Caution

There are also additional issues introduced by some Windows NFS clients that use nonstandard daemons on the server. See the section "Locking Options" in Appendix A, "Samba on Solaris."

Without NFS Clients

Without NFS services, locking considerations become a simple issue of local access versus SMB connections. If the majority of Windows clients are running recent versions, especially if they're running Windows NT, disabling strict file locking should improve performance without jeopardizing file integrity. Here's an example:

```
Strict Locking = No    # Fairly Safe on SMB-only servers
```

Opportunistic locks (*oplocks*) offer increased performance to shared file access (for example, databases and executables). Some UNIX kernels can handle the interaction between local, NFS, and SMB oplocks at the kernel level. Unfortunately, at this time,

FreeBSD does not (nor do NetBSD or OpenBSD) offer this support at the kernel level. Use the following on any OpenSource BSD UNIX Samba server:

```
Kernel Oplocks = No    # Not supported by Free/Net/OpenBSD
Oplocks = Yes          # Fairly Safe on SMB-only servers
```

Late versions of Samba 2.0 offer additional support for level 2 oplocks. Level 2 oplocks offer increased performance for Windows NT clients. If standard SMB oplocks are enabled and the Samba version in use is 2.0.5 or later, level 2 oplocks should also be enabled. Do this with the following:

```
Level2 Oplocks = Yes  # Use on Samba 2.0.5+
```

With NFS Clients

In addition to the global defaults, most of the locking options available in Samba can be defined on a per-share basis. As such, if interaction with NFS can be eliminated on a SMB share level (for example, a share containing only Windows executables or data), locking options can usually be set for performance.

When home directories are being mapped out via both NFS-to-UNIX clients and SMB-to-Windows clients, it's best to enable strict file locking:

```
Strict Locking = Yes   # Default and home directories
```

```
Strict Locking = No    # For Win9x/NT-only content shares
```

As discussed in the preceding section, BSD UNIX does not support oplocks at the kernel level. Additionally, using SMB oplocks will only benefit access to Windows-only executables and databases/repositories. The oplocks setting is also available as a per-share setting. Thus, on shares that are largely read/write, use:

```
Oplocks = No           # Default and home directories
```

For those shares that are read-only, largely comprised of executables, or shared files (such as "fat-client" databases which use Microsoft's Jet engine), use:

```
Oplocks = Yes          # For Win-only EXEs/DBs shares
Level2 Oplocks = Yes
```

Socket Options

FreeBSD version 3 supports a vast number of socket options for maximum Samba performance tuning.

Servers that mainly serve their local subnet clients should also minimize TCP and IP services (for example, NetBIOS/SMB) and delays (TCP_NODELAY and IPTOS_LOWDELAY), and they should reuse local addresses without repeat DNS lookups (SO_REUSEADDR=1, which FreeBSD supports). Use the following on servers that primarily serve local workstations:

```
Socket Options = TCP_NODELAY IPTOS_LOWDELAY SO_REUSEADDR=1
```

Servers with a great number of clients not on the local subnet (for example, enterprise backbone servers) should maximize throughput for IP services (IPTOS_THROUGHPUT). Enterprise and backbone servers should use something similar to this (in place of the preceding):

```
Socket Options = IPTOS_THROUGHPUT
```

FreeBSD supports a number of options that will benefit local subnets with a small-to-medium number of clients. Like other modern UNIX systems, FreeBSD sockets support the broadcast (SO_BROADCAST) and keepalive (SO_KEEPALIVE) options for optimal work-group server performance. Try enabling these options to increase performance (although enabling them on subnets with a large number of nodes may actually decrease performance):

```
Socket Options = ... SO_BROADCAST=1 SO_KEEPALIVE=1
Keepalive =
```

> **Note**
>
> If SO_BROADCAST is not enabled, WINS should be properly set up and operating (this is recommended for large subnets and likely required for access from external subnets). Usage of the SO_KEEPALIVE socket option removes any requirement and/or benefit of the smb.conf keepalive option.

As a boost for local LANs with few Windows clients (or a very powerful server), FreeBSD also supports the option to share port access among all Samba threads (SO_REUSEPORT). This improves efficiency because each smbd thread sees all incoming SMB traffic simultaneously (not requiring each thread to access the TCP/IP stack in turn), assuming the server has sufficient processing power to handle the slight additional overhead. If your server has processing power to spare, try enabling this option:

```
Socket Options = ... SO_REUSEPORT=1
```

If all SMB traffic is limited to the local subnet or if the SMB server has direct connections to all the subnets it serves SMB packets to (for example, via multiple network cards), routing can be completely bypassed by FreeBSD's sockets (SO_DONTROUTE). This saves a significant amount of overhead because packets can be immediately sent out on the appropriate interface instead of waiting for the destination IP to be resolved via the normal routing functions in the IP stack. Enable this only on Samba servers that serve their own subnet and no other:

```
Socket Options = ... SO_DONTROUTE=1
```

FreeBSD also offers socket options for setting thresholds before generating or accepting network traffic. These thresholds can apply to both packet size (LOWAT) and count (TIMEO).

The options for setting packet size thresholds are `SO_SNDLOWAT` and `SO_RCVLOWAT` for packets sent and received, respectively. Some basic network efficiency is implemented by default in setting the send threshold to a moderate number (`SO_SNDLOWAT=1024` in FreeBSD 3.4). This should be increased in heavily congested networks with a lot of SMB traffic. Again, here is the default in FreeBSD 3.4:

```
Socket Options = ... SO_SNDLOWAT=1024    #default in 3.4
```

By default, incoming packets are still processed as they are received (`SO_RCVLOWAT=1`). This setting should never need to be changed unless CPU utilization becomes abnormally high due to a high number of incoming packets. It is best to leave it at the default:

```
Socket Options = ... SO_RCVLOWAT=1       #default
```

The second and complementary set of socket options, the counters, are set with the socket options `SO_SNDTIMEO` and `SO_RCVTIMEO`. It's doubtful that settings different from the defaults for each will ever need to be explored.

The options for setting the size of the send and receive buffers (`SO_SNDBUF` and `SO_RCVBUF`) are available. By combining a high `SO_RCVBUF` setting with data shared on a softupdate-enabled file system (see the upcoming section, "FreeBSD 3.4 Softupdates Support"), high levels of SMB-only server performance can be achieved. Set the socket send and receive buffers with something similar to the following:

```
Socket Options = ... SO_SNDBUF=8192 SO_RCVBUF=32768
```

Fighting the Pro-Windows SMB Benchmark

Abnormally high throughput is achievable in a series of concentrated SMB client writes to a server running FreeBSD 3.4 using a combination of an extremely high `SO_RCVBUF` setting (1MB+) with a file system with softupdates enabled. Of course, storage requirements and other component configurations required to handle sustained levels of this kind of throughput put the server clearly outside the realm of "real-world" configurations. For example, it requires the use of raw, RAID-0 disk stripping over several dozen separate partitions. This is not exactly what one would want to do on a "mission-critical" (let alone what could be considered a "manageable") server.

> However, for marketing-driven studies (usually sanctioned by vendors or vendor-aligned publications) pitting Windows NT against NetWare and Linux, these settings will tilt the performance advantage in FreeBSD's favor on equivalent Intel hardware. Of course, you should not put much faith in the performance evaluations of these benchmarks since they unrealistically jeopardize system reliability and data integrity in favor of raw performance. In addition, they test only benchmark systems that serve only one purpose (for example: SMB-only, HTTPD-only, and so on). Most departmental servers are tasked with at least a dozen distinct but inseparable network services where UNIX has a heavy advantage over traditional PC network operating systems (NOS) such as NetWare and Windows NT.

In the case of issues arising from usage of some of the preceding options, full debugging is supported:

```
Socket Options = ... SO_DEBUG=1
```

Additional information and support for socket options in the FreeBSD operating system are available in the following man pages:

- `man 2 setsockopt`
- `man 5 socket`

Integration with NIS

Integrating Samba services on an NIS domain involves using a number of additional `smb.conf` options and considering many other files and factors outside the realm of Samba. These topics are discussed in some detail in Appendix A, "Samba on Solaris."

For the most part, FreeBSD's (and NetBSD/OpenBSD's) NIS capabilities and services for both client and server should be configured exactly as covered for Solaris in Appendix A, with three exceptions:

- FreeBSD does not support NIS+. Skip the section on the NIS+ GNU auto-`conf` option.
- The `yppasswd` password chat for FreeBSD is
  ```
  Password Chat = *Old*password* %o\n
      *New*password* %n\n *Reenter*password* %n\n \n
  ```
- FreeBSD does not use or offer compatibility with Sun's automounter and `auto.home` maps. Skip the section "SMB Redirection: Using Domain Logins and NIS Maps."

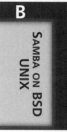

To minimize excessive additional network hops caused by following NFS mounted and automounted file systems in an NIS domain, follow the procedure in the section "No SMB Redirection: Limiting Shares to Physical Server." As a side benefit, the implementation will also eliminate any potential headaches created by Windows resources, such as icons, shortcuts, and links, that are not distributed file system (DFS) aware and do not know how to handle the same, remapped resources on different servers.

Non-Samba Configuration and Considerations

There has been one major new development that greatly affects client write performance to Samba servers running the latest release version of FreeBSD. This development is the use of the "softupdate" to replace traditional, overhead-costly journaling.

FreeBSD 3.4 Softupdates Support

Journaling file systems allow varying degrees of maintaining data integrity and crash recovery. Ideal journaling file system implementations provide optimal write-back file caching while always maintaining the file system's completely uncorrupted state, which can be recovered quickly in the event of a system crash. Although implementations vary from operating system to operating system and file system to file system, there are two universal constants among all journaling systems. One is the fact that development is not trivial. The second and more significant characteristic is the runtime overhead required for journaling.

Softupdates provide a new approach to maintaining data integrity while further optimizing cached writes. Where softupdates greatly differ from a traditional journaling file system is in the area of overhead. The softupdates approach has several times less overhead than journaling. The result is a performance increase of 50 to 200% in file system write throughput.

Although the softupdates algorithm is not new and was ported to the Fast File System (FFS) several months ago, FreeBSD 3.4-STABLE is the first widely used UNIX release to include the source in its kernel by default, and the tools to support it.

> **Note**
>
> NetBSD even has a development kernel (at the time of this writing) with softupdates support in its software RAID implementation.

To enable softupdates on an FFS slice in FreeBSD 3.4, run the following command on the unmounted (or read-only mounted) slice:

```
/sbin/tunefs -n enable /dev/slice
```

To view the current settings on an FFS slice, run

```
/sbin/tunefs -p /dev/slice
```

For more information on softupdates, see the files listed in the following section, "Additional Resources."

The Softupdates License

The license on the softupdates concept and associated source code has some interesting restrictions. The most significant (and restrictive) is that any redistribution of software (binary or source) that uses the softupdates algorithms and code must be completely available in source code form to the public. At the very least, assuming the operating system is modular, this would require the source code's entire file system module that uses softupdates to be made available (possibly the entire kernel itself).

Therefore, given the increase in SMB server write performance gained by the inclusion of softupdates in the OS kernel, it may very well be that the best-performing Windows servers of the near future will all be under Open Source licenses. Note that the softupdates license is not GPL or GPL-derived, so there may be some loophole that will allow it to be packaged in binary-only systems software.

Additional Resources

BSD UNIX Source and Documentation

Softupdates information (FreeBSD 3.4+):

- `/usr/src/sys/contrib/softupdates`
- `/usr/src/sys/ufs/ffs`

Online Resources for More Information

Ports collection (and source packages):

- `http://www.freebsd.org/ports/`
- `http://www.netbsd.org/Documentation/software/packages.html`

The history of BSD and NetBSD:

- `www.netbsd.org/Misc/history.html`

B

SAMBA ON BSD
UNIX

Samba Code Branches

by Steve Litt

On December 14, 1999, Andrew Tridgell issued his now famous "CVS rearrangement done—please read" message on the `samba-technical@samba.org` mailing list. In this email, Andrew described three CVS branches:

- The SAMBA_2_0 branch
- The head branch
- The SAMBA_TNG branch

These three CVS branches appear in increasing order of advanced features (and therefore decreasing order of stability). Andrew described the SAMBA_TNG branch as a continuation of the former head branch. He described the SAMBA_2_0 branch as the present stable version 2.0.*x*. He described the head branch as the branch containing code for the next major version, Samba 3.0. In the time since Andrew's email the head branch has often been described as the main branch. The most visible such reference is in the source/README file from the TNG branch. To reduce confusion, this appendix will continue using the name from Andrew's email, namely, the head branch.

CVS

CVS stands for *Concurrent Versions System*. It's a client/server version-control system originally from the UNIX world. The CVS server software is on the Samba.org server. Anyone with CVS client software can download the latest Samba source from the CVS server and have that source placed in a directory on his or her hard disk. Most modern Linux systems come packaged with CVS clients (and servers, for that matter). You can also obtain a CVS client for Windows.

A *CVS branch* (usually just called a *branch*) is a complete body of source code, documentation, and other files downloaded with CVS. The intent is to have the files of a branch compile and install into a working system. As described previously, you can download three different branches for Samba: The SAMBA_2_0 branch, the head branch, and the SAMBA_TNG branch. Each branch compiles and installs a different Samba version. You choose your branch according to your needs. For pure file serving on a production server, choose the SAMBA_2_0 branch. On the other hand, for a primary domain controller (PDC) on a noncritical system, choose the SAMBA_TNG branch.

A CVS client can also *upload* source code *to* the central repository. However, this is strictly controlled with security. According to the Samba.org Web site, approximately 20 people worldwide have the necessary permissions to upload source code. These people form the "inner circle" of the Samba team.

Instructions for downloading Samba via CVS are located at `http://samba.org/cvs.html`. Also, an HTML interface to CVS is located at `http://samba.org/cgi-bin/cvsweb/`. Chapter 5, "Installing Samba," has CVS download instructions as well.

> **Note**
>
> This appendix assumes you've read and understood Chapter 5. If you haven't yet, you should read that chapter.

Branch-Specific Information

The SAMBA_2_0 branch is the stable code branch—the 2.0.*x* Samba branch we're all used to. This branch yields an ultrareliable file server and is the only branch presently recommended for production environments. However, using the Samba yielded by this branch as a PDC, or with the Lightweight Directory Access Protocol (LDAP), is difficult or even impossible.

The SAMBA_2_0 branch is intended primarily for bug fixes, with few, if any, new features. New features primarily go in the other two branches.

The SAMBA_TNG branch is the heir to the old head branch (Samba 2.1). It's primarily experimental and is not presently recommended for production environments, although that will change as time goes on. It frequently experiences radical changes, meaning that features that work might break a day or a week later. However, the SAMBA_TNG branch is the only branch with a working, reliable primary domain controller functionality. It's also the branch recommended for LDAP interaction.

The SAMBA_TNG branch contains all of Luke Kenneth Casson Leighton's Samba Remote Procedure Call (RPC) system prototyping. It has many more daemons than the smbd and nmbd of previous branches. The exact names and functions of the daemons change frequently, so they're not described here. You can find up-to-date information on the technical@samba.org mailing list.

The head branch has been created to produce a stable Samba version to replace 2.0.*x*. It will probably be numbered Samba 3.*x.x*. Therefore, it's a sort of stand-in for the stable version that will eventually be built with SAMBA_TNG. At this point (February 2000), it seems unlikely that the SAMBA_TNG branch will become the stable version any time soon. This is why the head branch has been created. New features not involving PDC support or RPC will go in this branch so that Samba can progress beyond 2.0.*x* plus bug fixes. Additionally, the head branch has acquired the ability to interact with the additional daemons featured in the SAMBA_TNG branch, although the head branch contains code to fall back to the original two-daemon model if the additional daemons are not found. This allows better integration of head/TNG hybrids. It's quite likely the head branch will acquire a degree of PDC support by the time it goes stable.

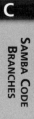

What's in a Name

The code for Samba 3.0 was named "the head branch" in Andrew Tridgell's December 14, 1999 email. Samba 3.0's branch name was subsequently described as "the main branch" in the source/README file from the SAMBA_TNG alpha 0.0 snapshot. This may reflect a changing attitude. Traditionally "main branch" has been a reference to code for the stable version, whereas "head branch" has been a reference to experimental code like SAMBA_TNG. It's possible that in the future SAMBA_TNG may acquire the "head branch" moniker.

The head/TNG hybrid is not a branch but instead is a mixture of executables from the SAMBA_TNG branch and the head branch. Specifically, the head/TNG hybrid is created by copying the head branch smbd and nmbd daemons to a SAMBA_TNG installation (remember that SAMBA_TNG has many daemons besides smbd and nmbd). This produces the most stable and reliable fileserver that can function as a PDC.

Note

Most information in this appendix has been gleaned from evaluating and summarizing the information on the Samba mailing lists.

Due to the nature of Open Source, there have been reports of people doing the "impossible" or the "not recommended" in various branches. For instance, many reports of 2.0.*x* PDCs and sporadic reports of 2.0.*x* LDAP implementations exist. Because the user can modify the source code, these things are possible.

All Samba code branches continually change. Instances have occurred in which tasks originally possible in the 2.0.*x* branch became impossible in later minor versions. Likewise, the SAMBA_TNG branch, heir to the old head branch (2.1.*x*), is becoming increasingly experimental.

The bottom line is that this appendix should be used as a starting point, not as an absolute authority, for evaluating which Samba branch to use. A thorough evaluation includes detailed attention to the technical@samba.org mailing list, personal experimentation, and perusal of the Kernel Cousin Samba Web site.

The Kernel Cousin Samba Web Site

The Kernel Cousin Samba Web site is an intelligently made weekly summary of the Samba mailing lists. For the regular subscriber, it offers a way to see the forest instead of the trees. For the occasional user or non-user of the Samba mailing list, it forms an excellent "cheat sheet." This Web site is excellent for spotting trends in Samba. You can access it at http://kt.linuxcare.com/KC/samba/.

Table C.1 shows some scenarios as well as branch choices.

TABLE C.1 Implementation Scenarios and CVS Branch Choices

Scenario	Samba CVS Branch Choice
An ultrareliable fileserver in a production or nonproduction environment, with no PDC	Samba 2_0 branch
A high-performance fileserver in a nonproduction environment, with no PDC	Head branch*
The most reliable Samba PDC in a production environment with NT or Windows 2000 servers	Windows NT/2000
A PDC not serving files in a network without NT Server PDCs	SAMBA_TNG branch
A PDC with reliable file service	TNG/head hybrid

The head branch may soon include its own PDC support.

Summary

To accommodate the dual goals of progress and stability, Samba, as of December 14, 1999, was split up into three branches: the stable SAMBA_2_0 branch (2.0.*x*), its successor, which is called the head branch (3.*x*.*x*), and the experimental SAMBA_TNG branch. SAMBA_TNG contains the PDC code and the most advanced RPC code, and it also implements many daemons besides the classic smbd/nmbd daemon pair.

Samba moves fast, so by the time you read this, the branches could have different names or different purposes. Also, it's entirely possible that the stable version will be 3.*something*. However, the principle will probably remain the same. The Samba CVS Web site, the Kernel Cousin Samba Web site, and the technical@samba.org mailing list are invaluable resources that define the branches and their purposes.

INDEX